ANNALS OF THE NEW YORK ACADEMY OF SCIENCES

Volume 345

STUDIES IN
CHILD LANGUAGE AND
MULTILINGUALISM

Edited by Virginia Teller and Sheila J. White

The New York Academy of Sciences
New York, New York
1980

Library of Congress Cataloging in Publication Data

Main entry under title:

Studies in child language and multilingualism.

(Annals of the New York Academy of Sciences ; v. 345)
Papers presented at meetings of the Linguistics Section of the Academy between Dec. 1976 and May 1979.
1. Language acquisition—Congresses. 2. Multilingualism—Congresses. I. Teller, Virginia. II. White, Sheila J. III. New York Academy of Sciences. Section of Linguistics. IV. Series: New York Academy of Sciences. Annals ; v. 345.
Q11.N5 vol. 345 [P118] 500s [401'.9]   80-16810
ISBN 0-89766-078-1
ISBN 0-89766-079-X (pbk.)

WP
Printed in the United States of America
ISBN-0-89766-078-1 (cloth)
ISBN-0-89766-079-x (paper)

ANNALS OF THE NEW YORK ACADEMY OF SCIENCES

VOLUME 345

June 16, 1980

STUDIES IN CHILD LANGUAGE AND MULTILINGUALISM*

Editors

Virginia Teller and Sheila J. White

━━━━━━◆━━━━━━

CONTENTS

* This *Annal* brings together a series of papers organized around the themes of child language and multilingualism that were presented at meetings of the Linguistics Section of The New York Academy of Sciences between December 1976 and May 1979.

PREFACE

The science of linguistics is by its very nature interdisciplinary, drawing active workers from fields ranging from anthropology through zoology. In arranging its monthly meetings at the Academy, the Linguistics Section attempts to invite speakers from a variety of fields that bear upon language behavior. The papers in this *Annal* offer examples of current work in two areas that recently have been represented strongly in our programs: child language and multilingualism. The current prominence of these two topics in relation to ongoing work in other facets of the discipline is not fortuitous. As researchers strive to understand how the child develops language in the first place, the development of multilingual skills in those who speak two or more languages with ease becomes a related area of concern. Conversely, as we understand more about how some people acquire language in the second and third place, we may indeed gain significant insights into how children acquire language initially. While the papers gathered here do not address this issue directly, it is in this spirit that they have been placed together.

We are grateful to the members of the Linguistics Advisory Committee for their active contributions throughout the period in which these papers were presented: Rosamond Gianutsos, Section Chair during 1977 and 1978, Doris Aaronson, Samuel W. Anderson, Edward H. Bendix, Eric Brown, Elaine Fenton, Louis Gerstman, Martin Gittelman, Herbert Klitzner, D. Terence Langendoen, Damien Martin, Judith Orasanu, Frances Podwall, Lawrence J. Raphael, Robert Rieber, and Kurt Salzinger. We wish to thank the staffs of the Meeting Services Department and the Editorial Department of the New York Academy of Sciences for the invaluable support and help they provided. Thanks are also due to Rosamond Gianutsos and Richard E. C. White for their insightful comments during the preparation of this material.

Virginia Teller, *Chair*
Sheila J. White, *Vice-Chair*

INTRODUCTION

Sheila J. White

Research Department
Lexington School for the Deaf
Jackson Heights, New York 11370

By following the "diary" tradition of longitudinal study, much of the early work in child language offered an essentially single-dimensional view of the child. This work consisted primarily of collecting characterizations of the phonological and lexical achievements of the child at particular ages. Events were recorded either by hand or, eventually, on tape and for the most part were divorced from the contexts in which they occurred. While this method can serve for the study of certain aspects of *phonological* development, it is questionable whether it can serve adequately for studies of *language* development. Problems inherent in the method include: (1) the view that the child-alone is the appropriate unit of study, (2) a confusion of language with speech, and (3) the lack of contextual information. In this section are examples of more wholistic approaches, and it is in this framework that I should like to introduce them.

Is the child-alone the unit to study? We are, biologically, social organisms with a long period of dependency relative to that of other social mammals. Infants who are abandoned do not survive; children who are not nurtured do not flourish. It is well documented that in extreme cases of isolation, such as exemplified by the "wild child" and the "institutional child," severe language delays and disorders are seen. The limited linguistic performance subsequently achieved by these children might best be regarded as being well adapted to their earlier isolation. The language problems presented by some handicapped children might also be the result of analogous processes— either brought about by the isolating nature of the deficit involved or imposed inadvertently by caregivers. Given all of this, a problem with the earlier approaches of studying language acquisition was that the child was *regarded* more or less in isolation. Since, normally, children exist in a context, it is crucial to study the acquisition process (at the very least) by looking at the dyad (mother-child, father-child, sibling-child, and so on). (Some workers are now beginning to look at triadic interactions as well.) The three authors in this section approach this issue in different ways: Nelson addresses this very directly by concentrating on techniques for relating input received by the child to the child's eventual syntactic output and by suggesting ways of observing and experimenting with the interaction. Pea addresses this by carefully setting his experimental stage within a dialogue framework, arguing that this is the most natural setting within which to show the child's logical

1

capacities. Horgan alludes to the possible consequences of mismatching maternal with child interaction styles. Each represents a significant advance over earlier procedures.

Language and speech are not synonymous. Data on the spoken language are, perhaps unfortunately, the easiest linguistic data to collect and analyze. However, we must not let this mislead us into thinking that language and speech are equivalent. The vocal and hearing faculties, which are jointly implied when we use the term "speech," make use of characteristic human input/output organs with clearly visible structures and well-defined embryologic and developmental pathways. Language is not an organ system; it is a function. No one has yet adequately defined what it is, let alone where it "lives." Language can be received and expressed by other modalities (for example, visual input-gestural output) which, of course, brings up the question of how to study *when* and *in what form* "language" is acquired. Although working with preverbal material is fraught with interpretive hazards, workers in the field in general have been pushing chronologically backwards from the collection of clear, connected strings of utterances, through holophrases and one-word productions, towards the collection and analysis of utterance-gesture pairs which seem to convey consistent, although idiosyncratic, meaning. Because of this trend, a child's language development has been shown to start much earlier than anyone (other than mothers!) had previously thought possible. It is this spirit that imbues Pea's work in showing that certain types of logic necessary for the understanding of negation can be demonstrated in children as young as 18 months of age—well before they could produce the actual utterances that would ordinarily have been required for their existential proof. Speech production does not exhaust the totality of the communication process, especially in the young child. Horgan shows our biases in the direction of regarding spoken output as the sign that a child "has language" by showing that judges rate children as precocious developers by the length of their utterances and not necessarily by the variety of their content or by their receptive abilities.

The centrality of contextual information. A child is considered to be saying a word *only* if someone else recognizes it as such. Contextual cues are often the key to that recognition. Aside from that simple truism, the failure to recognize the child as growing up within a web of conventions and shared social signals can lead to a serious underestimation, both of what is available and of what is necessary for a child to develop normally. It will also lead to a serious overestimation of children's achievements during the first few years of their lives. Horgan's paper addresses this issue to some extent by showing how large environmental influences, such as social class and birth order, may influence the degree of noun emphasis in the early stages of a child's language development. She suggests that, depending on the demands made on the child, this could have long-lasting effects on performance. Further, by making a plea for a healthy combination of experimental and observational/ethological techniques, all three authors in this section show their recognition of the relevance of events that surround any output.

Methodologic issues. The final link between these papers that stands in contrast to the informal diary methodology is the call for combining experimental and observational/ethological techniques. This is most explicitly stated in Nelson's paper, although Pea makes the sadly amusing observation that children's performance with logical negations had not been noticed sooner because the tasks given to them were inappropriate, and also because nobody had bothered to look at their spontaneous use of the forms. While Horgan maintains the longitudinal diary perspective for part of her work, she moves freely into the experimental realm as well, and argues cogently for the recognition of different, but equally valid strategies of development towards adult forms of language. Another direction of potential importance is signaled by Horgan's search for possible clusters of traits that are co-related to differences between her noun-lovers and noun-leavers.

Some final points of a general nature. Although it is true that the endpoint of child language is indeed well-formed adult language, it does not follow that the techniques used to examine the endpoint are adequate to an examination of the beginnings. The most parsimonious position that one can take with respect to the links between child and adult language is that the latter, in whatever form it is achieved, is both an outgrowth of and an adaptation to environmental forces. The achievement of a recognizable, socially acceptable, language system does not represent the end product of the unfolding of a linguistic template; rather, it is an adaptive achievement of the child growing up in a social world and interacting with both animate and inanimate objects within it. We have eyes to see with, ears to listen with, and minds to play with. If we are to make any sense of the "booming, buzzing confusion" of *child* language, we must use combinations of all our capacities, much the same way children do.

NOUNS: LOVE 'EM OR LEAVE 'EM

Dianne Horgan

Department of Psychology
Illinois State University
Normal, Illinois 61761

Chances are that if someone stopped you on the street and asked you what you thought about nouns, you'd be hard pressed for an opinion. A beginning language learner, however, may not be so indifferent. In fact, many beginning language learners have very definite ideas about nouns: they either love 'em or can leave 'em.

For the past decade the emphasis in child language research has been on similarities and universals in development. This emphasis was a natural result of close ties with transformational grammar. Individual differences were occasionally noted, usually with regard to speed of acquisition. When *qualitative* differences were found, they inevitably related to degree of noun emphasis. The two classic studies are those of Nelson[1] and Bloom, Lightbown, and Hood.[2]

THE CLASSIC STUDIES

Both Nelson and Bloom *et al.* believe that there are important differences in the extent to which children emphasize nouns, noun phrases, and pronouns in their language. Nelson studied vocabulary acquisition and found what appeared to be two different strategies in learning to talk: a referential one, characterized by a high proportion of common nouns among first words, and an expressive or personal-social strategy, characterized by a low proportion of common nouns.

Bloom *et al.* examined the two-word period and found what they called a nominal group, characterized by a high proportion of nouns in their early two-word sentences, and a pronominal group, who used more pronouns in their early two-word sentences. A nominal child, for example, might be expected to say things like "Mommy sock," while a pronominal child would be more likely to say something like "That ball." It is important to realize that these are not discrete types; children fall somewhere along a continuum of noun emphasis. Both Nelson and Bloom believe that although noun-emphasizers (we'll call them "lovers") *start* with a semantic emphasis, and non-noun-emphasizers (we'll call them "leavers") *start* with a syntactic emphasis, these two different strategies converge sometime between the ages of 2 and 3 years. Certainly all speakers must eventually gain control of both the semantic and the syntactic systems. If we look at qualitative differences that appear later, however, we find that if and when differences appear, they

5

0077-8923/80/0345-0005$01.75/2 © 1980, NYAS

too are often related to noun emphasis. The semantic-versus-syntactic distinction is obviously too narrow. In this paper we will explore other differences that characterize noun-emphasizers and non-noun-emphasizers.

OTHER STUDIES SHOWING NOUN EMPHASIS

The diversity of the other studies that have found noun-related differences suggests that noun emphasis has more than just an initial influence on language use. For example, Wepman and Jones[3] found that different types of aphasics could be distinguished by their noun-pronoun ratio. Bernstein's[4] well-known "elaborated" versus "restricted" codes reflect differences in noun-emphasis: middle-class speakers supposedly make greater use of nouns than do lower-class speakers. Middle-class speakers also, according to Bernstein, use more elaborated noun phrases. In a more recent study, Johnston[5] matched working- and middle-class 5-year-olds with respect to IQ and still found that middle-class children used more nouns, whereas working-class children used more pronouns. She, like others, suggests that there are different communication demands: middle-class children feel more pressure to use language that can be understood independently of the situational context. That is, middle-class children are expected to use linguistic means to indicate reference, whereas working-class children use language that is more tied to the immediate nonlinguistic context. These social-class differences that appear later in development are especially interesting with respect to Nelson's finding that all the first-born children of the most highly educated families were found in her referential (our lover) category. It appears then that although children's syntactic and semantic strategies may converge between the ages of 2 and 3 years, differences still occur later in development that are related to noun emphasis.

Since we find differences in noun emphasis cropping up at all stages of development and among diverse groups of subjects, we can use our lover/ leaver distinction as a preliminary way of organizing data. The rest of this paper will guide the reader through TABLE 1, which catalogues some of the differences relating to noun emphasis that have been found at different ages. As we pursue the differences we will consider whether they relate to the strategies that characterize children in the early stages of language development. A lover is simply defined in terms of more emphasis on nouns; leavers, in terms of less. "Lover" and "leaver" are convenient terms because they lack the connotations of previous terms. I simply want to group together differences in emphasis on nouns, and then see whether there is similarity in types of differences at different ages. Noun emphasis can be measured in different ways at different stages in development. For example, a lover at 14 months is defined by a high proportion of nouns among her first 50 words, whereas an adult lover might be defined in terms of using longer noun phrases and more noun phrases per utterance than do other subjects. Lover/ leaver status is thus always relative. In Wepman and Jones' study, for example, we would call one group of aphasics lovers *relative* to the other. Again, although TABLE 1 might suggest that lovers and leavers are discrete types, they actually should be seen as ends of a continuum. TABLE 1 simply represents an attempt at integration of some diverse findings and should be taken as a set of hypotheses, *not* conclusions.

TABLE 1
POSSIBLE CHARACTERISTICS OF LOVERS AND LEAVERS

Lovers	Leavers
Referential	Expressive, personal-social
More nouns	More pronouns
Objective language	Subjective language
Middle-class	Lower-class
Elaborated code	Restricted code
More frequently represented in literature	Less frequently reported in literature
More firstborns	More later-borns
Speaks more clearly	Suffers from "mush mouth"
Larger vocabulary before 30 months	Smaller vocabulary before 30 months
Goes clearly from one word to two	Utterances have variable morpheme length, more stereotyped phrases
Word order reflects meaning	More variable word order
Early sentences strongly semantic, even lexical; combination of substantive forms	Learns sentence frames, concentrates on relationships rather than specific concepts; pivot-open look
Rules operate on grammatical categories	Constant forms for constant functions
Precocious early language	Slow talker
Uses nonreversible instrumental passives	Uses reversible passives, word order often incorrect
At one-word stage, interprets question by content words	At one-word stage, interprets questions by form
Early questions seek information	Early questions used to initiate games
Right-handed	May be left-handed, precocious metalinguistic ability
Speaks in the here and now	More egocentric speech, echolalic speech, more use of register
Low tolerance for degraded stimuli	High tolerance for degraded stimuli

GENERAL CHARACTERISTICS OF LOVERS

Most of the literature on early language comes from diary studies of a few select children—first-born children of highly educated parents—who appear to be lovers. As Nelson[1] notes, many of the characteristics of early language thought to be universal may refer only to lovers. Let's start with a thumbnail sketch of the typical lover. The typical lover is also the "standard child" in the literature and we know what happens to the child only through the early stages of language development. This child speaks clearly—certainly an important quality for the subject of a long-term study. First, the child begins to talk by labeling the people, animals and objects in the personal environment. The lover's vocabulary is larger than a leaver's at the beginning of language acquisition. Language development follows an orderly and clearly discernible progression, from the one-word stage, to the two-word, to the telegraphic stage. A fairly rigid word-order is used to express semantic relations. Early sentences are strongly semantic, even lexical, and they combine substantive forms. In Nelson's words, the child "learns names for the objects that enter into and organize. . .conceptual relations. . . . Early sentences may be formed from these concepts by expressing a non-implicit concept relation in conjunction with the object name."[6] Thus "Mommy sock" would name the objects in a relationship, of say, ownership. According to Bloom *et al.*, our lover uses grammatical categories in functional relationships. This means that a lover encodes grammatical relations with categories of nominal forms, such as Agent, Object, Place, or Possessor. Thus, a lover might have a category Agent that would include nouns like "mommy," "daddy," and "doggie," and another category Object that might include "ball," "banana," or "cookie." Thus "Daddy ball" would encode the relationship of daddy acting upon a ball.

Language, for the lover, has a basis in communicative, pragmatic functions. She is strongly motivated to talk because language serves an instrumental function. Although the lover talks to herself and engages in word play, language grows out of the need to interact with, categorize, and control the world. The lover, like some philosophers, believes that language is primarily a referential system.

GENERAL CHARACTERISTICS OF LEAVERS

A few recent studies besides those of Nelson and Bloom *et al.*[7-10] have identified children whose approach to language is much different from that typically described in the literature. These leavers seem to belong to the "meaning as use" camp—they see sentences and not words as the conveyors of meaning. In Peters' words,[7] they take a more "gestalt" or global approach, "learning the tune before the words." Leavers look for patterns or shapes of constructions. They seem to be more sensitive to form, concentrating on sentence-frames and relationships rather than on specific concepts (concepts labeled by nouns). Thus the leaver's frequent use of pronouns allows her to express a relationship with a minimum of lexical information.[6] The lover can say "It big" without the burden of learning the specific names of a number of possible referents. "It big" may be used to refer to big dogs, big balls, and other big items. The leaver can concentrate his or her limited language skills on the *relationships* among things, while the lover would be concentrating on the names of things. Hence the lover will not yet be able to express as many relationships as a leaver.

The leaver's strategy involves using constant forms for constant functions.[2] For example, a leaver might have a constant form such as "allgone" that serves a constant function in the child's language: no matter what noun is combined with "allgone," it's all gone. The meaning of "allgone" determines the meaning of the sentence "Allgone cookie." Lovers, of course, sometimes say "Allgone cookie," too. The differences between lovers and leavers are ones of degree or emphasis. The utterances of both exhibit syntax and semantics in varying degrees of emphasis.

Leavers' early utterances have a more variable length than do those of lovers.[6] Their speech is peppered with "stereotyped" phrases (tourist-book talk).[6, 7] Their word order varies more than that of lovers[6] and they often suffer from "mush mouth."[7] Lovers seem to focus on the individual words, or the parts, whereas leavers focus on the whole or the gestalt. Lovers' strategy seems to be more analytic, whereas leavers' is more nonanalytic.

Our discussion of early language learners is beginning to make the child sound rather like a Little Philosopher than the Little Scientist who tests hypotheses. Before reaching the Little Scientist stage, the child apparently takes a philosophical stand, as it were, about the nature and purpose of language. The lover sees words as tags to denote objects. The leaver, on the other hand, somewhat resembles Gnat in *Alice in Wonderland*, who wonders about the use of objects' having names if they won't answer to them.[11]

We now have three tasks ahead of us: First, we want to see whether our lover/leaver distinction is related to other differences. Second, we want to know more about the language of the leaver. Third, we need to know about the continuity of noun emphasis: does the 18-month-old lover maintain a noun emphasis throughout development? We will begin by looking at several cross-sectional studies of children between the ages of 2 and 14 years. Then we will consider an ongoing longitudinal study of a leaver. Throughout our discussion we must keep in mind that lover/leaverhood should be seen as a continuum, not as a dichotomy.

RATE OF ACQUISITION AND NOUNS

Traditionally, if individual differences in language were considered at all, it was with respect to speed of acquisition. It is widely accepted that children vary tremendously in rate of acquisition. Studies of acquisition rates usually look at quantitative differences. The first study I will consider looks at differences in noun emphasis between fast and slow language acquisitors.[12] In this study, I matched fifteen pairs of 2- and 3-year olds on Mean Length of Utterance (MLU, a commonly used index of linguistic ability). The members of each pair differed by 6 months or more in age. Each pair, then, had a younger (precocious) member and an older (slower) member. The younger group and the older group each had equal numbers of boys and girls. MLUs ranged from 3.18 to 5.44, based on language elicited by asking the children to tell stories about pictures. All children were homogeneous with regard to social class and parents' educational level. To insure that members of each pair were well-matched in terms of language ability, adult judges were asked to decide, on the basis of protocols, which member of each pair was more advanced linguistically. Adults found this task exceedingly difficult, and their literally forced choices were almost exactly split between the younger and the older member in each pair. As a check of their classification as precocious or slower, parents were asked to rate their child's linguistic progress. Parents of the precocious children thought that they were developing faster than average, while parents of the slower children thought they were progressing at about average or slower-than-average rate.

Language from the younger (precocious) children was then compared with that of the older (slower) children with respect to a number of complexity measures and certain kinds of errors. Performance on a standard comprehension task was also compared. TABLE 2 shows the results. The precocious children appear to be lovers: they concentrated more on nouns and noun phrases. In addition, they may be more willing to make errors. (Ramer[13] also found a similar difference in risk-taking behavior among rapid

TABLE 2
CHARACTERISTICS OF PRECOCIOUS VERSUS SLOW TALKERS

Precocious talkers
  1. More noun phrases per utterance ($p < 0.01$).
  2. Longer noun phrases ($p < 0.05$).
  3. More pronoun errors of case, gender, and number; more verb errors of tense and agreement ($p = 0.11$).
Slower talkers
  1. More correct responses on a comprehension task ($p < 0.01$).
  2. Slightly more varied constructions, more main verbs per utterance, and more auxiliaries per verb phrase; not statistically significant.

---

and slow language learners.) The slower children performed better on the comprehension task, indicating superior receptive language ability. So even with closely matched MLUs, children well past the two-word stage differ in degree of emphasis on nouns and this is apparently related to speed of acquisition.* Nelson[6] also found a relationship between rate of acquisition and noun emphasis: leavers with low MLUs (1.0 to 2.5) spoke more like lovers at higher MLUs (2.5 to 4.5) in terms of using more sentences. This finding, like mine, suggests that if we use length (MLU) alone to judge linguistic ability, the leaver's language ability will be underestimated in terms of comprehension ability and sentence use. Indeed, the adult judges were asked which cues they used in making judgments of linguistic maturity and they indicated that length was the primary cue relied upon. If leavers' utterances tend to be shorter, even though more varied, then their language will be judged "slower." The fact that my subjects had higher MLUs and were older suggests that our lover/leaver distinction has implications beyond age 2½ or 3 when the two strategies appear to converge.

PASSIVES

The next study deals with children's spontaneous full passives.[14] This is rather a complex study, so I won't lead the reader through the linguistic argument, but essentially I looked at protocols from 234 children between 2 and 14 years of age and elicited passives from several hundred college students. The children were simply asked to describe or tell stories about pictures. I found that there were individual differences in the rules for producing passives. FIGURE 1 shows the different routes to acquiring the full use of the passive. Some children (until age 11) used reversible passives only, such as "The girl was chased by the dog." In a reversible passive either noun phrase could logically function as the subject or the object; girls can chase dogs and dogs can chase girls. Other children, until 9 years of age, used only

---

* Subjects were retested 3 months later, and the precocious children maintained their advantage relative to their agemates. We cannot, however, compare them with their matches for noun emphasis since their MLUs and their matches' MLUs were no longer close. MLU is, of course, highly correlated with any noun emphasis measure. In general, the slower children made larger gains over the 3-month period.

nonreversible passives with instruments as the logical subjects and always used the preposition "by," as in "The lamp was broken *by* the *ball.*" (This is nonreversible since it is unlikely that a lamp would break a ball.) Neither group used the common adult nonreversible passive where the logical agent is animate and the logical object is inanimate as in "The lamp was broken by the *girl.*" As the children got older, however, they added additional uses of the passive. The first group's reversible passives often had the word order incorrect (for example, they described a picture of a girl chasing a dog as "The girl was chased by the dog"). They gradually decreased the frequency of incorrect word orders. At about age 11, I saw the first appearance of "with" used in the instrumental case ("The lamp was broken *with* the ball") among children who also produced reversible passives, but not among the children who produced nonreversible *agentive* passives (for example, "The lamp was broken by the *girl*") or nonreversible instrumental passives using "by." The second group's development was very different. They start with the nonreversible instrumental passive. I found the first occurrence in children about age 9 of the nonreversible agentive passive ("The lamp was broken by the *girl*"). This occurred only among those children who also produced the instrumental passive and never in those who produced reversible passives. Presumably at some later age (past 14), both groups learn to use the full range of adult passives.

In preparing the present paper, I went back and checked the lover/leaver status of the passive-producing children. (Only a few of the total sample produced passives.) For every child who produced a passive, I computed the mean number of noun phrases per utterance and the mean length of noun phrase from the whole protocol. For children under 5, I compared these results with the means for all the non-passive-producing children whose MLUs were within ±0.5 of the passive-producing child. In each case, there were at least ten subjects whose MLUs fell into that range. For children over 5, I compared the means for each passive-producing child with the means for his or her age group (30 children at each age). The children who produced the nonreversible instrumental passives were lovers—that is, they had longer noun phrases and more noun phrases per utterance than did the non-passive-producing control subjects. The children who produced reversible passives fell into the category of leavers: they had shorter noun phrases and fewer noun phrases per utterance than did the comparison groups (p < 0.05).

If we look at the different kinds of passives in the context of our general knowledge of lovers and leavers, we see that they fit our expectations on the basis of what we know of younger children from the studies of Nelson and

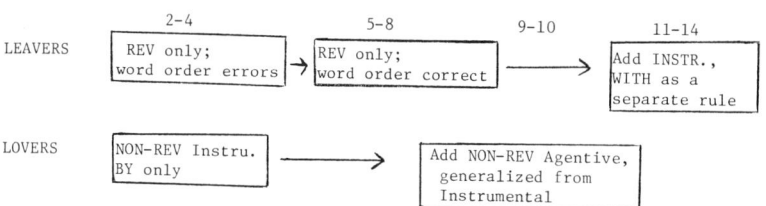

FIGURE 1. Alternative ways of learning the passive.

Bloom *et al.* The younger leavers had the form right, but often the word order (and hence the meaning) wrong. They produced perfectly well-formed passives—*syntactically*—but *semantically* they were incorrect. As we've seen, leavers emphasize form, patterns, and formal markings (in this case the past tense of the verb "to be" and the word "by") rather than meaning. Like leavers at earlier stages, our passive-producing leavers concentrate on relationships; in this case, the relationship of *reversibility* determines when a passive transformation may apply. What is more, the relationship of reversibility can be defined in personal-social terms as something like mutual activity. Lovers, on the other hand, seem to find the salient features of the passive *not* to be the *formal* markings, but rather the *semantic* features of the objects involved. In particular, they use the passive when the logical subject has the feature "plus instrument." Like the much younger lover whose rules operate on semantic categories like Agent and Object, the older lover's passive rule operates on the semantic category Instrument rather than the syntactic category Subject or Noun Phrase. That is, when an agent is the actor, the lover uses the active voice, but when an instrument is the cause of the action, the lover chooses the passive voice. This seems to reflect their semantic emphasis. According to most grammatical theories, transformations apply to syntactically defined categories, *not* semantically defined ones. In other words, the *syntactic* component of a grammar would have *one* passive rule that operates in a certain way whether the logical subject is an agent or an instrument. The *semantic* component, on the other hand, differentiates by semantic case, for instance, instruments versus agents. Lovers, then, have a passive rule that applies in a semantically restricted environment, namely, when an instrument is the logical subject. This is a semantic restriction since Instrument and Agent are semantic categories. This is a semantic constraint that does not appear in the adult syntax of passivization. Leavers, too, have a restricted passive rule. Their passives, however, apply only when objects are in a *relationship* of reversibility. Their restriction is not governed by syntax or semantics in the traditional sense. Reversibility is determined by real-world constraints, relating, for instance, to the ability of either object logically to function as the actor. In fact, the reversible passives that were formed involved mutual activity such as chasing, where both the chaser and the chased are involved in the activity. We saw that younger leavers are attuned to the social aspects of situations. Thus leavers' language in general, and their passives in particular, seem to be more heavily influenced by the nonlinguistic environment than is the lovers'. The pattern and the formal markings of the passive (syntactic elements) are salient to leavers, but their choice as to where to apply the rule is governed by real-world concerns of reversibility. Reversibility, as opposed to the semantic feature Instrument, seems, too, to relate to the distinction of "global" versus "analytic." To decide whether a rule applies on the basis of the relationship of the elements reflects a more gestalt or global approach, whereas to decide whether a rule applies on the basis of the semantic features of one word reflects a more analytic approach.

If this analysis is correct, it implies that the initial noun-emphasis strategy that a child adopts can influence the course of development. Even well past the stage where the syntactic/semantic strategies described by Bloom merge, speakers may still exhibit differences related to those strategies. The strategies have a broader basis than just that implied in the distinction of syntax versus semantics; global versus analytic approaches may be the most appropriate way to distinguish the strategies. We can, then, add to our list of characteristics of lovers versus leavers the fact that they produce different kinds of passives in different kinds of environments. We also see that although the paths may differ, leavers and lovers end up using the full range of passives.

THE COOKIE MONSTER AND NOUNS

I am currently studying noun-phrase elaboration by preschoolers. Children are retrospectively classified as lovers or leavers on the basis of their early one- and two-word utterances. Parents are questioned extensively about their child's first utterances. Some parents have shared with me tapes of their child's early language. On the basis of these data, I have been able to classify some children's first words as typical of Nelson's referential or expressive strategies, or their first sentences as corresponding to Bloom's nominal or pronominal types. So far I have been able to identify, test, and score only a few lovers and leavers, but the preliminary results look most interesting. (Interestingly, the few left-handers I've come across all appear to be leavers, supporting Peters'[7] suggestion that cerebral dominance may play a role in noun-emphasis strategies.)

To elicit noun phrases, we ask the child to tell Cookie Monster where a cookie is hidden. Pieces of felt, varying in size, shape and color, hide the cookie. A cookie is placed under one piece of felt among three others. The child describes to a Cookie Monster puppet which piece covers the cookie. The Cookie Monster (who has been hiding his eyes) provides feedback as to the effectiveness of the child's description. He will, for example, ask for clarification, as in "Which black one?" or "Which big one?" We are looking not just at length of noun phrase, but also at the appropriateness of the descriptions. In a similar task, Ford and Olson[15] found that children as young as 4 years did not give an invariant label or same-phrase designation to an object, but rather represented the object by using different adjectives depending on the context. In other words, they elaborated the noun phrase in ways appropriate to the context. For example, the same felt piece (a large black one) would be described as a large one in the context of small pieces and as a black one in the context of white pieces. In this sort of elaboration, the minimum redundancy hypothesis, as it is called, predicts that the noun phrase will be elaborated enough for a naive listener to pick out the appropriate object, but no unnecessary (redundant) information will be included.

The protocols from lovers versus leavers look quite different. Consider the following descriptions from a lover, aged 5 years, 6 months [5;6] "The big red square," "Under a big white square," "Under a little red square." A leaver, aged 5;4½ sounds very different: "It's red and it's a square," "It's the big one," "It is under the circle," "That one is black and it's a square." Both children are capable of giving information about shape, size, and color, but the lover appears to be able to do it within one noun phrase.

In terms of redundancy of information, lovers appear to differ from leavers. The same lover just mentioned, on nine trials out of the ten, described the target piece of felt in terms of all three features (size, color, and shape), although at least one aspect was redundant in each case. The leaver, however, never gave more than two pieces of information about each target. On three trials, he gave minimally redundant descriptions that uniquely described the target, on three other trials, he gave sufficient information that was redundant with respect to one aspect, and on another three trials, his descriptions were not sufficient to uniquely identify the objects. (He did not respond on one of the ten trials.) The lover, then, was not following the minimum-redundancy strategy at all, while the leaver was attempting to. This seems to fit our general lover/leaver pattern. The leaver is more sensitive to the nonlinguistic context and has a more personal-social emphasis; in this case, the leaver considers the social demands of the task. The lover's noun phrases are more elaborate, but independent of the nonlinguistic context. The lover, like Bernstein's middle-class speaker, uses linguistic devices to specify the referent. The leaver relies on the situational context.

More subjects have to be tested and scored to see whether these results hold for other preschoolers, but they suggest that early noun-emphasis affects later language use in predictable ways. These differences, like the differences in forming passives, reflect differential emphasis on the social and nonlinguistic context.

A LEAVER (LONGITUDINALLY)

To find out more about the language of leavers and to explore the question of continuity of noun emphasis during development, we need to follow leavers longitudinally. We've been talking as though once a lover, always a lover. This may well be false; children may shift back and forth from one emphasis to the other during development. Lovers may be able to become leavers and vice versa. Only longitudinal data can tell us.

The general strategy in our longitudinal study is to look for violations of alleged universals. If our leaver's language differs systematically from that which the literature leads us to expect, then we can look for an explanation in terms of our general knowledge about leavers' language. Thus, the additions to our catalogue of lover/leaver differences arising from this study should be seen as hypotheses since they are based on a single subject. Even if these differences do not reflect noun emphasis, they are results not accounted for (or even reported) in the literature. We can safely assume that processes found in this child's language operate in some other children's language as well. Looking at this child's language from the perspective of her as a leaver allows a preliminary analysis to be made.

Let's begin with some background on our leaver. Kelly is an extreme example of a leaver: less than 35 percent of her first 50 words were common nouns. Many of her first phrases were stereotyped social forms such as "Thank you," "Have a good day," "See you later," and "I like it." Most of her first sentences had a "pivot-open" look: "no," "hi," "bye," "it" and "that" were used with a wide variety of words. Kelly is the first-born daughter of a philosopher and a psycholinguist who provided a linguistic environment that was normal enough to produce a lover as a second child. Like that of other leavers, Kelly's early language was somewhat slower than most of the children reported in the literature. Like Peters' leaver, she was left-handed and had a gestalt strategy.[7] For example, at the age of 1;3, upon my return home, she would say something like "Hi, ah goo ga. Goo ga. Hi, hi." This was uttered apparently in response to my frequent questions about whether she'd been a good girl. Like the leavers in the passive study, Kelly produced reversible passives (often with the word order incorrect), but never nonreversible ones. Her early word order was variable. She seemed in all of her linguistic and nonlinguistic behavior to be very much a seeker of patterns. For example, at 1;4, she was taken to Churchill Downs where she observed the ritual of people standing in a crowd, and yelling "Go!" while waving their arms. For quite some time after that, she repeated this same pattern whenever she was in a crowd. It has always been important to Kelly that her breakfast consist of Wheat Chex *on top of* Cheerios and not the other way around. Of the children in the literature, Kelly's language development most resembled that of Kim, the adopted Vietnamese daughter in Doonesbury cartoons[16]: Kelly spoke "media-ese." Like the child described by R. Clark,[10] she incorporated whole undifferentiated phrases into a word slot. At the two-word stage, "poor precious Kelly" operated as a unit. Before she was 2, she frequently greeted strangers with "Hi, how ya doin'?" "Have a nice day!" "Hang in there," and "See ya later." Kelly could repeat verbatim dozens of long nursery rhymes and songs.

Kelly's general pattern of language development, then, shares similarities with those described according to Bloom's pronominal, Nelson's expressive, and Peters' gestalt views. What happens to Kelly's language after 2½ to 3 years of age should give us information about the later consequences of starting out as a leaver.

For Kelly, language was a way of engaging adults in some kind of game. Much of her language involved word games and jokes. First we will look at examples of her metalinguistic abilities and some of her jokes, then we will turn to her unusual production and comprehension of questions.

THE EMERGENCE OF KELLY AS COMEDIENNE

According to Slobin,[17] "the capacity to reflect on the form, meanings, and uses of language is clearly present at a very early age." He discussed his daughter's early metalinguistic awareness and suggested that being exposed to a series of foreign languages may have stimulated early attention to linguistic phenomena. Another way linguistic awareness may be stimulated is through language games. Kelly's awareness of language as play emerged very early. For example, at age 1;4, Kelly put her foot through an armhole in a nightgown, and said "Shoe," laughing hysterically. Later, she put her foot in a tennis ball container, and said "Shoe," again laughing. (It is hard to believe that this is an overgeneralization based on function!) At age 1;8, she said "Cow go moo. Mommy go mamoo. Daddy go dadoo." Her early jokes often involved violating semantic restrictions. "Bed cry" would be accompanied by shrieks of laughter.

When Kelly heard a new word, she would try it out, as when, at age 1;11, I told her I was proud of her:

Kelly: Daddy's proud of you. Grandma's proud of you. Uncle David's proud of you. Hamburger *not* proud of you. Ha, ha.

She often corrected our language, again demonstrating sophisticated linguistic knowledge. At age 2;9 I told her she was a good cook. She replied: "No, I'm a good cook*er!*" At age 2;11, this dialogue took place:

Mother: Do you have a donut half?

Kelly: Sorry! A half of a donut.

Kelly also "improved" songs. At 2;3 we heared that "Little Bo People had lost her steeple," and at 2;2, "Rudolph the red-nosed reindeer, you'll go down and get a hamburger." At 2;9 the following occurred:

Kelly [singing]: Mommy, listen: Somebody come and play with me [a Sesame Street song]. Somebody come and play with I.

Mother: Oh, that's silly. It's supposed to be "me."

Kelly: Somebody come and play with I----van! Ha, ha.

Somebody come and play with pee.

Somebody come and play with Pee----ter! Ha, ha.

Somebody and play with cheese.

Somebody come and play with Cheez----Whiz! Ha, ha.

Kelly also delighted in phonetic games. At age 3;3, she began starting the last syllable of every content word with a "t" and stressing that syllable: "banana" became "bana*ta*"; "penny" became "pen*tee*"; "dinner" became "din*ter*"; "strawberry" became "strawber*tee*"; "Kelly" became "Kel*tee*"; "Mommy" became "Mom*tee*"; "Alec" became "Al*tec*"; and so on.

Kelly was very much aware of language, as evidenced by her statement at 2;10 that her new baby brother couldn't think because he couldn't talk. She was also aware of multiple meanings for the same phonetic sequence, as when at 2;10 she explained that "There are two jeans: Jessica's mommy named Jean and jeans to wear."

At 4;0, I observed a nice example of Kelly's trying to figure out the meaning of a word based on the context. I explained that Bonnie and Kathy lived in the same dormitory. Kelly asked: "Is the mitory for Bonnie's door or Kathy's door?"

All of these examples demonstrate her attention to patterns, attention that no doubt contributed to her metalinguistic awareness. In addition, the more "subjective" use of language typical of leavers may have contributed to her willingness to engage in language games.

Kelly's early questions often demonstrated sophisticated metalinguistic knowledge, too. We turn now to a detailed examination of her questions.

QUESTIONS: COMPREHENSION†

Kelly's development of questions differs from that of the standard child in the literature, that is, the lover. In terms of comprehension, the standard view was expressed by Smith[18]: children between the ages of 1;6 and 2;0 can

† An expanded version of this section appears in the *Journal of Child Language.*[9]

handle only the high-stress content words that they can utter themselves. Thus, very young children respond to the familiar word in questions rather than to the form of a question. We would expect children to be able to distinguish questions from statements on the basis of intonation, but they should not be able to discriminate between different question forms at this age. Questions like *Where's your nose?* and *Is that your nose?* should elicit the same response—probably pointing at one's nose. When Kelly was 1;3 she had a spoken vocabulary of 11 words (uh oh, mm [- to kiss], hi, bye, ball [- to throw], see, mama [- a request for assistance from mother], Dadda [- a request for assistance from daddy and a general greeting], yeah, uh huh, and oh). At this point I asked her a number of questions.[9] We will look only at the naturally occurring questions. Kelly's responses to these are shown in TABLE 3. There were 84 yes-no questions, 77 wh-questions, and 54 tag questions. For comparison purposes, I looked at her responses to 50 statements. An affirmative response was given regardless of whether or not she understood the question. For example, when I asked her if she thought the bus would be on time, she said "Yeah." The negative responses included head shaking to questions like "Do you want more milk?" An example of a meaningful verbal response is the following:

Mother: Whatcha got?

Kelly: See. [holding up object]

An example of an appropriate nonverbal response would be the following:

Mother: Do you want juice?

Kelly: [goes to the refrigerator]

The differences between responses to all three types of question-forms were significant ($p < 0.05$). Yes-no questions and tag questions both differ significantly from statements; but responses to wh-questions and statements are similar. Kelly was more likely to respond verbally after questions than after statements: 56 percent of questions resulted in a verbal response, whereas only 26 percent of statements elicited a verbal response. Looking at types of questions separately, we see that yes-no questions elicited verbal responses 74 percent of the time, tag questions, 61 percent, and wh-questions only 31 percent.

TABLE 3
FREQUENCY OF RESPONSES TO ADULT UTTERANCES*

Child's response	Type of Adult Utterance			
	Yes-No Q	wh-Q	Tag Q	State-ments
None	11	46	18	32
Affirmative ("yeah" or "uh huh")	61	4	15	1
Negative (vigorous headshaking)	3	0	0	0
Other verbal expression (jargon or meaningful)	1	20	18	12
Appropriate nonverbal response	8	7	3	5
Totals	84	77	54	50

* From: Horgan.[9] Reproduced by permission.

Looking at Kelly's later language shows an interesting shift in focus. At 19 months, her vocabulary was just over 50 words. Suddenly her vocabulary increased dramatically when she discovered that everything had a name. Within a very short time, she knew the name of almost everything in her environment. The proportion of common nouns in her vocabulary increased to more than 70 percent. At the same point, three other things simultaneously occurred. (1.) Her comprehension increased dramatically. This was noticed independently by her mother, father, and babysitter. (2.) She no longer responded differentially to wh-questions and yes-no questions. A repeat of this study yielded no differential responses based on the form of questions. (3.) Kelly shifted to what Bloom *et al.* call the nominal reference system.[2] Kelly started combining substantive forms in her two-word utterances, and her language lost the characteristic "pivot-open" look.

The first two changes are probably related. During the earlier period, Kelly was more attuned to the form of utterances. Later, as she became more aware of nouns, she focused more on the content words—the nouns. Hence she no longer responded differentially to different question forms. Her comprehension increased dramatically since content words provide more informative clues to meaning than does the form of an utterance. So we see that Kelly's comprehension of questions seems to fit in with her leaver characteristics and again is different from that of the child typically reported in the literature. Crosby[19] reports that her leaver son also discriminated questions on the basis of their form. I repeated this study with my lover son several times and found no differential responses based on the form of questions: he treated "Is that your nose?" like "Where's your nose?" from the age of 12 months until the present (20 months).

From Kelly's question data, we can see that the merging of styles described for production occurs with comprehension as well. We see, too, that characteristics of the leaver strategy also apply to comprehension. Looking at Kelly's question production before and after the merging of her strategies should give us more information about the continuity of noun emphasis.

QUESTIONS: PRODUCTION

Kelly's question *production* also seems to differ from that of a lover. Jill and Peter De Villiers,[20] in discussing whether or not Washoe (the chimp) really asks questions, cite the kind of evidence we would need to credit Washoe with the semantic intent of "really" asking a question. To accept that Washoe asks questions, we would have to be satisfied that (1) she lacks information; (2) she seeks it; and (3) that she then acts in accordance with it. If we use the same criteria for Kelly, we would have to conclude that she did not "really" ask questions until age 3;6.

The final damning evidence against Washoe as a question-asker is that, despite the fact that she was asked "What's this?" thousands of times, there are no reports of her asking for the name of a new object. This, according to De Villiers and De Villiers, is the first, and for years the most prevalent, question that children typically ask. Indeed, Ingram[21] describes one landmark of Piaget's stage 6 of the sensorimotor period as the appearance of "What's that?" Leave it to a leaver: Kelly didn't ask "What's that?" until age

2;6. It wasn't that she didn't notice new objects, she just preferred her own labels for them. When she was barely 2 years, we took her to a gourmet store where she labeled odd cooking devices with nonsense words. I carefully recorded them all, trying to decide if they bore some phonetic similarity to some perceptually similar item. I took her back the next week and she relabeled them all with new "words." Kelly never asked us to do her labeling for her—she'd simply point at a new object and say "Oh! See kang!" or "Oh, a skime!"

Slobin reports that between 3 and 4 years his daughter was uncertain about the fixed or variable nature of word-referent relationships.[17] He suggests that her exposure to foreign languages may have contributed. Slobin's daughter believed that *"bread* really is 'bread,' though it may be called *Brot* or *hleb* or *ekmek* in certain special language games." Kelly, although not exposed to a variety of languages, *started* with the notion that the relationship between word and object is variable and up to the speaker to specify.

Most preschoolers believe words are immutably linked to their referents. Like early linguists they adhere to "Ding Dong" or "Bow Wow" theories. According to Vygotsky[22] words first function as a property of the referent and only later serve as symbols. Kelly's loose attitude about word-object relationships may reflect her extreme, characteristically leaver, lack of concern with nouns and her global approach to meaning. A lover, seeing language as primarily a referential system, would no doubt take the relationship between words and referents somewhat more seriously than Kelly does.

Kelly's first question form appeared at 2;0 and consisted of a stereotyped opener combined with an undifferentiated phrase or sentence, as "How about daddy go get a hamburger?" or, said the day after Christmas, "How about open more presents?" or even "How about what do you want to eat?" when she wanted *me* to ask *her* what she wanted to eat! Her early *how about-*questions serve as requests for actions, but not for information.

At 2;1, a handful of "typical" questions appeared, all locative, as in "Where Mommy can sit?" She quickly abandoned this conventional question after only a week and turned to using our questions to her: "Are you all done?" [while taking off her bib and telling us she had finished eating] or "Do you need to go potty? [telling us she needed to "go potty"]. These echolalic-type questions without pronoun reversal are often cited in the literature as examples of autistic speech, but they may occur among leavers. As in the Churchill Downs example, Kelly had extracted the social pattern in the situations and simply repeated verbatim the constant linguistic form that went with the situation.

Kelly, like some mothers, also used questions as prompts. This may reflect the social-control emphasis of the expressive/personal-social style. Like the mother who wants to control her child's behavior by questions such as "Can you say thank you?," Kelly used questions to control conversations. The following is a typical such conversation.

Mother: Hi, Kelly.
Kelly: Did you have fun with Daddy?
Mother: Did you have fun with Daddy?
Kelly: Yeah.

Mother: What did you do today?
Kelly: Did you ride on the blue horsey at the shopping center?
Mother: Oh, did you ride on the blue horsey?
Kelly: At the shopping center? Yeah.
Mother: That sounds like fun. What did you get at the shopping center?
Kelly: Did you get a nice ice cream cone?
Mother: I dunno, did you get a nice ice cream cone?
Kelly: Yeah.

These language games became increasingly complex. At 2;6:

Kelly: What does Jennifer have named Sheila?
Daddy: I dunno. What does Jennifer have named Sheila?
Kelly: A doggie named Sheila.
Kelly: What does Mary have named Alice?
Daddy: I dunno. What does Mary have named Alice?
Kelly: Does she have a pussycat named Alice?
Daddy: Does she have a pussycat named Alice?
Kelly: Yeah.

"Riddles" also occurred at 2;6:

Kelly: How do aspirins make?
Mother: Huh?
Kelly: How do aspirins make?
Mother: I dunno. How do aspirins make?
Kelly: They make you feel better.

and

Kelly: What did mommy woke?
Daddy: I dunno, what?
Kelly: Up.

At 2;7, these games often involved Kelly's setting up our linguistic expectations, then violating them.

Kelly: Do we kick Mary?
Mother: No, we don't kick Mary.
Kelly: Do we kick Jennifer?
Mother: No, we don't kick Jennifer.
Kelly: Do we kick the swimming pool?
Mother: No, we don't kick the swimming pool.
Kelly: We kick *in* the swimming pool. *Ha ha.*

and at 3;0:

Kelly: Mommy, do you love me?
Mother: Yes.
Kelly: Do you love me *to hit you? Ha ha.*

In all of these examples, we see her attention to form and patterns, the personal-social use of language rather than the referential use, and her emphasis on language as a game.

From 2;1 we heard Kelly, in solitary play, asking questions and answering them. For example at 2;4, in the bathtub: "I have an idea. Mommy has an idea. Do the soap have an idea? *No!!* Soap don't have ideas!"

She clearly had the syntactic ability to form questions, but at this stage, "How about X?" was still the only question that seemed to function pragmatically like a question. In other ways Kelly's grammar was quite complex: "Bunny has freckles, but monkey don't have any. Jessica's crying, but Kelly don't ever cry anymore. Bunny wants to go see Daddy who's typing. I wanna give the new baby to Uncle David because he don't have a baby."

At 2;5, *where*-questions reemerged, always referring to a lost object. *Where*-questions, thus, only appeared in a certain situation. At 2;6, a visit to Grandma sparked a new kind of situationally-specific question. During the visit, there was much looking at old pictures of daddy, Uncle David, Grandma, and so on. We would say "Do you know who this is?" or, if we had looked at the picture before, "Do you remember who that is?" Kelly would point at pictures of people—in magazines or anywhere—and ask "Do you remember who that is?" When we said "No, who is it?" she looked puzzled and didn't respond. Her use of "Do you remember?" questions, again like the Churchill Downs example, demonstrates her attention to the social pattern. Kelly learned the constant linguistic forms that go along with social situations and simply repeated them in similar situations.

Kelly's first "What's that?" questions appeared during this visit. Upon returning home, the "Do you remember?" questions fell out of her speech, presumably because the social, or nonlinguistic, context in which they occurred no longer existed. "Do you remember?" questions are used at Grandma's house. The "What's that?" questions remained, but decreased in frequency.

Kelly's question use demonstrates that she knew how to use the lover system, but she preferred her own system, which was linked more to the nonlinguistic social context. Again we see that although a speaker has control of both systems, she may still emphasize one.

At 2;7, tag questions appeared, usually referring to something she had done, as in "Kelly did a big jump, did she?" At about the same time, questions appeared that were actually offers for a command performance: "Do you wanna see me do a trick?" Or, playing with tongue depressors at the pediatrician's: "Dr. Schecter, do you wanna hear me play Beethoven on my stick instrument?"

During all this time, we heard increasingly complex questions in her solitary play, but in "real" interaction, no questions fitting the De Villiers' criteria appeared. At 2;11, we heard a few "Whatcha doing?" questions. At 3;0, tag questions with "Right" came in. (Kelly, naturally, felt compelled to answer these herself with "Right!") Finally at 3;2, Kelly began asking questions that seemed to request information. She did not, however, act on that information:

Kelly: Is this your right leg?
Mother: No, it's my left leg.
Kelly: Well, actually your left leg *is* your right leg.

Also at 3;2, she asked "Daddy, is this wrong side out or right side in?" Many of her questions at this age dealt with opposites: left-right, up-down, in-out. Also at this age, she began another question game: asking what letters words started with. Again, she did not act on that information.

After 3;2 Kelly began asking more questions, but they were not of the type described by the De Villiers. Questions like "Mommy, when you were a baby, were you in somebody's tummy?" were frequent, but questions like "What's for lunch?" simply did not occur. At 3;6 she finally began to ask questions that would satisfy even the De Villiers.

What can we conclude from all this? Kelly obviously had the linguistic competence to form questions. But clearly she was not motivated to use her syntactic forms to improve her communicative effectiveness. Kelly did not see language as a means; language was a game. Questions were a way of engaging in a social game, but not a means of acquiring information or labeling the world. Kelly was more concerned with controlling social interaction than with controlling and labeling the physical world around her. Much of the current work, like the De Villiers' question criteria, reflects pragmatic concerns that may not characterize all language learners. Such a focus is obviously too narrow. Because of the social and game potential of questions, questions may be a fruitful area in which to study such individual differences.

A LOVER/LEAVER FRIENDSHIP

In all aspects of her language, Kelly was not terribly interested in using language to communicate wants or needs. To appreciate how this noncommunicativeness or nonpragmatic approach contrasted with a lover's use of language, we can look at her in a free-play situation with a lover friend. At 2;8, I recorded Kelly playing with a little friend who was slightly older. Their MLUs were quite close: 4.62 (Jennifer) and 4.57 (Kelly). The differences in their use of language was striking. Jennifer, a classic lover, spoke clearly; her language to adults was primarily for communication. She asked and answered questions very appropriately. Jennifer was a child with whom you could have a meaningful dialogue. Jennifer's utterances were mostly well-formed and fairly uniform in length; her errors were highly predictable overgeneralizations. In cases where her speech was difficult to understand, it was easy to guess her intention from the context: Jennifer talked mostly in the here and now and was usually saying something both meaningful and appropriate to the situation. Jennifer differentiated between speech to herself and that directed to others; her egocentric speech was less well-formed. Jennifer's play was more complex and mature than Kelly's. For example, she "cooked dinner" in a very realistic way.

Kelly's language was much more animated and made greater use of intonation and register. Kelly's questions were rhetorical or games; she usually answered them herself. She talked in jargon, had a higher proportion of egocentric speech than did Jennifer, and sang to herself more, usually in rhymes. Kelly's syntax showed more variation—some of her sentences were extremely long and convoluted. Kelly made more errors of a less-predictable type. Kelly's language was harder to comprehend, at least partly because she often said completely nonsensical things, using words she couldn't possibly know the meaning of (corporation). She also made references to things that happened months ago or imaginary events. Her language to adults was very much like her egocentric speech. While Jennifer busied herself cooking with toy pots and pans on the toy stove, Kelly explained to me that "It's not really a stove, but actually it's a computational stove and potty chair." In her play, Kelly had a very high tolerance for degraded stimuli. At one point, she needed an umbrella and settled on a little plastic "G" for her umbrella. It was often impossible to figure out the theme of Kelly's game on the basis of her language and props. Jennifer tried doggedly to engage Kelly in a conversation or in her cooking; Kelly preferred her private conversations and games.

CONCLUSIONS AND IMPLICATIONS

We have seen that not all children follow the same course of language development. Much investigation remains to be done. Our lover/leaver distinction is too gross; we need to look at other kinds of individual differences to see how they affect noun emphasis. Much more longitudinal research is needed to find out about the continuity of noun emphasis. After making the "nominal shift," Kelly continued to show leaver characteristics. Other children may not. The social-class data suggest that environmental demands affect noun emphasis. Not only might differences in environment affect the course of language development, but also different environments might react to different language styles in different ways. In Kelly's middle-class, "progressive" environment, her language was interpreted as funny, charming, even poetic. Would there have been less acceptance of her language in a different environment? The interaction among speaker, listener, and linguistic style becomes even more complex when we consider how features of the speaker might evoke different responses in different environments. Would a less-bright, working-class leaver's language be accepted as readily as Kelly's?

We need, also, to explore language use in different situations. Throughout our discussion, we have seen that speakers learn to control both subsystems. How do they learn this code switching? In which situations do they emphasize one style over the other? The question data suggest that noun emphasis affects comprehension as well as production, even though the demands are quite different. We need controlled studies of leavers and lovers in different situations so that we can see if and at what ages their performances converge. All the data indicate that lovers and leavers concentrate on different aspects of the same situation. Preliminary data that I am collecting suggest that preschool lovers tend to make more mistakes on the grammatical object in comprehension tasks, whereas leavers tend to make more errors on the grammatical subject.[23] This suggests that lovers are attending more to the subject of a sentence, while leavers are paying more attention to the predicate. Thus, in a sentence like "The girl threw the frisbee," a lover would be especially concerned with who is doing the action, whereas a leaver would be especially concerned with what she's throwing.

Finally, we need to find out more about why children develop as lovers or leavers. Bloom et al.[2] argue that "variation in child speech is a function of individual cognitive development in interaction with different aspects of the linguistic code." Nelson[1] suggests that different parental interaction styles may influence that child's strategy. From our discussion here, it is clear that many factors interact to produce a lover or a leaver. First, there appear to be idiosyncratic preferences: we find lovers and leavers among all social classes, both sexes, in all types of families, and with mismatched siblings. Yet the environment must have some input since we find disproportionate numbers of lovers among first-born children of well-educated parents. The findings on handedness are suggestive; the right and left hemispheres of the brain process information in different ways. The left side, which is dominant for right-handers and some left-handers, processes incoming information in a sequential or analytic style. Research has shown a left hemisphere superiority in right-handed subjects for perception of language. The right hemisphere, which is dominant for about half of left-handers, appears to process input in a more gestalt manner and is superior in processing melodies and intonation contours of whole sentences.[7] Thus, cerebral dominance may affect whether one becomes a lover or a leaver.

The suggestion that leavers may often have their language ability underestimated underscores the practical importance of this work. We need to understand more about the leaver's language not just to complete our theories, but also to implement successful intervention programs for children with language problems. Lovers' language, because it is the norm among the middle class and the precocious child, is seen as superior. As a *reductio ad absurdum* argument against that, I submit the following noun phrase from an unnamed student's term paper: "Rehabilitative treatment of youngsters once involved in the formal criminal justice system using programs that have the primary goal of participation in the development of employment organization in interrelationships with agencies with the intention of rehabilitation of delinquent behavior." (Mercifully the sentence ended before coming to a verb.) Elaborated noun phrases are not inherently superior to unelaborated noun phrases. Referential language is not inherently superior to expressive language.

To use our evergrowing knowledge of the language acquisition process, we must know how generalizable our results and theories are, the range of differences that exist among normal children, and the differential effects of the environment on children with different language styles. It is time to explore the language of the leaver. After all, not everyone was born to be a lover.

REFERENCES

1. NELSON, K. 1973. Structure and strategy in learning to talk. Monogr. Soc. Res. Child Dev. **38** (1–2).
2. BLOOM, L., D. LIGHTBOWN & L. HOOD. 1975. Structure and variation in child language. Monogr. Soc. Res. Child Dev. **40** (2).
3. WEPMAN, J. M. & L. V. JONES. 1966. Studies in aphasia: Classification of aphasic speech by the noun-pronoun ratio. Brit. J. Dis. Comm. **1**: 46–54.
4. BERNSTEIN, B. 1962. Social class, linguistic codes, and grammatical elements. Lang. Speech **5**: 221–240.
5. JOHNSTON, R. P. 1977. Social class and grammatical development: A comparison of the speech of five year olds from middle and working class background. Lang. Speech **20**: 317–323.
6. NELSON, K. 1975. The nominal shift in semantic-syntactic development. Cognitive Psychol. **7**: 461–479.
7. PETERS, A. M. 1977. Language learning strategies: Does the whole equal the sum of the parts? Language **53** (3): 560–575.

8. BRANIGAN, G. 1977. Strategies for overcoming durational constraints during the one word period. Presented at a meeting of the Society for Research in Child Development.

9. HORGAN, D. 1978. How to answer questions when you've got nothing to say. J. Child Lang. **5:** 159–165.

10. CLARK, R. 1974. Performing without competence. J. Child Lang. **1:** 1–10.

11. HOLMES, R. 1959. The philosopher's *Alice in Wonderland*. The Antioch Review **XIX:** 133–149.

12. HORGAN, D. 1977. Individual differences in rate of language acquisition. Presented at the Boston University Language Development Conference.

13. RAMER, A. L. H. 1976. Syntactic styles in emerging language. J. Child Lang. **3:** 49–62.

14. HORGAN, D. 1978. The development of the full passive. J. Child Lang. **5:** 65–80.

15. FORD, W. & D. OLSON. 1975. The elaboration of the noun phrase in children's description of objects. J. Exper. Child Psychol. **19:** 371–382.

16. TRUDEAU, G. B. 1978. Doonesbury's Greatest Hits. Holt, Rinehart, and Winston. New York, N.Y.

17. SLOBIN, D. I. 1978. A case study of early language awareness. *In* The Child's Conception of Language. Sinclair, A., R. J. Jarvella & W. J. M. Levelt, Eds. Springer-Verlag. Berlin/Heidelberg/New York.

18. SMITH, C. 1970. An experimental approach to children's linguistic competence. *In* Cognition and the Development of Language. J. R. Hayes, Ed. Wiley. New York, N.Y.

19. CROSBY, F. 1976. Early discourse agreement. J. Child Lang. **3:** 125–126.

20. DE VILLIERS, J. G. & P. A. DE VILLIERS. 1978. Language Acquisition. Harvard University Press. Cambridge, Mass.

21. INGRAM, D. 1976. Sensorimotor intelligence and language development. *In* Action, Gesture, and Symbol: the Emergence of Language. A. Lock, Ed. Academic Press. New York, N.Y.

22. VYGOTSKY, L. S. 1962. Thought and Language. M.I.T. Press. Cambridge, Mass.

23. HORGAN, D. 1979. The importance of word order: Differences between comprehension and production and differences between individuals. *In* New Approaches to Language Acquisition. Ketteman, B. & R. E. St. Clair, Eds. Tübingen Beitrage Lingvistik, Germany.

LOGIC IN EARLY CHILD LANGUAGE*

Roy D. Pea†

*Department of Experimental Psychology
The Rockefeller University
New York, New York 10021*

This paper addresses one central aspect of the development of negation in early child language: the emergence of uses of negatives such as "no" and "not" for the purpose of logical denial. Insomuch as this concern touches on the use of negation for logical purposes, I will develop several issues concerning the origins of rudimentary logical competence as reflected in children's speech.

Logic is traditionally confined to distinguishing correct from incorrect arguments, and a great deal of psychological research has focused on the development of logical thinking as it involves such skills.[1, 2] The proposition is a central component of such arguments, and propositions constitute the premises and conclusion of arguments. Such propositions, unlike arguments themselves, are considered to be true or false rather than valid or invalid. Very little attention has been paid to the origins of the child's conception of the truth and falsity of propositions, yet the grasp of this binary distinction is a fundamental touchstone of reasoning and language cognition. The experimental study to be described provides a detailed investigation of children's conceptions of the truth-values of sentences expressing simple propositions; the children studied ranged in age from 1½ to 3 years.

What would such a study tell us? First, it would provide insights into the origins of logical abilities in early language and reveal how the child conceives of the language she uses. Since this knowledge of language incorporates features specific to language, such as truth-conditions, it would further our understanding on metalinguistic development.

Negation is the focus of such an inquiry into the origins of logic and knowledge of language because it is basic to all forms of logic since truth and falsity are related by the logical operation of negation. If a sentence p is true, then its negative, $\sim p$, is false, and vice versa. And the ability to logically negate is at the heart of our conceptualizations of the physical and social worlds, laying a necessary foundation for hypotheses and science by enabling us to posit what is not the case.[3, 4]

The development of logical negation, although not traditionally construed

* This research was supported by the Rhodes Trust and by Grant No. 15125 awarded by the National Institute of Mental Health.

† Present address: Department of Psychology, Clark University, Worcester, Massachusetts 01610.

27

0077-8923/80/0345-0027$01.75/2 © 1980, NYAS

in this vein, may be viewed as germane to the classic problem of establishing the emergence of sentences from the single words first produced by children. Preliminary to presenting an argument for this claim, however, I will outline the links between logical negation and predication. Sentences express relations of predication, and predications require the combination of two elements or ideas known as subject and predicate. Together these elements form a proposition that can, in two-valued logics, form a proposition that can be assessed as true or false. A proposition cannot be formed from either subject or predicate alone. The reason for this is that the subject points out some particular, such as " the ball," and the predicate applies a concept to that particular, like "is red." Thus, the predicative statement "the ball is red" is defined as true if the concept applies to the particular, and false if it does not. Since truth and falsity are mediated by the logical operation of negation, one can see that a fundamental tie exists between logical negation and predication. The set of rules that relate propositions to world-states are truth-conditions for utterances, and a substantial amount of what we know as speakers about language is captured in such rules.[5] The conception of the truth and falsity of propositions thus integrally involves an awareness of these truth-conditions, and the ultimate aim is to establish how and when very young children understand this important aspect of language.

The description of truth-conditions thus far has implied that only multi-word sentences can express predications. After all, how could both subject and predicate be expressed in a single word? But debates early in this century about the nature of the child's single-word speech challenged the rhetorical slant to this question.[6, 7] One contingent held that the child's single words were purely affective, expressing only internal states such as needs, whereas another claimed that the child could, with single words alone, emit "intellectual" speech that made rudimentary statements about the world. This latter group thought that the child speaking only single words could have a concept of predication even though not expressing it linguistically. For example, a child would approach a warm stove, say "hot", and be said to express a "holophrase" or rudimentary sentence, expandable into something like "the stove is hot." The subject was said to be implicit in the situation. Many reasons might underlie the child's curtailed expression, but one thing is clear: this controversy about single-word "predication" is fundamentally linked to whether the child is expressing propositions, which are subject to truth-conditions. The specific nature of this link is critical and will be defined later.

The controversy over "affective" and "intellectual" manifestations of thought in language has become topical once again upon the renewed interest in the language of the child since the 1960s. Oxford "ordinary language" philosophers, such as J. L. Austin, P. F. Strawson, and Paul Grice, focused their language studies on meaning as conveyed by utterances in the contexts of ordinary language use. Investigators into the language of the child have since discovered this work and have become convinced that the philosophers' techniques promised insights into early language meaning. The first studies with such an orientation dealt with children's single-word speech. Gruber[8] found that the child he studied first used words to indicate things and only later to predicate attributes of those things. Both Bates[9] and Bruner[10] have provided evidence that early words first convey requests and direct attention to aspects of the world before they are used in the construction of propositions for predication. And Dore[11] has developed a theory of the growth of speech acts according to which the child first conveys the force of an utterance (such as whether it is intended as a request, demand, or comment) before conveying propositions with her utterances.

All of these recent accounts place importance on the development of predication, yet no one has related the growth of predication to the truth-conditions basic to the assertion of propositions. Modern philosophical logic since Frege[12] is based on the principle that propositions are the bearers of truth-values. A basic tenet of this work is that the ability to conceive of propositions as true or false is one of the most central aspects of language comprehension and use. Marshall[13] anticipated the neglect of truth by the theories of predication development we have mentioned, and he pinned the problem down as one of deciding *what evidence* is relevant to the claim that the child has made the transition from the circumscribed ability of uttering appropriate single words on stimulus occasions (which the empiricist Quine[14, 15] sees as the nature of all early language) to creative and propositional language-use and the linguistic expression of judgments. The prototypes of linguistic judgment, in the writings of such philosophers as Kant who are concerned with this use of language, are judgments of the truth-values of sentences. One may consider statements that relate to stimulus-occasions or those that do not require a world-state for their verification, such as tautologies like "Either the ball is red or not red." Osherson and Markman[16] have found that being able to judge the truth or falsity of such analytic statements is a difficult task even for 7-year-olds. I will be considering only statements that relate to stimulus-occasions.

Statements such as "the ball is red" are true or false depending on the occasion when we use them. Judgments of the truth or falsity of such occasion-sentences reflect knowledge of the rule-governed and symbolic tie between statements and the world. We now return to Marshall's point. If a child can express judgments of truth or falsity about another's use of occasion-sentences, we could conclude that the child had made the major transition from affective language to truth-functional language. And we now return to the controversy of the "holophrase," for if the child has a concept of predication as revealed by the expression of truth-functional judgments, such as negations, we can infer that the child is asserting propositions in her use of single words.

PREVIOUS LITERATURE ON LOGICAL NEGATION

Several naturalistic studies of negation development and experimental studies of negation comprehension provide an empirical setting and some suggestive findings for an account of early logical negation.

Child-language diarists such as Leopold and Guillame observed that children as young as 18 months of age used negation to deny statements and to express the negative meaning "it is not so." These anecdotes cannot be independently assessed, however, because contexts of such one-word negative utterances were not provided. Clear examples of spontaneous negative use in sentences that deny propositions expressed by a previous speaker are provided by more recent studies of early language, such as the seminal observations of Bellugi[17] and Bloom.[18] In their data, exchanges such as the following are found in children's speech at age 2 years:

Adult: Daddy's getting old, huh?
Child: No, I get old[17] (p. 74)
Adult: Doesn't that look like scrambled egg? [referring to yellow wheel on a plate]
Child: That's not scramble[18] (p. 200).

Another common phenomenon observed at the same age is the practice of producing antithetical phrases.[7, 19-21] An example is provided by Snyder's child, who made the following antithetical statement about two different boats: "not that boat hot, that boat hot."[21] Weir[22] has also observed antithetical negations in the presleep monologues of her son. One of these consisted of a statement that is immediately contradicted and followed by an affirmative alternative:

Child: That light. No, is vacuum cleaner. Like vacuum cleaner here[22] (p. 107).

Examples such as these suggest that the 2-year-old child may be capable of utilizing negation for the logical purpose of denying a false statement and that he or she is highly aware of the contrast between affirmative and negative sentences. To firmly establish the soundness of these conjectures, though, substantial evidence is required from a controlled setting.

The first experimental attempt at asking children to judge the truth or falsity of sentences was published by Slobin[23] in 1966. Subjects ranging in age from 6 to 20 years verified simple passive and active sentences that varied in truth-value (either true or false) and that were either affirmative or negative in form. These two variables result in four types of sentences, which are presented in TABLE 1. These four types are true-affirmatives, false-affirmatives, false-negatives, and true-negatives, and simple examples (not the actual sentences Slobin used) are presented in the Table.

Slobin's research elaborated on a paradigm established by Miller[24] and Mehler[25] in which the difficulty of sentence comprehension was operationalized by the measures of reaction time and number of errors made. Subjects were asked to judge whether exemplars of a given statement-type were true or false with reference to a presented picture. Just as in the adult research, Slobin found that on average the affirmative sentences were verified more quickly and with fewer errors than were the negative sentences. He also found that the false-negative sentences were more easily comprehended than the true-negative sentences. The important finding for the issues of our concern is that significant agreement was displayed in the ranking of sentence-types for performance difficulty across the entire age-range of 6- to 20-year-olds studied: true-affirmatives < false-affirmatives < false-negatives < true-negatives. Slobin's study was the first direct test of children's comprhehension of logical negation, but since the 6-year-olds revealed a comprehension-difficulty hierarchy that matched that of the adults', the ontogenesis of this ability is still an open question.

TABLE 1
STATEMENT TYPES, EXAMPLES OF TYPES, AND THEIR DESCRIPTIONS

Abbreviation	Statement Type	Example*	Description
TA	True affirmative	"That is a ball"	Fact
FA	False affirmative	"That is a car"	Falsehood
FN	False negative	"That is not a ball"	Denial of a fact
TN	True negative	"That is not a car"	Denial of a falsehood

* Stimulus condition: referent = ball.

One additional remark that Slobin[23] makes in passing is central to the development of negation. Several of his youngest subjects refused to accept any of his negative statements in the experiment as true. The reason for this considerably complicates our enterprise to investigate the development of logical negation. Propositions are not usually denied without an affirmative context, even when such negatives would be true. In traditional formulations of this social constraint, a proposition is not negated unless someone has asserted or presupposed it.[26-30] The social conditions for negation thus interact with the logical conditions, and this fact suggests that we must consider both pragmatic and semantic aspects of negation for any developmental account of logical negation. It will be particularly important to consider the cognitive difficulty of the social aspects of negation since it would seem to require a considerable degree of nonegocentrism with regard to knowing about the belief system and presuppositions of others.

The first study to demonstrate dramatically these pragmatic factors in negation comprehension was carried out by Wason,[30] who set up an experimental context in which he could systematically provide "contexts of plausible denial." These contexts, he reasoned, would facilitate the understanding of the "true-negative" stimuli found to be most difficult in sentence-verification experiments such as Slobin's.[23] Wason specifically proposed the exceptionality hypothesis, which claimed that "it is more plausible to deny that an exceptional item possesses an attribute which makes it an exception, than to deny that any unexceptional item possesses the discrepant attribute of the exceptional item."

Wason's hypothesis is best understood in the context of FIGURE 1. The single dark circle differs from the seven similar white circles in only one important attribute, color. The exceptionality hypothesis thus claims that it is more plausible to assert that "Circle 7 is not white" than to assert that "Circle 6 is not black." Wason found support for this hypothesis in that his adult subjects took longer to complete negative sentences that were inplausible according to the hypothesis, such as "Circle 6 is not ____," than to complete ones that were plausible.

Donaldson[31] later did a similar experiment with 5- and 6-year-old children in which the exceptional item also only varied in color from the similar stimuli. She did not find that the exceptionality context aided the completion of negative sentences by the children. However, using a variation in method, de Villiers and Flusberg[32] experimentally demonstrated that 2½- to 4½-year-old children are aware of the pragmatic conditions for negation. These investigators tested Wason's exceptionality hypothesis by varying the stimuli

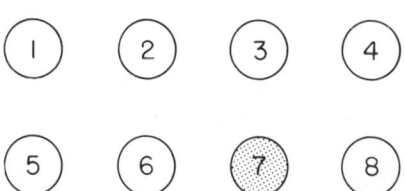

FIGURE 1. Wason's exceptionality hypothesis. It is more plausible to assert that "circle 7 is not white" than to assert that "circle 6 is not black." (After Wason.[30])

along easily-nameable class dimensions, with a typical stimulus set being made up from seven cars and one baby's bottle. Their 3½- and 4½-year-old subjects, like Wason's adults, took significantly longer to complete the implausible negative statements, such as "this is not a bottle" in the context of our example and they made more errors on them than on the plausible negative statements. Of the thirteen 2½-year-olds tested, only eight completed negative sentences at all. The responses of those who did carry out the task yielded differences between the two types of negatives; these differences were similar to those of the older children but nonsignificant. The error data for these 2½-year-olds, however, indicated that plausible negatives are understood earlier than implausible negatives since these subjects made errors for 36 percent of the implausible negatives compared with only 8 percent errors for plausible negatives. We can conclude from this study that apparently even 2½-year-olds are aware of the social, pragmatic conditions for negation. Results of this sentence-completion experiment, however, cannot be used as evidence for young children's knowledge of the logical conditions of negation because a sentence-completion task does not directly tap children's use of negatives to correct false statements. Instead, it only demonstrates their ability to complete true sentences, including negative ones.

Experiments have been devised by Donaldson and her colleagues[33-35] that do directly assess this logical aspect of negation performance. The feature of these studies of most interest for present purposes is a technique that was developed for eliciting judgments from preschool children as to whether statements were true or false. The investigator introduced the children to a talking "panda-bear" and they were told that he could learn to talk if they would only help him get better. The bear frequently made mistakes in describing situations the children could also see. Donaldson trained the children to press a bell when the panda said something "correct" and to press a buzzer when he said something "wrong." With this method she established that children as young as 3½ years could signal truth and falsity by noting a mismatch between a statement and the situation it describes. Younger children were unable to learn the contingencies between devices and judgments.

A talking-doll technique was also used in an unpublished study by De Villiers[36] in which children were explicitly told to tell the doll when he was right or wrong. As in the adult sentence-verification studies, stimuli were simple statements of the four types listed in TABLE 1. Detailed results were not presented in the paper, but De Villiers noted that 2-year-old children, when asked, "could accurately judge the affirmatives" as right or wrong and that 3-year-olds could "accurately label" false-negative statements as wrong, but did not correctly respond to true-negatives. Reaction-time data and error data for the 4- and 5-year-olds revealed the same ordering of statement-type difficulty that Slobin[23] found with older subjects. As one would expect, the greatest number of errors by far occurred in response to true-negative sentences.

In summary, previous experimental studies of children's performance with logical negatives have by and large either ignored very young children or provided only suggestive evidence that 2- and 3-year-olds utilize logical negation. Very young children were instructed to give responses of "right" or "wrong" and generally failed, and their spontaneous use of negatives was never studied. The difficulty of the task may also have contributed to a lack of competent performance for these young children, who had to follow experimental instructions. The usual language experience of such young children consists of extended dialogues, and, as mentioned previously, when children this age are allowed to spontaneously negate false statements in naturalistic settings, they appear to succeed. These discrepancies between experimental and ethological data make it especially important to study the emergence of logical negation by approximating the child's normal language experience of dialogue as much as possible and to simplify the task environment by using simple words and referent stimuli.

THE EXPERIMENTAL STUDY

Given the need to simplify the judgment task for the children, several modifications of the standard sentence-verification paradigm were made. In pilot studies, a technique was developed for eliciting and coding spontaneous logical judgments, particularly the children's use of affirmative, negative, and referent words, in response to sentences of the four types listed in TABLE 1. The technique was a dialogue format for sentence presentations, and the experimental session was composed of a counterbalanced series of two-turn sentence presentations.‡ For the first turn, the experimenter (E) asked the child to give or show him a particular referent from a full set of referents on a table at which the child and E sat. After the child retrieved the referent, E made one of four types of statements (TA, FA, FN, TN; TABLE 1) about their jointly attended referent. This technique proved very successful in eliciting responses from the children, who seemed to interpret the experimental statements as comments upon the retrieval task they had just been asked to perform. Pilot studies indicated that without this dialogue-like setting, children's interest waned rapidly from the isolated-stimulus sentence presentations not preceded by the give/show orientation phase of the current procedure.

The referents for the stimulus statements—real objects such as a toy ball, car, cat, and dog—were chosen because of their frequent appearance among toys and household objects for young children and because words for them are frequently among the first 50 words acquired by children.[37, 38]§

‡ This counterbalancing was pseudorandom, subject to the following constraints: the same truth-value or assertive-form never occurred more than twice in succession; the same referent word was never repeated in successive statements; and the same assertive-form/truth-value pairing was never repeated in successive statements.

§ The full set of referents was: apple, ball, car, cat, dog, hair, mouth, jumping, sitting, eating, drinking, big, little, red, and yellow. The hair and mouth belonged to a doll, and the actions could be executed with the doll. The colors and sizes applied to contrasting sets of balls (four total): small yellow, large yellow, small red, large red; only one ball was on the table for nonadjective-stimulus statement presentations, and the two relevant balls were presented for both the size and color statements. The

Forty children were the subjects of this study: five males and five females at 18, 24, 30, and 36 months of age. Subjects were first given a word-production pretest in order to find out whether they used the referent words. During the experimental session proper, subjects received a maximum of 48 two-turn sentence presentations, 12 of each of the four statement-types (TABLE 1). Children were tested individually, and the sessions were video-taped from a corner of the room.

The videotaped sessions were then transcribed into narrative form and used to determine, for example, the focus of the child's attention during our dialogues. Because the children's responses were often very complex, a detailed coding scheme was devised that classified responses into categories. This system captured the structural complexity of the responses and allowed very specific comparisons of response patterns to the different statement-types.

RESULTS AND DISCUSSION

The logic of analysis in discussing the children's responses is straightforward. The paradigm compares the relative frequencies of a particular kind of response to each of the four different statement-types, rather than the traditional method of tallying the number of correct answers by the experimenter's indices of judgement values, such as "right" or "wrong."[36] Since only minimal differences distinguish the four different statement types, differences in the children's response patterns to the different statement-types provide evidence of the ways in which the statements are differently interpreted by the children. For example, the FN statement in TABLE 1 only differs from the TA in that a negative morpheme occurs after the copula "is." The primary form of data presentation thus consists of comparisons between response-patterns to different statement-types as categorized in the response coding schemes already mentioned. The coding results that follow are presented in proportions rather than as absolute frequencies because the 18- and 24-month-old subjects received fewer overall test sentences. Specifically, 18-month-olds on average received 20 sentences each and 24-month-olds received 32, whereas the 30-month-olds received 46 and the 36-month-olds the full set of 48 sentences.

A brief review of the statement types as they relate to the questions raised earlier about the development of knowledge about the social and logical conditions of negation will usefully frame the results. The different statement types entail increasingly complex processing abilities for comprehension, as expected given the ordering of statement-type difficulty in sentence-verification studies with adults and older children. *True affirmatives* are correct assertions. *False affirmatives* are misnamings requiring correction. *False*

---

use of noun, verb, and adjective stimuli was motivated by Werner and Kaplan's[39] finding that predications emerge in this order, but since few of the 18- and 24-month-old children either produced or comprehended the verbs and adjectives, and since few differences occurred between the types for the 30- and 36-month-olds, the data presented are collapsed across these word categories.

negatives are perhaps the most important type of statement for our concerns about logical development because they not only require correction, but in addition, they involve understanding the negative internal to the sentence. The negative of the false-negative statement is also a denial, an opposition of a true statement. *True negatives*, the fourth type of sentence, also necessitate understanding the negative morpheme as oppositional, but they are removed from the usual affirmative context of denial. No one is proposing that the statement denied by a true negative is true since it is an obvious falsehood, so an understanding of true negatives involves transcending the communicational context of negation and focusing on logical form alone. As seen in studies involving children older than these, such implausible negatives are difficult to understand. To be made more comprehensible they require a plausible context, one not provided by the dialogue format of this experiment.

The results of primary interest concern the children's corrections of the false statement types. One prediction is that if the children are using the negative morphemes they produce to deny false statements, they will use these negations more frequently in response to false affirmatives than to true affirmatives. These statements differ only in truth-value as a result of the different lexical items. Results are presented in FIGURE 2. When the category of response is the use of all responses that contain negative morphemes, this prediction is confirmed most strikingly for the 30- and 36-month-old groups ($\alpha = 0.005$, Wilcoxon matched-pairs sign-rank test) and for the 18- and 24-month-old females ($\alpha = 0.05$, paired-difference t test). Children rarely negated true affirmatives at any age, yet they frequently denied false affirmatives. The complexity of such misnaming corrections radically changes during the period from 18 to 36 months, as one would expect, with

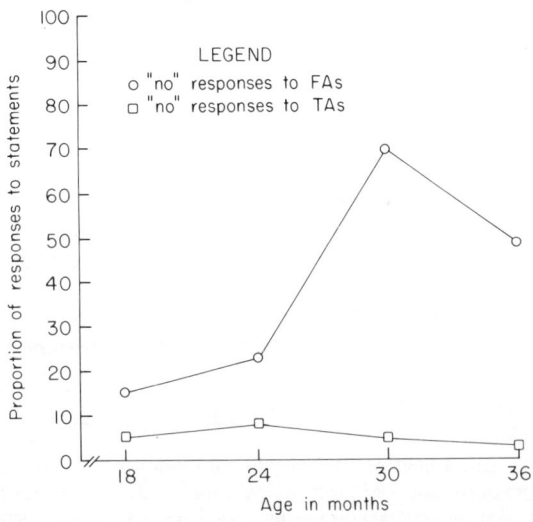

FIGURE 2. Proportion of "no" responses compared for false-affirmative and true-affirmative statements.

the youngest children almost always providing single-word "no" responses to false affirmatives. Children 24- to 36-months-old, however, often elaborated their corrections of false affirmatives by saying things like "no, it's a ball" or "that's not the car." Many responses to false affirmatives made by these older children consisted of conjunctions of two sentences, one right after another, that make explicit the logical relationship between denial, where the child corrects the false affirmative, and assertion, where the child is correctly naming either the referent, the thing referred to in the misnaming, or both. Such logical conjunctions are explicitly oppositional, so that in a typical example when E held up a ball and called it a car, a child said "that's not a car; that's a ball." Explicit oppositions were extremely rare at 18 months of age, but constituted responses to 21 percent of the false-affirmative statements by the 36-month-old children.

The other kind of false statements the children heard were false negatives, which falsely deny a true statement as in "that is not a car" when in fact it was a car. The prediction made earlier for the predominant negation of false-affirmative statements was straightforward because of the interaction of the statement type and the affirmation-negation response system. That is, "no" responses to true affirmatives would be rare, it was predicted, because such responses would be tantamount to falsely denying a true statement. But complications arise with false-negative statements, which can be corrected in two quite different ways. The example to be considered is the stimulus statement "that is not a ball" said in reference to a ball. One can correct this statement by saying "no, it is a ball" and negate the sentence as a whole with the negative morpheme, or one can say "yes, it is" and negate the negative morpheme internal to the false-negative statement with an affirmative morpheme, which serves an oppositional function. Given this two-choice set of correction devices, it becomes clear that any simple comparison of the relative frequency of single-word affirmative and negative responses is uninterpretable. In particular, if the child provides only a solitary "yes" in response to a false-negative statement, one should hesitate to conclude that such a child had "truth-functionally" denied the statement with an affirmative of opposition. Similar problems beleaguer interpretations of solitary "no" responses to false-negative statements, for one could not rule out the possibility that the child might be imitating the negative component of the sentence, an objection that cannot be pressed against the same response to the false-affirmative statements. Several predictions may be fruitfully proposed, however, when the children's responses are sentences rather than single words.

The analysis thus far has centered on "yes" and "no" responses, but the copula also plays a major role in the expression of judgments. The prototypical forms of assertion and denial, according to both classical and modern conceptions of language,[12, 40] are the predicate phrases "it is" and "it is not." These phrases are counterparts in logical function; one asserts, the other denies. The copula thus plays a pivotal role in the investigation of truth-functional assent and dissent, for while the single word "yes" is ambiguous with regard to its logical function in response to false-negative statements, the child's response of "yes it *is*" renders explicit the logical opposition to the false negative by the use of the copula. This is important in an analysis of responses to true-affirmative statements with false-negative statements, which differ only in the word "not." If the child is using the word "yes" oppositionally to deny the false-negative statement rather than to agree mistakenly with it, one would predict that the elaboration of such a response by means of the copula should be more frequent when the child is denying false-negative statements than when the child is agreeing with true-affirmative statements. In FIGURE 3, the data indicate that elaborated "yes" responses, consisting of "yes" and a predicative statement with the copula such as "yes, it *is* a ball," are more frequently used as responses to false negatives than to true affirmatives at both 30 and 36 months of age ($\alpha = 0.01$, Wilcoxon matched-pairs sign-rank test). Elaborated "yes" responses to any statement type at all are rare for the younger groups, so they cannot count as evidence for false-negative statement correction by such children.

However, if a child is using a statement to name the referent with the intent of correcting the false negative by oppositionally asserting its name, one would predict that naming statements with a denial function would frequently include the copula. The relevant comparison involves false negatives and true affirmatives again, and it is predicted that such elaborated referent naming phrases, such as "that is a ball," would be more frequent to false negatives than true affirmatives if they are in fact being used for denial. Analysis of the data presented in FIGURE 4 indicates that 24-month-old females, as well as the 30-month-olds ($\alpha = 0.005$, Wilcoxon matched-pairs sign-rank test) and 36-months-olds ($\alpha = 0.01$, Wilcoxon matched-pairs sign-rank test), frequently corrected the false-negative statements by asserting propositions with the referent name and the copula.

There are several reasons for emphasizing this last result. One is that the

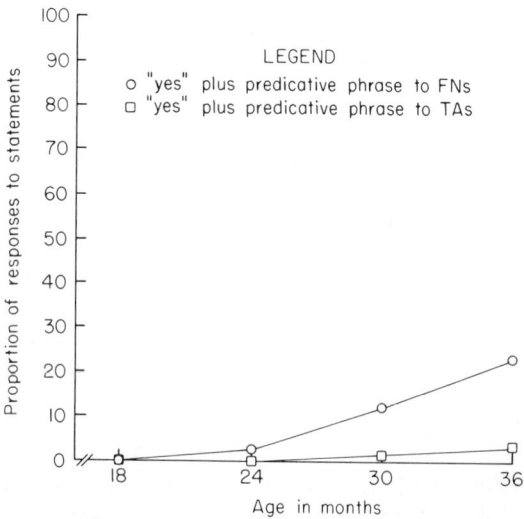

FIGURE 3. Proportion of "yes" plus predicative phrase responses compared for false-negative and true-affirmative statements.

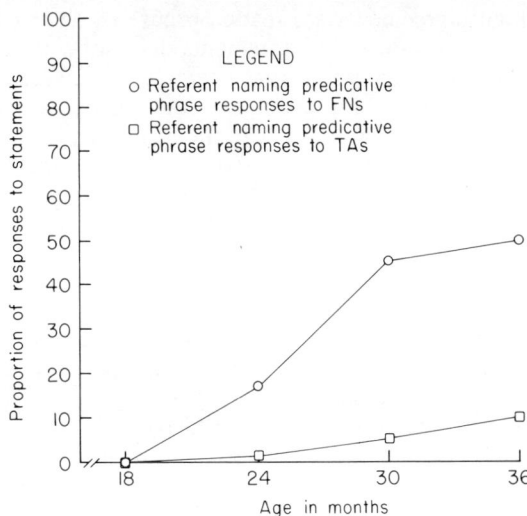

FIGURE 4. Proportion of referent-naming predicative phrase responses compared for false-negative and true-affirmative statements.

data provide another indication of the use of language by very young children to correct false statements. But just as importantly it demonstrates a comprehension of sentence-internal negation by the age of 2 years. This finding stands in contrast to suggestions made by Bellugi[17] that children at that age do not understand internal negation.

One additional finding of interest suggests that 18-month-olds are sensitive to negative morpheme of the false-negative statement type. Such subjects provided the name of the referent in response to 17 percent of the false-negative statements compared with 7 percent of the true-affirmative statements, even though these statement-types only differ in the presence of the word "not." Although still only uttering single words, these children seem to be asserting the referent name to correct the false negative, which suggests a preliminary resolution of the controversy over the nature of the child's knowledge of language and language use during this single-word utterance period. If the 18-month-old is asserting rudimentary propositions and if subsequent research supports this preliminary finding, controversies over whether such children are or are not predicating would be more profitably shifted to questions about *why* they are not expressing predications with sentences.

The children's spontaneous responses to true-negative statements were in general difficult to interpret. One child, a 30-month-old, was forthright in her agreement with such statements in responses such as "yes, it's not." Single-word negative responses were very common from all age groups, and given that the English assent-dissent system allows the use of "no" either in agreement or disagreement,[41] these responses are ambiguous in function. Given the predominance of single-word as opposed to elaborated "no" responses among the 18- and 24-month-old groups, the origins of true-negative statement agreements are made obscure by their brevity. But one form of response to true-negative statements does show that the 36-month-olds utilize negative agreement, in that negative-phrase repetitions, such as "it's not" (in response to, for example, "that is not a ball") are more frequently made to true negatives, where the negative phrase is true, than to false negatives, where it is false ($\alpha = 0.025$, Wilcoxon matched-pairs sign-rank test). It is also clear that the children found true negatives very difficult, for one kind of response was an emphatic and incorrect "yes it *is*!." This response occurred for 15 percent of the true negatives presented to 30-month-olds (compared with 7 percent at 24 months and 5 percent at 36 months) and has the appearance of disagreement. But the focus of disagreement is unclear, and no children offered reasons such as "that's a funny thing to say," which would suggest that the children were commenting on the pragmatic inappropriateness of true negatives.

The most unexpected responses occurred when 2- and 3-year-olds misnamed the stimulus objects, producing their own false statements. In a pretest, the children's use and understanding of the stimulus words from which the test statements were formed were assessed. Otherwise, the putative misnamings might be interpreted as imitations of words the children did not know. The importance of such misnaming responses is best placed in perspective with the findings of false-statement corrections. The children's denials of false statements demonstrate that they recognize the truth-conditions that regulate normal language use in our statements about the world. Such denials utilize truth-functional language, such as affirmation and negation, and express judgments concerning the language use of another person. The denials also reveal the children's implicit awareness of truth-conditions, much as our use of language demonstrates implicit awareness of the rules of grammer in Chomsky's[42] account of language knowledge. When these children also systematically break the correspondence rules of truth by spontaneously saying, as one child did during this study, "this is a garden" while pointing to a ball, they are explicitly showing a reflective knowledge of truth-conditions.

This new form of linguistic knowledge is an important development in the language and thought of the child. It broadens the scope of language cognition beyond the plane of interaction and immediate means-end satisfaction to allow a qualitatively new form of language cognition that is rule-regulated, and in this respect exemplifies critical features of the Soviet "second signal system."[43] Language theorists have thus dwelt upon the importance of lying, a distortion of reality by means of language, and the development of lying was once a topic of great interest. In the work of the Sterns[44] early in this century, lying was said to presuppose a stage of psychic development involving three components: "(1) a consciousness of falsity, (2) intentional deception, and (3) a distinct purpose in view." The children's explicit awareness of the contrast between truth and falsity in their intentional production of false statements in this study shares only the first of these components of lies, a consciousness of falsity. The children did not intend to deceive because the objects were in clear view, not displaced, and displacement is a critical feature of lying.[3, 45] In addition, their false responses were frequently accompanied by laughter, a very loud voice, accentuated intonation, and coy looks to their mothers. No one was being fooled. The children also had no distinct purpose or vested interest in having the experimenter believe their false responses, unlike the lying child who has broken a glass and disclaims herself as agent. But these instances of misnaming do show in an innocent way that the children realize that language can be used untruthfully, and that this realization presupposes a conception of truth and falsity.

IMPLICATIONS

These findings suggest a modification of our conceptualization of the modes of thought available to the very young child. The developmental theories of Piaget and Werner indicate a major development in representational intelligence at 18 months of age, in which a simultaneous differentiation and coordination occurs between signifiers (such as words or other symbols that serve only a representational function) and what they signify (such as objects or events). Language development in the several years after this onset of what has been called "the semiotic function" is typically construed as "preconceptual" and more idiosyncratic than collective in meaning.[46] This view is coincident with descriptions of the young child as egocentric, claims that have seriously eroded in recent years by research indicating that very young children take into account the linguistic, intellectual, and physical skills of other individuals.[47, 48] These previous research efforts focused upon social rule-cognition and were aimed at illuminating what competence children have when allowed to manifest their skills in the domain of simple tasks. The findings of this study indicate that the notation of a logical system, the conception of sentences as true or false, is yet another form of early rule-cognition that the 1½ to 3-year-old has available for conceptualizing the world. This idea should not be surprising when one considers that a capacity for understanding corrections is fundamental to any learning endeavor. This is particularly true in the case of language, where it is crucial to align, at least in part through negative sentences, the new and often idiosyncratic meanings held by the child with the conventional meanings held by the adult.

REFERENCES

1. OSHERSON, D. N. 1976. Logical Abilities in Children. Vol. 4. Erlbaum. Hillsdale, N.J.
2. FALMAGNE, R. J., ED. 1975. Reasoning: Representation and Process in Children and Adults. Erlbaum. Hillsdale, N.J.
3. ALTMAN, S. A.1967. The structure of primate social communication. In Social Communication Among Primates. S. A. Altman, Ed.: 325–362. University of Chicago Press. Chicago, Ill.
4. WILDEN, A. 1972. Structure and Function: Essays in Communication and Exchange. Tavistock. London.
5. EVANS, G. & J. McDOWELL, EDS. 1976. Truth and Meaning. Claredon Press. Oxford.
6. DE LAGUNA, G. 1963. Speech: Its Function and Development. Indiana University Press. Bloomington, Ind. (Originally published in 1927).

7. LEOPOLD, W. F. 1949. Grammar and General Problems in the First Two Years. Vol. 3. Northwestern University Press, Evanston Ill.
8. GRUBER, J. S. 1975. "Topicalization" revisited. Found. Language 13: 57–72.
9. BATES, E. 1976. Language and Context: The Acquisition of Pragmatics. Academic Press. New York, N.Y.
10. BRUNER, J. S. 1975. The ontogenesis of speech acts. J. Child Lang. 2: 1–19.
11. DORE, J. 1975. Holophrases, speech acts, and language universals. J. Child Lang. 2: 21–40.
12. DUMMETT, M. 1973. Frege: Philosophy of Language. Harper & Row. New York, N.Y.
13. MARSHALL, J. C. 1970. Can humans talk? In Biological and Social Factors in Psychlinguistics. J. Morton, Ed: 24–52. Logos Press. London.
14. QUINE, W. V. O. 1960. Word and Object. M.I.T. Press. Cambridge, Mass.
15. QUINE, W. V. O. 1974. The Roots of Reference. Open Court. New York, N.Y.
16. OSHERSON, D. N. & E. MARKMAN. 1974/5. Language and the ability to evaluate contradictions and tautologies. Cognition 3: 213–226.
17. BELLUGI, U. 1967. The Acquisition of the System of Negation in Children's Speech. Unpublished doctoral dissertation, Harvard University.
18. BLOOM, L. 1970. Language Development: Form and Function in Emerging Grammars. M.I.T. Press. Cambridge, Mass.
19. BLOCH, O. 1924. La phrase dans le langage de l'enfant. J. Psychol. (Paris) 21: 18–43.
20. DELACROIX, H. 1930. Le Langage et la Pensée. Paris.
21. SNYDER, A. D. 1914. Notes of the talk of a two-and-a-half year old boy. Pedagogical Semin. 21: 412–424.
22. WEIR, R. H. 1962. Language in the Crib. Mouton. The Hague.
23. SLOBIN, D. I. 1966. Grammatical transformations and sentence comprehension in childhood and adulthood. J. Verbal Learning Verbal Behav. 5: 219–227.
24. MILLER, G. A. 1962. Some psychological studies of grammar. Am. Psych. 17: 748–762.
25. MEHLER, J. 1963. Some effects of grammatical transformations on the recall of English sentences. J. Verbal Learning Verbal Behav. 2: 346–351.
26. BROWN, R. 1973. A First Language: The Early Stages. Harvard University Press. Cambridge, Mass.
27. KANT, I. 1963. Immanuel Kant's Critique of Pure Reason, N. K. Smith, trans. Macmillan. London. (Originally published in 1787).
28. LABOV, W. & D. FANSHEL. 1977. Therapeutic Discourse: Psychotherapy as Conversation. Academic Press. New York, N.Y.
29. STRAWSON, P. F. 1952. Introduction to Logical Theory. Methuen. London.
30. WASON, P. C. 1965. The contexts of plausible denial. J. Verbal Learning Verbal Behavior 4: 7–11.
31. DONALDSON, M. 1970. Developmental aspects of performance with negatives. In Advances in Psycholinguistics. G. B. Flores D'Arcais & W. J. M. Levelt, Eds. North-Holland. Amsterdam.
32. DE VILLIERS, J. G. & H. B. T. FLUSBERG. 1975. Some facts one simply cannot deny. J. Child Lang. 2: 279–286.
33. DONALDSON, M. 1972. Cognitive development in preschool children: The comprehension of quantifiers. British Social Science Research Council Report.
34. DONALDSON, M. & P. LLOYD. 1974. Sentences and situations: Children's judgements of match and mismatch. In Problems actuels en psycholinguistique. F. Bresson, Ed. C.N.R.S. Paris.
35. LLOYD, P. & M. DONALDSON. 1976. On a method of eliciting true/false judgements from young children. J. Child Lang. 3: 411–416.

36. DE VILLIERS, J. G. 1975. Some facts one simply cannot deny: Negation in child speech. Harvard University. Unpublished manuscript.
37. ANGLIN, J. M. 1977. Word, Object, and Conceptual Development. W. W. Norton. New York, N.Y.
38. NELSON, K. 1973. Structure and strategy in learning to talk. Monogr. Soc. Res. Child Dev. **38**(1–2, Serial No. 149).
39. WERNER, H. & B. KAPLAN. 1963. Symbol Formation: An Organismic-Developmental Approach to Language and the Expression of Thought. John Wiley. New York, N.Y.
40. STRAWSON, P. F. 1974. Subject and Predicate in Logic and Grammar. Methuen. London.
41. POPE, E. 1973. Question-answering systems. Papers from the Ninth Regional Meeting of the Chicago Linguistic Society. **9:** 482–492.
42. CHOMSKY, N. 1972. Language and Mind, 2nd ed. Harcourt, Brace & World. New York, N.Y.
43. VYGOTSKY, L. S. 1978. Mind in Society: The Development of Higher Psychological Processes. M. Cole, V. John-Steiner, S. Scribner & E. Souberman, Eds. Harvard University Press. Cambridge, Mass.
44. STERN, W. 1975. Psychology of Early Childhood up to the Sixth Year of Life, 3rd ed. A. Barwell, trans. Arno Press. New York, N.Y. (Originally published in 1924).
45. HOCKETT, C. F. 1963. The problem of universals in language. *In* Universals of Language. J. H. Greenberg, Ed.: 1–22. M.I. T. Press. Cambridge, Mass.
46. PIAGET, J. 1962. Play, Dreams, and Imitation. C. Gattegno & F. M. Hodgson, trans. W. W. Norton. New York, N.Y.
47. SHATZ, M. & R. GELMAN. 1973. The development of communication skills: Modifications in the speech of young children as a function of listener. Monogr. Soc. Res. Child Dev. **38**(5, Serial No. 152).
48. GELMAN, R. 1978. Cognitive development. Ann. Rev. Psychol. **29:** 297–332.

THEORIES OF THE CHILD'S ACQUISITION OF SYNTAX: A LOOK AT RARE EVENTS AND AT NECESSARY, CATALYTIC, AND IRRELEVANT COMPONENTS OF MOTHER-CHILD CONVERSATION

Keith E. Nelson

Department of Psychology
The Pennsylvania State University
University Park, Pennsylvania 16802

In acquiring a syntax or grammar governing sentence structures the young child encounters extensive conversational input. In this paper we will consider completed and proposed research that may help to reveal particular components of the input that directly affect the ease with which the child makes advances in language. Because the input is highly complex and because the child's language level and the caregiver's conversation usually will *mutually* influence each other, it appears that naturalistic analyses of child-adult conversations must be supplemented by experimental work controlling aspects of the adult's conversational behavior. In combination the outcomes of the observational and experimental studies may present a convergent pattern of evidence allowing powerful inferences to be drawn about the way in which input components are used by the child in constructing new syntactic rules. Thus, a broad goal of the discussion is to stimulate the gathering of more-differentiated and persuasive evidence than past work has provided on the relations between input components and syntactic progress. This evidence is expected to lead to more refined theoretical accounts of how the child processes and uses the input. Because the input the child receives must be used by the child to construct discourse rules and other language components, and because the processes involved may be related to those in syntax acquisition, the analysis here of theory and evidence will not be sharply restricted to syntax.

In the first section of the paper, naturalistic work on relationships between input and language growth are reviewed. The next section of the paper presents a theoretically motivated, systematic analysis of potential effects of various input components. A third portion discusses individual differences within this framework. These two middle sections give particular attention to possible "rare events"—infrequent, but important instances in which an adult, replying to a child's utterance, provides structural information not yet in the child's system that the child can code in relation to the structure of his or her original utterance. In the final part of the paper the discussion considers in some specificity the ways in which a theoretical account can be constructed through the use of convergent experimental and observational techniques.

45

0077-8923/80/0345-0045$01.75/2 © 1980, NYAS

NONINTERVENTION STUDIES ON RELATIONS BETWEEN LINGUISTIC INPUT AND 1- to 4-YEAR-OLDS' SYNTACTIC GROWTH

A discussion of major categories of input that might influence syntactic growth will be offered, rather than a study-by-study review of the research. Relevant studies cited are either naturalistic observations of parents speaking with their children or laboratory observations in which speech to real or imagined 1- to 4 year-olds was recorded.

Rate, Intonation, and Disfluencies

Many studies, in different languages, reveal that language input to 1- to 4-year-olds, as compared with speech to older children or adults, is slower, higher pitched, more altered in intonation pattern, more redundant, and less disfluent. A partial listing of such studies includes those of Drach,[1] Ferguson,[2] Garnica,[3] Rūke-Dravina,[4] Sachs et al.[5] and wide-ranging reviews by de Paulo and Bonvillian[6] and Snow.[7] In none of these studies, however, is there clear evidence that children's rate of syntactic growth or, indeed, rate of growth in any area of language is influenced by input rate, disfluency, or intonation. Nevertheless, these factors certainly could affect the child's attention to and processing of the well-structured utterances provided by any input source.

Imperatives and Imitations

Although research to date provides few clues about how *not* to speak to a child in the process of acquiring language, imperatives and imitations do recurrently appear among such clues. Heavy maternal use of imperative utterances directly imitative of the child's sentences have been shown to be negatively associated both with the child's concurrent language level and with the child's syntactic growth across 5 to 12 months or more after the measurement of the maternal input.[8–15]

Replies that Primarily "Extend" the Semantic Content of the Child's Utterance

It is almost certainly the case that many of the prosodic and syntactic characteristics of input language directed to young children reflect the mother's attempt to exchange semantic information successfully, as many observers have argued.[9, 14, 16–22] What is less agreed upon, and harder to establish on the basis of research reports in the literature, is whether particular semantic categories of reply by mothers may be associated with the child's progress in syntax. A major difficulty in judging this issue is that the possible categories of semantic "extensions" have not been highly differentiated. Moreover, different investigators have used many different categories and have labeled similar categories in contrasting ways. For these reasons the theoretical discussion here will not focus on adult forms defined primarily in semantic rather than syntactic terms. However, in future observational studies differentiated analyses will need to be made of both the semantic and syntactic overlap between children's utterances and adult replies. Such analyses may establish categories of semantic extension that are positively correlated with aspects of syntactic growth by the children, and these categories may then be incorporated in subsequent intervention experiments. For the moment, the clearest evidence that semantic extensions may facilitate syntactic growth is Cross's finding[23] that a group of children who reached certain levels of syntactic maturity earlier than a comparison group received more exposure to maternal input in the form of semantic extensions that were subsequently incorporated in the mother's exact or partial self-repetitions (a so-called "synergistic sequence"). However, even this result must be qualified—Cross does not provide adequate criteria for distinguishing such extensions from expansions and recasts (described later).

Expansions and Other Recasts

If the child produces a grammatically incomplete, incorrect sentence and the reply received uses all of the child's words in the same order and also adds additional morphemes that form a new grammatically complete utterance, then nearly all investigators, from Brown and Bellugi[24] onward, agree that the reply can be labeled an "expansion."[5, 7, 8, 23, 25-30, 48] Thus, the child's "Dog run" may receive the expansion "The dogs are running." However, I have argued that the function of displaying new syntactic information—new in relation to the child's particular sentence and possibly new in relation to some components of the child's current syntactic rule system—can be served not only by expansions of this sort, but also by many other utterances that, like simple expansions, maintain essential congruity with the semantic references of the child's utterance. The generic term "recasts"[11, 28, 31, 32] will be used to cover all such replies, but differentiations of subtypes have been sought and further differentiations will be made in the present analyses. Similarly, in the two most detailed projects by other investigators who examine maternal recasts and expansions as they relate to children's syntactic progress over time, subtypes of expansions and other recast replies have been included (under various labels). Published reports from each of these projects show positive relationships between subtypes of recasts and the child's rate of syntactic growth. Newport[29] differentiates two kinds of recasts: (1) "expansions," which include all of the child's words and add new lexical items (apparently regardless of perfect grammaticality in the reply); (2) replies that use some but not all of the child's words and add new lexical items. However, despite the fact that in initial language interviews only the second category was significantly related to the children's syntactic levels,* Newport et al.[14] report only on the first category in relation to the children's syntactic growth across 6 months. After partialling out age and initial language level for the children, mothers' frequent use of "expansions" was associated with increases over time in the children's use of auxiliaries ($r = 0.51$, $p < 0.08$, $n = 15$). Cross[23] measured language growth in a very different design; she compared 8 pairs of children who were *matched* on syntactic levels (and other relevant characteristics), but with one child in each pair "accelerated" by at least 5

---

* For eight measures of the child's syntax, including mean length of utterance and morphemes/verb, the correlation coefficient (r) ranged from $+0.65$ to $+0.88$, n $= 15$, $p < 0.01$.

months in terms of the age at which the syntactic level was achieved. However, different pairs were matched at *different* syntactic levels. This raises a problem, as does the widely varying syntactic levels of the children in the study by Newport *et al.* To the extent that different kinds of replies are useful to children at different stages of language growth, neither Cross's procedure nor the double partial correlation technique of Newport *et al.* can be considered a sensitive test of the relation between recasts and syntactic growth. Nevertheless, Cross[23] also finds that accelerated syntactic growth is related to maternal use of frequent recasts. "Accelerated" children compared with their matched counterparts, received about twice the proportion of recasts that changed the child's sentence type (for example, declarative to tag question) and about 50 percent more recasts that were "complete expansions" (using all of the child's words and maintaining the child's sentence type). Compared with their matched controls, children in the accelerated group also received a much higher proportion of sequences with *redundant* presentation of the syntactic information in recasts; in such sequences the mother used some form of recast reply ("complete expansion" or other subtype) and then repeated or paraphrased this recast within two conversational turns. Each of these findings was statistically significant. Additional data come from a sample of 19 children and their mothers (later expanded to 25 dyads) who were observed first when the children were 22 months of age. The project concerned, the Fiffin Project, and the sample have been described in more detail in previous reports on other facets of the data.[11-13, 33] The measures of language use relevant here are the 19 children's advances in language between 22 and 27 months, as correlated with the 22-month data on mother's language use with the children.[48, 49] Simple recasts were mother's replies (including expansions) that maintained reference to the same basic meaning in the child's preceding utterance, with structural changes that were confined to just one of three major sentence components— the subject, verb, or object. Complex recasts involved structural change in two or three of these components. This breakdown was made because it seemed probable that the 22-month-old's ability to analyze and make use of the structurally new information in recast replies would be higher for the simpler recasts. In line with this expectation, a high proportion of simple recasts in mothers' replies was correlated ($r = +0.47$, $p < 0.05$) with the children's rapid growth in MLU (mean length of utterance [in number of words]). Similarly, the same measure for the mothers was positively associated with auxiliary verb growth in the children's language ($r = +0.47$, $p < 0.05$). In contrast, the mothers' use of high proportions of complex recasts was negatively related to both measures of language growth; for auxiliary verbs $r = -0.61$, for MLU $r = -0.29$. It thus seems that the nature of the recasts is a crucial factor. Recasts displaying relatively *simple* structural changes appear useful to the child around 2 years of age.

Of course, in any particular correlational outcome, the directions of influence, mother to child or child to mother or both, cannot be proven. That limitation is one essential reason for the experimental work reported later in this paper. However, by picking up heuristic leads from the observational work and by sometimes discovering convergent results where the input has been controlled experimentally, we can build confidence in categorizations of some specific input components at specific developmental levels as important and others as less essential to the child's language growth (see the next section). In addition, in the data just reported, we gain additional clues by looking at the maternal predictor variables and the child language variables more closely at 22 months. When the children are 22 months of age, the children's language levels in terms of MLU or use of auxiliary verbs (auxiliaries per verb) show a pattern of weak and inconsistent correlations (two positive and two negative correlations) to the concurrent degree to which the mothers use simple or complex recasts. Thus, it is plausible to argue that the successful predictions from the mothers' recasts to the children's subsequent language growth after 22 months may reflect in part influences of available recasts.

A Classification of Possible Effects of Specific Input Components

In previous theoretical writing I have stated that some of the *necessary* conversational events for the child's advances in syntax may be relatively *rare* exchanges in which the child notices and codes discrepancies between his or her own recent sentence and a more advanced sentence given in reply by an adult.[11, 13, 32, 34] Similarly, for acquisition of discourse rules and other language sysems or subsystems[34] we need to specify which input components are necessary. And, among the necessary components some are likely to be infrequent in occurrence. I assume that in each system the essential consideration is whether the child actually notices and codes successfully new aspects of language. At the level of processing and comparing information, those events held to be necessary to the child's advances in syntax or discourse are the successful *comparisons* between input constructions and closely related constructions already in the child's language.

At a more refined level of analysis it may be possible to specify particular comparisons with input that are *necessary and sufficient* for the child's linguistic progress. For theory and for intervention approaches with language-delayed or language-deviant children, this category is clearly of special interest.

Confining ourselves for the moment just to necessary and necessary-and-sufficient input, the analysis of input, effects nevertheless becomes complicated because the particular new-sentence examples or replies required for advances in the child's system shift as one moves from one area or rule to another or from one stage to the next. As Table 1 illustrates, there are a number of *potential* candidates for necessary-and-sufficient input categories, in particular areas of language growth at specific periods of development. However, there are frequent gaps in Table 1 and many potentially relevant input components are not mentioned. These necessary omissions should make evident that we are only beginning to gain the data that will allow confident classification of the differential roles of specific input components.

This conclusion is buttressed by inspection of Tables 2 and 3, which address, respectively, input influences for questions and verbs and for requests and offers. The categories of possible influence for input elements

TABLE 1

SPECIFIC INPUT COMPONENTS (TABLE ENTRIES) CLASSIFIED BY THEIR POSSIBLE INFLUENCE IN THE LANGUAGE AREAS THEY MAY INFLUENCE

Category of Influence	Area of Child's Language Influenced		
	Tag Question Syntax	Auxiliary Rules for 1-Verb Sentences	Discourse Rules for Wh? Use
Necessary and sufficient/rare			
Early stages of mastery			
Late stages of mastery			
Necessary and sufficient/frequent			
Early stages of mastery	Recasts into tag question*		
Late stages of mastery			Wh? answer sequences between two input sources Wh? answer sequences between an input source and child
Necessary (not sufficient)/rare			
Early stages of mastery		Some auxiliaries in input only moderately more advanced than child's	
Late stages of mastery	Maternal declarative followed by maternal self-recasting into tag question	Auxiliary-fronted questions†	
Necessary (not sufficient)/frequent			
Early stages of mastery		Recasts with auxiliaries added	
Late stages of mastery		Auxiliary examples in nonrecast or recast input	

* See, for example, Nelson.[12, 13, 27, 28]
† See Newport, Gleitman, and Gleitman.[14]

TABLE 2

POSSIBLE ROLES OF INPUT COMPONENTS (TABLE ENTRIES) IN THE ACQUISITION OF
TAG QUESTIONS AND COMPLEX FUTURE-TENSE VERBS

	Area of Child's Language Influenced	
Category of Influence	Tag Questions	Future Tense 2-Verb Sentences
Necessary and sufficient/rare		
Early stages of mastery	Recasts into tag questions	
Late stages of mastery		Maternal recasting of child's utterance followed by maternal self-recasting into a 2-verb future-tense sentence
Necessary and sufficient/frequent		
Early stages of mastery		
Late stages of mastery		
Necessary (not sufficient)/rare		
Early stages of mastery		Maternal recasting of child's present-tense sentence into future-tense, 1-verb sentence; some sentence input sequences in future tense
Late stages of mastery	Maternal declarative followed by maternal self-recasting into tag question	
Necessary (not sufficient)/frequent		
Early stages of mastery		
Late stages of mastery		
Mild + catalyst		
Early stages of mastery	Input examples with "primitive tags," such as "OK?" and "Right?"	Maternal imitations of child's future-tense sentences
Late stages of mastery	Use of negative questions other than tags (for example, "Isn't that a nice turtle?")	Some sentence input sequences in future tense

TABLE 2—continued

	Area of Child's Language Influenced	
Category of Influence	Tag Questions	Future Tense 2-Verb Sentences
Strong + catalyst		
Early stages of mastery		
Late stages of mastery		
Irrelevant (neutral)		
Early stages of mastery	Maternal imitations of child's questions	
Late stages of mastery		
Mild − catalyst		
Early stages of mastery	Tags used only at the end of long, complex sentences	
Late stages of mastery	Maternal imitations of child's questions	Run-on input sequences, making relations between verb phrases difficult to track
Strong − catalyst		
Early stages of mastery		
Late stages of mastery	Primitive tags or ill-formed tags used where complete, well-formed tags would have clearer meaning	Tense used with great inconsistency in 2-verb input sentences
Veto variable		
Early stages of mastery		
Late stages of mastery		

are more differentiated than in any prior writing on this topic, with the categories systematically ordered from strong positive roles, such as necessary and sufficient or necessary but not sufficient, to neutral, to strong negative roles. These Tables may be treated as a theoretical outline of what we need to be able to say about the effects of specific input components on some specific areas of language development. In addition, the tentative specifications of input effects illustrate several characteristics that I expect will obtain when firmer, more extensive data are in hand:

1. Many of the necessary input components for specific language advances occur rarely.

2. The same kind of input component may play different roles in different areas of language development, as seen in TABLE 2 for maternal imitations in the areas of future tense verbs (positive catalyst) and questions (early stages, irrelevant; late stages, negative catalyst).

TABLE 3
POSSIBLE ROLES OF INPUT COMPONENTS (TABLE ENTRIES) IN THE ACQUISITION OF
APPROPRIATE REQUESTS AND APPROPRIATE VERBAL REPLIES TO OFFERS

	Area of Child's Language Influenced	
Category of Influence	Child's Use of Polite, Unambiguous Verbal Requests*	Child's Verbal Rejection or Acceptance of Other's Verbal Offers†
Necessary and sufficient/rare		
Early stages of mastery		
Late stages of mastery		
Necessary and sufficient/frequent		
Early stages of mastery		
Late stages of mastery		
Necessary (not sufficient)/rare		
Early stages of mastery		Adult verbal interpretation of child's nonverbal offer
Late stages of mastery	Child's observation of polite, complex request-compliance sequences between two input sources	
Necessary (not sufficient)/frequent		
Early stages of mastery	Adult compliance with 1 word and other simple requests, but with commentary on the actions, agents, et cetera that are involved and on the completion of the requested action	Some offers occur in very familiar routines (for example, baths, meals). Adult presentation of offer in redundant form (verbal plus sensorimotor offer)
Late stages of mastery	Adult sets conditions for compliance; for example, increased clarity about agent, use of polite form, etc	Some offers unaccompanied by supportive nonverbal context
Mild + catalyst		
Early stages of mastery		Politeness markings common in exchanges between two input sources
Late stages of mastery	Many open-ended questions as replies to requests; for example, "What do you want?"	Child's observation of complex offer-reply sequences between two input sources

TABLE 3—continued

	Area of Child's Language Influenced	
Category of Influence	Child's Use of Polite, Unambiguous Verbal Requests*	Child's Verbal Rejection or Acceptance of Other's Verbal Offers†
Strong + catalyst		
Early stages of mastery	Adult is responsive to child's insertion of request in familiar action sequence	Highly playful, stylized offer and request routines between parent and child's older sibling
Late stages of mastery	To a single request by child, many input utterances that explore the pragmatic and grammatical form possibilities that may best match the child's intentions in the request	
Irrelevant (neutral)		
Early stages of mastery	Adult commands	
Late stages of mastery		
Mild − catalyst		
Early stages of mastery	Adult interpretation of many requests as assertives	Frequent use of rhetorical questions by adults
Late stages of mastery		
Strong − catalyst		
Early stages of mastery		
Late stages of mastery	Repetitive, emotionally charged adult commands to child	Adult use of teasing when child fails to respond to initial offer
Veto variable		
Early stages of mastery		
Late stages of mastery	Adults' continued acceptance of nonverbal and 1-word requests, combined with adults' actions that oblige anticipated requests	

* See Bruner, Roy, and Ratner.[43]

† See Zukow, Reilly, and Greenfield[42]; Dore, Gearhart, and Newman[46]; and Garvey.[44] Concerning familiar routines and contexts in early linguistic development, see also Piaget[50] and Bates *et al.*[51]

3. Within an area of language, the same sort of adult reply may have a different effect at different stages in the child's development. Thus, in TABLE 2, input sequences expressed in future tense are assumed to be necessary in early future-tense acquisition stages in contrast to a merely facilitative (positive catalyst) influence in late stages of mastery.

4. Given a particular category of influence, such as a necessary and sufficient influence, it is often the case that different input components will be needed at different stages of development. This can be seen for necessary-and-sufficient input influences on future-tense verbs in TABLE 2 and for necessary input influences on offers as well as requests in TABLE 3.

5. Far from all input playing some positive (let alone necessary) role, much of the input will have effects ranging from irrelevant to so negative that acquisition will be blocked if the child must depend solely upon input sources whose conversations contain the component specified as a "veto variable."

6. The definition of input sequences must in part take into account the nonverbal and social contexts that accompany verbal acts. A good example in TABLE 3 is at the level of necessary (not sufficient) influences on the early stage for responses to offers: on the basis of work by Zukow, Reilly, and Greenfield[42] it is assumed that for acquisition children require some offers in the context of familiar routines and also some offers in verbal-plus-nonverbal form.

7. Included among the important components a child encounters will be *observed* exchanges between two more mature users of the language. Such exchanges allow the child to deploy attention and memory and strategies in different ways than if the burden of the child's own production is added. In addition, certain kinds of informative exchanges are likely to occur only between partners more linguistically mature than the child.

8. Although the classifications of TABLES 2 and 3 may seem intuitively most relevant to acquisition of a single, spoken first language, the same sorts of distinctions need to be made in theoretical accounts of second-language learning, of bilingual development, and of acquisition in sign language or any other nonspeech mode.[11]

ON INDIVIDUAL DIFFERENCES IN INPUT

To demonstrate persuasively that any component of input plays a specific role hypothesized in the foregoing classification system, it will be essential to secure converging data from different sources—multiple samples of an observational nature, experimental interventions, case studies, and so on. In the next section these combinations of approaches in the service of theory will be examined. Here we will present some data from one of the few large observational samples and will argue that the individual differences observed have important theoretical implications.

The individual differences under examination come from the Fiffin Project's[33] sample of 25 children, each observed at the age of 22 months with his or her mother. In the case of each variable the range in behavior across the sample will be discussed.

First, consider a simple discourse variable, "conversational parity," which is the number of total words attributable to the child rather than to the mother. For these young children all the mothers provided much more than half the conversation, but some mothers tended closer to parity (50 percent) than others. The range of scores for the mothers was from 78 percent to more than 99 percent. Even allowing for the limited speech skills of the children, it is clear that some mothers have a much stronger tendency to share in conversation, while others tend to "hog the floor." These differences are likely to have two consequences for the child's language learning that our theories should consider. First, the kind of discourse sequence displayed may be quite different for two children at the same language level if one mother provides 75 percent of the conversation and the second mother 95 percent—in short, the discourse input available will differ. If the second child, nevertheless, receives from conversations with the mother a necessary and sufficient set of discourse examples for acquiring appropriate discourse rules, then it is the second mother-child pair who may provide the more powerful evidence for acquisition theories. The additional consequence of conversations with a particular mother, who may or may not share much of the conversational "floor," is that a style of conversation may be set. In effect the child may be learning optional, stylistic rules to supplement the discourse rules essential for conversation. We should begin to include such stylistic rules in accounts of acquisition and the influences of input.

A second discourse measure for this group of mothers and children was the average "chain" of conversational turns on the same topic. For example, if a mother (M) and child (C) sustained the sequence of same-topic turns, C-1, M-1, C-2, M-2, C-3, M-3, the sequence would include six turns. The length of same-topic sequences averaged by a mother-child dyad ranged from 2.87 to 6.45. This wide a variation is very likely indeed to have consequences for the child's acquisition of discourse rules within the original time frame of the study of these children, 22 to 27 months of age. Checking this possibility is on the agenda. Already in hand is the information that the children in dyads with long conversational chains on a sustained topic at the early age period are children who at the age of 4½ years will use language well in a structured communication test ($r = +0.64$). Further evidence that early discourse skills are strongly associated with communication skills after the age of 4 years comes from recent work by Wells.[45] Still to be determined are the specific discourse components in the child's input that affect concurrent and long-term progress in discourse and related skills.

Wide input variations also emerge for syntactic measures. To give the general conclusion before any particulars, the present data indicate that there is *no simple pattern of input adjustment by mothers to the child's level of syntax.* Different mothers approach conversation with 2-year-olds in contrasting ways. This is shown, for example, by the fact that the 22-month-olds' MLU levels were correlated only very weakly ($r = +0.15$) with concurrent MLU for their mothers. And across measures it is clear that mothers' syntactic complexity levels may be below, matched with, or above the children's complexity levels.

Another illustration of the variation in input in the Fiffin Project sample is given by auxiliary verb use. The measure in this case is the *discrepancy* between mother and child in the average complexity of auxiliary verbs. Here the results indicate clearly that the level of auxiliary use by some mothers is not at the child's level and not slightly in advance of the child's level, but instead lies appreciably below or above the child's usage. The precise measure of auxiliary complexity, the average number of auxiliary elements per main verb, in this sample of mothers and children yielded scores between 0.00 and 0.50. Given this scale, the discrepancies between mother and child covered most of the possible relationships—from a mother whose auxiliary score was 0.19 *lower* than her child's score to a mother whose auxiliary score was 0.31 above her child's level. Elsewhere[32] I have reported that a positive discrepancy in this sample, more complex auxiliaries use by the mother than by the child, is associated with rapid growth in the use of auxiliaries for the child. In the context of the present discussion this finding may indicate that a fairly rich set of auxiliaries beyond the child's own level of use may at least be a *catalyst* to auxiliary development. But the additional fact that many children made progress in auxiliaries despite maternal input at or below the child's own level should lead us to a cautious interpretation about any *necessary* role of a rich set of complex auxiliary examples. What the child may require in input is a fairly small set of appropriately complex auxiliaries that lead to analysis, comparison, and then revision in the child's own auxiliary system. In other words, nearly all children may receive a relatively *rare* set of input auxiliary examples that they can and do process sufficiently to yield new information that can be built into the child's syntax system. However, these rare instances that really matter may for some children be embedded in a vast amount of irrelevant (neutral) or slightly confusing (negatively catalytic) auxiliary input, and for these children the pace at which the necessary instances are encountered will be relatively slow.

Recasts comprise another area of individual differences between mothers. As specified earlier, a mother who used many simple recasts when the child was 22 months of age tended to be paired with a child who made rapid syntactic growth during the 22- to 27-month age period. What is surprising and important for theory is that some of the children received very few simple recasts (less than 1% of their mothers' replies) while other children usually (50 to 67% of the mothers' replies) received a recast reply to their own utterance.

The individual differences discussed so far show that naturalistic samples can provide valuable clues about input influences on language acquisition. In the following section some additional ways in which the roles of input components may be differentiated empirically are discussed, and the importance of fitting naturalistic and supplemental techniques together in programmatic research is stressed.

CONVERGENT APPROACHES TOWARD BUILDING A THEORY OF SYNTAX ACQUISITION

So far recasts are the only components of input that have been shown in both experimental and observational studies to be positively associated with children's syntactic advances across time. First, we will briefly review the experimental data so far obtained. Then a sketch is offered of how further work on recasts and related components could in a programmatic fashion provide much of the essential information needed for a theory of syntax acquisition.

Experimental Recast Studies

Nelson, Carskaddon, and Bonvillian[31] used a broadly defined recast manipulation with one group of young nursery-school children. The outcome was encouraging to an experimental analysis of input effects. The children receiving "bonus input" in the form of recast replies to their own utterances showed stronger advances in syntax than did children in two comparison groups. Despite a relatively *limited number* of "bonus" recasts, the *rapid syntactic progress* made by children in this study, in the two intervention studies described below, and in similar naturally occurring situations, is highly compatible with central tenets of Nelson's "rare-event cognitive comparison theory" of syntax acquisition: (1) The child gains new information about differences between his or her current structures and input structures only when a discrepancy exists and is coded by the child; and (2) the number of codable discrepancy comparisons that are required before a child revises his or her system to incorporate the new form may vary from child to child and from form to form, but this number can be surprisingly low and may decline as development proceeds. Again, note that only those fairly *rare* discrepancies that are actually *noticed* and *coded* can be useful to the child.[11, 12, 13, 32, 39]

In another study of the influence of recasts, two children were followed intensively for a month.[13, 32, 35, 39, 48] Intervention periods involved conversations between child and experimenter, with the experimenter providing recasts into a particular target form—tag questions. The children both acquired tag questions. Further, because many nonintervention observation periods were scheduled between the sessions with recasts, it became possible to determine whether a child might store up information from a prior period of intervention input and then use this information in the formulation of original tag questions during an observation session. For one of the children the apparent "birth" of tag question usage did occur in an observation session. And since this original tag question by the child was spoken 20 hours and 37 minutes after the child had last heard an experimenter's use of a tag question (and because tags by the parents were virtually never used with the child), this result implicates fairly long-term storage and retrieval processes on the part of 3-year-olds. As we build theories of syntax acquisition, we need to look for more evidence of this kind, evidence that may tell us not only *which kinds* of input examples the child makes use of, but also *how many* examples on what *temporal schedule* are required. From very different angles, these are questions that concern other theorists.[36, 37, 40, 41] For example, de Villiers[36] considers how different input examples may have different influences, depending upon how they relate to prototypes of syntactical rules. And Maratsos and Chalkley[37] use a variety of data from many languages to explore theoretically how the child may find and form syntactic patterns within the input set received.

A third experimental study [28] demonstrated that specific recast forms could stimulate acquisition of corresponding forms by children. Thus, children who initially lacked complex question forms as well as complex verb forms generally acquired only those forms that they received in recast intervention. Recasts with verbs led to verb acquisition and recasts into question forms led to question acquisition.

These three experimental studies drew upon a naturally occurring mode of reply, "recasting," that was borrowed from analyses of mothers' natural speech to their children. So it is reasonable to expect that in the experimental work the experimenters were not the only possible sources of the recast replies that proved helpful to the children's progress in syntax, and that many of the outcomes rested on a *slightly increased availability* of the replies central to the child's cognitive comparisons of input structures with structures the child was using already. If this is so, then it should also be the case that in observational studies mothers who use relatively many recasts should make available more of the exchange information a child requires. In consequence, such mothers should have children who more rapidly progress in syntax than do children whose mothers use recasts relatively frequently. This is precisely what we reported early in this paper.

Although other studies have used experimental training to enhance the child's production of particular constructions,[36, 38] these studies have not tested whether such training leads children who initially lack any use of a form to begin to use the form in conversational contexts other than picture-labeling laboratory contexts.

General Considerations for Further Convergent Studies

Given the progress in understanding the facilitating role that recasts can play, we need now to move on to specify when recasts are *catalytic* and when they are *necessary* to syntactic advances by a child. In addition, much remains to be learned about recasts of different structural and complexity subtypes. For these reasons, the roles that expansions and other subtypes of recasts play in children's syntactic development should be analyzed differentially in future studies. At the same time, efforts should be made to identify other components of input that are positively associated with syntactic development. Accordingly, appropriate objectives of new research would be: (1) to complete observational, longitudinal studies of child-adult conversations during a period of rapid syntactic growth for the children; and (2) to conduct a complementary series of experimental intervention studies bearing on components of input shown in these observational studies and in prior observational work to be positively associated with advances in children's syntactic levels.

Both kinds of evidence are essential to any clear specification of how the conversational elements that children regularly encounter influence, or fail to influence, the course of their syntactic growth. Experimental evidence complementary to naturalistic evidence allows one to separate the influences of child on adult from the influences of adult on child. In addition, in some cases controlled experimental work with selected samples of children will allow determination that other covarying factors (such as the child's physiologic maturity) are not the primary explanations for changes both in input and in the child's syntactic levels.

Proposed Intervention Experiments

Listed here are examples of the kind of treatment interventions that need to be assessed. These examples are offered as a possible stimulant to further experimental work and to theory construction at a detailed level. As one heuristic method for finding useful theoretical contrasts, I suggest a basic experimental plan modeled on the 1977 recasting study of Nelson,[28] in which each treatment group: (a) received an intervention targeted on one syntactic construction; and (b) served as a control group (no intervention) for the construction targeted in the other group. Thus, if treatment interventions 1 and 2 are compared in a study, this comparison ought to involve four groups: (1) Treatment One targeted on Form One (say, tag questions); (2) Treatment One targeted on Form Two (say, passives); (3) Treatment Two targeted on Form One; and (4) Treatment Two targeted on Form Two. Similarly, when three different interventions are compared in a study six groups would be required. With this design, preintervention speech samples of all children (generally of ages between 20 and 36 months) would be assessed to determine which children lacked both kinds of targeted forms, and these children then would receive a series of conversational treatment sessions followed by assessment of postintervention language use of both kinds of forms. To the extent that a particular treatment boosts acquisition, children given the treatment should more often advance syntactically for their targeted than for their control form. In order to compare *degree* of effectiveness of different treatment interventions, of course, the groups of children would be matched on preintervention MLU, age, use of forms related to the target forms, and socioeconomic level.

Simple Recasts of the Child's Utterance

In this procedure, as in all the treatments to be described, the sentences provided by the experimenter would be fitted into the flow of the conversation. The heart of this simple recast procedure would be to provide an immediate reply to the child that not only indicates a target form, but that also minimizes the degree of difference between the child's utterance and the recast. For example, when the child says "Dog jump," the adult's reply might in simple fashion build in the future tense: "The dog will jump." This simple recast adds no new locative, object, agent, or main verb, even though these might be appropriate references to the nonverbal context. By selecting which of the child's utterances to recast, this condition could be satisfied for all recasts in this treatment. A simple recasting procedure of this sort gains theoretical interest when contrasted with the next variety of treatment.

Complex Recasts of the Child's Utterance

Here contextually appropriate recasts would be provided, with the complexity of the recasts set at a consistently higher level than in the case of simple recasts. Each of the complex recasts would add to the child's sentence both a target form and one of the following: a new object, main verb, or locative. An example would be "Jump fence" [child] followed by "The dog will jump the fence" [adult].

Because the observational evidence reviewed earlier indicates that mothers use recasts varying in their complexity and that at about 22 months simple recasts may be the more useful sort of input, a search for convergence naturally leads to an experimental comparison of complex and simple recasts used with children at each of two (or more) age levels. On grounds of limiting the child's processing task and drawing attention to the target forms one might expect simple recasts always to be more valuable input than complex recasts. However, an argument can be made for longer, more complex recasts. When these are provided, the additional information beyond the new target form may facilitate the child's analysis (particularly for children older than 30 months) of the form in two ways: (1) The child's general interest in the sentence may be heightened because there is more fresh information. (2) The child may see displayed across many recasts a broader variety of sentence constructions, and thus may acquire a better grasp of how the target form can be fitted correctly into many different overall sentences.

Experimenter's Self-Recasting with Simple Recasts

Once again the idea for this strategy of intervention is based upon observations [8, 23] of the behavior of some mothers with their children. If the child has just paused for a minute or two, the experimenter will take the initiative and present a pair of sentences: (1) a sentence much like the child's own sentences as recorded in prior taped sessions (for example, "Donkey eats flowers"); and (2) a simple recast of this sentence immediately after that includes a target form, such as a future-tense verb (for example, "The donkey will eat the flowers"). The child will thus be in a position to observe the same kinds of structural relations provided to children whose own sentences are given recasts, the crucial difference being that in this experimenter self-recasting group the child's own recent sentence is not one member of the sentences under comparison. To the extent that this treatment is less effective in facilitating syntactic progress than the "standard" recasting, we may infer that for the child having one's *own* sentence immediately recast aids in analyzing new syntactic information. Naturally, though, since this idea of adult self-recasting has had no prior experimental test, it is wise to be prepared also for another possible outcome; that the child's analysis of two contingent sentences may sometimes be facilitated by removal of the processing demands of sentence production. Either way, any experimental data on these questions will allow refinements in theories of how the child makes use of input examples in revising his or her syntax.

Proposed Observational Language Work

Naturalistic observations of children's language with their caregivers can be most revealing of language acquisition processes if the observations are part of a longitudinal or minilongitudinal design. In such designs advances in the children's language across time can be correlated with earlier aspects of the caregiver-child conversations, and this information is critical for the interpretation of any relationships between concurrent measures of input and the child's language. Moreover, in some cases a longitudinal design reveals "natural experiments" across time—instances in which particular forms are acquired, between two points of measurement, by one subsample but not by the remaining children, thereby setting up analyses of possible contrasts in input for the two groups. To take one example, children who acquired past-tense verbs in a limited time period were shown by Nelson *et al.*[47] to have received richer past-tense input than a contrasting group of nonacquirers. To enhance the probability that such natural experiments will occur and to give a better overall picture of language changes by the children and their caregivers, future work should space observational sessions more closely than has been the practice in most prior studies, with the exception of that of Wells.[45]

At least two categories of studies ought to be completed: the first with families in which the mother is the child's primary conversational partner and the second with families in which the mother works full-time and the child's primary conversational partner (at least 55% of total conversational time) is an adult babysitter (possibly a grandmother or other relative). As researchers and theory-builders, we ought to begin such latter extensions of our knowledge of input effects beyond data on maternal input. In order to avoid the serious problems of interpreting input-language-growth relationships when observational samples include children of widely varying age, in each study all the children at initial observation ought to be matched in age and/or language maturity. The measures of relationship between caregiver speech and child speech should be highly differentiated, including information on particular structural subtypes of expansions, recasts, and repetitions. When observational reports routinely include differentiated rather than just general measures, the construction and testing of a detailed theoretical model of language acquisition will become far easier.

One special measure is also worthy of consideration. It can be assumed that mothers differ in their abilities and tendencies to shift conversational levels appropriately, both when the child's utterances shift from hour to hour and also when the child's language advances across weeks and months. To obtain a *predictive* measure of how much adjustment a mother of (say) a 24-month-old may be expected to show over subsequent months, pairing each mother with other children may be useful. Accordingly, the degrees to which the mothers show conversational levels matched with those of 3 children— their own 24-month-old, a linguistically more advanced 26-month-old, and a yet more advanced 28-month-old—could be used as predictors of the following: the child's rate of language growth between 24 and 28 and between 24 and 32 months, and the degree to which the mother's shifts for the same periods are proportional to the child's changes in language levels.

If we can find effective predictors of what mothers are likely to do in their input over time, then we may learn to better recognize situations in which intervention or education may be appropriate to aid the mother and child. There is also a related question that our theories need to consider in greater detail: Why do some mothers make certain kinds of input shifts that other mothers fail to make? Our models of the child's language growth processes should be extended to account for the factors that influence how specific adults and older children speak to individual language learners. Put differently, what is the input for input?

Proposed Studies that Tailor Intervention to Prior Observational Analyses of Input

The idea underlying tailored language intervention is that conversations during a baseline period would be analyzed for many families and then interventions planned that take into account both the child's syntactic level and differences between families in the input structure provided the child. This procedure is best explained through example, although the following discussion merely illustrates the kinds of patterns that an observational phase could reveal. Suppose pairs of children from different families are identified in which the families fulfill the following criteria: (1) The child has not yet acquired passive constructions; (2) overall language level is equivalent for the two children; and (3) no instances of recasts into passive form have been identified in the parents' speech to the child. Intervention would then be tailored to match this information. One child in each pair would serve as a control for increased conversational time with adults and the other child would receive intervention incorporating recasts into passive constructions.

Another version of this paradigm could be employed when special input circumstances appear. For example, from preliminary observations it seems that when a child of 2 to 3 years of age undergoes extended hospitalization for non-life-threatening reasons (let alone for serious disease), such as certain forms of foot surgery, input drops in frequency and shifts in part from the parents to nurses. It would not be surprising to discover that the input during such hospitalization is completely devoid of certain components believed to be necessary or beneficial to next steps in the child's linguistic growth. By analyzing in combination the child's language level and any idiosyncracies in input, it should be possible to devise tailored interventions that would insure the child's progress in syntax despite the hospitalization.

A final category of study is intervention with language-delayed children. Again the basic idea would be to extensively sample the input as well as the child's language level in the first phase of a study. Then, on the basis of this information, intervention procedures with recasts or other techniques would be devised that introduce additional varieties of adult replies and examples into the mix of input the child already receives.

Tailored studies of this kind will add essential evidence to supplement the other intervention and observational investigations. With the full combination of paradigms, it may even prove possible to demonstrate some of the necessary and sufficient conditions for acquisition of particular syntactic constructions. Putting this possibility in language neutral as to particular outcomes, the necessary and sufficient conditions for the child's acquisition of construction A might be approached if the following results were obtained concerning adult Reply Form X: (1) In tailored intervention studies, control children who lacked Reply Form X in input did not acquire A across many months of observation; (2) Children in tailored intervention studies and in standard intervention studies acquired A when Form X was supplied in intervention conversations; and (3) Among many families who use Form X sometimes in conversations with children who lack A, there is a positive association between how frequently X occurs in input and how rapidly children acquire A. Given this combination of results, one interpretation, in line with the rare-event cognitive comparison theory discussed earlier, would be that to acquire A each child requires a certain number of instances in which X is both presented and attended to, and that as long as this threshold set of instances occurs, no further effect of frequency obtains. Under this interpretation, the correlational linking of the frequency of A with the rate of A-acquisition rests solely upon an increasing probability with increasing X frequency that the child will rapidly encounter the threshold set of attended-to instances. Another possible interpretation of the outcome combination just described is that the occurrence of Xs is necessary and sufficient to the child's acquisition of A, but the number of such Xs that are required by a child is directly related to the density of Xs in input—as the density of Xs increases, the child's analysis proceeds more rapidly, with the result that the more frequent the Xs, the fewer total Xs which the child must consider before incorporating form A into his or her syntactic system.

CONCLUSION

Any adequate theory of language acquisition will have to specify how the child utilizes particular aspects of linguistic input in the process of acquiring syntax. Moreover, the design of educational and therapeutic programs for children with difficulty in language mastery needs to draw upon a solid base of information about input effects in normal language acquisition.

The programmatic research discussed in this paper can generate data in a form that few previous projects have provided: Complementary evidence about the same elements of input analyzed through both intervention experiments and naturalistic observation. The coordinated use of observational and experimental paradigms carries the advantage that together they permit stronger inferences than either kind of paradigm alone about which input elements fall into each of these categories of influence on children's acquisition of particular syntactic structures: facilitative but neither sufficient nor necessary, sufficient, necessary and sufficient, irrelevant, or detrimental.

The evidence already in hand and that to be obtained are relevant to nearly any theory of language acquisition. In addition, information on when and how children make use of specific input components also has implications for ideas about the child's memory, attention, and general cognitive skills. For language-delayed or language-disordered children, the sort of focused intervention experiments discussed may provide not only directly relevant knowledge about input effects, but also a demonstration of concrete procedures that can be used effectively and selectively to enhance specific areas of syntactic growth. Similarly, as we learn more about how intervention can be tailored to gaps or idiosyncracies in a child's available input, prevention of certain language delays may become feasible.

Currently, we are beginning to know quite a bit about what adults say to young children. The great potential significance of more programmatic, convergent research is that it can add to this knowledge and go on to specify how some—but far from all—components of what we say influence the child's complex and rapid linguistic development.

REFERENCES

1. DRACH, K. 1969. The language of the parent: A pilot study. Working Paper 14, Language-Behavior Research Laboratory, University of California, Berkeley.
2. FERGUSON, C. 1964. Baby talk in six languages. Am. Anthropol. **66:** 103–114.
3. GARNICA, O. K. 1977. Some prosodic and paralinguistic features of speech to young children. *In* Talking to Children. C. E. Snow & C. A. Ferguson, Eds. Cambridge University Press. London.
4. RŪKE-DRAVINA, V. 1977. Modifications of speech addressed to young children in Latvian. *In* Talking to Children. (See Ref. 3.)
5. SACHS, J., R. BROWN & R. A. SALERNO. 1976. Adults' speech to children. *In* Baby Talk and Infant Speech. W. von Raffler-Engel & Y. Lebran, Eds. Swets & Zeitlinger. Lisse, the Netherlands.
6. DEPAULO, P. & J. BONVILLIAN. 1978. The effect on language development of the special characteristics of speech addressed to children. J. Psycholinguist. Res. **7:** 189–212.
7. SNOW, C. E. 1977. Mothers' speech research: From input to interaction. *In* Talking to Children. (See Ref. 3.)
8. CROSS, T. 1977. Mothers' speech adjustments: The contribution of selected child listener variables. *In* Talking to Children. (See Ref. 3)
9. NELSON, K. 1973. Structure and strategy in learning to talk. Monogr. Soc. Res. Child Dev. **38:** 1–2.
10. NELSON, K. 1975. Individual differences in early semantic and syntactic development. Ann. N.Y. Acad. Sci. **263:** 132–139.
11. NELSON, K. E. 1977. Aspects of language acquisition and use from age two to age twenty. J. Am. Acad. Child Psychiat. **16:** 584–607. (Also in Annual Progress in Child and Child Development, Volume 11. S. Chess & A. Thomas, Eds. Brunner/Mazel. New York.)
12. NELSON, K. E. Theories of language acquisition. Paper presented to The New York Academy of Sciences, March 1978.
13. NELSON, K. E. Toward a rare event cognitive comparison theory of syntax acquisition: Insights from work with recasts. Paper presented to The First International Congress for the Study of Child Language, Tokyo, August, 1978.
14. NEWPORT, L., H. GLEITMAN & L. GLEITMAN. 1977. Mother I'd rather do it myself: Some effects and non-effects of maternal speech style. *In* Talking to Children. (See Ref. 3.)
15. RINGLER, N. 1978. A longitudinal study of mothers' language. The Development of Communication. N. Waterson & C. E. Snow, Eds. Wiley. New York, N.Y.
16. BATES, E. 1976. Language and Context: The Acquisition of Pragmatics. Academic Press. New York, N.Y.
17. BROWN, R. 1973. A First Language: The Early Stages. Harvard University Press. Cambridge, Mass.
18. BROWN, R. 1977. Introduction. *In* Talking to Children. (See Ref. 3.)
19. CAZDEN, C. 1972. Child Language and Education. Holt, Rinehart, & Winston. New York, N.Y.
20. GLEASON, J. B. & S. WEINTRAUB. 1978. Input language and the acquisition of communicative competence. *In* Children's Language, Volume 1. K. E. Nelson, Ed. Gardner Press (Halsted/Wiley). New York, N.Y.
21. MENYUK, P. 1971. The acquisition and development of language. Prentice-Hall. Englewood Cliffs, N.J.

22. MOERK, E. 1972. Principles of interaction in language learning. Merrill-Palmer Q. **18:** 229–257.
23. CROSS, T. G. 1978. Mothers' speech and its association with rate of linguistic development in young children. *In* The Development of Communication. (See Ref. 15.)
24. BROWN, R. & U. BELLUGI. 1964. Three processes in the child's acquisition of syntax. Harv. Ed. Rev. **34:** 133–151.
25. BUSHNELL, F. W. & R. N. ASLIN. 1977. Inappropriate expansion: A demonstration of a methodology for child language research. J. Child Lang. **4:** 115–122.
26. CAZDEN, C. 1965. Environmental Assistance to the Child's Acquisition of Grammar. Doctoral dissertation, Harvard University.
27. NELSON, K. E. 1975. Facilitating syntax acquisition. Paper presented to the Eastern Psychological Association, New York, N.Y.
28. NELSON, K. E. 1977. Facilitating children's syntax acquisition. Development Psychol. **13:** 101–107.
29. NEWPORT, E. 1977. Motherese. Cognitive Theory, Volume 2. N. J. Castellan, D. B. Pisoni & G. R. Potts, Eds. Erlbaum. Hillsdale, N.J.
30. SNOW, C. E. 1972. Mothers' speech to children learning language. Child Dev. **43:** 549–565.
31. NELSON, K. E., G. CARSKADDON & J. D. BONVILLIAN. 1973. Syntax acquisition: impact of experimental variation in adult verbal interaction with the child. Child Dev. **44:** 497–504.
32. NELSON, K. E. 1979. Toward a rare event cognitive comparison theory of syntax acquisition. *In* Child Language: An International Perspective. D. Ingram & P. S. Dale, Eds. University Park Press. Baltimore, Md.
33. NELSON, K. E. & J. D. BONVILLIAN. 1978. Early language development: Conceptual growth and related processes between 2 and 4½ years of age. *In* Children's Language, Volume 1. (See Ref. 20.)
34. NELSON, K. E. & K. NELSON. 1978. Cognitive pendulums and their linguistic realization. *In* Children's Language, Volume 1. (See Ref. 20.)
35. NELSON, K. E. & M. DENNINGER. 1977. The shadow technique in the investigation of children's acquisition of new syntactic forms. Unpublished manuscript, New School for Social Research.
36. DE VILLIERS, J. G. 1980. The process of rule learning in child speech: A new look. *In* Children's Language, Volume 2. K. E. Nelson, Ed. Gardner Press (Halsted/Wiley). New York, N.Y.
37. MARATSOS, M. P. & M. A. CHALKLEY. 1980. The internal language of children's syntax: The ontogenesis and representation of syntactic categories. *In* Children's Language, Volume 2. (See Ref. 36.)
38. WILCOX, M. J. & L. B. LEONARD. 1978. Experimental analysis of Wh-questions in language-disturbed children. J. Speech Hearing Res. **21:** 220–239.
39. NELSON, K. E. 1980. Experimental gambits in the service of language acquisition theory: From the Fiffin Project to operation input swap. *In* Problems, Theories, and Controversies in Language Development: Syntax and Semantics. S. A. Kuczaj, Ed. Erlbaum. Hillsdale, N.J.
40. SHATZ, M. & R. GELMAN. 1977. Beyond syntax: The influence of conversational constraints on speech modifications. *In* Talking to Children. (See Ref. 3.)
41. SLOBIN, D. I. 1975. On the nature of talk to children. Foundations of Language Development, Volume 1. E. H. Lenneberg & E. Lenneberg, Eds. Academic Press. New York, N.Y.
42. ZUKOW, P. G., J. REILLY & P. M. GREENFIELD. Making the absent present: Facilitating the transition from sensorimotor to linguistic communication. *In* Children's Language, Volume 3. K. E. Nelson, Ed. Gardner Press (Halsted/Wiley). New York, N.Y. In press.

43. BRUNER, J. S., C. ROY & N. RATNER. The beginnings of request. *In* Children's Language, Volume 3. (See Ref. 42.)
44. GARVEY, C. 1975. Requests and responses in children's speech. J. Child Lang. **2:** 41–59.
45. WELLS, G. 1980. Apprenticeship in meaning. *In* Children's Language, Volume 2. (See Ref. 36.)
46. DORE, J., M. GEARHART & D. NEWMAN. 1978. The structure of nursery school conversation. *In* Children's Language, Volume 1. (See Ref. 20.)
47. NELSON, K. E., M. DENNINGER, B. J. KAPLAN & J. D. BONVILLIAN. Varied angles on how children progress in syntax. Paper presented to the Society for Research in Child Development, San Francisco, March 1979.
48. NELSON, K. E. Recasts and the introduction of new syntactic forms into the child's language. Paper presented to the Boston University Conference on Language Development, Boston, September 1977.
49. NELSON, K. E., M. DENNINGER, J. D. BONVILLIAN & B. J. KAPLAN. 1980. Maternal input adjustments and non-adjustments as related to children's linguistic advances and to language acquisition theories. Unpublished manuscript. Pennsylvania State University, University Park, Pa.
50. PIAGET, J. 1962. Play, dreams, and imitation in childhood. Norton. New York, N.Y.
51. BATES, E., I. BRETHERTON, C. SHORE & S. McNEW. Names, gestures, and objects: The role of context in the emergence of symbols. Children's Language, Vol. 4. K. E. Nelson, Ed. Gardner Press (Halsted/Wiley). New York, N.Y. In press.

INTRODUCTION

Virginia Teller

Department of Psychiatry
State University of New York
Downstate Medical Center
Brooklyn, New York 11203

South Beach Psychiatric Center
Staten Island, New York 10305

For many years research on multilingualism was dominated by those with a "monolingual mentality." The literature pointed repeatedly to deficits incurred by bilinguals on standard tests of "intelligence" and school achievement. Monolinguals generally performed better on verbal and nonverbal measures, and little advantage was seen, particularly in this country, in having early mastery of several languages. In retrospect, most of these early studies suffered from serious deficiencies. There were no consistent controls for such variables as socioeconomic status, age, sex and educational background, nor for degree of bilingualism. Often the tests were not standardized on a relevant population and were not administered in the speaker's dominant language. The papers in this section are evidence of a reversal of these tendencies. Not only is work conducted within the multilingual community itself, but also social and psychological factors not previously considered are now understood to be crucial. Consequently, research focuses more on understanding the complex set of social, psychological and linguistic variables that interact in a multilingual society.

Serpell and Southworth each investigate a community in a non-Western culture where trilingualism is not only the norm, but indeed a practical necessity of everyday adult life. Robert Serpell's study explores the trilingual capabilities of Grade 1 schoolchildren in Lusaka, the capital of Zambia. Although English is taught in school, the home language of these children is typically one of two Bantu languages, Nyanja or Bemba. Serpell takes a stand against the educational establishment, which prescribes Nyanja as the language of instruction in urban Lusaka and Bemba in outlying rural districts. If Zambian schoolchildren are to attain "a communicative competence adequate for Zambia's multilingual society," Serpell argues, then both teachers and pupils must be encouraged to use all three languages interchangeably in the classroom. He firmly believes that national unity depends on "fostering diversity within individuals rather than between different groups." Such statements are strongly reminiscent of the debates raging in many bilingual communities in this country over what combination of languages is best for educational purposes.

Franklin Southworth's investigation of the *when, why* and *how* of the code-switching behavior of Indian adults is set in Trivandrum, a city on the southwestern coast of India. Natives of this district usually claim either Malayalam or Tamil, both Dravidian languages, as their mother tongue; the better educated have a command of English as well. Southworth observes speakers combining all three languages in conversation, often in a single sentence, and finds that the factors governing such mixtures include the relative age and status of the speakers and the formality of the setting. He concludes that "switching appears to involve a kind of linguistic juggling or tightrope-walking, in which the speaker struggles to balance status, ethnic solidarity, subject matter, type of interaction, and a variety of communicative functions."

In Picurís, a native American language spoken in a northern New Mexico pueblo, Amy Zaharlick encounters a language struggling for survival. The pueblo children are educated in a nearby town, where they speak English in the classroom and Spanish to their classmates. As their competence in these languages increases, their knowledge of Picurís, the language of tribal functions and ceremonies, diminishes. This is a case of what Southworth calls "subtractive bilingualism," where languages of greater social and economic importance are gained at the expense of one's native tongue. Zaharlick's description of Picurís syntax, which won the Edward Sapir award* in 1979, falls squarely into the tradition of linguistic scholarship that Sapir actively engaged in. Fieldwork of this type is an important means by which the dying languages of native America can be preserved, for such grammars provide a potential source of instructional material for future generations.

Ruth Ramsay, the 1978 winner of the Sapir award, takes an ingenious approach to studying the special skills of accomplished adult multilinguals. A disbeliever in the "critical period" hypothesis, she tested her skepticism by asking ten multilingual and ten monolingual adults to learn a language with which all were unfamiliar. The target language, Euskera, a variety of the Basque language of northern Spain, was ideal for this purpose. Not only is Euskera virtually unknown throughout the world, but also Basque itself is unrelated to any other existing language. As Ramsay had predicted, most of the successful learners were multilinguals. The significance of Ramsay's study, however, lies less in revealing *who* succeeded than in showing *how* they succeeded. Her analysis reveals a set of attitudes, strategies, and styles related to language learning that clearly differentiate the successful from the unsuccessful learners.

The traits that Ramsay attributes to successful adult language learners are noticeably absent from the visually impaired population described by Leslie Clark and may be one reason for the recent decline of interest in braille. Like a foreign language, braille involves a unique symbol system that is used by a minority group within, in this case, a predominantly sighted population. Social and political forces both within and outside the braille

---

* The Edward Sapir award is given annually by the Linguistics Section for the outstanding paper submitted in a student competition. The chapters in this volume by Zaharlick and Ramsay are condensed versions of their award-winning dissertations.

community are converging on policies whose effect is to discourage the expansion of braille production and deemphasize braille instruction in school systems. Clark outlines a series of research projects that could be undertaken to ensure the future of braille, for example, simplifying and standardizing the grammar and studying the effects of age on ability to learn braille.

Despite the diversity of topics discussed by the authors in this section, the results of their work all hold clear implications for policy decisions affecting public life. Research on the capabilities of multilinguals cannot be divorced from the political, social and educational settings in which such studies are carried out. Nowhere is this more evident than in the schools, where early assessments can mold a child's future. It seems entirely appropriate for science to influence public policy in this way.

LANGUAGE-LEARNING APPROACH STYLES OF ADULT MULTILINGUALS AND SUCCESSFUL LANGUAGE LEARNERS

Ruth Marion Graeme Ramsay

Department of Communications
Hunter College of the
City University of New York
New York, New York 10021

INTRODUCTION

Communicative skills grow and change throughout life. Adults refine and develop their symbol-using skills for many years after school-leaving age. Not all adults, however, are equally creative or flexible in new modes of symbol use. Those who seem to feel less constrained in approaching and adopting new symbol-using systems may be regarded as worthy subjects of investigation by psychologists, linguists, communications scholars and others concerned with human mental processes. In the use of the symbol set that we call "language," one group—multilinguals—has notable facility.* Those who have learned more than a second language, especially if they have done so in their adult years, constitute one of the most promising subgroups for generating data on language and communicational skills.

Explorations of human language behavior and capacity must draw upon theoretical considerations from several fields—at the least, anthropology, psychology, education and communication theory. Too often, in research of language activity, complexity is reduced by the adoption of a linear or additive paradigm, although the multilayered nature of verbal communication is observable by any but the most unsophisticated adult. Interactions, cross-relationships, feedback loops and other processual concepts may be left out of the theoretical framework, which automatically distorts the inquiry, since to segregate a segment of "real life" from the whole for purposes of laboratory study tampers with the nature of the object of inquiry. The experiment to be reported here is heuristic and represents an attempt to take a more holistic and processual approach to the investigation of foreign language learning among adults. This study seeks elucidation of some of the processes that must go on in the categorization, semantic processing, and memorization of an unfamiliar language.

Two articles, one by Rubin[1] and the other by Stern,[2] appeared while this experiment was in progress. Both authors speculate that good language

---

* Throughout this study "multilinguals" will be distinguished from "bilinguals" by the requirement that conversational facility in at least three languages is the minimum for classification as a "multilingual."

73

0077-8923/80/0345-0073$01.75/2 © 1980, NYAS

learners supply their own motivations and create and use opportunities to interact in the target languages (TL, the language one is trying to learn); they are more willing to make linguistic guesses, are more able to tolerate confusion, uncertainty and shifting structures; and they can revise their expectancies without undue stress. All of this is indicative of a high degree of cognitive flexibility. Stern and Rubin further speculate that good learners actively employ memory strategies, constantly search for meaning while attending incidentally to form, and freely make and test inferences. The good learner sees language as having many functions and has a strong sensitivity to language use and style, and although the good language learner continuously self-monitors, he or she is not inhibited during the learning process. These impressions are closely akin to the hypotheses set down for the current experiment:

1. Despite predictions based upon the theory of a "critical period" for language learning, substantial learning (even in a brief timespan) can occur in full physiologic maturity and into advanced years.

2. In a foreign-language learning task set for adults, multilinguals will constitute a significant proportion of the successful learners.

3. Significant differences in cognitive style will differentiate multi- from monolinguals, and will also separate successful from unsuccessful learners.

4. There will be differences in approach styles between multi- and monolinguals; the same will hold for successful and unsuccessful learners.

5. The successful learners will be more field-independent,† but will show a balanced cognitive style (that is, they will tend to be closer to the center on this continuum).

6. Successful learners will evince more awareness of style in language and will perceive a broader range of language functions than unsuccessful ones.

7. Successful learners will sample a broad range of "learning sources" and will determine rapidly the techniques most productive for them.

8. Task and self-evaluational differences will appear in both groups.

9. Successful learners will not "fix" hypotheses and decisions until they compile a large data base in the TL. Multilinguals will show less rigidity as well.

10. Successful learners will make early efforts to use the language; the poorer learners will be reticent and fearful of making mistakes.

11. Information utilization, focus and points of entry will differ between groups.

There are questions in the sphere of language learning that need to be addressed: Are monolingual adults genetically condemned, in perpetuity, to monolingualism? Is multilingualism a genetic irregularity, or may its presence or absence be traced to social and cultural assumptions and attitudes? Is a "native-like pronunciation" the defining parameter for communication across languages? Is it reasonable to hope that the adult second- or third-language learner may be able to breach language barriers? The myth has

---

† Field-independence is a perceptual mode in which parts of complex presentations can be perceived separately from the whole, that is, "disembedded" from the surrounding field, and articulated as discrete entities. See the work of Witkin and Berry[3] and Witkin et al.[4]

somehow arisen that, beyond a certain age, humans cannot newly learn a foreign language to any degree of satisfying communicative competency. This myth shuts doors that need to be opened in a technologically expanding world. To assign to a biological component that which may be explainable by social components tends to a doctrinaire myopia. The impetus for this experiment came, then, from those who learned languages after their youth.

OPERATIONAL DEFINITIONS

Multilinguals (MLTs) are defined as adults, over 18 years of age, who are able to sustain an adult level of unspecialized social interaction in each of three or more languages. *Monolinguals* (MONs) are adults who have never in their lives been able to use any but their native tongue in extraacademic social interaction. *Successful learners* (SLs) are participants whose post-test scores were so high that, when ranked, these learners could be statistically defined as a separate group (somewhat on the analogy of a "scree test," as used by Cattell[5]). They are presumed to bear some resemblance to "good language learners" in the "real world." *Unsuccessful learners* (USLs) are those participants who were not able to demonstrate, whether by imitation, phrasal or single word responses, or syntactic patterning behavior, any ability to use the TL for communication of intentions or meanings.

Cognitive style refers to consistent individual tendencies in mental organization of complex phenomena. The literature on cognitive style‡ describes many similar, although not necessarily overlapping, dimensions. These are usually labelled in polar extremes, such as *levelling-sharpening,*[7] *field dependent-independent,*[3] and *analytic-relational.*[8] Three tests of cognitive style were selected as probes of a "part versus whole" mental processing style; test responses and scores were used to categorize cognitive styles of the participants.

Approach style refers to attitudes expressed by the participants towards the task, the TL, or towards themselves in relation to the task, as well as through the degree of commitment to the learning task. Criteria for commitment were: spacing of experiment sessions, degree of self-direction shown in the task, and extent of extraneous conversation by participants during time segments allotted to "study." These indicators are only weakly quantifiable, but they do reflect "style."

PARTICIPANTS

The minimum age of the participants (*P*s) was 21 years, the maximum age 61, and the average age 36½ (median 36). Occupations were broadly spanned. There were five academics (students or teachers), two dancers, one flight attendant, one housewife, one political worker, one waitress, and one *au pair* girl. All but one had some college education, ten had completed college, and five had degrees beyond the baccalaureate. TABLE 1 lists their language repertoires, and TABLE 2 lists *P*s' country of birth, travel history, and sex.

‡ For a judicious overview of the literature on "cognitive style," see Nisbett and Temoshook.[6]

TABLE 1
LANGUAGE REPERTOIRES OF PARTICIPANTS

Respon-dent	Native Language	Second Language	Third Language	Fourth Language	Fifth Language	Sixth Language	Seventh Language
01*	English	French	Col. Arabic	German	Swahili	Latin	
02*	Spanish	English	French	Italian	Latin	Russian	
03*†	English	French	German	Spanish	Greek	Russian	
04*†	French	English	Spanish	Modern Greek	Latin		
05	English	*French*	*Spanish*				
06	English	*Yiddish*	*French*				
07	English	*French*					
08	English	Hebrew	*French*	*Spanish*			
09*	Danish	English	German	Latin	French		
10	English	*French*	*Latin*				
11†	English	*French*	*Yiddish*	*Spanish*			
12*†	English and Spanish	Persian	French	Italian	Arabic	Turkish	Russian
13	English	*Latin*	*French*				
14	English	*Spanish*					
15*†	English and Spanish	French	Italian	Russian			
16*	German	Russian	English				
17	English	*German*		*Spanish*			
18	English	*German*	*Latin*	*German*			
19*†	English	Latin	French	German	Classical Greek	Italian	Sanskrit
20*	Danish	English	French	German			

NOTE: Italics indicate unsuccessful language attempts.
* = Multilingual.
† = Successful learner.

TABLE 2
SEX, COUNTRY OF BIRTH, AND TRAVEL EXPERIENCE OF RESPONDENTS

Respondent	Sex	Country of Birth	Travelled Where Native Languages Are Not Spoken
01	F	United States	Yes
02	F	Cuba	Yes
03	F	United States	Yes
04	F	France	Yes
05	M	United States	No
06	F	United States	
07	F	United States	No
08	F	United States	No
09	F	Denmark	Yes
10	F	United States	Yes
11	F	United States	Yes
12	M	Spain*	Yes
13	F	United States	Yes
14	F	United States	Yes
15	F	United States†	Yes
16	F	Germany	Yes
17	M	United States	No
18	F	United States	Yes
19	M	United States	Yes
20	F	Denmark	Yes

* Brought to United States immediately; bilingual household.
† Taken to Spain early; bilingual household.

Candidates for the MLT group were observed in conversation with speakers of languages in which they claimed competence, and they were judged to have little or no difficulty in social dialogue. The MON group was selected by self-report and on the basis of academic grades in foreign language classes. Ps were garnered by personal contact, word-of-mouth advertising, and by appeals to college teachers of foreign languages. All were volunteers; all were told that participation would require four separate time-blocks of testing, ranging from 1 to 3 hours each. All were willing to commit themselves to completing the four sessions. (Three additional Ps were recruited but were called back to their homelands before completing testing. Their data were dropped.)

EXPERIMENTAL CONDITIONS

Sessions I and II lasted about 75 minutes each. In the first hour there were 2 minutes of preliminary videotape viewing, 15 minutes of diverse testing (English language competency, cognitive style, phoneme recognition, and nonverbal comprehension), a 2-minute replay of the videotape, and 40 minutes of self-directed study. Putting away TL material and the after-session test periods were untimed, shaped by the *P*'s own pace. The first hour of Session III was like the others, but the complete session was longer and included a "final exam" and an interview. Sessions were held in small studios with fair-to-good lighting, carpets and reasonable quiet. Each *P* had a personal set of TL materials, kept in an envelope with *P*'s name on the front, boldly lettered. These were always in readiness on the work table prior to *P*'s entry. There were two chairs, one for *P* and one for the experimenter (*E*).

Each *P* worked individually, with the experimenter ("observer") present throughout. All activities were timed and directed by means of an audio cassette, but *P*s were informed that they could, at any time, ask questions of *E*.

On the work table were writing equipment, the envelope of TL materials and three cassette recorders: one for replaying an audio cassette of the videotape soundtrack, one with recorded instructions and timing reminders, and one with a microphone to record all vocalizations by *P*. To the right was a TV monitor for playing the videotapes. Testing materials were at the far end of the work table. As tests were used or completed, *P* placed these in the far right corner of the table, where they remained until *P* had departed. At the end of the study segments, *P*s placed all their notes and learning materials in the envelopes and put them away in a box provided for that purpose.

Within two weeks from the date of the third session, each *P* had a post-session and a debriefing. These were untimed, although some activities in the session were timed. The setting was informal, often in *P*'s home.

THE TASK

The task was introduced simply, in writing, as follows:

> Your task for the next 40 minutes will be to start to learn the language *Euskera*. There is so much material that it would be impossible for anyone to learn all of it in the time allotted. Do not worry about this. No one is expected to accomplish a great deal. Our interest is in what you do as you approach this new language experience.

After instructions on operation of the electronic equipment and handling of materials were given, instructions concluded:

> In the final session you will be asked to attempt some use of the language— writing a few sentences, asking and answering a few questions.

TARGET LANGUAGE MATERIALS

Materials were all derived from two basic sources: Experimental materials were based on C. de Arrigaray's *Gramatica del Euskera*[9] and an original script filmed on videotape. Consultation and corroboration for all material came from Mr. H. Arana, a native speaker of the TL.§ TL material may be assigned to four categories: direct, derived, obvious, and incidental.

§ Mr. Henry Arana, a native speaker of Euskera (Guipuzcoan Basque) and himself a multilingual, acted in the videotaping, served as informant, informal

DISCUSSION

This series of case illustrations was presented to emphasize the Janus-like quality of data obtained through hypnosis. Although it is possible with some people under some circumstances to elicit stunningly accurate information that is otherwise not available, conversely, it is quite possible to so contaminate the memory of the subject that he confuses the hypnotic implantations with his own knowledge. Then, by so fusing them, he cannot tell one from the other. Whether the subject does this for internal reasons of self-defense, because of benign external pressures, or because of blunt coercion to comply, the risk we take in using the hypnotic state to obtain information is that we may wittingly or unwittingly contaminate the memory of the subject in such a way that we cannot be certain of its credibility.

Therefore, the following conclusion is inevitably clear. All data obtained under hypnosis are vulnerable to the counterclaim of memory contamination or coercion (innocent or designed), even though incredibly accurate information can at times emerge. It is thus imperative to document all prehypnosis data as separate and distinct from information obtained during and after hypnotic interrogation. If this is not done, the prehypnosis testimony also risks losing its credibility. The most one can legitimately expect from hypnotic interrogation is further data, which may serve as *leads* for more conventional evidence gathering. Data elicited through hypnosis by itself deserve low or no priority until they are supported by other data. Even confessions of guilt made under hypnosis are vulnerable to counterclaims of coercion and deception, especially in demonstrably highly hypnotizable persons. This certainly does not hold for persons who are not hypnotizable and probably does not apply to those who test low on hypnotizability assessment tests.

However, this is not so simple an issue. It is easy to identify information elicited under *formal* trance interrogation; but it is not so easy to identify posthypnotic influences in testimony after the hypnotic interrogation has occurred and determine to what extent perspectives and facts are contaminated by the interrogation. So far, one could argue that if trance interrogation can be so vulnerable to contamination, why not simply ban all uses of hypnosis in the forensic sphere. That could certainly be done by legislative and judicial fiat but would eliminate only the *formal* use of hypnosis. In no way would it solve the actual dilemma. Such arbitrary orders cannot eliminate the spontaneous trance experience that most persons are prone to, especially under the stress of legal or police interrogation. The Janus-like features described with formal hypnosis can become monstrous perversions of due process when the witness or the accused under duress enters a spontaneous trance state as a desperate way to cope with the intrusion. Fact and fiction can become intertwined and even more confounded when neither the victim nor the interrogator knows that the victim is in trance. Thus, instead of trying to order hypnosis out of existence, it becomes our responsibility to be more knowledgeable about and sensitive to its occurrence.

The best defense against the innocent or calculated abuse of hypnosis is for every person engaged in the interrogation process to become sensitive to the subtle signs of emerging spontaneous trance in the subject being questioned. This requires some training and knowledge; but since trance occurs, is it not the obligation of the professional doing the interrogation to alert himself to it? Of course, the ideal would be for each person to know his own vulnerability to trance under duress and—with this foreknowledge—invoke appropriate safeguards for himself. The details of how this is done are not germane to the discussion here.

DIAGNOSTIC USES OF HYPNOSIS IN THE FORENSIC ARENA

A new and unexpected use of hypnosis has emerged in recent years; that is, using the assessment of hypnotic capacity by means of the Hypnotic Induction Profile (HIP)—a 5- to 10-minute clinical test.[1] The HIP not only determines the hypnotic capacity of the individual, but the configuration of the score also offers a presumptive indication of relative mental health or illness as well as a presumptive indication of personality style. This, in turn, yields information about which pathological syndrome is most likely to occur in that particular person under duress.

Following are actual case illustrations to indicate how this works.

The Reilly Case

Peter Reilly, a Connecticut teenager, was found guilty of murdering his mother.[4-6] The prosecution relied heavily upon a confession that Peter had signed after hours of interrogation and exposure to a lie detector test. Although he had signed a confession, Peter had stated that he still had no memory of killing his mother. The police had explained to him that he had an "amnesia." Peter had accepted this explanation. Friends in the small community who knew him well could not accept the jury's judgment of guilt. Knowing him to be a responsible yet gullible youth, they were perturbed that no medical or psychological testimony had been introduced in the trial. Events snowballed, leading to a hearing for a new trial. Upon examination, the HIP revealed a pattern that indicated that Peter was not the type of person likely to develop amnesia. Careful questioning indicated that he had a clear recall of the entire time span during which the murder had occurred. He had been at a church youth center meeting and had driven home during this time frame. When he had arrived home, he had found his mother dead. He had telephoned for medical help. The HIP pattern was also consistent with a borderline immature personality and poorly developed sense of self with ego diffusion. Peter's extreme modesty and uncertainty about himself along with his long-standing respect for police authority made him vulnerable to charges by the police that he had committed the crime. The polygraph situation was used to make him feel guilty enough to comply with

Obvious and Direct: The Videotape

Normally, language is actualized in either the oral or graphic mode. Even speech, however, has a strong visual component (facial expressions, eye focus, gestures, situational features, and articulatory movements). The social component is equally strong. For these reasons, and to keep presentation constant across all *P*s, videotape was selected as the primary mode of TL presentation, and playback control of each scene was made possible for all *P*s.

An English script was prepared. Scene I ostensibly took place in a customs area in an airport, with a male customs official and a female arriving passenger. Scene II was in the airport waiting room, with the female passenger awaiting the arrival of her host relative (male). Scene III was in the coffee shop in the airport, where the two characters stopped for refreshment. The roles were played by two adult native speakers of Euskera (the TL), with the man taking all the male parts, and the female playing one character throughout. All situations convey cultural messages and assumptions and therefore cannot be "culture-free." To hold down bias in favor of one or another *P*'s culture, these relatively "culture-common" situations were used. Non-United States-born *P*s had had some airport experience, while United States-born *P*s without this experience had some generalized or stereotypic sense of the milieu.

The TL speakers made lexical adjustments (reflecting their cultural experience), said they felt comfortable with the situations and roles, and translated, memorized, and acted the script. Then they were asked to replay the scenes, improvising, but using the content of the original script. This second videotape, because of its greater spontaneity, was the one ultimately used.

Obvious and Derived Materials

Scripts (Written)

A script of each scene was prepared; one was used in each session. The TL dialogue was given first, followed by an interlinear literal translation into English, with a free running, idiomatic English translation below. In addition an International Phonetic Alphabet (I.P.A.) transcription of the TL dialogue was supplied. All these versions of the script were checked and approved by the TL speakers, and were then made available to participants, each being given his/her own photocopy.

Vocabulary Cards

Three sets of vocabulary cards, based on 85 items drawn from the videotape, were prepared for each participant. Set 1 (TL-E) presented the 85 vocabulary items in the TL in bold print, centered, with an English gloss

teacher, and evaluator of the correctness of all TL material. Ms. Maria Luz Albizu played all the female roles in the tapes. Both contributed great effort, and my gratitude to them is immense.

beneath in smaller print. Set 2 (E-TL) presented the same items with the English dominant; Set 3 (PIC) had a cartoon of the concept in the center, with the relevant TL word in one upper corner and its English gloss in the other. One TL-E card had only the word *agur*|| with no English gloss.

Audio Cassette

Audio cassettes dubbed from the videotape's sound track were provided, along with a playback deck, to each participant.

Grammar Cards

Participants were also given 24 cards on which basic rules of TL grammar were written. Each card contained one rule (for example, a paradigm for declension or a conjugation) or one point of TL usage. Rules relevant to the videotape dialogue were excerpted from de Arrigaray's text.[9]

"Primer"

The participants were each given a small, 8-page "primer" constructed as a programmed instruction manual. This was designed to lead the reader through an introduction to the same TL lexicon and grammar, but was framed in a different narrative in order to vary the context.

The videotape, audio cassette, and printed scripts for Scene I were presented in the first session, as were the primer, the grammar cards, and the vocabulary sets. These cards were used instead of a bound list in order to give participants more flexibility in ordering and categorizing these elements and to permit the investigator to observe the approaches and use-styles of the participants as they searched for lexical items. In the second session, all the aforementioned items, plus script, videotape and cassette for Scene II were available; the procedure was repeated for Scene III, in session III. All the foregoing tools constituted the "apparent" TL learning materials.

Incidental Sources of TL Information

Five other sources of varying amounts of TL information were present during the experiment. First, all Ps were told that they could ask the investigator questions at any time. # Second, the "memory for vocabulary" test at the end of each session was designed to drill lexicon as well as to test it, since the same vocabulary was used each time. Third, there was a label on the box of vocabulary cards which had the word *iztia* ("repository of words") written upon it. The fourth source was the "Instructions to Participants," that is, the cassette tapes that guided each session. These always began and ended with the word *agur* (see footnote||); two tapes also contained the

---

|| This word is used in much of the same manner as *shalom* is in Hebrew, that is, for greetings, farewells, and rituals. It is closer in meaning, however, to the semantic field of the Spanish *reverencia*.

Long preparatory hours spent by the experimenter in working on TL materials assured that questions on the level that Ps were likely to use could be answered.

phrase *eskerik asko* ("thank you"). Finally, the "reading sequence" rehearsed script sentences.

TESTS ADMINISTERED

There were two broad testing areas; cognitive/psychological tests and those tests addressed to TL skill. (Competency in English was also tested.)

Psychological Tests

Personal language histories were collected. Three tests of "cognitive style" (embedded figures,** figure-ground,†† and generalizer-particularizer,‡‡ one per session) were assigned to determine whether there were commonalities of cognitive style among either MLTs or SLs. In the post-session, a category-width test§§ was given, which has been found to tap another postulated style of "broad" versus "narrow" categorizing. The form that was constructed for this experiment drew on the incidentally retained knowledge of the TL. A "flip test" of flexibility was also used as a tool to disclose speed of perceptual shift.‖‖

The cognitive style tests were selected from current literature on the basis of each test's applicability, common usage, and ease of administration. None yielded any significant results. They will not be discussed, except to comment that their inconclusiveness was not surprising, since the concept of cognitive style is not tightly defined. There is an intuition that the construct seems to hold much explanatory potential; at present it stands in need of clarification, conceptual unification and research.##

The flip test was an ad hoc test for speed, willingness, and flexibility in reorganization of perceptions. Six standard psychological drawings, each interpretable in two ways (for example, faces/vase or young woman/old crone), were presented to *P*s, who registered (1) their first interpretation; (2) the length of time required for the first "flip"; (3) the number of flips in a set time period.***

The category-width test used a set of 100 cards, with TL words and English glosses. *P*s were asked to sort these cards three different times, using different categories and labels of their own choosing. It was expected that the third sort would tax flexibility of perspective and motivate those least flexible to end the activity more abruptly. The test not only allowed patience, flexibility and creativity to be observed, but it also was aimed at seeing whether *P*s would show a pattern of response to surface characteristics or semantic features of the TL while categorizing.

** See Oltman *et al.*,[10] for the EFT test of figure-ground differentiation.

†† The "figure-ground" test of Kagan *et al.*[8] was adapted to use TL labels as probes in recalling ground or figure stimuli; for further explanation, see Ramsay.[11]

‡‡ The Schwarz[12] test for generalizer-particularizer was used, but the judgment categories were made more explicit for this experiment.

§§ See Bruner and Tajfel.[13]

‖‖ My thanks go to both Ron Erickson and Penny Liberatos for their input in the construction of this test.

See Riley and Denmark[14] for an extended discussion of these difficulties.

*** Graphics and basic background for this test came from Gregory.[15]

Target Language Tests

Throughout the experimental sessions, TL language skills were tested. Ps were tested for TL phoneme recognition, phonetic recall, lexical memory (using both TL and English probes), reading aloud, sentence recall or recognition, oral and written composition, and nonverbal comprehension. The "final exam" was similar in form to the final exam of the first semester in foreign language classes. There were ten questions of varying difficulty, designed to tap diverse language skills and linguistic levels. Before this test was given, Ps were asked to rank the questions in order of apparent difficulty. Ps' answering sequence was then checked to see whether difficulty correlated with answering sequence. Paraphrase, unscrambling, error correction, free construction of sentences, picture description, dictation and translation were all probed. Much of the test content drew heavily upon the videotapes and the primer; verbatim quotes were often used. Ps were told that they were permitted to use all their study aids; they were never told that they should not use verbatim phrases from the study materials.

In all sessions, a "memory for words" test was run in two parts. At first, given TL probes, Ps were asked to respond with English glosses (= recall), with any part of the gloss, or something about it (= partial), or to list when or where they had encountered it, if possible (= recognition). Then the test was re-run with English probes for TL responses. Responses were written.

After the testing was over, Ps were interviewed about their feelings at different stages of the self-instruction experience. Opinions about teaching methods in general were solicited. A final questionnaire was completed in the post-session including questions concerning motives for foreign language study and attitudes towards foreign languages.

SCORING AND REGROUPING INTO SL AND USL GROUPS

Each question of the final exam was scored by a weighted evaluation of the syntactic and communicative responses. A ratio of "answers attempted" to "correct responses" was computed for each question. (For details see Ramsay.[11]) Rank order for each question, for rank-of-all-ranks and for lexical memory was separately tabulated, as was total score. Those who were clearly the top performers were designated "successful learners" (SLs) and their data were searched for commonalities.

RESULTS

The first research task was the regrouping of Ps, according to their test scores, into SL and USL groups. TABLE 3 gives the ranking for summed scores (exclusive of memory scores). With the addition of memory scores (TABLE 4), shifts in the lower ranks occur, but the top group retains its integrity and distinctiveness. The rank-of-all-ranks score introduces a sixth candidate for consideration as an SL, the only monolingual P to score that well (TABLE 5).

All three scoring techniques yield a group of six who show distinctive patterns of "success." Using the Scree Test, which demarcates levels at the centerpoint of sharp slopes between graphed scores, there is one P superior

TABLE 3
SUMMED SCORES ACROSS NINE QUESTIONS AND RESPONDENTS' RANKING

Respon-dent	Question Number									Total	Rank
	1	2	3	4	5	7	8	9	10		
03*	0.709	0.700	0.500	0.500	0.200	0.500	1.0	0.726	1.925	11.341	1
12*	0.727	0.933	0.667	0.750	0.200	1.5	1.0	0.922	0.913	7.612	2
04*	0.650	0.467	0.917	0.722	0.200	1.250	0.0	0.832	1.918	7.599	3
15*	0.444	0.333	0.467	0.111	0.000	0.500	0.750	0.749	1.443	4.797	4
19*	0.144	0.600	0.167	0.694	0.350	0.000	0.000	0.959	1.201	4.115	5
11	0.350	0.000	0.000	0.139	0.000	0.500	0.750	0.844	1.327	3.820	6
07	0.260	0.000	0.917	0.444	0.000	0.500	0.000	0.645	0.671	3.437	7
08	0.623	0.600	0.000	0.000	0.000	0.000	0.000	0.777	1.237	3.237	8
01*	0.000	0.633	0.167	0.333	0.000	0.000	0.000	0.854	1.336	3.156	9
20	0.242	0.200	0.000	0.000	0.000	0.500	0.000	0.535	1.429	3.073	10
17	0.610	0.167	0.000	0.000	0.000	0.750	0.400	0.706	0.895	2.988	11
09*	0.009	0.000	0.167	0.083	0.000	0.500	1.0	0.425	0.535	2.718	12
02*	0.130	0.000	0.667	0.222	0.000	0.000	0.000	0.654	0.895	2.568	13
18	0.952	0.267	0.000	0.222	0.750	0.000	0.000	0.000	0.426	2.517	14
16*	0.000	0.000	0.000	0.111	0.000	0.000	0.000	0.730	1.565	2.406	15
06	0.305	0.267	0.000	0.000	0.000	0.250	0.500	0.335	0.680	2.337	16
13	0.233	0.133	0.167	0.000	0.000	0.000	0.000	0.819	0.730	2.082	17
10	0.623	0.367	0.000	0.000	0.000	0.000	0.000	0.418	0.633	2.041	18
05	0.386	0.000	0.000	0.000	0.000	0.000	0.000	0.402	0.802	1.590	19
14	0.117	0.000	0.000	0.222	0.000	0.000	0.000	0.298	0.817	1.514	20

* = Multilinguals.

TABLE 4
MEMORY SCORES, COMPOSITE SCORES, AND RANK ORDERS

Respondent	Memory Score	Rank	Total Score	Rank
03*	0.678	1	12.019	1
04*	0.600	2	8.199	2
12*	0.567	3	8.179	3
15*	0.543	4	4.797	4
19*	0.399	7	4.514	5
11	0.464	5	4.284	6
17	0.185	16	3.713	7
07	0.164	18	3.601	8
08	0.315	10	3.552	9
01*	0.340	8	3.496	10
20*	0.124	19	3.197	11
09*	0.281	11	2.999	12
18	0.250	12	2.767	13
02*	0.186	15	2.754	14
16*	0.206	13	2.612	15
06	0.189	14	2.526	16
10	0.423	6	2.464	17
13	0.322	9	2.404	18
05	0.171	17	1.761	19
14	0.093	20	1.607	20

* = Multilinguals.

to all others, two somewhat lower, and three other Ps who, although lower than the three top ones, are still above all other Ps by more than common variance (FIG. 1).

By any criterion, Ps 3, 4, and 12 are most successful, with 15 next. Numbers 11 and 19 shift in the hierarchy, depending on the scoring used, but are far ahead of the rest of the participants. Five, then, of the six SLs are MLTs, which supports the second hypothesis (significant at the 0.05 level).

Analysis of Successful Learners

English Language Ability; Cognitive Style

There were no significant differences in the test in English of structure and vocabulary. There were no significant differences between SLs and USLs on any of the cognitive style tests. The construct may not be formulated precisely enough as yet and is probably both multiplex and processual, as mentioned earlier.

Language Style: Memory for Detail; Inferencing; Evaluative Attitudes

The generalizer-particularizer technique[12] used three paragraphs from *The Golden Bough*[22] as a probe for the dimensions discussed in this section. Ps summarized each paragraph from memory and a panel of judges rated

TABLE 5

RANKS OF RESPONDENTS BY EACH QUESTION AND RANK-OF-ALL-RANKS

Respondent	\multicolumn{9}{Question}									Rank on Memory Test	Average Rank
	1	2	3	4	5	7	8	9	10		
12*	2	1	3	1	3	1	1	2	10	3	1
03*	3	2	5	4	3	4	2	10	1	1	2.5
04*	4	6	1	2	3	2	8	5	2	2	2.5
15*	8	8	6	11	6	4	4	8	4	4	4
11	10	14	11	10	6	4	4	4	7	5	5
09*	18	14	7	13	6	4	1	15	19	11	6
19*	15	4	7	3	2	11	8	1	9	7	7
01*	19	3	11	6	6	11	8	3	6	8	8
08	5	4	11	14	11	8	7	7	8	10	9
18	1	9	7	7	1	11	8	20	20	12	10
20*	13	11	11	14	6	4	8	14	5	19	11
10	5	7	3	14	6	11	8	16	18	6	12
02*	16	14	7	7	6	11	8	2	11	15	13.5
13	14	13	2	14	6	11	8	6	15	9	13.5
07	12	14	11	5	10	5	8	13	17	18	15
16*	19	14	11	11	6	11	8	9	3	13	16
17	7	12	13	14	6	3	7	11	11	16	17
06	11	10	11	14	6	10	6	18	16	14	18
05	9	14	11	14	6	11	8	17	14	17	19
14	17	14	11	7	6	11	8	17	13	20	20

* = Multilinguals.

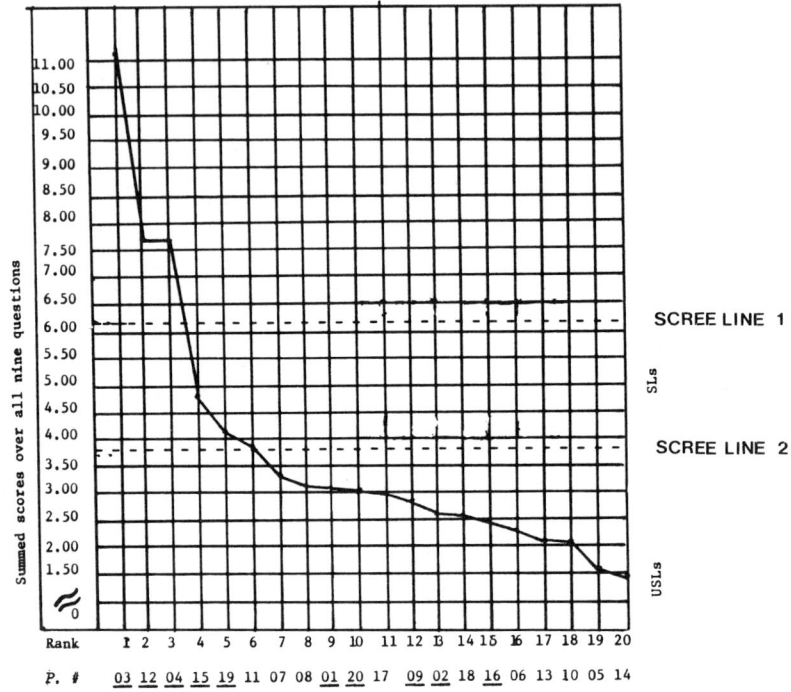

FIGURE 1. Scores graphed by rank in final exam. Underlined *P*s are MLTs. The Scree Line separates unique clusters from those clusters due to common variance. (See Cattell.[5])

each *P* on all four dimensions. (Inter-judge reliability was high; intraclass correlation was 0.8277.) "Concern for language style" was evaluated on a three-point scale of stylistic orientation. No criterion was given to the judging panel, but scoring was reliable across all judges. Differences did not reach a level of significance, but there was a trend for judges to rate the SLs as more concerned with style in their writing. "Evaluative attitude" was operationally defined as expression or lack of expression of a personal reaction toward the content of the original paragraphs. There was a strong trend ($p < 0.106$, df $= 18$, $t = 1.705$) among SLs to refrain from evaluating the texts and among USLs to include remarks evaluating the content or the activity. Inferencing was defined as including in a summary some extension beyond the information given. SLs tended to relate incoming or new material to prior knowledge and to express conclusions derived from implications in the original texts; the USLs did not ($p < 0.072$, df $= 18$, $t = 1.915$). "Memory for details" was determined by the number of actual distortions of textual details. Differences were not significant.

Memory as a Learning Factor

The lexical memory test, run in all three sessions, had several levels of response possible:

Level 1: a statement of *recognition* (such as source, length, form).

Level 2: a statement of *partial/displaced recall* (such as related terms interchanged, spelling errors, partial syllables).

Level 3: a statement of total and correct *recall*.

Level 0: no response.

Response changes to each probe were plotted over all three sessions to determine whether any patterns existed in lexical retention. Patterns of increment and decrement were found, which are shown in TABLE 6. Differences between successful and unsuccessful learners were determined by analyses of these patterns and are shown in TABLE 7.

Phoneme Tests: Nonverbal Interpretations

Initial attempts to imitate TL phonemes showed SLs more willing, overall, to try to produce these sounds ($p < 0.03$). Correctness was not measured; the focus was vocal shyness and auditory memory. However, SLs were shown to be more correct in imitating TL words after a single viewing ($p < 0.03$).

TABLE 6
RETENTION MEMORY PATTERNS

Category Name	Graph	Pattern
High consistency	—	Start level 2 and maintain
		Start level 3 and maintain
Low consistency	—	Start level 1 and maintain
		Start level 0 and maintain
Delayed increase	⌐/	Start level 1 or 2, maintain, and increase in Session 3
Orthogonal increase	╱	Increase in even steps across sessions
Early increase	⌐╱	Increase between sessions 1 and 2 and maintain
Delayed decrease	⌐╲	Maintain level between session 1 and 2; drop at least one level in session 3
Orthogonal decrease	╲	Decrease in even steps across sessions
Early decrease	╲⌐	Decrease between sessions 1 and 2; maintain thereafter
Equal recovery (positive bow)	∨	Start at some level in session 1; drop in session 2; return to initial level in session 3
Improved recovery	∨╱	Start at some level in session 1; drop in session 2; surpass initial level in session 3
Partial recovery	∨	Start at some level in session 1; drop sharply in session 2; rise to a level below the initial one in session 3; increase levels between sessions 1 and 2; drop back to original level
Relapse (negative bow)	∧	
Deep relapse	⌐╲	Increase levels between sessions 1 and 2; drop below original level in session 3
Partial relapse	╱⌐	Increase levels sharply between sessions 1 and 2; drop to a level above the initial one in session 3

* These were calculated for each word in the memory test for each subject.

TABLE 7
DIFFERENCES BETWEEN SUCCESSFUL AND UNSUCCESSFUL LEARNERS

Pattern	df	t test	Significance Level
High consistency	18	5.892	0.001
Orthogonal increase	18	2.698	0.015
Improved recovery	16	6.756	0.001
Equal recovery	16	2.662	0.018
Low consistency	18	−3.271	0.005

A focus on verbal versus nonverbal attention for SLs was seen:

1. USLs (and MONs) processed nonverbal information more in their initial efforts to understand the videotaped situations and they did so more accurately. Inaccurate interpretations predominated among SLs ($p < 0.06$).

2. USLs (and MONs) more often gained information from tone of voice, gesture, and situation.

Type-Token Ratio; Word Counts

Word counts and pronoun counts of all kinds proved nonsignificant. In the TL compositions and descriptions, the type-token ratio, when correction for length was applied, was significantly different for SLs ($p < 0.038$). SLs used a greater vocabulary and showed less hesitation in its use, as measured by the number of "accurate starts" (hesitationless utterances); ($p = 0.03$ for SLs and 0.15 for MLTs). SLs knew that vocabulary memory was important and spent as much time on vocabulary as on rules, often using words in phrases or sentences immediately.

Approach and Practice Styles

Testing schedules were set at the convenience of *P*s, but attendance spacing was examined and three classifications were made: "closely spaced" (no more than 2 days apart); "optional delay" (which never exceeded 7 days); and "unavoidable delay" (which did not, in any case, exceed 6 days between sessions). No SL had a gap of more than 4 days ($p = 0.03$); six MONs and three MLTs optionally delayed more than 5 days between sessions.

Of all the findings that may have practical application, perhaps the most significant is that none of the SLs failed to practice *viva voce* (accuracy would require the term *fortissimo*!). The amount of sound correlated almost directly to the final scores attained by all *P*s; the vocal activity of SLs differentiated them at the 0.03 level. Stevick's term *lathophobic aphasia*[17] (silence out of fear of making errors) has been used to account for the reluctance of adults to practice aloud or in the presence of others. The SLs (some immediately, some after a few moments) evinced no inhibition at all about practicing aloud; they also verbalized freely on the mental processes they were going through. The outstanding *P* spent the entire time in vocal TL activity, playing the tapes, following the dialogue while using the script and often cutting off the tape in mid-phrase and continuing the dialogue by himself. When he was displeased with some segment of his performance, he would return to following the videotape until he had reached some self-imposed criterion. A complacent acceptance that language-learning involves mistakes was evident in all SLs (and almost MONs), and kinetic involvement in the learning process was the rule. Walking around, spatially arranging cards, gesturing while vocalizing were conspicuous activities among SLs and notably absent among USLs. SLs spotted their errors often, but did not pause over them, and they did not appear to evaluate either the language or their own progress during the study sessions. They were totally absorbed in the ongoing TL task.

Use of Information Sources

In part, the success of the SLs must be attributed to their multiphased activity.[18] They used TL and PIC cards or grammar cards along with the scripts while listening to video or audio sources. Frequently the SLs used five sources at once. They used vocabulary creatively or in sentence frames. They noticed the "planted" words on the audiotapes, and used these thereafter. SLs noticed the label on the box of memory-test cards and assigned some meaning to the TL word. (One *P* assigned an inaccurate translation to the label, and was quite rueful when he found no use for the word "box.") SLs used various mnemonic tricks (spatial as well as verbal); no USLs reported any mnemonic activity.

Analysis of Unsuccessful Learners

The USLs had a radically different pattern of study and practice. They delayed in starting study activity; they lost further time in attempting to interact socially with the observer; whenever they discovered that they had made some error, they rehearsed the event not the correction; they commented on TL sounds, forms and materials; they reiterated that they were "not good at this" or said they were "stupid about languages." Most USLs used the E-TL vocabulary cards, but in a redundant manner, taking the PIC card and the TL-E card for each word and placing these behind the E-TL version of the same word. The result was an unwieldy pack of 254 cards, which they then read through silently. (This often used up the entire study segment.) Most of the USLs, when they realized that they were permitted to use these cards in answering final exam questions, asked to have the E-TL cards pulled out and rearranged alphabetically. USLs did not notice the greeting on the audio tape, did not pick up TL structural information from the primer, did not read any part but the English portion of the scripts, and never noticed that color vocabulary appeared on the TL cards *in ink of the color being named*. (One USL, in the third session, asked while working with these cards, "Did they run out of ink or something?") SLs preponderantly used phrasal memory drill, and appeared to use some process similar to "chunking." To recall, they disassembled the "chunk."†††

††† This concept of collecting numerous items under one supraordinate label for later retrieval or reconstruction, first articulated by Miller[16] in 1956, was evident both in physical arrangements of vocabulary cards and in errors in performance in the

[A final word on the statistical analysis‡‡‡: since each test explored some different skill, two-tailed tests using Fisher's t were applied throughout. The decision to use parametric tests was based on the small sample size. A one-tailed or nonparametric test could have been applied in many cases, with stronger significances resulting. With such a small sample, one should be wary about making sweeping generalizations, but some provocative trends in differences appeared on both MON/MLT and SL/USL axes.]

DISCUSSION

Certain assumptions have underlain this study, providing its rationale and directing the methodology: Language is a symboling system for human communication, and language learning is a social act than can be, and is, accomplished by some adults. Such activity involves social as well as personal factors, which are more accessible to investigation in multilinguals than in other adult populations. Under pressures of time and testing with no set instructions or routines, adults will approach tasks with strategies and behavior that they consider productive, and these strategies will be based on analogies drawn from past experiences. Past experience and perceptions of past experiences differ for all adults, therefore there can be no single method of language learning that can utilize the divergent conceptions of an adult population. However, there may be commonalities of effective processes, sequences, foci, and general attitudes that can be identified by looking at successful adult learners of foreign languages, for example, multilinguals. The goal may be attained through more than one instructional method and related to more than one instructional set of principles, and accomplishment will be influenced not only by individual abilities, but by social factors as well.

For practical purposes, it is worthwhile to look for a social impact on foreign-language learning before assigning a dominant role to a degenerating biological component to explain slower language acquisition by adults. It is also desirable to determine whether differences in individual approaches to language-learning accomplishments can indicate directions for change in teaching methods, social attitudes, and financial investments in foreign-language learning. Finally, treatment of language learning as a communicative and purposive activity, rather than as an isolable cultural and linguistic artifact may call for revision of language teaching methods for adults.

Given the foregoing assumptions, and the patterns found among SLs in the test circumstances, examination of the language-experience protocols is of interest. All the SLs had free choice of the languages they studied. Ten of the 14 USLs did not have real options about the language they studied in

lexical tests. Signs that this was the memory technique used also appeared in the reading sequence; Ps who did well in this test read in word and sometimes even phrase clusters.

‡‡‡ The statistician for these very extensive tests and analyses was a paragon of all the scientific virtues and none of the scientific flaws. I acknowledge my debt to Ms. Penny Liberatos for her painstaking assistance in preparing the statistical analysis.

school. In response to the question, "Did you, at the time of study, feel that learning a foreign language would be useful to you personally?", nine who later became multilinguals replied affirmatively, stating that their ability to speak other languages had always involved curiosity. None of the SLs knew how or where they had acquired the intense study habits they exhibited, but all attributed most of their ability to practice. With one exception, the SLs and the MLTs reported reading, solitary walks, daydreaming and puzzles as areas of interest from early childhood on. In contrast, USLs (and MONs) mention group games, active sports, photography and collecting as dominant areas of interest in childhood, adolescence, and young adulthood. No correlation was found between the number of languages spoken at home and identification as an SL (or MLT, for that matter), so the more introspective life-style of the SL or MLT may well be related to the opportunity, time, and relaxed attitude conducive to developing language-learning abilities, although this speculation tells us little about the components and processes of that skill.

The dominant community or social attitude toward interaction with outsiders probably resonates with other factors, both individual and societal, to facilitate or deter adult learning of languages. The massive commitment of time and energy demonstrated by the SL must be, at least, not disapproved of socially. For adults, and certainly in this experiment, *anomie* is unlikely to be a potent factor. In those national or cultural groups that demand a high level of language-learning proficiency, there are practical reasons for, and ample opportunity to use, this proficiency. In the United States, however, although language study in secondary schools is offered—and sometimes even mandatory—historically the climate is missing that encourages this skill as useful or socially desirable.§§§

The factor most often claimed as underlying poor language-learning ability was fear. (This was cited either as fear of failure or fear of being "humiliated" by a teacher. The answers to six of the questionnaires used this very word.) The second factor blamed for failure was the pedagogical emphasis on rules and perfection of utterances, rather than relevance of utterances. The third factor mentioned by USLs in relation to their poor history was the lack of opportunity to interact with speakers of the language, a factor *all* participants felt to be important. The need to talk with others is a compelling incentive. Finally, the USLs were fearful of guessing and of using unapproved sources for language information. They stuck to one text, one style, one vision of the task, and one level of language at a time. They were totally constrained in their earlier experiences and in this experiment. The SLs ranged freely among materials, levels, tasks, and forms of expression.

§§§ 1975 United States Census figures show that only one-tenth of the population of this country is able to speak a second language. Of that number, a great proportion are non-native speakers of English, which means that their second language is English. The balance of those who have the use of a second language are almost all students, formal or informal, of Spanish. Thus, learners of second languages other than English or Spanish in the United States constitute a negligible fraction of 1 percent of the population.

SLs operated on speaking, listening, reading, memorizing, producing, all in one whirling whole, stopping at each point of immediate need. They made quite clear their need for large amounts of input—more, in fact, than their immediate needs would have required. Perhaps censoring or editing what is doled out is not helpful to the adult learner. Certainly the SLs pursued a configurational approach much like that of young children, not limiting themselves in quantity of information or task boundaries and procedures. SLs often read through, or listened through some section, then "tabled" it in favor of some other item; however, the SLs would suddenly come back to the point at which they had stopped and resume work with the original material as if another source of information had enlightened some aspect of the study they put aside. The SLs gave the impression of analyzing for the purpose of synthesizing, whereas the USLs had too small a data base to analyze, and too little information to synthesize. Moreover, the USLs attempted these processes too early, then regarded their efforts as failures and *abandoned the data they had already processed*, attempting another approach *de novo*.

A new language is a phenomenon upon which the mind may operate, looking at both form and content. "Intent to learn" has been shown to lead to a heightened attention to *content* with an accompanying decrement in attention to *form*.[18] If these two aspects are reciprocals, then as content is beginning to be integrated into the mental organization, there may be small value in stressing form independent of content. Content may make the framework into which later formal information will be fitted.

The higher levels of storage and retrieval have been shown to operate on the basis of meaning—both lexical and syntactic.[19, 20] If a certain amount of content is processed for meaning and stored in memory before more formal information is taken in, the process of integration and linking to other existing mental structures becomes an ongoing one. This aids in creating criteria for selecting more pertinent information from the raw input. Demanding mastery of form over content may be likened to the type of jigsaw puzzle solver who sits with a group of pieces interlocked by chance and keeps randomly trying to add new pieces to the group. Other puzzle-solvers assemble pieces by some classification, thus increasing their chances of building up a segment of the puzzle. A third puzzle addict will gather all the "edge" pieces and make the frame into which all else must fit, and which gives clues to the logical connections. The overarching conceptual framework permits more freedom and shifting back and forth through the levels of input information. In language learning, freedom to move within an overall conceptualization should result in earlier integration of each new datum, giving earlier and better TL learning. The need to operate on many levels simultaneously is a hallmark of processing of "real life" phenomena. It aids conceptual development, precludes boredom, and counteracts "fatigue blindness," which often occurs in highly structured situations.

This would suggest that a greater volume of language input might be advantageous for the adult foreign-language student. At the same time, the social atmosphere within which these students operate should be one that encourages creativity and communication as the entry point as well as the goal of study. The ideal of perfection is not conducive to foreign-language learning for the adult. Constant evaluation, from any source, is also counterproductive. Grading may in itself be a negative factor.

CONCLUDING REMARKS

The emerging picture of the SL is of an early and avid reader, conscious of style and vocabulary (namely, TTR results), who draws information from any available source. The knowledge of one foreign language for the SL facilitates learning another. If the SL has been bilingual in his/her childhood, other social factors being equal, he/she is more of a potential candidate for successful language learning as an adult than any adult monolingual. The SL is likely to be the oldest, an only, or oldest of the same-sex child, with a finely balanced analytic and relational cognitive style.[21] The SL is accustomed to self-discipline and much practice, but is flexible in restructuring mental frameworks and is willing to "guess" (not randomly, but by testing a subconsciously sensed hypothesis). The SL relies less on nonverbal clues and for good reason—accuracy in these interpretations is low. It is probable that no matter what presentation methods are used, the SL will maximally adapt and integrate language information in several ways. This is the result of an ability to discern linguistic "noise" versus patterns, connections, and regularities. The SL is more concerned with the communicative goal than with structures or means. Not one SL asked the question, "What do you want me to do now?" Nine of the 14 USLs asked this question in one form or another. The SL is reasonably accurate in determining her/his capacities at any stage. [The SLs answered the "final exam" questions in much the order of ranking that they had made, based on perceived difficulty. The USLs answered or tried to answer questions in the order of their appearance. USLs both overrated and underrated their abilities to answer the questions.] SLs took pleasure in new symbol-using systems and most classed themselves as "xenophiles," without rejecting their own social groups. The USLs and MONs evinced differing degrees and forms of cultural rigidity, but all were openly unwilling to venture beyond the known set of perceptions. USLs and MONs were also highly negatively self-evaluative before and during the task. They were uninterested in symbol-using systems of most sorts, such as the mathematical and the musical, ciphers, codes, puzzles, and flags.

Both SLs and MLTs found symbol-using systems intriguing. Perhaps, rather than investigating "language ability" *per se*, research should focus on the construct of "communicative systems plasticity." At present, among the population at large, concentrated effort by a student or researcher in understanding symbol-using systems is supported only when a practical application seems probable. Expansion of symbol-using ability is not perceived as having intrinsic value. This bodes ill for adult language learning at the present; social acceptance and emotional conviction that alternate ways of life and thought are functional, viable, and demandingly meaningful are the *sine qua non* for rewarding language learning experiences for the adult.

Recapitulation of Hypotheses

1. Contrary to "critical period" theory, adult language learning, to a high level can and does occur. SUPPORTED.

2. Multilinguals are advantaged in the task of learning foreign languages in adult years. SUPPORTED.

3. Cognitive-style tests will distinguish multilinguals from monolinguals and will be predictive of success in adult language learning. NOT SUPPORTED. Data inconclusive; tests and definitions in need of sharpening and refining.

4. Differences in approach styles will mark monolinguals and multilinguals and distinguish between successful and unsuccessful learners. SUPPORTED.

5. Successful learners will sample more informational sources, but will find and pursue effective learning techniques sooner. SUPPORTED.

6. Successful learners will show more centrality on cognitive-style continua and more field-independence. NOT SUPPORTED. Data inconclusive.

7. Successful learners will defer judgment to a significant degree. SUPPORTED.

8. Task- and self-evaluation will differ between groups. SUPPORTED, but needs clarification.

9. Concern with style and functions of language is indicative of attitudes correlated with successful learning. SUPPORTED.

10. Early efforts to use the target language and lack of reticence in involvement with the target language predict greater probability of successful learning. SUPPORTED.

11. Multilinguals and successful learners will both differ with regard to the quantity of material memorized in lexical items and syntactic forms. STRONGLY SUPPORTED for SLs; evidence of trend in this direction for MLTs.

12. Self-direction and positive affective attitude toward the task will differ between groups. STRONGLY SUPPORTED for SLs; weakly supported for MLTs.

13. Information-utilization patterns and quantity, points of entry, and focus will distinguish successful learners from poor learners. SUPPORTED. Only point of entry and information utilization weakly separate MLTs from MONs.

SUMMARY

Twenty adults—ten multilinguals (users of three or more languages) and ten monolinguals (life-long users of only one language)—were given the task of learning, in a limited time period, a foreign language previously unknown to them. The language corpus was large, but finite, and no standards of accomplishment were given to participants. The choice of multilinguals for the test group was not arbitrary; free choice of target language, integrative versus instrumental motivation, anomie, and similar issues fade in studies of multilinguals, possibly providing a clearer picture of processes, behaviors, intuitions, and motivations of adult learners approaching a totally unfamiliar language. It was presumed that testing pressures would force each participant to resort to self-determined "optimal strategies" in the self-instruction task. Examination of results showed, as hypothesized, that multilinguals predominated in the group of "successful learners." The successful group was observed during the study process in an attempt to identify styles of task-approach and methods and other factors that might relate to their proficiency.

One original assumption was that cognitive style would be partially predictive of language-learning ability, but the concept was static and nonpredictive. The processual concept "approach style" yielded several insights into the relationship between active commitment and language-learning success in adult years. Strategies of memorization, learning, and ordering were discernible during the 4 hours of learning and may have implications relevant to the fields of psycholinguistics, language sociology and anthropology, communications, and foreign language pedagogy and requirements.

REFERENCES

1. RUBIN, J. 1975. What the "good language learner" can teach us. TESOL Q. **9** (1): 41–51.
2. STERN, H. H. 1975. What can we learn from the good foreign language learner? Canad. Mod. Lang. Rev. **31** (4): 304–318.
3. WITKIN, H. & J. BERRY. 1975. Psychological differentiation in a cross-cultural perspective. J. Cross-Cultural Psychol. **6** (1): 4–87.
4. WITKIN, H., A. DYK, H. FATERSON, H., D. GOODENOUGH & S. KARP. 1962. Psychological Differentiation. Wiley. New York, N.Y.
5. CATTELL, R. 1966. The Scree Test for the number of factors. Multivar. Behav. Anal. **I** (2): 245–273.
6. NISBETT, R. & L. TEMOSHOOK. 1976. Is there an external cognitive style? J. Pers. Soc. Psychol. **33** (1): 36.
7. GARDNER, R. W., P. S. HOLZMAN, G. S. KLEIN, H. B. LINTON & D. P. SPENCE. 1959. Cognitive control: A study of individual consistencies in cognitive behavior. Psychol. Issues **I** (4).
8. KAGAN, J., H. MOSS & I. SIGEL. 1963. Psychological significance of styles of conceptualization. Monogr. Soc. Res. Child Devel. **28** (2): 73–112.
9. DE ARRIGARAY, C. 1971. Gramatica del Euskera (dialecto Guipuzcoano), 2nd ed. Facsimil. Editorial Aunamendi. San Sebastian.
10. OLTMAN, P., E. RASKIN & H. WITKIN. 1971. Group Embedded Figures Test. Consulting Psychologists Press. Palo Alto, Calif.
11. RAMSAY, R. 1977. Multilinguals and Successful Language Learners: Cognitive Strategies and Styles of Approach to Language Learning in Adults.: 13. Unpublished Ph.D. dissertation. Graduate Center, CUNY. New York, N.Y.
12. SCHWARZ, F. 1972. Cognitive Style as a Parameter of Information Processing Activity. Unpublished Ph.D. disseration. Graduate Center, CUNY. New York, N.Y.
13. BRUNER, J. & H. TAJFEL. 1961. Cognitive risk and environmental change. J. Abnorm. Soc. Psychol. **62**: 231–241.
14. RILEY, T. & F. DENMARK. 1974. Field independence and measures of intelligence: Some considerations. Soc. Behav. Pers. **2** (1): 25–29.
15. GREGORY, R. L. 1970. The Intelligent Eye.: 15–17. McGraw-Hill. New York, N.Y.
16. MILLER, G. A. 1956. The magical number seven, plus or minus two. Psychol. Rev. **63**: 81–97.
17. STEVICK, E. Quoted in: Alatis, J. A. 1976. The urge to communicate vs. resistance

to learning in English as a second language. Eng. Lang. Teach. J. **XXX** (4): 226.

18. SCHNEIDER, F. & B. KINTZ. 1967. An analysis of the incidental-intentional learning dichotomy. J. Exp. Psychol. **73** (1): 85–90.

19. MORTON, J. 1970. A functional model for memory. *In* Models of Human Memory. D. A. Norman, ed. Academic Press. New York, N.Y.

20. REICHER, G. 1969. Perceptual recognition as a function of meaningfulness of stimulus material. J. Exp. Psychol. **81:** 275–280.

21. COHEN, R. 1969. Cognitive styles, culture conflict, and non-verbal tests of intelligence. Am. Anthropol. **71:** 828–865.

22. FRAZER, J. G. 1922. The Golden Bough (abridged edition). Macmillan. London. (Cited in Schwarz.[12])

LINGUISTIC FLEXIBILITY
IN URBAN ZAMBIAN SCHOOLCHILDREN*

Robert Serpell

*Institute for African Studies
University of Zambia
Lusaka, Zambia*

Discussions of language policy in multilingual nations often suffer from oversimplification. One factor that contributes to this trend is the temptation to impose on multilingual communities a compartmentalized mode of categorization whose validity is mainly confined to relatively homogeneous speech communities. In this mode, languages are construed as discrete and largely autonomous systems, and each individual is assumed to have a static, well-defined hierarchy of access to various languages, with the dominant position assigned to her mother-tongue, L_1, or native language. Yet in many multilingual communities the distinctions between various dialects and languages are blurred by fluid interchange, and an individual member of such a community may be more conscious of the various social connotations of different speech codes than of variations in her competence across them.

The present exploratory study was prompted by the feeling that the current national debate in Zambia concerning medium of instruction in primary schools has suffered from this type of conceptual bias. The speech community of Lusaka, Zambia's capital city, is characterized by (1) great diversity of ethnic origins, (2) a high incidence of individual multilingualism, and (3) a very fluid linguistic repertoire. The first of these features has tended to receive great emphasis in political and educational circles, often to the virtual exclusion of the other two equally important characteristics.

LINGUISTIC AND ETHNIC DIVERSITY

Hardman, for instance, in a brief to the Ministry of Education on "vernacular language teaching in Lusaka" attributed what he perceived as its "general inadequacy" to the following main causes:

> (a) the teacher's language may not be the same as the language of the zone in which he is teaching;
> (b) the teacher's language may not be the same as that of the readers which he and his class are using;
> (c) the teacher's command of any other language but his own may be inadequate for proper teaching;
> (d) it often happens that a child's language is neither that of his teacher nor that of the reader he has to use[18] (p. 1).

* This article is a revised and expanded version of a paper published in the *Journal of the Language Association of Eastern Africa.*[42]

In support of these observations Hardman appended the results of a survey of "home-language distribution in 26 Lusaka Grade 1 classes." This showed that the 17 teachers for these classes included only two whose home language was Nyanja† (the medium of instruction), one Tumbuka, six Bemba, five Tonga, one Lenje, one Lozi, and one Shona; whereas of the 1,044 pupils involved, 49 percent were classified as speaking Nyanja as their home language, 20 percent Bemba, 11 percent Tonga, 5 percent Lozi, and 15 percent other languages. In spite of certain classification anomalies, these latter figures on the children's home language-groups agree quite well with unpublished data collected as part of the 1969 National Population Census, which classified the total Lusaka primary school enrollment of 30,100 pupils by "major language group" as follows: 41 percent Nyanja, 19 percent Bemba, 14 percent Tonga, 5 percent Lozi and 22 percent other languages.‡

Hardman went on to remark that "points (a), (b), (c) and (d) give rise to situations which in purely educational terms are intolerable"[18] (p. 1). There can indeed be little doubt that the teaching of the indigenous Zambian languages in the urban schools left and still leaves a great deal to be desired. Chimuka, confirming the widespread view that "Zambian languages are the worst-taught subjects," writes that "the reasons for this situation may either be lack of material incentives, lack of self or internally imposed motivation, attitudes of mind or individual apathy towards Zambian languages"[3] (p. 24). What must be questioned, however, is whether diversity in itself is a cause of the poor teaching in this area. Carter presents a much more optimistic view of the educational consequences of linguistic diversity in Zambia's Western Province. He suggests three main reasons for the results—results that in view of the basic problem in the lower primary schools he considers to be "astonishingly good"[2] (p. 151). These reasons include the teacher's background and experience as well as the style of teaching. Furthermore, he adds "it seems possible ... that a polyglot atmosphere itself contributes something to the ease with which learning is acquired, linguistic as well as factual. The presence and interplay of many languages stimulates an alertness, almost an excitement, that opens the mind to learning in a way not found in the uniformity of the monoglot atmosphere"[2]

INDIVIDUAL MULTILINGUALISM

The background of the teacher is a multilingual one. Not only has she herself often grown up in a polyglot school environment, but she has also in most cases resided as an adult in two or more separate regions of the country and thus has had the opportunity to learn various different Zambian languages. Mytton included in his survey of 4,780 adults distributed over the whole of Zambia the following questions: "What language did you first speak as a child? What language(s) do you now speak at home? What

† Following the convention adopted by the Zambia Language Survey, prefixes of language names (as in Ci-Nyanja, IciBemba, SiLozi, and so on) have been omitted from this paper.

‡ I am grateful to the GRZ Central Statistical Office, Lusaka, for access to these data.

language(s) do you speak at work? [asked only of those with a job]. Besides these languages are there any others you can speak?"[29] (pp. 163–4). The answers to these questions were classified according to Kashoki and Mann's[22] criteria, which divide the more than 80 indigenous Bantu dialects into 14 groups sharing some "vocabulary and grammatical characteristics," so that variations within each group may be regarded conventionally as dialects of a single language. By these criteria Mytton's informants living in urban areas claimed *on average* to known about 2.8 different languages, whereas those in the rural area claimed an average of 1.9. We may conclude from these results that, in the statistical sense of the word, it is entirely *normal* in Zambia to be at least bilingual and, if resident in a town, to be trilingual.

Multilingual individuals vary, of course, in their degree of competence in each of the several linguistic codes to which they have access. Mytton's results show that the three most widely spoken languages in Zambia are Bemba (which 56 percent of his informants claimed to speak), Nyanja (42 percent), and Lozi (17 percent). It should be emphasized that these percentages included large numbers of people who did not learn these languages as the first language of their home. Indeed a *majority* of those claiming to speak Nyanja did not claim it as their "mother tongue." Oral traditions tell us that Nyanja is the main *lingua franca* of Lusaka, whereas Bemba is the main *lingua franca* of towns on the Copperbelt. These traditions are reinforced by official policy in matters of education, as well as various other activities in which official pronouncements are made. The Zambian language prescribed for use in Lusaka schools is Nyanja, whereas in Copperbelt schools it is Bemba. That this aspect of policy bears a relation to the social realities of the relevant speech communities is attested by Mytton's results showing that 96 percent of his informants living in Copperbelt towns claimed to speak Bemba and only 39 percent to speak Nyanja, whereas 95 percent of the Lusaka informants claimed to speak Nyanja and only 58 percent Bemba.

What Mytton's results do not tell us is the degree of competence of the various groups in the languages they claim to speak. Two studies that throw some indirect light on this question are available. Kashoki[21] obtained some useful baseline data on mutual intelligibility. Rural secondary school students who claimed *never* to have been exposed to languages other than their "mother tongue" listened to tape-recorded passages in Bemba, Nyanja Tonga, Lozi, Luvale, and Lunda. After each passage they answered a series of multiple-choice questions in English to test their comprehension of the passage. Students with Bemba as their home language scored an average of 99 percent correct on the Bemba passage and 42 percent correct on Nyanja. Students with Nyanja as their home language scored 98 percent on Nyanja and 25 percent on Bemba.

A study I carried out in Lusaka tested the aural comprehension of Nyanja by Grade 3 and Grade 6 primary-school pupils from Nyanja-, Bemba-, Tonga-, and Lozi-speaking families.[37] The children were also subdivided according to the length of time they had been living in Lusaka and their residential area. Each of these sampling variables was found to exercise a statistically reliable influence on the children's test scores. Children of Nyanja-speaking families scored higher than children of Bemba-speaking

families, who in turn scored somewhat higher than children of Tonga- or
Lozi-speaking families. Grade 6 pupils scored higher than Grade 3 pupils
with the same home language. But Grade 6 children born in Lusaka into
Bemba-speaking families scored about the same as the younger children of
Nyanja-speaking families enrolled in Grade 3. Finally, children of both
Nyanja- and Bemba-speaking families living in Matero (a relatively poor
residential suburb, where a large majority of families speak Nyanja at home)
scored slightly higher than children of the same home language living in
Libala (a wealthier suburb where Bemba-speaking families apparently
slightly outnumber Nyanja-speaking families). In an attempt to interpret this
last result it was suggested that residential communities in Lusaka may vary
in the extent to which they make use of one or another of the commonly
available linguistic codes.

THE SOCIAL MEANING OF CODE SELECTION

In a speech community where most individuals are multilingual, the
speaker's choice of linguistic code for a given utterance ceases to be dictated
primarily by her estimate of the audience's competence, and the selection of
one code in preference to another comes to carry social meaning. Multilingual speakers become extremely versatile at manipulating this aspect of
communication, the parameters of which are difficult to analyze from an
outsider's perspective. One dimension may be likened to a kind of social
stratification. The "superposition" of two dialects, which Ferguson[7] first
described as "diglossia," seems to find a parallel in the use of former colonial
languages in many Third World states.[8] The specific allocation of social
spheres to one rather than another varies, however, with the particular
historical circumstances. Thus, in Zambia English serves several of the
functions for which Ferguson found the H(igh) variety to be specialized in
Egypt, Switzerland, Haiti, and Greece: "speech in parliment; university
lecture; newspaper editorial; poetry."[7] And the various local languages in
Zambia serve most of the special functions listed for the L(ow) variety:
"instructions to servants, waiters, workmen and clerks; conversation with
family, friends and colleagues; folk literature"[7] (p. 328). Moreover, the
general description of H and L fits much of the Zambian usage of English
and the indigenous languages. English, as in the case of Ferguson's H, is
accorded higher prestige in Zambia than the indigenous languages. Most of
the nation's literary heritage is in English. Further, English is learned
through formal education rather than at home, is the subject of greater
standardization and "include(s) in its total lexicon technical terms and
learned expressions which have no regular L equivalents."[7] (p. 333). On the
other hand, two of the functions reserved in Ferguson's taxonomy for the H
variety are clearly assigned for the most part to the indigenous languages in
Zambia, namely "sermon in church"[30] and "personal letter."

Another dimension of social meaning in the choice of linguistic code is
social distance. Just as in Oakland California, "the use of Black English
promotes cohesion among Blacks"[23] (p. 148), so two urban Zambians from
the same minority ethnic group may express their solidarity by choosing to
converse in public in the code of their ancestral, rural home. Conversely, the

use of English by an African customer in the markets in Lusaka is often interpreted as a form of snobbery, much to the embarassment of visitors from distant African nations whose choice of this code is dictated solely by considerations of competence. Gumperz[12] has described a number of other types of code-specialization that may occur in multilingual communities.

The assignment of a given code to a single social function seems, however, to be too static a conception to do justice to the variety of social meanings expressed by code-selection in a multilingual community. "What one empirically observes ... is not customs so much as cases of verbal behaviour, illustrating very often processes of over- and under-communicating statuses (processes of impression management)"[32] (p. 300). Goffman, to whom this last expression is due, has pointed out that "it is not the attributes of social structure that are here considered, such as age and sex, but rather the value placed on these attributes as they are acknowledged in the situation current at hand"[10] (p. 134). Thus, Parkin reports from another multilingual African city, Nairobi, that:

> ..."in a particular conversation English is seen to express, say social exclusiveness, as against Swahili, which may express social inclusiveness. In another conversation, this set of values may be reversed ... people do not adhere rigidly to the stereotyped evaluations. They use the manifold behavioural connotations of different languages..."[31] (p. 212–214).

To this social-psychological potential of code-selection, we should add that the availability of these several speech registers puts at the speaker's disposal a remarkable range of nuances of meaning. This is particularly evident in the presentation of topics that concern the interaction between different cultures.[39] In both the social and the semantic field, the choice of code by multilingual speakers is often a highly creative exercise.

THE FLUIDITY OF MULTILINGUAL URBAN SPEECH

One further distinguishing feature of the Zambian speech community requires emphasis, and this is the fluidity of its verbal repertoire. In describing earlier the social significance of code-selection, I simplified the situation by implying that a whole message or conversation is transmitted in a single code. In practice, however, we find among Zambian multilinguals a great deal of switching to and fro between codes. Mkilifi[28] has described similar "language mixing" among Swahili-English bilinguals and trilinguals in Tanzania.

Theoretical linguistic analyses of these phenomena are still at a pioneering stage. Bautista[1] has proposed a generative grammatical model of bilingual competence for speakers in the Philippines who alternate between Tagalog and English. Her analysis suggests that there is "a qualitative difference between the insertion of L_2 words in L_1 utterences and the use of L_2 phrases and clauses in L_1 utterances...." Only the latter is truly "code-switching," which requires "activating two almost entire linguistic systems"[1] (p. 85). Reyes'[33] study of an American Chicano community alternating between Spanish and English suggests that a third, intermediary pattern needs to be distinguished. Single lexical items introduced from L_2 into an L_1 utterance may either be established loan-words, in which case we may speak of "incorporated borrowing," or a less standardized phenomenon of "spontaneous borrowing." The picture is further complicated by the fact that certain well-worn phrases may operate as tightly integrated units that are introduced in much the same "surface-structure" way as loan-words.[1]

Apart from the incorporation of such loan-words and loan-phrases, other forms of convergence seem to occur when two or more linguistic groups coexist over a long period. Gumperz and Wilson[16] have shown how in a multilingual community on the Indo-Aryan/Dravidian border in India the grammatical structures of Kannada and Urdu have shifted in the local dialects to parallel that of Marathi. The effect is that "while language distinctions are maintained" at the level of lexical forms, "actual messages show word-for-word or morph-for-morph translatability, and speakers can therefore switch from one code to another with a minimum of additional learning"[16] (p. 270). These authors go on to suggest that children growing up in this community probably start with the acquisition of a common core syntax, and only later superimpose on this the standard languages that each individual encounters in varying degrees according to her socioeconomic position. Speech patterns in urban areas of Zambia show a fluidity, or lack of clear compartmentalization of the various codes, throughout the three linguistic subsystems: lexical, grammatical, and phonological. Thus, in addition to lexical intrusions, we find constructions based on English word order imposed on a string of Nyanja or Bemba words, and extensive phonological restructuring of English words when they are "borrowed." The predominant patterns of intrusion seem to be from English into the Bantu codes for lexical items and grammar and from Bantu into English for phonology. But there are some reversals of these orders at all levels. These very varied patterns of code mixture pose a complex problem of criteria when it comes to identifying "errors" in the spoken or written usage of Zambian students.[39]

IMPLICATIONS FOR THE CLASSROOM

Language teaching is traditionally conceived as an exercise in instilling "correct" speech behavior. Yet a more important goal is to develop the student's articulacy. If, as I have suggested, the strategy of code-switching increases the range of a bilingual speaker's communicative competence, then educational practice should strive to encourage its utilization. The traditional emphasis on standards of correctness, however, tends to stigmatize the use of a fluid repertoire. Thus, Wingard, commenting on the use of English as a teaching medium in Uganda wrote: "the use of an indigenous language medium peppered with English words for which good indigenous language equivalents exist is a common but undesirable practice"[41] (p. 112). And Hardman states categorically that "such mixtures as "Town Nyanja" and "Ci-Copperbelt" should not be tolerated in the classrooms"[18] (p. 2). The notion of linguistic "purity," which underlies these value judgments, originates from speech communities where the different codes are strictly compartmentalized.

Compartmentalization also dominates most political thinking about language education. The decision to introduce English as the medium of instruction in Zambia's lower primary schools in 1965 was based on the dual premise that (1) children must learn either in English or in another language and that (2) a common linguistic code for all Zambians is a necessary tool for achieving political integration. The fallacy of assuming that a society must be homogeneous in order to be integrated has been exposed by Das Gupta[5] Kashoki,[19] and many others. Following up their pluralistic approach to language policy, I have suggested that "the key to planning for national unity through linguistic diversity . . . lies in fostering diversity within individuals rather than between different groups."[39]

The present study was conceived partly as a demonstration of the feasibility of using several languages concurrently in the classroom. It was hypothesized (1) that Lusaka schoolchildren would accept without question the switching by a teacher from one code to another, and that they would often reply to the teacher in a different linguistic code from that in which the question was phrased. A second purpose was to explore the situational and cognitive influences on children's communicative competence in the various codes. Here it was hypothesized (2) that different conceptual domains would be handled by the children more efficiently in one code than in another. More specifically the study predicted (2a) that Grade 1 children of Nyanja- and Bemba-speaking families in Lusaka would handle questions about home and playful interaction better in Nyanja and Bemba than in English, and (2b) that these children's command of English would be better in dealing with pictures than in answering questions about home or in the realm of play.

Two more hypotheses were concerned with the impact of the urban *lingua franca* on children who do not speak it as their "mother tongue." Advocates of the use of English in Zambia's urban primary schools often suggest that this is a beneficial policy for children whose home language is not the major indigenous language of that zone. Contrary to this view, it was hypothesized (3) that Grade 1 children from Bemba-speaking homes in Lusaka would have a better command of Nyanja than of English. Finally, in an attempt to show that this last phenomenon is not simply a result of structural similarity between the Nyanja and Bemba languages, it was hypothesized that (4) because Nyanja is the *lingua franca* of Lusaka, children from Nyanja-speaking homes in this city would have a less-good command of their second language, Bemba, than the command of Nyanja shown by the children of Bemba-speaking families.

METHOD

Subjects

Forty-two children attending Grade 1 in unscheduled§ schools in Lusaka were tested. The three schools sampled were situated respectively in the

§ Following the racial desegregation of the colonial schools of Northern Rhodesia, the better-equipped primary schools were renamed "fee-paying schools" in 1963 and when the fees were abolished in 1971, they were again renamed "scheduled" schools. The majority of Zambian schools are by contrast called "unscheduled."

center of the town, on the eastern periphery, and on the northern periphery. The centrally placed school draws most of its pupils from the adjacent police camp, which accommodates higher- and lower-ranking officers. All but a few of the pupils in the two outlying schools were living in the adjacent informal (or "shanty") housing areas. No attempt was made to verify the ages of the children. The ages that they stated ranged from 1 to 20 years, while their apparent age, as estimated by the researchers, ranged from 6 to 10 years with an average of about 8. The sample was roughly equally divided between boys and girls and between children who said they speak Nyanja or a related language at home and those who said they speak Bemba or a related language at home. The former group included one child from a Nsenga-speaking family and one from a Ngoni-speaking family, whereas the latter included three children from Mambwe-speaking families. Although Nsenga and Mambwe fall into distinct categories of the Kashoki-Mann taxonomy, the prevailing situation in the rural areas where these languages are widely spoken makes it clear that Nsenga-speakers are more likely to be familiar with Nyanja, whereas Mambwe-speakers are more likely to be familiar with Bemba.

For the purpose of statistical analysis, a balanced subsample of 24 subjects was selected at random with the restrictions that it should comprise one boy and one girl from each home-language group in each of the six testing sequences to be outlined later, and that two boys and two girls in each home-language group should come from each of the three schools. Although the class teachers assisted with the identification of subjects from appropriate language backgrounds, they were asked to refrain from selecting extremes of talent since it was emphasized that the study was concerned with the performance of "average" children.

Procedure

Each child was tested individually by an experienced female school teacher whose home-language was Nyanja and who was also fluent in Bemba and English. Although my home-language is English and I have only limited proficiency in Nyanja and Bemba, I was present throughout the session recording the child's responses and occasionally participating in the testing. Tester, child, and recorder were seated informally around the teacher's desk in a classroom or office at the child's school. The only formal apparatus was a small rubber ball (6 cm in diameter) and a copy of the English reader (entitled *In the House*) prescribed for the end of the second term in Grade 1 of the New Zambia Primary Course followed by all Lusaka schools. Testing was conducted in the last week of the second term of 1976.

Three tests comprising ten items each were administered in the same sequence to all children. The first test (Information) consisted of questions about the child and her home; the second test (Play) consisted of phrases, mainly simple commands, that might be used among children playing together (with a ball, and so on), and the third test (Picture) consisted of questions about the content of a picture such as might be asked by a teacher in the course of a lesson (FIG. 1). The full text of the tests is reproduced in the APPENDIX.

Father, Mother, Jelita
and Mulenga are
eating.
They are eating
nsima and fish.
They like nsima and
fish.
They eat nsima
every day.

FIGURE 1. Picture and text from Grade 1 reader entitled *In the House*. The Picture test consisted of questions about this picture's content. (Reproduced by permission of the National Educational Company of Zambia, Ltd.)

The six possible permutations of the three languages—Nyanja, Bemba, and English —define the six testing sequences followed. Thus, each child was tested successively in three different languages. The switches from one language to the next were not announced or explained, but followed a brief natural pause as the tester turned from one page of the schedule to the next and changed the topic from the conceptual domain of Information to Play or from Play to Picture. Supplementary remarks, instructions, and the like, were always phrased by the tester or recorder in the language allocated to the current test. In some cases, where the child's responses were unclear on first testing, clarification was sought in the child's home language after the end of the third test.

I recorded in longhand and verbatim the verbal responses by the children as well as the details of supplementary questions and remarks by the adults during testing.

RESULTS

Code-Switching and Problems of Scoring

Although Question 7 in the Information task explicitly inquired what language the child's family speaks at home, only 2 of our 42 subjects ventured explicitly to disclaim knowledge of one of the languages in which testing was conducted. In both cases it was a boy from a Nyanja-speaking family who interjected "sinizwa ci-Bemba" ("I don't know Bemba"). Neither of them registered any further protest when their remark was ignored and the test continued in Bemba. One of them shortly afterwards used the Bemba form *ng'anda* (house) rather than the Nyanja *nyumba*. The other proceeded to answer correctly all ten of the questions put to him in Bemba on the Picture test, but consistently phrased his replies in Nyanja or English. The former child further displayed his flexibility by replying in Nyanja to one of the Information test questions phrased in English, while replying in English to two of the Picture test questions phrased in Nyanja!

The fluidity of the speech repertoire in Lusaka posed considerable problems in categorizing the children's replies as "belonging" to one code rather than another. Adult informants were asked to specify whether a given word is an incorporated standard "loan-word" or a spontaneous switch to the vocabulary of another code. Judging by the uncertainty they expressed, it seems likely that only imperfect consensus would have been found if a comparative study had been made of judgments made by individuals on this issue. The arbitrariness of the classification scheme we adopted became particularly apparent when scoring responses to the Picture test. Consider for instance the following transcript of a boy from a Nyanja-speaking home who was given this test in Bemba:

Q. 5   T(tester): Ninani uyu?
         S(subject): Father.
Q. 6   T: Finshi balecita?
         S: Akumwa madzi.
Q. 7   T: Finshi balenwa?
         S: Madzi.

Q. 8   T: Cinshi ici?
         S: Table.
Q. 9   T: Cinshi ici?
         S: Shoes.
Q. 10   T: Cinshi ici?
         S: Ketan.

According to our criteria this subject's reply to Q. 5 was in English, to Q. 6 in Nyanja, Q. 7 Nyanja, Q. 8 Bemba, Q. 9 English. Q. 10 Bemba. But his replies to Qs. 8 and 10 could equally be regarded as English or Nyanja. In the absence of evidence to the contrary a child was always assumed to have replied in the same language as that in which the question was phrased. The replies to Qs. 5 and 9 are treated as English rather than Bemba because neither *father* nor *shoes* are considered standard loan-words in contemporary Bemba, whereas *table* (usually spelled *itebulu*) and *curtain* (or *iketan*) are standard urban Bemba, so that the child (who may well have felt that he was speaking English or Nyanja) was credited with using Bemba to answer Qs. 8 and 10. Theoretically one might wish to use phonological adaptation as an index of absorption of English-origin vocabulary into urban Bemba or Nyanja. But, even if the difficulties of recording the phonetic forms accurately could have been overcome, is it really appropriate to consider that a child who suppresses the initial *i* and/or the final *u* of *itebulu* is "using English" rather than speaking Bemba with an anglicized pronunciation?

These complexities are cited not because they were so frequent as to make consistent classification impossible, but in order to illustrate how artificial the distinction between these codes can become in a speech community with such a fluid repertoire. In order to quantify the incidence of code-switching by our subjects, the dividing line was set conservatively according to the principles outlined earlier. And in the subsequent analysis of communicative efficiency, responses judged to be correct but in a different code from that of the question were given a score of 1, whereas correct responses in the same code as the question were given a score of 2.

Another category of responses that were given a score of 1 was that which used the same code as the question, but seemed rather inappropriate. If the reply bore no sensible relation to the question (for example, T: "Who washes it for you?" S: "Yes"), a score of O was recorded; if it appeared a *bona fide* attempt to reply but was of dubious communicative adequacy (for example, T: "Who is this?" [a woman] S: "Man"), a score of 1 was recorded; and if the response was unorthodox in form but could not fail to communicate (for example, T: "What is he doing?" S: "A drinking"), a score of 2 was allowed. In some cases "errors" seemed to arise more from difficulties in pictorial perception than from limited linguistic competence. For instance, the artist has drawn such a large piece of *nshima* (stiff maize porridge) in the woman's hand (FIG. 1) that several children identified it as an egg or an orange. Likewise some children identified the man as a boy and one called the curtain a tree. When there was any uncertainty about the nature of the child's perception of the picture this was explored further at the end of the test in her home language. Where the error was found to originate from pictorial perception, a score of 2 was assigned. All scoring was done by me after consultation with several indigenous informants over doubtful cases.

A total of 82 code-switches (by these criteria) was recorded from the 42 subjects. Although these constitute only a small proportion (about 9 percent) of the 924 occasions on which switches could have occurred, it should be noted that many of the replies by the children took the form of only a single word so that conditions were not optimal for observing switching. Moreover, the switches were not confined to a few individuals, but were spread over most of the sample: 33 of the 42 subjects switched at least once. Our results therefore are consistent with the first hypothesis.

Three-quarters of all the switches recorded took place during the Picture test, a majority of these switches consisting of English words such as *man, woman, father, mother, girl, boy* as identifying responses to the question, phrased in Nyanja or Bemba: "Who is this?" The origin of the preference for an English word in this context is quite apparent. These children had during the past few months been asked by their teacher to identify figures in the pictures displayed on their classroom walls and in their schoolbooks. They had in all probability seldom been questioned about pictures by their parents, siblings, or friends in a social context in which the Nyanja and Bemba languages are predominantly used. Thus, although almost all of them were undoubtedly familiar with the appropriate Nyanja or Bemba words for identifying the people in the picture, it seemed appropriate to them in this context to use an English word in response to a question in Nyanja or Bemba. It is worth noting in this regard that more than half of these switches to English on the Picture test occurred when the child was being questioned in her home language.

The remaining 18 switches were spread evenly over most of the other conditions, the noteworthy exception being that only three were observed when a child was responding to the Information or the Play test in her home language. All three of these switches took the form of the child using the English word *years* in response to the question, phrased in Nyanja or Bemba, "How old are you?" This again is a question that children from this section of Lusaka society are very seldom asked outside the context of school.

Finally, of the 36 switches introducing a word in Nyanja or Bemba in response to a question in another language, all but four took the form of the child resorting to her home language in preference to the code of the tester's question.

Communicative Competence in Different Conceptual Domains

The research design permits nine different combinations among the three linguistic codes and the three conceptual domains. Each subject, however, was only tested in three of these combinations with the constraint that she must experience all three codes and all three domains. The statistical consequence of this design is a partial confounding of any interaction effects that might occur between the factors of code and domain with individual differences in competence between subjects. Winer[40] has described a method for analyzing the variance in this design so that the influences of the factors and their interaction are compared with residual variance within subjects.This method was followed in separate analyses for the two balanced subsamples of 12 children, one sample from Nyanja-speaking homes, the other from Bemba-speaking homes.

TABLE 1 summarizes the results of these analyses. In both cases a significant main effect was found from the factor of linguistic code and there was a significant interaction between linguistic code and conceptual domain, whereas the latter factor exercised no significant main effect. Mean scores for each of the nine conditions are represented graphically for the two samples in FIGURE 2, which also summarizes the results of comparisons between individual means. For the Nyanja home-language sample, scores in English were significantly lower than scores in Nyanja in all three domains. Scores in Bemba occupy an intermediary position, not significantly different from Nyanja scores on the Information test and not significantly different from English scores on the Play and Picture tests. Similarly for the Bemba home-language sample, scores in English were significantly lower than scores in Bemba in all domains, whereas scores in Nyanja were not significantly different from scores in Bemba on the Information and Play tests and not signficantly different from scores in English on the Picture test. The results for both samples thus provide strong confirmation of our hypothesis 2a that the children would handle questions about home better in Nyanja and Bemba than in English.

Regarding the specialization of competence in English, the results for the Bemba home-language sample reliably confirm our hypothesis 2b that these subjects' command of English would be better in dealing with pictures than in answering questions about home. For the Nyanja home-language sample

TABLE 1
ANALYSIS OF VARIANCE: SUMMARY TABLES FOR THE BALANCED SUBSAMPLES

Source	Sum of Squares	df	MS	F	p
Children from Nyanja-speaking families					
Between subjects:	182.23	11			
Groups	141.56	5			
Subjects within group	40.67	6	6.78		
Within subjects:	495.33	24			
A: Linguistic codes	303.40	2	151.70	32.84	<0.01
B: Conceptual domains	20.23	2	10.12	2.19	NS
A × B (adjusted)	97.77	4	24.44	5.29	<0.01
Residual	73.93	16	4.62		
Children from Bemba-speaking families					
Between subjects:	224.75	11			
Groups	164.92	5			
Subjects within groups	59.83	6	9.97		
Within subjects:	744.00	24			
A: Linguistic codes	454.17	2	227.09	45.69	<0.01
B: Conceptual domains	26.00	2	13.00	2.62	NS
A × B (adjusted)	184.33	4	46.08	9.27	<0.01
Residual	79.50	16	4.97		

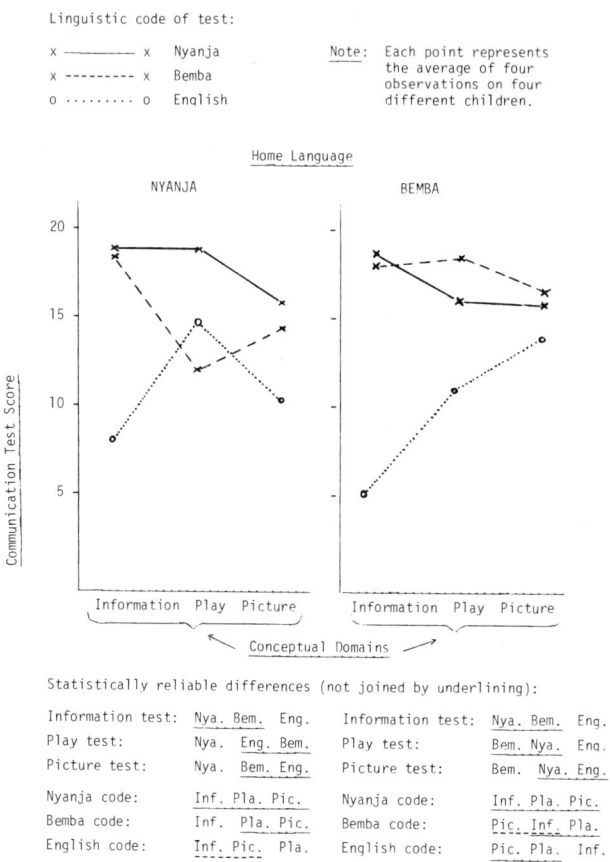

Linguistic code of test:

x ———— x   Nyanja

x -------- x   Bemba

o ········· o   English

Note: Each point represents the average of four observations on four different children.

Home Language

NYANJA   BEMBA

Communication Test Score

Information   Play   Picture   Information   Play   Picture

Conceptual Domains

Statistically reliable differences (not joined by underlining):

Information test:	Nya. Bem. Eng.	Information test: Nya. Bem. Eng.
Play test:	Nya. Eng. Bem.	Play test: Bem. Nya. Eng.
Picture test:	Nya. Bem. Eng.	Picture test: Bem. Nya. Eng.
Nyanja code:	Inf. Pla. Pic.	Nyanja code: Inf. Pla. Pic.
Bemba code:	Inf. Pla. Pic.	Bemba code: Pic. Inf. Pla.
English code:	Inf. Pic. Pla.	English code: Pic. Pla. Inf.

FIGURE 2. Communicative competence of two home-language groups in three conceptual domains in each of three codes.

the difference in English scores between the Information and Picture tests was in the predicted direction, but only reached a 10 percent level of significance (F = 3.47, df 1,16).

The main respect in which the results departed from the pattern of hypothesis 2 is the relatively high scores in English on the Play test. For both samples these scores were closer to the English Picture test scores than to the uniformly low English Information test scores. This result, like all the others outlined in FIGURE 2, appeared to be replicated in the larger sample when the scores of the remaining 18 subjects were inspected. Two complementary factors may help to explain this finding. First, the atmosphere of the Play test, although it elicited a number of smiles from the children, was clearly not truly analogous to the play situations with which they were familiar. Second, a number of the instructions in this test ("come here," "clap your hands," "show me ...," "bring me .. ") are almost certainly included in these children's Grade 1 English teaching exercises. On the first score we may suggest that the disposition to use English was enhanced by the formality of the testing situation, whereas the second factor may explain the fairly high level of English comprehension the children showed in this domain. It should also be noted that the Play test required much less language production by the child than did the other two tests.

Levels of Competence in the Different Codes

FIGURE 2 shows clear confirmation of the hypothesis 3 that the children from Bemba-speaking homes would have a better command of Nyanja than of English. The fact that on the Picture test the difference is too small to reach significance ($F < 2$, df 1,16) reflects the heavy penalty imposed by our scoring system for including English words in otherwise correct replies to questions in Nyanja.

The design of our study was not ideal for assessing relative competence across codes in the two home-language groups since each child was tested in a different domain for each language. Overall, however, the interactions between code and domain may be assumed to balance out roughly for the two subsamples. To test our hypothesis 4, therefore, a first-language (L_1) minus second-language (L_2) difference score was computed for each subject within the balanced subsamples. The mean $L_1 - L_2$ score for the Nyanja home-language group was 3.00, which is as predicted, significantly larger than the mean $L_1 - L_2$ score of 0.83 for the Bemba home-language group ($t = 2.52$, df 22, one-tailed $p < 0.01$). Overall, children from Nyanja-speaking homes were more disadvantaged by testing in Bemba than were children from Bemba-speaking homes by testing in Nyanja, the *major lingua* franca of Lusaka.‖

DISCUSSION

Methodological Constraints

The connotations of language choice in a multilingual community derive from the intuitions shared by members of the community. The present investigation sought to expose some of these intuitions within an explanatory framework.

A different approach to the same objective has been adopted by Scotton and her associates for the speech community of Kampala, Uganda. Initially a questionnaire was administered orally to a stratified sample of the population.[34] Respondents were asked to report on their own language usage and on their attitudes towards various language phenomena. The results of that

‖ An alternative explanation of this finding would be that Nyanja is an easier language for Bemba-speakers to follow than Bemba is for Nyanja-speakers. This hypothesis derives some support from Kashoki's [21] study of "naïve" listeners. A test of this possibility would be permitted by a replication of the present study among children living on the Copperbelt. Hypothesis 4 advanced earlier would generate the prediction for speech communities of the Copperbelt towns that children of Nyanja-speaking families would be *less* handicapped in their non-home language than would be children of Bemba-speaking families, since Bemba is the principal *lingua franca* of the Copperbelt.

study were used to generate predictions as to how a further Ugandan sample would interpret code-switching in a set of concocted conversations played on a tape-recorder.[35] The general success of those predictions demonstrates a consistency in that community between *language posture* ("what people claim they do with speech") and *language image* (" what people think they do with speech"). We cannot, however, infer from this an exactly corresponding pattern of *language usage*, since, as Khubchandani[25] has shown, the latter can deviate very substantially from the former two categories of sociolinguistic data.

The data for the present study are observations of actual language usage, but they were obtained within a controlled situation. These data display two minor limitations as evidence of how languages interact in urban Zambia. The first is the asymmetrical social framework in which the speech was elicited, and the second is the young age of the subjects in the experiment. We have already noted earlier that the issuing of commands and requests by a teacher-like figure probably invalidates the purpose implied by the title of the Play test. More generally, however, an interview to which one party brings a predetermined set of questions clearly constitutes a most atypical sequence of verbal utterances. As Erickson and Schultz[6] point out, the nature of social encounters normally generates a context out of interaction. The framework of discourse is negotiated between the participants.

The Meaning Potential of Code-Switching

There is reason to believe that conversational code-switching in multilingual communities often serves as a social cue to the interpretation of context. Gumperz[13] has analyzed tape-recorded conversations in three different bilingual communities: a village on the Austrian/Yugoslavian border; college students in Delhi, India; and Chicano students and professionals in the United States. In all three communities code-switches were observed that signaled each of the following meanings: quotation, addressee specification, interjection, and message qualification. Perhaps of greatest interest is a large remaining set of cases whose meaning seems to hinge on the contrast between the personal and the objective. In the examples that Gumperz cites, the appeal to this contrast seems to hark back to feelings of ethnicity: the speaker switches to the language of hearth and home to connote a greater personal involvement with that section of her utterance.[36]

The ethnic significance of different codes becomes paramount in the competitive verbal interactions described by Parkin[31] in Nairobi's markets. On these rather dramatic, public occasions it appears that members of different ethnic groups "use the manifold behavioural connotations of different languages to compete with each other or to make concessions"[31] (p. 214). Yet probably a commoner situation is that in which the ethnic origins of the codes are not consciously apprehended by speakers. Thus, Khubchandani remarks that "many speakers in the North-Central Region [of India] who are not native speakers of Hindi or Urdu in the strict linguistic sense but claim Hindi/Urdu as their mother-tongue in Census returns . . . are quite unaware of their bilingual or multilingual behaviour . . . for them

switching of linguistic codes from native speech to Hindi/Urdu is similar to
the switching of styles (such as formal, informal, intimate) in a monolingual
situation"[24] (pp. 11–12).

In our experiment we formally predetermined one-half of the utterances
and thereby lost the opportunity to observe a dynamic interchange. Moreover, it is debatable at what age children acquire the ability to use all the
subtleties of code-switching to communicative effect. Gumperz and Blom[14]
draw a distinction between "situational" and "metaphorical" code-switching.
In the former, the speaker's choice of linguistic form is "narrowly constrained
by linguistic norms"[14] (p. 295), whereas in the latter the speaker introduces
a word or phrase in an unconventional context and plays on the "flavour"
it has acquired from its "original setting"[14] (p. 296). Cook-Gumperz and
Gumperz cite evidence from an unpublished study of young Spanish-English
speakers[9] that "children, while using situational switching, have not yet, it is
presumed, developed sufficient communicative memory to use metaphorical
switching. Children cannot yet take off from the literal meaning of the
speech and diassociate this meaning from its situation in order to make
metaphorical use of semantic linguistic information"[4] (pp. 22–23).

Ecological Validity of the Experiment

Nevertheless, if our experiment is limiting in these respects, the limits it
incorporates are not without practical relevance. The authority structure of
Zambian classrooms is often fairly rigid, perhaps in part as a result of local
traditions' prescribing extreme deference by the young towards their elders.
Many of the teacher's speech acts are addressed to the class as a whole,
which in an urban area generally comprises children of very varied linguistic
home backgrounds. Both of these factors tend to limit the amount of detailed
feedback that the teacher actually receives to guide her in the choice of
linguistic forms. Our results on communicative competence in different
conceptual domains are thus derived from a social framework that approximates quite closely that of most Grade 1 teaching in urban Zambian schools.

Competence and Disposition

The communicative competence scores on which our statistical analysis
is based constitute a global measure for a complex underlying pattern. In
some instances a child responded to the teacher in a different language
because of what she perceived as appropriate to the context of the task.
Thus, most of those who were questioned further, after responding in English
to questions on the Picture test in either Nyanja or Bemba, were able on
request to provide equivalents in Nyanja or Bemba for their initial responses
in English. On the other hand, some children spontaneously translated some
of the questions put to them into their home language before replying. In
these and several other instances there were signs of the child's striving to
circumvent her limited competence by shifting the conversation to a more
familiar code. In practice, linguistic disposition and linguistic competence
are bound to interact. The degree of the child's competence affects her
disposition to use a particular code in a given situation, and the preferential

specialization of a code for certain realms of meaning restricts the range of topics on which she is exposed to new vocabulary that could extend her competence.

It would be possible experimentally to study the influences of topic and of social context as independent factors. But to do so might necessitate abandoning the attempt to simulate "realistic" situations. For, as Halliday points out, "in any social context, certain semantic resources are character-istically employed; certain sets of options are, as it were, 'at risk' in a given semiotic environment. These define the register"[17] (p. 126). As the child becomes adept in this dimension of communication, she will learn to express her purposive role in the "field" of discourse and her relationship to the addressee in the "tenor" of discourse. In contemporary Zambian society, English is often used to mark various specialized "fields," to mark a formal personal tenor, and to mark a didactic functional tenor. These several aspects of "diatypic variation"[11] are fairly autonomous in adult speech, but in the experience of Grade 1 children they tend to coincide a great deal of the time.

Educational Implications

Thus, English is presented to these children as a code more or less restricted in function to the formal exchanges between teacher and pupil on classroom topics. As a result, an almost ritual quality comes to characterize these children's early attempts to use the language. For instance, in the present study, some children began reading out the words beside the picture as soon as the book was opened, whereas others responded to questions about the picture by reciting long stock phrases without regard to their relevance (for example: T: "Have you seen this picture before?" S: "They are eating nshima"; and T: "Who is this?" S: "They are sitting on the chair"). Such responses seem to function as defensive strategies for dealing with a language that the child feels is required of her but that has only a tenuous connection with the rest of her intellect.

Such an attitude towards the officially designated medium of instruction constitutes a serious obstacle to learning. In recognition of this problem, a recent Government policy paper proposed the principle that "the child must be introduced to formal education through the medium of a familiar language in which he can communicate easily"[26] (p. 11). Pedagogically this principle is widely accepted, but in terms of practical policy it has often appeared very difficult to implement in multilingual cities. A priority system is needed to specify which languages shall be available as media of instruction in any given school. Rather than risking promoting strife between the various ethnic groups whose "mother tongues" are candidates for choice, the poli-cymakers have preferred the paradoxical option of an exogenous language because of its alleged impartiality.[27]

The political factors surrounding this contentious issue have been re-viewed elsewhere.[38] The main contribution of the present study concerns the psychological impact on Grade 1 pupils of English as compared with a Zambian language other than the child's "mother tongue." Whatever the fears of the politicians, it is clear from the present results that, among Grade

1 school children in Lusaka, Nyanja- and Bemba-speakers (as defined by their parents' ethnicity) find each other's languages more effective media of communication than they do English for a number of purposes. Our results also show a high degree of flexibility in the strategies of communication adopted by these children when dealing with linguistic forms over which their control is incomplete. These behavioral phenomena pose a challenge for policymakers to devise an educational curriculum that is flexible enough on the one hand to capitalize on the various language skills that Zambian children bring to school, and on the other to foster a communicative competence adequate for Zambia's multilingual society.

SUMMARY

A brief introductory account is given of the speech community of Lusaka, Zambia's capital city, which is characterized by a great diversity of ethnic origins, a high incidence of individual multilingualism, and a very fluid linguistic repertoire. This fluidity stands in marked contrast to the prevailing pattern of compartmentalization, which characterizes language policy in Zambian education. The present study was conceived partly as a demonstration of the feasibility of using several languages concurrently in Lusaka classrooms. Forty-two children attending Grade 1 in three Lusaka schools were given a series of questions and instructions by the same tester alternating among Nyanja, Bemba, and English. As expected, the children generally accepted this code-switching without question, and three-quarters of them replied at least once in a language other than that in which a question was posed.

The test material was divided into three conceptual domains (home, play, and picture) and these were paired according to a counterbalanced design with the three languages. Replies were scored in terms of appropriateness of content and consistency of code relative to the question. Statistical analysis confirmed the hypotheses that children from both Nyanja- and Bemba-speaking families would show greater communicative competence in Nyanja and Bemba than in English for the domain of concepts relating to their home and greater competence in English for the domain of concepts relating to a picture in a schoolbook than for the home domain. Results pertaining to the domain of play were less consistent—a finding that is attributed to the inadequacy of the test for this domain. A further hypothesis confirmed by the results was that the children of Bemba-speaking families would show less of a difference in communicative competence between Nyanja and Bemba than would children from Nyanja-speaking homes. The results are discussed in relation to current problems in Zambian educational policy and in relation to the broader issue of developing an adequate theoretical account of how codes are selected by speakers in multilingual communities.

ACKNOWLEDGMENTS

I am much indebted to Mrs. P. Nguluwe, without whose linguistic skills the study reported herein would have been impossible. Furthermore, in preparing the present version of this paper I have been greatly assisted by comments on the first report and by guidance to related literature from the following persons: Gloria Chan, Jim Dyal, Mubanga Kashoki, Ellen Kitonga, Jim Martin, Rogelio Reyes and Dolores Taylor. The faults that remain are, of course, my own responsibility.

REFERENCES

1. BAUTISTA, L. S. 1975. A model of bilingual competence based on an analysis of Tagalog-English code-switching. Philipp. J. Linguistics **6** (1):51–89.
2. CARTER, T. D. T. 1969. The question of language in Barotse schools. J. African Languages **8:** 141–152.
3. CHIMUKA, S. S. 1976. The teaching and learning of Zambian languages in secondary schools and teacher training colleges. Bull. Zambia Language Group **2** (2):22–30.
4. COOK-GUMPERZ, J. & J. J. GUMPERZ. 1976. Context in children's speech. *In* Papers on Language and Context. Working Paper No. 46. Language-Behavior Research Laboratory, University of California at Berkeley.
5. DAS GUPTA, J. 1968. Language diversity and national development. *In* Language Problems of Developing Nations. J. A. Fishman *et al.*, Eds.:17–26. Wiley. New York, N. Y.
6. ERICKSON, F. & J. SCHULTZ. 1977. When is a context? Some issues and methods in the analysis of social competence. Quart. Newsl. Inst. Comp. Human Dev. **1** (2):5–10.
7. FERGUSON, C. A. 1959. Diglossia. Word **15:** 325–340.
8. FISHMAN, J. A. 1967. Bilingualism with and without diglossia; diglossia with and without bilingualism. J. Soc. Issues **23** (2):29–38.
9. GENISHI, C. S. 1975. Rules for Code-Switching in Young Spanish-English Speakers: An Exploratory Study of Language Socialization. Unpublished Ph.D. dissertation. University of California at Berkeley.
10. GOFFMAN, E. 1964. The neglected situation. Am. Anthropol. **66** (6):133–136.
11. GREGORY, M. 1967. Aspects of varieties differentiation, J. Linguistics **3:** 177–198.
12. GUMPERZ, J. J. 1962. Types of linguistic communities. Anthropol. Linguistics **4** (1):28–40.
13. GUMPERZ, J. J. 1976. The sociolinguistic significance of conversational code-switching. *In* Papers on Language and Context. Working Paper No. 46. Language Behavior Research Laboratory, University of California at Berkeley.
14. GUMPERZ, J. J. & J. P. BLOM. 1971. Social meaning in linguistic structures: Code-switching in Norway. *In* Language in Social Groups. (Selected and introduced by A. S. Dil.) University Press. Stanford, Calif.
15. GUMPERZ, J. J. & E. HERNANDEZ. 1971. Bilingualism, bidialectalism and classroom interaction. In Ref. 14.
16. GUMPERZ, J. J. & R. WILSON.1971. Convergence and creolization: A case from the Indo-Aryan/Dravidian border in India. In Ref. 14.
17. HALLIDAY, M. A. K. 1975. Learning How to Mean: Explorations in the Development of Language. Arnold. London, England.
18. HARDMAN, J. M. 1966. Vernacular Language-Teaching in Lusaka. Ministry of Education, English Medium Centre (mimeographed memorandum VERN/L/2). Lusaka, Zambia.
19. KASHOKI, M. E. 1973. Language: A blue-print for national integration. Bull. Zambia Language Group 16F. (2): 19–49.
20. KASHOKI, M. E. 1975. Migration and language change: The introduction of town and country. African Soc. Res. **19:** 707–729.
21. KASHOKI, M. E. 1977. Between language communication in Zambia. Lingua **41:** 145–168.

22. KASHOKI, M. E. & M. MANN. 1978. A general sketch of the Bantu languages of Zambia. *In* Language in Zambia. S. Ohannessian and M. E. Kashoki, Eds.: 47–100. International African Institute. London, England.
23. KERNAN, C. M. 1973. Language behaviour in a black urban community. Monographs of the Language Behavior Research Laboratory, No. 2. University of California. Berkeley, Calif.
24. KHUBCHANDANI, L. M. 1972. Fluidity in mother-tongue identity. Paper presented at Third International Congress of Applied Linguistics, Copenhagen, August, 1972.
25. KHUBCHANDANI, L. M. 1980. Language and Communication in a Modern Setting: Implications of Cultural Pluralism and Modernization in South Asia. University Press of Hawaii. Honolulu, Hawaii.
26. MINISTRY OF EDUCATION. 1976. Education for Development: Draft Statement on Educational Reform. Government Printer. Lusaka, Zambia.
27. MINISTRY OF EDUCATION. 1977. Educational Reform: Proposals and Recommendations. Government Printer. Lusaka, Zambia.
28. MKILIFI, M. H. A. 1974. Triglossia and Swahili-English bilingualism in Tanzania. Lang. in Soc. **1:** 197–213.
29. MYTTON, G. 1974. Listening, Looking and Learning: Report on a National Mass Media Audience Survey in Zambia (1970–73). University of Zambia Institute for African Studies. Lusaka, Zambia.
30. NSONTA, P. M. 1975. Some observations on language use in churches in Zambia. Bull. Zambia Language Group. **2** (1):12–29.
31. PARKIN, D. J. 1974. Language switching in Nairobi. *In* Language in Kenya. W. H. Whiteley, Ed. Oxford University Press. Oxford, England.
32. PRIDE, J. B. 1970. Sociolinguistics. *In* New Horizons in Linguistics. J. Lyons, Ed. Penguin Books. Harmondsworth, England.
33. REYES, R. 1976. Studies in Chicano Spanish. Unpublished Ph.D. dissertation. Harvard University. Cambridge, Mass.
34. SCOTTON, C. M. 1972. Choosing a Lingua Franca in an African Capital. Linguistic Research, Inc. Edmonton, Canada.
35. SCOTTON, C. M. & W. URY. 1977. Bilingual strategies: The social functions of code-switching. Int. J. Sociol. Lang. **13:** 5–20.
36. SERPELL, R. 1977. Context and connotation: The negotiation of meaning in a multiple speech repertoire. Quart. Newsl. Inst. Compar. Human Devel. **1** (4): 10–15.
37. SERPELL, R. 1978. Comprehension of Nyanja by Lusaka school children. *In* Language in Zambia. S. Ohannessian and M. E. Kashoki, Eds.:144–181. International African Institute. London, England.
38. SERPELL, R. 1978. Some developments in Zambia since 1971. *In* Language in Zambia. S. Ohannessian and M. E. Kashoki, Eds.:424–447. International African Institute. London, England.
39. SERPELL, R. 1978. Learning to say it better: A challenge for Zambian education. *In* Language and Education in Zambia. L. N. Omondi and Y. T. Simukoko, Eds. Communication No. 14:29–57. Institute for African Studies, University of Zambia. Lusaka, Zambia.
40. WINER, B. J. 1962. Statistical Principles in Experimental Design. McGraw-Hill. New York, N. Y.
41. WINGARD, P. 1963. Problems of the media of instruction in some Uganda school classes. *In* Language in Africa. J. Spencer, Ed. Cambridge University Press. Cambridge, England.
42. SERPELL, R. 1979. Linguistic flexibility in a modern African city. J. Lang. Assoc. Eastern Africa **4** (1):55–76.

APPENDIX
THE TEST ITEMS IN ENGLISH, NYANJA AND BEMBA

Test 1: Information Language

1. (E) What is your name?
   (N) Dzina lako ndiwe ndani?
   (B) Ishina lyobe niwe nani?
2. (E) How old are you?
   (N) Ulindi zaka zingati?
   (B) Uline myaka inga?
3. (E) Where do you live?
   (N) Ukhala kuti?
   (B) Wikala kwi?
4. (E) Is your house far from school or nearby?
   (N) Kodi nyumba yanu ili kutali ndi sukulu kapena pafupi?
   (B) Bushe ing'anda yenu ili ukutali ne sukulu nangu ni mupepi?
5. (E) How many brothers and sisters have you got?
   (N) Ulindi alongo angati?
   (B) Wakwata bandume yobe banga?
6. (E) What language do you speak at home?
   (N) Mukamba citundu canji ku nyumba?
   (B) Chiliminshi musosa ku ing'anda?
7. (E) Who cooks your food at home?
   (N) Ndani amene akuphikira cakudya ku nyumba?
   (B) Ninani ukwipikila ifwakulya kung'anda?
8. (E) What's this? [pointing to child's uniform]
   (N) Ici ndi ciani?
   (B) Chinshi ici?
9. (E) Is it clean or dirty?
   (N) Kodi ndicoyera kapena ndi cadoti?
   (B) Bushe chili nefiko nangu na chibuta?
10. (E) Who washes it for you?
    (N) Ndani amene akucapira?
    (B) Ninani ukuchapila?

Test 2: Play Language

1. (E) Kick the ball [handing the child a ball]
   (N) Caya bola
   (B) Panta bola
2. (E) Leave it here [after repeating item 1 or item 10, when the child is about to act]
   (N) Isiye apo
   (B) Ishe apopene
3. (E) Come here
   (N) Bwera kuno
   (B) Isa kuno
4. (E) Clap your hands
   (N) Omba mumanja
   (B) Tota
5. (E) Jump up and down
   (N) Lumpa
   (B) Toloka
6. (E) Bend down

APPENDIX—continued

	(N)	Belama
	(B)	Kontama
7.	(E)	Show me your nose
	(N)	Ndionetse mphuno yako
	(B)	Nanga umona obe.
8.	(E)	What is your friend's name?
	(N)	Dzina la mzako ndi ndani?
	(B)	Ishina lyamunobe ninani?
9.	(E)	Where is your friend?
	(N)	Alikuti mzako?
	(B)	Umunobe alikwi?
10.	(E)	Bring me the ball
	(N)	Ndibweretsere bola
	(B)	Ndetele bola

Test 3: Picture Language

	(E)	Have you seen this picture before? [showing p. 14 of *In the House*]
	(N)	Kodi unaionapo kale iyi pikica?
	(E)	Bushe ici chikope walicimona kale?
1.	(E)	Who is this? [pointing to the girl]
	(N)	Uyu ndi ndani?
	(B)	Ninani uyu?
2.	(E)	Who is this [pointing to the woman]
3.	(E)	What are they doing?
	(N)	Acita ciani?
	(B)	Ninshi balechita?
4.	(E)	What are they eating?
	(N)	Akudya ciani?
	(B)	Ninshi balelya?
5.	(E)	Who is this [pointing to the man]
6.	(E)	What is he doing?
	(N)	Acita ciani?
	(B)	Finshi balechita?
7.	(E)	What is he drinking?
	(N)	Akumwa ciani?
	(B)	Finshi balenwa?
8.	(E)	What is this? [pointing to the table]
	(N)	Ici ndi ciani?
	(B)	Cinshi ici?
9.	(E)	What is this? [pointing to the woman's foot beneath the table]
10.	(E)	What is this? [pointing to one of the curtains in the window]

INDIAN BILINGUALISM: SOME EDUCATIONAL AND LINGUISTIC IMPLICATIONS

Franklin C. Southworth

Department of South Asia Regional Studies
University of Pennsylvania
Philadelphia, Pennsylvania 19104

INTRODUCTION

This paper contains two sections, which might at first glance appear unrelated, though they both deal with aspects of bilingualism. The first section reports on a comparative study of bilingual and monolingual schoolchildren, with regard to their performance on school examinations. The second part is a discussion of code-switching and code-mixing as practiced by adult speakers in the same part of India. The primary link between these two sections is that they are based on data collected as part of the same research project. I hope ultimately to integrate these materials with others into a more comprehensive picture of bilingualism in South Asia. (See the beginning of Section 2 for further discussion.)

1. ACADEMIC PERFORMANCE OF BILINGUAL AND MONOLINGUAL SCHOOLCHILDREN IN TRIVANDRUM (SOUTH INDIA)

Until relatively recently, most studies of the cognitive effects of bilingualism have concluded—indeed, they have in many cases presupposed—that the bilingual individual is at an intellectual disadvantage in comparison with a monolingual person, as evidenced by the former's generally lower scores on so-called "intelligence" tests and in school examinations.[1,2] There are numerous reasons why one might, *a priori*, expect this to be so. Apart from the presumed intellectual burden imposed by the learning of an additional language, a number of studies suggest that the bilingual or diglossic individual is under a certain amount of tension because of the need to make the right choice of language according to a variety of situational cues, and that there are (at least potentially) penalties for making the wrong choice.[3-6] This would seem to be especially true in situations of greater cultural or ethnic heterogeneity, and would apply particularly to upwardly mobile individuals.[6] In an important recent study, Sandra Ben-Zeev has claimed that it is "cognitively more difficult to become bilingual than to become monolingual," that bilingual children are required to exercise extra effort in language learning, and that the bilingual child is in a "position of uncertainty" and "subject to confusion and ... ridicule" because of the danger of making the wrong choice of language, or of producing unacceptable utterances as a result of linguistic interference[7] (pp. 39–40).

121

0077-8923/80/0345-0121$01.75/2 © 1980, NYAS

Notwithstanding all these potential problems for the bilingual, Lambert[2] claims on the basis of several recent studies (his own and those of others) that bilingual children, relative to monolingual controls, show definite advantages on measures of "cognitive flexibility," "creativity," and "divergent thought," and he concludes that the evidence for the superiority of verbal functioning of bilinguals (as compared with monolinguals of comparable background) is very strong. The key to this conclusion is "comparable background" since—as Lambert points out, and as many of us have no doubt observed—most of the earlier studies failed to control for important social factors such as class differences and neglected to measure the level of bilingual competence of the subjects. It should perhaps be added that most or all of these studies were carried out in Western countries where the monolingual subjects belonged to the dominant culture, and spoke a language that had both local and international prestige, whereas the bilingual subjects usually spoke a less prestigious language and often belonged to ethnic minority groups. I would add further that, since bilinguals in the West so often fall into this category, there exists a kind of implicit assumption among Western students of bilingualism (which we might call the "monolingual mentality") that monolingualism is the normal condition for a well-adjusted human being, and that any deviation from this norm implies an added burden. Although this viewpoint may have some limited justification in advanced Western societies, it is very inappropriate to apply it to many others, including most Asian societies. It should be unnecessary to point out that large monolingual nations like the United States (if, indeed, it can be considered such) are of very recent origin in terms of human history, and even today are the exception rather than the rule. Thus, any attempt to understand bilingualism as a general human phenomenon requires input from a variety of different societies.

Although Lambert has pointed to the need for controlling social class in comparing the performance of bilinguals and monolinguals, it is not clear that his own conclusions can be applied to any children except those of upper-middle-class background. Families belonging to this stratum of society are typically more geographically mobile, better-read, and more concerned about their children's intellectual development (as opposed to their training for a profession), than those of lower-middle-class or working-class backgrounds. As Ben-Zeev points out "Opportunity for language experience and the interest in language which comes with high educational level of the family may be an important factor in interaction with bilingualism"[7] (p. 33). Thus, the question remains to be answered whether carefully matched monolingual and bilingual subjects belonging to other social strata would give results comparable to those reported by Lambert.

A great deal of attention has been focused on the problems of educating the bilingual child, particularly the child who speaks a nonprestigious minority language, such as Spanish in many parts of the United States.[8, 9] The problems of such children may be compounded if their home environment also teaches them "rules of speaking" that differ greatly from those of the majority culture.[10-13] In addition to the pressure of language choice in particular situations, there may be a societal pressure on the individual to discontinue the use of the home language altogether, or pressure forcing an awkward choice between an inappropriate language and one that the individual does not control with confidence.[4] In addition to these intellectual burdens, there is also the emotional burden associated with belonging to a minority culture, whose members have an unfavorable image in the society as a whole,[14] or of feeling that one's linguistic usage is marked as inferior because of a foreign accent or "substandard" features.[15] The presence of such "nonlinguistic" ingredients as part of the "problem of bilingualism" raises an important question that has not yet been adequately answered, and has in fact rarely ever been asked, namely: to what extent is bilingualism per se an educational or intellectual problem, and to what extent is it part of the more general social problems of ethnic minorities and social class distinctions? Clearly this question cannot be answered without looking at the phenomenon of bilingualism in its total social context.

Furthermore, it must be recognized that the pattern of second- or third-generation attrition of the home language, so prevalent in the United States, is not a universal norm. If we look, for example, at families from India who have settled in the United States, we see a marked tendency for those of the younger generation to use the parents' language less and less as time goes on, just like other immigrant groups; however, Indians who move to other parts of India, or to other parts of the world, do not follow this pattern, at least not invariably. Thus, even if our goal is to understand the pressures on the bilingual person in our own society, it may be helpful to compare the situation in this country with that existing in other parts of the world.

Two major problems must be pointed out in Lambert's conclusion regarding the superior verbal functioning of the bilingual child. First, has the possibility been eliminated that the *successful* bilingual (to which many of these studies were apparently restricted) is successful by virture of some prior intellectual superiority? Ben-Zeev's claim is that the bilingual situation places the child in a dilemma that stimulates the child to develop strategies (such as increased sensitivity to feedback cues) that the monolingual child has no need to develop. An alternative possibility, which might be considered at least for some societies, is that, whereas the child is stimulated by the bilingual situation, there need not be any *dilemma* in the sense that the child's stimulus may be simply the need to communicate with a number of different people in different situations, without the anxiety postulated by Ben-Zeev. If in such circumstances, one child becomes bilingual, while another child of equal innate ability (whatever that means) does not, the difference may possibly be explained simply as the result of a different pattern of linguistic exposure.

The second problem to be noted is that, although the kinds of tests used in the studies reported by Lambert (which include Ben-Zeev's study) indicate that bilingual children are more adept at certain kinds of word-play and verbal manipulation than are monolinguals, these results do not tell us anything about the *practical* values of these skills. It would be reasonable to hypothesize that children showing this kind of superiority of verbal functioning would also show it in other kinds of verbal tasks, and it would be worthwhile testing this hypothesis by comparing the academic performance of bilinguals and monolinguals in such subjects as language, logic, or mathematics. Such a test would also perhaps tell us something about the implications of bilingualism for the individual's career preparation, professional development, and so on. If it should turn out that linguistic background has implications for these aspects of an individual's life, this conclusion would have important educational significance.

The literature on bilingualism contains many references to implications that go beyond the cognitive or educational. One problem often discussed is that of social identity. Several studies have suggested that situations that lead to compulsory use of a language other than the mother-tongue or that prevent a person from fully developing spoken and written command over the mother-tongue in some sense threaten that individual's "identity".[16] Related to this is the image of the minority-language group in the society at large.[17] Lambert, on the other hand—always the optimist—concluded from a carefully controlled study of the children of mixed Anglo-French marriages, that there was no basis for the view that bilingualism, or even biculturality, meant loss of identity[2] (pp. 19 ff.).

Lambert's encouraging words must, however, be tempered by the realization that the benefits of bilingualism are more easily available to some members of the society than to others. He makes this explicit when he points out that all of the studies that reported higher levels of verbal performance by bilinguals involved languages having "social value and respect in each of the settings. . . . In no case would the learning of the second language portend the slow replacement of it for the home-or other language, as would typically be the case for French-Canadians or Spanish-Americans developing high-level skills in English"[2] (pp. 18–19). He proceeds from this point to develop a distinction between *additive* bilingualism (in which one adds a new linguistic competence to that which one already has) and *subtractive* bilingualism (involving the attrition of one language in exchange for developing competence in one that appears to be important for economic and/or social reasons).

There is no doubt that additive bilingualism is more beneficial to the learner than subtractive bilingualism. The question is, which members of society have the option to choose the former rather than the latter? And what are the social factors that make it possible to choose? This is obviously another facet of the question posed before, namely, what contribution does bilingualism (or language competence in general) make to individual success or failure and what contribution is made by other factors? Presumably the answers to these questions will vary considerably from one society to another.

Although several of the studies just referred to have tried to identify factors that tend to promote or inhibit the acquisition of second languages, there appear to be hardly any cross-cultural studies of this subject. Yet it would seem to be of importance to understand why some bilingual nations have relatively low levels of individual bilingualism (Belgium, for example), whereas many others (such as many African and Asian nations) have very high levels. In various parts of Africa and South Asia, many cases can be found of individuals who have gone out of their way to develop multilingual competence beyond what would appear to be strict necessity. It would be useful to understand why this is so.

Before beginning this study, there was adequate evidence to support the view that bilingual children in India do *not* suffer from any intellectual or educational disadvantage as compared with their monolingual peers; in fact, they may well have certain advantages. In Kerala, where this study was conducted, the immigrant Tamil-speaking Brahmins (many of whom have lived in the area for generations) are renowned for their intellectual achievements. Of course, we may say, this is not surprising in an elite group which exhibits the same orientation to education and professional achievement, and the same attention to verbal performance, found among upper-middle-class Western people, such as those studied by Lambert or Ben-Zeev. Then what about those belonging to lower socioeconomic groups? If Ben-Zeev's hypothesis is correct, then we might expect that non-native speakers of Malayalam who belong to the working class would, by virtue of the extra sensitivity that she postulates, be able to transcend the features of lower-class dialect that appear to place many working-class individuals at a disadvantage in the educational system. This is one of the important aspects of this question that our study was intended to examine.

One further point should be raised before going on to discuss the details of the study. It seems possible that Indian bilingualism is a different *kind* of bilingualism than that found typically in Western countries. In the first place, bilingualism in India, as many researchers have pointed out, is very often associated with a type of diglossia which meshes closely with the cultural pluralism so prevalent in South Asia, especially in urban areas.[18–20] Thus, miltilingualism is an integral part of the social segmentation of life, to which many Indians adjust at a very early age. Different languages, dialects, or sharply distinct styles of speech are often complementarily distributed in the speech of individuals and groups in a way that minimizes their competition with each other. The fact that an individual uses English (or Hindi) in the office does not imply any pressure to use that language in preference to the home language (which might be, say, Bengali or Tamil) for domestic purposes. Just as a man "takes off his caste" when he changes from dhoti to trousers, he changes his social identity when he shifts from his home language to the language that is appropriate for the office. Thus, for many individuals, the question of "threatened identity" does not arise, and any additional competence attained in new languages will always be additive rather than subtractive.

Furthermore, it is possible to become bilingual in India without becoming bicultural to any great extent. This may come about, for example, in a domestic context where two languages are used by different sets of relatives. To a certain extent it is also true of formal learning in schools, even in the learning of English. Increasingly, English textbooks in Indian schools make use of Indian English grammer and lexicon, and tend to use local material (stories about Indian situations using Indian names, places, and so on) rather than the foreign models of a generation ago. "Pat has a hat" has now become "Mohan has a *topi.*" Thus, a child can develop competence in a language without the additional tension of dealing with a foreign culture, and he or she can begin to handle cultural differences only after basic linguistic competence has been attained.

A similar phonomenon of graduality can be seen in the learning of spoken language. Young children in middle-class Indian homes are often exposed to English by such means as the radio, phonograph records, and adult conversation, and they are able to learn passively for a long period of time before they are expected to perform in English. Even the first years in an English-medium school make few demands of performance. The rote learning that is so often criticized by western educationists may in this case serve the useful function of reducing the burden of anxiety that would be caused by pressure to perform. And although the pressure for academic performance later becomes very great, it is perhaps eased by the duality between formal and informal communication that characterizes Indian society.[20] Formal language can be said to be of almost ritual importance, whereas informal colloquial usage is extremely free by comparison. An obvious manifestation of this freedom is the kind of code-switching that many Westerners have found to be one of the most unusual features of verbal interaction in South Asia. A full explanation of the communicative functions and social motivations of this style of speech is still to be sought, but it seems possible that one of its *effects* is to reduce the strain of language learning. To the extent that speakers have a choice of language in a situation—if they can simply put in a Malayalam or Tamil word when the appropriate English word does not come to mind readily, for example—then they are free of the constraints that are found in some of the studies mentioned above.

SCOPE OF THE STUDY

On the basis of the kinds of assumptions that have been discussed here, the present study was planned. Its central focus is to test the hypothesis that if social class is kept constant, Indian bilinguals will perform better than, or at least as well as, monolinguals, on the usual tests of academic performance. As mentioned earlier, it is important to test the two groups on measures that have some validity within the culture rather than using tests of the types employed by Lambert and others, in order to find out the practical implications of any differences between them. It would also have been possible to carry out IQ tests, to see whether test performance deviated from verbal or nonverbal IQ in any characteristic way for the two groups. This was not done for several reasons. First, it was necessary to obtain a large sample, so that any differences in innate ability would be evened out. Secondly, the logistic problems of carrying out such tests even with a smaller sample were formidable. What is to be hoped, of course, is that there will be no significant differences between the two groups.

Although the study of academic performance was the main *raison d'être* of the study, several other kinds of data were also collected. First, it was necessary to have background data on the students we were studying so that other hypotheses that might be generated by the results could also be tested, for example, regarding the relationship between students' performances and their home situations, education of their parents, and so on. For the full sample of 1,300 children—half of them with Malayalam as their mother tongue and the other half claiming some other language as mother tongue—data were obtained on the occupation of the parent or guardian (which gives some indication of socioeconomic status) and the caste of the family (where this information was available in the school records). For a smaller sample of 500 (250 Malayalam speakers and 250 others), household surveys were conducted in order to obtain additional information on socioeconomic status, education of family members, and languages used in the home. In a still smaller sample of 125 (selected randomly, but evenly distributed among five socioeconomic levels) a rather long family interview was conducted. These interviews included questions on individual language histories, language use in the home, language attitudes, and parent's educational and career goals for their children. The interviews were recorded and transcribed; in addition, detailed notes were taken, which were then summarized in tabular form. The analysis of these interview materials is expected to provide a picture of what it means—emotionally, intellectually, and socially— to be a bilingual person in this society.

COMPARISON OF ACADEMIC PERFORMANCE OF MONOLINGUAL AND BILINGUAL SCHOOLCHILDREN

The population sample for the study of school performance comes from 16 schools, all located in the city of Trivandrum (the capital of the state of Kerala, on the southwest coast of India). It should be noted here that this is not an area of high bilingualism. According to the Census of 1961 (the latest that provides data on bilingualism), 95 percent of the population of Trivandrum District claim the state language, Malayalam, as their mother-tongue. This is close to the statewide average of 94 percent and compares with a high of 98 percent and a low of 90 percent in other districts. Of those claiming Malayalam as their mother-tongue in the State as a whole, only 4.7% claim knowledge of any second language. After Malayalam, the next language of numerical importance in Kerala is Tamil, claimed as mother tongue by 3 percent in the State as a whole, but by larger percentages in those districts that have easy communications with the adjacent State of Tamilnadu, namely Palghat and Trivandrum Districts. (Before Independence in 1947, the princely State of Travancore included both the present Trivandrum District and what is now Kaniyakumari District of Tamilnadu. Until states' reorganization in 1956, the southern part of Kerala, including Trivandrum District, was part of the old Madras State.)

The schools in the sample were selected to provide a good distribution from the point of view of socioeconomic class, and also to give adequate representation of minority ethnic groups, including the Tamils and the Kudumbis (who speak Konkani, an Indo-Aryan language). TABLE 1 lists some of the important characteristics of the schools selected. Some of the variables indicated in this list, particularly the medium of instruction, may well be crucial to academic performance, and must ultimately be tested for their significance. The preliminary conclusions that can be offered at present, which are presented in TABLE 2A, are based on hand tabulations, and can only include a limited number of variables. Thus, most of the interesting questions about the relative importance of factors such as social class, parents' education, sex, and the like, cannot be answered yet, but must await a thorough quantitative analysis.

Table 2A represents a comparison between those students claiming to be

TABLE 1

CHARACTERISTICS OF THE SCHOOLS IN THE STUDY

School Number	Medium of Instruction	Sex of Students	Grades	Type of Management	Total Number of Students
01	English	M	I–X	Private	816
02	Malayalam and English	M	V–X	State	1,501
03	Tamil	Mixed	V–X	State	840
04	Malayalam	F	V–X	State	923
05	Malayalam and Tamil	Mixed	I–IV	State	639
06	English	F	I–IV	Private	1,213
07	English	F	V–X	Private	1,161
08	Tamil	Mixed	I–IV	State	508
09	Malayalam	Mixed	I–X	State	1,820
10	Malayalam	F	V–X	State	1,057
11	Malayalam	Mixed	I–IV	State	426
12	Malayalam	Mixed	I–IV	State	189
13	English and Hindi	Mixed	I–XI	Central government	785
14	Malayalam	Mixed	I–IV	State	609
15	Malayalam	M	V–X	State	950
16	Malayalam	M	V–X	State	865

monolingual speakers of Malayalam and those claiming to speak Malayalam as a second language. (The majority of the latter claim Tamil as their mother tongue.) The dashes in the second column from the left, which represents the highest socioeconomic group, result from the fact that most students in this category, at least in the upper grades, would claim to speak English as a second language, and therefore we find few Malayalam monolinguals in this group. Furthermore, the students represented in this Table were all from Malayalam-medium schools, whereas children of the upper stratum mostly study in English-medium schools.

In this Table, any figure above 1.00 indicates that the monolingual subjects in that particular category scored higher on the average than did the bilingual subjects; scores less than 1.00 indicate that the bilingual students scored better. The numbers in parentheses indicate the number of subjects in each category; thus, 3/5 indicates 3 monolinguals and 5 bilinguals. As noted in TABLE 2B all individual scores are adjusted as percentages of the average scores of students in their schools. The rationale for this method is that schools vary considerably in their standards, but within schools this variation is less.

As one might expect, the fluctuations in TABLE 2A that appear in the individual categories (for example, 2.17, in standard IV for the lowest socioeconomic class, or 0.62 for standard VII in the second class) level out when we begin totalling them up: thus, the figures in the column at the right vary between 1.25 and 0.65, and the figures on the bottom line (the totals for each socioeconomic group) vary between 1.08 and 0.91. It is not yet clear what these fluctuations mean. In any case, the figure that matters most in the present context is the one at the bottom right of TABLE 2A, which represents the ratio of the average scores of 365 monolingual subjects and 302 bilingual subjects. This score of 0.93 would seem to leave standing the hypothesis that the bilinguals do as well or better than the monolinguals.

To anticipate one obvious question: our data for the linguistic competence of these students are primarily their own statements. In some cases, especially for the younger students, we sought corroboration from teachers, especially when a child claimed the ability to speak English. Given the prestige of English in India, it would be expected that many children would claim to speak it even if they could not. And in a number of cases, children were hooted down by their classmates when they did make this claim. (As Mrs. Isaac, the supervisor of data collection, put it, "How painful it was to see the faces of those children. . . .") If, in the older classes, where students wrote down their answers without being checked by the teachers, some students wrongly classified themselves as speakers of English, this error would not affect this particular table. The reverse, of course, is less likely to happen; that is, those speaking fluent English are very unlikely to deny it. Thus, this table compares students whose only *spoken* language is Malayalam with those who speak some other language *plus* Malayalam (and whose competence in Malayalam may range from near-native fluency to something much less).

Although further analysis of variables may well yield additional insights into the relative importance of socioeconomic class and other factors, TABLE

TABLE 2A

RATIO OF TOTAL AVERAGE SCORES OF MALAYALAM MONOLINGUALS COMPARED WITH MALAYALAM OT SPEAKERS (1977)

Standard (grade)	Socioeconomic Category*					
	1	2	3	4	5	All
I	0.94 (3/3)	1.13 (2/8)	1.41 (1/9)	— (6/0)	0.89 (19/6)	0.93 (31/26)
II	1.02 (3/5)	1.13 (8/10)	1.30 (6/7)	1.02 (13/12)	1.03 (23/7)	1.10 (53/41)
III	— (0/5)	1.41 (7/14)	0.94 (3/6)	0.63 (2/10)	0.76 (22/14)	0.88 (34/43)
IV	— (0/0)	1.36 (1/1)	— (0/0)	1.24 (4/5)	2.17 (6/2)	1.25 (11/8)
V	— (0/2)	1.19 (3/3)	0.93 (3/4)	1.02 (5/11)	1.43 (11/2)	1.00 (22/22)
VI	— (0/0)	1.11 (8/5)	1.05 (1/2)	0.78 (20/14)	0.82 (25/8)	0.65 (54/29)
VII	0.67 (1/1)	0.62 (4/4)	0.87 (1/6)	1.07 (15/19)	0.78 (25/5)	0.88 (46/35)
VIII	— (0/1)	0.89 (3/4)	0.84 (8/7)	1.35 (9/23)	1.17 (9/7)	1.04 (29/42)
IX	1.73 (2/2)	0.92 (7/9)	0.67 (5/13)	1.14 (17/22)	1.07 (34/4)	0.90 (65/40)
Totals	1.08 (9/19)	1.07 (43/58)	0.91 (28/56)	1.04 (91/116)	0.96 (174/55)	0.93 (365/302)

* Socioeconomic categories range from 1 to 5, with 1 being the highest.

TABLE 2B

Score†	School Average	Adjusted Score (a/b)	Average	Monolingual/ Bilingual Ratio
91 (M)	59.8	1.52		
47 (M)	56.8	0.83	1.09 (M)	
53 (M)	56.8	0.93		1.09/1.16 = 0.94
78 (B)	56.8	1.37		
76 (B)	56.8	1.34	1.16 (B)	
43 (B)	56.8	0.76		

* *Method of calculation*: These figures are calculated in two steps, as indicated here. First the individual scores are calculated as percentages of the average of scores for all students in the sample from the school in question. The ratios of these adjusted scores are then computed.

† M = monolingual; B = bilingual.

2 clearly *does not indicate any pattern of class differences* in the performance of bilingual and monolingual subjects. This evidence therefore is compatible with the hypothesis mentioned earlier that whatever the factors may be that influence individual performance, they are not correlated in any obvious way with the individual's class background.

2. ANALYSIS OF MULTILINGUAL INTERACTIONS (CODE-SWITCHING)

The data to be discussed below constitute a part of the normal speech behavior of educated Malayalis, and similar data can be obtained in all parts of South Asia. As Kachru[25] points out, this type of language has been until recently treated as a kind of "linguistica exotica," but is now beginning to receive serious attention as a linguistic and sociolinguistic phenomenon. The particular examples presented here are a by-product of the household interviews described above.

The relationship between code-switching and the acquisition of a second language is still unexplored. We do not know, for example, in what age range, or under what conditions, individuals acquire the ability to switch and mix languages, or the ability to distinguish between social contexts which permit mixed language and those where unmixed forms are appropriate. We do not know to what extent the observation of adult switching may facilitate or hamper children's acquisition of bilingual competence. We know nothing about the order of acquisition of different types of code-switching styles, or the way in which formal constraints on switching are learned (see below). These questions are mentioned here only to give some notion of the scope of investigations which still need to be carried out, and for which it will be necessary to obtain fairly extensive samples of linguistic data.

The switching phenomenon has been described in a number of papers by Fishman,[21] Gumperz,[22-23] McClure,[24] Kachru,[25] Southworth,[26] Valdes Fallis,[27] Zentella,[28] Marlos and Zentella,[29] and others. These discussions have generally tried to correlate code choice with features of the social situation (relationships among the participants, setting, subject matter, type of interaction, etc.), or have focused on the ways in which switching serves communicative functions (such as emphasis, focus, elaboration, clarification, etc.). While code-switching in South Asia shows both types of phenomena (correlations with social situation and metalinguistic functions), there is a great deal of switching taking place which cannot be accounted for by any of these explanations. We frequently find speakers switching rapidly back and forth within the same stretch of speech, even within the same sentence—even using more than two languages in the same sentence—in the *same* social situation, i.e., without any visible changes in subject matter, type of interaction, etc. I have suggested in an earlier paper that this kind of switching might be the result of a speaker's need to balance several different role relationships simultaneously.[26] One of the purposes of the present project was, in fact, to collect additional data to test this hypothesis. While I cannot prove this explanation to the exclusion of others, I believe that the data presented below will at least serve to show the plausibility of the hypothesis.

In the present context, the purpose will be to show that there are certain formal features of the linguistic data that correlate, in a rough way, with social characteristics of speakers and speaking situations. Broadly speaking, we can distinguish between *lexical switching*, in which lexical items of language A are inserted into constructions of language B, and *structural switching*, in which constructions (morphological or syntactic) of language A occur in the same discourse with constructions of language B. (By "constructions" is meant anything from inflected forms to full sentences.) The following examples will illustrate this distinction. (In all the examples given here, English forms appear in SMALL CAPITAL LETTERS, whereas Malayalam forms appear in lower-case Roman letters, and Tamil forms in lower-case italic letters. Each example is prefaced by a specification of (*1*) the interview number (1–125); (*2*) the speaker's socioeconomic category (see Table 2); and (*3*) the speaker's educational level: numbers I–IX for grades of school completed; SSLC for completion of high school; BA, MA, and so forth for higher degrees, with a plus sign (for example, BA+) indicating additional years of study beyond the degree specified).

Examples of lexical switching:

1. (#14, 3, II) enRe BROTHER untu. hindi samsaarikkum. ("There's my brother. He speaks Hindi.")

2. (#101, 3, IX) atu tanne CONTINUE ceyyanam. ("That [emphatic] should be continued.")

3. (#5, 3, SSLC) FAMILY aayi saadhaarana sinima kaanaan pookunna HABIT illa. ("I don't have the habit of going to see a movie with the family.")

4. (#89, 4, VII) COOKING aayittu boombee, puuna, delli-okke pooyittuntu. ("I have been to Bombay, Poona, Delhi, etc. for cooking" [working as a cook].)

5. (#90, 3, BA) oru INDIA maatRam ISOLATE ceytu irikkaan saadhikkilla. ("It is not possible for India to remain isolated.")

6. (#116, 2, BA) atu CONSCIOUS aayittaayirukkukayilla. ("It wouldn't be done consciously" [if we happened to use an English sentence while talking Malayalam].)

Examples of structural switching:

7. (#18, 2, BA) I HAVE WIDELY TRAVELLED IN NORTHERN PARTS BANK-nu veenti. avitokke pookumpool ii muRi hindi aanenkilum, muRi hindi WAS USEFUL TO ME. LANGUAGE pathikkaan budhimuttonnumilla PROVIDED YOU HAVE GOT INTEREST. ("... for the bank. When travelling there this broken Hindi, even though it was broken Hindi .... studying a language is not difficult provided ....")

8. (#11, 1, BA+) *appaavu peeciRatu inklish. naan tamizutaan peeciReen.* cila viittil anngane untu. *ippo oru* CRAZE *irukku. viittil inklish taan peecanam.* atu enkalukku FATHER-um collittaNNittilla. ñannagalute *ko-*

zantakaḷum appaṭi peecaRatu samatikka pooRatillai. atu SURE aa. tamiz tanne viiṭṭilu. AND WE NEVER SAID THAT THEY CALL 'MUMMY' OR 'DADDY'. viḷiccaal, YOU JUST CALL *'amma'* OR *'appa'.* atinRaavasyamilla. ("Father talks English. I talk Tamil. It is like that in certain houses. Now there is a craze. One should talk only in English in the house. Father has not advised us to do that, and we don't allow our children to do it. That is sure. Only Tamil in the house. And we never ... If you call, you just call *amma* ('mother') or *appa* ('father'). There is no need for that.")

9. (#15, 2, BA) MOTHER LEARNED MALAYALAM BECAUSE boombeeyil aayi-runnu aadyam. (" ... she was in Bombay previously.") [MALAYALAM is a slip of the tongue for HINDI here.]

10. (same) TEN YEARS boombeeyil aayirunnu. (" ... was in Bombay.")

11. (#13, 1, MA) *ezuta teriyaatu, vaacikke teriyaatu,* ONLY SPOKEN. ("Don't know how to write, don't know how to read, ...")

12. (#19, 2, BA) *appiṭi colla muṭiyaatu,* BECAUSE *paṭittattilu* I GOT GOOD MARKS. ("One cannot say that ... in studies ...")

13. (same) BECAUSE enikku hindiyooṭu kuuṭutal eṭuppam RIGHT FROM CHILDHOOD ... (" ... I had a lot of exposure to Hindi ...")

14. (same) SUPPOSE HE IS A TAMILIAN OR MALAYALI AND I HAVE THE FEELING THAT WE ARE INTIMATE; HE LIKES ME enna oru toonnalu vannu pooyaal, I TAKE THE LIBERTY TO USE TAMIL OR MALAYALAM ... ("If I get the feeling that (he likes me) ....")

15. (#100, 2, MA) OCCASIONALLY inglish upayoogikkum. (" ...(I) use English.")

16. (#17, 2, MA) WHEN I WAS A KID MOSTLY *tamiz taan.* (" ... [I spoke] Tamil.")

17. (same) *inklish paticcatu* MOSTLY BY MYSELF, *ennu collulaam.* ("I studied English ... one might say.")

18. (#106, 3, SSLC) *terincaalum,* WE TALK ONLY IN MALAYALAM BECAUSE HE IS MORE ACCUSTOMED TO MALAYALAM. ("Even though he knows [Tamil], ... ")

19. (#20, 2, MA+) *triccile* SHORT TERM *taan. atu oru* THIRTY YEARS BACK. ("(I was) in Trichy only for a short term. That was about .... ")

20. (#50, 3, BA) *ippom ille,* FOR THE TIME BEING. ("Not now ...")

21. (#52, 1, MA+) FIFTH STANDARD *vare tamiz taan,* atu kaziññi inglish. ("Up to fifth standard Tamil only, after that English.")

22. (#17, 3, SSLC) *inklish taan.* LETTER WRITING PURELY ENGLISH *taan.* ("English only ... only.")

23. (#72, 3, BA+) *avaRkku raṇṭu peeRkkum,* THEY CAN SPEAK TAMIL. ("Both of them .... ")

24. (#75, 2, BA) UP TO SSLC *vare* IT WAS TAMIL ... (" ... up to .... ")

25. (#13, 1, MA) *ippom,* CHILDREN *vantu,* THEY ARE LEARNING HINDI ... ("Now, as to the children, ...")

26. (#9, 3, SSLC+) anke ROMAN HINDUSTANNI-*nnu oru itu irukku.* THAT IS, *hinti-nnu collapaṭṭatu* ROMAN ALPHABET-le *ezuturatu,* NOT IN hindi lipi-le alla. ROMAN—ROMAN HINDUSTANI. ("There is a thing there called Roman Hindustani ... what is called Hindi is written in the Roman alphabet, not in Hindi script ....")

The following cases may appear at first glance to be like examples 1–6:

27. (#48, 4, SSLC+) [In answer to the question: entu CONTRACT aa? 'What kind of contract?"]—MAINTENANCE. ceRu raayiṭṭu keṭṭaṭam. saadan-annga SUPPLY ceyyaṇam. (" ... Some building construction. [We] have to supply materials.")

28. (#44, 5, VI) EMPLOYMENT EXCHANGE-ile CARD REGISTER ceytiRRuṇṭu. ("I have registered at the ... ")

29. (#89, 4, VII) ñanngaḷ paalakkaaṭṭil ninnu TRANSFER aayi ... ("When we were transferred from Palghat ....")

30. (#84, 3, BA) tamiz TEST paas aayaal INCREMENT kuuṭṭikiṭṭum. ("If one passes the Tamil test, one gets an extra increment.")

However, the view taken here is that such cases do not involve switching at all, on the grounds that lexical items of English origin such as CONTRACT, SUPPLY, TRANSFER, and the like are the normal words used in conversational Malayalam to express these particular meanings. Although in some cases there are Malayalam equivalents for such words, they would be appropriate only in official writing or very formal speech. Thus, sentence 28 would be regarded as a pure Malayalam sentence, even though most of its morphological raw material is of foreign origin, whereas sentence 1, containing the word BROTHER, would qualify as switching because there is clearly a Malayalam equivalent that would not be stylistically inappropriate in this context. (See Reference 26 for a discussion of some of the social functions of this kind of switching.) In another set of cases, words of English origin can be considered to be the only words in use in the language to express their referents: for example, *bassu* (bus), *skuuḷu* (school), *sinima* (cinema).

The aforementioned examples are drawn from the transcripts of the 125 family interviews. Almost all of these interviews involved encounters between people who had not previously met each other, and were thus rather formal. (The few exceptions were cases in which the main interviewer had some previous acquaintance with the interviewees.) Those interviewed included monolingual Malayalis, Malayalis who knew English, Tamil speakers who knew Malayalam and in some cases also English, and a few families from outside of the State, most of whom knew both Malayalam and English. The main interviewer was a middle-aged Malayali woman who is fluent in English, a very vivacious and articulate speaker in both languages, who frequently switches between the two. The junior interviewers included one

Malayalam speaker and one Tamil-Malayalam bilingual (both of whom also knew English).

Three languages (Malayalam, English, and Tamil) appear in the corpus. As the preceding examples indicate, we find mixtures of Tamil and English, Malayalam and English, and all three. (Mixtures of Malayalam and Tamil also occur, but have not been included in the earlier examples.) Since Malayalam and Tamil are closely related languages, a number of lexical items (such as *atu* [that], *oru* [one], *ippo* [now]) could be assigned to either one, and the decision must be made on the basis of context: in example number 8, for instance, the first instance of *atu* is assigned to Tamil and the second instance to Malayalam, on the basis of the other items in the sentences in which the form occurs. Almost all cases are decidable in this way.

Whereas switching between two Indian languages is common, switching between an Indian language and English is of a different nature, because of the position of English as the language of education, national government, and elite status generally. The following discussion will be concerned primarily with cases of switching involving English, though it will be possible to comment also about the roles of Tamil and Malayalam in these examples.

The interesting questions about switching seem to come under three headings: *when, why,* and *how?* By *when,* we mean what are the settings and situations in which switching takes place? What are the social cues and the social structural constraints that affect this type of behavior? By *why,* we mean what are the communicative functions of this style of speech? What does the speaker communicate when he or she switches? And by *how,* we are asking, what is the linguistic structure of code-switching? What are the formal constraints (if any) that determine the structural points at which switching is possible? These questions are of course all interrelated, and although they cannot be covered completely here, some impressions can be given.

First, regarding the *when* question: explicit statements by informants (including materials from language diaries collected for the project), supplemented by casual observation, provide a general picture. Ordinary domestic conversation among family members involves minimal switching (either lexical or structural), except for special effects, for example, to express particular emotional states such as anger, or for avoidance of loaded terms.[26] (There is variation among families, of course: for example, families who have lived in other parts of India or abroad for long periods make more use of languages other than the home language than do other families.)

The main exception to the general statement is that among families knowing English, when the interaction taking place is one that can be called a "discussion," switching into English becomes frequent. (The term "discussion" is our senior interviewer's term, and it refers to a conversation—usually with the participants sitting down—and usually about events outside the home, in which participants present their opinions and interpretations of those events.)

At the other extreme is the office situation, particularly that of the large business firm or bank, which reaches outside of the language region, or the Central Government offices, which employ people from different language regions. Officers in these establishments are highly educated, and even those of local origin have often spent considerable parts of their lives in other language regions. They have frequent contact with non-Malayalis, and conduct much of their professional lives in English. Their higher education has invariably been through English, and the more privileged among them usually attended English-medium schools from the beginning. The same would apply to the faculty of the Kerala University and to scholars working in research institutes, where the environment and the subject matter (which all have learned through English) serve to encourage frequent use of English. Whether because of the subject matter, the colonial heritage, or for other reasons, business conversations among officers in establishments of these kinds are primarily in English, although personal interactions may be entirely in Malayalam, or in one of the two switching styles illustrated here.

Now obviously enough, a basic constraint on a person's ability to use the structural switching style is competence in English. That is, only those people who can produce English sentences can produce the type of sentences shown in items 7 to 26. Thus, the most obvious message conveyed by this style of speech is that the speaker knows English; and at the same time, the use of this style implies the recognition that the hearer knows English. This does *not* necessarily imply that the speaker is highly educated. For example, utterances 18 and 22 were produced by individuals who had only a high school education and had learned their English while working outside of Kerala.

Conversely, some speakers who can be presumed to have had the requisite competence in English failed to do any structural switching (as defined earlier) in the interview situation. For instance, those individuals who produced the following utterances were certainly competent, according to their own statements as well as other evidence, to produce English sentences:

31. (#33, 2, BA+) illa. kaaraṇam ñaan MSC-kku pooyiṭṭuṇṭu. MSC *examination* ezuti. VIVA-kku pooyilla. CLASS kiṭṭumennu tooNNiyilla. MATH-EMATICS aaṇu. pinne HOPELESS aayi. B. ED-nu paṭhiccu. ("No. Because I went for M.Sc. I wrote the MSc. examination. I didn't go to the oral. I didn't expect to get a good rank. It's mathematics. So it was hopeless. I studied for B.Ed.")

32. (#5, 3, SSLC) pinne IAS-kaaru, IPS-kaarokke cila SUBJECTS eṭuttu samsaarikkaaRuṇṭallo, cila SPECIAL PROGRAMS. atokke keeḷkkaaRuṇṭu. ("Then the IAS and IPS people speak about certain subjects, you know, there are some special programs. I listen to all those.")

The first speaker here is, as the quote indicates, studying for an advanced degree. He uses words like VIVA (Indian English for "oral examination") and HOPELESS, which would not be used by speakers without a spoken command of English. The second speaker is a man who retired from a clerical job with the Indian Air Force, and who had worked for many years outside of Kerala. One might, in fact, raise the question whether this speaker's use of an English plural (SUBJECTS) and the phrase SPECIAL

PROGRAMS would not qualify as structural switching; and, in fact, we find that with one exception, speakers who used English plurals in Malayalam sentences also used full English sentences at other times in the interview. The single exception to this statement was a woman employed in a hospital dining room, who produced the following utterance:

33. (#69, 4, V) PATIENTS-okke samsaarikkunnatu namakku koRaccokke manasilaakum. ("We can understand a little of what the patients say.")

It seems possible that in this case, the word PATIENTS may have been learned as an unanalyzed whole, since this speaker dealt with patients as a group, rather than as individuals, in her professional capacity. Regarding the phrase SPECIAL PROGRAMS in example 32, this might also have been learned as an unanalyzed whole, but perhaps this is less likely than in the case of PATIENTS. The following is a similar case in which the decision between lexical and structural borrowing may be difficult, but in this case the speaker is one who used many English sentences in the interview:

34. (#121, 1, MA) *anta* TAMIL ACCENT pookukilla. ("That Tamil accent won't go away.")

Regarding sentence 31, it should be further commented that the word HOPELESS is an extremely unusual example of lexical switching. Almost all lexical borrowings from English in Malayalam and Tamil are borrowed as nouns, that is, they function as nouns in the surface structure of the borrowing language, regardless of their status in English. This is true even of English verbs, for example, CONTINUE in example 2, ISOLATE in 5, REGISTER in 28. (This illustrates what is apparently an all-India, or all-South Asia, pattern in which the English verb is compounded with an all-purpose verb such as Malayalam *ceyy* [do] or Tamil *pan* [do] to produce phrases like ISOLATE *ceyy* [isolate], and so on.) Thus, it would be reasonable to regard any instance of an English word functioning as anything other than a noun in Tamil or Malayalam as a case of structural borrowing. This would also include cases like SURE in 8, BECAUSE in 12, or OCCASIONALLY in 15. And in fact we do find that function words of this kind are only used in our data by speakers who also use full English sentences in the interviews.

Thus, the speakers who produced sentences 31 and 32 seem to be in a transitional stage between those who do only lexical switching and those who also do structural switching. Whether or not such speakers would use the switching style in other contexts cannot be determined from the data now available, but it is significant that these individuals, although educated, belong to a markedly lower social category than the person who interviewed them and that in fact the interviewer never used the switching style in addressing them during the interview, whereas she did in other cases. (One individual was of low caste, substantially younger than the interviewer, and with no professional or social standing; the other was employed in a very junior clerical position.) On the other hand, the two less-educated speakers who did use the structural switching style were both older than their respective interviewers (these two men were interviewed by the two junior interviewers), and were Brahmins who, in spite of their lower educational level, held fairly responsible positions. In both these cases, it was the interviewees who took the initiative in switching or in using full English sentences.

Although additional cases need to be brought into this analysis, it could be said tentatively that the use of the switching style relates to, and in fact signals, the social variables of (absolute) status, relative status of speaker and hearer, and social solidarity. Those who use structural switching in the interviews all belong to the first or second socioeconomic categories (mostly the first). Those who *initiate* switching are equal to, or higher than, their hearers in status. Social solidarity is indicated by the freedom and frequency with which switching occurs on both sides of the interaction; we found that when the senior interviewer interviewed people of her own class (category 1) whom she had not met before, the interviews began mostly in Malayalam, but structural switching increased as the conversation proceeded and rapport developed between the interviewer and the interviewees. When she interviewed people already known to her, there was frequent structural switching on both sides throughout the interview.

A further factor of importance is what might be called ethnic solidarity. We might ask, for example, why people who are fluent in English bother to use Malayalam at all. The answer seems to be that to carry on a conversation entirely in English would create an extremely formal atmosphere. Making excessive use of English is, in fact, a way of keeping a person at a distance.[26] It is appropriate to certain kinds of formal lectures, but not to conversations. This point can be further illustrated by the following example, which is not from the project data, but was observed by me in the office of a professor at Kerala University. During this conversation, the professor was talking to a Ph.D. student about a paper that the latter had handed in. The substance of the discussion was in English—appropriately so, since that is the language of instruction at the University—but it was punctuated with occasional Malayalam syllables as in the following case:

35. [from memory] YOU HAVE NOT DONE WHAT WAS EXPECTED OF YOU. EVEN AN M.A. STUDENT COULD HAVE DONE BETTER. keṭṭoo? ("Did you hear?")

The effect produced was that of a speaker who wished to remind his hearer from time to time that, even though they were speaking English, they still identified with each other as Indians (and as Malayalis). A similar example was provided by the project's Tamil-speaking assistant, who noted in his language diary that he felt obliged to use Tamil in speaking to a coffee-shop waiter whom he knew to be a Tamilian, even though the man was fluent in Malayalam and the other people at his table were Malayalis. This same phenomenon also appears in the interviews. When our Tamil assistant was present for the interviews, those interviewees who knew Tamil produced a number of mixed Malayalam and Tamil sentences, or trilingual sentences like 8 or 21, even when they were not addressing the Tamil assistant directly. One might tentatively suggest a rule that if a person who is an ethnic speaker of language X is a participant in an interaction, then other participants who know X will exhibit some structural switching into X. Not to do so would be considered standoffish. This rule would seem to apply regardless of the relative status of the two participants involved.

In general, this attempt to answer the *when* and the *why* questions about switching leads to the notion that the domains and functions of different languages in this society overlap to an extent that in many situations *it is not only possible, but socially necessary, to use more than one language* in the course of an interaction. Thus, rules of formality may indicate English, whereas ethnic solidarity demands Tamil or Malayalam. In other cases, informality (in a domestic context, for example) may require Tamil or Malayalam, but subject matter may require English. The presence of individuals of different ethnic backgrounds may require some speakers to add a certain proportion of another language to the mix.

From this perspective, switching appears to involve a kind of linguistic juggling or tightrope-walking, in which the speaker struggles to balance status, ethnic solidarity, subject matter, type of interaction, and a variety of communicative functions. But it can be put another way. As long as a speaker is interacting with a person or group of persons who know only one of the speaker's languages, one is constrained to the limits of that language system. Any idea that comes into one's head must be encoded within that system. On the other hand, in interacting with a person who shares more than one of one's languages, there is a greater degree of flexibility in expressing ideas. One thing that is clearly visible in the interview transcripts is that when the interviewer did not know the interviewees before the interview, structural switching became much more frequent in the later parts of the interview, as the conversation got going and rapport developed among the participants. This situation can be opposed to formal communication situations, in which one is constrained to use all sorts of outlandish expressions (in Malayalam or Tamil or Hindi, for example) to express notions that can be easily conveyed in English. I also found that after I had been in Kerala for some time, Malayalis who knew me often switched into Malayalam when talking with me, sometimes without apparent awareness that they were doing so.

John Gumperz has pointed out, in several of his papers, the parallelism between the style-switching that monolinguals (such as monolingual Americans or French speakers) do, and the code-switching of bilinguals. It seems necessary to comment that the kind of code-switching that we are talking about here seems to go beyond the style-switching of monolinguals and allows the individual a flexibility of expression that could not be obtained within any single system. If the kinds of social meanings that are signalled by code-switching in Indian society have their counterparts in monolingual groups, a comparative study of the devices used for encoding them would be of great sociolinguistic interest.

STRUCTURAL CONSTRAINTS ON CODE-SWITCHING

In examining the question of *how* these mixed sentences are produced, it may be useful to explore the possibility of formulating generative rules for their production. No attempt will be made here to present a set of formal rules; rather, some general requirements of such rules will be discussed. The purpose will be to attempt to answer the question whether there are constraints on mixed sentences that can be stated in general grammatical terms. (We will assume, for the present purposes, that the constraints on longer stretches of speech can be stated in terms of the constraints on individual sentences—that is, longer stretches of speech are considered to be composed of sentences that conform to the constraints to be discussed. Ultimately, this assumption will have to be modified to conform to statements such as those made in the preceding section: for example, the variation in the proportions of mixed sentences in different contexts, and so on.)

What we have called lexical switching earlier clearly involves insertion of a form from language B in the bottom level of a structure that is generated by rules of language A, as illustrated in item 36. Cases that we have listed under structural switching, however, involve higher constituents, as illustrated in items 37 and 38. (In these examples, the switched constituent is enclosed in brackets.) In a case like that illustrated in item 40, even though the switched constituent involves a single lexical item, it is dominated by a high-level node, and therefore can be considered a case of structural switching. Most of the mixed sentences in the data could be generated by a rule that allows any constituent, at any level, to be switched. Even a seemingly complex case like that illustrated in item 39 can be accounted for by the same procedure. (In this case, the matrix sentence is in English, but the segment shown here follows Malayalam rules except for the embedded sentence HE LIKES ME.) Thus, both types of switching can be accounted for by essentially the same mechanism.

36. (see 1)

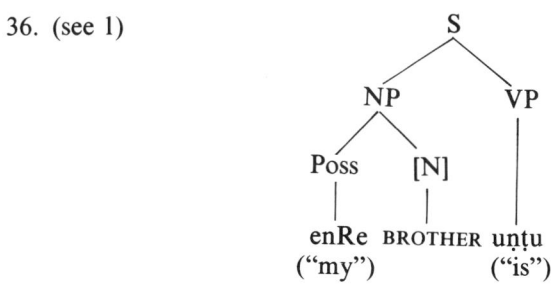

37. (see 7)

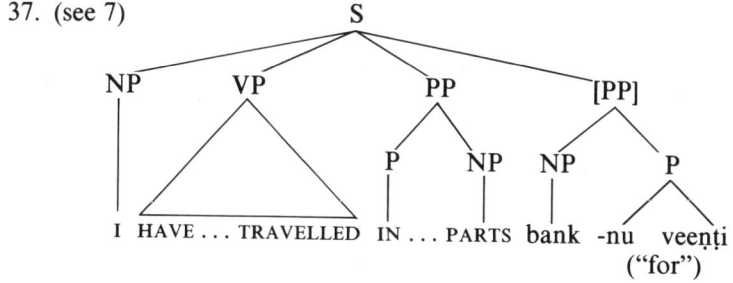

38. (see 10)

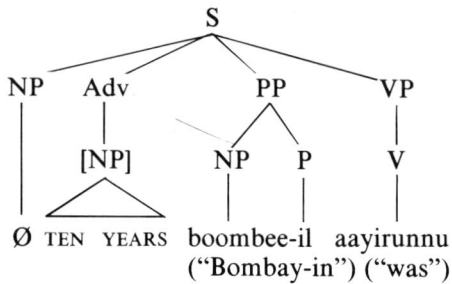

39. (see 14)

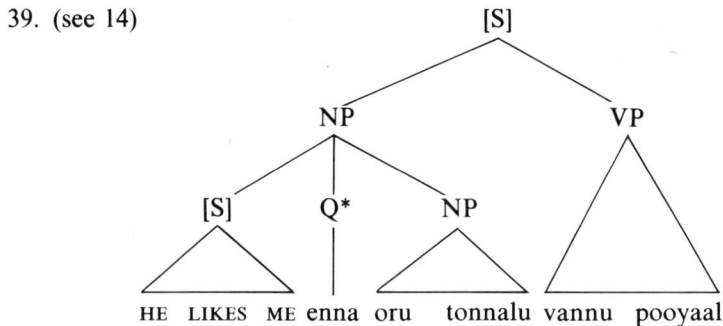

* Q = quotative marker.

Two important questions can now be asked, although they cannot be answered fully on the basis of the data now available: (1) Is the switching rule stated earlier applicable, without constraint, to any utterance? (2) Do all mixed sentences clearly follow the rules of one language in their overall structure, or are there indeterminate or mixed cases?

With regard to the first question, we are hampered not only by the lack of adequate data, but by certain social attitudes with regard to language mixing. Our switching rule would not only predict the acceptability of sentence 40 (a), which was given earlier as sentence 9, but also of 40 (b-f):

40. (a) MOTHER LEARNED MALAYALAM BECAUSE boombeeyil aayirunnu aad-yam.
    (b) MOTHER LEARNED MALAYALAM kaaraṇam boombeeyil aayirunnu aadyam.
    (c) MOTHER LEARNED MALAYALAM kaaraṇam SHE WAS IN BOMBAY BE-FORE.
    (d) amma malayaaḷam paṭhiccu kaaraṇam SHE WAS IN BOMBAY BEFORE.
    (e) amma malayaaḷam paṭhiccu BECAUSE SHE WAS IN BOMBAY BEFORE.
    (f) amma malayaaḷam paṭhiccu BECAUSE boombeeyil aayirunnu aad-yam.

The rule would also predict the acceptability of variants with switching within the larger constituent sentences (for example, MOTHER malayaaḷam paṭhiccu, boombeeyil aayirunnu BEFORE). Why not simply test these with informants for acceptability? The problem is that for most speakers in this society none of these sentences are "acceptable." They are not considered to be proper use of language, and even those who make extensive use of this style of speech tend to ridicule it when they become aware of others using it. Of course, we can simply wait around to see which sentences actually occur in spontaneous speech. As it happens, our data include the sentence "*appiṭi colla muṭiyaatu,* BECAUSE *paṭittattilu* I GOT GOOD MARKS" (given above as sentence 12), which has the same basic bilingual structure as sentence 40(f). But unless we can devise new data collection techniques, we are reduced to the statement that we do not know whether all possibilities occur, but that there is no obvious pattern of constraints in this particular type of sentence.

41(a). (see 7)

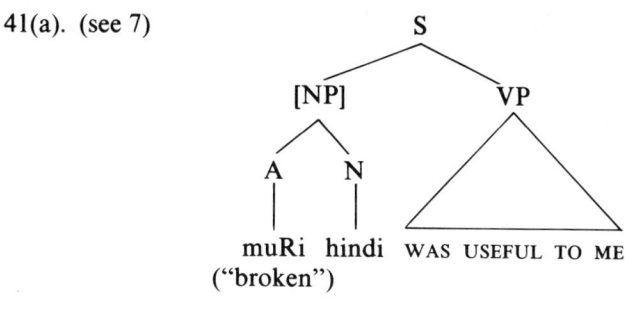

muRi hindi WAS USEFUL TO ME
("broken")

41 (b).

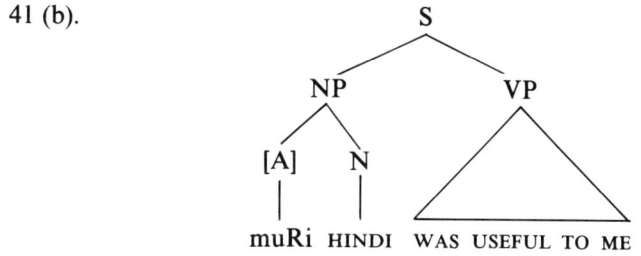

muRi HINDI WAS USEFUL TO ME

Searching through our examples, however, we do find some gaps. For example, sentences with the subject NP and the predicate VP in different languages are very rare. The only case in the examples presented here is the sentence "muRi hindi WAS USEFUL TO ME" (from example 7). This could, however, have been transcribed as "muRi HINDI WAS ...," that is, the word HINDI could have been considered as English, which would affect our analysis of the bilingual structure of the sentence, as illustrated in sentences 41(a) and (b). In this connection, we also find sentences like 23: "*avaRkku raṇṭu peeRkkum,* THEY CAN SPEAK TAMIL." Here the English pronoun THEY is redundantly inserted before the VP, and in fact we find no cases in our data where a subject *pronoun* appears with a switched predicate. Whether this is a general constraint on code-switching, or possibly a feature of interview style, cannot be determined on the basis of the present data. (Since this paper was written, the following sentence was noted, spoken by a

Malayali man resident in the United States, and addressed to his 9-year-old daughter:

41(c). *appa* [father] WILL STAY HOME TOMORROW, OK?)

Regarding the second question, there are clearly many mixed sentences whose basic structure could be generated by either Malayalam or English rules, and the decision as to which constituents are "switched" is arbitrary. Of the examples here, this is true of the sentences in 40, as well as 20 and 23. In a small number of cases, there are overlapping structures that appear to result from applying the rules of two languages at the same time. For example, in sentence 26 the sequence "NOT IN HINDI lipi-le alla" occurs. The bilingual structure of this sequence is shown in item 42. This overlapping structure is made possible by the different ordering of surface-structure elements in the two languages: in Malayalam, the negative verb is normally sentence-final. A similar case is illustrated in item 43; here the overlapping is made possible by the preposition + noun order in English, and the noun + postposition order in Tamil.

42. (see 7)

43. (see 24)

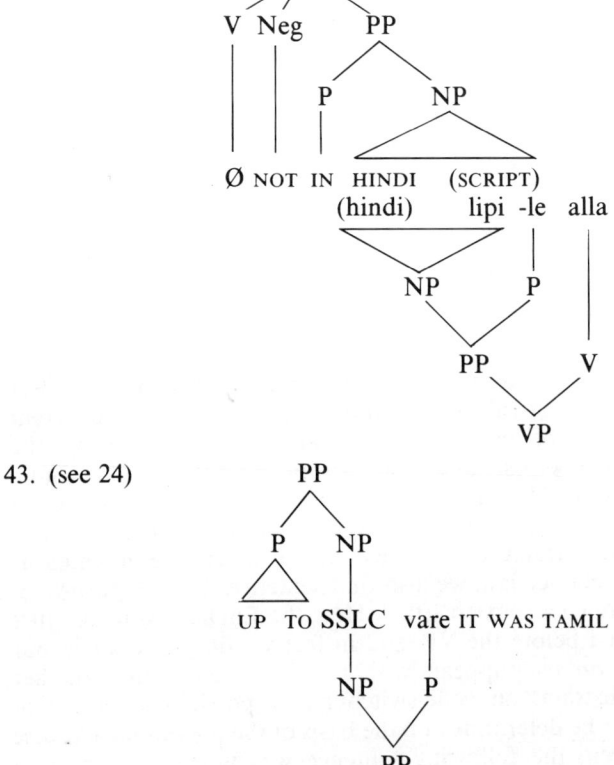

If we were to take the foregoing remarks seriously in terms of language production, we would conclude that for the bilingual speaker in societies of this kind, a decision is required at every point in speech production that corresponds to a node in a phrase-marker, including the topmost node for every sentence. The speaker thus requires constant access to both the lexicon and the grammatical rules of two (or more) languages while speaking. It would seem possible to construct two models to account for the output of such a speaker. One model would be that of a multichannel device, such as that used for international conferences where different translations are produced simultaneously on different channels. The speaker would then be in the position of a person who controls a channel selector switch, which he moves at will, thus causing different portions of the message to be broadcast in different languages. Such a model implies that there is a single original message (a single "deep structure"), which for social reasons is broadcast in a variety of surface forms. The alternative model, for which a mechanical analog seems more difficult to find, would involve switching in the "deep structure" itself. That is, the speaker would be viewed as switching from the grammar and lexicon of one language to that of another, more or less as the spirit moves him or her, that is, as various social, semantic, or other factors impinge on the speaking process. Although the first model may appear to be intuitively more realistic, an interesting project for future sociolinguistic and psycholinguistic research will be the evaluation of the relative merits of these (and possibly other) models.

REFERENCES

1. MacNamara, J., Ed. 1967. Problems of Bilingualism. J. Social Issues **23** (2).
2. Lambert, W. E. 1977. The effects of bilingualism on the individual: Cognitive and sociocultural consequences. *In* Bilingualism: Psychological, Social, and Educational Implications. P. A. Hornby, Ed. Academic Press. New York, N.Y.
3. Hunt, C. L. 1967. Language choice in a multilingual society. *In* Explorations in Sociolinguistics. S. Lieberson, Ed. Internat. J. Am. Linguistics **33** (4):112–125.
4. Herman, S. 1971. Explorations in the social psychology of language choice. *In* Readings in the Sociology of Language. J. Fishman, Ed.:492–511. Mouton & Co. The Hague, the Netherlands.
5. Blom, J. P. & J. Gumperz. 1972. Social meaning in linguistic structures: Code-switching in Norway. *In* Directions in Sociolinguistics. J. Gumperz & D. Hymes, Eds.:407–434. Holt, Rinehart & Winston. New York, N.Y.
6. Rubin, J. 1971. Bilingual usage in Paraguay. See Ref. 4:512–530.
7. Ben-Zeev, S. 1977. Mechanisms by which childhood bilingualism affects understanding of language and cognitive structures. See Ref. 2.
8. Gaarder, A. B. 1970. The first seventy-six bilingual education projects. *In* Report of the Twentieth Annual Round Table Meeting on Linguistics and Language Studies. J. A. Alatis, Ed.:163–178. Georgetown University Press. Washington, D. C.
9. Bernstein, B. 1971. Some sociological determinants of perception: An inquiry into sub-cultural differences. See Ref. 4:223–239.
10. Philips, S. U. 1970. Acquisition of rules for appropriate speech usage. See Ref. 8:77–102.
11. Gumperz, J. J. 1970. Verbal strategies in multilingual communication. See Ref. 8:129–148.

12. HYMES, D. 1970. Bilingual education: Linguistic vs. sociolinguistic bases. See Ref. 8:69–76.
13. ERVIN-TRIPP, S. 1967. An Issei learns English. See Ref. 1:78–90.
14. LAMBERT, W. E., R. C. GARDNER, R. OLTON & K. TUNSTALL. 1971. A study of the roles of attitudes and motivation in second-language learning. See Ref. 4: 473–491.
15. LABOV, W. 1970. The study of language in its social context. Studium Generale 23: 30–87.
16. TAYLOR, D. M. 1977. Bilingualism and intergroup relations. See Ref. 2.
17. TUCKER, G. R. 1977. Some observations concerning bilingualism and second-language teaching in developing countries and in North America. See Ref. 2.
18. GUMPERZ, J. & R. WILSON. 1971. Convergence and creolization: A case from the Indo-Aryan/Dravidian border. In Pidginization and Creolization of Languages. D. Hymes, Ed.:151–168. Cambridge University Press, Cambridge, U.K.
19. FERGUSON, C. & J. GUMPERZ. 1960. Linguistic Diversity in South Asia. Internat. J. Am. Linguistics 26 (3) (Part 2).
20. SRIVASTAVA, R. N. 1977. Indian bilingualism: Myth and reality. In Indian Bilingualism. P. G. Sharma & S. Kumar, Eds.:57–87. Kendriya Hindi Sansthan. Agra, India.
21. FISHMAN, J. A. 1971. Introduction. See Ref. 4:5–13.
22. GUMPERZ, J. J. 1964. Hindi-Punjabi code-switching in Delhi. In Proceedings of the Ninth International Congress of Linguists. 1115–1247. Mouton & Co. The Hague, the Netherlands.
23. GUMPERZ, J. J. 1972. Introduction. See Ref. 5:1–25.
24. McCLURE, E. 1977. Aspects of code-switching in the discourse of bilingual Mexican-American children. In Georgetown University Annual Round Table on Languages and Linguistics. Georgetown University Press. Washington, D. C.
25. KACHRU, B. B. 1977. Toward structuring code-mixing: An Indian perspective. See Ref. 20:188–209.
26. SOUTHWORTH, F. C. 1977. Functional aspects of linguistic heterogeneity. See Ref. 20:210–31.
27. VALDES FALLIS, G. 1976. Social interaction and code-switching patterns: A case study of Spanish/English alternation. In Bilingualism in the Bicentennial and Beyond. G. Keller, R. Teschner, & S. Viera, Eds.:53–85. Bilingual Press, Jamaica, New York.
28. ZENTELLA, A. Code switching and interactions among Puerto Rican children. Working Papers in Sociolinguistics, Southwest Educational Development Laboratory, Austin, Texas. Paper No. 50 (no date).
29. MARLOS, E., & A. ZENTELLA. 1978. A quantified analysis of code switching in four Philadelphia Puerto Rican adolescents. Penn. Rev. Ling. 3(4):46–59. University of Pennsylvania, Philadelphia.

AN OUTLINE OF PICURÍS SYNTAX*

Amy Zaharlick

Department of Anthropology
The Ohio State University
Columbus, Ohio 43210

This paper is a brief summary of my dissertation research on the Picurís language. Fieldwork was conducted in New Mexico between September 1974 and August 1975. Using a transformational approach, I described the syntax by 15 base rules and 21 transformational rules.

THE PUEBLO

The pueblo of Picurís is situated more than 8,000 feet above sea level in the Sangre de Cristo Mountains of northern New Mexico. It is a village of single-storey adobe homes nestled in a valley bounded on the north and west by the rugged Picurís Range, on the northeast by the Tres Ritos hills, on the southeast by the Truchas Mountain Range, and on the south by the Peñasco Plateau. The nearest town is the small Hispanic community of Peñasco, 2 miles east of the pueblo. Due in part to its relatively isolated location, Picurís is one of the least studied of the pueblos.

It appears that the Spanish expedition in 1540 into the Southwest did not encounter the Picurís. The first known contact by Europeans was the expedition of Gaspar Castaño de Sosa in 1590. The Spaniards were given one of the coldest receptions in the history of the Southwest.[1] Expedition records reveal that the pueblo was seven to nine stories tall, the greatest number of stories attributed to any pueblo mentioned in Spanish documents.

In 1598, Don Juan de Oñate, the first colonizer of New Mexico, referred to Picurís Pueblo by name, the "Gran Pueblo de los Picurís."[1] During this early historic period, the pueblo was a major link in an extensive, yet informal, system of trade and commerce between Pueblo and Plains Indians.[1] Oñate reported that the Picurís people formed alliances and traded with the Apaches.[2] In 1621, Fray Martín de Arvide established a Franciscan mission at Picurís.

The pueblo of Picurís and its powerful leader, Don Luis, played a major role in the Pueblo Revolt of 1680. The pueblo, with a population estimated by Vetancourt[3] (p. 318) at 3,000, joined Taos Pueblo and the Apaches de Achos on August 10. The Picurís killed their local clergy, profaned the church, and plundered the Spanish houses and fields. Then with the Taos,

* This study was supported by grants from The American University and The National Science Foundation.

the Picurís joined the Tewas, Tanos, and Pecos Pueblo Indians to lay seige to Santa Fe.[4]

Twelve years later, in 1692, Diego de Vargas won a bloodless victory in his reconquest of the Pueblos. Less than 2 years later, the northern Pueblos began to rebel again. When Governor Diego de Vargas marched north from Santa Fe to put down the revolt, he found Picurís completely deserted. The Picurís returned to the village after the governor's departure, but then they learned from the Apaches of a new threat. They heard that the French in the east were forcing the Apaches westward. Worn thin by the Spanish pressures and demands, the Picurís, together with some Tanos and Tewas, joined the Apaches on the plains. Again the governor visited Picurís and found it deserted. He took out in pursuit and managed to capture 84 women and children, who were given to his soldiers as servants. The remainder of the fleeing Indians took refuge at Cuartelejo, in territory that today is part of Kansas[4] (p. 281).

Evidently some of the Picurís returned to their pueblo for it is recorded that Picurís had about 300 people in 1706. It is also reported that the Picurís on the plains kept coming in and bringing word that their people were enslaved and wished to be freed. They wanted to return to their village. In response, in 1706 Juan de Ulibarrí went onto the plains and brought back 62 Picurís[5] (pp. 60–61).

This historical overview indicates the former size and importance of Picurís Pueblo. In the short space of 26 years, the Picurís population was reduced to one-tenth of its strength prior to the Pueblo Revolt. Despite this devastating event, Picurís has continued to exist, retaining many of its cultural traditions and, most significantly, its language.

The most recent census data available for Picurís Pueblo is that obtained in the summer of 1974 when I updated a revised version of a 1968 census list compiled by the United Pueblos Agency, Albuquerque, New Mexico. In 1974 there were 214 persons of Picurís descent on the tribal rolls. However, only 86 of these, representing 21 households, actually lived in the village. In most cases the residents were either under 21 or over 65. Grandchildren living with grandparents was a usual arrangement.

The same situation exists today. Adults leave the village in order to seek employment, for there are very few jobs either in the village or in neighboring Hispanic towns. Some recently completed Federal housing has enabled a few families to move back to the pueblo. The number of residents has not increased significantly, however, because of the present high death rate. Most nonresident Picurís believe that some day they will have a house built at the pueblo and move back, probably when they retire.

LINGUISTIC SETTING

The Picurís consider their language to be *the* language of the pueblo. It is used in all religious and ceremonial contexts, in conducting tribal council meetings, and in everyday conversation between adults. All residents of the community also speak English and a few are fluent in Spanish, English, and Picurís.

The children attend school in Peñasco, where they use English in the classroom and learn or expand their Spanish through interactions with their classmates and other members of the local population. Adults have explained that for a number of years now the children of the village have been increasing their use of English and are no longer learning Picurís. Several years ago a number of adults began to express great concern for maintaining the Picurís language as a part of their Indian identity. This concern became so great that a "bilingual" program for Picurís children was started at the Peñasco Elementary School.[†]

Picurís belongs to the Tanoan branch of the Kiowa-Tanoan language family. Tanoan is subdivided into Tiwa, Tewa, and Towa. There are four distinct languages that comprise the Tiwa branch—Taos, Picurís, Isleta, and Sandía—each associated with a separate pueblo community in New Mexico.

Prior to the work upon which this paper is based, relatively little research had been done on the Picurís language. The available materials consist of *Picurís Children's Stories* by John P. Harrington,[6] the recording of vocabulary items by George L. Trager,[7] and the work of Felicia Harben Trager.[8-10] In her unpublished Ph. D. dissertation, "Picurís Pueblo, New Mexico: An Ethnolinguistic "Salvage" Study,"[8] Felicia Harben Trager presented a description of the phonemic structure and made a preliminary analysis of the word constructions of the language. Her subsequent articles include a discussion of some morphemic-level changes within the traditional noun class system[9] and a summary statement of Picurís phonology.[10]

DATA COLLECTION

Systematic data collection began in September 1974. Sessions with consultants (informants) consisted of eliciting words, phrases, and sentences, which were tape recorded for later transcription and analysis. Prior to each session, English vocabulary lists and grammatical constructions were prepared. During the recording sessions, the nearest Picurís equivalents were elicited. As different types of words in the language were recognized, questions could be asked about the components of each word type. Later, once rules were determined that appeared to govern the formation of particular constructions, the consultants would be offered additional examples for verification or modification. This procedure was used with three residents of Picurís from September 1974 through January 1975. The primary consultant at this time was a 71-year-old woman.

At first this technique proved satisfactory, but as more details of the syntax became apparent, there arose two reasons for concern. First, it was

[†] With the consent and backing of the Picurís Tribal Council and the Picurís Education Committee, I have worked with this program to provide materials, teaching aids, and some preliminary linguistic training for the two Picurís teacher aides employed by the school. Fourteen Picurís students are involved in this program, of whom only a few actually speak or understand any Picurís. The program at this stage in its development is primarily a language-teaching program rather than a bilingual one.

becoming more and more difficult to elicit important kinds of syntactic distinctions that were believed to exist in the language. Frequently Picurís consultants would give several ways of saying the same thing. In these instances they were able to convey the idea, but not produce the distinction. Efforts to force the response usually resulted in confusion. For example, despite the fact that passive constructions do exist in the language, efforts to elicit passive constructions resulted, as often as not, in active ones. This confusion led to the second reason for dissatisfaction. It was suspected that the procedure did not allow the natural syntax of the language to fully emerge. There appeared to be a filtering effect due to the kinds of questions being asked—admittedly, questions based upon a knowledge of English syntax.

In February 1975, with a new consultant, it was decided that a different approach should be tried. Since little progress had been made in directly eliciting syntactic distinctions, it was thought that texts might provide grammatical constructions necessary to proceed with the analysis. It was felt that much time could be saved by using Harrington's *Picurís Children's Stories* instead of formulating new text material.

Since Harrington did not provide a description of the symbols he used, the first task was to determine the sounds his symbols represented.[‡] This completed, the consultant was asked to read the Picurís version of the stories and provide an English translation as she went along, morpheme by morpheme. Every so often her translations were checked against Harrington's. In nearly all cases the meaning was similar. In a few instances where the consultant encountered unfamiliar expressions, she either misinterpreted the Picurís, thereby arriving at a different meaning or, not recognizing the expression, she could offer no response. In each of these cases Harrington's translation provided enough information for her to identify the unfamiliar expression and assign the intended meaning.

This process was continued until four texts had been completed. It was felt that sufficient data for a syntactic analysis had been obtained since new types of constructions were no longer being encountered. However, since the study was bounded by the types of constructions included in the texts, it in no way could claim to include all syntactic processes in the language. One of the texts is included as an appendix in order to permit the reader to see

[‡] The Picurís language has a total of 35 phonemes: 14 consonants, 6 oral vowels, 96 nasal vowels, 3 stresses, 3 tones, and 3 kinds of transitional phenomena. The consonants are p, t, č, k, ', s, ł, x, h, m, n, l, w, and y. The oral and nasal vowels are i, į, e, ę, ə, ə̨, a, ą, o,; ǫ, u, ų. The three stresses are primary / ́/, secondary / ̀/, and weak /-/; tones are low, middle, and high; and the three phonemes of transition are plus /+/, sustained /,/, and final /./.

In Picurís, a syllable has the following structure: $C_1V_1(C_2)$, where C denotes any nonvowel, V any vowel, and the numerals 1 and 2, the position of accompanying segmentals in a syllable. C_1 may consist of any single consonant phoneme in the language or of any of the permissible consonant clusters (p', t', č', k', ph, th, kw, xw, k'w). V_1 may consist of any one of the 12 vowel phonemes or it may consist of the vowel cluster /ia/. C_2 is optional and may consist of one of the following consonants: /m, n, l, w, y/.

some Picurís syntactic constructions in context and to call attention to embedding, an important characteristic of the grammar. Embedding, the process of incorporating more than one base into a single verb construction, is observable in the ordering of surface-level, morphemic components.

ANALYSIS

An important source of data used in the analysis phase of the study was the work by other researchers on the Tiwa languages. These materials included the published and unpublished research and analyses of George L. Trager, [7, 11-16] who has worked on the Taos language since the 1930s, and the published and unpublished materials of Felicia Harben Trager,[8-10] who was the first to undertake a systematic investigation of the Picurís language. Also important were the studies by William L. Leap on Isleta [17-19] and Elizabeth A. Brandt on Sandía.[20] Since Taos, Isleta, and Sandía are closely related to Picurís, the linguistic details of these Tiwa languages were drawn upon to predict the processes operative in Picurís syntax today.

In the analysis phase each construction in the texts was categorized according to the types of grammatical elements it contained. The data in each category were analyzed, starting with the most basic constructions and progressing to the more complex. For each category of constructions, for example, negative expressions, a deep structural display was presented. These displays were compared with surface-level forms in order to determine how the latter were derived. The resulting transformational rules were sequentially applied to each deep structure string, starting with the most deeply embedded, until the surface-level forms were obtained. This process was continued until all of the constructions in the four texts were considered.

In the study, *syntax* was defined as the sentence-level arrangements and the underlying processes involved in the formation of grammatical constructions. In order to discern the sentence-level arrangements, it was necessary to delineate the patterns of combinations between bases and affixes in specific words, phrases, clauses, and sentences. The processes underlying the formation of grammatical constructions were revealed as a result of discovering the language-wide rules and constraints that govern the possible combinations permitted in specific constructions.

SYNTACTIC RULES

A linguistic analysis is an attempt to describe language regularities by recognizing both pattern and structure. Rules or principles express the regularities, and the grammar, therefore, is the compilation of its rules.

The grammar of Picurís can be summarized by two sets of rules. The base or phrase-structure rules describe the underlying structures of the language. These rules also specify the options and the possibilities for the expansion of each deep-structural component. The second set of rules, the transformational, account for the configurational differences between deep and surface structures. Both sets of rules attempt to capture the regularities implicit in the linguistic data.

Base Rules

The textual analysis has revealed the following base rules for the Picurís language:[§]

B1 $\#S\# \longrightarrow \#S\#$ $(\#S\# + Cl_1)$

B2 $\#S\# \longrightarrow$ (PartP)   (NP)   Aux   VP (Cl_1) (Cl_2) (Q)

B3 $Cl_1 \longrightarrow \left\{ \begin{array}{l} Cl\ \text{subordinate} \\ Cl\ \text{coordinate} \end{array} \right\}$

B4 $Cl_2 \longrightarrow$ Emphatic

B5 $Q \longrightarrow \left\{ \begin{array}{l} Q\ \text{sentence} \\ Q\ \text{word} \end{array} \right\}$

B6   PartP $\longrightarrow$ (NP)   Part $\left\{ \begin{array}{l} NP \\ PartP \end{array} \right\}$ (Cl_2)

B7   VP $\longrightarrow$ V   (NP)   (NP)   (PartP)

B8   V $\longrightarrow$ base   prefix

B9   Aux $\longrightarrow$ Tense   Aspect   Mode   Voice

B10   Tense $\longrightarrow \left\{ \begin{array}{l} \text{Past} \\ \text{Present} \\ \text{Future} \end{array} \right\}$

B11   Aspect $\longrightarrow \left\{ \begin{array}{l} \text{Perfective} \\ \text{Durative} \end{array} \right\}$

B12   Mode $\longrightarrow \left\{ \begin{array}{l} \text{Indicative} \\ \text{Imperative} \\ \text{Stative} \end{array} \right\}$

B13   Voice $\longrightarrow \left\{ \begin{array}{l} \text{Active} \\ \text{Passive} \end{array} \right\}$

B14   NP $\longrightarrow \left\{ \begin{array}{l} (S) \quad (PartP) \quad (Cl_2) \\ \qquad\qquad\qquad S \\ (PartP) \quad (N \quad Ns\ (\ )) \\ \qquad\qquad\qquad Cl \end{array} \right\}$

B15   N $\longrightarrow$ (NP)   Nb

[§] The abbreviations used in the rules are as follows: S = sentence; Ś = primary sentence; # = boundary marker; ( ) = optional element(s); Cl = clitic; PartP = particle phrase; Part = particle; NP = noun phrase; Aux = auxillary; VP = verb phrase; Q = question; V = verb; N = noun; Nb = noun base; Ns = noun-class suffix; Vpre- = verb prefix; Pass = passive; Poss = possessive.

A Picurís sentence may be a basic sentence or a coordinated structure composed of two or more basic sentences linked by a clitic. Recursiveness is an important property of the grammar because it accounts for the possibility of generating an unlimited number of basic sentences within one complex sentence. Base Rule 1 permits recursiveness. The #Ś# in Base Rule 2 represents a basic sentence, which must contain an auxiliary component and a verb phrase. These two elements are optionally preceded by a particle phrase or a noun phrase or both and optionally followed by one or two clitics or Q (interrogation) or both.

Certain elements have been deliberately omitted from Base Rule 2 because additional data will be required before they can be adequately treated. These elements include intonation, junctures, and stress patterns, which are required elements in every sentence.

The first type of clitic, Cl_1, may be rewritten as either a coordinating or subordinating clitic (B3). The second type of clitic, Cl_2, is rewritten as an emphatic clitic (B4). By Base Rule 5, Q may be rewritten as either an interrogative sentence or as an interrogative word. Base Rule 6 expands a particle phrase into a required particle, optionally preceded by a noun phrase and optionally followed by either a noun phrase or another particle phrase. These particle phrases may be moved rather freely within a sentence.

Base Rule 7 expands a verb phrase into a required verb and one or two optional noun phrases or a particle phrase or both. In Base Rule 8 the verb is divided into two required components—a base and a prefix. The Aux element in Base Rule 9 is expanded into its four components, each of which is expanded in the next four Base Rules, 10–13.

There are several different options for the rewriting of a noun phrase (B14). It may be expanded as a sentence or particle phrase, or both, optionally followed by a Cl_2. Or, it may be expanded as a noun and noun suffix optionally followed by either a clitic or a sentence. By convention, at least one of these options must be chosen, although two or three may be selected simultaneously. The four possibilities are the following: a sentence and a particle phrase; a particle phrase and a noun and noun suffix; a particle phrase, a noun and noun suffix (NP), and a sentence; or, a noun and noun suffix with clitic (NP + Cl). Base Rule 15 expands a noun to a required base preceded by an optional noun phrase.

It was noted earlier that recursiveness is an important property of the grammar. This recursive property is derived from the interaction of S, NP, and N according to the following rules:

$$S \rightarrow (NP) \quad Aux \quad VP \qquad (B2)$$
$$NP \rightarrow (S) \quad (N \quad Ns) \qquad (B14)$$
$$N \rightarrow NP \quad Nb \qquad (B15)$$

Every sentence can contain one or more noun phrases, which in turn may contain a noun or a sentence, which in turn contains a noun phrase, and so on. These rules predict that, in principle, there is no limit to the length of a sentence or noun phrase in the language.

Transformational Rules

The following transformational rules were derived for Picurís. An example is provided after each rule to indicate deep and surface-level forms and to provide the reader with data appropriate to that rule. Other examples are found in the short text, The Woman and the Wolf, included as an Appendix to this paper.

T_1 Compound-Noun-Phrase-Word

SD: $\begin{bmatrix} N & Ns & N & Ns \end{bmatrix}_{NP}$ ➤
       1   2   3   4

SC: 1 - ∅ - 3 - 4

This rule combines two nouns into one in surface structure.

Example: p'e'emę   +   p'a'ane   =   p'ep'a'anę
        "head"   "water"   "Christians"

T_2 Particle-Noun-Phrase-Word

SD: $\begin{bmatrix} Part & N & Ns \end{bmatrix}_{NP}$ ➤
      1   2   3

SC: 2 - 1 - 3

This rule combines a particle with a noun to form a new surface-level noun.

Example: ƛum   +   p'a'ane   =   p'aƛum'ene
        "warm"   "water"   "warm water"

T_3 Sentence-Noun-Phrase-Word

SD: $\begin{bmatrix} \begin{bmatrix} Aux & Vb & Vpre- & NP \end{bmatrix}_S & (N) & Ns \end{bmatrix}_{NP}$ ➤
       1   2   3   4   (5)   6
                               (5)

SC: 4 - 2 - (5) - 6

This rule combines an underlying sentence with a noun to form another type of surface-level noun.

Example: p'įkuy   +   ča'amǫ   =   p'įkuyča'amǫ
        "lay the road"   "song"   "making the road song"

T_4 Noun-Clitic

SD: N   Ns   Cl ➤
      1   2   3

SC: 1 - ∅ - 3

This rule produces a noun phrase by combining a noun with a clitic.

Example: če'enę   +   -ta   =   četa
        "eyes"   "in"   "in his/the eyes"

T_5 $Q_{Sentence}$

SD: #,   X   NP   Aux   VP, $(Q_{Sentence})$ ➤
      1   2

SC: 1,   (hoko),   2 $Q_{Intonation}$

This rule changes a declarative statement into an interrogative one.

Example: The declarative statement 'ạxiamǫ "you are ready" is transformed into a question by a final rise in intonation and the addition of the optional hoko.
       (hoko)   'ạxiamǫ ⌐   "Are you ready?"

T_6 Q_{Word}

SD: #,   X,   NP   Aux   VP, Q_{Word} ➤
      1   2   3   4

SC: 1 Q_{Word} 2   3 $Q_{Intonation}$

This rule changes a declarative statement into an interrogative one by the addition of a question word and by a rise in the intonation pattern.

Example: 'at'ahu   +   heyo and ⌐   =   heyo 'at'ahu?⌐
       "you are doing it"   "what"   "What are you doing?"

T_7 **Imperative**

SD: NP   Aux (Imperative)   Vb   Vpre-
    1   2   3   4   5
SC: 1   5 - 4 - Ø
This rule transforms a declarative statement into an imperative
statement by deleting the auxiliary element from surface structure.
Example: 'asǫhu   -   -hu   =   'asǫy
           "you are drinking" present   "Drink"

T_8 **Object Movement**

SD: (NP)   Aux [Vb   Vpre-   N   Ns]$_{VP}$

    1   2   3   4   5   6
SC: (1)   2   5 - Ø - 3   4
This rule embeds a verb object in a verb construction by moving
the verb object to a position immediately before the verb base.
Example: titayhu   +   p'a'ane   =   tip'atayhu
          "I am dipping it"   "water"   "I am dipping water"

T_9 **Reflexivization**

SD: (NP) Aux [Vb   Vpre-   NP   ([N   Ns   Cl]$_{NP}$)]$_{VP}$

    1   2   3   4   5   6   7   8
SC: (1)   4$_{+Reflexive}$ - (6 - Ø - Ø) - 3 - 2
This rule transforms a regular verb prefix into a reflexive
verb prefix when the subject and object are the same.
Example: xwiwehu   becomes   mǎxwiwehu
          "she is getting it up"   "she gets up"
  and   p'a'ophuy   becomes   mǎp'a'ophuy
          "he plunged it into the water"   "he plunged into the
                              water"

T_{10} **Particle Movement**

SD: (NP)   Aux [Vb   Vpre-   PartP   (N   Ns)]$_{VP}$
    1   2   3   4   5   6   7
SC: (1)   2   5 - (6   Ø) - 3   4
This rule embeds a particle into a verb phrase by moving it to
a position immediately before the verb base or before a
relocated noun object.
Examples: 'ixwia'ǎn   +   pǫha   =   'ipǫhaxwia'ǎn
          "he called them"   "all"   "he called all of them"
  and   anpumele'əlhemmia   + pǫha = 'anpǫhapumele'əlhemmia
      "his bees were sent out"   "all" "all of his bees were
                            sent out"

T_{11} **Passivization**

SD: NP$_1$ Aux Pass [Vb   Vpre-   (N   Ns)$_{NF_2}$]$_{VP}$
    1   2   3   4   5   6   7
SC: 1   5 - (6 - Ø) - 4 - <u>Cia</u> - 2
This rule transforms an active statement into a passive one by
the addition of a passive morpheme.
Example: k'uhu   becomes   k'učiahu
          "she is laying it down"   "it is laid down"

T_{12} **NP-Cl Movement**

SD: NP$_1$ Aux (Pass) [Vb   Vpre-   N   Ns   Cl]$_{VP}$
    1   2   3   4   5   6   7   8
SC: 1   6 - Ø - 8   5 - 4 - (<u>Cia</u>) - 2
This rule moves a verbal noun phrase to a position before the
verb construction.
Example: wan'ayxǫn   +   p'a'ay   =   p'a'ay wan'ayxǫn
          "when he came"   "to the river"   "when he came to
                            the river"

T_{13} Wia Deletion

SD: Vpre- (Part) N (Part) - <u>wia</u> - $\emptyset$ Aux
    1   (2)   3   (4)   5   6 ➡

SC: 1 - (2) - 3 $\left\{ \begin{matrix} (Ns) \\ (4) \end{matrix} \right\}$ Condition: <u>wia</u> is in final position.

This rule optionally deletes <u>wia</u> "to be" from surface structure when it occurs in final position.
Example: 'akiawia   becomes   'akiane
      "she is his mother"   "she is his mother"

T_{14} Aux Suffixation

SD: (NP) Aux (N) Vb Vpre-
    1   2   3   4   5
SC: (1) 3 - 4 - 2 5 ➡
This rule positions the auxiliary element in suffix position in surface structure. It is applied after verbal objects and particles are relocated (embedded).
Example: -hu   mɐn $\emptyset$ becomes   mɐnhu
       present   "see"   3Sing/Class A "he sees him"

T_{15} Verb Prefixation

SD: (NP) (N) - Vb - Aux Vpre-
    1   2   3   4   5
SC: (1) 5 - 2 - 3 - 4
This rule positions the pronominal prefix in its appropriate surface-level position. It also is applied after other elements are embedded.
Example: ʎiwmɐn'ɐn   + ti-   =   tiʎiwmɐn'ɐn
     "saw the woman" ISing/Class A "I saw the woman"

T_{16} Possessive

SD: (X) (NP) Aux [<u>wia</u>$_{+Poss}$ Vpre- N Ns N Ns]$_{VP}$ (Y)
    (1) (2)   3   4   5   6 7 8 9   (10) ➡
SC: (1) 5$_{+Poss}$ - 6 - $\emptyset$ - <u>wia</u> (10)
This rule transforms a regular verb prefix into a possessive verb prefix when <u>wia</u> + Poss is present in deep structure.
Example: kiawia   becomes   'akiawia
     "she is a mother"   "she is his mother"

T_{17} Prefix-Deletion

SD: X [Vpre-$_1$ - Vb] Vb Aux Vpre-$_2$
    1   2   3   4   5   6 ➡
SC: 1 $\emptyset$ - 3 - 4 - 5 6 Condition: Vpre-$_1$ = Vpre-$_2$ (2=6)
This rule deletes one of the identical prefixes when two verb constructions are transformed into one in surface structure.
Example: 'imɐhu   +   'itukehu   = 'itukemɐhu
    "they are going" "they are bathing" "they go to bathe"

T_{18} Relativization

SD: NP$_1$ # X NP$_2$ Aux VP #
    1   2 3   4   5   6 7 ➡
SC: 1 3 6 - 5$_{Set II}$ - 'e Condition: NP$_1$ = NP$_2$
This rule transforms **two sentences** having the same noun subjects or noun objects into one sentence containing a relative clause.
Example: pɐhan t'ayenɐ # pɐhan t'ayene č'ɐn piwene   kuytha #
    "all" "people" "all" "people" "come in""dead""lay there"
becomes pɐhan t'ay'enɐ piwene kuytha 'ič'ɐn'e ....
     "all the people who have been in where the dead
     person was lying ...."

T_{19} <u>Negation</u>

SD: NP_1 Aux_1 Vb_1 $Vpre_{-1}$ NP_2 Aux_2 $[Vb_2$ $Vpre_{-2}$ $(NP)]_{VP}$
       1   2   3   4   5   6   7   8   9 ➡

SC: 1 - 4 - <u>wa</u> - (9) - 7 - $6_{subordinate}$

       Condition: $NP_1 = NP_2$ and $Vb_1 = \square$

This rule transforms a positive statement into a negative one.

Example: 'uwəlehu   +   negation   =   'uwawəlemę̓

           "they are going out."   "they do not go out"

T_{20} <u>NP Conjunction Reduction</u>

SD: X_1 NP_1 VP_1 # X_2 NP_2 VP_2 # Cl_{coord}
      1   2   3   4   5   6   7   8   9 ➡

SC: (1)   2   3   (5)   7   (9)

Condition: $NP_1 = NP_2$

            $VP_1 \neq VP_2$, but are of the exact same grammatical
                                nature.

This rule combines two sentences having the same subject into one.

Example: Ⱡiwene   miyaxwiwemę̓   +   Ⱡiwene   'a'o'ophil
          "woman"   "she does not get up"   "woman" "her child with

          yokuy   =   Ⱡiwene miyaxwiwemę̓ 'a'o'ophil yokuy
          "she lay"   "The woman does not get up but lies there
                         with her child."

T_{21} <u>VP Conjunction Reduction</u>

SD: NP_1 VP_1 # (X) NP_2 VP_2 # Cl_{coord}
      1   2   3   4   5   6   7   8 ➡

SC: (4)   1   5   6

Condition: $VP_1 = VP_2$, and, if the VPs contain NPs, then the
            NPs in the verb phrases must have the same referent.

This rule combines two deep-structure sentences having the same
verb complex into one in surface structure.

Example: Ⱡiwenę̓ 'uwəlehu   +   sənenę̓ 'uwəlehu   =
          "women" "they are going out"   "men"   "they are going out"

          Ⱡiwenę̓ sənenę̓ 'uwəlehu
          "The men and women are going out."

Each of the first four transformational rules produces a type of surface-level noun phrase. T_1 produces a *compound-noun-phrase word* by combining two nouns in underlying structure. T_2 combines an underlying particle with an underlying noun phrase to produce a surface-level *particle-noun-phrase word*. A *sentence-noun-phrase word* is formed by T_3 from an underlying sentence and noun phrase. T_4 gives additional specification to a noun phrase by adding a clitic to yield an expression that is similar in meaning to a prepositional phrase in English.

Transformations 5 and 6 change a declarative sentence into an interrogative statement, while T_7 transforms an indicative statement into an imperative one.

Transformations 8, 10, and 12 move elements from deep-structural object position. If an element found in object position in deep structure contains a clitic, it is moved before the verb construction in surface structure. If it does not contain a clitic, then it is incorporated into a surface-level verb construction. T_8 incorporates NP objects, while T_{10} incorporates particles.

If an underlying subject is the same as an underlying object, *reflexivization*, T_9, changes the surface-level verb prefix to a special reflexive prefix. A surface-level prefix change also occurs from the application of the *possessive* transformation, T_{16}.

An active sentence is transformed into a passive sentence by T_{11}. By T_{13}, the verb *wia* is optionally deleted from surface structure when it is in final position. Verb prefixes and suffixes assume their proper surface-level order by means of transformations 14 and 15.

The last five transformations, 17–21, combine two deep-structural clauses into one surface-level sentence. T_{17} deletes one of the prefixes when two verbs are combined; T_{18} subordinates one clause to the other in the form of a surface-level relative clause, and T_{19} changes a positive statement into a negative one. Transformations 20 and 21 delete identical elements from surface structure when two like clauses are conjoined.

The transformational rules delete, insert, and/or rearrange grammatical material. The *compound-noun-phrase word*, the *noun clitic*, the *prefix deletion*, and the *conjunction reduction* rules are deletion rules for Picurís. These rules limit the redundancy of underlying structures by allowing the deletion of repeated or unnecessary elements. Insertion rules have the opposite effect. Such rules insert into sentences elements that have no independent meaning. The inserted elements do not occur in the deep structure, but they mark in surface structure the fact that a transformation has occurred. The $Q_{sentence}$ transformation is an example of this type of rule.

Rearrangement rules change the order of elements in underlying structures. The *particle-noun-phrase word*, the *particle movement*, the *aux suffixation* and *verb prefixation* rules are all examples of simple rearrangement rules. More complex rearrangement rules apply under special conditions. Examples of this type are the *sentence-noun-phrase word*, the *reflexivization*, the *possessive*, and the *negation* transformations. These rules are quite common and account for many of the striking differences between underlying and surface structures.

The *imperative* and the *object movement* rules employ both deletion and rearrangement. The Q_{word} transformation utilizes both insertion and rearrangement. In the case of embedded noun phrases, the *wia deletion* rule involves both deletion and insertion. The *passivization, NP-clitic*, and *relativization* rules employ a combination of all three. Most of these transformational rules are obligatory when applied. Others, such as *wia deletion*, are applied optionally.

The syntactic derivation of a sentence involves the sequential application of transformational rules. After each rule's application, an intermediate structure results that serves as input for the next rule. Many of the rules must be applied in a specified order. A good example is the ordering of the *object movement* and *verb prefixation* rules. The *object movement* rule must precede the *verb prefixation* rule so that the prefix can be correctly affixed to the relocated noun base rather than to the verb base. Of course, it must be remembered that sequential relationships are purely structural, not ones that a speaker consciously considers when constructing a sentence. Through this process, transformations yield the modified or derived structures that more closely resemble surface structure forms.

A complex sentence is one that consists of more than one clause. The clauses of a complex sentence may be bound together by means of embedding or conjoining. When one clause functions as a constituent of another, the relationship between them is referred to as subordination. The "lower" or subordinate clause of such a sentence is said to be embedded in the "upper" or main clause. All subordinate clauses can be derived from regular, deep-structure sentences through the use of appropriate transformations.

The source of all subordinate constructions lies in the rewriting of NP as #S#. The subordinate constructions that occur in Picurís are complement clauses, relative clauses, locative clauses, and possessive expressions.

If the NP under the VP node (the direct object NP) is rewritten as #S# by Base Rule 14, the resulting construction is a complement clause. A complement clause construction is the source of all surface-level expressions in the language containing more than one verb base, as well as the source of all negative expressions. A complement clause, by itself, functions as an object. In surface structure it contains a specific subordinate suffix to indicate its dependent status.

Whenever NP is rewritten as noun and noun suffix followed by #S#, the #S# is a relative clause modifying the rewritten NP. In surface structure the #S# always follows the NP. #S# together with NP may occur in either subject or object position in a sentence. A relative clause can be identified by its subordinate suffix and the clitic 'e in final position.

Locative clauses result from the rewriting of NP as #S# followed by a clitic. In surface structure locative clauses are recognized by the presence of subordinate suffixes and a special set of final clitics. Each of these clitics, consisting of one or more morphemes, has a translational meaning of "where" or "when." The choice of clitic depends upon the place and time characteristics associated with the verb that the locative clause modifies.

Possessive expressions in Picurís result from the rewriting of the optional NP of N as #S# followed by a noun base. In surface structure these expressions are indicated by a change in prefix form.

Coordination, or conjoining, is another common syntactic device used to combine two or more independent clauses into a complex sentence. In a coordinated construction neither clause is a constituent of the other. The source of all coordinated constructions derives from Base Rule 1, which rewrites #S# as #Ś# and a coordinating clitic. Frequently, coordination is implied in surface structure rather than expressed by the coordinating clitic.

Grammatical units, other than clauses, may be conjoined, resulting in many noun or verb phrases, or both, occurring in a single conjoined structure. These conjoined structures differ from conjoined clauses only in surface structure, for in deep structure all are derived from underlying clauses. The surface-level forms of conjoined phrases are the result of the application of the *conjunction reduction* rules. These rules can be applied optionally whenever the conjoined clauses are identical in all but one corresponding constituent. The effect of these rules is to collapse the clauses into a single clause and to conjoin the nonidentical constituents. If the clauses that are to be conjoined have no identical elements in deep structure, conjunction reduction cannot take place. The result in surface structure is a complex sentence consisting of two sentences juxtaposed to one another.

SUMMARY

On the whole, the transformational model used in the study proved satisfactory. It allowed for the identification and determination of different ways in which underlying sentences are raised to surface constructions. It permitted a distinction to be made between underlying structural differences and surface-level manifestations of the same underlying structure. The model provided a framework for discerning the properties that all sentences have in common and the ways in which they can differ. Finally, it revealed covert aspects of the grammar, which brought to light some of the relationships within, and between, sentences.

REFERENCES

1. SCHROEDER, A. H. 1974. A Brief History of Picurís Pueblo: A Tiwa Indian Group in North Central New Mexico. Adams State College. Alamosa, Colorado.
2. HAMMOND, G. P. & A. REY. 1953. Don Juan de Oñate, Colonizer of New Mexico, 1595–1628. Vol. 5–6. Coronado Cuarto Centennial Publications. Albuquerque, N.M.
3. VETANCOURT, A. 1871. Teatro Americana. Mexico.
4. HODGE, F. W., G. P. HAMMOND & A. REY. 1945. Fray Alonso de Benavides' Revised Memorial of 1634. Vol. 4. Coronado Cuarto Centennial Publications. Albuquerque, N.M.
5. THOMAS, A. B. 1935. After Coronado: Spanish Exploration Northeast of New Mexico, 1696–1727. University of Oklahoma Press. Norman, Okla.
6. HARRINGTON, J. P. & H. H. ROBERTS. 1928. Picurís Children's Stories. Annu. Rep. Bur. Am. Ethnol. **43:** 289–447.
7. TRAGER, G. L. 1937. Picurís Vocabulary Items. Unpublished slips from field notes of G. L. Trager.
8. TRAGER, F. H. 1968. Picurís Pueblo, New Mexico: An Ethnolinguistic "Salvage" Study. State University of New York at Buffalo. Buffalo, New York. Unpublished Ph.D. dissertation.
9. TRAGER, F. H. 1970. Morphemic change in Picurís: A case of culture contact? Southern Methodist University. Dallas, Texas. Unpublished ms.
10. TRAGER, F. H. 1971. The phonology of Picurís. Int. J. Am. Linguistics **37** (1): 29–33.
11. TRAGER, G. L. 1946. An outline of Taos grammar. *In* Linguistic Structures of Native America. Viking Fund Publication in Anthropology **6:** 184–221.
12. TRAGER, G. L. 1961. Taos IV: Morphemics, syntax, semology in nouns and in pronominal reference. Int. J. Am. Linguistics **27** (3): 211–222.
13. TRAGER, G. L. 1962. Some thoughts on "juncture." Studies in Linguistics **16:** 11–22.
14. TRAGER, G. L. 1963. Linguistics is linguistics. Studies in Linguistics (Occasional Papers, 10).
15. TRAGER, G. L. 1965. Taos. *In* Non-Western Languages. Unpublished manuscript.
16. TRAGER, G. L. 1972. Language and Languages. Chandler Publishing Company. Scranton, Pa.
17. LEAP, W. L. 1970. The Language of Isleta, New Mexico. Southern Methodist University. Dallas, Texas. Unpublished Ph.D. dissertation.
18. LEAP, W. L. 1973. An Overview of Isletan Tiwa Syntax. Washington, D.C. Unpublished manuscript.

19. Leap, W. L. 1975. On Negation in Isletan Tiwa. Washington, D.C. Unpublished manuscript.
20. Brandt, E. A. 1970. Sandía Pueblo, New Mexico: A Linguistic and Ethnolinguistic Investigation. Southern Methodist University. Dallas, Texas. Unpublished Ph.D. dissertation.

Appendix

The Woman and the Wolf

Nąk'uthęke,　　　　 čoxomęn　P'inweltha
Once upon a time　 once　　　mountain-some-there
　　　　　　　　　　　　　　　　 "Picurís"

'it'aythə.　　　　 čoxomęn　Xiwenẽ
they-people-live　 Once　　 women

nąnąk'emǫpupun'ayte　　　　　　 phaltahęnyo
time-as-get-dark-happen-after　 inside-there-emph.

'inęxuy.
they-there-stay.

čoxomęn　węn　Xiwene　nǫwian　　 hele　'ap'awia.
Once　　 one　woman　 night-be　 no　　she-not-
　　　　　　　　　　　　　　　　　　　　　 water-have

'Ip'amolokolehęn,　　　　　　　　　 P'aynǫn
She-them-water-jars-pick-up-dur.　Picurís creek

p'axayXiw.　　　 K'olomate　　 p'ataymęn
water-get-down　 Gourd-in-form　water-put in-dur.

'aKalwan.　　　　 "Heyo　'ąt'ahu?"　 čoxomęn
to her-Wolf-come.　What　you-do-pres.　once

'ǫmmia.　　　　　 "Tip'atayhu,"　　　 Xiwene　Kal'ǫmę,
he-say-passive　 I-water-pour-pres.　woman　 Wolf-tell

"'Ą'əlXayxuy,"　　　　 čoxomęn　Kalene pa 'ǫmmia.
you-get on back-then　once　　 Wolf　 by tell-passive.

"Hattą 'ąnthəmmakwil　 tip'a'olemęko,"　　　　　 čoxomęn
Then　 my-house-up to　 I-water-take up-go-now　 once

Xiwene tǫhu.　　　 "'Ą'əlXay　　　　 'a'ǫmęhu,
woman　 say-pres.　Get on my back　 I-you-tell-pres.

howe'ąn yǫhotayo　 'ąhąnnęči."　　　 Xiwene
or else right here　I-you-eat up-will.　Woman

'ąnąpixokwęn,　　　 'ip'amolomądo　　　 'ayhęn
she-afraid-became　 she-water-jar-leave　and then

Kalene 'ay mą'əlXay.
Wolf-on   she-got on his back

    Čoxomęn Kalene pa Xiwene p'immakwil
    Once   Wolf   by woman   mountain-go up

'owlia.   P'ikk'ətha
he-her-take up-passive   Mountain-top-there

kaliahęn,   Čoxomęn Kalene təpupa tə'opa
bring-passive-dur.   then   Wolf   east   north

tənǫn təkwetha wel 'okalxwiawele.
west south   other he-them-wolves-call-go-out

Xiwene męnčoho 'it'awtįlįkimmakwil
Woman then   she-pinyon tree-tall-there-go up

wile.
climb

    'Asəttthə'e   Čoxomęn 'akwęnXiw-
    Her-husband   then   his-not-quickly-wife

wilemę'epa,   thək'əčitate
come up-dur.-rel.-because house-top-there-from

mąXawia'ąn.   Xęwtęnyo sənenX̌ 'unąxəlkamphil
he-signal-past   Later on men   their-weapons-with

'iwan.   KalXoXe wa
they-came.   Wolf-Old over there

mątǫhęmęmępun'awte,   wan'ayhęn
he-signal-go-dur.-place-there-from   come-after

Xiwene t'awk'əta   yo 'ę'aṇ.   SənenX̌
woman pinyon-tree-top-in one sit-past   Men

'imąnǫt'ilephale.   Męnčoho
they-look-for-spread out-finished.   Then

nopin'aw   węn sənene pa Xiwene thęmia.
night-middle-in one man   by woman find-passive.

Hanko sənene mątǫhęmę.   Wel 'iwan'aytęn,
Then man   give yell-past   Other they-came-after

'iXiwXəwe   wewe thəppe. Liwene
they-woman-bring down-past again house-to Woman

sənenX̌   pa t'əphaliahu.
men   - by mad-really-passive-pres.

    Hokeyo   Čoxomęn XiwenX̌ thoXan'ayhęn
    That is why   then   women   evening-after

```
phal'awte                      wetąn    'uwaweleme
inside-the houses-from         alone    they-not-go out-dur.

hetęn          'ipučiko.
something      to them-happen-will-because
```

◆

Once upon a time the people were dwelling at Picurís. The women, after it got dark, were to remain inside their houses.

And one woman in the night had no water. She took the water jar and went down to P'aynon to get water. As she was pouring the water with her gourd, a Wolf came to her. "What are you doing?" he said. "I am pouring water," the woman said to the Wolf. "Get on my back, then," the Wolf said to her. "I am already about to take the water to my house," said the woman. "Get on my back, I said to you, or I will eat you up right here." The woman got afraid, left the water jar, and got on the Wolf's back.

And the Wolf took the woman up to the mountains. When he had brought her to the mountain top, the Wolf went northeast, northwest, southwest, and southeast, to call the other wolves. The woman then climbed a tall pinyon tree.

Her husband, when his wife did not come up from below quickly, yelled as a signal from the top of the house. And shortly men with their weapons arrived.

When the Old Wolf arrived from his summoning [the other wolves], the woman was sitting in the top of the pinyon tree.

The men all gathered for a search. And then at about midnight one man found the woman. Then the man gave a yell. After the rest came they took the woman home again. The woman was scolded very much by the men. And that is why the women, after it gets dark, do not go forth from inside the houses alone, for something might happen to them.

THE FUTURE OF BRAILLE

Leslie L. Clark

*Baruch College of the
City University of New York
New York, New York 10003*

For more than a century, the significance of braille has been reinforced and emphasized by every organization serving the blind. Its importance as a primary medium of achieving literacy and its capacity to provide random access to reference information were established early. These features were strongly reinforced by the two major causes of blindness—congenital blindness and industrial accidents—which at the turn of the century established the twin foci of the blindness rehabilitation community: the educable young and the employable adult.

Today the situation has altered. Talking books and synthetic speech systems are becoming primary sources of information. Furthermore, the proportion of the blind and visually impaired has changed: there are more persons with poor vision who do not require braille, more elderly who do not seem to want it, and more adults who do not use it. Changes in the use of braille have been accelerated by major increases in the cost of its production and deployment. In an ever more cost-conscious society, the Federal government is searching for ways to limit expenditures for materials of uncertain usefulness and effectiveness, and volunteer producers are looking for even more extensive methods of subsidizing products at a price that state agencies are willing and able to pay.

A variety of traditional approaches has been employed to find solutions to the complicated problems of providing braille material.[1] For the past 15 or 20 years, the primary emphasis has fallen upon technological innovation, and the pace of technological development increases steadily.

The primary challenges to braille are the talking book and, potentially, synthetic speech. But the talking book is basically a passive medium; it does not require the learner's active participation in the same way that braille or inkprint does.

Synthetic speech offers attractive possibilities for generating easily understood output from machine-readable sources, and its rate of presentation, like that of natural speech, is more than double the rate achieved by the average braille reader. Yet the periods of enjoyable listening it provides may be limited because of the relatively monotonous quality of the output. Furthermore, the current design of equipment for converting inkprint to synthetic speech (for example, the Kurzweil Reading Machine) requires manipulations that result in net reading speeds that are only slightly higher than those achieved with braille. (Average rates for both media range

0077-8923/80/0345-0165$01.75/2 © 1980, NYAS

between 80 and 100 words per minute.) Finally, the current cost of this equipment is prohibitive: for instance, the Kurzweil machine now costs $20,000, and even its proposed cost of $5,000 will probably preclude its mass adoption as a personal mode of reading unless major Federal subsidies are forthcoming.[2]

Recent research indicates that long-term use of synthetic speech may cause additional difficulties.[3] Because normal speech contains much redundancy in the information-carrying elements of the speech signal, it is extremely resistant to interference. The classic illustration of this is the so-called "cocktail party effect," in which one can concentrate on a single voice in a hubbub of voices and understand what the individual is saying. Because the amount of redundancy in synthetic speech is inherently low, the listener must pay greater attention to the speech signal. Moreover, the lack of redundancy places a greater burden on short-term memory. Thus errors in comprehension accumulate in short-term memory, and the intelligibility of the speech stream may decline after a person listens for long periods.

For these and other reasons, braille remains an important medium of communication and is a primary medium through which the blind achieve literacy. As a method of random access, it is unequalled for use with reference material and for rapid recall of previously read material. Yet, the use of braille has been declining. The main reason for this decline has not been a technical one, but one that is best characterized as benign neglect. One possible end result of this neglect—gradual deterioration of the braille production and deployment system for the small hard-core of some 30,000 to 60,000 users—is viewed in this article as an unsatisfactory outcome.

Much of the discussion that follows implies that if more braille materials were available, the use of braille would increase. Similarly, if braille was easier to learn, was taught better, and was supported by technological innovation, it would penetrate the everyday world of work and leisure and its use would increase. Are these assumptions valid? Little evidence exists to confirm or disconfirm them. By analogy, one might inquire whether the sighted have been reading more since speed-reading techniques were introduced.

THE CHANGING MIX OF READERS

Among the congenitally blind, the percentage who use braille may be as high as 90 percent. For example, braille remains an important medium of instruction for the 25,000 blind students in the United States. But among the 1.7 million Americans of all ages who cannot see well enough to read ordinary inkprint, this is not the case. A nationwide survey of severely visually impaired persons conducted by the American Foundation for the Blind (AFB), under contract to the Library of Congress, found that only 3 or 4 percent of those who learned braille at some time in their lives continued to use it.[4] There is also evidence that adventitiously blinded adults who learned braille in rehabilitation centers (where braille is routinely taught) seldom use it: indeed, many use it only for making brief notes, labeling tin cans, or identifying clothing rather than for vocational or recreational reading.[5]

Over the past five years, the number of individuals who use the Library of Congress braille book program has increased by about 20 percent (or an average of 4 percent each year). But the number of persons who use talking books and other audio materials has grown by about 20 percent *each year* over the same period.[6] The number of young braille readers registered with the American Printing House for the Blind, which produces textbooks and other educational materials in braille, has also declined slightly each year.[7] At best, one can say that the number of braille readers has reached a plateau. With respect to the increased population of the blind and visually impaired and individuals who use talking books, however, braille readership has declined.

There are two main reasons for this decline; one is concrete, the other abstract. First, because of significant increases in the cost of paper, labor, and distribution, the cost of producing braille materials has risen sharply, and the main purchaser of braille, the Federal government, is becoming more and more cost-conscious. Second, a combination of factors has culminated in the view that braille is a dying cause. As a result, actions that would enhance the availability of braille, insure the competence of both teachers and learners, and increase the value of braille for personal and vocational use are delayed.

UNCERTAIN MARKET AND LACK OF AVAILABILITY

Several problems related to the availability of braille may stem from ignorance of the real and potential market for braille. For example, there is no assurance, beyond the acceptance of materials now available, that what the braille production system is delivering is in fact what readers want. What they probably want is a mix of press and short-run braille, of changing as well as reference information, of textbooks and books read for pleasure, of material they are willing to pay for and material they cannot afford (as in the case of some on-the-job manuals).

The current braille production system cannot keep up with the inkprint publications issued each year. Although estimates vary, only 300 to 400 titles among the 40,000 or so published each year in English are issued in braille. If titles issued in talking-book form are added, the total is about 1,200 to 1,300 titles. Access to inkprint literature is increased by a small, unknown amount with aids such as the Optacon® reading aid (Telesensory Systems, Inc.) and the Kurzweil Reading Machine. But the contribution to the blind person's access to inkprint with all these aids is minor and is likely to remain so until additional technical breakthroughs occur in optical character reading and in microcomputers. (As mentioned earlier, the so-called reading machines may create a different set of problems; consequently they deserve careful and detailed examination.)

The unavailability of timely information in braille probably reduces to a significant degree the motivation of the blind to master braille. The primary gaps in braille materials are usually discussed in terms of non-job-related inkprint publications found on sale at newsstands or bookstores. But the problem is also critical in relation to the specialized needs of blind professionals. For example, the lawyer must have ready access to briefs and court decisions. The computer analyst or computer scientist must have access to new code manuals and user manuals. The blind psychologist must keep abreast of experiments and programs in his special area of interest. The electrical engineer must keep up with the latest circuit designs and components. Unable to locate this information in the mass of published materials, these professionals are forced to depend on sighted persons as readers and scanners, and unlike sighted professionals, they cannot rely on abstract services.

Pilot projects mounted in England to supply monthly abstracts in engineering, computer science, and other professions have been greeted with enthusiasm.[8, 9] Each user submits a profile of his interests, which is then used to identify and print out abstracts each month that match those interests. Printouts in braille are obtained by feeding the digital tapes used to produce inkprint output into a braille translator and a high-speed embosser. These printouts contain minor departures from braille standards and have been supplied free during the trial phase. So far, the number of users has been small—about 20 in the United States and 20 in the United Kingdom. Although the market for this service is not well defined, there may be 1,000 to 3,000 persons for whom braille abstract services would be useful.

In the case of blind computer programmers and systems analysts, the availability of translation programs and embossing devices has made job advancement possible. Furthermore, the availability of embossers that can be linked to hard-copy computer outputs have made it feasible for the blind to obtain jobs such as tax information officer with the Internal Revenue Service.

The ordinary blind citizen fares no better than do most blind professionals. Although his bank statements may be written in braille, he is unlikely to receive his bills in braille. Occasionally, he may find a restaurant that prints its menus in braille, but rarely will he find information about cultural events, transit systems, public services, and government buildings and services written in braille. Remedies for this situation are not easy to come by because the market is small.

Finally, among the most tragic victims of the unavailability of braille is the student who must wait for textbooks for months or even years after his sighted classmates receive their inkprint versions. If textbooks in braille were provided simultaneously with inkprint versions, blind students might perform as well as their sighted classmates. The issue, however, is debatable.[10]

UNEVEN QUALITY OF INSTRUCTION

Research in education, the psychology of learning, and the art of communication has indicated overwhelmingly that individuals can learn symbol systems such as foreign languages, typing, stenography, and Morse code with relatively little difficulty—if they are motivated. Most of these systems are probably as difficult—or even more difficult—to learn as braille. It is also true that a broad relationship exists between skill and intelligence. But supportive measures, such as review texts and programmed learning techniques for learning languages and codes, are more highly developed. Finally, when perfected, these symbol systems often yield salable skills. From the viewpoint of sheer learning, however, self-fulfilling prophecies are intimately involved: that is, if people expect a skill to be difficult to learn, the skill will be difficult to learn.

Over the past few years, the place of braille instruction in the blind child's curriculum has been de-emphasized. This has occurred as residential schools, which, until recently, were attended by most blind children who had no additional impairments, declined in importance. Now taught in classes together with sighted students, the blind child is immersed in an environment where most teachers, classmates, and other significant persons do not share his need for information in braille and thus may devalue it. This learning environment demands increasingly greater use of the spoken word, including sighted readers, special tape recordings, and talking books. Although first- and second-graders receive instruction in braille for about 1 hour each day, 5 days a week, older students usually are not given regular instruction during the school day. Instead, itinerant teachers instruct them in school resource rooms, generally for about 2 to 4 hours a week, and maintain and support the reading skill achieved in the first two grades (when reading speed is approximately 30 to 40 words per minute). In subsequent grades, increases in speed accrue from the same processes of practice and overlearning that are involved in learning to read inkprint. According to most authorities, the average reading rate among blind ninth-graders is 90 to 100 words per minute.[11]

Students are provided with approximately five to ten textbooks in braille each year. The majority come from volunteer sources. Exceptions are the basic reading texts and textbooks supplied by the American Printing House for the Blind, which remain unchanged from year to year. Talking books, normally containing recreational material, do not figure significantly in the normal school environment. For high school, college, and graduate students, books on cassette tapes or flexible disks are available through Recording for the Blind, Inc.

According to anecdotal evidence obtained from skilled teachers of braille, the relatively poor performance in braille of today's blind students—which reduces their motivation to use braille during and after school hours—results either from poor teaching methods or from inadequate time spent on instruction. Poor methods of teaching may be compounded by ineffectual organization of the teaching of braille. In fact, organizational issues may be more important than technical concerns. such as the best way to teach specific skills. Even the best methods will fail when staff and administration are not oriented toward common goals.

Similar problems occur in the teaching of the adventitiously blinded adult. Indeed, few adults who receive instruction in braille probably learn it well enough to use it for anything but note-taking and labeling. Anecdotal evidence tends to confirm this suspicion. Granted, the blinded adult's motivation to learn braille is critical. When braille will help to restore or reconstruct their work and family life, blinded adults will learn it. In the meantime, however, pressure increases to curtail training in braille among adult rehabilitants.

There are 40 comprehensive rehabilitation centers in the United States, all of which teach braille. (Not every state operates a comprehensive training center program.) All these centers have at least one teacher on staff; the largest have two or more, and Arkansas Enterprises for the Blind, one of the largest, has six. There are perhaps 60 teachers in these rehabilitation centers in total. Many small programs, such as the day programs in Florida, also provide instruction in braille. This brings the total number of braille teachers to about 200. Instruction is provided by these centers for periods varying between 6 and 9 months. Most use the "Standard Braille Series," Books I, II, and III, but there seems to be widespread dissatisfaction with this text. Alternative methods of teaching braille have been developed by Stocker in Kansas and Bankovics in Minnesota, among others.[12] Some methods emphasize the recognition of braille dot by dot, but the majority concentrate on recognition of characters and words. None focuses on pattern recognition—the meaning of units such as phrases or sentences.

Apparently no universal standards exist either for teacher competency or for the competency of students. Yet 40 or more clients are often taught at one time in the largest rehabilitation centers. Because most centers are funded locally within states, the existent wide variation in standards is not surprising. (Excellent instruction is provided in some large centers and in regional centers of the Veterans Administration.)

Generally speaking, the rehabilitation and special-education teachers now emerging from universities and other training institutions seem ill-prepared to teach braille. The result is a lack of motivation among students to learn it. The low financial rewards for teachers learning braille and the secondary role it is assigned in special education and in rehabilitation aggravate the effect of this lack of training standards. In contrast to teachers of sign language, who are regarded as skilled specialists, teachers of braille apparently do not think of themselves as such, for they do not involve themselves in transcribing or reading braille. Instead, they view themselves as carriers of a strange code for reading and writing that has little relevance to the spoken language.

Little has been done to develop methods of teaching braille that complement mainstreaming or rehabilitation effectively. For example, segmented teaching (the breaking down of teaching units so that braille skills are acquired step by step in reading and writing) is rarely used to motivate students. Nor has programmed instruction ever had much impact on the teaching of braille. Because, other things being equal, skill in braille seems closely linked to intelligence, more effort should be devoted to matching rote learning, programmed methods, and expectation of success to the capacities of students and adults.

One final problem: A recent estimate from the Bureau for the Education of the Visually Handicapped of the United States Office of Education indicates that 300 teachers of braille are needed immediately and that several thousand more will be needed in the next several years. What will they teach?

According to conventional wisdom, individual needs and capabilities are so varied that teachers must craft an individualized method for each student, drawing a mix from the available repertory. Sensitive and creative teachers, who surely ought to be rewarded by success in matching a student's capabilities with the desired outcome of making reading interesting, easy, and pleasant, will probably spend much of their energy trying to decide which method is most effective. Yet no one method seems better than the others, nor is there any combination of current methods that seem best. One reason is that each new method of teaching that has appeared over the past few decades has been the object of claims for increased speed and accuracy in reading braille. In reality, however, these claims are supported only by the success of exceptional students who seem to learn well no matter what method of instruction is employed. This phenomen is illustrated best by the recent enthusiasm for teaching speed-reading in braille, using techniques adapted from teaching speed-reading to the sighted. As Spungin[13] recently pointed out, the main reason for large increases in reading speed may be that many blind individuals who participate in these programs may have had, for the first time, information on specific braille reading techniques, and an actual step-by-step method to follow. In other words, their reading speed was likely to increase, regardless of the method used. The clear inference is that increases are a function of good teaching.

Therefore, good teaching will depend on knowledge of the processes and conditions under which optimal instruction occurs. Olsen[14, 15] has outlined a method of instruction that incorporates past and present research. Her conceptual framework calls for the following: (1) changing students' attitudes toward reading; (2) improving the coordination of their hand movements; (3) optimizing return sweeps and page-turning; (4) increasing the sensitivity of their fingers; (5) expanding their tactual-perceptual window; (6) reducing their lip movements and subvocalizations; (7) eliminating their regressive hand movements; (8) increasing their concentration and comprehension by using contextual and structural cues; (9) helping the student develop flexibility in reading rate; and (10) establishing rate and comprehension goals in order to increase reading speed.

Although it may appear that a disproportionate amount of attention has been devoted here to the teaching of braille, it is merited by the fact that the potential user's attitudes toward the medium are shaped by the teacher. Consequently, creating an environment in which ease of learning and enjoyment of skill can occur sets the stage for interest in making currently available braille materials more accessible and in establishing a demand for increased production and availability in the future. Curent methods of teaching braille, especially in the mainstreaming situation, rely heavily on the notion that there are similarities in reading inkprint and braille. Yet the differences, stemming from the special characteristics of the braille medium (dual spelling of words; use of symbols in multiple ways; confusion arising from lower-cell, one-cell, and two-cell signs and contractions; positioning of cells within a phrase or sentence; and the nonphonetic nature of the code) may frustrate nonspelcialists' attempts to use braille. New knowledge will minimize the effect of these differences, make instruction more efficient, increase the motivation of both teachers and students to achieve competence, and, it is hoped, alter public attitudes about the medium.

MISMATCH BETWEEN PRODUCTION AND MARKETS

Textbooks represent approximately 80 percent of the braille materials produced in the United States. The majority of them are still produced manually using braillewriters and vacuum-forming duplication systems. Preparation of stereograph plates is almost entirely manual, and most long-run materials are produced on ancient rotary and flatbed presses. Even the small percentage of computer-assisted systems require relatively large amounts of human intervention to assure a product that conforms closely to the rules of braille transcription and format. Add to this the fact that the cost of paper has increased four-fold over the past few years and it is not surprising that placing orders for large press runs has become more and more difficult.

The amount of human intervention required with computer-assisted systems is one important factor that determines the extent to which the computer can be used to generate larger quantities of braille at a reasonable cost. If an unlimited amount of volunteer labor were available, the amount of human intervention would not matter. But the number of qualified braillists and proofreaders is declining slowly, as is the number of volunteers in general. Neither the social nor administrative network necessary for the deployment of computer-assisted system exists, nor is there sufficient agreement about how to make such schemes possible.

The relative absence of computer-assisted production systems is in part related to the slow diffusion of technological information since the 1960s. Most braille presses, however, are ill-prepared to use computer technology to an optimal degree. Typical of computer applications in general, lack of standardization is the rule rather than the exception among the few presses that now use computer-assisted production methods. The computer programs used for translation, the input media, and methods of editing and proofreading braille are different from those used to produce inkprint material. Although advances in stereotype plate-making from digital tapes or punched paper tapes have been made in the United States and West Germany, the high cost of this equipment and uncertainty concerning the flow, magnitude, and continuity of production orders, have hampered dissemination of this technology.

It is encouraging to note that the physical plant for braille production is not necessarily inadequate. Together, the five or six major braille producers and a few dozen minor houses have about 50 presses. The age of a press is not necessarily a drawback since studies indicate that these machines, adapted from container folding systems, are mechanically overdesigned.[16] They are also mechanically simple. The major difficulty is that braille production is labor-intensive—tasks include capturing keystrokes on a stereotyper, loading the plates on the press and pulling the embossed copy from the press, stacking the copy for stapling, stapling and binding it, and shipping it out. These operations consume a tremendous amount of time. As mentioned earlier, in comparison to the flood of inkprint, the number of titles published in braille in small. A more serious consequence, however, is the chronic delay of textbook deliveries, especially for blind students who attend regular schools. In addition, production costs remain high because the economies made possible by automation are compromised.

Thus, a system that must strain to meet the needs of its primary audience, schoolchildren, has neither the resources nor the time to consider special groups such as diabetics and the aged, whose tactual sensitivity is typically less than normal and who might benefit from "jumbo braille," whose characters are larger than those of standard braille. The system is also unable to meet the immediate need of professionals for short runs of material essential to their work or the need of the blind citizen for access to timely information about cultural events, financial news, and so forth.

Unlike most books that are used in public schools and are available in libraries and bookstores, braille materials are usually paid for by the Federal government and state governments or by church-related groups. Therefore, an examination of the policies and priorities of these bodies in relation to braille is critical to understanding and interpreting trends in financing. Larger per-copy allowances or increased subsidies to major producers seems necessary.

On the basis of informal analyses, Schoof, Maure, and others have concluded that, without subsidies, the cost of producing one volume in braille is about $100 (four braille volumes are equivalent to one 250-page inkprint book).[17] When produced by volunteers, each volume costs about $50, including overhead and materials. But the cost of production is inescapably entwined with the decision whether to provide braille in the quantity, variety, and depth that is wanted or needed. Assuming, as the results of surveys indicate, that most braille materials currently produced are oriented toward recreational reading, it is possible to infer that in order to enhance braille usage, much nonrecreational material is called for.

MODERNIZING THE BRAILLE CODE

Because braille reading is linearly related to intelligence and few users fully master braille, simplifying its grammar might increase the number of skilled readers. But until fairly recently, changing the rules of braille would have been impossible, except for minor modifications in the code manuals that would allow for difficulties in special areas of knowledge, such as mathematics or music. Only within the last decade have any major international efforts been devoted to making braille less complicated.

Any effort to modify the grammar of braille must be understood in the context of the medium's history. In the English-speaking community, agreement about the need for compatible codes was reached in the 1920s, but only after an intense and bitter struggle among competing systems, each having articulate, competent champions among users. Surely this is one reason for the atmosphere of custodianship and protective management of change that characterized the activities of the "authorities" on braille in all countries. It also may explain the lack of interest in the impact of technology on the deployment of braille that has existed over the past two decades.

At present, braille authorities apparently believe that since the reader community's need for protection from capricious changes in braille is now appreciated, it is time to discuss changes that will make learning easier, make production faster, cheaper and adequate in amount, and increase reading speed.

In some countries, the portal for change may have in some instances opened too wide too soon: changes have been made in the braille code that are suited to the needs of the computer, but do not ease the task of the reader. Regrets are now being voiced about the lack of technical understanding and lack of control over the use of technology that have resulted in radical revisions in the rules.

The English-speaking community has tried to profit from the experiences of these countries as well as from countries such as the United States that have not moved quickly enough. Efforts have also been made to bring about some accomodation—between those who seek changes in the code and those who seek to produce it automatically with computer-assisted transcription— concerning the flexibility of a living medium and the consistency of the computer program. Meetings in this atmosphere of debate have been held since 1962 under the auspices of the major presses and universities to discuss the implications of computer-assisted production. Special committees within the Association for Computing Machinery, the World Council for the Welfare of the Blind, the Braille Authority of North America, and several publications are also devoting time and space to the problem.

In June 1976, the American Foundation for the Blind (AFB) and the Association for Computing Machinery sponsored a meeting that proved to be a milestone in the interaction between braille authorities and the technological community. The proceedings of that meeting demonstrate the open and interested attitude toward meaningfully managed change that marks the 1970s.[18]

Because of growing dissatisfaction with the difficulties of braille, general concern for improving reading efficiency through special techniques such as speed-reading, and the growing attention that technologists are paying to the handicapped, Douce and Tobin[19] proposed a comprehensive study of the grammatical rules of braille that would include the following:

1. An analysis of a comprehensive body of textual material in machine-readable form for optimal allocation of symbol codes in braille.

2. The use of a wide range of users and experts in evaluating proposed changes based on this analysis.

3. Statistical studies to assess effects of reduction in the number of rules and of space-saving.

4. Careful evaluations of how proposed changes would affect learning time, reading speed, and general acceptability.

5. Iterative use of feedback from these studies to improve proposals and refine experiments and to obtain definitive results that would either support or weaken the case for modifying the rules of braille.

This effort has received an initial push from the United Kingdom's Science Research Council. But the problem of expanding the scope of inquiry and extending its benefits to more users remains.

SOLUTIONS

The presence of the following material in a discussion of systematic factors affecting the availability, variety, and deployment of braille may seem curious at first to the general reader. Some parts of the discussion might appear better suited to a proposal submitted to a Federal or other source for funding. Yet the time seems appropriate to let the general reader share those special perspectives that inform proposals for change, and to try to open up the discussion of solutions to the difficult problems treated in the foregoing section. The poverty or richness of our conceptual resources in suggesting change, and our considerate, shared concern with their quality, will alter significantly the ways in which braille can be used in the decades that lie ahead.

The following sections describe research and demonstration projects that will aid in solving the problems just described. In addition to an estimate of the funds required to carry out each project, each is ranked according to its relative priority: 1 = highest priority; 2 = medium priority; 3 = lowest priority. Although all the projects are viewed as important, they are listed, in most instances, according to their priority to indicate the sequence in which they should be carried out.

CHANGE PUBLIC ATTITUDES

Foremost among the methods of changing public attitudes toward braille would to be hold a well-publicized international conference on braille touching on the problems discussed earlier. Many of the studies described throughout the remainder of this article need not, and probably should not, be delayed until the conference is held. Indeed, the information generated by these studies would contribute materially to the value of the conference. A second method would involve the publication of a series of articles about the problems of deploying braille. A third would be to involve both producers and consumers of braille in writing Federal funding proposals.

1. *Hold an international conference on braille* (priority 1; cost, $50,000; one-time effort). The entire direction of this 2- or 3-day conference would be to produce an intensive working summary containing firm recommendations for action in all areas affecting the future of braille. Whether the conference would result in solutions would, of course, depend on whether the studies described in the remaining pages had been undertaken. Because the American Foundation for the Blind has sponsored many conferences oriented toward both research and practice, it should be able to organize a successful meeting.

To accomplish the goal of attracting the public's attention, the conference would include the presentation of commissioned papers on major issues; demonstrations of current practice, proposed practice, and technological innovations; and reviews of evaluative and market studies already in progress. In addition, workshops would be conducted on current and future practice, and films and other graphic exhibits would be presented, and terminal facilities would be available for demonstrating on-line computer-assisted translation and embossing techniques. During luncheon breaks, those developing new methods and innovative practice methods would have an opportunity to describe their work. Presenters and discussants would represent purchasers, administrators, researchers, producers, consumers, and consumer advocates.

2. *Publish a series of articles on braille* (priority, 2; cost, $10,000; duration, 2 years). Several articles about the problems associated with braille have already been published in specialized publications such as the *Journal of Visual Impairment and Blindness* and the *Braille Research Newsletter*. To carry this information to a larger public, a series of six to twelve articles, costing about $1,000 each, should be commissioned for publication in more widely read magazines and journals such as *Scientific American, Science*, the *Harvard Educational Review*, and *Today's Education*.

Because these articles could bring the problems associated with braille to the attention of specialists in education, engineering, and administration, they should not only examine the problems and evaluate proposed solutions, but should confront the difficult questions of whether braille is truly useful, and why it is so.

These articles would not replace studies of the kind described later; they would be based on already-existing literature or on data derived from fresh research. Futhermore, they would be relatively free of jargon and written for nonspecialists in braille.

3. *Involve consumers and producers in Federal contracts for necessary studies and demonstration projects* (priority, 3; cost, $120,000; duration, 2 years). Solutions to the problems of production and deployment through the mechanism of Federal contracts, such as research funding proposals, could be solicited from two groups, producers of braille and users of braille. For example, producers might be asked to design a new braillewriter that is inexpensive, silent, and portable. In this case, the contract would be let in two stages: first, competition would be encouraged among designers to develop the best model of this device; second, the winning design would be translated into a production-engineering and marketing plan.

Another example would be to encourage designers to develop competitive schemes for capturing photocomposition tapes used to produce books and magazines and make the tapes available quickly for short runs of automatically produced braille, synthetic speech, and large print that would attract the interest of special segments of the blind population. This effort could in turn be divided into two stages: a study on the feasibility of using photocomposition tapes from one large publisher, and a national plan for the timely capture of the national output of these tapes.

The research funding proposal, or a similar mechanism, could be used to elicit plans from consumers for evaluating braille devices, new methods of production, or alternatives to the standard braille product. One could even consider asking user groups to write the proposals, evaluate the acceptability of changes in the rules and format of braille, hire their own researcher to help them evaluate their findings, and contract for braille material in nonstandard codes.

Define The Market and Enhance Availability

Five studies are proposed here. Because little is known about the market for braille, the first study focuses on defining this market. An initial effort has already been initiated by the American Foundation for the Blind and Baruch College, City University of New York. But two additional steps are required to obtain more comprehensive data. The focus of the other studies is to enhance the availability of braille by supplying publishers of textbooks with tapes for conversion to braille, making abstract services available to professionals, providing short-run services in schools, and supporting short-run production by regional centers.

1. *Undertake studies of demand* (priority, 1; cost, $50,000–$100,000; duration, 1½ years). Fundamental to understanding the use of braille and to planning for the future are the size and characteristics of the market for braille as well as the market for the allied media of large print and synthetic speech. A joint undertaking by AFB and Baruch College represents a beginning and should result in comprehensive information about the characteristics of readers, their reading behavior, comparative use of braille and large print, and the areas in which the unavailability of braille is most severe. Telephone interviews will be conducted with 500 or more braille readers drawn from a pool of 12,000 recipients of AFB's braille catalog, *Aids & Appliances for the Blind & Visually Impaired*, plus a sample of school-age blind children. The data obtained from this survey will be supplemented by interviews with 500 persons who receive a popular mass-circulation magazine in large print. The costs associated with this study, including direct expenditures and matching volunteered time of academic staff and survey specialists, are being borne by both organizations. (It should be noted that the major Federal purchasers of braille have not established ongoing market research programs.)

Because the sample used in the AFB/Baruch study is limited, it may not represent users of braille and large print nationwide. Thus, this effort should be supplemented in some way. For example, lists of braille users might be gathered from the Library of Congress, volunteer braillists, braille press houses, and service and consumer groups. Ideally, additional samples of user populations would be taken until the aggregate responses to questions included in the AFB/Baruch survey remained constant as the size of the sample is increased. Here again, interviews could be conducted by telephone (or in person, which might be preferable, but is more expensive).

This effort could be mounted in two steps: (1) interview an additional 500 respondents over 12 months at a cost of between $25,000 and $50,000; and (2) interview another 500 respondents over 18 months at a cost of roughly $50,000 to $100,000. After step 1 was completed, it would be necessary to decide whether the additional information obtained altered the conclusions based on the results of the AFB/Baruch study and step 1.

2. *Let contracts to textbook publishers to prepare tapes for conversion to braille* (priority, 1; cost, $20,000; duration, 1 year). Since most textbooks are prepared from automatic typesetters, contracts could be let to major textbook

publishers for preparation of tapes for conversion to braille. For example, with a contract of $20,000, the Houston Educational Computer Center could purchase duplicate tapes of texts in inkprint for 1 year and convert these tapes to ones capable of driving braille embossers. This experiment could yield data that might justify a continuing program of tape duplication as well as test the premise that braille textbooks can be produced at costs little higher than those of inkprint versions.

3. *Supply abstract services to professionals* (priority, 1; cost $50,000; duration, 3 years). This study would identify persons with a strong "need to know," subsidize the production of braille abstracts, and seek evaluations from users. When the study was completed, braille versions of abstracts could be produced at cost by contracting with distributors of abstracts for the major data bases involved.

4. *Evaluate the effectiveness of providing short-run services in schools* (priority, 2; cost, $100,000–$150,000; 2-year trial). Since short-runs (duplication runs of 2 to 25 copies) of braille copy are produced locally, the local solutions must be sought. The availability of inexpensive computer-translation packages, such as DOTSYS III and COBOL-compatible computer facilities in school systems, as well as relatively inexpensive braille embossers, costing $4,000 to $14,000, depending on speed, make it possible to set up an experimental program for testing the usefulness of local production.[20] Specifically, a pilot project could be set up in six to twelve schools to evaluate the effectiveness of almost simultaneous provision of braille materials for 2 years in mainstreamed classes. This effort could yield valuable data on how well blind students perform when they are not deprived of information that is accessible to their sighted classmates.

5. *Support short-run production by regional centers* (priority, 2; cost, $60,000; one-time grant). Pending development of small local terminals capable of translating inkprint to braille, greater dependence must be placed on regional facilities to produce braille versions of inkprint material. Regional centers that undertook contracts with transit systems, Federal agencies, restaurant chains, banks, and utility companies to provide subway maps, menus, bank statements, and the like in braille could become self-supporting within a few years. Start-up funds to support regional facilities such as the Baruch College Center in New York City would encourage their proliferation. One-time grants of $10,000 to six regional centers would provide an opportunity to test the hypothesis that the need is sufficient to continue these services.

Standardize Criteria for Teacher Competence and Conduct Management Audit

Because most individuals who are capable of reading braille seldom use it and an extremely active minority enthusiastically accept it, it seems prudent to obtain as much information as possible about current teaching practices before making policy decisions that involve funding and are therefore difficult to reverse.

To provide the backdrop for technical studies of teaching methods, two organizational/management audit studies are suggested: one on the school system; the other on the rehabilitation center system. Data about what is taught, who is teaching, and how effective the instruction is should give a realistic picture of current teaching practices. A second set of studies would focus on the cost structure of teaching braille. A third would focus on process and method (for example, diagnostic methods, the potential of programmed learning, and techniques for increasing speed and comprehension) and the impact of effect of age on the ability to learn braille.

1. *Conduct two organization studies on current teaching practices* (priority, 1; cost, $150,000; duration, 2 years). Two management-audit type studies are needed immediately to survey the syllabi, curriculum, and methods of training teachers; to determine the degree of their commitment to teaching braille; and to measure the competence and skill of teachers placed in schools and rehabilitation centers. In addition, the organizational arrangements for teaching, the number of teachers, and the number of hours of instruction provided would be defined. Both studies would also seek to clarify the administrative context in which teachers teach, that is, the role of braille in the curriculum and the standards of skill expected from both children and adults.

These studies are needed to establish what *is* versus what *could be* if innovative practice was introduced into the teaching of braille—information that is clearly lacking at present. For example, if the degree of skill acquired by adults in rehabilitation center training programs in braille were established, this information could be used as a benchmark for testing the efficacy of methods of self-instruction such as cassette- and hard-copy kits, which are now in use in the United Kingdom.[21]

The first study could be conducted at a university, but by faculty who are not involved in training of teachers in braille, or by a consulting firm with expertise in conducting organizational studies. Its purpose would be to gather information about the student population, currently and over the next few decades; to discover and identify the levels of competence that teachers attain during training; to determine the optimal number of teachers in relation to pupils; and to help define the nature of a core curriculum based on the goal of enhancing competence in braille skills and the creative use of available technologies. This study would cost about $75,000.

The second study would attack the serious issue of whether current training of adventitiously blinded adults in braille is helpful, useful, and cost-effective. It would not only focus on the level of competence of teachers and the nature of teaching methods, but would also attempt to evaluate the match between what is taught and what is needed or desired by the majority of blinded adults. Because current practice seems to be relatively ineffective, it will be important to determine whether the current allocation of funds for braille instruction in rehabilitation centers would be better spent on contract services for the few adults who would benefit.

2. *Determine the economic structure of braille teaching* (priority, 1; cost, $25,000; duration, 1 year). This study might well be subsumed under the organizational/management-audit studies mentioned earlier. Its focus would be the economics of different organizational arrangements for teaching braille and the specific levels of competence achieved by students. For example, little is currently known about the cost-effectiveness of braille

instruction in rehabilitation centers with respect to the level of skill acquired. Furthermore, until more is known about optimal strategies for instructing children, little will be known about the costs of braille instruction in the regular schools.

3. *Examine the techniques for optimizing the teaching of braille* (priority, 2; cost, $150,000; duration, 2 years). An investigation of process and method would support and enhance trends toward competence of teachers and students and reduce the variability of performance. First, because detecting and solving problems in reading as they occur reduces learning time and reinforces achievement, good diagnostic tests are critically important. Those incorporated in a series of stepped readers recently published by the American Printing House for the Blind and the *Neale Analysis of Reading Ability*, recently published in the United Kingdom, offer considerable promise for diagnostic and evaluative use, testing achievement, and identifying problems that impede achievement.[22]

Second, although the potential of machine-assisted, individually paced learning of braille has been documented by several investigators, the lack of suitable, inexpensive equipment until recently has impeded the use of this approach.[23] Thus, the forthcoming availability of braille reading machines using digitally encoded braille on cassette tapes provides an important avenue for exploration.

It has long been observed that those who read braille rapidly and with good comprehension use both hands rather than two fingers to scan and follow text. Furthermore, a number of investigators claim that reading speeds can increase up to 1,000 percent when several braille cells rather than individual cells are used as the basic unit of meaning.[24]

A separate study would concentrate on the influence of age on the ability to learn braille and thus illuminate the factors that affect teaching in rehabilitation centers and clarify the potential market for braille among the "advancing army of the aged" confronting rehabilitation centers.

Introduce Innovative Methods of Production

The uses of recent technological advances to enhance production of braille are limited only by one's imagination. As mentioned earlier, a multistep approach is needed to ameliorate the problems of production and deployment. Such an approach would mean (1) infusing technological advances into existing braille publishing houses; (2) altering the current braille code so that it approximates a "fully programmable" grammar; (3) using machine-readable input to braille translation systems; (4) developing efficient transcription programs that satisfy the standards of the code; and (5) using computer output to generate or set press plates automatically for driving a press braille system, creating digital braille tapes for read-only devices, and providing master tapes used in local multicopy production.

Four of the six studies proposed here deal with methods that hold promise of increasing production at a cost that is comparable to that of the existing system. These studies deal with the use of photocomposition tapes, a microprocessor-based inkprint-to-braille translator, mini- and microcomputer-based packages, and the upgrading of flatbed presses.

Because little is known about the comparative costs associated with alternative methods of production and deployment, studies 3 and 4 focus on the impact of several existing and projected technologies. Both are based on alternative assumptions about the market for braille.

1. *Investigate the use of photocompositor's tapes* (priority, 1; cost, $30,000; duration, 1 year). This project would involve upgrading a braille press to accept a variety of relatively error-free photocomposition tapes as direct input to a translation program. As a source of already-captured printed materials, compositor's tapes are a valuable means of increasing the range, depth, and variety of braille. In error-free form, these tapes are now commonly used by book publishers such as Cambridge University Press, and most magazines use them in relatively error-free form. At least one American newspaper is now produced using advanced laser technology, which reduces the inkprinted page to a digitally encoded form while the page mock-up is made in the editorial room. This method, too, is error-free and directly applicable to braille production systems as machine-readable input.

Most funds allocated for this project would be spent on developing a set of preprocessor programs to input photocomposition tapes. The remainder would be reserved for equivalent machine-readable input (for example, on floppy discs) capable of producing test material for replication in other press houses. A press already fitted with a computer-assisted translator, such as the one at National Braille Press, would be a good choice for this project.

The output of braille equivalent can also be used to test the acceptability and pricing of new silk-screen processes (see study 6), which may produce a product that is superior in quality to embossed copy and lower in cost. In addition, the output of braille equivalent can also be recorded in a form usable by current and forthcoming reading machines that accept digitally encoded cassettes of braille text. This approach will help determine the optimal design of these devices based on human factors, length of display, and the like.

2. *Develop a microprocessor-based braille production system* (priority, 2; cost, $100,000; duration, 2 years). Microprocessor-based terminals offer great potential for local production of short-run braille in hard copy or refreshable (line- or page-at-a-time) displays. This project would be divided into two phases. Phase 1 would focus on developing a "compiler-compiler"-based approach to the translation of braille that is independent of natural language. Consequently, an individual who is unfamiliar with the details of the translation program could modify the rules of translation from inkprint to braille. When he identified a contraction error, for example, he could key in the correct translation and the program would automatically modify its translation software.

In phase 2, a complete microprocessor-based "package" would be designed for braille and a limited variety of tactual graphic materials. Holman[23] has suggested an integrated package consisting of a graphic microcomputer— a general-purpose interface buss based on data cartridges or floppy discs and programmed in BASIC.[25, 26] As demonstrated during experimental production of braille and tactual pictures, this system can function in the braille universe and has been used to train teachers in the rudiments of braille. A feasibility study, using blind consumers and Comprehensive

Employment and Training Act (CETA) programmers, could result in a desktop system capable of producing Grade I braille and tactual graphics, with clear specification of the requirements for transient braille displays, for driving hard-copy embossers, for generating synthetic speech, and so on.

The costs of memory in microprocessors will undoubtedly continue to drop. For example, a two-kilobit core plus analog-to-digital converter and an eight-bit (64-word) register are currently available on one $10 chip. With machine-readable versions of inkprint as input, it should be possible to develop a video terminal fitted with a microprocessor-based translator for, at most, $500 more than the cost of the terminal alone.

3. *Investigate the impact of existing technologies under different conditions* (priority, 2; cost, $50,000; duration, 1 year). This exercise would begin with the current market and might predict a gradual, asymptotic decline in the demand for braille to a size representing the deaf-blind population only. Or it might assume that no changes will occur in current levels of production accuracy defined by the braille code. Or it might assume a modest mix of press runs and short-run document services, with and without changes in the braille code. At one extreme, it might consider as completely automated a system as possible for a small number of markets.

If contracted for with a prominent marketing research consultant, this study would help guide decisions by pricing alternative strategies of deploying needed braille materials. It would include methods and associated costs of equipment, labor, and amortization for the range of current methods of producing and distributing braille. It would begin with the use of manual slate and stylus and the Perkins braillewriter master/Thermoform® copy system, progress to intermediate machine-assisted systems such as the PCBS (Triformations, Inc.), and end with the computer-assisted systems now in existence (for example, APH, Duxbury, ARTS, DOTSYS III, and suitable input/output and CPU support systems).

In addition to fixing present costs predicated in all cases on producing a specific number of titles (400, for example) in braille, this investigation could provide information that would be useful to potential producers of all braille material, nonrecreational as well as recreational, with regard to time periods for production, the amount of capital investment required, the amount and extent of human labor, and the degree of human intervention in the production process in unsubsidized form.

4. *Investigate the impact of innovative technologies* (priority, 3; cost, $50,000; duration, 1 year). This study, a companion to the preceding one, would examine in a similarly structured way the impact of forthcoming technologies on the production of braille, both for press-run and short-run markets. Here, the focus would be projected systems such as laser scanning, multifont optical readers, automatic scanning, and recognition of previously brailled material. It would investigate the potential usefulness of translators, such as the one proposed by Fortier et al.—a syntax-based linguistic model capable of translating at extremely high speeds at low cost per page, but requiring a large general-purpose computer and, for languages other than English, a compiler-compiler microprocessor system.[25, 26] The study would also examine the effect of the wide availability of microprocessor and integrated-circuit braille-reading and -writing devices such as the ELINFA

Digi-Cassette, the West German Braillocord and Braillex systems, the "paperless braille" device under development at Telesensory Systems, Inc., and the braille-reading machine produced by Triformations, Inc. Finally, it would assess the cost-effectiveness of methods such as the optical-recognition-to-braille-conversion scheme under development at Kurzweil Computer Products. Engineering would be emphasized more heavily in this study than in the preceding one.

5. *Examine the usefulness of automatic-press braille systems* (priority, 3; cost, $100,000; duration, 1 year). One attractive alternative to labor-intensive flatbed presses would be the use of resettable computer-controlled stereotype plates that allow pages to be printed in sequence and automatically folded and cut into book form. Stapling could be incorporated into the paperflow system so that the press output would consist of books ready for shipment. With this method, labor costs are radically reduced, and speed of production is comparable to that of standard methods. According to a feasibility study conducted by Maure in 1976, this system might be cost-effective once development was amortized.

6. *Evaluate the cost-effectiveness and acceptability of silk-screen-based production systems* (priority, 3; cost, $100,000; duration, 1 year). Silk-screen-based production systems, which use methods shared in large measure with standard inkprint processes, have been studied for years concerning their adaptability to braille production. Techniques recently developed in the United States, West Germany, and Japan insure high-quality braille, with fixed dots, that is acceptable to readers because of its "feel" and durability. Cost studies conducted by AFB indicate that these processes may be competitive with press runs of all but the largest publications in braille. This study would explore the cost of production and the acceptability of the product.

Revise the Braille Code

This final proposal involves a collaborative study among representatives of the English-speaking communities to revise the braille code (priority, 2; cost, $150,000; duration, 3 years). The purpose of the study would be two-fold: (1) to simplify the rules and grammar of braille, while retaining the advantages of compactness and speed, so that a larger population could learn the code; and (2) to approach the ideal of a fully programmable set of rules and thus make possible faster and cheaper transcription by computer. It would be necessary to conduct this work in stages approximating those outlined by Douce and Tobin.

During stage 1, large bodies of text would be examined in machine-readable form to discover how symbol codes could be allocated to save space. Buckley has suggested using the so-called Brown Corpus, a data base of more than 1 million words drawn from a variety of sources, and the American Heritage Corpus, a data base of more than 5 million words drawn from the literature written for 3- to 9-year olds. To these could be added Weber's and Markson's comprehensive data base covering modern English literature from 1600 to the present.

The emphasis of stage 2 would be to standardize the signs, formats, and contextual rules of braille. Because of their expertise in contriving these original analyses and their sensitivity to the need for consistency, psycholinguists such as Francis and Giannutsos could provide important aid during this stage.

Stage 3, involving the examination of statistical data to assess the effects of number of rules and space-saving devices, can be conducted simultaneously with stages 1 and 2.

Steps 4 and 5 would concern proposed changes in the rules of grammar and syntax and evaluation of the effect of these changes on learning time, reading, and writing speed, and acceptability requires a carefully designed detailed experimental design and sensitive interpretation of the results. Among those who have long been interested in the readability of braille are a number of excellent investigators.[27]

CONCLUSION

The expectations of Americans for equal treatment are among the highest found in any country and in fact have been reinforced by recent changes in public law. An important segment of the reading public (potentially as many as 65,000) are readers of braille. Yet the basic premise of this article is that the use of braille has gradually declined, primarily because of benign neglect.

This article has identified several problems that explain this neglect. Some of these can be solved by generating new knowledge; others may yield to innovative applications of what is already known. But these remedies require a commitment to the current braille-reading public and to a view of braille as an important alternative method of communicating with and among the blind.

The money required to carry out all the activities proposed would be approximately $1.4 million, spread over a three-year period. This represents an investment of about $24 per user, which seems extremely modest since it would not only enrich the leisure of braille users but would most likely open up new job opportunities for them. In other words, the investment is cost-effective to the nation.

What is essential now is some national consideration of how to reverse the current trend—consideration at high levels, with a clear focus on developing a concensus about desirable directions. I share the conviction of many of my colleagues that there is a large, untapped sentiment for a commitment to solving the problems. The article represents one earnest expression of that commitment.

REFERENCES

1. CLARK, L. L. 1977. A funny thing happened to braille on the way to deployment. J. Visual Impairment & Blindness 71 (4):181–183.
2. KURZWEIL, R. 1978. The Kurzweil report: Technology for the handicapped. 1 (1). Kurzweil Computer Products Corp. Cambridge, Mass.
3. LAMPTON, D. R. 1978. Comprehension and intelligibility of synthetic speech as a function of exposure duration. Perceptual Alternatives Laboratory, University of Louisville, Louisville, Ky.
4. BERKOWITZ, M., L. SNYDER, P. DE TOLEDO & J. SHAPIRO. A Report on the

Survey to Determine the Extent of Eligible User Population not Currently Being Served or not Aware of the Programs of the Library of Congress Division for the Blind and Physically Handicapped. American Foundation for the Blind. New York, N. Y. (1978 Report on contract with the Library of Congress, (L1283). To be published.

5. STOCKER, C. S. & M. J. WALTON. 1967. Exploring a more efficient method of teaching braille. New Outlook for the Blind **61:**151–154.

6. EVENSEN, R. H. 1978. Braille readership in the United States and distribution of braille materials. Braille Res. News. **8:**10–16.

7. EVENSEN, R. H. 1974. Report on braille reader survey. Library of Congress, Division for the Blind and Physically Handicapped. Washington, D.C.

8. GILL, J. M. 1978. Psychological abstracts in braille. Rev. Europ. Blind **1:**28–30.

9. GILL, J. M. & M. D. MARTIN. 1976. INSPEC in braille. IEE News June: 3.

10. GEIL, J. 1977. History and status of the computer-generated braille project. Braille Res. Newsl. **7:**35–44.

11. NOLAN, C. Y. & C. J. KEDERIS. 1969. Perceptual factors in braille word recognition. Research Series No. 20. American Foundation for the Blind, New York, N. Y.

12. BANKOVICS, J. 1974. English braille in forty lessons. State Services for the Blind and Visually Handicapped. Minneapolis, Minn.

13. SPUNGIN, S. J. Rapid reading in braille. Paper presented to the Sixth Quinquennial Conference of the International Council for Education of the Visually Handicapped, Paris, France, August 1977.

14. OLSON, M. R. 1976. Easter braille reading: Preparation at the reading readiness level. New Outlook for the Blind October: 341–343.

15. OLSON, M. R. Teaching faster braille reading in the primary grades. Visual Impairment & Blindness **71** (3):112–124.

16. CLARK, L. L. 1977. The braille press and its future. Braille Res. Newsl. **6:**26–34.

17. MAURE, D. R. 1976. A proposal to enhance production and stabilise costs of press braille. American Foundation for the Blind. New York, N. Y. (Library of Congress Proposal RFP 76–17, May 1976.)

18. GILDEA, R. A. J. & M. BERKOWITZ (Eds.) 1976. Computerised braille: Proceedings of a workshop on the compliance of computer programs with english braille (American edition). American Foundation for the Blind. New York, N. Y.

19. DOUCE, J. L. & M. J. TOBIN. 1976. Discussion paper on the desirability of a joint research project on the braille code, extending the use of braille, and the improvement of reading skills. Braille Automation Newsl. **1:**5–8. (Reprinted in New Outlook for the Blind **70** (5):215.)

20. CLARK, L. L. Baruch Computer Research Center for the Visually Impaired. Braille Res. Newsl. **8:**2–9.

21. TOBIN, M. J. 1976. Beginning Braille. University of Birmingham. Birmingham, England.

22. LORIMER, J. 1977. Neale analysis of reading ability: adapted for use with blind children. NFER Publishing Co. Windsor, England.

23. ASHCROFT, S. C. & F. M. HENDERSON. 1963. Programmed instruction in braille. Stanwix House. Pittsburgh, Pa.

24. GRUNWALD, A. P. 1978. On braille and braille machines. Sensory World **30:**4–8, 30–31; **31:**11–14.

25. HOLMAN, P. C. 1978. 4051 Prints and teaches braille. Tekniques **2** (6):13–14.

26. SLABY, W. A. 1975. A Universal Braille Translator. SIGCAPH Newsl. **15** (March):

27. CLARK, L. L. Research perspectives on the braille code. J. Visual Impairment & Blindness **72:**75–77.

ADDITIONAL REFERENCES NOT CITED IN TEXT

ASHCROFT, S. C. 1960. Errors in oral reading at elementary grade levels. Doctoral dissertation, University of Illinois. Normal, Ill.

BIGGS, I. 1950. The introduction of Grade 2 braille in the primary grades. New Outlook for the Blind 44:103–105.

BUCKLEY, J. E. 1977. The efficiency of braille as a medium of communication. Braille Res. Newsl. 6:11–25.

CARDINALE, J. 1973. Methods and procedures of braille reading. Am. Found. Blind, Res. Bull. 26:171–183.

CATON, H. R. 1975. The development and evaluation of a tactile analog to the boehm test of basic concepts. Doctoral dissertation, University of Kentucky, 1975.

CLARK, L. L. 1961. Report of proceedings of conference on research needs in braille. American Foundation for the Blind. New York, N. Y.

CLARK, L. L. 1977. Microprocessors, microcomputers, and braille readers. J. Visual Impairment & Blindness 71 (8):366–367.

CONCANNON, J. 1970. A review of research on haptic perception. J. Education. Res. 63:250–252.

CRANDELL, J. M. & D. H. WALLACE. 1974. Speed reading in braille: An empirical study. New Outlook for the Blind 68:13–19.

CRONIN, B. 1972. A new technique using braille to teach print reading to dyslexic children. New Outlook for the Blind 66:71–74.

EATMAN, P. F. 1956. An analytic study of braille reading. Doctoral dissertation, University of Kentucky.

FERTSCH, P. 1946. An analysis of braille reading. Outlook for the Blind & Teacher's Forum 40:128–131.

FLANIGAN, P. J. 1966. Automated training and braille reading. Outlook for the Blind 60:141–146.

FLANIGAN, P. J. & E. S. JOSLIN. 1969. Patterns of response in the perception of braille configurations. New Outlook for the Blind 63:232–244.

GILL, J. M. 1978. Bibliography on braille automation and related research. Braille Res. Newsl. 7:25–35.

GILL, J. M. The use of digitally-stored text for braille production. Presented at National Computer Conference, New York, June 1976. (Reprinted in Braille Automation Newsl. August 1976: 6–10.

GILL, J. M. & J. HUMPHREYS. 1976. A feasibility study on a braille transcription service for short documents. Braille Automation Newsl. August: 19–24.

GILL, J. M. & J. HUMPHREYS. 1977. An analysis of braille contractions. Braille Res. Newsl. 5:50–57.

GRAHAM, M. D. 1962. Braille: Its characteristics, its actual uses, its potential uses: A suggested research and development program. American Foundation for the Blind. New York, N. Y.

HANLEY, L. F. 1961. A brief review of the research on braille reading. Internat. J. Education Blind, 10:65–70.

HANLEY, L. F. 1965. A diagnostic test of grade 2 braille misperceptions: A pilot study. Unpublished report.

HARLEY, R. K. & R. RAWLS. 1976. Comparison of several approaches for teaching braille reading to blind children. Am. Found. Blind Res. Bull. 23:63–91.

HENDERSON, F. M. n.d. Analysis of errors in braille word recognition. Unpublished report, George Peabody College for Teachers, Nashville, Tenn.

HENDERSON, F. M. 1967. The effect of character recognition training on braille reading. Specialist in education thesis, George Peabody College for Teachers, Nashville, Tenn.

HOFFMAN, P. M. & J. G. COOK. 1970. Design for introducing reading in braille to multi-impaired visually handicapped children. Master's thesis, University of Texas, Austin, Texas.

KEDERIS, C. J. 1964. Training for increasing braille reading rates: Final Report. American Printing House for the Blind, Louisville, Ky.

KEDERIS, C. J. & C. Y. NOLAN. 1972. Braille codes pilot project: Final Report. American Printing House for the Blind, Louisville, Ky.

KEDERIS, C. J. & C. Y. NOLAN. 1972. A pilot study of recognition thresholds for braille words. American Printing House for the Blind, Louisville, Ky.

KEDERIS, C. J., J. R. SIEMS & R. L. HAYNES. 1965. A frequency count of the symbology of English braille Grade Two: American usage. Int. J. Education Blind 15:38–46.

KUSAJUMA, T. 1974. Visual reading and braille reading: An experimental investigation of the physiology and psychology of visual and tactual reading. American Foundation for the Blind. New York, N. Y.

LOWENFELD, B. 1945. Braille and talking book reading: A comparative study. American Foundation for the Blind. New York, N. Y.

MANGOLD, S. S. 1977. The effects of a developmental teaching approach on tactile perception and braille letter recognition based on a model of precision teaching. University of Microfilms. Ann Arbor, Mich.

MORGAN, R. W. 1969. Instruction in braille writing: Its effects on some of the language arts skills. Specialists in education thesis, George Peabody College for Teachers.

NOLAN, C. Y., J. E. MORRIS, & C. J. KEDERIS. 1971. Bibliography of research on braille. American Printing House for the Blind.

REX, E. J. 1970 and 1971. A study of basal readers and experimental supplementary instructional materials for teaching primary reading in braille. Part I: An analysis of braille features in basal readers. Part II: Instructional materials for teaching reading in braille. Education Visually Handicapped 2:97–107; 3:1–7.

RUSSELL, H. K. 1970. The effect of order of presentation on the programmed learning of braille. Doctoral dissertation, Washington State University, Pullman, Wash.

UMSTED, R. G. 1970. Improvement of braille reading through code recognition Training. Doctoral dissertation, George Peabody College for Teachers, Nashville, Tenn.

UMSTED, R. G. 1972. Improving braille reading. New Outlook for the blind 66:169–177.

WEINER, L. 1963. The performance of good and poor braille readers on certain tests involving tactual perception. Int. J. Education Blind 12:72–77.

ANNALS OF THE NEW YORK ACADEMY OF SCIENCES
Volume 346

APPLICATIONS OF PHOTOCHEMISTRY IN PROBING BIOLOGICAL TARGETS

Edited by Andrew M. Tometsko and Frederic M. Richards

The New York Academy of Sciences
New York, New York
1980

Library of Congress Cataloging in Publication Data

Main entry under title:

Applications of photochemistry in probing biological targets.

(Annals of the New York Academy of Sciences; v. 346)
"This series of papers is the result of a conference entitled Applications of photochemistry in probing biological targets, held by the New York Academy of Sciences from May 30 to June 1, 1979."
1. Photochemistry—Congresses. 2. Biological chemistry—Congresses. 3. Photobiology—Congresses.
I. Tometsko, Andrew M., 1938–   II. Richards, Frederic Middlebrook.   III. New York Academy of Sciences.   IV. Series: New York Academy of Sciences. Annuals; v. 346.
Q11.N5   vol. 346   [QH345]   500s   [574.19′285] 80-15368

SP
Printed in the United States of America
ISBN 0–89766-080-3 (Cloth)
ISBN 0–89766-081-1 (Paper)

ANNALS OF THE NEW YORK ACADEMY OF SCIENCES
VOLUME 346
June 17, 1980

APPLICATIONS OF PHOTOCHEMISTRY
IN PROBING BIOLOGICAL TARGETS

Editors and Conference Cochairmen
ANDREW M. TOMETSKO AND FREDERIC M. RICHARDS

Advisory Committee
BARRY S. COOPERMAN, JOHN A. KATZENELLENBOGEN,
JEREMY R. KNOWLES, AND ASER ROTHSTEIN

———————◆———————

CONTENTS

*This series of papers is the result of a conference entitled Applications of Photochemistry in Probing Biological Targets held by the New York Academy of Sciences from May 30 to June 1, 1979.

Applications of Photochemicals in the Study of Cells and Complex Cellular Components

Financial assistance was received from:
- HOFFMANN-LA ROCHE, INC.
- ICI AMERICAS, INC.
- MERCK, SHARP & DOHME RESEARCH LABORATORIES
- MERCK, SHARP & DOHME RESEARCH PROGRAM
- NATIONAL INSTITUTE OF GENERAL MEDICAL SCIENCES—NIH
- RIKER LABORATORIES, INC.
- SMITH KLINE & FRENCH LABORATORIES
- U.S. ARMY RESEARCH OFFICE
- U.S. AIR FORCE OFFICE OF SCIENTIFIC RESEARCH

GENERAL INTRODUCTION AND WELCOME

Andrew M. Tometsko

Litron Laboratories, Ltd.
Rochester, New York 14620

On behalf of Dr. Richards, the Advisory Committee, and myself, I would like to welcome you to this New York Academy of Sciences Conference on Applications of Photochemistry in Probing Biological Targets. This conference is possible because of the New York Academy of Science's policy of supporting meetings that will advance scientific research. The Academy's conference committee has played a key role in the development of the conference. We appreciate particularly the efforts of Dorothy Cunningham, Charlotte Russell, Ellen Marks, Ann Collins, and their staffs, who have worked with us on the technical details of this conference. They have offered advice and worked hard to make this conference a success.

A special thanks is due the Advisory committee for the conference: Barry Cooperman, John Katzenellenbogen, Jeremy Knowles, and Aser Rothstein. Even though they have very busy schedules, they have always been available when problems and difficulties arose during the preparation. We appreciate their making this conference a high priority item in their scientific activities this year.

The seeds for this conference were sown almost two decades ago in the laboratory of Dr. Frank Westheimer at Harvard University, where experiments were carried out in which light was used to activate chemicals that, subsequently, labeled target enzyme molecules. Those early experiments suggested that light could play an important role in controlling and modulating the reactivity of chemical agents and, thus, provide special advantages in probing biological targets. The years since have seen a tremendous growth in the use of photochemical techniques and their application to an ever-greater variety of biological systems.

As public acknowledgement of his fundamental contributions, we are pleased to dedicate this conference to Dr. Frank Westheimer. Dr. Westheimer will deliver a keynote address at tonight's dinner.

As in any rapidly developing field, there exist technical problems, which can best be resolved at a conference such as this. In developing the format for the conference, we have attempted to evolve from more chemical to more biological considerations over the course of the three days. Thus, you will notice that the target systems become more complex as we move through the program. By providing this multidisciplinary flavor, it was our hope that there will be opportunities for chemists and biologists to meet and discuss technical problems and new research approaches.

We hope that this conference will contribute to the further growth and development in this blossoming area of science where photochemistry and biology merge, and that all of you will find it intellectually stimulating, and, to use the jargon of photochemistry, illuminating.

STRUCTURE AND DYNAMICS OF IMPORTANT REACTIVE INTERMEDIATES INVOLVED IN PHOTOBIOLOGICAL SYSTEMS *

Nicholas J. Turro

Department of Chemistry
Columbia University
New York, New York 10027

MOLECULAR PHOTOCHEMISTRY OF ORGANIC MOLECULES[1]

Molecular photochemistry is a science concerned with the description of physical and chemical processes induced by the absorption of photons in terms of a concrete mechanistic model based on molecular structures and their implied properties. Molecular organic photochemistry is a very broad discipline, embracing an extensive range of energetic, structural, and dynamic processes. The "molecular" part of molecular photochemistry emphasizes the use of the molecule as a crucial, unifying intellectual unit to parameterize, systematize, and visualize photochemical processes at the microscopic level from their very start (absorption of a photon) to their termination (isolation of products). The "photo" part of molecular photochemistry is a historical prefix and is now too restrictive. It is now clear that *electronically excited* states of molecules are at the heart of all "photoprocesses." Although photons are a most convenient means of initiating photochemistry, the absorption of light is not *required* to produce electronically excited states, i.e., thermal pathways may produce excited states and can therefore cause photoreactions to occur "in the dark."

PHOTOCHEMICAL REACTIONS

Photochemical reactions differ from thermal reactions in several important respects.

1. The initiating activation of a photoreaction is mainly provided by the absorption of light; activation of a thermal reaction is mainly provided by heat.

2. The electronic distribution and nuclear configuration of a photochemically activated molecule generally differ substantially from those of a thermally activated molecule so that the excited molecule is really an *electronic isomer* of the corresponding ground state molecule.

3. The thermodynamically favorable products accessible to a photoexcited molecule are far greater than those accessible to a ground state molecule, since the excited molecule possesses an excess energy content as a result of photon absorption.

The fact that light absorption, rather than heat, activates a photoreaction allows for both selectivity of activation (since only light-absorbing molecules are excited) and the ability to initiate reactions even at very low temperatures in all three phases. In fact, certain photoreactions are known to occur even at temperatures near 0 °K!

*This research was supported by the National Institutes of Health, grant no. 1 R01 GM25523-01.

1

The chronology of photoreactions may be conveniently divided into three stages:

1. The *absorptive act,* which consists of the interaction of a photon and a molecule, resulting in the absorption of the photon and the formation of an *electronically excited molecule.*

2. The *primary photochemical processes,* which involve electronically excited molecules.

3. The *secondary* or *"dark" processes,* which occur in the intermediates produced by the primary photochemical processes.

A "complete" understanding of a photoreaction requires knowing what happens at the molecular level from the absorptive act to the isolation or identification of its products. Molecular photochemistry is concerned with defining, through the interplay of theory and experiment, the spatiotemporal choreography of molecular structure (electrons, nuclei, and spins) that occurs in a photoreaction.

THE ELECTRONIC EXCITATION AND DE-EXCITATION OF ORGANIC MOLECULES

The absorption of ultraviolet or visible light by an organic molecule causes the excitation of an electron from an initially occupied, low energy orbital to a high energy, previously unoccupied orbital. The energy of the absorbed photon is used to energize an electron and cause it to jump to a higher energy orbital. Two excited electronic *states* derive from the *electronic orbital configuration* produced by light absorption. In one state, the electron spins are paired (antiparallel) and in the other state, the electron spins are unpaired (parallel). The state with paired spins has no resultant spin magnetic moment; it remains a single state in the presence of a (laboratory) magnetic field, and is termed a *singlet state.* A state with unpaired spins interacts with a (laboratory) magnetic field and splits into *three* quantized states; it is termed a *triplet state.*

The three states that are most crucial to an understanding of organic photoreactions are:

1. S_0 = ground, singlet state
2. S_1 = lowest energy excited, singlet state
3. T_1 = lowest triplet state.

In many cases, a single electron configuration is adequate to approximate a state. In some cases, however, a combination of two or more electronic configurations will be required to achieve a good approximation of a state. As a shorthand, we describe electronic *configurations* in terms of the key molecular *orbitals* that are expected to dominate the energy and/or chemistry of the configuration. Thus, for formaldehyde, we explicitly consider only the π_{CO}, n_O, and $\pi_{CO}*$ orbitals in discussing electronic configurations, and, hence, in discussing states. As a result of the above discussion, we may state the following rule: Each electronic state may be described (a) in terms of a *characteristic electronic configuration,* which in turn may be described in terms of two or three *characteristic orbitals,* and (b) in terms of a characteristic spin configuration.

For example, the S_0, S_1, S_2, T_1, and T_2 states of formaldehyde are described in TABLE 1. Of these states, only S_1 and T_1 are significant in the solution photochemistry of formaldehyde.

The photochemistry of most organic molecules is conveniently discussed with reference to these three states in terms of a *state energy diagram*.

STATE ENERGY DIAGRAMS: ELECTRONIC AND SPIN ISOMERS

An energy diagram is a display of the relative energies of the ground state, the excited singlet states, and the triplet states of a molecule for a given, fixed nuclear geometry (FIGURE 1). It is generally assumed that the nuclear geometries of all states displayed in a single state diagram are not very different from the equilibrium nuclear geometry of the ground state. Each excited state is different from the ground state, even though their molecular constitutions are identical, i.e., all the states in an energy diagram are *isomeric*. What is the basis of the isomerism? It is the *electronic* differences or the *spin* differences between the displayed states. Thus, the S_n states are electronic isomers of each other and the T_n states are electronic isomers of each other. The S_n and T_n states are related as spin-electronic isomers.

Photophysical processes may be defined as transitions that interconvert excited states with each other or excited states with the ground state. The important

TABLE 1

ELECTRONIC STATES OF FORMALDEHYDE

State	Characteristic Orbitals	Characteristic Spin—Electronic Configuration	Shorthand Description of State
S_2	π, π^*	$(\pi\uparrow)\ (n\uparrow\downarrow)\ (\pi^*\downarrow)$	$^1(\pi, \pi^*)$
T_2	π, π^*	$(\pi\uparrow)\ (n\uparrow\downarrow)\ (\pi^*\uparrow)$	$^3(\pi, \pi^*)$
S_1	n, π^*	$(\pi\uparrow\downarrow)\ (n\downarrow)\ (\pi^*\downarrow)$	$^1(n, \pi^*)$
T_1	n, π^*	$)\pi\uparrow\downarrow)\ (n\uparrow)\ (\pi^*\uparrow)$	$^3(n, \pi^*)$
S_0	π, n	$(\pi\uparrow\downarrow)\ (n\uparrow\downarrow)$	$\pi^2\ n^2$

photophysical processes, in turn, are classified as *radiative* and *radiationless* processes.

The commonly encountered photophysical radiative processes, as shown in FIGURE 1, are:

1. "Allowed" or singlet-singlet absorption ($S_0 + h\upsilon \rightarrow S_1$), characterized experimentally by an extinction coefficient ϵ ($S_0 \rightarrow S_1$)

2. "Forbidden" or singlet-triplet absorption ($S_0 + h\upsilon \rightarrow T_1$), characterized experimentally by an extinction coefficient ϵ ($S_0 \rightarrow T_1$)

3. "Allowed" or singlet-singlet emission, called *fluorescence,* ($S_1 \rightarrow S_0 + h\upsilon$), characterized by a radiative rate constant k_F

4. "Forbidden" or triplet-singlet emission, called phosphorescence, ($T_1 \rightarrow S_0 + h\upsilon$), characterized by a radiative rate constant k_P

5. "Allowed" transitions between states of the same spin, called *internal conversion* (e.g., $S_1 \rightarrow S_0 +$ heat)

6. "Forbidden" transitions between excited states of different spin, called *intersystem crossing* (e.g., $S_1 \rightarrow T_1 +$ heat), characterized by a rate constant k_{ST}

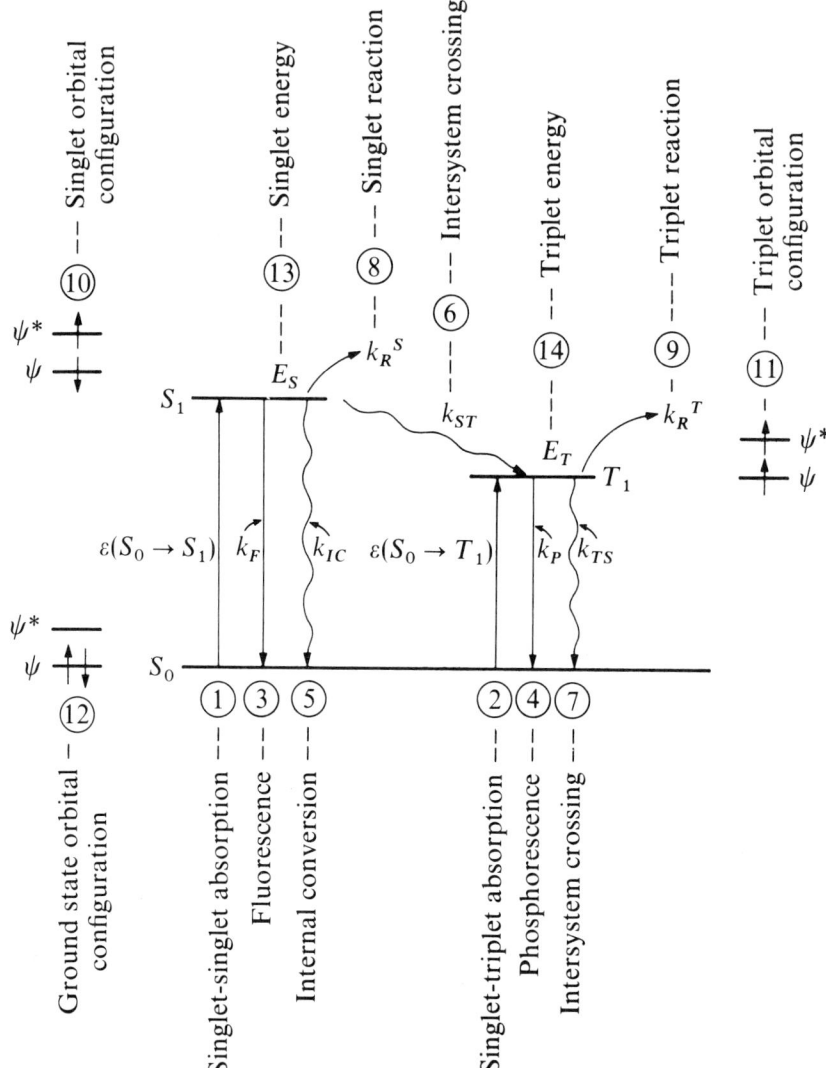

FIGURE 1. The three state energy diagram. A standard paradigm of organic photochemistry.

7. "Forbidden" transitions between triplet states and the ground state, also called *intersystem crossing* (e.g., $T_1 \rightarrow S_0$ + heat) and characterized by a rate constant, k_{TS}.

Photochemical processes may be defined as transitions from an electronically excited state to yield structures of different constitution or configuration than S_0. The commonly encountered photochemical processes are relatively few in number. In general, these reactions will be initiated by molecules in (8) S_1, or (9) T_1, and these reactions will be characterized by rate constants k_R^S and k_R^T, respectively.

The velocity of an electron making one complete circuit in a Bohr orbit is $\sim 10^{16}$ Å/s. Thus, an electron may move on the order of 10 Å in 10^{-15} s. Since the size of many commonly encountered groups of atoms (*chromophores*) responsible for absorption of light is on the order of 10 Å, we deduce that the time scales of photon interaction and electron motion are on the order of 10^{-15}–10^{-16} s.

Thus, the time period of $\sim 10^{-16}$ s sets a lower limit to the scale of chemical events, since no chemistry can occur before electron motion has occurred. It thus serves as a calibration point for the fastest events of chemical or photochemical interest.

What are calibration points for the *slowest* processes of direct photochemical interest? These are limited by the *radiative lifetimes* of electronically excited molecules. The *longest* fluorescence (S_1) lifetimes known for organic molecules are $\sim 10^{-6}$ s, and the *longest* phosphorescence (T_1) lifetimes are on the order of 30 s. Let us compare these times to those for nuclear motions such as vibrations, collisions, diffusions, and reactions. The fastest vibrations of organic molecules occur with a frequency of $\sim 10^{13}$ s^{-1} (e.g., a C—H stretching motion) and the slowest occur with a frequency of $\sim 10^{12}$ s^{-1} (e.g., a C—C bending motion). This means that it takes $\sim 10^{-12}$ to 10^{-13} s to complete a typical vibration. In 10^{-6} s (the longest fluorescence periods), an organic molecule will have executed $\sim 10^6$–10^7 vibrations and in 30 s, an organic molecule will have executed $\sim 10^{13}$–10^{14} vibrations.

The point of this comparison is to show that there is plenty of time for extensive nuclear motion during the lifetime of an electronically excited molecule. FIGURE 2 compares the spread of time for events of photochemical interest (from 10^{-15} s to 1 s) with the same spread of time ranging from 1 s to 10^{15} s. When compared in this manner, the history of a photoreaction passes through as many decades of time as the history of the universe!

The *minimum* energy required for electronic excitation of organic molecules is ~ 30–40 kcal/mole and corresponds to red light (700–800 nm). The *maximum* energy commonly employed by organic photochemistry corresponds to ~ 140 kcal/mole and corresponds to ultraviolet light (~ 200 nm).

Photoreactions must always occur in competition with radiationless and radiative processes, which limit excited state lifetimes to values that, generally, are much less than one second. It can be appreciated that, as the lifetime of an excited state becomes shorter, the amount of activation energy that can be accumulated by the excited state decreases.

Consider a photoreaction for which $A = 10^{13}$ s^{-1} and a second for which $A = 10^8$ s^{-1}. The former is representative of a unimolecular photoreaction and the latter is representative of a bimolecular photoreaction at room temperature. A rate of 10^8–10^9 s^{-1} would be feasible if $E_a = 6$ kcal/mole and $A = 10^{13}$ s^{-1}, but a reaction with $E_a = 6$ kcal/mole and A factor of 10^8 s^{-1} would proceed with a rate of only 10^3–10^4 s^{-1}. Since lifetimes of excited states are generally *much less* than a second, activation energies for photoreactions generally must be less than 20 kcal/mole. Furthermore, photoreac-

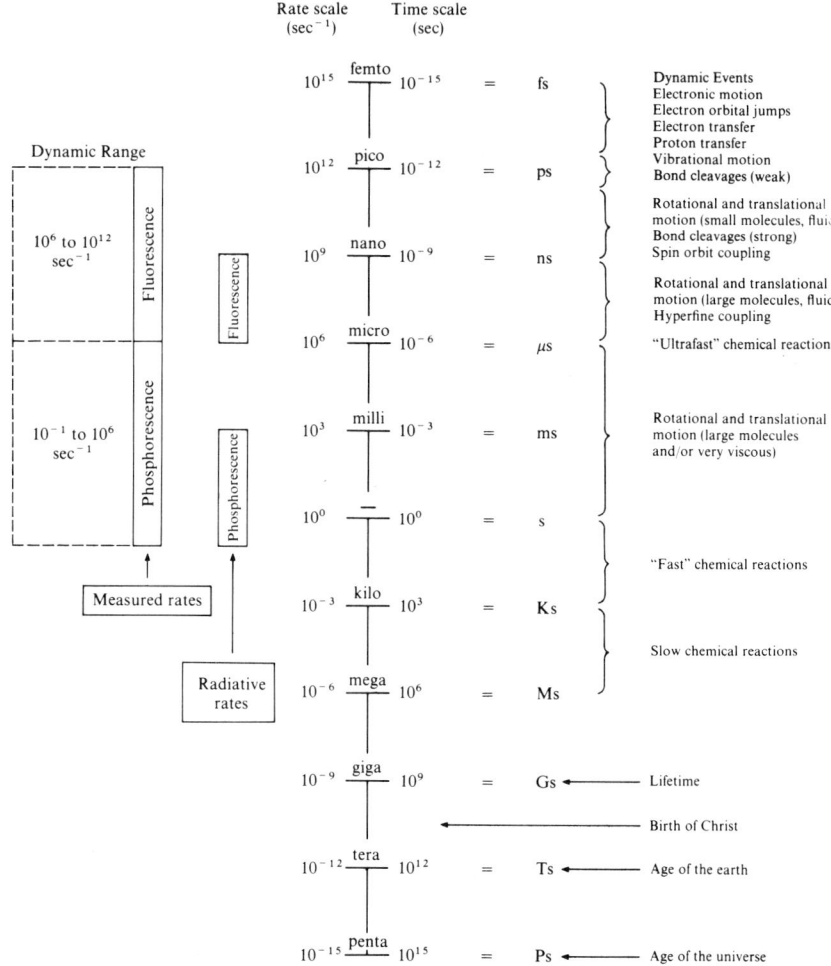

FIGURE 2. Comparison of times scales of events of importance in organic photochemistry to large-scale events.

tions of singlet states will rarely be able to compete with fluorescence if they possess E_a values larger than 10 kcal/mole.

PHOTOAFFINITY LABELING[2]

An ideal photoaffinity label would possess numerous properties, which can be divided into the following groups of classes: those that relate to the thermal chemistry of the receptor-ligand system and those that relate to the photochemistry of the receptor-ligand system. Only the latter properties are of interest to us here: (1) the ligand should possess an absorption band that will allow selective photoexcitation of the ligand in the presence of the receptor, (2) the photoexcited ligand should react efficiently with its "immediate" environment (or "instantaneously" produce a reactive intermediate that reacts "immediately" with its environment) to form a covalent bond, (3) the reactive species should not be readily deactivated by water. The terms "immediately" and "instantaneously" refer to the time period associated with the lifetime of the receptor-ligand complex. The lifetime of the latter may be associated with a rate of "escape" of the ligand from the complex.

It is useful to think of reaction efficiency in terms of the rates of deactivation of the excited state or of the reactive intermediate, compared to either the rate of reaction with the receptor or the rate of (irreversible) escape from the receptor. So we could write:

$$\text{Efficiency} = \frac{\text{rate of reaction}}{\text{rate of reaction} + \text{rate of deactivation} + \text{rate of escape}}.$$

From this expression it is clear that high efficiency requires that (rate of reaction) $\gg$ (rate of deactivation). By deactivation, we mean all irreversible processes that remove reactive species from the system.

The remainder of this article reviews the photochemistry of several systems that could, potentially, be developed into efficient photoaffinity labels.

PHOTOELIMINATION OF NITROGEN FROM DIAZO COMPOUNDS[3] AND AZIDES[4]
TO PRODUCE CARBENES AND NITRENES

The most characteristic photoreaction of diazo compounds and azides is photo-elimination of a molecule of N_2 followed by reaction of the resulting *carbene* or *nitrene*.

The photochemistries of both diazo compounds and azides are nicely parallel, as are the chemistries of carbenes and nitrenes. From analyses of the photochemistry of diazo compounds and of the reactions of carbenes, we may infer the photochemistry of azides and reactions of nitrenes by the use of the *isoelectronic analogy principle*, i.e., since carbenes and nitrenes are isoelectronic species (six valence electrons) their chemistries are expected to be qualitatively similar.

PHOTOCHEMISTRY OF DIAZO COMPOUNDS AND AZIDES:
CARBENES AND NITRENES

In order to understand the photochemistry of diazo compounds, one must understand the chemistry of carbenes, because the most characteristic photoreacton of diazo compounds is the loss of nitrogen to form carbenes. Use of the Wigner spin rule (spin conservation in an elemental chemical step) suggests that the following pattern should occur:

$$\text{Diazo compound} \rightarrow \text{carbene} + N_2$$

$$S_1 \rightarrow \text{singlet carbene}$$

$$T_1 \rightarrow \text{triplet carbene}$$

$$S_0 \rightarrow \text{singlet carbene.}$$

An interesting and important general feature of carbenes is the occurrence of two energetically proximate states, a singlet and a triplet state. Let us consider methylene as a prototype for analysis of the electronic structure and chemical reactions of carbenes.

In the extreme cases of sp^2 and sp hybridization of the carbene carbon atom, we predict that the bent form of CH_2 will be a singlet because its orbital occupancy will be $(sp^2)^2$, whereas the orbital occupancy for the linear form of CH_2 will be triplet $(p_x)^1$ $(p_z)^1$. For a nitrene, the nuclear shapes will be linear for both the singlet and the triplet, but the orbital configurations will be different, i.e., singlet = $(sp^2)^4$ $(p_z)^0$ and triplet = $(sp)^2$ $(p_x)^1$ $(p_z)^1$.

$$R_2CN_2 \xrightarrow{h\nu} R_2\ddot{C} + N_2$$
diazocompound → carbene

triplet   singlet

$$RNN_2 \xrightarrow{h\nu} R\ddot{N} + N_2$$
azide → nitrene

triplet   singlet

REACTIONS INVOLVING DIRADICAL AND ZWITTERION INTERMEDIATES

The majority of known photoreactions of organic molecules are probably not *concerted* in nature; i.e., they tend to involve intermediates along the reaction pathway between reactant (photoexcited molecule) and product. The most common photochemical intermediates are species that are not fully bonded, i.e., diradicals and zwitterions. An electronically excited state may generally be viewed in terms of two characteristic half-filled orbitals. Motion along a reaction coordinate due to stretching a σ-bond or twisting a π-bond may bring the representative point to a geometry for which the two half-filled orbitals are nearly degenerate. In this geometry, the molecule is termed a "diradicaloid." Interactions between the orbitally unpaired electrons of the diradicaloid generate *four* states: a diradical singlet ^1D; a diradical triplet ^3D; and two zwitterionic singlets, Z_1 and Z_2. The postulate that an electronically excited state tends toward a D or Z primary product as a reaction proceeds is an exceedingly powerful device for interpreting the photoreactions of organic molecules.

In the case of carbenes, we shall use the symbols R_2C: and $R_2\dot{C}\cdot$ to represent the singlet, with paired orbitals and electron spins, and the triplet, with unpaired orbitals and electron spins, respectively. In the case of nitrenes, the symbols are RN: and $R\dot{N}\cdot$ for the singlet and triplets. SCHEMA 1 outlines these ideas in terms of simple orbital notation and indicates the basis for the pronounced two electron, or electron paired, chemistry of singlet carbenes (and nitrenes) and the pronounced one electron chemistry of triplet carbenes (and nitrenes).

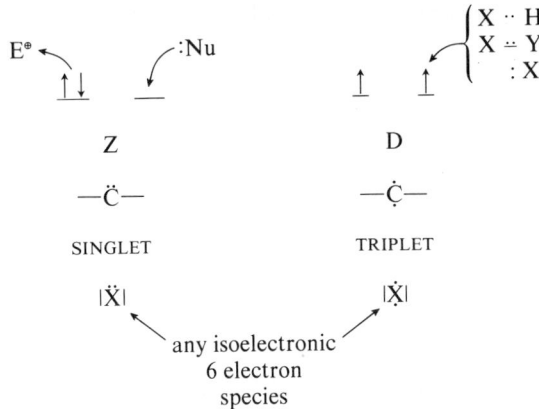

SCHEMA 1. The zwitterion/diradical paradigm of carbene/nitrene chemistry.

The chronological sequence of an organic photoreaction may be represented schematically as follows:

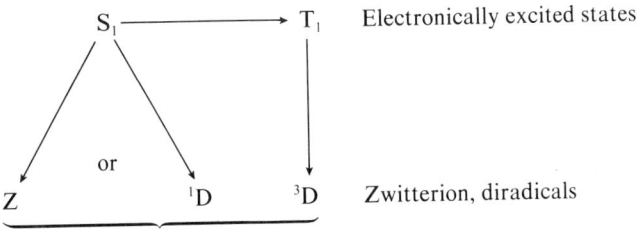

We shall now show that (a) the qualitatively distinct reactions of Z, ^{1}D and ^{3}D are very limited in number, and (b) the photochemistry of ligands commonly employed for photoaffinity labeling (azo compounds and azides) proceed by means of the production of carbenes, nitrenes, and radicals that affect covalent attachment via one of the reactions of a D or Z intermediate.

TYPICAL REACTIONS OF Z AND D IINTERMEDIATES

The typical reactions of Z intermediates may be either nucleophilic (addition of an electrophile) or electrophilic (addition of an electron pair). In the case of singlet carbenes, which generally react as Z intermediates, electrophilic (electron pair) reactions tend to dominate. The commonly encountered reactions of singlet carbenes are:

  1. Electrophilic attack of σ electron pairs (e.g., insertion into a C—H bond)
  2. Electrophilic attack of π electron pairs (e.g., insertion into a C=C double bond)
  3. Electrophilic attack of a nonbonding electron pair of low ionization potential (e.g., attachment to a sulfur atom of a sulfide)

4. Electrophilic rearrangement to a fully bonded molecule (e.g., rearrangement of a ketocarbene to a ketene).

The typical reactions of D intermediates are completely analogous to the reactions of radicals (one electron reactions). In the case of a triplet carbene, which generally reacts as a D intermediate, the following reactions are typical:

1. Radical attack on σ bonds (e.g., hydrogen atom abstraction to a triplet radical pair)

2. Radical attack on π bonds (e.g., addition to a C=C bond to form a triplet diradical)

3. Radical attack on a nonbonding electron pair of low ionization potential (e.g., electron abstraction from the nitrogen atom of an amine).

In contrast to singlet carbenes, triplet carbenes are much less likely to undergo rearrangements.

Via the isoelectronic principle, each reaction of R_2C: (singlet carbene) may be mapped on a reaction of R—N̈: (singlet nitrene) and each reaction of $R_2\dot{C}\cdot$ (triplet carbene) may be mapped onto RṄ· (triplet nitrene). Thus, we need not explicitly consider any nitrene chemistry in a general discussion. The general outline of carbene and nitrene production is given in SCHEMA 2.

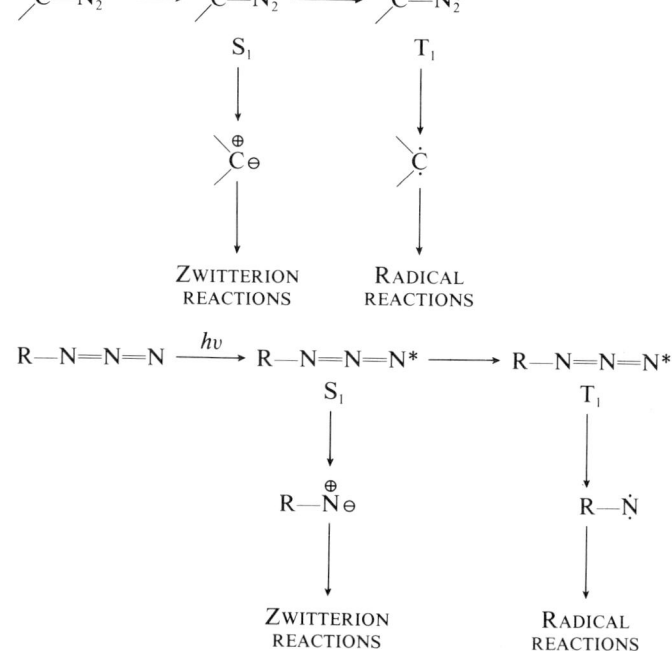

SCHEMA 2. Outline of typical reaction pathways involved in the photochemistry of diazo compounds and azides.

HYDROGEN INSERTION AND ABSTRACTION REACTIONS OF CARBENES

The abstraction or insertion of hydrogen by carbenes is very general. However, depending on the spin state, the mechanism of insertion is qualitatively different. Singlet carbenes insert into H—X bonds in a one- or two-step process involving the initial formation of a singlet radical pair that undergoes "cage" recombination to yield products.

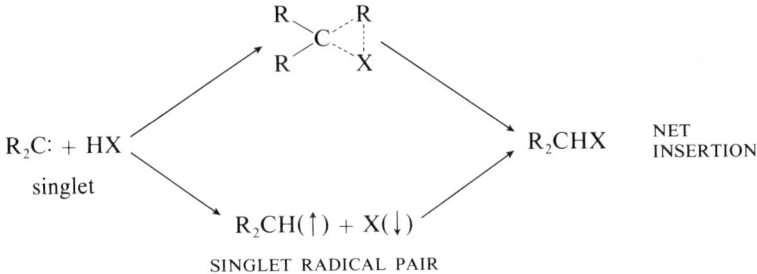

Triplet carbenes first abstract a hydrogen atom to produce a triplet radical pair that can produce the insertion product only after intersystem crossing. If the latter process is slow, diffusion of the radical pair may compete with net insertion.

$$R_2\dot{C}\cdot \ + HX \longrightarrow R_2CH(\uparrow) + X(\downarrow) \longrightarrow R_2CHX$$

triplet   TRIPLET RADICAL PAIR   NET INSERTION

Regrettably, very little quantitative data is available concerning even relative reactivities of carbenes toward hydrogen insertion and abstraction reactions. Furthermore, most of the available data do not distinguish the individual reactivities of singlet and triplet carbenes.

The following tentative statements may be made:

1. Singlet carbenes insert hydrogen into C—H bonds and triplet carbenes abstract hydrogen from C—H functions in a relatively indiscriminate manner (e.g., the ratio of tertiary CH to primary CH reactivity is generally less than 10).

2. The singlet carbene insertion reaction leads directly to a covalent attachment, while the triplet carbene reaction leads to a triplet radical pair that cannot result in a covalent attachment by bond formation until an intersystem crossing to a triplet radical pair occurs.

3. The singlet carbene insertion reaction competes with intersystem crossing to triplet carbene and other intramolecular (e.g., rearrangement) or intermolecular (e.g., addition to π bonds) reactions; the triplet carbene (generally the carbene ground state) does not tend to undergo unimolecular rearrangements, so only other triplet carbene reactions compete for its deactivation.

4. Insertion into C—H bonds dominates insertion into saturated OH and NH

bonds; abstraction from CH groups dominates abstraction from saturated OH and NH groups.

5. Vinyl and aryl C—H bonds are not abstracted, although net insertion into such bonds may occur via a π-bond addition-rearrangement sequence, e.g.,

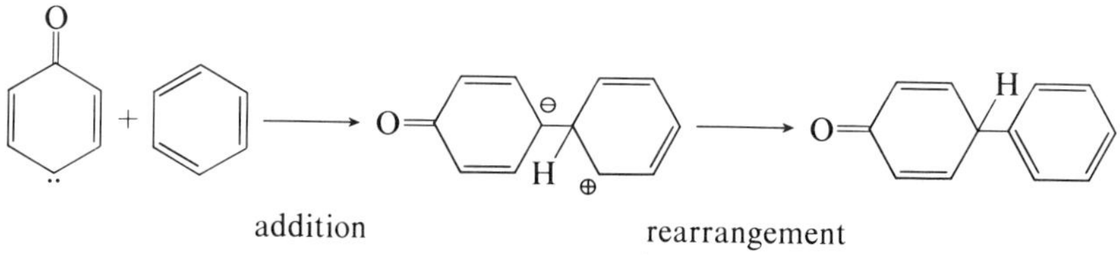

addition   rearrangement

ADDITION OF CARBENES TO C=C MULTIPLE BONDS

The addition of carbenes to C=C bonds is a very general reaction. Alkenes, polyenes, and even aromatic systems are substrates for this reaction.

The following general statements may be made concerning the addition of carbenes to C=C bonds:

1. Singlet carbenes add stereospecifically to ethylenes that are not symmetric along the C=C axis:

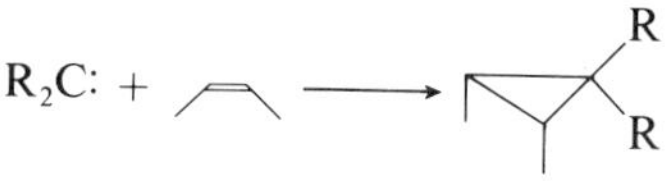

2. Triplet carbenes add nonstereospecifically to ethylenes that are not symmetric along the C=C axis (via a triplet diradical intermediate):

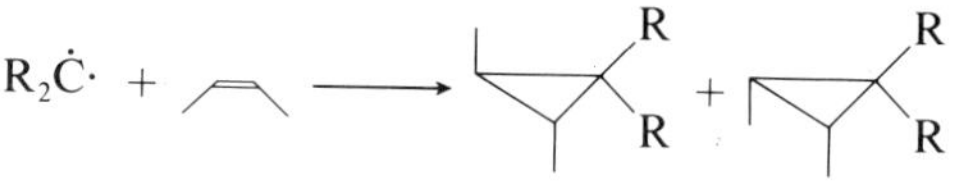

3. Singlet, but not triplet, carbenes add to aromatic rings to yield an initial cyclopropane that rearranges to cycloheptatrienes:

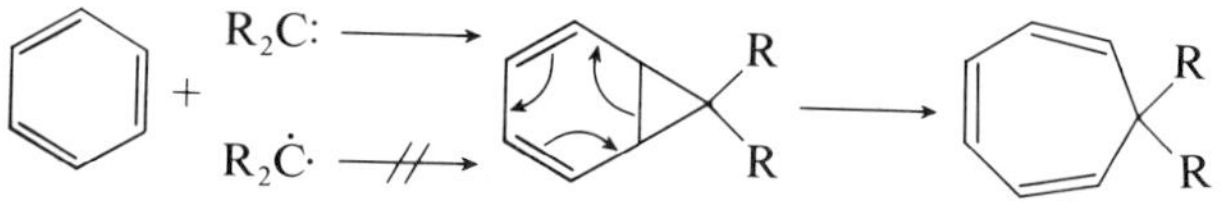

RATES AND SELECTIVITIES OF TRIPLET CARBENE REACTIONS

Absolute rate constants of carbene reactions are almost nonexistent, except for one report.[5] TABLE 2 lists some reported rate constants for reactions of Ph$_2$C·. The important point to notice is that a variation of rates over 10^4 is observed. Thus, this

TABLE 2

RATE CONSTANTS FOR SOME REACTIONS OF DIPHENYL CARBENE[5]

Reactions	K (M^{-1} s^{-1})
(1) Ph$_2$C: + Ph$_2$C: $\rightarrow$ Ph$_2$C=CPh$_2$	5×10^9
(2)* Ph$_2$C: + O$_2$ $\rightarrow$ Ph$_2$C=O	1×10^9
(3) Ph$_2$C: + CH$_3$OH $\rightarrow$ Ph$_2$CHOCH$_3$	$>10^7$
(4) Ph$_2$C: + PhCH=CH$_2$ $\rightarrow$ [triangle with Ph, Ph, Ph]	5×10^5

*This reaction is a singlet reaction, the others are triplet reactions.

carbene exhibits a considerable range of reactivity toward different substrates. This is probably true in general for triplet carbenes. In fact, the reactivity pattern R$_3$CH > R$_2$CH$_2$ > RCH$_3$ is generally observed in hydrogen abstraction reactions. Furthermore, abstraction of hydrogen from HO, HN and HC=C groups does not occur. These reactivity patterns are precisely those expected of carbon radicals.

SPECTROSCOPIC DETECTION OF CARBENES AND NITRENES

Carbenes and nitrenes have been fully characterized by their absorption and emission spectra at low temperatures in rigid matrices.[6] More recently, the absorption

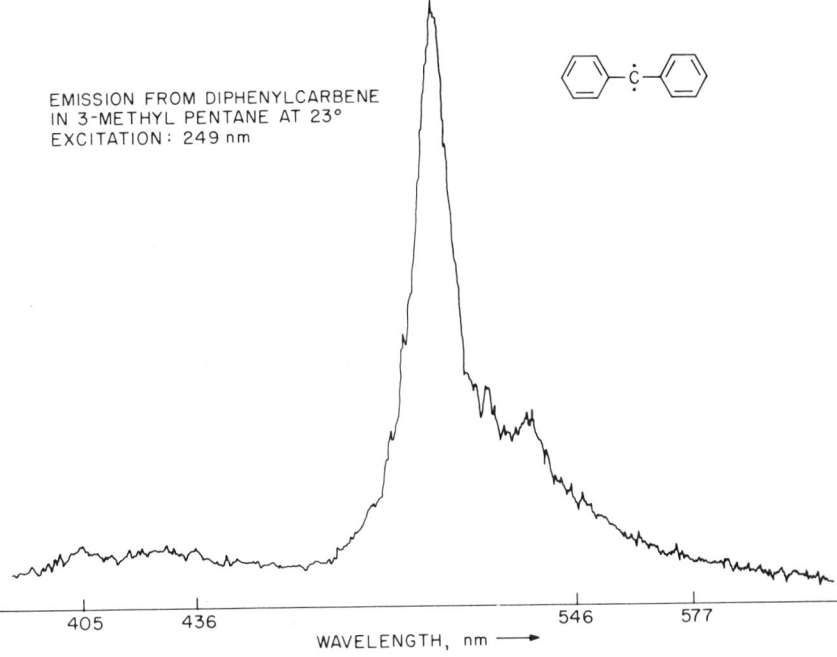

EMISSION FROM DIPHENYLCARBENE
IN 3-METHYL PENTANE AT 23°
EXCITATION: 249 nm

WAVELENGTH, nm $\longrightarrow$

405   436   546   577

FIGURE 3. The fluorescence spectrum of diphenyl carbene at room temperature in a fluid solution.

and emission spectra of carbenes have been observed in fluid solution at room temperature. For example, the fluorescence emission spectrum[7] of $Ph_2C\cdot$ in 3-methyl-pentane is shown in FIGURE 3. The point to be stressed here is that carbenes and nitrenes are real, if transient, chemical entities; they are not merely hypothetical structures created for convenience in mechanistic bookkeeping.

THE IMPORTANCE OF TIME SCALES AND MOVEMENT IN SPACE

Photochemical processes are limited in time by the rates of fluorescence (emission from S_1) and phosphorescence (emission from T_1) of excited molecules. FIGURE 2 schematizes the dynamic range of fluorescence (10^{12} s^{-1} to 10^6 s^{-1}) and phosphorescence (10^6 s^{-1} to 10 s^{-1}). Efficient production of D or Z intermediates requires that reactions of S_1 and/or T_1 compete with emission from these states. Efficient initial site

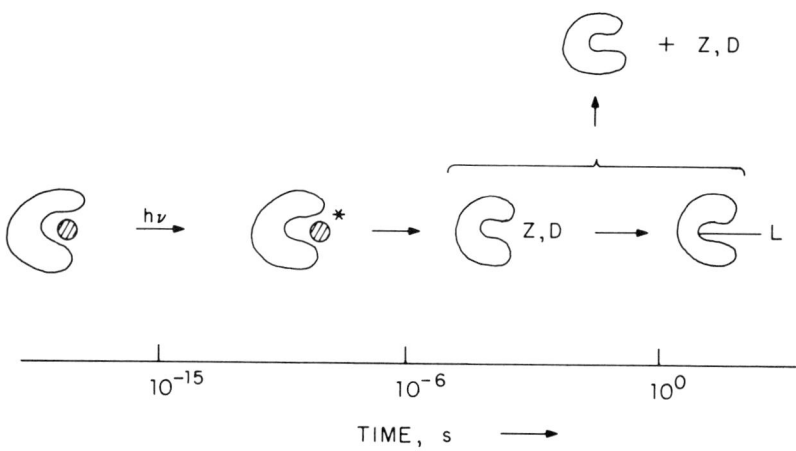

FIGURE 4. Schematic of time scales of probe-receptor complexes.

photoaffinity labeling requires that the net bond formation occurs in the environment in which the excited molecule is produced, i.e., the production of D and/or Z and the reaction of the latter to form covalent bonds must compete with escape of the ligand from the "hydrophobic pocket." Thus, it is not the absolute rates of reaction of excited states or intermediates that are important in determining labeling efficiencies. It is the competition between reaction rates and the rates of escape from the "hydrophobic pocket" that determines efficiency.

In FIGURE 4 the situation is shown schematically. It is likely that the ligand remains in the hydrophobic pocket for a time on the order of 10^{-6} s (or longer). Generally, Z or D will have been produced during this time period. Whether labeling will occur in an initial site now depends on the competition between the attack of D or Z on the environment relative to irreversible escape into the aqueous medium or some other portion of the receptor.

Summary

Some general principles (the Three State Paradigm and the Zwitterion/Diradical Paradigm), together with simple electron orbital and molecular structure considerations, allow the chemistry of carbenes and nitrenes to be elucidated. In terms of photoaffinity labeling, it is crucial to possess not only knowledge of the chemistry of these species but also information on dynamic processes such as reaction rates and escape rates of ligands from hydrophobic pockets of receptors.

References

1. For an elementary and thorough review of principles and examples of the photochemistry of organic molecules see: Turro, N.J. 1979. Modern Molecular Photochemistry. Benjamin/Cummings Publishing Co. Menlo Park, California.
2. Knowles, J. 1972. Acc. Chem. 5(4): 155–60.
3. Kermse, W. 1971. Carbene Chemistry (2nd ed.). Academic Press. New York.
4. Lwowski, W., Ed. 1970. Nitrenes. Interscience. New York.
5. Closs, G. & B. Rabinow. 1976. J. Am. Chem. Soc. 98: 8190.
6. For a review of nitrene spectroscopy see Reference 3, p. 13ff; for a review of carbene spectroscopy see Trozzolo, A.M. 1968. Acc. Chem. Res. 1(11): 329–35.
7. Aikawa, M. & J. Butcher. Private communication. Columbia University. New York.

Discussion

Unidentified Speaker: I want to ask you about the diradical mechanism. Have you tried to take an AB-molecule, which generates less stable radicals and would abstract hydrogen from the micelle itself, and see whether either A or B could insert itself into the micelle?

Dr. N. J. Turro: This has been done by Professor Breslow at Columbia. He has generated benzophenone-type molecules in micelles and he does get attachment to the various positions. He has also looked at selectivity along the carbon chain.

Unidentified Speaker: If that happens, then the problem with photoaffinity labels for reagents is that you could generate a diradical, but the radicals might migrate before bond insertion (bond formation) occurred. So you could wind up with a bond formed at a distance from the place of generation.

Turro: Sure. In this particular case, the type of thing that is happening is this. Our micelle contains a hydrogen, which is abstracted. Now this radical can induce abstraction somewhere else or it can add to a double bond or bond to another radical. The bonding process between radicals is a very facile one, with very little activation energy, and it is mainly going to compete with diffusion. Because of diffusion, you get into an entropy problem when you try to get the radicals together.

If your material is in a site in which the radicals can interact for a long enough period of time, then you have a triplet state reaction and, therefore, the radical pair is generated in a triplet and it is going to take about 10^{-8} seconds for the spins to rotate around to give you a singlet. Let's just say, for the sake of argument, that this is the one that rotates around so they can recombine.

One of the types of things you might try to do with a label of this type is facilitate this process, and there are mechanisms by which you can do that by various substitutions on the ring. That would be a rational approach. I don't know anybody who has done that. This process can be induced by magnetic nuclei. It turns out that triplet-singlet crossings can be made faster by putting carbon 13 at the proper center.

UNIDENTIFIED SPEAKER: Is there a problem with the radical center migrating down the chain?

TURRO: No. Radicals don't move very fast. Carbonium ions move like a shot along a chain, but radical centers will be, for most intents and purposes, fixed at the initial carbon until the reaction is over. So when you make a radical on a chain it stays there, unlike carbonium ions, which would move around, giving you the more stable carbonium ions. The radical would not rearrange to another radical very readily on this type of time scale. That would be one of the last things it would do.

I mentioned that the singlet carbene rearranges because that is a carbonium ion reaction, but the triplet carbenes don't rearrange because they have a radical type of chemistry. Radicals don't undergo any rearrangements very rapidly.

DR. D. E. HAYON (*Queens College*): You mentioned the zwitterion properties of singlet excited states, but you haven't mentioned such properties for triplet states. Does it follow that you have intentionally left out triplet states?

TURRO: With respect to zwitterion properties? Absolutely. If we want to talk about singlets and triplets in terms of two orbitals, the triplet state is a state in which the electron spins are parallel. What I mean by a zwitterion is a situation in which two electrons are paired in an orbital. Two electrons cannot be paired in an orbital in the triplet state. So, by my definition, it's excluded. This is basically, a conservation rule: you can't easily go from a zwitterion to a diradical. It takes time.

HAYON: What's your definition, then, of a charge character of an excited state as compared to a zwitterion character?

TURRO: Well, I can imagine charge-polarized excited triplets. You see, a triplet can have a polarity to it but I wouldn't call it a zwitterion on that account. If I measured electronic distribution and space in a triplet, it may have more positive character at one point, more negative character at another point, and have a net dipole moment. But I wouldn't call it a zwitterion because what I want to mean by "zwitterion" is something in which two electrons are always paired in the same orbital. It is possible to define "zwitterion" in other ways; that is the way I happen to be defining it. I think that this is a useful definition because it automatically gives you a certain kind of characteristic reactivity to think about.

HAYON: Should one not include the charge character, then, of triplet states, since they do interact by charge separation in some cases?

TURRO: Okay. What we will be talking about here is the two centers at which we will assume you can localize each of the electrons. A center A and a center B, forming a whole unit, but, if the electrons are localized on a given atom, then we can talk about the nucleophilic or the electrophilic tendencies of that half-filled orbital. In other words, a carbon radical is nucleophilic relative to an oxygen radical. They are both neutral, but an oxygen radical will tend to react with electron-rich hydrogen-carbon-hydrogen bonds faster, whereas a carbon radical will tend to react with electron-poor carbon-hydrogen bonds faster.

So your notion of polarity basically has to wait a little bit longer in these reactions. Only when you go into the transition state does it become important whether the radical center wants to take electrons or give them up. Then the radical gets much closer to the ideas of the zwitterion, except it is still one-electron rather than two-electron chemistry.

DR. T. I. KALMAN (*State University of New York at Buffalo*): Can you comment on the similarities and differences between the reactivities of aromatic ketones and of thioketones?

TURRO: The general types of reactions of benzophenone and thiobenzophenone are similar. They undergo hydrogen abstraction, which is your typical radical reaction, and they undergo additions to carbon-carbon bonds. There are some special reactions that thioketones undergo (I'm talking about the photochemically excited species now), as benzothiophenone will react with oxygen, generating benzophenone. If that happens with benzophenone, you don't notice it. The qualitative reactions are similar to, but the rates are usually much slower than, those of thioketones. And you have ground state chemistry, which is also a problem. The material isn't all that stable in the presence of electrophiles and nucleophiles.

DR. H. A. LESTER (*California Institute of Technology*): I'd like to answer the challenge issued to us to come up with some examples of how long the excited states stay in the catcher's mitt. One can think of two. The first is the experiment in which one flashes ligands off hemoproteins. There are a large number of experiments on this sort of thing. I'm not familiar with the latest literature, but I believe that the fastest spectral changes are seen within 100 ps. The excited state of the ligand is, in this case, I think, carbon monoxide. It seems to undergo some sort of change within 100 ps.

TURRO: The question is, does it escape the crucial environment? That I doubt. I don't think you can move that far in space in that period.

LESTER: The problem is whether it moves out of its well, as I understand it. The energy barriers don't seem to be real energy barriers. They seem to be distributed on humps so you can't really say when it is that the ligand has completely escaped the influence of the protein.

The other example doesn't really concern an excited state. It concerns the metastable state, a *cis*-isomer of a drug that started out *trans*. One can change the lifetime of the ligand by at least a factor of 100, depending on whether the ligand is in the *cis* or the *trans* form, and probably by a factor of 1000 or 10,000. So there again, it is not an excited state but it might as well be.

TURRO: I don't think the excitation energy is going to have too much to do with the lifetime in these species unless there's a tremendous polarity change in the excited state.

Another interesting concept is to change the polarity of something upon photoexcitation and have it go to the hydrophobic region. Then the ground states would not be reactive and the excited states might be.

PHOTOSENSITIVE STEROIDS AS PROBES OF ESTROGEN RECEPTOR SITES*

John A. Katzenellenbogen, Michael R. Kilbourn,
and Kathryn E. Carlson

School of Chemical Sciences
University of Illinois
Urbana, Illinois 61801

INTRODUCTION

Receptors for steroid hormones are those proteins found in the cytoplasm of target tissue cells that have the ability to bind steroids with high affinity and great selectivity. The initial steroid-receptor complex, which forms in the cytoplasm, undergoes an activation process, after which it moves into the nucleus and interacts with chromatin. This chromatin interaction, while still poorly understood, is thought to result in changes in gene expression that are ultimately reflected in the biochemical and physiological alterations that are characteristic of the tissue's response to the hormone.[1]

Affinity labeling stands to make a substantial contribution to our understanding of the intricacies of both the interaction between steroid hormones and receptors and the actions of the receptors themselves.[2] Steroid receptors, even in the richest tissue sources, are minor cellular constituents, whose purification is complicated by their thermal lability and their tendency to aggregate. Thus, a radiolabeled ligand that could be covalently attached to the receptor would be of great assistance to efforts directed toward the purification and characterization of receptors. Steroid receptors also exist in different states (unliganded, liganded and unactivated, liganded and activated), and move between different subcellular compartments. A process such as photoaffinity labeling, whereby a steroid derivative could be induced to attach covalently to a receptor at some time subsequent to its initial binding to the receptor, would provide a unique way of following the dynamic features of steroid receptor interaction: activation, subcellular redistribution, chromatin interaction, receptor recycling, and receptor degradation.

Finally, steroid receptors have a great tendency towards association, with the result that their apparent physicochemical properties may change upon purification. This causes one to doubt that attempts at reconstituting the cellular interactions between steroids, receptors, and chromatin binding sites *in vitro,* using purified elements, will result in accurate representations of the *in vivo* interaction. Photoactivated steroid analogs capable of covalent labeling may prove to be an important avenue for the exploration of receptor action in certain intact systems (e.g., cells in culture). Thus, the ultimate goal of efforts to develop affinity labeling agents for steroid receptors should be to obtain agents with sufficient selectivity and efficiency to provide adequate means for covalent labeling of receptors in systems that are

*This research was supported by the National Institutes of Health, grant no. AM 15556.

18

sufficiently intact or "physiological" so as to retain their responsiveness to hormones.

A Systematic Approach to Evaluating Photoreactive Estrogen Analogs as Affinity Labeling Agents for Uterine Estrogen Receptors

In earlier publications from our laboratory, we have outlined a systematic method for developing photoaffinity labeling agents for the estrogen receptor.[3] Candidate compounds, synthesized[4] on the basis of their potential for high receptor binding affinity and synthetic accessibility, are first evaluated in nonradiolabeled form by measuring their affinity for the estrogen receptor in a competitive binding assay.[5] The results from this assay are conveniently expressed as the ratio of association constants (RAC compound versus estradiol) × 100%, which is essentially a percent scale of binding affinity relative to estradiol. The capacity of the unlabeled compounds to photoinactivate the receptor is then determined through a photolysis-exchange assay.[6,7] This establishes that the photointeraction of the compound with the receptor is chromophore-dependent and site-specific, and it places an upper limit on the efficiency of covalent attachment.

These two assays, conveniently done on the photosensitive estrogens in unlabeled form, provide a rationale for selecting only the most promising agents for preparation in tritium-labeled form.[8] The reversible and irreversible (covalent) interaction of the radiolabeled compounds with receptor and nonreceptor proteins can be studied directly.[9]

Studies on the Uterine Estrogen Receptor

Binding Affinity and Inactivation Efficiency Studies With First Generation Photosensitive Estrogens

The receptor binding affinity and inactivation efficiencies of the first set of photosensitive estrogens that we prepared are shown in TABLE 1. The selection of this first generation of reagents was guided mostly by chemical accessibility, since, at the time of their conception, there was little to guide us in terms of the effect that structural changes would have on binding affinities and inactivation efficiencies.

The derivative with the highest affinity for the receptor is 3-azidohexestrol (**4**). The 3,3'-diazidohexestrol (**5**) also has relatively good affinity, but the binding of the 2- and 4-azido steroidal estrogens (**6** and **7**) is much lower. We explained this phenomenon on the basis of the higher symmetry and conformational flexibility of the hexestrol ligand as compared to the tetracyclic steroids and by the possibility that the monosubstituted hexestrols were projecting their functional group into the D-ring binding site of the receptor.[5] The binding affinity of all the diazoketones was relatively low, which is not surprising, considering the fact that, in most cases, a relatively bulky function is attached at or near a hydroxyl or keto group that is important in binding.

The photoinactivation efficiencies of the azide and diazo compounds in TABLE 1 showed an interesting pattern.[7] Regardless of their affinity, the steroidal A-ring

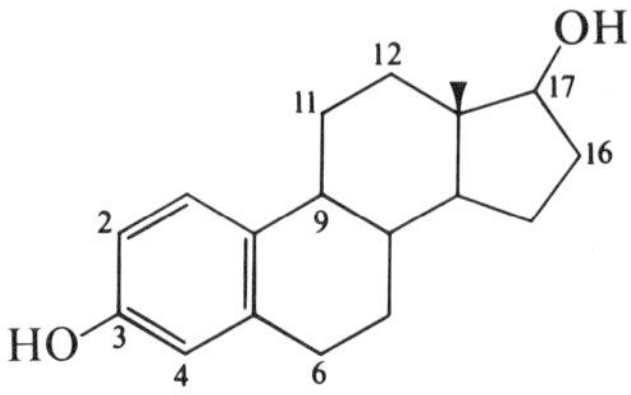

Estradiol

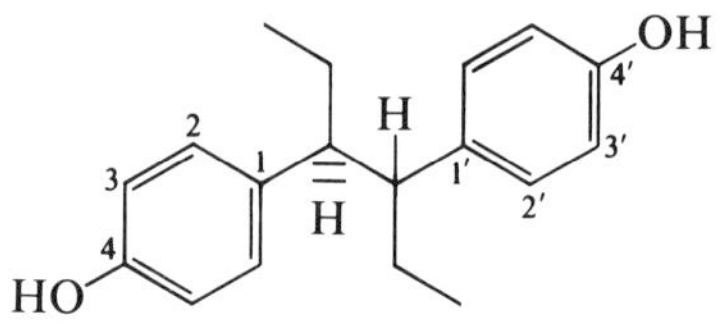

Hexestrol

TABLE 1

RECEPTOR BINDING AFFINITY AND INACTIVATION EFFICIENCY
OF PHOTOSENSITIVE ESTROGENS.*

Compound	No.†	Binding Affinity (RAC × 100%)‡	Inactivation Efficiency (%)§
Hexestrol 4-0-(3-diazo-2-oxopropyl) ether	1	1.8	15
Estradiol 3-0-(3-diazo-2-oxopropyl) ether	2	1.4	5
16-Diazoestrone	3	0.5	21
3-Azidohexestrol	4	70	15
3,3'-Diazidohexestrol	5	12	16
2-Azidoestradiol	6	3	0
4-Azidoestradiol	7	0.9	0
6-Oxoestradiol	8	20	—¶
$\Delta^{9(11)}$-12-Oxoestradiol‖	9	10	44

*From Reference 5. All experiments are with immature rat uterine cytosol.
†Compound numbers are shown in bold face throughout the text.
‡RAC is ratio of association constants $K_a^{compound}/K_a^{estradiol}$; for details, see Reference 5.
§At 254 nm; for details, see Reference 7.
¶Inactivation (at >315 nm) is first order, see text and Reference 7.
‖R. L. Neeley and J. A. Katzenellenbogen, unpublished. Inactivation efficiency is 66% at >315 nm.

derivatives, the azides **6** and **7,** and the diazoketo ether **2,** had little or no photoreactivity towards the rat uterine estrogen receptor, while the one D-ring derivative, 16-diazoestrone (**3**), though a low affinity binder, showed a relatively high inactivation efficiency. As we have mentioned, the precise manner in which the hexestrol derivatives are bound by the receptor is ambiguous because of the symmetry and conformational mobility of the ligand;[5] therefore, we were not too surprised to find that the same functional groups (azidophenol and diazoketopropyl ether) that were photoinert in the A-ring of the steroidal system (compounds **2, 6,** and **7**) showed, in the hexestrol system (compounds **1** and **5**), photoreactivity akin to that of the D-ring diazo compound (**3**). This suggests again that substituents on the rings of hexestrol may be accommodated in the D-ring binding site of the receptor.[7]

There are a number of reports of the use of aromatic[10] and unsaturated ketones[11] as attaching functions in photoaffinity labeling. Thus far, we have investigated two ketonic estrogens (**8** and **9**). The aromatic conjugated enone **9,** which has been described in the literature,[12] has interesting fluorescent properties[13] and a good affinity for the receptor; it is also an efficient inactivator both at 254 nm and at >315 nm. 6-Oxoestradiol (**8**) is a potent photoinactivator that consumes binding activity in a first order process. This suggests that inactivation is the result of a reaction from an electronically excited state that decays to starting material if it fails to react with a receptor.[7]

Studies with New Photoreactive Estrogens

More recently, we have prepared two additional photosensitive hexestrol analogs. We prepared 4-azido-4-deoxyhexestrol (**10**) to assess the photoreactivity of a simple aromatic azide; the other azide derivatives (**4–7**) were *o*-azidophenols, and we suspected that the relatively low inactivation efficiencies of these compounds might be due, in part, to the tautomerization of the *o*-hydroxyphenyl nitrene to an ortho-quinone imine (SCHEMA 1).[8] The 4-azido-4-deoxyhexestrol has a lower binding affinity than 3-azidohexestrol; nevertheless, its photoinactivation efficiency is nearly three times as great.

Also recently prepared is the hexestrol analog incorporating a *m*-nitroanisole function (**11**). Extensive investigations by Havinga and Cornelisse[14,15] have demonstrated that systems such as these undergo photoassisted nucleophilic aromatic substitution in which the methoxy group can be replaced by a variety of nucleophiles. In the excited state, the orientational effects are the reverse of those in the ground state; hence, the nitro group activates the methoxy group in the meta position.

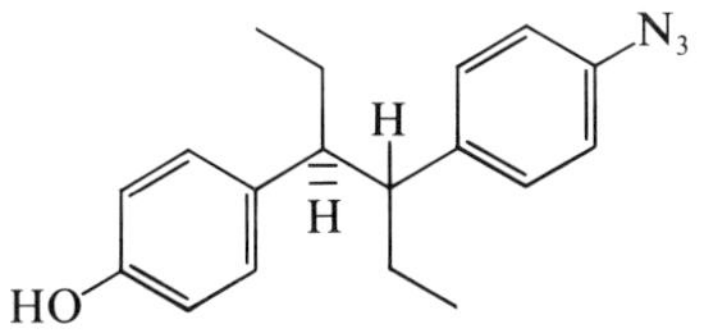

Binding Affinity   5.7%
Inactivation Efficiency   40%

4-Azido-4-Deoxyhexestrol (**10**)

Arylnitrene

o-Quinone Imine

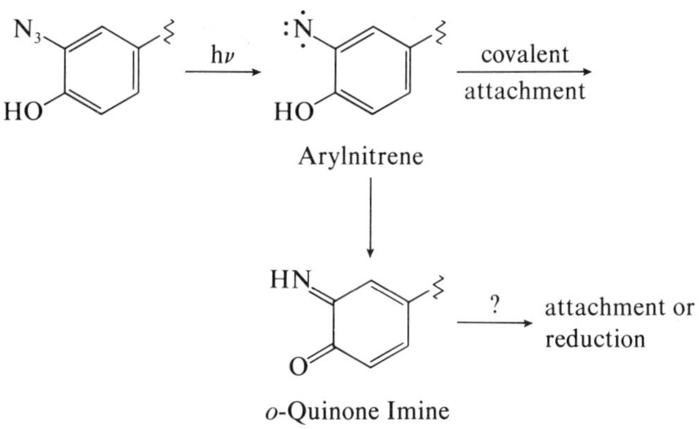

SCHEMA 1.

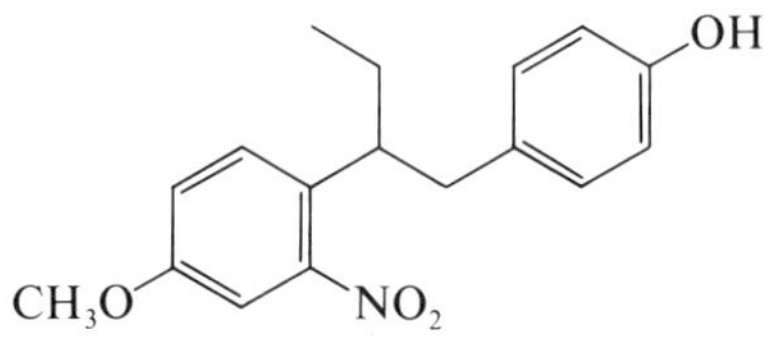

Binding Affinity   1.4%
Inactivation Efficiency 55%
(at >315 nm)

2-Nitrobisnorhexestrol
4-Methyl Ether (11)

SCHEMA 2.

Reaction proceeds from a short-lived excited state, often with high chemical yield. Thus, the *m*-nitroanisole group appears ideally suited for exploitation as an attachment function in photoaffinity labeling (SCHEMA 2).[16]

FIGURE 1 shows the photoinactivation time course of an estrogen receptor with nitrobisnorhexestrol methyl ether (11). Since this compound has a relatively long-wavelength chromophore, it can be irradiated with uv light filtered to remove radiation below 315 nm. Under these conditions, sites filled with estradiol are completely unaffected, while 55% of those filled with the nitroanisole derivative are inactivated. (The inactivation proceeds at a rate that closely parallels the rate at which this compound undergoes reaction with high concentrations of butylamine when irradiated under the same conditions.) The site specificity of inactivation is demonstrated by the fact that sites that are prefilled with estradiol (hence protected) are unaffected by the same concentration of the nitroanisole derivative that inactivates 55% of the sites when present by itself.

This *m*-nitroanisole derivative is the first of a series that we are currently preparing. While its affinity for the estrogen receptor is relatively low, introduction of a second alkyl group to give a more complete "hexane" backbone may produce a compound with increased affinity. In this system, however, we do not have the option of having both phenolic hydroxyl groups free, since *m*-nitrophenols do not undergo photoassisted nucleophilic aromatic substitution.

Studies with Tritium-Labeled Photosensitive Estrogens: Binding Selectivity and Receptor Labeling

Preliminary assessment of the receptor binding affinity and photoinactivation efficiency of the photosensitive estrogen analogs, as was done indirectly with the compounds in nonradiolabeled form, allows one to make a rational selection of those compounds that are worth preparing in tritium-labeled form for direct studies of binding selectivity and covalent attachment. Because of the low concentration and high affinity of the estrogen receptor, labeled compounds must be prepared with specific activities approaching the "carrier-free" level.

To date, a number of the compounds listed in TABLE 1 have been tritium labeled.[8] In several cases, compounds that had demonstrated substantial photoinactivation failed to show even marginal photocovalent attachment to proteins (e.g., 1, 8). While it is clear that compounds that covalently attach to receptor will show photoinactivation activity, we had recognized that the converse is not necessarily true. One can imagine certain reactions (atom transfers, photoreductions) that might occur in the binding site that would result in receptor inactivation but not in covalent attachment of the ligand.[9]

Of the compounds currently prepared in tritium-labeled form, 3-azidohexestrol (**4**) appears most interesting. FIGURE 2 shows an analysis of the binding of [^{3}H]-3-azidohexestrol in rat uterine cytosol preparations by sucrose gradient sedimentation.[9] The binding of estradiol is seen to be highly selective, since it is confined to the 8S region of the gradient, where the receptor sediments as an aggregated form under hypotonic conditions; there is no detectable binding in the 4S region, where most of the nonreceptor proteins sediment. 3-Azidohexestrol does bind to the 8S receptor, but it shows greatly elevated binding in the 4S region. Competition studies have demonstrated that the 4S binding is not estrogen specific. Thus, while this compound has

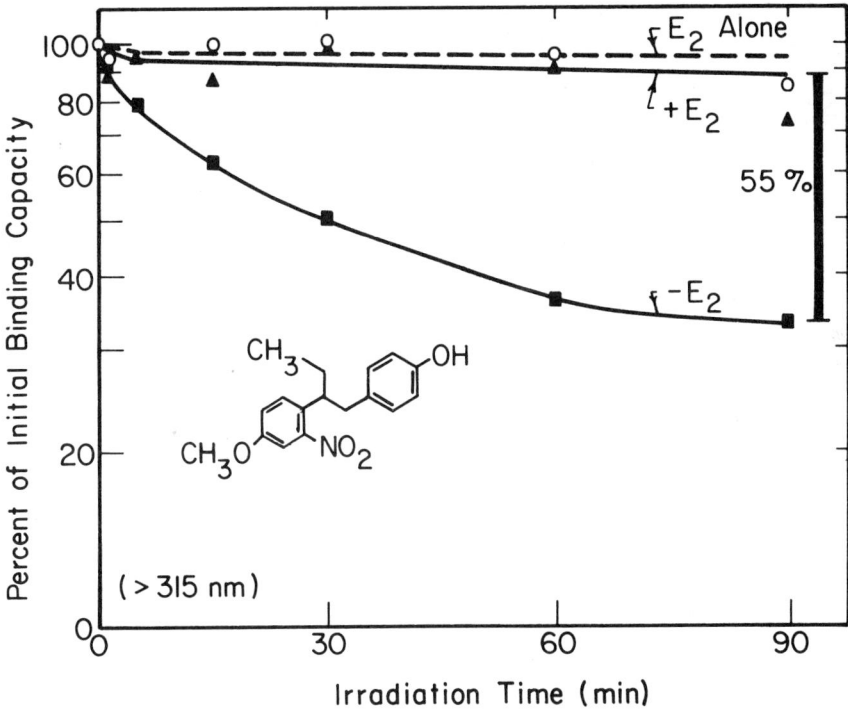

FIGURE 1. The time course of the photoinactivation of the estrogen receptor from lamb uterine cytosol with 2-nitrobisnorhexestrol 4-methyl ether (**11**). The receptor was incubated for 60 min at 0 °C with either estradiol at 30 nM (O) or compound **11** at 2133 nM (■), or it was preincubated with estradiol at 3000 nM for 15 min, followed by 2133 nM compound **11** for 60 min (▲). Irradiation was conducted at >315 nm in an apparatus previously described.[7] At the indicated times, aliquots were removed and binding capacity was measured by an exchange assay.[7] The inactivation efficiency was calculated as the difference between the ultimate inactivation observed with compound **11** alone versus that seen with compound **11** after the receptor sites were protected with estradiol.

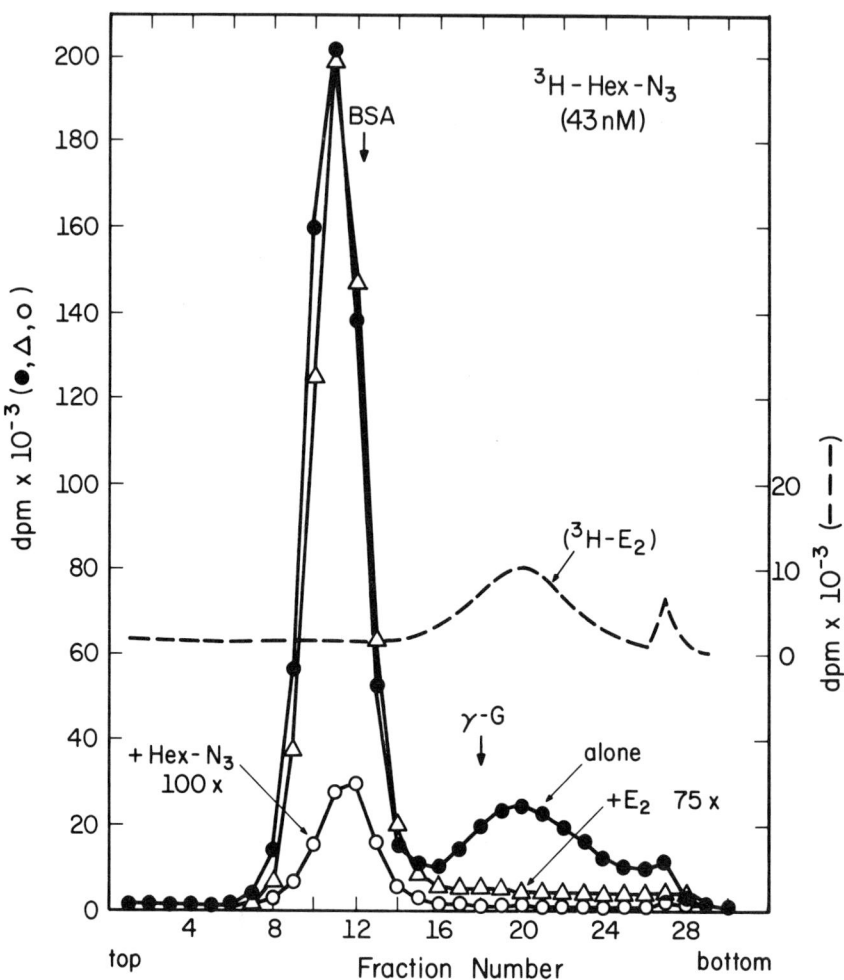

FIGURE 2. Sucrose density gradient profiles of [³H]-3-azidohexestrol (**4**) labeled cytosol. The rat cytosol was incubated with 43 nM 3-azidohexestrol alone (●) or after preincubation with either a 75-fold excess of unlabeled estradiol (△) or a 100-fold excess of unlabeled 3-azidohexestrol (○). The cytosol complex was charcoal-treated to remove unbound ligand and centrifuged for 13 h at 246,000 × g through gradients of 5–20% sucrose. Bovine serum albumin (4.5S) and γ-globulin (7.0S) were added as internal markers. The dashed line, with the displaced scale on the right vertical axis, is the binding profile for 30 nM [³H]estradiol alone.

excellent affinity for the estrogen receptor, its affinity for nonreceptor binding sites has been amplified to the point that its binding selectivity is poor.

To clarify the binding of this compound, we resorted to a partial purification (about thirty-fold) of estrogen receptor preparations from lamb uteri by ammonium sulfate precipitation and Sephadex G-200 chromatography. The receptor was also subjected to a brief trypsin treatment that did not affect its steroid binding properties, but eliminated problems of aggregation and greatly assisted purification.[17] Partially purified, trypsin-treated lamb uterine estrogen receptor preparations could be electrophoresed on polyacrylamide gels under conditions in which receptor binding activity is retained.[17]

FIGURE 3 shows the polyacrylamide gel electrophoretic profiles of lamb uterine estrogen receptor with [^{3}H]-3-azidohexestrol. With this partially purified preparation, a large amount of estrogen-specific binding is evident in the region of fractions 26–32 (FIGURE 3B). This stands in contrast to the large degree of nonreceptor binding seen with this compound prior to purification (see FIGURE 2). (The profiles of free [^{3}H]-3-azidohexestrol both before and after photolysis in the absence of protein are shown in FIGURE 3A; there are no peaks in the receptor region.)

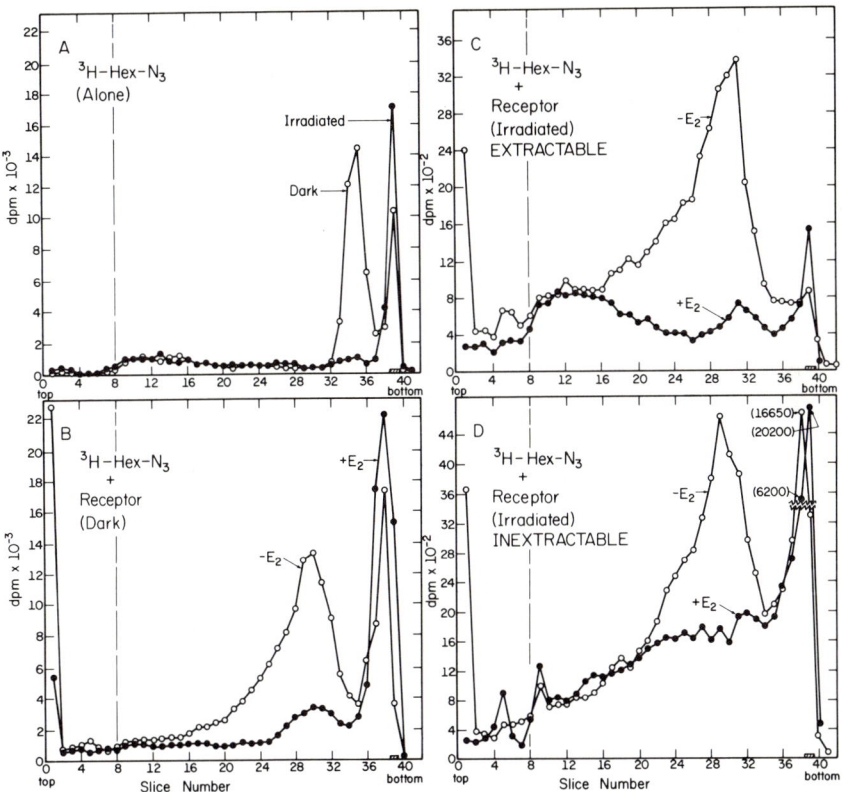

FIGURE 3. Polyacrylamide gel electrophoresis of [^{3}H]-3-azidohexestrol. FIGURE 3A shows the electrophoretic profile of [^{3}H]3-azidohexestrol before (○) and after (●) irradiation in the absence of protein. FIGURES 3B, 3C, and 3D are electrophoretic profiles of partially purified lamb uterine receptor preparations incubated with 4.3 nM [^{3}H]-3-azidohexestrol in the absence (○) and presence (●) of a 1000-fold excess of unlabeled estradiol. Samples for FIGURES 3C and 3D were irradiated for 5 min at 254 nm before electrophoresis. The radioactivity extractable with toluene (FIGURE 3C) represents [^{3}H]-3-azidohexestrol that is not covalently attached to the protein, while the inextractable radioactivity (FIGURE 3D) may indicate covalent binding.

A simple solvent extraction procedure was devised to follow the progress of covalent attachment of photosensitive estrogens to proteins by polyacrylamide gel electrophoresis.[9] Slices of gels, as normally prepared for scintillation counting, are preincubated in a small volume of toluene for two hours at room temperature. This quantitatively extracts from the gel slice those small organic molecules that are only reversibly bound to protein, but those that are covalently attached remain with the protein in the aqueous fraction (gel slice). After the extraction period, the gel slice (inextractable fraction—covalently attached) is removed and counted separately from the organic phase (extractable fraction—reversibly bound). In this manner, two profiles—one for reversibly bound and the other for covalently bound radioactivity—can be obtained from a single electrophoresis.

If the lamb uterine estrogen receptor complex with [³H]-3-azidohexestrol is kept in the dark prior to and during electrophoresis, all the radioactivity associated with the receptor region is solvent-extractable (FIGURE 3B). If the complex is photolyzed prior to gel separation, however, nearly half of the radioactivity that migrates in the receptor region is no longer solvent-extractable and thus appears to be covalently bound; the extractable fraction is shown in FIGURE 3C, and the inextractable fraction in FIGURE 3D. The estrogen specificity of the attachment process is ascertained by a parallel experiment in which attachment to the receptor is blocked by preincubation with an excess of unlabeled estradiol. As an additional control, [³H]-3-azidohexestrol was irradiated alone and then added to the receptor preparation and electrophoresed; no radioactivity at all was found in the receptor region of the gel (data not shown), indicating that the photoproducts have no affinity at all for the receptor.

Simple calculations show that the quantity of radioactivity in the receptor region of the gel that is nonextractable after photolysis corresponds to approximately 15–20% of the material bound at the time of photolysis. This is the maximum incorporation that would be expected on the basis of the 15% inactivation efficiency of 3-azidohexestrol.

Some additional experiments have been done with the lamb uterine receptor covalently labeled with [³H]-3-azidohexestrol. Radioactivity in the receptor region of the gel can be extracted efficiently with aqueous buffers. This activity is protein-associated, as is shown by its coprecipitation with protein upon treatment with hot trichloroacetic acid and boiling ethanol.

CONCLUSION

Photoaffinity labeling of estrogen receptors, particularly if applied in intact preparations, demands both high binding selectivity and high labeling efficiency of the photoreactive hormone analog. We have developed a rational method for assessing the potential of photosensitive estrogens as receptor photoaffinity labeling agents. Preliminary studies can be done on unlabeled candidate compounds to determine their affinity for the receptor and their capacity for site-specific photoinactivation of the receptor. On the basis of these preliminary results, compounds were selected for preparation in carrier-free, tritium-labeled form and were then investigated directly in terms of their binding selectivity and covalent attachment efficiency and selectivity. Of the compounds that have been fully investigated, 3-azidohexestrol is the most promising; it has high affinity for the receptor, although its interaction with nonreceptor proteins is elevated to the point of making selective labeling in intact systems impractical. Nevertheless, covalent attachment of the receptor can be demonstrated in partially purified preparations with an efficiency that corresponds to that estimated from its inactivation activity. Further refinements in ligand structure and photoattaching functions should lead to reagents with both higher binding selectivity and attachment efficiency that will prove to be valuable in photoaffinity labeling studies of intact, hormone-responsive systems. In this regard, the estrogen analogs incorporating the photoreactive *m*-nitroanisole function appear particularly interesting.

ACKNOWLEDGMENTS

We are grateful for the contributions of Drs. Harvey N. Myers, Howard J. Johnson, Jr., Robert J. Kempton, Robert J. McGorrin, Jr., Richard L. Neeley, and Donna W. Payne to the work described in this report. John A. Katzenellenbogen is a Camille and Henry Dreyfus Teacher-Scholar.

REFERENCES

1. For a review, see: GORSKI, J. & F. GANNON. 1976. Annu. Rev. Physiol. **38**: 425–50.
2. KATZENELLENBOGEN, J. A. 1977. *In* Biochemical Actions of Hormones, Vol. 4. G. Litwack, Ed.: 1–84. Academic Press. New York.
3. For a review, see: KATZENELLENBOGEN, J. A., H. J. JOHNSON, JR., H. N. MYERS, K. E. CARLSON & R. J. KEMPTON. 1978. *In* Bioorganic Chemistry, Vol. 4. E. E. van Tamelen, Ed.: 207–37. Academic Press. New York.
4. KATZENELLENBOGEN, J. A., H. N. MYERS & H. J. JOHNSON, JR. 1973. J. Org. Chem. **38**: 3525–33.
5. KATZENELLENBOGEN, J. A., H. J. JOHNSON, JR. & H. N. MYERS. 1973. Biochemistry **12**: 4085–92.
6. KATZENELLENBOGEN, J. A., H. J. JOHNSON, JR. & K. E. CARLSON. 1973. Biochemistry **12**: 4092–99.
7. KATZENELLENBOGEN, J. A., H. J. JOHNSON, JR., K. E. CARLSON & H. N. MYERS. 1974. Biochemistry **13**: 2896–94.
8. KATZENELLENBOGEN, J. A., H. N. MYERS, H. J. JOHNSON, JR., R. J. KEMPTON & K. E. CARLSON. 1977. Biochemistry **16**: 1964–70.
9. KATZENELLENBOGEN, J. A., K. E. CARLSON, H. J. JOHNSON, JR. & H. N. MYERS. 1977. Biochemistry **16**: 1970–76.
10. GALARDY, R. E., L. C. CRAIG, J. D. JAMIESON & M. P. PRINTZ. 1974. J. Biol. Chem. **249**: 3510–18.
11. MARTYR, R. J. & W. F. BENISEK. 1973. Biochemistry **12**: 2172–78.
12. BODENBERGER, A. & H. DANNENBERG. 1971. Chem. Ber. **104**: 2389–94.
13. NEELEY, R. J. 1977. Ph.D. Thesis, University of Illinois. Urbana, Illinois.
14. CORNELISSE, J. & E. HAVINGA. 1975. Chem. Rev. **75**: 353–88.
15. CORNELISSE, J., G. P. DE GUNST & E. HAVINGA. 1975. Adv. Phys. Org. Chem. **11**: 225–66.
16. JELENC, P. C., C. R. CANTOR & S. R. SIMON. 1978. Proc. Nat. Acad. Sci. USA **75**: 3564–68.
17. CARLSON, K. E., L-H. K. SUN & J. A. KATZENELLENBOGEN. 1977. Biochemistry **16**: 4288–96.

DISCUSSION

DR. J. KALLOS *(Hospital for Joint Diseases):* I would like to ask you whether you have any idea what the mechanism of receptor inactivation by 6-oxoestradiol is.

DR. J. A. KATZENELLENBOGEN: While we haven't looked at this in great detail, we believe that the receptor is inactivated by a photoredox process: the photoexcited ketone abstracts a hydrogen atom from the receptor. This is, essentially, an oxidative event that results in the destruction of the receptor's ability to bind the ligand. Thus, the receptor is inactivated but the ligand is not covalently bound. This theory predicts that the ligand would be reduced, but, so far, we have not investigated the nature of the photoproducts of 6-oxoestradiol under these conditions.

DR. F. H. WESTHEIMER *(Harvard University):* I think the progress that Dr. Katzenellenbogen has made is heartwarming. The final problem is, however, even more difficult than he admits. In their native state, many receptors are membrane-bound, and photolabeling reagents dissolve in the membrane, causing all sorts of difficulties. We have been trying to photolabel the dopamine receptor site and have experienced great difficulties with the problem of reagent solubility in the membrane.

KATZENELLENBOGEN: That's a very good point. There are many receptors for drugs, neurotransmitters, and protein hormones that are membrane bound. However, most work that has been done on steroid receptors and receptors for thyroid hormones has shown these receptors to be intracellular. While there are a few experiments that indicate that there may be binding sites for steroids on cell surfaces, I think the major receptor activity of steroids and thyroid hormones is going to be with cytoplasmic proteins. The labeling of membrane receptors is, perhaps, a still greater challenge.

DR. V. CHOWDHRY *(DuPont):* In the steroid series, I wonder whether the higher covalent attachment you observe with the 16-diazocompound, as compared to the A-ring compounds, is due to a higher level of nonspecific attachment, since this compound does not have a 17-hydroxyl group. Perhaps labeling with A-ring derivatives, though lower, is more specific.

KATZENELLENBOGEN: I want to re-emphasize the fact that those data were inactivation efficiencies, not covalent attachment efficiencies. We were measuring the extent to which the receptor is inactivated by photolysis in the presence of an unlabeled estrogen derivative, and we were measuring the survival of the sites by exchange with tritium-labeled estradiol subsequent to the photolysis. Thus, by this assay, we have no measure of the selectivity with which either the A-ring or the D-ring derivatives are affecting covalent attachment; such studies require tritium-labeled derivatives. However, because of the controls that are built into the inactivation assay method, we do know that the inactivation we are seeing is due to the destruction of the binding site by photolysis of a compound bound at that site. To get at the information you are interested in, we would need these compounds in tritium-labeled form, but since these steroid derivatives bind with such low affinity, we did not think that it would be fruitful to pursue them further.

CHOWDHRY: The 16-diazocompound, which gives a 21% inactivation efficiency, could be reacting by two processes, the carbene and the less reactive epoxide.

KATZENELLENBOGEN: That's certainly possible.

CHOWDHRY: Have you gone back and reinvestigated the diazoacetyl estrogens? You said these were hydrolytically unstable in your unpurified system, but they might be more stable in your purified system because α-diazoesters, particularly unsubstituted ones, are indeed more stable toward hydrolysis than esters.

KATZENELLENBOGEN: That is a good suggestion. Actually, while the 3-diazoacetates are labile phenolic esters, the 17-diazoacetate is reasonably hydrolytically stable;

it is a pretty good inactivator in the 15 to 20% range, but its binding affinity is relatively low.

DR. F. SWEET *(Washington University School of Medicine)*: When you have affinity labeling steroids of either the photochemical type or the electrophilic type in a heterogeneous system, the protein you want to label is in a mixture with many other proteins. These nonspecific proteins can give you nonspecific covalent labeling and deplete your reagents. Can you comment on how you get around these problems?

KATZENELLENBOGEN: Well, first of all, I think that the depletion of reagent by nonreceptor proteins is probably a process that is more serious with electrophilic affinity labeling reagents than photoaffinity labeling, since, in the former case, you may have a derivative that is a good electrophile and may be efficiently scavenged by any contaminating sulfhydryl compound, such as glutathione.

I am not so worried about the photoaffinity labels in terms of consumption of the agent by nonreceptor proteins, because these compounds are not reactive in the dark. Prior to photolysis, these agents are in reversible equilibrium with the desired and undesired (nonspecific) sites; upon photolysis, at least in the receptor systems, there is very little redistribution of ligand during the time of irradiation, because that takes just a few minutes, while dissociation, at least from the sites of interest, takes hours under the conditions we operate at.

Now the labeling of other (nonreceptor) proteins is, of course, a major problem, but it is one that we have dealt with by partial purification and further refinement of our reagents.

DR. B. FORBUSH, III *(Yale University School of Medicine and Physiology)*: I wonder if you have studied any of your compounds that have high binding specificity but low inactivation efficiency in the hopes that they would, perhaps, be equally inefficient in labeling the nonspecific background.

KATZENELLENBOGEN: Which compound are you referring to?

FORBUSH: None in particular. You pointed out that you always prepared tritium-labeled derivatives of the compounds with high inactivation efficiency, but these are ones that often may have a lot of nonspecific labeling. I wonder if there are any that have very high binding specificity and affinity, which, though they have a low labeling efficiency, may still label selectively?

KATZENELLENBOGEN: That is a good point, and one that we haven't fully pursued. We are looking at the question of binding selectivity in great detail, however, in connection with another project in which we are trying to make γ-emitting estrogen derivatives to image human breast tumors. In this case, binding specificity is even more critical than in affinity labeling. Recent studies we have done have encouraged us to look at some estriol derivatives because they are more hydrophilic and thus may prove to be more selective in their interaction with receptors in heterogeneous binding systems.

DR. H. BAYLEY *(Massachusetts Institute of Technology)*: We found that dithiols reduce azides. Since you have very tight binding sites in your experiments, I wonder if it would be possible to use dithiols to reduce the azides outside the binding site before photolysis and thus eliminate the nonspecific labeling you encounter?

KATZENELLENBOGEN: That is a very good suggestion. We will try it.

DR. D. BRADLE *(University of Florida)*: Are you aware of any studies that have been done on steroid receptor sites in plants or attempts to use this technique to study the function of steroids in plants?

KATZENELLENBOGEN: I am not aware of any studies on steroid receptors in plants. People have tried to make derivatives to label auxin binding sites in plants, but it is my impression that it is actually very difficult even to demonstrate the existence of these sites by reversible binding measurements. I think the studies have not progressed very far in terms of actual photoaffinity-labeling of these sites.

UNIDENTIFIED SPEAKER: In your experiments in which you saw receptor inactivation but no covalent attachment, have you considered whether the label might be exchanging with solvent? If this occurs, you may be binding but be unable to see your label.

KATZENELLENBOGEN: I think that is a possibility, but an unlikely one. We have seen inactivation without attachment in two cases with compounds labeled in multiple sites. With the 6-oxoestradiol, tritium labels were at positions 2 and 4, and with hexestrol diazoketopropyl ether, labels were at four positions in the hexane chain. There may be some exchange of the label with solvent protons during the experiment, but I am certain that it is not extensive enough to cause a complete loss of the label.

DIRECT PHOTOAFFINITY LABELING OF PHOSPHOFRUCTOKINASE USING ADENOSINE DERIVATIVES *

James J. Ferguson, Jr. and Mark MacInnes

Department of Biochemistry/Biophysics
University of Pennsylvania School of Medicine
Philadelphia, Pennsylvania 19104

INTRODUCTION

We have been concerned with reactions between cyclic nucleotides and cytoplasmic receptor proteins that recognize and interact with these biologically important effector molecules. In 1974, we reported[1] that ultraviolet (uv) irradiation of testicular cyclic nucleotide binding proteins in the presence of radioactive cyclic 3′,5′-adenosine monophosphate (cAMP) or cyclic 3′,5′-guanosine monophosphate (cGMP) results in a time-dependent incorporation of the isotope into the binding proteins. We gave evidence for the specificity of this reaction, both in terms of the protein and cyclic nucleotide involved. We also demonstrated that the cyclic nucleotide molecule was incorporated intact, as evidenced by the fact that [8-^{3}H]cAMP, [U-^{14}C-adenine]cAMP and [^{32}P]cAMP were equally effective as labels. Incorporation of both cAMP and cGMP was found to be a saturable process, with half-maximal incorporation occurring at a ligand concentration comparable to the dissociation constants of these compounds and the regulatory subunits of cyclic nucleotide responsive protein kinases. Action spectra of the reactions indicated that peak photoincorporation occurred at a wavelength of 280 nm on irradiation with either cAMP or cGMP.[2] Ability to photoincorporate these ligands paralleled the measured noncovalent binding capacity for the ligands in a number of tissues studied.[3]

We here describe a similar photoincorporation reaction using labeled cAMP, adenosine monophosphate (AMP), and adenosine diphosphate (ADP) as probe ligands, and the enzyme phosphofructokinase (PFK) as the "receptor protein."

Skeletal muscle phosphofructokinase is a well-characterized enzyme that normally exists as a tetrameric molecule. Its monomeric subunits, each with a molecular weight of about 90,000 daltons, are catalytically active. They are inhibited by adenosine triphosphate (ATP), one of the substrates of the reaction catalyzed by the enzyme. This inhibition is released in the presence of AMP, ADP, or cAMP, each of which presumably competes for binding at the site at which ATP binding causes inhibition. The kinetics of noncovalent binding of each of these ligands to PFK has been well characterized.[4] The known high affinity between cAMP and PFK ($K_d \sim 1\ \mu M$), as well as the commercial availability of the purified enzyme, prompted us to evaluate PFK as a model "binding protein" in our studies on direct photoaffinity labeling using these adenosine derivatives as ligands. Brunswick and Cooperman used PFK for

*This research was supported by the National Institutes of Health, grant no. 5 R01 HD 05507.

31

affinity labeling studies with the photoactivatable cAMP derivative $O^{2'}$-(ethyl-2-diazomalonyl) cAMP.[30]

MATERIALS AND METHODS

The incorporation of labeled ligands into PFK was estimated by measuring radioactivity in washed trichloroacetic precipitates of uv-irradiated reaction mixtures.[5] All incubations were carried out at least in duplicate, the values of which varied by no more than 10% of their mean. Irradiations were performed in either phosphate or glycylglycine buffer at pH 7.0 in a volume of 1 ml. Reaction mixtures were contained in 10 ml beakers suspended in a Dewar flask in which temperature could be maintained at 0 °C (ice in water) or at lower temperatures (dry ice in ethanol). The assembly was slowly rotated, with the solutions positioned 13 cm directly beneath a stationary Mineralite R-52 uv light source, in order to produce equivalent irradiation to each sample. This lamp emitted predominantly at 254 nm, with an intensity of about 0.6 mW/cm^2 in this configuration, measured on a J-260 Digital Radiometer (Ultra-Violet Products, Inc. San Gabriel, California). Light-shielded controls were always assayed and subtracted from experimental values. Variations from this procedure are indicated in the text. Noncovalent binding of radioactive ligands to PFK was evaluated by the centrifugation method of Hayes and Velick,[6] with overnight sedimentation of the enzyme through 5 μM cAMP in a Beckman SW 56Ti swinging bucket rotor spinning at 28,000 rpm. Enzymatic activity was completely sedimented under these conditions. Catalytic activity of PFK was assayed at pH 8 at room temperature using the method of Bergmeyer.[7]

[8-^{3}H]cAMP was purchased from Amersham, with a stated radioactivity of 28 Ci/mmol. [^{32}P]cAMP was purchased from the New England Nuclear Corp. [8-^{3}H]AMP, [8-^{3}H]ADP and [8-^{3}H]ATP were Amersham products. Ethanol solvent was evaporated from these ligands just prior to irradiation. Nonradioactive ligands were purchased from Sigma. Rabbit muscle PFK (EC 2.7.1.11, i.e., ATP: D-fructose-6-phosphate-1-phosphotransferase) was purchased in several batches from Sigma. It was routinely treated with charcoal before use, in order to remove the ATP used as stabilizer.[8] Bovine serum albumin was purchased from Sigma; whale myoglobin was a product of Miles Laboratories, Inc.

RESULTS

FIGURE 1 illustrates the time course of incorporation when irradiation was performed at 0 °C using PFK at 0.1 mg/ml and cAMP at a concentration of 0.2 μM. Incorporation was typically linear for about 40 min. FIGURE 2 illustrates the elution pattern obtained on gel filtration (Sephadex G-25) of the reaction product in buffer containing 0.03% sodium dodecycl sulfate. Rechromatography of the radioactive protein peak in the same solution on Biogel A-1.5 showed it to elute with an apparent molecular weight in the range of 90,000 daltons. Disc gel electrophoresis of the reaction product in sodium dodecyl sulfate/mercaptoethanol likewise revealed radioactivity to be congruent with a protein monomer of this size.

On irradiating cAMP in the presence of boiled PFK, Pronase-digested PFK, bovine serum albumin, or whale myoglobin, no incorporation into protein could be demonstrated. Incorporation of cAMP was directly proportional to PFK concentrations up to about 0.1 mg/ml in reaction mixtures. A decrease in specific incorporation was noted above this protein concentration, probably resulting from the filtering effects of uv-absorbing materials, which prevent incident light from reaching the reactive chromophore.[9] [3H]cAMP and [32P]cAMP incorporated at identical rates when irradiated at equal concentrations. When the ligand and protein reactants were rapidly mixed after separate irradiation, no incorporation could be demonstrated. [3H]cGMP at concentrations up to 1 μM did not photoincorporate into PFK.

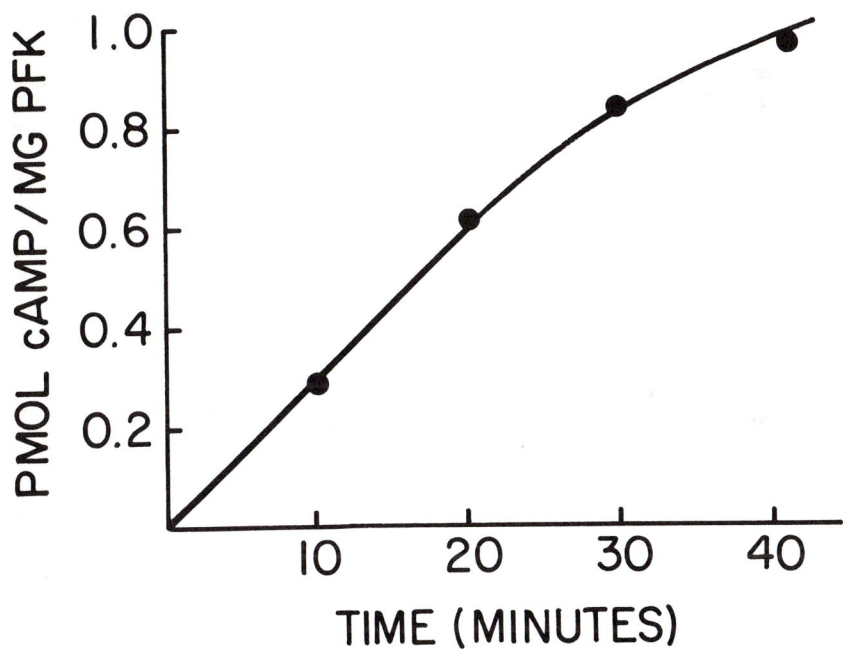

FIGURE 1. Incorporation of [3H]cAMP into PFK. PFK (0.5 mg/ml) was irradiated in the presence of 0.2 μM cAMP at a fluence of 0.5 mW/cm^2, and samples were removed at the indicated times for an assay of isotope incorporation into protein.

The action spectrum of photoincorporation of [3H]cAMP into PFK is illustrated in FIGURE 3. These studies were performed using a xenon light source and an Oriel Model #7320 monochromator. Slits were adjusted to provide a 2 nm band pass. Reaction mixtures were contained in a quartz cuvette with a 1 cm light path, and the entire solution was irradiated. The cuvette was chilled to 11 °C in a cooled aluminum block. Samples were irradiated for 30 min. Ferrioxalate actinometry[10] in identical cuvettes permitted calculation of the incident light at the indicated wavelengths. Based on the optical density of the irradiated solutions, a correction was made for the filtering effect of uv-absorbing components.[9] At least four measurements were made

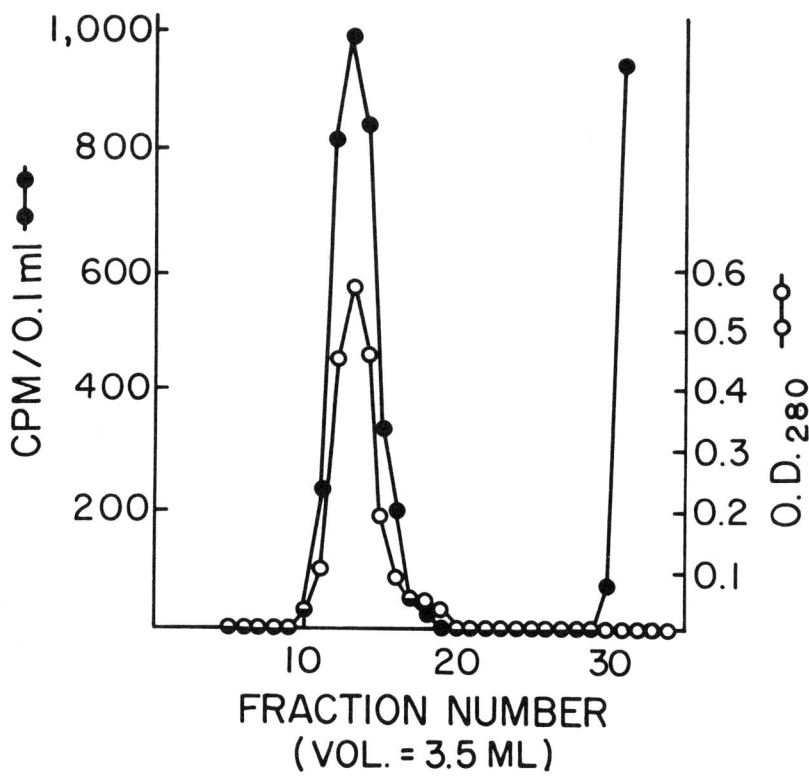

FIGURE 2. Gel filtration of labeled PFK. PFK (2.2 mg) in 5 ml buffer was irradiated for 20 min in the presence of 0.4 μM cAMP. The reaction mixture was made 0.1% (w/v) in sodium dodecyl sulfate, applied to a 2.5 cm × 35 cm Sephadex G-25 column, and eluted with a sodium phosphate buffer (pH 7.2) containing 0.03% detergent.

at each wavelength. The data recorded indicate peak incorporation at 255 nm, with a curve nearly coincident with the absorption spectrum of cAMP, and distinctly different from that of PFK. This curve is also clearly different from the action spectra of cAMP and cGMP photoincorporation into testis cyclic nucleotide binding protein, both of which showed peaks at about 280 nm.[2]

The kinetics of photoincorporation into PFK were evaluated as a function of total cAMP concentration. These studies were performed by varying the amount of radioactive cAMP added and by adding varying amounts of nonradioactive cAMP to a constant amount of radioactive cAMP. (This precaution was taken to ensure that the photoincorporated molecule was in fact cAMP and not a radioactive contaminant. Such proved to be the case when [8-³H] adenine was used as the probe ligand.) The results were identical, and representative data from one experiment are illustrated in FIGURE 4 in double reciprocal form. From this graph, we estimate that half-maximal incorporation occurred at a total ligand concentration of approximately 4 μM, a figure not greatly different from the K_d of 0.6 μM found by Kemp and Krebs,[4] and the

1.6 μM reported by Parmeggiani, *et al.*,[8] both under somewhat different conditions. We can further calculate that maximal photoincorporation occurred at a rate of about 0.5 pmol/min/mg PFK under our conditions of irradiation. From this figure, we can estimate that 0.005% of available binding sites (1 per 90,000 daltons) were covalently filled per minute of irradiation at this intensity.

TABLE 1 shows the effects of adding unlabeled ATP, ADP, and AMP to irradiated mixtures containing radioactive cAMP. Also shown are reciprocal experiments in which unlabeled cAMP was added in the presence of labeled ADP and AMP. It can be concluded that ADP and AMP are efficiently photoincorporated into a site that also recognizes cAMP. This is compatible with the known affinity of these ligands for PFK.[4] The failure of ATP to incorporate into PFK or to compete for cAMP incorporation was surprising and remains unexplained. Under these conditions of irradiation, 1.0 mM citrate, 0.1 mM fructose-6-phosphate, and 0.1 mM fructose-1,6-diphosphate did not affect incorporation of cAMP.

Photoincorporation of radioactive ADP and AMP were measured at varying ligand concentrations (data not shown). In each instance, the rate of incorporation was

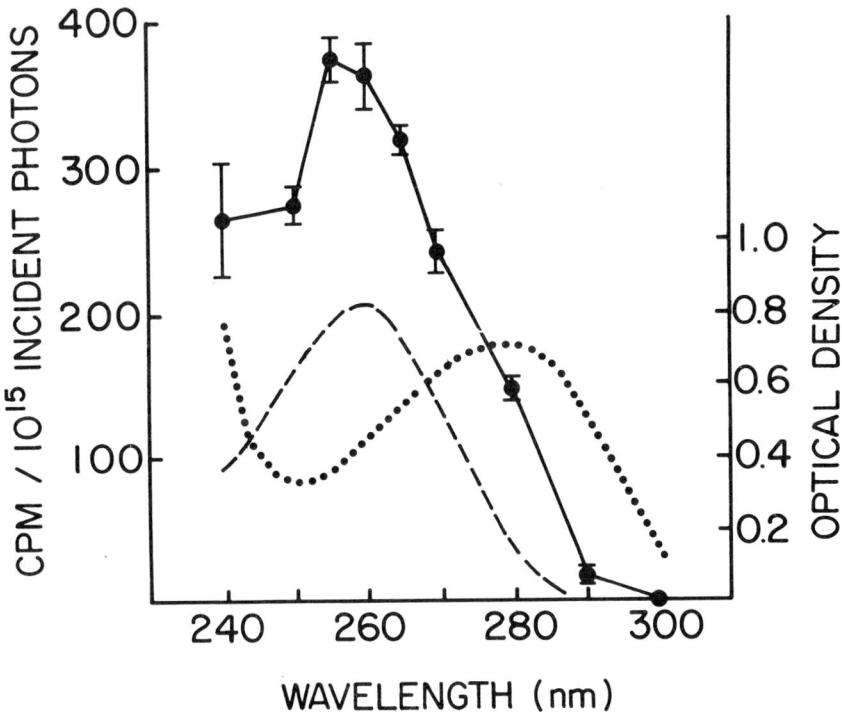

FIGURE 3. Action spectrum of [³H]cAMP incorporation into PFK. PFK (0.26 mg/ml) was irradiated 20 min at varying wavelengths in the presence of 1.67 μM [³H]cAMP at 11 °C. See text for details. ——●—●——: photoincorporation; ——: OD of cAMP; · · · · ·: OD of reaction mixture.

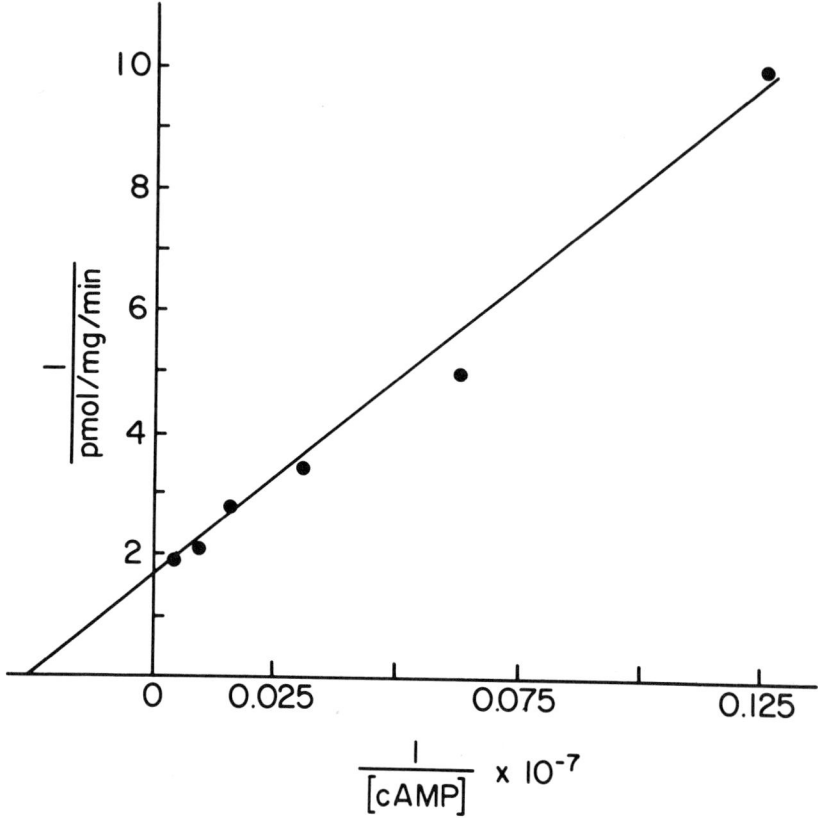

FIGURE 4. Concentration dependence of [³H]cAMP photoincorporation. PFK (0.05 mg/ml) was incubated 20 min at 0 °C in the presence of [³H]cAMP (0.2 μM), to which were added varying concentrations of unlabeled cAMP.

TABLE 1

NUCLEOTIDE INCORPORATION INTO PFK

Radioactive Ligand	Nonradioactive Ligand	Photoincorporation (pmol/mg/min)
[³H]cAMP (0.167 μM)	—	.093
[³H]cAMP (0.167 μM)	AMP (15 μM)	.027
[³H]cAMP (0.167 μM)	ADP (15 μM)	.025
[³H]cAMP (0.167 μM)	ATP (5 μM)	.086
[³H]AMP (0.20 μM)	—	.028
[³H]AMP (0.20 μM)	cAMP (15 μM)	.002
[³H]AMP (0.20 μM)	ADP (5 μM)	.003
[³H]ADP (0.26 μM)	—	.052
[³H]ADP (0.26 μM)	cAMP (10 μM)	.002
[³H]ATP (2 μM)	—	.001

half-maximum in the range from 1 to 4 μM total ligand concentration. This range of concentration also produced half-maximal incorporation when PFK and radioactive cAMP, ADP, or AMP were irradiated in the frozen state (see below).

If we assume that the adenine nucleotide is the light-responsive chromophore, and that its concentration during irradiation is sufficient to produce incorporation at the maximal rate, the minimal quantum yield of product formation can be calculated to be

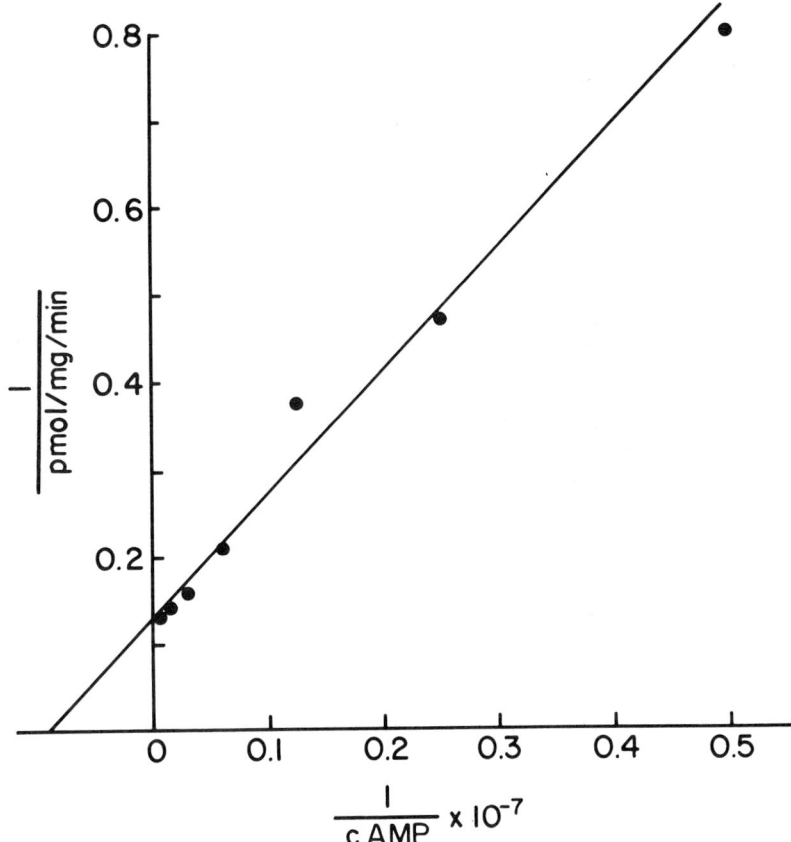

FIGURE 5. Concentration dependence of [³H]cAMP photoincorporation in the frozen state. Conditions as in FIGURE 4, except that irradiation was performed at −77 °C.

approximately 0.0001. Since there are multiple nonphotochemical determinants of the rate of photoincorporation in this system and we are not yet certain that we have kinetically optimized the reaction, it should be emphasized that the true quantum yield of the reaction may be considerably higher than this figure.

We have evaluated several variables that might be expected to alter the rate of ligand photoincorporation into PFK. Deoxygenation (accomplished by adding glucose,

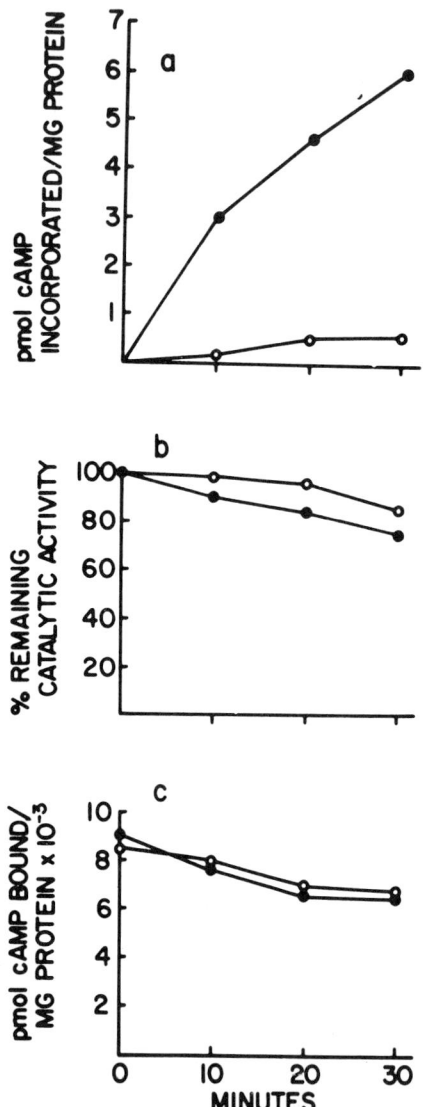

FIGURE 6. Irradiation effects at 0 °C and −77 °C. PFK (0.5 mg/ml) and 0.2 μM [³H]cAMP were irradiated at either 0 °C (—o—o—) or −77 °C (—•—•—). Samples were removed at the indicated times and assayed for isotope incorporation (top), catalytic activity (middle), and noncovalent binding (bottom).

glucose oxidase, and catalase, with irradiation under argon) had no effect on the rate of photoincorporation. Likewise, addition of 5 m*M* mercaptoethanol or 1 m*M* dithiothreitol had no effect. Incorporation was comparable in tris and phosphate buffers, with optimal incorporation at approximately pH 7.0. The presence of 10 m*M* ethanol had no effect on incorporation in the standard aqueous-state irradiation (see below). Temperature was not an important variable when irradiations were performed between 1 °C and 25 °C. However, irradiation in the frozen state dramatically increased the efficiency of incorporation of each of the three ligands into PFK.

Our studies at subzero temperatures stemmed from the observations of Wang[11] and Beukers and Berends,[12] who demonstrated the heightened reactivity of pyrimidines irradiated in the frozen state. We have found that incorporation of labeled cAMP, ADP, and AMP into PFK can be enhanced up to forty-fold if the reaction mixture is irradiated while frozen.[13] The characteristics of this increased incorporation were, in general, qualitatively similar to those seen in the aqueous state. As was the case at 0 °C, each nucleotide competed for incorporation of the others. ATP was again found to be inert both as labeling and as competing ligand. FIGURE 5 illustrates the kinetics of incorporation of varying concentrations of cAMP in the frozen state. A total ligand concentration of about 1 μM produced half-maximal incorporation of both AMP and ADP in ice. Deoxygenation had no effect on incorporation in the frozen state. Of interest was the *lack* of effect of freezing on the rate of PFK photodestruction when irradiation was carried out in ice. The catalytic activity and the noncovalent binding capacity of PFK were measured during the course of uv irradiation in both the aqueous (0 °C) and frozen (−77 °C) state, as illustrated in FIGURE 6. While freezing greatly enhanced the rate of photoincorporation, changes in these two parameters, which reflected the structural integrity of the protein, were unaltered by irradiation while frozen. Frozen-state irradiation did not result in incorporation into boiled PFK, whale myoglobin, or bovine serum albumin. Irradiation in ice equally enhanced both [³H]cAMP and [³²P]cAMP incorporation into PFK, indicating that the phenomenon involves the complete ligand molecule. The presence of ethanol (10 mM) inhibited frozen-state enhancement by more than 50%.

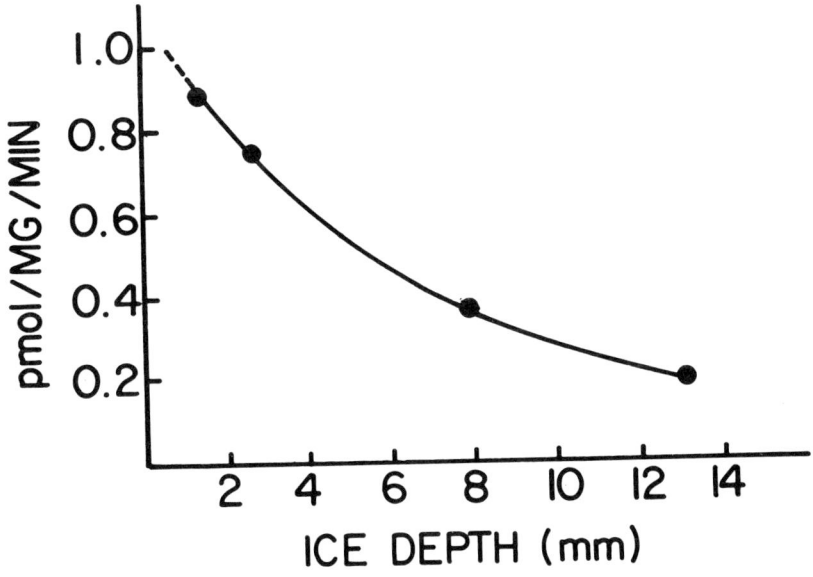

FIGURE 7. Photoincorporation at varying ice depths. PFK (0.05 mg/ml) and 0.16 μM [³H]cAMP were frozen and irradiated for 20 min in varying volumes in 10 ml beakers.

The depth of the frozen solutions affected the rate of incorporation, as shown in FIGURE 7. Preliminary studies on the effect of temperature of photoincorporation in ice suggest a discontinuity in temperature dependence. The results of two such experiments are illustrated in FIGURE 8.

We have carried out pilot studies to evaluate the use of direct photoaffinity labeling as a means to study the primary structure at the adenine nucleotide binding site of PFK. To this end we have isolated and characterized cyanogen bromide fragments of the enzyme after direct photoaffinity labeling. PFK, labeled with [³H]cAMP while frozen, was separated from excess free ligand by gel filtration (Sephadex G-25) in the presence of 0.03% sodium dodecyl sulfate. The labeled protein was treated with iodoacetamide[14] and chromatographed on Biogel A-1.5, where it eluted in the volume predicted for a molecule with a molecular weight of about 90,000 daltons. This labeled protein was subjected to reaction with cyanogen bromide[15] to cleave at methionine residues, and was again chromatographed on Biogel A-1.5 in sodium dodecyl sulfate. Radioactivity eluted almost exclusively in a peptide peak having a molecular weight of about 14,000 daltons. These elution patterns are illustrated in FIGURE 9. This labeled peptide has not yet been characterized further. These observations are compatible with the conclusion that a single circumscribed region on the PFK monomer is labeled in this process. This conclusion can, of course, only be validated by further exhaustive degradation of the labeled peptide and identification of the involved amino acids.

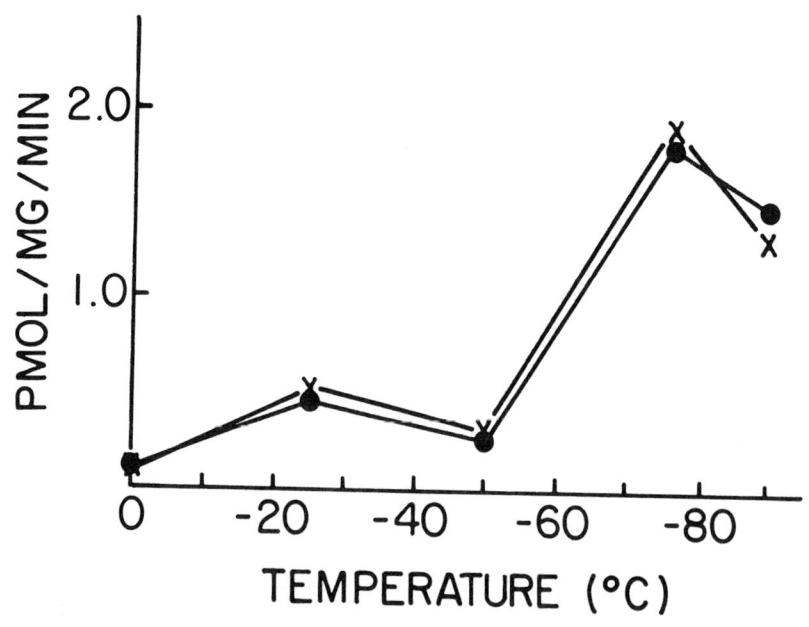

FIGURE 8. Photoincorporation as a function of ice temperature. PFK (0.07 mg/ml) and 0.16 μM [³H]cAMP were irradiated 20 min. A temperature of 0 °C was obtained in a water-ice bath; −25 °C, −50 °C, and −77 °C were obtained in dry ice–ethanol; −90 °C was obtained with liquid nitrogen–acetone.

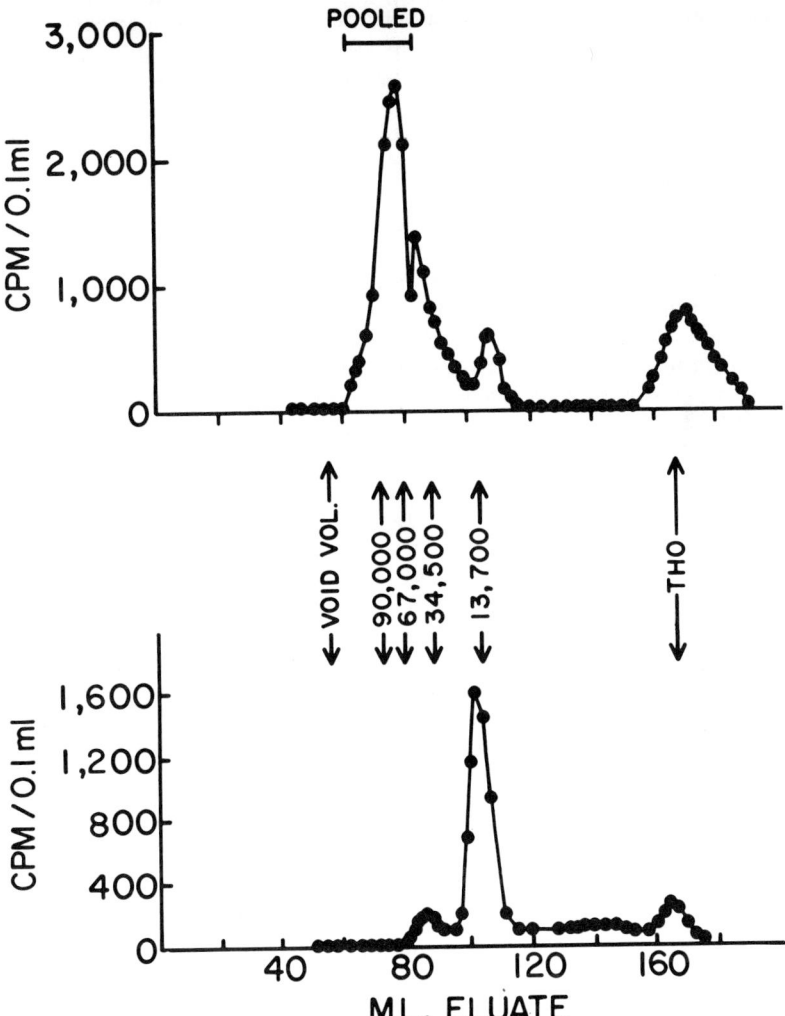

FIGURE 9. PFK peptide labeling by [³H]cAMP. See text for details. Chromatography performed on Biogel A-1.5 in buffered 0.05 *M* sodium phosphate containing 0.03% sodium dodecyl sulfate.

DISCUSSION

The nature of the photochemical reaction we have described is not yet established. The shape of the action spectrum of incorporation suggests that the adenine portion of the nucleotide is the light-responsive chromophore, but this interpretation is debatable. We do not yet know the chemical structure at the site of attachment of adenine nucleotides to PFK, though this information should be accessible when we degrade the labeled enzyme to the di- or tri-peptide level and subject the product to mass spectroscopy. We can, with reasonable confidence, eliminate the adenine C-8 as the point of attachment, since tritium attached to this carbon is retained during incorporation. This suggests that photocoupling of nucleotides to protein may be inherently different from the light-induced reaction of purine derivatives with alcohols,[16] amines,[17] and amino acids,[18] all of which are thought to involve covalent coupling at C-8.

Enhancement of incorporation in the frozen state is an interesting and potentially useful phenomenon, but its mechanism, too, is not yet explained. Freezing is known to produce aggregates of pyrimidine and purine solutes,[19] and this aggregation is thought to contribute to enhanced reactivity. Aggregate formation is known to be inhibited by the presence of ethanol,[20] and this may explain the observed inhibitory effect of ethanol. Chemical reactivity is known to be increased in the frozen state in several systems.[21,22] Likewise, certain uv-related phenomena *in vivo* are known to be enhanced in ice. Hill and Rossi[23] first described the increased sensitivity to uv light demonstrable in frozen bacteriophage. Irradiation in the frozen state is known to increase both the mutagenic[24] and lethal[25] effects of uv light on *E. coli, B. subtilis,* and other microorganisms. Smith and O'Leary[26] have shown that the rate of formation of cyclobutane-type pyrimidine dimers in *E. coli* exposed to uv light actually *decreased* at subzero temperatures, as did the production of photoreactivatable damage. In these studies, though, the formation of DNA-to-protein linkages did correlate with increased sensitivity to uv irradiation. We believe that nucleotide-protein interactions, analogous to those here described, may in part explain this phenomenon.

We suspect that frozen-state irradiation may enhance reactions like the protein-nucleotide coupling, which has been described between ATP and isoleucine-tRNA synthetase in Schimmel's laboratory[27] and between uridine 2' (3'),5'-diphosphate and RNase reported by Sperling's group.[28]

It is yet to be determined if, in the intact eukaryotic cell, ligands like nucleotides can be induced to react covalently with biologically important receptor proteins when irradiated with uv light.

The measured efficiency of uv-induced covalent reactions between PFK and biological effector nucleotides is clearly not great, as estimated by traditional quantum yield calculations. However, the considerable enhancement of reactivity that can be induced by an environmental modification such as freezing emphasizes the fact that a determination of quantum yield may in no way reflect reactivity in a different set of circumstances.

The degree of ligand incorporation into receptor sites on PFK and on cyclic nucleotide receptor proteins, while limited, should be adequate for analysis of the primary structure of these binding sites. In fact, the low reactivity of these nonderivatized affinity labels may be advantageous when they are compared to the more highly reactive conventional photoactivated derivatives, i.e. nitrenes and carbenes. These latter, because of their great chemical reactivity, may be less selective in their attachment sites, and, consequently, label binding peptides at multiple loci. Fine-structure analysis of proteins labeled by nonderivatized ligands and by photoactivated ligands will resolve this question. The use of electrophilic affinity labels for PFK has been described,[29] and this approach should prove valuable, not only for the comparative data it will provide, but for its intrinsic analytical properties, as well.

ACKNOWLEDGMENT

The authors acknowledge the excellent technical assistance of Mrs. Barbara Uschmann.

REFERENCES

1. ANTONOFF, R. S. & J. J. FERGUSON, JR. 1974. J. Biol. Chem. **249:** 3319–21.
2. ANTONOFF, R. S. & J. J. FERGUSON, JR. 1978. Photochem. Photobiol. **27:** 499–501.
3. ANTONOFF, R. S., J. J. FERGUSON, JR. & G. IDELKOPE. 1976. Photochem. Photobiol. **23:** 327–29.
4. KEMP, R. G. & E. G. KREBS. 1967. Biochemistry **6:** 423–34.
5. ANTONOFF, R. S., T. OBRIG & J. J. FERGUSON, JR. 1977. *In* Methods in Enzymology, Vol. 46. W. Jackoby, Ed.: 335–39. Academic Press. New York.
6. HAYES, J. E., JR. & S. F. VELICK. 1954. J. Biol. Chem. **207:** 225–44.
7. BERGMEYER, H. U. 1974. Methods of Enzymatic Analysis (2nd ed.). Academic Press. New York.
8. PARMEGGIANI, A., J. H. LUFT, D. S. LOVE & E. G. KREBS. 1966. J. Biol. Chem. **241:** 4625–37.
9. MOROWITZ, H. J. 1950. Science **111:** 229–30.
10. CALVERT, J. G. & J. N. PITTS. 1966. *In* Photochemistry.: 783–98. John C. Wiley and Sons. New York.
11. WANG, S. W. 1960. Nature (London) **188:** 844–46.
12. BEUKERS, R. & W. BERENDS. 1960. Biochim. Biophys. Acta **41:** 550–51.
13. FERGUSON, J. J., JR. 1980. Photochem. Photobiol. In press.
14. NELSON, C. A., M. E. NOELKEN, C. E. BUCKLEY III, C. TANFORD & R. L. HILL. 1965. Biochemistry **4:** 1418–26.
15. GROSS, E. 1967. *In* Methods in Enzymology, Vol. 11. C.H.W. Hirs, Ed.: 238–55. Academic Press. New York.
16. STEINMAUS, H., I. ROSENTHAL & D. ELAD. 1971. J. Am. Chem. Soc. **91:** 4921–23.
17. SALOMON, J. & D. ELAD. 1974. Photchem. Photobiol. **19:** 21–27.
18. ELAD, D. & I. ROSENTHAL. 1969. Chem. Commun.: 905–8.
19. MONTENAY-GARESTIER, T., M. CHARLIER & C. HÉLÈNE. 1976. *In* Photochemistry and Photobiology of Nucleic Acids, Vol. 1. S. Y. Wang, Ed.: 381–417. Academic Press. New York.
20. HÉLÈNE, C. 1966. Biochem. Biophys. Res. Commun. **22:** 237–42.
21. BUTLER, A. R. & T. C. BRUICE. 1964. J. Am. Chem. Soc. **86:** 313–19.
22. GRANT, N. H., D. E. CLARK & H. E. ALBURN. 1966. J. Am. Chem. Soc. **88:** 4071–74.
23. HILL, R. F. & H. H. ROSSI. 1954. Radiat. Res. **1:** 282–93.
24. ASHWOOD-SMITH, M. J. & B. A. BRIDGES. 1966. Mutation Res. **3:** 135–44.
25. ASHWOOD-SMITH, M. J. & B. A. BRIDGES. 1967. Proc. Roy. Soc. London Ser. B **168:** 194–202.
26. SMITH, K. C. & M. E. O'LEARY. 1967. Science **155:** 1024–26.
27. YUE, V. T. & P. R. SCHIMMEL. 1977. Biochemistry **16:** 4678–84.
28. HAVRON, A. & J. SPERLING. 1977. Biochemistry **16:** 5631–35.
29. MANSOUR, T. E. & R. F. COLMAN. 1978. Biochem. Biophys. Res. Commun. **81:** 1370–76.
30. BRUNSWICK, D. J. & B. S. COOPERMAN. 1971. Proc. Nat. Acad. Sci. USA **68:** 1801–4.

DISCUSSION

DR. B. S. COOPERMAN (*University of Pennsylvania*): About six years ago, we showed that a diazoderivative of cyclic AMP would specifically incorporate into about

30% of the binding sites in PFK on a single trial. The quantum yield for the reaction was roughly 0.3 to 0.5, which is some 3000 times your calculated quantum yield. The quantum yield that you report is actually very similar to the quantum yield for photodestruction of adenine nucleotides in solution. So I think your findings are expected, on the basis of what we know about simple adenine photochemistry, if one makes the assumption that it is the photodestruction process that generates the species capable of inserting into the protein. One of the things that I think your work demonstrates dramatically is that, if your compound is sufficiently radioactive, you can do site studies at very low levels of incorporation, provided you have adequate controls.

Dr. J. J. FERGUSON, JR.: One comment on that quantitation. We estimate that we can fill between 1 and 10% of the binding sites with an exposure of ten minutes at the fluence we use. With cytoplasmic cyclic AMP receptor proteins, which are presumably the regulatory subunits of protein kinase, this efficiency is much higher. We have been able to get 50% of the potential binding sites labeled in the same ten minute period. I think this difference in efficiency reflects the higher affinity in this latter system.

Dr. J. KALLOS: I would like to make a comment also regarding the affinity labeling of cyclic AMP receptor protein, which we were interested in a few years ago. At that time, we compared the efficiency of affinity labeling with cyclic AMP to labeling with dibutyryl cyclic AMP, using the cytoplasmic system. We found that the latter ligand was 3 or 4 times more efficient than was the cyclic AMP. I was wondering whether or not you have tried any analogs in your system.

FERGUSON: I have not tried the dibutyryl cyclic AMP radioactive derivative with PFK. I've used it with the testicular binding proteins, which we have studied, and it photoincorporates perfectly well there. That is encouraging, since it suggests that we can do similar studies on intact cells and get better ligand concentrations within the cells.

Dr. J. OFENGAND (*Roche Institute of Molecular Biology*): Dr. Ferguson, you showed that the radiation does not cause very much damage to the enzyme—some 20% in activation in 20 min—but your photoincorporations are much less than that. Do you have any experiments or any results that would show that the incorporation is, in fact, into a native molecule and not into a uv-damaged molecule?

FERGUSON: No. I can't tell whether a uv-damaged molecule will continue to photoincorporate. You are right that the absolute amount of photodestruction going on is greater than the amount of photoincorporation. We are, however, getting to the point where the rates of the two processes approach within an order of magnitude of each other. But you are absolutely right that there is considerable photodestruction.

PHOTOGENERATED, HYDROPHOBIC REAGENTS FOR INTRINSIC MEMBRANE PROTEINS*

Hagan Bayley† and Jeremy R. Knowles

Department of Chemistry
Harvard University
Cambridge, Massachusetts 02138

INTRODUCTION

Our present understanding of the structure of biological membranes is embodied in the fluid mosaic model.[1] In this model it is hypothesized that intrinsic (or integral) membrane proteins are embedded in a fluid lipid bilayer. A membrane also contains extrinsic (or peripheral) proteins bound, by noncovalent association, either to intrinsic proteins or, perhaps, to the lipid headgroups. The intrinsic proteins may be deeply buried in the bilayer (e.g., bacteriorhodopsin[2]) or they may be strongly bound to the bilayer through single short hydrophobic peptides (e.g., glycophorin A[3]). It is likely that structures intermediate between these two extremes exist (e.g., the anion transport protein of the human erythrocyte membrane[4]). In this paper we review our work on photogenerated, hydrophobic reagents designed to label those segments of membrane proteins that are buried in the hydrocarbon region of the lipid bilayer.

METHODS FOR LABELING HYDROPHOBIC PEPTIDES

Although it is possible, under favorable circumstances, to label hydrophobic sites with chemical reagents,[5] we decided to pursue the photochemical approach for several reasons.

1. The reagent can be activated *after* binding to the membrane. Therefore, no reaction will occur with functional groups on the membrane surface before the reagent has penetrated into the bilayer, and the extent of binding of the reagent to the bilayer can easily be measured.

2. Highly reactive, short-lived intermediates can be generated photochemically (see below).

3. The use of photogenerated reagents should, eventually, allow more sophisticated experiments, such as time-dependent studies using flash photolysis.

Three approaches towards the development of hydrophobic, photoactivatable reagents have been taken. In the first, which was originally described by Klip and Gitler,[6] a radiolabeled, chemically inert, hydrophobic molecule is allowed to bind to the membrane, where it is subsequently activated by irradiation. The photogenerated intermediate is intended to react covalently with the membrane constituents located between the two faces of the bilayer. A second approach is to perform an analogous

---

*This research was supported by the National Institutes of Health, grant no. GM22961.
†Present address: Department of Chemistry, Massachusetts Institute of Technology, Cambridge, Massachusetts 02139.

45

experiment with an amphipathic molecule that contains a hydrophobic photolabile group. Experiments along these lines have recently appeared in the literature.[7] A third, and a considerably more involved, approach is to use phospholipids containing photolabile groups.[8,9] The first approach, which is that taken here, has the advantages of being rapid and simple, although the other methods may provide more detailed information in the long run.

THE CHOICE OF PHOTOLABILE GROUP

Those sections of the polypeptide chains of membrane proteins that are exposed to the hydrocarbon core of the bilayer contain uncharged or hydrophobic amino acids that possess chemically unreactive groups, including a considerable proportion of hydrocarbon residues. We therefore resolved that we would use a reagent capable of insertion into carbon-hydrogen bonds. The most likely candidates were aryl nitrenes or carbenes, generated photochemically from azides or diazirines. Since there are no well-documented cases of photochemical *inter*molecular carbon-hydrogen bond insertion reactions for aryl nitrenes and because it was unclear whether the reactions we were attempting to perform were more akin to intra- or intermolecular chemistry, we decided to test the capability of nitrenes and carbenes for insertion into carbon-hydrogen bonds in model membranes.[10,11] It was not initially obvious that even a carbene would so react, since migration of the photogenerated intermediate into the solvent and reaction there with water or with buffer components was a real possibility.

Phenyl azide and phenyl diazirine bound to phosphatidylcholine vesicles were irradiated to generate the isosteric reactive intermediates, phenyl nitrene and phenyl carbene. In the case of dimyristoylphosphatidylcholine, phenyl carbene gave a 5% yield of products deriving from insertion into the carbon-hydrogen bonds of the saturated fatty acyl chains of the lipid. The insertion products were characterized by gas chromatography–mass spectroscopy. The nitrene gave only 0.25% reaction with liquid, and the products could not be shown to have derived solely from carbon-hydrogen bond insertion. Furthermore, when glutathione was added as a water-soluble scavenger of reactive intermediates, we found that the labeling of lipid by phenyl nitrene was greatly reduced, while labeling by the carbene was hardly changed. This indicated that, even when phenyl azide is largely bound to a membrane before irradiation, the photogenerated nitrene might be scavenged by reactive groups outside the bilayer, such as the thiol groups of extrinsic proteins. We therefore chose a carbene precursor as our reagent. It is important to note that our experiments did not exclude the possibility that an aryl azide very tightly bound to the bilayer might be capable of carbon-hydrogen bond insertion. However, the experiments of Gupta *et al.*[12] with arylazidophospholipids and our work (unpublished) with amphipathic aryl azides do appear to rule this out. Neither did we eliminate the possibility that a very tightly bound aryl azide might be used selectively to label groups other than carbon-hydrogen bonds within the bilayer. Reactive intermediates generated from azides more tightly bound than phenyl azide are not scavenged by water-soluble scavengers[13,14] and certainly react with membrane constituents.[15,16]

THE SYNTHESIS AND PROPERTIES OF A RADIOLABELED REAGENT

We chose spiro[adamantane-2,2'-diazirine] (FIGURE 1) rather than phenyl diazirine for more detailed evaluation. This molecule also had excellent prospects as a hydrophobic reagent[11] and had several advantages over other diazirines. First, radiolabeled adamantane diazirine of high specific activity is more amenable to synthesis than most aryl diazirines.[17] Further, from the literature on the solubilities of hydrocarbons, it seemed likely that adamantane diazirine would partition more strongly into the lipid bilayer than phenyl diazirine. Finally, adamantane diazirine is stable in the dark, it absorbs in the near ultraviolet (λ_{max} = 372.5, ϵ = 245) at wavelengths that do no damage to most biological systems, and it is reasonably small.

[³H]Adamantane diazirine was synthesized as outlined in FIGURE 2. The synthesis is so designed that a specific radioactivity of several thousand mCi mmol^{-1} can easily be achieved. The hydrophobicity of the radiolabeled diazirine was determined by estimating its partition coefficient between buffer and pure phospholipid bilayers using equilibrium dialysis. In experiments with dimyristoylphosphatidylcholine and dioleoylphosphatidylcholine vesicles at temperatures above the phase transition of

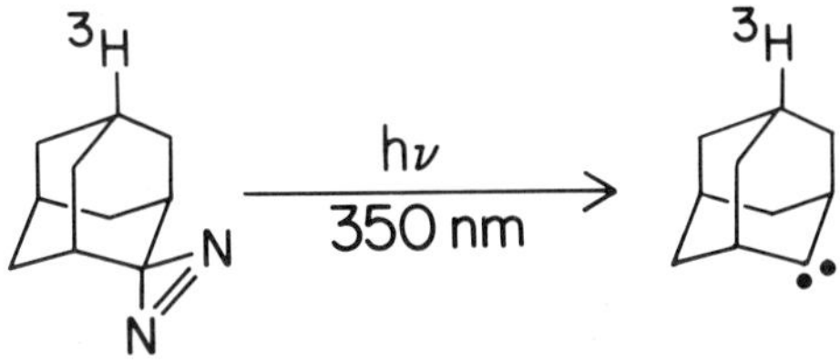

FIGURE 1. 1-[³H]Spiro[adamantane-4,4'-diazirine] yields the highly reactive carbene 1-[³H]adamantyl-4-idene on irradiation with near ultraviolet light.

these lipids, the concentration of reagent in the hydrocarbon part of the bilayer was found to be 5000 and 6000 times higher than that in the surrounding buffer. The corresponding values for phenyl azide (those for phenyl diazirine were not determined) were both 450.

HUMAN RED BLOOD CELL MEMBRANES LABELED WITH ADAMANTANE DIAZIRINE

[³H]Adamantane diazirine was tested on the human erythrocyte membrane, which is the best understood of all moderately complex biological membranes. In these experiments, our aim was to determine whether the intrinsic proteins could be selectively labeled.

The extent of binding of the diazirine to erythrocyte membranes (ghosts) was such that the concentration of the reagent in the bilayer was 1500 times that in the surrounding buffer. On irradiation, the tritiated adamantyl group was incorporated into the membranes and the covalently attached label was completely stable to further irradiation. Of the 38% of label that could not be removed by extensive washing, 80% was bound to lipid molecules and 20% to protein.

The distribution of radiolabel among the polypeptides of erythrocyte membranes labeled with [³H]adamantane diazirine after separation by sodium dodecyl sulfate/polyacrylamide gel electrophoresis is shown in FIGURE 3. This pattern .contrasts markedly with that obtained with [³H]phenyl azide, in which the extrinsic proteins (primarily spectrin) were heavily labeled (results not shown) and that obtained with [¹²⁵I]iodoazidonaphthalene,[15] from which it was concluded that it was "difficult to ascribe labeling to single [protein] bands." In the case of adamantane diazirine, the major intrinsic proteins [the anion channel (Band 3), glycophorin A (PAS I and II), the Band 4.5 region and glycophorin B (PAS III)] are clearly the most heavily labeled components of the membrane. An extrinsic protein, spectrin (Bands 1 and 2) is also labeled, but to a lesser extent on a weight-for-weight basis, since it comprises 30% by weight of the total membrane protein.

Numerous control experiments, which indicate that the peaks of radioactivity on the gels do represent labeled proteins, have been performed. When labeled membranes were extracted with organic solvents [e.g., chloroform-methanol (2:1)] before electrophoresis, the large peak of radioactivity near the dye front (FIGURE 3, region F) was no longer observed, but the rest of the pattern was largely unaltered. This suggests that the large peak of radioactivity represents labeled lipid. This peak may also contain some noncovalently bound photolysis products, although the larger part of these run in this gel system with an R_f of 0.85 and are completely removed by the washing procedure (FIGURE 3, legend). That the first major peak on the gel (FIGURE 3, region B) represented both Band 3 and PAS I (glycophorin A dimer) was shown as follows. First, trypsin-treated cells[18] were converted to ghosts and then labeled. In such preparations, glycophorin A was degraded but Band 3 was intact. The peak of radioactivity in region B was diminished but not eliminated. Second, after electrophoresis at high acrylamide concentrations, the radioactivity in region B separated into two radioactive peaks, corresponding to Band 3 and PAS I. Finally, both glycophorin A and Band 3 have been extracted from labeled membranes and purified to homogeneity without loss of radioactivity.[19] Another important control showed that the labeling pattern of erythrocyte ghosts was unchanged by "prelabeling" the membranes with high concentrations of unlabeled reagent. This eliminates the possibility that tight, efficiently labeled diazirine binding sites exist.

The low extent of spectrin labeling (FIGURE 3, region A) was independent of

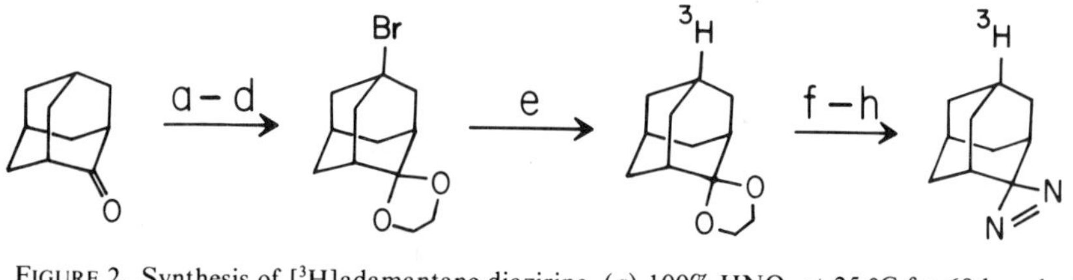

FIGURE 2. Synthesis of [³H]adamantane diazirine. (a) 100% HNO_3 at 25 °C for 69 h and at 60 °C for 2 h. (b) 25% H_2SO_4 at 95 °C for 2 h. (c) 48% HBr refluxed for 7 h. (d) $HOCH_2CH_2OH$, TsOH, in benzene refluxed for 14 h. (e) ³H₂, 10% Pd/C, K_2CO_3, in ethanol at 25 °C for 20 h. (f) KIO_4, H_2SO_4, in dioxane-water at 25 °C for 6 hr. (g) NH_3/CH_3OH and NH_2OSO_3H at 10 °C for 16 h. (h) CrO_3/H_2SO_4 in acetone at 20 °C for 30 min. Full details and relevant references will be given elsewhere.[22]

FIGURE 3. Membranes (3-4 mg ml^{-1} of protein in 5 mM sodium phosphate buffer, pH 8.0) were incubated under N$_2$, with [^{3}H]adamantane diazirine (15 μCi, 837 mCi mmol^{-1}; added as a solution in ethanol—final ethanol concentration 1.5%) for 1 h at 4 °C. After irradiation (3 cm from the center of a single Rayonet RPR 3500 Å lamp) for 15 min at 4 °C with thorough stirring, the membranes were diluted with a solution of bovine serum albumin (10 mg ml^{-1} in 5 mM sodium phosphate, pH 8.0 containing 1 mM EDTA), incubated for 15 min at 4 °C and recovered by centrifugation. After a total of four such washes the membranes were washed four more times with buffer. Polyacrylamide gel electrophoresis of portions of the sample was performed essentially as described by Fairbanks et al.[34] The gels were fractionated into 2 mm slices that were then assayed for tritium. Full details will be published elsewhere.[22] Numbers 1 to 7 indicate Coomassie Blue (CB) stained bands and numbers I to III periodic acid–Schiff reagent (PAS) stained bands.[34] The position of the tracking dye is shown by TD. The letters A to F indicate regions of the gels discussed in the text.

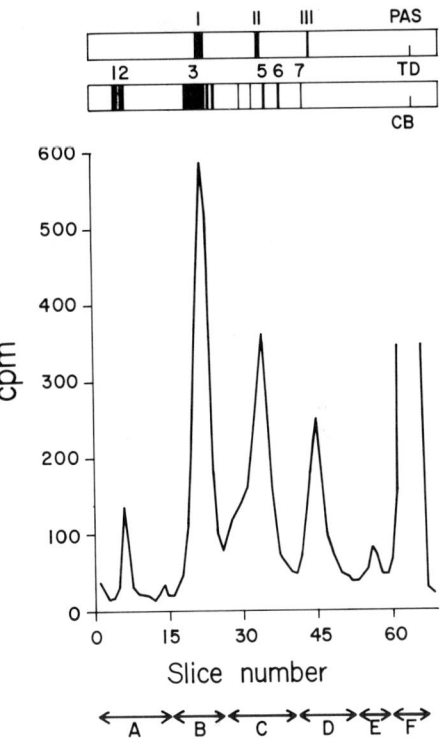

whether the protein was membrane bound or solubilized in the presence of membranes at low salt concentrations. We therefore concluded that a small amount of nonspecific labeling was occuring from the aqueous phase. Another experiment that demonstrated this is illustrated in FIGURE 4. Here, ghosts to which a substantial quantity of lysozyme had been bound (30% by weight of the total membrane protein) were labeled as before. A small increment of radioactivity in region E (FIGURE 3) was observed. That this increment was due to the incorporation of radioactivity by lysozyme was demonstrated by removing this protein and the other extrinsic proteins from the labeled membrane with 0.1 M NaOH[20] (FIGURE 4b). Only about 5% of the covalently incorporated label was removed by this procedure, and part of this was the contribution from spectrin. In experiments with the exogenous extrinsic protein aldolase, which binds tightly to Band 3,[21] similar results were obtained even when aldolase comprised 25% w/w of the membrane protein.

Since the intrinsic proteins of erythrocyte ghosts are labeled far more strongly with [^{3}H]adamantane diazirine than are the extrinsic proteins, the reagent is effective in distinguishing between these classes of proteins. The fact that extrinsic proteins that are present in large numbers of copies per cell may be labeled to a small extent must be born in mind when evaluating the results from membranes not previously characterized. A detailed report of our study of erythrocyte membranes will be published elsewhere.[22]

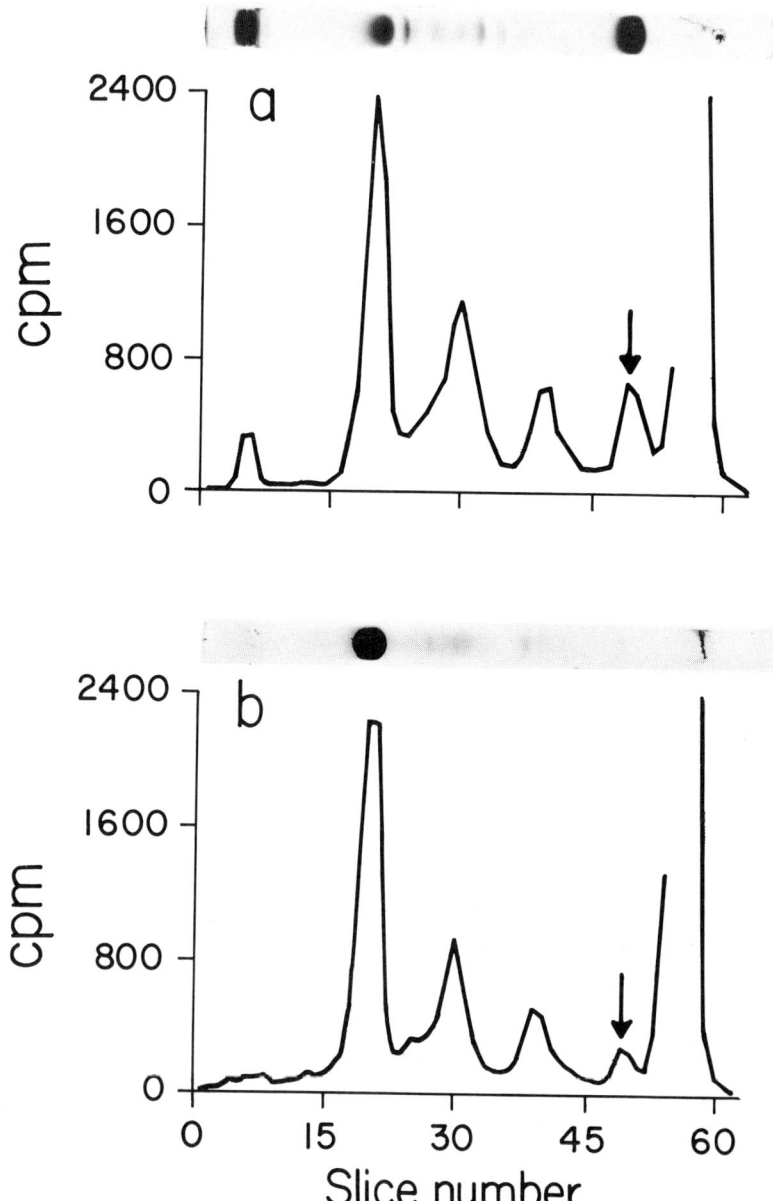

FIGURE 4. (a) Electrophoresis profile of erythrocyte membranes labeled with [³H]adaman-tane diazirine in the presence of lysozyme (~ 30% of the total membrane protein).
(b) The same as (a), but the membranes were treated with 0.1 M NaOH after labeling to remove extrinsic proteins, including lysozyme. The arrow shows the position to which lysozyme migrates.

FURTHER ANALYSIS OF THE LABELED PROTEINS

To confirm that adamantane diazirine labeled the hydrophobic regions of integral membrane proteins, we examined the distribution of radioactivity within the polypeptide chains of several membrane proteins that have been well-characterized by independent methods. This work is exemplified here by our study of the large chains of the human major histocompatibility antigens, HLA-A2 and -B7.[23] These two polypeptides are highly homologous[24] and have the same overall structure, which is illustrated in FIGURE 5. Each possesses a large N-terminal extracellular sequence of amino acids (~280 residues), a central hydrophobic sequence (26 residues), and a C-terminal hydrophilic sequence (32 residues).[25,26] The C-terminus is exposed to the cytoplasm of the cell;[27] therefore, the hydrophobic region is likely to lie within the interior of the membrane.

The HLA-A2 and -B7 polypeptides and the associated small subunit, β_2-microglobulin, were copurified from JY lymphoblastoid cells labeled with [^{3}H]adamantane diazirine by immunoadsorption into anti-human β_2-microglobulin IgG coupled to Sepharose beads. The eluted product was digested with papain. This

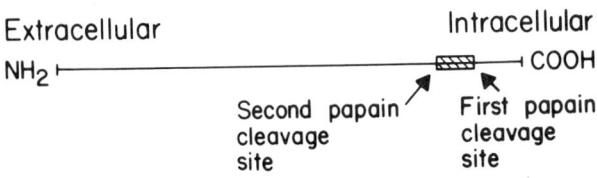

FIGURE 5. Schematic diagram of the heavy chains of HLA-A2 and −B7 antigens. The hydrophobic region of the polypeptide is in the cross-hatched box.

enzyme first cleaves most of the C-terminal domain from the bulk of chain, and, in a slower second step, removes the hydrophobic sequence and a small number of adjacent amino acids (see FIGURE 5). The distribution of radioactivity in the cleavage products is shown in FIGURE 6. The first product (39,000 daltons, lacking the C-terminus) contains ~ 85% of the label, but the second product (~ 34,000 daltons) contains < 15% of the original radioactivity. The label must, therefore, lie in or close to the transmembrane sequence of these antigens. Analogous results have been obtained with glycophorin A and the hemagglutinin (HA$_2$) from influenza virus.[23] In a control experiment, it was shown that the water-soluble scavenger glutathione did not affect the distribution of label within glycophorin A.[10,11,28]

FUTURE DEVELOPMENTS

From the above discussion it is clear that adamantane diazirine may be used with high confidence to distinguish extrinsic proteins from intrinsic proteins, and to identify those segments of intrinsic proteins that lie within the lipid bilayer. Nevertheless, we stress that hydrophobic reagents are not yet perfected and that more research in this area is desirable.

First, more reactive reagents may be required. Adamantane diazirine itself

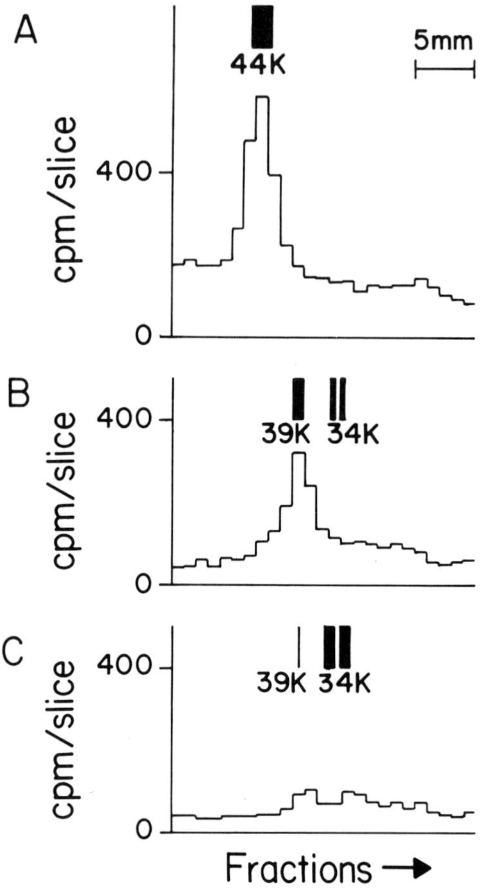

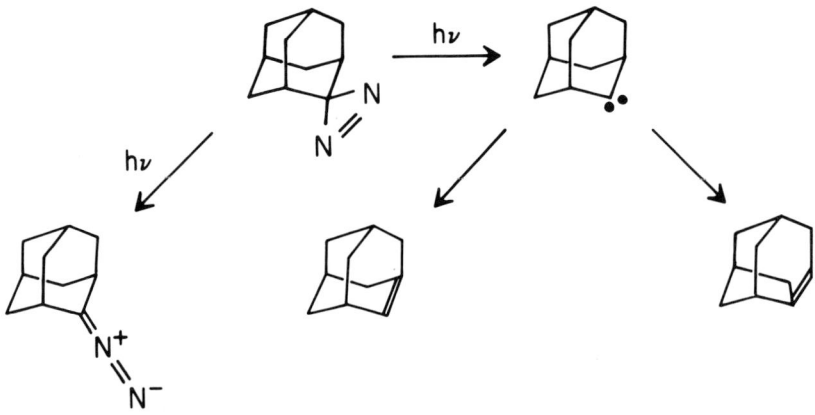

A 44K

5mm

cpm/slice

400

0

B 39K 34K

cpm/slice

400

0

C 39K 34K

cpm/slice

400

0

Fractions →

FIGURE 6. The distribution of label in the heavy chains of HLA-A2 and -B7 antigens labeled with [³H]adamantane diazirine, as determined by SDS-gel electrophoresis (cf. FIGURE 3; here only the relevant portions of the gels are shown). (a) Intact heavy chains. (b) Partial papain digest. About half the antigen has been converted to the 39,000 dalton form, which still contains the hydrophobic segment (FIGURE 5). Half has been further digested to the 34,000 dalton form (the HLA-A2 and -B7 specificities are separated here, hence the doublet of bands). (c) 34,000 dalton form generated by papain treatment. A trace of the 39,000 dalton intermediate remains. The shaded areas above the radioactivity profiles represent Coomassie Blue stain. Full details will be published elsewhere.[23]

hν

FIGURE 7. Photochemistry of adamantane diazirine. The generation of 2-diazoadamantane and the possible formation of highly strained olefins from adamantylidene.

52

rearranges, in part, to 2-diazoadamantane[11] and it is also conceivable that strained olefins may be involved in some of the subsequent reactions of the carbene (FIGURE 7). While these intermediates are extremely reactive, they are not capable of carbon-hydrogen bond insertion. Further, the carbene itself is likely to exhibit some chemical selectivity,[29,30] favoring electron-rich functional groups. A logical extension of our work would be to sequence the labeled regions of intrinsic proteins and so ascertain whether the amino acids containing the more reactive functional groups had been selectively labeled. But before such effort is expended, the reagent might be further improved.

Only a few other possibilities exist for relatively simple, highly unselective reagents. For instance, while aromatic diazirines have some attraction,[11,17] they cannot be made in high yield, and the diazo rearrangement products from these compounds are less reactive than diazoadamantane. Perhaps the highly indiscriminate carbenes formed from diazocyclopentadienes[29,31] are the most promising possibilities. Furthermore, adamantane diazirine is not of optimal hydrophobicity. Although the reagent of Bercovici et al.,[15] [125I]iodoazidonaphthalene, is likely to be more selective in its chemistry after photoactivation, it does bind extremely tightly to membranes. A carbene precursor that binds as tightly should also be tested.

Concurrently with the search for better reagents, the possible applications of lipophilic photogenerated reagents can be profitably explored. The development of photochemical protein-protein crosslinking reagents to study interactions with the bilayer is feasible. Nearest-neighbor interactions within the bilayer should be less complex than those outside it, simply because fewer proteins penetrate into the hydrocarbon region than are present at the membrane surface. A reagent based on carbene chemistry should produce more interpretable results than the earlier experiments with aryl azides.[32] Amphipathic reagents based on carbene chemistry should also be useful for the rapid exploration of transmembrane protein topography. Using suitably designed headgroups,[33] it may be possible to direct such reagents to one or both sides of a membrane. One of the most attractive possibilities for lipophilic photogenerated reagents is their application to time-dependent phenomena using flash photolysis. In theory, microsecond resolution might be achieved with carbenes, and such a technique could be used to study rapid conformational changes. On a longer timescale, such phenomena as membrane protein biosynthesis might be investigated. Our investigations and those of others show that these experiments are within reach.

NOTE ADDED IN PROOF

Adamantane diazirine has recently been used for studies of Band 3 (D. Goldman, submitted for publication), (Na-K)-ATPase (Farley, R. A., D. W. Goldman & H. Bayley. 1980. J. Biol. Chem. **255:** 860), and the HLA-D antigens (Kaufman, J. F. & J.) L. Strominger. 1979. Proc. Nat. Acad. Sci. USA **76:** 6304).

ACKNOWLEDGMENTS

We are especially grateful to D. Goldman, J. Pober, and J. White for their collaboration in the experiments on glycophorin A, the histocompatibility antigens, and hemagglutinin.

REFERENCES

1. SINGER, S. J. 1974. Annu. Rev. Biochem. **43:** 805.
2. HENDERSON, R. & P. N. T. UNWIN. 1975. Nature (London) **257:** 28.
3. SEGREST, J. P., R. L. JACKSON, V. T. MARCHESI, R. B. GUYER & W. TERRY. 1972. Biochem. Biophys. Res. Commun. **49:** 964.
4. DRICKAMER, L. K. 1978. J. Biol. Chem. **253:** 7242.
5. PICK, U. & E. RACKER. 1979. Biochemistry **18:** 108.
6. KLIP, A. & C. GITLER. 1974. Biochem. Biophys. Res. Commun. **60:** 1155.
7. WISNIESKI, B. J. & J. S. BRAMHALL. 1979. Biochem. Biophys. Res. Commun. **87:** 308.
8. CHAKRABARTI, P. & H. G. KHORANA. 1975. Biochemistry **14:** 5021.
9. RADHAKRISHNAN, R. et. al. This volume.
10. BAYLEY, H. & J. R. KNOWLES. 1978. Biochemistry **17:** 2414.
11. BAYLEY, H. & J. R. KNOWLES. 1978. Biochemistry **17:** 2420.
12. GUPTA, C. M., R. RADHAKRISHNAN, G. E. GERBER, W. L. OLSEN, S. C. QUAY & H. G. KHORANA. 1979. Proc. Nat. Acad. Sci. USA **76:** 2595.
13. GITLER, C. Personal communication.
14. BAYLEY, H. Unpublished work.
15. BERCOVICI, T., C. GITLER & A. BROMBERG. 1978. Biochemistry **17:** 1484.
16. GITLER, C. & T. BERCOVICI. This volume.
17. SMITH, R. A. G. & J. R. KNOWLES. 1973. J. Am. Chem. Soc. **95:** 5072.
18. DRICKAMER, L. K. 1976. J. Biol. Chem. **251:** 5115.
19. GOLDMAN, D. & H. BAYLEY. Unpublished work.
20. STECK, T. L. & J. YU. 1973. J. Supramol. Struct. **1:** 220.
21. STRAPAZON, E. & T. L. STECK. 1976. Biochemistry **15:** 1421.
22. BAYLEY, H. & J. R. KNOWLES. Submitted for publication.
23. GOLDMAN, D., J. POBER, J. WHITE & H. BAYLEY. 1979. Nature **280:** 841.
24. TERHORST, C., P. PARHAM, D. L. MANN & J. L. STROMINGER. 1976. Proc. Nat. Acad. Sci. USA **73:** 910.
25. ROBB, R. J., C. TERHORST & J. L. STROMINGER. 1978. J. Biol. Chem. **253:** 5319.
26. ROBB, R. J. 1978. Ph.D. Thesis, Harvard University.
27. POBER, J. S., B. C. GUILD & J. L. STROMINGER. 1978. Proc. Nat. Acad. Sci. USA **75:** 6002.
28. STANDRING, D. N. & J. R. KNOWLES. In press.
29. JONES, M., JR. & R. A. MOSS. 1973. Carbenes, Vol. 1; MOSS, R. A. & M. JONES, JR. 1975. Carbenes, Vol. 2. Wiley Interscience. New York.
30. ISAEV, S. D., A. G. YURCHENKO, Z. N. MURZINOVA, F. N. STEPANOV, G. G. KOLYADA & S. S. NOVIKOV. 1974. Zh. Org. Khim. **10:** 1338.
31. KANG, U. G. & H. SCHECHTER. 1978. J. Am. Chem. Soc. **100:** 651.
32. MIKKELSON, R. B. & D. F. H. WALLACH. 1976. J. Biol. Chem. **251:** 7413.
33. SHEETZ, M. P. & S. J. SINGER. 1974. Proc. Nat. Acad. Sci. USA **71:** 4474.
34. FAIRBANKS, G., T. L. STECK & D. F. H. WALLACH. 1971. Biochemistry **10:** 2606.

DISCUSSION

DR. N. J. TURRO: I have some general comments. The phenyl nitrene is, presumably, rearranging rather than hydrogen abstracting. One could, therefore, do one of two things: either make it longer-lived or get it to cross to the triplet, where one might be able to get hydrogen abstraction. You commented that no scavenging by glutathione occurred with 5-iodonaphthyl azide. I think you ascribed this to hydrophobicity. There are two possibilities that I can think of, one is that the iodine is coming off and you are labeling by a mechanism irrelevant to the nitrene. A photochemical mechanism is that iodine causes what is known as the heavy atom effect and, in that paradigm, instead of going from the excited azide singlet to the nitrene singlet you go to the S1 state, then to T1, and finally to the triplet nitrene. Now the triplet nitrene can abstract hydrogen as the carbene can, and you may get labeling that way.

The point I want to emphasize here is that there are known ways to get intersystem crossings from S1 to T1 to become more rapid and this might be a way out of some of the problems you have in labeling that are due to rearrangement of the singlet. It is a potentially general solution if you can find something compatible with everything else. Heavy atoms, bromine and iodine, and aryl ketones tend to help. I cannot give you a simple answer, but that is one possibility.

DR. H. BAYLEY: May I respond to that? First of all, the iodine is not coming off. This is really Professor Gitler's work and he is going to talk about that tomorrow. But we have made 5-iodonaphthyl azide and, as Professor Gitler has shown, it is incorporated photochemically into erythrocyte membranes. Iodine will detach from the naphthalene ring if you photolyze long enough, but that is not the mechanism by which labeling occurs here. We actually hydrolyzed the proteins we labeled with that reagent and showed, for instance, that there is no iodotyrosine. Photolysis of the azido group is clearly faster than C—I bond cleavage under our conditions.

Second, I'm not sure that I would like to use triplets, which are essentially radicals, in this situation. I think that it may be asking for trouble. You might get radical chain reactions and consequent damage to the membrane, such as protein cross-linking. Here we have the very loosest type of binding site; if the guy with this mitt was playing for the Yankees there would be real trouble. I wonder if this would be true if triplets are formed and they abstract hydrogen atoms?

TURRO: It may be true in some cases, but it is not necessarily true in all cases. I believe that, if you tried it, you would be likely to find something interesting. I don't see the possibility of a chain reaction. Free radicals are unreactive until you get high concentrations of olefins, which have very fast rates of reaction.

BAYLEY: I'm not saying that, I mean that if you create a radical and abstract a hydrogen atom in the bilayer, you then have two radicals that would diffuse all over the place.

TURRO: This is, I guess, what we are not so sure about: how far they will diffuse before they react.

The other comment I wanted to make is that what one would really like in this area is a way to analyze the reaction intermediates. It turns out that NMR is very sensitive under a very special set of circumstances. When you take an NMR spectrum during photolysis you can, sometimes, see incredibly low concentrations of material; this is because of a phenomenon called chemically induced nuclear polarization. Under certain circumstances you can produce products in which nuclear polarization occurs to the extent that you can see NMR even at 10^{-6} to 10^{-7} M concentrations, and it sounds to me like this is an area that is right for us to do some experiments in NMR with a light on, just in the hope that we can get some products that happen to have this polarization. It is, again, a hit or miss type of affair. But if you see it, you see it. You'd actually be getting direct information on the radicals in the labeling sites.

DR. M. E. DOCKTER (*St. Jude Children's Research Hospital*): My question is a simple one and I hope it has a simple answer. Because you are able to wash noncovalently bound probe away from erythrocyte membranes with BSA, why don't you see more covalent attachment to hydrophobic pockets of peripheral membrane proteins?

BAYLEY: It is not clear to me that peripheral proteins do have hydrophobic pockets that bind the diazirine tightly. Spectrin is labeled lightly whether it is bound to the bilayer or not. If you incubate ghosts at 37 °C at very low salt concentrations, the spectrin is removed from the bilayer and we've shown, in that circumstance, that spectrin is still labeled to a low extent. Well, there are two possibilities: either the protein is scavenging reactive intermediates present in the solution or there are hydrophobic pockets. But the hydrophobic pocket formed by the lipid bilayer is much larger than that formed by any protein, and we certainly haven't found any strong labeling of extrinsic proteins with this reagent. If BSA alone were photolyzed with the diazirine it might well be strongly labeled, but perhaps not in the presence of the lipid bilayer, which acts as a sink for the reagent. In any case BSA is hardly representative of soluble or extrinsic proteins.

DR. C. GITLER (*The Weizman Institute of Science*): It's nice to show that your compound will insert into a carbon-hydrogen bond in a model system but I think that what we are dealing with in a mixture such as a membrane is not whether a possibility of the model system will apply, but what happens in the membrane. I wonder if you have done the experiment in the liposome in which you simply give a choice to the carbene. In other words, if you put it into a liposome where it has no choice, it will insert into whatever is there. If you give it a choice, will it show you selectivity or nonselectivity? Have you done a liposome experiment where you have double bonds available for rapid reaction and still get insertion into carbon-hydrogen bonds?

BAYLEY: Yes, we have done that (1978, Biochemistry **17**: 2420). Adamantylidene will insert into a carbon-hydrogen bond in the presence of a double bond but, of course, the double bonds are much more reactive. I agree with you in that sense. I can think of a better example. For instance, if it were possible to take a lipid that had a hydroxyl group on an acyl chain that lay within the bilayer I'd be willing to bet that almost all of the reaction would be with the hydroxyl group. I'm not disputing that. All I'm saying is that this reagent is capable of inserting into a carbon-hydrogen bond and I have indicated that there may be circumstances where this is necessary.

GITLER: Yes, but by inference you are making the point that the nitrenes are no good because they don't have exactly that type of high insertion. I think that after we get through analyzing what really happens in the membranes it is not going to be as critical as you are making it today that one has to have insertion into carbon-hydrogen bonds to label apolar regions of membranes. As you have said, we have threonines, tryptophans, phenylalanines, and tyrosines within the bilayer. There are quite a few choices that, I think, make the labeling less stringent in the sense that you've made it.

BAYLEY: I agree with you in some ways but certainly, looking at the hydrophobic amino acid sequences I put up on my second slide, I doubt very much that a nitrene could label them (1979, Bacteriorhodopsin residues 92-101, Proc. Nat. Acad. Sci. USA **76**: 227;1978, Isomaltase hydrophobic segment, FEBS Lett. **96**: 183; 1978, Ovomucoid signal peptide, J. Biol. Chem. **253**: 9018).

GITLER: Well, you will see tomorrow the pattern that we get in the ghosts and, in fact, we can have beautiful resolution in experiments with nitrenes, which you tend to imply is not apparently possible; you'll see that we get exactly the same pattern as you get with your carbene. Except that we probably get about tenfold more incorporation efficiency in the sense that we have higher counts and when you have higher counts your patterns become more complicated. If you put in very few counts you can get very clean results.

BAYLEY: You imply that your results are quite different from those you published recently (1978, Biochemistry **17**: 1484).

DR. T. I. KALMAN: Perhaps in addition to remarks on the naphthalene reagent reacting differently, one could also consider differences other than hydrophobicity, as you mentioned, between the other reagents and naphthalene derivatives, by considering that stacking directs a naphthalene reagent to form some structure domains of its own. With respect to the reduction of azides by thiols, I'd like to ask you whether you would care to comment on the biological half-life of azides. Could we expect azido compounds to survive, *in vivo* and intracellularly?

BAYLEY: I guess what you are saying is that naphthalenes could orient within a liquid crystalline environment and this might affect the reactivity of these compounds in some way.

KALMAN: I thought that perhaps, with a naphthalene derivative, you could have stacking interactions that you wouldn't expect with the other compounds.

BAYLEY: Yes, I would expect that compound to have some orientation in the bilayer and that is one reason that we looked at nitrenes at all. It is not obvious that nitrenes won't insert under certain circumstances; for instance, the bilayer might correctly orient reactive intermediates for insertion. Stoffel's group in Germany has claimed, although I haven't seen hard data, that even alkyl nitrenes will insert into carbon-hydrogen bonds in bilayers—an unprecedented reaction, but a possibility.

We published a paper that showed that dithiols, for instance, DTT (Staros *et al.,* 1978, Biochem. Biophys. Res. Commun. **80:** 568), reduced aromatic azides. They do that very rapidly: about 1000 times more rapidly than monothiols, e.g., glutathione.

I believe that you are implying that these azides may not survive long *in vivo* because of the reducing environment. I think that is possible: I believe someone should look at that. For instance, in some of the early work with antibodies, rabbits were immunized with azidoaryl haptens, which, it was claimed, were stable *in vivo*. The thiol reduction was not known at that time and it would be interesting to reinvestigate that point.

DR. W. LWOWSKI (*Mexico State University*): Congratulations on your reagent, but a word of caution as to the applicability of nitrenes. I think that, somehow, you've manged to select the worst possible class of nitrenes. Aryl nitrenes go to the triplet state extremely quickly and otherwise rearrange. They are really very poor, especially for reaction with hydrocarbons. There are three other classes of nitrenes, which are excellent in carbon-hydrogen bond insertion and which you can make rather hydrophobic. Alkyloxycarbonyl nitrenes, especially, are very good at CH insertion. This form of nitrene strikes me as very suitable and there are others, which I can give you a list of, but I want to point out that the preference for aryl nitrenes is something a pot boiling organic nitrene chemist can hardly understand. But there might be good reasons for it.

BAYLEY: The reason aryl nitrenes have been used is, on the whole, because you can photolyze them in the visible or in the near uv; but I agree with you that sulfonyl nitrenes and others are much more reactive and they should be investigated.

LWOWSKI: You can photolyze those also in the very near uv at 300 nm and everybody seems to use 254 nm, so often there is no problem at all.

BAYLEY: I feel it is a very bad practice to irradiate biological systems at 254 nm unless you do the appropriate controls. . .

LWOWSKI: Oh, I agree, but the other nitrenes can be photolyzed at longer wavelengths.

BAYLEY: We've certainly shown with red cell ghosts that, if you irradiate in the presence of oxygen at 254 or 300 nm, you see massive cross-linking of membrane proteins. But you can get away with photolyzing at 254 or 300 nm under nitrogen or argon.

UNIDENTIFIED SPEAKER: I have a comment on your question about the stability of the azides in mammalian systems. We've done some work with azides and, in mammalian cells, if you add the compound to the cells and irradiate immediately or if you wait 24 hours and irradiate there is no difference in the biological effect. That is, they are equally toxic, so they do seem to survive for 24 hours. We haven't looked at it for longer than that.

BAYLEY: Well, I should just briefly point out that, as we showed in our paper, some azides are much more reactive than others. Aryl azides with electron withdrawing groups are reduced very rapidly indeed by dithiols and more slowly by monothiols whereas, for instance, alkyl azides are reduced much more slowly (Bayley et al., 1978, Tetrahedron Lett. 3633). I think the question of stability should be examined for each compound that you look at.

I would like to make one further comment on Dr. Lwowski's remark. It strikes me that the azidoadenine derivatives have been very useful reagents. I wonder whether that is because the derived nitrenes are more akin to carbonyl nitrenes than to aryl nitrenes.

UNIDENTIFIED SPEAKER: We have studied the effects of azides in cells for long periods of time and haven't seen these effects of sulfhydryls, and it seems to me that it is very important that the limits of sulfhydryl effects are defined. If it is there, what are the concentration parameters? Your concentrations were quite high in your studies, were they not? I mean compared to physiological conditions.

BAYLEY: No, they were not. You should look at the papers I mentioned. They have rate constants, show the range of reactivity of different thiols and azides and discuss the pH dependence of the reaction.

APPLICATION OF LIGHT SENSITIVE CHEMICALS TO PROBE PROTEIN STRUCTURE AND FUNCTION*

Michael C. DeTraglia, John S. Brand, and Andrew M. Tometsko

*The University of Rochester
Department of Radiation Biology and Biophysics
and
Litron Laboratories Ltd.
Rochester, New York 14620*

INTRODUCTION

The most powerful aspect of the photoaffinity labeling technique is the ability to generate, through photolysis, an intermediate of such high reactivity that covalent attachment to a ligand binding site can be achieved even when there are no nucleophilic residues at the site. By comparison, conventional affinity labeling techniques are very limited, in that requirements for nucleophile reactivity often dictate narrow ranges of pH, temperature, and concentration within which labeling experiments must be conducted. The present work will seek to demonstrate that the extreme reactivity of diradical intermediates generated during photolysis can be used to advantage in allowing conditions such as pH to be varied during photoaffinity labeling experiments. Thus, it is possible to probe the pH dependence of binding site affinity using certain photolabeling reagents and to interpret changes in affinity in terms of alterations in the conformation of protein components comprising the binding site.

In order to implement the photoaffinity labeling technique to sense protein conformation, a number of variables must be carefully considered. For instance, relationships between probe photolysis rate, binding site affinity, and photolabeling efficiency must be well understood. The interpretation of differential photoinactivation with pH as a reflection of changes in target site affinity relies, of course, on the assumption that neither probe photolysis rate nor nitrene insertion rate are pH dependent. Attempts to independently quantitate each of these events will be described. In order to utilize a particular photoaffinity reagent over a broad range of pH, the stability of the photoreactive species at extremes of pH must also be documented. A final point that will be considered is that, under somewhat fortuitous circumstances, it may be possible to photolyze a particular probe species, such as probe bound to the target site, while not affecting the bulk of probe in solution. This phenomenon can greatly enhance the selectivity of target site labeling.

In pursuing these studies, trypsin has been chosen as a model enzyme target. In addition to providing a convenient assay system for reversible and irreversible inactivation studies, the bulk of structural data available for this enzyme has

*This work was supported in part by the Department of Energy, contract no. EY-76-C02-3490, assigned report no. UR-3490-1629; the National Cancer Institute, contract no. NO1-CP-45611; and the National Institutes of Health, Research Career Development Award no. 1K04AM00101-05, to John S. Brand.

facilitated both the design of effective photoaffinity inhibitors and the interpretation of results relative to documented conformational transitions. Inhibitor and substrate binding contacts in the active site of trypsin have been identified by x-ray crystallography (FIGURE 1).[1] Two types of interactions are believed to contribute most of the binding free energy. The first is an electrostatic interaction between the carboxyl moiety of ASP-189 and the cationic side chains of amine, guanidine, and amidine ligands. A second contribution is believed to arise via contacts between the hydrophobic aliphatic or aromatic portions of inhibitors and substrates[2] and the peptide backbones of residues 190 through 191 and 214 through 216.[1] The catalytic charge relay complex composed of ASP-102, HIS-57, and SER-195 is analogous to that in chymotrypsin.

Benzamidine has been well characterized as a competitive inhibitor of tryptic proteases and has served as the basis for the synthesis of two photoaffinity inhibitors, meta- and para-azidobenzamidine (m-ABA, p-ABA). In addition to the azidoben-

zamidines, a more hydrophobic compound, 4-fluoro-3-nitrophenylazide (FNPA), and a five-membered ring nitrogen heterocycle, 3-azido-1,2,4-triazole (3-AT), have been studied. 3-AT is capable of undergoing both protonation and deprotonation; thus, its charge structure can vary drastically within the normal pH range of study.

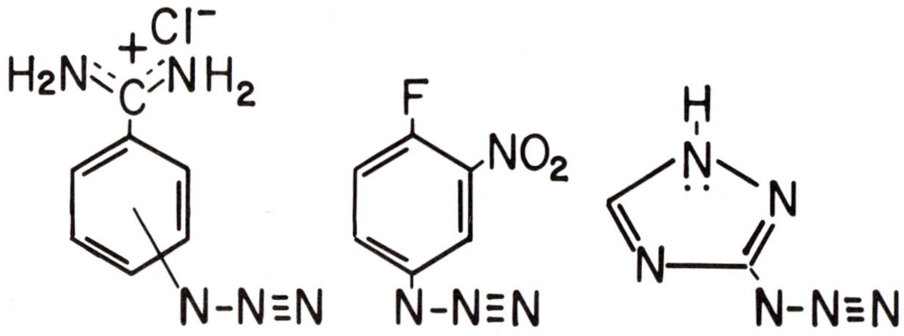

RESULTS AND DISCUSSION

Relationships Between Probe Photolysis Rate, Binding Site Affinity, and Photolabeling Efficiency

As with conventional affinity labeling, the success of a photoaffinity labeling experiment relies on a combination of binding site selectivity, reagent reactivity, and orientation. A photogenerated reagent should be generated (1) at its intended interaction site, (2) in an orientation that facilitates covalent insertion, and, most importantly, (3) at wavelengths that do not damage the target system.

The studies reported here have been conducted with a photolysis system consisting

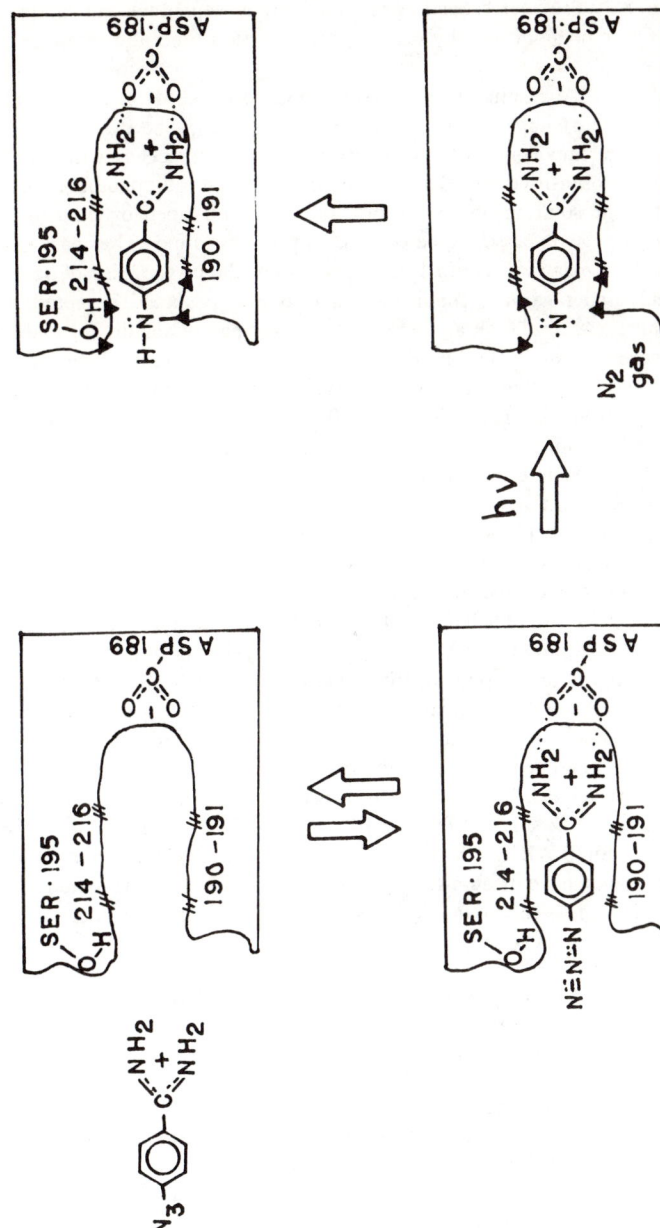

FIGURE 1. A schematic representation of the interaction of *p*-azidobenzamidine with the substrate binding cleft in trypsin. Reversible (dark) binding of benzamidine derivatives is governed by an electrostatic interaction between the amidine cation and the negatively charged carboxyl of ASP-189 and hydrophobic contacts with the peptide backbone of residues 190, 191, and 214–216.[1] Photolytic activation of the azide moiety generates a diradical nitrene species that covalently[4] attaches, probably by an insertion mechanism.[13,14] The exact site of covalent attachment has not yet been determined.

of a high intensity xenon flash lamp, the output of which is filtered to cutoff wavelengths below 290 nm.[3,4] Typically, the system is operated at 4 °C with a repetition rate of 14 pulses per second. The time course of photolysis of a typical photoaffinity label can be monitored by scanning the uv spectrum of the compound as a function of photolysis time.[5]

Photolysis of m-ABA results in a decrease in absorbance at 230 nm and a corresponding increase at approximately 290 nm (FIGURE 2). The existence of an isosbestic point at 267 nm confirms that solution photolysis proceeds with smooth conversion of the photosensitive precursor to a single predominating photoproduct. A first order rate for the solution photolysis process can be obtained by plotting the logarithm of the change in absorbance at 230 nm against time. This parameter provides a convenient means of comparing the solution photolysis rates of various photoaffinity labels under varying conditions, such as pH. It should be noted that certain photoaffinity reagents, such as the azidobenzamidines, which do not undergo protonation or deprotonation in the range from pH 3 to 10, seem to produce spectral patterns and photolysis rates that show little variation with pH. The photolysis rate for m-ABA determined from this result is 7.4×10^{-5} per pulse, irradiating only with wavelengths above 290 nm.

A comparison of rates determined for meta- and para-azidobenzamidines reveals that the para isomer, with a photolysis rate constant of 4.2×10^{-4} per pulse, photolyzes six times more rapidly than the meta form. Inhibition studies at pH 6.2 performed using carbobenzyloxy-L-lysine nitrophenyl ester as substrate reveal that both m- and p-ABA are competitive reversible inhibitors under nonphotolyzing conditions (TABLE 1). Meta-ABA has a tighter binding constant, 4×10^{-5} M, than does p-ABA, 6×10^{-4} M. Following 10 min of irradiation, the inhibition kinetic plots for both inhibitors appear to be noncompetitive with the substrate. Interestingly, the compound that more efficiently inactivates the enzyme under photolytic conditions is p-ABA, in spite of its lower binding affinity. Thus, the influence of photolysis rate and the orientation of the photogenerated intermediate can have a pronounced effect on the efficiency of photoactivated attachment processes. The observed noncompetitive inhibition constant of 2.7×10^{-4} M for m-ABA reflects less efficient photoinactivation than does that for p-ABA, 1.8×10^{-4} M. Substrate protection and nitrene scavenging experiments have been used to confirm that the enzyme inactivation observed with each of these compounds is subsequent to an affinity interaction.

Ability of Photolabeling Reagents to Sense Binding Site Conformation as a Function of pH

Having noticed that the rates of photolysis of such probes as the azidobenzamidines do not show a pH dependency, we became interested in determining whether or not the photoaffinity labeling technique can be applied to sense structural changes in binding sites on proteins. An experiment can be performed in which a series of enzyme solutions are irradiated in the presence of a photoaffinity inhibitor at varying pH values. After readjusting all of the solutions to a common pH and assaying the enzyme activity, differential effects of photoaffinity labeling as a function of pH can be assessed. A dark control, which does not undergo irradiation, can be used to judge

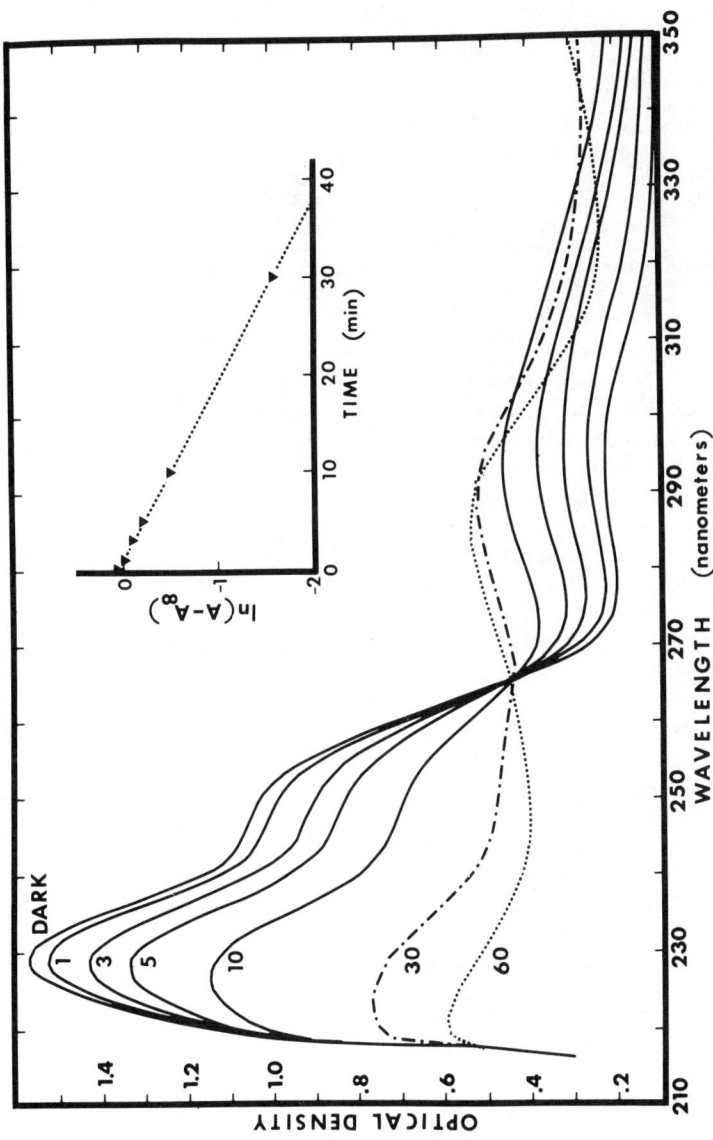

FIGURE 2. The ultraviolet absorption spectrum of *m*-azidobenzamidine (1.87×10^{-4} *M*). Solid lines for 0 (dark), 1, 3, 5, and 10 min of photolysis. Dashed and dotted lines represent 30 and 60 minutes, respectively. Photolysis rate (inset) is $k_p = 7.4 \pm 0.9 \times 10^{-5}$ per pulse. The synthesis of azidobenzamidines and the apparatus for photolysis have been described in detail previously.[4]

TABLE 1

INACTIVATION OF TRYPSIN BY AZIDOBENZAMIDINES*

	Meta-ABA	Para-ABA
Photolysis Rate k_p (per pulse)	$7.4 \pm 0.9 \times 10^{-5}$	$4.2 \pm 0.5 \times 10^{-4}$
Substrate Competitive Reversible Inhibition-Dark—K_{Ic} (M)	$4.0 \pm 0.2 \times 10^{-5}$	$6.0 \pm 0.1 \times 10^{-4}$
Irreversible Inhibition- 10 min Photolysis—K_{Inc} (M)	$2.7 \pm 0.1 \times 10^{-4}$	$1.8 \pm 0.1 \times 10^{-4}$
Substrate Protection TAME conc. for 50% Protection	~5.5 mM	~3.5 mM
Nitrene Scavengers 50 mM Tris 25 mg/ml Chymotrypsin	No effect	No effect

*Summarized from DeTraglia et al. 1978 J. Biol. Chem. **253**: 1846–52.

whether or not irreversible enzyme denaturation occurs at the pH extremes. A differential inactivation as a function of pH, using a photoaffinity label whose photolysis rate is not pH dependent, must then be attributed either to the pH dependence of nitrene insertion or to a conformational pH dependence of orientation or affinity at the binding site.

The pH dependence for the inactivation of trypsin by m-ABA and FNPA has been determined using the experiment described.[3,4] The optimum acidity for inactivation by m-ABA occurs in the neutral pH region, with inactivation occurring to a lesser extent at both pH extremes (FIGURE 3). This profile is not unexpected, considering that the enzyme's optimum activity is also at neutral pH.[6] By contrast, tryptic inactivation by FNPA is most effective at the extremes of pH.[3] Again, this is not inconsistent with the known hydrophobicity of FNPA. It is quite probable that the interaction of trypsin with FNPA involves an affinity interaction with a hydrophobic region of the protein, which is exposed at extremes of pH as the enzyme undergoes conformational denaturation. An important inference that can be drawn from these results is that pH extremes do not seem to deter the nitrene insertion process. Further studies should be undertaken to measure the pH dependence of the covalent attachment process directly.

The upper frame of FIGURE 3 shows the pH dependence of the enzyme's optical rotation at 436 nm both in the absence and presence of n-butylamine, a competitive inhibitor. As an indication of gross conformational changes in the enzyme, these data correlate very well with the FNPA result just described. The acidic cutoff for photoinactivation with m-ABA correlates well with the protonation of the catalytic histidine residue at the active site. The pK_a of this residue has previously been determined from the pH dependence of k_3, the deacylation of the enzyme-substrate complex. For benzoylarginine ethyl ester, the deacylation pK_a is 6.15.[6-8]

As an independent assessment of the pH dependence of m-ABA binding to trypsin, we have performed a series of equilibrium binding affinity measurements under nonphotolytic conditions. In this experiment, a trypsin solution is maintained in a spectrophotometer and is titrated by addition of precisely measured aliquots of m-ABA to both sample and reference cuvettes (FIGURE 4). As the ligand concentration is increased, a difference spectrum, which saturates as all of the available binding sites become occupied, is recorded. This saturation phenomenon, quantitated by measurement of the absorbance at 317 nm, can be treated by standard techniques to determine an equilibrium binding constant.[9] By repeating this experiment across a broad range of pH, a profile of equilibrium affinity versus pH can be constructed. This series of experiments confirms that the optimum pH for the interaction of *m*-ABA

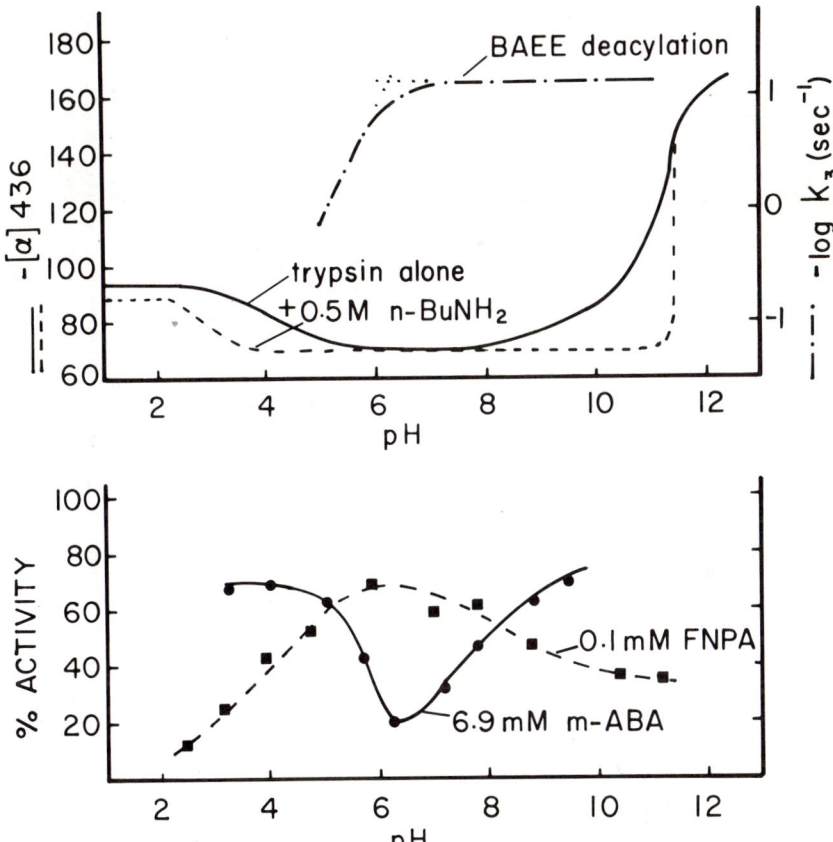

FIGURE 3. (Lower frame) The pH dependence of the inactivation of trypsin by 6.9 m*M* *m*-azidobenzamidine (*m*-ABA) (solid line) and 0.1 m*M* 4-fluoro-3-nitrophenyl azide (FNPA) (broken line) after 10 min of photolysis. Unphotolyzed controls incubated at each pH retained constant activity. All samples were assayed following readjustment to pH 6.2. Data from De Traglia, *et al.*[4] (*m*-ABA) and Tometsko and Turula[3] (FNPA).

(Upper frame) The pH dependence of conformational transitions in trypsin, marked by changes in optical rotation at 436 nm in the absence (solid line) and presence (dashed line) of 0.5 *M* n-butylamine, a competitive inhibitor. (Based on D'Albis and Bechet[7].) The pH dependence for deacylation of benzoylarginine ethyl ester (BAEE), believed to represent the pK_a of the catalytic histidine-57 residue, is shown in alternating dots and dashes. (After Inagami.[6]) The acidic cutoff for *m*-ABA photoinactivation appears to correlate with protonation of HIS-57. Enzyme denaturation correlates both with loss of substrate-competitive *m*-ABA interaction at alkaline pH and with increased FNPA binding at pH extremes.

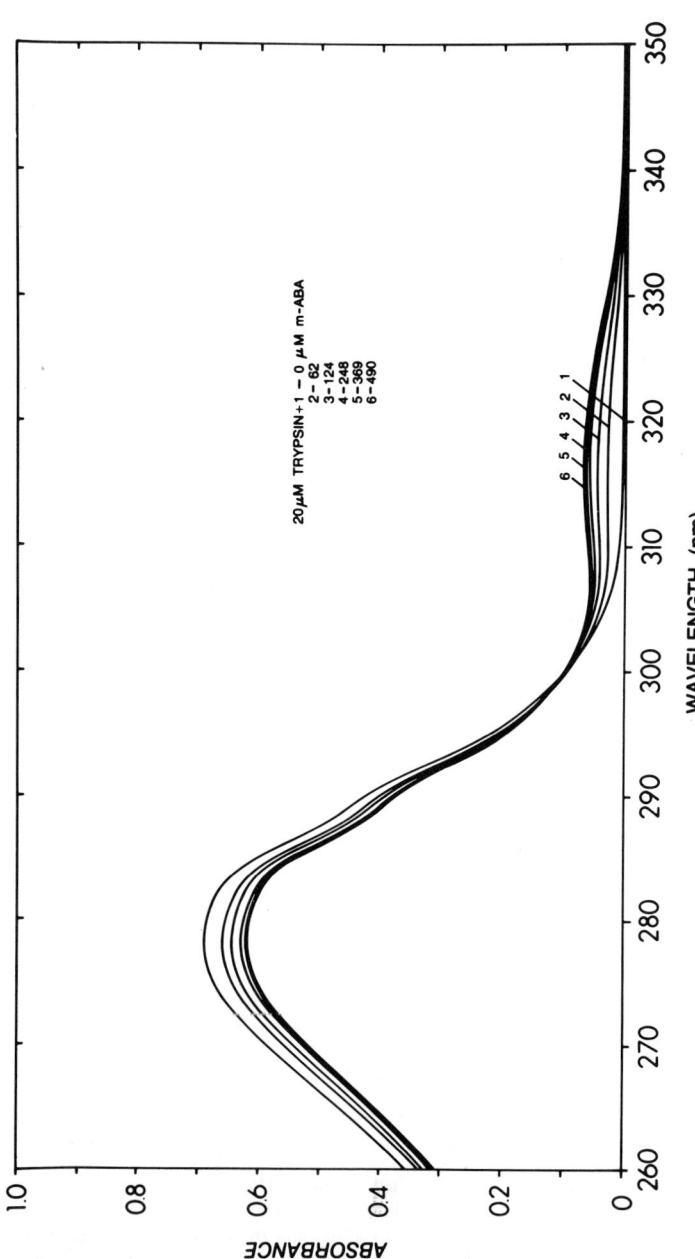

FIGURE 4. The difference spectrum for the equilibrium titration of trypsin by *m*-azidobenzamidine at pH 7. Spectral curves represent 20 μM trypsin in the presence of 0, 62, 124, 248, 369, and 490 μM *m*-ABA (1–6, respectively). Meta-ABA titrant was added to both sample and reference cuvettes. The buffer was 50 mM NaSuccinate, 50 mM Tris, and 20 mM CaCl$_2$, adjusted to the desired pH with conc. HCl. Titrations were conducted at room temperature (22 °C).

Spectral saturation curves were used to compute binding affinity constants by the method of Rose and Drago.[9] At pH 7.0, $K_d = 1.30 \times 10^{-4}$ M.

with trypsin is in the range from pH 6 to 7 (FIGURE 5). Immediately below pH 6, and in the range from pH 7.5 to 9, the binding affinity measured by equilibrium titration decreases appreciably. These data are in good correspondence with the results of the photoinactivation experiments described previously. Thus, it seems quite likely that the pH dependence of photoaffinity inactivation can be interpreted as an indication of binding site conformation.

A similar series of titration experiments can be performed to determine the pH

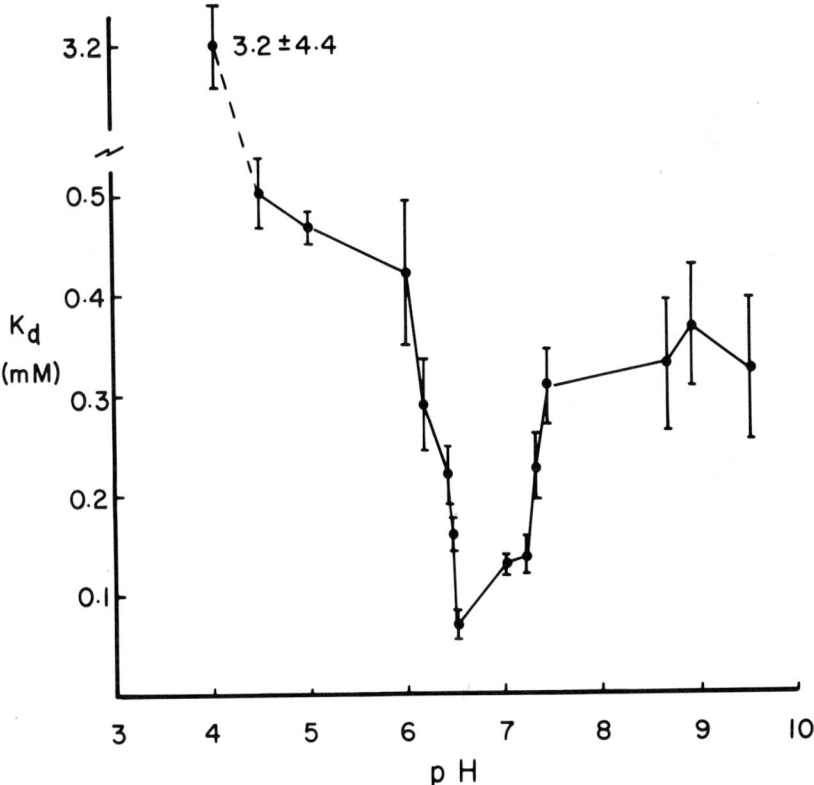

FIGURE 5. The pH profile for the binding of *m*-azidobenzamidine to trypsin determined by equilibrium spectral titrations (see FIGURE 4). The affinity dependence correlates well with the level of inactivation attained at each pH in photoaffinity inhibition experiments (FIGURE 3).

dependence of the binding of β-napthamidine to trypsin. As shown in FIGURE 6, the titration of trypsin by β-napthamidine produces a difference spectrum[2] with a maximum at 250 nm and isosbestic points at 244 and 261 nm. Quite unlike the interaction of *m*-ABA, the binding of β-napthamidine does not decrease in affinity at alkaline pH (FIGURE 7). Although β-napthamidine is a bulkier, more hydrophobic inhibitor than is *m*-ABA, it binds roughly ten-fold tighter than *m*-ABA even at neutral pH. These data suggest that a steric interaction of the azide substituent on

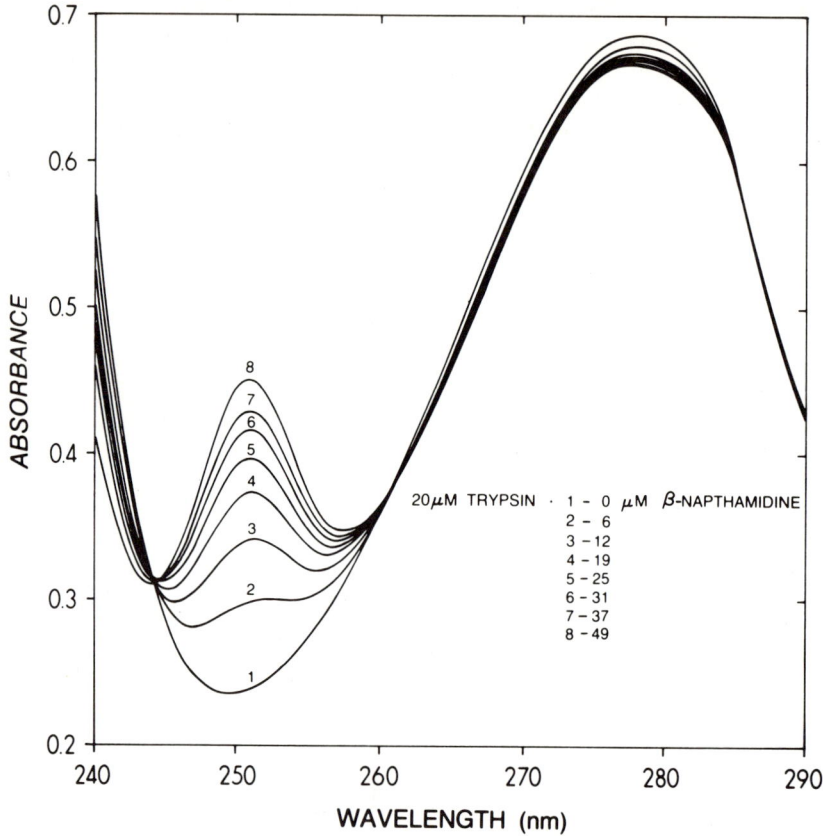

FIGURE 6. The difference spectrum for the equilibrium titration of trypsin by β-napthamidine at pH 6.5. Spectral curves represent 20 μM trypsin in the presence of 0, 6, 12, 19, 25, 31, 37, and 49 μM β-napthamidine (1–8, respectively) against a reference without enzyme. The buffer was 50 mM NaSuccinate, 50 mM Tris (20 mM Ca^{+2} added in some experiments, see FIGURE 7). Titrations were conducted at room temperature (22 °C). The binding constant computed from saturation curves at pH 6.5 was $K_d = 8.00 \times 10^{-6}$ M. β-Napthamidine was prepared by reacting β-cyanonapthalene (ICN) with anhydrous ethanol to form the imido ester, which was subsequently reacted with anhydrous ammonia to form the free unsubstituted amidine (method of Pinner and Klein[15]).

m-ABA may account for its decreased affinity relative to β-napthamidine and that this steric interaction may become more critical at alkaline pH. It is noteworthy that the presence of Ca^{+2} in the equilibrium titration increases the affinity of β-napthamidine binding.

Aryl Azide Stability at pH Extremes

A further requirement that must be satisfied before a photoaffinity labeling experiment can be performed across a broad pH range is that the photosensitive reagent must be chemically inert and stable throughout the range of interest. Analysis of the reagent's ir, nmr, and uv spectra under various conditions is often sufficient to determine whether instabilities exist. Often a compromise in temperature or time of exposure is sufficient to provide the required stability. For instance, FNPA, which couples to amines by a displacement reaction when warmed at alkaline pH, can be used as a photoaffinity label at pH 10 when short exposures and low temperatures are maintained.[3] Nonphotolyzed controls may be used to verify inertness during dark incubations with the photolabel.

It is known that organic azides decompose rapidly after protonation by mineral acids.[10] However, the required acidity for this reaction may be far stronger than that encountered in most biological studies. Studies of 3-azido-1,2,4-triazole have confirmed that, in acidic media, the molecule protonates on the ring and not on the azide (FIGURE 8).[11] The center frame of FIGURE 8 presents the infrared spectrum of uncharged 3-AT. The free azide band occurs at 2140 cm^{-1}. The upper frame, presenting the spectrum of the hydrochloride form of the molecule, indicates that the azide group is present in its free form, again at 2140 cm^{-1}. In fact, the molecule is stable when stored in 95% sulfuric acid. There are also indications in the literature that azide substituents present on electron donating ring systems may tautomerize to a less photosensitive tetrazole.[10,12] As shown in the lower frame of this figure, the anionic

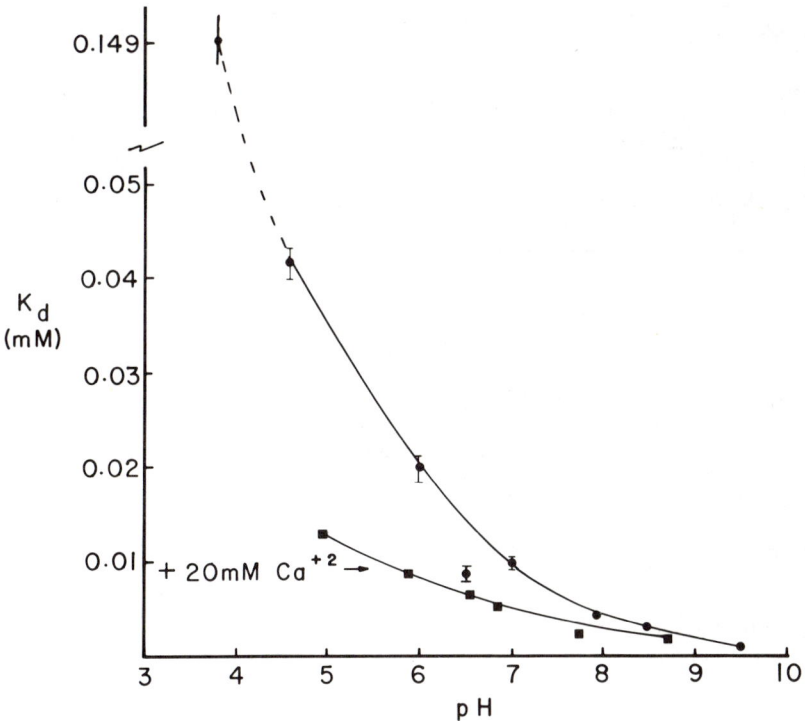

FIGURE 7. The pH profile for the binding of β-napthamidine to trypsin in the absence (circles) and presence (squares) of 20 mM Ca^{+2}.

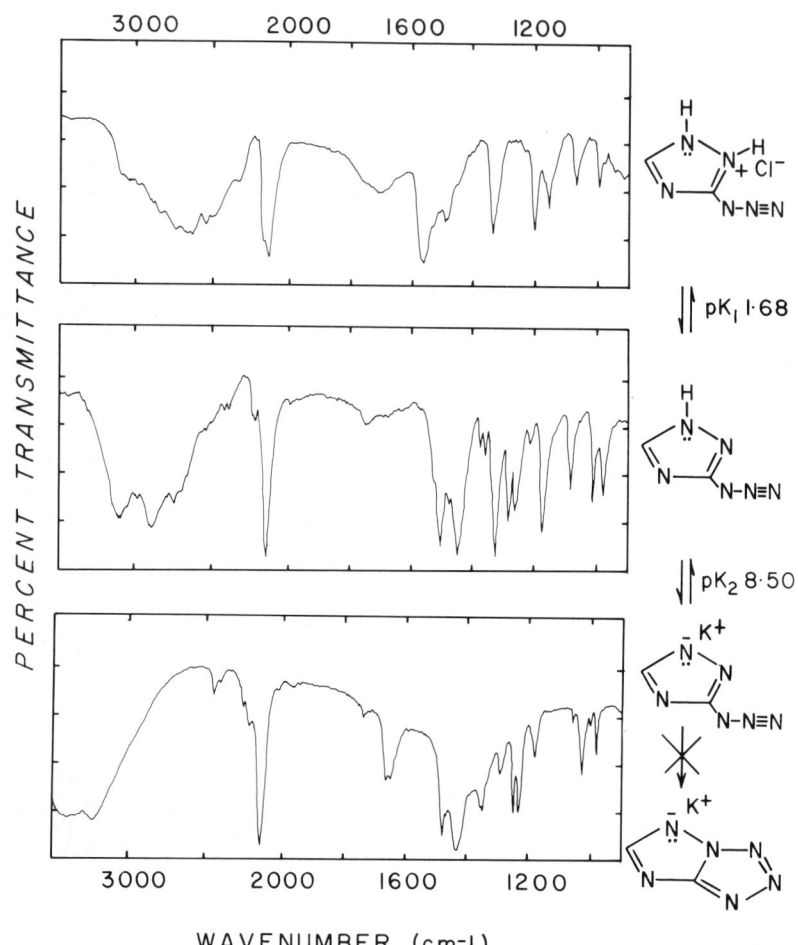

FIGURE 8. Infrared spectra for 3-azido-1,2,4-triazole (3-AT) as a hydrochloride salt (upper spectrum), uncharged (middle spectrum), and as an anion (lower spectrum). At acid pH, the molecule protonates on the ring, not on the azide; this is evidenced by the unchanged frequency of the azide stretch (2140 cm^{-1}) in both uncharged and protonated forms.[16] At alkaline pH, deprotonation to an anionic form is not accompanied by a tautomeric conversion of the azide to a tetrazole, which is again evidenced by the unchanged azide frequency at 2140 cm^{-1}. Protonation and deprotonation pKs were determined by aqueous titration with KOH. Infrared spectra were recorded as KBr pellets. The 3-AT was prepared by the method of Heitke and McCarty.[12]

azidotriazole also possesses a free azide band at 2140 cm^{-1}. The existence of a tetrazole tautomer for this molecule is, therefore, highly unlikely. The pK$_a$ values shown for protonation at pH 1.68 and deprotonation at pH 8.5 have been determined by aqueous titration of 3-AT with KOH.

From the example of 3-AT, one cannot overemphasize the need to fully examine the chemistry of photoaffinity labels before applying them to biological systems.

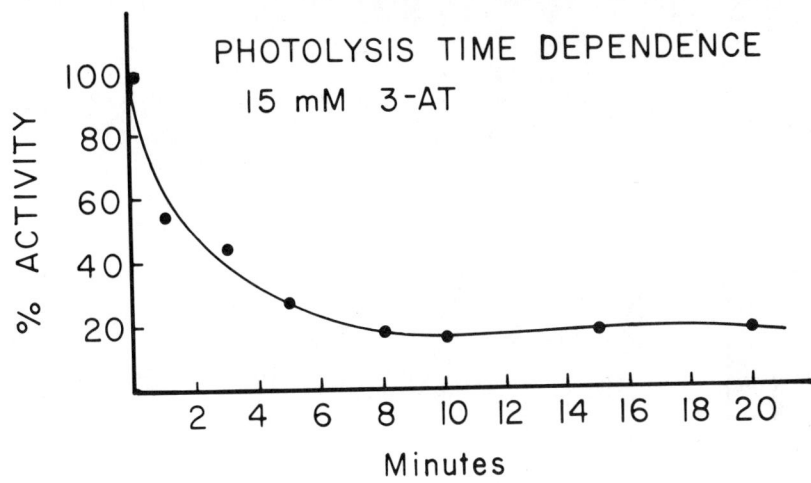

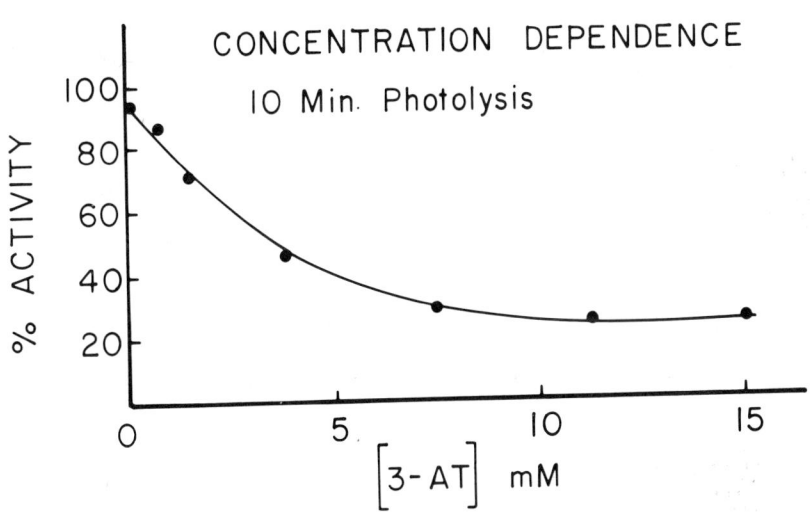

FIGURE 9. (Upper frame) The photolysis dependence of inactivation of trypsin by 15 m*M* 3-AT at pH 6.5 (photolysis conditions described previously). Half maximal inactivation is obtained with approximately two minutes photolysis time.

(Lower frame) Concentration dependence for inactivation by 3-AT using 10 min photolyses. Half maximal inactivation occurs with ~4 m*M* 3-AT.

All samples contained 0.2 mg/ml trypsin plus appropriate concentrations of 3-AT in Tris-Succinate buffer with 20 m*M* Ca^{+2}. Activity was measured by a modification of the method of Erlanger, *et al.*,[17] using benzoyl-L-arginine-p-nitroanilide as the substrate.

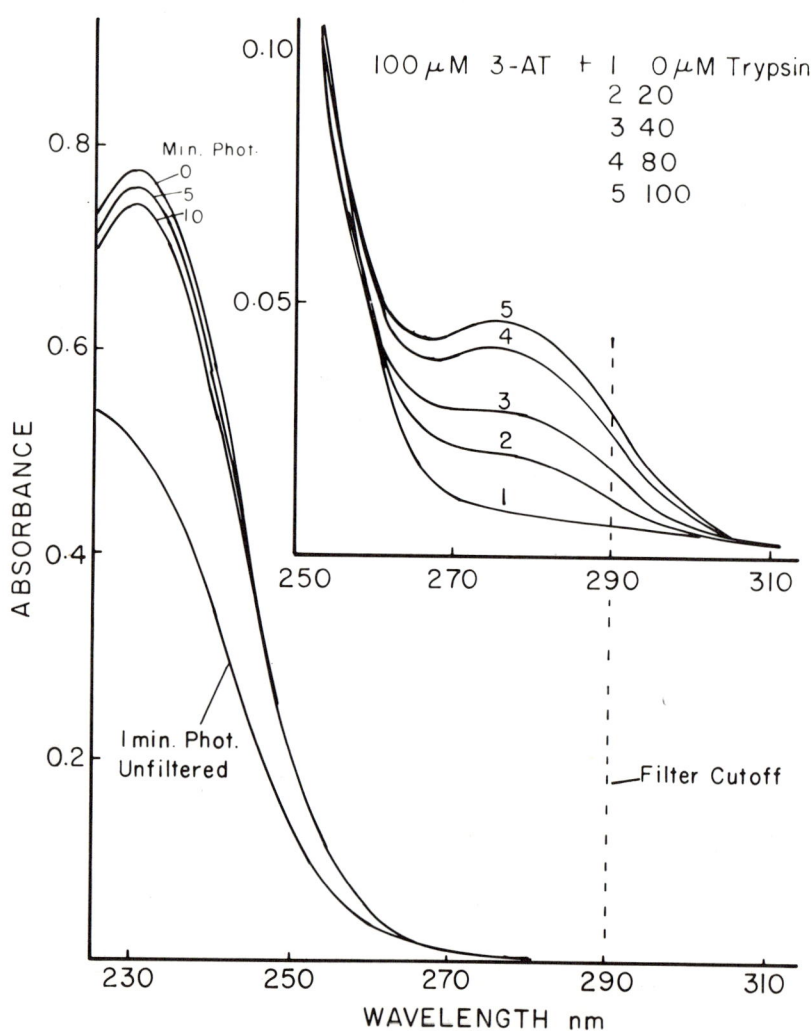

FIGURE 10. The ultraviolet absorption spectrum of 3-AT (100 μM) dark (0 min) and after 5 and 10 min of photolysis using the system previously described, with a 290 nm cutoff filter. Less than 5% of the compound is photolyzed in 10 min under these conditions. Also shown is a spectrum following one minute of unfiltered irradiation.

    (Inset) The absorption difference spectrum for the binary complex of trypsin with 3-AT, obtained by titration of 3-AT (100 μM) with increasing amounts of trypsin (0–100 μM; 1–5 respectively). The binary complex absorption, which extends to wavelengths above 290 nm, probably accounts for acceleration of the photolysis of 3-AT when it is bound to trypsin.

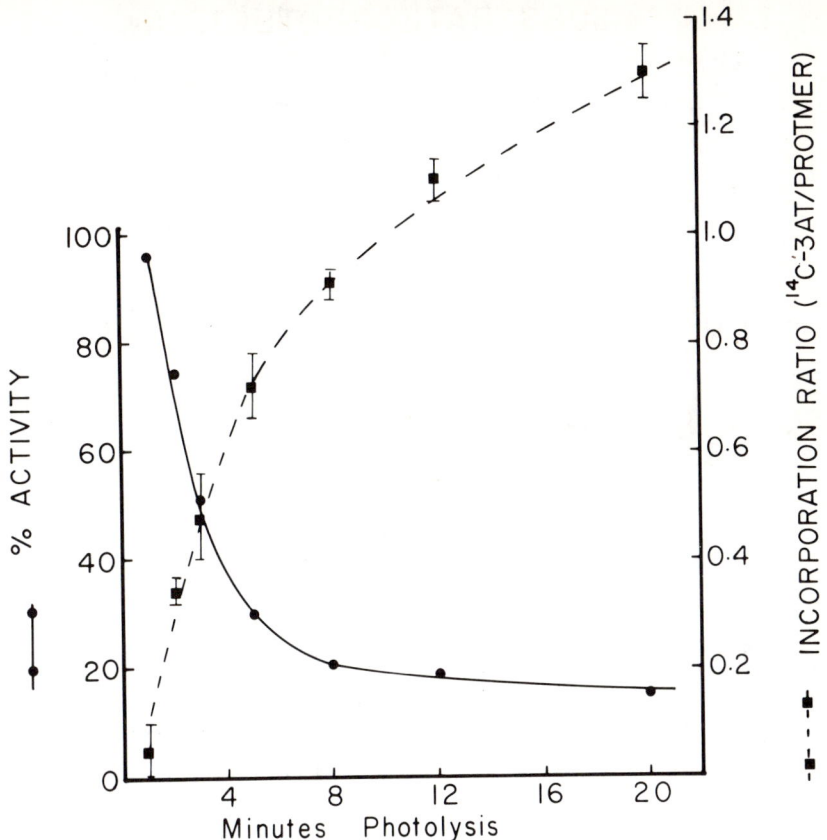

FIGURE 11. Incorporation ratio (squares) and percent activity (circles) as a function of photolysis time for photoaffinity labeling of trypsin by ^{14}C-3-AT. For the first 10 min, decreasing activity corresponds directly with a single probe molecule incorporated per protomer. Irradiation and activity measurements were conducted as previously described. Radiolabeled 3-AT was prepared from 5-^{14}C-3-amino-1,2,4-triazole (ICN) by the same procedure as the unlabeled reagent. The method for incorporation ratio determination has been described in detail elsewhere.[18]

Selective Photolysis of a Desired Photoreactive Species

A phenomenon that is not often considered in studies with photoaffinity labels is that the absorption characteristics of the bound probe may differ from those of the probe in free solution. Red or blue shifts in absorption due to differing environments encountered by the affinity label can alter its photolysis characteristics. In our studies of the interaction of 3-AT with trypsin, we have made some interesting observations.

The concentration dependence of tryptic photoinactivation by 3-AT at pH 6.5 using 10 min photolyses is shown in the lower frame of FIGURE 9. Fifty percent inactivation is achieved at approximately 4 mM 3-AT. Note that, in the upper frame,

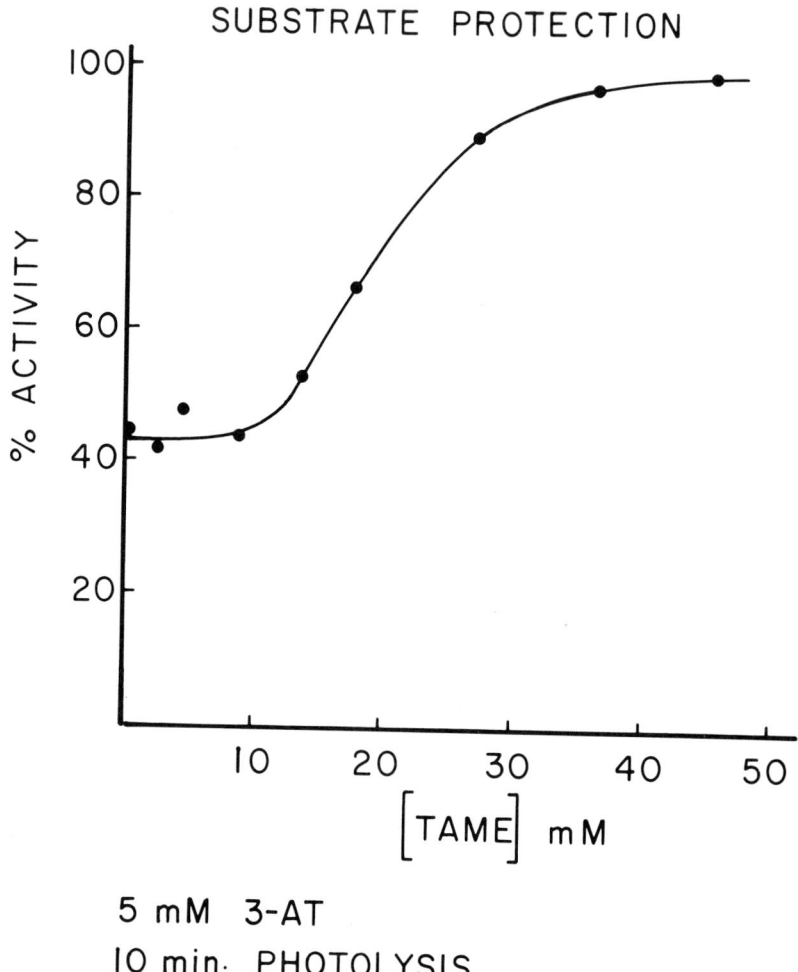

FIGURE 12. Protection of trypsin against photoinactivation by 5 mM 3-AT using *p*-tosyl-L-arginine methyl ester (TAME) as a competing substrate. The experimental method has been described elsewhere.[4]

the time required to photoinactivate half of the enzyme is only about 2 min and the maximal inactivation is achieved by 10 min. This rapid rate of photoinactivation seems paradoxical when compared with the rate of photolysis of 3-AT in solution. As shown in the left portion of FIGURE 10, 3-AT has an absorption maximum at 233 nm. When it is irradiated with a 290 nm cutoff filter, less than 5% of the compound is photolyzed during a 10 min exposure. Thus, there seems to be no correspondence between the rate of photolysis of 3-AT and its rate of photoinactivation of trypsin. A possible explanation, however, is that the probe species bound to trypsin is more susceptible to photolysis than is the unbound probe. That this may, in fact, be the case is illustrated in the inset.

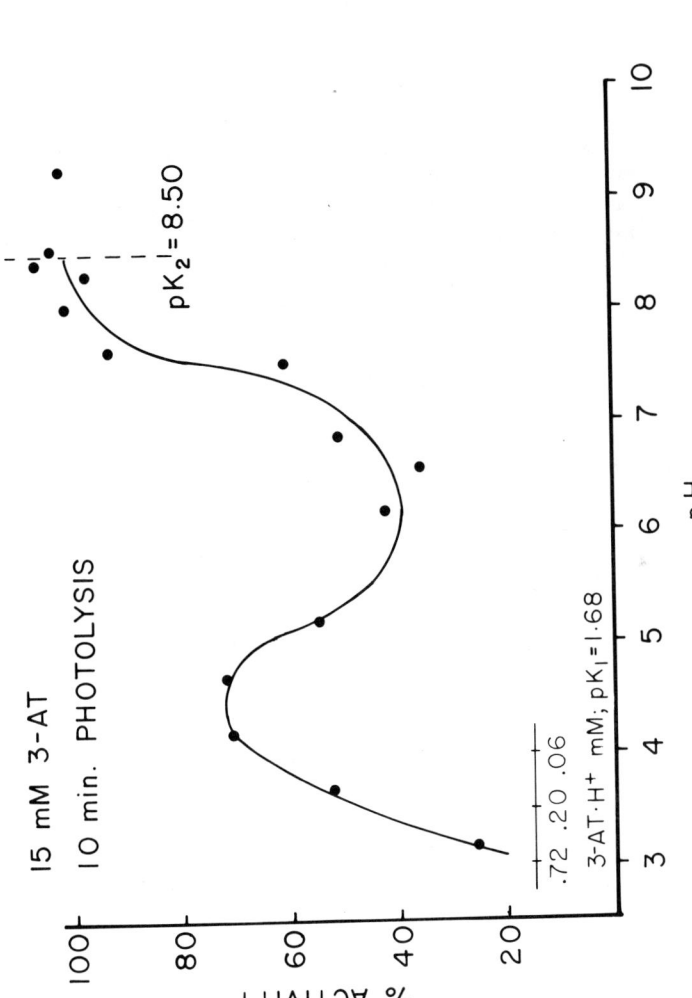

FIGURE 13. The pH dependence of the inactivation of trypsin by 15 mM 3-AT with 10 min photolysis. Alkaline cutoff agrees with the deprotonation of 3-AT at pH 8.5. At pH values below 4, the increased photoinactivation may result from protonation of 3-AT (pK_1 = 1.68), generating a cationic species that binds very tightly to the enzyme.

A difference spectrum for the bound probe can be obtained by titration in a manner similar to that described earlier for *m*-ABA. In this case, a 100 μM 3-AT solution is titrated by the addition of trypsin aliquots to both the sample and the reference. The resulting spectrum represents that of the bound probe species and shows a second maximum at 275 nm. The absorption of this new band extends beyond 290 nm and, therefore, accounts for the increased photolytic susceptibility of the enzyme-bound probe seen in photoinactivation time studies.

An examination of the rate of incorporation of ^{14}C-labeled 3-AT into trypsin at pH 6.5 reveals that, within the first 10 minutes of photolysis, the ratio of probe incorporated into enzyme approaches 1:1. Thus, the species that is most rapidly photolyzed and that accounts best for the enzymatic inactivation probably binds to a discrete functionally related site on the enzyme (FIGURE 11). Recall that, at pH 6.5, 3-AT is an uncharged molecule. In spite of the fact that it does not bear a cationic structure at neutral pH, our data indicate that the photoinactivation of trypsin results subsequent to interaction of 3-AT at the substrate binding site. In the presence of *p*-tosyl-L-arginine methyl ester (TAME), complete protection against photoinactivation can be achieved (FIGURE 12).

Considering its variable charge structure and the fact that uncharged 3-AT binds reversibly to the substrate recognition site on trypsin, we find it is interesting to examine the pH profile for inactivation of the enzyme by this probe. This experiment is somewhat the opposite of that performed using the azidobenzamidines (FIGURE 13). Meta-azidobenzamidine retains the same charge structure throughout the pH range and may, therefore, be used to sense the conformation of its complementary binding site on the enzyme. In contrast, the result obtained with 3-AT suggests that the probe's charge structure dictates its inactivation profile. As the pH approaches the alkaline pK of 8.5, the probe attains a net negative charge, and does not interact with the enzyme. As the pH decreases below 6, the probe loses its ability to bind to the enzyme until the pH reaches approximately 4. Below pH 4, the concentration of protonated azidotriazole begins to approach the millimolar range. This distinctly cationic species interacts very strongly with its binding site on trypsin and is able to produce significant levels of inactivation in the region from pH 3 to 4.

SUMMARY

These results suggest that important information regarding the conformation of complementary binding sites and the behavior of various charged states of inhibitors can be obtained from studies of the pH dependence of photoaffinity labeling experiments. This information may assist in identifying the pK_as of key residues controlling the binding interaction. This technique should prove very useful in probing binding site structure on nonfunctioning targets, such as enzyme zymogens, as well as complicated receptor interactions.

REFERENCES

1. BODE, W. & P. SCHWAGER. 1975. The refined crystal structure of bovine B trypsin at 1.8 Å resolution. II. Crystallographic refinement, calcium binding site, benzamidine binding site, and the active site at pH 7.0. J. Mol. Biol. **98**: 693–717.

2. MARES-GUIA, M. 1968. Hydrophobic interactions in the trypsin active center. Arch. Biochem. Biophys. **127:** 317–22.

3. TOMETSKO, A. M. & J. TURULA. 1976. Evaluating the stability and reactivity of a light sensitive probe by enzyme analysis. Photochem. Photobiol. **24:** 579–85.

4. DETRAGLIA, M. C., J. S. BRAND & A. M. TOMETSKO. 1978. Characterization of azidobenzamidines as photoaffinity labels for trypsin. J. Biol. Chem. **253:** 1846–52.

5. BAURIAN, R., J.-F. LAROCHELLE & F. LAMY. 1976. Photolysis of desmosine and isodesmosine by ultraviolet light. Eur. J. Biochem. **67:** 155–64.

6. INAGAMI, T. 1972. Trypsin. *In* Proteins: Structure and Function. Funatsu *et al.,* Eds.: Chapter 1. John Wiley & Sons. New York.

7. D'ALBIS, A. & J.-J. BECHET. 1967. Effet du pH sur la fixation d'inhibiteurs competitifs synthetiques par la trypsine. Biochim. Biophys. Acta **140:** 435–58.

8. CAPLOW, M. & W. P. JENCKS. 1962. The effect of substituents on the deacylation of benzoyl-chymotrypsins. Biochemistry **1:** 883–93.

9. ROSE, N. J. & R. S. DRAGO. 1959. Molecular addition compounds to iodine. I. An absolute method for the spectroscopic determination of equilibrium constants. J. Am. Chem. Soc. **81:** 6138–45.

10. PATAI, S. 1971. The Chemistry of the Azido Group, Chapter 4. Wiley (Interscience). New York.

11. PEVZNER, M. S., M. N. MARTYNOVA & T. N. TIMOFEEVA. 1974. Acid-base properties of 3(5)-azido-1,2,4-triazoles. Chem. Heterocycl. Comp. **9:** 1121–23.

12. HEITKE, B. T. & C. G. MCCARTY. 1974. Synthesis of C-amino and C-azido-1,2,4-triazoles. J. Org. Chem. **39:** 1522–26.

13. BAYLEY, H. & J. R. KNOWLES. 1977. Photoaffinity labeling. Methods Enzymol. **46:** 69–114.

14. DARFLER, F. & A. M. TOMETSKO. 1978. Applications of light sensitive chemicals for probing biological processes. *In* Chemistry and Biochemistry of Amino Acids, Peptides, and Proteins, Vol. 5. B. Weinstein, Ed. 31–93. Marcel Dekker, Inc. New York.

15. PINNER, A. & F. KLEIN. 1877. Umwandlung der Nitrile in Imide. IV. Mittheilung. Chem. Ber. **10:** 1889–97.

16. MEL'NIKOV, V. V., L. F. BAEVA, V. V. STOLPAKOVA, M. S. PEVZNER, M. N. MARTYNOVA & B. V. GIDASPOV. 1974. Vibrational spectra and structure of 1,2,4-triazole derivatives. V. 3-Azido-1,2,4-triazole derivatives. Chem. Heterocycl. Comp. **9:** 1117–21.

17. ERLANGER, B. F., N. KOKOWSKY & W. COHEN. 1961. The preparation and properties of two new chromogenic substrates of trypsin. Arch. Biochem. Biophys. **95:** 271–78.

18. DETRAGLIA, M. C., J. S. BRAND & A. M. TOMETSKO. 1979. Anal. Biochem. **99:** 463–73.

PHOTOAFFINITY PROBES IN THE ANTIBODY COMBINING REGION

Frank F. Richards and John Lifter

Department of Internal Medicine
Yale University School of Medicine
New Haven, Connecticut 06510

INTRODUCTION

The structure and function of the antibody combining region has been the subject of intensive chemical, physical, genetic, and biological study over the last decade.

Antibodies are ligating proteins that have binding regions complementary to a very large number of dissimilar chemical structures. The structural basis of this capacity to bind ligands has excited considerable interest. It is known that the overall three-dimensional structure of the combining region containing Fv domains has strong similarities in several antibodies. Thus, the polypeptide backbone of both the light and the heavy chain components of the Fv region consist of β pleated antiparallel regions. It has three loops at the free solvent exposed end of the domain joining these β pleated regions. The solvent exposed loops and, perhaps, their immediate neighboring structures are believed to constitute the binding region.[1] There is at present only a little direct evidence concerning the extent of the antigen-complementary region. More indirect evidence has suggested that an area of approximately $20 \times 12 \times 8$ Å is involved in the ligation process.[2] The extent of the binding region is of particular interest, since there is evidence that the combining region of a single immunoglobulin molecule will bind a number of structurally diverse ligands.[3,4] Such ligands are not necessarily small; some are large enough to occupy most of the presumed combining region. One interpretation of such data is that the combining region is composed of numerous ligand-binding subsites, forming a mosaic. There is evidence that binding of one large ligand takes place over that extensive region of its surface in contact with the immunoglobulin. It has been postulated that structurally diverse ligands may bind in a number of different ways to the mosaic of subsites. Thus, there is an alternative to the idea first postulated by Paul Ehrlich that antibody molecules contain cavities shaped like the antigen—the classic model of the lock and the key. The alternative possibility is that point-to-point interaction occurs between a number of dissimilar ligands and the mosaic of subsites in the combining region, but that interaction sufficiently well matched to give high affinity binding is relatively rare. There is some experimental evidence supporting this suggestion.[5] (For these and many other reasons, affinity and photoaffinity reagents have been used for a number of years to map the binding sites of a number of ligands that bind to homogeneous antibodies[6-8] and populations of antibodies with known ligand-binding specificities.)[9]

My colleagues and I began work several years ago on a mouse IgA myeloma protein derived from a mouse myeloma cell line named MOPC 460. This homogeneous immunoglobulin binds both menadione ($K_0 = 2 \times 10^4$ L/M at 20 °C) and ϵ 2,4

0077-8923/80/0346-0078 $1.75/1 © 1980, NYAS

dinitrophenyl lysine ($K_0 = 1 \times 10^5$ L/M at 20 °C). These ligands are bound competitively and there are certain structural resemblances between both ligands. For instance, the distance between the oxygen molecules on both the menadione and the Dnp portions are approximately equal. Also, many antibodies raised against the dinitrophenyl group also bind menadione, while many antibodies raised against menadione also bind Dnp.[10] One interpretation of these findings has been that the same site binds both Dnp and menadione.[10]

Earlier studies with the menadione and Dnp binding protein 460 showed, however, that it was possible to denature and partially renature this protein in such a fashion that the Dnp binding activity was retained while the menadione binding was nullified. Other chemical modification conditions were found that resulted in the reciprocal differential inactivation—menadione binding was left intact and Dnp binding was abolished. Later direct and indirect measurements on protein 460 confirmed that the menadione and Dnp binding sites were spatially separated and that the distance separating the centers of these two binding sites is approximately 14 Å.[11–13]

It became of interest, therefore, to study the combining region of protein 460 with reagents that were based on the structures of menadione and Dnp, but that were capable of modifying protein 460 by covalent interactions. We decided to synthesize one menadione-based and two types of Dnp-based photoaffinity reagents. We reacted these with protein 460 and located and characterized the modified amino acid residues. At the same time, other research groups were studying Dnp- and menadione-binding IgA mouse myeloma and protein MOPC 315, as well as protein 460, with Dnp-based haloketones.[8]

Heterogeneous anti-Dnp immunoglobulins had already been examined with nitrophenyl based diazonium salts. Such reagents are limited in their reactivity to a few amino acid residues, and we felt that an approach using reagents capable of being inserted into a wide range of heteroatomic carbon linkages as well as reacting, after rearrangement, as an acylating agent would increase considerably the choice of potentially reactive groups at or near the ligation site. Unfortunately, the menadione-based photoaffinity reagent, 1 methyl-2:4-naphthaquinone-^{3}H-3-thioglycolyldiazoketone:[14]

proved to be a powerful photosensitizer. After this compound was reacted with protein 460 in the presence of light, a number of new N-terminal amino acid residues were detected by the dansyl-Edman sequence analysis method, suggesting that the peptide chains had been split in a number of places. Unfortunately, the pattern of peptides produced was not easily reproduced from experiment to experiment. We decided, therefore, to work with the Dnp-based photoaffinity reagents. One reagent was a diazoketone, the other an azide.[15]

Principles

[3]H-2,4-dinitrophenylalanyldiazoketone (^{3}H-DnpAD) reacts according to the following scheme. DnpAD undergoes photolysis to a carbene, which may insert into heteroatomic (containing N, O, or S) side chains of amino acid residues.[16] Analogous carbenes with ester rather than ketene linkages also insert into tyrosine and histidine[17] and insertion by carbenes into C—H bonds has also been reported.[18] The carbene undergoes Wolff rearrangement to a ketene, which may acylate nucleophilic carboxyl, hydroxyl, amino, and thiol functions. Lysine, tyrosine, cysteine, and perhaps also histidine, aspartic, and glutamic acid may be acylated by ketenes.[16]

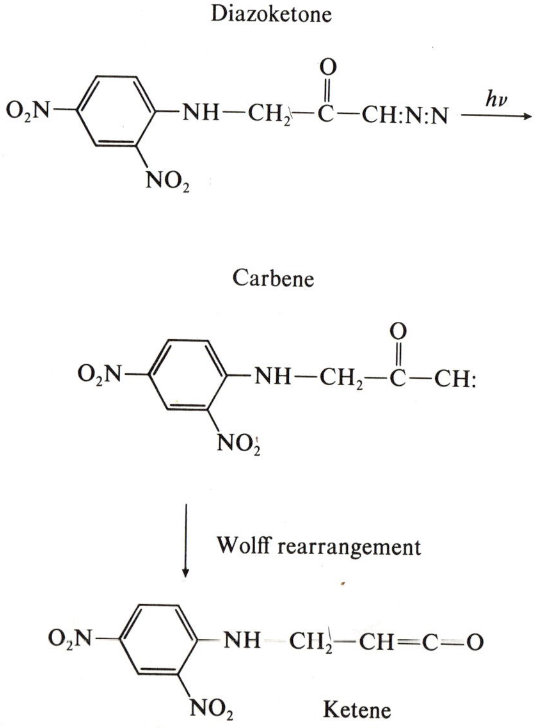

Diazoketone

Carbene

Wolff rearrangement

Ketene

[3]H-2,4, dinitrophenyl-1-azide (DnpN$_3$) generates a nitrene on photolysis, which has the potential of inserting into heteroatomic linkages such as C=O, C—S—, C—N, C—H, or N—H.

The reactive intermediate[19]

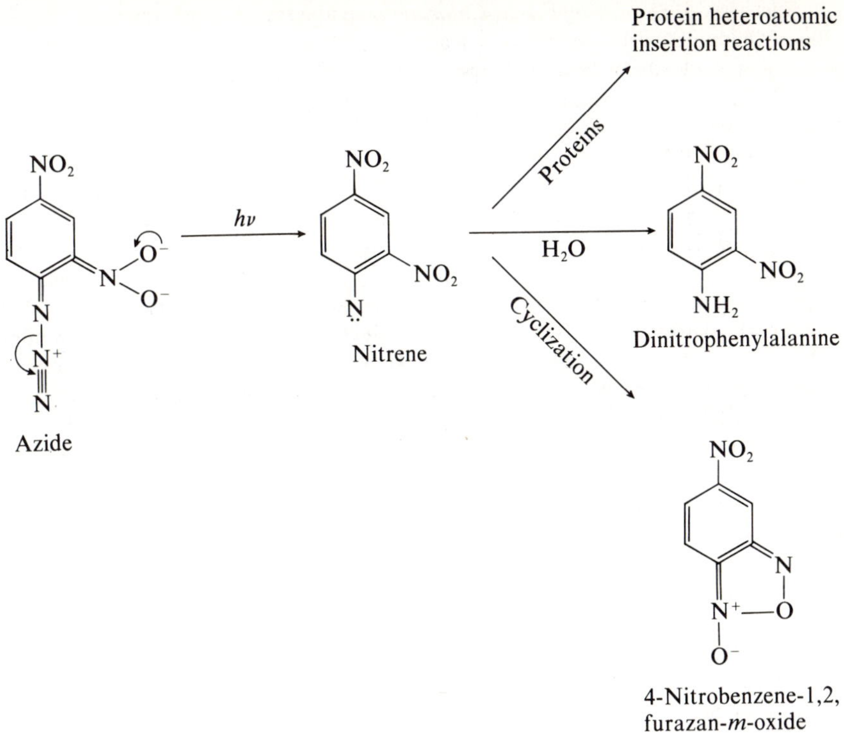

Protein heteroatomic
insertion reactions

Azide

$h\nu$

Nitrene

Proteins

H_2O

Cyclization

Dinitrophenylalanine

4-Nitrobenzene-1,2,
furazan-m-oxide

may hydrolysize to dinitrophenylaniline or cyclize to an n-oxyfurazan derivative. There is no information on the reactivity of this derivative, but the relatively high incorporation of the reagent into protein suggests that it is not a rapidly formed major intermediate.

Synthesis of Reagents

DnpAD and ³H-DnpAD

Synthesis of Dnp Alanine. 1-Fluoro-2,4-dinitrobenzene (20 ml) in 30 ml absolute dried ethanol was added over 20 min to 11 g L-alanine and 42 g Na_2CO_3 in 250 ml water and stirred at 20 °C in the dark for 2 h. The yellow precipitate was filtered, washed with ether, and redissolved in a minimal volume of water; the resulting solution was acidified to pH 1.0 with HCl and the reprecipitated Dnp alanine was filtered and dried in the dark. ³H-Dnp L-alanine was prepared by similar methods from (3,5,6 ³H) 1-fluoro-2,4-dinitrobenzene on a 1–2 mg scale, except that centrifugation in 1-0 ml vials replaced the filtration steps. Pure Dnp L-alanine should give a single component either on polyamide thin-layer chromatography in benzene 80: acetic acid 20 v/v (Solvent I); or in t-amyl alcohol saturated with pH 6.0: 0.2 N sodium phthalate buffer (Solvent II); or by electrophoresis at pH 1.8 and pH 6.0.

Synthesis of Dnp Alanyl Acid Chloride. Dnp alanine (0.25 g) was suspended in 300 ml thoroughly dried benzene (Dnp alanine); 1.0 ml redistilled SO Cl_2 in 20 ml dry benzene was added slowly over 20 min,[20] the mixture was refluxed for 2 h, and stored at −20 °C overnight, moisture being carefully excluded at all stages. Synthesis was followed by the rosaniline reaction.[21]

Synthesis of Dnp Alanyl Diazoketone. Dnp alanyl acid chloride (40 μg) was made up to 100 ml of anhydrous diethyl ether at 0 °C and added slowly to 10 ml dry ether containing 1×10^{-2} moles diazomethane at 0 °C. (For preparation of ethereal diazomethane, see Reference 22.) The resulting mixture was stored in a moisture-proof container in the dark at 4 °C for 12 h. During large-scale preparations, the DnpAD was precipitated from the ether solution and washed with ether at 4 °C. For small-scale synthesis of ^{3}H-DnpAD, the product was purified on a basic alumina column 1×15 cms (Brockman activity I), which was eluted with dry dioxane. Ultraviolet absorption Δ max were at 255 and 342 nm; ir spectra gave a 2115 cm^{-1} diazo stretch band. Mass spectroscopy gave no molecular ion, but two major peaks at m/e 210 and 69 are consistent with the two halves (Dnp-NH CH CH_3)$^+$ and (O=CCH=N=N)$^+$.

Synthesis of DnpN$_3$ and ^{3}H-DnpN$_3$. DnpN$_3$ and ^{3}H-DnpN$_3$ were synthesized by direct displacement of fluorine in 1-fluoro-2,4-dinitrobenzene or the (3,5,6 ^{3}H) analog.[23] Fluorodinitrobenzene (14.7 mg) was dissolved in 0.25 ml redistilled by dimethylformamide; 10 mg solid sodium azide was added and the mixture was stirred in the dark at 20 °C for 2 h and then dried *in vacuo*. The dried film was then redissolved in a minimal volume of dioxane and streaked onto the origin of thin-layer (TLC) polyamide plates (Chen-Ching Trading Co., Ltd., Taiwan). The polyamide plates were prechromatographed with chloroform and dried prior to sample application. The plate was exposed to ammonia gas for 5 s after sample application, but prior to chromatography, so as to convert unreacted fluorodinitrobenzene to dinitroaniline. The TLC plate was developed with chloroform. DnpN$_3$ ran at the front; dinitroaniline, the major contaminant, had an R_f of 0.5. DnpN$_3$ was eluted from the TLC plate with dry ethanol and was stored dry or as an ethanolic solution in the dark at −10 °C. The melting point of dry DnpN$_3$ is 65 °C (uncorrected). High resolution mass spectrometry gave a high intensity M—N$_2$ ion peak at m/e 181.01252, corresponding to a composition $C_6H_3N_3O_4$ (Calculated to be 181.01236). The ir spectrum gave an N$_3$ stretching band at 2145 cm^{-1}, indicating that the azide rather than the corresponding 4-nitrobenzo-1,2-furazan-n-oxide was present. The nmr spectrum in CD Cl_3 showed two doublets at 7.55 and 8.47 ppm and a singlet at 8.97 ppm.

Reaction Conditions

Modification of Protein 460 with Photoaffinity Reagents

The choice of optimal reaction condition will depend on the nature of both the photoaffinity label and the immunoglobulin chain that is to be labeled. Thus, Dnp reacts predominantly with the light chain of protein 460 and requires a larger concentration of DnpAD and a longer irradiation time than the reaction of DnpN$_3$, which reacts predominantly with the heavy chain. The considerations for a choice of reaction conditions are complex and will differ for each protein. The reader is referred to References 15, 24, and 25 for the conditions employed with protein 460.

Controls

It is common practice to check the fact that the label is "site-directed" by inhibiting the covalent attachment of the affinity label (for instance, a Dnp-based reagent) by an excess of a nonreactive analog (i.e., Dnp Lysine). It should be stressed that this control is, by itself, insufficient evidence for attachment of the label to a single binding site and is based on circular reasoning. Few, if any, affinity reagents are universally reactive and, if labeling outside the most strongly binding ligand site occurs, it is almost certainly based on weaker interactions between protein and ligand at specific loci. A high concentration of analog bearing the same binding group (i.e., Dnp) will inhibit in both the strongly binding site and the more weakly binding sites. Small changes in the specific radioactivity of the protein after the addition of low concentrations of analog (i.e., on the order of the concentration needed to half saturate the high affinity site) is much better evidence of reaction with that avid site than is the abolition of all labeling by 10^{-2} molar concentration of the ligand or its analog. Control experiments are also needed to answer the following questions:

1. Are photoaffinity labels catalyzed to reactive intermediates by the protein in the absence of light?

2. Are the number of attached affinity label molecules matched by the number of ligating sites lost?

3. Do all the affinity reagent-protein complexes involve covalent bonds?

4. Is radioactivity released by high concentrations of nonradioactive analog under protein-ligand dissociating conditions?

SUMMARY OF RESULTS

After the reaction of protein 460 with ^{3}H-DnpAD, 85% of the total radioactivity was found on the light chain and 20% on the heavy chain. The light chain had 70% of the total radioactivity in a single peptide spanning residues 25–85. All the radioactivity of this peptide was in a single modified residue, lysine 54 of the L chain. The remaining 30% of the total radioactivity outside this peptide appeared to be distributed among several different sites, but there was no evidence of a second single residue containing a substantial proportion of radioactivity. The heavy chain contained 15% of the ^{3}H-DnpAD radioactivity. The amount of radioactivity in any one peptide of the heavy chain was insufficient to make isolation of the labeled residue(s) a rewarding procedure. Most of the 15% radioactivity was scattered over 3 peptides spanning residues 29–58, 62–77, and 78–108. In contrast to the DnpAD, DnpN$_3$ reacted mainly with two tyrosine residues, 33 and 88, in the heavy chain of protein 460. This was shown by isolating a CNBr fragment containing 60% of the total radioactivity in the H chain and by further degrading to show the location of the radioactivity. Although no other major locus of radioactivity was identified, sequential automated Edman degradation released some radioactivity into the chlorobutane washes during the first three cycles of degradation, suggesting that there may have been other acid, unstable photoaffinity reagent-protein adducts present.

Our photoaffinity labeling experiments are consistent with the following conclusions.

[3]H-DnpAD labels preferentially the light chain reacting by nucleophilic attack on Lys 54. It seems likely, therefore, that DnpAD underwent Wolff rearrangement to a ketene prior to reaction. A smaller quantity of radioactivity was, however, widely spread over the heavy chain. ^{3}H-DnpN$_3$ reacted principally with two tyrosines in positions 33 and 88.* The distance from the center of the ring to the reactive portion of the photolyzed intermediate derived for DnpAD is 5.6 Å and, for DnpN$_3$, 3.6 Å. The positions of residues analogous to those labeled have been discovered by x-ray crystallographic models of protein NEW, a human IgG myeloma protein. Unless the overall arrangement of the combining region of protein NEW differs substantially from that of protein 460, it seems unlikely that all the residue modifications observed could have occurred if the Dnp portion was bound to a single locus on the protein. Even when allowance is made both for the 2 Å difference in the ring-center-to-reactive-portions distance in the two reagents and for the uncertainty that the provisional assignation of Tyr 88 is correct, the distances separating the modified residues are too large. The data on which these conclusions are based have been published in more detail.[15,24-26]

DISCUSSION

It is encouraging that a large number of studies with affinity and photoaffinity reagents have reported labeling patterns that, with minor differences, suggest that the hypervariable, solvent-exposed loops of the Fv domain contain the modified amino acid residues. TABLE 1 gives a list of some of the modified residues that have been described in the literature.

However, care must be taken in the interpretation of all affinity labeling experiments. It cannot be assumed, without independent evidence, that amino acid residues modified by affinity reagents are necessarily in a single ligation site. Such sites may be visible on x-ray diffraction analysis of protein-ligand complexes and probably represent that mode of association of protein and ligand that is energetically most favorable. It does not exclude other, less favorable, modes of interaction that may be transiently present. The probability of interaction between a photoaffinity label and a potentially modifiable amino acid residue depends both on the reaction rate of the activated residue and on the proximity of a modifiable amino acid residue. Thus, it is possible that covalent reactions may occur not only at a high affinity binding site, but

---

*Dr. Eduardo Padlan and Dr. Elvin Kabat have drawn our attention to the possibility that another assignment to the residue we tentatively identify as Tyr 88 can be made. The primary amino acid sequence of this region of protein 460 is not known. If, however, the cysteine residue normally found at or near position 96 were displaced, or if there were unexpected deletions present, it would be possible that our isolated peptide could be homologous with residues 49–60 of a related myeloma protein derived from MOPC 315. In this event, the modified tyrosine residue would be homologous to Tyr 53 of protein 315. When the amino acid sequence of protein 460 is known, we will be able to choose between these two possibilities.

TABLE 1

SUMMARY OF AFFINITY LABELING EXPERIMENTAL RESULTS ON SOME IMMUNOGLOBULINS

Affinity Reagent	Protein	Ligand Binding Set of Proteins	H Chain Residue(s) Modified	L Chain Residue Modified	Effect of Reaction on Ligand Binding	Reference(s)
BADL	Protein 315 IgA mouse myeloma	Dnp, menadione	Lys-54			27, 28
BADE	Protein 315 IgA mouse myeloma	Dnp, menadione		Tyr-34		27, 28
MNBDF‡	Protein 315 IgA mouse myeloma	Dnp, menadione		Tyr-34	Reduces association constant from 7.5×10^5 to 1.5×10^4; no effect on valence	29, 30
BADE	Protein 460 IgA mouse myeloma	Dnp, $K_0 = 1 \times 10^5$ 1/mol; menadione, $K_0 = 2 \times 10^4$ 1/mol	Tyr; Cys	Lys-54; Cys	Not reported	28
Dnp-AD	Protein 460 IgA mouse myeloma	Dnp, $K_0 = 1 \times 10^5$* 1/mol; menadione, $K_0 = 2 \times 10^4$ 1/mol		Lys-54	Stoichiometric loss of binding with incorporation	15, 24
Dnp-N$_3$	Protein 460 IgA mouse myeloma	Dnp, $K_0 = 1 \times 10^5$ 1/mol; menadione, $K_0 = 2 \times 10^4$ 1/mol	Tyr-33 Tyr-88 (or Tyr-53)		Loss of binding activity; remaining binding at reduced association constant	15, 24, 25
MNBDF‡	Guinea pig IgG	Dnp	Tyr		Not reported	31
MNBDF‡	HPC-3 IgG mouse myeloma	Dnp, $K_0 = 8.4 \times 10^4$ 1/mol	Tyr			32
DPPC†	TEPC-15 IgA mouse myeloma	Phosphorylcholine, $K_0 = 2.2 \times 10^5$ 1/mol	Tyr-34	Loss of binding with incorporation		33
MNBDF‡	Porcine IgG	Dnp	Tyr 1st hypervariable	Tyr-33 (λ) 83 chain	Not reported	34, 35
MNBDF‡	Mouse and rabbit IgG	Dnp	Tyr	Not reported		36

*Labeling reported, modified residue unidentified.
†DPPC, p-diazoniumphenylphosphorylcholine.
‡MNBDF, m-nitrobenzenediazonium fluoroborate.

also at reactive residues close to lower affinity transient complexes. X-ray crystallography has demonstrated that multiple low affinity binding sites for a single ligand occur in an immunoglobulin combining region.[37] If, in addition to a high affinity binding site, a combining region contained additional low affinity binding sites, this might be difficult to detect by conventional hapten binding techniques, such as equilibrium dialysis or fluorescence quenching.

Since covalent bond formation with an affinity label depends on both geometric considerations and reactivity, it does not necessarily follow that the most avidly binding site will be the most extensively modified. Ruoho *et al.*[38] expected that covalent bond formation between an azide affinity reagent and acetylcholinesterase would occur during the lifetime of the reagent-protein complex, but they demonstrated, with the use of a scavenger molecule (*p*-aminobenzoic acid), that this probably does not occur. In another instance, these workers used 4-azido-2-nitrophenyl-L-lysine as a photoaffinity reagent for anti-Dnp antibodies and concluded that, in this system, reaction had occurred prior to the dissociation of the hapten-antibody complex.

It is unlikely that many predictions about the rates or mechanisms of either conventional affinity or photoaffinity reagents can be made without detailed knowledge of the geometry of the interaction and the lifetimes of the intermediates. Kinetic measurements of the association of Dnp-based ligands and another mouse IgA myeloma immunoglobulin, protein 315, suggests that there are multiple binding sites in this immunoglobulin combining region. The data support the existence of an initial "encounter complex," followed by the formation of a "final" complex in which a distinct subsite for the Dnp ring and three other ligand-binding subsites may be identified.[39]

More recently, Lancet and Pecht have examined the kinetics of the binding of protein 460 with a Dnp-based ligand by chemical relaxation methods. Their results support a mechanism in which two interconvertible conformational states of the protein bind the hapten with different association constants. Hapten binding shifts the equilibrium to an energetically more favored state.[40] Hapten ligation of antibodies is, therefore, probably not a simple process involving a single second-order interaction between one group of spatially juxtaposed residues forming a single binding site and one region of the hapten. A more likely interpretation of the available data suggests that there may be other low affinity binding sites present, as well as high affinity binding sites. Whatever the details of the mechanism, recent independent evidence suggests that at least one photoaffinity reagent, $DnpN_3$, reacts in the antibody-combining region of both protein 460 and protein 315, which latter is another mouse IgA myeloma protein binding both Dnp and menadione.

Anti-idiotypic antibodies have been prepared against the combining regions of both these proteins. When both protein 315 and protein 460 are modified with $DnpN_3$, the modified amino acid residues interfere strongly with the binding of the myeloma protein to the anti-idiotypic antibodies.[41,42]

It seems likely that the use of photoaffinity reagents, together with the development of independent methods to check that the covalent protein-photoaffinity ligand complex resembles the protein-ligand complex, will remain important tools in the study of macromolecule-ligand interactions.

ACKNOWLEDGMENTS

The authors wish to acknowledge their collaborators and coauthors, Drs. W. Konigsberg, Choy-Leong Hew, Masanori Yoshioka, Carolyn Converse Cooper, J. M. Varga, R. W. Rosenstein, and Martine Y. K. Armstrong. This paper is based on their studies.

REFERENCES

1. NISONOFF, A., J. E. HOPPER & S. B. SPRING. 1925. The Antibody Molecule, Chapter 5: 209. Academic Press. New York.
2. KABAT, E. A. 1966. J. Immunol. **97:** 1.
3. EISEN, H. N. 1971. Progress in Immunology: 243. Academic Press. New York.
4. RICHARDS, F. F., W. H. KONIGSBERG, R. W. ROSENSTEIN & J. M. VARGA. 1975. Science **187:** 130.
5. VARGA, J. M., S. LANDE & F. F. RICHARDS. 1974. J. Immunol. **112:** 1565.
6. WOFSY, L., H. METZGER & S. J. SINGER. 1962. Biochemistry **1:** 1031.
7. RICHARDS, F. F. & W. H. KONIGSBERG. 1978. Methods in Enzymology, Vol. 46: 508. Academic Press. New York.
8. GIVOL, D. 1974. Essays in Biochemistry, Vol. 10: 73. Biochem. Soc. London.
9. FRANEK, F. 1973. Eur. J. Biochem. **33:** 59.
10. JOHNSTON, M. & H. N. EISEN. 1973. J. Immunol. **117:** 1189.
11. ROSENSTEIN, R. W., R. A. MUSSON, M. Y. K. ARMSTRONG, W. H. KONIGSBERG & F. F. RICHARDS. 1972. Proc. Nat. Acad. Sci. USA **69:** 877.
12. MANJULA, B. N., F. F. RICHARDS & R. W. ROSENSTEIN. 1976. Immunochemistry **13:** 929.
13. ROSENSTEIN, R. W. & F. F. RICHARDS. 1976. Immunochemistry **13:** 939.
14. ROSENSTEIN, R. W. & F. F. RICHARDS. 1972. J. Immunol. **108:** 1467.
15. YOSHIOKA, M., J. LIFTER, C.-L. HEW, C. A. CONVERSE, M. Y. K. ARMSTRONG, W. H. KONIGSBERG & F. F. RICHARDS. 1975. Biochemistry **12:** 4679.
16. KIRMSE, W. 1964. *In* Carbene Chemistry. Academic Press. New York.
17. SHAFER, J., P. BARONOWSKY, R. LAURSEN, F. FINN & F. H. WESTHEIMER. 1966. J. Biol. Chem. **241:** 412.
18. VON E. DOERING, W. & L. H. KNOW. 1956. J. Am. Chem. Soc. **78:** 4947.
19. FLEET, G. W., J. R. KNOWLES & R. R. PORTER. 1969. Nature (London) **224:** 511.
20. Vogel, A. I. 1956. A Textbook of Practical Organic Chemistry (3rd ed.): 189, John C. Wiley. New York.
21. CONVERSE, C. A. & F. F. RICHARDS. 1969. Biochemistry **8:** 4431.
22. DEBOER, TH. J. & H. J. BACKER. 1963. Organic Syntheses Coll., Vol. 4: 250. John C. Wiley. New York.
23. GRIECO, P. A. & J. P. MASON. 1967. J. Chem. Eng. Data **12:** 623.
24. HEW, C.-L., J. LIFTER, M. YOSHIOKA, F. F. RICHARDS, W. H. KONIGSBERG. 1973. Biochemistry **12:** 4685.
25. LIFTER J., C.-L. HEW, M. YOSHIOKA, F. F. RICHARDS & W. H. KONIGSBERG. 1974. Biochemistry **13:** 3567.
26. RICHARDS, F. F., J. LIFTER, C.-L. HEW, M. YOSHIOKA & W. H. KONIGSBERG. 1974. Biochemistry **13:** 3572.
27. HAIMOVICH, J., D. GIVOL & H. N. EISEN. 1970. Proc. Nat. Acad. Sci. USA **67:** 1656.
28. HAIMOVICH, J., H. N. EISEN, E. HURWITZ & D. GIVOL. 1972. Biochemistry **11:** 2389.
29. GOETZL, E. J. & H. METZGER. 1970. Biochemistry **9:** 1267.
30. GOETZL, E. J. & H. METZGER. 1970. Biochemistry **9:** 3682.
31. RAY, A. & J. J. CEBRA. 1972. Biochemistry **11:** 3647.

32. MARTIN, H., N. L. WARNER, P. E. ROEDER & S. J. SINGER. 1972. Biochemistry **11:** 4999.
33. CHESEBRO, B. & H. METZGER. 1972. Biochemistry **11:** 266.
34. FRANEK, F. 1971 Eur. J. Biochem. **19:** 176.
35. FRANEK, F. 1973. Eur. J. Biochem. **33:** 59.
36. THORPE, N. O. & S. J. SINGER. 1969. Biochemistry **8:** 4523.
37. AMZEL, L. M., R. J. POLJAK, J. M. VARGA & F. F. RICHARDS. 1974. Proc. Nat. Acad Sci. USA **71:** 1427.
38. RUOHO, A. E., H. KIEFER, P. E. ROEDER & S. J. SINGER. 1973. Proc. Nat. Acad. Sci. USA **70:** 2567.
39. HASELKORN, D., S. FRIEDMAN, D. GIVOL & I. PECHT. 1974. Biochemistry **13:** 2216.
40. LANCET, D. & I. PECHT. 1977. Proc. Nat. Acad. Sci. USA.
41. ROSENSTEIN, R. W., J. B. ZELDIS, W. H. KONIGSBERG & F. F. RICHARDS. 1979. Mol. Immunol. In press.
42. ZELDIS, J. B., W. H. KONIGSBERG, F. F. RICHARDS & R. W. ROSENSTEIN. 1979. Mol. Immunol. In press.

DISCUSSION

DR. F. M. RICHARDS *(Yale University):* I think of immunoglobulins as highly specialized ligating proteins. Pecht and his associates have shown that, even for a single ligand, there may be more than one binding site on a single immunoglobulin molecule. If you had a single, specific high-affinity binding site surrounded by a number of specific low-affinity binding sites, you might never detect the low-affinity sites by binding studies unless these were carried out at very high ligand concentrations. Such an arrangement might, however, increase the local concentration of ligand and, hence, the apparent binding contrast of the high-affinity binding site. A sufficiently reactive photoaffinity label may be able to react both at the high- and low-affinity binding sites. It is this model I have in mind, rather than a site that is at once loose and specific.

DR. C. GITLER: There seems to be a very different way in which a molecule like, say, butane or pentane combines to a protein, as is shown very nicely by a protein in which you get saturation binding very rapidly. I think that's one of the reasons why we think that some of our hydrophobic azides do not label most proteins: most proteins have crevices—hydrophobic crevices—that would be too small. For example, BSA is labeled very beautifully. Now the question is: Is your antibody combining site closer to a BSA type of situation than it is to a usual protein binding site?

DR. F. F. RICHARDS: Dr. Gitler, you've asked a very perspicacious question to which there is, as yet, no answer. The essential mystery appears to be this: Why does binding of many ligands occur at one part of the surface of a molecule and not at another? If one looks at the three-dimensional model of the immunoglobulin molecule, one can see several regions that look as if they might be antigen-binding cavities, yet the majority of ligand binding takes place at the solvent-exposed end of a variable region.

One person who has thought deeply about the physical characteristics of a ligand binding site is Dr. F. M. Richards. Perhaps it has to do, as he suggests, with atomic packing densities and, perhaps, with the vibrational freedom permitted to certain surface amino acid residues, also. We have no definite answers to these questions as yet.

DR. H. F. E. ESCHER *(University of Sherbroome):* I would like to know what the mechanism by which this tyrosine was labeled by the azide is. That means isolating this insurgent compound, or whatever it is.

F. F. RICHARDS: I'm afraid to say that we haven't done that. We had considered doing some mass spectroscopy to determine the structure of the tyrosine-azide adduct but, one way or another, it never got done. It's one thing, I think, that is really missing in the story and should be done.

ESCHER: I think it's really important, especially since you mentioned the inability of the azides to make CH insurgence and, if tyrosine is labeled, you start to . . .

F. F. RICHARDS: I really am aware of the difficulties, since quantities are very low and one is dealing with radioactive compounds. Most mass spectroscopists become unhappy if you put radioactive compounds into their high-resolution machines. We would need to make the adduct again, using non-radioactive reagents. That's an expensive and long job. I am afraid we have not yet done this.

THE USE OF PHOTOLABELS TO PROBE THE OUABAIN BINDING SITE OF THE (Na, K)-ATPase*

Arnold E. Ruoho and Clifford C. Hall

Department of Pharmacology
University of Wisconsin
Madison, Wisconsin 53706

INTRODUCTION

Digitalis glycosides are specific inhibitors of the ion transport (Na, K)-ATPase (ATP phosphohydratase, EC 3.6.1.3).[1,2] It has been suggested that this enzyme is the receptor through which the cardiac glycosides produce their inotropic effect on the heart.[3-5]

The (Na, K)-ATPase, purified from several sources,[6-9] consists of at least two polypeptides: a catalytic subunit (α), $M_r = 100,000$, and a glycoprotein (β), $M_r = 50,000$. Structural studies indicate that the enzyme probably contains an $\alpha_2\beta_2$[10] or $\alpha_2\beta_4$[11] structure.

During the hydrolysis of ATP, the terminal phosphate is transferred to the α subunit of the enzyme as an aspartyl phosphate.[12] This phosphorylation is dependent upon the simultaneous presence of Na^+ and Mg^{++}.[13] Cardiac glycosides bind to this phosphorylated form of the enzyme,[14,15] which has been described as a type I complex.[16,17] The enzyme can be phosphorylated with inorganic phosphate *in vitro* with the simultaneous presence of Mg^{++} and cardiac glycosides.[18] This latter cardiac glycoside-enzyme complex has been referred to as the type II complex.[16,17]

Cardiac glycoside derivatives that are capable of covalent bond formation in the binding site are useful for several reasons:

1. To allow analysis of peptide fragments of the binding site, which will be exposed to denaturing conditions

2. To identify structural relationships between the various binding sites of the enzyme (e.g., ATP site and glycoside binding sites)

3. To probe the cardiac glycoside binding site with compounds that can also be used in intact atria to assess the similarity of the (Na, K)-ATPase binding site with the *in situ* cardiac glycoside receptor.

We prepared 3-haloacetyl derivatives of strophanthidin and hellebrigenin for affinity labeling of the binding site,[19] but they lacked sufficient specificity for structural work (FIGURE 1). One disadvantage of these reagents is the requirement for a suitably positioned nucleophile in the active site. Since the 3-haloacetyl compounds (which were inhibitors and therefore did bind to the enzyme at the specific binding site) did not result in measurable yields of covalent bond formation, it appeared that suitable nucleophilic residues were beyond bond forming distance at the 3-hydroxyl position of the steroid binding site. It was clear from these experiments that affinity probes would require either derivation at positions other than the 3-hydroxyl in order to seek out appropriate functional groups in the protein that are suitably positioned in

*This work was supported by a National Institutes of Health grant, no. NS12392.

90

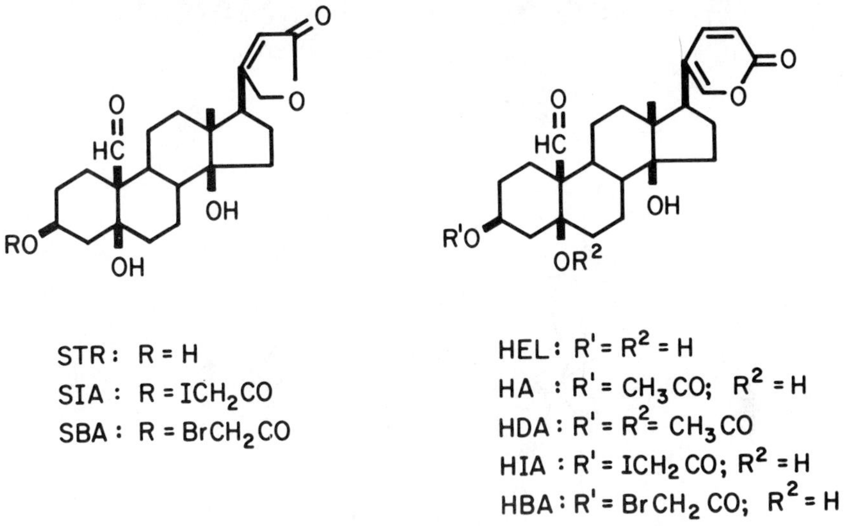

STR: R = H

SIA: R = ICH$_2$CO

SBA: R = BrCH$_2$CO

HEL: R' = R^2 = H

HA : R' = CH$_3$CO; R^2 = H

HDA: R' = R^2= CH$_3$CO

HIA : R' = ICH$_2$CO; R^2 = H

HBA: R' = BrCH$_2$CO; R^2 = H

FIGURE 1. The structure of haloacetyl derivatives. STR: strophanthidin; SIA: strophanthidin-3-iodoacetate; SBA: strophanthidin-3-bromoacetate; HEL: hellebrigenin; HA: hellebrigenin-3-acetate; HDA: hellebrigenin-3,5-diacetate; HIA: hellebrigenin-3-iodoacetate; HBA: hellebrigenin-3-bromoacetate.

the binding site to allow reaction to occur (in effect, a molecular "fishing expedition") or incorporation of groups that formed covalent bonds in a much more nonselective fashion and that were more reactive. This latter requirement is very effectively met by the use of ligands, which can be converted by photolysis into exceedingly reactive intermediates and, under appropriate conditions, insert into C—H bonds.[20] Compounds that generate carbenes of nitrenes upon photolysis have been used for the photoaffinity labeling of a variety of ligand binding sites.[21] The use of these compounds, therefore, allows a greater opportunity for covalent bond formation in a binding site, since the presence of specific reactive centers (e.g., N—H, O—H, S—H) is probably not necessary.

In addition to the photolabels described in this paper, other photoactivatable compounds have been reported for photolabeling of the ouabain binding site of this enzyme.[22-25]

LABELING OF THE α SUBUNIT OF THE ENZYME

^{14}C-Diazomalonyl Cymarin

Cymarin (FIGURE 2) is a cardiac glycoside containing the 2-deoxy, 3-methoxy sugar, cymarose, in glycosidic linkage to the 3-hydroxyl of the aglycone, strophanthidin. Cymarose contains, therefore, only one secondary hydroxyl that can be acylated with ease. ^{14}C-diazomalonyl (^{14}C-DAM) chloride was prepared at a specific activity of 5 mCi/mmol.[26] When this carbene generator was photolyzed with a medium pressure

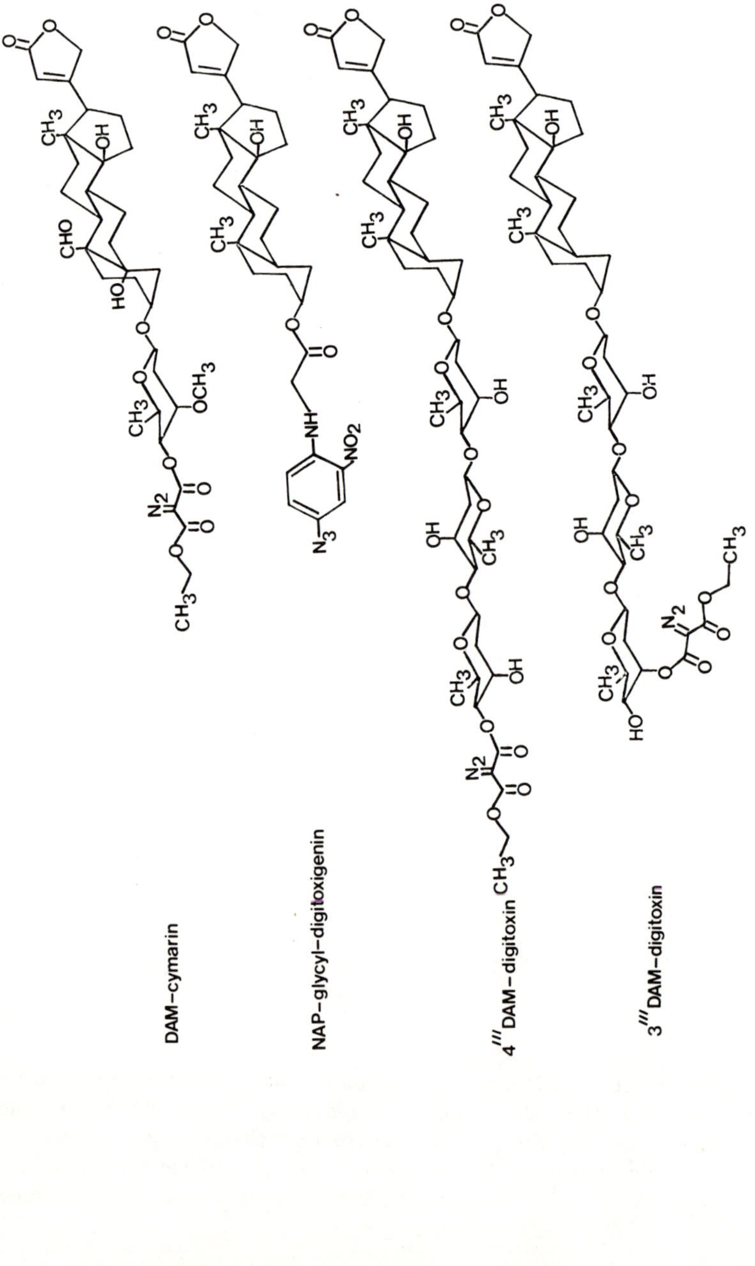

FIGURE 2. Structures of photolabels.

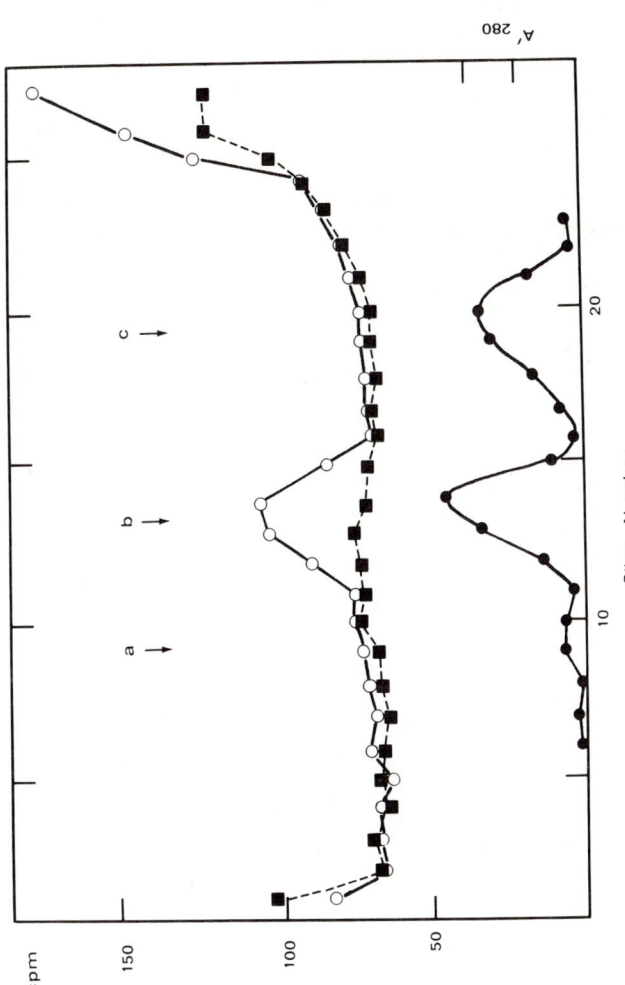

FIGURE 3. The distribution of radioactivity covalently attached to (Na, K)-ATPase that had been photolyzed in the presence of ^{14}C-DAM cymarin. Samples of dog kidney enzyme that had been photolyzed either in the presence of the complete MgATP phosphorylating system (○) or in the complete system plus a 25-fold excess of cymarin as protector (■) were run on SDS gels, which were scanned, sliced, and counted. The A_{280} trace from the gel with the unprotected sample was divided into segments exactly as the gel had been sliced. The mean A_{280} of each of these segments was calculated and the values plotted (●). The units of A_{280} are arbitrary, since the scanner was uncalibrated. The three protein components are: (a) cross-linked $\alpha\beta$ dimer, (b) large chain, and (c) small chain. (From A. E. Ruoho and J. Kyte[26]; by permission of the *Proceedings of the National Academy of Sciences*.)

mercury lamp in the type I complex with the deoxycholate (DOC) purified dog kidney (Na, K)-ATPase, specific photolabel insertion was observed into the α subunit of the enzyme only (FIGURE 3). This data leads to two conclusions:

1. The α subunit contained at least a portion of the cardiac glycoside binding site.

2. The α subunit must span the bilayer since it has been shown that cardiac glycosides inhibit only from the outside surface of the membrane and ATP phosphorylates only from the inside.[27]

Primarily because of the low specific radioactivity of this compound, however, it was not possible to unequivocally eliminate the possibility that the β subunit contributes to the binding site as well. If the ratio of labeling $\alpha:\beta$ was 10:1, radioactivity would not have been detectable in the β subunit region.

NAP Glycyl Digitoxigenin and NAP Glycyl Strophanthidin

The synthesis of these photolabels was accomplished in the following fashion. Nitrofluorophenylazide was reacted with glycine to produce N-nitrophenylazidoglycine.[28] The acyl halide of this compound was produced with oxalyl chloride. The 3-hydroxyl of digitoxigenin or strophanthidin was then acylated in pyridine and dioxane. The tritiated compound was synthesized by reacting ^{3}H-digitoxigenin (7–17 Ci/mmol; derived by purification of the acid hydrolysate of ^{3}H-digitoxin on thin layer chromatography) with N-nitrophenylazidoglycyl chloride (NAP glycyl chloride), as described above. The product, ^{3}H-NAP glycyl digitoxigenin, was 99% radiopure in three solvent systems on thin layer silica gel G.

Derivation of the 3-hydroxyl of the cardiotonic steroid aglycones does not compromise their inhibition of the action of (Na, K)-ATPase. NAP glycyl digitoxigenin (FIGURE 2) and NAP glycyl strophanthidin (FIGURE 4) retain the same potency for inhibition of (Na, K)-ATPase activity as digitoxigenin. The I_{50} (concentration for half maximal inhibition) for these two photolabels was found to be $1-3 \times 10^{-7}$ M (FIGURE 4), which was similar to that determined for digitoxigenin under the same experimental conditions. The nitrene generated on photolysis (as estimated from molecular models) is positioned slightly beyond the second glycosidic bond of digitoxin, the parent glycoside, and will, therefore, probe that area of the glycoside binding site. Since ^{3}H-digitoxin could be readily purchased at high specific radioactivity (7.4–12.2 Ci/mmol), the digitoxigenin derivative was synthesized in a tritiated form as a photoaffinity label for the binding site.

Photolysis of the enzyme-photolabel complex resulted in ouabain protectable covalent labeling of the α subunit (FIGURE 5); no labeling was observed if the enzyme-photolabel complex was not photolyzed. This specific photoincorporation into the large polypeptide agrees with experiments previously reported.[23,24,26] The labeling pattern was found to be virtually identical for both type I and type II complexes. No specific labeling could be detected with either type of complex in the glycoprotein (β) subunit (slices 15–17, FIGURE 5). Because of the very high specific radioactivity of the photolabel, even 10% of that incorporated into the α subunit would have been readily detected. No more than 5% of the site-bound label was photoincorporated into the α subunit.

Some cross-linking of the α subunit was observed in these experiments but none of

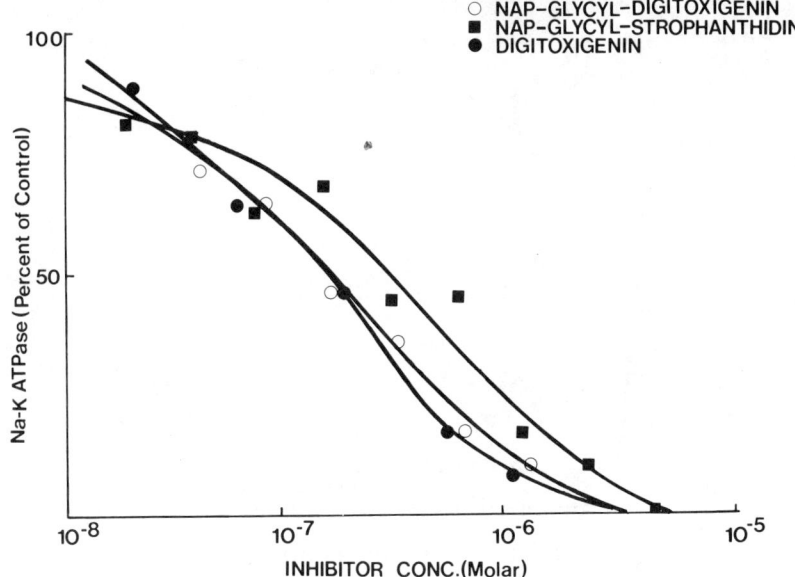

FIGURE 4. Inhibition of enzyme activity with photolabels. Eel enzyme (6 μg/tube) was mixed with various concentrations of photolabel (added in dimethyl sulfoxide (DMSO)) and incubated 30 min at room temperature in 1 ml of 1% DMSO, 60 mM NaCl$_2$, 2.0 mM MgCl$_2$, 2.0 mM Na$_2$ATP, 0.1 mM ethyleneglycol-bis-(β-aminoethyl ether) N, N'-tetraacetic acid (EGTA), and 92 mM Tris (pH 7.4). After 30 min, 0.1 ml of the same medium was added to one set of tubes (minus K$^+$), and 0.1 ml of the same medium containing 53 mM KCl was added to another set of tubes (plus K$^+$). The tubes were allowed to incubate 4 min at 38 °C, and then 1 ml of 10% TCA was added to stop the reaction. DMSO alone was added to the control tubes with no photolabel. The difference in inorganic phosphate production between plus and minus K$^+$ at a given photolabel concentration was used to calculate the enzyme activity.

the β subunit. Under the least favorable conditions, 20% of the α subunit was cross-linked to the top of the gels in 10 s. In some experiments, no cross-linking was observed. Variations in photolytic cross-linking were due primarily to the reduction in light intensity with lamp usage. Under all conditions in these experiments, the β subunit remained resistant to photolytic cross-linking. This is an important observation, since lack of NAP glycyl digitoxigenin photoincorporation into the β subunit cannot be due to the removal of this subunit to the top of the gel in a cross-linking reaction.

LABELING OF THE β SUBUNIT OF THE ENZYME

4'''-Diazomalonyl Digitoxin

In order to probe the binding site further to determine whether the β subunit could be photolabeled if the photoactive group was placed in a position more distal from the aglycone than was the case with NAP glycyl digitoxigenin, the 4'-diazomalonyl

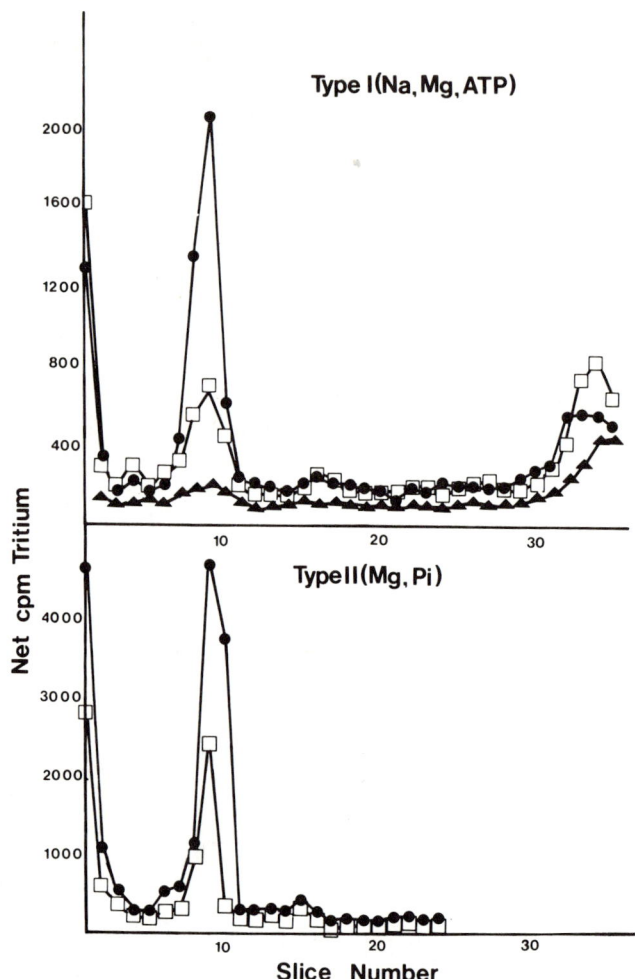

FIGURE 5. SDS polyacrylamide gel patterns of ^{3}H-NAP glycyl digitoxigenin covalent label-ing.

Upper panel (type I complex): ^{3}H-NAP glycyl digitoxigenin (10^{-6} M) was incubated with the enzyme for type I complex binding. After 90 s of photolysis at 0–2 °C, the eel enzyme was dissolved in 0.1 ml of 2% SDS and 5% β-mercaptoethanol and electrophoresed on 10% acrylamide ethylene diacrylate cross-linked gels. ●: $10^{-6}M$ ^{3}H-NAP glycyl digitoxigenin; □: 10^{-6} M ^{3}H-NAP glycyl digitoxigenin and 10^{-3} M ouabain; ▲: 10^{-6} M ^{3}H-NAP glycyl digitoxigenin bound to the enzyme but not photolyzed. Coomassie staining indicated the presence of the α subunit at slices 7–10 and of the β subunit at slices 15–18.

Lower panel (type II complex): ^{3}H-NAP glycyl digitoxigenin (10^{-6} M) was incubated with the enzyme for type II complex binding. Photolysis and electrophoresis methods are as described above. ●: 10^{-6} M ^{3}H-NAP glycyl digitoxigenin; □: 10^{-6} M ^{3}H-NAP glycyl digitoxigenin and 10^{-3} M ouabain. Coomassie staining indicated the presence of the α subunit at slices 7–11 and of the β subunit at slices 14–17.

derivative of digitoxin was synthesized (FIGURE 2). Yoda and Yoda[29] have demonstrated that acetylation of the various hydroxyls of digitoxin by the method of Satoh and Morita[30] affects the dissociation rate of the enzyme-glycoside complex. Increased rates of dissociation were seen with several acetylated derivatives but most notably with the 3'-monoacetyl digitoxin in both type I and type II complexes and the 3''-monoacetyl digitoxin in the type I complex. The least affected, in terms of dissociation rate, was the 4'''-digitoxin. This implied that the 4'''-position on the third digitoxose is sufficiently distant from the aglycone that one might expect "exo" labeling[31]; that is, probing the immediate environment of the binding site by placing the reactive group (in this case, a carbene) at a suitable distance from that portion of the molecule involved in the primary binding site (the aglycone and probably the first sugar of the glycoside).

It was found that the 4'''-diazomalonyl digitoxin was as potent as digitoxin in inhibiting the (Na, K)-ATPase activity (FIGURE 6). The I_{50} for 4'''-diazomalonyl digitoxin was found to be 4×10^{-7} M and, for digitoxin, 8×10^{-7} M. The binding isotherms determined for ^{3}H-4'''-diazomalonyl digitoxin and ^{3}H-digitoxin were very

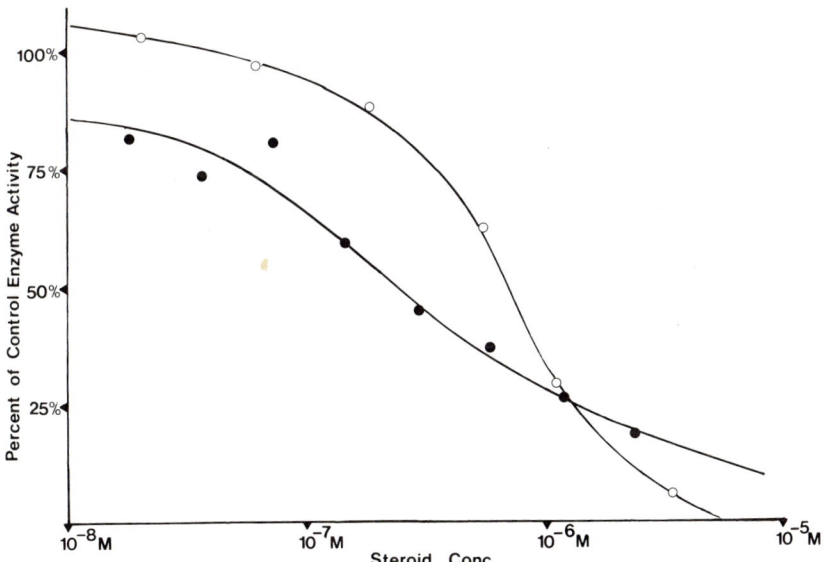

FIGURE 6. Inhibition of (Na, K)-ATPase with 4'''-diazomalonyl digitoxin and digitoxin. Eel enzyme (6 μg/tube) was mixed with various concentrations of photolabel and digitoxin and incubated 30 min at room temperature in 1 ml of 1% DMSO, 60 mM NaCl, 2.0 mM MgCl$_2$, 210 mM Na$_2$ATP, 0.1 mM EGTA, and 92 mM Tris (pH 7.4). After 30 min, 0.1 ml of the same medium was added to the minus K$^+$ tubes, and 0.1 ml of the same medium containing 53 mM KCl was added to the plus K$^+$. The tubes were allowed to incubate 4 min at 38 °C, after which 1 ml of 10% TCA was added to stop the reaction. DMSO alone was added to the control tube with no photolabel. The difference in inorganic phosphate production between plus and minus K$^+$ at a given photolabel concentration was used to calculate the enzyme activity. ●: 4'''-diazomalonyl digitoxin; O: digitoxin.

similar. The value estimated for the parent digitoxin and ^{3}H-photolabel in the type I complex was 8–10 × 10^{-8} M.

The stability of the type I enzyme-photolabel complex was compared to the stability of the type I enzyme-ouabain complex at 4 °C. As shown by Yoda,[32] rhamnosides such as ouabain possess the slowest dissociation rate of the common glycosides used as inhibitors of the (Na, K)-ATPase. ^{3}H-ouabain binding was stable for at least 2 h at 4 °C when complexed to the purified eel enzyme. Similarly, within 2 h at 4 °C an insignificant amount of ^{3}H-4‴-diazomalonyl digitoxin had dissociated from the binding site. In all binding experiments, nonspecific binding of ^{3}H-4‴-diazomalonyl digitoxin never exceeded 5% of the total binding.

FIGURE 7 (upper panel) shows the photolytic labeling profile obtained for the type I photolabel-enzyme complex after sodium dodecylsulfate (SDS) disc gel electrophoresis. The 4‴-diazomalonyl derivative demonstrated ouabain protectable incorporation

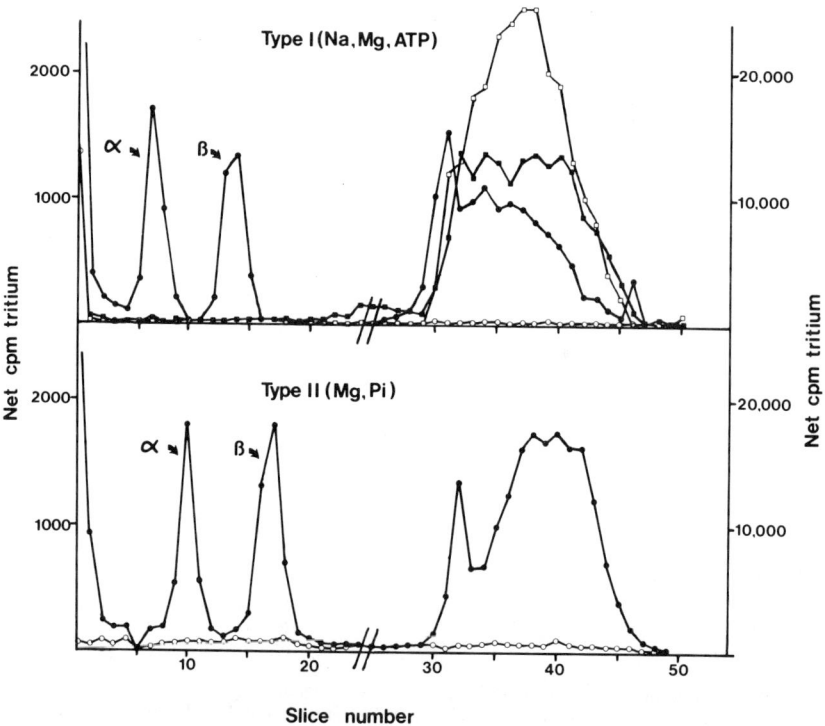

FIGURE 7. The ^{3}H-4‴-diazomalonyl digitoxin labeling pattern of eel enzyme on SDS polyacrylamide gels.

Upper panel (type I complex): ●: 1.5 × 10^{-6} M photolabel; ○: 1.5 × 10^{-6} M photolabel and ouabain 10^{-5} M; ■: 3 × 10^{-6} M photolabel not photolyzed; □: 3 × 10^{-6} M photolabel prephotolyzed for 10 s and then bound to the enzyme under type I conditions.

Lower panel (type II complex): ●: 8.3 × 10^{-7} M photolabel; ○: 8.3 × 10^{-7} M photolabel and ouabain 10^{-5} M. The slash at slice 25 indicates a change to the right hand side ordinate. Binding of the 4‴-derivative was more than 95% specific.

into the α subunit of the enzyme, as previously noted for NAP glycyl digitoxigenin and other photolabels.[23-26] However, specific incorporation into the β subunit was also noted with this compound. This incorporation was not detected if the enzyme-ligand complex was not photolyzed or if the ligand was prephotolyzed before being added to the enzyme. These data support the conclusion that 4'''-diazomalonyl digitoxin is a photoaffinity label for the cardiac glycoside binding site.

The absolute amount of photoincorporation varied, in the α subunit, from 1 to 5% and, in the β subunit, from 0.5 to 2%. Photolytic cross-linking of the enzyme was confined entirely to the α subunit, as estimated by Coomassie staining.[26] No major cross-linking of the β subunit could be detected. It is likely that a portion of the radioactivity that did not penetrate the gel was photoincorporated into the α subunit in a cross-linked state. Since the tritium in the peak region of the dye marker (slice 40) was also present in the prephotolyzed and unphotolyzed dark controls, we conclude that it was mainly unreacted photolabel.

A similar photoincorporation pattern was detected with the type II photolabel complex of the enzyme (FIGURE 7, bottom panel). Again, covalent labeling could readily be detected in the β subunit as well as in the α subunit, suggesting that these two complexes (type I and type II) of cardiac glycoside with the enzyme probably do not involve gross conformational dissimilarities, although subtle conformational changes probably do occur, as evidenced by different dissociation rates of cardiac glycosides from the type I and type II complexes.[17] Cross-linking of the α subunit also routinely reduced the absolute amount of radioactivity detected at this position on the gels. No cross-linking of the β subunit could be detected.

It was noted that, for both complexes, a radioactive peak could be reproducibly detected on the gels at slice 32 (FIGURE 7). Although poorly resolved from the broad unreacted photolabel peak at the bottom of the gel, this peak of radioactivity was consistently on the gels. Utilizing soluble standard protein markers (data not shown), it was determined that this peak corresponded to a molecular weight of approximately 12,000, which is the size estimated for a proteolipid component reported to be photolabeled in the enzyme purified from pig kidney[23] and from electric eel.[24] Further experiments, however, are needed to clarify the labeling with the diazomalonyl digitoxins in this region of the gel.

3'''-Diazomalonyl Digitoxin

This compound was prepared by very facile acyl migration of the diazomalonyl group, as was described by Satoh and Morita for acetyl derivatives.[30] Since the 4'''-hydroxyl of digitoxin is equatorial, the 3'''-hydroxyl is axial,[33] and the digitoxose rings are held in the preferred C-1 (D) configuration,[33] substituents on the 4'''-hydroxyl and 3'''-hydroxyl will be projected in the binding site in significantly different directions. If the residues on the β subunit that interact with the carbene generated at the 4'''-position are accessible to the carbene generated at the 3'''-position, then the labeling patterns between the 4''' - and 3''' -isomers should be at least qualitatively similar. If, on the other hand, a very specific "cut off" exists in this region of the binding site, then it is possible that labeling of the β subunit would be either undetected or greatly reduced. In fact, when the enzyme–^{3}H'3'''-diazomalonyl digi-

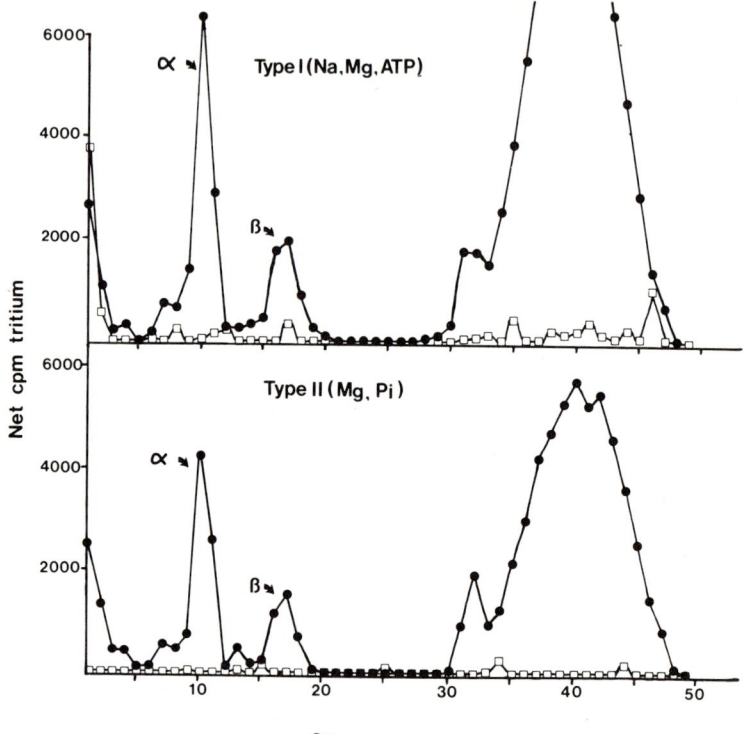

FIGURE 8. The ^{3}H-3'''-diazomalonyl digitoxin labeling pattern of eel enzyme on SDS polyacrylamide gels.
Upper panel (type I complex): ●: 5.5×10^{-7} M photolabel; □: 5.2×10^{-7} M photolabel and 10^{-5} M ouabain.
Lower panel (type II complex): ●: 5.27×10^{-7} M photolabel; □: 2.2×10^{-7} M photolabel and 10^{-5} M ouabain. Binding of 3'''-derivative was greater than 98% specific.

toxin complex was photolyzed, label could again be detected in the β subunit as well as in the α subunit (FIGURE 8). Covalent labeling efficiencies were similar to those found for the ^{3}H-4'''-derivative. Since light flux and binding site occupancy varied, it was not possible to make accurate quantitative comparisons concerning covalent incorporation between these isomers in these experiments.

These data indicate that, within a very short distance in the "sugar specific"[32] binding site region, type I and type II complex β-chain residues and α-chain residues are within at least 15 Å of each other.

DISCUSSION

Four light-activatable photolabels for (Na, K)-ATPase have been prepared. Two of these compounds have been prepared as tritiated derivatives at specific radioactivities ranging from 7.4 to 12.2 Ci/mmol. The nitrophenylazido derivatives of digitoxigenin and strophanthidin retain the same potency for inhibition of the enzyme as the aglycone, digitoxigenin. Specific binding to both type I and type II complexes was demonstrated utilizing radiopure tritiated NAP glycyl digitoxigenin (12.2 Ci/mmol). Both of these complexes were prepared with approximately 1 mole of cardiac glycoside/mole of enzyme. Photolysis of the enzyme-photolabel complex resulted in ouabain protectable covalent incorporation only into the 100,000 dalton polypeptide (FIGURE 5). Specific labeling was not detected in the glycoprotein (β) subunit regardless of the time of photolysis. This is consistent with the results of the use of other photolabels[23–26] on the ATPase, in which either the photoactivatable group extends to the general region of the second sugar residue (as estimated from molecular models) or the photoactivatable group is attached to the A/B ring junction of the aglycone.[25] No detectable photolytic cross-linking of the β subunit occurred in these photolysis experiments. This is an important observation, since one could argue that the lack of tritium in the region of the β subunit is due to the removal of this subunit to the top of the gel. Some photolytic cross-linking of the α subunit was found to occur, however, and this accounts for the radioactivity found at the top of the gel. The experiments performed with ^{3}H-NAP glycyl digitoxigenin were designed to focus exclusively on the α and β subunits. No attempt was made to scrutinize the gels in the region of the dye marker for the labeling of the proteolipid reported by Forbush et al.[23] and Rogers and Lazdunski.[24] At this point, it can be concluded from our data and the data of others[23–25] that the α subunit contains the primary aglycone portion of the ouabain binding site. The β subunit is not directly involved in binding either the aglycone or the first and second sugars of the glycosides.

Based on the experiments with 4′′′-diazomalonyl digitoxin and 3′′′-diazomalonyl digitoxin, it can be concluded further that the β subunit does reside close to the "sugar-specific" site. Yoda has shown that specific interactions, presumably in the form of hydrogen bonds, occur with the hydroxyls of the digitoxose portion of digitoxin.[32] This interaction has been shown to stabilize the steroid-enzyme complex by, primarily, decreasing the dissociation rate. From acetylation studies, Yoda and Yoda concluded that the 4′′′ hydroxyl was not involved in the formation of a stable cardiac glycoside-enzyme complex.[25] The 3′ and 3′′′ hydroxyls were involved to varying degrees in the type I and type II complexes. Acetylation of the 3′ hydroxyl greatly increased the dissociation rate of digitoxin in the type I complex, suggesting that this hydroxyl may be involved in a binding reaction crucial to the maintenance of the stability of this complex. If the hydroxyl at the 4′′′ position is not integrally involved in hydrogen bonding to the protein surface, it might be expected that the reactive carbene will be "exo" labeling and thus probing the immediate environment of the sugar-specific site.[31] It is possible that the area accessible to the carbene at the 4′′′ position contains large amounts of water. This may account partially for the low levels of incorporation, since the insertion of carbenes into water would serve as a competing reaction.[20] Another possible side reaction of the carbene is insertion into the oxygen of the 3′′′ hydroxyl, resulting in a stable six-membered ring. This possibility has not been experimentally investigated by, for instance, analyzing the photolysis products of 4′′′-diazomalonyl digitoxin or 3′′′-diazomalonyl digitoxin.

Photoincorporation into the β subunit (FIGURE 7) with the ^{3}H-4′′′-diazomalonyl digitoxin was specific and did not occur if the enzyme-photolabel complex was not photolyzed. This subunit was labeled in both type I and type II complexes. It is likely that the labeling of the α subunit occurs in an area different from that observed with NAP glycyl digitoxigenin, since the photoactive groups are at quite different positions relative to the aglycone portion of the molecule. The tritium at the bottom of the gel (FIGURE 7) is probably unreacted photolabel, since a peak in this region of the gel is seen in the dark control. It is possible that some portion of the photolabel has inserted into the lipid that borders the sugar-specific site.

Our results are consistent with the hypothesis that the α subunit is the locus of the primary cardiac glycoside binding site. However, the secondary area of the binding site, which interacts with the sugars, borders closely with some portion of the β subunit. This implies that, in the region of the sugar-specific site, the α and β subunits of the detergent-purified (Na, K)-ATPase of *Electrophorus electricus* are very intimately associated. If one compares structures utilizing molecular models of NAP glycyl digitoxigenin, nitroazidobenzoyl-ouabain (NAB-ouabain),[23] NAP-ouabain,[24] and 4'''-diazomalonyl digitoxin, the diazo group of 4'''-diazomalonyl digitoxin extends approximately 10 Å further from the aglycone than does the azido group of NAP glycyl digitoxigenin and 5 Å further than the azido groups of NAB-ouabain and NAP-ouabain. Since specific labeling of the β subunit could not be detected with NAP glycyl digitoxigenin but did occur with 4'''-diazomalonyl digitoxin, β subunit residues must border the region of the third digitoxose. This β subunit labeling cannot be detected with reactive groups placed in the region of the second sugar. Forbush *et al.* reported some incorporation (1%) into the β subunit with NAB-ouabain in which the photoactive azide extends to the third glycosidic bond.[23] This labeling probably reflects exo labeling of the β subunit, also, but it is difficult to make a comparison with the 4'''-diazomalonyl digitoxin labeling because the microenvironment of the hydrophobic azidophenyl group may be much different from that of the more polar diazomalonyl group.

Our results show that there is a possibility of systematically studying the sugar-specific region of the binding site by using 4'''-, 4''-, and 4'-diazomalonyl (or other photoactivable) derivatives of digitoxin. These compounds are synthesized by deriving the terminal equatorial hydroxyl of digitoxin, bisdigitoxoside, and monodigitoxoside.[20] Acyl migration of the diazomalonyl group to the 3''' and 3'' positions will allow the facile preparation of additional compounds to probe the site. This series of compounds will be useful because the same photoactive group can be compared at different positions on the molecule. The smaller diazomalonyl functional group is also less likely to produce those local perturbations in structure that may occur with the bulkier hydrophobic nitrophenylazido group.

REFERENCES

1. SCHATZMANN, H. J. 1953. Helv. Physiol. Pharmacol. Acta **11**: 346.
2. GLYNN, I. M. 1964. Pharmacol. Rev. **16**: 381.
3. AKERA, T. 1977. Science **198**: 569.
4. PETERS, T., R. H. RABEN & O. WASSERMAN. 1974. Eur. J. Pharmacol. **26**: 166.
5. SCHWARTZ, A., G. E. LINDENMAYER & J. C. ALLEN. 1975. Pharmacol. Rev. **27**: 3.
6. KYTE, J. 1972. J. Biol. Chem. **247**: 7642.
7. HOKIN, L. E., J. L. DAHL, J. D. DEUPREE, J. F. DIXON, J. F. HACKNEY & F. PERDUE. 1973. J. Biol. Chem. **248**: 2593.

8. LANE, L. K., J. H. COPENHAVER, G. E. LINDENMAYER & A. SCHWARTZ. 1973. J. Biol. Chem. **248:** 7197.
9. JORGENSEN, P. L. 1974. Biochim. Biophys. Acta **356:** 53.
10. PETERSON, G. L., R. D. EWING, S. R. HOOTMAN & F. P. CONTE. 1978. J. Biol. Chem. **253:** 4762.
11. HASTINGS, D. F. & J. A. REYNOLDS. 1979. Biochemistry **18:** 817.
12. ALBERS, J. W. 1976. *In* The Enzymes of Biological Membranes, Vol. 3. A. N. Martonosi, Ed.: 283–301. Plenum Press. New York.
13. DAHL, J. & L. E. HOKIN. 1974. Annu. Rev. Biochem. **43:** 327.
14. MARTSUI, H. & A. SCHWARTZ. 1968. Biochim. Biophys. Acta **151:** 655.
15. SCHWARTZ, A., H. MATSUI & A. H. LAUGHTER. 1968. Science **160:** 323.
16. VAN WINKLE, W. B., J. C. ALLEN & A. SCHWARTZ. 1972. Arch. Biochem. Biophys. **151:** 85.
17. YODA, A. 1973. Mol. Pharmacol. **9:** 51.
18. SCHWARTZ, A., G. E. LINDENMAYER, J. C. ALLEN & J. L. McCANS. 1974. Ann. N.Y. Acad. Sci. **242:** 577.
19. RUOHO, A. E., L. E. HOKIN, R. J. HEMINGWAY & S. M. KUPCHAN. 1968. Science **159:** 1354.
20. KNOWLES, J. R. 1972. Acc. Chem. Res. **5:** 155.
21. JAKOBY, W. B. & M. WILCHEK. *In* Methods in Enzymology, Vol. 46. Academic Press. London.
22. TOBIN, T., T. AKERA, T. M. BROSDY & H. R. TAREJA. 1976. Eur. J. Pharmacol. **35:** 69.
23. FORBUSH, B., J. KAPLAN & J. F. HOFFMAN. 1978. Biochemistry **17:** 3667.
24. ROGERS, T. B. & M. LAZDUNSKI. 1979. Biochemistry **18:** 135.
25. ROGERS, T. B. & M. LAZDUNSKI. 1979. FEBS Lett. **98:** 373.
26. RUOHO, A. & J. KYTE. 1974. Proc. Nat. Acad. Sci. USA **71:** 2352.
27. GARRAHAN, P. J. & I. M. GLYNN. 1967. J. Physiol. **192:** 159.
28. FLETT, G. W. J., J. R. KNOWLES & R. R. PORTER. 1972. Biochem. J. **128:** 499.
29. YODA, A. & S. YODA. 1975. Mol. Pharmacol. **11:** 653.
30. SATOH, D. & J. MORITA. 1969. Chem. Pharm. Bull. **17:** 1456.
31. BAKER, B. R. 1967. *In* Design of Active Site-Directed Irreversible Enzyme Inhibitors: 17–22. John Wiley and Sons. New York.
32. YODA, A. 1974. Ann. N.Y. Acad. Sci. **242:** 598.
33. SESSA, G. & G. WEISSMANN. 1970. J. Biol. Chem. **245:** 3295.

BIFUNCTIONAL ARYL AZIDES AS PROBES OF THE ACTIVE SITES OF ENZYMES*

Susan H. Hixson. Tracey F. Brownie, Cynthia C. Chua,
Barbara B. Crapster, and Lisa M. Satlin

Department of Chemistry
Mount Holyoke College
South Hadley, Massachusetts 01075

Stephen S. Hixson, C. O'Donnell L. Boyce, Marion Ehrich,
and Edward K. Novak

Department of Chemistry
University of Massachusetts
Amherst, Massachusetts 01003

INTRODUCTION

A series of five inhibitors was used in a continuing investigation of the use of aryl azides to label the active site regions of isolated enzymes in solution. In each case, photolysis of the enzyme-inhibitor system while the inhibitor was at the active site should have produced a nitrene from the aryl azide portion of the inhibitor. This nitrene was expected to insert into a nearby portion of the protein chain. Identification of the insertion sites provides information about the three-dimensional structure of the active site of the enzyme in solution. The initial three inhibitor-enzyme systems studied provided useful general information about the possibilities and problems involved in this general method, while the last two systems are being pursued to the point of identifying the insertion sites.

3-AZIDOPYRIDINE ADENINE DINUCLEOTIDE (1)—YEAST ALCOHOL DEHYDROGENASE

The NAD$^+$ analog, 3-azidopyridine adenine dinucleotide (1),[1] was synthesized by the action of pig brain diphosphopyridine nucleosidase on a mixture of 3-azidopyridine and adenosine-labeled [^{3}H]NAD$^+$. Inhibitor 1 has ultraviolet absorption maxima at

(1)

*This research was supported by grants from the National Science Foundation, the National Institutes of Health, the Research Corporation, and the Petroleum Research Fund, administered by the American Chemical Society.

0077–8923/80/0346–0104 $1.75/1 © 1980, NYAS

256 nm ($\epsilon = 2.86 \times 10^4$ M^{-1} cm^{-1}, water) and 303 nm ($\epsilon = 4.75 \times 10^3$ M^{-1} cm^{-1}, water). It binds noncovalently to yeast alcohol dehydrogenase (YADH, EC 1.1.1.1) with a $K_i = 2.4 \times 10^{-4}$ M. A typical 1-YADH photolysis solution contained 2.88×10^{-4} M (11.51 $\times$ 10^{-4} M in active sites) YADH and 4.00×10^{-4} M **1**, a molar ratio at which 84% of the **1** present is initially at the active site of the enzyme. The photolyses were carried out with light of wavelengths greater than 310 nm.

When a simple 1-YADH solution was photolyzed, 7% of the inhibitor became covalently bound to the enzyme. In separate experiments in which a 4.8-fold molar excess of NAD$^+$ relative to **1** was added in order to displace most of the **1** from the active site of the YADH, photolysis led to covalent attachment of 4% of the **1** to the enzyme.[1] The extent of insertion of **1** into YADH is low. Another serious problem is that **1** clearly is able to insert into YADH even when it is displaced from the active site prior to photolysis. Since only 84% of the **1** is present at the active site of YADH even when no NAD$^+$ is present in the photolysis mixture, this nonactive site (random) labeling would complicate the interpretation of any labeling results that might be obtained.

PARA-AZIDOBENZENESULFONAMIDE (2)—CARBONIC ANHYDRASE

In an attempt to increase the extent of insertion and to minimize the complications arising from random labeling, a system was designed in which the binding between the enzyme and the noncovalently bound inhibitor prior to photolysis was stronger. Para-azidobenzenesulfonamide (**2**)[2] was synthesized either from [^{35}S]sulfanilamide or

$$N_3 \text{—}\!\!\!\bigcirc\!\!\!\text{—} SO_2NH_2 \qquad\qquad (2)$$

from [^{3}H]sulfanilamide that had been obtained in tritiated form by exposing cold sulfanilamide to tritium gas (the Wilzbach method, New England Nuclear). Inhibitor 2 proved to be a potent inhibitor of bovine erythrocyte carbonic anhydrase (EC 5.2.1.1) with a $K_i = 1.3 \times 10^{-6}$ M. The ultraviolet absorption maximum of **2** was at 261.5 nm ($\epsilon = 1.98 \times 10^4$ M^{-1} cm^{-1}, water). Photolysis with 254 nm light of a 4.05×10^{-4} M carbonic anhydrase solution containing 2.18×10^{-4} M **2** led to covalent attachment of 24–26% of the **2** residues to the protein under conditions in which more than 99% of the **2** was bound to the active site of the enzyme at the start of photolysis. When a 2-carbonic anhydrase mixture containing a 20-fold molar excess (42.5×10^{-4} M) of another benzenesulfonamide inhibitor of carbonic anhydrase, *p*-toluenesulfonamide ($K_i = 3.8 \times 10^{-6}$ M), was irradiated, 29–30% of the **2** residues became bound to protein. Clearly, the **2**, when photoactivated, is capable of inserting into the enzyme in good yield, even when it is displaced from the active site.

The 24–26% insertion seen in the 2-carbonic anhydrase system may reflect only active site labeling if the nitrene both formed and inserted while at the active site. However, some portion of the insertion product instead may reflect nonactive site labeling were the nitrene sufficiently long-lived to allow for diffusion away from the active site and insertion elsewhere in the protein chain.

Two procedures were used to compare the labeling pattern of **2** in the 2-carbonic anhydrase mixture with that of **2** in the **2**-carbonic anhydrase-*p*-toluenesulfonamide system. First, labeled protein from each system was maleylated, digested with trypsin, and then chromatographed on Sephadex G-75. Each preparation gave the same peptide elution profile, but the distribution of radioactivity among the eluted peptides differed in the two cases. Although some radioactivity was eluted in most fractions, a major peak containing significantly more radioactivity than any of the others was observed for the **2**-carbonic anhydrase preparation, while the radioactivity was uniformly distributed throughout the various peptide fractions in the case of the **2**-carbonic anhydrase-*p*-toluenesulfonamide preparation. This result suggests that the sites labeled by **2** do depend on whether the **2** is displaced from the active site prior to photolysis.

In a second approach to differentiating the labeling patterns, affinity chromatography was used in an attempt to separate active site labeled carbonic anhydrase from nonactive site labeled enzyme. Two columns specific for carbonic anhydrase were used. Whitney[3] had previously separated active human erythrocyte carbonic anhydrase B (full sulfonamide binding ability), monocarboxamidomethyl human erythrocyte carbonic anhydrase B (low sulfonamide binding ability), and apoenzyme (no sulfonamide binding ability) on a column prepared by coupling *p*-aminomethylbenzenesulfonamide with cyanogen bromide-activated Sepharose 4B. When a photolyzed **2**-carbonic anhydrase preparation was eluted with a pH-salt gradient from a similar column, the unbound **2** residues eluted immediately, but all protein, both labeled and unlabeled, eluted in a single peak (S. Burroughs, unpublished work). A second affinity column was prepared by coupling sulfanilamide to carboxymethyl Sepharose 4B (CH-Sepharose 4B). Again, all protein was eluted in a single peak by a pH-salt gradient (A. Lowrie, unpublished work). Likewise, elution with a buffer containing an increasing *p*-toluenesulfonamide concentration gradient afforded no separation of labeled and unlabeled protein (S. Burroughs, unpublished work). The results of these affinity columns indicate that either carbonic anhydrase was labeled with **2** at points other than the active site or that, when **2** inserts via the nitrene end of the molecule at the active site, the benzenesulfonamide binding site on the protein is not sufficiently well-blocked to interfere at all with the binding of the enzyme to the affinity columns. Because the latter possibility seems remote, it is likely that **2** residues migrate from the active site prior to insertion.

PARA-AZIDOPHENACYL BROMIDE (3)–GLYCERALDEHYDE-3-PHOSPHATE
DEHYDROGENASE

Since the **2**-carbonic anhydrase system indicated that even with tightly bound noncovalent inhibitors random labeling must still be a serious consideration, we since have used only inhibitors bound covalently to the active sites of enzymes prior to photolysis. One such inhibitor, *p*-azidophenacyl bromide (**3**), was designed to be useful

$$N_3-\text{\large$\bigcirc$}-{}^{14}\overset{\displaystyle O}{\overset{\|}{C}}CH_2Br \qquad\qquad (3)$$

with enzymes containing essential cysteine or lysine residues. This inhibitor is easily synthesized from [*carboxyl*-^{14}C]-*p*-aminobenzoic acid. It is thermally stable and has an ultraviolet absorption maximum at 300 nm (ϵ = 2.01 × 10^4 M^{-1} cm^{-1}, 2% methanol in water).[4] Rabbit muscle glyceraldehyde-3-phosphate dehydrogenase (GPDH, EC 1.2.1.12) was readily inactivated by 3 with the rate of incorporation of radioactivity into the enzyme paralleling the rate of loss in activity, and, at low incubation ratios of 3 to GPDH, the reagent appeared to be specific for cysteine-149, the sulfhydryl residue required for enzymatic activity.[4] The labeled GPDH (nonphotolyzed) was reduced, carboxymethylated, digested with trypsin, and chromatographed on Sephadex G-25. The radioactivity eluted in two peaks, a major one corresponding to a large tryptic peptide, as is reasonable for labeling of cysteine-149, which is found in a 17 amino acid tryptic peptide, and a second, smaller peak eluting later. (Separate experiments showed that prolonged incubation of the major peak with trypsin gave rise to the smaller peak.) Similar treatment of the photolyzed 3-labeled GPDH produced a single radioactive peak corresponding in elution volume to that of the major peak obtained from the nonphotolyzed material. This result is compatible with (a) insertion of the nitrene from 3 at a site within a small tryptic peptide so that the cross-linked peptide is not appreciably larger than the cys-149 peptide, (b) insertion of the nitrene into the enzyme chain at a site that is part of the same cysteine-149 tryptic peptide, or (c) no insertion at all so that what is being seen is simply the cysteine-149 tryptic peptide with decomposed 3 residue still bound.

Two approaches generally useful for identifying nitrene insertion sites have been investigated. In the first, any cross-links formed by 3 residues between the cysteine-149 binding site and the insertion sites are left intact. In this case, radioactive label found in the protein is of two kinds, that which is involved in cross-links and represents interesting products, and that which is in the form of decomposed but noninserted 3 residues still attached to the cysteine-149 and is not of interest. Since the majority of the radioactive label is expected to be of this uninteresting sort, and since the tryptic digest results suggest that both interesting and uninteresting products are comprised of peptides of similar size, the purification of cross-linked products is likely to be difficult. As the work below with inhibitors 4 and 5 suggests, the analytical problems are sufficiently difficult without these complications, so we have directed our efforts to a second approach for identifying insertion sites.

In this approach, the α-keto thioether bond formed between the 3 residues and cysteine-149 is cleaved after photolysis of the 3-labeled GPDH. Now all radioactivity remaining with the protein will represent sites of insertion, the products of interest. Several methods have been used to cleave this bond, and current work is aimed at obtaining quantitative cleavage with sufficient recovery of intact protein to allow for identification of the sites of insertion within the primary sequence of GPDH.

The final two inhibitor-enzyme systems to be discussed were designed to alleviate both of the major problems seen thus far. First, to avoid random labeling, each inhibitor is covalently bound at the active site of the enzyme prior to photolysis. Second, to minimize analytical problems, the enzyme-bound inhibitors possess a bond that can be cleaved easily following photolysis.

PARA-AZIDO-α-DIAZOACETOPHENONE (4)–PEPSIN

Para-azido-α-diazoacetophenone (4) was synthesized by reacting [*carbonyl*-^{14}C]-*p*-azidobenzoylchloride with diazomethane. Inhibitor 4 was expected to react

$$N_3-\langle\!\!\!\bigcirc\!\!\!\rangle-{}^{14}\overset{\overset{\displaystyle O}{\|}}{C}CHN_2 \tag{4}$$

with porcine pepsin by esterifying aspartic acid-215 to form p-azidophenacyl pepsin by analogy with the reaction of pepsin with p-bromo-α-diazoacetophenone[5,6] and with other α-diazo carbonyl compounds.[7-9] In a typical reaction mixture, 6.25×10^{-5} M porcine pepsin (EC 3.4.4.1), 1.7×10^{-3} M cupric chloride, and 2.43×10^{-4} M 4 were incubated for 24 h at pH 5 and room temperature. The protein was found to be more than 90% inactivated (hemoglobin assay) and to have incorporated 4 in a ratio of nearly one mole of 4 per mole of enzyme. More than 97% of the bound label could be released from the enzyme by treating the labeled protein with hydroxylamine at pH 9. These data indicate that 4 almost certainly esterified specifically aspartic acid–215, as expected.

Inhibitor 4 itself has an absorption maximum at 314 nm, but this peak reflects, in part, the absorption of the diazo group. To determine the absorption characteristics of the inhibitor after it had become bound to pepsin, a small amount of hydrochloric acid was added to a solution of 4 in 10% ethanol. The acid served to decompose the diazo group to yield, presumably, p-azido-α-hydroxy(and ethoxy)acetophenone. Following the acid addition, the absorption maximum of the inhibitor shifted from 314 nm to 291 nm. The extinction coefficient of decomposed 4 at 278 nm, useful for determining the ratio of 4 bound to pepsin, was found to be 1.12×10^4 $M^{-1}cm^{-1}$.

The 4-labeled pepsin was photolyzed with light of wavelengths greater than 310 nm and then was treated with hydroxylamine to cleave the 4-pepsin ester linkage. The photolyzed enzyme so obtained retained 32% of the original label. Since a similar nonphotolyzed preparation retained less than 4% of the label, the photochemical decomposition of the azide leads to formation of insertion products in good yield.

Two approaches were taken to identify the site(s) of nitrene insertion. In the first, the original 4-pepsin ester bond was cleaved with hydroxylamine after photolysis and the labeled pepsin was treated with thermolysin. Chromatography of the digest on Sephadex G-25 led to one major radioactively labeled peptide peak (FIGURE 1). When this fraction was subjected to further purification by anion exchange chromatography on DEAE-Biogel A, all radioactivity again eluted in one peptide peak (FIGURE 2). This fraction, in turn, was subjected to high voltage paper electrophoresis at 2700 V for 2 h in a 5% acetic acid-pyridine buffer, pH 3.5, and one major radioactive band was obtained, with some separation of this band from unlabeled peptides. The results of the amino acid analysis of the peptide(s) eluted from this band revealed an extremely high molar ratio of several individual amino acids to radioactive label. Clearly, a substantial amount of unlabeled peptide(s) cochromatographed with the labeled one(s).

A variety of purification steps, including cation exchange chromatography on CM-Biogel A (BioRad Laboratories), anion exchange chromatography on AG 1-X2 (BioRad Laboratories), and descending paper chromatography prior to electrophoresis, did not noticeably enhance the purity of the labeled material finally isolated.

A second approach was tried in order to improve the purity of the final product. The photolyzed 4-labeled pepsin was not treated with hydroxylamine but was reduced, carboxymethylated, and treated with thermolysin directly. After Sephadex chroma-

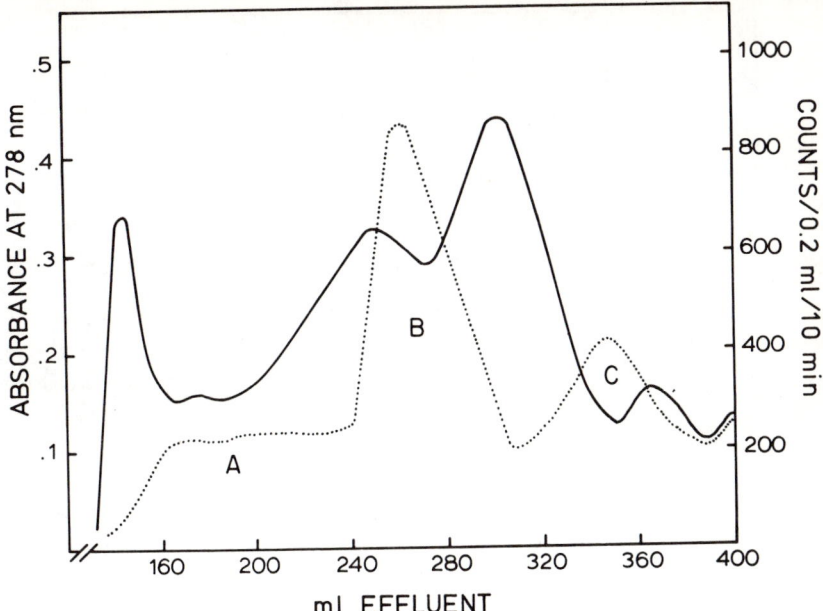

FIGURE 1. Sephadex G-25 chromatography of the thermolysin digest of photolyzed **4**-labeled pepsin. Immediately prior to use, porcine pepsin (Worthington Biochemical Corporation) was purified by gel filtration on a 2.5 × 65 cm Sephadex G-25 (fine) column at 4 °C with 0.006 M sodium acetate buffer, pH 3.4, as eluent. Protein concentration was determined by using an ϵ_{278} = 5.17 × 10^4 M^{-1}cm^{-1}. A solution containing 6.25 × 10^{-5} M pepsin, 1.7 × 10^{-3} M cupric chloride, and 2.43 × 10^{-4} M ^{14}C-**4** (0.322 Ci/mol, added as a solution in 10% ethanol–0.006 M sodium acetate buffer, pH 5) in 0.006 M sodium acetate, pH 5, was stirred 24 h at room temperature in the dark. The mixture then was dialyzed for 24 h at 4 °C against water. The **4**-labeled pepsin solution was added to a 6 in. Pyrex tube, which, in turn, was placed in a beaker of ice water, and the solution was irradiated in a Rayonet Photochemical Reactor with the 350 nm lamps (light output 310–420 nm, λ_{max} = 350 nm); the progress of the reaction was monitored by following the decrease in absorbance at 278 nm that occurred as the azide group decomposed. Following photolysis, the protein sample was stirred at room temperature for 18 h with one-fifth its volume of 5 M hydroxylamine, pH 9, and then was dialyzed against water, lyophilized, retreated with hydroxylamine for 18 h, dialyzed, and lyophilized. The protein was reduced and carboxymethylated,[10] dialyzed 24 h against water, lyophilized, and redissolved in 0.02 M Tris buffer, pH 8, containing 0.002 M calcium acetate and thermolysin (Sigma) in an amount equal to 10% by weight of the pepsin substrate. The solution was incubated at 40 °C for 2.5 h, lyophilized, taken up in 2 ml of 0.1 M ammonium bicarbonate solution and applied to a 1.8 × 2000 cm column of Sephadex G-25 (fine), equilibrated, and run at 4 °C with 0.1 M ammonium bicarbonate as buffer. The flow rate was 10 ml/h. Fractions of 3.3 ml were collected and analyzed for A_{278} (——) and counted for radioactivity (· · · ·).

tography, the major radioactive peak was treated with hydroxylamine and rechromatographed on Sephadex. Unfortunately, the one major radioactive peak obtained in this second Sephadex column coincided with the one major peptide peak, an indication that the original cross-link formed by **4** upon photolysis is between thermolysin peptides of similar size. This fact defeats part of the rationale for leaving the cross-link

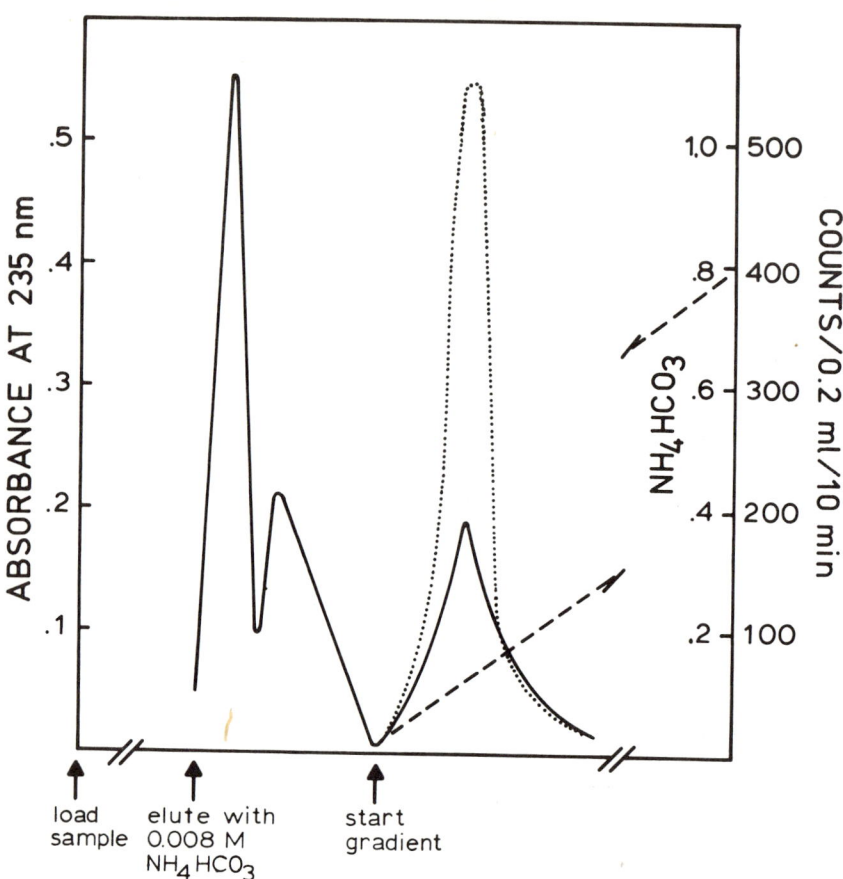

FIGURE 2. Anion exchange chromatography of the thermolysin digest of photolyzed **4**-labeled pepsin. The fractions comprising the major radioactive peak obtained from Sephadex chromatography of the thermolysin digest (FIGURE 1, peak B) were pooled, lyophilized, taken up in 50 ml of water and relyophilized; this procedure was repeated five times. The final sample was taken up in sufficient water to give absorbance readings of about 0.7 and 0.3 at 235 and 278 nm, respectively, and then was applied to a 1.5 × 10 cm column of DEAE-Biogel A (BioRad Laboratories). The column previously had been washed sequentially with water, 0.01 *M* sodium hydroxide, water, and 0.5 *M*, 0.1 *M*, and 0.008 *M* ammonium bicarbonate. The column was eluted for 2.5 h with 0.008 *M* ammonium bicarbonate and then with a linear bicarbonate gradient made from 200 ml each of 0.008 *M* and 2 *M* ammonium bicarbonate until the salt concentration in the eluent was 0.5 *M*. The flow rate was 45 ml/h. Samples of 1.5 ml were collected and analyzed for A_{235} (———) and counted for radioactivity (· · · ·).

intact until smaller, unlabeled peptides had been removed. Further anion exchange chromatography of the labeled peptide fraction on AG 1-X2 followed by high voltage paper electrophoresis again afforded a mixture of labeled and unlabeled peptides.

Digestion of photolyzed **4**-labeled pepsin with pepsin rather than thermolysin prior to hydroxylamine treatment, followed by a series of further chromatography steps, also gave only a mixture of labeled and unlabeled peptides.

The 4-pepsin system, then, has good photochemical labeling properties. The difficulties have come only in the purification of insertion sites. More powerful analytical methods may prove successful at separating the labeled peptide(s) from unlabeled peptide(s) of such similar size and charge although the results to date are not encouraging.

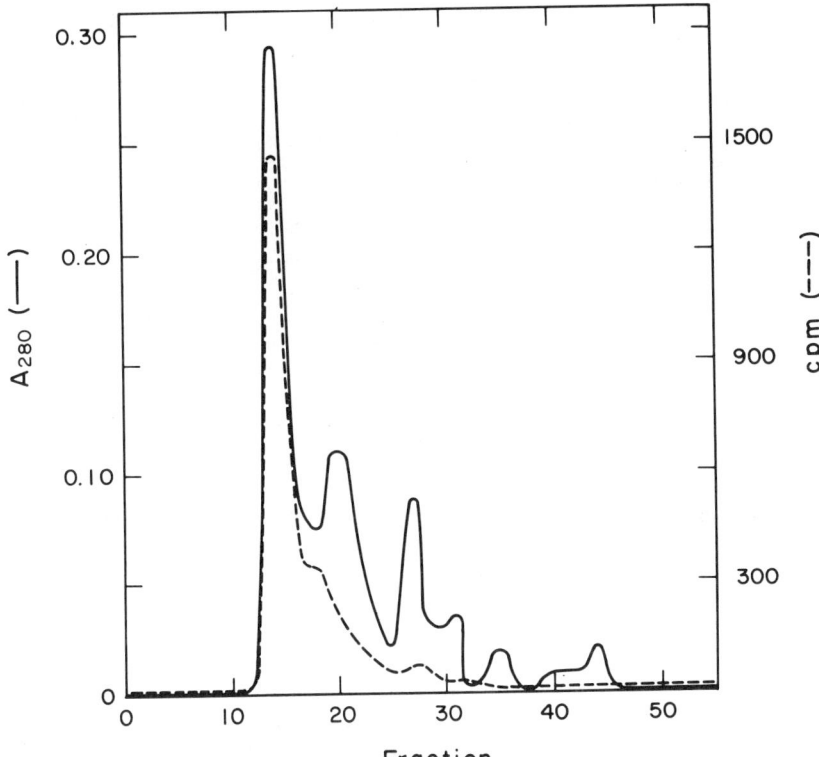

FIGURE 3. Sephadex G-25 chromatography of the tryptic digest of photolyzed **5a**-labeled carboxymethylated YADH. Carboxymethylated YADH was treated with one molar equivalent of **5a**, dialyzed, photolyzed, treated with hydroxylamine, and dialyzed as described previously.[12] The resulting protein solution was made 6 M in guanidine hydrochloride and 0.002 M in EDTA, and the pH was adjusted to 8.1. The solution was flushed with nitrogen and incubated at 35 °C for 1.5 h, then treated with an 800-fold molar excess of dithiothreitol relative to YADH, flushed with nitrogen, and incubated at room temperature with stirring for 4 h. A 20-fold molar excess of iodoacetic acid relative to dithiothreitol was added and the solution was incubated at room temperature with stirring for 1.0 h. The solution was dialyzed against water and then against 0.001 M hydrochloric acid until all precipitate had redissolved. The sample was lyophilized to dryness, dissolved in 0.1 M ammonium bicarbonate buffer, pH 8.0, and treated with a 1:50 molar ratio of trypsin (Worthington TPCK) to YADH for 8 h with stirring at room temperature. Any solid remaining was removed by centrifugation. The sample was added to a 0.8 × 112 cm Sephadex G-25 (fine) column and was eluted with 0.1 M ammonium bicarbonate buffer, pH 8.0. The flow rate was 14.0 ml/h. Fractions were collected every 8 min and analyzed for A_{280} (———). A 0.05 ml aliquot of each fraction was counted for radioactivity (----).

PARA-AZIDOPHENACYL IODOACETATE (5)–YEAST ALCOHOL DEHYDROGENASE

Para-azidophenacyl iodoacetate (5) is a bifunctional inhibitor designed to be useful with a variety of enzymes containing particularly reactive nucleophilic residues at their active sites. Radioactive form 5a of 5 was synthesized by reacting ^{14}C-3 with bromoacetic acid and treating the product with sodium iodide, while form 5b was synthesized in an analogous manner, starting with cold 3 and [2-^{14}C]bromoacetic acid.[11] Inhibitor 5 has an ultraviolet absorption maximum at 287 nm in methanol (ϵ = 2.35 × 10^4 M^{-1}cm^{-1})[11] and at 292 nm in water (ϵ = 2.35 × 10^4 M^{-1}cm^{-1}).[12]

$$N_3-\!\!\!\bigcirc\!\!\!-\overset{O}{\overset{\|}{^{14}C}}CH_2O\overset{O}{\overset{\|}{C}}CH_2I \qquad \text{(5a)}$$

$$N_3-\!\!\!\bigcirc\!\!\!-\overset{O}{\overset{\|}{C}}CH_2O\overset{O}{\overset{\|}{C}}{}^{14}CH_2I \qquad \text{(5b)}$$

When carboxymethylated YADH (YADH inactivated by treatment with excess iodoacetate) was treated with one molar equivalent of 5, the inhibitor appeared to bind specifically to cysteine-153,[12] one of two essential cysteine residues found at each active site of the tetrameric enzyme. The 5-labeled carboxymethylated YADH was photolyzed, treated with hydroxylamine to cleave the ester bond within the 5 residues, and found to retain 22% of the label. Similar treatment of nonphotolyzed material left less than 4% of the label still bound to protein.[12] Therefore, as in the 4-pepsin system, the p-azidophenacyl chromophore proved able to decompose with good levels of insertion.

In work aimed at identifying the sites of insertion of the nitrene, the 5-labeled carboxymethylated YADH was photolyzed, treated with hydroxylamine, reduced, totally carboxymethylated, and digested with trypsin. On Sephadex G-25 chromatography of the digest, one major radioactively labeled peak was seen (FIGURE 3). When the fractions in this peak were combined, treated with chymotrypsin, and rechromatographed, again only a single major radioactive peak was obtained. Chromatography of the original tryptic digest on Sephadex G-50 likewise produced one major labeled peak, which eluted early although several smaller labeled peaks eluted later.

For further purification studies, the tryptic digest was subjected to chromatography on Sephadex G-25. Fractions in the major radioactive peak were combined and subjected to two-dimensional separation on cellulose thin layer plates. Electrophoresis at pH 6.3 was carried out in the first dimension, followed by thin layer chromatography in the second. A typical chromatogram is shown in FIGURE 4. In similar runs, the number of spots containing significant radioactivity varied from six to eight.

The peptides in several of the radioactive spots were eluted from the cellulose and subjected to amino acid analysis. In this case, as opposed to the 4-pepsin case, the quantities of individual amino acids detected were reasonable in relation to the radioactivity present. However, the quantities of amino acids obtained in the sample analyses were not consistently high enough above the blank analyses to allow for definitive determinations of amino acid decompositions. The cellulose plate separations are to be repeated with larger quantities of material.

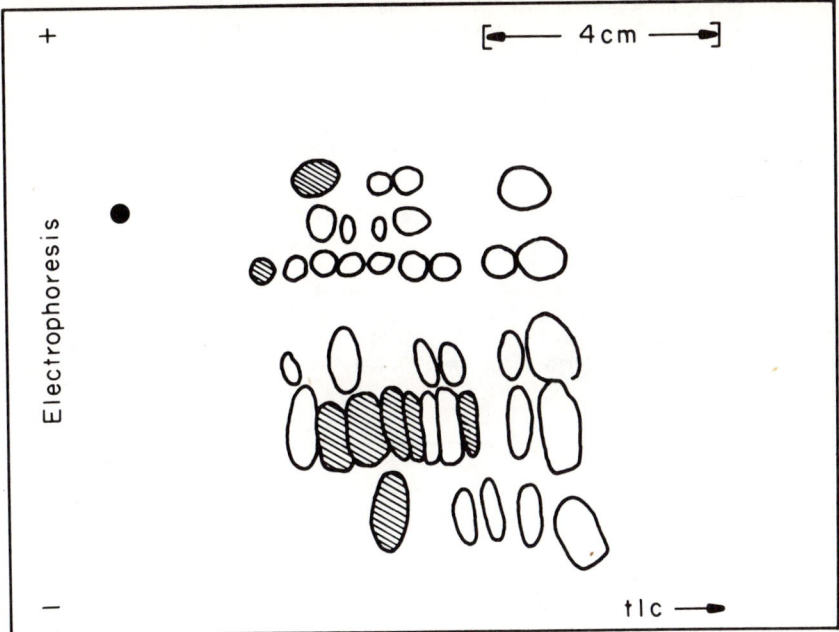

FIGURE 4. Two-dimensional analysis of the tryptic peptides from photolyzed **5a**-labeled carboxymethylated YADH. Fractions from the major radioactive peak in FIGURE 3 were combined, lyophilized to dryness, and resuspended in 2% ammonium hydroxide. An aliquot was spotted (●) on a 20 × 20 cm EM Cellulose Pre-Coated TLC plastic sheet, 0.10 mm layer thickness. The plate was sprayed with the electrophoresis solvent, 25:1:225 pyridine–acetic acid–water, pH 6.3, and run for 35 min at a constant voltage of 1000 V and a current of 35 mA in a Desaga TLE-Double Chamber Thin Layer apparatus. The plate was dried and subjected in the second dimension to thin layer chromatography in a 33:1:40:50 pyridine–acetic acid–water–1-butanol solvent for 3.5 h. The plate was dried and the peptides were visualized with fluorescamine.[13] To detect radioactivity, the cellulose from each area containing peptide was scraped from the plate, added to scintillation fluid, and counted. When amino acid analyses were to be performed, duplicate plates were run. One plate was used to count for radioactivity while peptides were eluted from the second and then hydrolyzed.

The pattern of radioactivity on the chromatograms indicates that several labeled peptides are being isolated. The multiple radioactive spots can be simply a result of nonspecific cleavage by trypsin. On the other hand, they may arise from insertion of **5** residues into different amino acids within the same ultimate tryptic peptide, into different points in the same amino acid, or into amino acids nearby in the tertiary structure but located in different tryptic peptides. Once meaningful amino acid analyses are obtained, these possibilities can be distinguished.

REFERENCES

1. HIXSON, S. S. & S. H. HIXSON. 1973. Photochem. Photobiol. **18:** 135–38.
2. HIXSON, S. S., S. H. HIXSON & C. O. L. BOYCE. 1973. Abstracts of Papers, 166th National American Chemical Society Meeting: BIOL 90.
3. WHITNEY, P. L. 1974. Anal. Biochem. **57:** 467–76.

4. HIXSON, S. H. & S. S. HIXSON. 1975. Biochemistry **14:** 4251–54.
5. ERLANGER, B. F., S. M. VRATSANOS, N. WASSERMAN & A. G. COOPER. 1967. Biochem. Biophys. Res. Commun. **28:** 203–8.
6. ERLANGER, B. F. 1974. Private communication to E. T. Kaiser; cited in CHEN, H. G. & E. T. KAISER. 1974. J. Am. Chem. Soc. **96:** 625–26.
7. BAYLISS, R. S., J. R. KNOWLES & G. B. WYBRANDT. 1969. Biochem. J. **113:** 377–86.
8. FRY, K. T., O. K. SIM, J. SPONA & G. A. HAMILTON. 1970. Biochemistry **9:** 4624–32.
9. STEPANOV, V. M. & T. I. VAGANOVA. 1969. Biochem. Biophys. Res. Commun. **31:** 825–30.
10. CRESTFIELD, A. M., S. MOORE & W. H. STEIN. 1963. J. Biol. Chem. **238:** 622–27.
11. OFENGAND, J., I. SCHWARTZ, G. CHINALI, S. S. HIXSON & S. H. HIXSON. 1977. Methods Enzymol. **46:** 683–702.
12. HIXSON, S. H., S. F. BURROUGHS, T. M. CAPUTO, B. B. CRAPSTER, M. V. DALY, A. W. LOWRIE & M. L. WASKO. 1979. Arch. Biochem. Biophys. **192:** 296–301.
13. LAI, C. Y. 1977. Methods Enzymol. **47:** 236–43.
14. GRACY, R. W. 1977. Methods Enzymol. **47:** 195–204.

DISCUSSION

DR. W. LWOWSKI: You speak of insertion; my question is, do you mean CH insertion or any linkage formation?

DR. S. H. HIXSON: Any covalent bond attachment that allows the radioactive label to remain attached to protein throughout the rest of our procedures. We did discover one thing about the type of linkages formed in the pepsin work. If you are familiar with the literature reporting the sequencing of pepsin, you know that that work was based on initial cyanogen bromide cleavage of the protein. We found that, on cyanogen bromide cleavage of our labeled pepsin, we lost the majority of the radioactivity. So this radioactivity was clearly not bound through CH insertion of the nitrene.

LWOWSKI: What nitrenes can do best is add to an unshared electron pair on nitrogen, oxygen, or sulfur and go on from there. The organic chemists have neglected to study these reactions separately in solution, for which I apologize.

HIXSON: Actually, Dr. S. S. Hixson, one of the coauthors, is also a mechanistic photochemist. In some early cases, his group tried photolyzing some model aryl azides in solution and got a huge variety of products.

RECENT STUDIES ON STEROID ISOMERASES FROM *PSEUDOMONAS TESTOSTERONI* AND *PSEUDOMONAS PUTIDA**

William F. Benisek, John R. Ogez, and Stephen B. Smith

Department of Biological Chemistry
School of Medicine
University of California
Davis, California 95616

INTRODUCTION

In 1955, Paul Talalay reported the occurrence and partial purification of a Δ^5-3-ketosteroid isomerase (EC 5.3.3.1) in *Pseudomonas testosteroni* grown in the presence of testosterone.[1] By 1959, the isomerase was available in essentially pure crystalline preparations.[2] The reaction catalyzed by the isomerase has been shown to consist of an allylic isomerization of steroidal 5-ene-3-ones to their conjugated 4-ene-3-one isomers with concomitant 4β to 6β intramolecular proton transfer. This reaction is shown in FIGURE 1. The enzyme has been the object of numerous investigations of its structure and function. Much of this work has been the subject of a recent review.[3] Δ^5-3-Ketosteroid isomerase has attracted interest because of its rather large turnover number, its moderate size, and the fact that it is obtainable in a pure state in large quantities. In addition, because it binds steroids as substrates or competitive inhibitors, albeit with less affinity than mammalian intracellular steroid receptors, some effort has been made to elucidate the structural bases for steroid binding by the isomerase. The primary structure of the constituent polypeptide chain has been reported by Benson *et al.*[4] and a crystallographic study of its three-dimensional structure is reported to be underway.[5]

Below a concentration of approximately 2 mg/ml, the *testosteroni* isomerase is a dimer of identical 13,394 dalton subunits. Each subunit consists of a single polypeptide chain. The dimer probably has two independent functioning steroid binding sites,[6,7] although Vincent *et al.*[8] have reported that, in their experiments, the dimer exhibits a "half-of-the-sites" binding stoichiometry. Considerable variation of the steroid structure can be tolerated without exceeding the ability of the enzyme to bind the steroid. In a recent comprehensive survey, Weintraub *et al.*[9] found that a wide variety of estrogens, androgens, and progestins were competitive inhibitors of the catalytic process. Many of the enzyme's competitive inhibitors are steroidal Δ^4-3-ones, the products of the enzymatic reaction when it is conducted in the thermodynamically favored direction.

Over the past several years, we have sought to exploit the inherent photochemical reactivity of the Δ^4-3-one competitive inhibitors of the enzyme in an effort to identify, by photochemical modification techniques, important functional groups of the steroid binding active sites of this enzyme.[10–12] The most detailed work has been conducted

*This research was supported by the National Institutes of Health, grant no. AM-14729.

115

using the competitive inhibitor 19-nortestosterone acetate (19-NTA) as the light-activated reagent.

To briefly summarize this work, it was found that the *P. testosteroni* isomerase was subject to a 19-NTA-dependent ultraviolet light-stimulated inactivation that appeared to be the result of a reaction at the active site, since nonchromophoric steroids protected the enzyme from 19-NTA-dependent photoinactivation. Chemical studies of the photoinactivated enzyme have shown that, contrary to our first report,[10] only about 0.08 mole of 19-NTA became covalently linked to protein per mole of isomerase active sites inactivated.[13] Instead of covalent linkage, the inactivating reaction causes the destruction of one residue of aspartic acid per subunit[11,12] by means of a 19-NTA sensitized photodecarboxylation of aspartic acid–38, leaving a residue of alanine. The fate of the side chain carboxyl has not yet been clarified. One possibility is that it appears as CO_2, although there is still no evidence for this.

In the present report, we wish to describe our recent studies on the active site of the steroid isomerase from another bacterial species, *Pseudomonas putida,* which, like *testosteroni,* produces a steroid isomerase when grown in the presence of certain

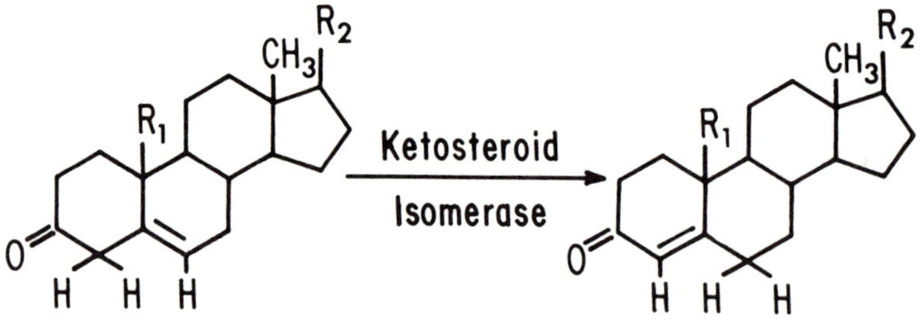

FIGURE 1. The reaction catalyzed by Δ^5-3-ketosteroid isomerases.

steroids. In addition, we shall describe some light-independent chemical modification studies of the *testosteroni* isomerase that lend support to our previous conclusion, based on photochemical labeling studies,[12] that aspartate 38 is part of the active site of the enzyme.

EXPERIMENTAL PROCEDURES

P. testosteroni steroid isomerase was purified from progesterone-induced cells following the procedure of Jarabak et al.,[14] as modified by Benson et al.[20] *P. putida* steroid isomerase was purified to near homogeneity by the procedure of Smith et al.[15] This procedure involves cell rupture, freeze-thaw of the cell extract, precipitation of nucleic acids by Mn^{2+}, $(NH_4)_2SO_4$ precipitation, diethylaminoethyl (DEAE) cellulose gradient elution chromatography, affinity chromatography on 19-NTA-succinyl-ethylenediamine-agarose, and exclusion chromatography on Sephadex G-100. The purified isomerase exhibits one major Coomassie Blue staining band in several different gel electrophoresis systems and in analytical gel isoelectric focusing. Details of the purification and of the general properties of this isomerase are published elsewhere.[15,23]

N-ethyl-N'-(3-dimethylamino) propyl carbodiimide hydrochloride (EDAC) was purchased from Calbiochem. Cystamine dihydrochloride was a product of Aldrich Chemical Co. Para-mercurianiline-agarose was prepared according to Sluyterman and Wijdenes.[16] 19-Nortestosterone acetate, 1,4,6-androstatrien-3-one-17β-ol, deoxycholic acid, and cholic acid were purchased from Steraloids, Inc. Dithioerythritol was obtained from Pierce Chemical Co. Iodoacetic acid was a product of Sigma Chemical Co., and was recrystallized from ethanol. 4-[^{14}C]-1,4,6-androstatrien-3-one-17β-ol (TEO) was synthesized from 4-[^{14}C]-testosterone by the procedure of Caspi *et al.*[17] Alpha chymotrypsin, 47 U/mg was a product of Worthington Biochemical Corp.

Amidation of *P. testosteroni* isomerase with cystamine was performed by a modification of the procedures of Hoare and Koshland,[18] which were used with other amines. In a typical reaction, enzyme (28 μM in subunits), in 0.1 M pyridine-HCl (pH 4.75) containing 0.5 M cystamine and 2.5% v/v methanol, was treated with 5 mM EDAC-HCl at 25 °C. At intervals, aliquots were removed and the reaction was quenched by addition to 0.5 M cystamine–1M sodium acetate (pH 4.75) in order to consume unreacted EDAC. Residual enzyme activity was assayed by our modification[10] of the method developed by Kawahara *et al.*[21] Exhaustive dialysis was used to remove cystamine; protein-bound cystamine was determined by acid hydrolysis of the performic acid oxidized protein,[19] followed by amino acid analysis for taurine. Thus, two taurines are recovered per cystamine. The disulfide bond of protein-bound cystamine was cleaved reductively by treating the dialyzed protein derivative with 1 mM dithioerythritol in 0.1–0.2 M potassium phosphate buffer (pH 7.0) for 8–12 h at 4 °C in a nitrogen atmosphere. Excess reagents were removed by anaerobic dialysis, first against 0.1 M potassium phosphate (pH 7.0) and then against water. The thiol-bearing protein was digested for 6 h with α-chymotrypsin, which was dissolved in 1 or 2% NH$_4$HCO$_3$, and 1 mM 2-mercaptoethanol at pH 8.5 and 37 °C under N$_2$, added to the substrate in three, 0.75% by weight, portions at 0, 2, and 4 h. The digest derived from 490 nmol of native isomerase polypeptide chain was applied to a 0.3 ml bed-volume column of *p*-mercurianiline-agarose equilibrated with 0.1 M sodium phosphate, pH 8.0. The column was washed with several milliliters of 0.1 M sodium phosphate (pH 8.0) and the retained peptides were recovered by elution with 0.9 ml of 0.1 M 2-mercaptoethanol in 0.1 M sodium phosphate, pH 8.0. The mercaptoethanol eluate was treated with a 1 molar equivalent of iodoacetic acid, while the pH was maintained at 8.0 by the continual addition of NaOH. When the demand for NaOH ceased, indicating that the alkylation was completed, the peptide material was separated from the reagents and buffer species by exclusion chromatography on Sephadex G-15, which was equilibrated and eluted with 0.1 M pyridine-HOAc, pH 5.0. Fractions containing peptide material were located by amino acid analysis of acid hydrolysates of fraction aliquots. A single peptide peak was found, which eluted at the excluded volume of the column. Fractions contiaining this material were pooled and lyphilized. The resulting residue was examined by amino acid analysis and N-terminal amino acid sequence analysis.

Amino acid analysis was performed on 24 h/110 °C constant boiling HCl hydrolysates using a Durrum D-500 amino acid analyzer.

N-terminal sequence analysis of peptides was carried out with a Beckman Model

890C sequencer, which employed dimethylallylamine as the coupling buffer and was controlled by Beckman Program 102974. Acetic anhydride treated horse heart cytochrome *c* was used as a carrier to reduce extractive losses of the peptide.[12]

Cysteine thiol groups of *P. putida* isomerase were determined by colorimetric analysis using 5,5'-dithio-bis-(2-nitrobenzoic acid) (DTNB) in 8 *M* urea.

The light source for the photolyses of *P. putida* steroid isomerase was a 100 watt Hanovia medium pressure mercury vapor discharge lamp housed in a Pyrex immersion well. The lamp was located 40 cm from the sample tubes. The reaction mixtures were contained in 5 mm o.d. Pyrex nmr tubes and consisted of isomerase in 10 mM potassium phosphate, 1 mM Na_2 EDTA, 1 mM sodium azide, 1 mM dithiothreitol, 10% (v/v) methanol and the amounts of TEO, deoxycholate (DOC), or cholate indicated in the appropriate table or figure. All samples were maintained in an atmosphere of argon. Prior to irradiation experiments, the stock solution of isomerase was treated with 20 mM dithioerythritol and then dialyzed under argon in an effort to ensure that all enzyme half-cystine residues were in the reduced form. In experiments in which the effect of irradiation on enzyme thiol content was investigated, dithiothreitol was omitted from the photoreaction mixture.

RESULTS

Carbodiimide Promoted Amidation of P. Testosteroni Isomerase

When *P. testosteroni* steroid isomerase was treated with EDAC in the presence of the amines (glycine ethyl ester, taurine, and cystamine) or ammonium ion at pH 4.75, rapid inactivation reactions ensued in each case that followed pseudo-first order kinetics for more than 90% of the reaction. The first order rate constants for the various reactions were calculated from the plots of the logarithm of the percent of activity versus time. In all cases, the inactivation reactions were greatly retarded by the presence of the competitive inhibitor, 19-NTA, the same inhibitor that sensitizes the enzyme to ultraviolet photoinactivation. The rate constants are summarized in TABLE 1. Comparison of these rate constants with the kinetic data of Hoare and Koshland[18] revealed the interesting fact that all of the inactivation reactions proceeded

TABLE 1

KINETICS OF INACTIVATION OF STEROID ISOMERASE BY EDAC AND VARIOUS AMINES

Amine	[EDAC] (mM)	[19-NTA] (μM)	K_{obs} (min^{-1})
0.6 *M* taurine	50	0	−0.63
0.6 *M* taurine	50	37	−0.29
0.6 *M* taurine	50	410	−0.03
1.0 *M* gly OEt	5	0	−0.53
1.0 *M* gly OEt	5	34	−0.13
1.0 *M* gly OEt	5	410	−0.015
0.5 *M* cystamine	5	0	−0.42
0.5 *M* cystamine	5	410	−0.02
1.0 *M* NH_4Cl	5	0	−0.17
1.0 *M* NH_4Cl	5	410	−0.012

NOTE: Buffer = 0.1 *M* pyridine-HCl, pH 4.75.

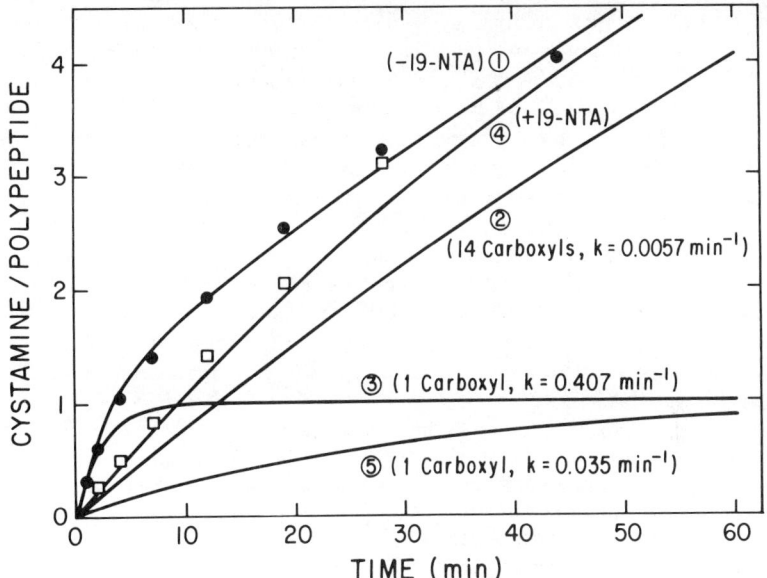

FIGURE 2. The kinetics of cystamine incorporation.

at much more rapid rates than did the reactions of low molecular weight carboxylic acids with amines studied by Hoare and Koshland. For example, it can be estimated from the data of Hoare and Koshland that the reaction of *m*-nitrohippurate with 1.0 *M* glycine methyl ester in the presence of 5 m*M* carbodiimide would proceed with a first order rate constant of 0.005–0.006 min^{-1}, whereas isomerase was inactivated by 1.0 *M* glycine ethyl ester in the presence of 5 m*M* EDAC with a first order rate constant approximately 100-fold greater. With the possible exception of taurine, similarly large rates of inactivation were obtained with 0.5 *M* cystamine (1.0 *M* in amino groups) and 1.0 *M* NH$_4$Cl. These results suggest that the isomerase might possess one or a limited number of carboxyl groups that are hyperreactive towards carbodiimide/amine derivatization. Thus, the possibility of selective chemical modification at a steroid binding site was not unlikely, since the rapid inactivation was suppressed by 19-NTA.

The reaction with cystamine was selected for detailed study because of the ease with which peptide fragments containing cystamine-modified amino acids could be isolated, as well as other practical considerations. The kinetics of cystamine incorporation into the enzyme for a reaction performed with 0.5 *M* cystamine, 5 m*M* EDAC at pH 4.75—the same conditions as those used for the inactivation kinetics measurements of TABLE 1—are given in FIGURE 2. The filled circle data points are the experimental measurement to which a theoretical curve (curve 1), which is calculated for a kinetic model in which one carboxyl group per subunit is amidated at a rate constant of 0.407 min^{-1} and 14 other carboxyl groups per subunit each react with a rate constant of 0.0057 min^{-1}, is fitted. The preparations of isomerase used possess 15 carboxyl groups per subunit. For reference, curve 3 is the theoretical incorporation curve for one carboxyl coupling to cystamine at 0.407 min^{-1}, while curve 2 shows the calculated incorporation kinetics for 14 carboxyls coupling at a rate constant of 0.0057 min^{-1}. Thus, curve 1 = curve 3 + curve 2. In the presence of the activity protecting steroid, 19-NTA, the kinetics of cystamine incorporation are given by the filled square data points. These were fitted by theoretical curve 4, which is calculated for a kinetic model in which one carboxyl reacts with a first order rate constant of 0.037 min^{-1} and 14 other carboxyls react at 0.0057 min^{-1}. The composite theoretical curves are curve 5 and curve 2, that is, curve 4 = curve 5 + curve 2. Thus, the effect of 19-NTA is to greatly reduce the rate of the rapid amidation reaction and not to affect the normally reactive carboxyl group's reactions. A comparison of the inactivation rate constants with the rapid amidation rate constants in the presence and absence of 19-NTA is given in TABLE 2. So we see that rate constants for inactivation and rapid amidation are similar, suggesting that the rapid amidation reaction is the reaction responsible for enzyme inactivation.

Since one carboxyl group was much more reactive with the cystamine/EDAC treatment than the others, it was feasible to attempt to identify the site of rapid amidation by peptide isolation and subsequent sequence analysis. Therefore, we set up a preparative scale reaction in which 490 nmol of isomerase subunits were subjected to

TABLE 2

KINETICS OF INACTIVATION AND RAPID CYSTAMINE INCORPORATION

	First Order Rate Constant (min^{-1})	
	Inactivation	Rapid Incorporation
−19 NTA	0.42	0.407
+19 NTA	0.02	0.037

NOTE: Conditions are given in EXPERIMENTAL PROCEDURES.

0.5 M cystamine–5 mM EDAC inactivation for 2.0 min—a time judged to be close to optimum for maximal amidation of the hyperreactive carboxyl with acceptably low levels of modification of the normally reactive 14 other carboxyls. Following the termination of the reaction, chymotryptic fragments of the polypeptide, which contained sites of cystamine amidation, were isolated and characterized as described in detail in EXPERIMENTAL PROCEDURES and outlined in FIGURE 3.

Material that represented the sum total of peptides containing cystamine amidated carboxyls was eluted from the organomercurial column and examined by amino acid analysis and sequence analysis. The amino acid composition of the peptide material eluted by 2-mercaptoethanol-containing buffer is given in TABLE 3. With the exception of the presence of 0.8 residues of S-carboxymethyl cysteamine, the composition of the eluted peptide fraction is close to that expected for chymotryptic peptide C-7, which comprises residues 31–48.[4] The site of amidation was identified by sequence analysis of this peptide without further purification steps, as described in EXPERIMENTAL PROCEDURES. The sequence obtained and its comparison with the corresponding portion of native isomerase[4,12] is given in FIGURE 4. The sequence obtained for the eluted peptide was identical to that expected for residues 31–48 (peptide C-7[4]) except that a blank was found at the position corresponding to residue

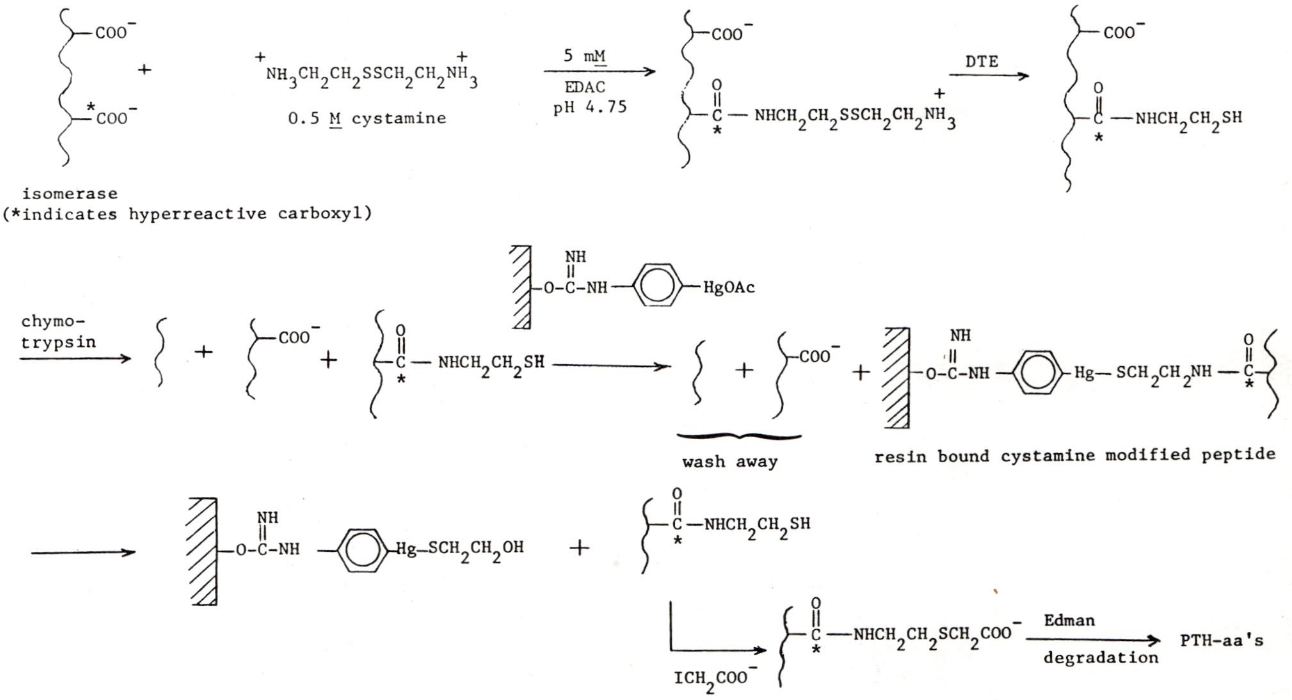

FIGURE 3. The amidation of carboxyl groups by cystamine/EDAC and the isolation of amidated peptide fragments by thiol-specific covalent chromatography.

TABLE 3

AMINO ACID COMPOSITION OF CYSTAMINE-MODIFIED CHYMOTRYPTIC PEPTIDE MATERIAL

Amino Acid	Residues	Theory for C-7 (Residues 31–48)
ala	2.98	3
thr	1.90	2
ser	1.97	2
glu	2.06	2
pro	1.97	2
gly	2.0*	2
ala	2.24	2
val	2.05	2
met	0.08	0
ile	0.11	0
leu	0.16	0
lys	0.09	0
arg	1.00	1
S-carboxymethyl cysteamine	0.78	0

*Taken as the basis for the calculation of molar ratios.

asp-38. Though negative in character, these data suggest that asp-38 is the site of rapid amidation. It should be noted that Ogez and Benisek[12] obtained a clear positive identification of aspartic acid at position 38 in their Edman degradation of peptide C-7. No trace of phenylthiohydantoin (PTH)-asp was obtained from the Edman degradation in the modified C-7.

TEO-Dependent Photoinactivation of P. Putida Steroid Isomerase

The purification and properties of the Δ^5-3-ketosteroid isomerase of *Pseudomonas putida* Biotype B have been reported by Smith *et al.*[15,23] A comparison of some of the properties of the *P. putida* isomerase and its *P. testosteroni* congener is made in TABLE 4.

The amino acid compositions of the two isomerases are somewhat similar, except that the *putida* isomerase possesses four residues of cysteine per subunit and the *testosteroni* isomerase does not contain this amino acid. The sequence of the N-terminal 50 residues of the *putida* isomerase is compared with the corresponding sequence of the *testosteroni* isomerase in FIGURE 5. In order to bring the sequences into register, a two-residue gap has been inserted into the *testosteroni* sequence. The sequences are homologous from the N-terminus through *putida* residue 32, although many structurally conservative substitutions are present. The sequences are identical between *putida* residues 33 and 41, perhaps reflecting a critical function for this portion of the polypeptide. The significance of the fact that four of these nine residues are anionic in both proteins is not known. Perhaps the hyperreactivity of aspartate 38 towards EDAC-cystamine, both cationic molecules, is due to the proximity of aspartate 38 to three other negatively charged residues.

residue	31	32	33	34	35	36	37	38	39	40	41	42	43	44	45	46	47	48
C-7	ala	asp	asp	ala	thr	val	glu	asp	pro	val	gly	ser	glu	pro	arg	ser	gly	thr
cystamine modified peptide	ala	asp	asp	ala	thr	val	glu	•	pro	val	gly	ser	glu	pro	*	*	*	

• no PTH identified

* degradation terminated after residue 44

FIGURE 4. The sequence of organomercurial resin-retained peptide and its comparison with chymotryptic peptide C-7. Sequence analysis was performed for 14 cycles of Edman degradation, as described in EXPERIMENTAL PROCEDURES. PTH amino acids were identified by gas/liquid chromatography[25] and two-dimensional thin layer chromatography.[26]

TABLE 4

COMPARISON OF PROPERTIES OF STEROID ISOMERASES FROM
P. Putida AND *P. Testosteroni*

Property	P. Putida	P. testosteroni
Molecular weight	~27,000	26,788
Subunits	2	2
Steroid binding sites	Yes	2
K_d	10^{-5}–10^{-4}	10^{-6}–10^{-4}
Amino acid composition	Similar to *P.t.*, except 4 cysteines present	No cysteine
Primary structure	N-terminal 50 residues homologous to *P.t.*	Known[4,12]

In initial attempts to achieve an active-site-selective steroid-dependent photoinactivation of the *putida* isomerase, we were frustrated by the fact that our preparations of the enzyme were much less stable under irradiation by ultraviolet light than was the *testosteroni* isomerase. The instability appears to be related to a tendency of solutions of the enzyme to accumulate disulfides when stored in the presence of air. Such solutions exhibit a very rapid loss of enzyme activity upon irradiation, even in the absence of absorbing steroids. In order to minimize this presumably nonspecific photoinactivation, several modifications of our standard conditions and apparatus[24] were adopted. These include a large reduction in light intensity (a 100 watt lamp at 40 cm versus a 450 watt lamp at 4.5 cm), a strict anaerobicity maintained by an argon atmosphere, the inclusion of azide ions as a singlet oxygen trap, and the prereduction of adventitious protein disulfide bonds, followed by anaerobic dialysis to remove low molecular weight disulfides. A systematic study to evaluate the relative importance of these modifications has not been made.

Because of the great reduction in light intensity, a steroid that absorbs light of $\lambda >$ 300 nm more efficiently than Δ^4-3-one steroids was selected for further attempts to obtain a photochemical reaction at the steroid binding site. The steroid used for this work was 1,4,6-androstatrien-3-one-17β-ol (TEO), a competitive inhibitor of the isomerase that has strong absorption bands at 223 nm ($\epsilon = 1.16 \times 10^4$), 260 nm ($\epsilon = 9.8 \times 10^3$), and 310 nm ($\epsilon = 1.06 \times 10^4$). The 310 nm band is nicely overlapped by

```
             I              5               10              15              20              25
putida      H met asn leu pro thr ala gln glu val glu gly leu met ala arg tyr ile glu leu val asp val gly asp ile

testosteroni H met asn thr pro     glu his met thr ala val val gln arg tyr val ala ala leu asn ala gly asp leu
             I              5               10              15              20


                  30              35              40              45              50
putida      glu ala ile val glx met tyr ala asp asp ala thr val glu asp pro phe gly glu pro pro ile his gly lys---

testosteroni asp gly ile val ala leu phe ala asp asp ala thr val glu asp pro val gly ser glu pro arg ser gly thr---
                  25              30              35              40              45
```

FIGURE 5. A comparison of the N-terminal sequences of *P. putida* isomerase and *P. testosteroni* isomerase. The sequence analysis of the *putida* isomerase was determined for the intact polypeptide after derivatization of SH groups with 4-vinyl pyridine or iodoacetamide. PHT amino acids were identified as described in FIGURE 4 as well as, in some cases, by amino acid analysis of SnCl₂/HCl hydrolysates.[27]

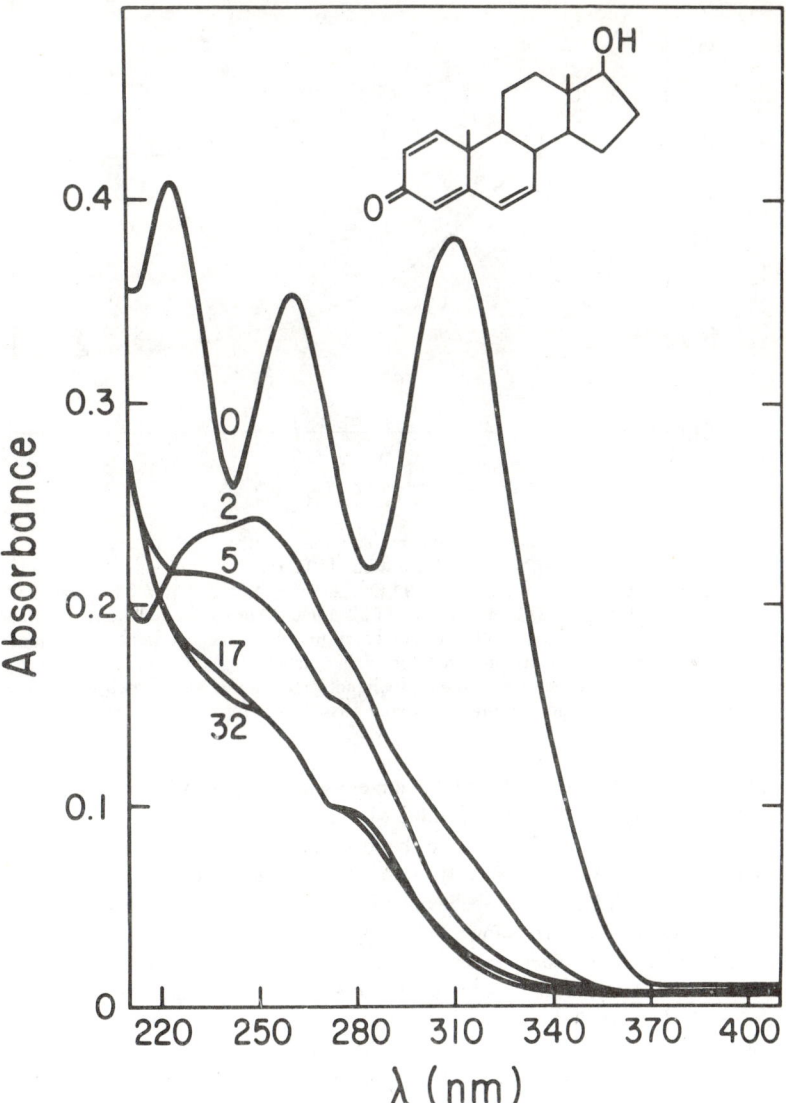

FIGURE 6. The ultraviolet absorption spectrum of TEO and the effect of irradiation upon the spectrum. 353 μM TEO was irradiated under the conditions described for enzyme photoinactivation in EXPERIMENTAL PROCEDURES. At various times, aliquots were withdrawn, diluted with 10% aqueous methanol, and the spectra were recorded. The numbers near the spectra are the times of irradiation in minutes.

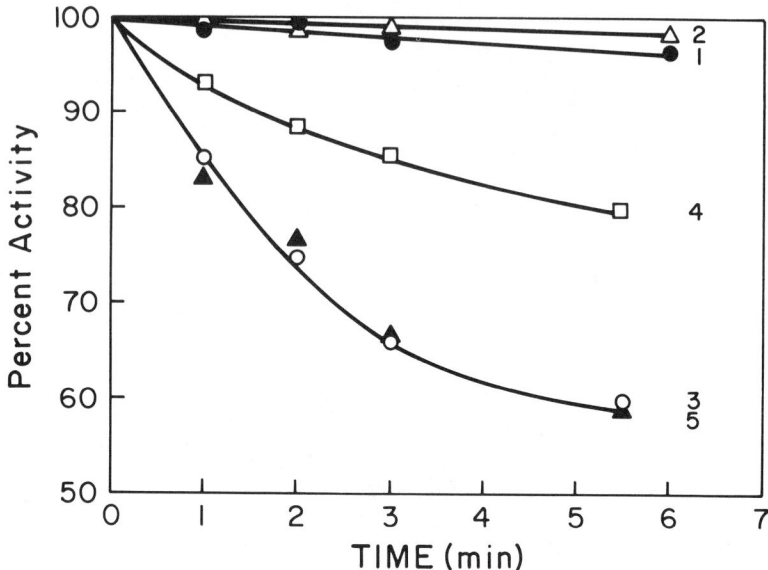

FIGURE 7. The kinetics of TEO-dependent photoinactivation of *P. putida* isomerase. All reaction mixtures contained 277 n*M* isomerase subunits. Curve 1, no additions; Curve 2, plus 282 μ*M* deoxycholate; Curve 3, plus 272 μ*M* TEO; Curve 4, plus 272 μ*M* TEO and 282 μ*M* deoxycholate; Curve 5, plus 272 μ*M* TEO and 282 μ*M* cholate. Other reaction conditions are described in EXPERIMENTAL PROCEDURES. In order to ensure the maintenance of anaerobic conditions, a separate tube was prepared for each time point. After each sample tube was withdrawn from the photochemical reactor, an aliquot was removed and diluted with 1% bovine serum albumin (pH 7.0) and the diluted enzyme was assayed for enzyme activity.

the 289.4, 296.7, 303, 313, 334, and 366 nm emission maxima of the medium pressure mercury discharge lamp. TEO is unstable when irradiated by Pyrex filtered light from such a lamp (FIGURE 6). The 310 nm band rapidly disappears during the first few minutes of irradiation by a 100 watt mercury discharge lamp 40 cm away.

The effects of TEO on the behavior of the *putida* isomerase's enzyme activity towards ultraviolet light are shown in FIGURE 7. Curves 1 and 2 show that enzyme irradiated alone or in the presence of the nonchromophoric competitive inhibitor, deoxycholate (DOC), is not photoinactivated under these conditions. However, the enzyme suffers rapid photoinactivation in the presence of TEO (curve 3). The enzyme activity does not go to zero because of the photoinstability of TEO. With fresh additions of TEO, the enzyme activity can be brought to levels approaching complete inactivation. Curve 4 shows that the rate of the TEO-dependent photoinactivation is significantly reduced if the competing steroid, DOC, is included in the reaction mixture. The protection by DOC is unlikely to be the result of DOC-scavenging reactive species generated by light from TEO because cholate, which is not a competitive inhibitor of *putida* isomerase,[23] affords no protective effect, as shown by curve 5. This pattern of results suggests that the inactivating reaction occurs at the enzyme's active site.

Further evidence that a site-specific photoreaction is involved comes from quantitative studies, which demonstrate a good correlation between the initial rate of enzyme inactivation and the occupancy of the active site by TEO. In these experiments, enzyme was irradiated in the presence of a fixed concentration of TEO and variable concentrations of DOC. One can calculate, for any particular concentration of TEO, the ratio of the initial velocity of photoinactivation in the presence of DOC to the initial velocity in its absence. This ratio can be called the calculated relative velocity, ν_{calc}^{rel}, and is given by:

$$\nu_{calc}^{rel} = \frac{^{DOC}K_1[TEO] + {^{DOC}K_1}{^{TEO}K_1}}{{^{DOC}K_1}{^{TEO}K_1} + {^{DOC}K_1}[TEO] + {^{TEO}K_1}[DOC]},$$

where [TEO] and [DOC] are the initial concentrations of TEO and DOC and $^{TEO}K_1$ and $^{DOC}K_1$ are the kinetically determined competitive inhibition constants for TEO and DOC, respectively.

Thus, ν_{calc}^{rel} is solely determined by equilibrium binding considerations. This analysis assumes that free enzyme and enzyme-DOC complex do not photoinactivate at a significant rate, and this is borne out by FIGURE 7. TABLE 5 gives the results of the calculations and compares the calculated relative rates with those measured experimentally, ν_{obs}^{rel}. It is found that the observed and calculated rates are nearly equal, lending some support to the theory that the TEO-enzyme complex is the species through which photoinactivation proceeds.

The chemical process or processes responsible for TEO-dependent photoinactivation is still under investigation, but some features of the change in the enzyme structure have been uncovered. When isomerase was photoinactivated in the presence of 4-[^{14}C]-TEO and this reaction mixture subjected to gel filtration under denaturing conditions (8 M urea), no significant radioactivity was found to be associated with the polypeptide-containing fractions, indicating that the photoreaction does not involve significant stable covalent bond formation between the steroid and the protein.

A comparison of the amino acid compositions of native and 80% photoinactivated isomerase is presented in TABLE 6. No significant decrease in the amount of any amino acid is apparent, although an apparent 0.83 increase in glycine is observed. However, more detailed studies will be necessary in order to substantiate this change, since its statistical significance is marginal. The analyses in TABLE 6 were not designed to measure the cysteine residues in the enzyme. Therefore, cysteine thiol groups were measured for a series of photoinactivated enzyme samples whose photoinactivation level varied from 0 to 80%. DTNB colorimetry was used as the assay reaction for thiol groups. As shown in FIGURE 8, a good correspondence between the extent of photoinactivation and the loss of one out of four thiol groups per polypeptide chain is obtained, suggesting that the inactivating reaction involves the loss of a thiol group.

TABLE 5

INHIBITION OF TEO-DEPENDENT PHOTOINACTIVATION BY DEOXYCHOLATE

Number	[TEO] (μM)	[DOC] (μM)	ν_{calc}^{rel}	ν_{obs}^{rel}
1	272	0	1.0	1.0
2	272	70	0.79	0.77
3	272	164	0.61	0.63
4	272	282	0.48	0.49

TABLE 6

AMINO ACID COMPOSITIONS OF NATIVE AND TEO-DEPENDENT
PHOTOINACTIVATED ISOMERASE

Amino acid	Native*	Photoinactivated†
asp	11.08	10.88
thr	4.36	4.58
ser	4.06	4.67
glu	16.65	16.54
pro	8.04	7.96
gly	11.62	12.45
ala	11.83	12.16
val	9.90	9.93
met	4.29	4.18
ile	5.43	5.21
leu	8.00‡	8.00‡
tyr	3.50	3.43
phe	3.96	4.05
his	2.79	2.70
lys	1.93	2.32
arg	7.61	7.99

*Average of 4 samples.
†Average of 3 samples; residual enzyme activity 20% of native.
‡Leu = 8 taken as the basis for the calculation of molar ratios.

DISCUSSION

The conclusion by Ogez and Benisek[12] that residue 38 of *P. testosteroni* isomerase is an aspartic acid and that this residue is important for enzyme function because its photodecarboxylation to alanine results in an inactive enzyme has been supported by

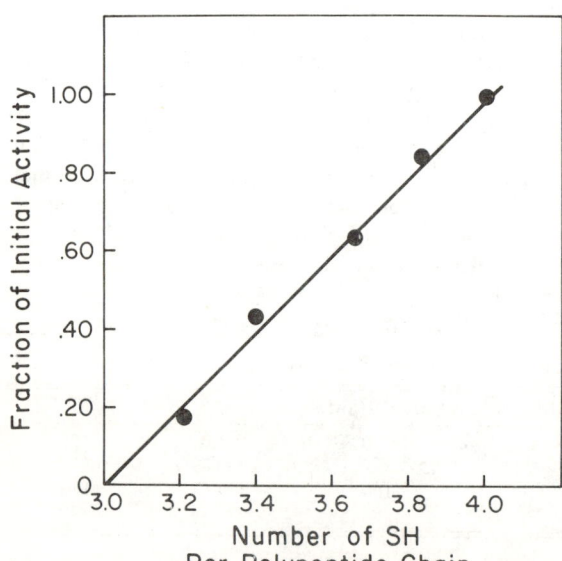

FIGURE 8. The effect of the extent of TEO-dependent photoinactivation on the thiol content of isomerase. Samples of isomerase were irradiated in the presence of TEO to varying extents of inactivation under the conditions described in EXPERIMENTAL PROCEDURES, except that dithiothreotol was omitted from the reaction mixtures. Aliquots were withdrawn and assayed for SH content with DTNB in 8 *M* urea following the procedure described in Means and Feeney.[22]

the carboxyl amidation studies employing cystamine as the derivatizing amine reported here. Had residue 38 been an asparagine, as found by Benson *et al.*[4] in the original sequencing work, coupling of residue 38 would not have been expected. The fact that the aspartate 38 amidated enzyme has very low, if any, catalytic activity indicates some important role for aspartate 38 in enzyme function. However, the large size of the derivatizing amine makes it impossible to determine whether inactivation is the consequence of side chain bulk or of the abolishment of the charge and/or the basic character of aspartate 38. We,[11] and others,[3] have suggested that a carboxyl group of aspartic acid may be the base responsible for the transport of the 4β proton of the 5-ene-3-one enzyme substrate to the 6β position of the 4-ene-3-one product. It may, therefore, be significant that, when NH_4^+ is the amidating amine, the enzyme is rapidly inactivated in a 19-NTA inhibited reaction, as shown in TABLE 1. It is tempting to suggest that the site of amidation by NH_4^+ is the same as that by cystamine, since both inactivations are protected by 19-NTA. If subsequent studies prove this to be the case, it would indicate that the basicity or charge of the aspartate 38 side chain is the important chemical property modified, which would support the earlier speculations[3,11] based on the photochemical modification sensitized by 19-NTA.

The TEO-dependent photomodification of *P. putida* steroid isomerase still needs further clarification with regard to the identification of the specific cysteine whose thiol group is modified and to the chemistry of the thiol loss reaction. It is interesting to note that, in this reaction, as well as in the *testosteroni* isomerase decarboxylation, photoaffinity reagent attachment is not a feature of the major chemical modification process. This phenomenon is both a help and a hindrance. Certainly, when covalent attachment fails to occur, identification of the site of reaction is made much more difficult. On the other hand, the absence of a permanently attached, bulky, inevitably inactivating affinity reagent allows the investigator to make deductions regarding the functional role of the modified amino acid residue when that modification involves only a sterically mild perturbation. Thus, in photoaffinity modification studies of purified enzymes and binding proteins, photoreactions that do *not* lead to covalent coupling of reagent to protein should provide more information about the functional significance of specific amino acid residues than those photoreactions that do result in covalent bond formation between reagent and protein.

ACKNOWLEDGMENTS

We wish to acknowledge the contributions of Mr. Al Smith and Ms. Kathy Kanagaki in determining the amino acid sequences and composition, respectively.

REFERENCES

1. TALALAY, P. & V. S. WANG. 1955. Biochim. Biophys. Acta **18:** 300–1.
2. KAWAHARA, F. S. & P. TALALAY. 1959. J. Biol. Chem. **235:** PC1–PC2.
3. BATZOLD, F. H., A. M. BENSON, D. F. COVEY, C. H. ROBINSON & P. TALALAY. 1976. *In* Advances in Enzyme Regulation, Vol. 14, G. Weber, Ed.: 243–67.
4. BENSON, A. M., R. JARABAK & P. TALALAY. 1971. J. Biol. Chem. **246:** 7514–25.
5. WESTBROOK, E. M. 1976. J. Mol. Biol. **103:** 659–64.
6. WANG, S. F., F. S. KAWAHARA & P. TALALAY. 1963. J. Biol. Chem. **238:** 576–85.

7. OGEZ, J. & W. F. BENISEK. 1977. Biochem. Biophys. Res. Commun. **85**: 1082–89.
8. VINCENT, F., H. WEINTRAUB, A. ALFSEN & E. E. BAULIEU. 1976. FEBS Lett. **62**: 126–31.
9. WEINTRAUB, H., F. VINCENT, E. E. BAULIEU & A. ALFSEN. 1977. Biochemistry **16**: 5045–53.
10. MARTYR, R. J. & W. F. BENISEK. 1973. Biochemistry **12**: 2172–78.
11. MARTYR, R. J. & W. F. BENISEK. 1975. J. Biol. Chem. **250**: 1218–22.
12. OGEZ, J. R. & W. F. BENISEK. 1977. J. Biol. Chem. **252**: 6151–55.
13. MARTYR, R. J. & W. F. BENISEK. 1974. Unpublished results.
14. JARABAK, R., M. COLVIN, S. H. MOOLGAVKAR & P. TALALAY. 1969. Methods Enzymol. **15**: 642–51.
15. SMITH, S. B., J. W. RICHARDS & W. F. BENISEK. 1980. J. Biol. Chem. **255**. In press.
16. SLUYTERMAN, L. AE. & J. WIJDENES. 1974. Methods Enzymol. **34**: 544–47.
17. CASPI, E., E. CULLEN & P. K. GROVER. 1963. J. Chem. Soc.: 212–17.
18. HOARE, D. G. & D. E. KOSHLAND. 1967. J. Biol. Chem. **242**: 2447–53.
19. HIRS, C. H. W. 1967. *In* Methods in Enzymology, Vol. 9. C. H. W. Hirs, Ed. 197–99.
20. BENSON, A. M., A. J. SURUDA, R. SHAW & P. TALALAY. 1974. Biochim. Biophys. Acta **348**: 317–20.
21. KAWAHARA, F. S., S. F. WANG & P. TALALAY. 1962. J. Biol. Chem. **237**: 1500–6.
22. MEANS, G. E. & R. E. FEENEY. 1971. Chemical Modification of Proteins.: 155–57, 220. Holden-Day, Inc. San Francisco.
23. SMITH, S. B., J. W. RICHARDS & W. F. BENISEK. 1980. J. Biol. Chem. **255**. In press.
24. BENISEK, W. F. 1977. Methods Enzymol. **46**: 469–79.
25. PISANO, J. J., T. J. BRONZERT & H. B. BREWER, JR. 1972. Anal. Biochem. **45**: 43–59.
26. KULBE, K. D. 1974. Anal. Biochem. **59**: 564–73.
27. MENDEZ, E. & C. Y. LAI. 1975. Anal. Biochem. **68**: 47–53.

FRANK H. WESTHEIMER: AN APPRECIATION

Barry S. Cooperman

Department of Chemistry
University of Pennsylvania
Philadelphia, Pennsylvania 19104

Great men may be compared to torches shining at long intervals, to guide the advance of science. They light up their time, either by discovering unexpected and fertile phenomena which open up new paths and reveal unknown horizons, or by generalizing acquired scientific facts and disclosing truths which their predecessors had not perceived.
Claude Bernard
Introduction to a l'Etude de la Medecine Experimentale, 1865.

This conference deals with the applications of photochemistry to the study of a variety of biochemically important structures, and it is altogether fitting that it honors Frank Westheimer, the originator of one of the most important of these applications, photoaffinity labeling. It is striking that, in this era of big science and many scientists, the seminal experiment in this field may be clearly attributed to one person. The first publication on the use of photolabile groups to explore enzyme active sites is Singh, Thornton, and Westheimer's 1962 paper on the photolysis of diazoacetyl chymotrypsin.[1] A follow-up article appeared in 1966,[2] but, as late as 1967, Singer,[3] in a review of affinity labeling, could only write that "the approach devised by Singh *et al.* (1962) might be exceedingly useful." The use of the conditional was dictated by the paucity of published results. Indeed, it was not until 1969, with the work of Frank Richards at Yale[4] and Jeremy Knowles at Oxford,[5] that other groups entered the field. Of course, use of this approach has grown enormously since 1969, as this meeting bears witness.

It is thus clear that Frank Westheimer was ahead of his time, but not, I submit, by chance. I asked Ed Thornton to recall his work with Frank Westheimer, and he writes:

"I met F. H. Westheimer while a postdoc with C. G. Swain at MIT. Swain's postdocs were eligible to attend the famed Bartlett-Westheimer seminars. I wanted to work with Westheimer because of his towering intellect and his special blend of humor, cynicism, and sense of irony. He somehow found space in then-new Conant Lab. As we discussed a project, he smiled a little and said, approximately, that he had a "crazy" idea but, after all, my NIH postdoctoral fellowship left me free to work on anything, and it would certainly be a challenge. He then proceeded to outline the preparation of diazoacetylchymotrypsin and the exciting—if outlandish—possibility that photogenerated intermediates might insert into peptide groups and thus provide a means for identifying residues in the neighborhood of the active site.

"Never having worked with an enzyme before, I was both interested and apprehensive. No enzyme's tertiary structure was known, and the first x-ray structure of a protein had only recently been reported. It seemed possible then that the α-diazo group might give enough substrate analogy to lead to rapid deacylation, but diazoacetylchymotrypsin was, in fact, as Westheimer expected, even more stable than

0077–8923/80/0346–0131 $1.75/1 © 1980, NYAS

acetylchymotrypsin. I departed after a year, in 1961, having just shown that there was some incorporation of radiolabel into the photolyzed protein even after treatment with hydroxylamine, which completely removed label from unphotolyzed ^{14}C-diazoacetyl-chymotrypsin. It was more than could reasonably have been expected. The path, as far as I had taken it, had followed Westheimer's predictions exactly! Enzyme tertiary structure seemed easily accessible.

"Some years later, after he came to believe the results, and after many more photoaffinity labeling experiments, he told me he had decided that photoaffinity labeling wasn't really quite as easy as it had seemed in 1961."

I think that it can be fairly said that the innovative diazoacetylchymotrypsin experiment arose as the logical product of the application of Frank Westheimer's rigorous intellect, which, throughout his whole career, has been focused on the problem of the nature of chemical reactivity, to the problem of the determination of the three-dimensional structure of enzymes in solution. Indeed, innovative, seminal experiments have been Frank Westheimer's hallmark from his early work on electrostatic and steric effects on chemical reactivity[6–10] to his current studies on nucleophilic substitution on phosphate esters.[11,12]

In recalling my days in Frank's group, two impressions are most lasting. First, on the experimental level, was his enormous dedication to good data, to proving a hypothesis true by at least two or three different routes. He believes, with Aristotle, that "the least initial deviation from the truth is multiplied later a thousand times," and continually emphasized the need for scrupulous care in reporting one's results. Second, on the intellectual level, was his active interest in virtually every domain of science. I well recall the weekly group seminar, which always started with a wide-ranging discussion on practically anything before getting down to a more traditional discussion of a particular topic. These opening discussions were often speculative, and Frank encouraged us to take a position and defend it, so the discussions provided excellent training for applying scientific logic to problem solving. Because they were speculative, differences of opinion were common. As beginning students, when we differed with Frank the weight of his arguments forced us, eventually, to defer to him, but after several years in his group, we were trained to the point where we could validly stand our ground when we differed with him, a development he both fostered and welcomed. I remember my satisfaction when, toward the end of my thesis work, Frank concluded such a matching of wits with me by saying, "Barry, I think you're ready to leave."

I conclude this appreciation with a listing of the references indicated in the text, as well as a complete list of the publications of Frank Westheimer in the area of photoaffinity labeling.

REFERENCES

1. SINGH, A., E. THORNTON & F. H. WESTHEIMER. 1962. The photolysis of diazoacetylchymotrypsin. J. Biol. Chem. **237**: PC3007.
2. SHAFER, J., P. BARONOWSKY, R. LAURSEN, F. FINN & F. H. WESTHEIMER. 1966. Products from the photolysis of diazoacetylchymotrypsin. J. Biol. Chem. **241**: 421.
3. SINGER, S. J. 1967. Covalent labeling of active sites. Adv. Protein Chem. **22**: 1–54.
4. CONVERSE, C. A. & F. F. RICHARDS. 1969. Two-stage photosensitive label for antibody combining sites. Biochemistry **8**: 4431–36.

5. FLEET, G. W. J., R. R. PORTER & J. R. KNOWLES. 1969. Affinity labeling of antibodies with aryl nitrene as reactive group. Nature (London) **224:** 511–12.
6. KIRKWOOD, J. G. & F. H. WESTHEIMER. 1938. The electrostatic influence of substituents on the dissociation constants of organic acids (I). J. Chem. Phys. **6:** 506.
7. WESTHEIMER, F. H. & J. G. KIRKWOOD. 1938. The electrostatic influence of substituents on the dissociation constants of organic acids (II). J. Chem. Phys. **6:** 513.
8. WESTHEIMER, F. H. & M. SHOOKHOFF. 1940. The electrostatic influence of substituents on reaction rates (I). J. Am. Chem. Soc. **62:** 269.
9. WESTHEIMER, F. H. 1940. The electrostatic influence of substituents on reaction rates (II). J. Am. Chem. Soc. **62:** 1892.
10. WESTHEIMER, F. H. 1948. A quantitative theory of steric effects. Rec. Chem. Prog. **10:** 11.
11. WESTHEIMER, F. H. 1968. Pseudorotation in the hydrolysis of phosphate esters. Acc. Chem. Res. **1:** 70.
12. WESTHEIMER, F. H. 1977. The hydrolysis of phosphate esters. Pure Appl. Chem. **49:** 1059.

OTHER PHOTOAFFINITY LABELING PUBLICATIONS

CHAIMOVICH, H., R. VAUGHAN & F. H. WESTHEIMER. 1968. Rearrangement accompanying the photolysis of diazoacyl esters. J. Am. Chem. Soc. **90:** 4088.

VAUGHAN, R. J. & F. H. WESTHEIMER. 1969. A method for marking the hydrophobic binding sites of enzymes: An insertion into the methyl group of an alanine. J. Am. Chem. Soc. **91:** 217.

BROWNE, D. T., S. S. HIXSON & F. H. WESTHEIMER. 1971. A diazo compound for the photochemical labeling of yeast alcohol dehydrogenase. J Biol. Chem. **246:** 4477.

HEXTER, C. S. & F. H. WESTHEIMER. 1971. Intermolecular reaction during photolysis of diazoacetyl α-chymotrypsin. J. Biol. Chem. **246:** 3928.

HEXTER, C. S. & F. H. WESTHEIMER. 1971. S-carboxymethylcysteine from the photolysis of diazoacetyl trypsin and chymotrypsin. J. Biol. Chem. **246:** 3934.

STEFANOVSKY, Y. & F. H. WESTHEIMER. 1973. Diazoacetyl subtilisin. Proc. Nat. Acad. Sci. USA **70:** 1132.

CHOWDHRY, V., R. VAUGHAN & F. H. WESTHEIMER. 1976. 2-Diazo-3,3,3-trifluoropropionyl chloride: Reagent for photoaffinity labeling. Proc. Nat. Acad. Sci. USA **73:** 1406.

GOLDSTEIN, J., C. MCKENNA & F. H. WESTHEIMER. 1976. α-Diazobenzylphosphonate dianion. J. Am. Chem. Soc. **98:** 7327.

CHOWDHRY, V., F. H. WESTHEIMER. 1978. p-Toluenesulfonyldiazoacetates as photoaffinity labeling reagents. J. Am. Chem. Soc. **100:** 309.

WESTHEIMER, F. H. 1978. Photoaffinity labeling: Marking the receptors for biologically active molecules. Proc. Am. Philos. Soc. **122:** 355.

CHOWDHRY, V. & F. H. WESTHEIMER. 1978. p-Toluenesulfonyldiazoacetates: Reagents for photoaffinity labeling. Bioorg. Chem. **7:** 189–205.

CHOWDHRY, V. & F. H. WESTHEIMER. 1979. Photoaffinity labeling of biological systems. Annu. Rev. Biochem. **48:** 293–325.

PHOTOAFFINITY LABELING—RETROSPECT AND PROSPECT

Frank H. Westheimer

The James Bryant Conant Laboratory of Chemistry
Harvard University
Cambridge, Massachusetts 02238

This conference brings together many of the investigators who have made especially significant contributions to the field of photoaffinity labeling. Let me say a few words about the origin of photoaffinity labeling, and then try to see what it's good for. Why do we need it at all? What new things can we achieve with this method that we haven't already exploited?

Photoaffinity labeling had a hazardous birth. The first experiments were designed to illustrate and establish the method by chemically determining the groups in the close neighborhood of the active site of chymotrypsin. The idea of attaching a photolabile diazo group at the reactive serine of chymotrypsin, producing a carbene by photolysis, and finding out what group the carbene would bite is illustrated in SCHEMA 1. At the beginning, I discussed the idea with E. J. Corey. He encouraged me, but at the same time warned me that the photochemical Wolff rearrangement might spoil it all. At that time, although the photochemical Wolff rearrangement of diazoketones was well known, the photochemical Wolff rearrangement of diazoesters had never been observed, so I knew we were safe. We weren't, but perhaps it's worth noting that, even after we had discovered the photochemical Wolff rearrangement with diazoacetylchymotrypsin, a famous visiting chemist assured me that our work must be in error, since prior research had shown that the rearrangement did not occur with diazoesters. If only he had been correct!

The project was almost stillborn. E. R. Thornton, who is now at the University of Pennsylvania, carried out the original experiments, and was then joined by Ajaib Singh. When they photolyzed diazoacetylchymotrypsin, most of the radioactivity from our sample appeared in solution; the protein recovered the majority of its enzymic activity. The recovery of enzymic activity wasn't complete, but we assumed that that was because we had somehow denatured some of the enzyme. After all, chymotrypsin isn't stable: it hydrolyzes proteins; in essence, it eats itself. The loss in enzymic activity could have been caused by the hydrolytic self-destruction of the enzyme. We decided, therefore, that our experiment was a failure, and we had better do something else. Fortunately, they pushed the idea further, and found that radioactivity had indeed been incorporated into the protein. We celebrated, and, in 1962, published a paper in the *Journal of Biological Chemistry* announcing the method.

Before we celebrated too much, however, our research group looked to see where the radioactivity had been incorporated, and received a rude shock. The product was largely that of Wolff rearrangement. Wolff rearrangement leads to marking of the same serine residue to which the diazoacetyl group had been attached in the first place. Nothing new had been learned. Once again, we were on the verge of giving up the project, but we looked still further, and found, miracle of miracles, that some of

134

0077–8923/80/0346–0134 $1.75 © 1980, NYAS

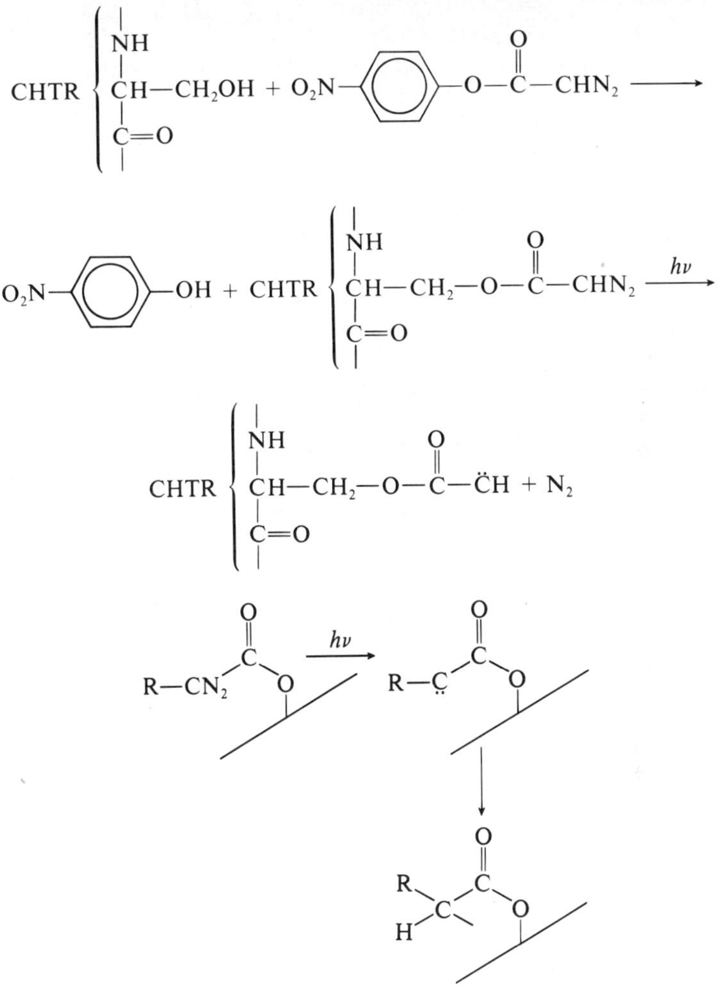

SCHEMA 1.

the radioactivity was present in products that represented new chemistry, that came from the attack of the carbene, generated photochemically, on nearby amino acid residues. The camel had gone through the eye of the needle, and we could enter the Kingdom of Heaven.

When our research group finally achieved this desirable result and we were celebrating again, our "friends" came to help us. What we had achieved, we were informed, was pointless; everything we had done could more easily be done, and be better done, by x-ray crystallography. We had argued that x-ray crystallography deals with crystals, that is to say, with the solid state, whereas we were finding out what happens in solution. Not so, they informed us. The syllogism came straight from

Gilbert and Sullivan. You will recall that Ko-Ko had told the Mikado that he had beheaded Nanki Pooh, and later had to explain to the monarch why he had misinformed him. Ko-Ko said, "It's like this: When your majesty says, let a thing be done, it's as good as done—practically it is done—because your majesty's will is law. Your majesty says, kill a gentleman, and a gentleman is told off to be killed. Consequently, that gentleman is as good as dead—practically he *is* dead—and if he is dead, why not say so?" Well, crystalline proteins contain so much bound ester that they are as good as in solution; practically, they *are* in solution, and if they are in solution, why not say so? On the basis of this reasoning, we realized that our work in solution merely duplicated that of the x-ray crystallographers on the solid state. And they got much more information than we did. I became convinced that we had tried to reinvent the wheel and come up with a square one.

At this point, others rescued the situation. In 1967, S. J. Singer looked at the little bit of published work, realized its potential, publicized the method in a review, and, some years later, christened it photoaffinity labeling. It's easy to underestimate the importance of nomenclature, but, in science, success is enhanced by an appealing name.

In 1969, Jeremy Knowles, then at Oxford, utilized aryl azides as reagents for photoaffinity labeling and applied them to the problem of identifying the binding sites for antigens on antibodies (SCHEMA 2). The work signaled two important advances.

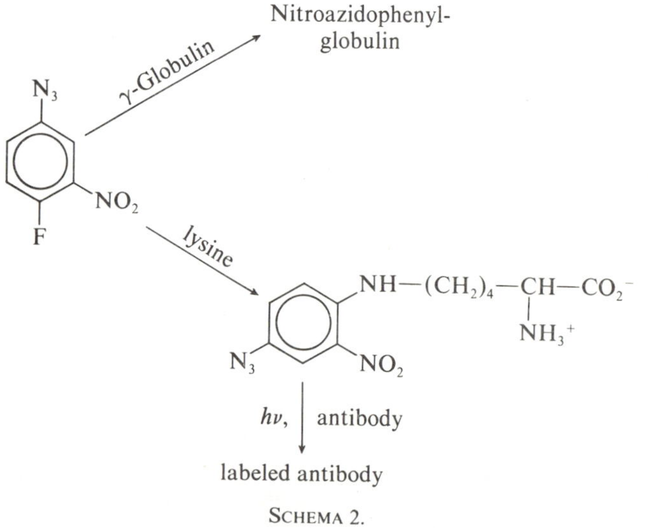

SCHEMA 2.

First, of course, was the introduction of a new and potentially useful class of reagents for photoaffinity labeling. Second, he applied the method to a problem—the structure of antibodies—in which x-ray crystallography, although useful, may not be entirely satisfactory; thus, he opened the way for most of the important work that followed.

At the same time, at Yale, Frank Richards and Caroline Converse introduced diazoketones as reagents with which to label the binding site in antibodies. Of course, our group was much more sophisticated than theirs; we knew that diazoketones would undergo Wolff rearrangement to ketenes and that they would not react quickly enough to label anything. We were so smart that we didn't try the experiment; Richards and Converse showed that it worked beautifully. Joseph Mayer once said that the advantage of young chemists over older ones is that older chemists know too many things that won't work.

Barry Cooperman, at the University of Pennsylvania, attached a carbene reagent to cyclic AMP (SCHEMA 3) and used photoaffinity labeling to identify the protein that

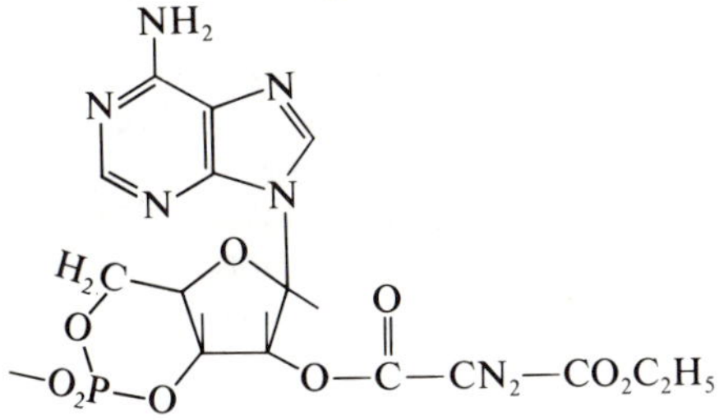

SCHEMA 3.

binds it. That was an important step forward. With a couple of notable exceptions, membranes have numerous different proteins imbedded in them; these proteins slowly float around, as if in a viscous two-dimensional liquid. Since the proteins are not arranged in definite patterns, the membranes generally show no x-ray crystallographic structure. Here was an area where the x-ray crystallographers couldn't follow.

Among those who later applied the general method of photoaffinity labeling were some biochemists and biologists who tried to label ribosomes and receptor sites with antibiotics and similar compounds without bothering to attach any photolabile group. This sort of nonsense is outrageous, and the most outrageous aspect of it is that the method sometimes works. In particular, labeling has been achieved with chloramphenicol and puromycin on ribosomes, by a chloromalonyl derivative on the ouabain binding site of Na^+-K^+ ATPase, and by cyclic AMP on phosphofructokinase. Perhaps we should elevate Mayer's aphorism to the status of a law of chemistry.

Enough of looking backward. What are the characteristics of an ideal photolabeling reagent? What can we do that we have neglected in the past?

A good reagent for photolabeling should be easy to make; stable, at least in the dark and in diffuse daylight; have a handle with which it can be bound to the substrate; and decompose readily on photolysis, preferably with light of wavelengths long compared to those that can destroy the receptor site. It should be stable over a wide range of pH to permit studies of the effect of acidity on protein conformation. The decomposition should lead to a species that reacts rapidly and indiscriminately with anything and everything in its environment, but it should not undergo rearrangement if that rearrangement leads to loss of reactivity. Some progress has been made toward developing reagents with this list of properties.

The first reagents used—esters of diazoacetic acid—contain a photolabile group that decomposes to yield a carbene, which is indeed highly reactive and indiscriminate in its attack on chemical bonds. But the reagent has only a weak absorption band at

TABLE 1
DESIRABLE PROPERTIES FOR REAGENTS FOR PHOTOAFFINITY LABELING

1. Stability to heat and acid.
2. Rapid photolysis at long wavelengths.
3. Rapid insertion of intermediate.
4. Little or no rearrangement.

long wavelengths, with an ϵ of about 15 at 340 nm, and although the principal absorption band, at 240 nm, has a large extinction coefficient, many sensitive organic molecules, including proteins, decompose when subjected to light of that wavelength. Furthermore, diazoesters, on photolysis, undergo Wolff rearrangement to a considerable extent. And when a diazoacetate is attached to a sulfhydryl group, the rearrangement is complete: no carbene escapes the rearrangement to perform useful chemistry. The same criticisms apply to the diazomalonates.

More recently, Vinay Chowdhry has invented some superior reagents. 3,3,3-Trifluoro-2-diazopropionates are stable to strong acid at room temperature and undergo photolysis with little rearrangement. Even the thioesters of trifluorodiazopropionic acid are not completely lost to rearrangement, so the reagents can, presumably, be attached to the thiol groups of enzymes and then photolyzed to yield interesting chemistry—although this has not yet been tried. Joseph Stackhouse has recently prepared a potentially useful reagent related to dansyl derivatives (SCHEMA 4).

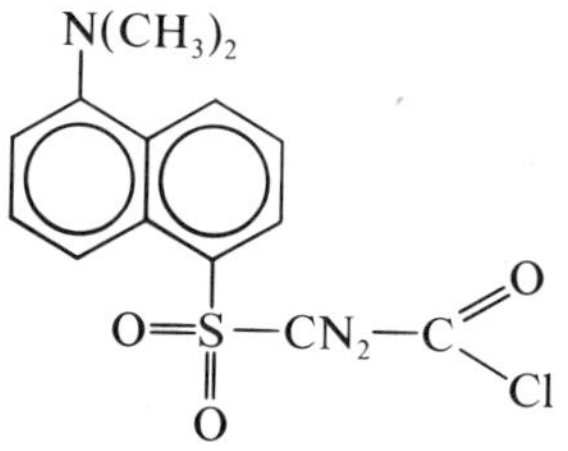

SCHEMA 4.

Another such reagent is Chowdhry's 2-diazo-2-tosyldiazoacetylchloride. 2-Diazo-2-tosyldiazoacetates not only decompose with relatively little rearrangement, but they also show an enhanced absorption spectrum at 340 nm. The extinction coefficient is only about 250—we could do with a band 100 times as intense—but the absorption is, nevertheless, sufficient to allow reasonably rapid photolysis at wavelengths that are safe for most compounds.

Why do reagents that contain electron withdrawing substituents rearrange less than simple diazoesters do? A possible reason is suggested by some of Chowdhry's work: perhaps the rearrangement is stereoselective; the nature of the products may be controlled by the conformation of the starting material.

The idea of two conformers for diazoesters and ketones was introduced by F. Kaplan and G. K. Meloy, who found that nmr spectra of diazomethyl ketones gave two signals for the hydrogen atom attached to the diazo carbon atom; they ascribed the doubling to hindered rotation about the carbon-carbon single bond, as shown in SCHEMA 5, in which only the double-bonded structures that contribute to the

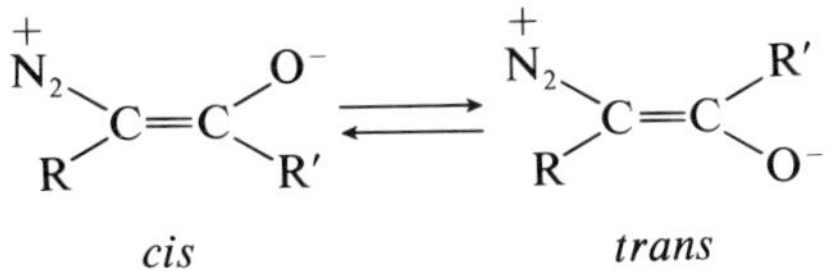

SCHEMA 5.

resonance hybrids have been drawn. In his investigations, Chowdhry found two signals for the trifluoromethyl group in ^{19}F nmr spectroscopy at low temperatures, but only one at room temperature. One example of his spectra is presented in FIGURE 1.

Presumably, then, the resonance interaction between the diazo group and the carbonyl group introduces partial double bond character to the bond between them. Rotation about this partial double bond is sufficiently hindered at low temperatures that the *cis* and *trans* structures give rise to separate nmr signals, whereas, at room temperature, they are interconverted rapidly; rapidly, that is, on an nmr time scale. One can devise a reasonable explanation—not necessarily the correct explanation— why the conformer of the trifluoromethyl compound with the diazo group and the alkoxy group of the ester in *cis* position predominates, that is, why the conformer that does *not* rearrange is the more abundant.

The reagents discussed above were prepared in my laboratory; many others were developed elsewhere; some of these have already been mentioned. Among the more interesting examples is that of R. J. Martyr and W. L. Benisek, who photolyzed a naturally occurring α,β-unsaturated steroid in the active site of Δ^5-ketosteroid isomerase. If the photoactivated molecule reacts, it binds to the enzyme; if it doesn't, it isn't destroyed, but reverts to the starting material and can be activated again: it will, eventually, react. J. Katzenellenbogen has used a similar approach. If, however, the photoactivated molecule is converted by intersystem crossing to a relatively long-lived triplet, it may fall out of the receptor site before it undergoes effective photochemistry.

Another excellent reagent, or class of reagents, has been introduced by Charles Cantor and his collaborators, who have found that the amino groups of proteins will react photochemically with nitroanisoles. Additional types have been introduced by J. Henkin, Knowles, and others. More photoaffinity labeling reagents, with their own special properties, have been and will be invented.

In a number of cases, photoaffinity labeling has failed; the early failures include one of Singer's and one of ours. At a Harvard Commencement some years ago, the University preacher prayed that the graduating class would enjoy a modicum of failure; presumably, he was anxious that they avoid excessive arrogance. That sermon was more appropriate to Harvard seniors than to research chemists, who customarily enjoy a modicum of failure without even the need to pray for it. Singer tried to label acetylcholine esterase in erythrocyte membranes, but found only indiscriminate labeling. He named this particular variety of failure "pseudophotoaffinity labeling."

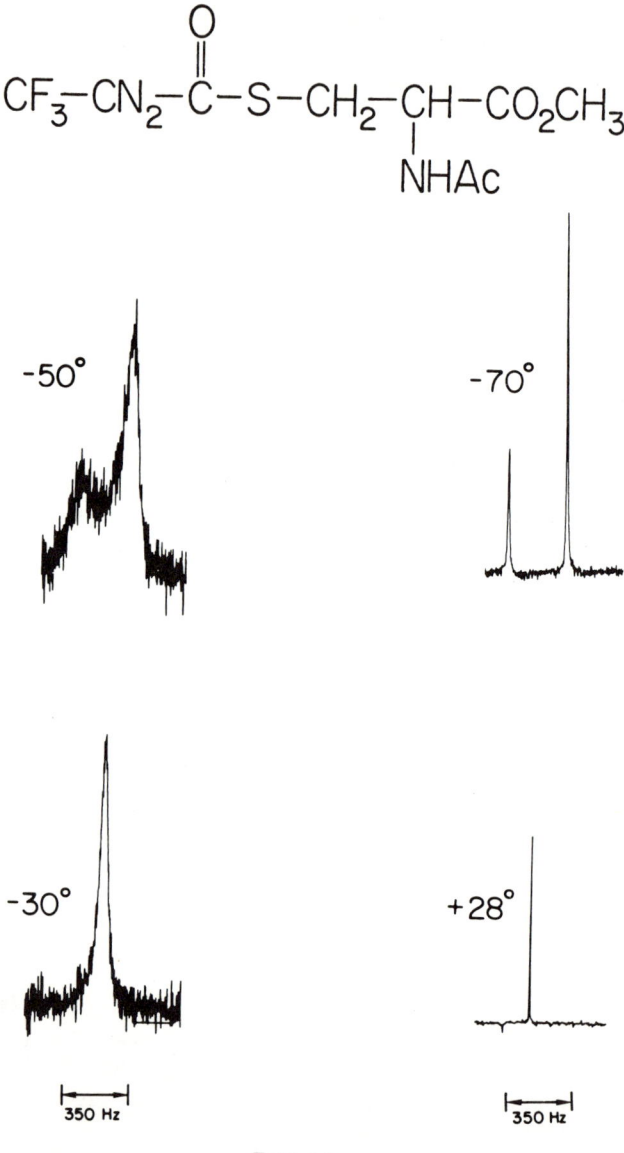

$$CF_3-CN_2-\overset{\overset{\textstyle O}{\|}}{C}-S-CH_2-\underset{\underset{\textstyle NHAc}{|}}{CH}-CO_2CH_3$$

FIGURE 1.

We tried to label lactate dehydrogenase with a diazoketone analog of DPN. Since this diazoketone has an especially strong electron withdrawing group attached to the reactive center, the tendency of the diazoketone to undergo Wolff rearrangement is considerably reduced, though not be any means eliminated. The reagent was, however, completely ineffective in labeling the enzyme.

H. Bayley and Knowles compared the reactivity of a carbene with that of a nitrene for labeling the fatty acid chains in a synthetic membrane and found that the former was superior; in fact, labeling with the nitrene was, in this instance, notably unsuccessful.

Aside from weeping, what can one do about such experiments? Obviously, learn from them. What is missing is a firm understanding of the chemistry involved. Since, as this conference shows, biochemists and biologists are imaginatively applying photoaffinity labeling to a myriad of biological problems, chemists should explore and understand the fundamental chemistry involved.

Veronica Vaida at Harvard is making a start. Although the chemistry of CH_2 in the gas phase has been investigated extensively, and although Gerhart Closs has measured rates of reaction of diphenyl carbene in solution, almost nothing is known about the stability of carboethoxycarbene. It isn't even known whether the Wolff rearrangement of diazoesters is a concerted process; whether the photolysis leads to a carbene that then rearranges; whether such a rearrangement proceeds by way of a cyclic intermediate, as shown in SCHEMA 6; or whether the process occurs in some

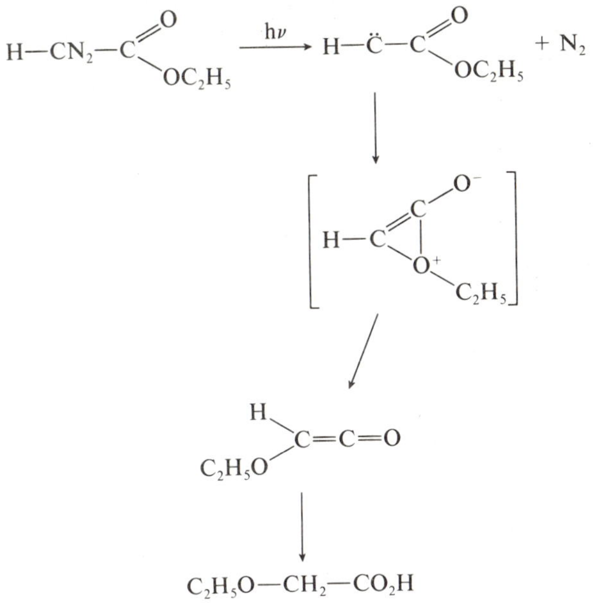

$$H\!-\!CN_2\!-\!C\!\!\underset{OC_2H_5}{\overset{O}{<}} \quad \xrightarrow{\ h\nu\ } \quad H\!-\!\ddot{C}\!-\!C\!\!\underset{OC_2H_5}{\overset{O}{<}} \quad + \ N_2$$

$$\left[\ H\!-\!C\!\!\underset{O^+}{\overset{C\!\!=\!\!O^-}{<}}\!\!-\!C_2H_5\ \right]$$

$$\underset{C_2H_5O}{\overset{H}{>}}C\!=\!C\!=\!O$$

$$C_2H_5O\!-\!CH_2\!-\!CO_2H$$

SCHEMA 6.

instances by one route and in some by another. The rates of reaction of carboethoxy-carbene with solvent, with C–H bonds, with –O–H bonds, etc. are unknown.

Similarly, the chemistry of nitrenes is insufficiently understood. Arylazides react, on photolysis, as if they produce nitrenes that sometimes rearrange to expand the ring to form azepines, sometimes couple, and sometimes undergo other chemistry. The lifetimes of some arylnitrenes are reported to be relatively long—perhaps 0.001 s. Most of the arylazides used in photoaffinity labeling, however, have been derived from Knowles's nitroarylazide. The chemistry of the nitroarylazides and the corresponding nitroaryl nitrenes has yet to be explored. Furthermore, in no instance has the detailed structure of the chemical product of photoaffinity labeling with an aryl azide been identified. Presumably, Vaida will answer many of the relevant questions. She is using nanosecond laser flash photolyses to explore the chemistry of nitrenes and carbenes.

But what can we do with the pseudophotoaffinity experiments? We can, as a matter of fact, use them as a kind of chemical clock with which to measure the lifetime of carbenes and nitrenes and, perhaps, to measure the residence time of substrates bound at the active sites of enzymes. Large numbers of experiments have recently established that the binding of many small molecules to proteins often takes place at rates near the diffusion limit, that is, with rate constants of about 10^8–10^9 $M^{-1} s^{-1}$. When we know the dissociation constant for a reaction in which a reagent binds with the speed of diffusion, we can then calculate the rate constant for the dissociation of the reagent from the receptor. If the rate at which the reagent escapes from its binding site is large compared to that at which the carbene or nitrene reacts with its chemical surroundings, no specific labeling will occur. If the rate of escape is small relative to the rate of chemical reaction, photoaffinity labeling should succeed. This statement isn't quite accurate, since the rate of escape calculated by the method outlined above is that of the photoaffinity reagent and the rate of reaction is that of its photolysis product, but perhaps the statement is a useful approximation to the truth.

To illustrate the possibilities, we may wish to make some semiquantitative estimates. To the best of my knowledge, the tightest binding of any small molecule to a protein is that of biotin to avidin. That dissociation constant is reported to be in the range of 10^{-15} M. If that is correct, then the constant for the "off" rate will be equal to or less than 10^{-7} s^{-1}, with a half-time of four months or more. Obviously, the biotin-avidin complex is stable enough that even a relatively slow reagent—say, a ketene produced by the rearrangement of a diazoketene—could react completely before it was released from the binding site.

In our laboratory, recently, Richard Brody and Howard Levine have been investigating inhibitors for orotidine-5'-phosphate decarboxylase, an enzyme we purified. The barbiturate analog of the substrate binds with a dissociation constant in the neighborhood of 10^{-13} M, and the half-time for the dissociation is about 2 h, measured at 25 °C. If any photoactive derivative has anything like these properties, it need not react rapidly in order to tag the protein before it leaves the active site.

But what is the situation for the examples of pseudoaffinity labeling, i.e., the failures that we and Singer experienced? The dissociation constants for our analogs were about 10^{-5} M. If the rate constant for the association process has the value of 10^9 $M^{-1} s^{-1}$, then the off rate constant is 10^4 s^{-1} and the half-time for residence of the inhibitor on the protein is only about 0.1 ms. If the reagent fails to react in a few tenths of a millisecond, the reactive intermediate will have left the site. Of course, it may have left anyway, for the binding of, say, a carbene to the receptor site need not be as tight as that of the diazo compound. Nevertheless, the hypothesis that carbenes require on the order of a tenth of a millisecond to react with their surroundings is interesting.

But if this is so, Singer, we, and others have missed a bet, one that we can now explore. If the rate constant for the dissociation of an inhibitor to an enzyme is in the range of $10^4 s^{-1}$, and if the reaction is one with a normal pre-exponential factor, then it has an activation energy of about 12 kcal/mol. Of course, the pre-exponential factor needn't be normal; for many reactions in aqueous solution it is not. Levine found that the activation energy for the dissociation of our barbiturate inhibitor from orotidine-5'-phosphate decarboxylase is only about 8 kcal/mol. But *if* the activation energy is as large as 12 kcal/mol, then, at -50 °C, the rate constant would have fallen to about 10 s^{-1}, and the half-time for dissociation extended to 0.1 s. That might well be sufficient for reaction with a carbene to occur; we might be able to convert a pseudoaffinity labeling to a true photoaffinity labeling. The dramatic effect of change in temperature on the rate of dissociation of cyclic AMP from its receptor has been presented at this conference by Boyd Haley.

That such experiments are possible has been shown by the work of P. Douzou, who showed us all how to prepare native enzymes in solution at low temperatures. Using his techniques, we should be able to explore photoaffinity labeling at extremely low temperatures. Of course, there are many ways in which such experiments could fail. The equilibrium constants for binding may be less favorable at low temperatures than at room temperature. Alternatively—or additionally—the reaction of carbenes with electrophiles or with carbon-hydrogen bonds will also be temperature dependent, so the rate at which carbenes and nitrenes react with their surroundings will also be diminished. What is critical, of course, is the rate of chemical reaction as compared to the rate at which the carbene or other reactive intermediate is liberated from the receptor site. But we should behave like young chemists, who haven't yet learned what won't work. No experiments succeeds unless it is tried.

If the experiment works, one will be able to time the loss of the carbene and the rate of the chemical reaction. In an ideal and lucky case, with slow separation of the carbene from the active site, one might even be able to use the chemical reaction of the carbene to detect other reactants at the active site. For example, a water molecule must be absorbed into the active site of hydrolytic enzymes; measuring its rate of reaction would at least be interesting.

Although these excursions into the fundamental chemistry of carbenes and nitrenes will supply fascinating and useful information, the number of possible applications of photoaffinity labeling continues to grow. Many of the new applications are described in this volume, providing both an overview of the past and a glimpse of the future.

GENERAL LABELING OF MEMBRANE PROTEINS*

Frederic M. Richards and Josef Brunner

Department of Molecular Biophysics and Biochemistry
Yale University
New Haven, Connecticut 06520

Introduction

Probes designed to give information on aspects of membrane structure not directly related to specific functions are called general labeling reagents. Many fluorescent and ESR probes, which report the properties of lipid bilayers, would fall into this category. Reagents that covalently modify proteins have been used to estimate the position of various components with respect to the bilayer in many membrane systems. The conclusions have usually been restricted to such descriptions as inside, outside, transmembrane, etc. A more detailed extension of such studies would be, for example, an attempt to estimate the areas of various molecules that are in contact either with the external or internal aqueous phases or with the nonpolar portion of the bilayer. To correctly reflect such structural geometry, the reagents' properties must be very carefully defined. The location of the reagent must be known. Specific binding must not occur. Both steric and electrostatic exclusion must either not occur or be clearly definable. The reagent must be truly nonselective in its reactivity. Such stringent requirements have yet to be met. Looking over the past few years, it appears that the design and construction of a covalent general label may, in fact, be more difficult than the design and construction of specific affinity labels.

Some Experiences with Phenyl Azide Reagents

Some years ago, Staros[1] synthesized the nitro-azidophenyl derivative of taurine, NAP-taurine, as a candidate for a general labeling reagent. The rationale was clear: the strong sulfonic acid group would make the compound very soluble in water, restricting it to an aqueous compartment. The negative charge should prevent penetration through intact membranes, thus restricting the reagent to either the external or internal aqueous compartment, as required. The compound contained a photoactivatable group in the form of an aryl azide that, on photolysis, yielded a nitrene, which was assumed to be highly reactive and nonspecific. This activated probe would then react indiscriminately with whatever was in its immediate vicinity. If the reagent had all of these characteristics, the extent of labeling of the protein components on the external surface of a cell or vesicular membrane system would depend on the contact area between the protein and the aqueous compartment.

A summary of some of the experiments on the application of NAP-taurine to the study of human erythrocytes is shown in FIGURE 1. Reaction at the external surface of

*This research was supported by the United States Public Health Service, grant no. GM-21714, to the Membrane Research Center at Yale University, and by a Swiss National Foundation Fellowship given to Josef Brunner.

0077-8923/80/0346-0144 $1.75/1 © 1980, NYAS

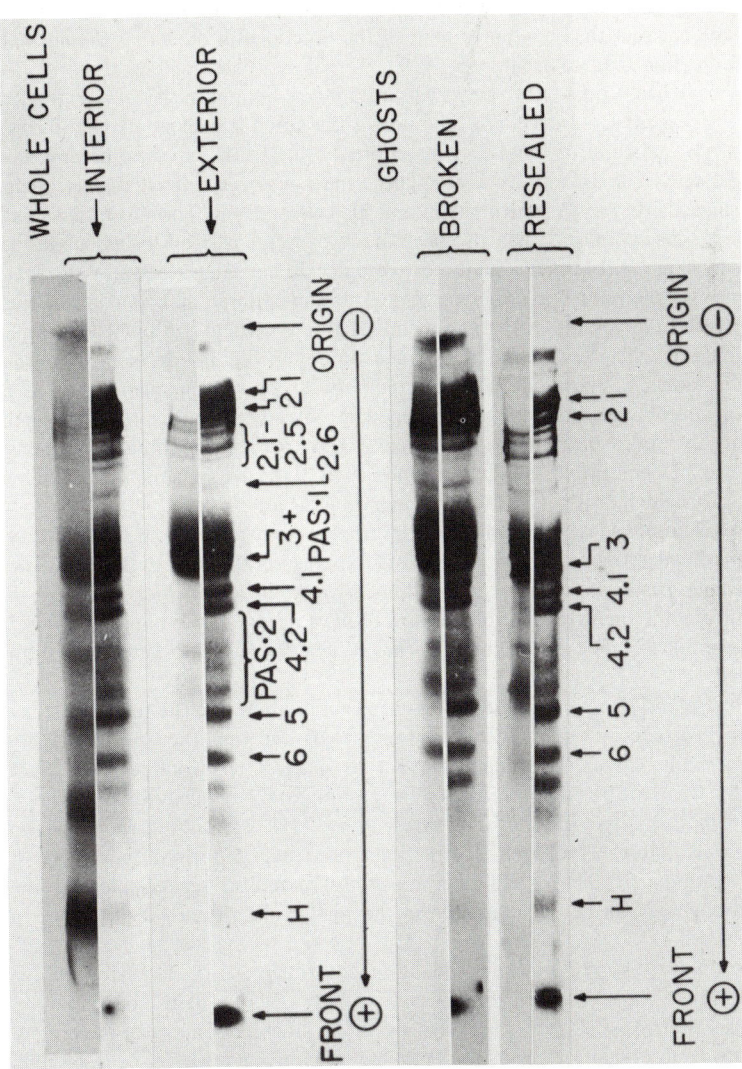

FIGURE 1. Labeling of erythrocyte membrane proteins (RBC) with ^{35}S-NAP-taurine. SDS gels run from right to left. The lower half of each panel is the Coomassie Blue stained gel, the upper half the autoradiogram of the same gel. The generally accepted numbering scheme is used for the protein bands, with H showing the position of a monomer chain of hemoglobin. The resealed ghosts were stained from the external side. This figure is a composite of data from References 1 and 2.

either whole cells or resealed ghosts showed very intense labeling of the band 3 region and less intense, but perfectly detectable, reaction in the PAS staining regions. Those data confirmed similar results obtained with a variety of other reagents. The new observation was the labeling of the bands in the 2.1 to 2.6 region, which was not detected by the other reagents. It was concluded, on the basis of the presumed characteristics of NAP-taurine, that these materials protruded on the external side of the membrane but that they contained none of the functional groups that the normal protein modification reagents required.

NAP-taurine has turned out to be very useful indeed, but not in the way originally planned. This reagent is an excellent inhibitor of the anion transport channel in red cells. The strong labeling of band 3 is undoubtedly due to this specific binding, as would be expected for an affinity label. This aspect was recognized and is being intensively investigated by Aser Rothstein and his colleagues in Toronto (see Knauf and Rothstein, this volume). It has also been found by Semenza and his associates in Zurich,[3] by Dockter[4] in Memphis, and, more recently, in our laboratory at Yale, that NAP-taurine is, apparently, a minidetergent. The non-sulfonic acid portion of the molecule is very lipid-soluble, and the reagent partitions strongly in favor of simple synthetic liposomes. The position of the reagent in any particular experiment is not confined to an aqueous phase but is distributed between dilute aqueous solution and the outer portions of one monolayer of the membrane. On photoactivation, the reagent is capable of labeling in either location. It seems likely, at this time, that the proteins of bands 2.1 to 2.6 penetrate deeply into the bilayer from the cytoplasmic side but may not emerge on the external surface of the membrane at all.

The curious failure to label certain of the internal protein components, particularly band 5, the red cell actin, even in broken ghosts remains unexplained to this day. The active nitrene is perfectly capable of labeling any protein with which it comes in contact. Failure of a small reagent of this size to have access to the band 5 material seems highly unlikely, since the reaction of other reagents of comparable size has been demonstrated.

Problems for aryl nitrenes, in the context of general labels, are the facts that they may not be very reactive by photochemical standards and that they can be highly selective. In many cases, they appear to act as general electrophiles and react preferentially with the range of nucleophilic groups attacked by ordinary protein modifying reagents. These nitrenes only insert into C—H bonds when they have no other option available. Hydrogen abstraction with radical formation can be a significant reaction. Radical recombination is, presumably, responsible for the cross-linked oligomers of hemoglobin seen in the whole cell interior labeling pattern shown in FIGURE 1.

Bahn[5] synthesized several phenyl azides attached to alkyl chains of varying lengths (FIGURE 2). These were intended to partition strongly in favor of the lipid bilayer, which they do: when applied to erythrocytes, extensive labeling of many of the protein components was observed. However, the problems of interpretation are considerable. If reaction with nucleophiles is highly favored over CH insertion, then the labeling may occur with such groups during the relatively rare appearances of the reagent in the aqueous phase. Conversely, there is no reason to suppose that the protein surfaces in contact with the aqueous phases are devoid of nonpolar binding sites. The well-known binding of alkanes to serum albumin[6] and of various straight-chain alkyl derivatives to chymotrypsin[7] serve to emphasize this possibility. Gitler and Bercovici discuss the behavior of a different set of lipophilic azides later in this volume.

One possible solution for this problem is the use of scavengers for the photoactivated species. However, the same set of problems arises again. The requirements for the properties of the scavenger are the mirror image of those for the labeling reagent: rigorous containment in the compartment to be scavenged, absence from the reaction volume intended for the probe, high reactivity for the photoactivated species, and zero or low reactivity for any component of the system other than the activated probe. Even with all these requirements fulfilled, the probe might bind tightly to a protein and cause the scavenging to fail for purely steric reasons. Scavenging effects are best examined as a function of scavenger concentration. As with most probes, binding of the scavenger may affect the properties of the system under study.

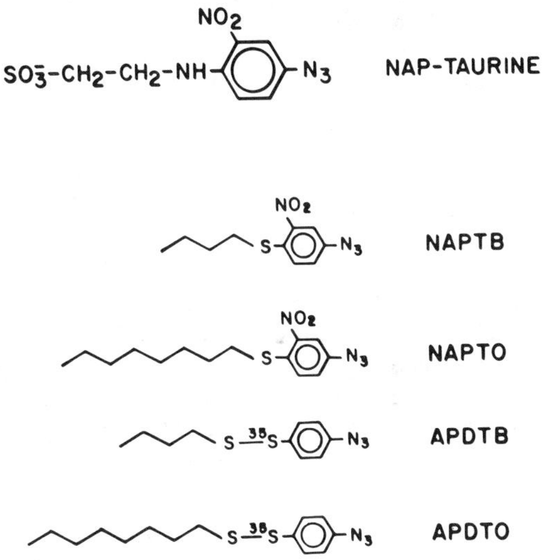

FIGURE 2. The structural formulae of NAP-taurine[1] and some nonpolar phenyl azides.[4]

CROSS-LINKING AND THE REACTION RATE PROBLEM

The problems are the same for the application of bifunctional cross-linking reagents, as far as the individual functional group behavior is concerned. However, in many applications, the formation of a link between two macromolecules is the only significant result. The nature and location of the coupled groups are not of concern, and the difficulties discussed above can be set aside. If spatial localization is important or if the absence of a cross-link is considered significant, then all of the problems must be considered for the reaction of each end of the reagent. These issues and some of the earlier work are discussed by Peters and Richards,[8] by Das and Fox,[9] and, with special reference to heterobifunctional photoactivatable reagents, by Ji.[10] An example of one such reagent, showing the initial dark loading reaction prior to the photolysis step, is shown in FIGURE 3.

For membrane protein cross-linking studies in particular, molecular motion

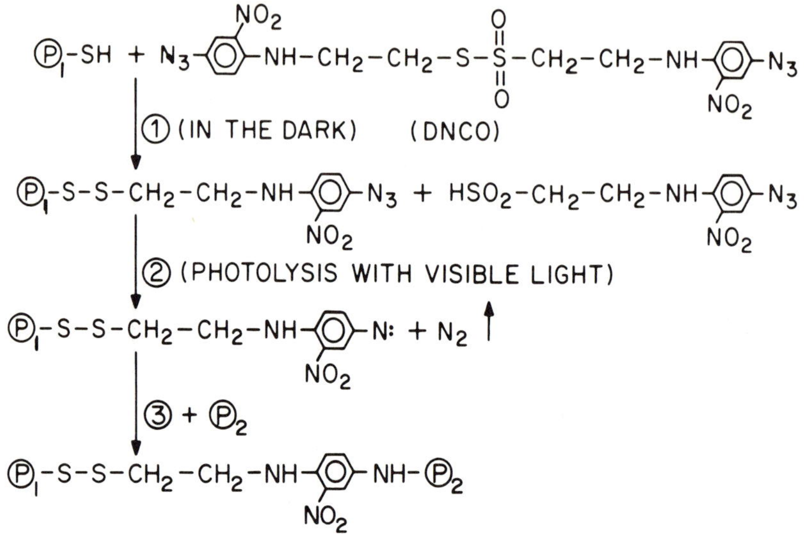

FIGURE 3. A two-step reaction scheme with an unsymmetrical, cleavable, cross-linking reagent, di(nitrophenylazido) cystamine dioxide (DNCO). (From Huang and Richards,[11] with permission.)

introduces a special complication because of the very concentrated systems represented by natural membranes. To distinguish between stable and collision complexes is, in general, very difficult. Homo- or heterocomplexes of proteins present in small amounts can be established with some certainty, but cross-linking studies have not been able to confidently determine the state of aggregation of major species in general.

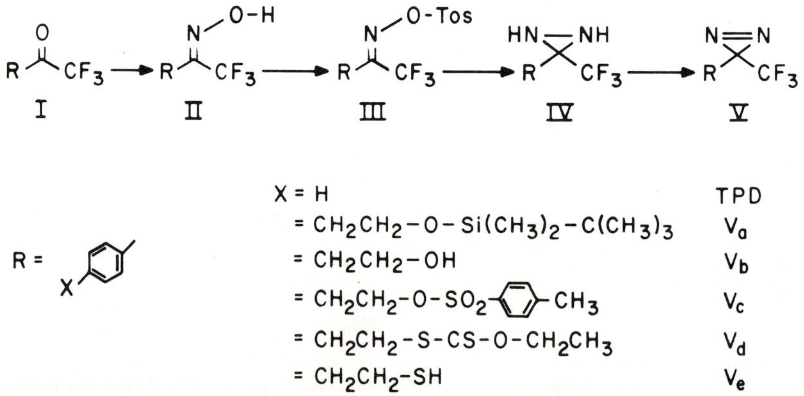

FIGURE 4. The synthesis of 3-trifluoromethyl, 3-phenyl diazirines (V). The diaziridine (IV) was prepared according to the procedure of Zeifman et al.[15] Oxidation of IV was achieved with a 95% yield with freshly prepared silver oxide in absolute ether. Para-substituted analogs of TPD (Va–Ve) were obtained similarly: Dimethyl-tert.butyl-silyl ether was used as a protective group for the hydroxyl function during the introduction of the trifluoroacetyl group (formation of Ib) and the subsequent reactions leading to Vb.

The situation would be markedly improved by the development of reagents whose reaction time is short compared to the time necessary for molecular diffusion in the plane of the membrane. Kiehm and Ji[12] have suggested that a millisecond reaction time is appropriate and have reported studies with heterobifunctional reagents containing nitrene generating groups. The present authors feel that the microsecond range is preferable, since it assures minimum movement even in fluid membranes; therefore, they are concentrating on carbene generating systems.

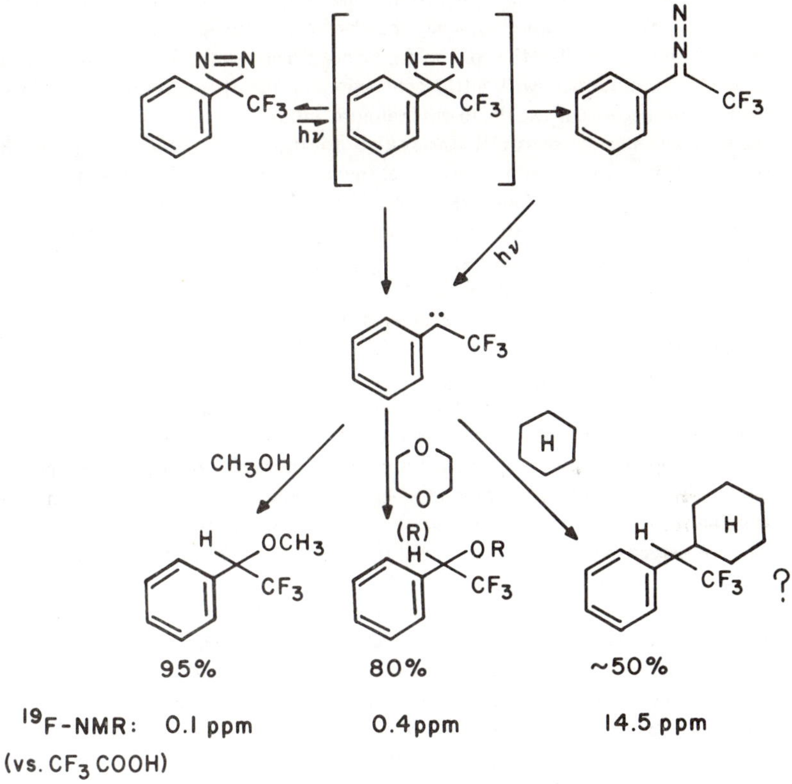

FIGURE 5. The photolysis scheme for trifluoromethyl-phenyl-diazirine (TPD), showing the formation of the diazoisomer and direct and indirect formation of the carbene. Possible products of the reaction of the carbene in three pure solvents are shown. The product from methanol has been positively identified. There is strong evidence for the identity of the dioxane and cyclohexane products, but the identification is not complete.

REAGENTS BASED ON A TRIFLUOROMETHYL DIAZIRINE

Brunner et al.[13] have described the synthesis of 3-trifluoromethyl-3-phenyl diazirine (TPD). This compound has some potentially desirable characteristics, which are now being examined in detail. The precursor diaziridine is easily synthesized by a sequence of reactions that appears to be unique for perfluoroalkyl-substituted ketones.[14,15] The intermediate diaziridine was isolated with high yields. Some para-substituted derivatives (FIGURE 4) have been synthesized; they were designed to permit either the introduction of high specific radioactivity (e.g., by methylation of the alcohol) or the incorporation of this functional group into phospholipids.

The photolysis and reaction scheme for TPD is shown in FIGURE 5 and its absorption spectrum in FIGURE 6. The peak at 353 nm permits rapid photolysis at wavelengths well above 300 nm. On photolysis, 65% of the diazirine is converted to the carbene and 35% to the diazoisomer. The diazo compound is also photosensitive and, when photolyzed in various solvents, gives a product profile essentially identical to that obtained with the diazirine. This conclusion is based on ^{19}F-nmr spectroscopic analysis of the reaction mixtures. However, since the absorption coefficient of the diazoisomer at 300 nm is much less than that of the diazirine, a nearly complete photolysis of the diazirine can be obtained with little conversion of the diazo compound. Thus, a transient accumulation of the diazo compound occurs.

The diazoisomer is relatively insensitive to protonation and the subsequent substitution of the nitrogen by a nucleophile. In cyclohexane or dioxane containing one molar acetic acid, less than 2% degradation of the diazo compound was observed in two hours, a period of time sufficient for complete photolysis of the diazoisomer. This might represent a significant improvement in the design of highly photosensitive carbene precursors that, upon photolysis, are not detectably rearranged to an intermediate that could lead to photochemically irrelevant labeling of a protein.

The diazirine has been photolyzed in three pure solvents and the products have been examined by ^{19}F-nmr spectroscopy (FIGURE 5). In methanol, the O—H insertion product was obtained with a yield of about 95%. The peaks were identified by comparison with an authentic sample of the methyl-ether synthesized by a different route. There appears to be one principal product in dioxane, which is presumed to be the result of either C—O insertion or a C—O displacement reaction.[16] In cyclohexane, the principal product, shown by the signal at 14.5 ppm, represents more than 50% of the starting reagent (FIGURE 7a). The splitting of this signal appears to be due to a proton on the carbon atom adjacent to the CF_3 group. The disappearance of the doublet when the reaction was carried out in deuterocyclohexane confirmed the fact that this proton originated in the solvent (FIGURE 7b). The reaction of the carbene in cyclohexane is complex, as indicated by the appearance of a number of minor components that can be related to the reaction with the secondary C—H of cyclohexane, since, again, the splitting of the signals disappears when photolysis is performed in deuterocyclohexane. One nmr signal with no detectable fine structure appeared at 5.6 ppm. Among various possibilities azine formation is very likely to occur.[17]

These data reflect the general electrophilic nature of the carbene, which implies that reaction with a biological target is not a random process but a rather selective one. Thus, functional groups such as SH, OH, NH_2, the thioether of methionine, and all aromatic ring systems found in amino acids represent preferential sites for reaction with the carbene. However, the data also indicate that, if no nucleophiles are available, attack at aliphatic residues of proteins may occur. This may be of particular significance if the diazirine is intended to be used in labeling the hydrophobic core of a membrane. The chemical selectivity of the intermediate carbene is critical in the context of general labeling of membranes. Whether labeling from a hydrophilic compartment or from within the hydrophobic core of a bilayer, reaction with nucleophiles may be orders of magnitudes faster than the insertion of the carbene in

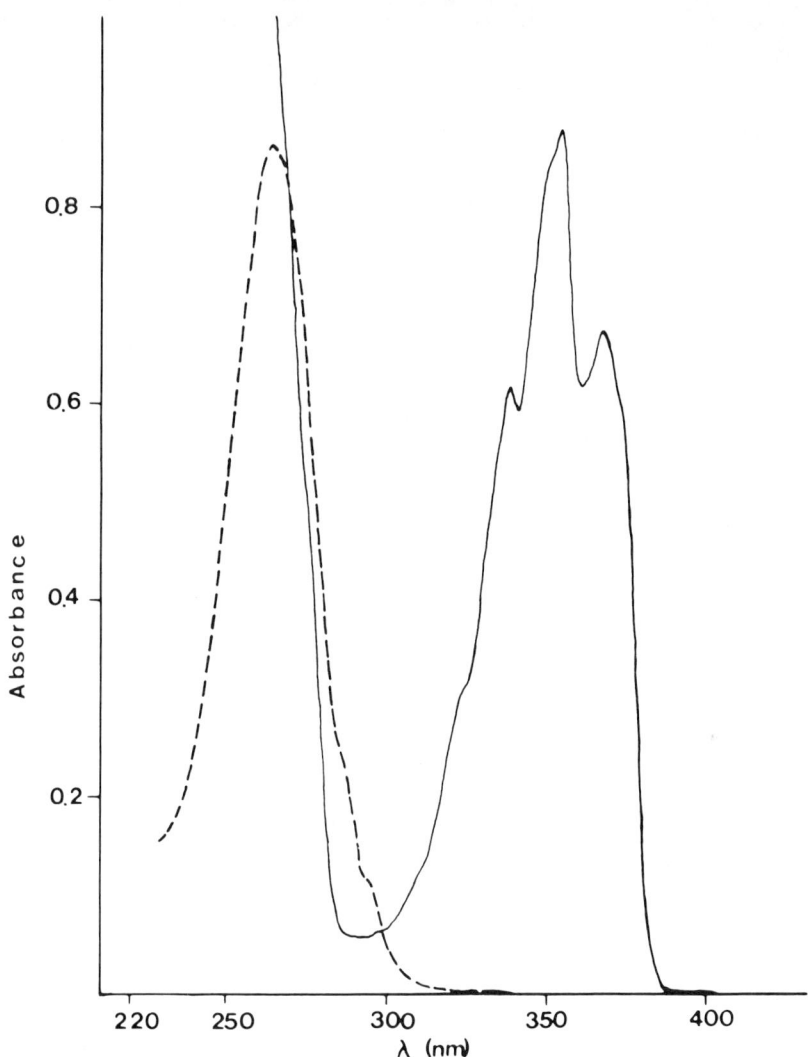

FIGURE 6. The ultraviolet spectra of 3-trifluoromethyl 3-phenyl diazirine, 3.3 m*M* in cyclohexane (————), and of the isomeric 1-phenyl-2,2,2-trifluorodiazoethane, 0.053 m*M* in cyclohexane (-----). The spectra were recorded on a Cary model 15 spectrometer.

λ_{max} (diazirine) 353 nm: $\epsilon_{353} = 266$
λ_{max} (diazo) 264 nm: $\epsilon_{264} = 16200$
λ_{max} (diazo) 467 nm: $\epsilon_{465} \simeq 20$

the C—H bond of an aliphatic amino acid side chain. Since the reaction of nitrenes and carbenes with olefins is well documented,[18,19] it is plausible that the unsaturated lipids, as well as the water in the external phases, can compete efficiently with saturated residues of proteins in their reaction with a carbene or nitrene.

No internal rearrangement of the carbene has yet been detected and, particularly,

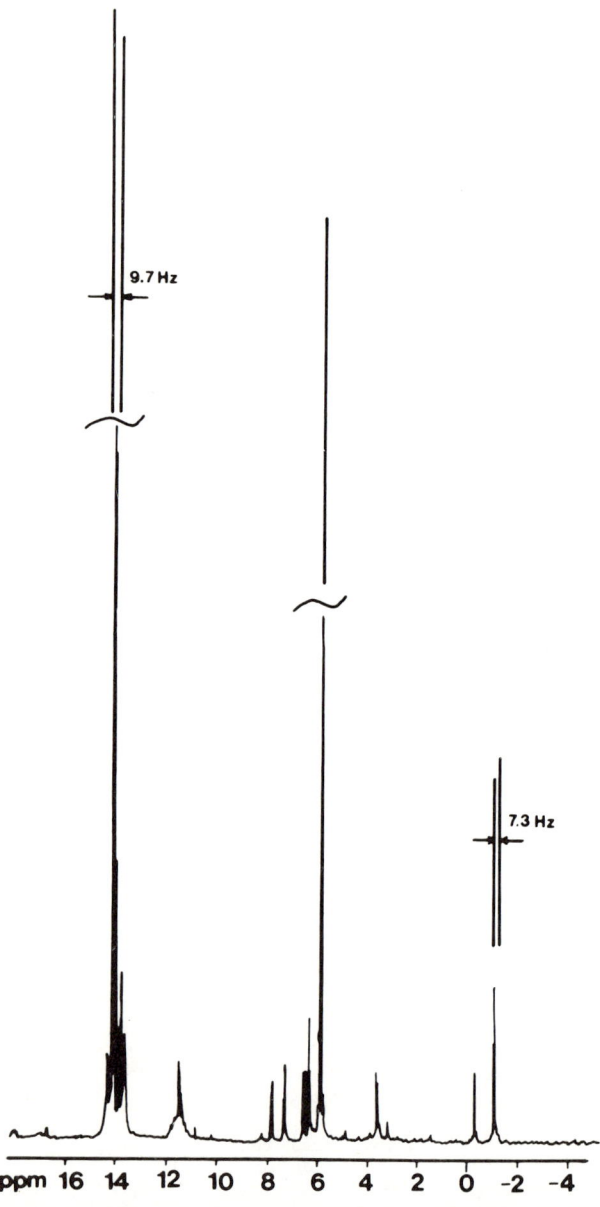

FIGURE 7a. Fluorine nmr spectra of the products of photolysis of 3-trifluoromethyl-3-phenyldiazirine in cyclohexane. The samples were photolyzed in pyrex tubes for 90 min using a medium pressure mercury lamp. The principal signals were also recorded on an expanded scale and are shown above the corresponding resonances in the full trace.

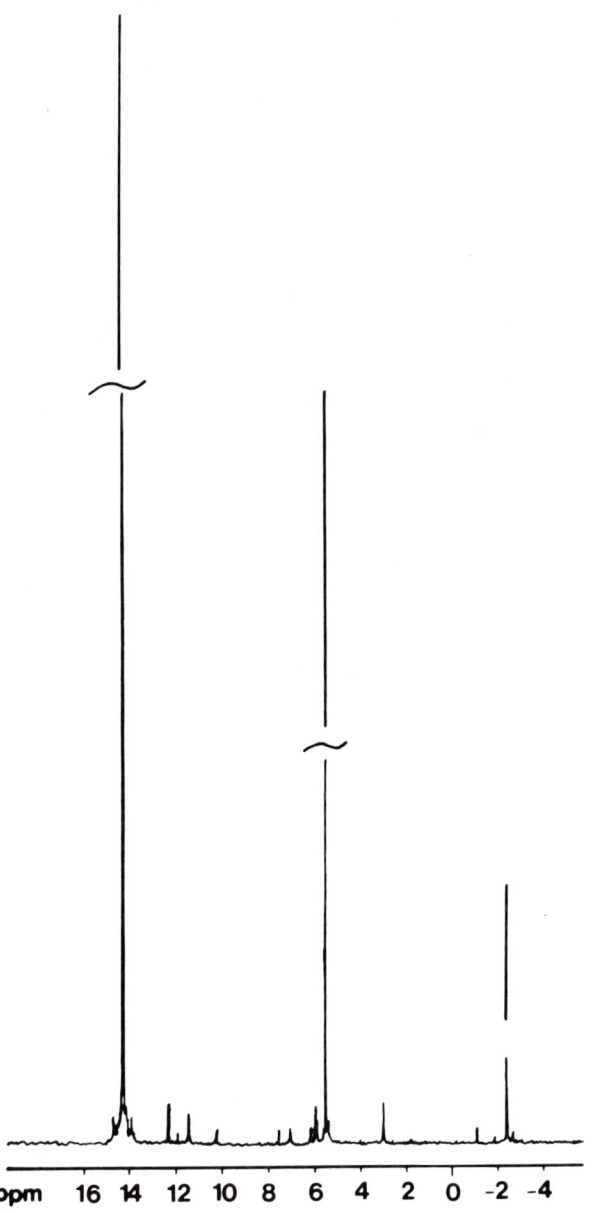

FIGURE 7b. Fluorine nmr spectra of the products of photolysis of 3-trifluoromethyl-3-phenyldiazirine in deuterated cyclohexane. See caption of FIGURE 7a.

1,2-fluorine migration does not occur. No fluorine resonances were detected that would correspond to the chemical shifts of trifluorostyrene, the presumed product of internal rearrangement.[20]

LABELING GROUPS INCORPORATED IN PHOSPHOLIPIDS

The para-substituted trifluoromethylphenyl diazirines were designed to be incorporated into phospholipids. That such modified phospholipids can form bilayers has been shown by Chakrabarti and Khorana.[21] More recently, the same laboratory reported a substantial improvement in the technique of synthesizing phospholipids,

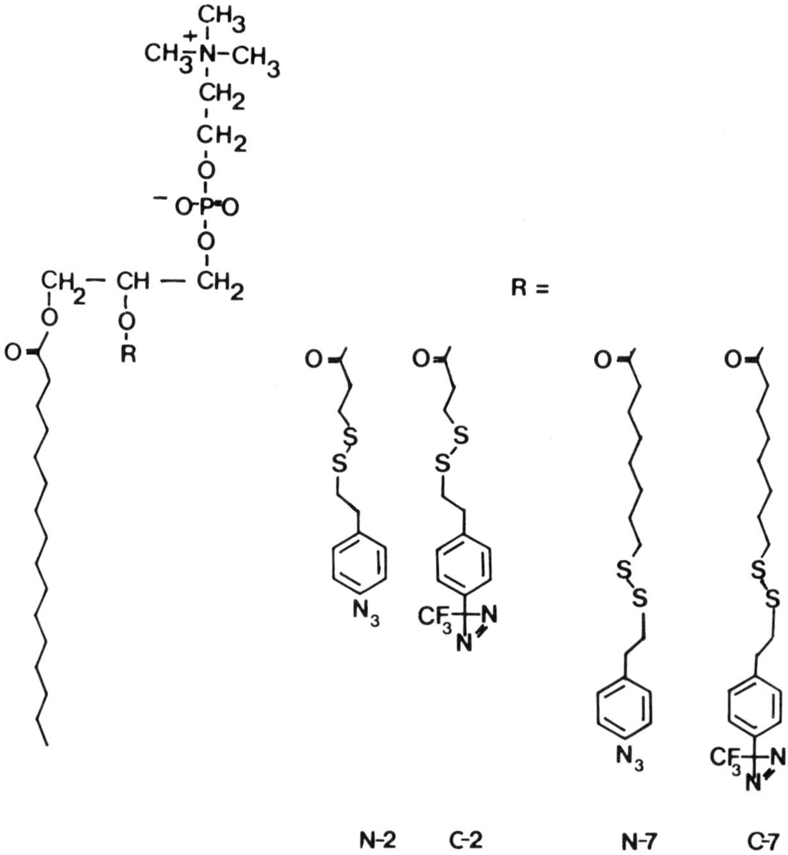

FIGURE 8. Lecithin analogs containing the azidophenyl (N-2, N-7) or 3-trifluoromethyl,3-phenyl-diazirine (C-2, C-7) photosensitive groups and an S—S bond. These were synthesized by acylation of palmitoyl-lysophosphatidylcholine with the anhydrides of the modified fatty acids, in accordance with Gupta et al.[22] The asymmetric disulfides were prepared by the thiol induced fragmentation of sulfenylthiocarbonates of 3-thiopropionic acid and 8-thiooctanoic acid.[37] The length of the modified fatty acids in N-7 and C-7 corresponds closely to that of a palmitoyl chain; N-2 and C-2 fatty acids are shorter by approximately 6.5 Å.

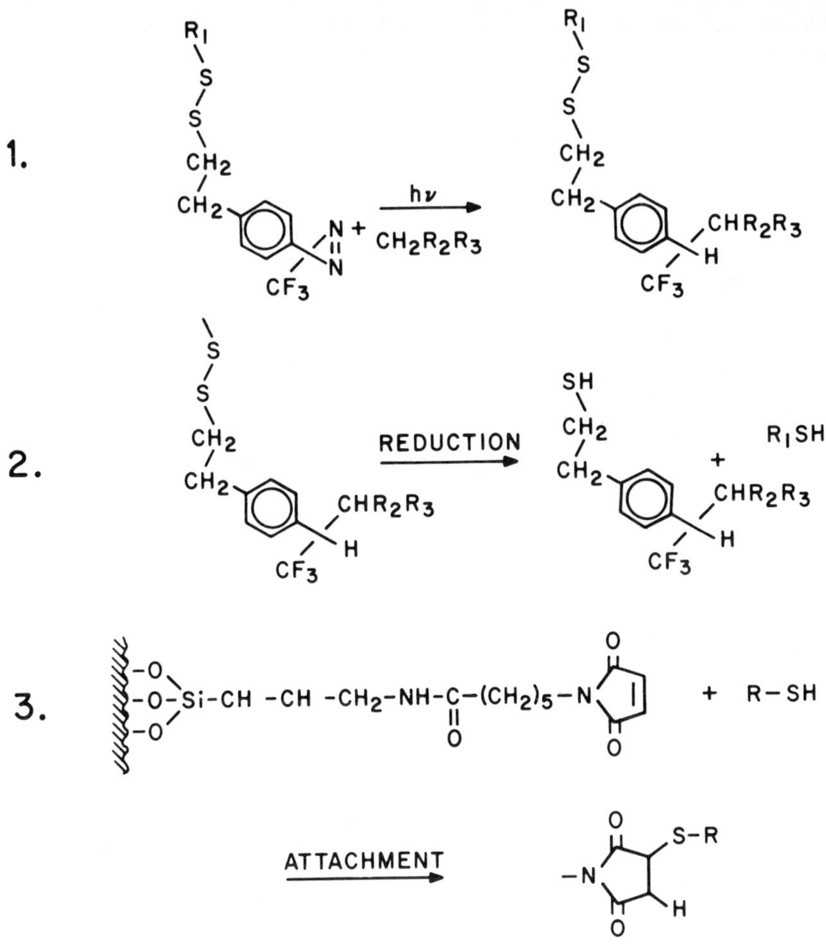

FIGURE 9. The covalent attachment of a photolabeled target, based on the sulfhydryl function generated by cleavage of the disulfide bond of the probe. Reduction was performed in 95% n-propanol with tributyl-phosphine. Porous glass (70 Å) containing N-substituted maleimide arms was prepared by reacting aminopropyl glass with maleimidocaproic acid N-hydroxisuccin-imide ester[38] in acetonitrile.

which allows convenient preparation of phospholipids containing modified fatty acid chains.[22] The ability of phospholipids containing photosensitive groups to form bilayer structures is extremely valuable, since this clearly defines and restricts the position of the photosensitive unit within the bilayer of a membrane or to domains of proteins that play a role in binding phospholipids. Hydrophobic compounds, such as azidophenyl-alkyl sulfides,[5] azidonaphthalenes,[23] and TPD, presumably are not only rapidly exchanged between membranes, but also, as pointed out earlier, nonspecific binding to hydrophobic sites of externally located proteins can take place, causing interference with the expected labeling pattern.

We have synthesized various lecithin analogs (FIGURE 8). The photoactivatable groups, *p*-phenyl azide and TPD, are linked to the terminal carbon of the 2-fatty acyl-chain by a disulfide bridge. These lipids, when in the pure state and when mixed with dipalmitoyl lecithin or egg lecithin, readily form small liposomes by sonication, as determined by high resolution ^{1}H-nmr spectroscopy. Furthermore, we have been able to show that these lipids (as yet investigated only with N-7) can serve as a substrate for the phospholipid exchange protein.[24,25] Thus, natural membranes can be doped asymmetrically with the photoactivatable lipids. The different chain lengths of the probes should permit labeling at different depths in a membrane.

Disulfide bonds are easily cleaved by a number of reducing agents, such as dithiothreitol or tributyl-phosphine.[26,27] After a membrane protein has been labeled, the entire phospholipid molecule is covalently bound to the protein. The presence of an S—S bond close to the photosensitive group offers a means of removing most of the phospholipid, leaving only a fragment of the whole probe and simultaneously creating a thiol function. This reduction should facilitate the analysis of the cross-linking site on the protein or on a peptide derived from the protein. Furthermore, the formation of a sulfhydryl function allows highly selective manipulations at only those proteins, peptides, or amino acids that have been cross-linked.

LABELING IN VESICLES WITH PHOSPHOLIPID REAGENTS

Liposomes prepared from various radioactively labeled lipids and a photolabeling reagent (the molar ratio of lipid to reagent was 20:1) were photolyzed. The disulfide bond was then cleaved by reduction and photolabeled products were trapped with glass beads containing N-substituted maleinimide arms (FIGURE 9). Covalently bound radioactivity was measured. Only 50–90% of the S—H–containing products were bound to the beads, presumably due to competition with glass adsorption and reoxidation reactions.

The reagents shown in FIGURE 5 were placed in synthetic vesicles prepared from ^{14}C-oleyl-palmitoyl phosphatidylcholine and a trace of ^{3}H-dipalmitoyl-lecithin and photolyzed. Reaction of the nitrene or carbene with saturated lipid can be estimated from the amount of bound ^{3}H. Since the principal ^{14}C-labeled lipid contained an equimolar ratio of saturated and oleyl chains, the ratio of ^{14}C to ^{3}H in the immobilized products can be used to estimate both insertion and addition. The results are given in TABLE 1. Both reactions are seen with both reagents, but the carbene shows a greater tendency to react with the saturated ligands than does the nitrene. In all cases, the absolute yield of products is about 5–10%. Quenching of the reactive intermediates by intermolecular reactions between probe molecules is probably responsible for these low yields.†

By varying the position of the double bond along the fatty acyl chain, different insertion-addition ratios are expected. From such changes, a function could be derived

†The concentration of TPD in the various solvents was in the range from 10 to 15 m*M*. The estimated concentration of the TPD function in the liposome experiments varied, depending on the assumed volume of the occupied portion of the bilayer. The thickness of the entire lipid region was assumed to be 35 Å, while the TPD group might reasonably be restricted to a 10 Å thick layer in the middle. The effective reactive group concentrations would be 70 to 250 m*M*, depending on the thickness chosen. Thus, the liposome labeling was carried out at effective reagent concentrations 5 to 25 times as high as those of the solution measurements.

expressing the probability of reaction of the reagent within the layer of membrane that is occupied by the double bond.

LABELING OF GRAMICIDIN A IN LIPOSOMES

Dipalmitoyl lecithin and egg lecithin multilamellar liposomes containing lipid, reagent, and Gramicidin A in a 20:1:1 molar ratio were photolyzed above the phase transition temperature. The extent of labeling was determined after separation from unreacted Gramicidin A either after reduction, by trapping on glass beads, or by separation on thin layer chromatography (TLC) plates. Data for the nitrene and carbene generating reagents are given in TABLE 2. Photolysis of the azidophenyl group is complete after 15 min in the apparatus used; the slight decrease in yield after 60 min

TABLE 1

REACTION OF THE NITRENE (N-7) AND CARBENE (C-7) PHOSPHOLIPID PROBES
WITH PALMITOYL-OLEYL-PHOSPHATIDYLCHOLINE (POPC) LIPOSOMES*

| | Total Counts Recovered (%)† | | Labeling Yields (%) | |
| | | | Reaction with Saturated Chains | Reaction with Double Bonds |
Photolabel	^{14}C	^{3}H		
N-7	7.7	1.9	1.9	5.8
C-7	10.7	6.4	6.4	4.3

*10 mg of [^{14}C]-POPC, a trace of [^{3}H]-DPPC (<1 mol%), and probe N-7 or C-7 (POPC:label molar ratio = 20:1) were freeze-dried from 95% benzene and 5% methanol, dispersed in 2 ml water at 45 °C, and photolyzed for 45 min at a wavelength >300 nm. After freeze-drying, the lipids were dissolved in 800 μl of 95% n-propanol and extensively flushed with nitrogen. Disulfide was reduced with a 2–3 fold excess of tributylphosphine and sulfhydryls trapped with 100 mg porous glass containing the N-alkyl-maleimido group. Adsorbed radioactivity was removed by repeated extraction of the beads with methanol:formic acid (98:2). Bound radioactivity was determined after release from glass by acid-hydrolysis.
†If every reagent molecule reacted with a lipid and if the binding of the SH groups in the reduced samples was quantitative, the expected number of ^{3}H or ^{14}C counts bound to the beads was defined as 100%. The actual recoveries are listed.

may be due to photolytic decomposition of the reaction product. The diazirine is photolyzed faster than the nitrene (not shown); the increase in labeling yields from 15 min to 60 min must be assigned to the carbene derived from the diazo compound that is generated from the diazirine during the initial period of photolysis and then photolyzed slowly.

The three-fold higher overall efficiency of the nitrene in labeling Gramicidin A compared with the carbene does not conform with the general view that carbene insertion into C—H bonds is more probable than nitrene insertion. Assuming that all C—H bonds in the entire Gramicidin A have reactivities identical to those of the C—H bonds of a saturated fatty acyl chain, we can estimate that, in the case of the carbene, approximately ten times more cross-linking with Gramicidin A was found than was expected. The labeling yield with the nitrene-generating reagent was two orders of magnitudes higher than the predicted value. Reaction with the terminal CH$_3$

TABLE 2

REACTION OF THE NITRENE (N-7) AND CARBENE (C-7) PHOSPHOLIPID PROBES
WITH GRAMICIDIN A IN DIPALMITOYLPHOSPHATIDYLCHOLINE (DPPC) LIPOSOMES

| | Observed Labeling Yields (%)* | | Expected Yields (%)† (Assuming equal insertion probabilities in all lipid and peptide CH groups.) |
Photolabel	Photolysis Time 15′	Photolysis Time 60′	
N-7	14.2	12.3	0.15
C-7	3.5	5.4	0.52

*Dipalmitoyl lecithin, ^{14}C-Gramicidin A, and label (N-7 or C-7) (molar ratio = 20:1:1) were freeze-dried from benzene:methanol 95:5 and dispersed in water (10 mg lipid/ml) at 45–50 °C. Photolyses were performed at >300 nm. Photolabeled Gramicidin A was separated from unreacted peptide by thin layer chromatography (Kieselgel 60) using chloroform:methanol:water (65:25:4) as the solvent. The labeling yield is the percentage of the total Gramicidin A that was modified. This value is identical to the percentage of photolabel that reacted with the peptide, assuming one label per Gramicidin A.

†The fatty acid chains of one DPPC molecule have 62 C—H bonds, and 20 molecules 1240 bonds. One Gramicidin A molecule has 100 aromatic and aliphatic C—H bonds. From TABLE 1, the expected extent of insertion of N-7 into saturated bonds is 1.9% × 100 ÷ 1240 = 0.15%, and, of C-7, 6.5% × 100 ÷ 1240 = 0.52%.

groups of the aliphatic amino acid side chains cannot account for these values. Moreover, CH_3 groups are generally less reactive than are secondary C—H bonds, so most of the C—H bonds in the Gramicidin A are relatively unreactive towards either the carbene or the nitrene. As discussed earlier, photolytically derived species are less selective than are ordinary reagents but they are not nonselective. Thus, multiple and nonstoichiometric modifications in a variety of amino acid residues are expected.

Fragments of proteins have been produced by chemical cleavage or by proteolysis and then analyzed[28,29] for relative label content. Almost all analytical approaches measure labeling of biological systems by techniques that involve separation of proteins by gel electrophoresis and the determination of the label associated with individual bands.[30–33] To what level of resolution can this procedure be extended? In the case of Gramicidin A, it is not yet possible to generate useful smaller fragments by proteolysis or limited hydrolysis. As an alternative approach, we have subjected the labeled Gramicidin A to the Edman degradation procedure up to 15 cycles.

Since this peptide is very soluble in most organic solvents, a routine program for automated degradation did not appear promising. Indeed, during the degradation of Gramicidin A in a spinning cup sequenator in the presence of the carrier polybrene, the peptide is completely extracted after two to three cycles.[34] Alternative methods, such as manual operation involving product separation by ion-exchange chromatography after each step,[35] appeared very time consuming and, in addition, the reproducibility is considerably worse than that of the automated systems. Since the carboxyl terminal COOH group is blocked, covalent attachment to a solid support by either one of the established coupling reactions was not possible and several attempts to find an appropriate modification of the OH of the ethanolamide group failed. The Gramicidin A was finally bound to glass beads by the sulfhydryl group of the label itself; thus, the peptide was attached at the photolabeled amino acid. The low extent of the labeling reaction guaranteed that essentially all of the bound molecules contained only one modified amino acid. Binding to the glass was shown to depend on photolysis and on the free sulfhydryl groups formed by reduction. Treatment of the attached polypeptide with 1.5 molar HCl in methanol in order to remove the N-terminal formyl group did not release any significant peptidic material from the beads.

Degradation was performed with a sequenator equipped with a spinning cup. In addition to the standard program, each step of the degradation involved an extraction with methanol to assure the removal of any released material. Between 25 and 55 nmols of Gramicidin A could be attached per 100 mg of glass. Thus, detection and quantitation of the Edman degradation products involved conventional analytical techniques such as gas chromatography of the PTH amino acids and amino acid analysis of the back-hydrolysates. Only a brief summary of the results will be given here:

1. Through cycle 8, excellent repetitive yields (>95%) were obtained and very

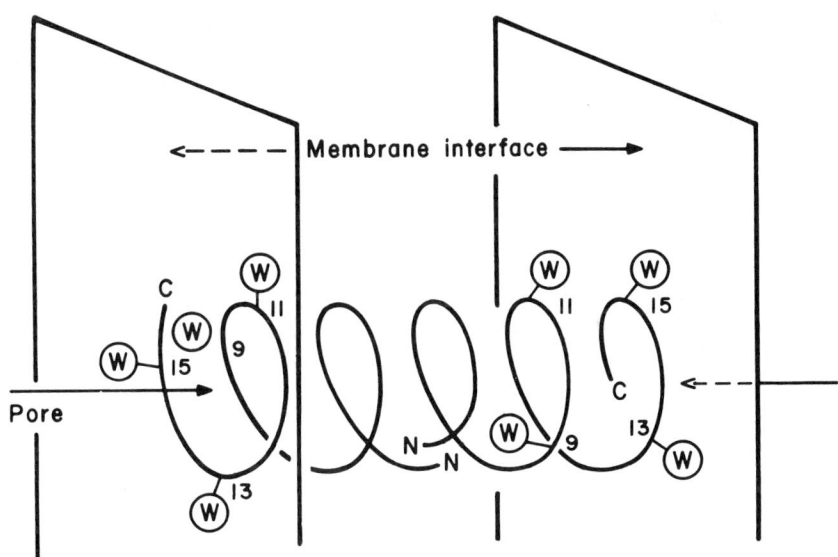

Arrangement of the Gramicidin A channel
in the membrane

(W) symbolizes tryptophan side chains

HCO Val-Gly-Ala-Leu-Ala-Val-Val-Val-Trp-Leu
    1   5   10

Trp-Leu-Trp-Leu-Trp NHCH$_2$CH$_2$OH
11   15

FIGURE 10. A schematic diagram of the dimer of Gramicidin A in the head to head helical model[39] (adapted from Miroshnikov *et al.*[40]). The tryptophan residues, W, in positions 9, 11, 13, and 15 in the C-terminal portion of the peptide, are shown near the bilayer surfaces. The peptide sequence is shown below.

little background was measured, the sequence derived being consistent with that in the literature.

2. Significant drops of the yields were found after cycles 9, 11, and 13.

3. Additional material was extracted from the anilinothiazolidine (ATZ) amino acids from cycles 9, 11, and 13, which, after back-hydrolysis, gave substantial amounts of leucine.

Inspection of the Gramicidin A sequence (FIGURE 10) shows that there are tryptophans at positions 9, 11, 13, and 15. The appearance of leucine in the material eluted from those cycles after the back-hydrolysis steps is consistant with the release of peptides 10–15, 12–15, and 14–15 during the cleavage of bonds 9—10, 11—12, and 13—14. Thus, the sequence data indicate that the attack by the reagent on Gramicidin A has occurred predominantly at the tryptophan residues. This analytical technique is not very sensitive and the possibility that a minor fraction of the reagent has modified aliphatic amino acid residues cannot be excluded. Since it was shown that the photolysis conditions did not produce any significant changes in the spectroscopic behavior of Gramicidin A by itself, the reactive species within the polypeptide are the intact tryptophan residues rather than degradation products. However, we have not been able to discriminate between insertion into N—H and reaction with the hydrocarbon ring portion of the indole ring. Reaction with the amide N—H bonds of the polypeptide backbone is rather unlikely according to the current model of the pore, in which the amide groups are sterically well protected (FIGURE 10). Such a reaction would also make the observed specificity for the tryptophan residues difficult to explain.

These results are in accord with the general view that (singlet) carbenes and nitrenes are electrophilic species and that reaction with an aromatic system may be much faster than with an aliphatic C—H bond. We expect that a similar chemical selectivity would be observed for other amino acid side chains containing any of the functional groups or aromatic systems. Detailed interpretation of such labeling patterns is difficult, since the intrinsic reactivities, as well as conformational effects of the individual amino acid residues, have to be considered.

Geometrical localization through this probing procedure has another problem. The membrane probes N-7 and C-7 were both intended to label the Gramicidin A pore in the N-terminal half of the peptide, according to Urry's model. However, all four tryptophan residues are located in the C-terminal half and are presumed to be in a layer of the membrane close to the lipid-water interface (FIGURE 10). If the pore model is correct, and the evidence is very strong, reaction with the tryptophans requires the chain(s) of the phospholipid reagent to loop back towards the membrane interface (FIGURE 11). This need not be a permanent conformation; only a rare transient fluctuation. If the lifetime of the reactive intermediate is long enough, tryptophan may continuously trap the small fraction of the reactive species that reaches one of the indole rings.

It has yet to be proved that Gramicidin A is in the pore state at the time the labeling occurs. As an alternative to the reagent loop-back possibility, the monomer form of Gramicidin A may randomly diffuse within and across the membrane and be attacked by the reagent during this process. Experiments are planned in which the native peptide is substituted by 0-pyromellitoyl–Gramicidin A, which has been shown not to diffuse across the membrane[36] and with which the integrity of the pore structure is better preserved.

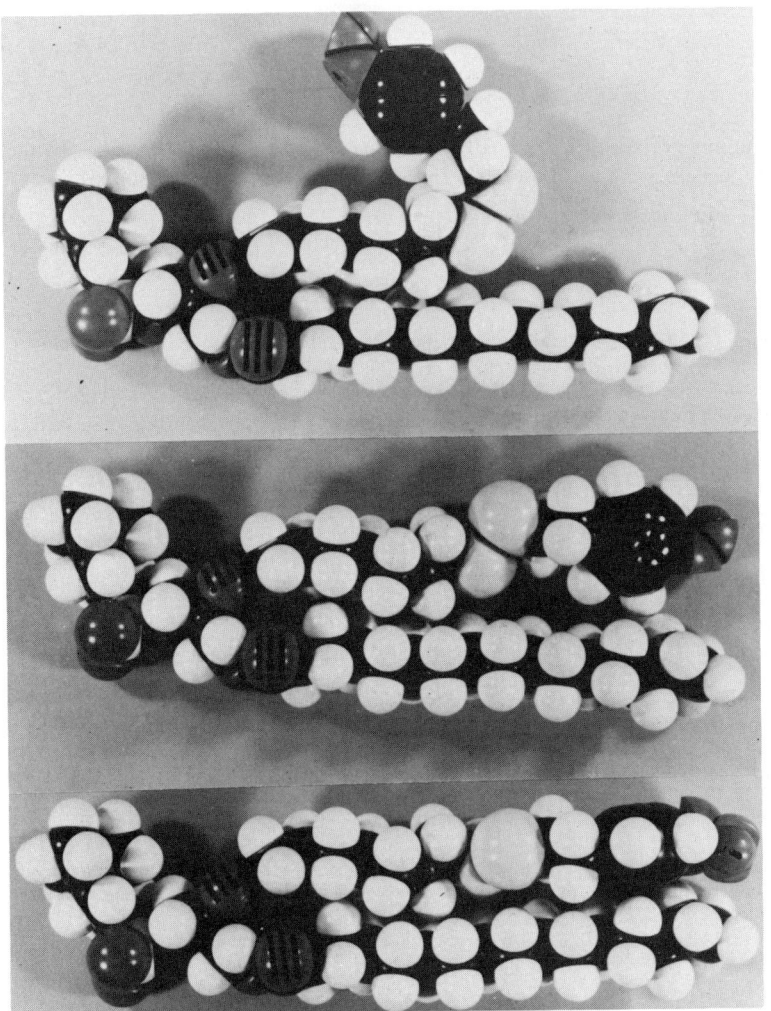

FIGURE 11. CPK models of N-7, with fully extended chains showing equivalence in length and with a looped-back reagent chain showing access, in terms of chain flexibility, to the surface area of the bilayer.

The relative reactivity with each type of side chain, as well as the main chain, will have to be known for any reagent to be used as a probe of protein geometry at the detailed level of single amino acid residues. Where kinetic as well as equilibrium processes are involved, a knowledge of absolute reaction rates will be important. Comprehensive data of this sort is not yet available for any probe. As a result, there are, at present, severe limitations on the structural resolution at which labeling results can be interpreted with confidence.

ACKNOWLEDGMENTS

The authors gratefully acknowledge the help of Dr. Paul Fletcher, in the peptide sequence analysis, and J. Mouning and M. Lane, in the preparation of the manuscript.

REFERENCES

1. STAROS, J. V. & F. M. RICHARDS. 1974. Photochemical labeling of the surface proteins of human erythrocytes. Biochemistry **13**: 2720–26.
2. STAROS, J. V., B. E. HALEY & F. M. RICHARDS. 1975. Photochemical labeling of the cytoplasmic surface of the membranes of intact human erythrocytes. J. Biol. Chem. **250**: 8174–78.
3. NÄF, F., J. BRUNNER, H. WACKER, & G. SEMENZA. 1979. In preparation.
4. DOCKTER, M. E. 1979. Fluorescent photochemical surface labeling of intact human erythrocytes. J. Biol. Chem. **254**: 2161–64.
5. BAHN, P. R. 1978. Hydrophobic photochemical probes of erythrocyte membrane structure. Ph. D. dissertation, Yale University.
6. WISHNIA, A. 1962. The solubility of hydrocarbon gases in protein solutions. Proc. Nat. Acad. Sci. USA **48**: 2200.
7. BROWN, W. E. 1975. Alkyl isoiyanates as active site-specific reagents for serine proteases. Location of alkyl binding site in chymotrypsin by x-ray diffraction. Biochemistry **14**: 5079–84.
8. PETERS, K. & F. M. RICHARDS. 1977. Chemical cross-linking: Reagents and problems in studies of membrane structures. Annu. Rev. Biochem. **46**: 523–51.
9. DAS, M. & C. F. FOX. 1979. Chemical cross-linking in biology. Annu. Rev. Biophys. Bioeng. **8**: 165–94.
10. JI, T. H. 1979. The application of chemical cross-linking for studies on cell membranes and the identification of surface receptors. Biochim. Biophys. Acta Biomembranes **559**: 39–69.
11. HUANG, C.-K. & F. M. RICHARDS. 1977. Reaction of a lipid-soluble, unsymmetrical, cleavable, cross-linking reagent with muscle aldolase and erythrocyte membrane proteins. J. Biol. Chem. **252**: 5514–21.
12. KIEHM, D. J. & T. H. JI. 1977. Photochemical cross-linking of cell membranes. J. Biol. Chem. **252**: 8524–31.
13. BRUNNER, H., H. SENN & F. M. RICHARDS. 1979. The synthesis and properties of 3-trifluoromethyl-3-phenyl diazirine. J. Biol. Chem. In press.
14. SMITH, R. A. G. & J. R. KNOWLES. 1975. The preparation and photolysis of 3-aryl-^{3}H-diazirines. J. Chem. Soc. Perkin Trans. **2**: 686–94.
15. ZEIFMAN, YU. V., E. G. ABDUGANIEV, E. M. ROKHLIN & I. L. KNUNYANTS. 1972. Derivatives of hexafluoroacetone oxime. Translation from Izv. Akad. Nauk SSSR Ser. Khim. **12**: 2737–41.
16. KRIMSE, W., Ed. 1971. Carbene Chemistry. Academic Press. New York, London.
17. GALE, D. M., W. J. MIDDLETON & C. G. KRESPAN. 1966. Perfluorodiazo compounds. J. Am. Chem. Soc. **88**: 3677–23.

18. LWOWSKI, W. 1970. Nitrenes. Interscience Publishers. New York, London.
19. MCMANUS, S. P., Ed. 1973. Organic Reactive Intermediates. Academic Press. New York, London.
20. DEWAR, M. J. S. & J. KELEMEN. 1968. Ground states of conjugated molecules. X. ^{19}F nmr chemical shifts in aryl fluorides. J. Chem. Physics 49(2): 499–508.
21. CHAKRABARTI, P. & H. G. KHORANA. 1975. A new approach to the study of phospholipid-protein interactions in biological membranes. Synthesis of fatty acids and phospholipids containing photosensitive groups. Biochemistry 14: 5021–33.
22. GUPTA, C. M., R. RADHAKRISHNAN & H. G. KHORANA. 1977. Glycerophospholipid synthesis: Improved general method and new analogs containing photoactivatable groups. Proc. Nat. Acad. Sci. USA 74: 4315–19.
23. BERCOVICI, T. & C. GITLER 1978. 5-^{125}I-iodonaphthyl azide, a reagent to determine the penetration of proteins into the lipid bilayer of biological membranes. Biochemistry 17: 1484–89.
24. WIRTZ, K. W. A., L. M. G. VAN GOLDE & L. L. M. VAN DEENEN. 1970. The exchange of molecular species of phosphatidylcholine between mitochondria and microsomes of rat liver. Biochim. Biophys. Acta 218: 176–79.
25. KAMP, H. H. & K. W. A. WIRTZ. 1974. Phosphatidylcholine exchange protein from beef liver. In Methods of Enzymology, Vol. 32. S. Fleischer & L. Packer, Eds.: 140–46. Academic Press. New York.
26. MEANS, G. E. & R. E. FEENEY. 1971. Chemical Modifications of Proteins. Holden-Day, Inc. San Francisco.
27. RÜEGG, U. T. & J. RUDINGER. 1977. Reductive cleavage of cysteine disulfides with tributylphosphine. In Methods in Enzymology, Vol. 47. C. H.-W. Hirs & S. N. Timasheff, Eds.: 111–26. Academic Press. New York.
28. KAHANE, I. & C. GITLER. 1978. Red cell membrane glycophorine labeling from within the lipid bilayer. Science 201: 351–52.
29. GOLDMAN, D. W., J. S. POBER, J. WHITE & H. BAYLEY. 1979. Selective labeling of the hydrophobic segments of intrinsic membrane proteins with a lipophilic photogenerated carbene. Nature. 280: 841–43.
30. BRETSCHER, M. S. 1971. Human erythrocyte membranes: Specific labeling of surface proteins. J. Mol. Biol. 58: 775–81.
31. STAROS, J. V., B. E. HALEY & F. M. RICHARDS. 1974. Human erythrocytes and resealed ghosts. A comparison of membrane topology. J. Biol. Chem. 249: 5004–7.
32. SIGRIST-NELSON, K., H. SIGRIST, T. BERCOVICI & C. GITLER. 1971. Intrinsic proteins of the intestinal microvillus membrane. Iodonaphthylazide labeling studies. Biochim. Biophys. Acta 468: 163–76.
33. WISNIESKI, B. J. & J. S. BRAMHALL. 1971. Labeling of the active subunit of cholera toxin from within the membrane bilayer. Biochem. Biophys. Res. Commun. 87: 308–13.
34. FLETCHER, P. Personal communication.
35. SARGES, R. & B. WITKOP. 1965. Gramicidin A. The structure of valine- and isoleucine-gramicidin A. J. Am. Chem. Soc. 87: 2011–20.
36. APPELL, J.-H., E. BOMBERG, H. APES & P. LÄUGER. 1977. J. Membr. Biol. 31: 171–88.
37. BROIS, S. J., J. F. PILOT & H. W. BARNUM. 1970. A new pathway to unsymmetrical disulfides. The thiol-induced fragmentation of sulfenyl thiocarbonates. J. Am. Chem. Soc. 92: 7629–31.
38. KELLER, O. & J. RUDINGER. 1975. Preparation and some properties of maleimide acids and maleoyl derivatives of peptides. Helv. Chim. Acta 58: 531–41.
39. URRY, D. W. 1971. The Gramicidin A transmembrane channel: A proposed $_{(L,D)}$helix. Proc. Nat. Acad. Sci. USA 68: 672–76.
40. MIROSHNIKOV, A. I., ST. LORDANOW, E. N. SHEPEL, V. T. IVANOV & YU. A. OVCHINNIKOV. 1972. Structure-activity relationship and physicochemical properties of Gramicidin A and its synthetic analogues. In Peptides 1972. H. Hanson & H. D. Jakube, Eds.: 341–45. North Holland Publ. Co. Amsterdam.

DISCUSSION

DR. W. LWOWSKI: Is there any hint as to which groups your probe actually attaches to in the peptide? You said it's not predominantly CH; is there any good guess as to what it is?

DR. RICHARDS: The only evidence that we have shows that it is likely to be a tryptophane residue, but we do not exactly know where it is reacting on the indole system. Probably on the nitrogen function, but we don't know that for certain. I think the fact that the Edman degredation did work as well as it did indicates that this reagent is not reacting with the main peptide chain. That would almost certainly cause much more interference with the degradation than was observed.

DR. L. BASKIN (*College of Medicine and Dentistry of New Jersey*): Dr. Richards, you mentioned that the average distance between the surfaces of proteins in the membrane is about 10 Å. Is there any hope, even with a photochemical reagent, for cross-linking these and retaining the type of information that might be required to understand the structure?

F. M. RICHARDS: I let the 10 Å slip out quicker than I should have. It's more likely to be 20 or 30, on the average. Since some of these components are oligomers, we squeeze them together in one place and get slightly longer distances in other places. You're talking about distances on the order of 50 Å, let's say, for diffusion, and, in principle, we can stop that on a photochemical time scale. The carbenes might be shown to react in the microsecond region; I'm sure that that would be fast enough for cross-linking studies.

The nitrenes that Ji, in Wyoming, has used probably react in the millisecond time range. I don't think that's fast enough to be sure about the interpretation.

DR. E. LONDON (*Cornell University*): Have you ever tried cross-linking of sarcoplasmic reticulum dissolved in detergents in which you might have a reasonable oligomer that couldn't aggregate?

F. M. RICHARDS: Yes; I think it is still tetrameric if you pick the right detergent.

DR. F. H. WESTHEIMER: Although I certainly agree that methyl groups are the worst things to label I can't resist reminding the audience that Vaughn managed to insert from a diazomalonyl derivative into the methyl group of alanine to produce a glutamic acid residue in trypsin.

DR. M. E. DOCKTER: As you mentioned, we've been synthesizing some fluorescent compounds, the precursors of which are azides. In your talk, you mentioned the need to look at the spectroscopy of these reactions more carefully. I would like to point out to the audience that you can easily monitor the reaction because the azide itself is not fluorescent and the product formed is highly fluorescent. If you use reagents with appropriate chromophores, you can shift the fluorescence out far enough into the red to easily monitor the actual reaction sequence in membrane systems.

DR. A. M. TOMETSKO: I'm concerned that, in looking at membranes, the partitioning between the aqueous phase and the membrane phase is an important parameter when using these different probes. The partition coefficient (e.g., octanol and water) could provide useful base line data for comparing probes from different labs. Have you looked at the partition coefficients?

F. M. RICHARDS: I think you're absolutely right. One should study the partitioning and we did. We use hexane and water as a reference system.

PHOSPHOLIPIDS CONTAINING PHOTOACTIVABLE
GROUPS IN STUDIES OF
BIOLOGICAL MEMBRANES*

R. Radhakrishnan, C. M. Gupta, B. Erni, R. J. Robson,
W. Curatolo, A. Majumdar, A. H. Ross,
Y. Takagaki, and H. G. Khorana

*Departments of Biology and Chemistry
Massachusetts Institute of Technology
Cambridge, Massachusetts 02139*

INTRODUCTION

Membranes perform a variety of important biological functions. Their ubiquitous components are proteins and phospholipids. An understanding of the dynamics of specific interactions between phospholipids and membrane proteins is important to studies of their structural and functional relationships. A variety of physicochemical, biochemical, and chemical approaches have been introduced for this purpose with varying degrees of scope and success; the information thus far obtained remains limited. The development of new organochemical approaches to the study of the above problems is highly desirable, and the work reviewed here represents initial studies in this general area. The most prominent and unique feature of integral membrane proteins is their hydrophobicity, which allows strong and specific interactions with phospholipids. Therefore, the principle aim in this work is the study of hydrophobic interactions between proteins and phosopholipids. Currently available approaches usually involve the addition of reagents, which may serve either as noncovalently linked probes or as covalent cross-linking agents to the membrane. Both are likely to perturb normal interactions, and their distribution in the membrane may be biased against the regions of specific contacts between phospholipids and proteins. Therefore, the main procedure used in the present work has been to covalently incorporate suitable photoactivable groups into the fatty acyl chains of synthetic phospholipids. Secondarily, since the aim is to explore the points of contact between the chemically inert phospholipid hydrocarbon chains and the exposed hydrophobic amino acid side chains in proteins, clearly the large body of chemistry that relies on the presence of the usual functional groups is excluded. An attractive alternative is to use suitable photoactivable groups as probes, an approach pioneered by Frank Westheimer and colleagues.[1,2]

In this article we review our work on:

1. The synthesis of a variety of fatty acids containing nitrene and, in particular, carbene precursors and the synthesis of defined phospholipids by incorporating the above fatty acids

*This investigation was supported by the National Institute of Allergy and Infectious Diseases, grant no. AI11479; the National Cancer Institute, grant no. CA11981; the United States Public Health Service; and the National Science Foundation, grant no. PCM78-13713.

0077–8923/80/0346–0165 $1.75/1 © 1980, NYAS

2. Demonstrating the formation of intermolecular cross-links between fatty acyl chains upon the photolysis of unilamellar and multilamellar liposomes

3. Studies on the sites of the intermolecular cross-links as a function of the length of the fatty acyl chain carrying the photoactivable group

4. Attempts to devise new and more versatile photoactivable carbene precursors that can form components of fatty acyl chains

5. Photoaffinity labels for the polar headgroups in phospholipids

6. The use of the above phospholipids in studies of phospholipid-phospholipid interactions

7. Results of the initial studies on interactions between phospholipids and a number of polypeptides and membrane proteins.

SYNTHESIS OF FATTY ACIDS CONTAINING PHOTOACTIVABLE GROUPS

The photoreactive azido group, a nitrene precursor, can easily be introduced at any desired position along a hydrocarbon chain and, in initial work, a variety of fatty acids of this type were synthesized[3] (e.g., VII and VIII in FIGURE 1). As described below, these were incorporated synthetically into phospholipids. However, extensive photo-

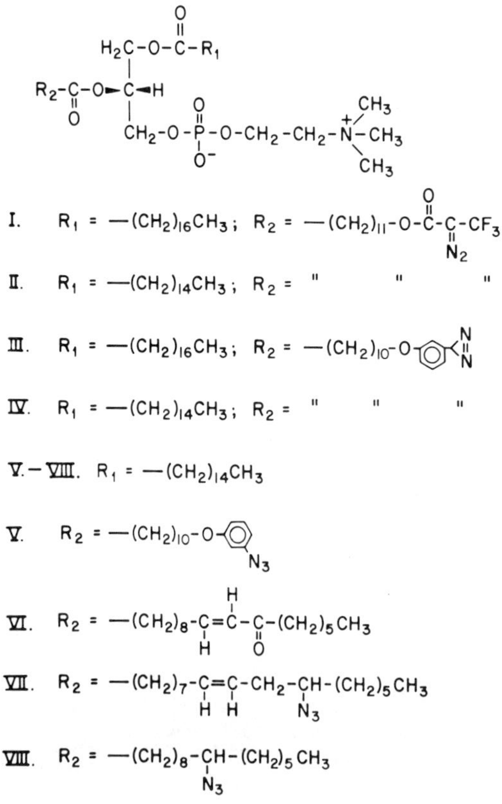

FIGURE 1. Synthetic mixed 1,2-diacylphosphatidylcholines carrying different photoactivable groups in the acyl substituents on the sn-2 position of the glycerol backbone. The phospholipids were prepared from 1-acyl-sn-glycero-3-phosphorylcholines by acylation with fatty acyl anhydrides containing photoactivable groups in the hydrocarbon chains.

lytic studies with vesicles prepared from these phospholipids showed that the nitrene intermediates formed displayed very few, if any, intermolecular insertion reactions into C—H bonds.[4] It seems probable that the cross-linking reactions previously observed with aliphatic nitrenes involved reactions with double bonds in unsaturated fatty acids; it is also probable that, in the case of aromatic nitrenes (generated from groups such as V in FIGURE 1), reactions occur with either nucleophilic groups, e.g., SH on a protein surface, or double bonds, resulting in the formation of aziridines and other products. Some of these reactions carried out by irradiation at certain wavelengths could also proceed via a radical mechanism. Diazo and diazirine groups are the familiar photoreactive carbene precursors. These, as incorporated into groups shown in fatty acids of types I and III (FIGURE 1), have proved to be the most useful in the present work. The two groups are different in regard to their chemical character and may, in fact, prove to be complementary in many ways. Aryl diazirines have, in particular, the advantages of remarkable chemical stability,[5,6] longer wavelength absorption, and relative ease of photolysis.

SYNTHESIS OF MIXED ACYL GLYCEROPHOSPHOLIPIDS

In this work, mild and efficient methods for the chemical synthesis of 1,2-diacyl and mixed diacyl glycerophospholipids are essential because the synthetic photoreactive fatty acids are sensitive—without such mild conditions these phospholipids would not be easily accessible. A satisfactory method for acylation has been developed;[7] it is illustrated by the three general cases in FIGURE 2. Of the different approaches to the synthesis of glycerophospholipids,[8-12] the one involving acylation(s) of a preformed phospholipid backbone, such as *sn*-glycero-3-phosphorylcholine (GPC) (FIGURE 1) is particularly attractive. The resulting diacyl product may, when necessary, be converted to the 2-lysophospholipid by treatment with phospholipase A$_2$. Subsequent acylation of the 2-OH group (FIGURE 2) then yields the mixed diacyl phospholipid. Commonly used reagents for acylation of GPC and lysophospholipids are fatty acyl chlorides,[13] anhydrides,[14,15] and mixed anhydrides.[11,16] The reagents are usually used in great excesses (3- to 10-fold) because the acylation of the 2-OH group is particularly sluggish. Further, the use of fatty acyl chlorides is often accompanied by the formation of significant amounts of several side products.[17] The yields of acylation products have been, most often, unsatisfactory.

N,N-Dimethyl-4-aminopyridine, which has been shown to be a powerful catalyst in many acylation reactions in organic synthesis,[18,19] has proved to be a very efficient catalyst in phospholipid synthesis as well. Acylations of GPC, lysolecithins, N-protected lysophosphatidylethanolamines, and *sn*-glycero-3-phosphate (FIGURE 2) all could be accomplished in 75–90% yields at room temperature with moderate amounts (1.2–1.5 mol equiv per OH group) of fatty acyl anhydrides.

INTERMOLECULAR CROSS-LINKING ON PHOTOLYSIS OF PHOSPHOLIPIDS CONTAINING PHOTOACTIVABLE CARBENE PRECURSORS

Using the above general method, a variety of phospholipids containing diazo and diazirine carbene precursors in the fatty acyl chains were prepared (FIGURE 3). With

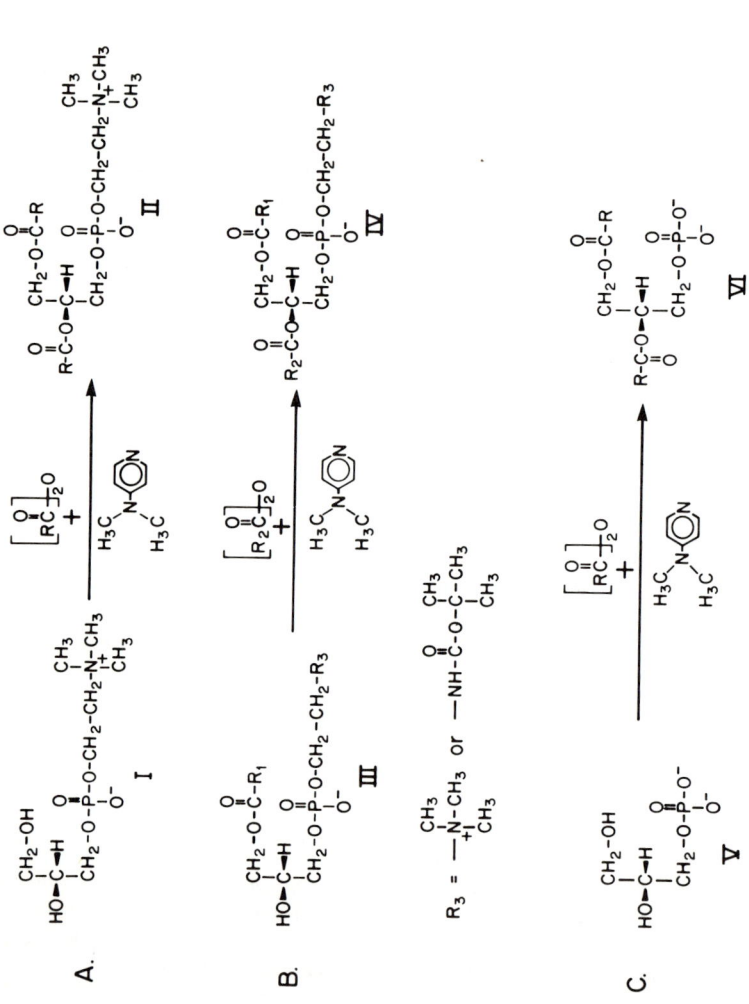

FIGURE 2. N,N-Dimethyl-4-aminopyridine-catalyzed acylation reactions in the synthesis of phospholipids. (A) Acylation of *sn*-glycero-3-phosphoryl-choline (GPC). (B) Acylation of 1-fatty acyl-*sn*-glycero-3-phosphorylcholines and N-protected ethanolamines. (C) Synthesis of phosphatidic acids by acylation of *sn*-glycero-3-phosphate.

Variation in Chain Length of Phospholipids Containing Photoactivable Groups

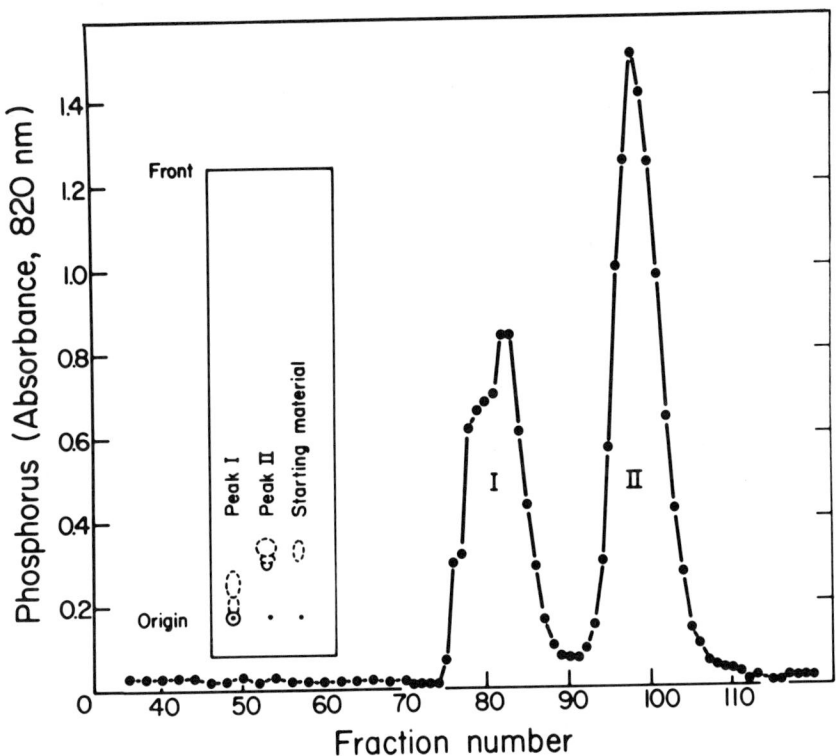

1. Variables n_1, n_2; $n_1 = 14$, 16; $n_2 = 11$, 13, 15; 10, 12, 15
2. Varying location of fatty acids with photoactivable groups (c-1, c-2, c-1,2)

FIGURE 3. The structures of the synthetic mixed acyl phosphatidylcholines, incorporating the carbene precursors β-trifluoro-α-diazopropionate and phenoxydiazirine at the ω-positions of the *sn*-2 fatty acyl chain.

FIGURE 4. The elution pattern from a Sephadex LH-20 column (2.5 × 100 cm) of the products obtained from the photolysis of 1-palmitoyl-2ω-(trifluorodiazopropionyl)lauroyl-*sn*-glycero-3-phosphorylcholines. Peak I, the intermolecularly cross-linked products, accounted for 38% of the total phosphate-containing material. Peak II results from intramolecular insertion products and side reactions of the carbene intermediate.

both sets of phospholipids, sealed vesicles were prepared by sonication. Photolysis at wavelengths greater than 315 nm yields products formed by intermolecular cross-linking reactions. These were analyzed after separation on gel permeation columns. Two representative separations of reaction products from the two types of phospholipids are shown in FIGURES 4 and 5.[4] The earlier elution of the first main peaks shows that these peaks consist of materials with molecular weights higher than those of the starting materials. The average yield of cross-linked products is 40–45% for the diazophospholipid (FIGURE 4) and 50–60% for the diazirinophospholipids (FIGURE 5). Several lines of evidence establish that these products arise by a covalent attachment of the carbene to the saturated fatty acyl chain of a second phospholipid molecule.

An experiment carried out with both types of phospholipids containing photosensitive carbene precursors uses a mixture of the photoactivable phospholipid and a

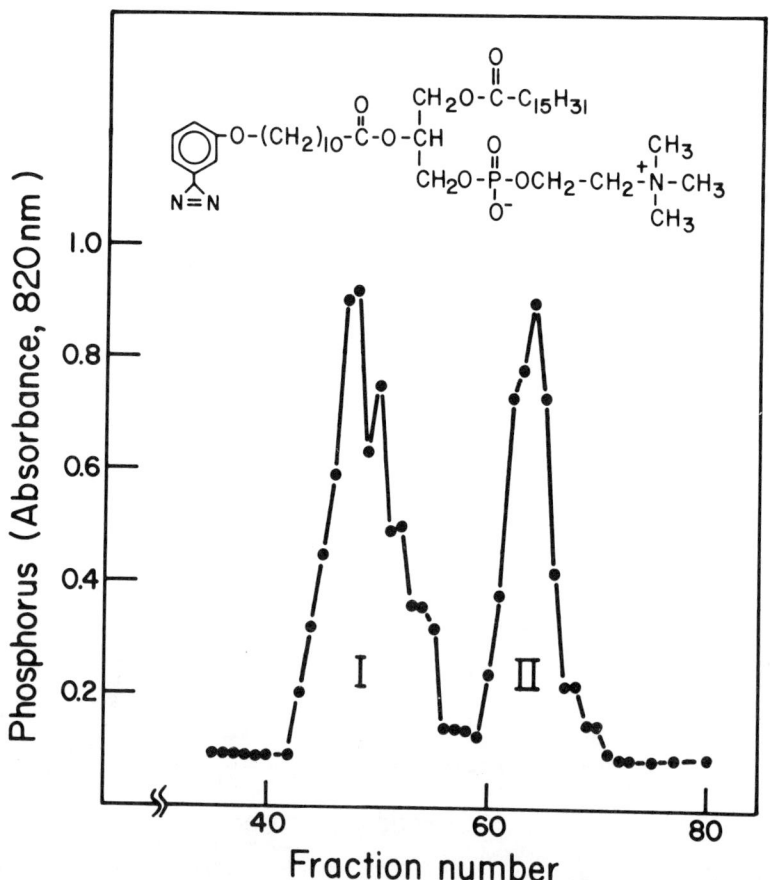

FIGURE 5. A Sephadex LH-20 column elution profile (2.5 × 100 cm) of the products obtained from the photolysis of 1-palmitoyl-2-ω-(diazirinophenoxy)undecanoyl phosphatidylcholine. Peak I accounted for 55% of the total phosphate-containing material and peak II, the remainder.

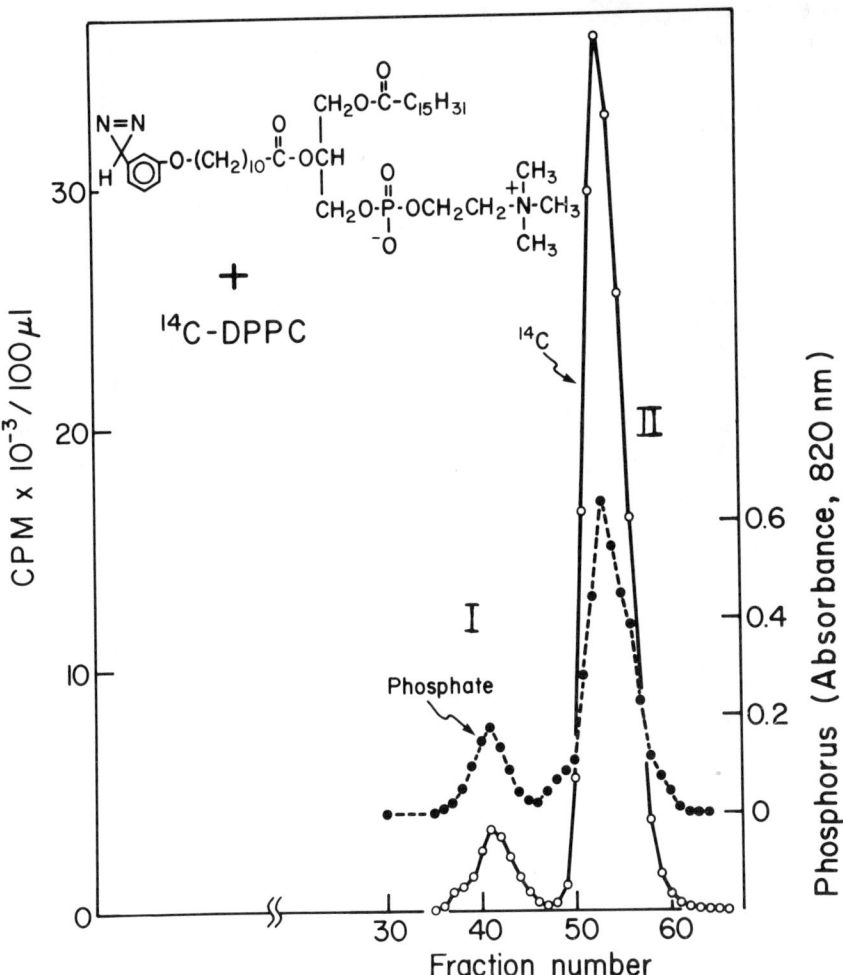

FIGURE 6. A Sephadex LH-20 column elution profile of the products obtained from the photolysis of vesicles prepared from an equimolar mixture of the diazirinophospholipid and [^{14}C]DPL. Peak I accounted for 11% of the total radioactivity.

radioactively labeled phospholipid such as [^{14}C]-dipalmitoyl phosphatidylcholine (DPL), which can serve only as the "acceptor" of the generated carbene. Cross-linking to the radioactive phospholipid should give a radioactively labeled dimer that can be analyzed. Results of a typical photolysis experiment are shown in FIGURE 6. (Conditions for the maximal amount of formation of the radioactive dimer by adjusting the ratio of the two phospholipids have not been worked out.) Peak I contains the dimer, which has been studied by a number of degradative methods, as shown in FIGURE 7. The radioactivity was distributed in the multiple products, as was expected. Attention should be drawn to the products formed on methoxide-catalyzed

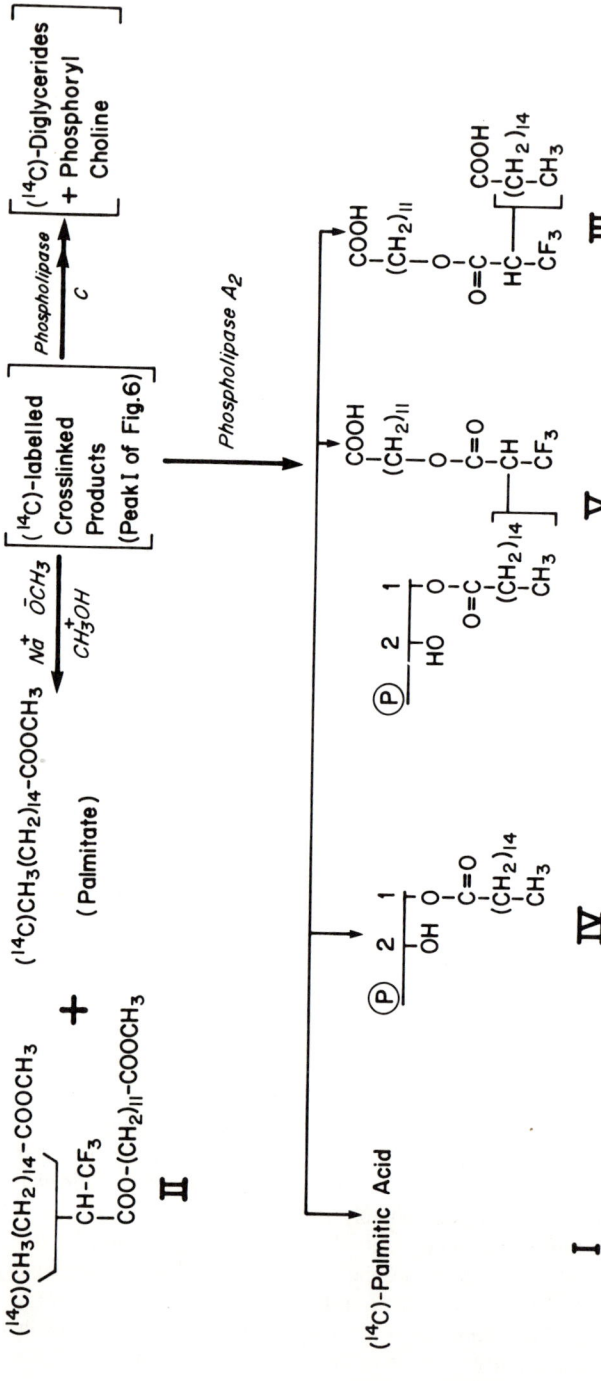

FIGURE 7. The methods of degradation used for the analysis of cross-linked phospholipids. Only the [^{14}C]-palmitic acid and products containing this radioactive residue are shown. P stands for phosphoryl choline.

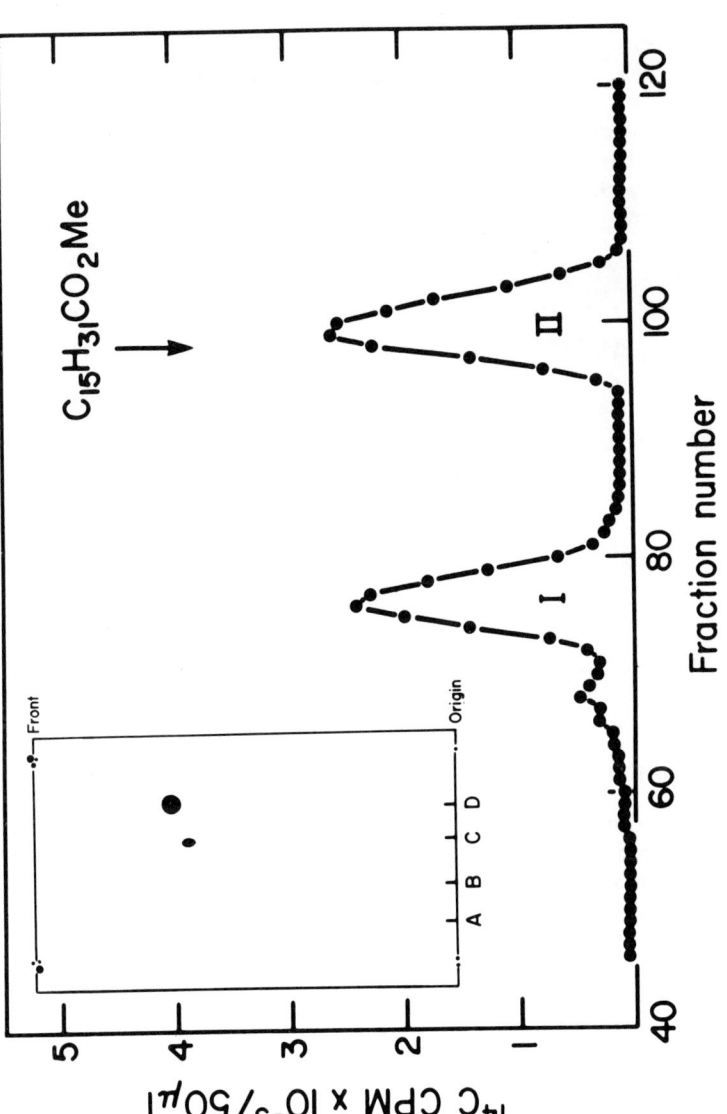

FIGURE 8. A Sephadex LH-20 chromatogram of the products obtained after the transesterification of Peak I (FIGURE 3). Fractions 72–81 (Peak I) and 95–105 (Peak II) were pooled for analysis. The inset is the autoradiogram of silica gel TLC (chloroform: ether (9:1 v/v) of Peaks I and II. A: mixture as present in Peaks I and II; B: Peak II; C: Peak I; and D: methyl palmitate standard.

transesterification of the cross-linked products. As expected, [^{14}C]-methyl palmitate and the ^{14}C-labeled dimeric fatty acid ester were produced and their ratio, as judged by their radioactivity, was 1:1 (FIGURE 8). The results of corresponding sets of experiments with the diazirinophenoxy phospholipids were identical.

Further experiments on the demonstration of intermolecular cross-linking were carried out by including [^{14}C]-cholesterol in phospholipid vesicles and, again, the formation of products containing the phospholipids and radioactive cholesterol was demonstrated.

From these studies and those reported below, the general structures of the cross-linked products of the diazo and diazirine derivatives after transesterification are shown in FIGURE 9.

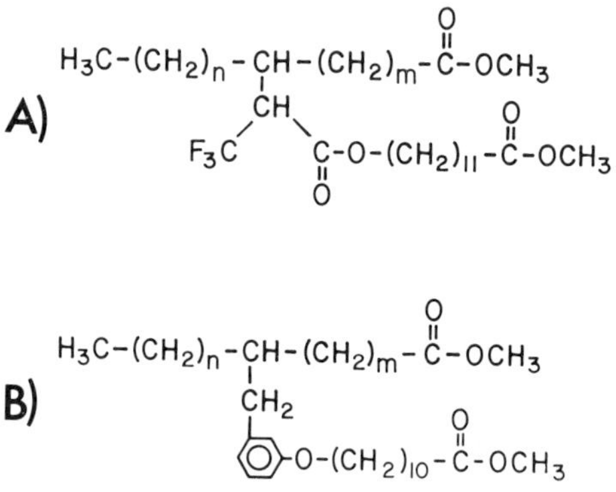

A)
$$H_3C-(CH_2)_n-CH-(CH_2)_m-\overset{\overset{\textstyle O}{\|}}{C}-OCH_3$$

B)
$$H_3C-(CH_2)_n-CH-(CH_2)_m-\overset{\overset{\textstyle O}{\|}}{C}-OCH_3$$

FIGURE 9. The general structures of the cross-linked fatty acid esters obtained using (A) the diazo and (B) the phenyldiazirine phospholipid systems.

DETERMINATION OF THE SITES OF CROSS-LINKS IN INTERMOLECULAR REACTIONS

Having demonstrated the occurrence of photocatalyzed intermolecular insertion reactions, it is important to ask if there is any relationship between the sites of cross-links in the acceptor hydrocarbon chain and the chain carrying the carbene group. Because of the ordered packing and the cooperation in hydrophobic interactions between the fatty acyl chains, a correlation may indeed hold. If a pattern could be seen in the points of cross-links, then, in principle, a potentially useful approach to the study of the topography of interactions between membrane components would become available. As described below, a correlation has indeed been demonstrated, with respect to the sites of cross-links, for both the diazo and diazirino phospholipids and, further, the results are consistent with the recent conclusion that the sn-1 and sn-2 fatty acyl chains are out of step by a few carbon atoms.[20,21]

Finding a method for the quantitative analysis of the sites of intermolecular cross-linking between the two fatty acyl chains was of critical importance. Fortunately, this was made possible by the use of mass spectrometry in work with both series of cross-linked products.

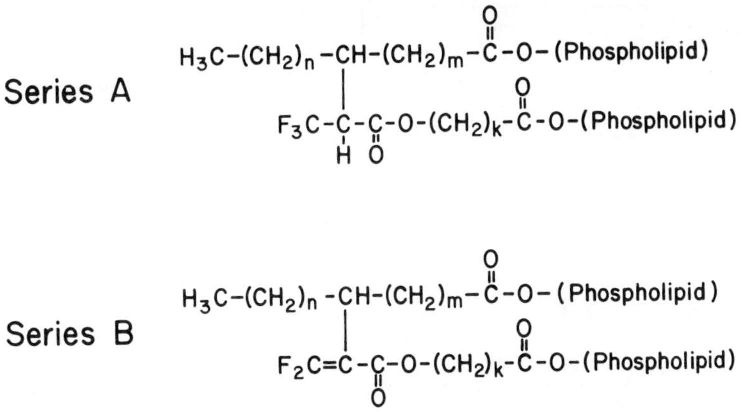

Series A

$$H_3C-(CH_2)_n-CH-(CH_2)_m-\overset{\overset{\displaystyle O}{\|}}{C}-O-(Phospholipid)$$

$$F_3C-\underset{\underset{\displaystyle H}{|}}{\overset{}{C}}-\underset{\underset{\displaystyle O}{\|}}{C}-O-(CH_2)_k-\overset{\overset{\displaystyle O}{\|}}{C}-O-(Phospholipid)$$

Series B

$$H_3C-(CH_2)_n-CH-(CH_2)_m-\overset{\overset{\displaystyle O}{\|}}{C}-O-(Phospholipid)$$

$$F_2C=C-\underset{\underset{\displaystyle O}{\|}}{C}-O-(CH_2)_k-\overset{\overset{\displaystyle O}{\|}}{C}-O-(Phospholipid)$$

FIGURE 10. The general structures of the two series of cross-linked products obtained by the photolysis of phospholipids containing a β-trifluoro-α-diazopropionyl group in the *sn*-2 fatty acyl chain.

Determination of Sites of Cross-Links in Phospholipids Containing β-Trifluoro-α-Diazopropionyl Groups

The fragmentation patterns of the cross-linked structures shown in FIGURE 9 would have been difficult to interpret (for Series B) had not two modifications of the experimental strategy for cross-linking reactions enabled us to use mass spectrometry reliably. For phospholipids carrying the diazo group it was found that, when photolyses are performed using the highly ordered multilamellar structures, the primary products formed are exclusively those shown in Series B (FIGURE 10),[22] while

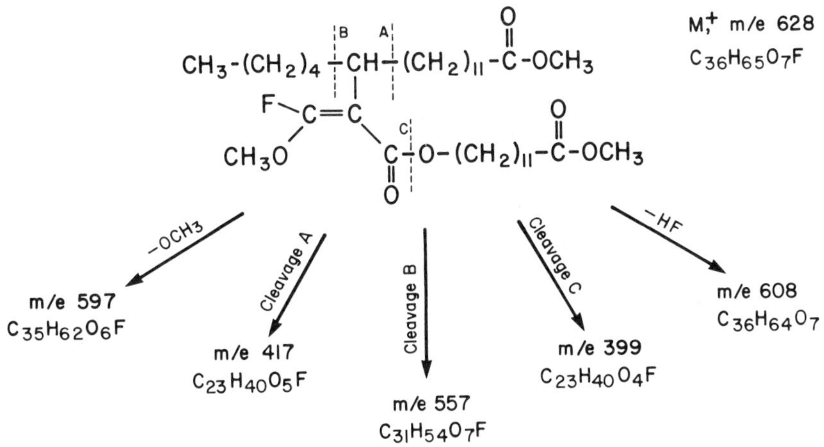

FIGURE 11. The major modes of mass spectral fragmentation observed in compounds of the B series after transesterification.

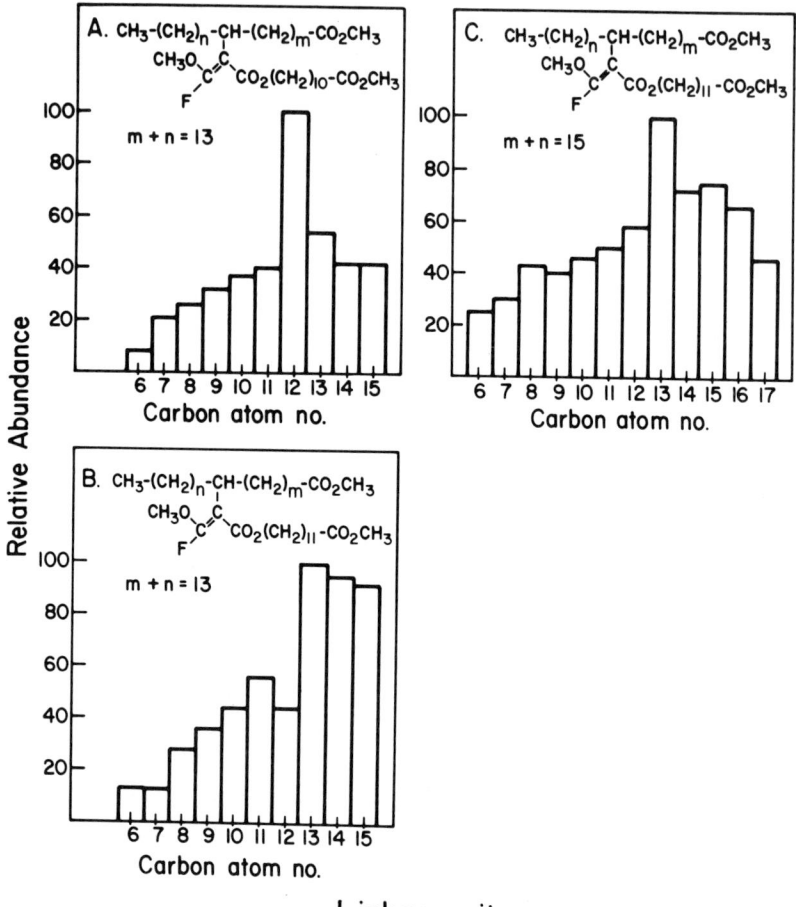

FIGURE 12. The distribution of linkage sites for cross-linking in the diesters obtained from the transesterification of the series B compounds, calculated on the basis of the abundance of the fragment ions arising from cleavage A (FIGURE 11).

photolysis of unilamellar vesicles prepared by sonication gives the adducts shown in Series A (FIGURE 10). The products shown in FIGURE 9 would arise from phospholipids of Series A (FIGURE 10) by transesterification. The presence of the double bond in Series B, which is allylic to the point of the cross-link, influences the fragmentation pattern (FIGURE 11) and the spectra are more readily interpretable.

The relative abundance of the ions was obtained from the low-resolution electron impact spectra; this information indicates the distribution of the positions of cross-linking. As seen in FIGURE 12, the position of maximal cross-linking varies with the chain length of the fatty acid containing the diazo group. There is a broad distribution of cross-linking, with the amount decreasing toward the polar headgroup of the phospholipid. The point of maximum cross-linking in each case is approximately three carbons shorter than the length of the photolabeled chain.

Determination of the Sites of Cross-Links in Phospholipids Carrying Diazirinophenoxy Groups

For the cross-linked products of the diazirinophospholipids, the major mode of fragmentation was, as expected, a cleavage at the benzylic site (FIGURE 13). The benzylic cation appeared with *m/e* at 306 instead of 305 due to γ-hydrogen abstraction. The mass spectrum also exhibited a peak at 307, a contribution from the natural abundance of the ^{13}C isotope. If selected carbon atoms in the acceptor chain were to be dideuterated, one at a time, a study of the abundance ratio of 306 peaks to 307 peaks would determine the extent of deuterium transfer to the benzylic position by carbene insertion to the C—H bond. It is assumed that the short-lived carbene inserts into the C—H bond in a concerted fashion and that the isotopic effect that would pertain in all cases is minimal. Thus, a series of phospholipids, which were specifically deuterated in the *sn*-1 chain and carried the diazirinophenoxy group in the *sn*-2 chain, were prepared (SCHEMA 1) and the unilamellar vesicles composed of the deuterated phospholipids were photolyzed. The cross-linked phospholipids were transesterified and the dimeric fatty esters were analyzed by low-resolution electron impact ionization mass spectrometry. The relative abundance of peaks at *m/e* 306, 307, and 308 were determined and used to calculate the extent of deuterium transfer to different cross-linking sites. The results to date are summarized in TABLE 1.

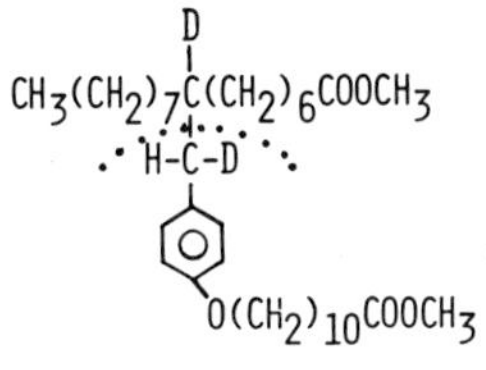

$$\overset{\displaystyle D}{\underset{\displaystyle }{CH_3(CH_2)_7C(CH_2)_6COOCH_3}}$$

$$H-C-D$$

$$O(CH_2)_{10}COOCH_3$$

$$C_{36}H_{60}D_2O_5 \quad M^+ \; 576.472$$

	DEUTERATED		NON-DEUTERATED	
	MOL. WT. OF FRAGMENT	INTENSITIES OF IONS	MOL. WT. OF FRAGMENT	INTENSITIES OF IONS
BENZYLIC	306.22	(4556)	306.22	(3832)
	307.22	(3550)	307.22	(1344)
TOP ACYL CHAIN	269.245	(2528)	269.24	(832)
	270.254	(3756)		
	271.259	(3676)		

FIGURE 13. The major modes of mass spectral fragmentation observed in cross-linked diazirino fatty esters. For comparison, the high-resolution mass spectral data with the nondeuterated compound is shown on the right side of the figure.

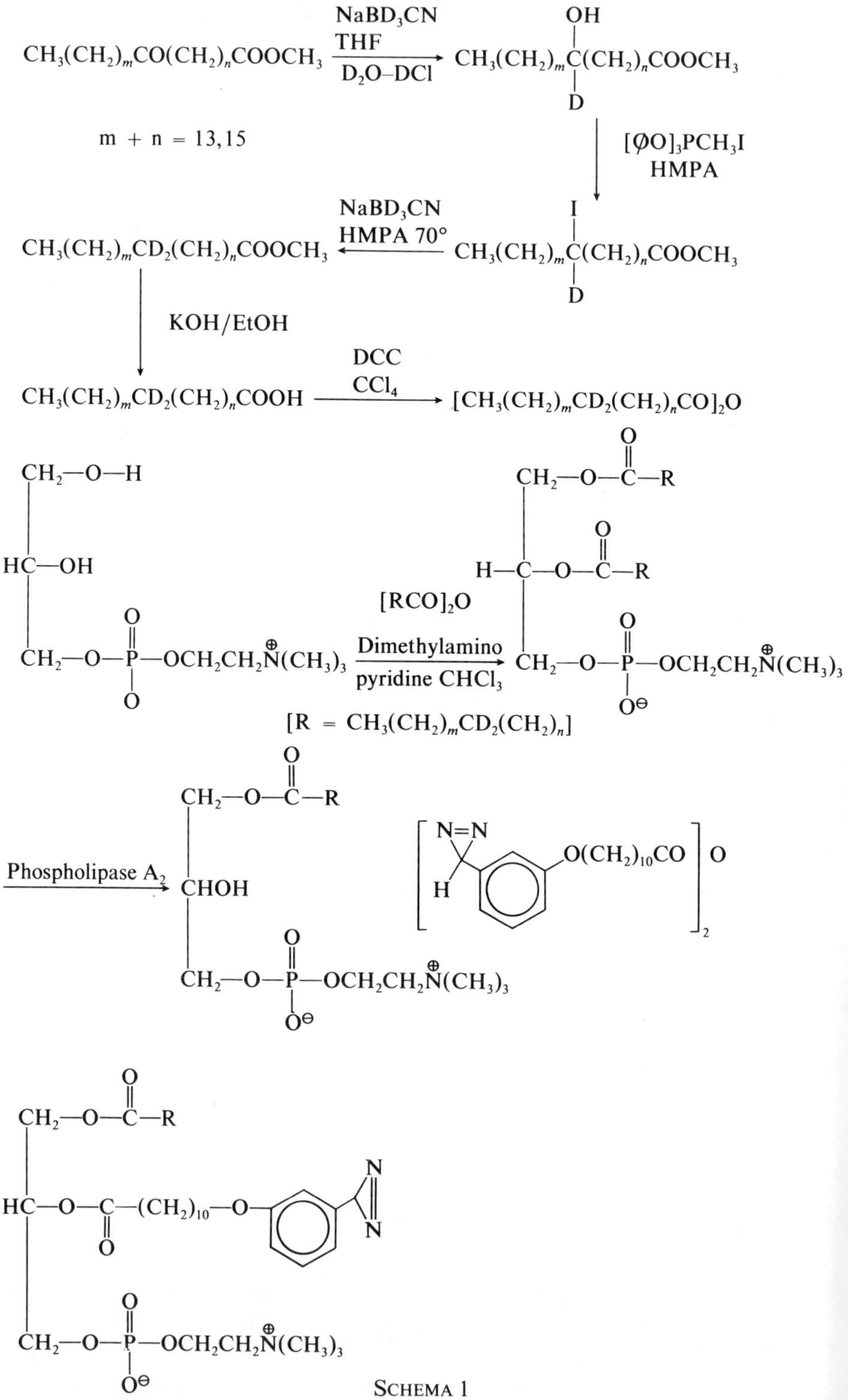

$$CH_3(CH_2)_mCO(CH_2)_nCOOCH_3 \xrightarrow[\text{D}_2\text{O–DCl}]{\text{NaBD}_3\text{CN} \atop \text{THF}} CH_3(CH_2)_m\underset{\underset{D}{|}}{\overset{\overset{OH}{|}}{C}}(CH_2)_nCOOCH_3$$

m + n = 13,15

$$\downarrow \begin{array}{c}[\emptyset O]_3PCH_3I \\ \text{HMPA}\end{array}$$

$$CH_3(CH_2)_mCD_2(CH_2)_nCOOCH_3 \xleftarrow[\text{HMPA 70°}]{\text{NaBD}_3\text{CN}} CH_3(CH_2)_m\underset{\underset{D}{|}}{\overset{\overset{I}{|}}{C}}(CH_2)_nCOOCH_3$$

$$\downarrow \text{KOH/EtOH}$$

$$CH_3(CH_2)_mCD_2(CH_2)_nCOOH \xrightarrow[\text{CCl}_4]{\text{DCC}} [CH_3(CH_2)_mCD_2(CH_2)_nCO]_2O$$

$$\begin{array}{c} CH_2\text{—O—H} \\ | \\ HC\text{—OH} \\ | \\ CH_2\text{—O—}\overset{\overset{O}{\|}}{\underset{\underset{O}{\|}}{P}}\text{—OCH}_2CH_2\overset{\oplus}{N}(CH_3)_3 \end{array} \xrightarrow[\text{pyridine CHCl}_3]{\text{Dimethylamino}} \begin{array}{c} CH_2\text{—O—}\overset{\overset{O}{\|}}{C}\text{—R} \\ | \\ H\text{—C—O—}\overset{\overset{O}{\|}}{C}\text{—R} \\ | \\ CH_2\text{—O—}\overset{\overset{O}{\|}}{\underset{\underset{O^\ominus}{|}}{P}}\text{—OCH}_2CH_2\overset{\oplus}{N}(CH_3)_3 \end{array}$$

$$[\text{RCO]}_2\text{O}$$

$$[R = CH_3(CH_2)_mCD_2(CH_2)_n]$$

$$\xrightarrow{\text{Phospholipase A}_2} \begin{array}{c} CH_2\text{—O—}\overset{\overset{O}{\|}}{C}\text{—R} \\ | \\ CHOH \\ | \\ CH_2\text{—O—}\overset{\overset{O}{\|}}{\underset{\underset{O^\ominus}{|}}{P}}\text{—OCH}_2CH_2\overset{\oplus}{N}(CH_3)_3 \end{array}$$

$$\left[\begin{array}{c} N=N \\ \diagdown \diagup \\ \underset{H}{C} \end{array} \!\!\! \text{—} \bigcirc \text{—O(CH}_2)_{10}CO \right]_2 O$$

$$\begin{array}{c} CH_2\text{—O—}\overset{\overset{O}{\|}}{C}\text{—R} \\ | \\ HC\text{—O—}\underset{\underset{O}{\|}}{C}\text{—(CH}_2)_{10}\text{—O—}\bigcirc\text{—}\begin{array}{c}N\\ \diagup \\ C \\ \diagdown \\ N\end{array} \\ | \\ CH_2\text{—O—}\overset{\overset{O}{\|}}{\underset{\underset{O^\ominus}{|}}{P}}\text{—OCH}_2CH_2\overset{\oplus}{N}(CH_3)_3 \end{array}$$

SCHEMA 1

178

TABLE 1

ANALYSIS OF CROSS-LINKING POSITIONS

	Excess Intensity versus D_0^*	D_1 Transfer (%)
D_0	0	0
D_2-C_7	11	9.9
D_2-C_8	9	8.3
D_2-C_9	15	13.0
D_2-C_{10}	18	15.3

*The intensity of the 307 peak is obtained by normalizing with respect to the intensity of the 306 peak.

So, in this set of experiments, there is a distribution of cross-linking such that the extent of cross-linking increases toward the more hydrophobic methyl terminus of the fatty acyl chain, as might be expected from the length of the chain carrying the diazirine group. It is clear from what has been shown with the two sets of phospholipids that cross-linking does not occur at single site. Rather, a distribution of cross-linking is observed, with the maximum at the position most consistent with the molecular structures of phospholipids in bilayers.[20,21] These studies need to be extended further, but the results offer promise for cross-linking reactions at roughly predetermined distances from the exterior of the bilayer.

ATTEMPTS TO DESIGN MORE VERSATILE CARBENE-GENERATING GROUPS

The results described above, which used the aryl diazirine and the diazopropionyl system, encouraged us to design new groups that would insert into C—H bonds with minimal intramolecular rearrangements and that could be placed anywhere along the fatty acyl chains. In the work described above, the diazo or diazirino groups are at the ω positions of the fatty acyl chains, and their positions can be varied only by altering the length of the fatty acyl chain that carries them. Ideally, it should be possible both to retain the desired length of the fatty acyl chain and to shift the photoactivable group up and down the chain as required. Other important considerations are perturbations in the packing of hydrocarbon chains and the presence of polar groups, such as the ester and the ether linkages, in the above phospholipids; such structural effects should be kept to a minimum. These considerations seem to suggest an aliphatic diazirine, but the carbene thus derived has been shown to undergo an extensive 1,2-hydride shift, resulting in olefinic products.[23] However, the possibility exists that the ordered packing of hydrocarbon chains in phospholipid bilayers would restrict the conformational mobility of the carbene and promote intermolecular insertion. Therefore, we prepared a phospholipid that contained 10-azistearic acid in position *sn*-2 and [^{14}C]-labeled palmitic acid in *sn*-1. When multilamellar liposomes prepared from it were photolyzed, the formation of some (7%) phospholipid dimer was observed. However, further analysis showed that the dimer did not arise by insertion of the carbene into the C—H bonds of the radio-labeled palmitic acid but by dimerization of two photoreactive fatty acids to form an azine.

It seemed logical to replace the hydrogens, α and α', on the carbenic site by

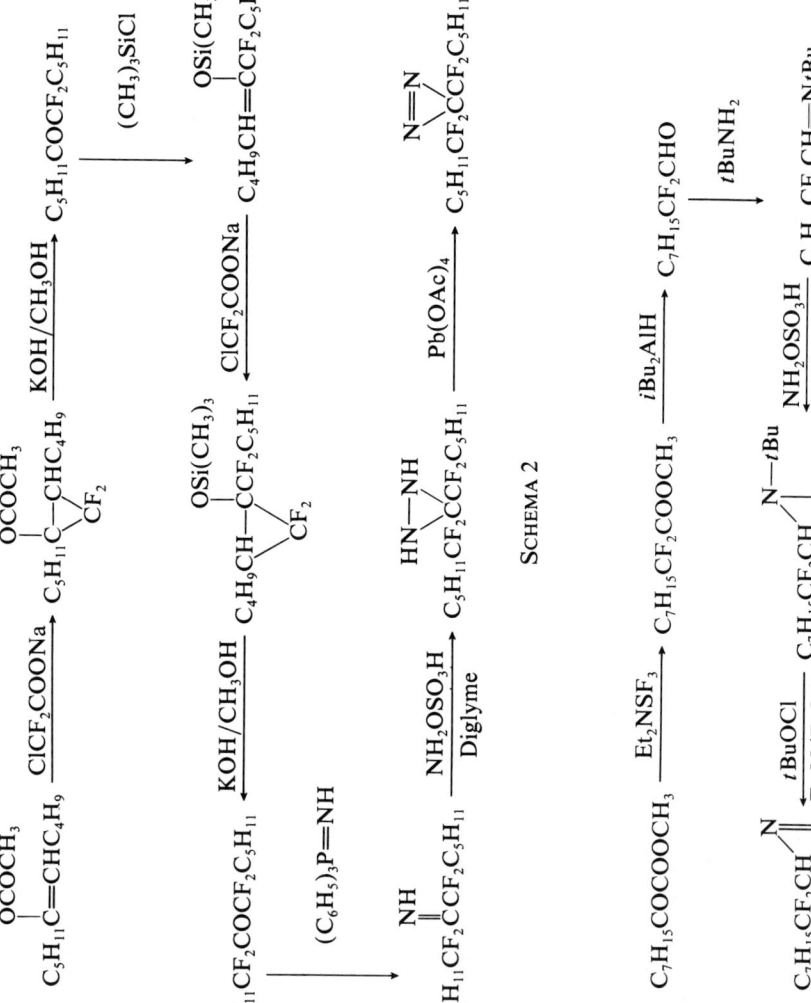

SCHEMA 2

SCHEMA 3

fluorines. Because the length and Van der Waals radius of a C—F bond are close to those of a C—H bond,[24] these structures should remain relatively small. The replacement of hydrogen by fluorine was suggested by reports that showed that photogenerated carbenes from the β-trifluoro-α-diazopropionyl group,[25] perfluoro-diazo compounds,[26] and diazirines[27] are capable of insertion into C—H bonds without any significant intramolecular rearrangement involving fluorine migration. The syntheses of two simple aliphatic fluoroalkyl diazirines are shown in SCHEMATA 2 and 3.

The key intermediates in the diazirine syntheses were the α-perfluorocarbonyl compounds. The α,α'-tetrafluoroketone in SCHEMA 2 was prepared by a homologation reaction brought about by the addition of difluorocarbene to an enolic double bond, followed by solvolytic opening of the difluorocyclopropanol.[28] The α-difluoroester (SCHEMA 3) was obtained by fluorination of an α-ketoester with diethylamino sulfur trifluoride.[29] The syntheses of the fluorodiazirines (SCHEMATA 2 and 3) were achieved[30] by combining and modifying methods used for the syntheses of related diazirines.[5,27,31]

The photochemical reactions brought about by irradiating these diazirines in cyclohexane or methanol are shown in SCHEMA 4.

Upon irradiation at 310 nm, both the diazirines undergo rapid photoisomerization to the stable linear diazo compounds and photofragmentation to the carbene. The carbenes, however, did not insert to any extent into the C—H or O—H bonds of the solvents but reacted intramolecularly, i.e., they formed a cyclopropyl derivative, which resulted from insertion into the C—H bond β to the carbene, and a difluoro olefin, which resulted from alkyl chain migration. One remarkable property of the tetrafluoro diazirines is that isomerization between the diazirine and the diazo compound is reversible and wavelength-dependent. Upon irradiation at 310 nm, the diazirine isomerizes to the diazo compound and the diazo compounds revert to the diazirine at

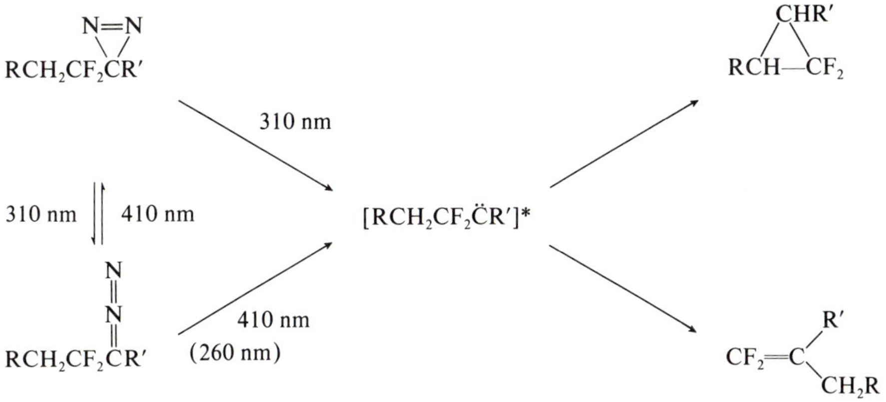

a)   R = —C$_4$H$_9$ R' = —CF$_2$C$_5$H$_{11}$

b)   R = C$_6$H$_{13}$ R' = H

SCHEMA 4

410 nm. No such isomerization is observed with the difluorodiazirine, nor does it occur if the tetrafluoro diazo compound is irradiated at 260 nm.

Photoreactive Carbene Precursors as Components of Polar Headgroups in Phospholipids

In addition to understanding the interactions of the acyl chains of phospholipids with each other and with membrane proteins within the bilayer, it is desirable to probe the interactions between the polar headgroups and the nonembedded parts of membrane proteins. There is a great heterogeneity in the natures of lipid headgroups in biological membranes, the meaning of which is not clear. Membrane enzymes may show varying degrees of specificity with respect to the polar headgroups. For example, the activity of inner mitochondrial enzyme β-hydroxybutyrate dehydrogenase shows an absolute requirement for the choline headgroup.[32-34]

It would be very desirable to have a series of phospholipids with photoactivable carbene precursors located in the headgroup region. A number of derivatives can be envisaged, two of which, prepared some time ago, are shown in Figure 14. It is interesting that one of these has already proved of interest in the study of phospholipase A_2 from snake venom.[35] Another particularly attractive carbene precursor is the 3-aryl-3H-diazirine. Photogenerated carbenes would be expected to insert into N—H, C—H, or O—H bonds of membrane proteins and, perhaps, headgroups of neighboring phospholipid molecules. Cross-linking studies of this type would help determine the amino acid residues in the parts of the membrane proteins that lie at the hydrocarbon-water interface. Such a study could also aid our understanding of the nature of the highly specific interactions between phospholipids and certain membrane enzymes, such as β-hydroxybutyrate dehydrogenase.

Another potentially useful headgroup label is a quaternized diazirino pyridine, which could replace choline. The positive charge is preserved and the size of the label approximates that of an N-propyldimethylammonium group. The synthesis of pyridyl-3H-diazirines has been reported[5] and methods have now been developed to

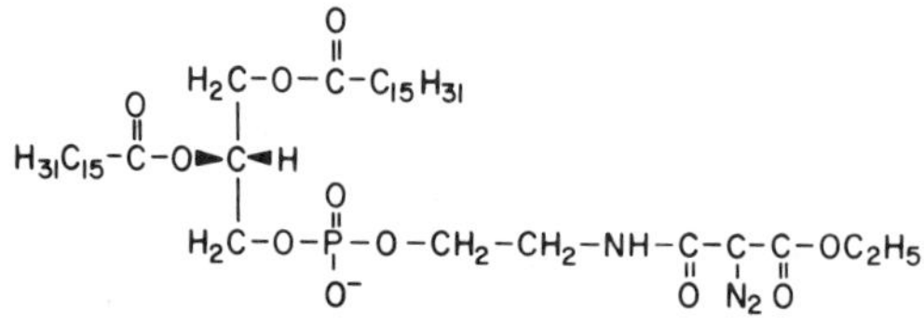

XXIV

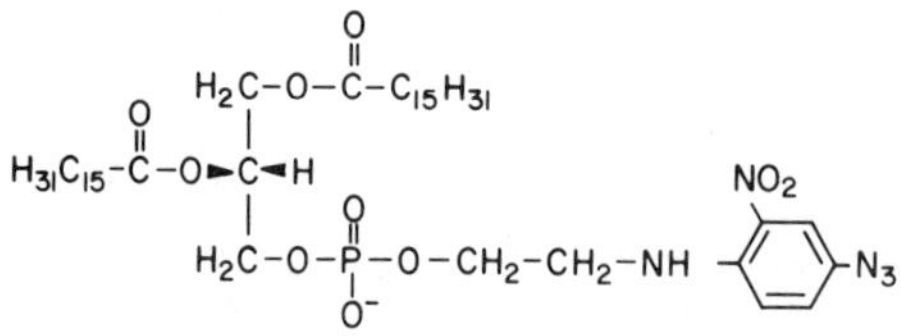

FIGURE 14. Structures of phosphatidylethanolamines carrying photoreactive polar headgroups.

XXV

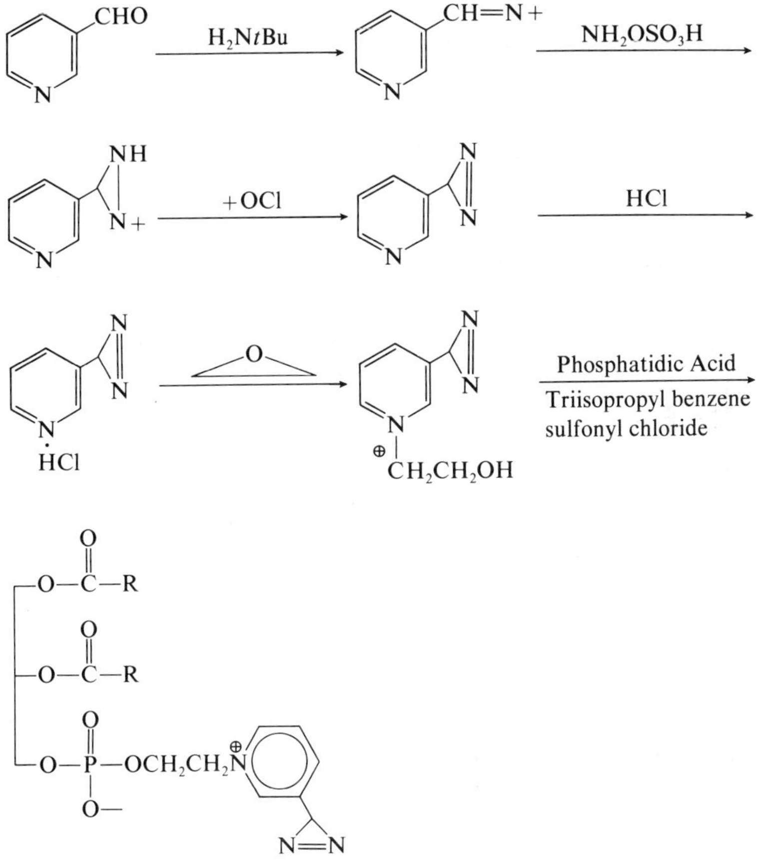

SCHEMA 5

quaternize this group with a β-hydroxyethyl group. The synthetic methodology presently being used is shown in SCHEMA 5. The diazirine substituted at the 4-position of the pyridine ring is also being synthesized.

PHOSPHOLIPIDS CONTAINING CARBENE PRECURSORS IN THE STUDY OF MODEL MEMBRANES

Cross-Linking in Mixed Phospholipid Systems

An important consideration in the development of the photochemical probes is to see whether functional groups like double bonds can scavenge the carbenes in the bilayer and thus prevent random insertion into membrane components. A series of competitive experiments were done to determine the extent, if any, of such effects. A typical experiment is outlined in FIGURE 15. Competition between dipalmitoyl lecithin

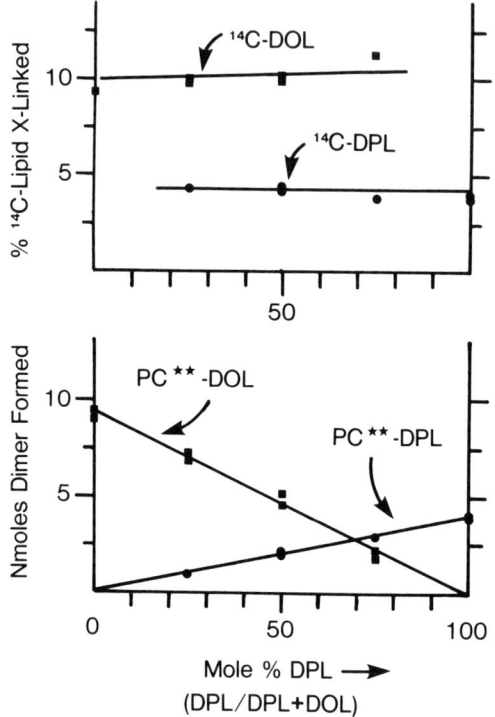

FIGURE 15. The competition between DPL and DOL for cross-linking to the diazirine phospholipid (denoted PC**). The mole ratio of diazirine phospholipid to (DOL + DPL) was 1:1 in all cases. Top panel: the percentage of DPL or DOL cross-linked as a function of (DPL/DPL + DOL). Bottom panel: nmol of dimeric products formed.

(DPL) and dioleyl lecithin (DOL) for cross-linking to the diazirine phospholipid IV (FIGURE 1) was studied by photolyzing various mixtures of IV/[^{14}C]DPL/DOL and IV/DPL/[^{14}C]DOL. The results show that there is some preference for cross-linking to DOL, presumably due to some specificity of the carbene for the double bond in the 9–10 position of the acyl chains in DOL. However, significant cross-linking to DPL is also observed in the presence of DOL. Phospholipids containing linolenoyl chains (double bonds in 9–10, 12–13, and 15–16 positions) or acyl chains with ω-phenyl groups have been shown not to act as carbene scavengers.

Cross-Linking in Phase Separation Studies

Synthetic diacyl phospholipids are known to undergo a phase transition at a characteristic temperature commonly known as the order-disorder transition. This transition consists of the cooperative melting of the bilayer acyl chains from a relatively ordered to a more disordered state. Differential scanning calorimetry (DSC) recordings are presented in FIGURE 16 for multilamellar dispersions of the diazirino phospholipid, DPL, and a 1:1 mixture of DPL and DOL. The 1:1 DPL/DOL mixture exhibits a broad transition with peak maxima at ~30 °C and a second transition at ~ –19 °C, indicating that lateral phase separation (a two-phase zone) occurs at certain temperatures. Thus, as the 1:1 mixture is cooled, a broad transition, which consists of acyl chain solidification in a DPL-rich phase, accompanied by lateral

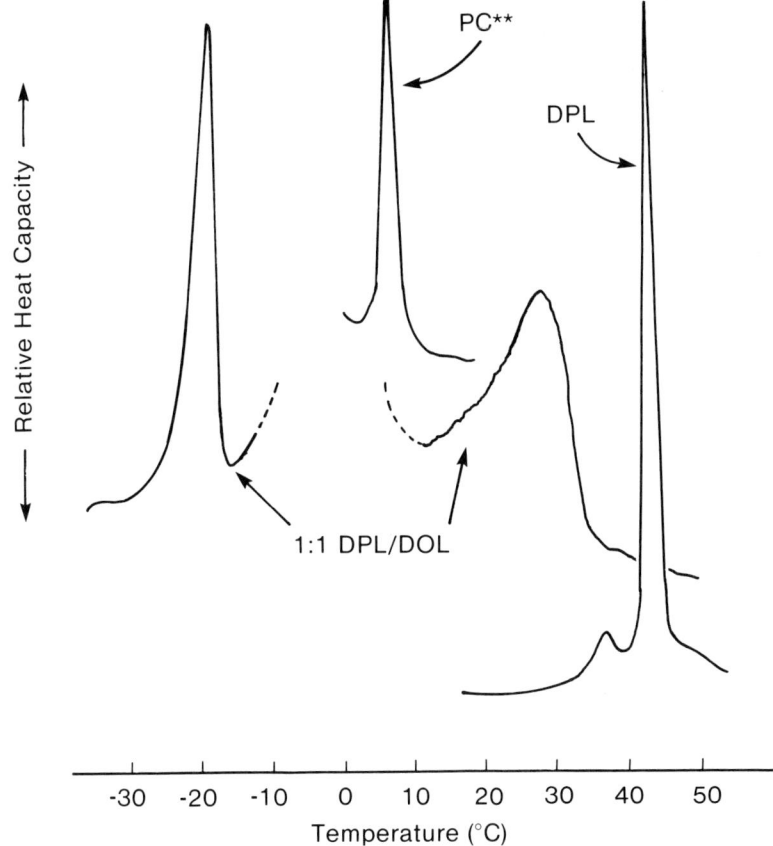

FIGURE 16. Differential scanning calorimetry (DSC) recordings of diazirino phospholipid, DPL and a 1:1 mixture of DOL and DPL. The heating rate was 5 °C/min.

separation of a fluid DOL-rich phase occurs over the range 10–32 °C. As the temperature is decreased further, the acyl chains in the DOL-rich phase solidify at −19 °C. In order to determine whether the distribution of carbene insertion products is sensitive to the physical states of the phospholipids, the temperature dependence of cross-linking was studied for a DPL/DOL/diazirino lipid mixture (1:1:0.2 molar ratio). The results obtained are shown in FIGURE 17. Above ~30 °C, the distribution of dimeric products remains invariant with temperature. However, at temperatures below ~30 °C, the production of diazirino phospholipid-DOL dimer increases, while the diazirino phospholipid-DPL dimer production decreases. It appears that, at temperatures below ~30 °C, the diazirino phospholipid partitions preferentially into the more fluid DOL-rich phase. Thus, the cross-linking method can detect lateral phase separations and, more importantly, has the capability of indicating which particular molecular species is undergoing phase separation. Studies aimed at determining whether this approach can be used to detect lateral phase separation in biological membranes are currently underway.

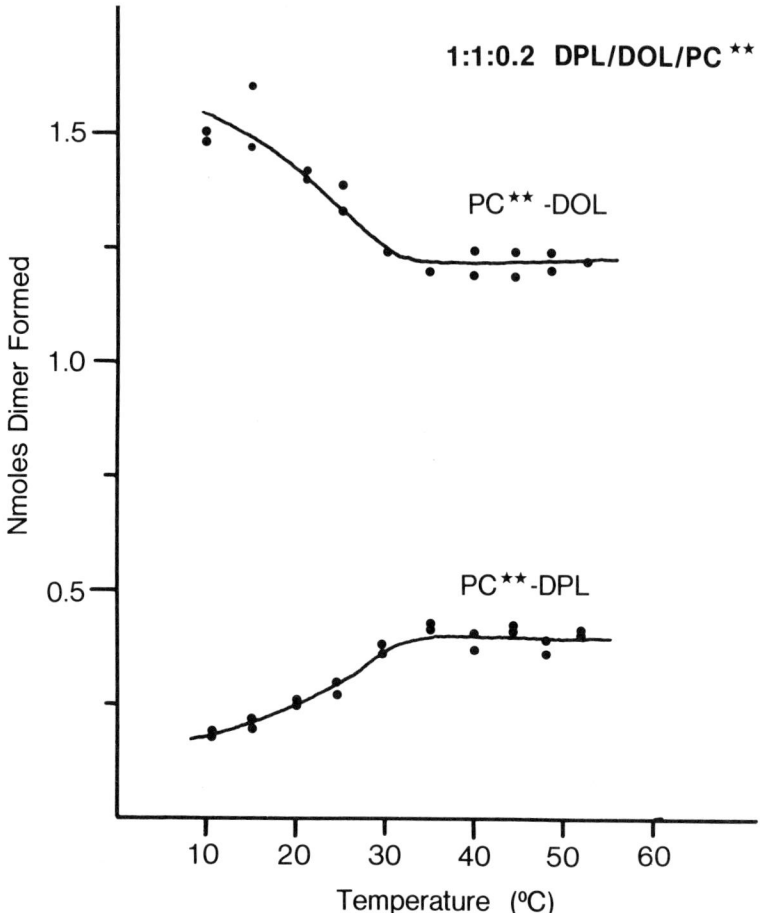

FIGURE 17. The distribution of cross-linked dimeric products generated by photolysis of a DPL/DOL/diazirino phospholipid mixture (1:1:0.2) as a function of temperature.

STUDIES OF INTERACTIONS BETWEEN MEMBRANE PROTEINS AND PHOSPHOLIPIDS

In recent years, it has become clear that there are at least two major classes of membrane proteins. Peripheral proteins,[36] which have a relatively weak association and can be separated from membranes relatively easily, form one broad group. The second class, designated "integral proteins" by Singer,[36] have strong hydrophobic associations with membranes and are usually very difficult to isolate and purify. Solubilization without inactivation requires carefully chosen detergents; even so, significant amounts of phospholipid, which is difficult to remove completely, may remain.

When without phospholipids, membrane enzymes often lose their activity, but they may be reactivated by adding phospholipids. Thus, membrane proteins display strong interactions with phospholipids. Since these proteins undergo lateral motion and since they often interact with other proteins in the membranes (e.g., the activation of adenyl cyclase after the formation of the hormone-receptor complex), it is clear that the study of interactions between phospholipids and proteins is important to the understanding of membrane functions. It is hoped that the present organochemical approach will yield some insights regarding the topology of the membrane-embedded proteins, the nature of the surface contacts between phospholipids and the proteins, and, finally, the nature of the interactions among proteins within the membranes.

A number of considerations influenced our choice of membrane proteins. The most important consideration was the availability of a reliable purification procedure so that the protein's function could be reconstituted by the synthetic phospholipids. Secondly, the amino acid sequence of the proteins had to be known. Thirdly, as will be evident below, the proteins chosen were such that the main classes of membrane-associated proteins were represented.

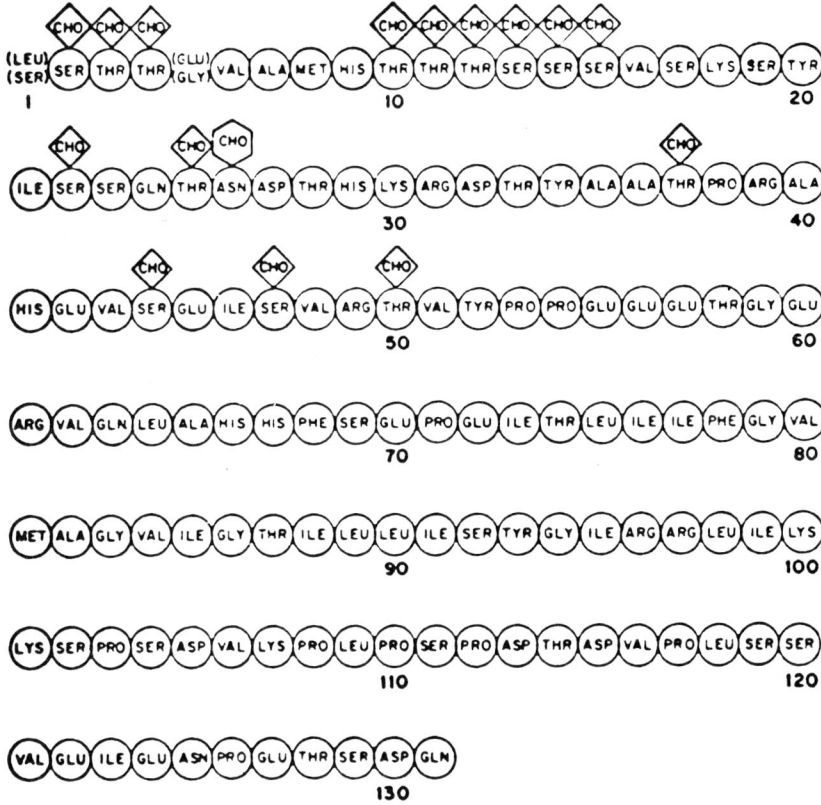

FIGURE 18. The amino acid sequence of human erythrocyte glycophorin A.[39] Boxes above certain residues indicate the attachment of oligosaccharides at these sites.

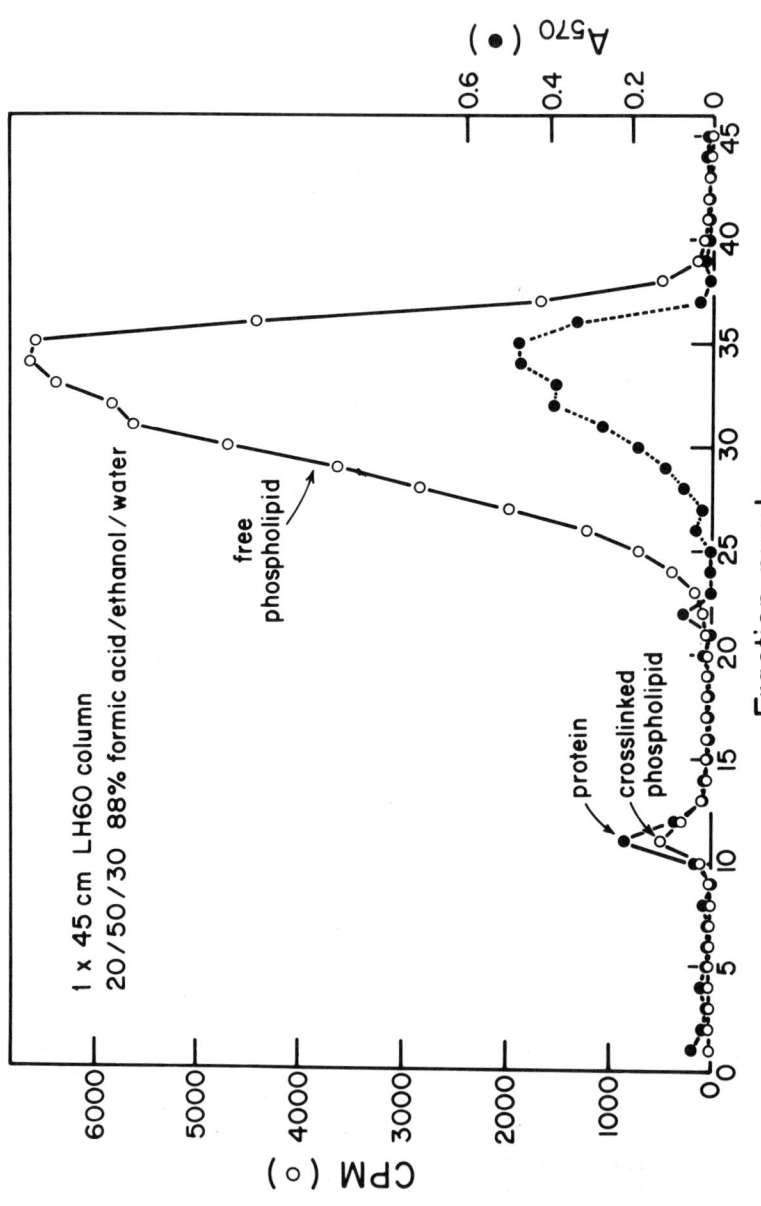

FIGURE 19. A Sephadex LH-60 column (1 × 45 cm) separation of cross-linked glycophorin from excess diazirino phospholipid. The solvent system used was 88% formic acid:ethanol:water (20:50:30, v/v/v). The A_{570} (ninhydrin assay) in fractions 30–35 is due to trisma buffer and not protein.

Glycophorin A

This protein, the major sialoglycoprotein of human erythrocyte membranes, is one of the most studied and best understood.[37] It is known that glycophorin A assumes a transmembrane conformation with the sugar-bearing N-terminus on the outer face and the C-terminus protruding into the cytoplasmic side.[38] The amino acid sequence, which is known, contains a very hydrophobic segment (residues 73–91, FIGURE 18), which may be associated with the lipid bilayer.[39] The structural characteristics of this protein render it amenable to the photoaffinity labeling technique. Thus, the aim would be to determine the identity and structure of the intramembranous portion of glycophorin A and, hopefully, to learn how membrane proteins fold within the bilayer. Glycophorin A was isolated according to Furthmayer *et al.*,[40] and reconstituted into synthetic phospholipid vesicles using the cholate dialysis method.[41] Using this method, there was only 1 residual cholate molecule for every 800 phospholipids in the reconstituted vesicles. The lipid and protein from these vesicles appeared together as a single band on a sucrose gradient; the vesicles were found to be asymmetric with ~75% of the glycophorin sugars facing outward. Photolysis of the vesicles was carried out under nitrogen using the 366 nm line from a 1000 W HgXe arc lamp. The half-time for photolysis of the diazirine under these conditions was 2 s. To separate the phospholipids from glycophorin A, the photolysis mixture was chromatographed on a Sephadex LH-60 column equilibrated with 88% formic acid/ethanol/water (20:50:30 v/v/v). FIGURE 19 shows the elution profile from such a column. The phospholipid cross-linked to glycophorin A appeared with the latter at the excluded volume.

TABLE 2 shows the percentage of [14C]-diazirine phospholipid cochromatographing with the protein. Only a negligible amount of the phospholipid appeared at the void volume in the following controls: (1) vesicles that had not been irradiated, (2) vesicles in which the lipid and the protein were separately photolyzed, and (3) vesicles with the [14C] label in dimyristoyl lecithin (DML) rather than in the diazirine phospholipid.

The cross-linked glycophorin from the LH-60 column was analyzed by sodium dodecylsulfate-polyacrylamide gel electrophoresis. The radioactivity from the labeled diazirino phospholipid appeared with glycophorin A on electrophoresis. Cleavage of

TABLE 2

RADIOACTIVITY (%) COCHROMATOGRAPHING WITH GLYCOPHORIN A
ON SEPHADEX LH-60 COLUMN*

	Irradiation	C-6 Diazirine†	C-11 Diazirine†
[14C]-DML	+	N.D.	0.007
[14C]-Diazirine lipid	−	0.31	0.21
[14C]-Diazirine lipid	+	2.6	1.8
[14C]-Diazirine lipid and protein photolyzed separately and mixed	+	0.25	0.13

*All photolysis mixtures contained DML:diazirine lipid:protein in the ratios 277:30:1 and the radioactivity was in either of the two phospholipids.
†C-6 diazirine:1-palmitoyl-2-ω-diazirinophenoxyhexanoyl phosphatidylcholine; C-11 diazirine:1-palmitoyl-2-ω-diazirinophenoxyundecanoyl phosphatidylcholine.

the cross-linked glycophorin with cyanogen bromide and trypsin, followed by gel electrophoresis, showed the sites of cross-linking to be within the tryptic fragment 62–96 and the cyanogen bromide fragment 9–81. Therefore, the cross-linking sites must lie between residues 62 and 81. Work is in progress to determine, by Edman sequencing, which amino acids are involved in cross-links.

Cytochrome b_5

Cytochrome b_5 is an amphipathic membrane protein that consists of a hydrophilic segment containing a heme-bearing catalytic site and a hydrophobic membranous segment anchoring the protein to the membrane. The primary structure of the hydrophobic segment of cytochrome b_5 of several species is known.[42-45] Cytochrome b_5 is a protein component of a system that converts saturated fatty acid to unsaturated fatty acid. This conversion involves an electron transport sequence from cytochrome b_5 reductase to cytochrome b_5 to the terminal cyanide-sensitive oxidase, the desaturase, which brings about the conversion of stearoyl-coenzyme A (CoA) to oleoyl-coenzyme A.

NADH $\rightarrow$ Cytochrome b_5 $\rightarrow$ Cytochrome b_5 $\rightarrow$ Cyanide-sensitive desaturase
reductase

O_2

Stearoyl-CoA   Oleoyl-CoA

Various studies indicate that the membranous segment of cytochrome b_5 is inserted into the hydrophobic region of the lipid bilayer. Cytochrome b_5 and cytochrome b_5 reductase have been reconstituted with liposomes and it has been shown that the protein-protein interactions in this model system are dependent upon the lateral diffusion of the membranous segments of these proteins in the hydrocarbon region of the phospholipid bilayer.[46] Addition of the desaturase to this system reconstituted oxygen- and NADH-dependent desaturation of stearoyl-CoA to oleoyl-CoA.[47]

Purified rabbit liver cytochrome b_5 (sequence shown in FIGURE 20) was found to insert into liposomes consisting of 1-palmitoyl-2-ω-(β-trifluoro-α-diazopropiony-loxy)lauroyl-sn-glycero-3-phosphorylcholine. The phospholipid was diluted ten-fold with DPL and irradiated after the incorporation of cytochrome b_5. Gel permeation chromatography (on Sephadex LH-60) of the irradiated sample is shown in FIGURE 21. Radioactively labeled phospholipid is associated with the absorption peak of cytochrome b_5. The water-soluble fragment of cytochrome b_5 polymerizes upon irradiation, even in the absence of photoactivable phospholipids or in the presence of tryptophan in the photolysis medium. This polymerized cytochrome b_5 elutes at the void volume from the above column (FIGURE 21, fraction 12). Both monomeric and polymeric cytochrome b_5 were combined and subjected to cyanogen bromide cleavage. The radioactivity was found to be associated with the fragment comprising residues Glu (96) to Met (125). Further work is in progress to determine the precise sites of cross-linking.

```
                91              96              101             106             110
PORCINE    ILE ALA LYS PRO SER GLU THR LEU ILE THR THR VAL GLU SER ASN SER SER TRP TRP THR...

HORSE      ILE ALA LYS PRO VAL GLU THR LEU ILE THR THR VAL ASP SER ASN SER SER TRP TRP THR...

BOVINE     ILE THR LYS PRO SER GLU SER ILE ILE THR THR ILE ASP SER ASN PRO SER TRP TRP THR...

RABBIT     LEU SER LYS PRO MET GLU THR LEU ILE THR THR VAL ASP SER ASN SER SER TRP TRP THR...

                111             116             121             126             131
PORCINE  ..ASN TRP VAL ILE PRO ALA ILE SER ALA LEU VAL VAL SER LEU MET TYR HIS PHE TYR THR SER GLU ASN

HORSE    ..ASN TRP VAL ILE PRO ALA ILE SER ALA VAL VAL ALA LEU MET TYR ARG ILE TYR THR ALA GLU ASP

BOVINE   ..ASN TRP LEU ILE PRO ALA ILE SER ALA LEU PHE VAL ALA LEU ILE TYR HIS LEU TYR THR SER GLU ASN

RABBIT   ..ASN TRP VAL ILE PRO ALA ILE SER ALA LEU ILE VAL ALA LEU MET TYR ARG LEU TYR MET ALA ASP ASP
```

FIGURE 20. A comparison of the primary sequences of the hydrophobic C-terminal of cytochrome b_5 from pig, horse, cattle, and rabbit livers. The sequences from the first three sources were elucidated by Ozols et al.[42,43] and Fleming et al.[44] Rabbit liver cytochrome b_5 was sequenced in this laboratory.[45] Nonhomologous amino acids are underlined.

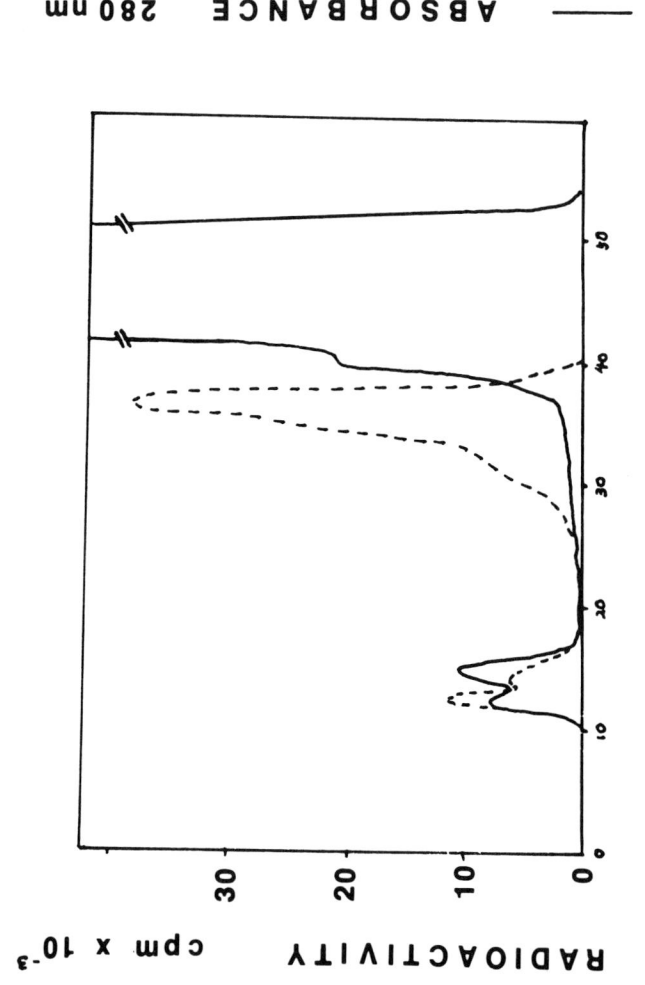

FIGURE 21. A Sephadex LH-60 column elution profile of the products obtained from the photolysis of cytochrome b_5 and a 1:9 molar ratio mixture of diazophospholipid and DPL. Tryptophan was added to minimize the photodamage to the protein. The solvent system used for the gel permeation chromatography was ethanol:88% formic acid (4:1 v/v).

Gramicidin A

Gramicidin A, a pentadecapeptide ionophore produced by *B. brevis,* forms channels selectively permeable to monovalent cations in biological and artificial membranes. The primary structure of the ionophore has been reported.[48] A dimeric structure is involved in the formation of the channel, for which two models have been proposed: (1) N-terminal to N-terminal dimerization of the π^4_{LD} helix proposed by Urry[49] and (2) the double-helix–type model proposed by Veatch *et al.*[50] (FIGURE 22). While the present evidence[51] strongly favors Urry's model, the use of photoactivable phospholipids can offer convincing evidence in support of one of the models.

The photoaffinity labeling approach involves the following considerations. A sequence analysis after the irradiation of gramicidin reconstituted into photoactivable phospholipid vesicles would reveal which amino acid residues can cross-link to the phospholipid molecules. Varying the chain length of the photolabeled phospholipids and repeating the above analysis should provide information about the topology of gramicidin in the lipid bilayer.

Sonicated vesicles were prepared from mixtures of gramicidin and photolabeled phospholipids. Both 1-palmitoyl-2-ω-diazirinophenoxy undecanoyl-*sn*-glycero-3-phosphorycholine and 1-palmitoyl-2-ω-trifluorodiazopropionyloxy lauroyl-*sn*-glycero-3-phosphorylcholine were used for these studies. Photolysis of vesicles containing a 50:1 molar ratio of phospholipid to gramicidin resulted in approximately 40–60% cross-linking of gramicidin to the phospholipid. The rate of the formation of cross-linked products corresponded to the rate of the disappearance of photoactivable groups in the phospholipids. Cross-linked products were separated from the unreacted gramicidin either by thin layer chromatography (TLC) on silica gel H plates or by Sephadex LH-20 column chromatography in methanol. A typical elution profile is shown in FIGURE 23. In a control experiment, photolysis of gramicidin in vesicles composed of DPL or DML gave no cross-linked material detectable either by TLC or by Sephadex column chromatography. Since gramicidin is extremely hydrophobic, sequencing methods have been developed that involve attaching the labeled peptide to a solid phase or solubilization by derivatization with a high molecular weight water-soluble polymer, such as polylysine.

SUMMARY

Photoactivable carbene precursors, aryl diazirines and trifluorodiazopropionates, were incorporated synthetically into the ω-positions of fatty acids, which were used to synthesize phospholipids. Extensive intermolecular C—H insertion reactions were demonstrated by photolysis of liposomes prepared from the above phospholipids. Structural analysis of the cross-linked products showed that the predominant sites of cross-linking were in the expected positions within the bilayer. Studies on the topography of a number of membrane proteins using the above phospholipids were initiated. Cross-linking of the photoactivable phospholipids to membrane-embedded proteins, glycophorin A, cytochrome b_5, and gramicidin A, was demonstrated.

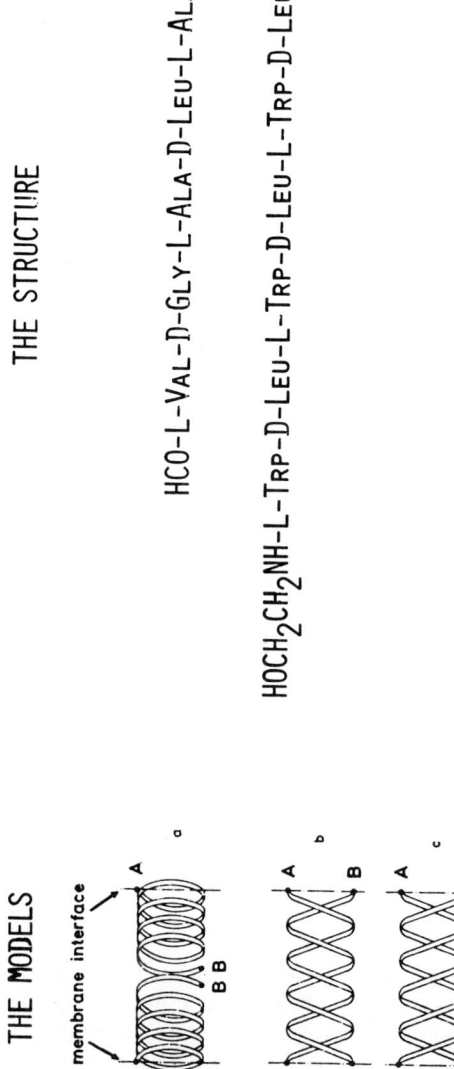

THE STRUCTURE

HCO–L–VAL–D–GLY–L–ALA–D–LEU–L–ALA–D–VAL–L–VAL

HOCH₂CH₂NH–L–TRP–D–LEU–L–TRP–D–LEU–L–TRP–D–LEU–L–TRP–D–VAL

THE MODELS

membrane interface

FIGURE 22. The primary structure of gramicidin[48] and the proposed models for the action of gramicidin as an ionophore are shown. In the model proposed by Urry,[49] two molecules of gramicidin align as shown to form the channel. The N-formyl terminus is B, while the C-terminal ethanol is A. In the second model, proposed by Veatch et al.,[50] parallel or antiparallel helices formed from two molecules span the membrane forming the channel (shown in the bottom panel).

LH-20 ELUTION PROFILE OF [^{3}H] T$_{RP}$ GRAMICIDIN BEFORE
AND AFTER PHOTOLYSIS WITH
1-C$_{18}$-2-ω-PHENOXYDIAZIRINO UNDECANOYL PC VESICLES

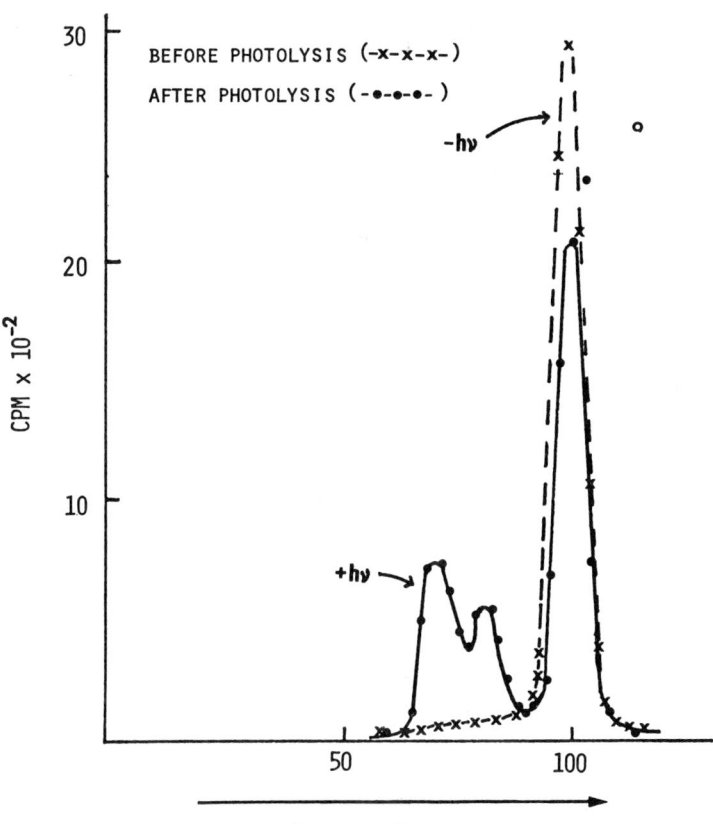

FIGURE 23. A Sephadex LH-20 (1 × 118 cm) column separation of the products obtained before and after photolysis of mixed vesicles from diazirino phospholipid and gramicidin. The elution was performed with methanol.

ACKNOWLEDGMENTS

Drs. A. Ross and R. Robson are postdoctoral fellows supported by the Damon Runyon–Walter Winchell Cancer Fund (DRG-144-F and DRG-301-F, respectively). Dr. W. Curatolo was supported by an N.I.H. Postdoctoral Traineeship (No. T32 CA09112). Dr. B. Erni was a postdoctoral fellow supported by the Stiftung für Stipendien auf dem Gebiete der Chemie, Basel, Switzerland.

This work was greatly aided by the High Resolution Mass Spectrometry facility at M.I.T., which is supported by the National Institutes of Health Research Grant No.

RR00317 from the Biotechnology Resources Branch, Division of Research Resources (Principal Investigator: Prof. K. Biemann). We thank Prof. Biemann for his valuable suggestions throughout the course of this work, and Dr. C. E. Costello for the mass spectral determinations and interpretations. We also thank Dr. D. M. Small of the Boston University Medical School for the use of his differential scanning calorimeter.

REFERENCES

1. SINGH, A., E. R. THORNTON & F. H. WESTHEIMER. 1962. J. Biol. Chem. **237:** 3007–8.
2. For recent reviews see: CHOWDHRY, V. & F. H. WESTHEIMER. 1979. Annu. Rev. Biochem. **48:** 293–325; BAYLEY, H. & J. R. KNOWLES. 1977. Methods in Enzymology, Vol. 46. W. B. Jakoby and M. Wilchek, Eds.: 69–114. Academic Press. New York; PETERS, K. & F. M. RICHARDS. 1977. Annu. Rev. Biochem. **46:** 523–51.
3. CHAKRABARTI, P. & H. G. KHORANA. 1975. Biochemistry **14:** 5021–33.
4. GUPTA, C. M., R. RADHAKRISHNAN, G. E. GERBER, W. L. OLSEN, S. C. QUAY & H. G. KHORANA. 1979. Proc. Nat. Acad. Sci. USA **76:** 2595–99.
5. SMITH, R. A. G. & J. R. KNOWLES. 1975. J. Chem. Soc. Perkin Trans. 2: 686–94.
6. BRADLEY, G. F., B. L. EVANS & I. D. R. STEVENS. 1977. J. Chem. Soc. Perkin Trans. 2: 1214–20.
7. GUPTA, C. M., R. RADHAKRISHNAN & H. G. KHORANA. 1977. Proc. Nat. Acad. Sci. USA **74:** 4315–19.
8. SLOTBOOM, A. J., H. M. VERHEIJ & G. H. DE HAAS. 1973. Chem. Phys. Lipids **11:** 295–317.
9. ROSENTHAL, A. R. 1975. Methods in Enzymology, Vol. 35, Part B. J. M. Lowenstein, Ed.: 429–528. Academic Press. New York.
10. KATES, M. 1977. Methods in Membrane Biology, Vol. 8. E. D. Korn, Ed.: 219–90. Plenum Press. New York.
11. KEANA, J. F. W. & A. R. ERTLE. 1976. Chem. Phys. Lipids **17:** 402–6.
12. BOSS, W. F., C. J. KELLEY & F. R. LANDSBERGER. 1975. Anal. Biochem. **64:** 289–92.
13. BAER, E. & D. BUCHNEA. 1959. Can. J. Biochem. Physiol. **37:** 953–59.
14. LAPIDOT, Y., I. BARZILAY & J. HAJDU. 1969. Chem. Phys. Lipids **3:** 125–34.
15. ROBLES, E. C. & D. VAN DEN BERG. 1969. Biochim. Biophys. Acta **187:** 520–26.
16. PUGH, E. & M. KATES. 1975. J. Lipid Res. **16:** 392–94.
17. ANEJA, R. & J. S. CHADHA. 1971. Biochim. Biophys. Acta **239:** 84–91.
18. STEGLICH, W. & G. HÖFLE. 1969. Angew. Chem. Int. Ed. Eng. **8:** 981.
19. REESE, C. B. 1973. In Protective Groups in Organic Chemistry. J. F. W. McComie, Ed.: 95–143. Plenum Press. New York.
20. HITCHCOCK, P. B., R. MASON, K. M. THOMAS & G. G. SHIPLEY. 1974. Proc. Nat. Acad. Sci. USA **71:** 3036–40.
21. BÜLDT, G., H. U. GALLY, A. SEELIG, J. SEELIG & G. ZACCAI. 1978. Nature (London) **271:** 182–84.
22. GUPTA, C. M., C. E. COSTELLO & H. G. KHORANA. 1979. Proc. Nat. Acad. Sci. USA **76:** 3139–43.
23. BARON, W. J., M. R. DE CAMP, M. H. HENDRICK, M. JONES, R. H. LEVIN & M. B. JOHN. 1973. In Carbenes, Vol. 1. M. Jones, Jr. and R. A. Moss, Eds.: 20. Wiley. New York.
24. SHEPPARD, W. A. & C. M. SHARTS. 1969. Organic Fluorine Chemistry.: 18–51. W. A. Benjamin. New York.
25. CHOWDHRY, V., R. VAUGHAN & F. H. WESTHEIMER. 1976. Proc. Nat. Acad. Sci. USA **73:** 1406–8.
26. FIELDS, R. & R. N. HASZELDINE. 1964. J. Chem. Soc.: 1881–89.
27. MIDDLETON, W. J., D. M. GALE & C. G. KRESPAN. 1968. J. Am. Chem. Soc. **90:** 6813–16.
28. CRABBE, P., A. CERVANTES., A. CRUZ, E. GALEAZZI, J. TRIARTE & E. VELARDE. 1973. J. Am. Chem. Soc. **96:** 6655–65.
29. MIDDLETON, W. J. 1975. J. Org. Chem. **40:** 574–78.

30. ERNI, B. & H. G. KHORANA. 1980. J. Am. Chem. Soc. In press.
31. ZEIFMAN, Y. V., N. P. GAMBARYAN & I. L. KNUNYANTS. 1963. Dokl. Akad. Nauk SSSR. **153:** 1334–37.
32. COLEMAN, R. 1973. Biochim. Biophys. Acta **300:** 1–30.
33. GROVER, A. K., A. J. SLOTBOOM, G. H. DE HAAS & G. HAMMES. 1975. J. Biol. Chem. **250:** 31–38.
34. GAZZOTTI, P., H. G. BOCK & S. FLEISCHER. 1975. J. Biol. Chem. **250:** 5782–90.
35. HUANG, K. S. & J. H. LAW. 1978. *In* Enzymes of Lipid Metabolism. S. Gatt, L. Freysz, and P. Mandel, Eds.: 177–83. Plenum Press. New York.
36. SINGER, S. J. 1971. *In* Molecular Biology. L. I. Rothfield, Ed.:145–222. Academic Press. New York.
37. FURTHMAYR, H. 1977. J. Supramol. Struct. **7:** 121–34.
38. COTMORE, S. F., H. FURTHMAYR & V. T. MARCHESI. 1977. J. Mol. Biol. **113:** 539–53.
39. TOMITA, M., H. FURTHMAYR & V. T. MARCHESI. 1978. Biochemistry **17:** 4756–70.
40. FURTHMAYR, H., M. TOMITA & V. T. MARCHESI. 1975. Biochem. Biophys. Res. Commun. **65:** 113–21.
41. KAGAWA, Y. & E. RACKER. 1971. J. Biol. Chem. **246:** 5477–87.
42. OZOLS, J. & C. GERARD. 1977. Proc. Nat. Acad. Sci. USA **74:** 3725–29.
43. OZOLS, J. & C. GERARD. 1977. J. Biol. Chem. **252:** 8549–53.
44. FLEMING, P. J., H. A. DAILEY, D. CORCORAN & P. STRITTMATTER. 1978. J. Biol. Chem. **253:** 5369–72.
45. TAKAGAKI, Y., G. E. GERBER, K. NIHEI & H. G. KHORANA. 1980. Submitted for publication.
46. STRITTMATTER, P. & M. J. ROGERS. 1975. Proc. Nat. Acad. Sci. USA **72:** 2658–61.
47. STRITTMATTER, P., L. SPATZ, D. CORCORAN, M. J. ROGERS, B. SETLOW & R. REDLINE. 1974. Proc. Nat. Acad. Sci. USA **71:** 4565–69.
48. SARGES, R. & B. WITKOP. 1965. J. Am. Chem. Soc. **87:** 2009–19.
49. URRY, D. W. 1971. Proc. Nat. Acad. Sci. USA **68:** 672–76.
50. VEATCH, W. R., E. T. FOSSEL & E. R. BLOUT. 1974. Biochemistry **13:** 5249–56.
51. BAMBERG, H. J. & H. A. APELL. 1977. Proc. Nat. Acad. Sci. USA **74:** 2402–5.

DISCUSSION

DR. H. A. LESTER: Both your comments and those of Dr. F. M. Richards concerning gramicidin raise the question of the exact cause of its ion selectivity in membrane channels. It could be hoped that probes of the sort that you mentioned with gramicidin could be used to probe the open state of the water-lined membrane channel. One experiment, for instance, that could be done relatively simply by your group would be to examine the labeling of gramicidin in liposomes whose membrane potential you control. The reasoning here is that the gating of the gramicidin channel is supposed to be dependent on membrane potential because, presumably, the monomer/dimer equilibrium depends on the membrane potential. So the dimerization should take place only under conditions in which the membrane potential was established and not under conditions in which it is not. It would be very interesting to see whether you would get different kinds of labeling patterns under those conditions. Hopefully, this sort of technique could then be refined to the point where you could actually produce the labels rapidly enough using flash lamps, which, indeed, will produce as many photons in a millisecond as your oriel source will in two seconds. Then you could actually probe the very brief open states of channels in biological membranes.

DR. R. RADHAKRISHNAN: Thank you for the suggestion and we'll think more about it along these lines.

DR. V. CHOWDHRY: I'm curious if you would like to speculate on the mechanism of the HF elimination?

RADHAKRISHNAN: We think it could be a result of the packing in the more ordered liposomes. The two chains probably come together and the carbene thus generated somehow undergoes a reaction in a bimolecular fashion and causes the elimination of hydrogen fluoride. We do not know, of course, exactly. It is just speculative at this stage and I wouldn't want to get into any discussion of it.

CHOWDHRY: In our model studies in free solution, we did not detect any HF eliminated product. So if it is present at all, it is present in very small quantities and that is consistent with your speculative mechanism of bimolecular process. I'm curious whether you've tried to interrupt the photolysis early on and see whether the subsequent HF elimination is actually a much slower process, one which you might pick up early in the event and not through the mechanism that you just suggested?

RADHAKRISHNAN: No, we haven't done that but, in solution in cyclohexane, we do not get into that complication at all. I mean, there is no elimination of HF and the structure is consistent with what you would expect on the basis of a true insertion reaction. So we suspect that it is characteristic only of multilamellar dispersions and that it has to do with the packing in the bilayer.

CHOWDHRY: I'd like to add that, in our studies in cyclohexane, the reaction leading to the insertion product yielded more than 95% and was satisfyingly clean. We really don't see other products, as you apparently do with the trifluoro-methyl-phenyldiazirine.

DR. H. BAYLEY: Yesterday, I talked about my prejudice for carbenes but today Dr. F. M. Richards has claimed that nitrenes will insert into carbon hydrogen bonds and Dr. Stoffel has claimed that aliphatic azides on photolysis will insert into carbon hydrogen bonds. At the beginning of your talk, you stated that neither of those two classes of reagents would do that. I was wondering if you'd like to state your evidence for that and perhaps Dr. Richards would like to say how he characterized his insertion products?

RADHAKRISHNAN: We have carried out a series of photolyses in mixed vesicles with radioactive saturated lecithins and saturated azidophospholipids and unsaturated phospholipids and phospholipids that contain phenylazide. In all cases when the photolysis was carried out at 300 nm with filtered radiation, there was no appreciable cross-linking; I should say, probably, 0.2%, on the basis of the radioactivity, but nothing more. And the cross-linkings that are observed by others could be a result of the photolysis conditions. But we could not detect any of these agents inserting into a C—H bond of a saturated fatty acid chain. Maybe, if you use an unsaturated lecithin as the acceptor or substrate, you will get products that result from the insertion of the nitrene into a carbon-carbon double bond or somewhere else in the molecule. So, for our studies, we find, especially for the kinds of things we want to do—probing the hydrophobic surface of the membrane proteins—that it would be advisable to have a label that is capable of insertion even into a saturated, I mean, a C—H bond.

BAYLEY: Could I ask Dr. Richards to comment on the azide experiments?

DR. F. M. RICHARDS: I'm not sure that I have the question exactly correct. In the work that Dr. Brunner has done so far, he has only attempted to specifically identify the products when they were done in the various pure solvent systems. The work that has been done in the liposomes is simply a covalent attachment. We have no idea of the specific nature of the attachment. And there is very little in a saturated lipid chain that could react. Yet, it certainly does react covalently. However, we do not have the product identified in the same sense that the MIT group does.

USE OF LIPOPHILIC PHOTOACTIVATABLE REAGENTS TO IDENTIFY THE LIPID-EMBEDDED DOMAINS OF MEMBRANE PROTEINS*

Carlos Gitler and Tuvia Bercovici

Department of Membrane Research
The Weizmann Institute of Science
Rehovot, Israel

INTRODUCTION

In 1973, Klip and Gitler were concerned with the fact that the reagents available at that time to label membrane proteins only indirectly allowed the identification of the segments of the polypeptide chains in contact with or embedded within the membrane lipids.

They set out, therefore, to design a reagent that would label the lipid-embedded domains of membrane proteins directly. Prior to this, Shinitzky and Gitler, while in G. Weber's laboratory, had been involved in the development of a method to estimate membrane lipid microviscosity by measuring the polarization of the fluorescence emission of aromatic molecules dissolved in the liquid hydrocarbon regions of the membrane lipids.[1,2] These results indicated that aromatic molecules, such as perylene, would readily partition into the membrane lipids, and that they would monitor the state of the lipid chains while dissolved near the center of the bilayer (the lipid core). This conclusion was derived from the fact that the observed freedom of motion of the fluorescent molecules showed them to be embedded in a nearly isotropic environment.[1] It was reasoned, therefore,[3,4] that labeling reagents, which could readily locate in the lipid core, could be designed by the simple expedient of making them sufficiently apolar in nature. However, such reagents would have to meet three additional requirements:

1. They would have to be unreactive until they are located in the liquid lipid core

2. Once located within the lipid bilayer, they would have to be readily activatable by a procedure that would not damage the membrane components

3. The activated species would have to be sufficiently reactive to interact with the side-chains of the amino acids embedded in the lipid core.

Once these criteria were defined, the choices were narrowed to photoactivatable aromatic carbene and nitrene precursors. The initial studies were performed with diazoacetate derivatives that generated highly reactive carbenes upon irradiation.[4] Aromatic azides were also studied, since they have the quality that, upon irradiation, highly reactive nitrenes are formed by energy that is first absorbed in the aromatic system as a whole, and then transferred from the hydrocarbon to the azido group.[5] Molar absorptivities for the conversion to the reactive species two orders of magnitude higher could be obtained with aromatic azides rather than with carbene precursors. For this reason, we chose to concentrate on aromatic azides.

*This research was supported by a grant from the Israel Academy of Sciences.

199

For the initial experiments, we used two reagents, [³H-U]-naphthalene-1-azide and [¹²⁵I]-4-iodobenzene-1-azide.[3,4] It could be shown that these aromatic azides readily partitioned into the lipid core and, upon photoactivation, labeled only those domains of membrane proteins adjacent to the membrane lipids and the lipids themselves.[3,4,6-8]

Attempts to prepare [³H-U]-naphthalene-1-azide with a specific radioactivity of 3 Ci/mmol resulted in marked autoactivation during storage and the generation of artifacts during irradiation. Furthermore, since the [¹²⁵I]-4-iodobenzene-1-azide had an absorption maximum at 258 nm, it had to be irradiated at the edge of the absorption band in order to avoid damaging irradiation of the membrane proteins. Taking these limitations into account, we synthesized a new reagent, [¹²⁵I]-5-iodonaphthalene-1-azide (INA), which overcame these disadvantages.[9]

As will be discussed below, INA labels both membrane lipids and proteins while dissolved in the lipid core. By means of this reagent, those proteins adjacent to the membrane lipids can be readily identified. In addition, the discrete peptide segments embedded in or spanning the lipid bilayer can be directly labeled, enabling their subsequent isolation and characterization.

Since 1974, when our first results were presented, other compounds that dissolve in the bilayer and can then be photoactivated have been developed.[10-14] Independently, a different approach was taken both by Chakrabarti and Khorana[15] and by Stossel et al.,[16] which involved the synthesis of fatty acids containing photoactivatable groups, which could then become incorporated into phospholipids in order to probe their contiguity with the membrane protein.

Since these various reagents will be discussed by other participants in this meeting, we will concentrate on the properties of [¹²⁵I]-5-iodonaphthyl-1-azide.

General Properties of [¹²⁵I]-5-Iodonaphthyl-1-Azide

Several procedures to prepare highly radioactive [¹²⁵I]-5-iodonaphthyl-1-azide are available. Of these, the procedure of choice is based on the reduction of 5-nitronaphthyl-1-azide with sodium dithionite† to give 5-aminonaphthyl-1-azide, which can then be diazotized and the diazonium group displaced by ¹²⁵I-sodium iodide.[9] Specific radioactivities of 10–15 Ci/mmol can readily be obtained. The [¹²⁵I]-INA is stable in an ethanol solution for four days and, after that time, breakdown products can be removed by chromatography in silicic acid prior to its further use.[3]

INA has an absorption maximum at 310 nm with a molar extinction, ϵ, of 21,400 M^{-1} cm^{-1}, which allows its photoconversion into the reactive nitrene by exposure to the 314 nm line of a mercury lamp, using very short times of exposure (see below).

The partition coefficient of INA into n-octanol can be calculated, according to Fugita et al., to give a log P value of ~5.[17] This is due to the high hydrophobic contribution of the iodide portion coupled to the naphthalene group. [¹²⁵I]-INA

---

†It should be noted that sodium dithionite forms complexes with amines that preclude its extraction into ether. For this reason, this reaction is carried out in a solution of ethanol containing 10% water, to which an excess of solid sodium dithionite is added. The solution is then filtered to remove excess dithionite prior to its purification.

partitions more than 99.9% into different membranes, even at concentrations lower than 10^{-7} M and membrane lipid levels less than 1 mg. This high lipid solubility is important because there are negligible levels of INA in the aqueous phase that could bind to apolar pockets of proteins. As will be described below, the incorporation of INA into membrane proteins is not affected by the presence, in the aqueous phase, of solutes that bind to the active sites of enzymes, transport proteins, or receptors. This apolar nature of INA is also important in precluding the exit of the nitrene to the aqueous phase following photolysis.

RATE AND EFFICIENCY OF INCORPORATION OF INA INTO MEMBRANE PROTEINS
AND PHOSPHOLIPIDS: EFFECT OF AQUEOUS NITRENE SCAVANGERS

Exposure of the membrane-containing INA to low light fluxes results in the rapid conversion of INA into a reactive nitrene that attaches covalently both to membrane proteins and to lipids. TABLE 1 shows that, within very short periods of photolysis, complete conversion of INA into the nitrene ensues with very high efficiencies of incorporation of the label into the membrane proteins. At the same time, the label is incorporated into the lipids. The total incorporation varies, in different membranes, from 20 to 58% of the INA originally dissolved in the lipids. This high efficiency is probably due to the fact that the nitrene resides in the bilayer and mainly interacts with the components present there.

In order to further test whether the photogenerated 5-iodonaphthyl-1-nitrene (INN) might label components external to the bilayer, labeling experiments were performed[21] in the presence of p-aminobenzoic acid, an effective nitrene scavenger.[22] No differences in the extent or the pattern of incorporation of INN into the membrane

TABLE 1

COVALENT INCORPORATION OF [^{125}I]-INA INTO THE PROTEINS
OF DIFFERENT CELLS AND ISOLATED MEMBRANES

Membrane Source	Concentration	Time of Irradiation*	Covalent Incorporation into Proteins (% of total INA)	Reference
Human erythrocytes	10% suspension	30	20	9
Lymphocytes	5×10^7/ml	6	30	not published
Tetrahymena pyriformis	10^7/ml	6	35	not published
Erythrocyte ghosts	1.8 mg prot/ml	6	18	9
Sarcoplasmic reticulum	4.0 mg prot/ml	2	38	9
Purified (Na^+, K^+)-ATPase	0.6 mg prot/ml	0.6	18–35	18
Brush border	2.0 mg prot/ml	2	30	19
AChoR-rich membranes	2.0 mg prot/ml	2	31	20

*Conditions of irradiation as in Reference 9.

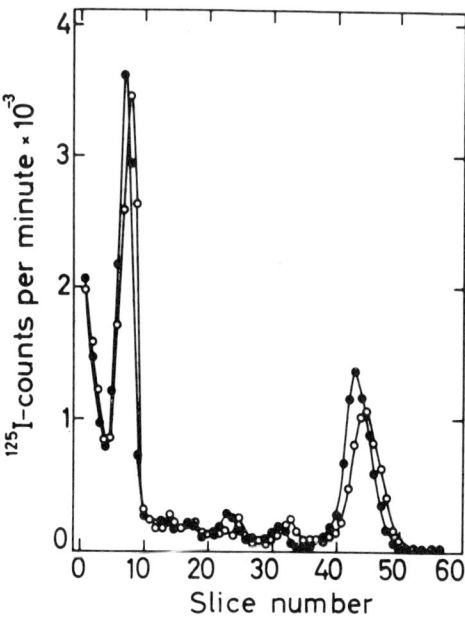

FIGURE 1. The effect of reduced glutathione on the pattern of incorporation of 5-iodonaphthyl-1-nitrene into the sarcoplasmic reticulum (SR) membrane components. SR membranes (8 mg protein in 2 ml) in the absence (•) and in the presence (○) of 15 mM GSH were labeled with [^{125}I]-INA by the procedure of Bercovici and Gitler.[9] Sodium dodecyl sulfate (SDS)-polyacrylamide gel electrophoresis tube gels were then run, fixed, stained, and sliced into 1.5 mm slices and the ^{125}I content determined.

proteins were observed in the presence of the scavenger. Bayley and Knowles recently reported a marked reduction in the incorporation of the photolysis products of phenylazide dissolved in phospholipid liposomes when 15 mM glutathione (GSH) was present in the external solution.[13] These results indicated that the phenylnitrene, even though generated within the bilayer, must diffuse out into the aqueous solution. We therefore further tested whether GSH had a similar effect on INN labeling.

The results obtained indicate that the photolysis of 5-iodonaphthyl-1-azide dissolved in the lipid phase of sarcoplasmic reticulum membranes leads to the formation of a nitrene that does not exit from the phospholipid bilayer. Thus, the pattern and extent of labeling of the sarcoplasmic reticulum intrinsic membrane proteins by INN are not modified by high levels of nitrene-reactive GSH in the aqueous phase (FIGURE 1). Furthermore, the presence of the nitrene scavenger decreases, but only slightly (by 12%), the level of incorporation of the label into the membrane lipids of the sarcoplasmic reticulum. Equivalent findings (Karlish, unpublished results) have been obtained upon labeling the (Na$^+$, K$^+$)ATPase of kidney microsomes. That is, the presence of GSH does not modify the INN labeling of the protein component and slightly decreases that of the lipid.

The photolysis of INA dissolved in phospholipid liposomes results (TABLE 2) in a remarkably high percentage of the incorporation of the label into the phospholipid molecules, both in the absence (44–49%) and in the presence of 15 mM GSH (31–34%). Furthermore, both the extent of INN incorporation and the decrease induced by GSH were insensitive to the varying nucleophilic character of the polar head-groups of the phospholipid molecules used. Therefore, it seems highly unlikely that the INN reacts as an *aqueous* electrophilic reagent.

It is known that intact erythrocytes contain some 5–8 mM internal GSH. Labeling of both intact erythrocytes and erythrocyte ghosts leads to the same labeling pattern, again suggesting that INN is unaffected by the presence of aqueous scavangers.

PATTERN OF INCORPORATION OF INA INTO MEMBRANE PROTEINS: INTRINSIC AND EXTRINSIC PROTEINS

The definition of intrinsic and extrinsic proteins was an operational one, based on the ease of and means required for solubilization of the various proteins from the membrane. Intrinsic proteins, in general, require detergents for their solubilization while extrinsic proteins can be solubilized without detergents. The studies of Helenious and Simons[23] and of Clark[24] gave a further criterion, namely that intrinsic proteins strongly bind detergent while extrinsic proteins do not. The available evidence suggests that regions of polypeptide chains of intrinsic proteins are in contact with or embedded in the lipids of the membrane. Clearly, then, the best method of distinguishing intrinsic from extrinsic membrane proteins would be to label them from *within* the lipid bilayer. This labeling would be best if it could be performed in intact cells with little disturbance of the membrane components. The discoveries that low levels of INA ($10^{-7} M$) readily partition into the lipid core and that a few minutes of exposure to light result in a highly efficient incorporation into the membrane proteins make it an ideal reagent to identify those intrinsic proteins that exist adjacent to the membrane lipids.[9]

We have identified the intrinsic proteins of several membranes, including intestinal brush border membranes;[19] sarcoplasmic reticulum membranes;[9] erythrocyte membranes;[9] T- and B-lymphocytes; *Tetrahymena pyriformis* ciliary, pellicle, and endoplasmic reticulum membranes (paper in preparation); and acetylocholine

TABLE 2

EFFECT OF REDUCED GLUTATHIONE ON THE INCORPORATION
OF THE PHOTOLYSIS PRODUCTS OF INA INTO PHOSPHOLIPID LIPOSOMES

Phospholipid in Liposomes*	GSH†	% of Total INA Incorporated‡	With GSH / Without GSH
Egg phosphatidylcholine	—	44	
	+	32	0.73
Egg phosphatidylethanolamine (PE)	—	49	
	+	32	0.65
Bovine phosphatidylserine (PS)	—	46	
	+	34	0.75
Phosphatidylinositol	—	44	
	+	31	0.72

*The phospholipid (4 mg/ml) was sonicated for 20 min in a solution of 125 mM NaCl and 30 mM sodium phosphate buffer, pH 7.4, under N_2.

†The final reduced glutathione concentration was 15 mM.

‡The radioactivity associated with the labeled phospholipid is reported as a percentage of the total applied. PE and PS include small amounts of those lyso-derivatives and fatty acids that are also labeled.

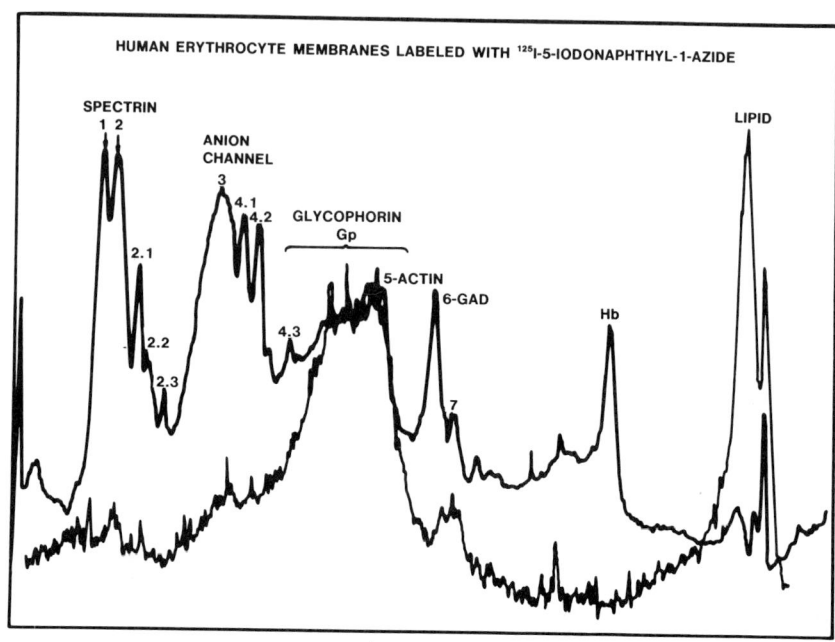

HUMAN ERYTHROCYTE MEMBRANES LABELED WITH ^{125}I-5-IODONAPHTHYL-1-AZIDE

FIGURE 2. The pattern of incorporation of [^{125}I]-INA into human erythrocyte membranes. Heavy line: a densitometric tracing of the slab gel electrophoretic run stained with Coomasie Brilliant Blue. Light line: a densitometric tracing of the radioautogram of the same gel. Labeling as in Bercovici and Gitler.[9]

receptor-rich membrane fragments.[20] Several general findings have been obtained. Those proteins (with the exception of spectrin) that can be released readily by mild nondetergent methods, that is, behave as extrinsic proteins, are not found to be labeled by INA. An interesting case is that of actin. It has not been labeled, neither in brush border membranes, in lymphocytes, nor in erythrocytes. Thus, it appears unlikely that it directly interacts with the membrane lipids.

The findings obtained by INA labeling of erythrocyte membranes are of interest because of the extensive knowledge available regarding the different proteins of this membrane. FIGURE 2 shows the pattern of incorporation of INA into erythrocyte ghosts. Labeled proteins include bands 2 and 3, the PAS positive bands, band 7, and a strong labeled band of 20,000 daltons. No label is found in band 1, 4.1, 4.2, 5, or 6 (after their solubilization using different treatments[25,26]). With the exception of band 2 (spectrin includes bands 1 and 2), this shows that extrinsic proteins are not labeled while those behaving like intrinsic proteins are readily labeled. Band 2 shows a consistent low level of incorporation, which is a regular finding. This suggests that the bulk of this protein is not in contact with the bilayer. However, a small segment might be embedded in the lipid. Further characterization is required to clarify this interesting finding.

When erythrocyte ghosts are labeled with the reagent of Bolton and Hunter,[27] which is an amino-specific reagent soluble in benzene, the labeling pattern is completely different from that found in FIGURE 2. All polypeptides are strongly labeled with band 3, which contains the highest incorporation. Actin, spectrin, glyceraldehyde-3-P-dehydrogenase, and bands 4.1, 4.2, and Hb are strongly labeled. This shows clearly that INA is not behaving as a general, nonspecific label reacting with amino groups of membrane proteins.

PATTERN OF INA INCORPORATION INTO SPECIFIC MEMBRANE PROTEINS: THE LIPID-EMBEDDED DOMAINS

It has been generally found that, after INA labeling of different membranes, exhaustive proteolysis results in the release of appreciable amounts of membrane protein without any concomitant release of radioactivity.[3,4,9,18-20]

This indicates that the labeled lipid-embedded domains remain associated with the lipids after proteolysis. This allows for their initial characterization with regard to number and approximate molecular weight prior to the determination of their sequence. Enough experiments with purified proteins have now been performed to enable us to see a general trend, which is discussed below.

ANCHORING LIPID-EMBEDDED DOMAINS

It is likely that the role of many of the proteins that exist in membranes is mainly to present to the aqueous surface of the cell an adequately positioned series of determinants, which probably play an important role in cell-extracellular matrix and cell-cell recognition. These include proteins like glycophorin,[28] and the virus coat proteins.[29] These proteins are characterized by the presence of a sequence of some 23 mainly apolar amino acids (FIGURE 3), which are thought to form an α-helical segment that is embedded in the bilayer and allows the protein to span the lipid bilayer.[28,29] No other function is known for these apolar segments other than that of anchoring the protein to the membrane (see, however, Reference 30).

```
                    5                          10
NH₂ → VAL - GLN - LEU - ALA - HIS - HIS - PHE - SER - GLU - PRO - GLU
      62


                    15                         20
      ILE - THR - LEU - ILE - ILE - PHE - GLY - VAL - MET - ALA - GLY
      73


          25                   30                        35
  - VAL - ILE - GLY - THR - ILE - LEU - LEU - SER - TYR - GLY - ILE - ARG - ARG → COO⁻
                                                           95      97
```

FIGURE 3. The amino acid sequence of the T_6 segment of glycophorin A. This segment contains 80-90% of the radioactivity incorporated into glycophorin during [^{125}I]-INA photolabeling of human erythrocyte membranes.

We have photolabeled human erythrocyte membranes with [^{125}I]-INA (as in FIGURE 2) and, after isolating the labeled glycophorin, have determined the distribution of the label within the polypeptide chain. Our results[31] indicate that the sequence shown in FIGURE 3, the so-called trypsin-insoluble segment (TIS or T$_6$), contains nearly all of the incorporated label (80–90% in each of four separate experiments). The TIS or T$_6$ (33 amino acids) represents 25% of the glycophorin polypeptide chain and 10% of the total molecule (60% carbohydrate and 40% protein[28]). The discovery that it contains between 80–90% of the radioactivity derived from [^{125}I]–INA directly supports the concept that glycophorin is anchored in the lipid of the membrane through its hydrophobic domain (residues 73–95), which is inserted into the lipid bilayer. These results also indicate that INA essentially only labels from within the bilayer.

The lipid-embedded domain of the type discussed in this section may play a further role. It may confine proteins to the membrane surface, increasing the probability of collision between different molecules. Thus, the effectiveness of the cytochrome b_5 interaction with the NADH-cytochrome b_5 reductase may be markedly enhanced by their confinement—by the anchorage segment—to the membrane surface. The availability[32] of the primary sequence of the membranous segment of cytochrome b_5 makes it an interesting protein to study by means of lipophilic photoactivatable labels, such as INA.

It is interesting that the apolar leader peptide of nascent polypeptide chains may also play an anchorage role in these proteins until processing for secretion may result in its removal.

IONOPHORIC LIPID-EMBEDDED DOMAINS

It is likely that the lipid-embedded domains of membrane proteins will be involved in the formation of channels leading to the diffusion of the ions down their concentration gradients. In the case of the acetylcholine receptor (AChoR) it is believed that agonist binding leads to the transient formation of transmembrane channels. In nerve depolarization, such a channel opening would be induced by the presence of a transmembrane potential. It is also likely that ligand-induced encounter channels may be formed in many cells. These could induce transient channels permeable to Ca^{++}, which may lead to phenomena such as mast cell histamine release. In attempts to identify the manner in which channels form, it is important to first identify those polypeptides that are in contact with the membrane lipids.

We have recently[20] carried out experiments of this type with AChoR-rich membranes obtained from the electric organ of *Torpedo californica*. FIGURE 4 shows that these membranes contain two main components, which are labeled with [^{125}I]-INA, of 90,000 and 40,000 daltons; minor labeling is also observed in the region of 55–65 kilodaltons. Purification of the acetylcholine receptor by affinity chromatography using Sepharose-bound *Naja naja siamensis* toxin showed the receptor to be labeled exclusively in the 40,000 daltons subunit (FIGURE 5, top). Exhaustive trypsin digestion resulted in the formation of an unlabeled 27,000 dalton fragment and a labeled 13,000 dalton polypeptide (FIGURE 5, bottom). INA labeling was not affected by the presence of α-bungarotoxin, GSH, or carbamylcholine. The labeled membranes and the receptor derived from them bound α-bungarotoxin normally. If, however, the AChoR was labeled after purification while dissolved in Triton X-100 solution, all four subunits were labeled by INA. These results may indicate that the receptor interacts differently with Triton X-100 micelles than with the lipids in which it is embedded in the membrane.

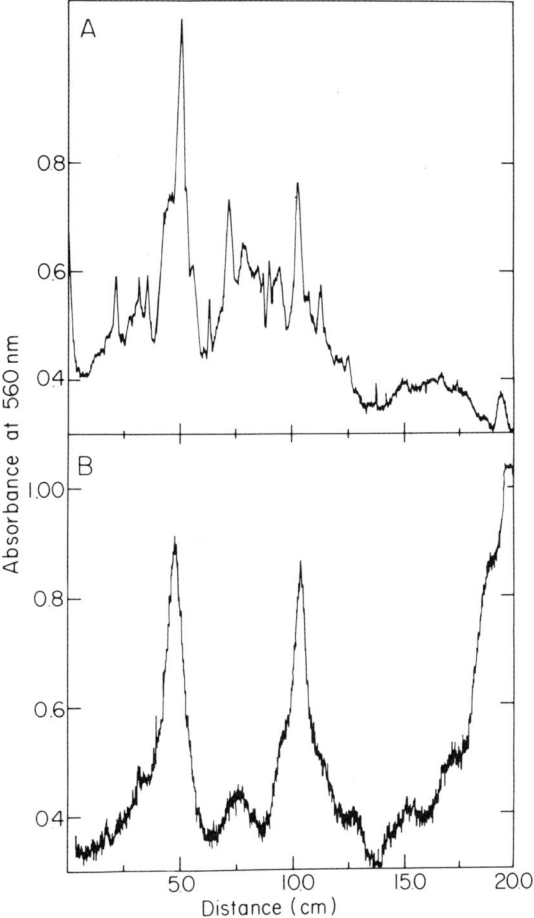

FIGURE 4. The pattern of photolytic incorporation of [^{125}I]-INA into AChoR-rich membranes from the electric organ of *Torpedo californica*.[20] Upper figure: a densitometric tracing of the SDS-electrophoretic slab gel stained with Coomasie Brilliant Blue. Lower figure: a densitometric tracing of the radioautogram from the same gel.

IONOPHORIC LIPID-EMBEDDED DOMAINS OF TRANSPORT PROTEINS

We have, also, recently identified the lipid-embedded domains of the (Na^+,K^+)-ATPase and the Ca^{++}-ATPase. Labeling with INA shows that the 100,000 dalton polypeptides of both carrier proteins are the near-exclusive site of label incorporation. Exhaustive trypsinization of the (Na^+, K^+)-ATPase results in a polypeptide of 12,300 daltons containing all the INA-derived radioactivity.[18] Prior proteolysis and subse-

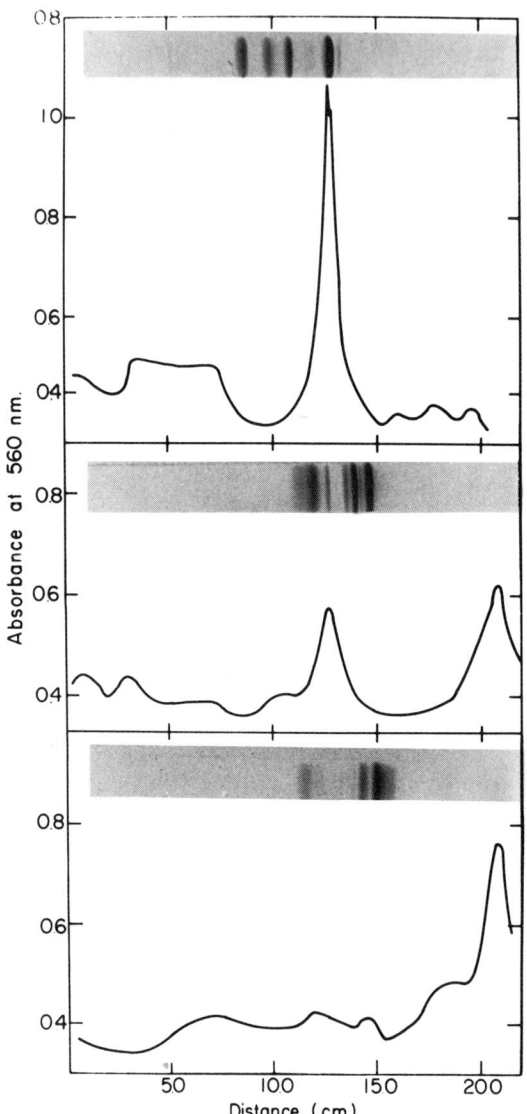

FIGURE 5. The pattern of distribution of radioactivity in the acetylcholine receptor purified from membranes photolabeled with [^{125}I]-INA (upper figure). The effect of trypsin digestion on the distribution of label in the derived peptides. Short time incubation (middle figure) and exhaustive incubation (lower figure) with trypsin.

quent INA labeling results in essentially the same amount of label incorporation into the 12,300 dalton peptide. Equivalent experiments with the Ca^{++}-ATPase result in the formation of *two* labeled polypeptides of 13,800 and 12,200 daltons. This confirms our original finding that the Ca^{++}-ATPase has at least two segments of its polypeptide chain embedded in or spanning the lipid bilayer.[9]

TABLE 3 gives the apparent molecular weights of those peptides derived from ion translocator proteins identified through INA labeling and proteolysis. In addition, it includes those polypeptides that represent one of the subunits of the H^+-ATPase that is active in the H^+-translocation step labeled by the lipophilic dicyclohexylcarbodiimide (DCCD) (see Reference 37 for a discussion). The DCCD-binding proteolipid derived from chloroplasts has been shown to retain its function when it is reconstituted into phospholipid liposomes.[36] Proteolytic fragments of the Ca^{++}-ATPase have been shown to retain ionophoric properties.[38] It will be interesting to test the INA-labeled peptides to determine whether they, also, retain ionophoric functions upon reconstitution.

NATURE OF THE RESIDUES LABELED BY INA UPON PHOTOLYSIS

We have, as yet, no evidence as to the chemical nature of the residues that are the site of INA incorporation. The high lipid labeling shown in TABLE 2 is probably due to the interaction of INN with the double bonds of the fatty acids. Equivalent photolysis of INA in phospholipid liposomes containing saturated fatty acids (dipalmitoyl lecithin or dimyristoyl lecithin) resulted in the incorporation of much lower amounts of the label into the phospholipids. This indicates that the nitrene is not capable of efficient direct insertion into the secondary and primary carbons of the fatty acid chains.

Studies on the incorporation of INN into the gramicidin A present in the phospholipid indicated significant incorporation of the photolysis products into this peptide. It will be of interest to determine the nature of the reactive moieties. The tryptophan residues would seem likely candidates. The efficient incorporation of INN into the T_6 peptide of glycophorin indicates that it can label some of its apolar residues. The results of the INA labeling of erythrocyte membranes indicate that band 3, even though it is present in high concentrations, is not labeled as well as the glycoproteins of this membrane. When the anion-carrier protein (band 3) is subjected to tryptic digestion it is degraded to give a 17,000 dalton peptide[39,40] (and a smaller second peptide[41]), which retains full functional properties as an anion carrier. This could imply that the lipid-embedded peptides retain their quaternary structure upon proteolysis. Such a quaternary structure could shield some of the peptides from the lipids and thus from lipophilic photoactivatable labels. Bacteriorhodopsin is believed

TABLE 3

IONOPHORIC MEMBRANE-EMBEDDED DOMAINS

Protein	Apparent Molecular Weight of the Embedded Peptide
Identified by INA labeling and trypsin digestion	
Ca^{++}-ATPase	13,800, 12,200
(NA^+, K^+)-ATPase	12,300[18]
AChoR	13,000[20]
DCCD binding component isolated as proteolipids	
H^+-ATPase	
Mitochondria	10,000,[33] 11,000,[34] 13–14,000[35]
Chloroplast*	8,300[36]

*Has been shown, upon reconstitution, to function as a proton channel.[36]

to contain seven helical segments normal to the bilayer such that nearly all the protein is embedded in the lipid.[42] It is readily labeled with INA and studies are in progress to determine if all the helical segments are labeled. This steric hindrance could also explain why not all the proteolytic segments of the (Na^+, K^+)-ATPase are labeled with INA.[18]

Further detailed analysis is required to define the chemical nature of the attachment sites of INA. It is clear, however, that it is an excellent reagent with which to identify intrinsic proteins and the lipid-embedded segments of those proteins.

ACKNOWLEDGMENTS

We would like to acknowledge that the results presented are the fruits of an enjoyable collaboration with A. Bromberg, A. Yanovsky, R. Tarrab-Hazdai, S. J. D. Karlish, I. Kahane, P. L. Jorgensen, K. Sigrist-Nelson, and H. Sigrist.

REFERENCES

1. SHINITZKY, M., A. C. DIANOUX, C. GITLER & G. WEBER. 1971. Biochemistry **10:** 2106–13.
2. RUDY, B. & C. GITLER. 1972. Biochim. Biophys. Acta **288:** 231–36.
3. KLIP, A. & C. GITLER. 1974. Biochem. Biophys. Res. Commun. **60:** 1155–62.
4. KLIP, A. 1974. Master's Degree Thesis. Center for Research and Advanced Studies, National Polytechnic Institute. Mexico D. F., Mexico.
5. REISER, A. & R. MARLEY. 1968. Trans. Faraday Soc. **64:** 1806–15.
6. GITLER, C. & A. KLIP. 1974. *In* Perspectives in Membrane Biology. S. Estrada-O. & C. Gitler, Eds.: 149–78. Academic Press. New York.
7. KLIP, A. & C. GITLER. 1976. *In* Mitochondria: Biogenesis, Structure, and Function. L. Packer & A. Gomez-Puyou, Eds.: 315–35. Academic Press. New York.
8. KLIP, A., A. DARSZON & M. MONTAL. 1976. Biochem. Biophys. Res. Commun. **72:** 1350.
9. BERCOVICI, T. & C. GITLER. 1978. Biochemistry **17:** 1484–89.
10. MIKKELSON, R. B. & D. F. H. WALLACH. 1976. J. Biol. Chem. **251:** 7413–16.
11. NIEVA-GOMEZ, D. & R. B. GENNIS. 1977. Proc. Nat. Acad. Sci. USA **74:** 1811–15.
12. ABU-SALAH, K. M. & J. B. C. FINDLAY. 1977. Biochem. J. **161:** 223–28.
13. BAYLEY, H. & J. R. KNOWLES. 1978. Biochemistry **17:** 2414–19.
14. BAYLEY, H. & J. R. KNOWLES. 1978. Biochemistry **17:** 2420–23.
15. CHAKRABARTI, P. & H. G. KHORANA. 1975. Biochemistry **14:** 5021–33.
16. STOFFEL, W., K. SALM & U. KÖRHEMEIR. 1976. Hoppe-Seyler's Z. Physiol. Chem. **357:** 917–24.
17. FUJITA, T., T. IWASA & C. HAUSCH. 1964. J. Am. Chem. Soc. **86:** 5175–86.
18. KARLISH, S. J. D., P. L. JØRGENSEN & C. GITLER. 1977. Nature (London) **269:** 715–17.
19. SIGRIST-NELSON, K., H. SIGRIST, T. BERCOVICI & C. GITLER. 1977. Biochim. Biophys. Acta **468:** 163–76.
20. TARRAB-HAZDAI, R., T. BERCOVICI & C. GITLER. 1980. J. Biol. Chem. In press.
21. SIGRIST-NELSON, K., H. SIGRIST, T. BERCOVICI & C. GITLER. 1976. Unpublished results.
22. RUOHO, A. E., H. KIEFER, P. E. ROEDER & S. J. SINGER. 1972. Proc. Nat. Acad. Sci. USA **70:** 2567–71.
23. HELENIOUS, A. & K. SIMONS. 1975. Biochim. Biophys. Acta **415:** 20–79.
24. CARK, S. 1975. J. Biol. Chem. **250:** 5459–69.
25. STECK, T. L. & J. YU. 1973. J. Supramol. Struct. **1:** 220–32.

26. YU, J., D. A. FISHMAN & T. L. STECK. 1973. J. Supramol. Struct. **1:** 233–46.
27. BOLTON, A. E. & W. M. HUNTER. 1973. Biochem. J. **133:** 529–39.
28. FURTHMAYER, H., R. E. GALARDY, T. MOTOWO & V. T. MARCHESI. 1978. Arch. Biochem. Biophys. **185:** 21–29.
29. NAKASHIMA, Y., R. L. WISEMAN, W. KONIGSBERG & D. A. MARVIN. 1975. Nature (London) **253:** 68–71.
30. TIEFTENBERG-TOSTESON, M. 1978. J. Membr. Biol. **38:** 291–309.
31. KAHANE, I. & C. GITLER. 1978. Science **201:** 351–52.
32. OZOLS, J. & G. CRAIG. 1977. Proc. Nat. Acad. Sci. USA **74:** 3725–29.
33. STECKHOVEN, F. S., R. F. WAITKUS & H. VAN MOERKERK. 1972. Biochemistry **11:** 1144–50.
34. SIGRIST, H., K. SIGRIST-NELSON & C. GITLER. 1977. Biochem. Biophys. Res. Commun. **74:** 178–84.
35. CATTELL, K. J., C. R. LINDOP, I. G. KNIGHT & R. B. BEECHEY. 1971. Biochem. J. **125:** 169–77.
36. NELSON, N., E. EYTAN, B.-E. NOTSANI, H. SIGRIST, K. SIGRIST-NELSON & C. GITLER. 1977. Proc. Nat. Acad. Sci. USA **74:** 2375–78.
37. GITLER, C. 1977. *In* Bioenergetics of Membranes. L. Packer, Ed. Elsevier/North Holland Biomedical Press. Amsterdam.
38. SHAMOO, A. E., T. C. RYAN, P. S. STEWART & D. H. MACHENNAN. 1976. J. Biol. Chem. **251:** 4147–55.
39. GRINSTEIN, S., S. SHIP & A. ROTHSTEIN. 1978. Biochim. Biophys. Acta **507:** 294–304.
40. CABANTCHICK, Z. I., P. KNAUF & A. ROTHSTEIN. 1978. Biochim. Biophys. Acta **515:** 239–302.
41. ROTHSTEIN, A. Personal communication.
42. HENDERSON, R. & P. N. T. UNWIN. 1975. Nature (London) **257:** 28–32.

DISCUSSION

DR. H. F. E. ESCHER: You mentioned that your naphthyl azide was degrading before you were using it. I think that this is a common feature with radioactive aromatic azides. We have researched the same thing with peptides containing para-azidophenyl-alanine. When it was stored at high specific activity, the peptide showed altered spectral patterns after one week.

DR. C. GITLER: We agree with you. We found that high specific activity tritium-labeled naphthyl azide (3Ci/mmol) decomposed quite rapidly upon storage and generated artifacts in the electrophoretic gels. So we went to iodine-labeled compounds, since the gamma emission should cause less ionizing radiation damage. But, unfortunately, our compound, (^{125}I)-5 iodonaphthyl-1-azide, is not stable in storage and can only be used some three to four days after synthesis. To solve this problem, we made a precursor that readily allows incorporation of iodine just prior to use.

DR. A. W. NICHOLSON (*University of Pennsylvania*): This is in reference to comments on the stability of tritium-labeled azides. I've been working with tritium-labeled aromatic azide for some time now and I've found that there has been no problem with radiodecomposition when it is stored in a liquid state at four degrees with a small amount of ethanol to act as a scavenger. But I might add that the tritium label is not on the aromatic azide section. It's on another part of the molecule, on the purine ring system; I have found no problems with these.

USE OF NAP-TAURINE AS A PHOTOAFFINITY PROBE FOR THE HUMAN ERYTHROCYTE ANION EXCHANGE SYSTEM*

Philip A. Knauf and Aser Rothstein

Research Institute
The Hospital for Sick Children
Toronto, Ontario, Canada M5G 1X8

INTRODUCTION

For over 100 years it has been known that the membrane of the red blood cell contains a system that is capable of exchanging cellular HCO_3^- for plasma Cl^- or vice versa.[1] This system permits CO_2 to be carried by the blood in the form of plasma HCO_3^-,[2] thus increasing the CO_2 carrying capacity of the blood, just as hemoglobin increases its oxygen carrying capacity. To be physiologically effective, this anion exchange system must operate very rapidly, so that the exchange will take place during the time of passage through a capillary (less than one second). Recent measurements indicate that the half-time for anion exchange at body temperature (measured by exchange of the isotope ^{36}Cl) is only about 50 ms.[3] The exceptional speed of the exchange suggests that the red blood cell membrane may be specialized for this particular transport function. The process does not involve energy input, but simply permits the anions to mutually equilibrate, in accordance with their concentration gradients.

The transport system seems to be restricted to a very tightly coupled one-for-one exchange of anions, with net flow across the membrane being at least ten thousand times slower.[4-7] This tight coupling of influx and efflux, together with other properties of the system, suggests that anions do not simply diffuse across the membrane, but rather that they must first combine with a membrane site (C in FIGURE 1) and only then are translocated across the membrane.[2,7,8] If it is assumed that the unloaded carrier (C) cannot cross the membrane unless it is complexed with an anion, then the system will be forced to transport one anion out for every anion that goes in. Although the model is shown in FIGURE 1 as a diffusible carrier system, the translocation of the carrier-anion complex (CA) could just as well involve a change in conformation of a transport protein, so that an inside-facing site is converted to an outside-facing site and vice versa, as in the model presented later in this paper.

The observation that the flux of chloride is inhibited at high chloride concentrations led Dalmark[9] to postulate that the transport system contains a second, lower-affinity, anion binding site, the modifier site (FIGURE 1). While the substrate site is half-saturated with chloride at 65 mM,[10] the modifier site is half-saturated only at the much higher concentration of 335 mM.[9] When an anion is bound to the modifier site (M), translocation of the anion-substrate site complex is inhibited.

A clue to the molecular identify of this transport system was first provided by

*This research was supported by two Canadian Medical Research Council grants, no. MT-5149 and no. MT-4665.

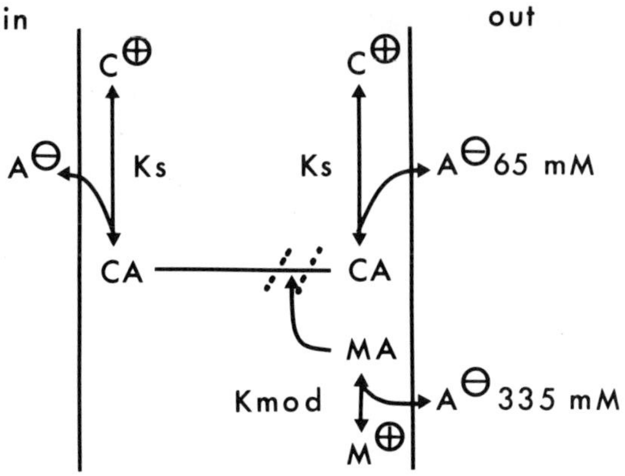

FIGURE 1. A carrier model for the anion exchange system. Anions bind to the transport carrier (C) and cross the membrane as a carrier-anion complex (CA). When anions are bound to the modifier site (M), transport is inhibited. The substrate (transport) site is half-saturated with chloride at $65 mM$ (K_s);[10] the modifier site at 335 mM (K_{mod}).[9] (From Knauf,[7] by permission of Academic Press, Inc.)

experiments with chemical probes, in particular the aromatic disulfonate, 4,4'-diisothiocyano-1,2-diphenylethane-2,2'-disulfonate (H$_2$DIDS). At low temperatures, this compound binds reversibly and with high affinity ($K_i \simeq 10^{-7}M$) to the substrate site of the transport system.[11] At higher temperatures, the isothiocyano groups at the two ends of this probe can react with amino acid side chains near the transport site.[12,13] When cells are exposed to tritium-labeled H$_2$DIDS, the label is found almost exclusively in a 93,000 dalton protein known as band 3,[12-14] suggesting that this protein contains the substrate site of the transport system. The substrate site displays considerable asymmetry in its interactions with compounds such as H$_2$DIDS: they inhibit transport when present at the extracellular side of the membrane, but not when present on the cytoplasmic side.[15,16]

The photoreactive reagent, N-(4-azido-2-nitrophenyl)-2-aminoethylsulfonate (NAP-taurine) has also proven to be a useful chemical probe for the red cell anion exchange system. This reagent (FIGURE 2) was originally synthesized by Staros and Richards[17] to serve as a general label for surface proteins. Because of its sulfonic acid moiety, however, NAP-taurine seems to interact preferentially with anion binding sites. The aryl azide of NAP-taurine does not react with proteins or lipids in the dark; therefore, the kinetics of its reversible interactions can be conveniently studied. After exposure to light, the azide is converted to a very reactive aryl nitrene, which can react covalently with virtually any biological molecule in its vicinity.[17,18] Therefore, NAP-taurine can be used to covalently label the sites to which it was reversibly bound in the dark.

This paper will focus on three aspects of the interactions between NAP-taurine

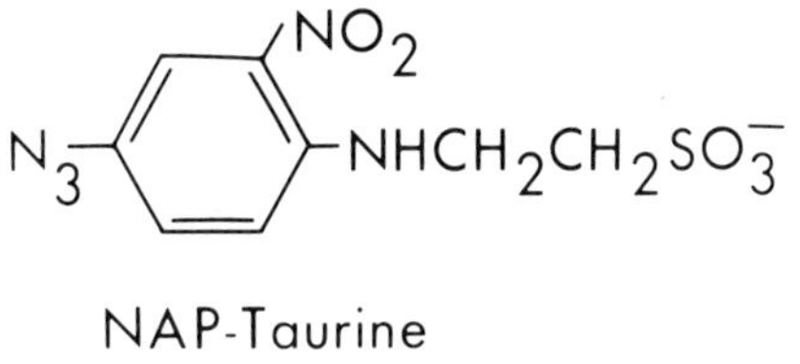

FIGURE 2. The chemical structure of NAP-taurine.

NAP-Taurine

and the anion exchange system:

1. The functional nature of the sites labeled by NAP-taurine.
2. The use of extracellular NAP-taurine as a photoaffinity label.
3. The use of NAP-taurine to detect conformational changes related to the transport of anions in the substrate and modifier sites of the band 3 protein.

RESULTS AND DISCUSSION

Site of Action of NAP-Taurine

In considering the possible interactions between NAP-taurine and the anion exchange system, it is natural first to ask whether or not NAP-taurine can be transported by the system. Experiments with ^{35}S-labeled NAP-taurine demonstrate that this probe does cross the membrane at 37 °C.[19,20] Moreover, its flux is very strongly inhibited by 4,4′-diisothiocyano-stilbene-2,2′-disulfonate (DIDS), an analog of H_2DIDS, and also by dipyridamole (Persantin).[20] As both of these compounds are rather potent inhibitors of the anion exchange system, which probably inhibit transport by different mechanisms,[7] this supports the idea that NAP-taurine, like many other organic anions,[21] is transported by the anion exchange system. At 0 °C, the flux of NAP-taurine across the membrane is so slow that it is difficult to detect.[19] This would be expected if NAP-taurine is transported by the anion exchange system, since this system has an extraordinarily high sensitivity to changes in temperature[7] (an activation energy of about 30 kcal/mol). In addition to providing further evidence that NAP-taurine is a substrate for the transport system, this slow penetration at 0 °C allows the effects of NAP-taurine at the cytoplasmic (inside) and extracellular (outside) faces of the membrane to be studied independently.

If NAP-taurine is a substrate for the anion exchange system, it should act as a competitive inhibitor of the exchange of other anions, such as chloride. When NAP-taurine is present inside resealed red cell ghosts (which were used to avoid complications due to the binding of NAP-taurine to hemoglobin), this prediction is borne out. The data for the effect of cytoplasmic NAP-taurine on chloride exchange are shown by a Hunter-Downs plot in FIGURE 3.[22] On the y-axis is plotted $I(1 - i)/i$, where I is the inhibitor (NAP-taurine) concentration and i is the fractional inhibition. This is equivalent to plotting the apparent K_i, that is, the concentration of NAP-taurine required to inhibit chloride exchange by 50%. This plot has the advantage that a straight line is obtained over the entire chloride concentration range, despite the presence of two anion binding sites: the substrate site and the modifier site. The y-intercept gives the K_i at zero chloride concentration, which, for intracellular NAP-taurine, is about 730 μM, indicating that internal NAP-taurine is a rather weak inhibitor of chloride exchange. As the chloride concentration is increased, more NAP-taurine is required to inhibit chloride exchange by 50%; that is, chloride and NAP-taurine compete with each other. The x-intercept of the plot, which corresponds to the chloride concentration required to half-saturate the NAP-taurine binding site, is only 36 mM. Because of the scatter in the data, this is not significantly different from the value of 65 mM reported for half-saturation of the substrate site. The results are significantly different ($p < 0.001$) from those expected if NAP-taurine were acting at the modifier site or at some other site with an even lower chloride affinity.[22]

These data, therefore, suggest that internal NAP-taurine inhibits by acting at the substrate site, a conclusion reinforced by the finding that NAP-taurine, as a substrate, has a low affinity for the anion exchange system, similar to that displayed by internal NAP-taurine as an inhibitor.[22]

In contrast to internal NAP-taurine, external NAP-taurine is a far more potent

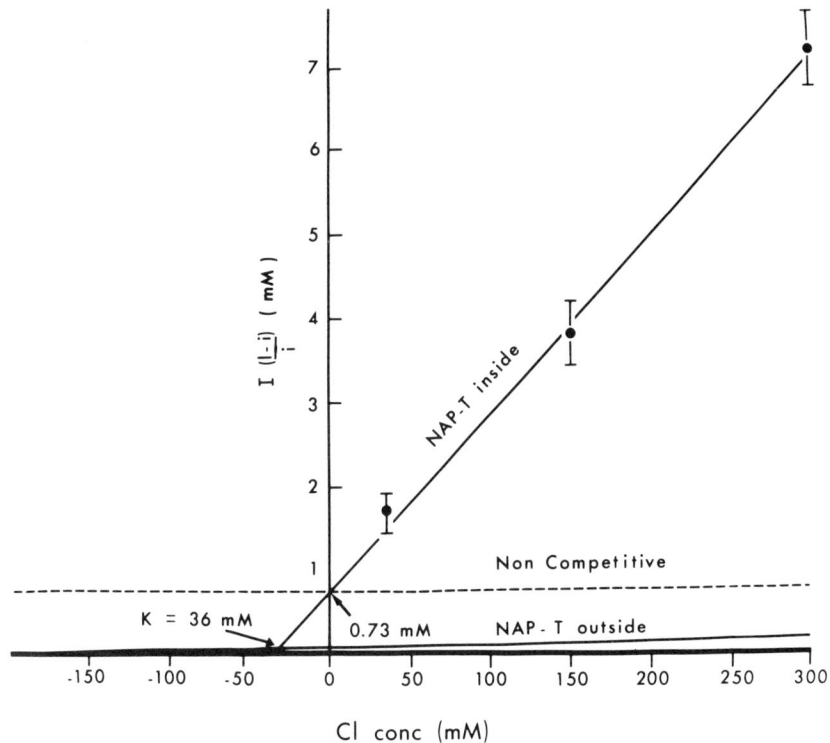

FIGURE 3. A Hunter-Downs plot of the effects of intracellular NAP-taurine on chloride exchange in resealed red cell ghosts at pH 7.2 and 0 °C. $I (1 - i)/i$ is plotted against the external chloride concentration in mM, where I is the inhibitor (NAP-taurine) concentration in μM and i is the fractional inhibition. $I(1 - i)/i$ is equivalent to the apparent K_i, the concentration of NAP-taurine required to inhibit Cl exchange by 50%. The upper solid line represents the least-squares best fit to the data for internal NAP-taurine. The lower solid line shows the extracellular NAP-taurine data for comparison. The broken line represents the expected result for noncompetitive inhibition. To avoid possible complications due to chloride or membrane potential gradients, the chloride concentrations in the ghosts and in the medium were kept nearly equal. (From Reference 25).

inhibitor. As can be seen from FIGURE 4, more than 50% inhibition is caused by 100 μM NAP-taurine, even at high chloride concentrations. The effect of chloride on external NAP-taurine inhibition is also different from its effect on internal NAP-taurine. When the data for low chloride concentrations are plotted on a Hanes plot, as in FIGURE 5, the results are clearly different from those expected for competitive

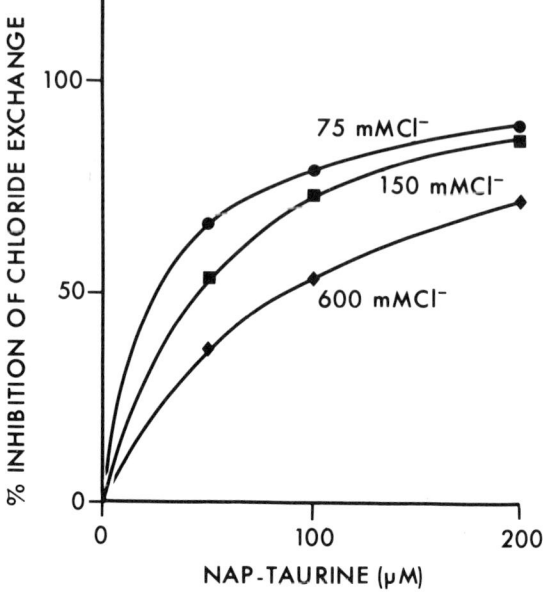

FIGURE 4. The inhibition of chloride exchange in red blood cells at 0 °C by extracellular NAP-taurine. Cells were loaded with various KCl concentrations by the nystatin technique so that internal and external chloride concentrations would be nearly equal.[22] The same is true for the experiments described in FIGURES 5, 6, and 10.

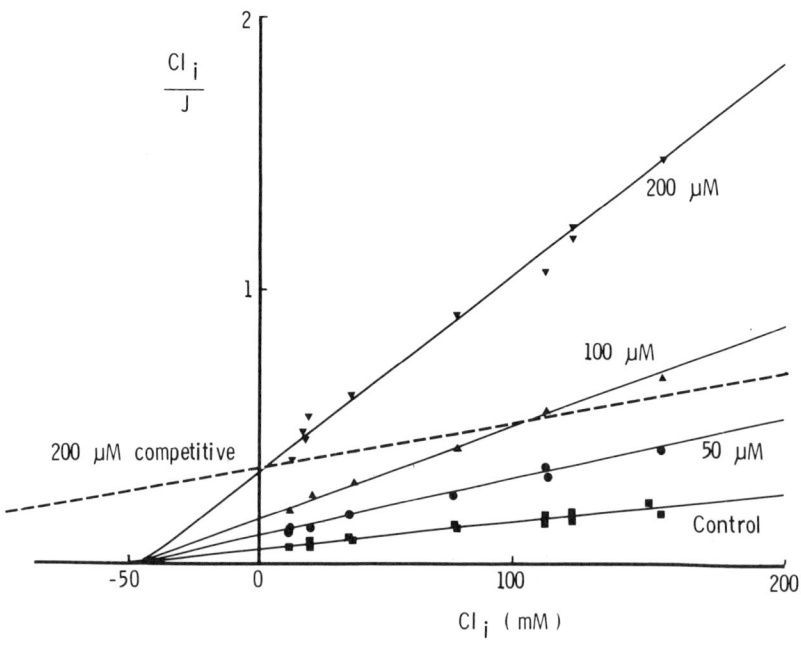

FIGURE 5. A Hanes plot of the effect of external NAP-taurine on chloride exchange in red blood cells at pH 7.2–7.5 and 0 °C. The internal chloride concentration (Cl_i) in mM divided by the chloride flux (J) in mmol/(kg cell solids-min) is plotted against Cl_i. The solid lines were calculated from the data of three experiments by the least squares method. The broken line shows the expected result for competitive inhibition with 200 μM NAP-taurine. (From Reference 22.)

inhibition at the substrate site (indicated by the broken line for 200 μM NAP-taurine). When data at higher NAP-taurine concentrations are plotted on a Hunter-Downs plot (FIGURE 3),[22] the results are significantly different ($p < 0.001$) from those predicted for action at the substrate site, and are also different ($p < 0.001$) from those expected for completely noncompetitive inhibition. The data suggest that external NAP-taurine acts at a site that has a lower affinity for chloride than does the substrate site, possibly the modifier site.

To test this possibility, the data for chloride flux as a function of chloride

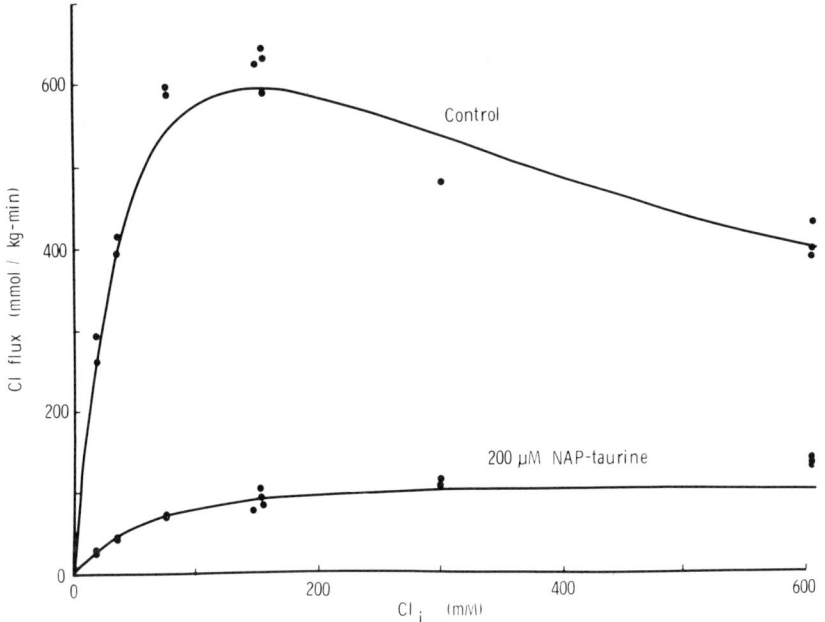

FIGURE 6. Chloride flux as a function of internal chloride concentration in nystatin-treated red cells at pH 7.2 and 0 °C. The upper curve was calculated from the model shown in FIGURE 1. The lower curve was calculated from the same model, assuming that extracellular NAP-taurine inhibits chloride exchange by binding to the modifier site. The points are experimental. (From Reference 22.)

concentration in the presence of 200 μM NAP-taurine were compared with the predictions of the modifier site model (FIGURE 6). As can be seen from the figure, the data fit well to this model, with the possible exception of the points at 600 mM chloride, where the large change in ionic strength may affect the inhibition. At present, it is impossible to rule out more complex models involving sites other than the substrate and modifier sites, but the data so far are consistent with the concept that extracellular NAP-taurine inhibits chloride exchange by acting at the modifier site.

A comparison of the inhibitory properties of external and internal NAP-taurine is given in TABLE 1. The modifier site seems to be asymmetric, in that it is accessible to

TABLE 1

SIDE-DEPENDENT EFFECTS OF NAP-TAURINE ON CHLORIDE EXCHANGE

	Outside	Inside
K_i (0 mM Cl$^-$)	20 μM	730 μM
K_i (140 mM Cl$^-$)	37 μM	3600 μM
K_{Cl}	165 mM	36 mM
Probable site	Modifier	Substrate

NOTE: K_i is the concentration of inhibitor required to inhibit chloride exchange by 50%; K_{Cl} is the concentration of chloride required to half-saturate the inhibitory site. K_i at 0 mM Cl$^-$ was determined by extrapolation from Hunter-Downs plots.

external, but not to internal, NAP-taurine. Recent data of Schnell et al. suggest that the modifier site is affected only by external Cl$^-$ and not by intracellular Cl$^-$.[23] On the other hand, the substrate site is probably available to external as well as internal NAP-taurine, since NAP-taurine appears to be transported by the anion exchange system. Inhibition of chloride transport due to the binding of external NAP-taurine to the substrate site is difficult to observe, however, because of the much stronger inhibitory effect produced by the higher affinity interaction with the modifier site.

Use of NAP-Taurine as a Photoaffinity Label for the Modifier Site

If external NAP-taurine acts as an ideal photoaffinity reagent, it should be possible to label its binding site (the modifier site) after exposure to light, as shown in FIGURE 7. To determine whether or not NAP-taurine acts in this fashion, its effects on anion exchange after exposure to light were measured, using sulfate fluxes as a convenient test for the activity of the anion exchange system. As shown in FIGURE 8 (first column), sulfate exchange is strongly inhibited in the presence of NAP-taurine. When, however, the cells were washed twice with a medium containing 0.5% albumin, the sulfate flux returned to the control value (FIGURE 8, second column). If the cells were exposed to intense light in the presence of NAP-taurine and then washed, sulfate flux was inhibited (third column), demonstrating that exposure to light is capable of making the inhibition irreversible. That this effect was not due to some long-lived photoproduct of NAP-taurine is evident from the last two columns, which show that, if NAP-taurine is exposed to light before the cells are added, it has no significant effect on sulfate flux either when present in the dark or after exposure to light.

These results are consistent with the action of NAP-taurine as a photoaffinity label. It could be possible, however, that NAP-taurine in the medium is activated by light and that the nitrene then collides with the membrane and reacts with it, thereby causing inhibition unrelated to reaction with the reversible binding site. To test this alternative, the nitrene scavenger p-aminobenzoic acid (PABA) has added to the medium to scavenge activated nitrenes.[24] The addition of PABA had no effect on the ability of light to convert the reversible inhibition in the dark to an irreversible inhibition.[25] This suggests that the nitrene moiety of NAP-taurine, whose reaction results in irreversible inhibition, is hidden in some cleft in the membrane structure where it is inaccessible to scavengers present in the external medium.

If the irreversible inhibition of anion exchange after exposure to light in the presence of NAP-taurine is due to the covalent reaction of NAP-taurine molecules already reversibly bound to the modifier site, then one would expect a close correlation between the reversible inhibition produced by NAP-taurine in the dark and the irreversible inhibition produced after exposure to light. Theoretically, if the rates of photoactivation for NAP-taurine in solution and bound to the cells are identical, and if the cells are irradiated for a sufficient time, then the reversible and irreversible inhibition should be exactly the same.[25] From the data in FIGURE 8, as well as from other experiments,[25,26] the reversible and irreversible inhibitions are similar for low (<100 μM) NAP-taurine concentrations. The irreversible inhibition is, however, slightly but significantly higher than the reversible inhibition.[25] This difference probably does not reflect additional inhibition caused by the reaction of photoactivated NAP-taurine in the medium with the membrane, since the difference persists in

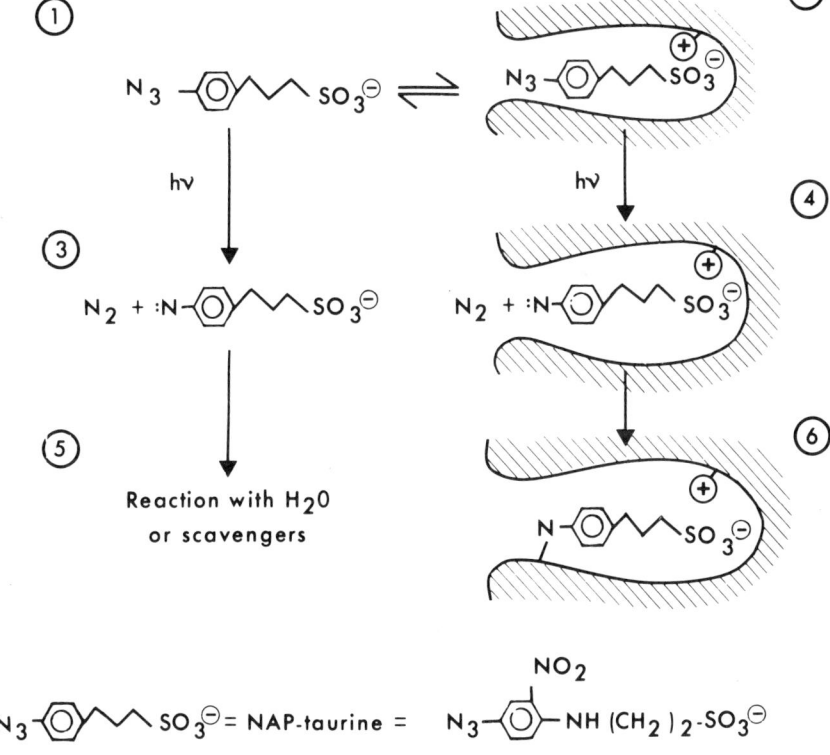

FIGURE 7. Photoaffinity labeling by NAP-taurine. NAP-taurine in solution (1) in the dark can reversibly bind to anion binding sites (2), such as the modifier site in the case of extracellular NAP-taurine. Exposure to light converts the aryl azide of NAP-taurine to an aryl nitrene (3 and 4). This highly reactive intermediate is rapidly removed from solution by reaction either with water or with added scavenger substances, such as PABA (5). The nitrene can also react with membrane components near the site of reversible binding, thereby labeling the binding site (6). (From Reference 25.)

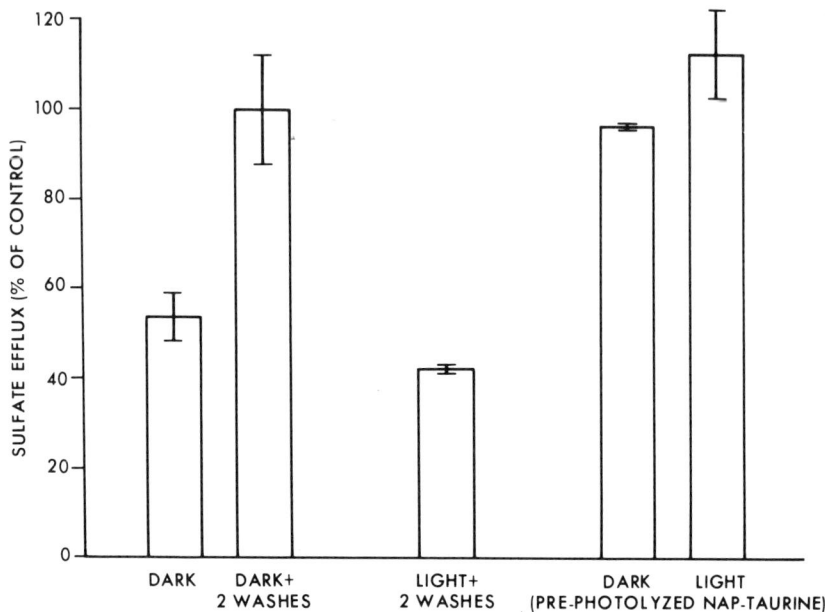

FIGURE 8. Inhibition of sulfate exchange by extracellular NAP-taurine at 27 °C and pH 7.4. Cells were loaded with ^{35}S-sulfate in a buffer containing 5 mM Na_2SO_4, 20 mM NaCl, 200 mM sucrose, and 25 mM tris(hydroxymethyl)aminomethane (Tris), and then the efflux of the isotope was measured as described in Reference 25. In the columns labeled "Dark," 50 μM NAP-taurine was present during the flux measurement, except where otherwise indicated ("Dark + 2 washes"). For the columns labeled "Light," cells at 5% hematocrit were irradiated for 20 min with light from a General Electric DX8 Photospot at a distance of 10 cm in the presence of 50 μM NAP-taurine. The cells were then washed twice in a buffer containing 0.5% bovine serum albumin and the sulfate flux was measured. For the two columns at the right, the NAP-taurine was prephotolyzed by exposure to sunlight before being used in the flux experiments. Bars indicate the standard error of five and three experiments for columns 1 and 3, respectively, and the range of two experiments for the other columns.

the presence of PABA, which should inhibit such nonspecific reactions. Because of the geometry of the irradiation apparatus, it is possible that the NAP-taurine bound to the cells is more efficiently irradiated than that which is in the medium. This could account for the slight excess of irreversible over reversible inhibition.[25] Regardless of the origin of this small difference, it is clear that NAP-taurine is a very efficient photoaffinity label, one that reacts with all, or nearly all, its reversible binding sites.

This high efficiency is seen only for low NAP-taurine concentrations and only after sufficiently long irradiation times. Because of the absorption of light by hemoglobin inside the red blood cells, rather long irradiation times are necessary. If the cell concentration is increased, the efficiency of photoactivation is drastically reduced.[20,25] Similarly, much longer irradiation times are necessary at high NAP-taurine concentrations because the NAP-taurine in solution absorbs much of the incident light. Because of these technical problems, it is rather difficult to prepare large quantities of highly labeled cells.

When intact red cells are exposed to light in the presence of extracellular ^{35}S-labeled NAP-taurine, and when ghosts are prepared from these cells, solubilized in sodium dodecyl sulfate (SDS), and then electrophoresed on polyacrylamide gels,[27] most of the label is found in the 93,000 dalton band 3 protein,[17,20,25,26,28] the same protein that is labeled by DIDS or H_2DIDS.[12-14] As shown in FIGURE 9, the band 3 protein is arranged asymmetrically in the lipid bilayer.[29-33] At the outside of the membrane, there is a site (1) of cleavage by pronase[34,35] or chymotrypsin[31,32,35] which generates a 55,000 dalton nonglycosylated segment (A + B) and a 38,000 dalton C-terminal segment (C) that contains all the carbohydrate of band 3.[36] Both of these segments are tightly associated with the membrane. Cleavage at the internal surface of the membrane (site 2) with trypsin or chymotrypsin[32,37] releases a water soluble[32] N-terminal[31,36] fragment of about 40,000 daltons (A). Cleavage at both sites produces a membrane-associated fragment of about 17,000 daltons (B), which must span the membrane, since it is produced by proteolytic cleavages at opposite sides of the membrane.[32,37]

To determine which of these segments contains the NAP-taurine labeling site, NAP-taurine treated cells were exposed to external pronase to produce cleavage at site 1. As can be seen from FIGURE 10, most of the label is found in the region of the gel corresponding to the A + B segment, and very little label is seen in the 38,000 dalton region. Both the NAP-taurine inhibition of chloride exchange and the labeling of the A + B segment (FIGURE 10) were reduced at high chloride concentrations; this is consistent with the concept that the site labeled by NAP-taurine after exposure to light is the same chloride-sensitive site to which NAP-taurine binds in the dark. The correlation between the inhibition of chloride exchange and the binding of NAP-

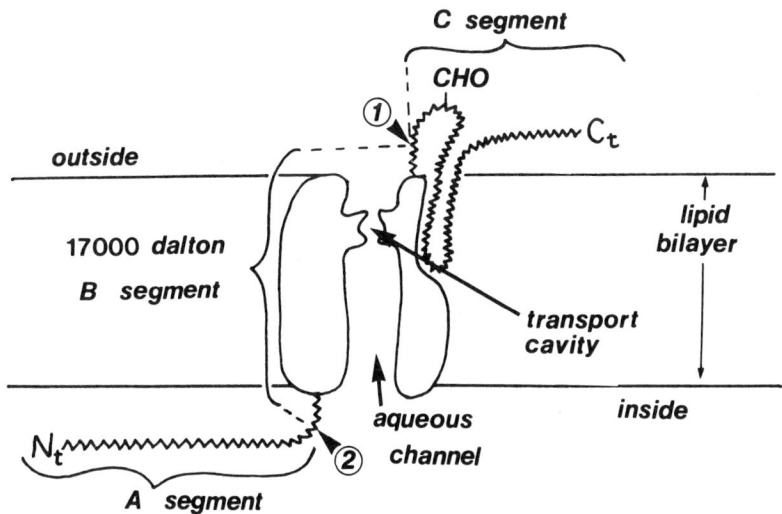

FIGURE 9. The arrangement of band 3 in the erythrocyte membrane. Sites of proteolytic cleavage at the outside and the inside of the membrane are labeled 1 and 2, respectively. N_t and C_t are the N and C-termini of the polypeptide; CHO is the site of glycosylation. The size of the membrane-associated segment of band 3 is somewhat exaggerated for the sake of clarity. (From Reference 50.).

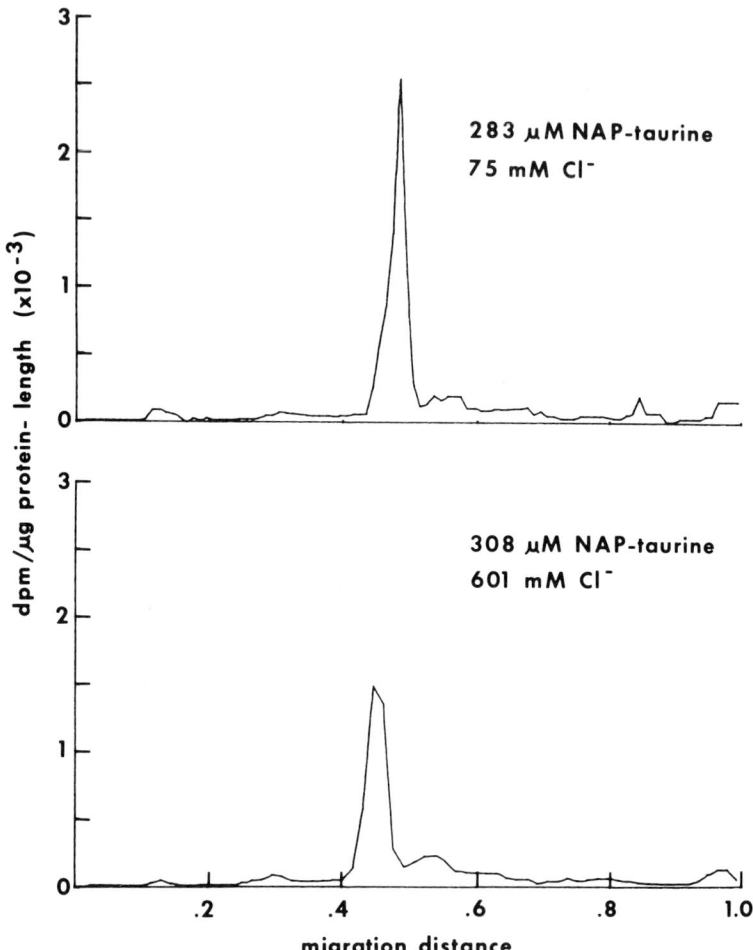

FIGURE 10. The labeling of membrane proteins by ^{35}S-labeled external NAP-taurine in high and low chloride media after treatment of intact labeled cells with pronase. The number of disintegrations per minute of ^{35}S in each gel slice divided by the amount of protein applied to the gel (in micrograms) and by the length of the slice relative to the migration distance of the tracking dye, Pyronin Y, is plotted against the distance of the slice from the top of a polyacrylamide gel, relative to that of Pyronin Y. The major labeling peak corresponds to the A + B segment of band 3, as shown in FIGURE 9. Very little labeling is seen in the region (between 0.6 and 0.8) where the C segment is found. (From Reference 25.)

taurine to the A + B segment was good ($r^2 = 0.96$), and the least-squares best fit to the data indicated that about 9×10^5 molecules per cell are required for 100% inhibition.[25] This is similar to the values for the number of band 3 monomers[27] and the number of H$_2$DIDS binding sites per cell,[12,13] suggesting that each band 3 monomer contains one H$_2$DIDS binding site (substrate site) and one NAP-taurine binding site (modifier site).

If the orientation of band 3 shown in FIGURE 9 is correct, then one would expect to find the extracellular NAP-taurine label in the 17,000 dalton B region, since this is the only portion of the A + B segment accessible from the outside of the membrane. If cells are labeled with external NAP-taurine and if ghosts are prepared and electrophoresed on SDS-polyacrylamide gels, the results shown in Figure 11A are obtained, with most of the label in the band 3 region. If the ghosts are treated with 10

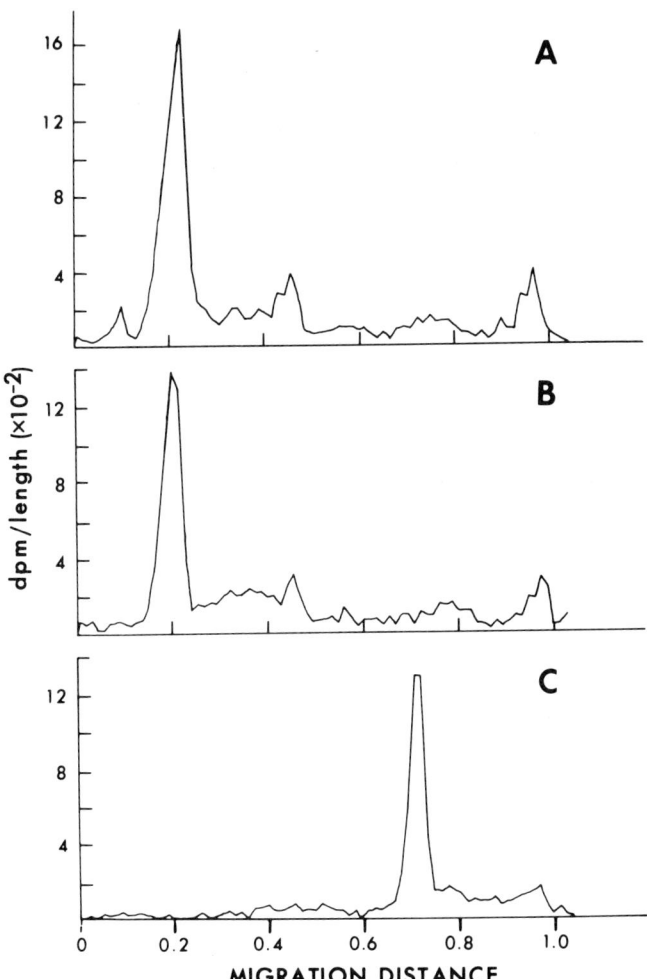

FIGURE 11. The effects of alkali and chymotrypsin treatment on membrane proteins labeled by extracellular NAP-taurine. A: untreated ghosts; B: Ghosts "stripped" of peripheral proteins by incubation with ice-cold 10 mM NaOH, as described in Reference 25; C: Stripped ghosts treated with chymotrypsin. Proteins were separated on 7.5% polyacrylamide gels. Results are plotted as in FIGURE 10. The positions of the major peaks correspond to band 3 in A and B ("3") and to the 17,000 dalton B fragment ("17K") in C. (From Reference 25.)

mM NaOH to remove loosely bound "peripheral" proteins,[37,38] as in FIGURE 11B, the labeling pattern is very similar, except that a minor labeling peak in the high molecular weight region towards the top of the gel (bands 2.1–2.6[17]) is removed. When these ghosts are treated with chymotrypsin to cleave the band 3 protein at sites 1 and 2, the 17,000 dalton (B) fragment of band 3 is produced (FIGURE 11C). Almost all the label that was present in the band 3 region is quantitatively recovered in the region of the gel corresponding to the 17,000 dalton segment, demonstrating that this segment contains the NAP-taurine labeling site (and therefore contains part or all of the modifier site).

When red cells are labeled with H$_2$DIDS at neutral pH, most of the label is also found in this 17,000 dalton fragment,[37] suggesting that this fragment contains at least part of the substrate site, as well as the modifier site. At higher pH, H$_2$DIDS also labels a portion of the 38,000 dalton C segment,[39] demonstrating that this segment may also be at or near the substrate site. There is, as yet, no evidence to indicate that the C segment is adjacent to the modifier site, since it is not labeled by external NAP-taurine. Recent experiments have located the principal site of H$_2$DIDS binding at neutral pH at a 4,000 dalton subfragment located near the middle of the B segment.[40] While not yet conclusive, similar experiments with NAP-taurine are consistent with the hypothesis that external NAP-taurine labels the same fragment. Other portions of the 17,000 dalton segment may be labeled as well.

Use of NAP-Taurine to Detect Conformational Changes in the Transport System

In addition to its usefulness as a label for the modifier site, NAP-taurine can also be used to test models for the transport mechanism. For instance, a model with a single transport site that oscillates between an inside-facing and outside-facing conformation, such as the model shown in FIGURE 1, predicts that the transport site cannot face both sides of the membrane at the same time. Thus, if the transport site has reacted with H$_2$DIDS or DIDS at the external surface of the membrane, it will not be available to react with NAP-taurine at the cytoplasmic surface. Such transmembrane effects on the accessibility of the substrate site are predicted by the single transport site (ping-pong) model shown in FIGURE 1, but are not predicted by models in which there are two noninteracting transport sites on opposite sides of the membrane, both of which must bind anions before transport of the two anions can take place simultaneously.

Grinstein et al. reacted intact cells with DIDS, washed away the unbound DIDS, made ghosts from the cells, and prepared inside-out vesicles from the ghosts.[16] They then compared the binding of NAP-taurine to the cytoplasmic surface of these DIDS-pretreated vesicles with its binding to untreated vesicles. As can be seen from TABLE 2, pretreatment of the external surface of the membrane with DIDS greatly reduced the binding of NAP-taurine to the cytoplasmic side of the band 3 protein. In addition, some unexpected effects on the labeling of other proteins by NAP-taurine were observed, indicating either interaction between band 3 and other proteins or, possibly, disruptive effects of DIDS pretreatment on the structure of the membrane. In spite of these complications, the results are consistent with the hypothesis that the band 3 protein possesses a single transport site, which is accessible either to DIDS or

H_2DIDS from the outside of the cell or to NAP-taurine from the cytoplasmic side of the membrane, but not to both at the same time. Such a model is also favored by recent kinetic evidence.[7,30,41]

A potentially less disruptive method for inducing conformational changes in the transport system involves the use of the substrate, chloride, itself. For a model such as that shown in FIGURE 1, the ratio of outside-facing to inside-facing unloaded carriers in a chloride medium will be related to the Donnan ratio (Cl_i/Cl_o). For the particular case of a carrier with equal chloride affinities at the two sides of the membrane and equal translocation rates in the two directions, the ratio of outside-facing unloaded carrier to inside-facing will be exactly equal to Cl_i/Cl_o.[7,30,42] This redistribution of unloaded carrier has nothing to do with the membrane potential, since it is predicted by a model that assumes that potential has no effect whatsoever on the anion exchange process.

This feature of the mechanism can be used to examine the question of whether or not the substrate site conformation affects the modifier site. If the external chloride

TABLE 2

EFFECT OF EXTRACELLULAR DIDS PRETREATMENT ON THE BINDING OF NAP-TAURINE
TO THE CYTOPLASMIC SIDE OF THE RED BLOOD CELL MEMBRANE
AFTER EXPOSURE TO LIGHT

	Band 3 Region	Total
Control	5,761	10,802
DIDS pretreated	2,603	6,432
Difference	3,158	4,370
% of total difference	72.2	100

NOTE: Cells were pretreated with 5 μM DIDS. Inside out vesicles prepared from these cells or from control cells were irradiated in the presence of 0.23 mM tritium-labeled NAP-taurine for 5 min at 0 °C and were then solubilized in SDS and electrophoresed on 7.5% polyacrylamide gels. Numbers represent the average of four determinations of the number of counts in the gel regions for a single preparation of vesicles. The effect of DIDS on the total and band 3 labeling was significant at the $p < 0.001$ level. (From Reference 16.)

concentration (Cl_o) is reduced, then more of the unloaded carriers will be in the outward-facing conformation. If NAP-taurine binds to the modifier site only when the substrate site is in this conformation, then lowering the external chloride concentration should enhance the inhibitory effect of NAP-taurine. This effect should be far greater than the small enhancement of inhibition that is seen when the chloride concentration is reduced on both sides of the membrane. In fact, when the external chloride concentration is reduced and the internal chloride concentration is kept constant, the inhibitory potency of NAP-taurine (measured by its effect on sulfate exchange[20,22,26,28]) is greatly enhanced. Similarly, in cells with 58 mM internal Cl and 10 mM external Cl, chloride exchange was 50% inhibited by only 13.5 μM NAP-taurine, even less than the K_i for NAP-taurine extrapolated to zero chloride (20.2 μM ± 1.7 S.E.M.) from data with $Cl_i = Cl_o$. While not conclusive, these data suggest that the modifier site may be accessible to external NAP-taurine only when the substrate site is in the outward-facing conformation.

Interaction between the substrate and modifier sites is not unexpected, in view of the evidence that these sites may be adjacent. Although on the basis of competition with chloride, H_2DIDS (or DIDS) and NAP-taurine seem to act at different sites, they do display some mutual interference. DIDS inhibits NAP-taurine binding to band 3,[20] and NAP-taurine reduces DIDS inhibition of sulfate flux[20] and inhibits binding of H_2DIDS to band 3.[26] This may indicate that the very large DIDS molecule overlaps at least part of the modifier site and therefore interferes with NAP-taurine binding, so that DIDS and NAP-taurine mutually compete, even though they are affected differently by chloride. An overlap of H_2DIDS onto the modifier site would be difficult to detect kinetically, however, because the competitive effect of chloride would be dominated by its much stronger interaction with the substrate site. Although it is, perhaps, simplest to think of such interactions between DIDS and NAP-taurine in terms of steric hindrance, it is also possible that an allosteric effect may be involved, since there is good evidence that DIDS can cause conformational changes in the membrane.[7,16,30,43] It should be noted that the interaction of inhibitors that bind to different sites is not without precedent. The potency of the noncompetitive inhibitor niflumic acid is strongly affected by a disulfonic stilbene (similar to DIDS) that probably binds to the substrate site.[44]

Model for the Transport System

A model that takes into account the information obtained with the photoaffinity probe, NAP-taurine, as well as other kinetic and biochemical information rgarding the transport system and the band 3 protein is shown in FIGURE 12. The transport site probably contains a positive charge, due to the presence of a guanidino group of arginine. This positive site is likely to be arginine, both because the transport system is insensitive to changes in pH from 7 to 11[45] and because a guanidino group would account for the observed selectivity of the transport system for the binding of the various halide anions.[9,46] In addition, there is a second ,titratable group (probably amino) that can be protonated at low pH and that converts the monovalent carrier to a divalent anion carrier. The modifier site is shown near the outer portion of the transport site, since it appears to be accessible to both NAP-taurine and chloride only from the outside, and since, from the evidence discussed above, it is probably adjacent to the substrate site.

The conformational change involved in the actual translocation of anions probably involves neither rotation of the band 3 protein, since the protein is arranged asymmetrically in the membrane, nor "diffusion" of a loop of the band 3 protein, since such a process would disrupt the membrane structure and would probably not explain the very rapid rate of transport (about 5×10^4 ions per site per second at body temperature).[3] More likely, the change of the transport site from inside-facing to outside-facing involves a very subtle conformational change, which actually does not involve much physical movement of the anion binding site, but rather a change in the position of the diffusion barrier, as originally suggested by Patlak (FIGURE 12B, panels 1–4).[47] The transport site is probably formed at the interface between two domains of the same band 3 monomer, since all the evidence so far indicates that each band 3 monomer functions as an independent transport site,[7] despite the fact that most of the band 3 protein seems to be associated as dimers in the membrane.[7,30]

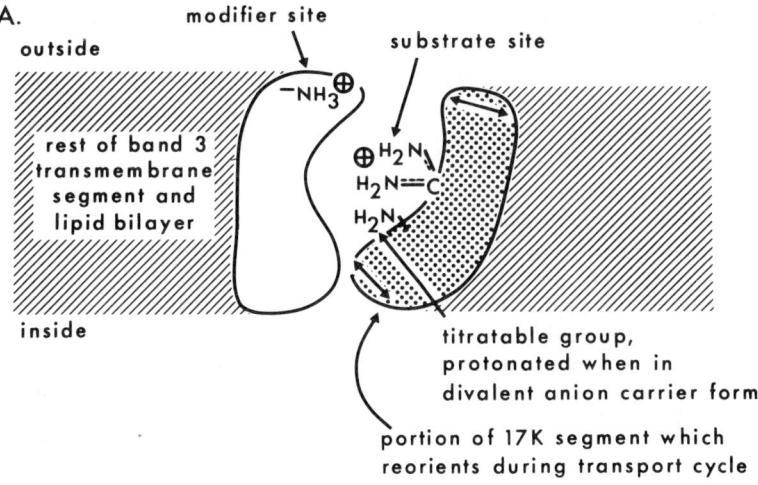

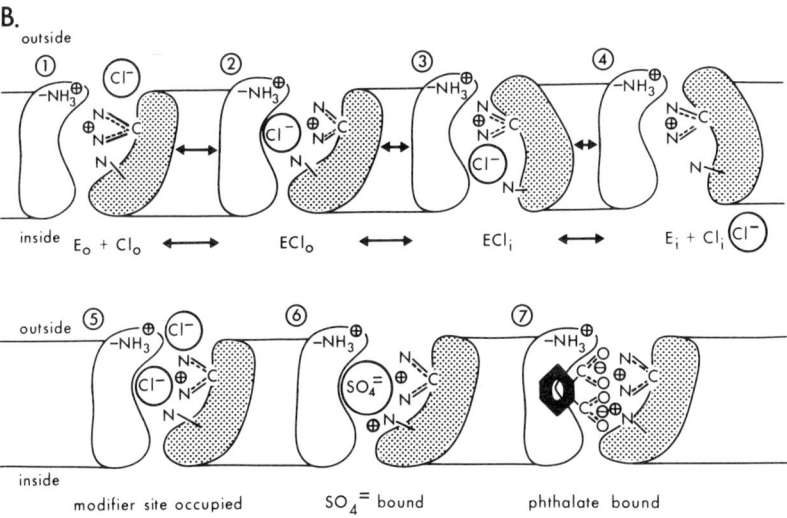

FIGURE 12. A model for the structure of the transport site (A) and for the mechanism of the red cell anion exchange system (B). (From Knauf,[7] by permission of Academic Press, Inc.)

According to this model (FIGURE 12B), transport occurs when an anion in the external solution binds to the transport site when it is in the outside-facing (E_o) conformation (panel 1). This permits a spontaneous conformational change to occur (panels 2 and 3), so that the transport site faces inward, after which the anion is released into the internal solution (panel 4). The system then binds another anion from the inside solution, and the steps are repeated in the opposite direction. If it is assumed that the conformational change can only occur when the anion is bound, then the model will exhibit the tight coupling of anion influx and efflux that is experimentally observed.

If an anion is bound to the modifier site, as in panel 5, the system is locked in the outward-facing conformation and cannot transport anions. Conversely, if the system is in the inward-facing conformation, the modifier site is not accessible (panels 3 and 4) to anions or to NAP-taurine. Physiologically, the presence of a positively charged site (modifier site) adjacent to the substrate site may increase the local concentration of anions by electrostatic attraction and, thereby, facilitate the operation of the transport system. Inhibition by binding to this site may only be a consequence of the unusually high anion concentrations used to probe the system experimentally.

As shown in panel 6, when the amino group in the transport site is protonated, the system can transport divalent anions such as sulfate,[2,7,8,48] but its rate of transport is much lower than that of chloride. Even organic anions with relatively large hydrophobic groups, such as phthalate (panel 7), can be accomodated.[21,49] The apolar moiety probably passes through a hydrophobic region near the interface between the two protein domains that form the transport cavity. The existence of such a hydrophobic region is also suggested by structure-activity studies with inhibitors.[7,30] Although large hydrophobic moieties are tolerated, divalent organic anions are only transported if the distance between the charges in the hydrophilic region is less than about 4 Å.[21,49] This suggests that the size of the transport cavity itself is rather limited, and that it certainly is not large enough to span the lipid bilayer. It seems likely, therefore, that anions reach the transport site by diffusing through a hydrophilic channel formed by portions of the 17,000 dalton (B) and 38,000 dalton (C) segments of band 3, as shown in FIGURE 9.

In summary, the photoaffinity probe, NAP-taurine, has contributed greatly to our understanding of the anion transport mechanism. It has been particularly useful for locating the modifier site in the band 3 protein, for detecting the asymmetric orientation of the modifier site, and for observing conformational changes in the substrate site, as well as the effects of these changes on the accessibility of the modifier site. Despite these advances, the potential of NAP-taurine to provide information is not yet exhausted. Although the nitrene moiety produced by photoactivation of NAP-taurine is chemically unspecific, it seems to be relatively restricted in the sites it can label due to the binding of NAP-taurine within some cavity in the membrane. Thus, it may be possible, in the future, to determine much more precisely the segment of band 3 and, perhaps, the actual amino acid residues to which external NAP-taurine binds, and which are, therefore, at or near the modifier site. Internal NAP-taurine may also provide additional information regarding segments of band 3 that are adjacent to the substrate site, but are not labeled by DIDS or H_2DIDS because of the chemical specificity of those probes.

ACKNOWLEDGMENTS

The authors gratefully acknowledge the contributions of W. Breuer, W. Furuya, S. Grinstein, L. McCulloch, S. Ship, and T. Tarshis to the experiments described in this paper.

REFERENCES

1. NASSE, H. 1878. Pfluegers Arch. Gesamte Physiol. Menschen Tiere **16:** 604–34.
2. GUNN, R. B. 1979. *In* Membrane Transport in Biology, Vol. 2. G. Giebisch, D. Tosteson & H. H. Ussing, Eds. : 59–79. Springer Verlag. New York.
3. BRAHM, J. 1977. J. Gen. Physiol. **70:** 283–306.
4. HUNTER, M. J. 1971. J. Physiol. (London) **218:** 49P–50P.
5. HUNTER, M. J. 1977. J. Physiol. (London) **268:** 35–49.
6. KNAUF, P. A., G. F. FUHRMANN, S. ROTHSTEIN & A. ROTHSTEIN. 1977. J. Gen. Physiol. **69:** 363–86.
7. KNAUF, P. A. 1979. *In* Current Topics in Membranes and Transport, Vol. 12. F. Bronner & A. Kleinzeller, Eds.: 249–363. Academic Press. New York.
8. GUNN, R. B., M. DALMARK, D. TOSTESON & J. O. WIETH. 1973. J. Gen. Physiol. **61:** 185–206.
9. DALMARK, M. 1976. J. Gen. Physiol. **67:** 223–34.
10. BRAZY, P. C. & R. B. GUNN. 1976. J. Gen. Physiol. **68:** 583–99.
11. SHAMI, Y., A. ROTHSTEIN & P. A. KNAUF. 1978. Biochim. Biophys. Acta. **508:** 357–63.
12. SHIP, S., Y. SHAMI, W. BREUER & A. ROTHSTEIN. 1977. J. Membr. Biol. **33:** 311–24.
13. LEPKE, S., H. FASOLD, M. PRING & H. PASSOW. 1976. J. Membr. Biol. **29:** 147–77.
14. CABANTCHIK, Z. I. & A. ROTHSTEIN. 1974. J. Membr. Biol. **15:** 207–26.
15. KAPLAN, J. H., K. SCORAH, H. FASOLD & H. PASSOW. 1976. FEBS Lett. **62:** 182–85.
16. GRINSTEIN, S., L. MCCULLOCH & A. ROTHSTEIN. 1979. J. Gen. Physiol. **73:** 493–514.
17. STAROS, J. V. & F. M. RICHARDS. 1974. Biochemistry **13:** 2720–26.
18. KNOWLES, J. R. 1972. Acc. Chem. Res. **5:** 155–60.
19. STAROS, J. V., F. M. RICHARDS & B. E. HALEY. 1975. J. Biol. Chem. **250:** 8174–78.
20. CABANTCHIK, Z. I., P. KNAUF, T. OSTWALD, H. MARKUS, L. DAVIDSON, W. BREUER & A. ROTHSTEIN. 1976. Biochim. Biophys. Acta **455:** 526–37.
21. MOTAIS, R. 1977. *In* Membrane Transport in Red Cells. J. C. Ellory & V. L. Lew, Eds.: 197–220. Academic Press. New York.
22. KNAUF, P. A., S. SHIP, W. BREUER, L. MCCULLOCH & A. ROTHSTEIN. 1978. J. Gen. Physiol. **72:** 607–30.
23. SCHNELL, K. F., E. BESL & A. MANZ. 1978. Pfluegers Arch. Gesamte Physiol. Menschen Tiere (Eur. J. Physiol.) **375:** 87–95.
24. RUOHO, A. E., H. KIEFER, P. E. ROEDER & S. J. SINGER. 1972. Proc. Nat. Acad. Sci. USA **70:** 2567–71.
25. KNAUF, P. A., W. BREUER, L. MCCULLOCH & A. ROTHSTEIN. 1978. J. Gen. Physiol. **72:** 631–49.
26. ROTHSTEIN, A., P. A. KNAUF & Z. I. CABANTCHIK. 1977. *In* Biochemistry of Membrane Transport. G. Semenza & E. Carafoli, Eds.: 316–27. Springer Verlag. Berlin.
27. FAIRBANKS, G., T. L. STECK & D. F. H. WALLACH. 1971. Biochemistry **10:** 2606–17.
28. ROTHSTEIN, A., Z. CABANTCHIK, & P. A. KNAUF. 1976. Fed. Proc. Fed. Am. Soc. Exp. Biol. **35:** 3–10.
29. BRETSCHER, M. S. 1971. J. Mol. Biol. **59:** 351–57.
30. CABANTCHIK, Z. I., P. A. KNAUF & A. ROTHSTEIN. 1978. Biochim. Biophys. Acta **515:** 239–302.
31. DRICKAMER, L. K. 1976. J. Biol. Chem. **251:** 5115–23.
32. STECK, T. L., B. RAMOS & E. STRAPAZON. 1976. Biochemistry **15:** 1154–61.
33. STECK, T. L. 1978. J. Supramolec. Struct. **8:** 311–24.
34. BENDER, W. W., H. GARAN & H. C. BERG. 1971. J. Mol. Biol. **58:** 783–97.
35. CABANTCHIK, Z. I. & A. ROTHSTEIN. 1974. J. Membr. Biol. **15:** 227–48.
36. DRICKAMER, K. 1978. J. Biol. Chem. **253:** 7242–48.
37. GRINSTEIN, S., S. SHIP & A. ROTHSTEIN. 1978. Biochim. Biophys. Acta **507:** 294–304.
38. STECK, T. L. & J. YU. 1973. J. Supramol. Struct. **1:** 220–32.
39. JENNINGS, M. L. & H. PASSOW. 1979. Biochim. Biophys. Acta. **554:** 498–519.
40. ROTHSTEIN, A., M. RAMJEESINGH, S. GRINSTEIN & P. A. KNAUF. 1980. Ann. N.Y. Acad. Sci. **341:** 433–43.

41. GUNN, R. B. & O. FRÖHLICH. 1979. J. Gen. Physiol. **74:** 351–74.
42. DALMARK, M. 1975. J. Physiol. (London) **250:** 39–64.
43. SNOW, J. W., J. F. BRANDTS & P. S. LOW. 1978. Biochim. Biophys. Acta **512:** 579–91.
44. COUSIN, J. L. & R. MOTAIS. 1979. J. Membr. Biol. **46:** 125–53.
45. FUNDER, J. & J. O. WIETH. 1976. J. Physiol. (London) **262:** 679–98.
46. DIAMOND, J. M. & E. M. WRIGHT. 1969. Annu. Rev. Physiol. **31:** 581–646.
47. PATLAK, C. S. 1957. Bull. Math. Biophys. **19:** 209–35.
48. GUNN, R. B. 1978. *In* Membrane Transport Processes. J. F. Hoffman, Ed.: 61–77. Raven Press. New York.
49. AUBERT, L. & R. MOTAIS. 1975. J. Physiol. (London) **246:** 159–79.
50. KNAUF, P. A. & S. GRINSTEIN. 1979. Fed. Proc. Fed. Am. Soc. Exp. Biol. In press.

DISCUSSION

DR. RUSSELL (*City College of New York*): Can I assume that you used butane dione or some other specific inhibitor to identify the guanidino group in the binding site?

DR. P. A. KNAUF: No; we haven't done that as yet. The location of the guanidino group is postulated on the basis of kinetic data. For one thing, the transport system is insensitive to pH over the range from pH 7 to pH 11. So, if the transport site is positively charged, which at least seems plausible, then guanidino seems to be about the only candidate that won't be titrated over this pH range.

Secondly, the system exhibits selectivity in the binding of the different halides. The selectivity series is that for binding to a weak positive site that would, in fact, correspond to the binding affinities expected for guanidino groups.

RUSSELL: Well, there are quite a few very selective reagents for identifying it. Since you can check with chloride to see if you're protecting that inhibition, you would be able to pinpoint its identification.

KNAUF: Yes, we would like to do that. We are concerned about the possible amino reactivity of these reagents since it's known that amino reagents are effective inhibitors.

DR. M. E. DOCKTER: Is it possible to tell whether or not the NAP-taurine and the DIDS are acting on the same polypeptide chain of the dimer or on opposite polypeptide chains of the dimer?

KNAUF: I think the question really doesn't exist because Jennings and Passow have recently shown, in a series of very elegant experiments, that the DIDS binding to band 3 is not just stoichiometric in the sense that there are the same number of DIDS binding sites as band 3 monomers, but rather that there is actually one DIDS molecule bound to each band 3 monomer, since H_2DIDS can quantitatively cross-link individual monomers of band 3 after proteolytic cleavage. That is, you can cleave each band 3 monomer with chymotrypsin at the outer surface and you can then glue the molecule back together again. With H_2DIDS, Jennings and Passow were able to glue back together more than 95% of the band 3 monomers, suggesting that there is one H_2DIDS bound to each band 3 monomer. Since there are few, if any, monomers that don't have DIDS-binding sites, the question really can't be asked.

I am not certain that each monomer also has one NAP-taurine binding site, but that would seem most likely.

DOCKTER: Just so I understand—in order to get 100% inhibition by DIDS you have to have one label bound per monomer, not one label per dimer.

KNAUF: That's exactly right. Also, the kinetics appear to be linear, as shown by Dixon plots. There doesn't appear to be any cooperativity, at least none that is detectable in the kinetic experiments that have been done so far.

DR. H. A. LESTER: You mentioned that NAP-taurine seems to bind best to the substrate site from the internal surface of the erythrocyte. Is that correct?

KNAUF: I don't think that's really correct. It probably binds to the substrate site from the outside surface as well. You would expect that because it appears to be a transported substrate for the system. I think, however, that, at the outside surface, NAP-taurine binds to the modifier site with such a high affinity that it is difficult to pick up inhibitory effects that are due to the much weaker binding to the substrate site. In fact, if we go up to very high NAP-taurine concentrations, we do observe a slight upward curvature in Dixon plots, which suggests that we may be seeing an interaction with a second, lower affinity, site that might be the transport site. However, the effect is very small because the inhibition is almost completely dominated by effects at the modifier site.

LESTER: Would you obtain different labeling patterns depending on whether you labeled with NAP-taurine from the inside or from the outside or under conditions in which you think that the substrate site would be mostly facing the inside or the outside?

KNAUF: We would like to see whether the site of labeling by NAP-taurine at the outside, which, kinetically, at least, seems to be the modifier site, is different from its site of labeling from the inside, presumably the substrate site. We may, in fact, try to do those experiments. Again, they're complicated by the low affinity of NAP-taurine for the substrate site, so we would expect a fair amount of nonspecific labeling. From the outside it's much more specific.

PHOTOAFFINITY LABELING
OF ANION TRANSPORT COMPONENTS
IN HEPATOCYTE PLASMA MEMBRANES*

Daniel Levy and Shirley Cheng

Department of Biochemistry
School of Medicine
University of Southern California
Los Angeles, California 90033

INTRODUCTION

Recent studies have suggested that membrane-associated carrier proteins mediate the transport of various solutes across the plasma membrane.[1,2] The photoaffinity labeling technique has been used in an effort to characterize these transport systems. This technique has been shown to be a particularly valuable tool for the study of complex biological systems[3] and has afforded many insights into the nature of binding and transport sites in plasma membranes.[4-10] A photoreactive reagent, N-(4-azido-2-nitrophenyl)-2-aminoethylsulfonate (NAP-taurine), has been successfully used to identify the plasma membrane component that is involved in the erythrocyte anion transport system.[11] The functional properties of this transport protein have been characterized by purification and liposome reconstitution procedures.[12,13]

Isolated hepatocytes have been shown to possess specific transport sites for amino acids,[14] sugars,[15] and anions such as cholic acid,[16] taurocholic acid,[17] and bromosulfophthalein.[18] As opposed to erythrocytes, in which the processes of anion and glucose transport have been extensively investigated, the nature and disposition of the membrane components involved in the transport of these solutes in hepatocytes remain undefined. This report describes the interaction of a fluorescent anion, 1-anilinonaphthalene-8-sulfonate (ANS), and sodium sulfate with intact hepatocytes and hepatoma tissue culture (HTC) cells and the use of NAP-taurine for the photoaffinity labeling of membrane-associated proteins that may be components of the anion transport system.

METHODS

Preparation of Isolated Hepatocytes and HTC Cells

Isolated hepatocytes were prepared, using a collagenase perfusion technique,[19] from male Sprague Dawley rats (200–250 g), which were fed *ad libitum*. The cells were incubated in Krebs-Ringer bicarbonate buffer, at pH 7.4, saturated with 95% O_2 and 5% CO_2 with 10 mM glucose for 30 min at 37 °C. Following this treatment, the cells were washed and resuspended in 0.25 M sucrose–5 mM Tris·HCl at pH 7.4. HTC cells were grown in suspension cultures in Swim's 77 medium supplemented with

*This research was supported by a National Science Foundation grant, no. PCM 76-23852, and by a National Institutes of Health grant, no. CA-14089.

0077–8923/80/0346–0232 $1.75/1 © 1980, NYAS

5% fetal calf serum and 5% calf serum.[20] The cells were washed with phosphate-buffered saline, washed with 0.25 M sucrose–5 mM Tris · HCl at pH 7.4, and then resuspended in the Tris-sucrose buffer. Cell viability was estimated by Trypan blue exclusion and the cell number was determined with a hemocytometer. All experiments were carried out on cell suspensions with viabilities of 85–95% for hepatocytes and greater than 95% for HTC cells. Experiments were done within 3 h of cell isolation. Cell viability was checked upon completion of each experiment; it was shown to decrease less than 2% during the course of the experiment.

Fluorescence Measurements

Fluorescence measurements were performed on a Perkin-Elmer MPF-4 fluorescence spectrophotometer.[27] Aliquots of ANS were added to the cell suspensions (1 × 10^6 cells/ml) in 0.25 M sucrose–5 mM Tris·HCl at pH 7.4 and quickly mixed, and the fluorescence intensity at 470 nm was recorded. Light scattering effects were insignificant under the conditions used in these studies.

Transport Assay

Transport was initiated by the addition of the cell suspensions (8–10 × 10^6 cells/ml) to an equal volume of a solution containing 20 mM Na_2SO_4, 250 mM sucrose, 5 mM Tris·HCl (pH 7.4) and radioactive sulfate (4.0 μCi $^{35}SO_4^{-2}$/ml), yielding final concentrations of 4–5 × 10^6 cells/ml, 10 mM Na_2SO_4, and 2 μCi $^{35}SO_4^{-2}$/ml. When the effects of sulfate concentration on sulfate uptake were investigated, isotonicity was maintained by altering the sucrose concentration. At various time intervals, aliquots (200 μl) of the incubation mixture were removed and placed into a 1.5 ml centrifuge tube containing dibutylphthalate (0.5 ml). The cells were separated from the medium within 3 s by centrifugal filtration in a Brinkmann 3200 microfuge. Following centrifugation, the aqueous medium and dibutylphthalate were removed with a pasteur pipet and the cell pellet was resuspended in water (200 μl) and transferred to a counting vial. Radioactivity was measured using a scintillation fluid consisting of 16% BBS-3 Biosolv and 0.33% Butyl-PBD fluoralloy in toluene. Estimation of trapped extracellular sulfate in the cell pellet was made using [methoxy-^{3}H] inulin.[22] Similar results were obtained when the incubation step was terminated immediately after the addition of the cells.

Photoaffinity Labeling of Hepatocytes and HTC Cells with NAP-Taurine

Photolysis of NAP-taurine in the presence of intact hepatocytes, HTC cells, or the corresponding plasma membrane preparations was carried out in a glass water-jacketed vessel maintained at 24 °C by means of a circulating pump. The isolated cells (1 × 10^8) in 0.25 M sucrose–5 mM Tris·HCl (pH 7.4) were irradiated in the presence of [^{35}S]NAP-taurine (50 μCi). Following irradiation, the cells were washed three times with the incubation buffer; plasma membranes highly enriched in 5'-nucleotidase activity and substantially free of contamination by mitochondria and endoplasmic reticula were isolated.[23] Plasma membranes (300 μg) were also irradiated in the presence of [³⁵S]NAP-taurine (10 μCi) in 50 mM Tris·HCl at pH 7.4. Cells and plasma membranes were maintained in suspension during the photolysis procedures by means of a magnetic stirrer. Irradiation was effected for 20 min with a General Electric medium-pressure 400 W mercury arc lamp located 4 cm from the reaction vessel. Plasma membranes were dissolved in 1% sodium dodecyl sulfate and analyzed by slab gel electrophoresis.[24]

Miscellaneous

4-Fluoro-3-nitrophenylazide and NAP-taurine were obtained from Pierce Chem. Co., dibutylphthalate from Aldrich Chem. Co., collagenase from Worthington Biochem. Corp., Butyl-PBD from Beckman, carrier free ³⁵SO₄⁻² as Na₂SO₄ from ICN, [³⁵S]taurine (52.9 mCi/mmol) from Amersham-Searle Corp. [³⁵S]NAP-taurine was prepared as discribed in Reference 25. Protein concentrations were determined by Lowry's method,[26] as modified by Hartree.[27] Radioactivity measurements were performed on a Beckman LS-245 liquid scintillation counter.

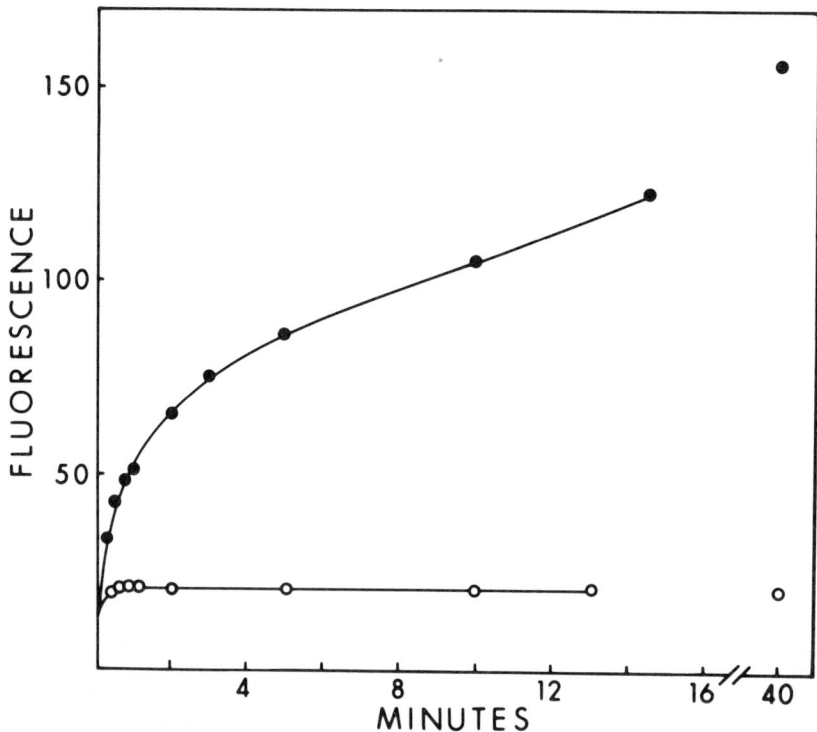

FIGURE 1. The kinetics of the interaction of ANS with intact hepatocytes (●) and HTC cells (O). The cells (10^6 cells/ml) were incubated with ANS (20 mM) at 25 °C in 0.25 M sucrose–5 mM Tris·HCl (pH 7.4). The fluorescence emission was measured at 470 nm.

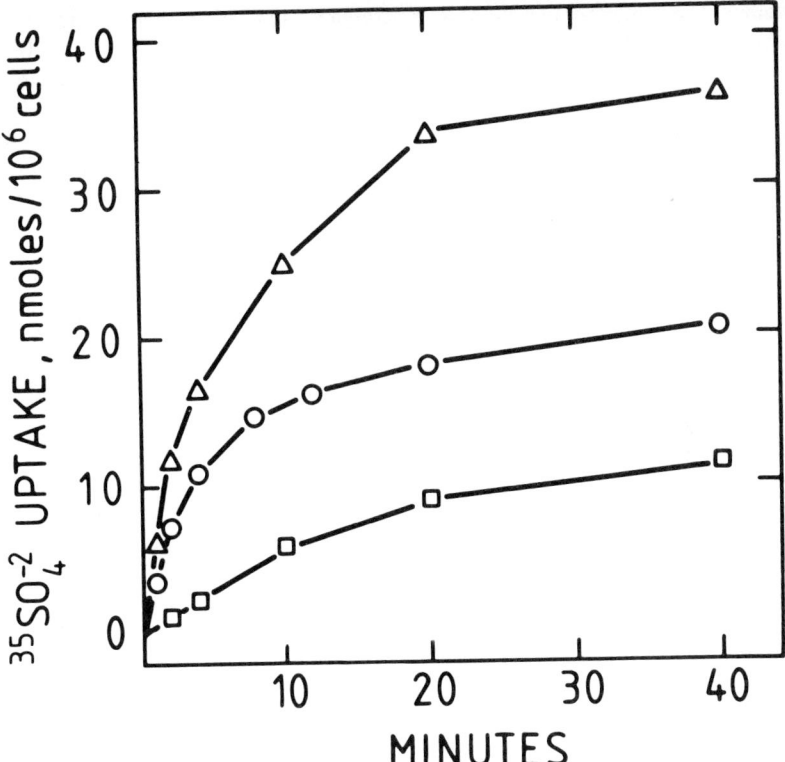

FIGURE 2. The effect of temperature on the time course of the uptake of sulfate by isolated hepatocytes. The cells (5×10^6/ml) were incubated with 10 mM Na$_2$SO$_4$ and 2 μCi ^{35}SO$_4^{-2}$ in 0.25 M sucrose–5 mM Tris · HCl (pH 7.4), as described in the section entitled "Methods," and the uptake was evaluated at different time intervals and temperatures. (△): 37 °C; (○): 25 °C; (□); 4 °C.

RESULTS

Anion Transport Properties of Hepatocytes and HTC Cells

The interaction of ANS with intact hepatocytes resulted in a fluorescence enhancement that was biphasic in nature, as shown in FIGURE 1. A rapid initial increase, which suggested ANS binding to the plasma membrane, was followed by a slower component, which reflected ANS transport into the cell with subsequent binding to intracellular sites. In contrast, the interaction of ANS with HTC cells was characterized only by a rapid initial increase in fluorescence, which was complete in 15 s. The absence of the second slow component, which was observed in hepatocytes, suggested that ANS transport into HTC cells was greatly reduced. This characteristic was also demonstrated upon direct observation of the ANS-treated cells using fluorescence microscopy.[21]

Several studies have suggested that ANS interacts with the sulfate anion transport system in the membranes of erythrocytes[28] and in Ehrlich ascites cells.[29] In an effort to further characterize the anion transport system in hepatocytes, a kinetic analysis of sulfate transport and its inhibition was made. The time course of sulfate uptake by isolated quiescent hepatocytes as a function of temperature is shown in FIGURE 2. The uptake is linear for 2 min and approaches a plateau after approximately 40 min, reflecting the attainment of an equilibrium between influx and efflux. The temperature dependence (uptake was significantly higher at 37 °C than at 25 °C) suggested

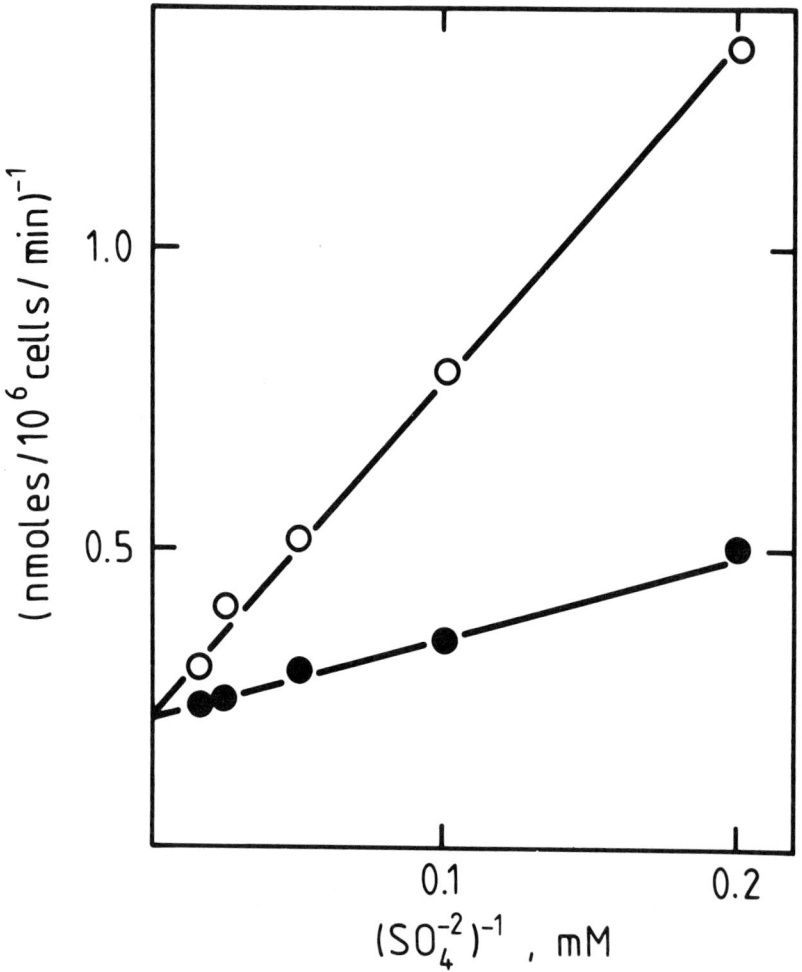

FIGURE 3. The effect of NAP-taurine on sulfate uptake by isolated hepatocytes. The cells (5 × 10^6/ml) were incubated with sulfate, as described in the section entitled "Methods," in both the presence and the absence of NAP-taurine (2 mM) at 37 °C for 2 min. A double reciprocal plot for sulfate uptake (●) indicates an apparent K_m of 6.5 mM and a V_{max} of 4.8 nmol/10^6 cells^{-1}/min.$^{-1}$. In the presence of NAP-taurine (○), a K_i of 0.65 mM was calculated.

TABLE 1

THE EFFECT OF NAP-TAURINE ON SULFATE UPTAKE*
BY HEPATOCYTES AND HTC CELLS

NAP-taurine (mM)	(% Uptake)§	
	Hepatocytes	HTC Cells
0	100	100
0.5	65	70
1.0	50	50
2.0	45	40
1.0 (dark) + wash†	100	
1.0 (light)‡ + wash	50	

*Experiments were performed in the dark unless indicated. 10 mM sulfate was added to 5 × 10^6 cells/ml, as described in the section entitled "Methods," in the presence of various concentrations of NAP-taurine, and uptake was measured at 37 °C for 10 min.

†Cells were washed three times with the incubation buffer prior to the addition of sulfate.

‡Irradiation was carried out for 20 min, as described in the text.

§Standard error is ±5%.

the existence of a facilitated transport process. After 40 min, an uptake of 35 ± 1.5 nmol sulfate/10^6 cells was measured at 37 °C. A ratio of 1.05 was calculated for the intracellular to extracellular sulfate concentrations, using a value of 3.35 μl/10^6 cells for the intracellular water volume,[30] indicating that there was no transport against a concentration gradient. The transport process was concentration-dependent, reaching saturation at a sulfate concentration of 60 mM. When these data were analyzed by a Lineweaver-Burke plot (FIGURE 3), a linear relationship was obtained from which was derived an apparent K_m of 6.5 mM and a V_{max} of 4.8 nmol/10^6 cells/min.

NAP-taurine, which is a photosensitive inhibitor of sulfate efflux in erythrocytes,[11] has been shown to be a competitive inhibitor of sulfate uptake by the isolated hepatocytes (FIGURE 3) in the dark. A 50% inhibition of sulfate transport was obtained in the presence of 2 mM NAP-taurine (TABLE 1). The inhibition in the dark was essentially reversible when the hepatocytes were washed with the incubation buffer in either the presence or the absence of bovine serum albumin (TABLE 1); however, the inhibition became irreversible when the cells were photolyzed in the presence of NAP-taurine.

Initial studies with the fluorescent anion (ANS) suggested the existence of an anion transport defect in HTC cells. This problem was further explored with the sulfate transport assay described for quiescent hepatocytes. The time course of uptake as a function of temperature is shown in FIGURE 4. Again, as was the case with hepatocytes, uptake is significantly higher at 37 °C than at 25 °C; however, the extent of sulfate uptake is greatly diminished in the HTC cell system. This process, also, was concentration-dependent, reaching saturation at 40 mM sulfate. Analysis of the transport data by a Lineweaver-Burke plot (FIGURE 5) indicated an apparent K_m of 7.1 mM and a V_{max} of 0.34 nmol/10^6 cells/min; the latter figure was only 7% of that obtained in the hepatocyte system. NAP-taurine was also shown to be a competitive inhibitor of sulfate transport in the HTC cell system (FIGURE 5), in which a 50% inhibition was obtained at a concentration of 1.0 mM NAP-taurine (TABLE 1).

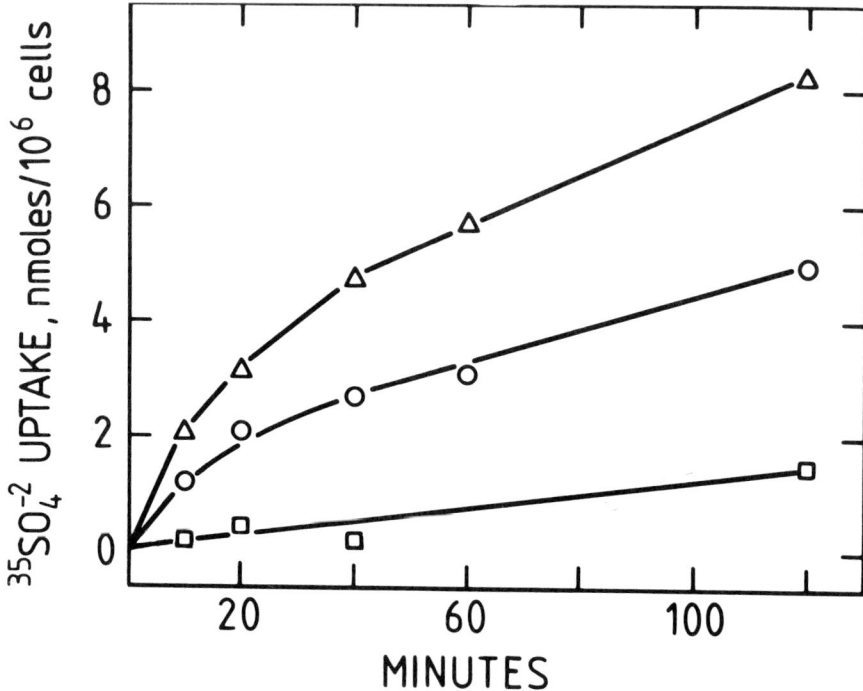

FIGURE 4. The effect of temperature on the time course of the uptake of sulfate by HTC cells. The cells (5 × 10⁶/ml) were incubated with sulfate, as described in FIGURE 2, and the uptake was evaluated at different time intervals and temperatures. (△): 37 °C; (○): 25 °C; (□): 4 °C.

Photoaffinity Labeling Studies

Intact hepatocytes and HTC cells were irradiated with visible light in the presence of NAP-taurine. Following this, the cell suspensions were washed, the plasma membrane fractions were isolated, and covalent incorporation of the radioactive photoprobe into membrane components was analyzed by sodium dodecyl sulfate–polyacrylamide gel electrophoresis. As shown in FIGURE 6, there were, primarily, only two membrane components, with apparent molecular weights of 43,000 and 54,000, that were labeled in hepatocyte plasma membranes. Identical results were obtained when NAP-taurine was photolyzed in the presence of hepatocyte plasma membranes. There was only negligible labeling of plasma membrane components in the absence of photolysis or with preirradiated NAP-taurine. Irradiation of the cell systems or plasma membranes for periods up to 30 min in either the presence or the absence of NAP-taurine had no effect on the gel patterns when they were stained with Coomassie Blue. When photolysis was carried out in the presence of 100 mM sulfate, a 50% inhibition of the incorporation of NAP-taurine into the 43,000 and 54,000 dalton components was observed. When photolysis of NAP-taurine was carried out in the presence of HTC cells, however, no significant labeling of those membrane components was observed (FIGURE 6). Inspection of the Coomassie Blue stained gels indicated that the 43,000 dalton protein was a component of both membrane systems, while the 54,000 dalton component was almost completely absent from the HTC cell plasma membranes.

DISCUSSION

In this study, the anion transport properties of intact isolated hepatocytes and HTC cells have been characterized and membrane-associated proteins that may be

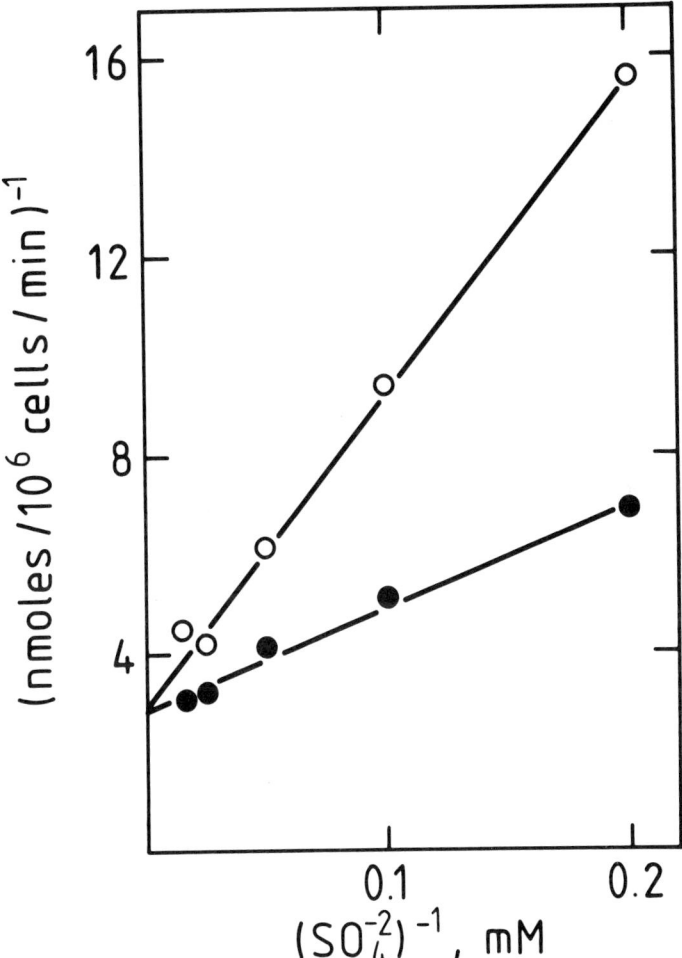

FIGURE 5. The effect of NAP-taurine on sulfate uptake by HTC cells. The cells were incubated with sulfate, as described in the section entitled "Methods," in both the presence and the absence of NAP-taurine (2 mM) at 37 °C for 2 min. A double reciprocal plot for sulfate uptake (O) indicated a K_m of 7.1 mM and V_{max} of 0.34 nmole/10^6 cells^{-1}/min.$^{-1}$ In the presence of NAP-taurine (O), a K_i of 1.0 mM was calculated.

involved in this transport process have been identified by a photoaffinity probe, NAP-taurine. Initial studies[21] with a fluorescence anion, ANS, suggested that there was a much smaller capacity for the transport of anions in HTC cells than in hepatocytes. These observations were corroborated by studies on sulfate transport, which process was characterized by concentration and temperature dependence in both cell systems, suggesting a carrier-mediated transport mechanism. The intracellular and extracellular sulfate concentrations at equilibrium were equal, indicating

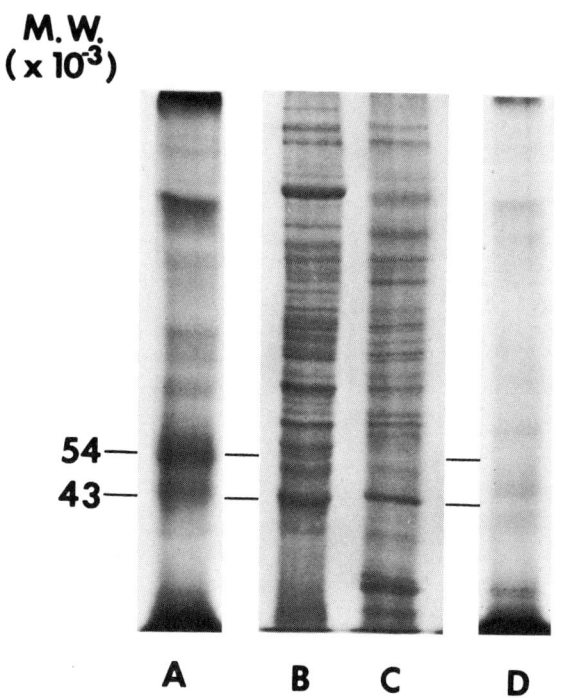

M. W.
(x 10^{-3})

54—
43—

A   B   C   D

FIGURE 6. Sodium dodecyl sulfate–polyacrylamide gel electrophoresis (10%). A: An autoradiogram of plasma membranes (B) derived from intact hepatocytes that have been photolyzed for 20 min in the presence of 2 mM [^{35}S]NAP-taurine. B: A Coomassie Blue stained gel of 150 μg purified hepatocyte plasma membrane. C: A Coomassie Blue stained gel of 150 μg purified HTC cell plasma membrane. D: An autoradiogram of plasma membranes (C) derived from HTC cells that have been photolyzed for 20 min in the presence of 2 mM [^{35}S]NAP-taurine.

that this process did not occur against a concentration gradient. Double reciprocal plots of the transport data indicated that the K_m values were quite similar for both hepatocytes and HTC cells; however, a 93% reduction in the V_{max} value was observed in the HTC cell system.

NAP-taurine has been shown to be a competitive inhibitor of sulfate transport in hepatocytes and HTC cells (FIGURES 3 and 5); this has been previously demonstrated in erythrocytes.[11] In the presence of 1 mM NAP-taurine, similar values were obtained for reversible inhibition of transport in the absence of light and for irreversible inhibition after irradiation (TABLE 1), suggesting a high degree of labeling specificity. Electrophoretic analysis of the radioactive photoaffinity probe incorporated into hepatocyte plasma membrane constituents indicated that most of the probe was associated with membrane proteins with molecular weights of 43,000 and 54,000. This incorporation could be inhibited by 50% in the presence of excess sulfate, suggesting that labeling was specific for the anion transport system. Identical labeling results were obtained when the photolabeling reaction was carried out on isolated plasma membranes where one would expect the membrane proteins to be more accesible to the photoprobe, again suggesting a site-specific membrane modification. Additional support for the specificity of the labeling reaction was derived from the lactoperoxidase-catalyzed iodination of hepatocytes[31] and HTC cells,[32] in which the modification of a large number of surface components was observed; in contrast, only two proteins were labeled by NAP-taurine. The greatly decreased anion transport capacity in HTC cells appears to be associated with the loss of the 54,000 dalton membrane component (FIGURE 6). The failure of NAP-taurine to label the 43,000 dalton membrane component suggests that a functional anion transport system is required for the binding of NAP-taurine to the transport sites, and that, in the absence of the 54,000 dalton protein, the 43,000 dalton protein now has altered binding properties, or accessibility, to the photoprobe. These studies suggest that the 54,000 and 43,000 dalton proteins may be components of a transmembrane assembly, creating a hydrophilic channel[33] through which anions can be transported. Further studies, which will characterize the structure and function of these membrane proteins, are being made in an effort to understand the architecture, dynamics, and regulation of this transport system.

REFERENCES

1. SINGER, S. J. 1974. Annu. Rev. Biochem. **43:** 805–33.
2. GUIDOTTI, G. 1977. J. Supramol. Struct. **7:** 489–97.
3. BAYLEY, H. & J. R. KNOWLES. 1977. *In* Methods in Enzymology, Vol. 45. W. B. Jakoby & M. Wilcheck, Eds.: 69–114. Academic Press. New York.
4. HUCHO, F., P. LAYER, H. R. KIEFER & G. BANDINI. 1976. Proc. Nat. Acad. Sci. USA **73:** 2624–28.
5. YIP, C. C., C. W. T. YEUNG & M. L. MOULE. 1978. J. Biol. Chem. **253:** 1743–45.
6. BREGMAN, M. D. & D. LEVY. 1977. Biochem. Biophys. Res. Commun. **78:** 584–90.
7. DAS, M., T. MIYAKAWA, C. F. FOX, R. M. PRUSS, A. AHARONOV & H. R. HERSCHMAN. 1977. Proc. Nat. Acad. Sci. USA **74:** 2790–94.
8. LEVY, D., E. GLOVER & S. CHENG. 1977. Biochim. Biophys. Acta **469:** 194–201.
9. TROSPER, T. & D. LEVY. 1977. J. Biol. Chem. **252:** 181–86.
10. ROSENBLIT, P. D. & D. LEVY. 1977. Biochem. Biophys. Res. Commun. **77:** 95–103.
11. CABANTCHIK, R. I., P. A. KNAUF, T. OSTWALD, H. MARKUS, L. DAVIDSON, W. BREUER & A. ROTHSTEIN. 1976. Biochim. Biophys. Acta **455:** 526–37.
12. ROSS, A. H. & H. M. MCCONNELL. 1978. J. Biol. Chem. **253:** 4777–82.
13. CABANTCHIK, Z. I., P. A. KNAUF & A. ROTHSTEIN. 1978. Biochim. Biophys. Acta **515:** 239–302.
14. SEGLEN, P. O. & A. E. SOLHEIM. 1978. Eur. J. Biochem. **85:** 15–25.
15. BAUER, H. & H. W. HELDT. 1977. Eur. J. Biochem. **74:** 397–403.
16. ANWER, M. S., R. KROKER & D. HEGNER. 1976. Hoppe-Seyler's Z. Physiol. Chem. **357:** 1477–86.
17. SCHWARZ, L. R., R. BURR, M. SCHWENK, E. PFAFF & H. GREIM. 1975. Eur. J. Biochem. **55:** 617–23.

18. VAN BEZOOIJEN, C. F. A., T. GRELL & D. L. KNOOK. 1976. Biochem. Biophys. Res. Commun. **69:** 354–61.
19. ZAHLTEN, R. N., F. W. STRATMAN & H. A. LARDY. 1973. Proc. Nat. Acad. Sci. USA **70:** 3213–18.
20. MACKENZIE, C. W., III & R. H. STELLWAGEN. 1974. J. Biol. Chem. **249:** 5755–62.
21. CHENG, S. & D. LEVY. 1978. Biochim. Biophys. Acta **511:** 419–29.
22. LIVINGSTON, J. N. & D. H. LOCKWOOD. 1974. Biochem. Biophys. Res. Commun. **61:** 987–96.
23. CHENG, S., H. M. MCQUEEN & D. LEVY. 1978. Arch. Biochem. Biophys. **189:** 336–43.
24. O'FARRELL, P. H. 1975. J. Biol. Chem. **250:** 4007–21.
25. STAROS, J. V. & F. M. RICHARDS. 1974. Biochemistry **13:** 2720–26.
26. LOWRY, O. H., N. J. ROSEBROUGH, A. L. FARR & R. J. RANDALL. 1951. J. Biol. Chem. **193:** 265–75.
27. HARTREE, E. F. 1972. Anal. Biochem. **48:** 422–27.
28. FORTES, P. A. G. & J. F. HOFFMAN. 1974. J. Membr. Biol. **16:** 79–100.
29. LEVINSON, C. & M. L. VILLEREAL. 1975. J. Cell. Physiol. **86:** 143–54.
30. LE CAM, A. & P. FREYCHET. 1977. J. Biol. Chem. **252:** 148–56.
31. EVANS, W. H. 1974. Nature **250:** 391–94.
32. TWETO, J., E. FRIEDMAN & D. DOYLE. 1976. J. Supramol. Struct. **4:** 141–59.
33. SINGER, S. J. 1977. J. Supramol. Struct. **6:** 313–23.

DISCUSSION

DR. P. A. KNAUF: Your inhibition studies with NAP-taurine seemed to indicate that you might have a component of sulfate flux that is insensitive to NAP-taurine. Is that correct?

DR. D. LEVY: Yes, there were no cases in which we were able to completely inhibit the transport. It is possible that the accessibility of NAP-taurine to some of the sulfate transport sites is being blocked and, therefore, that there is a transport component that we have not been able to inhibit.

KNAUF: Have you looked at the two components in terms of possible sensitivity to temperature or to other factors to see if they might be different transport processes?

LEVY: We have carried out the transport studies at various temperatures and have not observed differential sensitivity. We have not, however, preloaded hepatocytes with NAP-taurine and then carried out the labeling studies at 4 °C, where the probe would be unable to efflux, in an attempt to differentially label the two membrane components that appear to be involved in the transport process.

KNAUF: Have you tried looking at the effects of proteases added to the intact cells to see if they alter the mobility of any of your labeled components?

LEVY: Those are studies that are now being carried out.

DR. B. E. HALEY (*University of Wyoming*): Do you think all the band 3 anion transport proteins are identical or are there some that are fairly specific for carrying different ions?

KNAUF: I think it's possible that cyclic A is transported by the inorganic anion transport system.

There are hydrophobic regions that Carlos Gitler has sited and there are other hydrophobic regions. I think there are—there's band 3 and there are other things that may just happen to run the same region of the gel as band 3 but may, in fact, be totally different proteins in terms of their primary structure. An example of this is the catalytic site of the ATPase, sodium potassium ATPase, which sort of runs in the tail band 3 region, but is clearly a separate and very distinct protein. You can show this very readily by proteolytic susceptibility under conditions in which you cleave band 3 at the outside.

DR. C. GITLER: I'm quite interested in your findings that there is a water-soluble component and an integral component. You know that, in the protein ATPase, there are the so-called Fl, which can be released to water soluble, and the so-called proteolytic, which remains within the membrane. And one real question is—where does the specificity come from? Is the specificy in the water-soluble component? Is the portion that you have in the membrane a simple channel that is nonspecific and is there a binding outside? Do you have any kind of information on the specificity—is it specific for the sulfate when you reconstitute? Or is it simply a water channel?

LEVY: I hope that, in the next few weeks, we will have reasonably purified both components and we can then address those questions in our reconstitution experiments.

DR. M. E. DOCKTER: Your talk today raised a problem in my own mind because, earlier this morning, we heard Dr. F. M. Richards' talk about NAP-taurine as a more general surface label; it's certainly been used in a lot of systems. Today, in your talk, you talked about using NAP-taurine apparently under approximately the same concentration, the same conditions as a specific label for an anion transport protein. Would you comment on that?

LEVY: I think that in both the hepatocyte and the red cell system, under the conditions that we've been using, there is a very high degree of specificity and it is certainly not acting as a general surface label.

DR. F. M. RICHARDS: I had no intention of suggesting that NAP-taurine is a useful general label. Precisely the opposite. I'm delighted that it is useful for something. (Laughter.) To the best of my knowledge, nobody has developed what I would call a general label that is suitable for labeling proteins from the aqueous components.

DOCKTER: Do you know if the labeling that you saw at the bottom of the gels, which appeared to be the greatest majority, was phospholipid labeling?

LEVY: There was some phospholipid labeling. However, most of the radioactivity at the bottom of the gel was photoproducts of NAP-taurine that had not covalently attached themselves to membrane proteins.

CURRENT APPLICATIONS
OF THE PHOTOAFFINITY TECHNIQUE
TO THE STUDY OF THE STRUCTURE OF COMPLEX I

Richard J. Guillory, Stella J. Jeng, and Shiuan Chen

John A. Burns School of Medicine
University of Hawaii
Honolulu, Hawaii 96822

INTRODUCTION

Gottikh and his group showed that the use of carbodiimidazole to facilitate the formation of activated carboxylic acids is applicable to the synthesis of a wide spectrum of nucleotides, amino acyl nucleotides, nucleoside di- and triphosphates, and tRNA derivates.[1,2] Interestingly, the particular solvent system used was found to effectively influence the esterification pathway.[2] Extending this work, we have described the utilization of imidazolide intermediates of N-4-azido-2-nitrophenyl-β-alanine in synthetic methods resulting in the esterification of adenosine[3] and diphosphopyridine nucleotides.[14] In these studies, the dimethylformamide:water mixture (1:5 v/v) used restricted reactivity to the ribose hydroxyl groups without acylating the 6-amino group of the adenine base (SCHEMA 1).

In addition, biologically active analogs of coenzyme A, palmitoyl CoA, and flavin mononucleotide have been prepared by identical procedures.[4] Also, the general utility of this method for the formation of nucleotide analogs by substitution at the ribose hydroxyl group is indicated by the synthesis of spin-labeled analogs of ATP, ADP, AMP, and NADP having 3-carboxy-2,2,5,5-tetramethylpyrroline-1-oxyl coupled to this position.[3] The synthetic procedure has also been successfully applied to the synthesis of a photoaffinity analog of tetrodotoxin that retains the biological activity of the parent compound.[5] This reagent can be covalently bound to receptor sites associated with the sodium pores of excitable membranes.

In the synthesis of the ATP photoaffinity probe, the esterification step can provide 2' or 3' isomers. In the case of amino acid esters of nucleotides,[1,2] these can be resolved chromatographically, a resolution not readily accomplished with the arylazido-β-alanyl esters of ATP. In the esterification of ATP with N-t-butoxycarbonyl-α-alanine (SCHEMA 2), the reaction products can be shown to be resolved into three components by paper chromatography using n-butanol:water:acetic acid (5:3:2) as an eluent.[3] The two minor components, with R_f values of 0.45 and 0.69, were converted to the major component ($R_f = 0.37$) after standing at room temperature. Because of the lesser polarity, it is assumed that the component with $R_f = 0.69$ represents the 2',3' disubstituted ATP analog. The component with $R_f = 0.45$ is the 2' isomer and the component with $R_f = 0.37$, the 3' isomer. This assessment was made for two reasons: that conversion of the 2' to the 3' isomer via acyl migration is well supported by a number of studies[7,8] and that the 2' hydroxyl groups of both adenosine and uridine are more open to electrophilic attack than their 3' hydroxyl groups.[9] Thus, the 2' hydroxyl group is kinetically more reactive for substitution, but such substitution is relatively

0077–8923/80/0346–0244 $1.75/1 © 1980, NYAS

less stable than the thermally more favorable esterification at the 3′ hydroxyl group.[7] From such considerations, the 3′ isomers are considered to be the specific components isolated under our synthetic conditions. Such a conclusion is supported by the observation that the esterification of adenosine with fluorosulfonylbenzoylchloride results in the preferential formation of 3′-*p*-fluorosulfonylbenzoyladenosine.[10] Conclusive evidence for this assignment is presented below, in the form of an analysis of nmr spectra of pyridine nucleotide probes.

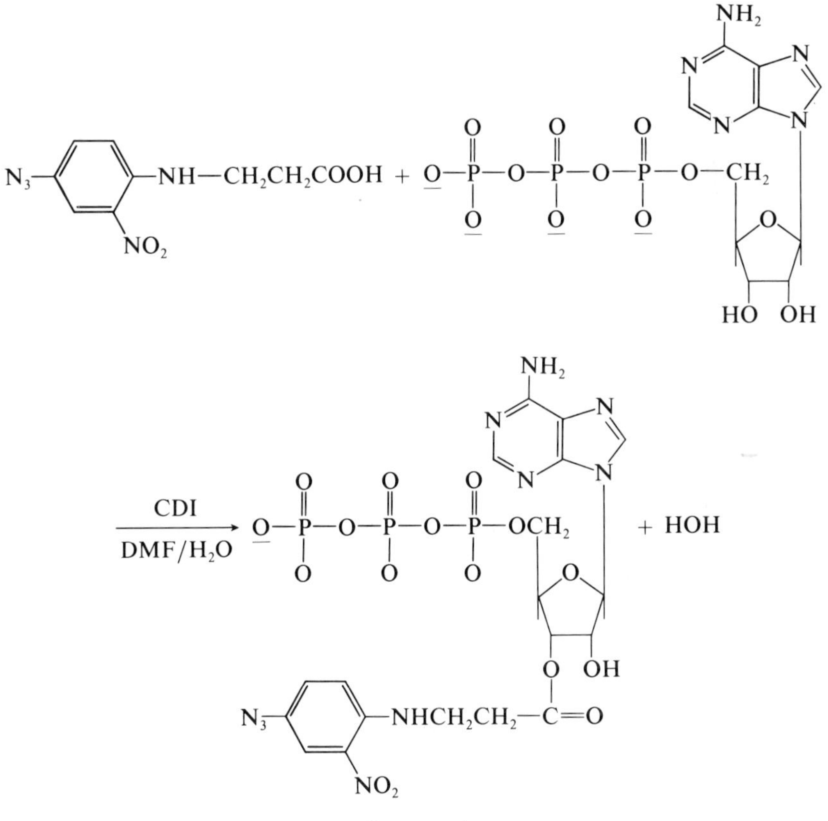

SCHEMA 1

PYRIDINE NUCLEOTIDE PHOTOAFFINITY PROBES

The first synthesis of a photoaffinity analog of pyridine nucleotides was reported in 1971 by Westheimer and his colleagues.[11] This compound, the 3-diazoacetoxymethyl analog of NAD$^+$ (SCHEMA 3), is a carbene generating analog. The synthesis of a nitrene generating analog of NAD$^+$ was subsequently described by Hixson and Hixson.[12] They showed that the latter compound, 3-azido-pyridine adenine dinucleotide (SCHEMA 4), is a competitive inhibitor of NAD$^+$ reduction by yeast alcohol dehydrogenase. Upon photolysis of the ^{3}H-labeled analog with the enzyme, a limited amount (7%) of the nucleotide analog was covalently bound to the enzyme. The authors made the important point that photochemical labeling reagents would be most profitably used when they can first be strongly bound to ligand sites via noncovalent interactions with K_i on the order of 10^{-6} M.

Koberstein has described the synthesis of the 8-azido adenine analogs of NAD$^+$ from 8-azidoadenosine-5'-phosphate and NMN (SCHEMA 5).[13] Evidence was presented that indicated that this derivative has a folded structure. The K_m (azido NAD$^+$) demonstrated for lactate, glutamate, and alcohol dehydrogenase was 1.7-, 3.7-, and 3-fold higher than that for NAD$^+$.

The potential pyridine nucleotide photoaffinity probes reviewed above have yet to be systematically examined with respect to possible interactions with the mitochondrial electron transport system. In contrast to those analogs that have the photoreactive azido group on the adenine or nicotinamide ring are those prepared using the methodology developed by Jeng and Guillory for carbodiimidazole-catalyzed esterification of arylazido-β-alanine to the ribose of adenine nucleotides.[3]

In this paper, we wish to concentrate initially on the structural assignment for an NAD$^+$ and an NADP^1 arylazido-β-alanyl photoaffinity probe. Secondly, we shall describe certain experiments that indicate that these two compounds act as specific

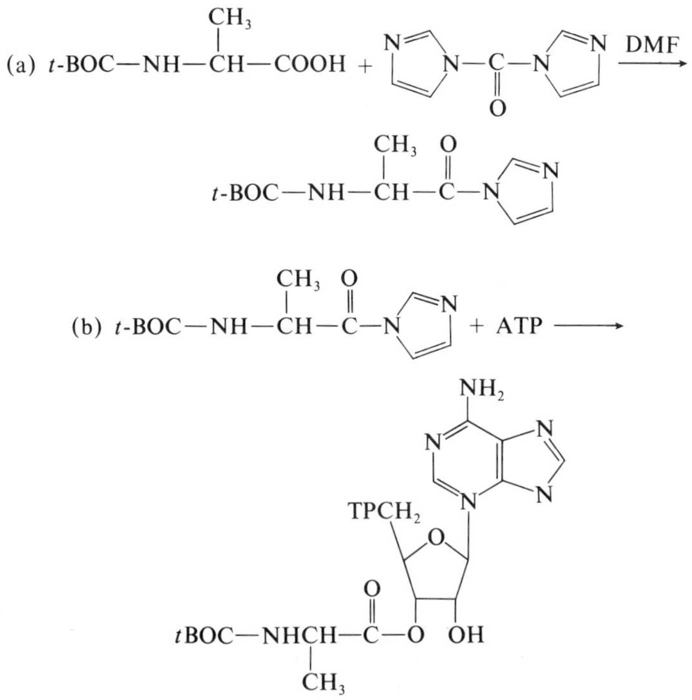

SCHEMA 2

3-Diazoacetoxymethyl-pyridine
  adenosine dinucleotide

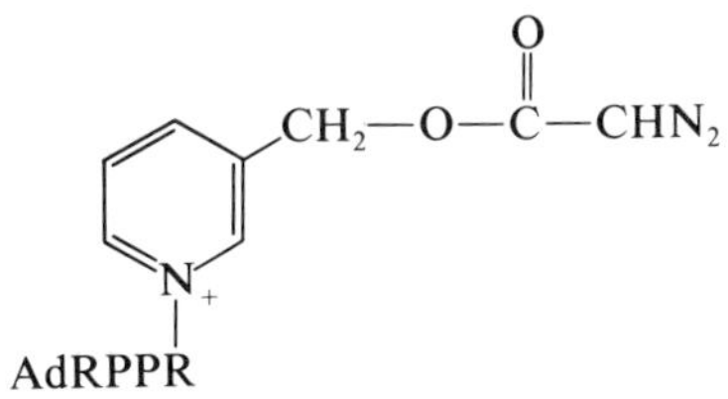

3-Azido-pyridine adenine dinucleotide

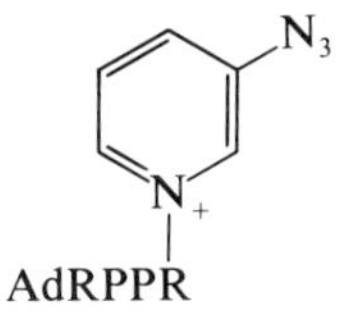

AdRPPR

SCHEMA 3

AdRPPR

SCHEMA 4

8-Azido NAD$^+$

NRPPR

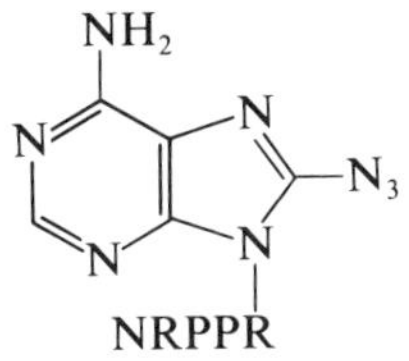

SCHEMA 5

site-directed photoaffinity probes for individual enzymatically active peptides of Complex I of the electron transport chain.

EXPERIMENTAL

Arylazido-β-Alanyl NAD$^+$

Structural Determination

Controlled incubation of N-4-azido-2-nitrophenyl-β-alanine and carbodiimidazole in the presence of nicotinamide adenine dinucleotide, followed by chromatography on Whatman 3MM paper in the solvent system composed of *n*-butanol, water, and acetic acid in the ratios 5:3:2, revealed the presence of two reaction products containing the arylazido adjunct (R_f = 0.61 and 0.49). The material with an R_f of 0.49 (arylazido-β-alanyl NAD$^+$) was eluted with water and found to be capable of undergoing reduction in the presence of ethanol and yeast alcohol dehydrogenase; this was indicated by the development of an absorption band at 340 nm.[14]

The initial report on experiments with arylazido-β-alanyl NAD$^+$ presented evidence for the structural assignment, represented by A3'-0-{3-[N-(4-azido-2-nitrophenyl)amino]propionyl} NAD$^+$ (SCHEMA 6).[24]

The presence of a single arylazido-β-alanyl group per pyridine nucleotide unit in this assignment was verified by base hydrolysis resulting in cleavage of arylazido-β-alanine from the nucleotide analog, followed by isolation and quantitative assessment of the hydrolyzed components.

Jeng and Guillory have shown that the ester linkage that couples nucleotides with the arylazido-β-alanine function is base-labile.[3] This bond is cleaved after short periods of incubation at pH values greater than 8. In addition, the absorbance of the nucleotide analog at 260 and 475 nm is consistent with a 1:1 stoichiometry for the combination of the arylazido-β-alanyl and nicotinamide-adenine dinucleotide portions.

The site of the esterification of the arylazido-β-alanyl group to the NAD$^+$ was revealed through the study of the hydrolytic products formed upon treatment of arylazido-β-alanyl NAD$^+$ with nucleotide pyrophosphatase from *Crotalus adamanteus* venom (Sigma Chemical Company, Type II). Two products were obtained, as determined by chromatography in the solvent system 1-butanol:water:acetic acid

Arylazido-β-alanyl NAD$^+$
(A3'-O-{3-[N-(4-azido-2-nitrophenyl)amino]propionyl} NAD$^+$)

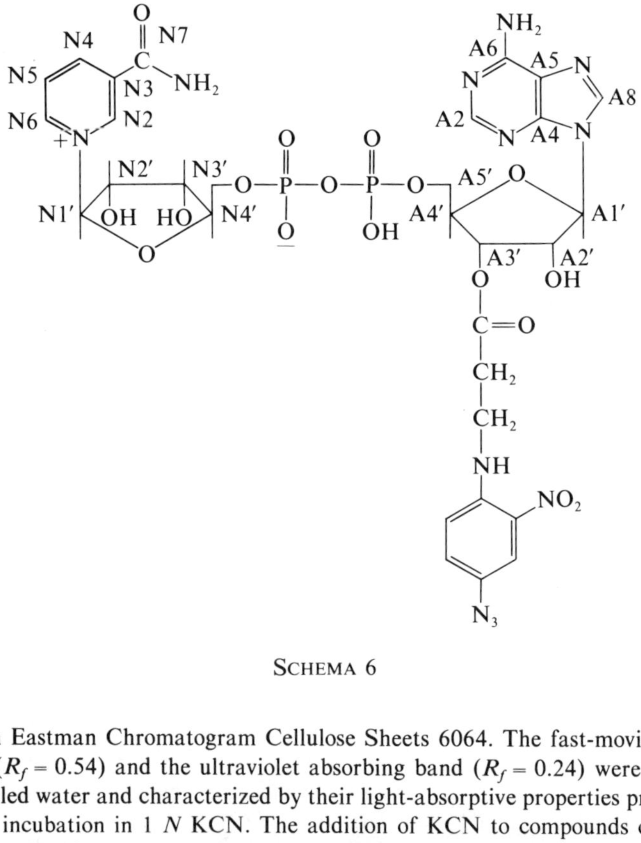

SCHEMA 6

(5:3:2) on Eastman Chromatogram Cellulose Sheets 6064. The fast-moving orange material ($R_f = 0.54$) and the ultraviolet absorbing band ($R_f = 0.24$) were extracted with distilled water and characterized by their light-absorptive properties prior to and following incubation in 1 N KCN. The addition of KCN to compounds containing pyridine nucleotides is characterized by the appearance of a 325 nm absorption peak and a decrease in 260 nm absorbance.[15,16] When the uv absorbing material ($R_f = 0.24$) is treated with 1 N KCN, there is the definite production of an absorption band at 325 nm and a decrease in the 260 nm absorbance. Similar treatment of the orange material ($R_f = 0.54$), which has the characteristic arylazido-β-alanine absorption at 475 nm, resulted in no clear spectral band changes.

The spectral and chromatographic characteristics of the products resulting from enzymatic cleavage of arylazido-β-alanyl NAD$^+$ were compared with those for synthesized arylazido-β-alanyl NMN and arylazido-β-alanyl AMP. This comparison makes it clear that enzymatic hydrolysis of arylazido-β-alanyl NAD$^+$ results in the formation of products having the absorptive and chromatographic characteristics of NMN and of a yellow material having the absorptive and chromatographic characteristics of the synthetic arylazido-β-alanyl AMP.

Base hydrolysis of the material containing arylazido-β-alanyl resulted in the formation of equimolar quantities of a material that comigrates with AMP and of a yellow material that comigrates with arylazido-β-alanine. It is, consequently, concluded that the ribose associated with the adenine of NAD$^+$ is specifically esterified under our synthetic conditions and that the ribose associated with the nicotinamide portion of the dinucleotide is not attacked.

Reactivity with Alcohol Dehydrogenase

Alcohol dehydrogenase has been used to assess the effectiveness of arylazido-β-alanyl NAD$^+$ in comparison with the previously mentioned pyridine nucleotide photoaffinity probes. The pyridine nucleotide analog acts as a substrate for yeast alcohol dehydrogenase (EC 1.1.1.1) when incubated with the enzyme in the dark ($K_m = 0.052$ mM, $V_{max} = 4.4$ μmol mg^{-1} min^{-1} at pH 7) and inhibits reduction of the natural substrate. Upon photolysis in the presence of the enzyme, the analog is converted into a potent inhibitor of the dehydrogenase. A 4 min irradiation in the presence of a 45-fold molar excess of arylazido-β-alanyl NAD$^+$ resulted in an 80%–90% photodependent inhibition, while a similar period of irradiation in the presence of a 110-fold molar excess arylazido-β-alanine did not influence enzymatic activity. Since arylazido-β-alanine itself does not inhibit the dehydrogenase activity, it is clear that the NAD$^+$ portion of the arylazido-β-alanyl NAD$^+$ is required in order to direct the reagent to the catalytic site of the enzyme.

A further indication of the rather specific reactivity of the pyridine nucleotide analog was the limited degree of photodependent labeling of the enzyme by arylazido-[3-^{3}H]-β-alanyl NAD$^+$. Yeast alcohol dehydrogenase was irradiated for 4 min in the presence of a 46-fold molar excess of arylazido-[3-^{3}H]-β-alanyl NAD$^+$ (3.6×10^7 cpm μmol^{-1}), resulting in a 91% inhibition of enzymatic activity. The inhibited preparation (0.5 ml) was dialyzed for 24 hrs against 2 liters of 1% sodium dodecyl sulfate and the dialyzed preparation was applied to a Sephadex G-50 column (20 $\times$ 1 cm) equilibrated with 1% sodium dodecyl sulfate. Only in the case of the photoirradiated preparation did the protein emerge at the void volume associated with a sizable quantity of radioacitvity. Photodependent inhibition was associated with covalent labeling of 1.9 mol arylazido-β-alanyl NAD$^+$ to 1 mol yeast alcohol dehydrogenase (MW 141,000).

Reactivity with Complex I

The NADH-CoQ reductase (Complex I) of ox heart mitochondria represents one of the major enzyme complexes of the mitochondrial electron transport system.[17] In addition to NADH-CoQ reductase activity, the purified preparation catalyzes both

NADPH-CoQ and ferricyanide reductase activity as well as both forward (NADH-NADP$^+$) and reverse (NADPH-NAD$^+$) pyridine nucleotide transhydrogenase activities.[18] Since the transhydrogenase activities are not detected in other respiratory chain complexes, it has been assumed that the transhydrogenase protein is an integral component of Complex I preparations.

The reduced arylazido-β-alanyl NAD$^+$, formed by reaction with alcohol and yeast alcohol dehydrogenase, was tested for its substrate and photoaffinity reactivity with the membrane-bound NADH dehydrogenase.

The rate of CoQ$_1$ (coenzyme Q with 1 isoprenoid unit in the side chain) reduction catalyzed by the arylazido-β-alanyl NADH analog was found to be 73.5% of that with the natural NADH substrate.[14] In addition, the reduction of CoQ$_1$ by arylazido-β-alanyl NADH catalyzed by Complex I is rotenone-sensitive, supporting the specificity of action of the nucleotide analog as a substrate for the dehydrogenase. The K_m of arylazido-β-alanyl NADH used as a substrate for NADH-CoQ reductase was determined to be 33 μM, which is of the same order of magnitude as the value of 7 to 20 μM determined for NADH. These values are similar to those reported for NADH by Hatefi and Stempel.[19] In addition, the maximum velocity (2.6 μmol min^{-1} mg^{-1}) was identical for both the natural cofactor and the arylazido analog. Following a 5 min irradiation of the NADH-CoQ reductase–arylazido-β-alanyl NAD$^+$ mixture, which contained 1 mg Complex I and 0.11 mM arylazido-β-alanyl NAD$^+$ in 0.25 M phosphate buffer at pH 7, there was a 60 to 70% inhibition of activity.

Under identical conditions, there was only a small inhibition of the activity of a sample irradiated in the absence of arylazido-β-alanyl NAD$^+$ and no inhibition in a sample incubated with arylazido-β-alanyl NAD$^+$ in the dark.

FIGURE 1 shows that incubation with the reduced form of the analog following a 4 min irradiation results in a greater than 95% inhibition of the NADH-CoQ$_1$ reductase, while an equal concentration of the oxidized form of the analog results in a 75% photodependent inhibition; the reduced analog is more effective as a photoaffinity inhibitor. The presence of NADH during an irradiation equivalent to that of arylazido-β-alanyl NAD$^+$ was able to completely prevent both photodependent inhibition and enzymatic activity.

Arylazido-β-alanyl NAD$^+$ brings about a sizable inhibition of NADH-CoQ$_1$ reductase activity when incubated with the enzyme complex in the dark. The addition of higher substrate concentrations results in a reversal of this inhibition (5.3 $\times$ 10^{-2} mM NADH is able to completely reverse the inhibitory influence of 1.1 $\times$ 10^{-2} mM arylazido-β-alanyl NAD$^+$). On the other hand, when Complex I is subjected to photoirradiation in the presence of 1.1 $\times$ 10^{-2} mM arylazido-β-alanyl NAD$^+$, the addition of higher concentrations of the natural substrate (NADH) is not able to reverse the inhibitory effect. Arylazido-β-alanyl NAD$^+$ thus acts as a competitive inhibitor of NADH-CoQ reductase in the dark and is converted into a noncompetitive irreversible inhibitor upon photoirradiation in the presence of the enzyme complex.

In view of its apparent specificity with regard to the NADH-CoQ$_1$ reductase activity, an analysis of the kinetic effects of arylazido-β-alanyl NAD$^+$ on the various activities dependent upon pyridine nucleotides present in the Complex I preparation was carried out.[30] In particular, we were interested in answering two basic questions: (1) Are the NADH and NADPH oxidoreductase systems identical? (2) What is the relationship, if any, between pyridine nucleotide oxidations and the transhydrogenase activity?

NADH-CoQ₁ Reductase

As anticipated from the preliminary results described above, arylazido-β-alanyl NAD⁺ is a competitive inhibitor with respect to NADH. Surprisingly, the analog is also a competitive inhibitor with respect to CoQ₁. In both cases, the evaluated apparent K_i, $K_{i,app}$ (arylazido-β-alanyl NAD⁺), 68 μM and 171 μM, respectively, is higher than the $K_{m,app}$ values for the substrates, 7.5 μM (NADH) and 11.2 μM (CoQ₁), in this activity. The $K_{m,app}$ value for NADH is approximately one-ninth the $K_{i,app}$ value for arylazido-β-alanyl NAD⁺. The $K_{i,app}$ of arylazido-β-alanyl NAD⁺ with respect to the dependence of reaction velocity on CoQ₁ concentration is 15 times

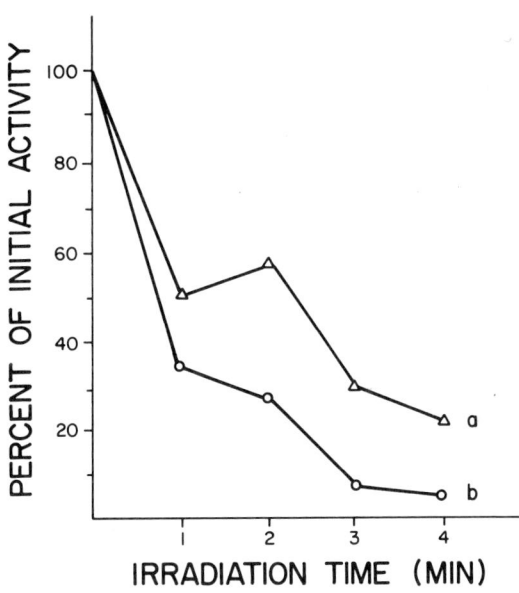

FIGURE 1. A comparison of the photodependent inhibition of NADH-CoQ₁ reductase by arylazido-β-alanyl NAD⁺ and arylazido-β-alanyl NADH. (a) During photolysis, 0.2 ml of 0.25 M phosphate buffer (pH 7.0) containing 4.68 × 10⁻⁵ mmol of arylazido-β-alanyl NAD⁺ was irradiated with 0.18 × 10⁻⁵ mmol of NADH-CoQ reductase. (b) Arylazido-β-alanyl NAD⁺ (4.68 × 10⁻⁵ mmol) was preincubated in 0.12 ml of 0.25 M phosphate buffer (pH 7.6) containing 0.71 mM ethanol and 200 μg of yeast alcohol dehydrogenase; 0.18 × 10⁻⁵ mmol of NADH-CoQ₁ reductase (in 0.1 ml) was added and the mixture was subjected to photoirradiation. At the appropriate times, 4 μl aliquots were removed and assayed for NADH-CoQ₁ reductase activity.[14] NADH-CoQ reductase (Complex I) (EC 1.6.5.3) was isolated from ox heart mitochondria according to the procedure of Hatefi.[20] Activity was assayed as described by Hatefi and Rieske.[27] Protein was measured by the method of Jacobs *et al.*[28] with versatol-4 (from Warner-Chilnott Laboratories, Morris Plains, N.J.) as standard.

greater than the $K_{m,app}$ for CoQ₁ itself, indicating a rather weak effect of the analog on CoQ₁ interaction with NADH-CoQ₁ reductase. This competitive inhibitor effect of arylazido-β-alanyl NAD⁺ with respect to CoQ₁ might be considered to be due to an indirect effect, i.e., an interaction at other than the CoQ₁ binding site. If arylazido-β-alanyl NAD⁺ binds to the CoQ₁ site, then CoQ₁ would be expected to provide more effective protection against the analog-photodependent inhibition of CoQ₁ reduction than NADH. However, experimentally, CoQ₁, even at concentrations well over twice those of NADH, protects against inactivation to only 10%.[30] Thus, the competitive inhibitor effect by arylazido-β-alanyl NAD⁺ against CoQ₁ in the NADH-CoQ reductase reaction is difficult to explain simply. It is possible that the added hydrophobicity of the arylazido-β-alanyl NAD⁺ influences the reactivity of the analog at the CoQ site. The kinetic analysis of the influence of arylazido-β-alanyl NAD$^+$ on the other Complex I reactions dependent upon pyridine nucleotides is summarized in TABLE 1.

NADH-AcPyAD$^+$ Transhydrogenase

For the NADH-AcPyAD$^+$ (3-acetylpyridine adenine dinucleotide) transhydrogenase of Complex I, arylazido-β-alanyl NAD$^+$ is a noncompetitive inhibitor with respect to NADH. This noncompetitive inhibition is interesting in view of the competitive effect exhibited with the NADH-CoQ$_1$ reductase. The noncompetitive inhibition may have an explanation in terms of the structure of the analog—since the arylazido-β-alanyl NAD$^+$ has its photoaffinity adjunct attached to the ribose of the AMP portion of the molecule, the NADH-AcPyAD$^+$ transhydrogenase may "recognize" the photoaffinity reagent as an NADP$^+$ analog. In this assay, AcPyAD$^+$

TABLE 1

THE EFFECTS OF ARYLAZIDO-β-ALANYL NAD$^+$ ON PYRIDINE NUCLEOTIDE–DEPENDENT ACTIVITIES OF COMPLEX I FROM OX HEART MITOCHONDRIA[30]

Reaction	Concentration of Fixed Substrate (μM)	Concentration of Arylazido-β-Alanyl NAD$^+$ (μM)	Inhibitory Kinetic Effect	$K_{m,app}$ (μM)	$K_{i,app}$ (μM)
NADH-CoQ$_1$	30 (CoQ$_1$)	147	Competitive	7.5 (NADH)	68
reductase	80 (NADH)	140	Competitive	11.2 (CoQ$_1$)	171
NADH-AcPyAD$^+$	200 (AcPyAD$^+$)	19	Noncompetitive	16.7 (NADH)	—
transhydrogenase	120 (NADH)	21	Competitive	278 (AcPyAD$^+$)	9.5
NADPH-CoQ$_1$ reductase	30 (CoQ$_1$)	14	Mixed	385 (NADPH)	—
NADPH-AcPyAD$^+$ transhydrogenase	300 (AcPyAD$^+$)	157	Competitive	71 (NADPH)	384

substitutes for NADP$^+$ and one would expect, therefore, that arylazido-β-alanyl NAD$^+$ would be a competitive inhibitor with respect to AcPyAD$^+$ for transhydrogenation. Experimentally, this possibility is borne out, i.e., arylazido-β-alanyl NAD$^+$ is a competitive inhibitor with respect to AcPyAD$^+$ with a $K_{i,app}$ of 9.5 μM.

NADPH-AcPyAD$^+$ Transhydrogenation

In contrast to its effectiveness on NADH-AcPyAD$^+$ transhydrogenation, the analog had only a minor effect on NADPH-AcPyAD$^+$ transhydrogenation. While the indications are that the inhibitory effect is of a competitive nature, the $K_{i,app}$ being 5 times the $K_{m,app}$ (71 μM) for NADPH, the low level of inhibitory activity prevents an accurate evaluation of the kinetic order. A competitive reaction with NADPH would support the hypothesis that the reagent is "recognized" by the enzyme as an NADP$^+$ analog. In view of the small inhibitory effect, though, it would appear that the bulky arylazido-β-alanyl group presents a major steric hindrance, preventing firm binding to the enzyme. This may be indicative of a restrictive interaction within the adenine binding region, as well.

NADPH-CoQ₁ Reductase

Arylazido-β-alanyl NAD$^+$ had a complex kinetic influence on NADPH-CoQ₁ reductase activity in the dark. This kinetic effect can be explained if the photoaffinity probe acts initially as a substrate for transhydrogenation:

NADPH + Arylazido-β-alanyl NAD$^+$ $\rightarrow$ NADP$^+$ + Arylazido-β-alanyl NADH,

and then secondly as a substrate for CoQ₁ reduction by NADH-CoQ reductase:

Arylazido-β-alanyl NADH + H$^+$ + CoQ₁ $\rightarrow$ Arylazido-β-alanyl NAD$^+$ + CoQ · 2H.

There is thus a simultaneous expression of a transhydrogenation and a CoQ₁ reductase action in the presence of the pyridine nucleotide analog, which complicates the analysis of NADPH-CoQ₁ reductase. The discovery that palmitoyl CoA only inhibits CoQ₁ reduction in this system in the presence of arylazido-β-alanyl NAD$^+$ supports this proposal.[30]

In summary, the kinetic analysis shows that arylazido-β-alanyl NAD$^+$ is a potent inhibitor of the Complex I activities dependent upon pyridine nucleotides, except for NADPH-AcPyAD$^+$ transhydrogenation.

PHOTODEPENDENT EFFECTS OF ARYLAZIDO-β-ALANYL NAD$^+$

Upon photolysis, the NAD$^+$ analog (at a 26 molar excess over Complex I) is a potent, irreversible inhibitor of NADH-CoQ reductase, NADPH-CoQ₁ reductase, and NADH-AcPyAD$^+$ transhydrogenase. Under the same conditions, there was no influence on the NADPH-AcPyAD$^+$ transhydrogenase activity. The photodependency of the inhibitions was demonstrated by a combination of light and dark control experiments. When the enzyme solution was photolyzed in the absence of arylazido-β-alanyl NAD$^+$, all four of the above activities were maintained at their maximum rates. The dark control, an unphotolyzed solution containing the same amount of analog and enzyme, indicated that arylazido-β-alanyl NAD$^+$ did not bring about significant inhibition without photolysis. When the enzyme complex was photolyzed in the presence of either NAD$^+$ or arylazido-β-alanine, there was no significant inhibition, showing that the photodependent inhibition due to arylazido-β-alanyl NAD$^+$ is not simply a result of nonspecific labeling by arylazido-β-alanine or of a photosensitive effect of NAD$^+$.

The photodependent effect of arylazido-β-alanyl NAD$^+$ on the different Complex I activities dependent upon pyridine nucleotides was studied as a function of the concentrations of the photoaffinity analog. As can be seen from FIGURE 2, the two NADH-dependent reactions (A and B) were inhibited by up to 70% when photoirradiated in the presence of a 25-fold molar excess of arylazido-β-alanyl NAD over that of Complex I. A molecular weight of 570,000 was taken for Complex I.[20]

The maximum inhibition of the NADPH-CoQ₁ reductase activity was also 70% at a 25-fold molar excess of arylazido-β-alanyl NAD$^+$ (FIGURE 2C); however, this

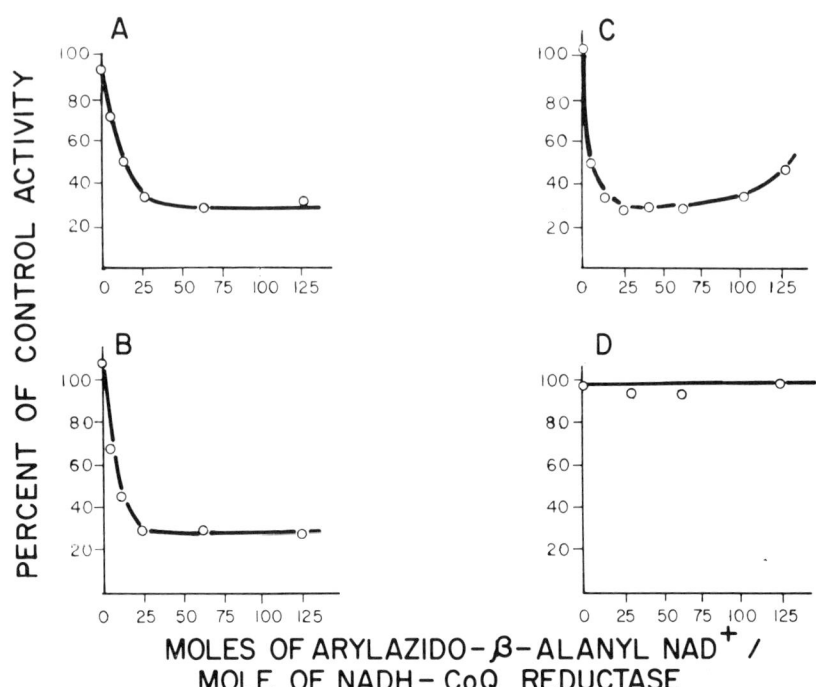

MOLES OF ARYLAZIDO $-\beta-$ ALANYL NAD$^+$ /
MOLE OF NADH $-$ CoQ REDUCTASE

FIGURE 2. The photodependent inhibition of arylazido-β-alanyl NAD$^+$ on the various activities present in NADH-CoQ reductase (Complex I) preparation. The samples were assayed both before and after a one minute period of photoirradiation; the activity prior to photolysis was taken to represent 100% activity. Assays were performed as described in Reference 30. For A (NADH-CoQ$_1$ reductase) and B (NADH-AcPyAD$^+$ transhydrogenase), the irradiation mixture contained 0.147 nmol of Complex I and arylazido-β-alanyl NAD$^+$ at the molar excess above the enzyme concentration indicated in the respective figures. The volume of the irradiation mixture was 0.24 ml. The reduced form of AcPyAD$^+$ has a molar extinction coefficient of 5100 at 375 nm.[29] For C (NADPH-CoQ$_1$ reductase), the irradiation mixture contained 0.441 nmol of Complex I and a concentration of NAD$^+$ analog at the molar excess over the enzyme concentration indicated in the figure. The irradiation volume was 0.18 ml. For D (NADPH-AcPyAD$^+$ transhydrogenase), the irradiation mixture contained 0.294 nmol of Complex I and an analog concentration at the molar excess over the enzyme indicated in the figure. The irradiation volume was 0.27 ml.[30]

inhibition decreased as the NAD$^+$ azido analog concentration was increased. Presumably, at the higher arylazido-β-alanyl NAD$^+$ concentrations, additional nonbound analog is present in solution and becomes a substrate for coupled NADPH–arylazido-β-alanyl NAD$^+$ transhydrogenation and arylazido-β-alanyl NADH-CoQ$_1$ reductase. In contrast to the above reactions, the NADPH-AcPyAD$^+$ transhydrogenase activity was not inhibited, even at a 125-fold molar excess of arylazido-β-alanyl NAD$^+$ (FIGURE 2D).

Of the two pyridine nucleotides, NADH was found to be more effective than NADPH in protecting against arylazido-β-alanyl NAD$^+$ photodependent inhibition of both NADH-CoQ$_1$ and NADPH-CoQ$_1$ reductase activities (FIGURES 3A and 3B).

The effectiveness of NADH as a protective agent (100% protection at a concentration two-fifths that of arylazido-β-alanyl NAD$^+$) indicates both a high specificity for the interaction of the analog and a comparatively lower affinity than that of NADH.

This result suggests that the two CoQ$_1$ reductase activities originate from the same pyridine nucleotide binding site. If there were two independent nucleotide binding sites for these activities, then one would expect that NADPH, as the natural substrate, would be more effective in protecting NADPH-CoQ$_1$ reductase activity against arylazido-β-alanyl NAD$^+$ photodependent inhibition.

Covalent Labeling Pattern of Arylazido-β-Alanyl NAD$^+$

A kinetic analysis indicated that the photodependent inhibition of the Complex I reactions dependent upon pyridine nucleotides brought about by the NAD$^+$ analog is noncompetitive. Under identical conditions, neither arylazido-β-alanine nor NAD$^+$ alone or in combination significantly inhibited the above activities. During photoirra-

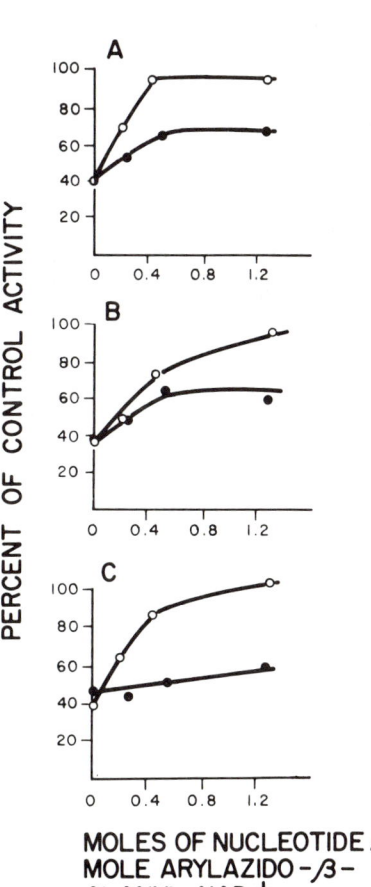

FIGURE 3. NADH and NADPH protection of the arylazido-β-alanyl NAD$^+$ photodependent inhibition of pyridine nucleotide–dependent activities present in the NADH-CoQ reductase (Complex I) preparation. For A (NADH-CoQ$_1$ reductase) and C (NADH-AcPyAD$^+$ transhydrogenase), the irradiation mixture contained 0.147 nmol of Complex I and 3.47 nmol of arylazido-β-alanyl NAD$^+$ and NADH (or NADPH) at the indicated molar excess over arylazido-β-alanyl NAD$^+$. The irradiation volume was 0.24 ml. For B (NADPH-CoQ$_1$ reductase), the irradiation mixture contained 0.441 nmol of Complex I and 11.2 nmol of arylazido-β-alanyl NAD$^+$ and NADH (or NADPH) at the indicated molar excess over arylazido-β-alanyl NAD$^+$. The irradiation volume was 0.18 ml. All other conditions are as described in FIGURE 1.[30] NADH: o-o-o; NADPH: •-•-•.

PERCENT OF CONTROL ACTIVITY

MOLES OF NUCLEOTIDE / MOLE ARYLAZIDO-β-ALANYL NAD$^+$

diation, an arylazido-β-alanyl NAD$^+$ concentration of 8.6 μM provided a 50% inhibition of the NADH-CoQ$_1$ reductase. This concentration is only 12.6% of the $K_{i,app}$ value for arylazido-β-alanyl NAD$^+$ as a competitive inhibitor of NADH (68 μM). In addition, as a result of the dilution of the photolyzed preparation during the enzymic assay, the free titer of the nucleotide analog was less than 0.34 μM. This low inhibitory titer following photolysis and the specificity of the interaction are strong indications of the covalent nature of the photodependent interaction.

This point is further supported by an examination of the radioactive labeling of the gel electrophoresis pattern of a sample of Complex I photolyzed in the presence of arylazido-[3-^{3}H]-β-alanyl NAD$^+$ (FIGURE 4).

In this particular experiment, the NADH-CoQ reductase and NADH-AcPyAD$^+$ transhydrogenase were inhibited some 40%. The resultant labeling pattern indicates that, of the twelve to fourteen peptides of Complex I resolved by this procedure, only three peptide bands appear to have been significantly labeled by the photoaffinity

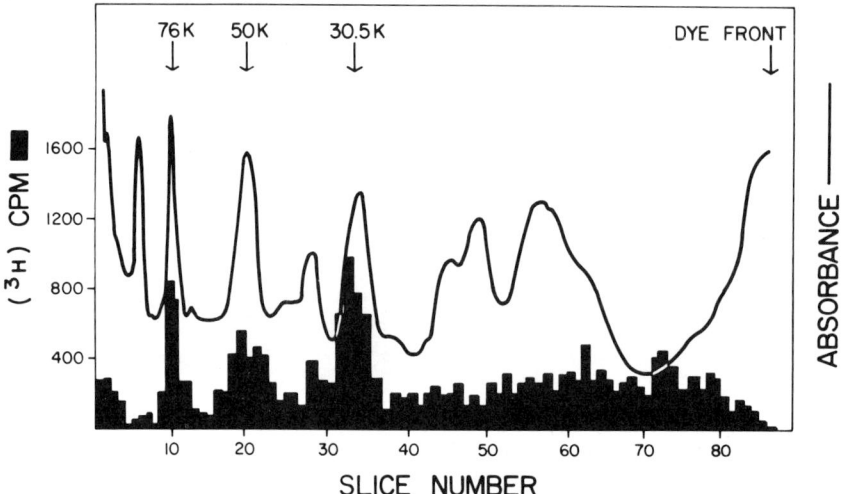

FIGURE 4. Sodium dodecyl sulfate–polyacrylamide gel electrophoresis of Complex I following irradiation with arylazido-[3-^{3}H]-β-alanyl NAD$^+$. Six hundred micrograms of Complex I in 0.18 ml 0.25 M phosphate buffer pH 7.0 were photolyzed (2 min) in the presence of 0.14 mol arylazido-[3-^{3}H]-β-alanyl NAD$^+$, specific activity 7.3 $\times$ 10^7 cpm/μmol. The photoirradiated sample was dialyzed against 1 liter of a solution containing 1% (w/v) sodium dodecyl sulfate and 1% (v/v) β-mercaptoethanol. Following overnight dialysis in the dark at 25 °C, the solution was applied to 10% polyacrylamide sodium dodecyl sulfate (SDS) gels for electrophoresis, according to the procedure described by Weber and Osborn.[21] The gels stained with Coomassie Blue were scanned at 550 nm and sliced with a multi-blade slicer. The combined slices (1 mm) from twelve gels were digested overnight with 0.3 ml of 30% H$_2$O$_2$ at 65 °C, and the radioactivity of each sample was measured by liquid scintillation in 5 ml of Aquasol (New England Nuclear).

Molecular weights were evaluated on sodium dodecyl sulfate gels using glucose-6-phosphate dehydrogenase (104,000; EC 1.1.1.49), pyruvate kinase (57,000; EC 2.7.1.40); liver alcohol dehydrogenase (41,000; EC 1.1.1.1), lactate dehydrogenase (37,000; EC 1.1.1.27), and cytochrome C (12,300), as standards.[23] The evaluated molecular weights for the major labeled peptides are indicated by a postscript above each band.

FIGURE 5. The photodependent effect of arylazido-β-alanine on the NADH-CoQ$_1$ reductase and the NADH-K$_3$Fe(CN)$_6$ reductase activities of complex I. The irradiation mixture contained 125 mM phosphate buffer (pH 7.0), 1.16 × 10^{-10} mol enzyme complex, and arylazido-β-alanine at the concentrations indicated in the figure. The final volume during irradiation was 0.4 ml and irradiation lasted 4 min at 15°C. The activities prior to photoirradiation were taken as 100%. NADH-CoQ$_1$ reductase: o-o-o; NADH-K$_3$Fe(CN)$_6$ reductase: •-•-•.

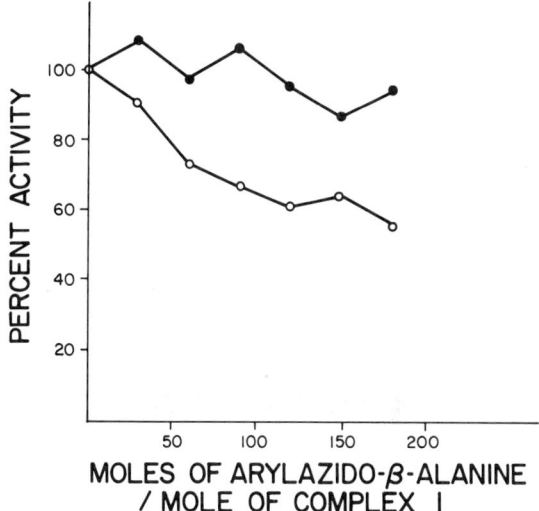

MOLES OF ARYLAZIDO-β-ALANINE / MOLE OF COMPLEX I

probe. Specifically, those peptides that band at the 7.6, 5.0, and 3.05 × 10^4 molecular weight levels.

ARYLAZIDO-β-ALANINE

Arylazido-β-alanine, even at concentration levels above 100-fold molar excess above the enzyme, has no influence on the activity of yeast alcohol dehydrogenase either in the dark or following photoirradiation.[14] Also, at a 50-fold molar excess, a concentration at which arylazido-β-alanyl NAD$^+$ is maximally effective in inhibiting NADH-CoQ reductase, arylazido-β-alanine has no effect on this activity. At a 200-fold molar excess, the NADH-CoQ$_1$ reductase is inhibited by arylazido-β-alanine to a maximum of 40%. Under the same conditions, the NADH-K$_3$Fe(CN)$_6$ reductase is not influenced (FIGURE 5). This result would seem to indicate that arylazido-β-alanine has a certain specificity towards the different activities of Complex I dependent upon pyridine nucleotides. However, the photodependent inhibition in the presence of arylazido-β-alanine could not be prevented by the presence of either NADH or CoQ$_1$ in the irradiation mixture, indicating that the observed inhibition is probably not due to interaction at the reactive site of either of these cofactors.

When Complex I was photoirradiated in the presence of arylazido [3-^{3}H]-β-alanine, the radioactive labeling pattern found was that illustrated in FIGURE 6. It is clear that there is no major specificity for labeling by arylazido-β-alanine. At this concentration of arylazido-β-alanine, there was no inhibition of NADH-CoQ reductase, NADH-AcPyAD$^+$ transhydrogenase, or NADPH-AcPyAD$^+$ transhydrogenase. Consequently, it is reasonable to assume that the labeling pattern observed for arylazido-β-alanyl NAD$^+$ (FIGURE 4) is a primary result of the active site binding specificity for the pyridine nucleotide portion of arylazido-β-alanyl NAD$^+$. Further

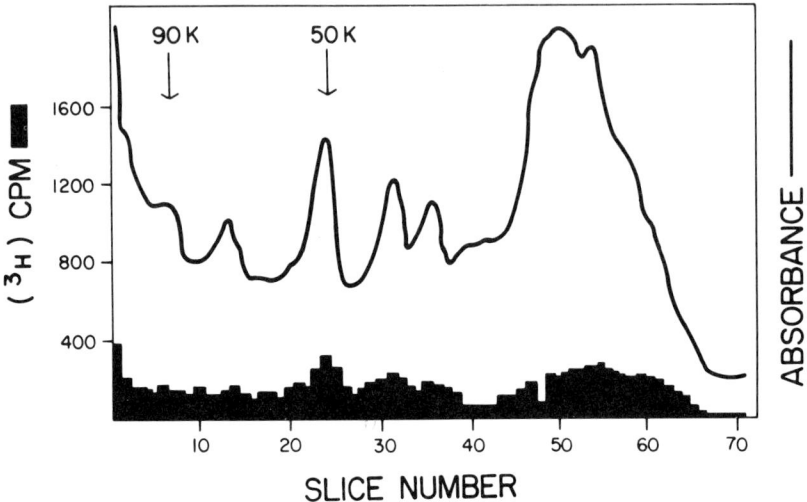

FIGURE 6. Sodium dodecyl sulfate–polyacrylamide gel electrophoresis of Complex I following irradiation with arylazido-[3-³H]-β-alanine. The conditions were identical to those described for FIGURE 4, except that arylazido-[3-³H]-β-alanyl NAD⁺ was replaced by 0.211 μmol arylazido-[3-³H]-β-alanine (specific activity 6.9×10^7 cpm μmol⁻¹).

labeling experiments at higher concentrations of arylazido-β-alanine in both the presence and the absence of NAD⁺ and CoQ₁ are in progress.

ARYLAZIDO-β-ALANYL NADP⁺

Low levels of NADPH-CoQ₁ and NADPH-ferricyanide reductase activities are detected in submitochondrial particles and purified preparations of NADH-CoQ₁ reductase.[18] The NADPH oxidation is not associated with pyridine nucleotide transhydrogenase activities; nor is it detected in other respiratory chain complexes. The NADPH oxidation of submitochondrial particles occurs with a phosphate to oxygen ratio of 2.4:2.9.[22]

In addition to arylazido-β-alanyl NAD⁺, an NADP⁺ analog has been prepared, using the same methods developed for the adenine nucleotides and for arylazido-β-alanyl NAD⁺.[23] This analog was considered a potential photoaffinity reagent for NADP⁺-dependent enzyme systems and was, consequently, used in a study of the Complex I activities dependent upon pyridine nucleotides.

THE STRUCTURE OF ARYLAZIDO-β-ALANYL NADP⁺

Two orange ultraviolet-absorbing reaction products were observed when the products formed by interacting NADP⁺ with arylazido-β-alanine in the presence of carbodiimidazole were subjected to chromatography with n-butanol, water, and acetic acid in the ratios 5:3:2. That product, which had an R_f of 0.40, was recovered from the paper by elution with H_2O; it had an absorption spectrum characterized by maxima at 475 nm, 290 nm (Shoulders), and 260 nm (FIGURE 7). This material was subjected to structural analysis using the same procedure applied to the elucidation of the structure of the NAD$^+$ analog. Base hydrolysis of the arylazido-β-alanyl group from the nucleotide analog, followed by a quantitative evaluation of the NADP$^+$ and arylazido-β-alanine that were formed, indicated a ratio of 1.09 for the concentration of NADP$^+$ to that of arylazido-β-alanine. This material has an apparent molar extinction coefficient of 5.67×10^3 (475 nm) and 45.4×10^3 (260 nm).

The determination of the site of esterfication of arylazido-β-alanine on NADP$^+$

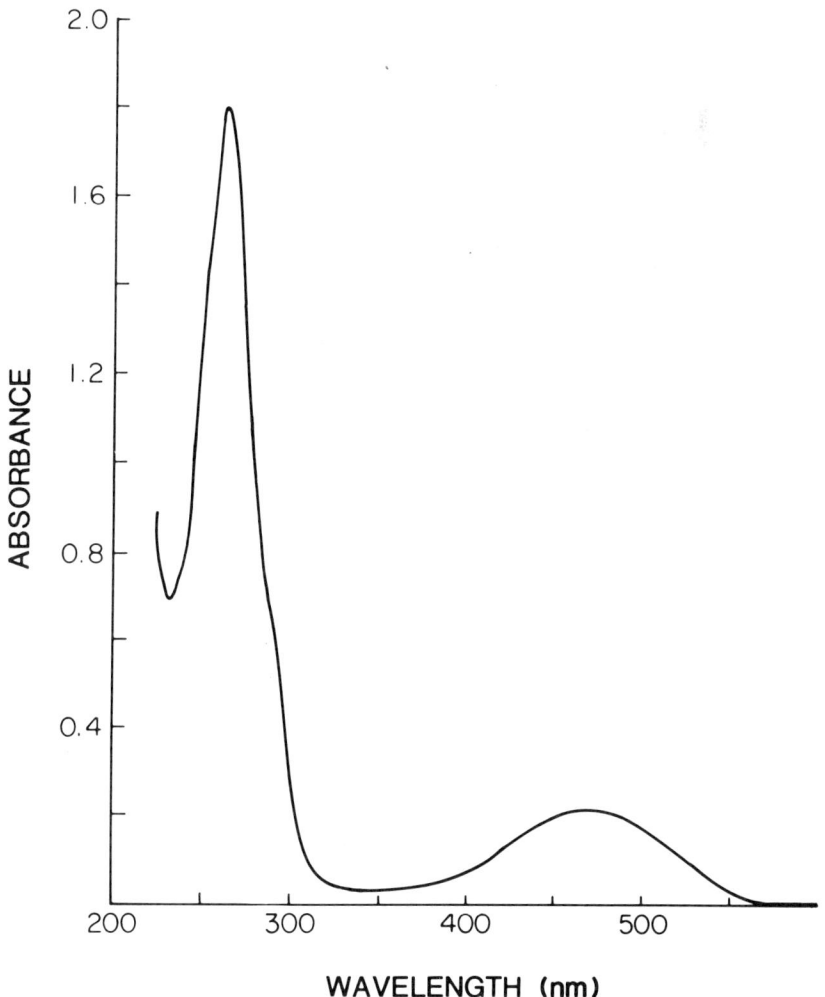

FIGURE 7. The absorption spectrum of arylazido-β-alanyl NADP$^+$. Arylazido-β-alanyl NADP$^+$ (39 nmol) in 1 ml distilled water.

was initiated by the enzymatic cleavage of the analog with nucleotide pyrophosphatase. The expected enzymatic hydrolytic products of NADP$^+$ are nicotinamide mononucleotide and adenosine-2',5'-diphosphate, and one would, therefore, expect that the arylazido-β-alanyl group would be on the ribose either of the NMN or of the 2',5'-ADP. An orange material ($R_f = 0.61$) that was formed upon enzymatic hydrolysis had an R_f value similar to that of arylazido-β-alanyl NMN$^+$, while an ultraviolet absorbing material ($R_f = 0.11$) had chromatographic characteristics different from those of either NMN or AMP. This result suggested that the arylazido-β-alanyl group is on the NMN portion of the analog.

N3'-O-{3-[N-(4-Azido-2-nitrophenyl)amino]propionyl} NADP$^+$

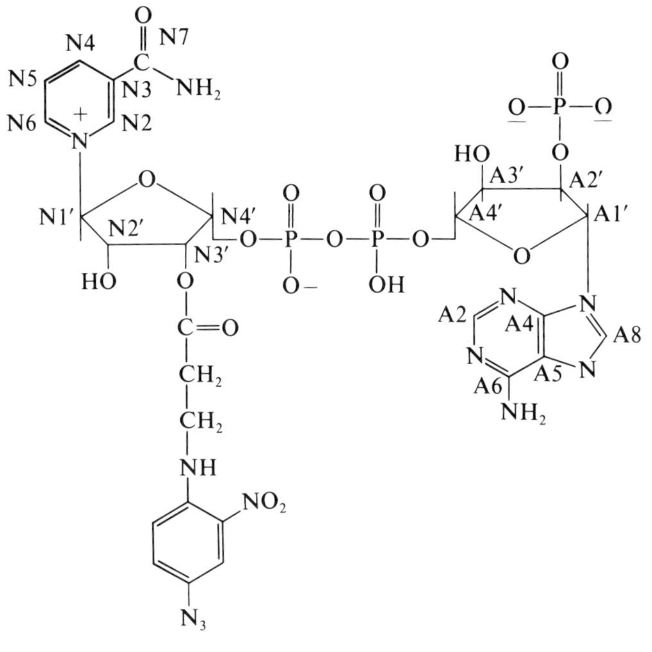

SCHEMA 7

The two enzymatically formed products were subjected to incubation in 1 N KCN. Under these conditions, the orange material developed a 325 nm absorption band concomitant with a decrease in its 260 nm absorbance, while the ultraviolet-absorbing hydrolytic product gave no indication of a spectral shift in KCN. These results indicate that the orange material is an NMN derivative containing a single arylazido-β-alanyl adjunct. From the overall analysis, it is clear that the nucleotide analog has a single arylazido-β-alanyl group associated with the NMN portion of NADP$^+$. The proposed structure of this analog is indicated in SCHEMA 7.

NUCLEAR MAGNETIC RESONANCE SPECTRA OF THE PHOTOAFFINITY PROBES

Nuclear magentic resonance spectra of $NADP^+$ and NMN reveal that the majority of the protons of the ribose portion of the nucleotides are positioned at high field regions relative to HDO. The exceptions are the H'_1 protons of both and the H'_2 proton of the adenine ribose of $NADP^+$, which appear at a lower field relative to the HDO peak (FIGURES 8 and 12). The nuclear magnetic resonance spectra of arylazido-β-alanyl derivatives of these molecules (FIGURES 9 and 13) reveal that an extra proton signal has been shifted from the higher field region to the lower (relative to the HDO peak). FIGURE 9, a spectrum of arylazido-β-alanyl NADP, shows the resolved H'_1 and esterified linked proton resonances clearly. In this case, the H'_2 resonance is obscured by the water peak. This unique downfield shift of one proton signal can be explained by the deshielding effect of the ester group introduced through the formation of the photoaffinity analog. Double irradiation experiments have been carried out to determine which of the hydroxyl groups (2' or 3') has been deshielded due to esterification.

In FIGURE 10, the results of an irradiation of the $NADP^+$ analog within the water peak or at the H'_1 proton resonance (FIGURE 11) are presented. A restricted region of these spectra in the vicinity of the H'_1 proton resonance clearly shows the downfield shifted resonance and the water peak. Consequently, the proton resonance under the water peak is clearly coupled to both H'_1 and the ester-linked protons, indicating that this must be the H'_2 proton and that the ester-linked proton must be the H'_3 specie. This is corroborated by an experiment in which the region associated with the H'_1 proton signal was directly irradiated. In this last experiment, the splitting pattern of the ester-linked proton was not significantly modified, indicating that the H'_1 proton is not directly adjacent to the ester-linked proton, and that the latter must be the H'_3 protein.

The NMN spectra also clearly shows the resonance corresponding to the H_1 proton; there is, of course, no resonance corresponding to the shifted resonance of the H'_2 proton of $NADP^+$ (FIGURE 12). In comparison, the spectra of arylazido-β-alanyl NMN (FIGURE 13A) indicates a resonance between the H'_1 proton and the water peak. This shifted resonance is the result of the deshielding effect of esterification. When this preparation undergoes H'_1 decoupling (FIGURE 13B), there is, as expected, no change in the splitting pattern of ester-linked proton signals. Since the ester-linked proton is not directly adjacent to the H'_1, it must be in the H'_3 position. This assignment is consistent with previous considerations based upon kinetic reasoning.[3]

INTERACTION OF ARYLAZIDO-β-ALANYL $NADP^+$ WITH COMPLEX I

A kinetic analysis of the nonphotodependent effects of arylazido-β-alanyl $NADP^+$ was carried out on a number of pyridine nucleotide–dependent activities present in the NADH-CoQ reductase preparation.[23] Among the activities, $NAD(P)H$-CoQ_1 reductase, NADH-$AcPyAD^+$ transhydrogenase, and NADPH-$AcPyAD^+$ transhydrogenase, only the latter was competitively inhibited in the dark (with respect to NADPH) by arylazido-β-alanyl $NADP^+$.

In contrast to its ineffectiveness in the NADH-$AcPyAD^+$ transhydrogenation,

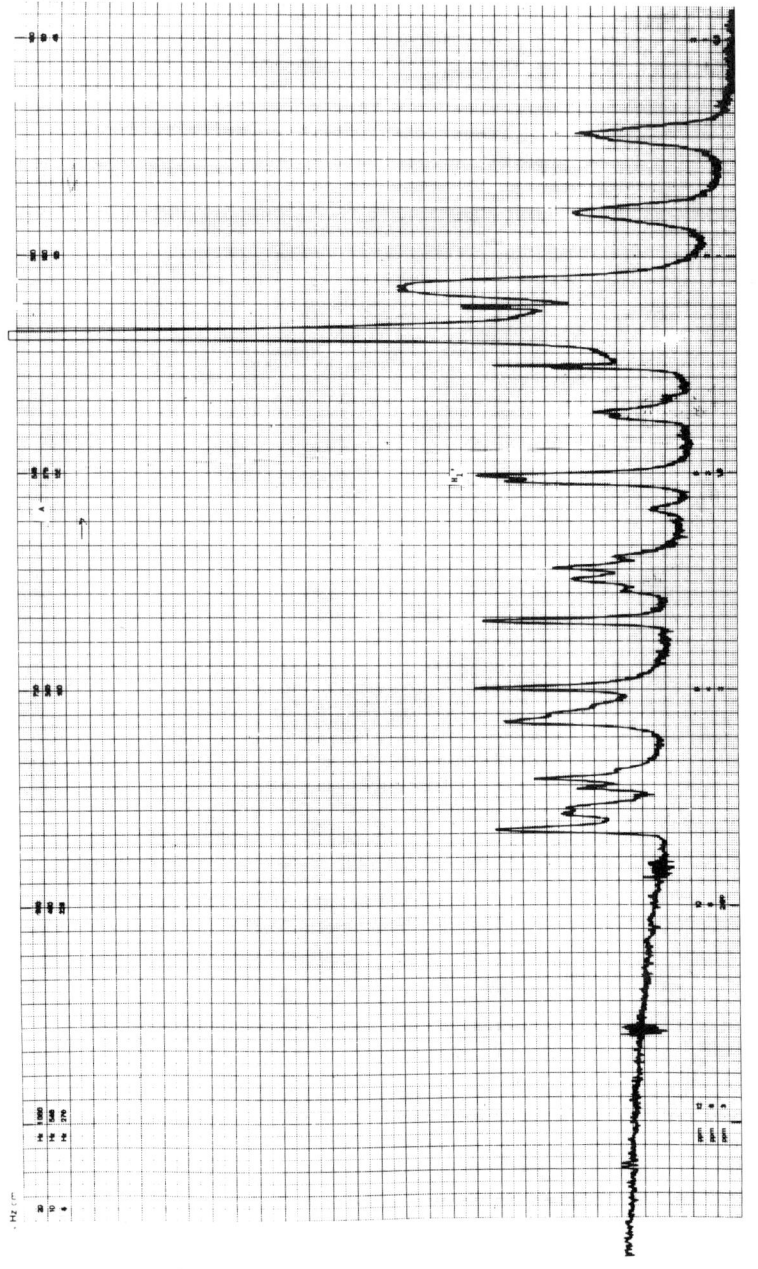

FIGURE 8. The nmr spectrum of NADP⁺.

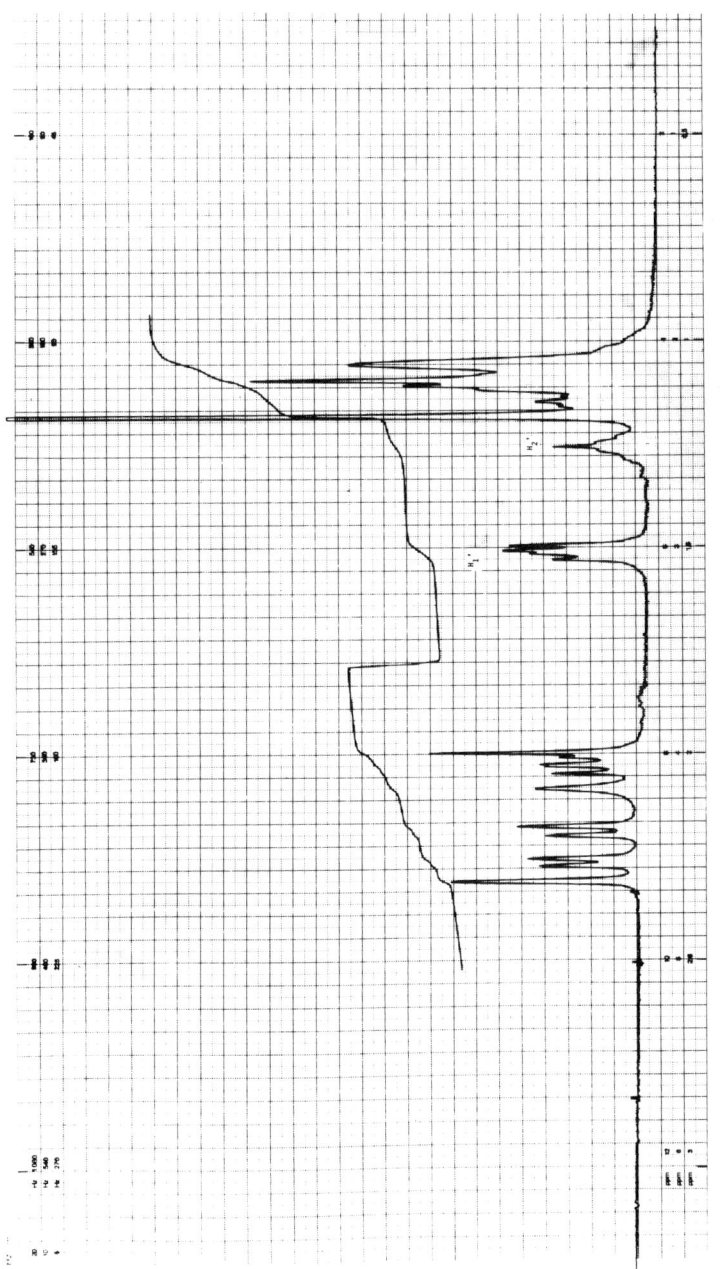

FIGURE 9. The nmr spectrum of arylazido-β-alanyl NADP⁺.

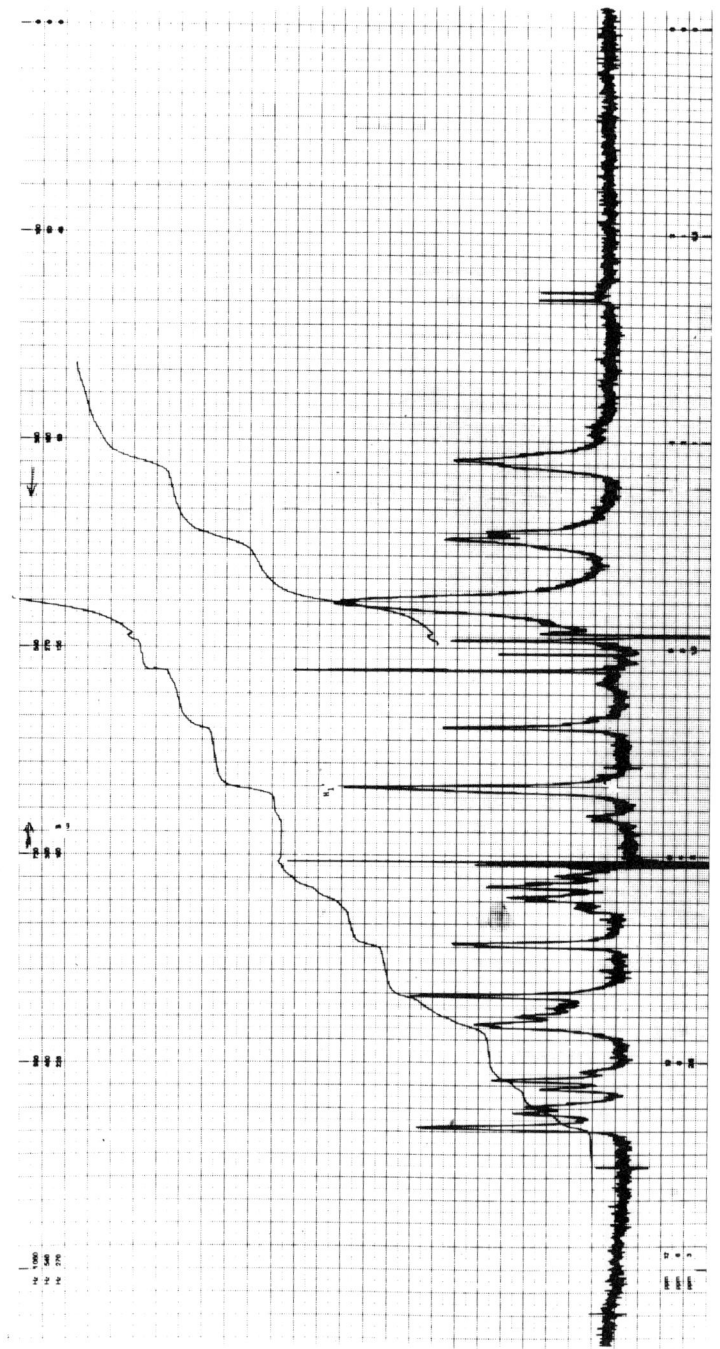

FIGURE 10. The nmr spectrum of arylazido-β-alanyl NADP with H_2O decoupling.

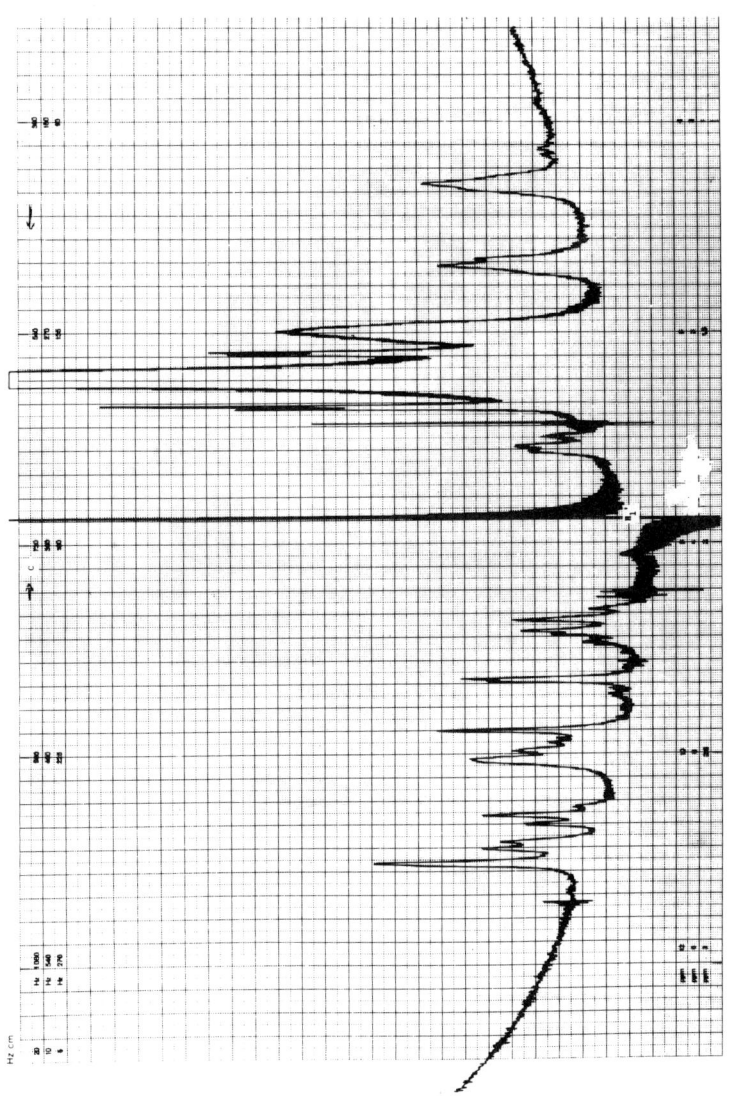

FIGURE 11. As with FIGURE 10, but with decoupling at the H_1' proton resonance.

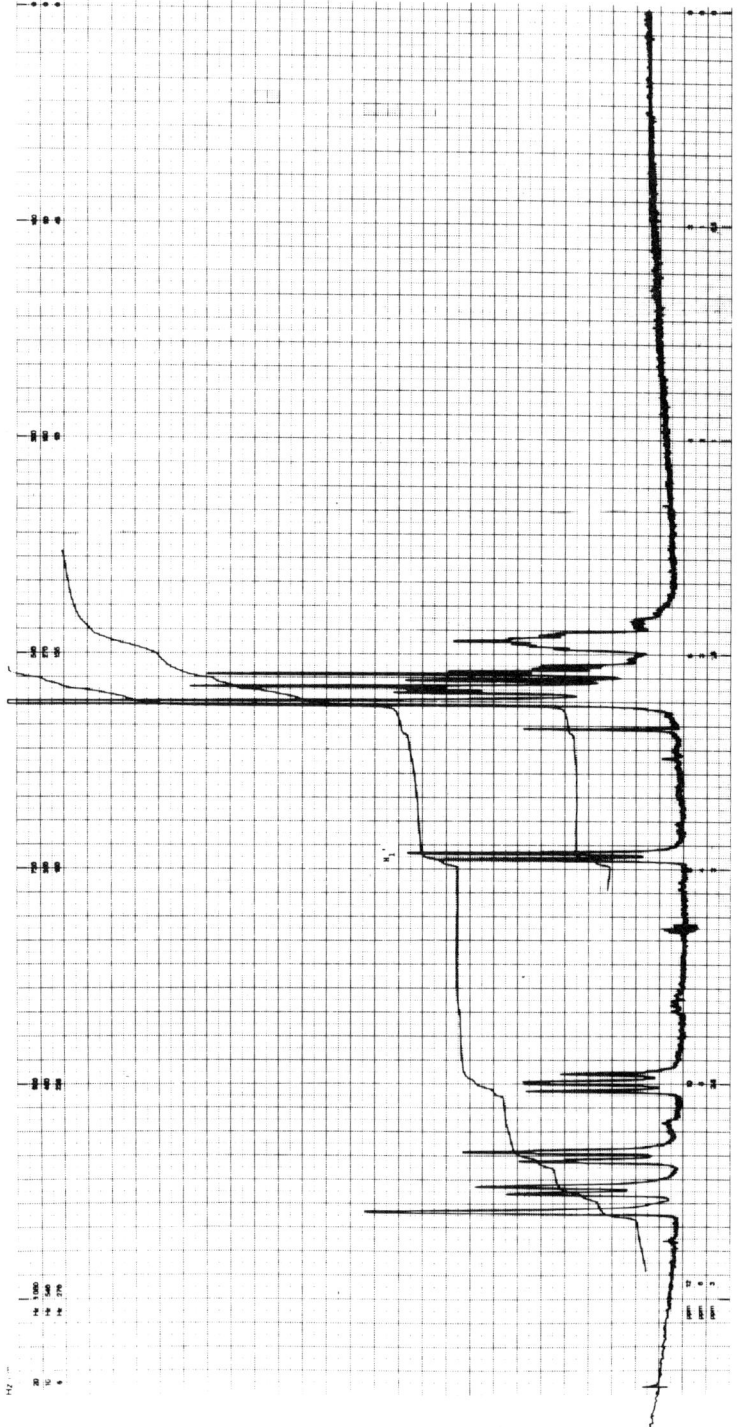

FIGURE 12. The nmr spectrum of NMN.

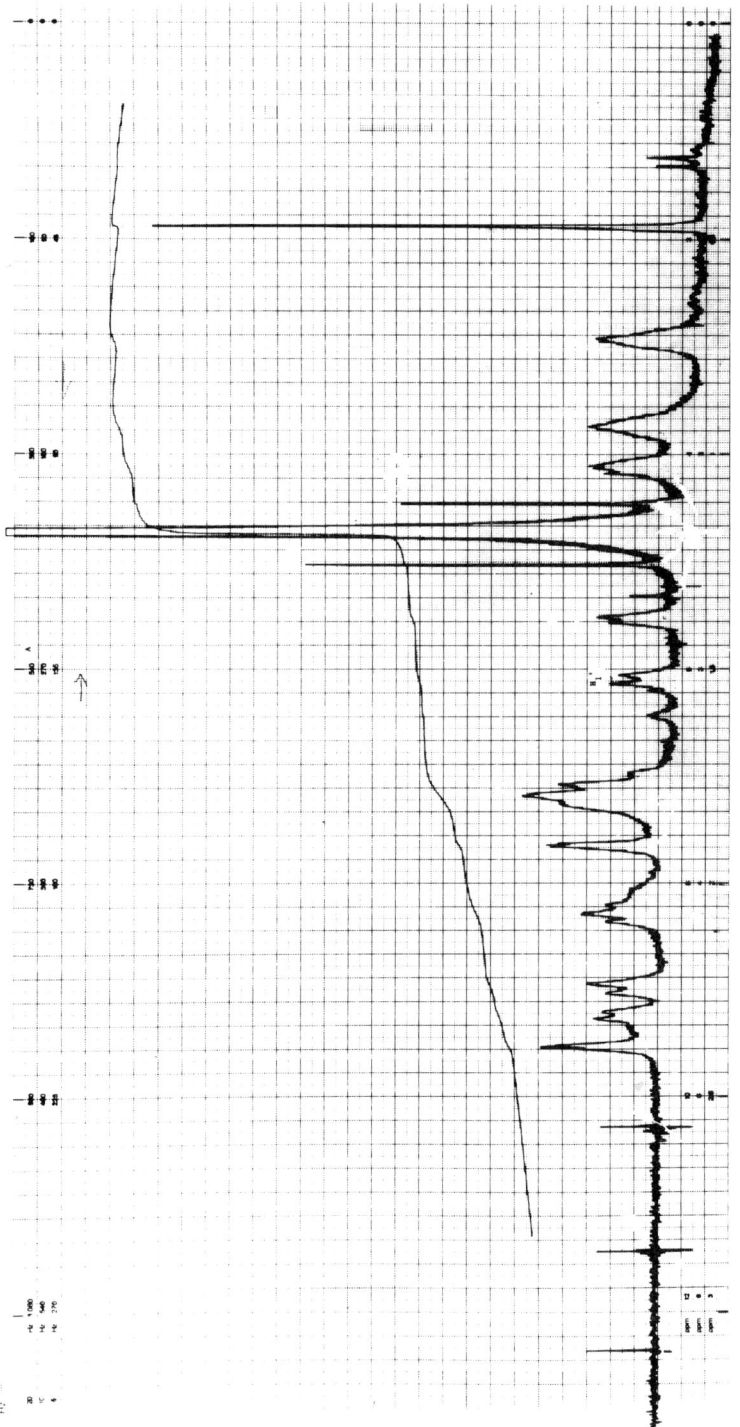

FIGURE 13A. The nmr spectrum of arylazido-β-alanyl NMN.

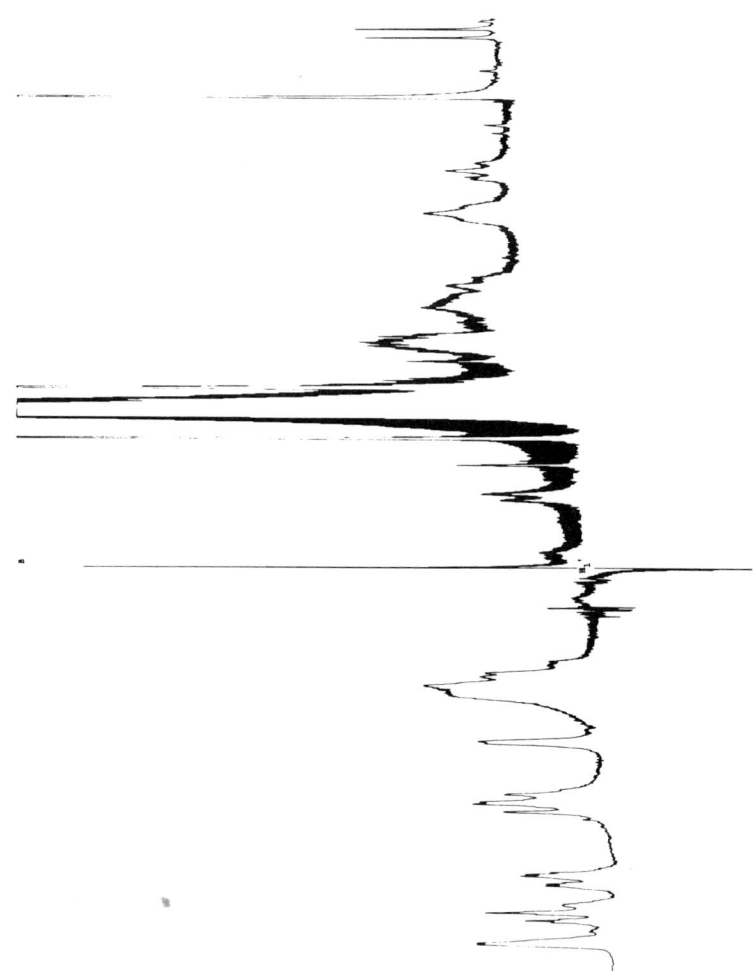

FIGURE 13B. The nmr spectrum of arylazido-β-alanyl NMN decoupled by irradiation at the H_1 resonance.

arylazido-β-alanyl NADP$^+$ is shown in FIGURE 14A to be a very potent competitive inhibitor (with respect to NADPH) of NADPH-AcPyAD$^+$ transhydrogenation. The evaluated $K_{i,app}$ value for the NADP$^+$ analog in the latter reaction was 6.0 μM. This low value can be compared to the $K_{m,app}$ for NADPH of 161 μM. For this activity, the arylazido-β-alanyl NADP$^+$ is a noncompetitive inhibitor with respect to AcPyAD$^+$

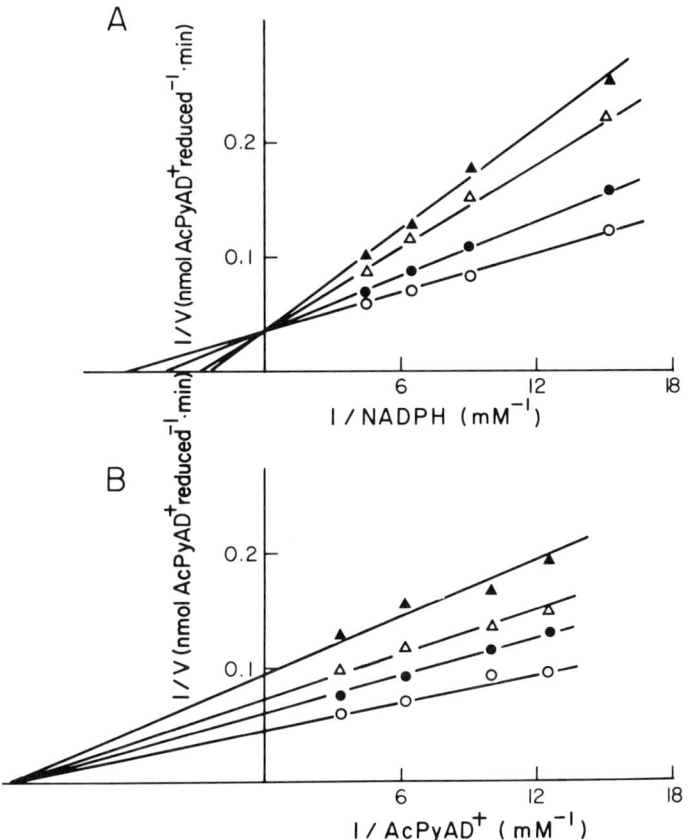

FIGURE 14. A kinetic analysis of the inhibition by arylazido-β-alanyl NADP$^+$ of the NADPH-AcPyAD$^+$ transhydrogenase activity present in NADH-CoQ reductase (Complex I) preparation.[23] (A) In the presence of 0 (o), 3.2 (•), 6.4 (△), and 9.5 μM (▲) arylazido-β-alanyl NADP$^+$ the concentration of AcPyAD$^+$ was 300 μM. (B) In the presence of 0 (o), 4.2 (•), 8.3 (△), and 16.9 μM (▲) arylazido-β-alanyl NADP$^+$ the concentration of NADPH was 195 μM. The noninhibited activity was assayed at 0.87 μmol of AcPyAD$^+$ reduced per min per mg protein.

(FIGURE 14B). TABLE 2 summarizes the kinetic results of the effect of arylazido-β-alanyl NADP$^+$ on the measured activities present in the Complex I preparation. The fact that only the NADPH-AcPyAD$^+$ transhydrogenation is inhibited contrasts with the action of arylazido-β-alanyl NAD$^+$, which is a potent inhibitor of all the measured activities of Complex I *except* the NADPH-AcPyAD$^+$ transhydrogenation.

Arylazido-β-alanyl NADP$^+$ shows no significant effect on the NADH or NADPH-CoQ$_1$ reductase activities at concentrations above 183 μM. This is in contrast to arylazido-β-alanyl NAD$^+$, which is a strong competitive inhibitor at this level.

PHOTODEPENDENT EFFECTS OF ARYLAZIDO-β-ALANYL NADP$^+$ ON THE
COMPLEX I ACTIVITIES DEPENDENT UPON PYRIDINE NUCLEOTIDES

Following a one minute photolysis of the enzyme complex (0.45 mg) with 44 nmol arylazido-β-alanyl NADP$^+$, the NADPH-AcPyAD$^+$ transhydrogenase activity was inhibited 54% compared to the untreated preparation. (None of the other pyridine nucleotide–dependent reactions were influenced.) However, the dark control, an enzyme complex mixed with an identical concentration of arylazido-β-alanyl NADP$^+$ but not subjected to light irradiation, was also inhibited (41%). In view of the potent

TABLE 2

THE EFFECT OF ARYLAZIDO-β-ALANYL NADP$^+$
ON THE PYRIDINE NUCLEOTIDE–DEPENDENT ACTIVITIES PRESENT
IN THE NADH-CoQ REDUCTASE (COMPLEX I) PREPARATION
FROM OX HEART MITOCHONDRIA[23]

Reaction	Concentration of Fixed Substrate (μM)	Concentration of Arylazido-β-Alanyl NADP$^+$ (μM)	Inhibitory Kinetic Effect	$K_{m,app}$ (second substrate) (μM)	$K_{i,app}$ Arylazido-β-Alanyl NADP$^+$ (μM)
NADH-CoQ$_1$ reductase	30 (CoQ$_1$)	183	None	12.3 (NADH)	—
NADH-AcPyAD$^+$ transhydrogenase	300 (AcPyAD$^+$)	155	None	13.3 (NADH)	—
NADPH-CoQ$_1$ reductase	30 (CoQ$_1$)	183	None	357 (NADPH)	—
NADPH-AcPyAD$^+$ transhydrogenase	300 (AcPyAD$^+$)	5.2	Competitive	161.0 (NADPH)	6.0
	200 (NADPH)	5.2	Noncompetitive	83.3 (AcPyAD$^+$)	—

competitive inhibition demonstrated for this activity ($K_{i,app} = 6.0$ μM with a K_m (NADPH) of 161 μM), the inhibition is not unexpected. Nevertheless, the inability to demonstrate a *major* photodependent effect is surprising and opens to question the role of arylazido-β-alanyl NADP$^+$ as a potential photoaffinity labeling reagent. While this inability to clearly demonstrate a photodependent inhibitory effect for arylazido-β-alanyl NADP$^+$ on the NADPH-AcPyAD$^+$ transhydrogenase could be explicable on a kinetic basis, there are alternative explanations. The analog may insert itself within the area of the active site but in such a way that it allows for sufficient flexibility, provided either by the nucleotide derivative or by the binding site itself, for reversible interaction of the natural nucleotide with the catalytic site. Thus, while the analog competes with the natural substrate for the catalytic site, the positioning of the photoaffinity group is not oriented properly to allow for complete insertion, although it effectively restricts entrance to the catalytic site. Consequently, the bound analog provides a steric hindrance to the reactivity of NADPH at the active site, thus accounting for the competitive type of inhibitior effect. Alternatively, there is the possibility that this enzyme has a secondary (allosteric) binding site with which the nucleotide analog binds preferentially, influencing reactivity at the catalytic site. The arylazido-β-alanyl NADP$^+$ does, in fact, interact with and covalently label Complex I in a photodependent manner, as indicated by experiments using arylazido-[3-^{3}H]-β-alanyl NADP$^+$.

Complex I (6 mg) was subjected to a 4 min irradiation period in the presence of 0.272 mM arylazido-[3-^{3}H]-β-alanyl NADP$^+$. Under these conditions, the NADPH-AcPyAD$^+$ transhydrogenation was inhibited 46%, while the NADH-AcPyAD$^+$ transhydrogenase and NAD(P)H-CoQ$_1$ reductase activities were not significantly influenced. Following photolysis, the enzyme mixture was mixed to a 1% sodium dodecyl sulfate concentration and chromatographed on a Sephadex G-75 column equilibrated with the same solution. As can be seen from FIGURE 15A, a substantial portion of the radioactive pyridine nucleotide analog remains associated with the protein eluted at the void volume. When a nonirradiated mixture containing the same quantity of enzyme as the tritium analog was subjected to the same chromatographic procedure, there was a major reduction in the radioactivity associated with the eluted protein (FIGURE 15B).

In the photolyzed preparation, 2.91 nmol of arylazido-[3-^{3}H]-β-alanyl NADP was bound per mg protein, representing a molar ratio of nucleotide to Complex I protein of 1.66. In the case of the dark control, 0.96 nmol of analog was bound per mg Complex I, representing a molar ratio of 0.548.

Thus, the photolyzed preparation had a sizable quantity of radioactive nucleotide associated with protein following the disruption of the protein structure by sodium dodecyl sulfate. Such results provide us with clear evidence for photodependent labeling of Complex I by arylazido-β-alanyl NADP$^+$. This labeling pattern is surprising, since the dark control exhibits an inhibition of the NADPH-AcPyAD$^+$ transhydrogenase, which is, in general, only 10 to 15% less than that of the photolyzed preparation. At a 400-fold molar excess of analog over Complex I, there is an 80% inhibition of enzymatic activity following photolysis and a 65% inhibition in the absence of photoirradiation.

The experiment illustrated in FIGURE 16 indicates that arylazido-β-alanyl NADP$^+$ may, primarily, covalently label Complex I on a limited number of peptides and on the one associated with the NADPH-AcPyAD$^+$ transhydrogenase. It is clear that, under the photolytic conditions of the recognized resolved peptides, only those of molecular weights of 90,000, 76,000, 37,000, and 26,500 are significantly labeled. The mitochondrial pyridine nucleotide transhydrogenase has been purified by Anderson and Fisher[24] and by Hojekerg and Rydstrom;[25] both reports indicate that the transhydrogenase has a molecular weight of 90,000 to 110,000. One of the peptides labeled by arylazido-[3-^{3}H]-β-alanyl NADP$^+$ has a molecular weight of 90,000 and, since the NADPH-AcPyAD$^+$ transhydrogenase activity is the only enzymatic activity inhibited by this analog, this might suggest that this peptide is indeed the transhydrogenase protein. The NAD$^+$ analog, arylazido-β-alanyl NAD$^+$, does not label the 90,000 molecular weight peptide. This is consistent with the lack of an inhibitory effect of this analog on NADPH-AcPyAD$^+$ transhydrogenase activity.

The specific labeling pattern is distinctly different from that exhibited by arylazido-β-alanyl NAD$^+$ (FIGURE 4) and from the obviously nonspecific pattern observed for arylazido-β-alanine (FIGURE 6).

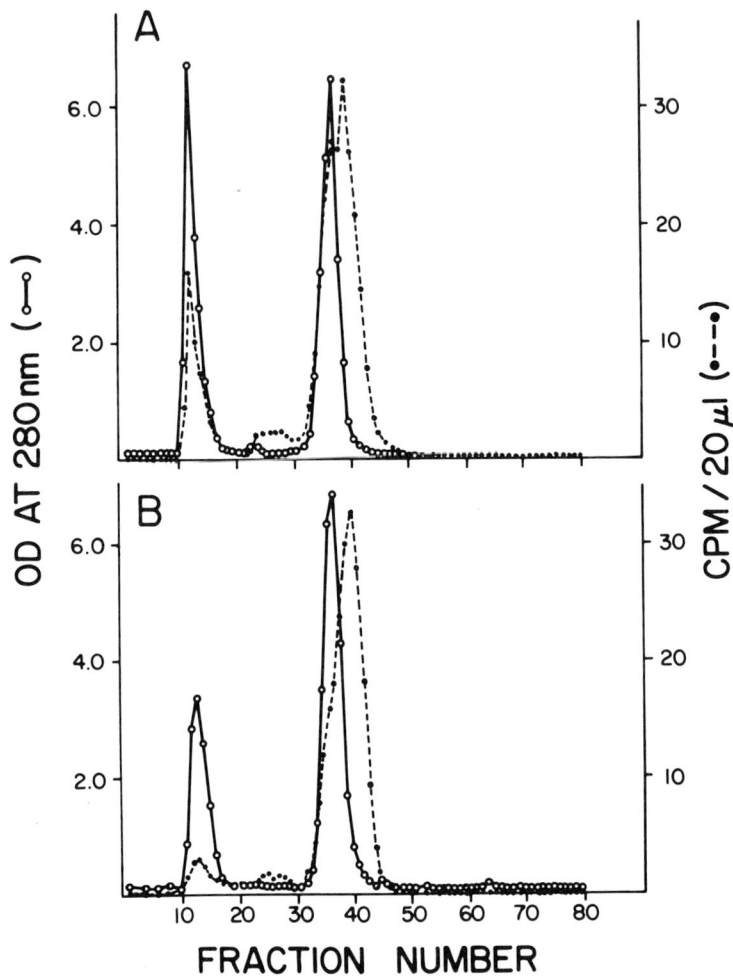

FIGURE 15. Sephadex G-75 sodium dodecyl sulfate chromatography of complex I–arylazido-[3-³H]-β-alanyl NADP⁺ mixtures.[23] (A) The elution pattern of a photolyzed Complex I–arylazido[3-³H]-β-alanyl NADP⁺ mixture. Six milligrams of Complex I in 0.77 ml of buffer was photolyzed (4 min) in the presence of 0.21 μmol arylazido-[3-³H]-β-alanyl NADP⁺ (specific activity 4.83×10^7 cpm/μmol). An aliquot (0.4 ml) of this mixture was incubated overnight in the dark at 37 °C with 1% (w/v) sodium dodecyl sulfate and 1% (v/v) 8-mercaptoethanol. The mixture was applied to a Sephadex G-75 column (44 × 0.7 cm) equilibrated with a 1% sodium dodecyl sulfate solution. The protein was eluted with an identical solution. (B) The elution pattern of an unirradiated mixture of Complex I and arylazido-[3-³H]-β-alanyl NADP⁺. The procedure was that described above, except that the enzyme-analog mixture was not photolyzed.

That the interaction of arylazido-β-alanyl NADP⁺ with the catalytic site responsible for NADPH-AcPyAD⁺ transhydrogenase is not a simple ligand interaction is indicated by an interesting time-dependent change in the kinetic order of the inhibitory effect of arylazido-β-alanyl NADP⁺. As can be seen in FIGURE 11A, a competitive inhibition with respect to NADPH is observed following irradiation of the analog with Complex I. In this experiment, the $K_{i,app}$ values for arylazido-β-alanyl NADP with and without light irradiation were 1.04 μM and 1.94, respectively. When the analog was photolyzed prior to mixing with the enzyme complex, the kinetics of this interaction with respect to NADPH were also of a competitive nature ($K_{i,app}$ 7.33

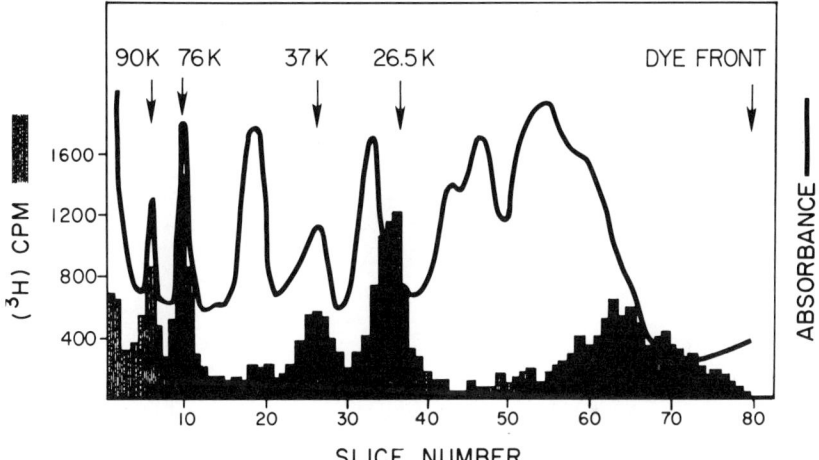

FIGURE 16. Sodium dodecyl sulfate–polyacrylamide gel electrophoresis of Complex I following irradiation with arylazido-[3-³H]-β-alanyl NADP⁺. Two hundred and fifty microliters of an irradiated mixture of Complex I and arylazido-[3-³H]-β-alanyl NADP⁺, as described in FIGURE 15, was dialyzed against one liter of a solution containing 1% (w/v) sodium dodecyl sulfate and 1% (v/v) β-mercaptoethanol. Following overnight dialysis in the dark at 25 °C, the solution was applied to a 10% polyacrylamide sodium dodecyl sulfate gel for electrophoresis, according to the procedure described by Weber and Osborn.[21] The gels stained with Coomassie Blue were scanned at 550 nm and sliced with a multi-blade slicer. The slices (1 mm) were digested overnight with 0.3 ml of 30% H_2O_2 at 65 °C, and the radioactivity of each slice was measured by ligand scintillation in 5 ml of Aquasol (New England Nuclear). Molecular weights were evaluated as described in FIGURE 4.

μM). It is observed that a major proportion of the inhibitory profile is of a photodependent nature; it is, however, also obvious that there is a large non-photodependent inhibitory effect.

When the assays for transhydrogenation are carried out following an extended incubation of the Complex I-analog mixture at 0 °C (following photoirradiation), the kinetic profile indicated in all cases (FIGURE 17B) is that of noncompetitive inhibition. The dark control (the nonphotolyzed Complex I-analog mixture) and the control in which arylazido-β-alanyl NADP⁺ was photolyzed prior to its addition to the enzyme now exhibited a rate of transhydrogenation only slightly less than that of the light

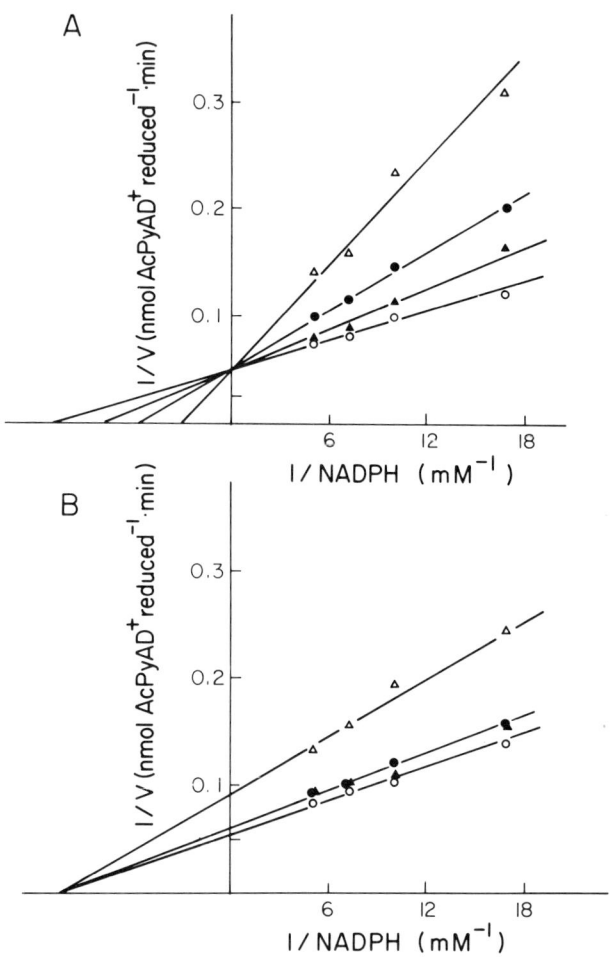

FIGURE 17. A kinetic analysis of the arylazido-β-alanyl NADP[+] inhibition of the NADPH-AcPyAD[+] transhydrogenase activity associated with NADH-CoQ reductase (Complex I).[23] (A) In addition to a control sample (o) containing 0.5 mg of complex I in a final volume of 0.2 ml, three other samples were prepared containing, in addition to complex I, 56.4 nmol of arylazido-β-alanyl NADP[+]. One of the latter samples was subjected to photoirradiation for 3 min (△), a second was covered with aluminum foil and maintained in the dark (•), and the arylazido-β-alanyl NADP[+] in the third sample (▲) was photolyzed for 3 min prior to mixing with complex I. For an analysis of enzymatic activity, a 10 μl aliquot of each mixture was assayed for enzymatic activity at different NADPH concentrations in the presence of 300 μM AcPyAD[+]. (B) The samples from A were incubated at 0–4 °C for 5 hr and then assayed as outlined above.

control. The photolyzed Complex I-analog preparation was, on the other hand, still 42% inhibited with respect to NADPH-AcPyAD$^+$ transhydrogenation. Neither the presence of arylazido-β-alanine or NADP$^+$ either alone or in combination induced this time-dependent change in the kinetic profile. In this manner, a clear analog-photodependent inhibition is observed. This interesting result is tentatively ascribed to a conformational change induced by the nucleotide analog that occurs at the active site of the NADPH-AcPyAD$^+$ transhydrogenase. Experiments using the pyridine nucleotide probes with the purified mitochondrial transhydrogenase protein may explain this action.

The Variable Enzymatic Activities Associated with Complex I

While it appears certain that both the NADH-CoQ$_1$ reductase and the NADPH-CoQ$_1$ reductase activities are manifestations of a single enzyme, the relationship of the NADH-AcPyAD$^+$ and NADPH-AcPyAD$^+$ transhydrogenations to each other and to the CoQ$_1$ reductase activities is less certain. The different degree of inhibition of the two transhydrogenase activities by arylazido-β-alanyl NAD$^+$ and arylazido-β-alanyl NADP$^+$ indicates that the reactions are the results of different enzymes.* The biological significance of the two transhydrogenase activities is, however, still uncertain.

None of the mitochondrial complexes other than Complex I are associated with transhydrogenation.[26] It is, consequently, generally assumed that the protein responsible for this enzymatic activity is actually an intrinsic component of the arrangement of Complex I within the intact mitochondrial electron transport chain. There is, however, the possibility that the solubility characteristics of the transhydrogenase protein are responsible for its apparent specific association with Complex I only. This association may, in fact, occur as a result of a redistribution of the protein from its *in vivo* associations due to the disruptive procedures required for the separation of Complex I from other electron transport components.

Table 3 lists the specific activities of the principal enzymatic reactions of Complex I for four different preparations recently isolated in this laboratory. While the specific activities for the enzymes assayed are all quite varied, the ratio of the two transhydrogenase activities is relatively constant for each of the preparations. In contrast, there is no such ready correlation with respect to the amount of transhydrogenation relative to the NADH-CoQ$_1$ reductase activities. The relative amount of reductase to transhydrogenation varies from 2.3 to 0.41 (average 1.05 ± 0.75), while the relative amount of NADH-AcPyAD$^+$ transhydrogenation to NADPH-AcPyAD$^+$ transhydrogenation varied from 14.6 to 10.3 (average 12.1 ± 1.4).

Complex I preparation 3 had a much higher NADH-CoQ$_1$ reductase activity relative to transhydrogenation than did the other three preparations. A comparison of the electrophoretic pattern for this preparation (Figure 18) with those used for the arylazido-β-alanyl NAD$^+$ and arylazido-β-alanyl NADP$^+$ labeling experiments reported in this paper (preparation 2) is revealing. Associated with the difference in

---

*Recent work on the photoinhibition of Complex I reactions by arylazido-β-alanyl ATP has shown that, of the three enzymatic activities investigated, only the NADH-AcPyAD$^+$ transhydrogenase activity was not greatly influenced. This supports the above concept.

TABLE 3

ENZYMATIC LEVELS* OF THE PYRIDINE NUCLEOTIDE–DEPENDENT REACTIONS OF COMPLEX I

| Preparation | NADH-CoQ$_1$ Reductase (A) | Transhydrogenation | | Relative Activities | |
		NADH-AcPyAD (B)	NADPH-AcPyAD (C)	(A) / (B) + (C)	(B) / (C)
1	10.0	8.3	0.8	1.1	10.3
2	15.8	35.9	2.9	0.41	12.3
3	25.0	10.0	0.9	2.3	11.1
4	5.1	11.7	0.8	0.41	14.6
Average	14.0 ± 6.4	16.4 ± 9.7	1.35 ± 0.77	1.05 ± 0.75	12.1 ± 1.4

*Enzymatic activity is reported as μmol min^{-1} mg^{-1} of Complex I at infinite CoQ$_1$ (for NADH-CoQ$_1$ reductase) or infinite AcPyAD$^+$ concentration (for transhydrogenation).

enzymatic activity for preparation 3 are much reduced levels in the 90,000 and 76,000 molecular weight peptides relative to those of mw 50,000 and 30,500. The data indicate that the transhydrogenase and the NADH-CoQ$_1$ reductase activities are not in constant proportion in every Complex I preparation isolated.

SUMMARY

Chemical and physical studies of two pyridine nucleotide photoaffinity probes have shown that the structural assignment for arylazido-β-alanyl NAD$^+$ is represented by A3'-0-{3-[N-(4-azido-2-nitrophenyl)amino]propionyl} NAD$^+$ and, for arylazido-β-alanyl NADP$^+$, by N3'-0{3-[N-(4-azido-2-nitrophenyl)amino]propionyl} NADP$^+$.

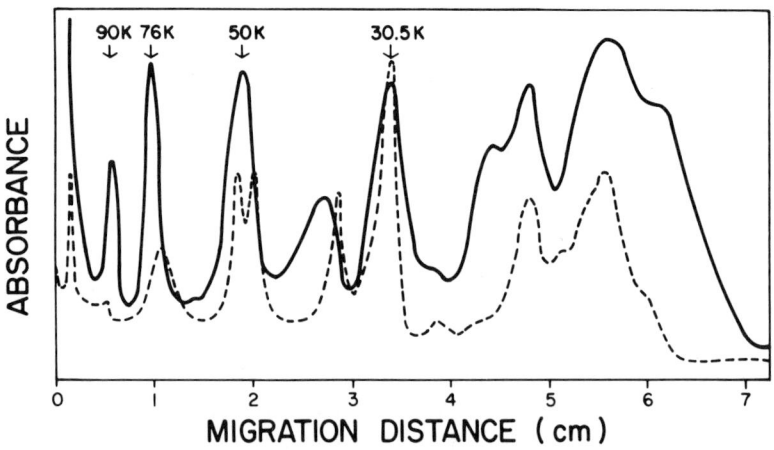

FIGURE 18. Sodium dodecyl sulfate–polyacrylamide gel electrophoresis of Complex I. Electrophoresis of two Complex I preparations with large relative differences in the NADH-CoQ$_1$ reductase and NAD(P)H transhydrogenase activity. See TABLE 3 and text for details. Complex I preparation 2: —; Complex I preparation 3: ---.

Arylazido-β-alanyl NAD^+ is an active phototaffinity probe for enzyme systems requiring NAD^+. It is a potent inhibitor of $NAD(P)H$-CoQ_1 reductase and NADH-$AcPyAD^+$ transhydrogenase activity in Complex I. The photodependent inhibitions could be prevented by the presence of the natural substrate (NADH) during irradiation. Arylazido-β-alanyl NAD^+ has a minimal effect on NADPH-$AcPyAD^+$ transhydrogenation. In contrast to the inhibitory profile of the NAD^+ analog, arylazido-β-alanyl $NADP^+$ is, in Complex I, only effective against NADPH-$AcPyAD^+$ transhydrogenation.

Since the photodependent inhibitory profiles of arylazido-β-alanyl NAD^+ for both NADH-CoQ reductase and NADPH-CoQ reductase are identical at low arylazido-β-alanyl NAD^+ concentrations, we assume that these two activities use the same enzymatic site. Both oxidoreductase activities were photodependently inhibited (greater than 70%) in the presence of a 25-fold molar excess of the analog over the enzyme complex. The fact that NADH is more effective than NADPH in protecting against inhibition of *both* activities is taken as a further indication of the identity of the nucleotide binding site for these two activities. One would expect, in the case of different binding sites, that NADPH would be much more effective in protecting the NADPH-CoQ_1 reductase activity against photodependent inhibition in the presence of arylazido-β-alanyl NAD^+.

In the dark, arylazido-β-alanyl NAD^+ is a noncompetitive inhibitor with respect to NADH and a competitive inhibitor with respect to $AcPyAD^+$ of NADH-$AcPyAD^+$ transhydrogenation. This is taken to indicate that this activity represents a pyridine nucleotide reaction site of Complex I independent of that for the oxidoreductase activities. The possibility of an identical catalytic site being responsible for NADH-$AcPyAD^+$ transhydrogenation and NADH dehydrogenation is ruled out by the fact that arylazido-β-alanyl NAD^+ is a competitive inhibitor, with respect to NADH, of the oxidoreductases, but not of the NADH-$AcPyAD^+$ transhydrogenase. Since arylazido-β-alanyl NAD^+ is not an effective inhibitor of the NADPH-$AcPyAD^+$ transhydrogenase either in the dark or after photoirradiation, this activity is taken to represent a third independent nucleotide binding site.

Thus, three distinct pyridine nucleotide reactive sites are present within Complex I, those for $NAD(P)H$-CoQ reductase, NADH-$AcPyAD^+$ transhydrogenase, and NADPH-$AcPyAD^+$ transhydrogenase. The findings also suggest that NADH and NADPH oxidations take place at an identical site, distinct from that responsible for the pyridine nucleotide transhydrogenase activities of Complex I.

The specificity of the two photoprobes, which was evaluated by kinetic and photodependent inhibitory studies, has its counterpart in the labeling pattern of the peptides of Complex I following photoirradiation in the presence of the tritium-containing photoprobes. It is anticipated that further resolution of Complex I with the aid of the pyridine nucleotide photoprobes will assist in characterizing the relationship of these enzymatic activities to the different protein subunits of Complex I.

REFERENCES

1. GOTTIKH, B. P., A. A. KRAEVSKII, P. P. PURYGIN, T. L. TSILEVICH, Z. S. BELOVA & L. N. RUDZITC. 1967. Izv. Akad. Nauk. SSSR Ser. Khim. (Engl.): 2453.
2. GOTTIKH, B. P., A. A. KRAYEVSKY, N. B. TARUSSOVA, P. P. PURYGIN & T. L. TSILEVICH. 1970. Tetrahedron **26:** 4419.

3. JENG, S. J. & R. J. GUILLORY. 1975. J. Supramol. Struct. **3**: 448–68.
4. GUILLORY, R. J. Unpublished observations.
5. GUILLORY, R. J., M. D. RAYNER & J. S. D'ARRIGO. 1977. Science **196**: 883–85.
6. JENG, S. J. Unpublished observations.
7. ZAMCENIK, P. C. 1962. Biochem. J. **85**: 257.
8. MCLAUGHLIN, C. S. & V. M. INGRAM. 1965. Biochemistry **4**: 1442–48.
9. GRIFFIN, B. E., M. JARMAN, C. B. REESE, J. E. SULSTON & D. R. TRENTHAN. 1966. Biochemistry **5**: 3638.
10. PAL, P. K., W. J. WECHTER & R. F. COLMAN. 1975. Biochemistry **14**: 707.
11. BROWNE, D. T., S. S. HIXSON & F. H. WESTHEIMER. 1971. J. Biol. Chem. **246**: 4477–84.
12. HIXSON, S. S. & S. H. HIXSON. 1973. Photochem. Photobiol. **18**: 135–38.
13. KOBERSTEIN, R. 1976. Eur. J. Biochem. **67**: 223–29.
14. CHEN, S. & R. J. GUILLORY. 1977. J. Biol. Chem. **252**: 8990–9001.
15. NISHIZUKA, Y. & O. HAYAISHI. 1963. J. Biol. Chem. **238**: 3369–77.
16. BURTON, R. M. & N. O. KAPLAN. 1963. Arch. Biochem. Biophys. **101**: 139–49.
17. HATEFI, Y. 1960. In Comprehensive Biochemistry, Vol. 14. M. Florkin and E. Stolz, Eds.: 199–231. Elsevier. Amsterdam.
18. HATEFI, Y. & W. G. HANSTEIN. 1973. Biochemistry **12**: 3515–22.
19. HATEFI, Y. & K. E. STEMPEL. 1969. J. Biol. Chem. **224**: 2350–57.
20. HUENNEKENS, F. M. & B. MACKLER. 1971. In Electron and Coupled Energy Transfer in Biological Systems, Vol. 1, Part A. T. E. King and M. Klingenberg, Eds.: 135–57.
21. WEBER, K. & M. OSBORN. 1969. J. Biol. Chem. **244**: 4406–12.
22. HATEFI, Y., L. DJAVADI-OHANIANCE & Y. M. GALANTE. 1945. In Electron Transfer Chains and Oxidative Phosphorylation. E. Quagliariello, S. Papp, F. Palmieri, E. C. Slater, and N. Siliprandi, Eds.: 257–63. North Holland Publishing Co.
23. CHEN, S. & R. J. GUILLORY. J. Biol. Chem. In press.
24. ANDERSON, W. M. & R. R. FISHER. 1978. Arch. Biochem. Biophys. **187**: 180–90.
25. HOJEBERG, B. & J. RYDSTROM. 1977. Biochem. Biophys. Res. Commun. **78**: 1183–90.
26. HATEFI, Y., A. G. HAAVIK & D. E. GRIFFITHS. 1962. J. Biol. Chem. **237**: 1676–80.
27. HATEFI, Y. & J. S. RIESKE. 1967. Methods Enzymol. **10**: 235–39.
28. JACOBS, E. E., M. JACOBS, D. R. SANADI & L. B. BRADLEY. 1956. J. Biol. Chem. **223**: 147–56.
29. STEIN, A. M., N. O. KAPLAN & M. M. GIOTTI. 1959. J. Biol. Chem. **234**: 979–86.
30. CHEN S., & R. J. GUILLORY. 1979. J. Biol. Chem. **254**: 7220–27.

DISCUSSION

DR. Y. HATEFI *(Scripps Clinic and Research Foundation):* I'd like to elaborate a little bit on your comments, which, as a matter of fact, fully agree with our resolution of Complex I and our study of the enzymes involved. As you pointed out, there is a transhydrogenase enzyme present in Complex I with a molecular weight of 90,000 to 100,000 and this catalyzes transhydrogenation from NADPH to NAD$^+$ analogs. There is, also, an NADH dehydrogenase that has three subunits; this we have purified. The subunits have apparent molecular weights on SDS gels of about 50,000, 25,000, and 10,000. This enzyme catalyzes oxidation of NADH, oxidation of NADPH, and transhydrogenation from NADH to NAD$^+$. At low pH, it also catalyzes transhydrogenation from NADPH to NAD$^+$, but not at the pHs that you've been looking at. So these results clearly agree with yours, i.e., that you are looking at two different types of enzymes. Have you tried treating your preparation of Complex I with phenylchloroxal to inhibit the transhydrogenation enzyme and eliminate that portion of the reaction in order to see the NADH dehydrogenase activity more clearly?

DR. R. J. GUILLORY: No, we haven't done that specifically. What we have looked at are chase experiments in which the natural substrates are present during photoinhibiton in order to detect the possible loss of one of the binding sites for a particular analog. Those experiments haven't, as yet, been completely conclusive. Your suggestion is well taken and we shall attempt the experiment.

THE USE OF PHOTOAFFINITY PROBES
TO ELUCIDATE MOLECULAR MECHANISMS
OF NUCLEOTIDE-REGULATED PHENOMENA*

Patricia B. Hoyer, James R. Owens, and Boyd E. Haley

Department of Biochemistry
University of Wyoming
Laramie, Wyoming 82071

INTRODUCTION

The purpose of this paper is to describe results, techniques, problems, and new experimental approaches that involve the use of nucleotide photoaffinity probes. It is our contention that photoprobes such as 8-azidoadenosine-3',5'-cyclic monophosphate (8-N$_3$cAMP), 8-azidoguanosine-3',5'-cyclic monophosphate (8-N$_3$cGMP), 8-azido-adenosine-5'-triphosphate (8-N$_3$ATP), 8-azidoguanosine-5'-triphosphate (8-N$_3$GTP) and will be extremely useful in determining the mechanisms by which their natural analogs regulate biological phenomena. Regulation by such nucleotides can be effected either by conformational changes caused by binding to a receptor molecule or by phosphorylation of a substrate molecule. Both of these situations require that the nucleotide in question occupy a specific site on a specific macromolucule. It is the determination of the extent of interaction between the nucleotide and the receptor protein that is of prime importance, as well as how, when, and where such interactions occur.

Research in our laboratory has been directed at the mechanisms through which cAMP and ATP regulate cellular events and certain related biochemical reactions. Our approach has been to use the 8-azido derivatives of both of these compounds; our earlier emphasis was on cAMP. Use of [^{32}P]8-N$_3$cAMP has shown that it is specific for cAMP binding sites and efficiently photoincorporated into receptor molecules under optimal conditions.[1-3] The photolysis of 8-N$_3$cAMP probably generates a nitrene that has the ability to react with any amino acid residue within the active site (FIGURE 1). Also, 8-N$_3$cAMP is a good biological mimic of cAMP with regard to activating Type I and II protein kinases.[1,3] It is not a good substrate for most phosphodiesterases (PDE), showing no significant hydrolysis with mammalian PDEs, but it is hydrolyzed by *D. discoideum* PDE.[4,5]

Previous results obtained using [^{32}P]8-N$_3$cAMP have shown that it may be used to determine several kinetic and physical properties of cAMP receptor molecules, such as approximate molecular weights and ligand binding affinities.[1-3] It has been used to determine the cellular location of cAMP receptor proteins and when certain receptor proteins appear during a cell or life cycle.[4,6] It has also been used to determine the effects of cAMP on the membrane binding properties of Type I-M protein kinases' regulatory (R$_I$) and catalytic (C) subunits. These results indicate that this protein kinase is attached to the membrane through the R$_I$ subunit and that cAMP causes release of the C subunit, although the R$_I$-cAMP complex remains bound to the

*This research was supported by a National Institutes of Health grant, number GM-21998.

0077–8923/80/0346–0280 $1.75/1 © 1980, NYAS

membrane.[7] This tightly bound cAMP may be released from the membranes by the addition of MgATP, which appears to greatly increase its "off-rate" and, presumably, its hydrolysis by endogeneous PDEs.[7]

The results discussed herein will show that other parameters, such as ionic strength, may change both the percentage of photoincorporation of [^{32}P]8-N$_3$cAMP and the effects of MgATP. Data obtained using Type II-M protein kinase indicate that autophosphorylation appears to modulate MgATP effects on cAMP binding and may explain why such phosphorylation occurs. We will discuss a new technique, "cold trapping," that should enable us to evaluate both the specific "site-occupancy" of cAMP binding proteins in homogenates and whole cells and, perhaps, the ratio of R$_{II}$ to R$_{II}$-PO$_4$ that exists within a cell or tissue under various metabolic conditions. Also, photoaffinity labeling, coupled with two-dimensional gels, gives results that indicate that R may exist in several isoprotein forms called RIPs (regulatory isoproteins).

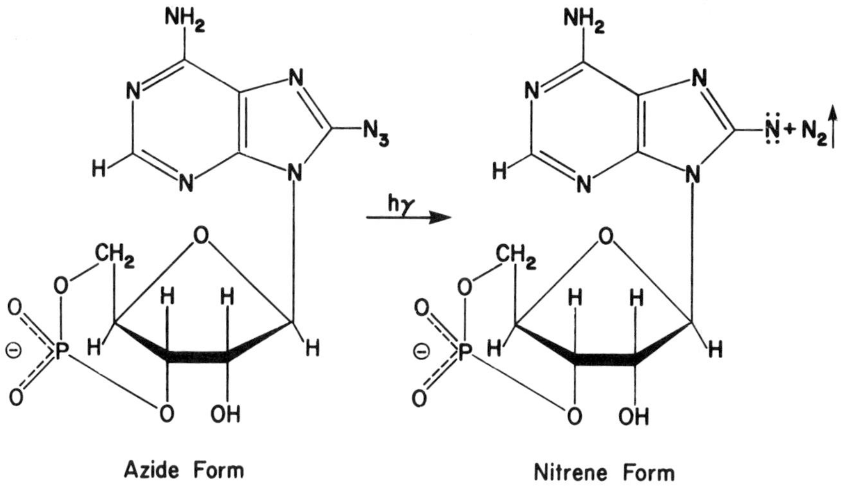

Azide Form   Nitrene Form

FIGURE 1. The photolysis of 8-N$_3$cAMP.

METHODS

[^{32}P]-8-N$_3$cAMP and [β-γ^{32}P]-8-N$_3$ATP were synthesized from [^{32}P]-cAMP and AMP by procedures reported in References 8 and 9. [γ^{32}P]-ATP was prepared as reported by Glynn and Chappel.[10]

Human blood samples (50 ml) were collected by vena puncture and immediately transferred to an Ehrlenmeyer flask containing 10 mg sodium heparin dissolved in 25 ml phosphate buffered saline solution (PBS) containing 13.6 mM phosphate and 150 mM NaCl (pH 7.4) at an osmolality between 308 and 315. The cells were washed three times with PBS (without heparin) by gentle mixing followed by centrifugation (10,000 × g for 30 s) and removal of the wash solution and white buffy coat by aspiration. Hemoglobin-free membranes were prepared from these cells by hemolysis and washing procedures described in Reference 11.

Membranes were stored frozen at $-20\,^\circ C$ and, on the day of use, were thawed and used immediately. Solutions were photolyzed for 5 min at $0\,^\circ C$ at 1 cm from a UVS 11 mineral light (UltraViolet Products, Inc.). Unless otherwise stated, the solutions photolyzed contained 700 μg membrane protein in 0.225 ml of a solution containing 0.1 μM 8-N_3cAMP, 80 mM NaCl, 40 mM KCl, 2.5 mM MgCl$_2$, and 20 mM Tris-HCl (pH 7.4).

To remove the catalytic subunits, red blood cells membranes containing 700 μg protein were washed twice with 5 ml of a solution containing 1 μM cAMP, 80 mM NaCl, 40 mM KCl, 0.5 mM ethylenediamine tetraacetic acid, 2.5 mM MgCl$_2$, and 20 mM Tris-HCl (pH 7.4). The membranes were washed by resuspension (by vortexing for 1 min), followed by centrifugation (for 10 min at 25,000 $\times$ g) and aspirating off the wash solution. To check for nucleotide binding protein in the wash solutions, the initial wash was mixed with [^{32}P]-8-N_3cAMP or [β,γ^{32}P]-8-N_3ATP in a quartz cuvette, photolyzed for 5 min at 2 cm, and mixed with 700 μg membrane protein (to assure a large enough pellet on PCA precipitation); the protein was precipitated by the addition of 5 ml 6% PCA (perchloric acid) at $0\,^\circ C$. Protein concentrations were determined by the method of Lowry et al.[12]

Rat brain homogenates and particulate fractions (crude membranes) were prepared from adult Wistar rats by homogenization in 4 ml 0.32 M sucrose/g wet brain. Cellular debris and nuclei were removed by centrifugation at 800 $\times$ g for 10 min, followed by filtration of the resulting supernatant through Miracloth. The filtrate was centrifuged at 18,000 $\times$ g for 30 min with subsequent removal of the supernatant (designated the soluble fraction). The pellet was resuspended in 0.32 M sucrose (designated the particulate fraction). The samples were either used immediately or stored frozen at $-20\,^\circ C$.

The precipitated membrane proteins were prepared for electrophoresis by dissolution in 0.20 ml of a protein solubilizing solution that consists of 25% sucrose, 2.5% SDS (sodium laurylsulfate), 2.5 mg% Pyronin Y, 25 mM Tris-HCl buffer (pH 8.0), 2.5 mM EDTA, and 15.4 mg dithiothreitol per ml or 0.25 ml 2-mercaptoethanol per 10 ml. Twenty five μl of solubilized membranes (67 $\pm$ 5 μg protein) were added to each gel slot. A slab gel electrophoresis system was used, employing a linear gradient (6 to 12%) of polyacrylamide with a 4% stacking gel. Both chambers of the gradient-making apparatus contained 0.36 M Tris-HCl buffer (pH 8.7), 0.1% SDS, 0.13 vol% N,N,N',N'-tetramethylethylenediamine, and 0.01 wt% ammonium persulfate. For a 6 to 12% gel, the first and second chambers contained 5.9 and 12.2 wt% acrylamide (1.5 wt% bisacrylamide), respectively; the second also contained 0.65 M sucrose. The stacking gel contained 0.1% SDS, 62.4 mM Tris-HCl (pH 6.7), 4 wt% acrylamide, 0.05 vol% N,N,N',N'-tetramethylethylenediamine, and 0.15 wt% ammonium persulfate. The gradient gel dimensions were 16.5 cm $\times$ 13.3 cm. $\times$ 1 mm; the stacking gel, 16.5 cm $\times$ 2 cm $\times$ 1 mm. Electrophoresis was done at 35 mA for about 4.5 h or until the tracking dye reached the bottom of the gel.

After electrophoresis, the gels were removed from the form, washed, and fixed for 1 h in a liter solution of aqueous 5% acetic acid and 10% 2-propanol. The gels were stained 1 h in 250 ml of a solution containing 25% 2-propanol, 10% acetic acid, and 0.05% Coomassie Brilliant Blue. The gels were destained with fixing solution for about 1.5 h in the presence of several pieces of synthetic packing foam to soak up the stain. All these steps were carried out at $50\,^\circ C$, with shaking. Gels were dried 2 h on a

Hoefer Scientific Instruments Model SE 540 slab gel dryer at 80 °C. Autoradiography was done as described in References 3 and 7. An Ortec Model 4310 densitometer was used for scanning dried gels and autoradiographs. The dried gels were sliced and counted in Beckman Ready-Solv Solution VI with a Beckman LS-250 Liquid Scintillation System.

The two-dimensional gel procedure was adapted from O'Farrell.[13] Three percent cylindrical polyacrylamide gels 10 cm in length containing 2% w/v ampholytes (BioRad; either 5–7 and 3–10 range ampholytes in ratios of 3:2 or 4–6, 6–8, and 3–10 in ratios of 2:2:1) were used for isoelectric focusing. For the second dimension, a 3 to 12% polyacrylamide gradient SDS slab gel was used with a 3% stacking gel. The unequilibrated cylindrical gel was held in place on top of the stacking gel by means of a 3% polyacrylamide gel containing 2% w/v SDS. (Isoelectric focusing gels not used immediately were frozen and stored at -80 °C in an SDS sample buffer containing 10% w/v glycerol, 2.3% w/v SDS, and 0.0625 M Tris-HCl, pH 6.8.) On either side of the isoelectric focused gel, wells were formed in the slab gel with teflon strips for separation of the appropriate erythrocyte membrane protein standard. The membrane protein was solubilized for isoelectric focusing by Ames and Nikaido's procedure[14] and 100 μg protein was added to each gel. The gels were stained by Righetti and Drysdale's method,[15] then dried and autoradiographed as described above.

RESULTS

The data shown in FIGURE 2 indicate that the binding and photoincorporation of [^{32}P]-8-N$_3$cAMP into CA-1 in both the presence and the absence of MgATP are very dependent upon monovalent metal ion concentrations. Both Na$^+$ and K$^+$ can cause a 25% increase in photoincorporation on going from 10 mM to 400 mM [M$^+$] without MgATP being present. Also, the inhibition of photoincorporation by 10 μM MgATP is greatly affected by [M$^+$]; 10 mM [M$^+$] allows a 72% decrease, whereas, at 400 mM [M$^+$], only a 5% decrease is observed.

The graph in FIGURE 3 shows the effects of varying [MgATP] and ionic strength on [^{32}P]8-N$_3$cAMP photoincorporation. MgATP concentrations in the 0.1 to 1.0 mM range are required for a significant inhibition of photoincorporation at ionic strengths similar to those found in living cells. The data plotted in the insets of FIGURES 2 and 3 show that increasing ionic strength decreases MgATP inhibition of photoincorporation linearly.

The graph shown in FIGURE 4 indicates that increasing [^{32}P]8-N$_3$cAMP concentrations cannot decrease the inhibitory effect of 10 μM MgATP. This specific cAMP receptor is saturated with [^{32}P]8-N$_3$cAMP at approximately 75–90 nM concentrations.[2,3] Also, 10 μM MgATP causes only a 50–65% decrease in maximal photoincorporation. Therefore, if the two nucleotides were competitive, increasing the concentration of [^{32}P]8-N$_3$cAMP from 80 to 800 nM should have increased the cpm photoincorporated. These results indicate that MgATP displaces cAMP from the receptor protein in a manner that is not competitive.

The autoradiograph of FIGURE 5 shows red cell membrane cAMP receptor proteins that have been photolabeled with [^{32}P]8-N$_3$cAMP and separated by SDS-PAGE (left side) or by a two-dimensional system of isoelectric focusing (IF)X

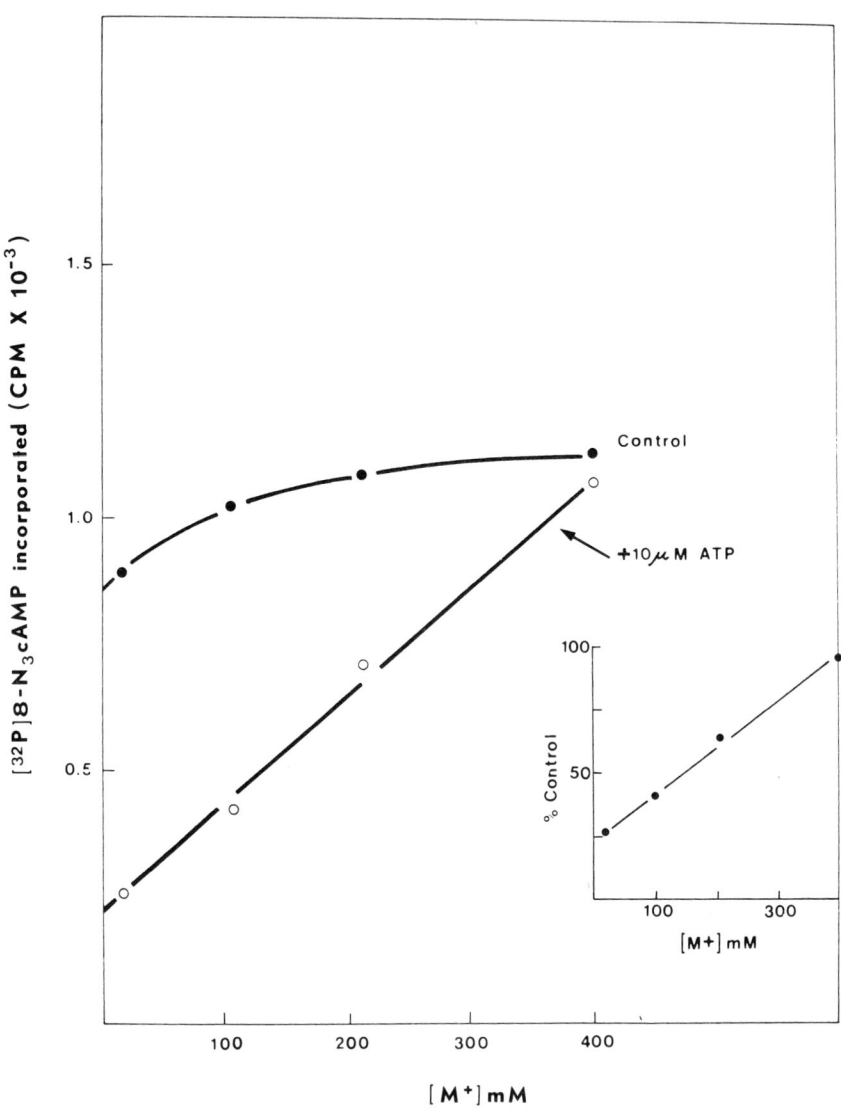

FIGURE 2. The variation in photoincorporation of 90 nM [^{32}P]8-N$_3$cAMP into CA-1 with increasing monovalent metal ion concentration in both the presence and the absence of 10 μM ATP. Both Na$^+$ and K$^+$ have been used with similar results in the presence of 10 mM Tris-Cl (pH 7.4) and 5 mM MgCl$_2$.

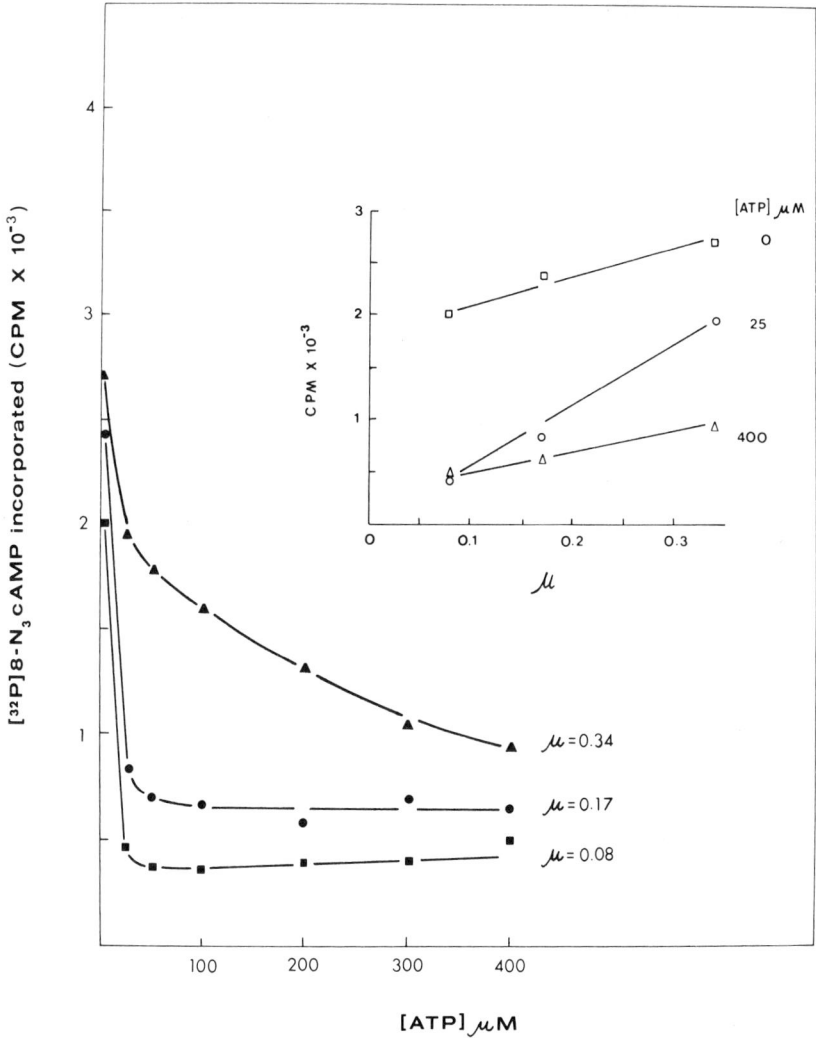

FIGURE 3. The effect of varying ionic strength (μ) and ATP concentration on the photoincorporation of [^{32}P]8-N$_3$cAMP into CA-1. Ionic strength was varied by adding a 1:1 mole to mole mixture of NaCl and KCl to a solution containing 10 mM Tris-Cl (pH 7.4) and 5 mM MgCl$_2$.

SDS-PAGE, as described in METHODS. CA-1 and CA-2 have the same migration rates as regulatory subunits of Types I and II protein kinases, respectively. CA-2 is separated into 3 or 4 isoelectric species that may represent different regulatory isoproteins (RIPs), assuming that no protein-charge modification has occurred during the electrophoresis procedure. CA-1 appears as one isoelectric spot in this autoradiography, but it has been resolved into two spots with lighter loading. Also, the complete

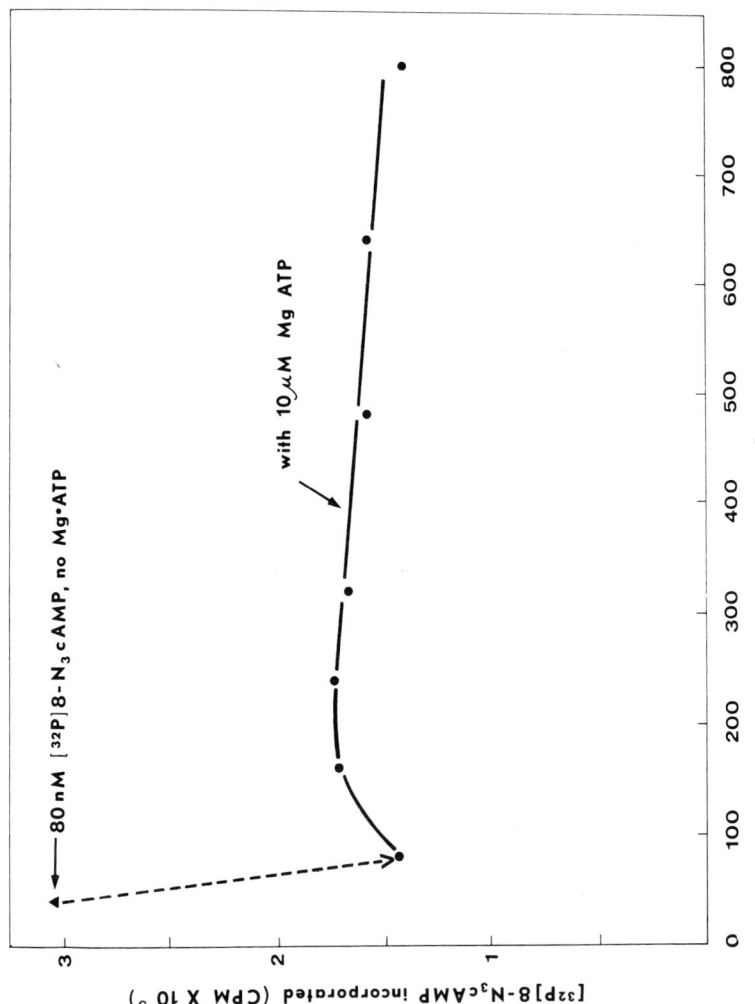

FIGURE 4. The effect of increasing $[^{32}P]8\text{-}N_3cAMP$ upon photoincorporation into CA-1 in the presence of 10 μM ATP. The medium contained 10 mM KCl, 10 mM Tris-Cl (pH 7.4), and 5 mM MgCl$_2$.

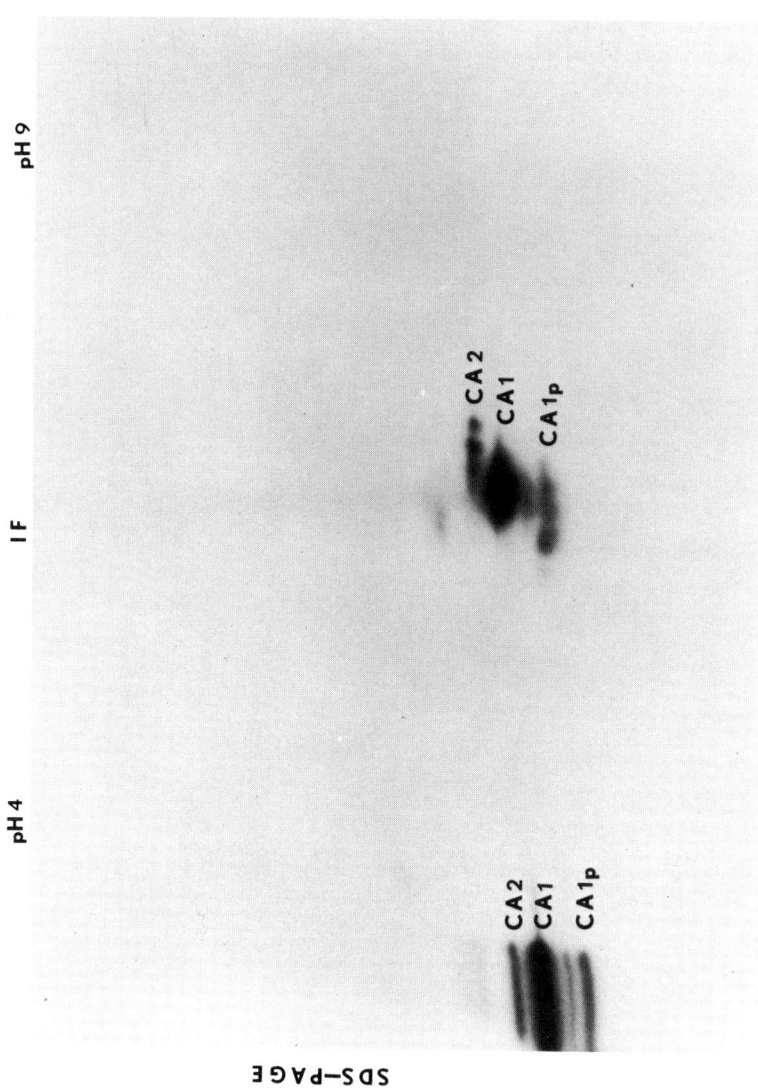

FIGURE 5. An autoradiograph of a dried two-dimensional slab gel on which [^{32}P]8-N$_3$cAMP photolabeled proteins have been separated, as described in METHODS. The left side of the gel shows a one-dimensional separation by SDS-PAG electrophoresis.

trypsinization of CA-1 results in 90% of the radioactivity being found in two spots of approximately equal labeling and equal molecular weights. CA-1p is an initial proteolytic product of CA-1 and migrates more to the acidic region of the IF gel, as does the lightly labeled protein that migrates at approximately 59,000 apparent molecular weight (just above CA-2), and that has properties similar to the phosphorylated regulatory subunit of Type II kinases.

The red cell membrane also contains proteins whose approximate molecular

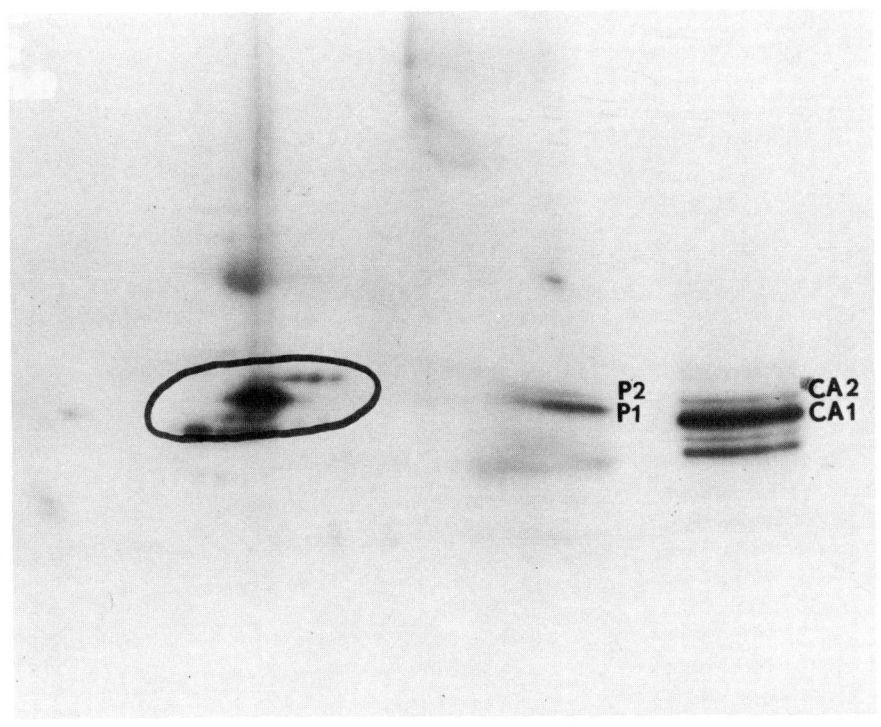

FIGURE 6. An autoradiograph of a dried two-dimensional gel on which both [^{32}P]8-N$_3$cAMP photolabeled proteins and proteins phosphorylated in the presence of [γ^{32}P]ATP plus 8-N$_3$cAMP have been separated, as described in METHODS. The [^{32}P]8-N$_3$cAMP photolabeled constellation is circled (see FIGURE 5), and P1 and P2 mark the phosphorylated proteins that migrate in the same way as CA-1 and CA-2. The right side of the gel shows a one-dimensional separation of [^{32}P]8-N$_3$cAMP photolabeled proteins by SDS-PAG electrophoresis.

weights are 49,000 and 54,000 that comigrate closely with CA-1 and CA-2 and whose phosphorylation is stimulated by cAMP. Earlier work has indicated that these two proteins are not the same as CA-1 and CA-2.[3,16] These phosphoproteins migrate to the high pH end (pI $\simeq$ 8.8) of the IF gel, approximately 5 to 6 cm from CA-1 and CA-2 (pI $\simeq$ 6.3 and 6.5, respectively), and do not appear in isoprotein form. FIGURE 6 shows the separation of a mixture of [^{32}P]8-N$_3$cAMP photolabeled proteins and [γ^{32}P]ATP phosphorylated proteins on a two-dimensional gel. The [^{32}P]8-N$_3$cAMP photolabeled constellation is circled and the cAMP stimulatable phosphoproteins are labeled P1 and P2. Also, the photolabeled profile is not changed by the addition of cold MgATP; nor is the phosphorylated profile changed by photolysis with unlabeled 8-N$_3$cAMP.

To support the two-dimensional gel results, we washed photolabeled and phosphorylated membranes with a Triton-borate solution and obtained results in agreement with those reported by others.[16] The results are shown in FIGURE 7; they indicate that CA-1 photolabeled with [^{32}P]8-N$_3$cAMP is more than 50% removed from membranes by one 3 ml wash with the Triton-borate solution, whereas no measurable phosphorylated protein is removed by this treatment.

In an earlier report, we described an experimental technique, "cold trapping," that may be used to measure relative site occupancy of the cAMP regulatory subunits of Types I and II protein kinases.[7] This technique is based on the observation that the first cyclic nucleotide (either cAMP or 8-N$_3$cAMP) to occupy the regulatory site may be trapped into that site by lowering the temperature to 4 °C. The "trapped" cyclic nucleotide will exchange only extremely slowly with any additional cyclic nucleotide, including cAMP, unless MgATP is present. A simple graphic description of this technique is shown in FIGURE 8. The effect of MgATP in greatly increasing the exchange of cold trapped [^{32}P]8-N$_3$cAMP (when cAMP will not) and the data presented in FIGURE 4 indicate that MgATP has an allosteric binding site that acts in other than a competitive fashion. Our observations of the synergistic effects of the catalytic subunit with MgATP, as well as data presented by others, indicate that the MgATP site may be placed between the regulatory and catalytic subunits. Also, Mg[β-γ^{32}P]8-N$_3$ATP, which mimics MgATP in dissociating cold trapped [^{32}P]8-N$_3$cAMP, photolabels the regulatory subunit lightly and the catalytic subunit to a much greater extent.[5]

Mg8-N$_3$ATP may be used to further investigate the mechanisms of nucleotide regulation of protein kinases as well as the partitioning of ATPases between the membrane and soluble fractions. The results of such an experiment are shown in FIGURE 9. This radiograph shows [^{32}P]8-N$_3$cAMP labeled proteins in slot 1. Slot 2 contains proteins that were washed from red cell membranes in the presence of cAMP and [β-γ^{32}P]8-N$_3$ATP and photolyzed after being separated from the membrane pellet. There are two very heavily labeled proteins, one of which migrates similarly to the catalytic subunit (slightly above band 5) and one of which comigrates with band 6. Neither of these photolabeled proteins have been purified or identified. Slot 3 contains proteins treated like those of slot 2 with one procedural exception. These proteins were taken from membranes that were prewashed with cAMP, which removes C (catalytic subunits). Proteins of slot 3 were then washed from these membranes in the presence of cAMP and [β,γ^{32}P]8-N$_3$ATP. In this situation there is greatly reduced photolabeling of both major bands, indicating that cAMP controls the partitioning of more ATP binding proteins than just protein kinase catalytic subunits. Slots 5 and 6 each contain a split of the membranes from which slot 2 proteins were isolated. Slots 7 and 8 contain like membranes separated from slot 3 proteins. These membranes were also photolyzed after the addition of 0.5 mM MgATP to the membranes of slots 5 and 7. The data indicate that MgATP does protect to a significant degree and that not all of the protein with sites that are photolabeled with [β,γ^{32}P]8-N$_3$ATP were removed from the membranes.

Our earlier published results described the MgATP-dependent decrease of photoincorporation of [^{32}P] 8-N$_3$cAMP into CA-1, the regulatory subunit of a Type

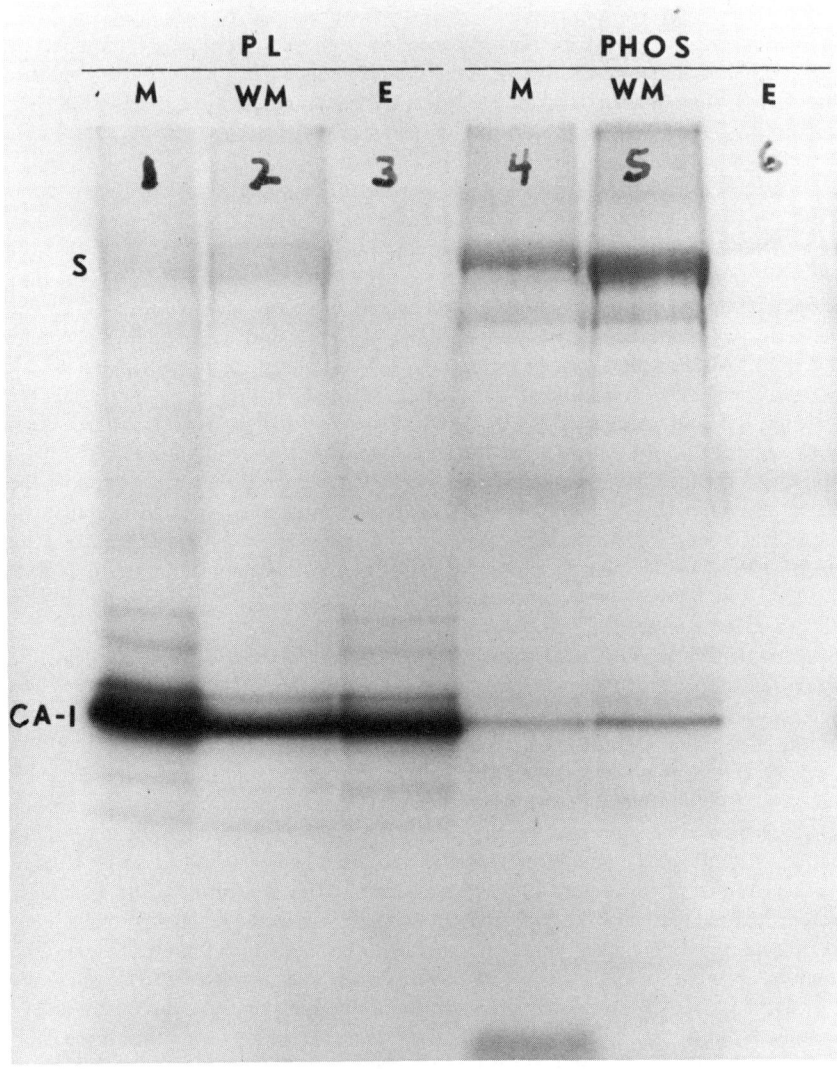

FIGURE 7. An autoradiograph of a dried SDS-PAG on which [^{32}P]8-N$_3$cAMP photolabeled proteins (PL) and proteins phosphorylated by [γ^{32}P]ATP in the presence of cAMP (PHOS) have been separated. Slots 1 and 4 contain unwashed membranes (M), slots 2 and 5 contain membranes washed once with 3 ml of a solution containing 0.5% Triton and 56 mM sodium borate at pH 8.0 (WM). Slots 3 and 6 contain the proteins eluted by the wash solution from the membranes in slots 2 and 5, respectively.

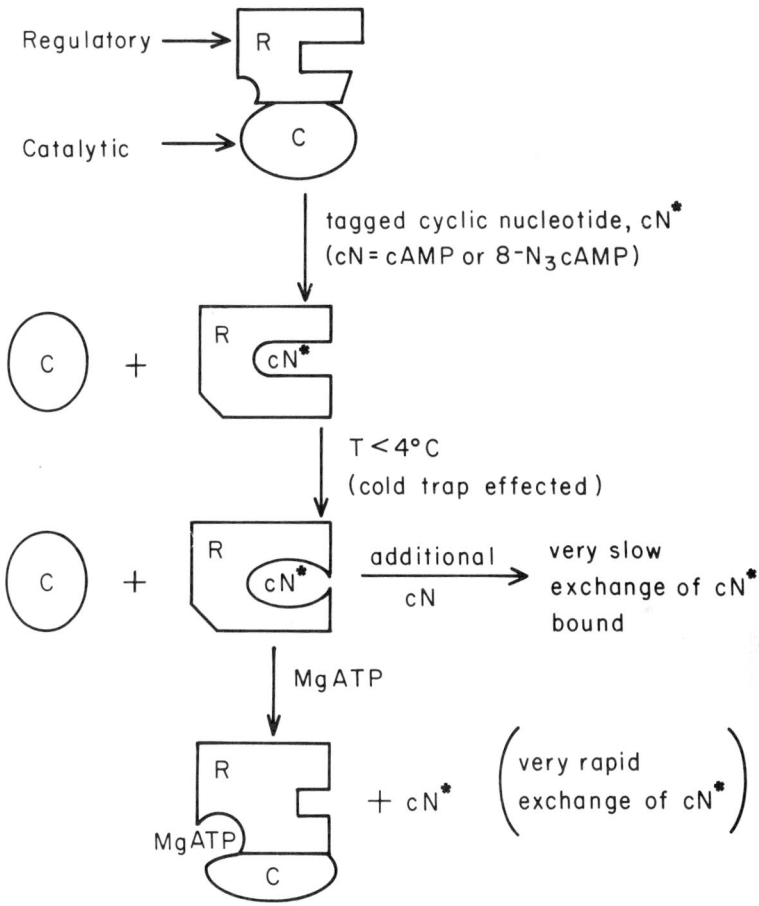

FIGURE 8. An illustration depicting the cold trap technique used in the study of cAMP-activated protein kinases.

I-M protein kinase. In the light of other published results, this was not too surprising.[17,18] On the same gels, however, we observed the same effect on CA-2, which migrates in the same way as the regulatory subunit of Type II protein kinases. This surprising result prompted us to look at the effects of MgATP on Type II kinases in rat brain homogenates, since this system appeared rich in this kinase. Using previously described procedures, we prepared and used fractions with and without catalytic subunit present.[7] The net effects of increasing MgATP on $[^{32}P]8$-N_3cAMP photoincorporation into R_{II} and $R_{II}PO_4$ in both of these preparations is shown in FIGURE 10. In

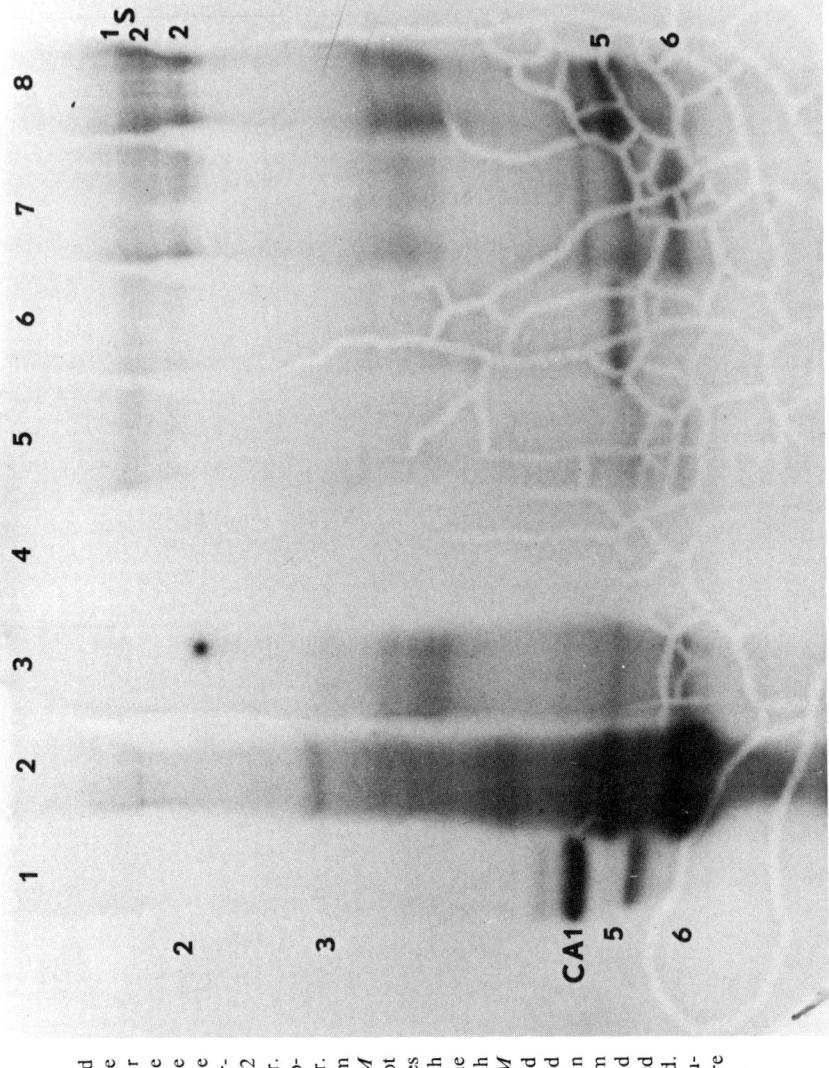

FIGURE 9. An autoradiograph of a dried SDS-PAG on which red cell membrane proteins photolabeled with either [^{32}P]8-N$_3$cAMP or [β,γ-^{32}P]8-N$_3$ATP have been separated. Numbers to the left of the figure represent the Coomassie Blue stained protein bands described in References 3 and 26. Spectrin (S) bands 1 and 2 are marked in the upper right hand corner. Slot 1 contains membrane proteins photolabeled with [^{32}P]8-N$_3$cAMP as a marker. Slot 2 contains proteins eluted from membranes in the presence of 90 nM cAMP and 88 μM [β,γ-^{32}P]8-N$_3$ATP. Slot 3 contain proteins eluted from membranes prewashed with 90 nM cAMP (which should remove the catalytic subunit of the protein kinase) by an additional wash containing 90 nM cAMP and 88 μM [β,γ-^{32}P]8-N$_3$ATP. Proteins of Slots 2 and 3 were photolyzed after being separated from the membranes. Slots 5 and 6 contain the membrane proteins separated from the membrane proteins separated from Slot 2 proteins and photolyzed. Slots 7 and 8 contain the membrane proteins separated from Slot 3 proteins and photolyzed. Membranes of Slots 5 and 7 were incubated 5 min with 0.5 mM ATP before photolysis. Nothing was added to Slot 4.

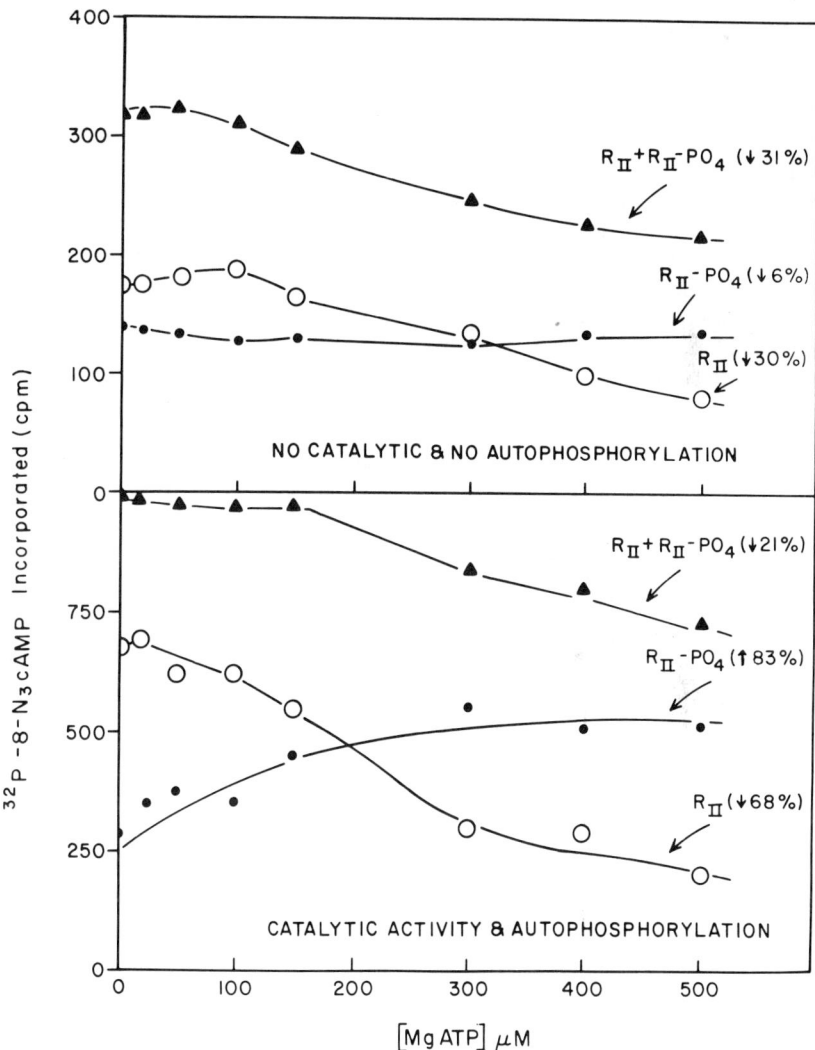

FIGURE 10. The effect of increasing MgATP concentrations on [³²P]8-N₃cAMP photoincorporation into the regulatory subunits of rat brain Type II protein kinase in both the presence and the absence of catalytic activity. Photolabeled proteins were separated by SDS-PAG electrophoresis. R_{II} and $R_{II}PO_4$ were identified by comigration with purified R_{II} and $R_{II}PO_4$ standards as well as by autophosphorylation, which was observed by autoradiography. Radioactive bands were sliced from the gel and counted by liquid scintillation.

the presence of the catalytic subunit, there is an increase in $R_{II}PO_4$ and a decrease in R_{II}, which are due, primarily, to autophosphorylation. There is also a net decrease in photoincorporation into $R_{II} + R_{II}PO_4$ of about 21%. In the absence of catalytic subunit, no autophosphorylation occurs and the level of photolabeling of $R_{II}PO_4$ remains essentially constant up to 0.5 mM MgATP. The photoincorporation into R_{II} decreases by 30% over the same range. This led us to propose a mechanism, shown in FIGURE 11, in which MgATP increases the "off rate" of cAMP from R_{II} while having little or no effect on cAMP bound by $R_{II}PO_4$ at similar MgATP concentrations. This modulation by autophosphorylation may be used to allow the release of catalytic subunit in the presence of inhibiting MgATP concentrations for a time span controlled by the rate of dephosphorylation by a previously described protein phosphatase.[19]

Current research in our laboratory is directed at measuring the "site occupancy" of cAMP receptor proteins in intact cells and tissues using an extension of the cold trap technique. Such data would allow one to answer specific questions concerning cAMP-mediated responses. For example, does the ratio of R_{II} and $R_{II}PO_4$ site occupancy change? Does a specific hormone cause production of cAMP for a specific intracellular receptor? That is, are Type I or Type II protein kinases specifically activated by specific hormones? Also, what percentage of maximum cAMP site occupancy is required to produce the desired biological effect?

A graphic description of these problems is shown in FIGURE 12, in which both hormone A (H_A) and hormone B (H_B) cause cAMP production in the same cell or tissue with the same or different biological effect subsequently occurring. This system could be tested by adding H_A and incubating until the second messenger effect has occurred. The cells or tissue would then be quick-frozen to fracture membranes and cold trap cAMP onto the receptor proteins involved. A mixture of $[^{32}P]8$-N_3cAMP (to occupy empty receptor sites) and EDTA (to chelate Mg^{2+}, which prevents MgATP from effecting an exchange of bound cAMP and $[^{32}P]8$-N_3cAMP) is added. The system would then be slowly thawed at 4 °C, incubated 15–20 min to allow $[^{32}P]8$-N_3cAMP to bind to empty sites, and photolyzed to incorporate the radioactive label. The use of isoelectric focusing, SDS-PAGE, and cell fractionation to separate receptor proteins, followed by liquid scintillation counting, will allow us to determine which receptors have been protected by having bound endogenously produced cAMP. The result obtained by the application of this technique to isolated ovine luteal cells was that 1 and 10 ng/ml of lutenizing hormone (LH) stimulated 75 and 100% of the maximal rate of synthesis of progesterone, respectively.[20] At these concentrations, there was no significant increase in detectable cellular cAMP levels using a radioimmunoassay technique.[21] However, the Type I regulatory subunit was protected by 15 and 30% ($\pm 5\%$), respectively, and the Type II subunits by 6 and 11% ($\pm 5\%$), respectively. Also, progesterone synthesis was maximal at 10 ng/ml of LH and so was the decrease in $[^{32}P]8$-N_3cAMP incorporation into receptor proteins. That is, the rate of progesterone synthesis at 1000 ng/ml LH was equivalent to that at 10 ng/ml LH and protection of the Type I regulatory subunit was 30% in both cases. Also, occupancy of the cAMP receptor preceded progesterone synthesis.[20]

Nucleotide triphosphates are one of the controls that regulate cAMP production and the activation of cAMP-stimulated kinases. Specifically, GTP regulates cAMP production by adenylyl cyclase and MgATP regulates its binding to cAMP-activated kinases. The use of photoaffinity probes of GTP and ATP to look at both of these

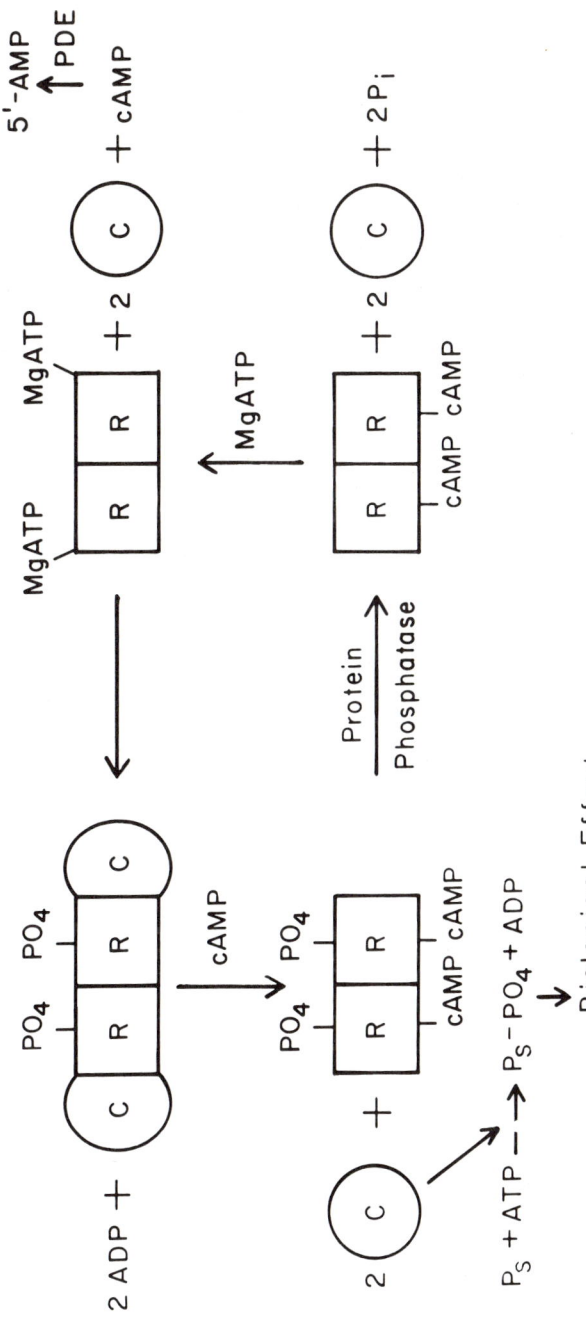

FIGURE 11. Mechanism proposing that autophosphorylation of the Type II regulatory subunit controls MgATP modulation of cAMP binding.

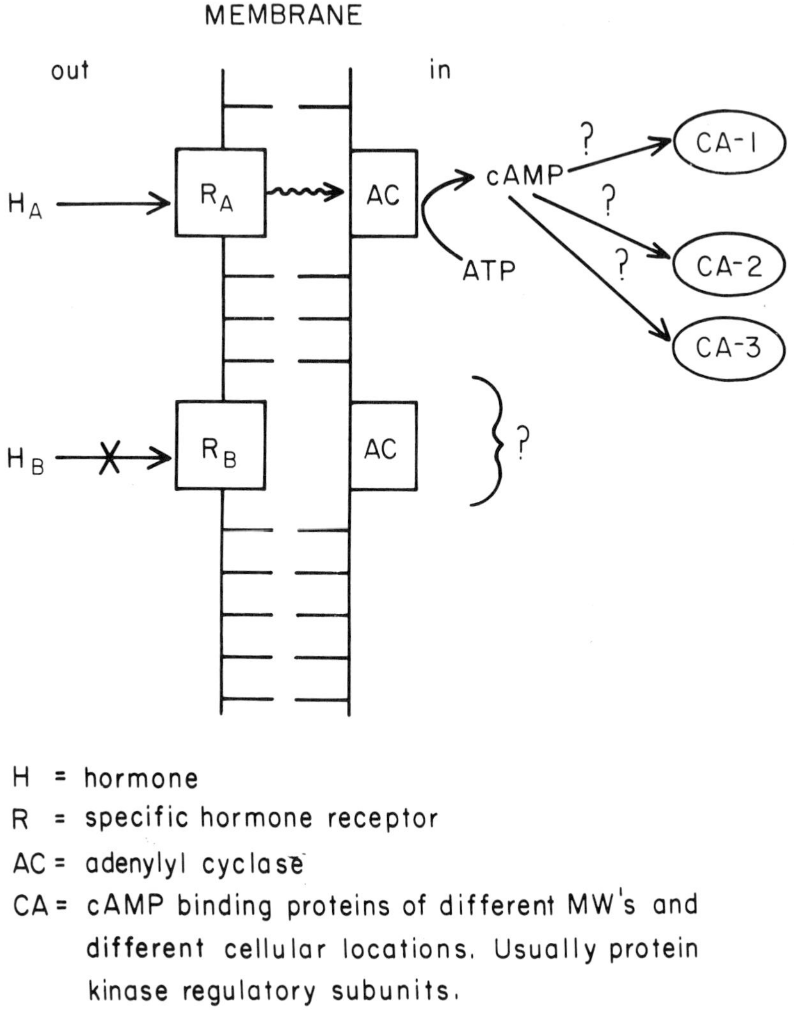

FIGURE 12. An illustration posing the question, "Does a specific hormone cause the production of cAMP for a specific intracellular receptor (e.g., Type I or Type II kinase)?"

systems should reveal some details of the molecular regulatory mechanisms. However, the triphosphate probes present special problems. For example, they may be able to phosphorylate certain proteins and they are hydrolyzed by various enzymes. It is also possible that the photoaffinity probe would not be a substrate but that the photolyzed product would be. Also, probes such as $[\beta\text{-}\gamma^{32}\text{P}]8\text{-}N_3\text{ATP}$ may supply $[^{32}\text{P}]$-Pi for ADP to ATP conversion. In the case of phosphorylation systems, this could lead to erroneous conclusions. In each biological or biochemical system, several control experiments must be carried out to resolve these problems. For example, incubation of red blood cells with $[\beta\text{-}\gamma^{32}P]8\text{-}N_3ATP$, without photolysis, results in radioactive label appearing in the spectrin 2 protein.

Another problem is graphically shown in FIGURES 13 and 14. FIGURE 13 is a dried SDS-polyacrylamide gel on which membrane proteins, photolabeled with varying concentrations of $[\beta,\gamma^{32}P]8\text{-}N_3ATP$ at two different KCl concentrations (10 and 200 mM), have been separated. FIGURE 14 is an autoradiograph made with the gel of FIGURE 13. A major difference between the protein profiles of the gel of FIGURE 13 is apparent in the region labeled 4, with more proteins being resolved at low KCl

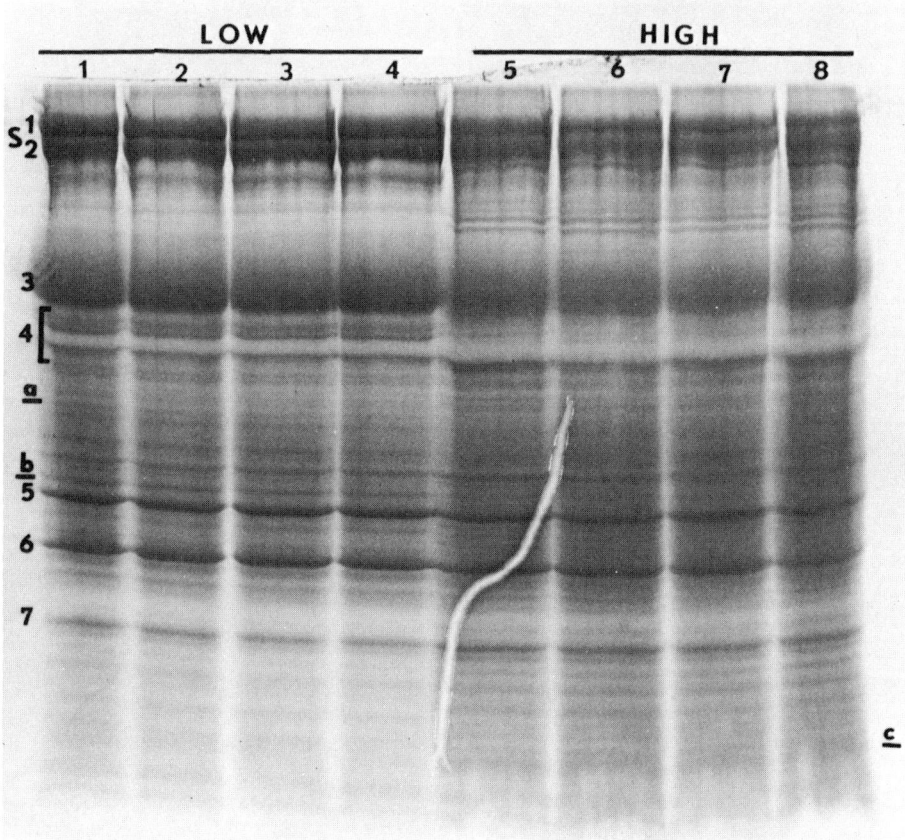

FIGURE 13. A Coomassie Blue stained SDS-PAG on which red cell membrane proteins have been separated. Slots 1–4 were incubated with 15 mM KCl, 0.5 mM MgCl$_2$, and 1 mM Tris-Cl (pH 7.4). Slots 5–8 were incubated with 200 mM KCl, 5 mM MgCl$_2$, and 5 mM Tris-Cl (pH 7.4). The slots were incubated for 5 min at 0 °C with $[\beta,\gamma^{32}P]8\text{-}N_3ATP$ concentrations in Slots 1 and 5, 2 and 6, 3 and 7, and 4 and 8 being 15, 37, 73, and 157 μM, respectively. After incubation, the membranes were photolyzed and solubilized, as described in METHODS, and immediately applied to the separating gel.

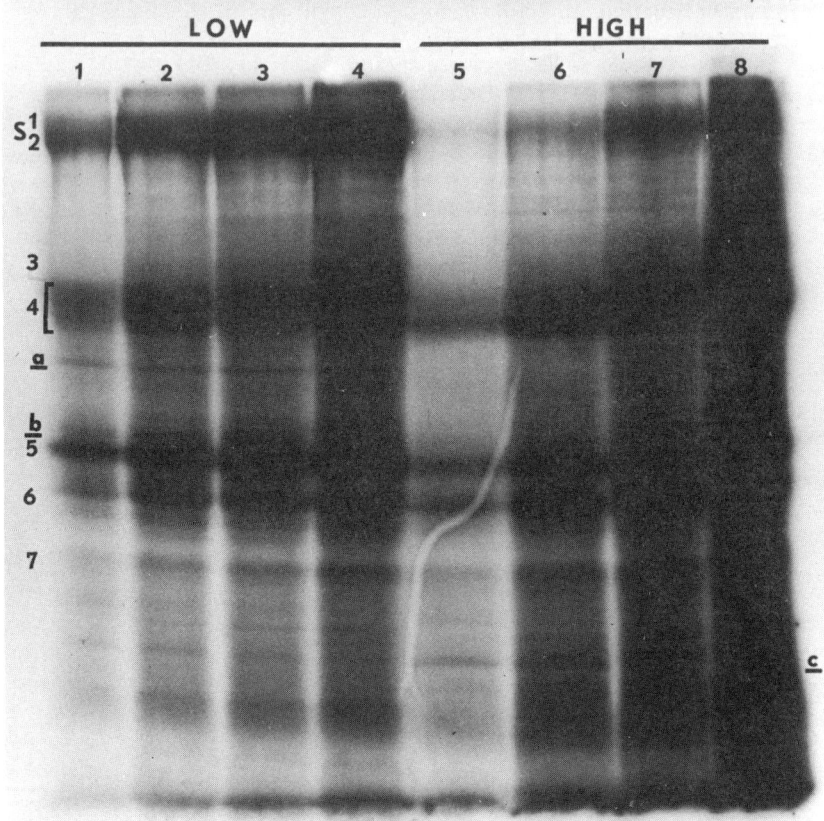

FIGURE 14. An autoradiograph made with the gel of FIGURE 13, showing protein bands that are photolabeled with $[\beta,\gamma^{32}P]8$-N_3ATP under the conditions given.

concentrations. This difference is also reflected in the autoradiograph of FIGURE 14. There are other significant differences between the photolabeled profiles: proteins at positions *a* and *b* are labeled only at low KCl concentrations and a protein at position *c* is significantly labeled only at high KCl concentrations. Therefore, one may obtain different results in using photoprobes to look at complex biological structures by merely changing ionic conditions. We have also observed different results on the same membrane preparation by such changes as sequential freeze-thawing and increasing buffer concentrations.

DISCUSSION

The development of photoaffinity probes as site-specific reagents for biological receptors is still in its infancy. We should be aware of the potential for the collection of both successful and misleading data using the photoaffinity approach. Discrepancies in data among laboratories will be common and will probably be based on slight differences among the system preparations and photolabeling procedures. The data and techniques presented in this paper were selected to show both the abilities of the photoaffinity approach and some of the potential problems.

[^{32}P]8-N$_3$cAMP is an excellent probe for cAMP binding sites; it has allowed us to measure the physical and kinetic properties of protein kinase regulatory subunits and to determine their location within a cell.[1-3,6] These protein kinases are "turned on" and "turned off" by binding and dissociating cyclic nucleotides, respectively. The use of [^{32}P]8-N$_3$cAMP to measure "site occupancy" through the cold trap technique[7] allows one to study the molecular mechanisms of the regulation of these enzymes.[7,22] In the case of Type II protein kinase, in which autophosphorylation of R$_{II}$ occurs, there appears to be a great advantage in using [^{32}P]8-N$_3$cAMP to measure the fluctuation in the R$_{II}$ to R$_{II}$PO$_4$ ratios under various conditions, e.g., increases in MgATP concentrations. The data in FIGURE 10 indicate that autophosphorylation modulates the MgATP effect on cAMP dissociation, as described in the mechanism of FIGURE 11. This mechanism is in agreement with the observations of others and supports the hypothesis that dissociation of R and C subunits of Type II kinases by cAMP occurs primarily through the phosphorylated form and reassociation occurs through the dephosphorylated form of the regulatory subunit.[23,24] We feel that autophosphorylation allows the Type II kinase, R$_{II}$PO$_4$, to bind cAMP in the presence of inhibitory MgATP concentrations. Dephosphorylation then allows MgATP to turn off the system by increasing the cAMP off-rate from R$_{II}$. This mechanism is probably oversimplified, since other factors may be involved. It also brings into question an aspect of MgATP regulation of Type I kinases. Since Type I does not autophosphorylate, what modulates the MgATP effect so that Type I kinases can be turned on in the presence of cellular levels of MgATP? We have searched unsuccessfully for the answer to this question.

We have shown, in FIGURES 1 and 2, that ionic strength affects the Type I kinase response to MgATP. The fact that MgATP has its maximum effect at micromolar concentrations at low ionic strength would indicate that the Type I protein kinase would find it quite difficult to bind cAMP under cellular conditions, i.e., m*M* MgATP concentrations; however, inhibition of the binding of [^{32}P]8-N$_3$cAMP by MgATP at isotonicity becomes more reasonable, in that the inhibitory concentrations approach ATP levels found in viable cells. That is, the MgATP concentration causing maximal inhibition increases from the micromolar range at low ionic strength to the near-millimolar range at isotonicity. The data in FIGURE 4 also show that MgATP inhibition of binding is not competitive and cannot be reversed by increasing cyclic nucleotide concentrations.

The data shown in FIGURES 5 and 6 indicate that the regulatory proteins may exist in isoprotein form—these are called "regulatory isoproteins" (RIPs). These RIPs may or may not represent functionally different kinases or kinases from different cellular locations. The autoradiographs of FIGURES 6 and 7 also indicate that the cAMP-stimulated phosphoproteins of red cell membranes, which migrate on SDS-PAGE like the [^{32}P]8-N$_3$cAMP photolabeled proteins, are not the same. The use of photoprobes in determining this is a unique application of the separation of a binding event and a phosphorylation event on the molecular level.

The use of the cold trap technique (FIGURES 8 and 12) to look at cAMP site occupancy in intact cells and tissues promises to be quite useful for answering several important questions concerning second-messenger mediated responses. It does present some specific problems; for example, we have found that $[^{32}P]8\text{-}N_3cAMP$ photolabels several proteins, including those tentatively identified as R_I, R_{II}, and $R_{II}PO_4$, in chick embryo heart.[25] Isolation of "beating heart" cells from this tissue using a collogenase technique gives viable cells whose cAMP levels appear to be elevated, since the sites corresponding to R_I, R_{II} and $R_{II}PO_4$ sites are no longer accessible to $[^{32}P]8\text{-}N_3cAMP$ photolabeling and the other proteins are still available. Incubation of these cells for 5 min with epinephrine prevents all photoincorporation, indicating the existence of active adenylyl cyclase.[25] It is possible that isolation of the cells causes activation of part of the adenylyl cyclase activity, e.g., by proteolysis, giving misleading results. In order to use $[^{32}P]8\text{-}N_3cAMP$ and cold trapping with this system, the apparent partial activation of adenylyl cyclase must be circumvented by cell culture techniques or by the use of protease inhibitors. Applying the cold trap technique to intact cells and tissues has been technically difficult and has presented special problems. However, its potential for revealing changes in cAMP site occupancy in viable cells could be quite significant and may help resolve questions such as why a cell has more than one type of cAMP-activated protein kinase.

The data of FIGURES 13 and 14 show that drastically different results may be obtained by changing the ionic strength when using a photoaffinity probe for ATP binding sites. Whether or not this is of physiological importance remains to be determined, but it certainly must be a consideration in the design of experiments and the interpretation of their results. The results of FIGURE 9 show that $[\beta,\gamma^{32}P]8\text{-}N_3ATP$ may be used to follow the membrane release of kinase catalytic subunit stimulated by cAMP. It appears that other ATP-binding proteins may also be released under these conditions. The significance and identity of these proteins is currently under investigation. However, the use of nucleotide photoaffinity probes to investigate the partitioning of specific proteins between particulate and soluble fractions should prove to be quite valuable in many membrane and cellular systems.

We have attempted to show some of the many applications of nucleotide photoaffinity probes to the study of nucleotide-regulated phenomena. Much of the data in this area is preliminary and requires much follow-up research; however, the development of these techniques will give researchers some unique approaches to special problems. These will allow the mechanisms by which living cells regulate their functions, environment, and development to be identified.

ACKNOWLEDGMENT

The authors thank Miss P. Young for technical assistance.

REFERENCES

1. POMERANTZ, A., S. A. RANDOLPH, B. HALEY & P. GREENGARD. 1975. Biochemistry **14** (17): 3858.
2. HALEY, B. 1975. Biochemistry **14** (17): 3852.
3. OWENS, J. R. & B. HALEY. 1976. J. Supramol. Struct. **5:** 91.
4. HAHN, G. L. 1978. Ph. D. Thesis, University of Wyoming. Laramie, Wyoming.
5. HALEY, B. Unpublished data.
6. SKARE, K., J. L. BLACK, W. L. PANCOE & B. HALEY. 1977. Arch. Biochem. Biophys. **180:** 409.

7. OWENS, J. R. & B. HALEY. 1978. J Supramol. Struct. **9**: 57.
8. HALEY, B. 1976. Methods in Enzymology, Vol. 46. W. Jacoby and M. Wilchek, Eds.: 339–46.
9. CZARNECKI, J., R. T. GEAHLEN & B. HALEY. 1979. *In* Methods in Enzymology, Vol. 56. S. Fleisher and L. Packer, Eds.: 642.
10. GLYNN, I. M. & J. B. CHAPPEL. 1964. Biochem. J. **90**: 147.
11. HALEY, B. & J. HOFFMAN. 1974. Proc. Nat. Acad. Sci. USA **71**: 3367.
12. LOWRY, O. H. & J. V. PASSONNEAU. 1966. J. Biol. Chem. **241**: 2268.
13. O'FARRELL, P. H. 1975. J Biol. Chem. **250**: 4007.
14. AMES, G. F. & K. NIKAIDO. 1976. Biochemistry **15**: 616.
15. RIGHETTI, P. G. & J. W. DRYSDALE. 1974. J. Chromatogr. **98**: 271.
16. RUBIN, C. S. 1975. J. Biol. Chem. **250**: 9044.
17. HADDOX, M. D., N. E. NEWTON, D. K. HARTLE & N. D. GOLDBERG. 1972. Biochem. Biophys. Res. Commun. **47**: 361.
18. BEAVO, J. A., P. J. BECHTEL & E. G. KREBS. 1974. Proc. Nat. Acad. Sci. USA **71**: 3580.
19. CHOU, C. K., J. ALFANO & O. M. ROSEU. 1977. J. Biol. Chem. **252**: 2855.
20. FLETCHER, P. W. 1978. Ph. D. Thesis, University of Wyoming. Laramie, Wyoming.
21. STEINER, A. L., C. W. PARKER & D. W. KIPNIS. 1972. J. Biol. Chem. **247**: 1106.
22. HOYER, P. & B. HALEY. 1979. Abstracts ICN-UCLA Conference on Covalent Modification of Proteins. Keystone, Colorado.
23. ROSEN, O. M. & J. ERLICHMAN. 1975. J. Biol. Chem. **250**: 7788.
24. RANGEL-ALDAO, R. & O. M. ROSEN. 1976. J. Biol. Chem. **251**: 3375.
25. JOHNSON, C. & B. HALEY. Unpublished results.
26. STECK, T. L. 1972. J. Mol. Biol. **66**: 295.

DISCUSSION

DR. H. BAYLEY: I'm presuming that there are two conformations of azido compounds; the structural description is not very good, so I just say "azide up" and "azide down"—maybe you can explain that better. Have you got any comments on that?

DR. B. E. HALEY: You mean, on the fact that the azido group doesn't stick out straight but is at an angle.

BAYLEY: Exactly.

HALEY: Well, I think that it's probably like most organic compounds that have several stereochemical possibilities. It's probably an equilibrium ratio. The other question is the anti-*syn* ratio. Here, I think, the azido derivatives are probably, primarily, in the *syn* form. I don't know what the approximate ratio of the angles of the azide would be.

DR. F. H. WESTHEIMER: You said that the half-time for the replacement of the azido reagent by cyclic AMP at 4 °C is on the order of days. What is it at 25 °C?

HALEY: Well, it's much more rapid. However, our information is not complete. We have done it at 37 degrees; at that temperature, it's a matter of about 20 minutes. It's very, very slow, though, and I think that that's the reason that this probe works so well. It's tied into a site from which it doesn't come off very fast. No matter how you photogenerate, it's going to remain there for several minutes and react, whether it's a carbon insertion or an interaction with another chemical group.

DR. J. A. KATZENELLENBOGEN: It must be more than that because our azido derivatives bind in the same range and they don't react as well as yours. It must be a good nitrene.

PHOTOLABILE ANTIBIOTICS AS PROBES OF RIBOSOMAL STRUCTURE AND FUNCTION*

Barry S. Cooperman

Department of Chemistry
University of Pennsylvania
Philadelphia, Pennsylvania 19104

INTRODUCTION

The *E. coli* ribosome is an organelle composed of a 30S subunit (molecular weight 0.9×10^6 daltons) and a 50S subunit (molecular weight 1.8×10^6 daltons). The 30 S subunit is composed of 21 proteins and a 16S RNA (~1540 bases long) and the 50 S subunit is composed of 33 proteins and a 23S RNA (~3000 bases long).[1,2] The goal of our current research is to use photoaffinity labeling to construct a structure-function map of the ribosome. Such a goal is challenging, because of the size and complexity of the ribosome, but feasible, both because of the variety of approaches that are open to us, and because of the large body of information obtained by other techniques with which our results can be correlated.

The potential utility of affinity labeling for studies of the ribosome was first recognized in the early 1970s, and many reports, which have been recently summarized in several reviews both by ourselves and others,[3-6] have appeared since that time. The ribosome has a large number of ligands that can serve as potential photoaffinity labels. These include tRNA, mRNA, and the several protein factors (at least 9 or 10) that are important for protein synthesis *in vivo* and bind to the ribosome at different stages of the ribosome cycle. In addition, a great variety of antibiotics act by inhibiting protein synthesis at the ribosomal level.[7,8] As a group, this class of antibiotics inhibits virtually every identifiable step of the ribosome cycle and displays a wide spectrum of structural diversity. Moreover, many of these antibiotics have been shown to have distinct binding sites on the ribosome, and there is a substantial body of literature, generated in large part by the pharmaceutical industry, on structure-activity relationships among these antibiotics and their derivatives. Thus, antibiotics, too, are potential photoaffinity labels, and it is with such compounds that most of our work has been concerned. Our object has been to correlate antibiotic binding sites with antibiotic inhibitory effects and thus provide information that will allow us to progress toward the desired structure-function map of the ribosome.

We are currently working with five antibiotics (or their derivatives): puromycin, lincomycin, blasticidin S, streptomycin, and tetracycline, the structures of which, along with those of the derivatives being studied, are shown in TABLE 1. The first three of these inhibit peptidyl transferase, a function that has been localized to the 50S subunit. The last two are antibiotics that interfere with normal tRNA-ribosome binding, and have been thought to act primarily on the 30S subunit. Our most definitive results have been obtained with puromycin and its derivatives, and our

*This research was supported by the National Institutes of Health, grants AM-13212 and AI-14717, and the National Science Foundation, grant PCM-84278.

302

TABLE 1

STRUCTURES OF REAGENTS, ANTIBIOTICS, AND ANTIBIOTIC DERIVATIVES

(1) Ethyl-4-iodo-2-diazoacetoacetate

$ICH_2C(O)CN_2CO_2Et$

(1a) Ethyl-4-chloro-2-diazoacetoacetate

$ClCH_2C(O)CN_2CO_2Et$

(2) 2-Carbethoxy-2-diazoacethydrazide

$NH_2NHC(O)CN_2CO_2Et$

(3) 4-Azido-2-nitrophenylhydrazine

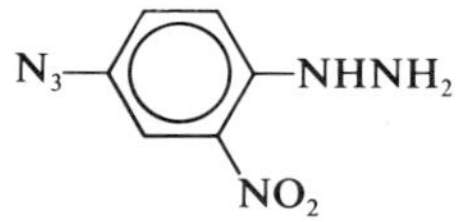

(4) 2,4-Dinitrophenylhydrazine

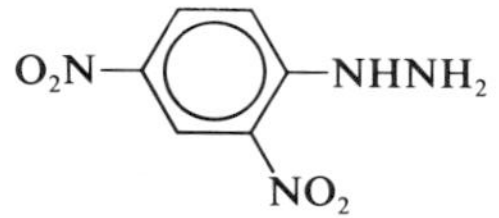

(5) Ethyl-2-diazomalonyl chloride

$ClC(O)CN_2CO_2Et$

(6) Puromycin

$R_1 = CH_3O; R_2 = H.$

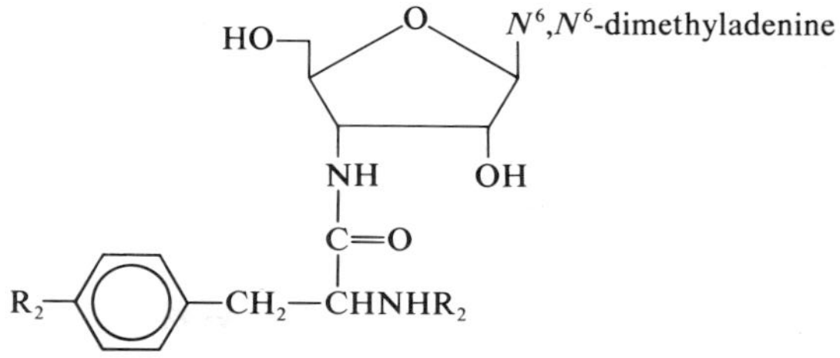

(7) p-Azidopuromycin

$R_1 = N_3; R_2 = H.$

(8) N-EDM-Puromycin

$R_1 = CH_3O; R_2 = C(O)CN_2CO_2Et$

TABLE 1 (*Continued*)

(9) Lincomycin

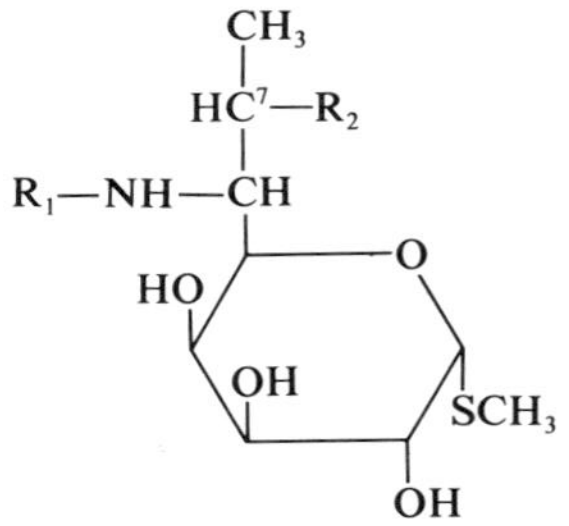

(10) Methyl (7S)-7-deoxy-7-mercapto-1-thio-α-lincosaminide R_1 = H; R_2 = —SH

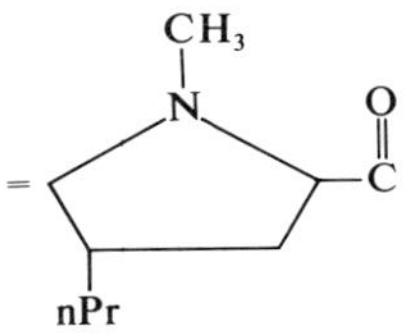

(11) S-(3-carbethoxy-3-diazo)acetonyl 7-deoxy-7-mercaptolincomycin

$R_1 = $ [structure] ; $R_2 = SCH_2C(O)CN_2CO_2Et$

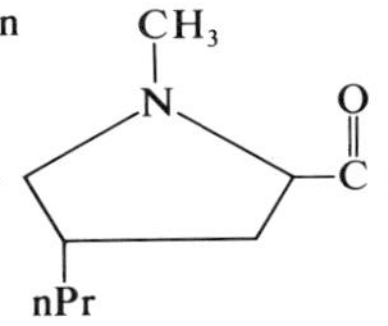

(12) Blasticidin S, R=H

(13) N-(3-carbethoxy-3-diazo)acetonyl blasticidin S

R = —$CH_2C(O)CN_2CO_2Et$

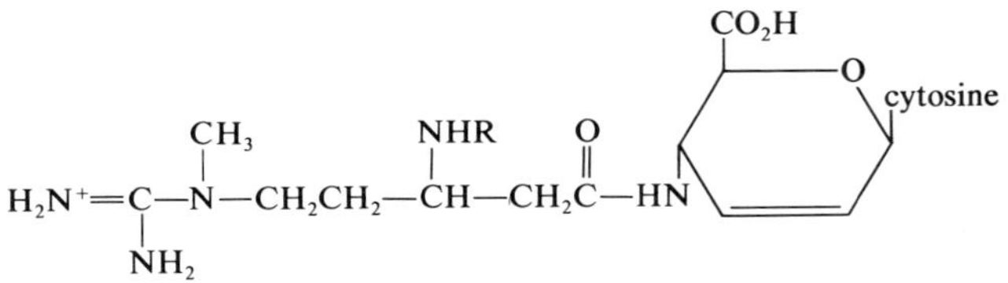

(14) Streptomycin, R = O

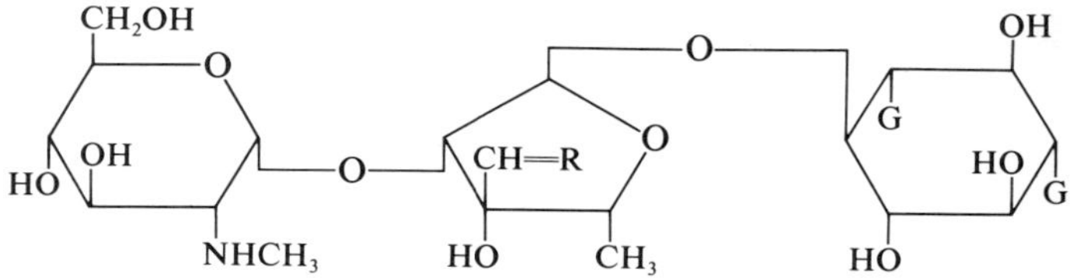

(15) N-(Ethyl-2-diazomalonyl)streptomycyl hydrazone,

R = NNHC(O)CN₂CO₂Et

(16) N-(2,4-Dinitrophenyl)streptomycyl hydrazone,

R = NNH— ⟨O₂N, NO₂⟩

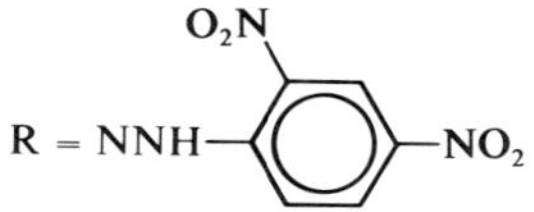

(17) N-(2-Nitro-4-azidophenyl)streptomycyl hydrazone,

R = NNH— ⟨O₂N, N₃⟩

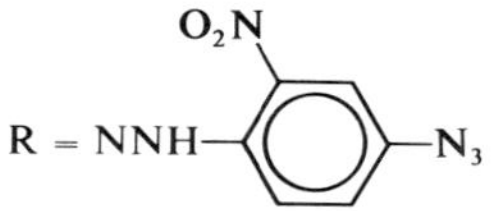

(18) Tetracycline

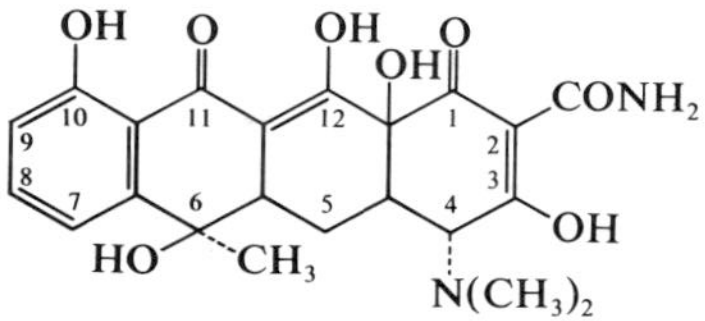

studies with this antibiotic point the way for further work with the other antibiotics. One reason for concentrating on puromycin is that it is unique among antibiotics in that it acts as a substrate for the ribosome; that is, it structurally resembles the 3' end of tyrosyl-tRNA, and functionally acts as an acceptor of the peptide from peptidyl-tRNA, thereby terminating protein biosynthesis.

LOCALIZATION OF IINCORPORATION SITES

Our work to date has been involved with determining the extent of covalent incorporation into individual proteins extracted from ribosomes irradiated in the presence of radioactive photolabile antibiotics in a Rayonet photochemical apparatus equipped with either 2537 Å or 3500 Å lamps. Our principal tools are one- and two-dimensional polyacrylamide gel electrophoresis (PAGE), and specific immunoprecipitation using antibodies to ribosomal proteins, performed in collaboration with W. A. Strycharz in Nomura's laboratory (University of Wisconsin). The one-dimensional gels do not fully resolve all the ribosomal proteins, but they do allow us to measure both a labeling pattern and its response to changes in the experimental protocol in a fairly rapid fashion. The two-dimensional gels resolve all the ribosomal proteins and can be employed to identify labeled proteins, but they are considerably more time-consuming. We generally use them to analyze labeled proteins from experiments shown to be particularly interesting by one-dimensional PAGE analysis. Since covalent incorporation of antibiotics can lead to altered electrophoretic mobility, even two-dimensional PAGE analysis is sometimes insufficient for their identification; the immunoprecipitation technique is particularly helpful in these cases. Fuller accounts of these procedures may be found in several recent articles from this laboratory.[9–12]

It should be noted that we have done little about localizing sites of RNA labeling, despite the fact that several of our antibiotic derivatives incorporate effectively into ribosomal RNA. The reason for this is the lack of a rapid scanning method for localizing labeling to limited RNA regions ($\sim$50 nucleotides). Work to develop such a method is currently underway at this laboratory.

INCORPORATION OF PHOTOLABILITY AND RADIOACTIVITY

Two major practical problems in photoaffinity labeling studies are the incorporation of both photolability and radioactivity into the ligands of interest. These problems will be discussed in the sections below devoted to results obtained with each antibiotic, but we would like to summarize some of our more interesting findings here.

First, two native antibiotics, puromycin and tetracycline, photoincorporate effectively into ribosomes.[13,14] Since these antibiotics are commercially available in radioactive form, work with them has proceeded straightforwardly.

Second, the 2,4-dinitrophenylhydrazone of streptomycin photoincorporates effectively into ribosomes.[15] The use of the nitrophenyl group in photoaffinity labeling studies was first introduced by Escher and Schwyzer,[16] but its general utility has recently been questioned.[17] We wish to point out that published photochemical syntheses involving nitrophenyl groups provide a rationale for their utility as photoaffinity labeling reagents.[18,19] Our work provides another example of such use and also raises the question as to whether, in the absence of direct proof, the assumption is always justified that photoaffinity labeling with a ligand carrying a p-azido-o-nitrophenyl group (prepared using the Fleet reagent[20]) proceeds solely via nitrene insertion.

Third, we have synthesized four new reagents: ethyl-4-chloro-2-diazoacetoacetate (1a) and ethyl-4-iodo-2-diazoacetoacetate (1), which we used to alkylate 7-thio-7-deoxylincomycin and blasticidin S, respectively,[12] and 2-carbethoxy-2-diazoacethydrazide (2)[12] and 4-azido-2-nitrophenylhydrazine (3),[15] which we used to derive the 3'-aldehyde in streptomycin.

Fourth, the known reagents 2,4-dinitrophenylhydrazine (4) and ethyl-2-diazomalonylchloride (5), as well as 2, have been synthesized in highly radioactive form, permitting the simultaneous introduction of radioactivity and photolability.[15]

Fifth, [³H]-dimethylsulfate at high specific radioactivity (4 Ci/mmol, New England Nuclear) has been used to introduce a radioactive methyl group in the synthesis of the lincomycin derivative (11).[21] Sixth, in collaboration with Dr. Richard Ehrenkaufer (Brookhaven National Laboratory), a microwave discharge technique using tritium gas has been used to prepare biologically active [³H]-streptomycin and [³H]-blasticidin S of high specific radioactivity.[22]

Puromycin

Photoaffinity labeling experiments have been carried out with native puromycin (6)[9-13] and with two photolabile derivatives, 6-dimethylamino-9[3'-deoxy-3'-(p-azido-L-phenylalanylamino)-β-D-ribofuranosyl]purine (p-azidopuromycin) (7)[12,23] and N-ethyl-2-diazomalonyl puromycin (N-EDM puromycin) (8).[13] We began our studies with N-EDM puromycin. This compound photoincorporated into E. coli ribosomes, although it exhibited an apparent low affinity and labeled 30 S proteins preferentially, particularly S14 and S18. Total incorporation as a function of light fluence was found to be biphasic; in particular, incorporation was seen to increase with fluence long after the diazo group was lost. This unexpected result led us, in turn, to examine the photoincorporation of puromycin itself, which examination has yielded a series of interesting results. Photolysis with either the 2537 Å or 3500 Å lamp leads to puromycin incorporation into both ribosomal protein and RNA. Protein L23 is labeled to the highest extent, by far, of any ribosomal protein. The labeling is site-specific, as shown by the saturation of L23 labeling as a function of puromycin concentration, as well as by the ability of structural and functional analogs of puromycin to markedly decrease the extent of [³H]-puromycin incorporation into L23. The saturation of L23 labeling allows us to calculate a K_d value of 0.7 mM, similar to the K_m value found for puromycin in the peptidyl transferase assay. That puromycin analogs decrease L23 labeling means that the extent of L23 labeling can be used to probe the ability of other peptidyl transferase inhibitors to compete for puromycin binding. By this criterion, chloramphenicol, blasticidin S, lincomycin, erythromycin, and sparsomycin all show no competition for the puromycin site. These results support the notion that the precise sites of the action of these antibiotics are different from those of puromycin, which is, perhaps, not surprising, since none of these antibiotics are close structural analogs of puromycin.

The protein labeled by puromycin to the second highest extent is S14. Although

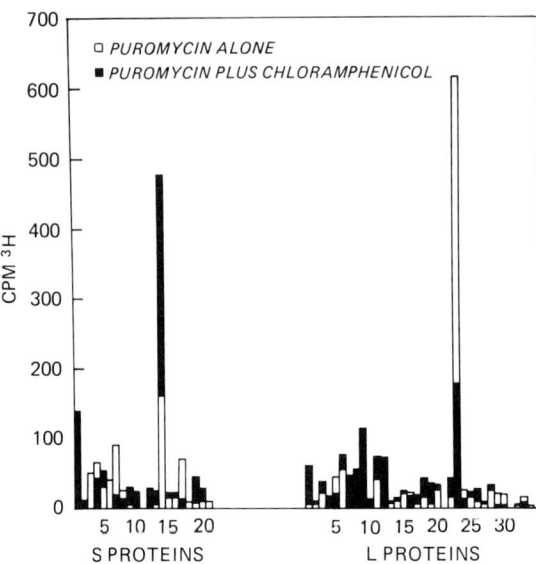

FIGURE 1. The pattern of ribosomal protein labeling with [8-³H] puromycin in both the presence and the absence of chloroamphenicol, as determined by two-dimensional PAGE. The values for proteins labeled with puromycin alone are the average of two gels and, for proteins labeled in the presence of chloramphenicol, the average of seven gels. In displaying the data, the lower radioactivity value is superimposed on the higher one. Experimental conditions: puromycin (0.1 mM) alone (□), puromycin (0.1 mM) plus chloramphenicol (0.1 mM) (■), photolysis with 3500 Å lamps. The absolute levels of counts reported are not directly comparable between the two experiments.

chloramphenicol does not compete for puromycin labeling of L23, the presence of chloramphenicol leads to a tremendous stimulation of S14 labeling, to the extent that it becomes the most highly labeled protein. FIGURE 1 shows the results of two-dimensional PAGE analyses on proteins labeled by puromycin in both the absence and the presence of chloramphenicol. Detailed studies have shown that S14 labeling depends on specific sites for both puromycin and chloramphenicol. Moreover, since L23 labeling by puromycin can be demonstrated for isolated 50S subunits, and since chloramphenicol-stimulated S14 labeling by puromycin can be demonstrated for isolated 30S subunits, there must be separate puromycin and chloramphenicol sites on each of the subunits.†

The photochemistry leading to puromycin incorporation is not, at present, understood. It has been shown that thiols effectively inhibit the incorporation, which is at least consistent with a radical coupling mechanism. The quantum efficiency for the photodestruction of N^6, N^6-dimethyladenine is quite low (<0.001), so this moiety does not appear to be sufficiently reactive to account for the labeling observed. The possibility that labeling involves 8-alkylation of the dimethyladenine[63] is excluded by the fact that the same results are obtained using [8-³H]-puromycin or [CH₃-³H]-puromycin. Moreover, in the immunoelectron microscopy studies described below, the N^6, N^6-dimethyladenine moiety is recognized, making it unlikely that this portion of the molecule is involved in the covalent linkage. Thus, incorporation presumably occurs in the 0-methyl tyrosine or 3-amino ribose portions of the molecule by an as yet unknown mechanism.

In any photoaffinity labeling experiment, the possibility exists that the receptor is being photodenatured during the course of the experiment, raising the question of

†Chloramphenicol binding to 50S subunits has been demonstrated previously.[62]

whether or not the labeling results obtained reflect ligand interaction with either native or denatured receptor. A straightforward approach to this problem is to measure labeling as a function of light fluence. In the absence of chloramphenicol, puromycin incorporation into L23 was found to increase almost linearly as a function of light fluence. Moreover, the fraction of label incorporated into L23 versus total incorporation was highest at the lowest light fluence used and decreased at higher light fluence. These results provide strong evidence that L23 labeling occurs on native ribosomes that have suffered no photodenaturation. In contrast, S14 labeling by puromycin in the presence of chloramphenicol shows a distinct lag in incorporation as a function of light fluence. This phenomenon is clearly demonstrated by the results in FIGURE 2, which show one-dimensional polyacrylamide gel electrophoresis patterns of labeled proteins. In the figure, the major peak in region IV corresponds to labeled L23, while that in region VI corresponds to labeled S14, and it is clear that it is only as light fluence increases that S14 labeling becomes dominant. These results were the first evidence for the existence of a photochemical event in addition to that required for

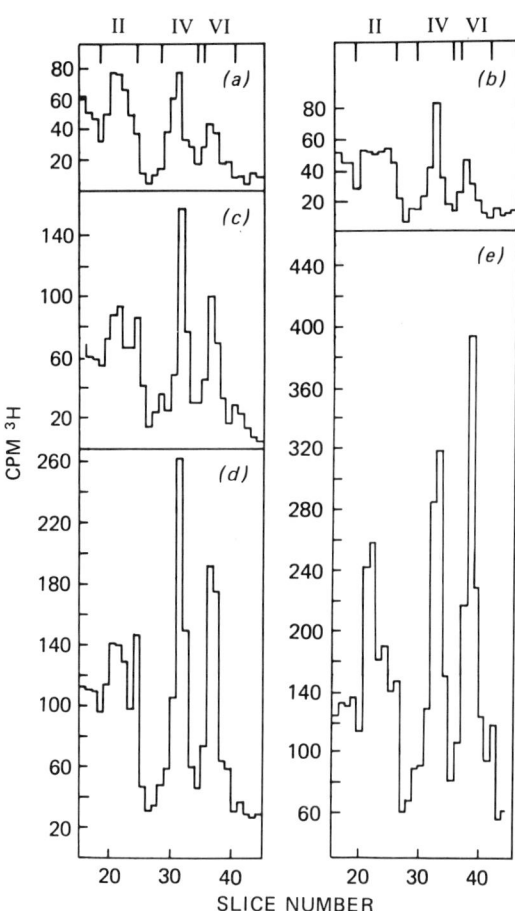

FIGURE 2. The light fluence dependence of one-dimensional polyacrylamide gel patterns of proteins from 70S ribosomes labeled with [8-^{3}H] puromycin in the presence of chloramphenicol. (a) 2 min photolysis; (b) 2 min photolysis; (c) 5 min photolysis; (d) 10 min photolysis; (e) 20 min photolysis. Experimental conditions: 100 A$_{260}$ units/ml ribosomes; 0.10 mM puromycin; (a) no added chloramphenicol, (b–e) 0.10 mM chloramphenicol added.

puromycin incorporation. Further investigation showed this event to be a chloramphenicol-dependent photoinduced alteration of the 30 S subunit, as shown by the results presented in TABLE 2. By contrast, note the lack of effect on L23 labeling.‡ In a formal sense, then, S14 labeling does occur on a photodenatured ribosome. However, we believe that the results are indicative of the presence of puromycin and chloramphenicol sites on the native 30S structure for the following reasons:

1. S14 is the second highest labeled protein, even in the absence of chloramphenicol

2. Enhancement of S14 labeling is found only in the presence of chloramphenicol and not in the presence of its biologically inactive diastereomer, implying a specific interaction site for chloramphenicol.

3. Irradiation causes only a minor loss of 30S subunit-dependent peptidyl transferase activity, and the extent of this loss is only minimally increased in the presence of chloramphenicol.

The results presented above are evidence for two puromycin sites on the ribosome: a 50S site, from which L23 is labeled, and a 30S site, from which S14 is labeled. In the

TABLE 2

RELATIVE LEVELS OF S14 AND L23 LABELING BY IMMUNOPRECIPITATION ANALYSIS

Conditions*	S 14	L 23
1. Puromycin alone	0.20	1.0
2. Puromycin plus chloramphenicol	(1.0)	1.9
3. Prephotolysis of 70S and chloramphenicol	5.8	1.9

*The photolyses were performed for 5 min with 0.1 mM [^{3}H]-puromycin, ± 0.1 mM chloramphenicol, and 100 A_{260}/ml of 70S ribosomes. In experiment 3, 70S ribosomes and chloramphenicol were combined and prephotolyzed for 20 min, puromycin was then added, and the complete reaction mixture was photolyzed for 5 min. Values reported are normalized to S14 labeling in line 2.

absence of a detailed knowledge of the photochemistry leading to incorporation, it is not clear to what extent the observed specificity of labeling reflects a special photochemical reactivity of L23 and S14 as opposed to a close proximity of these proteins to the puromycin binding sites. We have sought to resolve this ambiguity in two ways. First, we photolyzed solutions of extracted total ribosomal proteins and radioactive puromycin, subjected a sample to PAGE analysis, and compared the results obtained to those seen when the proteins are extracted from puromycin-photolabeled 70S ribosomes. Although the results obtained to date are preliminary, it is already quite clear that the former experiment gives a pattern of puromycin incorporation totally different from the latter. In particular, there is no marked labeling of either L23 or S14. In fact, radioactivity incorporated into the isolated proteins seem to follow protein density on the gel, i.e., it appears totally indiscriminate. This result is evidence that neither L23 or S14 is especially photoreactive, and

‡Separate experiments on isolated 30S subunits showed similar effects on S14 labeling. However, prephotolysis of either 30S or chloramphenicol separately did not lead to stimulation of S14 incorporation.

demonstrates that an intact ribosome structure is needed in order to get high L23 labeling. The effect of chloramphenicol on this control has not yet been evaluated.

The second approach was to use *p*-azidopuromycin (**8**) as a ribosome photoaffinity label so as to be able to compare the nitrene-dependent labeled proteins with the results obtained above. This compound is synthesized by condensation of N-tBOC-*p*-azidophenylalanine with puromycin aminonucleoside, followed by deprotection. It is, as expected, a very good functional analog of puromycin, displaying comparable activity in a peptidyl transferase assay. Photolyzed *p*-azidopuromycin, lacking the azido function, might photoincorporate into ribosomes by the same mechanism as puromycin itself. Thus, in order to make the desired comparison, it is important to demonstrate that the photoincorporation results obtained with *p*-azidopuromycin are truly nitrene-dependent. One approach is to compare results obtained with *p*-azidopuromycin that has been briefly prephotolyzed, just long enough to remove the azido function (pre-photolyzed *p*-azidopuromycin). A second approach is to compare the photoincorporation efficiency of *p*-azidopuromycin and puromycin. Because the photolysis of *p*-azidopuromycin leads to a complex mixture of products, some of which have limited solubility, the second approach has yielded the more clearly interpretable results. With the 3500 Å lamps and identical irradiation times, the extent of photoincorporation of *p*-azidopuromycin is >50-fold higher than that of puromycin itself. Thus, the use of limited light fluence gives a pattern of photoincorporation that is clearly azide-dependent, and so, inferentially, nitrene-dependent (FIGURE 3a and b). Two-dimensional PAGE and immunoprecipitation results show three major labeled proteins, L23, L18, and S18; the extent of *p*-azidopuromycin incorporation of all three are roughly comparable. This experiment, along with the results obtained with puromycin, demonstrates that two different photochemistries result in incorporation into L23. Added chloramphenicol stimulates *p*-azidopuromycin incorporation, but the identity(ies) of the newly labeled protein(s) have not as yet been determined.

During the course of our work with *p*-azidopuromycin, we encountered some methodological problems that, although now cleared up, are worth discussing for their possible relevance to other photoaffinity labeling studies. One of the classic controls in a photoaffinity labeling experiment is the measurement of the extent of background "incorporation" in the absence of irradiation, to make sure that the procedures used to remove excess radioactive affinity label in solution from receptor are effective, as well as to assess the possible importance of dark reactions leading to incorporation. In our earlier work, we found that repeated ethanol precipitation was effective in giving very low background levels of puromycin "incorporation" into ribosomes in the absence of irradiation, and that this procedure proved to be effective for *p*-azidopuromycin removal, as well. However, when we applied the ethanol precipitation procedure to our actual photoincorporation experiments, we obtained surprisingly inconsistent results, which, as we subsequently demonstrated, had arisen from the rather large background values obtained for the dark reaction of ribosomes with prephotolyzed *p*-azidopuromycin. These high background values are due, in part, to polymeric material formed upon the photolysis of *p*-azidopuromycin that coprecipitates with ribosomes upon ethanol addition. However, since the observed incorporation values were still 3–4 times higher in the irradiated samples as compared to the dark samples with prephotolyzed *p*-azidopuromycin, we originally thought our results from PAGE

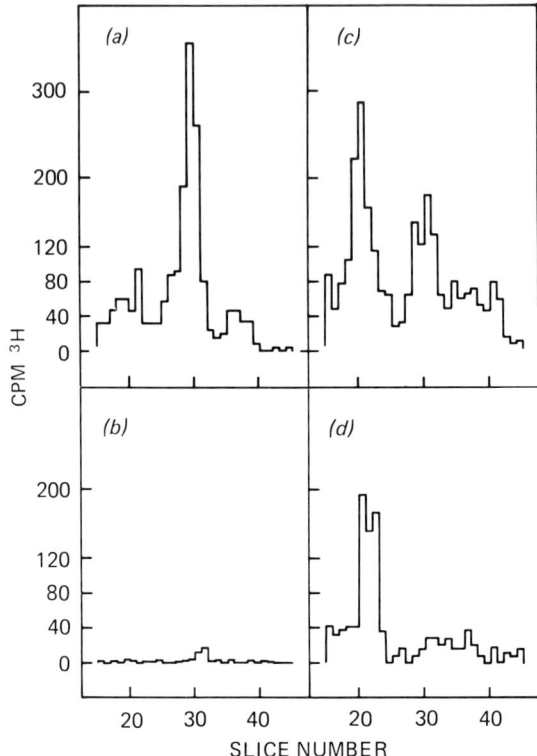

FIGURE 3. One-dimensional polyacrylamide gel patterns for 50S proteins labeled with *p*-azidopuromycin or puromycin. In experiments (a) and (b), 70S ribosomes were irradiated in the presence of *p*-azidopuromycin (50 μM) and puromycin (50 μM), respectively, with 3500 Å lamps for 10 min. After an initial low speed centrifugation, both samples were subjected to repeated ethanol precipitations, and 50S subunits were isolated by high-salt (0.4 M NaCl) sucrose gradient centrifugation.[10,11] In experiment (c), 50S subunits were irradiated in the presence of *p*-azidopuromycin (25 μM) with 2537 Å lamps for 4 min. In experiment (d), *p*-azidopuromycin (25 μM) was prephotolyzed with 2537 Å lamps for 1.8 min and incubated with 50S ribosomes in the dark. In experiments (c) and (d), there was no initial low speed centrifugation, and only repeated ethanol precipitation was used to remove nonbound *p*-azidopuromycin or photolyzed *p*-azidopuromycin.

In all four experiments, the protein was isolated by acetic-acid extraction.[65] Experiment (a) may be compared directly with experiments (c) and (d), since we have shown that irradiation with 2537 Å lamps instead of 3500 Å lamps, and of 50S particles instead of 70S particles, has little effect on the labeling pattern of 50S protein.

analysis of proteins extracted from ethanol-precipitated ribosomes could be considered at least qualitatively correct.[23] In this we were in error, and for two reasons:

First, our prephotolysis dark incubation control was performed by photolyzing a stock solution of *p*-azidopuromycin and adding an aliquot to a ribosome solution. Because of the polymerization reaction, however, the concentration of soluble prephotolyzed material is much less than the initial concentration of *p*-azidopuromycin. In consequence, the background value obtained with this control seriously underestimates the amount of noncovalently bound *p*-azidopuromycin present in the ethanol-precipitated ribosomes obtained following the irradiation of the *p*-azidopuromycin and the ribosomes.

Second, and more critically, some prephotolyzed material comigrates with ribosomal protein upon gel electrophoresis, which phenomenon has led us to mistakenly identify some ribosomal proteins as sites of the photoaffinity labeling by *p*-azidopuromycin. A proper procedure for the removal of noncovalently bound photolyzed *p*-azidopuromycin consists of an initial low speed centrifugation to precipitate polymeric, photolyzed *p*-azidopuromycin while leaving ribosomes in the supernatant, followed by repeated ethanol precipitation to remove soluble photoproducts and either high salt sucrose gradient or cushion centrifugation to remove residual noncovelently bound material. PAGE analyses of proteins extracted from ribosomes treated in this manner allow clear identifications of the covalently labeled material. Some representative data are shown in FIGURE 3a, c, and d.

After we began our work with *p*-azidopuromycin, we became aware that two other groups were working with the same compound. Their brief published accounts suggest that they were unaware of the problems of the high background from noncovalent labeling described above.[24,25]

Through the use of the technique of immunoelectron microscopy, our photoaffinity results can be used as a three-dimensional probe of ribosomal structure. The underlying idea here is to make a complex between a puromycin-labeled ribosome and an antibody to puromycin. When the complex is examined in the electron microscope, the position of the antibody's attachment to the ribosome indicates the location of the covalently bound puromycin, and thus of that portion of the ribosome to which the puromycin is attached. This technique was first applied to ribosomes using antibodies to ribosomal proteins to determine protein locations on the ribosome.[26,27] Subsequently, Glitz and Politz[28] showed that an antibody to N^6,N^6-dimethyladenosine could be used to locate the adjacent N^6,N^6-dimethyladenosines near the 3' end of 16S RNA within the 30S subunit. In their work, they used a 30S subunit isolated from the kasugamycin-resistant strain TPR 201 (which lacks N^6,N^6-dimethyladenosine in 16S RNA) as a control; they pointed out that their antibody interacted strongly with puromycin, as expected. Quite recently, Keren-Zur *et al.* used an antibody to the 2,4-dinitrophenyl group to locate the position of a dinitrophenyl group attached at the 3' end of aminoacylated tRNA^{Val}, which had been photochemically cross-linked to the 30S subunit, but at a position >80 Å away from the site of dinitrophenyl attachment.[29] In the present work, performed in collaboration with Glitz and Olson, we have examined the complex formed between anti-N^6,N^6-dimethyladenosine and a 30S subunit isolated from TPR 201 ribosomes that had been photoaffinity labeled with puromycin in the presence of chloramphenicol.[30] Some representative pictures are shown in FIGURE 4. Protein S14 is the major labeled site in the mutant 30S subunit, since it is in the subunit derived from Q13. What is striking about our results is that a composite diagram for anti-N^6,N^6-dimethyladenosine binding to puromycin-labeled 30S subunits is virtually identical to the composite diagram for anti-S14 binding to the 30S subunit determined previously by Lake and Kahan.[26]

The location of ribosomal proteins by immunoelectron microscopy is being actively studied by two different groups, and both of them agree on the location of S14. Thus,

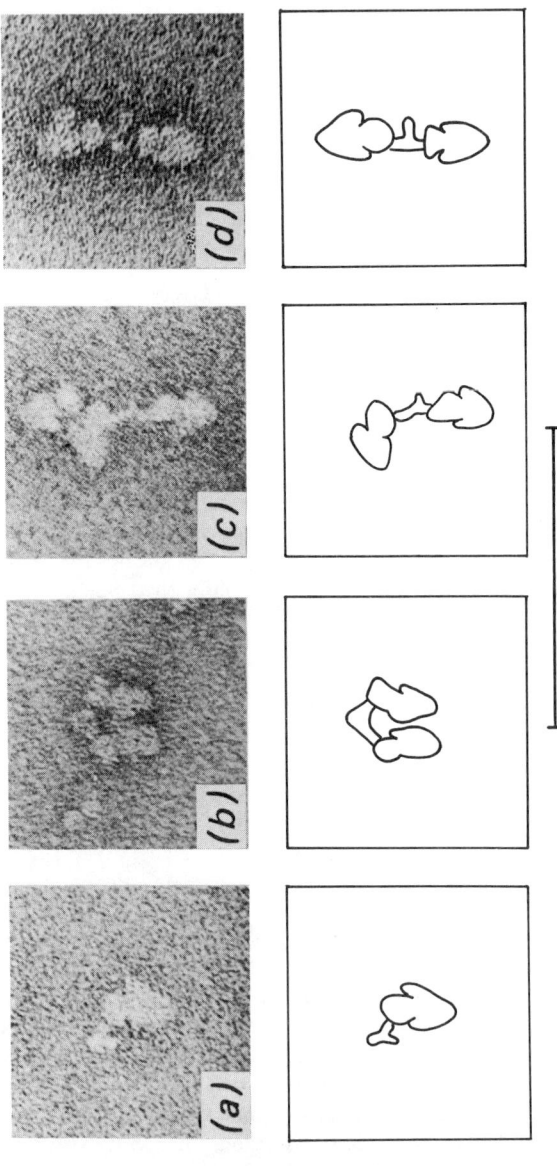

FIGURE 4.   Electron micrographs of puromycin-modified 30S ribosomal subunit-antibody complexes.[30] Below each frame is an interpretive drawing. The closed bar is 1000 Å long.

our present results, while demonstrating the power of the technique, are only confirmatory with respect to the S14 location. However, these groups do disagree over the locations of other ribosomal proteins, in particular L23,[27,31] so our further use of this technique should contribute interesting new information. In addition, some ribosomal proteins have apparent antigenic sites at widely different locations on the ribosome, but it is not known which part of the protein corresponds to which antigenic site. Since we have the inherent ability to locate the site of covalent attachment of the affinity label to a given amino acid residue, the combination of affinity labeling with immunoelectron microscopy should allow specific regions of elongated proteins to be located on the ribosome.

Lincomycin and Blasticidin S

Lincomycin is a peptidyl transferase inhibitor that appears to block binding of the 3' end of tRNA at both the A and P sites. Previous studies have shown that substitution is possible at C-7 with retention of antibiotic activity. Thus, both the R and S isomers of 7-chloro-7-deoxylincomyocin are active antibiotics,[32] as is (7S)-7-mercapto-7-deoxylincomycin and several of its S-alkylated derivatives.[33] Accordingly, we have synthesized **11** and shown it to be approximately as effective as lincomycin itself in inhibiting peptidyl transferase. Synthesis of the parent thiol involves condensation of the amine (**10**) with N-methyl-γ-propylproline. We are able to make the thiol in highly radioactive form by condensing γ-propylproline (kindly supplied by Dr. Brian Bannister at Upjohn) with **10** and methylating N-demethyl-7-mercapto-7-deoxylincomycin with [^{3}H]-dimethyl sulfate. The thiol is alkylated with reagent **1a**, as described elsewhere,[12,27] to yield **11** in radioactive form.

Photoincorporation of **11** into the ribosome occurs upon photolysis with either the 2537 Å or 3500 Å lamp. The incorporation is carbene-dependent, as shown by the lack of incorporation obtained with the prephotolyzed compound. Incorporation takes place into both 30S and 50S subunit proteins. The protein labeled to the highest extent, by far, appears, from two-dimensional PAGE analysis, to be L14. Proteins S4 and/or S5 and S15 are also labeled to significant extents. Firmer identification depends upon the results of specific immunoprecipitation experiments now underway. Despite the clean photochemistry and relatively specific labeling pattern, we have been unable to demonstrate good inhibition of photoincorporation of **11** by added lincomycin. This might only be a reflection of the rather low affinity constant of lincomycin for the ribosome, since there are indications from two other studies that the photoincorporation of **11** proceeds in a site-specific manner. First, a recent article by Hummel *et al.* describes the isolation of a lincomycin-resistant strain of *E. coli* having an altered L14.[34] This is, in itself, support for the significance of our photoaffinity labeling result. In the near future, we plan to examine whether or not ribosomes from this mutant strain are any different from ribosomes from a wild-type strain in photoaffinity labeling experiments with **11**. Second, the blasticidin S derivative (**13**), which contains the same photoreactive group as **11** and is also a peptidyl transferase inhibitor, gives a totally different protein labeling pattern from that obtained with **11**, as shown by one-dimensional PAGE analysis.[22] Thus, the labeling obtained depends on the structure of the molecule containing the diazo functionality, and not on the photochemistry of the diazo group alone.

Streptomycin

Streptomycin is an antibiotic that is known to affect tRNA-ribosome interaction. It has one tight site per 70S ribosome ($K_D \sim 0.1\ \mu M$), which is known to be located on the 30S subunit, ($K_D \sim 0.5\ \mu M$) and a number of other sites of lower affinity ($K_D = 10^{-4}\ M$) present on both the 30S and 50S subunits.[35–39] Streptomycin stimulates miscoding at very low concentrations ($<1\ \mu M$),[40] which is, presumably, a consequence of streptomycin binding to the tight site, and also interferes with several other ribosomal functions related to the ribosome-tRNA interaction.[41]

Streptomycin derivatives active both in stimulating miscoding and in inhibiting tight-site streptomycin binding may be prepared by deriving the single carbonyl function in the molecule, the 3'-aldehyde.[42] Accordingly, we have prepared three photolabile derivatives of streptomycin (15, 16, and 17) in radioactive form for testing as photoaffinity labeling reagents, by condensation of streptomycin with two new carbonyl reagents (2 and 3) and the known hydrazine (4).[12,15] Reagent 2 is synthesized by condensation of EDMCl with hydrazine. We have developed a simple microscale procedure that allows us to synthesize [^{14}C]-EDMCl from [^{14}C]-phosgene without adding carrier. Thus, [^{14}C]-EDMCl and, subsequently, 2 are available at 53 Ci/mol.

We have previously described a Dimroth rearrangement involving diazo to 1,2,3-triazole anion isomerization, as shown below.[43]

$$\underset{\text{RNHCCN}_2\text{CO}_2\text{Et}}{\overset{\text{O}}{\overset{\|}{}}} \rightleftharpoons R\text{—N} \underset{N}{\overset{\overset{O^-}{\underset{}{C}}=\overset{CO_2Et}{\underset{}{C}}}{\diagdown \diagup}} N \quad + H^+$$

Both reagent 2 and its streptomycin derivative (15) are subject to this isomerization.[15] Since the triazole is much less photolabile than the diazo isomer, and since it can be difficult to reverse the above equilibrium, we have developed synthetic procedures that maintain both 2 and 15 in their diazo forms, mostly by working at or below pH 4.5. The photoaffinity labeling of ribosomes is performed at pH 7 and 0 °C. In our apparatus under these conditions, photolysis of the diazo group of 15 in the presence of ribosomes is over in a time (<5 min) short compared to the $t_{1/2}$ for formation of the triazole (20–30 min). Thus, the diazo isomer of 15 can be tested as a photoaffinity label. However, functional assays of 15 are performed at higher temperatures, under conditions in which triazole formation is rapid compared to the assay procedure, so it is the effect of the triazole isomer that is being measured here. Reagent 4, 2,4-dinitrophenyl hydrazine, was prepared at 14 Ci/mmol by an efficient microscale condensation of [^{3}H]-2,4-dinitrofluorobenzene (Amersham) with hydrazine, and condensed with streptomycin to make radioactive 16. Reagent 3 was prepared by condensation of hydrazine with the Fleet reagent, 4-azido-2-nitro-fluorobenzene (Pierce). We do not, as yet, have this material available in radioactive form. Radioactive 17 has been made, using [^{3}H]-streptomycin (2–3 Ci/mmol), prepared in collaboration with Dr. Richard Ehrenkaufer (Brookhaven National Laboratory), by placing streptomycin dried on a cellulose nitrate filter into the microwave discharge tritium atom labeling system described in Reference 44.

The three streptomycin derivatives (**15–17**) have been found to be active both in stimulating miscoding in protein synthesis and in inhibiting tight-site binding of [³H]-dihydrostreptomycin, although with each, higher concentrations are required for maximal response than those required with streptomycin itself. In addition, **15** and **16** have been shown to be effective bacteriocides (**17** was not tested). Both **15** and **16** have been tested as potential photoaffinity labels for the ribosome.[15] Preliminary experiments have shown that both **15** and **16** photoincorporate using either the 2537 Å or the 3500 Å lamp. However, the photoincorporation of **15** is predominantly carbene-independent. As a practical matter, we have chosen to pursue photolabeling studies with **16** first, largely because it is available at a much higher specific radioactivity than **15** (14 Ci/mmol [³H] compared to 53 mCi/mmole [¹⁴C]). Most of this work has been done with the 3500 Å lamps, since they allow higher levels of incorporation to be achieved at lower levels of ribosomal activity loss. One- and two-dimensional PAGE analyses of labeled ribosomal protein have shown that a single 50S protein, which we have tentatively identified as either L18 or L22, is labeled to the highest extent and two 30S proteins (S1 and, tentatively, S13) are labeled to significant extents. Because streptomycin is a trication, the definitive identification of these proteins cannot be made with confidence from gel electrophoresis experiments alone, and must await the results of an immunoprecipitation analysis, which is currently underway.

However, it is already clear from one-dimensional PAGE analyses that the observed labeling does not arise from the unique, tight streptomycin site, since concentrations of streptomycin sufficient to saturate this site do not prevent labeling, and similar labeling patterns are obtained upon the photoincorporation of **16** into ribosomes isolated from either streptomycin-sensitive or streptomycin-resistant strains. However, even ribosomes isolated from streptomycin-resistant strains can be induced to misread at a high enough concentration of streptomycin,[45] and misreading is known to be stimulated by streptomycin-like molecules that bind to sites on the ribosome different from the unique streptomycin site.[36,39] Since **16** does stimulate misreading, the observed labeled proteins may correspond to such sites. In this connection, it is interesting that, at low concentrations of **16**, photoincorporation into distinct ribosomal proteins is stimulated by low concentrations of streptomycin. This parallels the effect of low concentrations of streptomycin in stimulating the tight-site binding of paromomycin, an aminoglycoside that induces misreading at low concentrations (<1 μM), does not inhibit tight-site streptomycin binding, and binds somewhat better to the 50S than to the 30S subunit.[39]

Tetracycline

Tetracycline (**18**) inhibits the binding of aminoacyl-tRNA to the ribosome, and binds more tightly to the 30S than to the 50S subunit. Several studies have indicated the presence of one tight binding site per 70S particle ($K_D = 5 \times 10^{-6}$ M–3×10^{-5} M) and a large number of weaker sites.[46–50] Since the mRNA binds to the 30S subunit, a likely site of action for tetracycline is at or near the codon-anticodon interaction. We are currently engaged in a collaborative effort with Drs. Cava and Flaks at the University of Pennsylvania to test a range of properties of tetracycline and tetracycline derivatives. Part of this effort involves the synthesis of photolabile derivatives of tetracycline for use in photoaffinity labeling studies with ribosomes. However, tetracycline is, itself, a photolabile molecule, as is evidenced by its rather high quantum yield for photodestruction,[14,51] its ability to photoinactivate virus particles,[52] and its photosensitization of organic reactions[64] and puromycin incorporation into ribosomes (mostly into protein L23), which we have recently demonstrated.[10] This photoreactivity and our previous results with puromycin incorporation have prompted us to test native tetracycline as a photoaffinity label. Irradiation of [3H]-tetracycline (New England Nuclear) in the presence of 70S ribosomes leads to the apparent incorporation of radioactivity into ribosomal proteins. 30S proteins show higher levels of labeling, and both two-dimensional PAGE and immunoprecipitation analyses show S4 and S18 to be the dominant labeled proteins. Significant radioactivity is also found in S7, S13, and S14.[14] Tritton has obtained similar results independently.[53]

As is typical in photoaffinity labeling experiments, one of the first controls we performed was to show that our isolation procedures were effective in removing noncovalently bound [3H]-tetracycline from ribosomal proteins prior to PAGE or immunoprecipitation analysis. Subsequently, the results with prephotolyzed *p*-azidopuromycin, described above, prompted us to perform the control of incubating ribosomes with prephotolyzed tetracycline, with no subsequent photolysis. This procedure does, in fact, apparently label ribosomal protein, which is similar to what is obtained in the normal photolysis experiment by one-dimensional PAGE analysis. Since both spectral and tlc analysis show that tetracycline is chemically altered during prephotolysis (although we have not identified the products), it is reasonable to suppose that one or more of the new compounds formed is responsible for this apparent labeling. These results have led us to attempt to answer the following questions in work that is currently in progress:

1. What portion of the labeling observed in a normal photolysis experiment results from a dark reaction of prephotolyzed tetracycline?

2. Is the labeling observed with prephotolyzed tetracycline covalent?

3. What portion of the observed labeling arises from the interaction of tetracycline with a specific site(s) on the ribosome?

In connection with these results, it should be noted that Katzenellenbogen and his coworkers have previously observed that noncovalently bound steroid analogs comigrate on PAGE electrophoresis with proteins from lamb uterine cytosol.[54]

COMPARISON OF ANTIBIOTIC PHOTOAFFINITY LABELING AND OTHER RESULTS

The results of the labeling studies reported in this paper are presented in TABLE 3. It is interesting to compare the results obtained with the two peptidyl transferase inhibitors, puromycin and lincomycin (or their derivatives), with results obtained from other studies of ribosomal structure, particularly those involving the mapping of antigenic determinants of ribosomal proteins on the ribosome by immunoelectron microscopy. Because of the remaining uncertainties discussed above, such a comparison is premature for the streptomycin and tetracycline labeling results.

The immunoelectron microscopy results should be considered with the following points in mind:

1. Two research groups have published all of the protein mapping studies. Both groups have reported mapping results for all 21 30S proteins. Stöffler and his

coworkers have reported results for 19 of the 33-odd 50S proteins and Lake and his collaborators have reported results for eleven 50S proteins.[54-56]

2. The two groups differ in their interpretations of the three-dimensional structure of the subunits, and, therefore, in the detailed positioning of the proteins. However, it is fair to say that, for most of the 30S proteins mapped in common, there is agreement between the two groups on the protein positions along the vertical axis of the 30S subunit. There is more obvious disagreement regarding the positions of the 50S proteins.

3. Some of the proteins appear to have more than one antigenic determinant on a ribosomal subunit, sometimes at widely separated positions.

4. The technique is extraordinarily sensitive to both the purity of the proteins used to generate antisera and the specificity of the antisera. As a result, there is, at present, controversy over the validity of at least some of the published antigenic assignments.[57] This is particularly important as it relates to point 3.

The major 50S proteins labeled by puromycin and its derivatives (6–8) and by the lincomycin derivative (11) are L14, L18, and L23. As can be seen in FIGURE 5, these

TABLE 3

A SUMMARY OF PHOTOLABELED PROTEINS

Antibiotic or Derivative	50 S proteins	30 S proteins
6	L23	S14*
7	L18, L23	S18
8	—	S14, S18
11	L14	S4 or S5
16	maybe L18 or L22	S1, maybe S13
18	—	S4, S18, S7, S13, S14

*Enhanced in the presence of chlormaphenicol.

three proteins are near neighbors, at least in the Stöffler model, thus providing evidence that the peptidyl transferase center is located in the region indicated by the dotted line. This region is shown to include L16, since this protein has been clearly implicated in peptidyl transferase activity by studies in other laboratories, and, in addition, cross-links to L23 upon treatment of the 50S subunit with 2-iminothiolane.[66]

There is a variety of evidence that the 3' end of aminoacyl-tRNA interacts directly with the 30S subunit in both the absence and, under some conditions, the presence of 50S subunits. Since puromycin is a structural analog of the 3' end of aminoacyl-tRNA, our results indicate that S14 is at or close to the 30S interaction site, which agrees both with the result of Girshovich et al.,[58] that S14 is the major labeled protein when an arylazido derivative of 3'-aminoacyl-tRNA is photoincorporated into 30S subunits, and with the postulated placement of the 3' end of aminoacyl-tRNA in the putative recognition (R) site for aminoacyl-tRNA binding.[59] The labeling results with N-EDM-puromycin suggest that acylation of the α-amino group in puromycin changes the relative affinities of puromycin for its binding sites so that the 30S subunit

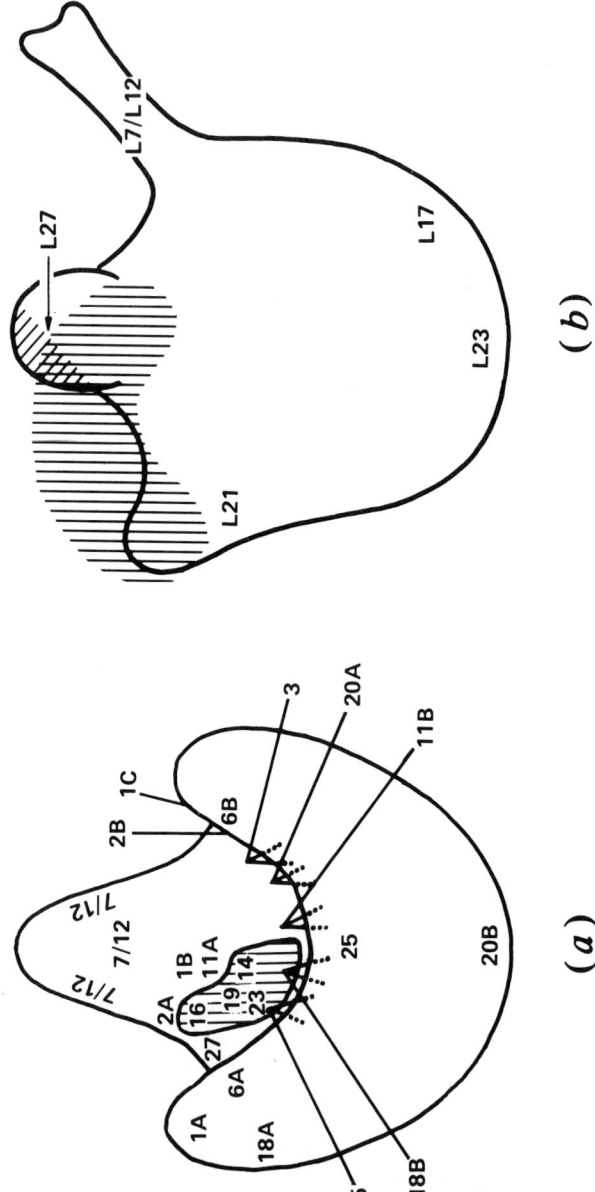

FIGURE 5. The structure of the 50S ribosomal subunit with the location of some proteins. (a) Stöffler and Wittmann,[1] (b) Lake.[31]

site is favored. Our finding, that both N-EDM-puromycin and *p*-azidopuromycin label S18 as a major product, suggests that this protein is close to S14 and is at least consistent with a recent three-dimensional computer modeling study of the 30S subunit.[60] However, S18 is known to contain a highly reactive SH group, and the proper controls to exclude the possibility that S18 is labeled as a result of its chemical reactivity have not yet been done.[61]

CONCLUSION

In summary, our studies have resulted in the development of new reagents and synthetic procedures for the introduction of both radioactivity and photolability into antibiotics; have provided examples of how PAGE analysis can be used to conveniently test various aspects of photoaffinity labeling of complex receptors, such as the ribosome; have revealed examples of unexpected photoreactivity, as in the case of puromycin; and have provided strong evidence regarding the three-dimensional location of the peptidyl transferase center and the site of the interaction of the 3' end of aminoacyl-tRNA with the 30S subunit. Work that is now in progress should provide similar detailed information regarding other functional sites in the ribosome.

REFERENCES

1. STÖFFLER, G. & H. G. WITTMANN. 1977. *In* Molecular Mechanisms of Protein Biosynthesis. H. Weissbach and S. Pestka, Eds.: 117–202. Academic Press. New York.
2. FELLNER P. 1974. *In* Ribosomes. M. Nomura, A. Tissieres, and P. Lengyel, Eds.: 169–91. Cold Spring Harbor Laboratory. New York.
3. COOPERMAN, B. S. 1978. *In* Bioorganic Chemistry: A Treatise to Supplement Bioorganic Chemistry, an International Journal, Vol. 4. E. van Tamelen, Ed.: 81–115. Academic Press. New York.
4. JOHNSON, A. E. & C. R. CANTOR. 1977. *In* Methods In Enzymology, Vol. 46. W. B. Jakoby and M. Wilchek, Eds.: 180–94. Academic Press. New York.
5. ZAMIR, A. 1977. *In* Methods in Enzymology, Vol. 46. W. B. Jakoby and M. Wilchek, Eds.: 621–37. Academic Press. New York.
6. KUECHLER, E. & J. OFENGAND. 1980. *In* Transfer RNA: Structure, Properties and Recognition. P. Schimmel, D. Söll and J. Abelson, Eds. 413–44. Cold Spring Harbor Laboratory. New York.
7. PESTKA, S. 1977. *In* Molecular Mechanisms of Protein Biosynthesis. H. Weissbach and S. Pestka, Eds.: 467–553. Academic Press. New York.
8. VAZQUEZ, D. 1974. FEBS Lett. **40:** S63–S84.
9. JAYNES, E. N., JR., P. G. GRANT, G. GIANGRANDE, R. WIEDER & B. S. COOPERMAN. 1978. Biochemistry **17:** 561–69.
10. GRANT, P. G., W. A. STRYCHARZ, E. N. JAYNES, JR. & B. S. COOPERMAN. 1979. Biochemistry **18:** 2149–54.
11. GRANT, P. G., B. S. COOPERMAN & W. A. STRYCHARZ. 1979. Biochemistry **18:** 2154–60.
12. COOPERMAN, B. S., P. G. GRANT, R. A. GOLDMAN, M. A. LUDDY, A. MINELLA, A. W. NICHOLSON & W. A. STRYCHARZ. 1979. *In* Methods in Enzymology, Vol. 59. K. Moldave and L. Grossman, Eds.: 796–815. Academic Press. New York.
13. COOPERMAN, B. S., E. N. JAYNES, D. J. BRUNSWICK & M. A. LUDDY. 1975. Proc. Nat. Acad. Sci. USA **72:** 2974–78.
14. GOLDMAN, R. A. & B. S. COOPERMAN. 1980. In preparation.
15. LUDDY, M. A. & B. S. COOPERMAN. 1980. In preparation.
16. ESCHER, E. & R. SCHWYZER. 1974. FEBS Lett. **46:** 347–50.
17. CHOWDHRY, V. & F. H. WESTHEIMER. 1979. Annu. Rev. Biochem. **48:** 293–325.
18. NEADLE, D. J. & R. J. POLLITT. 1967. J. Chem. Soc. 1764–66.

19. NAGUBASHAN, T. L., J. J. WRIGHT, A. B. COOPER, W. N. TURNER & G. H. MILLER. 1978. J. Antibiot. **31:** 43–54.
20. FLEET, G. W. J., J. R. KNOWLES & R. R. PORTER. 1972. Biochem J. **128:** 499–508.
21. MINNELLA, A. & B. S. COOPERMAN. 1980. In preparation.
22. GOLDMAN, R. A., M. A. LUDDY, R. EHRENKAUFER, E. PLOTZKER & B. S. COOPERMAN. 1980. In preparation.
23. NICHOLSON, A. W. & B. S. COOPERMAN. 1978. FEBS Lett. **90:** 203–8; 1980. In preparation.
24. SYMONS, R. H., R. J. HARRIS, P. GREENWELL, D. J. ECKERMANN & E. F. VANIN. 1978. *In* Bioorganic Chemistry: A Treatise to Supplement Bioorganic Chemistry, an International Journal, Vol. 4. E. van Tamelen, Ed.: 409–36. Academic Press. New York.
25. KRASSNIGG, F., V. A. ERDMANN & H. FASOLD. 1978. Eur. J. Biochem. **87:** 439–43.
26. LAKE, J. A. & L. KAHAN. 1975. J. Mol. Biol. **99:** 631–44.
27. TISCHENDORF, G. W., H. ZEICHHARDT & G. STÖFFLER. 1975. Proc. Nat. Acad. Sci. USA **72:** 4820–24.
28. POLITZ, S. M. & D. G. GLITZ. 1977. Proc. Nat. Acad. Sci. USA **74:** 1468–72.
29. KEREN-ZUR, M., M. BOUBLIK & J. OFENGAND. 1979. Proc. Nat. Acad. Sci. USA **76:** 1054–58.
30. OLSON, H. M., P. G. GRANT, D. G. GLITZ & B. S. COOPERMAN. 1980. Proc. Nat. Acad. Sci. USA **77:** 890–94.
31. LAKE, J. A. 1980. *In* Transfer RNA: Structure, Properties and Recognition. P. Schimmel, D. Söll, and J. Abelson, Eds.: 393–411. Cold Spring Harbor Laboratory. New York.
32. MAGERLEIN, B. 1971. Adv. Appl. Microbiol. **14:** 185–229.
33. BANNISTER, B. 1977. J. Chem. Soc. Perkin Trans 1: 1057–8.
34. HUMMEL, H., W. PIEPERSBERG & A. BOCK. 1979. Mol. Gen. Genet. **169:** 345–47.
35. KAJI, H. & Y. TANAKA. 1968. J. Mol. Biol. **32:** 221–30.
36. CHANG, T. N. & J. G. FLAKS. 1972. Antimicrob. Agents Chemother. **2:** 294–307.
37. GARVIN, R. T., D. K. BISWAS & L. GORINI. 1974. Proc. Nat. Acad. Sci. USA **71:** 3814–18.
38. SCHREINER, G. & K. H. NIERHAUS. 1973. J. Mol. Biol. **81:** 71–82.
39. LANDO, D., M. A. COUSIN, T. OJASOO & J. P. RAYNAUD. 1976. Eur. J. Biochem. **66:** 597–606.
40. DAVIES, J. & B. D. DAVIS. 1968. J. Biol. Chem. **243:** 3312–16.
41. PESTKA, S. 1971. Annu. Rev. Microbiol. **25:** 487–562.
42. HEDING, H. & A. DIEDRICHSEN. 1975. J. Antibiot. **28:** 312–16.
43. BRUNSWICK, D. J. & B. S. COOPERMAN. 1973. Biochemistry **12:** 4074–78.
44. EHRENKAUFER, R., W. C. HEMBREE & A. P. WOLF. 1977. J. Labeled Compd. **14:** 271–79.
45. TAI, P.-C., B. J. WALLACE & B. D. DAVIS. 1978. Proc. Nat. Acad. Sci. USA **75:** 275–79.
46. CONNAMACHER, R. H. & H. G. MANDEL. 1965. Biochem. Biophys. Res. Commun. **20:** 98–103.
47. MAXWELL, I. H. 1968. Mol. Pharmacol. **4:** 25–37.
48. FAY, G., M. REISS, & H. KERSTEN. 1973. Biochemistry **12:** 1160–64.
49. STREL'TSOV, S. A., M. K. KUKHANOVA, G. V. GURSKII, A. A. KRAEVSKII, I. V. BELYAVSKAYA, L. S. VIKTOROVA, A. D. TREBOGANOV & B. P. GOTTIKH. 1975. Molek. Biol. (English version) **9:** 729–38.
50. TRITTON, T. R. 1977. Biochemistry **16:** 4133–38.
51. HLAVKA, J. J. & P. BITHE. 1966. Tetrahedron Lett. **32:** 3843–46.
52. ESPARAZA, J., C. I. PINA & F. NOVO. 1976. Antimicrob. Agents Chemother. **10:** 16–178.
53. TRITTON, T. R. 1979. Private communication.
54. STRYCHARZ, W. A., M. NOMURA & J. A. LAKE. 1978. J. Mol. Biol. **126:** 123–40.
55. LAKE, J. A. 1978. *In* Advanced Techniques in Biological Electron Microscopy, Vol. 2. J. K. Koehler, Ed.: 173–211. Springer Verlag. New York.
56. LAKE, J. A. 1978. FEBS Lett. **43:** S121–30.
57. WINKELMANN, D. & KAHAN, L. 1978. Fed. Proc. Fed. Am. Soc. Exp. Biol. **37:** 1739.
58. GIRSHOVICH, A. S., E. S. BOCHKAREVA, V. M. KRAMOROV & Y. A. OVCHINNIKOV. 1974. FEBS Lett. **45:** 213–17.

59. LAKE, J. A. 1977. Proc. Nat. Acad. Sci. USA **74:** 1903–7.
60. GAFNEY, P. T. & G. R. CRAVEN. 1979. *In* Methods in Enzymology, Vol. 59. K. Moldave and L. Grossman, Eds.: 602–11. Academic Press. New York.
61. MOORE, P. B. 1971. J. Mol. Biol. **60:** 169–84.
62. VAZQUEZ, P. 1964. Biochem. Biophys. Res. Common. **12:** 409–13.
63. ELAD, D. 1976. *In* Aging, Carcinogenesis, and Radiation Biology: The Role of Nucleic Acid Addition Reactions. K. C. Smith, Ed.: 243–60. Plenum. New York.
64. WIEBE, J. A. & D. E. MOORE. 1977. J. Pharm. Sci. **66:** 186–89.
65. HARDY, S. J. S., C. G. KURLAND, P. VOYNOW & G. MORA. 1969. Biochemistry **8:** 2897–905.
66. KENNY, J. W. & TRAUT, R. R. 1979. J. Mol. Biol. **127:** 243–63.

DISCUSSION

DR. J. J. FERGUSON, JR.: I have some questions concerning the attachment of an unmodified molecule to its binding site. What's the affinity for puromycin binding to the transferase site? Do you know what the chromophor is? Are you sure that it's puromycin that's light sensitive? Could it possibly be the protein?

DR. B. S. COOPERMAN: Much has been made of the need for a tight site in order to do affinity labeling studies. The puromycin binding site revealed by our direct measurements of the saturation of puromycin labeling has a K_d of about one-half millimolar; a very weak site on a very complex receptor. That actually corresponds very well with the K_m value for puromycin as a peptidyl transferase substrate, which is about two-tenths millimolar, but then, with tRNA present, a change by a factor of three probably doesn't represent a serious discrepancy.

I think the reason we get away with it is that we can resolve the system. For instance, L23 labeling, which, from the gel pattern, looks to be very large, is only about 20% of the total labeling. The reason that it is so clear is that you can spread everything out and look at L23 alone.

Now, as to the photochemistry involved in the incorporation, I want to say, first, I don't know. It does not appear to be in the adenine portion of the molecule. One of the experiments showing that is, in fact, the immuno-electron microscopy experiment I just showed you. The antidimethyladenine antibody recognizes photoincorporated puromycin very well and one would not expect that to happen if the dimethyladenine moiety of puromycin were directly involved in the incorporation. Furthermore, we originally tried these experiments with the tritium in two different positions on the puromycin molecule, but the tritium at position 8, which is, in fact, one of the sites you might invoke for a reaction, gives exactly the same patterns at tritium elsewhere in the molecule. So dimethyladenine is not involved.

As to the possibility of photoincorporation from the protein—I don't think it is likely. There is an experiment we've done very recently, that I didn't talk about. We took the whole collection of ribosomal proteins and photolyzed them in the presence of puromycin to answer the question, "Is there any special photoreactivity that develops in L23?" The answer is "no." In that experiment, the labeling followed the protein staining essentially one for one. Furthermore, there are a lot of studies on photo-cross-linking of proteins to RNA and ribosomes. L23 is not a major protein photo-cross-link; it doesn't have much photoreactivity. L23 does not appear to be an especially reactive protein by the tests that have been used and, for that reason, I think that the reaction probably occurs with the tyrosyl group in puromycin, but I'm not sure.

TOPOLOGY OF THE RIBOSOMAL BINDING SITES FOR tRNA AS REVEALED BY PHOTOAFFINITY LABELING

James Ofengand, Fwu-Lai Lin, Lilian Hsu,*
Mordechai Keren-Zur,† and Miloslav Boublik

Roche Institute of Molecular Biology
Nutley, New Jersey 07110

INTRODUCTION

The existence of two functionally specific binding sites for transfer RNA (tRNA) on the ribosome, known for more than 20 years to be the site of protein synthesis, was first proposed by Watson in 1964.[1] Over the intervening 15 years, this model has been elaborated and refined through the efforts of many workers. The current concept of how the two sites function during peptide chain elongation is as follows:[2]

A protein called elongation factor Tu(EFTu), complexed with guanosine triphosphate (GTP), binds aminoacyl-tRNA (AA-tRNA) and directs it to one of the ribosomal sites, the A site. This is the codon translation step, in which the presence of a particular codon in the A site selects the appropriate tRNA bearing a matching anticodon. Peptide bond formation follows automatically when there is a peptidyl-tRNA in the other site, the P site. Then the process of translocation occurs, in which both the peptidyl-tRNA in the A site and its associated codon move to the P site. This process is catalyzed by another protein, elongation factor G (EFG), which also uses GTP. The ribosome is then in the same state as it was initially and a second cycle of amino acid addition begins. The protein chains are started by a special mechanism requiring three additional protein factors, called initiation factors,[17] which are thought to place the first AA-tRNA, which is always formylmethionyl-tRNA (fMet-tRNA), directly into the P site. Peptide chain termination likewise proceeds by a special mechanism, but, since tRNA is not involved, it does not concern us here.

Despite this seeming wealth of detail, the molecular mechanisms involved are still obscure. For example, both the way in which codon-anticodon base pairing triggers stable binding of AA-tRNA to the A site and the molecular mechanics of translocation are unknown. There is, as yet, no real understanding of how the ribosome works.

We have approached this question by first attempting to determine the location and nature of the two tRNA binding sites, the A and P sites, in the belief that the molecular processes will become more evident once the positions are known. The dimensions of the problem are illustrated in FIGURE 1, which shows tRNA and the ribosome on the same scale. As this figure amply demonstrates, there is still no universal agreement about the structure of even the exhaustively studied *E. coli* ribosome, although the only major point of disagreement is in the mutual orientation of the two subunits. Each tRNA is one-third the diameter of the ribosome, and two of

---

*Present address: Department of Biochemistry, University of Massachusetts, Amherst, Massachusetts 01003.
†Present address: Syva Research Institute, 3221 Porter Avenue, Palo Alto, California 94304.

them, one each in the ribosomal A and P sites, must be arranged in such a way that their amino acid ends are near to each other, as is necessary for peptide bond formation, and, probably, with their anticodons together as well, in order to translate sequential codons.

The way these two sites are arranged is, essentially, a topological question. Such problems are well suited to analysis by affinity labeling, a method that can provide an unambiguous determination of close contact points between two macromolecules. Bochkareva *et al.*,[8] Pellegrini *et al.*,[9] and Czernilofsky and Kuechler[34] introduced this approach to ribosome structure in their pioneering work on the peptidyl transferase center, which was subsequently greatly expanded upon by other workers, who studied not only the locale of the aminoacyl end of the tRNA, but also, indirectly, the

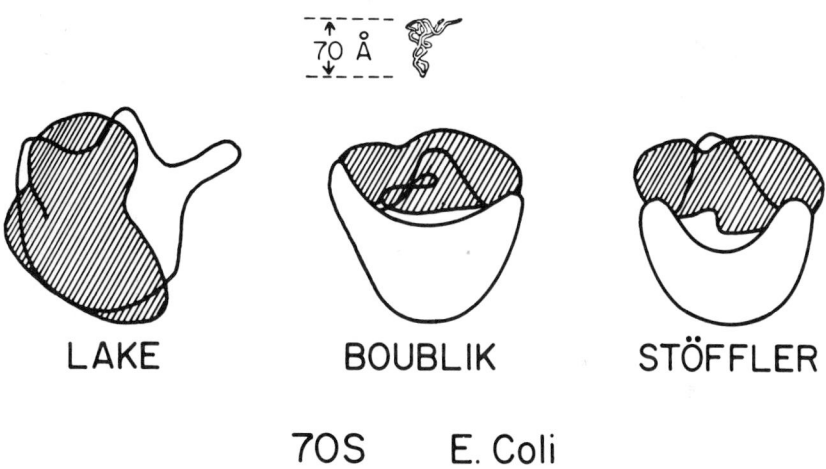

LAKE   BOUBLIK   STÖFFLER

70S   E. Coli

FIGURE 1. Postulated structures for the *E. coli* 70S ribosome. The three structural diagrams are taken from Lake,[3] M. Boublik *et al.*,[4,38] and Brimacombe *et al.*[5] The tRNA structure is the crystal structure of yeast tRNA^{Phe}.[6] All are drawn to the same scale. From Kuechler and Ofengand,[7] by permission.

anticodon, by the use of affinity and photoaffinity labeled mRNA analogs (for a recent compilation of these results, see Kuechler and Ofengand[7] and Ofengand[35]).

Instead of examining the two ends of the tRNA, which, perforce, must be close together in both the A and P sites, our laboratory has focused its attention on the central region, which is expected to show the maximum movement upon translocation. By modifying specific bases in this region with appropriate photoaffinity probes, we have been able to obtain information about its position when bound at either the A or the P site.

STEREOCHEMISTRY OF THE PROBES

The probes used are simple aryl azides, suitably activated to react readily with the functional groups of interest (FIGURE 2). APA- and APAA-Br were reacted with the

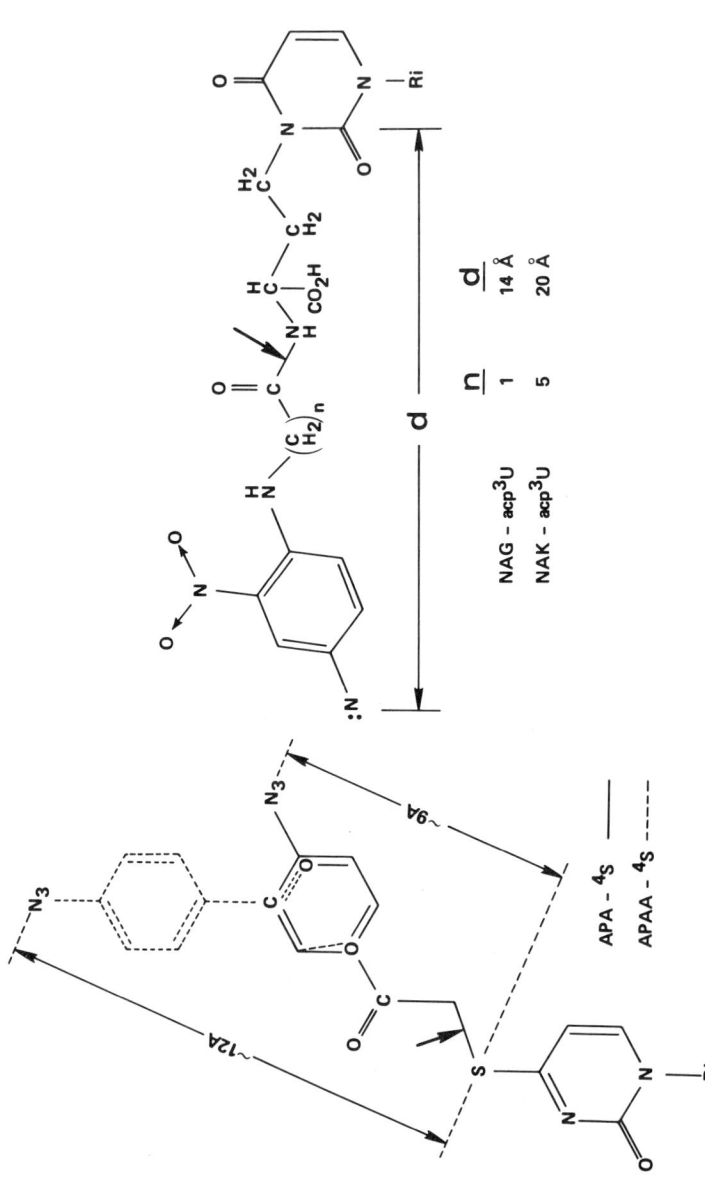

FIGURE 2. Structures of the aryl azide-modified minor bases. Left: S-(*p*-azidophenacyl)-4-thiouridine (APA-⁴S) (solid line) and its longer *p*-azidophenacylacetate analog (APAA-⁴S) (dashed line). Right: 6-(2-nitro-4-azidophenylamino)caproate (NAK) and N-(2-nitro-4-azidophenyl)glycine (NAG) derivatives of acp³U. The arrow shows the point of bond formation between the photoaffinity probe and the pyrimidine base.

-SH group of 4-thiouridine (^{4}S), while the N-hydroxysuccinimide-activated NAK and NAG were reacted with the free aliphatic NH_2 group of 3-(3-amino-3-carboxypropyl)uridine (acp^3U). The syntheses of these compounds and their reaction conditions are given in Ofengand *et al.*[10] The probes are located at a single site on a given tRNA molecule, since the particular minor bases we have chosen for study, ^{4}S and acp^3U, occur only once in a particular tRNA, and always at the same place in the sequence. In order to obtain some information about the distance relationships involved, we have used two probes at each site, which have the same reactive ends, but different lengths.

The stereochemistry of these probes in relation to the overall tRNA structure is shown in FIGURE 3. There are several points to note. First, the APA group fits readily into the tRNA structure, with the reactive nitrene pointed outward so that it can react with any nearby components. Second, its reactive end does not extend beyond the overall perimeter of the tRNA, so any cross-linking obtained must reflect a very close approach to the ribosomal surface. Third, although the APA probe is bound close to the body of the tRNA, it nevertheless defines one of its two topological surfaces, that on the right side in view b. Fourth, the reactive end of the NAG probe is freely available and defines the other topological surface of the tRNA, namely that to the left in view b. Fifth, since both nucleotides occur in the same tRNA, tRNA^{Phe} of *E. coli,* labeling each nucleotide separately should yield complementary information.

CROSS-LINKING WITH APA(A)-MODIFIED tRNA

Kinetics

When APA-modified Phe-tRNA (Phe-tRNA^{APA}) was bound to the ribosomal A site in the presence of EFTu and then irradiated, cross-linking occurred (FIGURE 4). Maximum cross-linking was reached in less than 5 min and was stable to further irradiation for at least 60 min. The analysis was performed by sucrose gradient centrifugation at 0.3 mM Mg^{++}, at which concentration the two ribosomal subunits separate and all noncovalently bound [^{3}H]Phe-tRNA is released. All of the observed cross-linking was to the 30S subunit (see FIGURE 5 below). Phe-tRNA^{APAA} also cross-links with the same kinetics (data not shown) and also only to the 30S subunit, but with one-half the yield (see TABLE 1).

Photochemical and Functional Specificity

As shown in TABLE 1, cross-linking at the A site was a true affinity probe–dependent reaction. There was no cross-linking in the absence of EFTu, and cross-linking required irradiation, polynucleotide, and the azido function on the probe, since phenacyl-modified (PA) tRNA was ineffective. Contrary to our expectations, the longer APAA probe did not give more covalent linking, but less. This may have resulted from the greater rotational freedom in the longer probe, which placed the reactive nitrene in an orientation less favorable for reaction.

Although the APA-modified tRNAs were always found to be more than 90% derivatized at the 4-thiouridine residue,[10] the low percentage of covalent linking

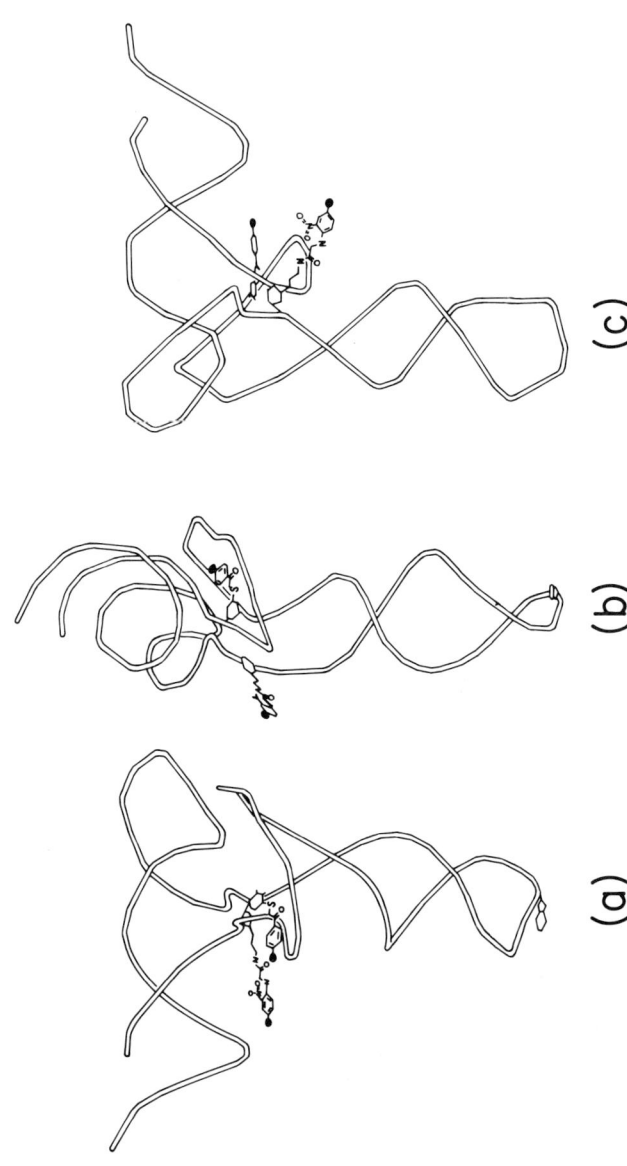

(a)   (b)   (c)

FIGURE 3. The stereochemistry of APA and NAG when attached to tRNA: three views of the structure of yeast tRNA$^{Phe 6}$ with NAG-acp^{3}U$_{47}$ in place of U$_{47}$ and APA-^{4}S in place of U$_8$. In views (a) and (b), APA-^{4}S is on the right and in view (C), it is the upper structure. The continuous double line shows the ribose phosphate backbone. APA and NAG, drawn to scale, are shown in their maximally extended forms. Other, less extended, conformations are also possible, as a result of bond rotations. The azide group (solid balls) is not to scale. The 5′ anticodon base, Gm$_{34}$, is shown in views (a) and (b). From Kuechler and Ofengand,[7] by permission.

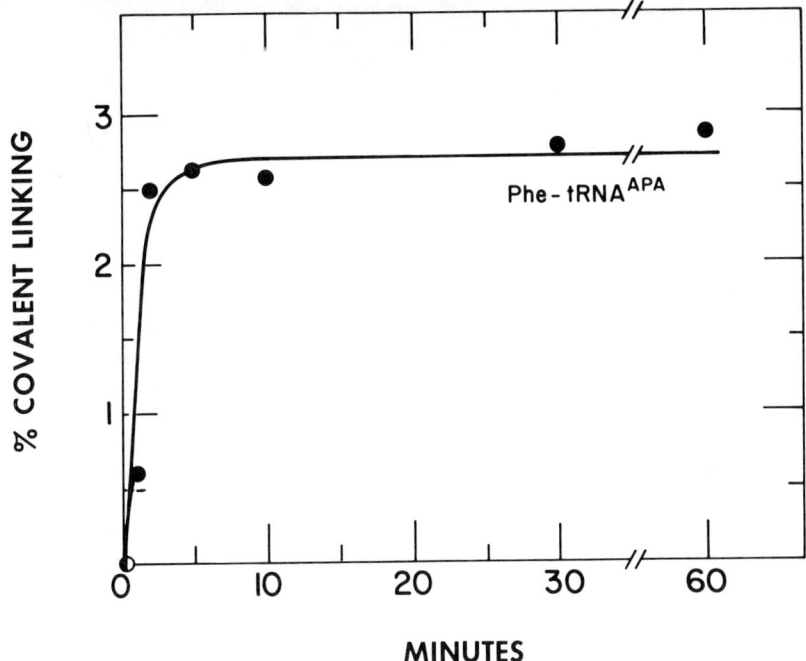

MINUTES

FIGURE 4. The kinetics of covalent cross-linking of Phe-tRNA^{APA} to the ribosomal A site. Noncovalent complexes of (^{3}H)Phe-tRNA^{APA} bound at the A site were prepared[10] and irradiated at 0 °C with the 300 nm lamps of a Rayonet Srinivasan-type photochemical reactor equipped with a Mylar filter.[11] The filter selects only wavelengths above 310 nm (1% transmission at 309.8 nm). This apparatus produces an incident light intensity at the reaction tube of 0.44 μEinstein min^{-1} ml^{-1} (see TABLE 4). The percentage of covalent linking, the ratio of covalent to noncovalent binding times 100,[13,18] was determined by sucrose gradient analysis at 0.3 mM Mg^{++}. All of the cross-linking observed was to the 30S subunit.

TABLE 1

REQUIREMENTS FOR COVALENT LINKING OF APA- OR APAA-MODIFIED
Phe-tRNA TO THE RIBOSOMAL A SITE

Reaction Mixture	Noncovalent Binding Percentage	Covalent Linking Percentage
Complete, APA	83	2.8 ± 0.3
− irradiation	87	<0.1
− EFTu	2	<0.1
− mRNA	—	<0.1
+ EFG	76	<0.1
Complete, APAA	80	1.3 ± 0.1
Complete, PA	89	<0.1
Complete, XL-APA	64	0.1 ± 0.1

NOTE: tRNA^{Phe} was derivatized and aminoacylated as described in References 10, 12, and 13. After noncovalent A site binding with EFTu in the presence of a 50–60-fold molar excess of uncharged yeast tRNA^{Phe} to block EFTu-independent binding,[10] samples were irradiated and analyzed by sucrose gradient centrifugation. APA, APAA, or PA: Phe-tRNA modified on its ^{4}S with either the APA, APAA, or phenacyl group, as in FIGURE 2. XL-APA: tRNA whose ^{4}S$_{8}$ was first blocked by irradiation at 350 nm to cross-link ^{4}S$_{8}$ to C$_{13}$[14] and then reacted with APA-Br and aminoacylated. All of the cross-linking was solely to the 30S subunit.

obtained does not preclude the possibility that covalent linking may have come from a minor modification at another site in the tRNA, a site from which the probe underwent cross-linking with high efficiency. To test this possibility, the 4-thiouridine residue was first chemically blocked by photo-cross-linking to cytidine-13 (XL-tRNA).[14] (This is a highly specific reaction.) The XL-tRNA was then subjected to APA-modification, bound to ribosomes, and irradiated. As shown in the table, XL-APA–modified Phe-tRNA yielded only residual levels of cross-linking, indicating that >96% of the covalent linking detected was coming from APA-^{4}S.

Val-tRNA$_1^{Val}$, the major tRNA^{Val} species in *E. coli,* also has a ^{4}S residue in the same position as tRNA^{Phe}. It was modified with the APA and APAA groups and studied in a similar way. Overall, the A site covalent linking patterns were very similar, both qualitatively and quantitatively (data not shown). Thus, the interactions we have observed may be general for all A site–bound tRNA.

To show that that tRNA which became cross-linked was in a functional A site, the ability to form dipeptide was tested. Ac[^{3}H]Phe-tRNA was first placed in the P site, after which [^{14}C]Phe-tRNA^{APA} was added, by EFTu, to the A site. After incubation for peptide bond formation, the mixture was irradiated. Both [^{3}H] and [^{14}C] were found to be cross-linked to the 30S subunit only, in a ratio of, approximately, 1 mole of [^{3}H]Phe to 2 moles of [^{14}C]Phe. If the [^{14}C]Phe-tRNA was unmodified, no cross-linked [^{3}H] was found. Thus, a minimum of one-half the cross-linkable Phe-tRNA^{APA} must have been bound to a functional A site (data not shown).

As noted above, all of the observed cross-linking was to the 30S subunit. This is shown in FIGURE 5, which also illustrates the EFTu dependence cited above. Interestingly, the substitution of GTP by guanylyl 5'-methylene diphosphonate (GDPCP), a nonhydrolyzable analog of GTP that prevents the release of EFTu from the ribosomal complex,[15] completely blocked cross-linking. This result, which shows that the ribosome AA-tRNA complex formed in the absence of GTP hydrolysis is structurally different from the normal one, could be explained by the existence of a distinctive pre-A site, such as the R site postulated by Lake.[16] However, it is also possible that, since EFTu is presumably still associated with the tRNA-ribosome complex, it may simply be in the way. A third possibility is that the presence of the EFTu-GDPCP complex perturbs the tRNA and/or the ribosome enough to move the APA group away from contact with the 30S.

Cross-linking appears to be specific for the A site. When the A site–bound tRNA was treated with EFG before irradiation, cross-linking was abolished (TABLE 1, line 5), although noncovalent binding (to the P site) was retained. Direct cross-linking to the P site in the presence of initiation factors (IF), which site should, more properly, be called the initiation, or I site, was also attempted, but without success (TABLE 2). There was a low level of cross-linking to both subunits that was dependent both on the probe and on irradiation (data not shown). However, it appeared to be largely nonspecific, as judged both by the lack of effect of omission of IF and polyuridylic acid (poly (U)) and by the lack of reactivity with puromycin (tRNA cross-linked at the P site showed reaction with puromycin, as in FIGURE 7 and TABLE 3).

All of the 30S cross-linked tRNA was to ribosomal protein (data not shown). This was demonstrated by SDS-sucrose gradient centrifugation[13] and by centrifugation after treatment with 6 M urea. All of the acid-precipitable radioactivity was found at the top of the gradient, whereas the 16S RNA had moved almost to the bottom. The

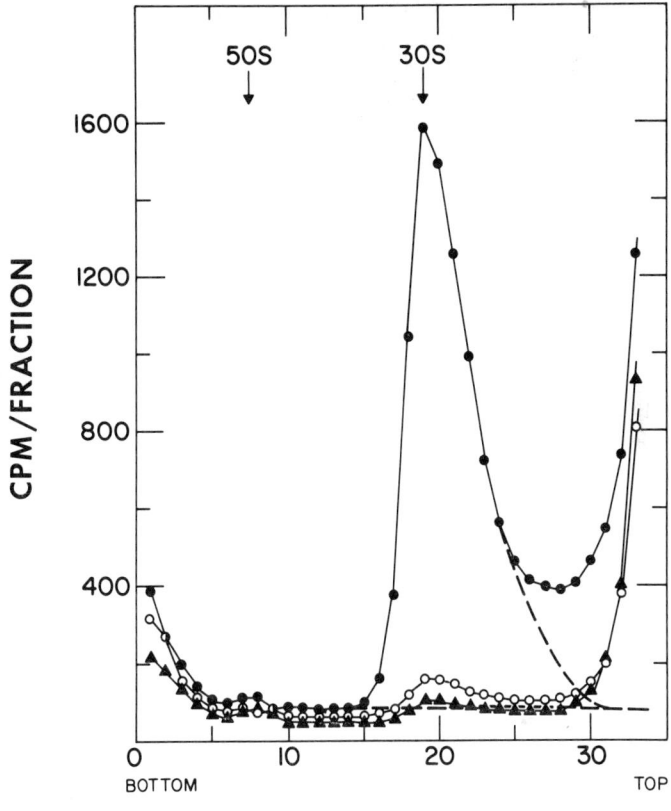

FRACTION NUMBER

FIGURE 5. The effect of replacement of GTP by GDPCP. Noncovalent complexes at the ribosomal A site were irradiated through the Mylar filter at 0 °C with 300 nm lamps. GTP (•), GDPCP (o), or no Tu-GTP (▲) were used as indicated. The sucrose gradient analysis was performed at 0.3 mM Mg^{++}. The dashed line indicates how the 30S peak (•) was quantitated. Noncovalent binding was 4.3, 2.0, and 0.38 pmol/A$_{260}$ unit of ribosomes for GTP, GDPCP, or no Tu-GTP, respectively. In the same order, the covalent cross-linking was 4.9%, 0.5%, and <0.1%.

cross-linked 30S protein was identified as solely S19 by immunological methods (L. Kahan and J. Ofengand, unpublished results).

CROSS-LINKING WITH NAK- OR NAG-MODIFIED tRNA

Photochemical Specificity

tRNA^{Phe} photoactivated by labeling with NAK on the opposite face of the tRNA (see FIGURE 3) could also be cross-linked to the ribosome. In this case, the labeling proceeded best from the I and P sites—both subunits were labeled. Cross-linking was

TABLE 2

ATTEMPTED CROSS-LINKING OF AcPhe-tRNA^{APA} TO RIBOSOMES
IN THE PRESENCE OF INITIATION FACTORS

	Covalent Linking Percentage			
	Without Puromycin		With Puromycin	
Reaction Mixture	30S	50S	30S	50S
Complete	0.8	0.4	0.5	0.2
Minus IF and poly (U)	0.9	0.2	0.9	0.2

NOTE: P site noncovalent binding at 5 mM Mg^{++} was performed at 30 °C for 20 min with initiation factors. 87% of the N-acetyl (Ac) Phe-tRNA^{APA} was noncovalently bound, of which 93% was released by puromycin incubation (1 mM, 15 min, 37 °C). In the absence of poly(U) and initiation factors, 13% binding occurred, none of which could be released by puromycin treatment. The extent of covalent linking was determined by sucrose gradient analysis.

dependent on the presence of the probe and on irradiation; prephotolysis of the probe blocked cross-linking (FIGURE 6). This experiment was done in the presence of the initiation factor required for tRNA binding to the I site, IF2, plus GTP, conditions that should lead to binding to the initiation site, since AcPhe-tRNA is known to be capable of mimicking fMet-tRNA in forming initiation complexes.[33]

Functional Specificity

The effect of binding AcPhe-tRNA^{NAK} to the P site in the absence of IF2 was examined, as was the use of GDPCP in place of GTP. Since GDPCP cannot be hydrolyzed, the release of IF2 from the ribosome is blocked.[17] The results are shown in FIGURE 7. As noted in the legend, noncovalent binding was equally effective with and without IF2, with either GTP or GDPCP. However, the cross-linking pattern was quite different: in the absence of IF2 (panel A), i.e., P site binding, roughly equal cross-linking to both subunits was obtained; when IF2 and GTP were added (panel B), cross-linking to both subunits decreased, but the 30S was most affected. On the other hand, when IF2 and GDPCP were used so that the IF2 molecule presumably remained ribosome-associated, there was a large increase in 50S cross-linking, with little or no effect on the 30S subunit. This situation is in direct contrast to that observed with APA at the A site, where the use of GDPCP blocked cross-linking. Most of the cross-linking was in a functional site, since the cross-linked tRNA could still react with puromycin, a characteristic of both P and I site binding.[10] The failure to achieve a better puromycin reaction with the cross-linked 50S in panel C is due to partial retention of IF2 on the ribosome under the conditions used. An extent of reaction comparable to that in panels A and B was obtained when IF2 was removed before puromycin treatment (data not shown).

A summary of the cross-linking results of FIGURE 6, FIGURE 7, and experiments not shown is given in TABLE 3, in which only the average values of several experiments are given for simplicity. We have noticed, however, that experiments involving IF2 with either GTP or GDPCP have given more variable results in quantitative terms than those without IF2, and IF2 plus GDPCP seems more variable than IF2 plus GTP. The reason for this is not clear.

TABLE 3 also shows that the NAG probe is similar to NAK, but with a 2–3-fold lower yield. This, again, contrasts with the APA experiments, in which the shorter probe gave more cross-linking.

Cross-linking was poly(U)-dependent, a test of functional specificity in addition to puromycin reactivity. This was true of both the 50S and the 30S cross-linking,

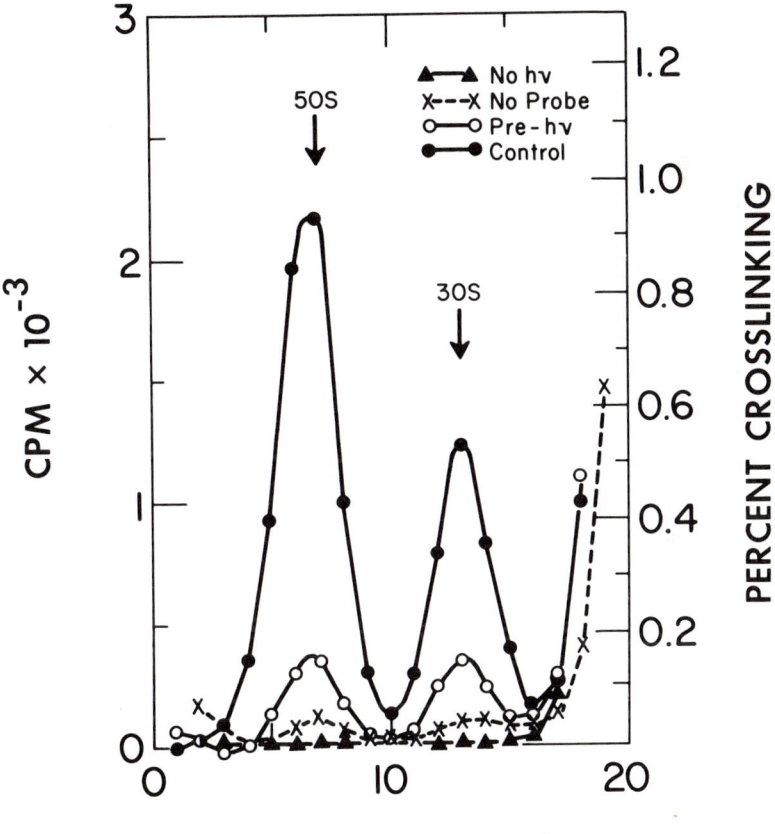

FRACTION NUMBER

FIGURE 6. Cross-linking of AcPhe-tRNA^{NAK} to both ribosomal subunits in the presence of IF2 and GTP. tRNA^{Phe}, derivatized with NAK just as for NAG,[10] aminoacylated, and acetylated,[13] was bound to the ribosomal P site.[10] The sample was irradiated for 20 min at 0 °C through a 4 cm solution filter of 1 M NaNO$_2$ with a 600 W incandescent lamp 6 cm away. Analysis was performed by sucrose gradient centrifugation at 0.3 mM Mg^{++}. ●——●: complete system containing IF2 and GTP; ▲——▲: complete system but unirradiated; x-----x: complete system irradiated but with unmodified AcPhe-tRNA replacing AcPhe-tRNA^{NAK}; o——o: complete system (ribosomes omitted) prephotolyzed for 60 min at 0 °C before addition of ribosomes, incubated at 30 °C for 60 min, and rephotolyzed for 20 min at 0 °C. The percentages of noncovalent binding were 86%, 86%, 52%, and 72%, respectively.

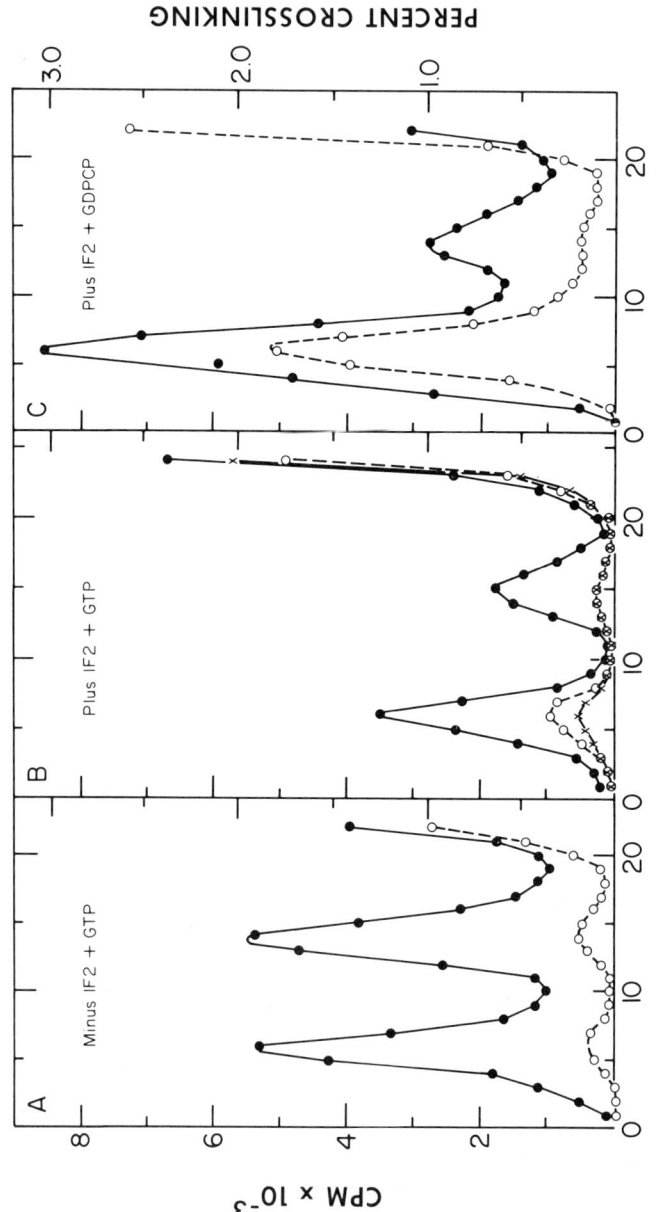

FIGURE 7. The effect of IF2, GDPCP, and puromycin on the extent of cross-linking. The binding, irradiation, and analysis were as described in FIGURE 6. Panel A: IF2 was omitted and GTP (0.2 mM) was present. Panel B: IF2 (0.14 μM) and GTP were present. Panel C: IF2 (0.27 μM) and GDPCP (0.4 mM) were present. ●: not treated with puromycin; ○——○: treated with 1 mM puromycin for 60 min (panels A and C) or 10 min (panel B) at 30°C *after* irradiation; x----x: treated with puromycin (1 mM, 10 min, 30°C) *before* irradiation. The percentages of noncovalent binding were 86, 80, and 81%, for panels A, B, and C, respectively.

although less obviously so for the 30S in the IF2 + GTP series. However, it should be noted that not only was the poly(U)-independent cross-linking four times greater than the puromycin-resistant fraction when poly(U) was present, but it was also largely puromycin-resistant as well. It seems likely that the 30S cross-linking observed in the absence of poly(U) is qualitatively different from that in its presence. The poly(U)-independent cross-linking to the 30S in the absence of IF2 was quite large, 62% of that in the presence of poly(U). However, as it is puromycin-resistant (data not shown), it probably is due to some type of nonspecific binding that is absent when poly(U) is present.

We also attempted to cross-link Phe-tRNA^{NAK} or Phe-tRNA^{NAG} to the A site.

TABLE 3

REQUIREMENTS FOR COVALENT LINKING OF NAK- OR NAG-MODIFIED
AcPhe-tRNA TO THE RIBOSOMAL P SITE

	Covalent Binding Percentage			
	Without Puromycin		With Puromycin	
Reaction Mixture	50S	30S	50S	30S
+ IF2 + GTP	4.2	2.4	1.0 (0.6)	0.4 (0.4)
− poly (U)	0.2	1.6	0.2*	1.3*
− NAK	0.1	0.1		
− NAK, + NAG	1.4	1.1	0.5 (0.2)	0.2 (0.1)
− light	<0.1	<0.1		
Prephotolyzed†	0.5	0.5		
+ IF2 + GDPCP	13.7	2.9	7.6‡	0.5‡
− polyU	0.3	0.8		
− IF2 + GTP	7.2	6.8	0.4	0.6
− polyU	0.4	4.2		
− IF2 + GDPCP	6.0	5.2		

NOTE: Binding, with additions or omissions as indicated; irradiation for 20 min; and sucrose gradient analysis were carried out as described above. After irradiation, samples were treated with puromycin (1 mM) at 30 °C for 10 min (IF2 + GTP series) or 60 min (others). Values in parentheses were obtained by carrying out the puromycin treatment *before* irradiation.
*Poly(U) was added back before puromycin incubation.
†As in the legend to FIGURE 6.
‡GTP, 2 mM, was added to the 0.4 mM GDPCP-containing solution at the same time as puromycin in order to attempt nucleotide exchange and release of IF2.

Noncovalent binding proceeded without difficulty, a fact established for NAG some years before.[10] However, there was no significant EFTu- or poly(U)-dependent cross-linking, although there was some apparently nonspecific reaction with both subunits that required the presence of the arylazide as well as photoactivation. At this stage of our work, we are inclined to believe that cross-linking from NAK- or NAG-acp^{3}U is largely a P and I site phenomenon.

Only preliminary studies have been done so far on the further location of the cross-linking site. All of the 30S cross-linking occurred to ribosomal proteins, not to the 16S RNA. The 50S cross-linking was to both 23S RNA and protein.

CROSS-LINKING OF UNMODIFIED tRNA

Photochemical and Functional Properties

Several years ago, we reported that Val-tRNA^{APA} in the P site could be cross-linked in rather high yield to 16S RNA by irradiation above 310 nm.[18] We assumed that the photoactive APA-^{4}S residue was the site of cross-linking in the tRNA because Val-tRNA^{PA} did not cross-link. Subsequently, however, it was found that the APA-^{4}S residue was not involved. Various nonphotoreactive derivatives of ^{4}S in tRNA^{Val}, including PA-^{4}S, did not block the cross-linking reaction, and, ultimately, we showed that ^{4}S-free Val-tRNA was as active as ^{4}S-containing tRNA.[13]

As illustrated in FIGURE 8, cross-linking occurred with single-hit kinetics both in the presence and in the absence of ^{4}S; the final yield, 60–70% of the noncovalently bound tRNA, was also the same.

A crude type of action spectrum analysis was then performed by measuring the rate of cross-linking with different cut-off filters and different lamps (TABLE 4). Shorter wavelengths were more effective in producing tRNA-ribosome cross-links. The 310 nm filter depressed the reaction rate 7-fold while only decreasing the incident light intensity by a third. Cross-linking was induced more than three times faster by 300 nm + M irradiation than by 350 nm + M irradiation, even though the longer wavelength lamps supplied six times more photons. When the 323–324 nm filter (N)

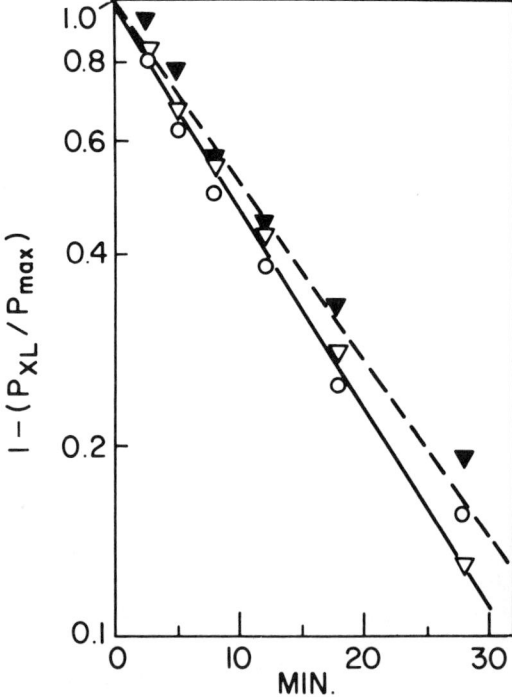

FIGURE 8. The kinetics of cross-linking of unmodified AcVal-tRNA to the ribosomal P site. Ribosomal P site complexes were formed; irradiated for the times indicated in the legend to FIGURE 4, but without the Mylar filter; and analyzed by cellulose nitrate filter adsorption in 0.1 mM MG^{++}.[11,13] o: AcVal-tRNA (preparation 1); ∇: AcVal-tRNA (preparation 2); ▼: thiouridine-free[13] AcVal–tRNA (preparation 2). Noncovalent binding was 44, 33, or 34 pmol/ml, and 67, 61, and 64% of each preparation, respectively, could be cross-linked. The data are plotted semilogarithmically, where P_{XL} is the percentage of cross-linking and P_{max} is the plateau level of cross-linking. From Ofengand *et al.*[11] Reprinted with permission from *Biochemistry*.

TABLE 4

RATE OF CROSS-LINKING UNDER DIFFERENT IRRADIATION CONDITIONS

Irradiation Condition	Light Intensity* μEinstein min^{-1} ml^{-1}	Initial Rate of Cross-Linking† Percentage of maximum/h
300 nm	0.63	408
300 nm + M	0.44	57
300 nm + M + N	0.39	5
300 nm + M + Pb	0.27	1
350 nm	2.9	58
350 nm + M	3.0	17
350 nm + M + N	2.1	4

*Measured by ferrioxalate actinometry. In this irradiation arrangement, photon absorption was proportional to the volume of solution irradiated over the range studied. 300 and 350 nm identify the two sets of lamps supplied with the photochemical reactor. M; Mylar plastic filter; N: 4% napthalene in hexane; Pb; 1.2 M lead nitrate in water. The wavelengths for 1% transmission (1 cm) were 310, 323, and 331 nm, respectively. For details, see Reference 11.

†The initial slope of the plots of the percentage of cross-linking at 0 °C versus time, divided by the maximum percentage of cross-linking obtained, times 100.

was used with the 300 nm lamps, the reaction rate decreased 80-fold, with only a 40% decrease in incident light intensity. Light above 331 nm (Pb filter) did not induce cross-linking. These results indicate that the optimum wavelengths for cross-linking lie below 310 nm and that wavelengths above 324 nm are ineffective. Since reasonable rates of reaction could be obtained at > 310 nm, we chose to conduct most of the subsequent experiments at these wavelengths in order to minimize any potential short wavelength uv damage to the tRNA or the ribosomes.

This direct cross-link between unmodified tRNA and 16S RNA is, in effect, a probe of zero length, and therefore, must give information about a very close encounter between tRNA and ribosomal RNA. Because there was no obvious nucleotide candidate for excitation by the active wavelengths other than the ^{4}S residue in either the reactive tRNAs or rRNA, some simple photochemical properties were examined. The first was sensitivity to prephotolysis (FIGURE 9).

This is usually done by irradiating the components separately. However, since no covalent linking occurs in the absence of polynucleotide, as was shown in Reference 13 and confirmed in FIGURE 9, the experiment could be done in a simpler way. A mixture of tRNA and ribosomes without poly(U$_2$,G) was irradiated, poly(U$_2$,G) was added, the mixture was incubated for 1–2 min to allow complex formation to occur, and reirradiated (solid circles). Clearly, the 140 min of prephotolysis had no effect on either the rate or yield of the reaction. It also had almost no effect on noncovalent binding (> 80% retained). Moreover, if the second irradiation was omitted (solid triangles), there was no cross-linking.

This experiment produced two important conclusions. First, the excitable residue was not decomposed by irradiation in the absence of an acceptor, but, apparently, simply returned to the ground state. This may account for the unusually high yields of covalent products—there is no destructive reaction. Second, because irradiation was needed at the second step, reaction did not occur via a long-lived chemical intermediate generated by irradiation that was only able to form a covalent bond when

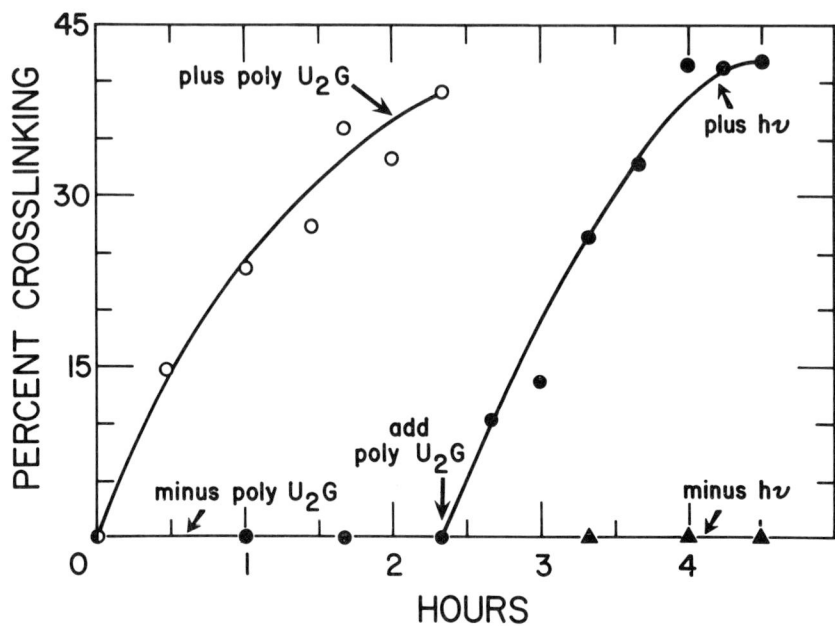

FIGURE 9. Prephotolysis of AcVal-tRNA plus ribosomes in the absence of poly(U₂,G). Ribosomal P site complexes were formed either with poly(U₂,G) (○) or without poly(U₂,G) (●), producing 76 pmol/ml and < 0.8 pmol/ml of noncovalent complexes, respectively. Both tubes were irradiated through a Mylar filter with 300 nm lamps for the indicated times. At 140 min irradiation, poly(U₂,G) was quickly added to the tube lacking poly(U₂,G) to give the standard concentration, the tube was incubated 5 min at 37 °C, and chilled to 0 °C. One part was reirradiated (●), while the other part was kept on ice in the dark (▲). Noncovalent binding for the second incubation corresponded to 62 pmol bound per ml (82% of the first incubation). The total 4.5 h irradiation had no effect (< 4%) on the TCA precipitability of the AcVal-tRNA in the mixture. From Ofengand *et al.*[11] Reprinted with permission from *Biochemistry*.

noncovalent complex formation was induced by the subsequent addition of poly(U₂,G).

Several other properties, photochemical and biochemical, are listed below. For details, see Ofengand *et al.*[11]

1. Only certain unmodified tRNAs could be cross-linked.

2. Cross-linking required the presence of the same mRNA codons as did noncovalent binding.

3. The cross-linked AcAA-tRNA could still react with puromycin; therefore, the cross-linked tRNA was in the P site.

4. The same AA-tRNA bound in the A site (by EFTu) did not cross-link.

5. Cross-linking was not affected by free radical or triplet state quenchers such as O₂, thiols, or ascorbate.

6. Cross-linking occurred exclusively to 16S ribosomal RNA.

Site of Cross-Linking in tRNA

The tRNA specificity cited above is shown in TABLE 5, in which cross-linking activity is correlated with the nucleotide sequence for each tRNA. From this, we have deduced the site of attachment by the following argument.[11] We assume that there is a single site that can cross-link and that it is located at the same place in all reactive tRNAs. The evidence for a single cross-link is circumstantial, being based on the single-hit kinetics of cross-linking that have been found in all our experiments, e.g., FIGURE 8. The evidence that the single cross-link is always in the same place is that the three most active tRNAs cross-link exclusively to 16S RNA, to the 8S fragment of 16S RNA, and to the same-sized denatured fragment of the 8S piece.[19] We also assume that 4-thiouridine is not involved. This has been tested only for *E. coli* tRNA$_1^{Val}$ (FIGURE 8; also Schwartz and Ofengand[13]), but if the first two assumptions are valid, then the lack of involvement of 4-thiouridine should be true for all tRNAs. It is clearly valid for FU-tRNA$_1^{Val}$, tRNA^{Val} (*B. subtilis*), and tRNA^{Thr} (*B. subtilis*), which do not contain 4-thiouridine.[20-22,35] We further assume that the observed specificity is due to the presence or absence of some common feature of nucleotide sequence and is not a consequence of a unique conformational property in some particular region of the tRNA molecule that is shared by a particular subset of tRNAs. The analysis has been done by two partially independent methods that are described in detail below.

Method A

The failure of FU-tRNA$_1^{Val}$ to react suggested that the reactive residue in the tRNA was uridine-derived, as all uridine and uridine-derived residues are replaced by 5-fluorouridine in this tRNA[20,21] and no gross conformational changes occur upon

TABLE 5

COMPARISON OF tRNA SEQUENCES TESTED FOR THE ABILITY TO CROSS-LINK
TO THE RIBOSOMAL P SITE

tRNA	Cross-Linking Percentage	Residue Number						
		7	29	34	47	59	64	65
Val$_1$ (*E. coli*)	45	U	U	cmo^{5}U	U	U	U	U
Val (*B. subtilis*)	45	U	U	mo^{5}U	U	G	U	U
Val$_2$ (*E. coli*)	1.3	G/A	A	G	acp^{3}U	C	C/A	G
Val$_1^{FU}$ (*E. coli*)	5.0	F	F	F	F	F	F	F
Phe (*E. coli*)	0.5	A	G	G	acp^{3}U	U	A	C
Met$_f$ (*E. coli*)	0.5	G	G	C	U	A	G	C
Ser$_1$ (*E. coli*)	24	G	G	cmo^{5}U	U	A	U	G
Thr (*B. subtilis*)	17	G	U	mo^{5}U	U	G	C	G

NOTE: The cross-linking activity given for each of the tRNAs is the maximum obtained under comparable assay conditions. Residues are listed according to a scheme in which the nucleotide positions common to yeast tRNA^{Phe} are numbered consecutively from the 5′ end.[23] tRNA sequence data was taken from Siddiqui *et al.*,[23] except for FU-tRNA$_1^{Val}$[20] and *B. subtilis* tRNA^{Val}.[34] From Ofengand *et al.*[11] Reprinted with permission from *Biochemistry*.

fluorouracil substitution.[20] When the 4-thiouridine and uridine residues also found in tRNA$_2^{Val}$ (inactive) were eliminated, the seven positions listed in TABLE 5 remained. Comparison with the inactive species, tRNA$_f^{Met}$ and tRNA^{Phe}, eliminated 47 and 59. Comparison of tRNA$_1^{Ser}$ (active) with tRNA^{Phe}, tRNA$_f^{Met}$, and tRNA$_2^{Val}$ for common residues eliminated all of the original seven positions except 34 and 64. A similar comparison of tRNA^{Thr} (active) versus the inactive tRNAs eliminated all but 29, 34, and 59. The only residue common to all three lists was 34.

Method B

We compared the sequence of *E. coli* tRNA$_1^{Val}$ with tRNA$_2^{Val}$, tRNA^{Phe}, and tRNA$_f^{Met}$, noting all those *positions* where the nucleotide found in tRNA$_1^{Val}$ was not found in one of the inactive tRNAs. There were twelve such positions. *B. subtilis* tRNA^{Val} had the same nucleotides at these positions as *E. coli* tRNA$_1^{Val}$. A similar comparison of tRNA$_1^{Ser}$ and *B. subtilis* tRNA^{Thr} with tRNA$_2^{Val}$, tRNA^{Phe}, and tRNA$_f^{Met}$ was then made, and the two lists so generated were compared with the list of twelve positions from the tRNA$_1^{Val}$ comparison. Only three positions, 6, 32, and 34, were found in all three lists. In two of these cases, A$_6$ and C$_{32}$, the same nucleotide was found in *E. coli* tRNA$_1^{Val}$ (active) as in FU-tRNA$_1^{Val}$ (inactive), leaving only residue 34 as the candidate for the reactive residue, the same as was determined by Method A. This residue is the 5'-anticodon base located at the tip of the anticodon loop. It corresponds to Gm$_{34}$ in FIGURE 3 and is the most exposed residue in that area of the molecule.

Site of Cross-Linking in Ribosomal RNA

Partial T$_1$ RNase digestion of the Ac[^{3}H]Val-tRNA–16S RNA covalent complex showed that all the cross-linking was to the 3'-one-third (8S) fragment of the 16S RNA molecule, but not to the 3'-terminal 48 nucleotides.[19] Colicin E3 treatment, which specifically cleaves the 3'-terminal 48mer from the 16S RNA, was also used to show that this fragment, which contains the mRNA recognition region,[24] was not involved.[19] Examination of the tRNA-8S fragment by denaturing gel electrophoresis to reveal hidden nuclease cuts showed only a single band, which corresponded in position to an oligonucleotide 150–200 residues in length. Since the tRNA must have been intact at least from the cross-link site to its [^{3}H]valine-bearing 3' end, the mRNA fragment must have been 75–150 residues long. This should be quite adequate for positioning in the now known sequence of 16S RNA.[25,26] This work is now in progress. The same results were also found for the *B. subtilis* Val-tRNA and Ser-tRNA covalent complexes.[19] Thus, it is likely that all of the reactive tRNAs are cross-linked to the same, or nearly the same, place on 16S RNA.

Is the tRNA Directly Linked to Ribosomal RNA?

In any complex system in which cross-linking occurs, it is important to ask whether the two components studied are attached to each other directly, or by a third,

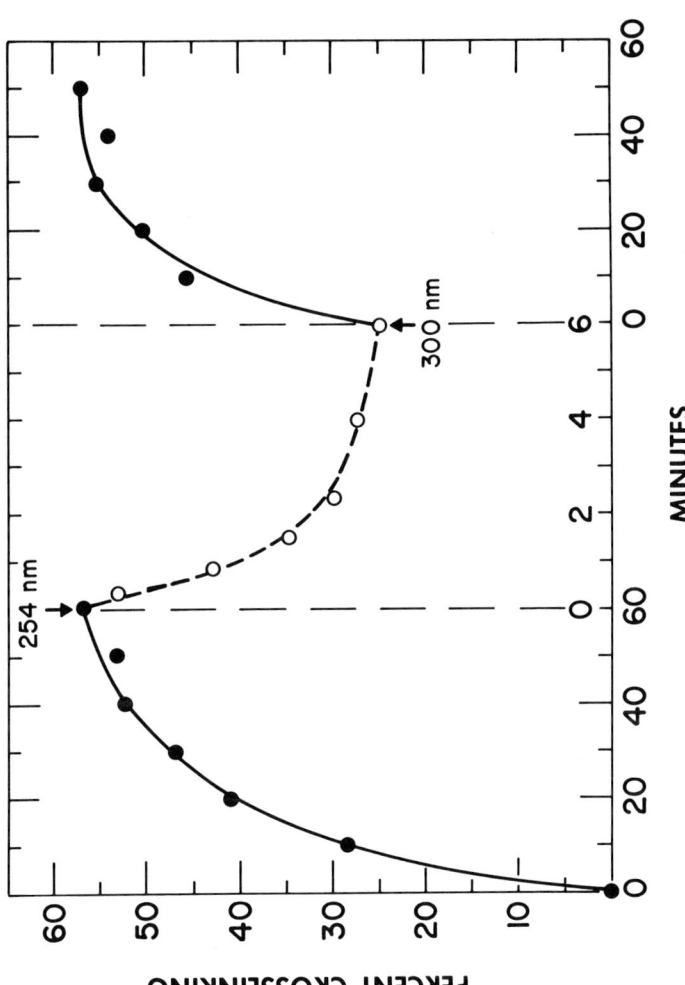

FIGURE 10. The reversibility of cross-link formation by uv light. Ribosomal P site complexes, formed with 8 A_{260} units/ml of tight couple ribosome and 84 nM AcVal-tRNA (66% noncovalently bound), were irradiated with 300 nm lamps without the Mylar filter. Samples (●) were assayed for cross-link formation. At 60 min, the sample was transferred to a 12 mm i.d. quartz tube placed in the center of a second Rayonet reactor with the glass cooling chamber removed and irradiated, with stirring, for up to 6 min with 254 nm lamps. The incident light intensity was 0.9 μEinstein min^{-1} ml^{-1}. Samples (○) were assayed as before. At 6 min, the samples were transferred back to the original irradiation system and reirradiated. the level of noncovalent binding remained constant throughout the experiment, being 56, 57, and 62 nM for the first, second, and third irradiations, respectively.

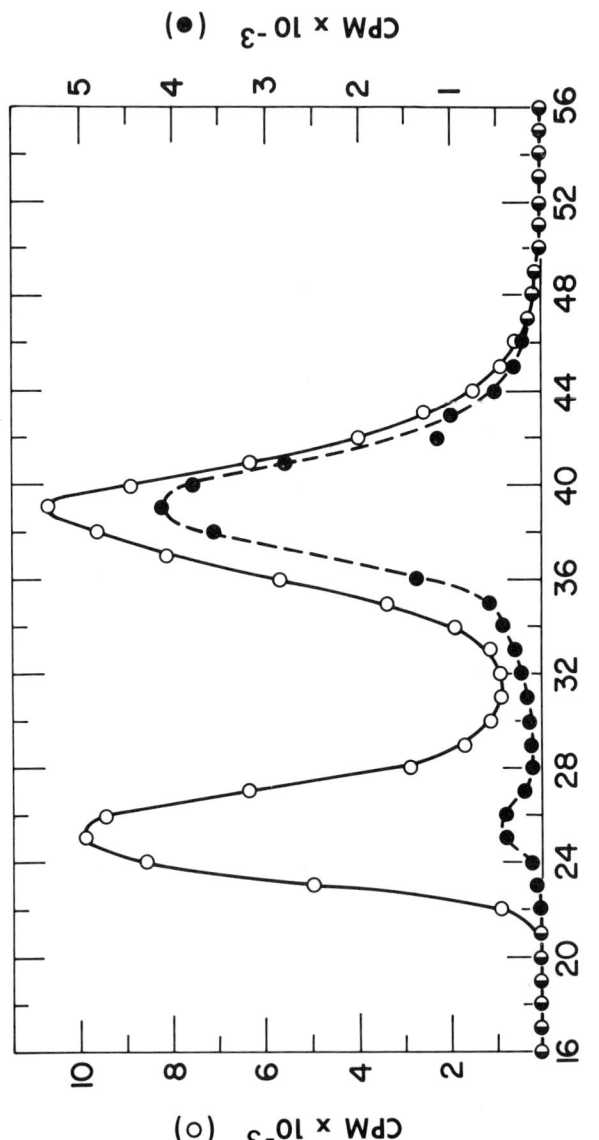

FIGURE 11a. Separation of cross-linked from un-cross-linked tRNA by gel filtration: Cross-linked ribosome-tRNA complexes were prepared by incubation and irradiation (300 nm lamps with a Mylar filter) for 2.5 h. The reaction mixture was chromatographed on Sephacryl S-200 with 50 mM Hepes (pH 7.5), 50 mM NH$_4$Cl, and 0.3 mM MgCl$_2$ (o). The first peak, the ribosome-tRNA complex, contained 42% of the total tRNA present. When unirradiated complex was examined (•), no peak of ribosome-associated tRNA was found.

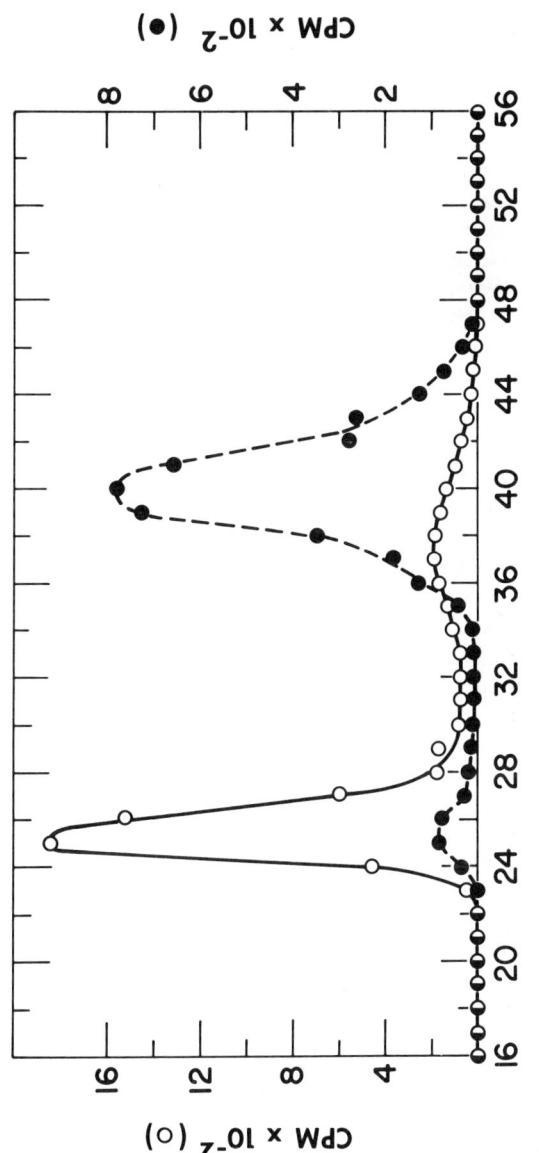

FIGURE 11b.   Separation by gel filtration of tRNA split off by uv irradiation from ribosome-tRNA complexes. After 10 min uv irradiation, as described in FIGURE 12, an aliquot of the ribosome-tRNA complex was chromatographed on Sephacryl S-200, exactly as in FIGURE 11a. (●): 10 min irradiation with 254 nm lamps; (○): sample not irradiated at 254 nm.

undetected, molecule (in our case, either ribosomal protein(s) or the polynucleotide mRNA). If mRNA were the spacer, it could be cross-linked to the 16S RNA at almost any site and little topological information about tRNA would be obtainable from this study. We tested this possibility by using the trinucleotide codon, GpUpU, as a substitute for the polynucleotide. Irradiation of both types of complexes gave the same rate and yield of cross-linking.[11] This experiment shows that, even if the codon is part of the covalent complex, the two linkage points can be, at most, two nucleotides apart. More recent experiments, using radioactive polynucleotide, have shown that no codons of mRNA are present in the complex.[36]

The tRNA-8S fragment described in the preceding section was used to show the absence of a protein linker, since we reasoned that a protease should have the best chance to reach the putative protein spacer in an already partially degraded RNA complex. Denaturing gel electrophoresis examinations of the products of digestion with either pronase or proteinase K (10 μg/ml, 25 °C, 60 min) showed no significant change from controls.[19] We conclude that there is no protein link between tRNA and 16S RNA.

Photolysis of the Covalent Link

Covalent bond formation could be reversed by short wavelength irradiation. We chose 254 nm light for this experiment because the well-known reversible cleavage of thymine dimers in DNA can be effectively carried out at this wavelength.[27] tRNA–16S RNA covalent complexes were prepared, from which the RNA was isolated and then irradiated in a denaturing buffer. Analysis was made by gel filtration. There was a rapid and virtually complete photolysis of the complex, which obeyed single-hit kinetics for at least 85% of the reaction.[11]

Photolysis of tRNA-ribosome covalent complexes could also be shown (FIGURE 10). Cross-linking was first performed at > 310 nm, as usual. Irradiation at 254 nm resulted in a rapid cleavage, although complete splitting was not obtained. Probably other nonreversible cross-links between the noncovalently bound tRNA and the ribosome were formed concomitantly with the splitting of the preformed cross-link. The covalent link could then be reformed by reirradiation at > 310 nm. This experiment shows not only that the covalent link could be broken by uv irradiation, but also that the ribosomes were not damaged by either the 310 or 254 nm irradiation, since they could not only rebind the tRNA but reform the cross-link, as well. The ribosomes were the limiting reagent in this experiment.

Was the tRNA regenerated also? Since excess tRNA was present, new tRNA may have been cross-linked during the second > 310 nm irradiation. This possibility was examined in a separate experiment. Covalent complex was freed of noncovalently bound tRNA by gel filtration in 0.3 mM Mg^{++} (FIGURE 11a). Note that there was no ribosome-associated tRNA if irradiation was omitted. Irradiation of this complex at 254 nm rapidly split out 95% of the AcVal-tRNA with first order kinetics (FIGURE 12). As shown by gel filtration before and after 254 nm irradiation (FIGURE 11b), the tRNA was no longer associated with ribosomes. This irradiated mixture was used as a source of regenerated AcVal-tRNA for cross-linking to fresh ribosomes (FIGURE 13). Clearly, the regenerated tRNA (solid circles) was as active as untreated control

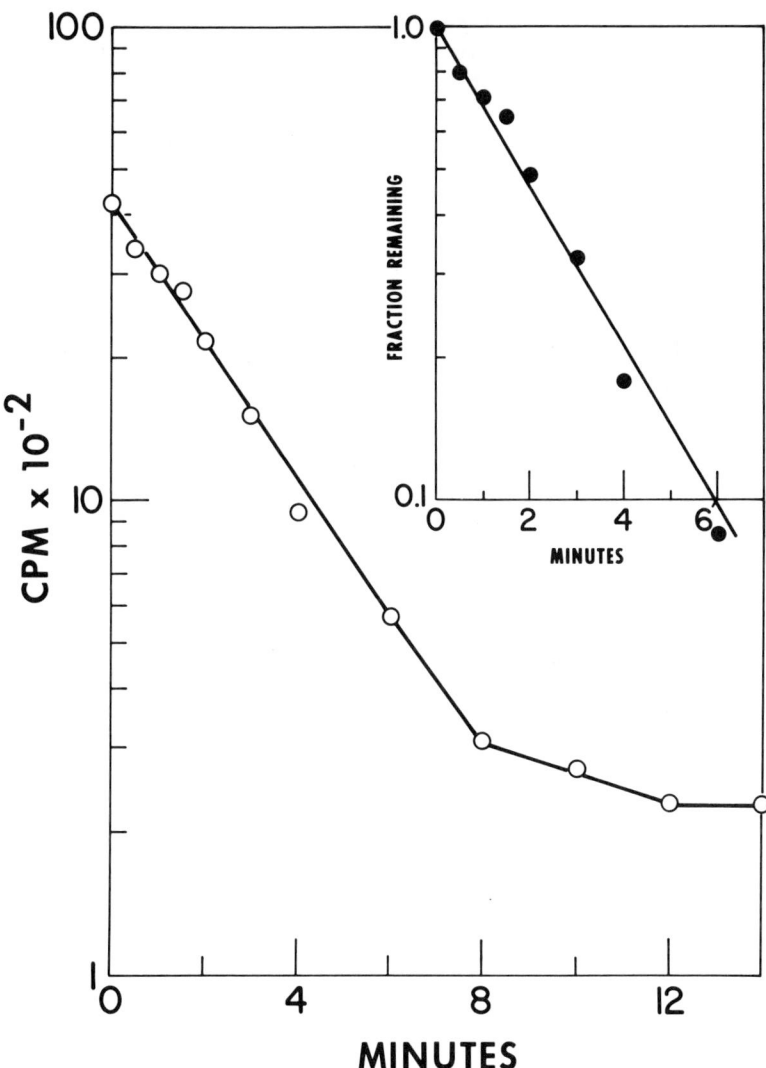

FIGURE 12. The kinetics of splitting of the ribosome-tRNA covalent link by 254 nm light. Fractions 23–27 from FIGURE 11a were pooled; the ribosome-tRNA complex (23.3 nM, A$_{260}$ = 3.0) was placed directly in a 12 mm i.d. quartz tube and irradiated with 254 nm lamps with stirring. The incident light intensity was 0.45 μEinstein min^{-1} ml^{-1}. Samples were assayed for covalently bound tRNA by filtration at 0.1 mM Mg^{++}. The open circles show the actual cpm found. The inset shows the same data corrected for the resistant fraction (4%). The T$_{1/2}$ was 1.9 min. There was no loss of TCA-precipitable cpm as a result of the 10 min irradiation.

tRNA (open circles) for cross-linking. Therefore, both the ribosome and tRNA are regenerated by uv-induced splitting of the covalent complex.

This result is important because the ability to be rapidly split by short wavelength uv light with regeneration of the original reactants is one of the characteristic features of Pyd-Pyd cyclobutane dimers that distinguish them from many other photochemically-induced nucleotide adducts. (See Reference 36 for further discussion). More recently, additional photochemical evidence for cyclobutane dimer formation has been obtained. Photolysis at 313 nm in the presence of various indole derivatives as sensitizer has shown that only those indoles which induce cyclobutane dimer cleavage are able to induce photolysis of the cross-link.[36]

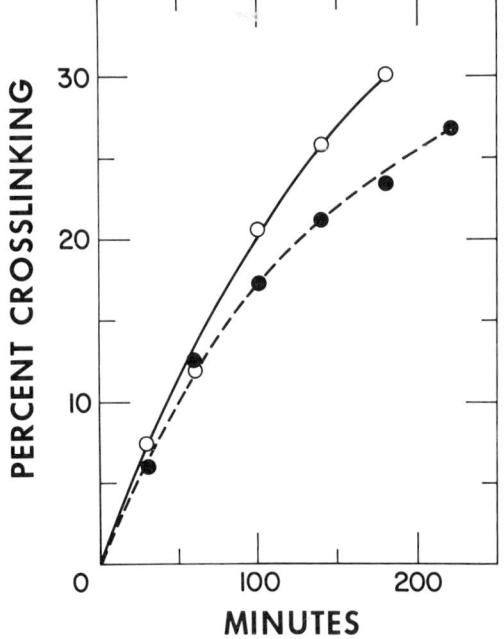

FIGURE 13. Cross-linking activity of AcVal-tRNA split off from the ribosome-tRNA complex by 254 nm light. Ribosome binding and irradiation with 300 nm lamps through the Mylar filter was done as described above. Control untreated AcVal-tRNA (o) was added at 28 nM and AcVal-tRNA that was split off from ribosomes by uv irradiation (•) was present at 22 nM. Regenerated AcVal-tRNA was prepared by irradiating the ribosome-tRNA complex fraction from the Sephacryl column of FIGURE 11a for 10 min under the conditions given in FIGURE 12. The irradiated mixture was used directly, without physically separating the split-off tRNA from the ribosomes, since FIGURE 11b showed that the splitting was almost complete. Additional ribosomes were added to ensure a ribosome excess. 61% of the control tRNA and 60% of the regenerated tRNA were noncovalently bound. There was no cross-linking after incubation without irradiation.

The common nature of the cross-link in each of the reactive tRNAs was examined by measuring the rate of photolysis of their respective tRNA-30S complexes. TABLE 6 shows that the rates of photolysis of three of the tRNA-ribosome complexes were essentially identical. In this connection, note that the reactive tRNA base is cmo^5U in *E. coli* $tRNA_1^{Val}$, but mo^5U in *B. subtilis* $tRNA^{Val}$. Also, while the codon for $tRNA_1^{Val}$

is GUG (poly(U_2,G) or GpUpU was used), that for Ser_1 is UCG (poly(U,C,A) was

used). The relatively constant rate of photolysis in all three cases suggests that the 5'-anticodon base of tRNA is directly connected to the same base of 16S RNA.

TABLE 6

RATE OF PHOTOLYSIS OF tRNA-RIBOSOME COVALENT COMPLEXES

tRNA	Rate Constant* min^{-1}
Val$_1$ (*E. coli*)	1.27
Val (*B. subtilis*)	1.18
Ser$_1$ (*E. coli*)	1.20

NOTE: Covalent ribosome-tRNA complexes were prepared by irradiation and freed of unreacted tRNA by gel filtration, as in FIGURE 11a. Photolysis with a light intensity of 0.22 μEinstein min^{-1} ml^{-1} was carried out as in FIGURE 12, and the rate constant was evaluated from a semilogarithmic plot of the data, after correction for the residual resistant fraction, as in the inset to FIGURE 12.

*The maximum rate constant obtained by photolysis of a sufficiently dilute sample.

Localization of the 30S Attachment Site by Electron Microscopy

Since the cross-link involves the anticodon of tRNA, it must mark the decoding region of the 30S subunit. Up to now, this site has only been visualized by affinity-labeling 30S proteins with mRNA analogs and then locating the antigenic sites for these proteins on the ribosome by immunoelectron microscopy. The ability to covalently attach tRNA to the 30S subunit via its anticodon (see above) created a unique opportunity to locate the decoding site directly.[28] The procedure used (FIGURE 14) was, first, acylation of the α-amino position of valine on Val-tRNA with the dinitrophenyl (DNP) group; second, linkage to the ribosome by irradiation, and third, after isolation of the 30S subunits, formation of 30S dimers by reaction with anti-DNP antibody. More than 97% of the attached DNP was on the α-NH$_2$ of valine; cross-linking was poly(U$_2$,G)-dependent, puromycin-sensitive, and exclusively to the 30S. No dimers were formed when an excess competing amount of free DNP was present or when the DNP group was left off the tRNA.

The dimers, which were 1:1 covalent complexes of tRNA and 30S, could then be separated from unreacted 30S by centrifugation. Upon examination in the electron microscope, monomers and dimers were found (FIGURE 15). The Y-shaped antibody served as a marker for the aminoacyl end of the tRNA, which is about 80 Å from the

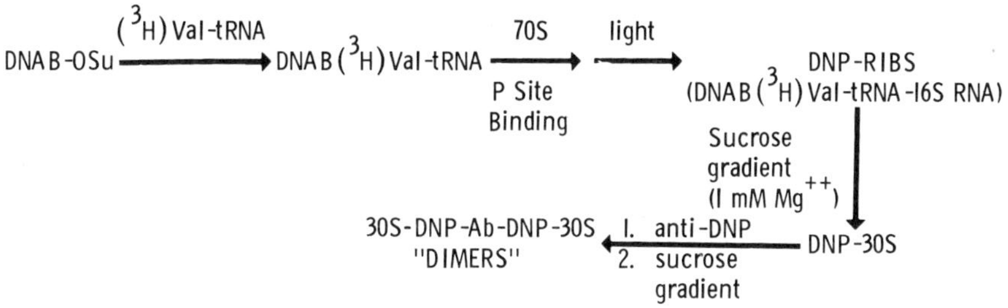

FIGURE 14. A flow diagram of the preparation of antibody-labeled 30S-tRNA complexes. DNAB: N-(γ-dinitrophenyl)aminobutyrate; OSu: N-hydroxysuccinimide.

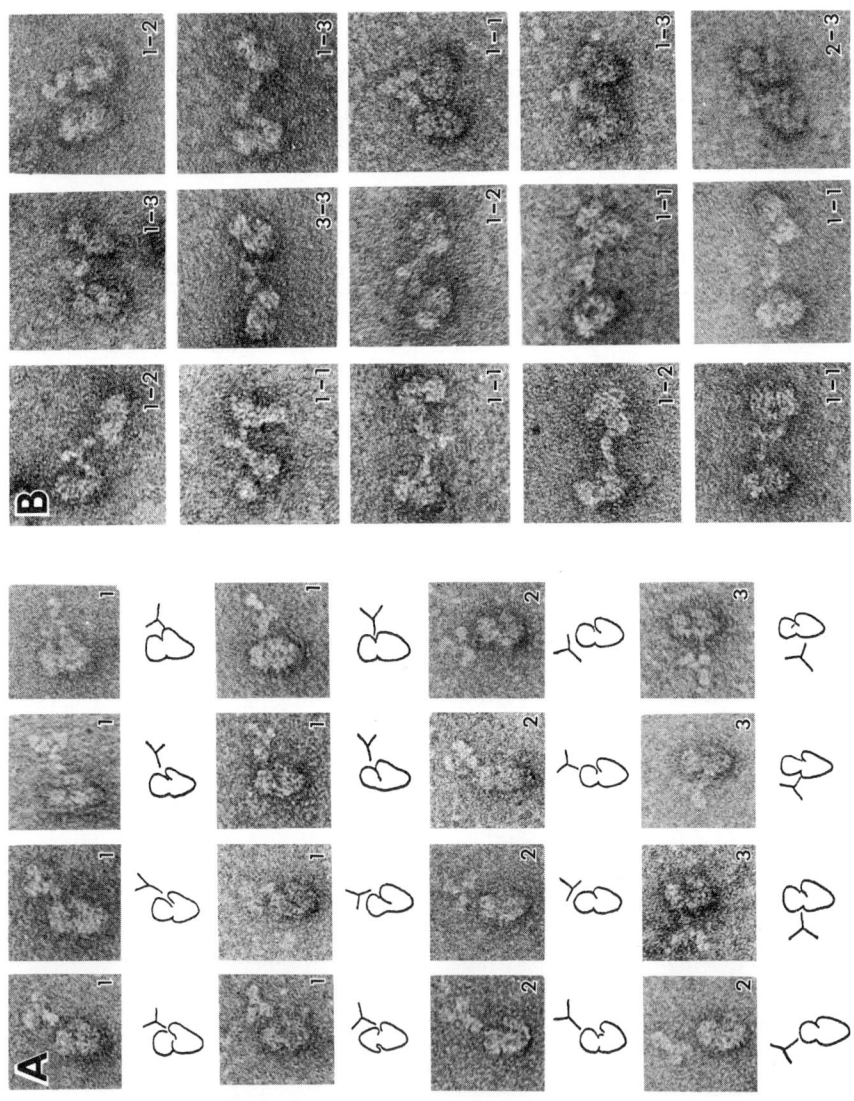

TABLE 7
DISTRIBUTION OF SITES OF ANTIBODY ATTACHMENT TO 30S SUBUNITS

Position	Percentage
1	61
2	21
3	15
4	3
5	<1

NOTE: The location of positions 1–3 on the 30S subunit is shown in FIGURE 15. Position 4 is below 3 on the same side of the subunit and position 5 is at the bottom tip of the 30S. A total of 500 particles were examined, 240 as antibody-30S monomers and 130 as antibody-30S dimers. Adapted from Keren-Zur *et al.*,[28] by permission.

actual site of cross-linking, assuming that the crystal structure of tRNA is preserved under these conditions (1 mM Mg^{++}). More than one attachment site for the antibody was found; they were distributed as shown in TABLE 7. Most of the antibody was attached to area 1, near the cleft and large projection, although some was also found attached to areas 2 and 3. By extrapolating 80 Å from each of the three major antigenic sites, the approximate common region of cross-linking was obtained. This area, in the cleft region, should be the decoding site.

DISCUSSION

Location of the Aminoacyl End and Anticodon Binding Regions

FIGURE 16 summarizes our current knowledge of the location of regions of the ribosome important for interaction with tRNA, as determined from affinity labeling experiments in combination with immunoelectron microscopy. The upper row shows the two current models of the 30S subunit. The proteins indicated by the circled numbers are the ones labeled by mRNA analogs and thus are presumptive markers of the decoding site. The Boublik[30] model of the 30S is similar to the Lake model, but is not shown because no protein locating has been done. The mRNA-associated proteins cluster on both models: on and around the platform in (a) and on the upper left crest in (b).

Our electron microscopic results are in good agreement with this localization to the upper one-third of the particle, and are particularly close to model (a). Our results also agree with the location of the 3'-third of 16S RNA, which was determined indirectly and indicated on the diagrams by plain numbers, since we found this region of the 16S RNA to be the one cross-linked to the tRNA anticodon. Thus, it seems

FIGURE 15. (*Facing page.*) Electron micrographs of 30S-tRNA covalent complexes with bound anti-DNP. The anti-DNP labels the aminoacyl end of the tRNA. A: monomers with interpretive drawings; B: dimers of 30S subunits with attached anti-DNP. The numbers on each electron micrograph identify the sites of antibody attachment. The magnification is 520,000× in every case. From Keren-Zur *et al.*,[28] by permission.

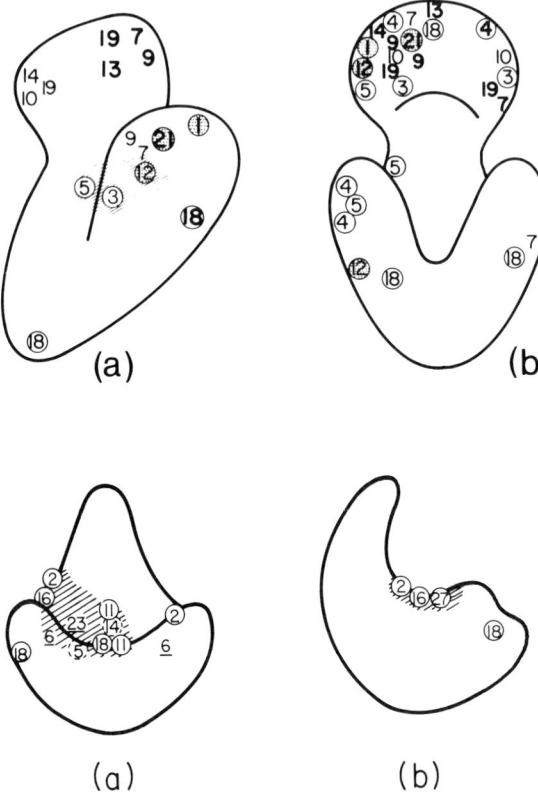

FIGURE 16. Proteins on the surface of the *E. coli* ribosome that are in the vicinity of tRNA, mRNA, or the 3′ segment of 16S RNA. Upper row: proteins of the 30S subunit that are near either mRNA or the 3′ region of 16S RNA. The location of the proteins and the overall shape of the particles were determined by immunoelectron microscopy according to (a) Lake[3] and Winkelmann and Kahan[29] and (b) Brimacombe *et al.*[5] The circled numbers locate proteins near mRNA, as determined by affinity and photoaffinity labeling with mRNA analogs. Plain numbers locate proteins associated with the 3′ third of the 16S RNA by affinity labeling as well as by other criteria, and stippled circles represent proteins with both properties. Boldface type signifies proteins on the surface toward the viewer and light type, those on the surface away from the viewer. Lower row: proteins of the 50S subunit that are in the vicinity of the peptidyl transferase center. The location of the proteins and shape of the particle are from Brimacombe *et al.*[5] (a) Front view. (b) Left side view. The numbers locate proteins near the peptidyl transferase center, as determined by affinity and photoaffinity labeling with analogs of aminoacyl-tRNA. The shaded area denotes the putative peptidyl transferase center. For further details and references, see Kuechler and Ofengand[7] and Ofengand.[39] Figures reproduced from Kuechler and Ofengand,[7] by permission.

fairly certain that the decoding region of the ribosome is located on or near the major cleft of the 30S particle.

The peptidyl transferase center (PTC) has been identified on the 50S particle by a similar localization of proteins affinity-labeled from the amino acid end of tRNA. This is indicated by the shaded areas in the diagrams in the bottom row of the figure. The arrangement of the decoding site and the PTC with respect to each other can be visualized by reference to FIGURE 1, from which it is clear that the distances involved can be spanned by a tRNA in the crystal structure conformation.

Arrangement of the Two RNAs on the Ribosome

What is the arrangement of the two RNAs with respect to each other? Where are their central regions located? Which is the P and which is the A site?

With respect to the first question, an important experiment has been recently performed by A. E. Johnson and C. Cantor.[37] By derivatizing the ⁴S of two different tRNAs with appropriate fluorescent groups and placing both tRNAs on the same ribosome, they were able to determine that the dyes were < 30 Å apart, that is, as close or closer than the thickness of a tRNA double helix. The simplest way to accomplish this while simultaneously keeping the amino acid ends close together and the anticodons adjacent is for the two tRNAs in the A and P sites to be side by side, and in the same orientation. This is an important conclusion. It can be easily visualized if one imagines FIGURE 3b in duplicate. It is then possible to ask which tRNA is in the P site and which is in the A site.

We suggest that the tRNA on the right in this imaginary figure is in the A site because the APA group could make contact with the ribosomal surface most readily from this tRNA. If the A site were on the left, the other tRNA would be in the way. The NAK probe results are in agreement with this notion. In this case, the tRNA on the left, i.e., in the P site, should be the one likely to make contact with the ribosome, since the probe is now on the opposite surface of the tRNA. Indeed, those were our

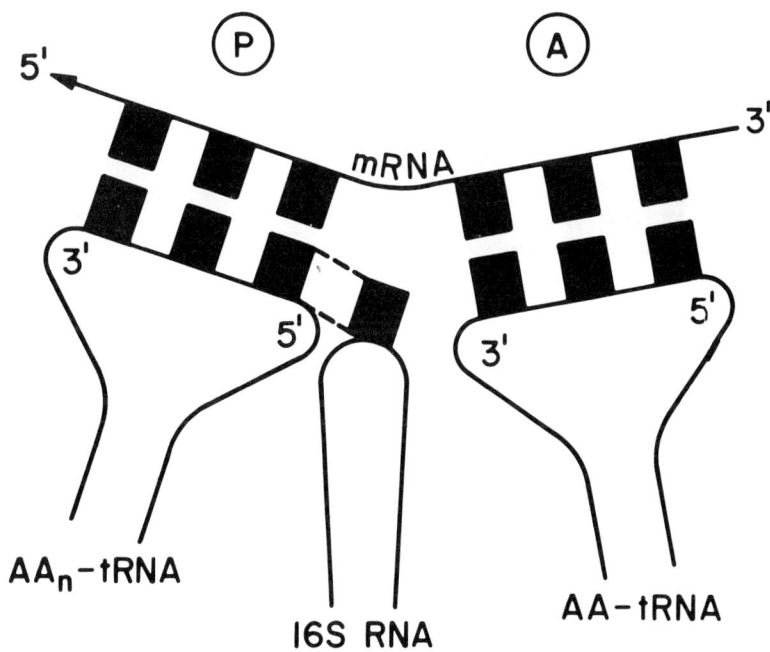

FIGURE 17. A schematic diagram of tRNAs in both P and A sites engaged in simultaneous translation of adjacent codons. AA$_n$-tRNA: peptidyl tRNA in the P site; AA-tRNA: amino-acyl-tRNA in the A site. The arrangement of tRNA and mRNA shown on the figure is dictated by the fact that mRNA is translated from the 5' to the 3' end,[31] and codon-anticodon base pairing is antiparallel.[32] The arrow shows the direction of mRNA movement past a stationary ribosome. A loop of 16S rRNA is inserted in such a way that one of its pyrimidine bases is brought sufficiently close to the 5' anticodon base of the P site–bound tRNA to allow cyclobutane dimer formation (dashed lines).

findings. P or I site–bound NAK-modified tRNA cross-linked readily, but A site–bound tRNA did not.

The facts that the APA (A site) probe was 30S specific and that the NAK (P site) probe was cross-linked to both subunits place additional strong constraints on how the two tRNAs can be arranged, but it is not possible to be more precise about the matter until some of the linkage points to the ribosome have been determined. It should also be noted here that our results with NAK-modified tRNA cross-linked both with and without IF indicate that there are structural differences between P and I sites even on the 70S ribosome. These differences have, so far, only been demonstrated at the quantitative level, but it is possible that they are a reflection of a qualitatively different pattern of cross-linking. The biggest difference was seen when IF2 dissociation from the ribosome was prevented. The presence of IF2, rather than quenching the cross-linking, potentiated it by somehow causing the NAK-acp^{3}U region of the P site–bound tRNA to more closely approach the 50S surface.

Rationale for the P Site–Specific Anticodon-Ribosomal RNA Interaction

The marked preference for cross-linking from the P site over that from the A site suggests that some special structural arrangement exists between the 5' end of the anticodon and 16S RNA at this site on the 30S subunit. A hypothesis for this interaction that would still allow codon-anticodon recognition to occur is shown in FIGURE 17. In this figure, we assume that base-pairing takes place at both the P and the A site simultaneously, although there is no strong evidence either for or against this (see Ofengand[39] for a further discussion of this point). The results obtained above show that a loop of 16S RNA must also be part of the decoding site, since cross-linking, probably by cyclobutane dimer formation, can occur (dashed lines). We suggest that it may be necessary to stabilize the anticodon of P site–bound tRNA either in addition to normal base-pairing or because of the lack of it. A loop of 16S RNA may have that specific function.

Conclusion

The unique feature of the photoaffinity labeling approach, which we have found very helpful, is the ability it confers to choose the time of covalent bond formation. This has allowed us to perform various functional tests before cross-linking and to select the point in the ribosome cycle to be examined. The identification of the ribosomal proteins or RNA cross-linked, and the exact placement of the cross-link, is then a straightforward, although tedious, process. However, while most of the ribosomal proteins have been located on the subunit by immunoelectron microscopy, the same is not true for ribosomal RNA. Moreover, many of the ribosomal proteins are elongated and have multiple antigenic sites on the ribosome (see the top row of FIGURE 16 for examples of this). Thus, it is not at all certain that an affinity probe cross-linked to a given protein is near any of its antigenic sites. Fortunately, the possibility of directly visualizing the point of cross-linking to the ribosome by the affinity immunoelectron microscopy approach (illustrated above for the anticodon cross-link) circumvents this problem. Thus, although we are still far from a complete understanding of how tRNA fits on the ribosome, there is every reason to believe that this approach will eventually provide the experimental basis for determining where the A and P sites are and how they function.

ACKNOWLEDGMENT

We wish to thank Richard Liou for his excellent technical assistance throughout this work.

REFERENCES

1. WATSON, J. D. 1964. Bull. Soc. Chim. Biol. **46:** 1399–425.
2. WEISSBACH, H. & S. PESTKA, Eds. 1977. Molecular Mechanisms of Protein Biosynthesis. Academic Press. New York.
3. LAKE, J. A. 1978. *In* Advanced Techniques in Biological Electron Microscopy II. J. K. Koehler, Ed.: 173–211. Springer-Verlag. Berlin and Heidelberg.
4. BOUBLIK, M., W. HELLMANN & A. K. KLEINSCHMIDT. 1977. Cytobiologie **14:** 293–300.
5. BRIMACOMBE, R., G. STÖFFLER & H. G. WITTMANN. 1978. Annu. Rev. Biochem. **47:** 217–49.
6. KIM, S. H., F. L. SUDDATH, G. J. QUIGLEY, A. MCPHERSON, J. L. SUSSMAN, A. H. J. WANG, N. C. SEEMAN & A. RICH. 1974. Science **185:** 435–40.
7. KUECHLER, E. & J. OFENGAND. 1980. *In* Transfer RNA: Structure, Properties, and Recognition. P. Schimmel, D. Soll, and J. Abelson, Eds.: 413–44. Cold Spring Harbor Laboratory. New York. In press.
8. BOCHKAREVA, E. S., V. G. BUDKER, A. S. GIRSHOVICH, D. G. KNORRE & N. M. TEPLOVA. 1971. FEBS Lett. **19:** 121–24.
9. PELLEGRINI, M., H. OEN & C. R. CANTOR. 1972. Proc. Nat. Acad. Sci. USA **69:** 837–41.
10. OFENGAND, J., I. SCHWARTZ, G. CHINALI, S. S. HIXSON & S. H. HIXSON. 1977. *In* Methods in Enzymology, Vol. 46. W. B. Jakoby and M. Wilchek, Eds.: 683–702. Academic Press. New York.
11. OFENGAND, J., R. LIOU, J. KOHUT, I. SCHWARTZ & R. A. ZIMMERMANN. 1979. Biochemistry **18:** 4322–32.
12. OFENGAND, J. & R. LIOU. 1978. Nucleic Acids Res. **5:** 1325–34.
13. SCHWARTZ, I. & J. OFENGAND. 1978. Biochemistry **17:** 2524–30.
14. OFENGAND, J., P. DELANEY & J. BIERBAUM. 1974. *In* Methods in Enzymology, Vol. 29. L. Grossman and K. Moldave, Eds.: 673–84. Academic Press. New York.
15. BERMEK, E. 1978. Progr. Nucleic Acid Res. Mol. Biol. **21:** 63–100.
16. LAKE, J. A. 1977. Proc. Nat. Acad. Sci. USA **74:** 1903–07.
17. GRUNBERG–MANAGO, M. & F. GROS. 1977. Progr. Nucleic Acid Res. Mol. Biol. **20:** 209–84.
18. SCHWARTZ, I. & J. OFENGAND. 1974. Proc. Nat. Acad. Sci. USA **71:** 3951–55.
19. ZIMMERMANN, R. A., S. M. GATES, I. SCHWARTZ & J. OFENGAND. 1979. Biochemistry **18:** 4333–39.
20. HOROWITZ, J., J. OFENGAND, W. E. DANIEL, JR. & M. COHN. 1977. J. Biol. Chem. **252:** 4418–20.
21. HOROWITZ, J., C.-N. OU, M. ISHAQ, J. OFENGAND & J. BIERBAUM. 1974. J. Mol. Biol. **88:** 301–12.
22. HASEGAWA, T. & H. ISHIKURA. 1978. Nucleic Acids Res. **5:** 537–48.
23. SIDDIQUI, M. A. Q., J. OFENGAND, J.-P. GAREL & H. DRABKIN. 1980. *In* CRC Handbook of Microbiology. A. I. Laskin and H. A. Lechevalier, Eds. In press. CRC Press. West Palm Beach, Florida.
24. STEITZ, J. A. & K. JAKES. 1975. Proc. Nat. Acad. Sci. USA **72:** 4734–38.

25. BROSIUS, J., M. L. PALMER, P. J. KENNEDY & H. F. NOLLER. 1978. Proc. Nat. Acad. Sci. USA **75:** 4801–5.
26. CARBON, P., C. EHRESMANN, B. EHRESMANN & J. P. EBEL. 1978. FEBS Lett **94:** 152–56.
27. FISHER, G. J. & H. E. JOHNS. 1976. *In* Photochemistry and Photobiology of Nucleic Acids, Vol. 1. S. Y. Wang, Ed.: 225–94. Academic Press. New York.
28. KEREN-ZUR, M., M. BOUBLIK & J. OFENGAND. 1979. Proc. Nat. Acad. Sci. USA **76:** 1054–58.
29. WINKELMANN, D. & L. KAHAN. 1978. Fed. Proc. **37:** 1739.
30. BOUBLIK, M. & W. HELLMANN. 1978. Proc. Nat. Acad. Sci. USA **75:** 2829–33.
31. SCHWEET, R. & R. HEINTZ. 1966. Annu. Rev. Biochem. **35:** 723–58.
32. OFENGAND, J. 1977. *In* Molecular Mechanisms of Protein Biosynthesis. H. Weissbach and S. Pestka, Eds. Chapter 1: 7–79. Academic Press. New York.
33. LUCAS-LENARD, J. & F. LIPMANN. 1967. Proc. Nat. Acad. Sci. USA **57:** 1050–57.
34. CZERNILOFSKY, A. P. & E. KUECHLER. 1972. Biochim. Biophys. Acta **272:** 667–71.
35. ISHIKURA, H. 1979. Personal communication.
36. OFENGAND, J. & R. LIOU. 1980. Biochemistry **19.** Submitted.
37. JOHNSON, A. F. & C. CANTOR. 1979. Personal communication.
38. BOUBLIK, M., 1979. Personal communication.
39. OFENGAND, J. 1980. *In* Ribosomes: Structure, Function, and Genetics. G. Chambliss, G. Craven, J. Davies, L. Kahan, and M. Nomura. Eds.: 497–529. University Park Press. Baltimore, Maryland.

LABELING OF NUCLEIC ACIDS WITH PSORALENS*

Pill-Soon Song and Ching-Nan Ou

Department of Chemistry
Texas Tech University
Lubbock, Texas 79409

INTRODUCTION

Recently, useful applications of psoralens (furocoumarins) (FIGURE 1) as photochemical probes of chromatin structure,[1-3] secondary structure in viral DNA and *Drosophila* ribosomal RNA,[4,5] satellite DNA structure,[6] bacterial and viral DNA repair mechanisms,[7,8] and viral DNA-RNA hybrid structure[9] have been reported.

The photoreactivity of coumarins and furocoumarins has been correlated with their cycloaddition to the pyrimidine bases of DNA.[10-13] Musajo[14] was the first to report on the photoreaction of psoralens with DNA. Apparently, psoralens interact in the dark with DNA in a manner similar to that of other polycyclic aromatic hydrocarbons (e.g., acridine orange, ethidium bromide, actinomycin). Upon subsequent irradiation with near-uv light, the intercalated psoralen molecule can form covalent bonds with nearby pyrimidine bases of the DNA.

Studies by many workers have shown that both the furyl and pyrone functional groups are involved in their photoreactions with nucleic acids. The most likely reaction involves the formation of interstrand cross-links in the DNA through the photocycloaddition of the 3,4- and 4',5'-double bonds of the furocoumarin molecules.[15-20] The photoreactivity of furocoumarins can be interpreted in terms of strong localization of the triplet excitation in the region of the $C=C$ bond of the pyrone portion.[13,21] Recent theoretical and EPR/ODMR calculations also suggest that the triplet excitation is located in the pyrone $C=C$ bond.[22-24] FIGURE 2 shows the energy level diagram for furocoumaryl compounds.[21] In all cases, the low-lying $^1\pi,\pi^*$ and $^3\pi,\pi^*$ states represent the photoactivated species that are capable of reacting with substrates such as DNA bases. In this review, we will describe applications of furocoumarins plus near-uv light to the structural probing of nucleic acids, with emphasis on results from this laboratory. Details of experimental procedures are not included here, as they have already been described elsewhere by the present authors.[15]

LABELING OF DNA

It is generally accepted that only the pyrimidine bases of DNA react with excited psoralens. Results obtained by several laboratories indicate that either the 3,4- or 4',5'-$C=C$ bond of psoralen adds across the 5,6-$C=C$ bond of the pyrimidine base to give a 3,4- or 4',5'-furocoumaryl pyrimidine cycloadduct.[10,11,25] Although several indirect results suggest that Thy is the preferred site of photobinding of psoralens, and ^{14}C-psoralen apparently photoadds to the $C_5=C_6$ bond of Thy in DNA through its

*This research was supported by a United States Public Health Service grant, no. CA13598, and by the Institute of Environmental Chemistry of Texas Tech University.

355

0077–8923/80/0346–0355 $1.75/1 © 1980, NYAS

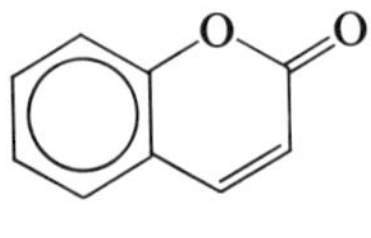

FIGURE 1. Chemical structures of coumaryl compounds. **1:** Coumarin; **2:** 5,7-dimethoxycoumarin (DMC); **3:** Psoralen (furocoumarin); **4:** 8-methoxypsoralen (R = —CH$_3$, 8-MOP), 8-hydroxypsoralen (R = H, 8-HP); **5:** Angelicin; **6:** 4,5′,8-trimethylpsoralen (R = H,TMP), 4′-amino-4,5′,9-trimethylpsoralen (R = —CH$_2$NH$_3$$^+Cl^-$, 4′-amino-TMP); **7:** cis-benzodipyrone; **8:** t-benzodipyrone.

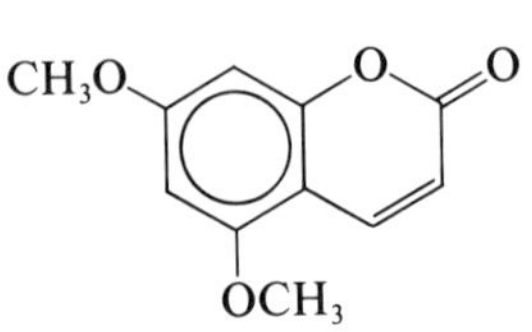

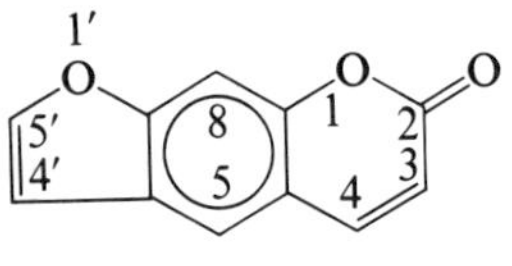

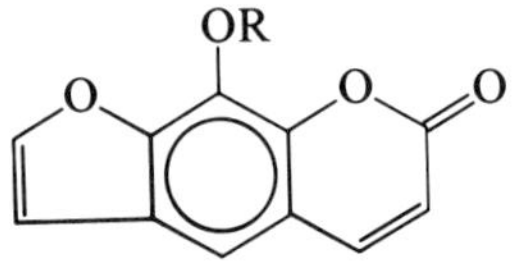

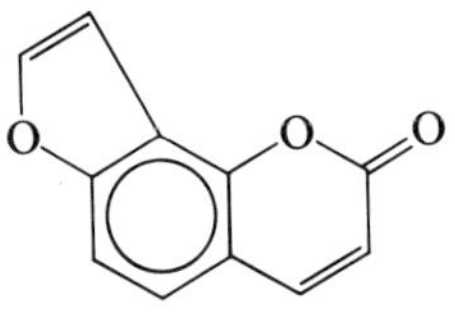

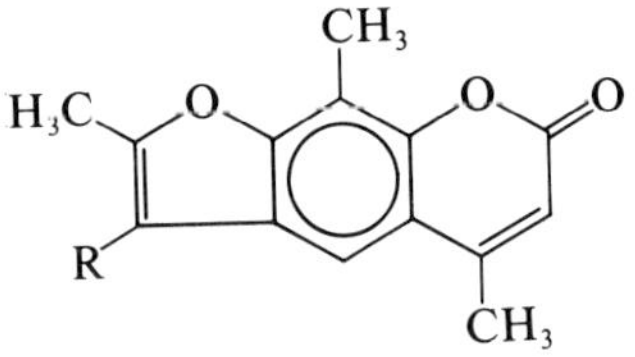

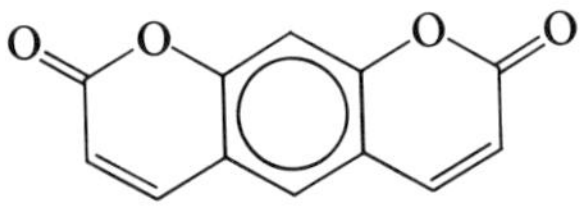

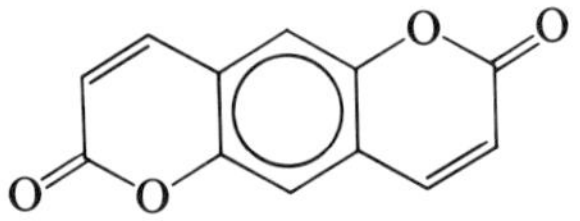

3,4-C=C bond,[11] definite chemical and structural characterizations of Thy adducts, as well as other base adducts of DNA, have yet to be established. FIGURE 3 illustrates these reactions.

There is convincing evidence that the formation of bifunctional adducts occurs in the photobinding of psoralens to DNA both *in vivo* and *in vitro*. A possible pathway for the formation of this bifunctional adduct is shown in SCHEMA 1.

In this regard, *t*-benzodipyrone (8, FIGURE 1) is, potentially, the most effective cross-linking agent, since it possesses two equally reactive C=C bonds for the photocycloaddition (SCHEMA 2).

Labeling of DNA by psoralens is thought to be a two-step process, the first step being the formation of a complex between psoralen and DNA, followed by formation of covalent bonds upon irradiation with light of $\lambda < 400$ nm. These steps are discussed separately below.

Formation of Complexes Between Psoralens and DNA

The formation of a molecular complex by weak forces plays an important role in the subsequent photoreaction between furocoumarin and DNA, since the short-lived excited state of the former can be effectively trapped (or reacted) by the DNA, thus eliminating the diffusive and solvent-quenching processes of the reactive species and substrate molecules. The molecular complexes between nucleic acids and psoralens are formed by intercalation of the planar psoralen chromophores between two base pairs of double-stranded DNA.[26] Single-stranded DNAs are less susceptible to intercalation than are double-stranded and supercoiled DNAs. DNA regions of alternating sequences of purine and pyrimidine bases are favorable for intercalation, but no preference for either A-T or G-C sequences has been found.[27]

Photoaddition

The DNA-intercalated psoralens (Ps) undergo cycloaddition to DNA bases, particularly Pyr bases, upon irradiation with near-uv light. The degree of photobind-

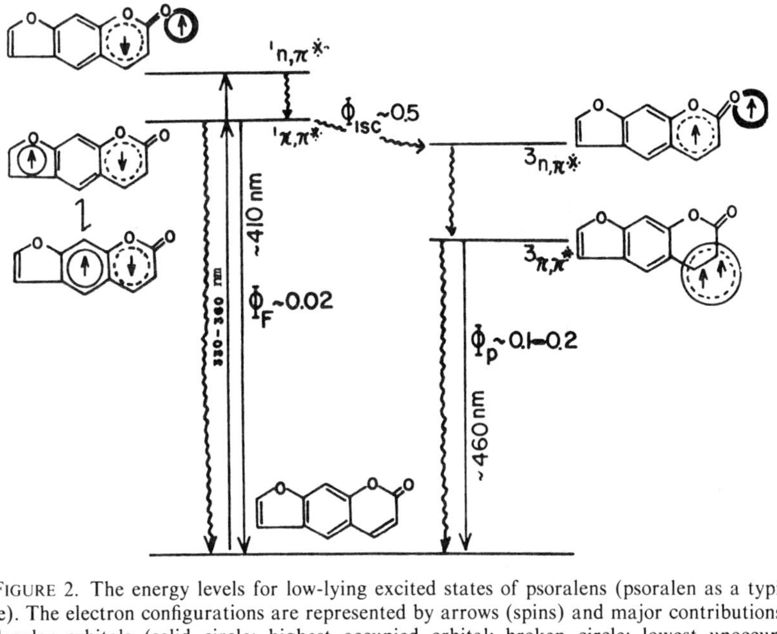

FIGURE 2. The energy levels for low-lying excited states of psoralens (psoralen as a typical case). The electron configurations are represented by arrows (spins) and major contributions of molecular orbitals (solid circle: highest occupied orbital; broken circle: lowest unoccupied orbital) for low-lying singlet and triplet configurations of the $^{1,3}n,\pi^*$, $^{1,3}\pi,\pi^*$, and $^{1,3}\pi,\pi^*$ states.

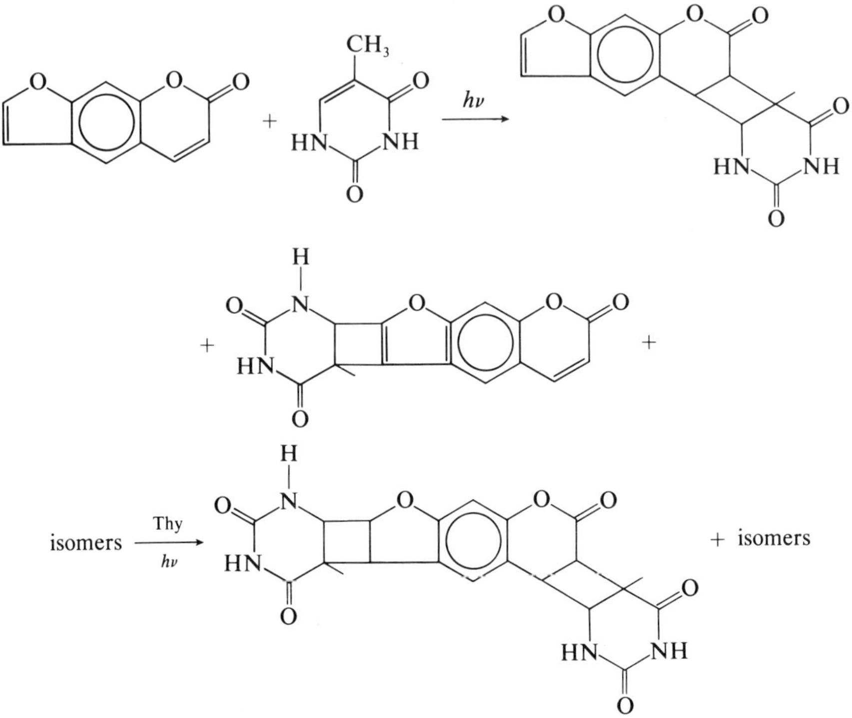

FIGURE 3. Photochemical formation of 3,4- and 4′,5′-monocycloadducts and 3,4,4′,5′-cross-link adducts. Both geometric (head-to-head and head-to-tail) and stereochemical (*anti* and *syn*) isomers are possible.

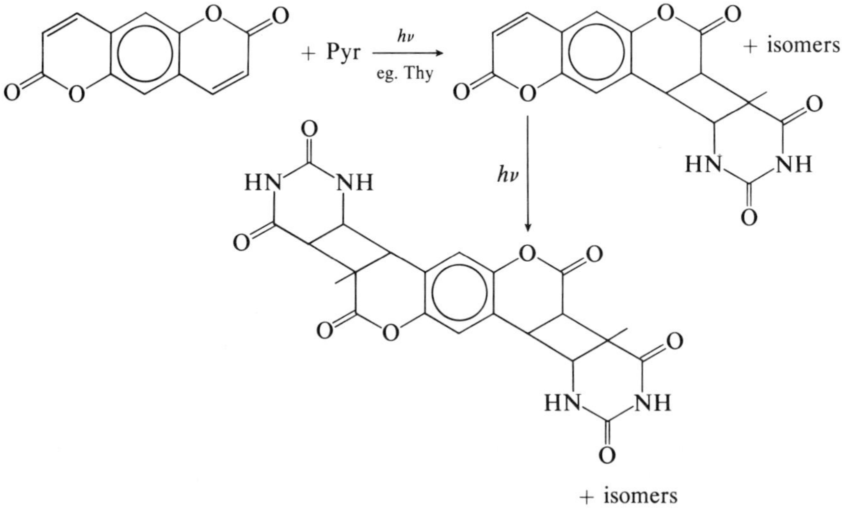

SCHEMA 1.

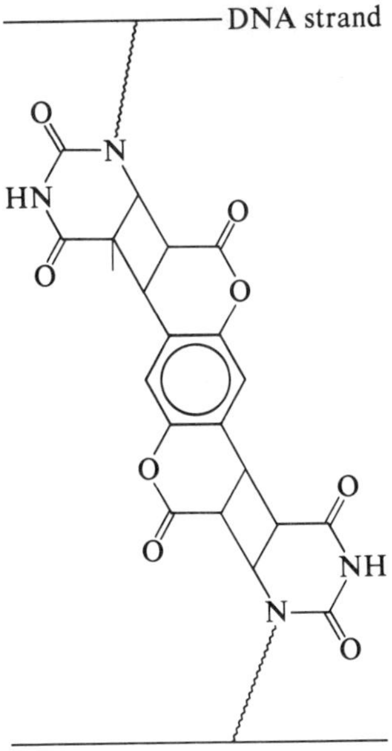

SCHEMA 2.

ing of Ps to DNA is roughly proportional to the degree of intercalation in the dark. The simplified reaction scheme is shown below:[28]

$$DNA + nPs \overset{K}{\rightleftharpoons} DNA\text{-}(Ps)_n$$

$$DNA\text{-}(Ps)_n \overset{h\nu}{\longrightarrow}$$

$$DNA\text{-}3,4\text{-}Ps \text{ (3,4-monoadducts)} + DNA\text{-}4'5'\text{-}Ps \text{ (4',5'-monoadducts)}$$

$$DNA\text{-}3,4\text{-}Ps \xrightarrow[\lambda \geq 300 \text{ nm}]{h\nu} DNA\!\!<^{4',5'}_{3,4}\!\!>Ps \text{ (cross-link adducts)}$$

$$DNA\text{-}4',5'\text{-}Ps \xrightarrow[\lambda \geq 300 \text{ nm}]{h\nu} DNA\!\!<^{3,4}_{4',5'}\!\!>Ps$$

Values of the quantum yield for photoaddition of Ps to DNA depend not only upon the amount of light absorbed by intercalated psoralens, but also upon the irradiation time. Thus, the corrected quantum yield for the photobinding of *intercalated* 8-methoxypsoralen (8-MOP) to calf thymus DNA is as high as 0.19, corresponding to a binding ratio of 1 8-MOP/13 base pairs.[28] After six consecutive additional treatments with trimethylpsoralen (TMP), 1 TMP/3–5 base pairs has been achieved with *Drosophila* main-band DNA.[29] The poly d[A-T] · poly d[A-T] sequence region is apparently the most favorable site for both intercalation and photocycloaddition of psoralens. Poly[G-C] sequences are not favorable for the photocycloaddition, although intercalation at the G-C sequence is not inhibited. The polynucleotide regions corresponding to the sequence of poly dA·poly dT or poly dG·poly dC are apparently not suited for optimal intercalation and subsequent photocycloaddition.[30] The photobinding of psoralen and 8-MOP increases with increasing (A, T) content of the DNA, and the number of 4′,5′-monoadducts and cross-link adducts is highest when the (A, T) content of the DNA is 50–60%.[27]

Since the coumaryl portion of psoralens is largely responsible for the photoactivation and monocycloaddition reactions of psoralens with nucleic acids, it is of interest to compare the photoreactivity of psoralens with that of hepatocarcinogenic aflatoxins (AF), which also possess the coumaryl chromophore.[31,32] However, AF_{B1} and AF_{G1} (FIGURE 4) bind preferentially to single-stranded DNA through their 8,9- and 9,10-C=C bonds, respectively, rather than through the coumaryl C=C bond. Upon irradiation with near-uv light and under identical conditions, AF_{B2} and AF_{G2}, containing the latter bond only, do not significantly bind to DNA. The photobinding sites on DNA include both G-C and A-T sequences, with somewhat preferred binding

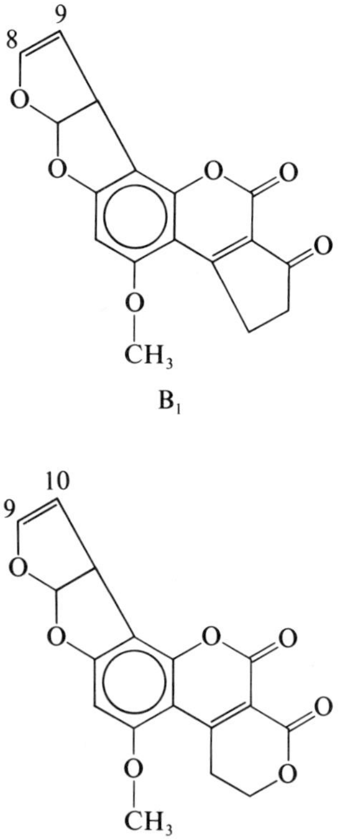

FIGURE 4. The chemical structure of aflatoxins B_1 and G_1.

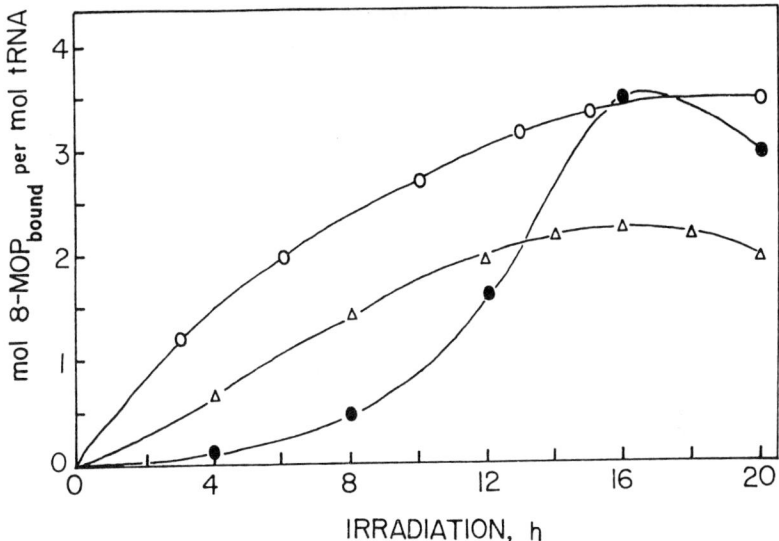

FIGURE 5. Photobinding of ^{3}H-8-MOP to 5-fluorouracil-enriched tRNA (–o–), native tRNA (–•–) and preirradiated (330 nm) tRNA (–△–). These unfractionated tRNAs were isolated from *E. coli* cells.[34] Note that the preirradiated tRNA binds 1–1.5 molecules less per molecule of tRNA, indicating that the preirradiation has destroyed one of the 8-MOP photobinding sites. Yeast phenylalanine tRNA showed photobinding kinetics essentially identical to those of 5FU-tRNA.[34]

at the latter, which contrasts with the guanine site for microsomally activated AF_{B1}.[33]

LABELING OF RNA

Psoralens form complexes with RNA, which results in covalent linking between them upon near-uv irradiation.[26] 8-MOP also intercalates into tRNA, as detected by the increase in fluorescence anisotropy of 8-MOP in the presence of tRNA.[34] One 8-MOP is intercalated for every 30 nucleotides of 5FU-enriched tRNA. The intercalation of 8-MOP into tRNA can only be detected by the fluorescence anisotropy method, since absorption and fluorescence changes are minimal, apparently due to very weak interactions between 8-MOP and tRNA.

The photobinding of psoralens to RNA occurs under near-uv irradiation.[35–38] For example, 8-MOP photobinds to yeast RNA *in vivo,* although its binding is only 4% of the photobinding to DNA. 3-Carbethoxypsoralen is, however, 3.6 times more reactive toward yeast RNA than 8-MOP.[38] Angelicin is known to bind equally well to DNA and RNA.[39] Cross-linking of rRNA has also been demonstrated.[36] There is an indication that uracil is the reactive base in the photobinding of psoralen to rRNA.[11] ^{14}C-labeled psoralen photochemically binds to various polynucleotides in a ratio of approximately 1:30 (nucleotides). It has also been shown that psoralen can bind not only to Pyr bases, but also to purine bases.

TABLE 1

NUCLEOSIDE COMPOSITION OF IRRADIATED tRNA (*E. coli*) AS DETERMINED BY THE CHEMICAL TRITIUM LABELING METHOD[34,41,43]

Nucleoside	Mole% ± S.D.	
	15 h irradiated tRNA	tRNA†
G	30.81 ± 0.10	30.60 ± 0.21
C	29.81 ± 0.21	29.47 ± 0.25
A	18.55 ± 0.11	19.12 ± 0.18
U	14.20 ± 0.08	14.30 ± 0.13
ψ	1.79 ± 0.03	1.80 ± 0.02
hU	2.33 ± 0.01	2.25 ± 0.03
m^5U	1.15 ± 0.04	1.13 ± 0.02
m^7G*	0.76 ± 0.02	0.75 ± 0.04
I	0.26 ± 0.02	0.25 ± 0.01
m^2A	0.22 ± 0.01	0.24 ± 0.02
m^6A	0.07 ± 0.01	0.09 ± 0.01
m^1G	0.11 ± 0.04	0.12 ± 0.01

*Corrected for 64% recovery.
†The control sample is the nonirradiated tRNA that is analyzed by this method without treatment with RNase T_1.

The photobinding of 8-MOP to tRNA with 365 nm light has been studied quantitatively.[34] The maximum photobinding is 3–4 mol of 8-MOP per mole of *E. coli* tRNA and 5FU-tRNA, with an overall quantum yield of 2.3×10^{-3}. The photobinding kinetics for 8-MOP-tRNA show an apparent induction period or sigmoidal kinetic curve (FIGURE 5), indicating a specific initial photobinding site on

TABLE 2

NUCLEOSIDE COMPOSITION OF IRRADIATED 5FU-tRNA AS DETERMINED BY THE CHEMICAL TRITIUM LABELING METHOD[34,41,43]

Nucleoside	Mole% ± S.D.	
	20 h irradiated 5FU-tRNA	5FU-tRNA†
G	29.80 ± 0.01	30.22 ± 0.29
C	28.24 ± 0.12	28.53 ± 0.23
A	19.17 ± 0.23	19.10 ± 0.30
U	1.46 ± 0.01	1.44 ± 0.02
5FU	18.36 ± 0.30	18.30 ± 0.14
ψ	0.10 ± 0.02	0.14 ± 0.01
hU	0.12 ± 0.01	0.13 ± 0.02
m^5U	0.20 ± 0.01	0.10 ± 0.01
$7G*$	0.76 ± 0.09	0.75 ± 0.05
I	0.26 ± 0.01	0.26 ± 0.02
m^2A	0.26 ± 0.02	0.25 ± 0.01
m^6A	0.09 ± 0.02	0.08 ± 0.02
5FC	0.74 ± 0.01	0.74 ± 0.03

*Corrected for 64% recovery.
†The control sample is the nonirradiated 5FU-tRNA that is analyzed by this method in the absence of RNase T_1.

tRNA that is identified as 4-thiouridine at position 8 from the 5′ end of tRNA. Photobinding of 8-MOP also occurs at the adenine bases in yeast tRNA[Phe]. The photobinding of 8-MOP changes the conformation (of secondary structures in particular) of tRNA.

Specific binding sites on tRNA and 5FU-tRNA are likely to be determined by two factors: (1) ground-state complex formation between 8-MOP and tRNA, which provides two or three possible intercalating base plates[40] and (2) reaction between excited 8-MOP and exposed bases. Both factors are probably involved in the photobinding of 8-MOP to tRNA and 5FU-tRNA.

TABLE 1 shows a nucleoside composition analysis of *E. coli* tRNA irradiated at

TABLE 3

NUCLEOSIDE COMPOSITIONS OF 8-MOP-tRNA PHOTOADDUCT AND CONTROL tRNA
AS DETERMINED BY THE CHEMICAL TRITIUM LABELING METHOD[34,41,43]

| | Mole% ± S.D. | |
Nucleoside	8-MOP-tRNA (15 h irradiated)†	tRNA‡
G	30.53 ± 0.25	30.81 ± 0.10
C	28.10 ± 0.16	29.81 ± 0.21
A	16.90 ± 0.10	18.55 ± 0.11
U	13.30 ± 0.12	14.20 ± 0.08
ψ	1.83 ± 0.02	1.79 ± 0.03
hU	2.33 ± 0.03	2.33 ± 0.01
m^5U	1.14 ± 0.02	1.15 ± 0.04
m^7G*	0.69 ± 0.01	0.76 ± 0.02
I	0.23 ± 0.01	0.26 ± 0.02
m^2A	0.21 ± 0.01	0.22 ± 0.01
m^6A	0.09 ± 0.01	0.07 ± 0.01
m^1G	0.12 ± 0.01	0.11 ± 0.04

*Corrected for 64% recovery.
†Corrected for the content of 8-MOP-nucleoside adduct.
‡The control sample is the 15 h irradiated tRNA that is analyzed by this method after treatment with RNase T_1.

365 nm in the absence of 8-MOP under anaerobic conditions. It can be seen that the anaerobic irradiation does not yield any significant photodecomposition of tRNA, as expected, and further insures that the chemical tritium labeling method yields reliable nucleoside composition data,[34,42,43] provided tRNA is first treated with RNase T_1 (a guanine-specific endonuclease) prior to the chemical tritium labeling. This is also true with 5FU-tRNA (TABLE 2).

TABLE 3 shows a decrease in cytidine, uridine, and adenine bases by approximately 1 mole% upon photoaddition of 8-MOP to tRNA, indicating that the binding sites involve these nucleosides. We are now examining the 8-MOP-nucleoside photoadducts that remain at the origin of the TLC chromatogram of enzyme-digested 8-MOP-tRNA. In the case of 8-MOP-5FU-tRNA, a significant decrease of 5FU is clearly seen (TABLE 4), suggesting that 5FU is the preferred photobinding site for 8-MOP. Apparently, at least one of the 8-MOP photobinding sites on 5FU-tRNA is at adenosine (TABLE 4), as in the case of tRNA (TABLE 3). These results clearly suggest that photoreaction occurs between 8-MOP and pyrimidine as well as between 8-MOP and purine bases, particularly the adenine base.

The preferential site for intercalation and photoaddition of 8-MOP to DNA is the region containing the poly d(A-T) sequence.[28,30] It is likely that the poly(A-U) sequence in tRNA is a preferential photobinding site for 8-MOP. The photolabeling of guanosine and cytidine in tRNA with 8-MOP is also evident (TABLE 5). Since *E. coli* tRNA[Phe] contains 17 G-C among a total of 21 base pairings in its secondary structure,[42] it is not surprising that guanosine and cytidine of 8-MOP-intercalating regions of tRNA[Phe] also photoreacted with 8-MOP (TABLES 3 and 5). In the case of 8-MOP-5FU-tRNA, more than 70% of the photobinding sites involve 5FU (TABLE 4).

TABLE 4

NUCLEOSIDE COMPOSITIONS OF 8-MOP-5FU-tRNA PHOTOADDUCT
AND CONTROL 5FU-tRNA
AS DETERMINED BY THE CHEMICAL TRITIUM LABELING METHOD[34,41,43]

| | Mole % ± S.D. | |
Nucleoside	8-MOP-5FU-tRNA†	Control 5FU-tRNA‡
G	30.30 ± 0.24	29.80 ± 0.10
C	28.31 ± 0.33	28.24 ± 0.12
A	17.82 ± 0.14	19.17 ± 0.23
U	1.68 ± 0.02	1.46 ± 0.01
5FU	14.60 ± 0.23	18.36 ± 0.30
ψ	0.23 ± 0.01	0.10 ± 0.02
hU	0.29 ± 0.01	0.12 ± 0.01
m^5U	0.14 ± 0.01	0.20 ± 0.01
m^7G*	0.70 ± 0.01	0.76 ± 0.09
I	0.27 ± 0.01	0.26 ± 0.01
m^2A	0.24 ± 0.02	0.26 ± 0.02
m^6A	0.13 ± 0.01	0.09 ± 0.01
5FC	0.67 ± 0.02	0.74 ± 0.01

*Corrected for 64% recovery.
†Corrected for the content of 8-MOP-nucleoside adduct.
‡The control sample is the 20 h irradiated 5FU-tRNA, which is analyzed by this method after treatment with RNase T₁.

The 8-MOP-tRNA and 8-MOP-5FU-tRNA photoadducts absorb light in the region of 320–500 nm.[34] This suggests that the predominant addition takes place at 4′,5′-positions, since 3,4-monoadducts absorb very little in this region. We have no evidence for or against intrastrand cross-linking of tRNA at the present time. From the CD study of the photoadducts,[34] it appears that the base stacking and helicity of the tRNA arms are disrupted to some extent.

CONCLUSIONS

The photolabeling of DNA and RNA with psoralens occurs with high efficiency without apparent photodynamic degradation of the nucleic acids if the reactions are carried out under anaerobic conditions. Both pyrimidine and purine bases are involved

TABLE 5

NUCLEOSIDE COMPOSITIONS OF E. coli tRNA^Phe, 15 H IRRADIATED tRNA^Phe, AND 8-MOP-tRNA^Phe PHOTOADDUCT AS DETERMINED BY THE CHEMICAL TRITIUM LABELING METHOD*[34,41,43]

Nucleoside	tRNA^Phe		15 h irradiated tRNA^Phe		8-MOP-tRNA^Phe			Expected§ in 74†
	Mole %	In 74*	Mole %	In 74†	Mole %	In 74†	Corrected Value in 74‡	
G	30.94	22.90 ± 0.15	30.96	22.91 ± 0.18	29.99	22.19	21.02 ± 0.24	23
C	28.95	21.42 ± 0.18	29.21	21.61 ± 0.21	28.54	21.12	20.01 ± 0.25	21
A	19.06	14.10 ± 0.13	18.52	13.71 ± 0.24	19.79	14.64	13.87 ± 0.11	14
U	12.17	9.00 ± 0.10	12.01	8.89 ± 0.13	12.15	8.99	8.51 ± 0.17	9‖
ψ	3.40	2.52 ± 0.02	4.00	2.96 ± 0.04	4.34	3.21	3.04 ± 0.02	3
hU	2.79	2.06 ± 0.03	2.93	2.16 ± 0.03	2.92	2.16	2.05 ± 0.03	2
m5U	1.42	1.05 ± 0.01	1.46	1.08 ± 0.02	1.46	1.08	1.02 ± 0.01	1
m7G¶	1.30	0.96 ± 0.03	0.92	0.68 ± 0.05	0.83	0.61	0.58 ± 0.02	1

*With RNase T₁ treatment.

†The chain length is 76 nucleotides; 2-methylthio-N^6-isopentenyl adenosine and 3-(3-amino-3-carboxypropyl) uridine were subtracted.

‡Corrected for the content of 8-MOP-nucleoside.

§See Reference 42.

‖ ^{3}H-Thiouridine is recovered mainly as (^3H)-U.[41]

¶Corrected for 64% recovery.

as the sites of photoaddition. Although the photoadducts have not been fully characterized, the photolabeling of biomolecules with psoralens provides a new tool for probing biopolymer structure. This tool is particularly promising because of the specificity of photoaddition as determined by noncovalent interactions (e.g., intercalation) in the ground state. For example, the photoaddition of psoralens and their derivatives show a degree of specificity with respect to the base sequence, single- versus double-stranded regions, and the helical structure of nucleic acids.

REFERENCES

1. HANSON, C. V., J. L. RIGGS & E. H. LENNETTE. 1978. J. Gen. Virol. **40**: 345.
2. WIESEHAHN, G. P., J. E. HYDE & J. E. HEARST. 1977. Biochemistry **16**: 925.
3. CECH, T. & M. L. PARDUE. 1977. Cell **11**: 631.
4. SHEN, C.-K. J. & J. E. HEARST. 1976. Proc. Nat Acad. Sci. USA **73**: 2649.
5. WOLLENZIEN, P. L., D. C. YOUVAN & J. E. HEARST. 1978. Proc. Nat. Acad. Sci. USA **75**: 1642.
6. SHEN, C.-K. J. & J. E. HEARST. 1977. J. Mol. Biol. **112**: 495.
7. COLE, R. S., D. LEVITAN & R. R. SINDEN. 1976. J. Mol. Biol. **103**: 39.
8. CASSUTO, E., N. GROSS, E. BARDWELL & P. HOWARD-FLANDERS. 1977. Biochim. Biophys. Acta **475**: 589.
9. SHEN, C.-K. J., T. S. HSIEH, J. C. WANG & J. E. HEARST. 1977. J. Mol. Biol. **116**: 661.
10. MUSAJO, L., F. BORDIN & R. BEVILACQUA. 1967. Photochem. Photobiol. **6**: 927.
11. KRAUCH, C. H., D. M. KRÄMER & A. WACKER. 1967. Photochem. Photobiol. **6**: 341.
12. KRÄMER, D. M. & M. A. PATHAK. 1970. Photochem. Photobiol. **12**: 333.
13. SONG, P. S., M. L. HARTER, T. A. MOORE & W. C. HERNDON. 1971. Photochem. Photobiol. **14**: 521.
14. MUSAJO, L. 1969. Ann. Ist. Super. Sanita **5**: 376 and references therein.
15. OU, C. N., C. H. TSAI & P. S. SONG. 1977. Research in Photobiology: 257–265. Plenum. New York.
16. COLE, R. S. 1970. Biochim. Biophys. Acta **217**: 30.
17. COLE, R. S. 1971. J. Bacteriol. **107**: 846.
18. DALL'ACQUA, F., S. MARCIANI & G. RODIGHIERO. 1970. FEBS Lett. **9**: 121.
19. CHANDRA, P., S. KRAFT, A. WACKER, G. RODIGHIERO, F. DALL'ACQUA & S. MARCIANI. 1971. Biophysik **7**: 251.
20. MARCIANI, S., M. TERBOJEVIC & F. DALL'ACQUA. 1972. Z. Naturforsch. **27b**: 196.
21. MANTULIN, W. W., & P. S. SONG. 1973. J. Am. Chem. Soc. **95**: 5122.
22. SONG, P. S., C. A. CHIN, I. YAMAZAKI & H. BABA. 1975. Int. J. Quantum Chem. Quantum Biol. Symp. **2**: 1.
23. HARRIGAN, E. T., A. CHARKRABARTI & N. HIROTA. 1976. J. Am. Chem. Soc. **98**: 3460.
24. MOORE, T. A., A. B. MONTGOMERY & A. L. KWIRAM. 1976. Photochem. Photobiol. **24**: 83.
25. MUSAJO, L., F. BORDIN, G. CAPORALE, S. MARCIANI & G. RIGATTI. 1967. Photochem. Photobiol. **6**: 711.
26. MUSAJO, L. & G. RODIGHIERO. 1972. Photophysiology **7**: 115 and references therein.
27. DALL'ACQUA, F., D. VEDALDI & M. RECHER. 1978. Photochem. Photobiol. **27**: 33.
28. OU, C. N., C. H. TSAI, K. J. TAPLEY & P. S. SONG. 1978. Biochemistry **17**: 1047.
29. SHEN, C.-K. J. & J. E. HEARST. 1978. Cold Spring Harbor Symp. Quant. Biol. **42**: 179.
30. MARCIANI, S., F. DALL'ACQUA, D. VEDALDI & G. RODIGHIERO. 1976. Farmaco Ed. Sci. **31**: 140.
31. SHIEH, J. C. 1978. M. S. Thesis, Texas Tech University. Lubbock, Texas.
32. SHIEH, J. C. & P. S. SONG. 1980. Cancer Res. **40**: 689.
33. CROY, R. G., J. M. ESSIGMANN, V. N. REINHOLD & G. N. WOGAN. 1978. Proc. Nat. Acad. Sci. USA **75**: 1745.
34. OU, C. N. & P. S. SONG. 1978. Biochemistry **17**: 1054.

35.   PATHAK, M. A., D. M. KRÄMER & T. B. FITZPATRICK. 1974. *In* Sunlight and Man. M. A. Pathak *et al.,* Eds.: 335. University of Tokyo Press, Tokyo.

36.   ISAACS, S. T., C.-K. J. SHEN, J. E. HEARST & H. RAPOPORT. 1977. Biochemistry **16:** 1058.

36.   MIZUNO, N., S. TSUNEISHI, S. MATSUHASHI, S. KIMURA, Y. FUZIMURA & T. USHIZIMA. 1974. *In* Sunlight and Man. M. A. Pathak *et al.,* Eds.: 389. University of Tokyo Press, Tokyo.

38.   AVERBECK, D., E. MOUSTACCHI & E. BISAGNI. 1978. Biochim. Biophys. Acta **518:** 464.

39.   RODIGHIERO, G., L. MUSAJO, F. DALL'ACQUA, S. MARCIANI, P. CHANDRA, H. FELLER, A. GÖTZ & A. WACKER. 1971. Biophysik **8:** 1.

40.   KIM, S. H. 1977. *In* Transfer RNA. S. Altman, Ed. MIT Press. Cambridge, Massachusetts.

41.   RANDERATH, K., E. RANDERATH, L. S. Y. CHIA & B. J. NOWAK. 1974. Anal. Biochem. **59:** 263.

42.   BARRELL, B. G. & B. F. C. CLARK. 1974. Handbook of Nucleic Acids Sequences. Joynson-Bravers. Oxford, England.

43.   OU, C. N. 1977. Ph.D. Dissertation, Texas Tech University. Lubbock, Texas.

DISCUSSION

UNIDENTIFIED SPEAKER: Did you locate exactly where in the sequence these sites are?

DR. P. S. SONG: All we have located are the bases, not the location of the bases in the sequence. We are now doing essentially what Professor Schimmel has done; that is, taking various fractions of the tRNA—I mean, nucleotides—and then locating the radioactive label.

UNIDENTIFIED SPEAKER: I wanted to ask you about the photoinduction. You implied that it was the incorporation of the first molecule that potentiated the succeeding molecules. But you also showed that the prephotolyzed tRNA had no induction and, of course, in that case, there was no prior incorporation of the molecule. So, it wasn't obvious that that was the unique interpretation of your induction experiment.

SONG: It is difficult to answer that; we need to know something about the ground state complexation. The ground state complexation that I refer to was with 5FU-enriched tRNA, the reason being that the 5FU-tRNA does not absorb and fluoresce and it is, therefore, possible to do fluorescence anisotropy based on 8-MOP fluorescence. But we were not able to do it with the normal tRNA and, therefore, in order to answer your question, I think we need to know how many 8-MOP are actually complexed.

UNIDENTIFIED SPEAKER: It wasn't obvious that it was 8-MOP complexation rather than a photochemical event on the tRNA itself that accounts for the lag period. That is, in principle, one can explain the lag by a change, a photochemical change in the tRNA independent of 8-MOP, which allows 8-MOP to bind; and the fact that you could prephotolyze tRNA and get that phenomenon (i.e., eliminate the lag in the absence of 8-MOP by prephotolysis of tRNA) suggests that that's at least a possible interpretation.

SONG: Certainly that's a possibility. Our thinking has been that their initial photoaddition had caused substantial changes in the conformation that then enhanced the photoreactivity of the subsequent binding. We may be incorrect in making that assumption, but we made that assumption on the basis that the largest CD change had occurred in the first binding without any substantial change in the subsequent photobinding.

PHOTOAFFINITY LABELING OF DNA

K. Lemone Yielding and Lerena W. Yielding

Laboratory of Molecular Biology
University of Alabama in Birmingham
Birmingham, Alabama 35294

INTRODUCTION

The resolution of ligand-nucleic acid interactions is a problem of great biological significance. Such interactions account for various types of normal regulatory loops and, in addition, represent major mechanisms for the therapeutic and toxic effects of drugs and other xenobiotic agents. Specific ligands also serve as useful tools for studying nucleic acid structure and function both *in vitro* and within intact cells.

Despite extensive studies on a number of important ligands, it is still not possible to define the precise interactions that account for structural and biological effects nor to design new reagents that interact predictably to produce the desired consequences. This is due partly to our incomplete knowledge of the complexity of nucleic acid structure and processes, and partly to our incomplete understanding of the nature and distribution of ligand binding. Biological effects are often provoked by very low drug concentrations, while binding studies must often be done using much higher levels of drug site saturation than those which provoke biological effects. It is also axiomatic that most potent ligands have multiple targets, making assignment of specific targets difficult. Furthermore, metabolic drug processing often makes it difficult to determine the biologically active form(s) of the ligand. The most formidable problem in studying ligand effects, however, is reversibility, which is characteristic of most interactions. Therefore, binding sites and their properties must be studied under steady state conditions, since the definitive complexes cannot be isolated from *in vivo* experiments and the relatively high levels of ligand saturation that must be used result in a rather high noise/specificity ratio.

Photoaffinity labeling is a powerful technique for studying reversible ligand-nucleic acid interactions, because noncovalent complexes may be converted to covalent adducts and retrieved for study. Many of the ligands of interest bind to nucleic acids with very high affinity, contain visible chromophores that absorb in the visible range, and have potential sites for photosensitive derivatization. Thus, the ligands of interest may be intrinisically photosensitive or may be derivatized. The chromophoric nature of the reagents permit irradiation at wavelengths at which the cell is transparent and immune to damage. Photoactivation *in situ* can bypass or avoid requirements for metabolic activation; the time and extent of ligand attachment can be controlled precisely. The conversion of a reversible complex to a covalent adduct may be expressed biologically either as an enhancement of the ligand effect or as a desensitization of the cell to the characteristic response to binding. A distinction must be made, of course, between covalent adduct formation and photosensitization and photodestruction of the target site.

An ideal photoaffinity probe should display the following properties:

0077–8923/80/0346–0368 $1.75/ © 1980, NYAS

1. The ligand should be photoactivatable at a light wavelength and light intensity that are nondestructive to the receptor site and to the cell.

2. Photolysis of the free ligand should not generate any molecular species that leads to complicating reactions.

3. The lifetime of the photoactivated state must be short enough to assure quenching by solvent interactions to the exclusion of any secondary perturbations of significant biomolecules and to assure adduct formation before dissociation or rearrangement occurs. Ideally, the "quenched" species should be biologically inert.

4. The photolysis process should be fast and efficient enough that the covalent labeling is representative of the ligand bound at equilibrium.

5. Photolytic adduct formation should be accompanied by distinguishable and characteristic biological effects. This may be enhancement in the case of nondestructive adduct formation or quenching of its effects when the attached ligand is substantially modified after photolysis.

6. Ligand derivatives prepared as photoaffinity probes must show equilibrium binding and biological effects that are characteristic of the parent compound and the photolytic adduct must be stable enough to permit isolation.

Ethidium and the acridines are classic ligands for nucleic acids whose detailed mechanisms of action are priority issues. These agents have potent biological effects and model studies of their binding have featured in the development of some important concepts in modern molecular biology. Both the acridines and ethidium have two recognized binding modes to DNA: an external, electrostatically oriented stacking mode and an internal or intercalation mode. It is the latter type of binding that has been considered the most important and to which has been attributed the major biological consequences. The concept of intercalation, first proposed by Lerman for acridines,[1] provided a straightforward explanation for frameshift mutagenesis and has been the model used for the subsequent interpretation of the binding of many other ligands. These frameshifts, furthermore, were useful in predicting the triplet nature of the genetic code. There is a compelling lack of consistent correlation, however, between intercalative drug binding and mutagenesis or other biological effects. Ethidium, which has been the intercalator most intensively documented, is not a mutagen for bacteria in the absence of metabolic activation,[2] and mutagenic and nonmutagenic acridine analogs appear to exhibit equally strong intercalative binding.[3] Therefore, the precise relationships between binding and the mechanisms for mutagenesis need resolution.

Definitive binding models have been developed for both ethidium and the acridines through crystallographic study of complexes with complementary dinucleotides.[4,5] Despite the elegance of these models, it still must be established that they exist as solution complexes in extended polynucleotides and, especially, that they produce *in vivo* binding. The inductive leap from crystal model to biological effect is quite difficult and will require some means of looking at complex formation at low levels of saturation within the restricted structure of intact chromosomes. The binding models for these two classes of drugs are very similar, but their biological effects present interesting differences. Both can be mutagenic for mitochondria in yeast. Acridines are effective *only* in growing cells; ethidium mutagenizes resting cells but only after metabolic activation. Certain acridines produce frameshift mutations in bacteria, but ethidium requires metabolic activation to act as a frameshifter and shows a different strain mutagenic specificity with respect to the nature of the frameshift. Thus, after metabolic activation, ethidium is effective mostly for *Salmonella* TA1538, while 9-NH$_2$ acridine *without* metabolic activation is active only for TA1537.[2] It is, therefore, not clear just what the relationship between DNA binding and mutagenesis is. Accounting for the other biological effects of these interesting compounds is equally indefinite. There is a real need to determine the roles for nucleic acid and other binding targets in biological drug *in vivo* effects and to establish the relationship between such targeted binding and definitive *in vivo* binding models.

Carcinogens are other examples of important DNA ligands. The complexity of metabolic activation and deactivation, the presumed requirement for covalent attachment, and the identification of multiple potential targets from *in vitro* studies must be sorted out in relation to the prolonged nature of the carcinogenic process, the distinction between "malignant" and "premalignant" states, and the roles of initiation and promotion. The precise targeting and fate of these ligands are critical issues.

This presentation will summarize some of our experiences with two successful attempts at photoaffinity labeling of nucleic acids. In the first example, a photosensitive derivative of ethidium bromide was prepared and studied for its DNA binding properties, and the consequences of its photolysis were examined both for covalent adduct formation and for their biological consequences. The second example involved direct photochemical attachment to DNA (*in vitro*) of the anticancer, anthracycline antibiotics: adriamycin, daunomycin, and rubidazone.

PHOTOAFFINITY PROBE STUDIES OF ETHIDIUM BROMIDE EFFECTS:
SUCCESSFUL USE OF A PHOTOSENSITIVE DRUG ANALOG

Background

Ethidium has become a classic reagent for studies of nucleic acid structure. It is routinely used to identify closed circular DNA duplexes because of its ability to affect the superhelical density predictably.[6] It is also well known for its biological effects. Although it binds tightly to all classes of nucleic acids *in vitro,* its ability to act as a powerful selective mutagen for yeast in mitochondria has made it important as a tool for studying cytoplasmic genetics.[7] Most importantly, ethidium is a major drug worldwide in the management of trypanosomiasis in livestock, although toxicity has limited its usefulness in treating parasitic diseases in humans. Its properties and uses make it an ideal candidate to serve as a prototype for studying drug–nucleic acid interactions by photoaffinity labeling. It is a significant drug, it is a useful tool for studying nucleic acid structure and function, it is a strong chromophore in the visible range, it binds to DNA with high avidity, and it has chemical properties that permit its derivatization.

Preparation of Ethidium Azides

The azide analog of ethidium was selected as a potential photosensitive probe for ethidium binding. Thus, ethidium azide was synthesized by diazotization of ethidium bromide, followed by direct substitution with sodium azide. Our early experiments demonstrated that the azide derivative was mutagenic for yeast mitochondria and that photolysis by visible light resulted in covalent attachment to DNA and a large increase in this mutagenesis.[8] Furthermore, photolysis provoked frameshift mutations in *Salmonella* with evidence for a repairable DNA lesion.[9] Because of these exciting findings, a revised synthesis, based on strict control of stoichiometry and separation of the products by carboxymethyl-cellulose chromatography, was developed. Both the monoazide and the diazide products were prepared and separated in good yields with crystalline purity.[10] NMR spectra and x-ray diffraction data established the mono-azido product as the 8-azido compound.[10,11] The synthetic scheme and product structure are presented in FIGURE 1. The additional synthesis of the radiolabeled product has made rigorous studies of the physical and biological properties of these photoaffinity probes possible.

Comparison of the Physical Properties and Binding of Ethidium and Ethidium Azides

Detailed comparisons of the properties of ethidium, ethidium monoazide, and ethidium diazide are presented in TABLE 1. Ethidium monoazide was found to be very

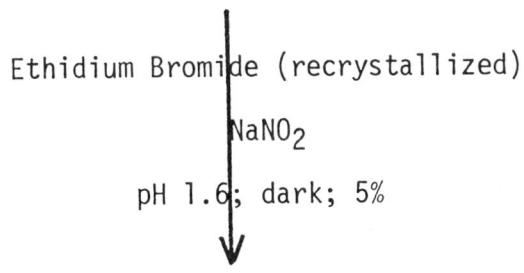

Ethidium Bromide (recrystallized)

NaNO$_2$

pH 1.6; dark; 5%

Diazonium salt of primary amine
(mono or bis-, determined by reactant stoichiometry)

NaN$_3$, pH 2.2, dark; 5^0

Azide substitution at diazonium salt of primary amine (mono- or di- depending on stoichiometry of reaction sequence)

ppt pH 12.0 (dark)

Purification on cellex at pH 2.8

FIGURE 1. Synthesis of ethidium azide.

similar to ethidium in crystal structure[11] and in absorption and fluorescence spectra.[12,13] The addition of DNA to ethidium or ethidium monoazide resulted in virtually identical shifts in absorption spectra and fluorescence enhancement from which identical binding parameters were calculated. Binding of ethidium diazide to DNA was only 1/10 as strong, with a decrease rather than an increase in fluorescence upon binding. The monoazide, therefore, was selected as a good candidate for photoaffinity labeling, while the diazide appeared less promising. Each azide derivative was quite photosensitive to visible light. Irradiation with a daylight fluorescence lamp (40 J m^{-2} sec^{-1} lamp^{-1}) gave the first order rate constants indicated in TABLE 1. Operationally, even very high concentrations could be photolyzed after brief exposures under conditions of irradiation that did not damage cells.

Photolytic Efficiency for Covalent Adduct Formation with DNA

The efficiency of photolytic conversion of a drug-DNA complex to a covalent adduct can be estimated quite simply from experiments employing a number of DNA concentrations with a single drug concentration. The simplifying assumption was made that, by extrapolating to infinite DNA concentration, all added drug was present as the complex. It followed that the ratio of covalent adduct to total drug at infinite DNA represented the extent of covalent conversion from irradiation, or the photolytic efficiency.[14] Such experiments were performed with ^{14}C ethidium mono-azide by mixing polynucleotide solutions with drug and measuring the TCA precipit-

TABLE 1

COMPARISONS OF ETHIDIUM BROMIDE, ETHIDIUM MONOAZIDE, AND ETHIDIUM DIAZIDE

Characteristic	Ethidium Bromide	Ethidium Monoazide	Ethidium Diazide
UV-visible spectrum and DNA titration (nonphotolyzed)			
λ_{max} free	5680/476 nm	5220/456 nm	5850/432 nm
λ_{max} bound	3874/516 nm	3760/495 nm	4100/445 nm
Specific hypochromic shift			
at λ_{max}	40 nm	39 nm	13 nm
K_d	4.4×10^{-7} M	4.6×10^{-7} M	4.81×10^{-6} M
Fluorescence spectrum and DNA titration (nonphotolyzed)			
Emission max (free)	600 nm	590 nm	500 nm
Emission max (bound)	590 nm	580 nm	507 nm
Relative intensity*			
(free)	1	1	1
(bound)	21	21	0.068
Rate of photolysis		$k = 5.72 \times 10^{-6}$ J^{-1} m^{-2} s^{-1}	$k = 6.07 \times 10^{-5}$ J^{-1} m^{-2} s^{-1}
Crystal properties	red, needle	red, needle	yellow, plate
Space group	P2$_1$/c; $Z = 4$	P2$_1$/c; $Z = 4$	
Density	1.376 g cm^{-3}	1.06 g cm^{-3}	

*Intensity relative to emission peak of free ligand.

TABLE 2

PHOTOLYTIC EFFICIENCY FOR CONVERSION OF NONCOVALENT COMPLEXES OF ETHIDIUM
MONOAZIDE AND POLYNUCLEOTIDES TO COVALENT ADDUCTS

Polymer	Efficiency of Photolytic Attachment @ Polymer $\rightarrow \infty$
Native DNA (Calf thymus)	0.23
Nucleoids (human lymphocyte)	0.19
Heat denatured DNA (Calf thymus)	0.26
Heat denatured & formaldehyde treated DNA (Calf thymus)	0.45
Poly A	0.42
RNA (yeast)	0.29

NOTE: Values for the covalent adduct were determined after photolysis with ^{14}C-labeled ethidium monoazide using a constant input level of 1×10^{-5} M ligand and by extrapolation to infinite polymer concentration. The extrapolated ratio of adduct to input ligand concentration was taken to represent the efficiency of covalent attachment from isolated high affinity ligand binding sites.[14]

able drug following photolysis. The values obtained for photolytic efficiency are given in TABLE 2. It should be noted that these are minimal values, since no corrections were made for either DNA recovery or the stability of the drug-adduct. Thus, we calculated that the minimum photolytic efficiencies with an ordinary fluorescent lamp range from 25 to 40%.[14] It appeared, therefore, that the photolytically provoked covalent adduct was reasonably representative of the noncovalent complex.

Mitochondrial Mutations by Ethidium Azide

The mutation processes for yeast mitochondria present several interesting problems in addition to the question of the identity of the drug binding sites. Ethidium can, at sufficiently high concentrations, convert virtually an entire cell population, either resting or growing, to mitochondrial (petite) mutants. Specific metabolic activation is required for EB mutagenesis; such activation can, apparently, be blocked by glucose repression.[15] The metabolic processes proposed include drug activation and covalent attachment,[16] and drug stimulation of DNase with degradation of mitochondrial DNA.[17] It has been emphasized that the initial processes are reversible and that the late steps, presumed to be DNA degradation, can be blocked and the cells "rescued" by high concentrations of ethidium.[18] Ethidium azide has provided a useful probe for studying ethidium mutagenesis in mitochondria.

Several important questions concerning mitochondrial mutagenesis by ethidium have been addressed with the photoaffinity probe technique using ethidium azide. The appropriateness of using such probes was confirmed by several findings. First, the induction of petite mutants by the monoazide derivative without photolysis was similar to that of the parent compound for time course, for concentration effectiveness,[8,19] and for the deletion of mitochondrial drug resistance markers.[20] Photolysis of an otherwise submutagenic concentration of the ethidium monoazide and, to a lesser extent, the ethidium diazide, however, provokes substantial numbers of petite mutants. Thus, a covalent attachment enhances the biological effect instead of producing a completely different effect or simply blocking the effect of the parent compound. Glucose-repressed cells were studied for two important questions, since glucose prevents ethidium mutagenesis. If the glucose-repressed cells simply exhibit an inability to produce metabolic drug activation, photolytic activation should bypass this block. In contrast, if glucose blocks a step following the covalent attachment of ethidium, photolytic mutagenesis by ethidium monoazide should also be prevented. Glucose-repressed cells were, in fact, readily mutagenized by photolytic activation of the photoaffinity probe, thus showing the inability to bypass the glucose-imposed metabolic block.[21] Furthermore, the inability of ethidium bromide to cause mutations in the presence of high concentrations of glucose made it possible to do straightforward competition studies between ethidium bromide and ethidium monoazide to determine the identity of the binding sites for these two agents. These experiments showed that ethidium bromide could successfully compete for and prevent ethidium azide mutagenesis in glucose-repressed cells.[22] Concomitant studies of the photolytic binding of the radioactive ethidium monoazide showed that, under conditions in which mutagenesis was prevented by competing concentrations of ethidium bromide, covalent attachment to mitochondrial DNA was also prevented.[22] Thus, the study of glucose-repressed cells confirmed that glucose prevents metabolic activation of the ethidium moiety to cause mutations and, at the same time, permitted confirmation of the identity of the binding sites for ethidium bromide and ethidium monoazide under conditions of monoazide mutagenesis.

Based on the binding of the molecules, as well as the fate of mitochondrial DNA during the mutagenesis process, it has been assumed that the target for mitochondrial mutagenesis by ethidium bromide has been mitochondrial DNA. The ethidium monoazide was also used to probe binding of the ethidium moiety to other subcellular fractions; it was shown that substantial binding occurred to nuclear DNA and to nuclear, cytoplasmic, and mitochondrial proteins and RNA. All binding factions were competed for partially by ethidium bromide—the definitive relationship of such binding loci to the mutagenic action to the drug must still be determined. It may be significant, however, that, based on the cellular content of DNA, substantially more attachment occurred to mitochondrial DNA than to nuclear DNA.[23]

Propidium is an ethidium analog that has been reported to differ considerably from ethidium in its mutagenic properties for mitochondria. Unlike ethidium, it is not mutagenic for resting cells[24,25] and is only moderately mutagenic for growing cells.[25] The lack of mutagenicity of propidium for cells could not be attributed to a lack of cell permeability because the addition of the drug to growing cells greatly accelerated the mutagenic effects due to the added presence of ethidium bromide.[25] Thus, the difference in metabolic handling represented a reasonable explanation for the difference in the mutagenic effectiveness of these two agents. Our studies with photoaffinity labeling also showed that propidium could compete effectively for mutagenic attachment of ethidium monoazide to mitochondria: This is additional evidence that propidium penetrates the cell and it provides an additional tool to distinguish among the different steps of ethidium mutagenesis. We were able, for example, to relate the rescue that has been reported for high concentrations of ethidium bromide to competition for the initial binding process, since either ethidium or propidium could prevent mutagenesis by ethidium azide when added prior to the photolytic step.[26]

The photoaffinity probe technique has, therefore, proved quite useful for beginning studies of the nature of mitochondrial mutagenesis and promises to answer a number of important questions that remain concerning this important biological process.

Ethidium Monoazide as a Probe for Frameshift Mutagenesis

Studies with *Salmonella* tester strains have produced three interesting types of findings, which argue that the ethidium photoaffinity probe will also be useful in studying the important question of the mechanisms for frameshift mutagenesis. First, the parent compound is not mutagenic unless it is activated by microsomal enzymes, despite its ability to intercalate.[2] Furthermore, ethidium monoazide was nonmutagenic in the dark.[9] Upon photolysis, however, it was an active mutagen for strain TA1538.[9] This specificity contrasts with that of 9-NH_2 acridine, with which it is often compared for binding to DNA, which is mutagenic, without metabolic activation, for strain TA1537.[2] The role of covalent attachment for the ethidium analog was suggested by the discovery that a repair-proficient strain was protected from mutagenesis.[9] In contrast, mutagenesis by 9-NH_2 acridine was not affected by whether or not the tester strain was repair-proficient.[2]

Second, covalent binding of the ethidium moiety to DNA was demonstrated, after intracellular photolysis of the ^{14}C-labeled monoazide, by isolation of the ^{14}C-labeled *Salmonella* DNA. This procedure was also used to show simple competition of ethidium bromide for ethidium monoazide binding, suggesting the identity of the bulk of the DNA binding sites.[27]

Third, the complex nature of frameshift mutagenesis was demonstrated by the discovery that ethidium bromide could enhance both photolytic mutagenesis and toxicity of the ethidium monoazide despite competition for total binding.[28] This seeming paradox should be resolvable by precisely identifying the covalent adducts formed both with and without added ethidium. Resolution of this problem should assist us in defining the natures of mutagenic and comutagenic effects.

Use of Ethidium Monoazide to Study DNA Repair

In addition to probing specific drug actions and mutagenic mechanisms, photoaffinity labeling can also provide readily measurable substrates for DNA repair processes. Due to the specificity of their binding, such labels can be directed to specific sectors of the genome.

Ethidium monoazide was used to study repair synthesis in human lymphocytes.[29] Irradiation of cells with drug concentrations as low as 1×10^{-6} M provoked active repair synthesis. The K_{dis} for the drug calculated from a dose response curve was 0.8 μM, in good agreement with values reported for drug binding to isolated DNA. The level of repair activity was not additive with uv at either saturating or nonsaturating levels of either insult. The ability to simultaneously measure both the extent and distribution of drug excision and the DNA bases inserted subsequently should provide an important approach for studying DNA repair processes. The photoaffinity probe should prove especially useful as an alternative insult to uv damage for studying repair processes in nondividing cell populations in which prelabeling of cellular bulk DNA is not possible.

Summary

Ethidium, a classic nucleic acid ligand, has been converted to a photosensitive derivative with minimal disruption of its binding and biological properties. Binding was shown to be not only identical to EB by physical studies, but also competitive with the parent drug. Photolysis produced covalent adducts *in vitro* and *in vivo* with a large enhancement of petite mutagenesis in yeast, production of frameshift mutagenesis in *Salmonella,* and DNA repair synthesis in human cells. Thus, this probe is presented as a promising tool for studying subcellular drug distribution in relation to biological effects, in defining mechanisms for mutagenesis, and as a measurable substrate for DNA repair processes. The success of this probe suggests that it is feasible to construct analogous probes for the study of other nucleic acid ligands, a task in which our laboratory is actively engaged.

ANTHRACYCLINE ANTIBIOTICS AS DIRECT ACTING PHOTOAFFINITY PROBES

The effectiveness of adriamycin in cancer chemotherapy has sparked considerable interest in its mechanisms of action. Its reported binding to DNA may account for its action, but its specific intracellular fates have not been determined. Photoaffinity labeling could provide the means of defining its distribution and actions. Anthracycline antibiotics were previously reported to show photosensitive effects with both viruses and DNA following irradiation in the uv range.[30,31] In view of its visible spectrum, we conducted studies with adriamycin and certain of its analogs to determine their photosensitivities in the visible range. Adriamycin, daunomycin, and rubidazone were all found to be sensitive to irradiation by a daylight fluorescent lamp. Furthermore, irradiation of the drugs with visible light in the presence of calf thymus DNA resulted in a protection against photolytic degradation. This was accompanied by covalent adduct formation between the DNA and drugs, as shown by loss of solvent and phenol extractability of the drug from DNA solutions, stability to alkaline and thermal denaturation of DNA and lack of separation by column chromatography.[32] TABLE 3 summarizes the formation of covalent adduct between the three drugs tested and native, denatured, or formaldehyde-denatured calf thymus DNA. At saturating drug levels, about one-third of the drug complexes with native calf thymus DNA were converted to covalent adducts. These preliminary studies suggest that chromophoric drugs with demonstrable photosensitivity should be considered as possible candidates for direct photoaffinity labeling without a requirement for derivatization.

SUMMARY AND CONCLUSIONS

Photoaffinity labeling is a powerful, relatively new approach to defining *in vivo* sites of interactions and mechanisms for biological effects of a variety of nucleic acid ligands. Reversible complexes can thus be converted to stable, covalent adducts with the potential for their precise molecular localization and description, for definition of their persistent biological effects following covalent fixation, and for competition studies with effective and ineffective drug analogs. The rational design of new ligands with predictable binding and biological properties will follow from such definitive studies of drug binding mechanisms. Photoaffinity labeling can be accomplished either by the use of the intrinsic photosensitivity and photoreactivity properties of ligands or by the process of photosensitive derivatization.

Ethidium monoazide has served as a prototype for the construction of a photosensitive derivative of a drug that retains the binding and biological properties of its parent. This probe should permit definitive localization and characterization of its specific biological effects: inhibition of nucleic acid processes, perturbation of nucleic

TABLE 3

PHOTOINACTIVATION OF ANTHRACYCLINE ANTIBIOTICS AND
PHOTOADDUCT FORMATION WITH DNA

	Percentage of Photodestruction of Drug (%)	Percentage of Drug Converted to Covalent Adduct (%)
Adriamycin alone	82	
+ native DNA	4	40
+ heat denatured DNA	7	15
+ formaldehyde treated DNA	19	3
Daunorubicin alone	85	
+ native DNA	5	35
+ heat denatured DNA	5	8
+ formaldehyde treated DNA	21	2
Rubidazone alone	66	
+ native DNA	8	30
+ heat denatured DNA	8	5
+ formaldehyde treated DNA	33	2

NOTE: Irradiation was for 6 h with a daylight fluorescent lamp at a flux of 40 J m^{-2} s^{-1}, with drug and DNA concentrations of 0.5 and 5 mM, respectively.

acid structure, mutagenesis, and antiparasitic action. Such probes will also prove useful for studying normal biological structures and processes, in addition to exploring pathological effects.

Preliminary studies with adriamycin, daunomycin, and rubidazone have provided examples of direct photolabeling with light-sensitive drugs without the complication and the consequent need to establish that such a drug analog is still representative of the parent compound.

REFERENCES

1. LERMAN, L. W. 1961. J. Mol. Biol. **3:** 18–30.
2. MCCANN, J. E., CHOI, E. YOMASAKA & B. N. AMES. 1975. Proc. Nat. Acad. Sci. USA **72:** 5135–39.

3. RIVA, S. C. 1966. Biochem. Biophys. Res. Commun. **23:** 606–11.
4. TSAI, C. C., S. C. JAIN, H. M. SOBEL. 1975. Proc. Nat. Acad. Sci. USA **72:** 628–32.
5. SAKORE, T. D., S. C. JAIN, C. C. TSAI & H. M. SOBEL. 1977. Proc. Nat. Acad. Sci. USA **74:** 188–92.
6. WARING, M. J. 1970. J. Mol. Biol. **54:** 247–79.
7. SLONIMSKI, P. P., G. PERRODIN & J. H. CROFT. 1968. Biochem. Biophys. Res. Commun. **30:** 232–39.
8. HIXON, S. C., W. E. WHITE, JR. & K. L. YIELDING. 1975. J. Mol. Biol. **92:** 319–29.
9. YIELDING, L. W., W. E. WHITE, JR. & K. L. YIELDING. 1976. Mutation Res. **34:** 351–58.
10. GRAVES, D. E., L. W. YIELDING, C. L. WATKINS & K. L. YIELDING. 1977. Biochim. Biophys. Acta **479:** 98–104.
11. STERNGLANZ, H., D. E. GRAVES, L. W. YIELDING & C. E. BUGG. 1978. J. Cryst. Mol. Struct. **8:** 93–103.
12. GRAVES, D. E., C. L. WATKINS & L. W. YIELDING. Biochemistry. Submitted.
13. YIELDING, L. W. To be published.
14. CANTRELL, C. E., K. M. PRUITT & K. L. YIELDING. 1979. Mol. Pharmacol. **15:** 322–31.
15. HOLLENBERG, C. P. & P. BORST. 1971. Biochem. Biophys. Res. Commun. **45:** 1250–54.
16. BASTOS, R. N. & H. R. MOHLER. 1974. J. Biol. Chem. **249:** 6617–27.
17. PAOLETTI, C. H. & M. GUERENEAU. 1972. Biochem. Biophys. Res. Commun. **48:** 950–58.
18. HALL, R. M., M. K. TREMBATH, A. W. LINNANE, L. WHEELIS & R. S. CRIDDLE. 1976. Mol. Gen. Genet. **144:** 253–62; and CRIDDLE, R. S., L. WHEELIS, M. K. TREMBATH & A. W. LINNANE. *Ibid.:* 263–72.
19. MORITA, M. & K. L. YIELDING. 1977. Mutation Res. **56:** 21–30.
20. FUKUNAGA, M. & K. L. YIELDING. 1979. Jpn. J. Med. Sci. Biol. **32:** 219–23.
21. HIXON, S. C., W. E. WHITE, JR. & K. L. YIELDING. 1975. Biochem. Biophys. Res. Commun. **66:** 31–35.
22. MORITA, T. & K. L. YIELDING. 1978. Mutation Res. **54:** 27–32.
23. FUKUNAGA, M. & K. L. YIELDING. 1979. Biochim. Biophys. Acta **585:** 293–99.
24. MAHLER, H. R. 1972. J. Supramol. Struct. **1:** 449–60.
25. FUKUNAGA, M. & K. L. YIELDING. 1978. Biochem. Biophys. Res. Commun. **84:** 501–7.
26. FUKUNAGA, M. & K. L. YIELDING. 1979. Mutation Res. **62:** 35–42.
27. YIELDING, L. W., D. E. GRAVES, B. R. BROWN & K. L. YIELDING. 1979. Biochem. Biophys. Res. Commun. **87:** 424–32.
28. YIELDING, L. W., B. R. BROWN, D. E. GRAVES & K. L. YIELDING. 1979. Mutation Res. **63:** 225–32.
29. CANTRELL, C. E. & K. L. YIELDING. 1977. Photochem. Photobiol. **25:** 189–91.
30. SANFILLIPPO, A., G. SHIOPPACASSI, M. MORVILLO & M. CHIONE. 1968. G. Microbiol. **16:** 49–54.
31. VERINI, M. A., A. M. CASAZZA, A. FIORETTI, F. RODENGHI & M. GHIONE. 1968. G. Microbiol. **16:** 55–66.
32. DAUGHERTY, J. P., S. C. HIXON & K. L. YIELDING. 1979. Biochim. Biophys. Acta. **565:** 13–21.

DISCUSSION

DR. V. CHOWDHRY: Have you seen any effect with the ethidium bromide photolysis itself?

DR. K. L. YIELDING: We've done the appropriate controls with irradiation of the parent compound and found no effects under the conditions of these experiments; ethidium is photosensitive if you put it in light for extended periods of time, but not under these conditions.

PHOTO-CROSS-LINKING STUDIES
OF NUCLEIC ACID STRUCTURE*

Charles R. Cantor

Barth Laboratory
Department of Chemistry
Columbia University
New York, New York 10027

INTRODUCTION

In contrast to the wide variety of photoaffinity labeling studies of protein targets reviewed in this volume, there have been very few studies of photochemical labeling of nucleic acid targets. This is not because of a lack of interesting targets. Instead, it probably reflects the fact that, until very recently, it was relatively difficult to locate sites of covalent modification on large nucleic acids. As a result, most photoaffinity labeling studies in nucleic acid systems have involved either the direct exploitation of the photochemical reactivity of occasional strange bases[1-3] or the use of strange bases or nucleic acid chain termini for the placement of photoactivatable groups.[4,5] The nucleic acid was then used as a photoaffinity reagent to identify components of its binding site in nucleoprotein complexes. Often, these components were proteins, and, although occasional nucleic acid targets were found, there was no systematic attempt to look for them.

A number of factors have sparked a renewed interest in nucleic acid photo-cross-linking and photoaffinity labeling. In one of the best-studied nucleoprotein systems, the ribosome system, it has become increasingly clear that the nucleic acid plays important structural and functional roles.[6] There are strong indications that particular nucleic acid structural features also play a role in various types of RNA processing in both prokaryotes and eukaryotes. There is a great need to prove the existence of these structures and show how they are recognized by various enzymes.

Techniques for handling nucleic acids have advanced significantly in the past few years; these will greatly facilitate nucleic acid photoaffinity labeling. Recombinant DNA techniques allow us to isolate usable amounts of particular DNA sequences. The availability of a myriad of restriction nucleases and new, rapid nucleic acid sequencing techniques have revolutionized our ability to obtain primary structure information. Inevitably, these techniques will also catalyze great improvements in the identification of sites of chemical modification on nucleic acids. The electron microscope has proved to be a remarkably effective tool for low resolution location of the sites of attachment of proteins, cross-linkers, and annealed nucleic acid pieces.[7,8]

These systems and advances set the stage for the development of productive photoaffinity labeling studies on nucleic acids—the missing ingredient is a suitable

*This research was supported by two United States Public Health Service Research grants, nos. GM 14825 and GM 19843 and by a National Science Foundation Research grant, no. PCM 7709254.

0077-8923/80/0346-0379 $1.75/1 © 1980, NYAS

arsenal of nucleic acid–specific photochemical reagents. From studies on proteins, it is clear that the most useful reagents will be those that lead to high yield specific reactions.[9-12] However, the typical photoactivatable groups used on proteins do not seem attractive for nucleic acid targets. A sensible approach is to start with nucleic acid photoreagents of proven effectiveness and adapt these for photoaffinity labeling studies. Psoralens stand out as the most promising class of reagents available.

Psoralens are intercalating agents that bind to double-stranded nucleic acids. They are efficient at photoadditions to pyrimidine bases and form double-strand nucleic acid cross-links where alternating purine-pyrimidine sequences exist.[13-16]

In this paper, I shall summarize the results of some of our recent studies, which used psoralens to examine the structure of ribosomal RNA. Then I will show how psoralens may be used as affinity labeling reagents. In these approaches, the unique feature of psoralens is their ability to make double-strand cross-links. Finally, I will comment on some of the limitations of psoralens. The structures of some of psoralen derivatives we used are shown in FIGURE 1.

RIBOSOMAL RNA CROSS-LINKING

The 30S subunit of the *E. coli* ribosome contains a single 16S rRNA molecule and 21 different proteins. A variety of spectroscopic, chemical modification, and hydrodynamic studies show that the free RNA must be folded intramolecularly into an extensive network of double-stranded regions. The extent of double strand must be similar in the free RNA and in the ribosome, but the exact pattern of double-stranded regions is unknown, nor is it known how much this pattern changes upon ribosome assembly. The nucleotide sequence of the 16S rRNA is known,[17-19] and if this sequence can be folded into a pattern of secondary structure far more stable than alternative patterns, manual and computer searches have, thus far, failed to find it.

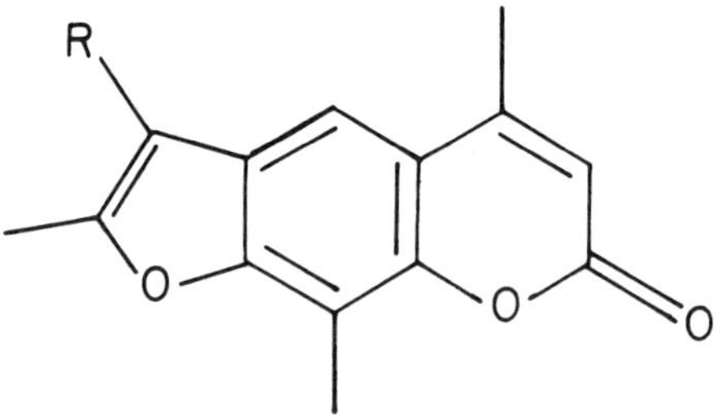

FIGURE 1. Structures and abbreviations of several psoralen derivatives.

Compound, R =	Abbreviation
$HO-CH_2-$	HMT
$NH_3^+-CH_2-$	AMT
$HS-(CH_2)_2-NH-CH_2-$	CMT

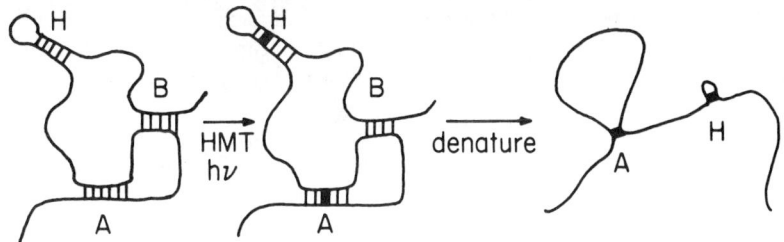

FIGURE 2. A schematic illustration of the analysis of RNA secondary structure by psoralen cross-linking and electron microscopy. A, B, and H refer to helical regions; the solid bar is a psoralen cross-link.

Even much smaller RNAs, such as the 5S rRNA, cannot be folded into uniquely stable structures on the basis of sequence information alone.

In collaboration with Pallaiah Thammana, Paul Wollenzien, and John Hearst, we have used psoralen cross-linking to examine the pattern of secondary structure of the 16S rRNA, both free and in the 30S particle. The type of experiment performed is shown schematically in FIGURE 2. After irradiating samples in the presence of the psoralen derivative, HMT, proteins, if present, were removed by phenol extraction; all RNA secondary structure was denatured by a formamide-formaldehyde procedure; the resulting molecules were examined in the electron microscope. At the resolution attainable by current techniques, cross-links between double-stranded regions distant in the primary structure appeared as open loops, as does feature A in FIGURE 2. Large cross-linked hairpins, such as feature H, will show up as bulges on the nucleic acid contour, while small hairpins will be visible only indirectly, as a decrease in the total length of the nucleic acid chain.

By simple inspection of fields of cross-linked molecules, the general character of the secondary structure of 16S rRNA is visible. Large loops are quite common and cross-linked molecules are shorter than controls. However, there is relatively little evidence for the presence of large hairpin loops. Thus, the types of structures proposed for the 16S rRNA on the basis of early sequence data, which consisted entirely of large hairpins,[20] will have to be discarded. The location of the large loops seen by electron microscopy can be determined by quantitative length measurements on many individual molecules. In this way, the positions of eleven cross-links in free 16S rRNA have been mapped to an accuracy of about ±50 bases.[21] Molecules containing more than one large loop are used to assign the relative polarity of various cross-linked features. However, an absolute assignment of specific cross-links, such as 3'-proximal or 5'-proximal, was possible only through more elaborate techniques.[22]

A statistical analysis of the frequency of occurrence of these eleven cross-links is consistent with the hypothesis that they represent a sampling of eleven secondary structure features that occur simultaneously in the 16S rRNA molecule. Relatively simple model construction indicates that these features constrain the 16S rRNA to a volume only two to three times that of the 30S ribosome itself. Thus, the results indicate that RNA molecules can be designed so as to fold into compact structures without the aid of proteins. When the 30S ribosome was examined by HMT cross-linking, the pattern of secondary structure observed closely resembled that of the free 16S rRNA, with the possible exception of some differences near the 3' end.[23] This suggests that the 16S rRNA may serve as a structural core for the 30S ribosome. The general nature of these results agrees well with recent hydrodynamic and electron microscopic studies.[24,25]

Further insights into the 16S rRNA structure will require more cross-links, as well as much more accurate locations for the cross-links obtained to date. The former problem cannot be solved simply by increasing psoralen or irradiation doses, since that simply leads to molecules that do not spread well enough on electron microscope grids to permit quantitative examination. One potentially promising approach is to find a method for the specific introduction of psoralens. For example, intact ribosomes are far less reactive than free rRNA. Thus, a ribosome sample in which one or more specific proteins had been deleted might show a markedly enhanced pattern of specific psoralen cross-linking. Other approaches involve the use of psoralens in a manner equivalent to affinity labeling; these will be described subsequently.

It may be possible to locate cross-links more accurately through improved electron microscopic techniques, but, in the long run, the most definitive information is sure to come from finding psoralens in the sequence. If the yield of an individual cross-link is high enough, brute force oligonucleotide mapping should suffice. In simple cases with a single cross-link, ladder sequencing techniques should be readily adaptable. With multiple cross-links in low average yields, however, it will be necessary either to purify molecules with individual features prior to analysis or to find ways of breaking the cross-link so that diagonal separation techniques can be used to analyze many cross-links simultaneously, just as they are used with complex protein assemblies.

Knowledge of an RNA structure implies knowing not only where individual double-stranded regions are but also where two single strands approach each other and where two duplexes approach each other. In principle, given appropriate single- and double-strand–specific reagents, such structural questions should be resolvable using the same general strategy as that described above for HMT.

NEW PSORALEN APPLICATIONS

The success of psoralen cross-linking in studies of 16S rRNA and various other nucleic acid structures provides a strong inducement to further characterize the photoreactions of psoralens with nucleic acids and, also, to prepare new psoralens with enhanced capabilities. A problem encountered in numerous psoralen studies is the need to have a relatively high concentration of reagent in order to ensure sufficient binding and subsequent photoreaction. One solution to this problem is the synthesis of psoralens with higher affinity for nucleic acid double strands.[13] With nucleoproteins, however, such compounds have the risk that their avidity for the nucleic acid may lead to displacement of the bound proteins and perturbation of the structure.

The need for high reagent concentrations in an actual experimental situation would be circumvented if psoralens could be covalently attached to one nucleic acid strand while retaining the ability to form a cross-link to the other strand of a duplex upon subsequent irradiation. The second irradiation could be performed in the absence of all free reagents. Using the fact that psoralen cross-linking involves two separate photoreactions, Hearst and his colleagues were able to form psoralen-DNA monoadducts by irradiation with a short laser pulse.[26] Subsequent reirradiation, after removing the unreacted psoralen, yielded cross-links. This procedure is elegant, but it is restricted to rather small extents of psoralen incorporation.

We recently found that if AMT or any other psoralen derivative is irradiated at 390 nm, just at their long wavelength absorption edge, in the presence of double-stranded DNA or RNA, psoralen monoadducts are formed very efficiently.[27] When these monoadducts are reirradiated at 360 nm after the unattached psoralen is removed, cross-links form readily. With DNA, the efficiency of cross-linking by psoralen monoadducts is nearly 50%. This is what is expected if each psoralen at an alternating pyrimidine-purine site is capable of quantitative photo-cross-linking. Thus, a sample of DNA or RNA containing psoralen monoadducts becomes a powerful photoaffinity reagent for any piece of nucleic acid to which it is base-paired.

Psoralen-monoadduct photoaffinity reagents have a wealth of potential applications. In ribosomes, for example, we are overcoming the unreactivity of 70S particles towards psoralens by forming monoadducts with separated 30S and 50S subunits. Then, after recombination to make 70S particles, subsequent irradiation yields cross-links.[28] Monoadducts should be especially useful in studies of the kinetics of conformational rearrangements in nucleic acids. They should also be useful in studies of DNA transcription, replication, and repair.

By forming a heteroduplex or an R-loop between two nucleic acids with limited homology, it should be possible to place monoadducts specifically in a restricted portion of a short nucleic acid. After purification away from its larger partner, the monoadduct-containing single strand could be used as a hybridization probe of either nucleic acid sequence or accessibility in numerous systems. Since the hybrid can be covalently trapped by subsequent irradiation, both electron microscopic analysis and purification of the target DNA sequence will be greatly facilitated.

Perhaps the most useful types of psoralens will be those containing additional functional groups. Several thiol-containing psoralens, including the compound CMT (shown in FIGURE 1) and others containing longer chains, have recently been prepared in our laboratory.[29] One can envision a number of different applications for such compounds, including bis-double-strand cross-linking, breakable double-strand cross-linking, and nucleic acid photoaffinity labeling.

If a folded nucleic acid superstructure is photolyzed in the presence of CMT or its analogs, numerous psoralen adducts are formed, but the thiol remains accessible for subsequent reaction. Oixdizing the thiols or bridging thiols by treatment with bis-maleimides produce cross-links wherever a double strand folds back on itself to form a close contact. The locations of the cross-links could be found by electron microscopy or by restriction nuclease analysis, exploiting the reversibility of the disulfide bond. Thus, one ought to be able to map the folding pattern of DNAs in viruses or condensed chromosomes.

In pilot studies,[29] larger analogs of CMT were diffused into bacteriophage λ, irradiated, and then oxidized. After the protein coat was removed, covalent loops of DNA were visible in the electron microscope. Subsequent reduction eliminated those loops. This strongly encourages the development of additional cross-linkable psoralens and bis-psoralens. Indeed, examples of the latter class of compounds have already been prepared by Peter Dervan and his group.[30]

The reactive thiol group in compounds like CMT could be used to attach the psoralen to a variety of nucleic acid–binding ligands, thus opening the way to many types of photoaffinity labeling. The main difficulty in nucleic acid affinity labeling in the past has been isolating and identifying the product. It is instructive to demonstrate how a thiol-containing psoralen can facilitate this process. Consider a ligand attached to the psoralen through a disulfide band. After affinity labeling and reduction, the thiol-containing psoralen will remain attached at the nucleic acid target site by either a monoadduct or a cross-link. The presence of the thiol will allow partial purification of the target nucleic acid by affinity chromotography on organomercurial columns.[31] If a cross-link is present, the location of the target on the nucleic acid will be visible by electron microscopy under denaturing conditions. A cross-link will also allow purification of the target by exploiting the rapid renaturability of cross-linked nucleic acids. Alternatively, if a monoadduct has been placed at the target, this would assist subsequent purification and analysis by the hybridization techniques sketched above.

Clearly, other chemically reactive analogs of psoralens are likely to appear on the scene for a variety of specific applications. Psoralens containing an attached protein-specific reactive moiety offer one solution to the serious problem of the lack of protein–nucleic acid cross-linking reagents.

LIMITATIONS OF PSORALENS

Many of the advantages of psoralens and their derivatives have been described, but psoralens are not without drawbacks. Probably, the most serious problem arises from the fact that psoralens are intercalating agents. As such, they are incapable of binding to a nucleic acid without perturbing its structure. Binding a psoralen in the absence of light is expected, by analogy with other intercalators, to cause a lengthening of its double-strand region of about 3 Å and an unwinding of that double strand of about 26°. In addition, a small kink and displacement of the helix's axis may occur.[32] When a monoadduct forms, a larger structural disruption is expected; still more disruption will occur with a cross-link.

These disruptions appear to be tolerated fairly well by extended nucleic acid structures and even by relatively folded structures like 16S rRNA. However, tight nucleic acid or nucleoprotein tertiary structures appear to be relatively resistant to psoralen. For example, intact ribosomes[23] and nucleosome cores[33,34] show very little psoralen reactivity. It appears that such particles are rather intolerant to the binding of intercalators, since they also exclude the binding of molecules like ethidium reasonably effectively.[28] Presumably, the unwinding that accompanies intercalation, while requiring only small local motions, would lead to such large motions at a distance from the binding site that the energetic cost is too great.

Psoralen monoadducts may allow cross-linking in such structures, since these could be attached to the nucleic acid prior to its condensation into a tightly folded structure. However, this entails the risk that a seriously distorted tertiary structure with little biological significance will result. What are badly needed are nonintercalative nucleic acid photoreagents. How difficult it will be to construct these remains to be seen. The advantage of intercalators like psoralens or ethidium azides[35] is that, once activated, the reagent has little choice but to react with the target nucleic acid. In contrast, a photoactivable group bound in a nucleic acid groove would still be exposed to solvent and, therefore, covalent reaction yields might be much lower than desired.

REFERENCES

1. KUECHLER, E. & J. OFENGAND. 1979. *In* Transfer RNA. P. Schimmel, D. Soll, and J. Ableson, Eds.: 413–44. Cold Spring Harbor Press. New York.
2. SCHWARTZ, I. & J. OFFENGAND. 1978. Biochemistry **17:** 2524–30.
3. YANIV, M., A. CHESTIER, F. GROS & A. FAVRE. 1976. J. Mol. Biol. **58:** 381–88.
4. SCHWARTZ, I., E. GORDON & J. OFENGAND. 1975. Biochemistry **14:** 2907–14.
5. HSIUNG, N., S. A. REINES & C. R. CANTOR. 1974. J. Mol. Biol. **88:** 841–55.
6. STEITZ, J. A. & K. JAKES. 1975. Proc. Nat. Acad. Sci. USA **72:** 4734–38.
7. WU, M. & N. DAVIDSON. 1978. Nucleic Acids Res. **5:** 2825–46.
8. WOLLENZIEN, P. L., D. L. YOUVAN & J. E. HEARST. 1978. Proc. Nat. Acad. Sci. USA **75:** 1642–46.
9. CHOWDHRY, V., R. VAUGHAN & F. H. WESTHEIMER. 1976. Proc. Nat. Acad. Sci. USA **73:** 1406–8.
10. FLEET, G. W. J., R. R. PORTER & J. R. KNOWLES. 1969. Nature (London) **224:** 511–12.
11. GALARDY, R. E., L. C. CRAIG & M. P. PRINTZ. 1973. Nature (London) New Biol. **242:** 127–28.
12. JELENC, P. C., C. R. CANTOR & S. R. SIMON. 1978. Proc. Nat. Acad. Sci. USA **75:** 3564–68.
13. ISAACS, S. T., C. J. SHEN, J. E. HEARST & H. RAPOPORT. 1977. Biochemistry **16:** 1058–64.
14. OU, C. N., C. H. TSAI, K. J. TAPLEY, JR. & P. S. SONG. 1978. Biochemistry **17:** 1047–53.
15. DALL'ACQUA, F., D. VELDALDI & M. RECHER. 1978. Photochem. Photobiol. **27:** 33–46.
16. HYDE, J. E. & J. E. HEARST. 1978. Biochemistry **17:** 1251–57.
17. BROSIUS, J., M. L. PALMER, P. J. KENNEDY & H. F. NOLLER. 1978. Proc. Nat. Acad. Sci. USA **75:** 4801–5.
18. CARBON, P., C. EHRESMANN, B. EHRESMANN & J. P. EBEL. 1978. FEBS Lett. **94:** 152–56.
19. SQUIRES, C. L. & C. L. SQUIRES. 1979. Unpublished results.
20. EHRESMANN, C., P. STIEGLER, B. A. MACKIE, R. A. ZIMMERMAN, J. P. EBEL & P. FELLNER. 1975. Nucleic Acids Res. **2:** 265–78.
21. WOLLENZIEN, P. L., J. E. HEARST, P. THAMMANA & C. R. CANTOR. 1979. J. Mol. Biol. **135:** 255–70.
22. WOLLENZIEN, P. L., J. E. HEARST, C. L. SQUIRES & C. L. SQUIRES. 1979. J. Mol. Biol. **135:** 285–92.
23. THAMMANA, P., C. R. CANTOR, P. L. WOLLENZIEN & J. E. HEARST. 1979. J. Mol. Biol. **135:** 271–84.
24. ALLEN, S. H. & K. P. WONG. 1978. J. Biol. Chem. **253:** 8759–66.
25. VASILIEV, V. D., O. M. SELIVANOVA & V. E. KOTELIANSKY. 1978. FEBS Lett. **95:** 273–76.
26. JOHNSTON, B. H., M. A. JOHNSON, C. B. MOORE & J. E. HEARST. 1977. Science **197:** 906–8.
27. CHATTERJEE, P. K. & C. R. CANTOR. 1978. Nucleic Acids Res. **5:** 3619–33.
28. CHU, Y. G. & C. R. CANTOR. 1979. Unpublished results.
29. GOLDENBERG, M., R. HAAS & C. R. CANTOR. 1979. Unpublished results.
30. DERVAN, P. Personal communication.
31. HILDEBRANDT J. & C. R. CANTOR. 1979. Unpublished results.
32. SOBELL, H. M., C. C. TSAI, S. C. JACN & S. G. GILBERT. 1977. J. Mol. Biol. **114:** 333–66
33. SHEN, C. K. J. & J. E. HEARST. 1978. Cold Spring Harbor Symp. Quant. Biol. **42:** 179–89.
34. CECH, T. R., D. POTTER & M. L. PARDUE. 1978. Cold Spring Harbor Symp. Quant. Biol. **42:** 191–98.
35. WHITE, J. R., W. E. YIELDING & K. L. YIELDING. 1977. *In* Methods in Enzymology, Vol. 46. W. Jakoby & M. Wilchek, Eds.: 644–49. Academic Press. New York.

PHOTOCHEMICAL CROSS-LINKING BETWEEN PROTEINS AND NUCLEIC ACIDS AS A PROBE OF NUCLEOPROTEIN INTERACTIONS*

Ruth Sperling,[†] Abraham Havron,[‡] and Joseph Sperling[‡]

The Weizmann Institute of Science
Rehovot, Israel

The tendency of proteins and nucleic acids to cross-link covalently as a result of irradiation by ultraviolet (uv) light can be used as a probe of nucleoprotein structure. This "zero-length" cross-linking agent presumably joins together amino acid residues and nucleic acid constituents, thereby "freezing" existing interactions in the native complex. The major advantage of this approach is that photochemical cross-linking can be performed on naturally occurring nucleoprotein complexes under optimal conditions in which maximum binding or maximum stability of the native complex occurs. It does not require decomposition, further introduction of foreign reactive groups, and subsequent reconstitution of the complex's components.

The validity of conclusions derived from such an approach regarding protein–nucleic acid contacts is based on the assumption that the uv-induced covalent cross-links are formed specifically either between interacting regions on the macromolecules or between residues that are in close proximity in the native complex. Compliance with this condition is necessary if the photochemical cross-linking is to freeze existing contact points in the irradiated protein–nucleic acid complex. It is apparent, therefore, that the reliability of the photochemical approach depends on the ability of both purines and pyrimidines to form covalent adducts with a large number of amino acids and, at the same time, requires that specific covalent bonds be formed only between neighboring residues in the native structure.

By analogy to photoalkylation reactions both of amino acids[1] (FIGURE 1) and of nucleic acid constituents[2] (FIGURE 2), it could have been anticipated that covalent adducts of amino acids to the heterocyclic base constituents of nucleic acids would be a major product of irradiation of their mixtures. This, however, was not the case, since only trace amounts of such cross-links could be identified (unpublished observations). On the other hand, significant yields (up to 60%) of cross-linked products were obtained whenever a nucleoprotein complex with an appreciable binding constant ($>10^5$ M^{-1}) was irradiated.[3] These observations provided the initial clue of the specific involvement of neighboring residues in the photochemical cross-linking. On the basis of the model reactions (FIGURES 1 and 2), it can be assumed that, at least in principle, all amino acid residues are capable of forming covalent adducts with the heterocyclic base constituents of the nucleic acids. Indeed, it has been reported that a large variety of amino acids are capable of forming covalent addition products with the pyrimidine constituents of DNA[4]; the involvement of purines in photochemical cross-linking to

*This research was supported by grants from the Israel Commission for Basic Research and the United States–Israel Binational Science Foundation, Jerusalem, Israel.
†Department of Chemical Physics.
‡Department of Organic Chemistry.

0077–8923/0346–0386 $1.75/1 © 1980, NYAS

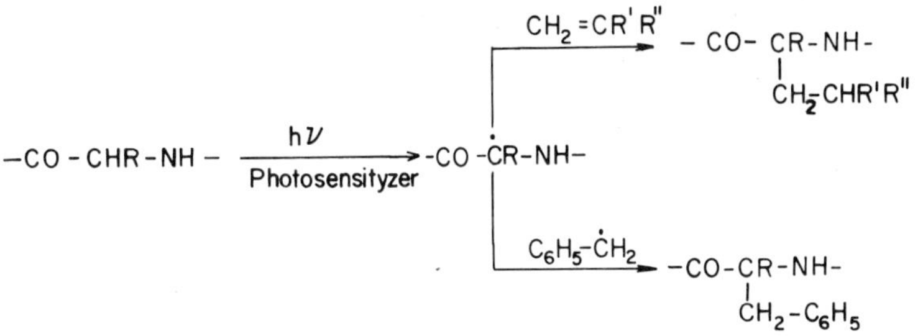

FIGURE 1.

proteins has been demonstrated in the complex of ATP with histone H4,[5] in the complex of ATP with Ile-tRNA synthetase,[6] and in the photoaffinity labeling of membrane proteins with cGMP.[7]

We verified the specificity of the cross-linking reactions and their confinement to interacting residues by identifying the amino acid residues that participated in cross-linking to a nucleotide in a protein-nucleotide complex of known structure. Hence, it was possible to ask whether the cross-linked regions on the protein were relevant to the binding site of the pyrimidine ring as mapped by x-ray diffraction. Thus, covalent bonds between RNase-A and either of its competitive inhibitors, cytidine 2′(3′), 5′-diphosphate (pCp) or uridine 2′(3′), 5′-diphosphate (pUp), were induced by uv irradiation of each of the stable enzyme-inhibitor complexes.[8] Analysis of the tryptic peptides of the modified protein revealed a single specific peptide, which became covalently linked to both nucleotide inhibitors. The amino acid residues that took part in the photochemical reaction were identified as Ser-80, Ile-81, and Thr-82.[9] These three consecutive residues, as can be seen in the three-dimensional x-ray model of the enzyme, are part of a β-sheet structure that forms the bottom of the binding site for the pyrimidine ring of the nucleotide inhibitor.[10]

In our subsequent work, we employed the photochemical cross-linking approach to study histone-DNA interactions within nucleosomes—the chromatin repeating sub-units. Rat liver mononucleosomes were irradiated either directly, with uv light of $\lambda = 254$ nm, or in the presence of a photosensitizer, with light of $\lambda > 290$ nm. The order of

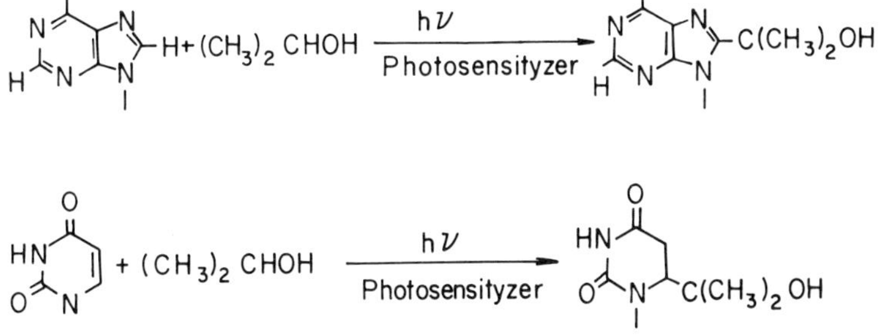

FIGURE 2.

the rates of disappearance of the histones from their normal migration positions on polyacrylamide gels was found to be: histone H1 > histones H2A and H2B ≫ histones H3 and H4. This disappearance of the histones, which was caused by the uv irradiation, can be accounted for by their involvement in histone-histone[11] and histone-DNA cross-links.[12] Using mononucleosomes that had been cross-linked with a low dose of uv light, we demonstrated,[12] with two independent labeling techniques, that, out of the four core histones,[13] only histones H2A and H2B, in equal amounts, were involved in cross-links with the DNA. Furthermore, a complex of histones H2A and H2B bound to one another through a short piece of DNA was also isolated and characterized.[12]

These results, combined with arguments concerning the nature of the photochemical reactions discussed above, led us to conclude that the four histones in the chromatin core are not positioned equivalently with respect to the surrounding DNA. This conclusion is compatible with a model of the histone core that was derived from structural studies of self-assembled histone fibers.[14]

A further product of the cross-linking of mononucleosomes were cross-linked particles that contained full length nucleosomal DNA (185 base pairs) covalently linked to histone H1. These particles, though devoid of the core histones, retained some properties of intact nucleosomes, as they were partially resistant to mild nuclease digestion and exhibited a CD spectrum similar to that of chromatin.[12] These observations led us to suggest that histone H1, which is located on the outside of the nucleosome,[15] is not bound only to the DNA linker,[16] but binds to the DNA at multiple sites. By doing so, it clamps the folds of the DNA once it has been coiled around the nucleosome core. Therefore, the photochemical cross-linking of H1 to the DNA freezes this fold. Thus, removal of the core histone subsequent to the cross-linking still leaves the structure partially intact.

REFERENCES

1. SPERLING, J. & D. ELAD. 1971. J. Am. Chem. Soc. 93: 3839.
2. LIVNEH-NOY, E., D. ELAD & J. SPERLING. 1978. Biochemistry 17: 3128.
3. SPERLING, J. & A. HAVRON. 1977. Photochem. Photobiol. 26: 661.
4. VARGHESE, A. J. 1976. In Aging, Carcinogenesis, and Radiation Biology. K. C. Smith, Ed.: 207–23. Plenum Press. New York.
5. SPERLING, J. 1976. Photochem. Photobiol. 23: 323.
6. YUE, V. T. & P. R. SCHIMMEL. 1977. Biochemistry 16: 4678.
7. ANTONOFF, R. S., J. J. FERGUSON, JR. & G. IDELKOPE. 1976. Photochem. Photobiol. 23: 327.
8. SPERLING, J. & A. HAVRON. 1976. Biochemistry 15: 1489.
9. HAVRON, A. & J. SPERLING. 1977. Biochemistry 16: 5631.
10. RICHARDS, F. M. & H. W. WYCKOFF. 1971. Enzymes (3rd ed.). 4: 467.
11. DELANGE, R. J., L. C. WILLIAMS & H. G. MARTINSON. 1979. Biochemistry 18: 1942.
12. SPERLING, J. & R. SPERLING. 1978. Nucleic Acids Res. 5: 2755.
13. KORNBERG, R. D. 1977. Annu. Rev. Biochem. 46: 931.
14. SPERLING, R. & E. J. WACHTEL. 1980. Adv. Protein Chem. In press.
15. BALDWIN, J. P., P. G. BOSELEY, E. M. BRADBURY & K. IBEL. 1975. Nature 253: 245.
16. WHITLOCK, J. P., JR. & R. T. SIMPSON. 1976. Biochemistry 15: 3307; SHAW, B. R., T. M. HERMAN, R. T. KOVACIC, G. S. BEAUDREAU & K. E. VAN HOLDE. 1976. Proc. Nat. Acad. Sci. USA 73: 505.

PHOTOENZYME PROBES OF PHOTODAMAGE
TO CELLS AND CELLULAR DNA*

B. M. Sutherland

Biology Department
Brookhaven National Laboratory
Upton, New York 11973

INTRODUCTION

Radiation, whether ionizing or nonionizing, induces a large number of photoproducts in living cells. At biological doses of radiation—those the cell has a reasonable chance of surviving—the principal target for radiation is DNA.[1] I shall deal exclusively with ultraviolet radiation (210 nm $< \lambda <$ 320 nm), as its effects on cells and cellular DNA are, perhaps, best understood. In addition, the principal enzyme probes available today recognize and act specifically on uv-induced damage in DNA.

When ultraviolet radiation impinges on a biological system, be it isolated transforming DNA, a bacterium, or a sunbather, a large variety of photochemical changes can be induced in DNA.[2] These changes include the formation of cyclobutyl pyrimidine dimers (between adjacent pyrimidines on the same DNA strand), pyrimidine hydrates, pyrimidine adducts, protein-DNA cross-links, and interstrand DNA-DNA cross-links (FIGURE 1). In double-stranded DNA at low uv doses, the principal photoproduct is the *cis, syn* cyclobutyl dimer shown in FIGURE 1. Dimers can be formed between any two adjacent pyrimidines in DNA, although the initial rate of formation differs for the three C[]T, T[]T, and C[]C.[3] By saturation of the 5,6 bond through dimer formation, the absorption of the pyrimidine can be greatly reduced, but not eliminated; thus, further irradiation can split dimers to produce the parent monomers. The equilibrium level of each of the three dimer types depends not only on the potential number of sites, but also on the relative absorbance of the dimer and the monomer at the irradiation wavelength.[4] Since the absorption of the dimer increases sharply at shorter wavelengths, reversal reactions are favored at 240 nm, while formation is favored at longer wavelengths ($\sim$290 nm).[1] Since neither the dimer nor the monomer absorb at wavelengths longer than about 320 nm, light in the 320–600 nm region cannot effectively alter dimer yields by direct absorption.

Photoproducts such as the dimer cause death and mutations in cells. It is, therefore, essential that an organism be able to remove or reverse lesions in its DNA; most organisms, in fact, from the bacteriophage T4 to man, have at least one pathway (and usually several) for removing dimers from DNA.[5] Two of these paths are photoreactivation and excision. I shall discuss each of these in turn, with emphasis on the enzymes useful as probes of dimer damage.

*This research was supported by a National Cancer Institute grant, no. CA 23096; by a Research Career Development Award, no. CA 00466; and by the United States Department of Energy.

0077–8923/0346–0389 $1.75/1 © 1980, NYAS

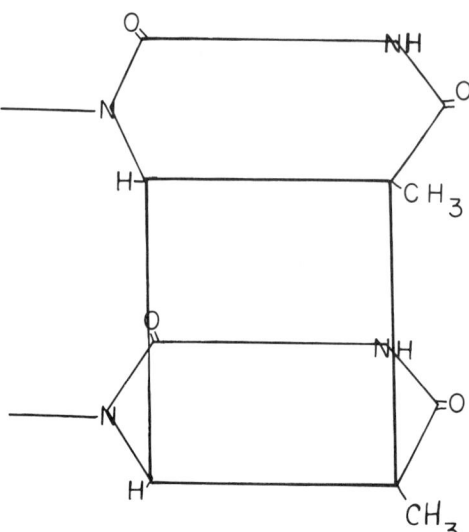

FIGURE 1. A thymine-thymine cyclobutyl pyrimidine dimer, formed in DNA between adjacent pyrimidines on the same DNA strand.

PHOTOREACTIVATION

Photoreactivation is a one-enzyme repair pathway. The photoreactivating enzyme (PRE) is present in almost all organisms, but the level of the enzyme may vary according to tissue,[6] individual genotype,[7] or, for *E. coli* and cultured mammalian cells, the composition of the growth medium.[8-10] The reaction mediated by the enzyme is shown schematically in FIGURE 2; the PRE binds to a dimer-containing region of DNA to form a stable (in the dark) enzyme-substrate complex.[11] Upon absorption of light in the wavelength range 300–600 nm, the dimer is monomerized and the enzyme is released. The enzyme does not nick the phosphodiester backbone, induce any new synthesis, or cause any biologically significant or otherwise detectable side reactions.[12] The enzyme cannot be "preactivated" with light; it must be complexed with the dimer substrate when the photoreactivating photon is absorbed. The requirement of the enzyme for light and the wavelength dependence of the photoreactivation reaction lend additional "handles" for its use as a probe. (The purified *E. coli* enzyme has no intrinsic absorption in the 300–500 nm range in which it is active; upon binding of the enzyme to dimer-containing DNA, there appears a new absorption band, which has the correct wavelength range, wavelength maximum, and molar extinction coefficient to account for photoreactivation.[13])

The PRE is specific for *cis, syn* cyclobutyl pyrimidine dimers in DNA. It will not act on dimers in RNA,[14] and, in fact, heavily-irradiated RNA does not compete with dimer-containing DNA for the PRE, even at a thousand-fold excess of RNA (Hausrath and Sutherland, unpublished data). It will not act on dimer-containing oligodeoxyribonucleotides of less than about ten nucleotides in length,[15] nor will it accept DNA containing addition products of thymine linked to a coumarin through a cyclobutyl ring (Sutherland and Song, unpublished data). The enzyme will act on all *cis, syn* cyclobutyl dimers formed in DNA (T[]T, C[]T, T[]C, C[]C, U[]U, U[]T, and T[]U; the uracil-containing dimers are formed either from uracil naturally occurring in the DNA or by deamination of a cytosine-containing dimer), although the rate may be affected both by the identity of the dimer and by the nondimerized, nearest-neighbor bases.[16]

Photoreactivating enzyme activities have been detected in many species, but only the PREs from *E. coli*,[17] human leukocytes,[18] baker's yeast,[19] and *Streptomyces griseus*[20] have been purified. These proteins differ in molecular weight, subunit structure, and composition,[21] thus (perhaps) pointing to convergent evolution of the protein moieties. These PREs also differ in wavelength response, in both maxima and range. The action spectra of the enzymes from yeast and *E. coli* have broad maxima for photoreactivation in the 360–380 nm range and extend from 300 nm to about 500 nm; the action spectrum of the PRE from *S. griseus* peaks at 436 nm and extends from 300 to 500 nm. Enzymes from human leukocytes, human fibroblasts, potorous (marsupial) fibroblasts, and the protozoan Blepharisma (Giese, personal communication), however, extend beyond 500 nm to at least 546 nm (obviating the use of yellow lights as safelights). Thus, by choosing the enzyme probe carefully, one can "design" a probe with a known wavelength response.

EXCISION

A second repair path is excision, in which dimer-containing oligonucleotides are removed from the DNA and replaced by new synthesis.[5] Enzymatic steps of this repair pathway include:

1. Incision adjacent to the damage
2. New synthesis by a polymerase, using the undamaged strand as a template
3. Excision of the damage-containing oligonucleotide by an exonuclease
4. Ligation of the newly synthesized region to the parental strand.

The same excision pathways seem to be able to remove damage inflicted by a wide variety of agents; specificity for kinds of damage seems to be imparted by the initial

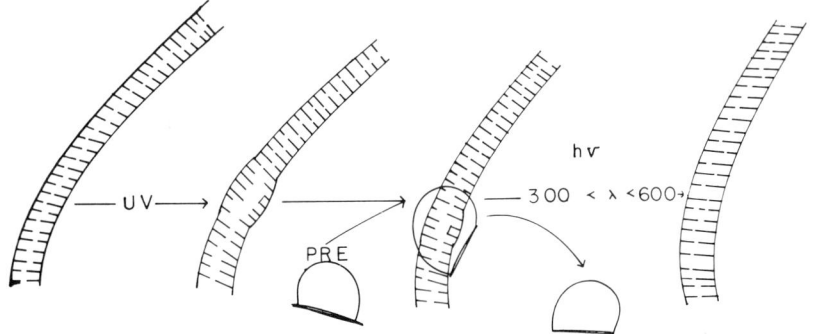

FIGURE 2. The action of the photoreactivating enzymes. Ultraviolet light (220–310 nm) irradiation produces dimers in DNA. The enzyme binds to the dimer-containing region of DNA, and, upon absorption of a photon, (300–600 nm) monomerizes the dimer and repairs the DNA.

incision enzymes. One such specific enzyme is the uv-endonuclease from *Micrococcus luteus*.[22,23] This enzyme makes a single-strand scission in the phosphodiester backbone adjacent to a dimer. Carrier and Setlow have shown that only the dimer-containing strand is nicked (and thus the enzyme does not recognize as substrate only the local denatured region induced by the dimer); unirradiated DNA is not a substrate for the enzyme.[23] RNA polymers, tRNA or ribosomal RNA, either irradiated or unirradiated, are not nicked by the enzyme. Although heavily irradiated poly rA:rU is attacked by the enzyme, it is attacked at a much lower rate than polydeoxyribonucleotides, whether DNA or poly dA:dT. Photoreactivation of uv-irradiated DNA with *E. coli* PRE removes about 98% of the sites for the *M. luteus* endonuclease. Recently, Ahmed and Setlow have shown that the distance between *M. luteus* endonuclease-sensitive sites is the same (1.89×10^6 daltons versus 1.94×10^6 daltons) as that between dimers. Thus, the *M. luteus* enzyme recognizes only dimers and nicks at the dimers.

PROBING DNA DAMAGE

How can we use these uv damage–specific enzymes (photoenzymes) as probes of damage to DNA? They are useful as probes of both the purified DNA extracted from irradiated cells and the intact cell. I shall first discuss their use in extracted DNA, then recent developments in probing mammalian cells.

Studies of extracted uv-irradiated DNAs have centered on two major areas: (1) quantitation of dimer damage and (2) reversal of dimer damage to allow examination of the effects of nondimer photoproducts. The specificity and action of the *M. luteus* endonuclease have enabled it to be used as a major research tool in the determination of dimer levels, especially at dimer concentrations too low for accurate radiochemical determination.[24] In these experiments, cells are treated with uv light, then allowed to undergo whatever repair processes are of interest. The cells are harvested and the DNA is extracted and treated with the *M. luteus* endonuclease. The (radioactive) DNA is sedimented in an alkaline sucrose gradient, and its molecular weight is calculated. Since the reduction in single-strand molecular weight of the DNA results from nicking adjacent to dimers, the dimer concentration can be calculated directly. Achey *et al.* have recently extended this technique to the use of nonradioactive DNAs by separation with alkaline agarose gel electrophoresis and visualization of the renatured DNA with ethidium bromide staining.[25]

A second *in vitro* use of the photoenzyme probe is the photoreactivation to completion of uv-irradiated DNAs to allow an assessment of the role of nondimer damage in DNA. Feldberg (personal communication) is currently employing this approach to determine the substrate of a binding protein that recognizes uv-irradiated DNA, but seems to be specific for a lesion other than the cyclobutyl dimer.

The photoenzymes can also be used as specific dimer probes in intact cells. These studies were initially undertaken to solve a perplexing problem in mammalian cell photobiology—that of the identification of the components of excision repair in both normal and deficient xeroderma pigmentosum (XP) cells. The XP cells, derived from patients with an inherited tendency to sunlight-induced skin cancer, had been divided into at least five complementation groups on the basis of intergroup cell fusion, which restored excision capacity.[26] Tanaka and his colleagues reasoned that the repair deficiencies in XP cells might be probed by the addition of exogenous enzymes and devised a method of Sendai virus permeabilization of the cell membrane that allowed the insertion of a uv-endonuclease.[27,28] They were able to show increased repair synthesis and uv-survival upon insertion of the incision enzyme into XP cells, and Smith and Hanawalt obtained similar stimulation of repair synthesis in isolated nuclei of XP cells.[29] A major puzzle remains, however; Tanaka et al. obtained stimulation of repair synthesis in all XP complementation groups, indicating that an exogenous

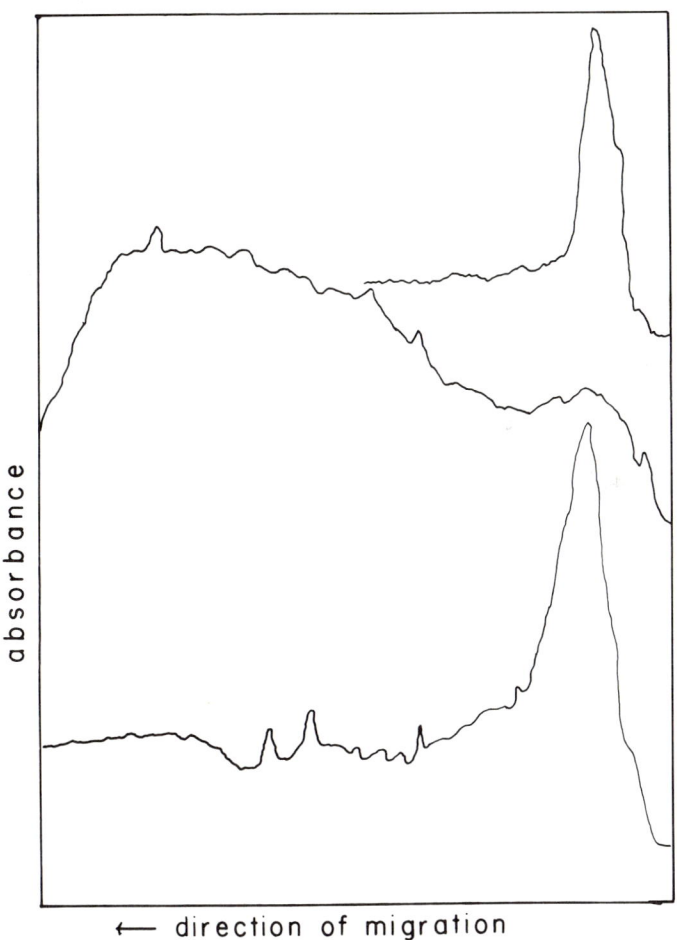

← direction of migration

FIGURE 3. DNA migration patterns from V79 Chinese hamster cells that were not irradiated (upper curve); were exposed to 10 J/m^2 of uv (middle curve); and were exposed to 10 J/m^2 of uv, then treated with PEG plus *E. coli* photoreactivating enzyme and exposed to visible light (30 min) (bottom curve). V79 cells contain little or no endogenous photoreactivating enzyme and excise dimers slowly from their DNA (~10% in 24 h).

uv-endonuclease could allow repair synthesis in cells with different biochemical defects.

We have developed another method of inserting repair enzymes into mammalian cells in culture.[30] Since our early attempts using Sendai virus to insert the *E. coli* PRE into Chinese hamster cells were unsuccessful, we tried polyethylene glycol (PEG), which is used to induce cell fusion, as is Sendai virus. Treating the cells with an insertion mixture of 30 g polyethylene glycol–60 ml minimal essential medium (MEM) without serum, washing them, and incubating them with *E. coli* PRE allows the *E. coli* photoreactivating enzyme to be inserted into the cells. FIGURE 3 shows that the inserted enzyme mediates reversal of dimers (as shown by the *M. luteus*

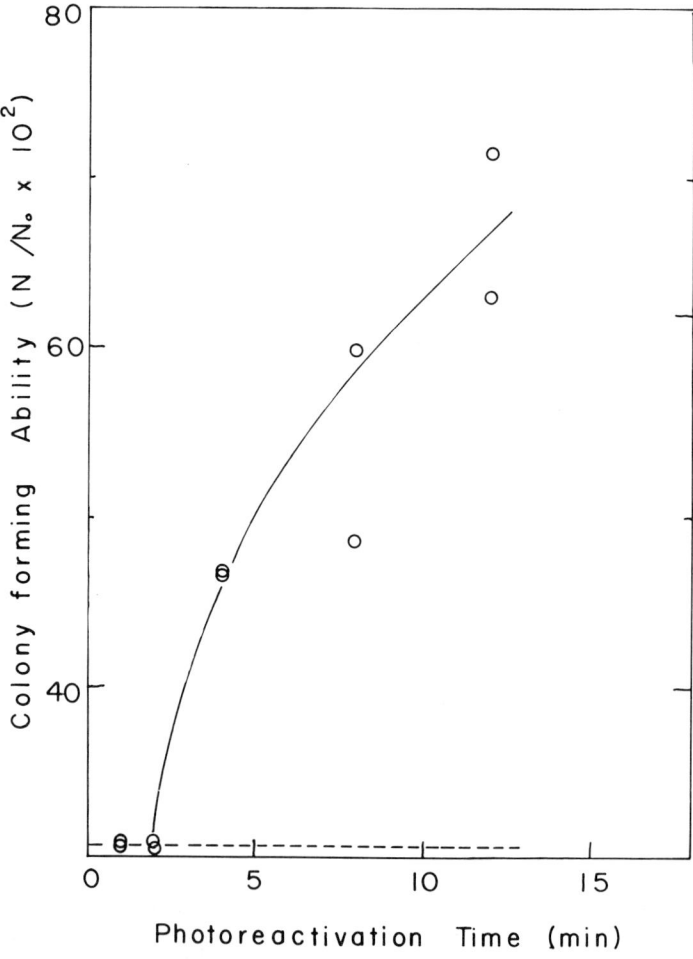

FIGURE 4. The recovery of colony-forming ability by V79 cells treated with ultraviolet light ($10 J/m^2$), treated with PEG plus *E. coli* PRE, and then exposed to photoreactivating light (solid line). The dashed line indicates that the colony-forming ability is unchanged if the treated cells are not exposed to photoreactivating light.

endonuclease-sensitive sites) in the presence of photoreactivating light. (V79s grown in MEM possess little or no endogenous PRE and excise dimers very slowly from their DNA.) FIGURE 4 shows that, in addition, the action of the enzyme restores biological activity to the cells, indicating that the inserted prokaryotic enzyme did not induce detrimental side reactions.

This method has two major immediate applications:

1. Although PRE activity is present in most mammalian tissues, the expression of the PRE gene seems to be controlled by the genotype of the cell[7] as well as by (unknown factors in) the medium.[9,10] Thus, the examination of cellular photoreactivation will be extended to genotypes and culture conditions unfavorable for PRE production. An especially important case is the "photoreactivation (PR) test"; since the PRE is specific for dimers, a true photoenzymatic reversal of potential biological damage would indicate that dimers were important in the production of that damage. This test has been used in bacteria, the simple eukaryote Paramecium, and the fish Poecelia to show that dimers are important in these organisms in the production of death and mutation by ultraviolet light.[31] The ability of the inserted E. coli enzyme to mediate dimer reversal in mammalian cells will allow the PR test to be used in cultured mammalian cells.

2. Since polyethylene glycol is easy to obtain and handle, is gentle to the cells, and does not induce latent or productive virus infection, it may provide a general method for the insertion of exogenous enzymes into mammalian cells. The size of protein able to enter the PEG-permeabilized cells is at least 35,000,[32] as that is the monomer molecular weight of the enzyme, which is present as higher aggregates.

Development of the use of photoenzyme probes depends on two major factors. The first is the development of a method for the insertion of exogenous enzymes into intact cells. The Sendai and PEG techniques show great promise here. The second is the isolation and characterization of enzymes specific for different kinds of damage in DNA. Several of these enzymes have been isolated, or their activities reported: one enzyme that nicks at apurinic sites in DNA,[33] one that removes uracil from DNA,[34] one that recognizes nondimer damage in uv-irradiated DNA (Feldberg, unpublished data) and one that is specific for DNA damage induced by ionizing radiation.[35] Certainly, many others are being studied at present or will be described in the near future. The development of a whole battery of protein probes for examining small numbers of specific lesions in DNA and determining their biological importance will open new vistas to our understanding of chemical and radiation damage to biological systems.

ACKNOWLEDGMENTS

I thank S. Hausrath for expert assistance.

This research was carried out at Brookhaven National Laboratory under the auspices of the United States Department of Energy.

REFERENCES

1. SETLOW, R. B. 1966. Cyclobutane-type pyrimidine dimers in polynucleotides. Science 153: 379–86.

2. SMITH, K. C., Ed. 1976. Aging, Carcinogenesis, and Radiation Biology: The Role of Nucleic Acid Addition Reactions: 1–561. Plenum Press. New York.

3. SETLOW, J. K. 1966. The molecular basis of biological effects of ultraviolet radiation and photoreactivation. *In* Current Topics in Radiation Research, Vol. 2. M. Ebert and A. Howard, Eds.: 195–248. North Holland. Amsterdam.

4. SETLOW, R. B. & W. L. CARRIER. 1966. Dimers in ultraviolet-irradiated DNAs. J. Mol. Biol. **17:** 237–54.

5. SETLOW, R. B. 1967. Physical changes and mutagenesis. J. Cell. Comp. Physiol. **64** (Suppl. 1): 51–68.

6. COOK, J. S. & J. R. MCGRATH. 1967. Photoreactivating enzyme activity in metazoa. Proc. Nat. Acad. Sci. USA **58:** 1359–65.

7. SUTHERLAND, B. M., M. RICE & E. K. WAGNER. 1975. Xeroderma pigmentosum cells contain low levels of photoreactivating enzyme. Proc. Nat. Acad. Sci. USA **72:** 103–7.

8. NISHIOKA, H. & W. HARM. 1972. Analysis of photoenzymatic repair of uv lesions in DNA by single light flashes IX. Excess production of photoreactivating enzyme in *E. coli* $B_{s_{-1}}$-160 under different growth conditions, and its suppression by adenine. Mutat. Res. **16:** 121–31.

9. SUTHERLAND, B. M. & R. OLIVER. 1976. Culture conditions affect photoreactivating enzyme levels in human fibroblasts. Biochim. Biophys. Acta **442:** 358–67.

10. MORTELMANS, S., J. E. CLEAVER, E. C. FRIEDBERG, M. C. PATERSON, B. P. SMITH & G. H. THOMAS. 1977. Photoreactivation of thymine dimers in uv-irradiated human cells: Unique dependence on culture conditions. Mutat. Res. **44:** 433–46.

11. RUPERT, C. S. 1962. Photoenzymatic repair of ultraviolet damage in DNA. II. Formation of an enzyme-substrate complex. J. Gen. Physiol. **45:** 725–41.

12. SETLOW, R. B. & J. K. SETLOW. 1962. Evidence that ultraviolet-induced thymine dimers in DNA cause biological damage. Proc. Nat. Acad. Sci. USA **48:** 1250–57.

13. WUN, K. L., A. GIH & J. C. SUTHERLAND. 1977. Photoreactivating enzyme from *E. coli:* Appearance of new absorption on binding to ultraviolet-irradiated DNA. Biochemistry **16:** 921–24.

14. SETLOW, J. K. 1966. The molecular basis of biological effects of ultraviolet radiation and photoreactivation. Curr. Top. Radiat. Res. **2:** 195–248.

15. SETLOW, J. K. & F. J. BOLLUM. 1968. The minimum size of the substrate for yeast photoreactivating enzyme. Biochim. Biophys. Acta **157:** 233–37.

16. SETLOW, R. B., W. L. CARRIER & F. J. BOLLUM. 1964. Nuclease-resistant sequences in ultraviolet-irradiated deoxyribonucleic acid. Biochim. Biophys. Acta **91:** 446–61.

17. SUTHERLAND, B. M., M. J. CHAMBERLIN & J. C. SUTHERLAND. 1973. Deoxyribonucleic acid photoreactivating enzyme from *Escherichia coli*. J. Biol. Chem. **12:** 4200–5.

18. SUTHERLAND, B. M. 1974. Photoreactivating enzyme from human leukocytes. Nature **248:** 109–12.

19. WERBIN, H. & J. J. MADDEN. 1977. The subunit structure of yeast DNA photolyase and the purification of a fluorescent activator of the enzyme. Photochem. Photobiol. **25:** 421–27.

20. EKER, A. & A. FICHTINGER-SCHEPMAN. 1975. Studies on a DNA photoreactivating enzyme from *Streptomyces griseus*. Biochim. Biophys. Acta **378:** 54–63.

21. SUTHERLAND, B. M. 1978. Photoreactivation in mammalian cells. Int. Rev. Cytol. Suppl. **8:** 301–34.

22. GROSSMAN, L., J. C. KAPLAN, S. R. KUSHNER & I. MAHLER. 1969. Enzymes involved in the early stages of repair of ultraviolet-irradiated DNA. Cold Spring Harbor Symp. Quant. Biol. **33:** 229–234.

23. CARRIER, W. L. & R. B. SETLOW. 1970. Endonuclease from *Micrococcus luteus* which has activity toward ultraviolet-irradiated deoxyribonucleic acid: Purification and properties. J. Bacteriol **102:** 178–86.

24. AHMED, F. E. & R. B. SETLOW. DNA repair in xeroderma pigmentosum cells treated with combinations of ultraviolet radiation and N-acetoxy-2-acetylaminofluorene. Cancer Res. **39:** 471–79.

25. ACHEY, P. M., A. D. WOODHEAD & R. B. SETLOW. 1978. Photoreactivation of pyrimidine dimers in DNA from thyroid cells of the teleost, *Poecilia formosa*. Photochem. Photobiol. **29:** 305–10.

26. ROBBINS, J. H., K. H. KRAEMER, M. A. LUTZNER, B. W. FESTOFF & H. G. COON. 1974. Xeroderma pigmentosum: An inherited disease with sun sensitivity, multiple cutaneous neoplasms, and abnormal DNA repair. Ann. Int. Med. **80:** 221–48.

27. TANAKA, K., M. SEKIGUCHI & Y. OKADA. 1975. Restoration of ultraviolet-induced DNA synthesis of xeroderma pigmentosum cells by the concomitant treatment with bacteriophage T4 endonuclease V and HVJ (Sendai virus). Proc. Nat. Acad. Sci. USA **72:** 4071–75.

28. TANAKA, K., H. HAYAKAWA, M. SEKIGUCHI & V. OKADA. 1977. Specific action of T4 endonuclease V on damaged DNA in xeroderma pigmentosum cells *in vivo*. Proc. Nat. Acad. Sci. USA **74:** 2958–62.

29. SMITH, C. A. & P. C. HANAWALT. 1978. Phage T4 endonuclease V stimulates DNA repair replication in isolated nuclei from ultraviolet-irradiated human cells, including xeroderma pigmentosum fibroblasts. Proc. Nat. Acad. Sci USA **75:** 2598–602.

30. SUTHERLAND, B. M. & S. G. HAUSRATH. 1980. Polyethylene glycol insertion of *E. coli* photoreactivating enzyme into mammalian cells. Submitted.

31. HART, R., R. B. SETLOW & A. WOODHEAD. 1977. Evidence that pyrimidine dimers in DNA can give rise to tumors. Proc. Nat. Acad. Sci. USA **74:** 5574–78.

32. FUSELIER, C. O. & R. M. SNAPKA. 1977. Photoreactivating enzyme from *E. coli*. Photochem. Photobiol. **25:** 415–20.

33. KUHNELEIN, V., S. PENHOET & S. LINN. 1976. An altered apurinic DNA endonuclease activity in Group A and Group D xeroderma pigmentosum fibroblasts. Proc. Nat. Acad. Sci. USA **73:** 1169–73.

34. LINDAHL, T. 1976. New class of enzymes acting on damaged DNA. Nature **259:** 64–66.

35. SETLOW, R. B. & W. L. CARRIER. 1973. Endonuclease activity toward DNA irradiated *in vitro* by gamma rays. Nature New Biol. **241:** 170–72.

MOLECULAR ASPECTS OF PHOTOTOXICITY

Andrija Kornhauser

Division of Toxicology
Food and Drug Administration
Washington, D.C. 20204
and
Harvard School of Dental Medicine
Boston, Massachusetts 02115

INTRODUCTION

One of the most potent environmental agents influencing life on earth is sunlight. Because of its ubiquity, the wide range of its chemical, biological, and medical effects is still not fully appreciated. That solar energy makes life possible is a generally accepted fact. It has, however, only recently become apparent that many of the effects of solar radiation are detrimental. Evolution of life, therefore, can be regarded as a continuous adaptation to light by a simultaneous process of utilization of solar energy and protection against its detrimental effects.

Modern civilization presents a challenge for basic photomedical and photobiological research. The challenge arises primarily from the alterations in living habits of a large portion of the population, such as holiday trips, clothing styles, and particularly, the fashion of suntanning among Caucasians. The possibility that the quality of light on the surface of the earth might be changed by environmental factors also has to be considered. Many of these factors lead to an essentially increased exposure to light for a large segment of the population.[1]

A phototoxic reaction can be described as a nonimmunological light-induced adverse skin response, its clinical appearance resembling that of a sunburn. Theoretically, everyone can be affected by this condition provided that light energy of the proper wavelength and enough molecules to absorb it are present. In the last decade, phototoxic reactions caused by drugs, cosmetics, and a large number of industrial and environmental chemicals have become a major health problem of the population.[1] Chronic phototoxic exposure can lead to neoplastic changes. It is established without doubt that the consequence of a life-long enhanced exposure to light is a rapid increase in skin tumors.[2] These include basal and squamous cell carcinomas and, to a certain extent, malignant melanomas. This fact is confirmed by the pronounced increase in frequency of skin cancers among that part of the population, particularly the Celtics and Teutonics, who, in the course of history, settled in regions with higher solar irradiation (Africa, Australia, North America).

Phototoxicity studies, particularly those related to human disorders, have, so far, predominantly been based on gross anatomical or histological procedures. Our knowledge of the molecular events that occur during these processes is still very limited. In this review, some molecular changes that take place in skin after light exposure will be discussed. Because of the magnitude of the topic, this paper will be limited to the reactions involving ultraviolet (uv) radiation; those toxic effects of

398

0077–8923/80/0346–0398 $1.75/ © 1980, NYAS

visible light commonly referred to as "photodynamic effects," which require oxygen participation, will not be covered.

LIGHT CHARACTERISTICS

The uv part of the electromagnetic spectrum covers wavelengths from 200 to 400 nm. Portions of the uv spectrum have distinctive features from both the physical and the medical points of view. The accepted designations for the biologically important part of the uv spectrum are uv-A, 400–315 nm; uv-B, 315–280 nm; and uv-C, 280–220 nm (FIGURE 1). Wavelengths of less than 290 nm do not occur at the earth's surface, since they are absorbed, predominantly by ozone, in the stratosphere.

Most photobiological reactions that occur in skin are induced by uv-B. This is the wavelength region that inhibits cell mitosis, makes vitamin D, and causes sunburn and skin cancer. Ultraviolet-A radiation causes only a few minor direct photobiological effects; however, this portion of the spectrum is responsible for the vast majority of the reactions produced by the exogenous photosensitizers that cause most of the phototoxic and photoallergic phenomena in humans.

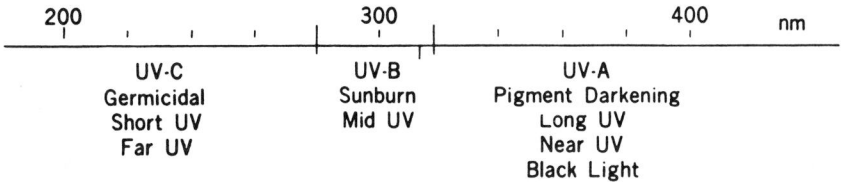

FIGURE 1. Biologically important regions of the uv spectrum.

SPECIFIC MOLECULAR ALTERATIONS IN CELLS

On the molecular level, DNA is the most sensitive target in a cell exposed to uv light. Other cellular constituents can also be affected, but to a lesser degree. Damage to cells through a photoreaction is initiated at the site where the chromophore absorbs specific wavelengths of light. Absorption of this energy results in an excited molecule; dissipation of this energy results in an adverse phototoxic effect upon the cell.

Thymine Dimers

Cyclobutane-type pyrimidine dimers in DNA are the most important and the best-studied lesions induced by uv in cells. They result from the formation of covalent bonds between adjacent pyrimidines of the same DNA strand and interfere with normal DNA function. Beukers and Berends first demonstrated the formation of these dimers in vitro,[3] and Wacker et al., in in vivo studies, found them in DNA from uv-irradiated bacteria.[4] These findings marked the beginning of a new era in molecular biology. Thymine dimers (TT) (FIGURE 2, I) were later shown to occur in a

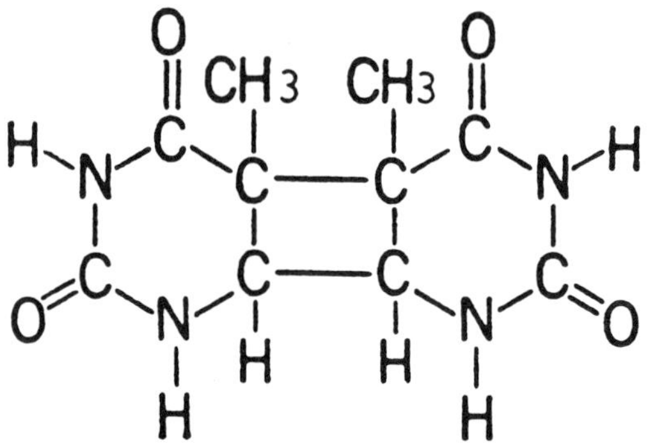

FIGURE 2. (I) The structure of the thymine dimer (*cis,syn*); (II) the hypothetical ketone-thymine intermediate.

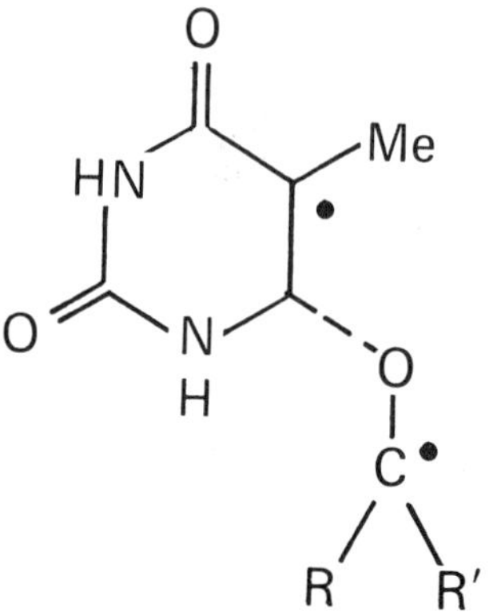

number of higher systems, and, more recently, in mammalian and human skin following uv irradiation.[5] Studies initiated by Cleaver and Trosko demonstrated the involvement of TT in xeroderma pigmentosum (XP);[6] this finding represents one of the rare cases in which a specific molecular lesion can be correlated with a malignant process. In another approach, Hart *et al.* used cell extracts from uv-irradiated Amazon mollies (small fish) and reported evidence that pyrimidine dimers in DNA gave rise to tumors.[7]

Several hypotheses about the reaction mechanism of the photodimerization of pyrimidines have been suggested;[8] these include population of the triplet state of thymine or uracil induced by energy transfer from the triplet state of a suitable sensitizer. In our earlier work, we proposed that photosensitized dimerization of pyrimidines involving acetone or acetophenone takes place by means of triplet energy transfer from the sensitizer to the substrate.[9] The essential hypothesis in this reaction mechanism, besides the triplet energy transfer, is the intermediate formation of a complex between the donor (e.g., a ketone molecule) and the acceptor (a pyrimidine molecule) that gives an unstable adduct of Type II (FIGURE 2), which can react with another pyrimidine molecule in its ground state. If this proposal is correct, only a few sensitizers could actively promote pyrimidine dimerization. To explore the validity of this hypothesis, we investigated the ability of several classes of compounds having triplet energies higher than or similar to that of thymine to act as photosensitizers in thymine dimer formation.[10,11] We also wanted to determine whether the energy transfer from the sensitizer to the substrate occurs through a simple physical mechanism[12] or whether it is restricted by some complex-forming reaction (Schenck's relay mechanism).[13]

During this study, the compounds shown in TABLE 1 were examined for their ability to induce formation of TT. Solutions of thymine-2-[14]C (2×10^{-3} M) with and without these potential photosensitizers (10^{-4} to 10^{-1} M) were irradiated in an open quartz cuvette in the presence of air with wavelengths of light longer than 300 nm (uv-A + uv-B; 1.2 J/cm^2). Thymine dimers obtained in this reaction were separated by paper chromatography and their radioactivity was assayed in a liquid scintillation counter.

As can be seen in TABLE 1, only a few of the potential sensitizers caused a measurable thymine dimerization. A small amount (1–2%) of thymine dimer was detected after uv irradiation, even in the absence of a sensitizer. Acetone, ethyl acetoacetate, and dihydroxyacetone were more potent sensitizers than acetophenone and benzophenone.

The question as to whether energy transfer in the case of sensitized photodimerization of pyrimidines occurs through a direct physical mechanism or through a kind of Schenck's relay mechanism is not merely academic.[13] In all biological systems that are exposed to light, it is of major importance whether a chromophore that absorbs light can transfer its energy of excitation to another important biological macromolecule in an unrestricted way or whether the energy transfer is somehow restricted by an intermediate complex formation between a donor and an acceptor. All these results, as well as some of our additional studies,[11,14] showed that the Schenck mechanism is highly favored under these experimental conditions.

The following conclusions can be derived from these results:

1. The sensitized energy transfer taking place during thymine dimerization most likely does not occur through a simple physical mechanism. The ability of the sensitizer in its excited state to form a complex with the pyrimidine molecule appears to be a prerequisite for this type of photosensitization.

2. Ethyl acetoacetate and dihydroxyacetone, types of molecules that are commonly present in any viable cell and that were not previously known to be photosensitizers, proved to be as effective as acetone or acetophenone. On the other hand, urocanic acid, a major uv-absorbing compound present in mammalian skin, did not show any sensitizing ability in inducing thymine dimerization. The uv energy

TABLE 1

FORMATION OF THYMINE DIMERS (TT) AFTER IRRADIATION OF THYMINE-2-^{14}C
IN THE PRESENCE OF DIFFERENT SENSITIZERS

Number	Sensitizer	TT Formed (%)
1	None	1–2
2	Acetone	30–40
3	Dihydroxyacetone	25–30
4	Acetophenone	5–10
5	Benzophenone	5–8
6	4-Methoxyacetophenone	2–4
7	Ethyl acetoacetate	35–45
8	Phenyl cyanide	1–3
9	Carbazole	3–6
10	Fluorene	2–3
11	Napthalene	1–3
12	Xanthene-9-one	1–3
13	Urocanic acid	1–3

NOTE: Solutions of thymine-2-^{14}C (2×10^3 M) and sensitizer (10^{-4} to 10^{-1} M) were irradiated with a total uv (>300 nm) dose of 1.2 J/cm^2. Irradiations were carried out in water (1, 2, 3, 13), in water/ethanol (3:1) (4, 6–12), and in water/dioxane (3:1) (5, 12).

absorbed by the urocanic acid molecule is believed to induce its *cis, trans* isomerization.[15]

3. Topical preparations containing acetone, dihydroxyacetone, or other acetone derivatives should be used cautiously, since they might damage the epidermal DNA when skin is exposed to uv radiation. The above studies have practical applications for correlating the structure of a potential phototoxic agent to its ability to induce pyrimidine dimerization or other molecular lesions in cells.

DNA-Protein Cross-Links

Heteroadducts to DNA, i.e., compounds formed by the covalent attachment of a large number of different types of compounds (both normal cellular constituents, such as proteins, and exogenous compounds, such as drugs, carcinogens, and cosmetics) have profound effects upon cells. The cross-linking of DNA and protein in bacteria was the first *in vivo* photochemical heteroadduct reaction to be reported.[16] Some studies on uv-induced DNA and protein cross-links in mammalian cells *in vitro* were based mainly on the reduced DNA extractability after uv irradiation.[17] Evidence that this lesion plays a significant role in killing uv-irradiated cells has been produced under several experimental conditions.

The chemical nature of the DNA-protein cross-links is not yet known. An *in vitro* photochemical reaction between thymine and cysteine has been observed and may be one of the possible mechanisms for the covalent linking of DNA to protein *in vivo*.[18] Furthermore, 11 of the common amino acids combine photochemically with uracil in different model systems.[18]

Mammalian (eukaryotic) cells, in general, represent a suitable model for the cross-linking reaction, since their DNA is closely packed with proteins that might facilitate the formation of uv-induced DNA-protein covalent bonds. Todd and Han studied the general features of uv-induced (254 nm) DNA-protein cross-links in both asynchronous and synchronous HeLa cells.[17] Cross-linking was demonstrated by the detection of unextractable DNA in irradiated cells. These investigators found that the uv-induced DNA-protein cross-linking in synchronously growing HeLa cells exhibited age-dependent variations; the maximum yield of cross-linking was observed during S-phase, while cells irradiated in G_1 or G_2 had much smaller amounts. Significantly, changes in the age-response pattern for the yield of cross-links varied throughout the cell cycle in the same way as the efficiency of uv light for cell killing. For at least the duration of the experiments (8 h post-exposure), no recovery (repair) from this damage was observed.

Cross-linking of DNA to proteins was originally studied only in chemical model systems, in bacterial systems, or *in vitro* tissue culture systems with various cell lines. In almost all cases, uv radiation of 260 nm, which does not normally occur at the earth's surface, was used. To study a possible role of the DNA-protein cross-links in an *in vivo* system, we focused our investigations on the isolation of chromatin from irradiated and nonirradiated guinea pig epidermis.[19,20] The backs of guinea pigs were irradiated with a moderate physiological dose (800 J/m²; 290–350 nm), which corresponds to approximately five times the minimal erythema dose (MED).*

---

*The MED is defined as the minimal dose of uv irradiation (290–320 nm) that produces definite, but minimally perceptible, redness 24 h after exposure.

Epidermis was obtained from both the irradiated and the control sites and homogenized. Chromatin was isolated from the homogenates by applying Sepharose B-4 and DEAE cellulose chromatography and density gradient centrifugation; its biological activity was analyzed by chemical methods and tests.[19,20]

FIGURE 3 shows a representative fractionation profile of epidermal chromatin on Sepharose B-4 columns both before and after uv irradiation. The major changes upon irradiation were seen in the first peak, which represents epidermal DNA. In the nonirradiated specimen (A), the absorbance ratio (260 nm/230 nm) was 1.99; in the irradiated specimen (B), it decreased to about 1. This decrease and the presence of proteins (8–11%) in this fraction, as determined by Lowry's test, indicated that cross-linking of DNA and protein had occurred.

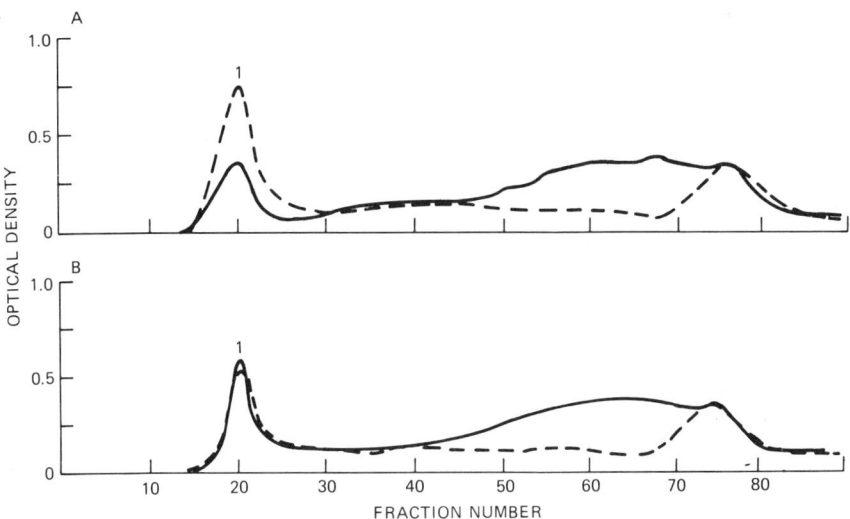

FIGURE 3. The fractionation profile of epidermal chromatin on a Sepharose B4 (2 × 40 cm) column before (A) and after (B) uv irradiation. The irradiation dose was 800 J/m^2 at 290–350 nm. The eluent was 2 M NaCl in 0.1 M EDTA, the fraction volume was 2.0 ml, and the flow rate was 1 ml/min. The absorbance ratio (260 nm/230 nm) of peak 1 in A is 1.99, in B, 1.0. (----: 260 nm; —: 230 nm.)

A comparison of the sucrose gradient centrifugation profiles of the uv-irradiated epidermal chromatin and the nonirradiated epidermal DNA, including a calf thymus DNA (molecular weight 1.3×10^6) as an internal standard, showed (1) a significant breakdown of the high molecular weight DNA fraction and the presence of small molecular weight DNA fragments on the top of the sucrose gradient after uv irradiation, and (2) an increment of the high molecular weight DNA at 60 min after irradiation (the regeneration or repair phase).

We were able, with our techniques, to obtain 4–5 mg extractable DNA free of protein from 1 g wet epidermal tissue. Immediately after uv irradiation, the yield of this extractable DNA was reduced by 20–30%, presumably as a result of DNA-protein cross-linking, and, possibly, of DNA strand breakage. This observation is consistent with our previously reported findings, as well as with the reported findings of single- and double-strand breakage of DNA upon uv irradiation (>290 nm).[21] We also suggested that epidermal DNA is the primary chromophore for uv absorption. Its main lesions are the result of direct absorption of uv radiation by skin DNA. Apparently, these lesions do not proceed substantially through a photosensitized reaction by triplet energy transfer from some other molecules.

The above results can be summarized as follows:

1. Ultraviolet irradiation, in physiological doses (5 MED) of 290–350 nm, decreased the actual amount of dissociable chromosomal DNA by 20–30% as a result of cross-linking of DNA to protein and DNA strand breakage

2. A comparison of the corresponding elution profiles from Sepharose columns of the dissociable DNA isolated from uv-irradiated and nonirradiated epidermal specimens indicated cross-linking of protein to DNA

3. Ultraviolet irradiation caused a significant breakdown of that high molecular weight DNA which was isolated after irradiation

4. In the regeneration phase, an active repair process was operating in the viable cells of the epidermis.

So far, no other evidence for the cellular repair of DNA-protein heteroadducts has been found. It is conceivable that, through evolution, cells exposed to light evolved a repair system for eliminating this type of heteroadduct; this system is different from photoreactivation, which is known to be specific for pyrimidine dimers.

All these findings suggest that uv radiation, even in moderate doses, can induce measurable alterations of the chromosomal material, chromatin. Skin chromatin has not yet been isolated and analyzed, however, except in our preliminary work.

Specific covalent attachments of DNA-binding proteins to their DNA substrate are of great potential usefulness for the identification of the DNA-binding sites of proteins and, possibly, for the isolation of the DNA region covered by the proteins. For mammalian cells especially, it may be useful to covalently attach chromosomal proteins to their specific sites by uv irradiation, before disruption of the cell or the nucleus. Thus, this method can provide us with a powerful tool for applying uv radiation to the probing of biological targets, as well as for obtaining new information on the regulation of gene expression in higher organisms.

Psoralen Phototoxicity

Furocoumarins, derivatives of which are commonly called psoralens, constitute a well-known group of naturally occurring and synthetic substances that, when added to any of several biological systems and irradiated with long-wave uv light (uv-A), produce various biological effects. These effects cannot be obtained with either psoralens or light alone.

The photobiological reactions of furocoumarins have received widespread attention in past years and are regarded as one of the most fascinating phenomena in nature. On the molecular level, the following facts are known at present.

Psoralens intercalate into DNA by forming molecular complexes involving weak chemical interactions ("dark reaction"). Upon uv-A irradiation of such a system, *in vitro* or *in vivo,* covalent bond formation between a pyrimidine base and the furocoumarin molecule takes place (C_4-cycloaddition). Because of their structure, psoralens in this reaction can react either at their 3,4-double bond or at their corresponding 4',5'-site, yielding monoadducts (the former product is not fluorescent and the latter is). Upon absorption of an additional photon, a further chemical reaction yielding a "cross-linked DNA" may take place. Thus, psoralens can behave as photoreactive bifunctional agents, one molecule reacting with two pyrimidines in *opposite* strands of DNA. The result is a cross-linked DNA in which the individual strands cannot be separated by the standard denaturation conditions. Both types of

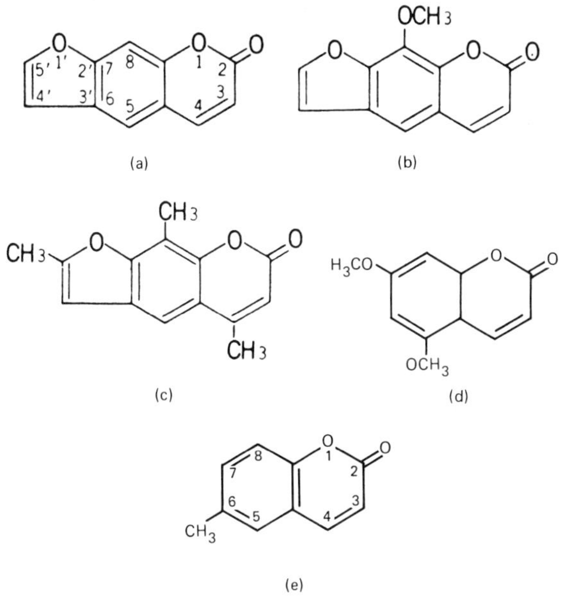

FIGURE 4. The structures of some furocoumarin and coumarin derivatives. (a) psoralen; (b) 8-methoxypsoralen (8-MOP); (c) trimethylpsoralen (TMP); (d) 5,7-dimethoxycoumarin (DMC); (e) 6-methylcoumarin.

these lesions, the monofunctional adduct and the cross-linked product, can be repaired *in vivo.*[22-25]

The structures of some furocoumarins and coumarins are shown in FIGURE 4. Psoralen reactions with thymine mono- and diadducts are shown in FIGURE 5. FIGURE 6 schematically shows DNA cross-linked by a psoralen molecule.

The covalent addition of furocoumarins to DNA, particularly the cross-linking reaction, is believed to be responsible for the major effects of psoralen photosensitization. These effects include mutation and lethality in prokaryotic and eukaryotic systems, inhibition of DNA synthesis, sister chromatid exchange, cutaneous phototoxicity, and carcinogenesis.

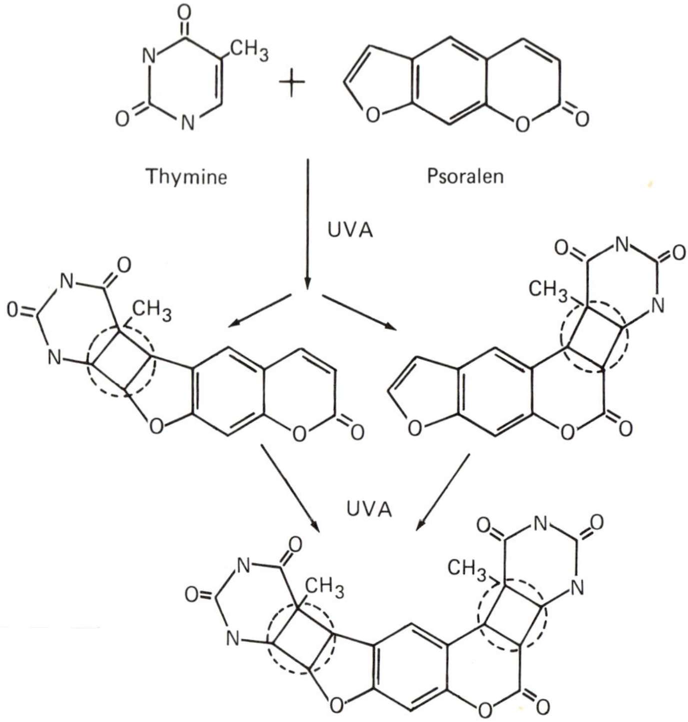

FIGURE 5. Photoaddition products of psoralen with thymine after uv irradiation *in vitro*.

Skin photosensitization is one of the most widely studied properties of some furocoumarins. Several clinical types of photodermatoses occur when skin comes into contact with plants or vegetable products and is later exposed to sunlight. Much less is known about potential adverse cutaneous effects after chronic ingestion of foods that contain furocoumarins (figs, limes).

Recently, Dall'Acqua[26] showed that the photoaddition of furocoumarins to DNA is not a random process. Specific sites exist in DNA for the photochemical interaction with psoralens; the sequences that can be considered specific receptors for the photobiological activity of psoralens are represented by alternate sequences of adenine and thymine (A and T) in each complementary strand of the polynucleotide. Psoralen has a greater photoreactivity toward thymine than it has toward cytosine. The receptor sites have a high capacity for intercalation and subsequent photoreaction with psoralens.[26]

The most interesting aspect of this subject is that, although furocoumarins are the most potent phototoxic compounds, they can be also used as therapeutic agents. They have been applied clinically to treat vitiligo (leukoderma) and to increase the tolerance of human skin to solar radiation. Recently, a new clinical discipline, photochemotherapy (PCT), was introduced for treatment of psoriasis and other skin disorders.[27–29]

PCT is defined as the interaction of light and an orally administered drug intended to produce a beneficial effect on a disease. One of its widest applications entered the medical terminology as PUVA (psoralen + uv-A).

Psoriasis is a chronic cutaneous disorder of unknown cause that afflicts up to 3% of the population in the United States. The consequences of the disease vary from inconvenience to disablement. PUVA is carried out by treating patients with oral 8-methoxypsoralen (8-MOP, FIGURE 4b) and a high intensity source of uv-A radiation. The therapy is highly effective, clean, and acceptable to patients. Some problems, however, persist; these include possible induction of cataracts, hematologic effects, alteration of the immune response, skin aging, and a possible increase of cutaneous cancers.

A thorough, well-directed clinical evaluation has just been published with the cooperation of 16 American clinical centers.[30] In 1978, about 35,000 patients in this country received PUVA treatment. The medical community is faced with a severe dilemma. Although PUVA therapy has alleviated the suffering of thousands of psoriasis victims since its recent introduction, it still must be considered experimental. Much more research and changes in some regimens of the procedure will be needed before PUVA can be regarded as safe and suitable for general use.

The metabolism of the photosensitizing furocoumarins is now under intensive

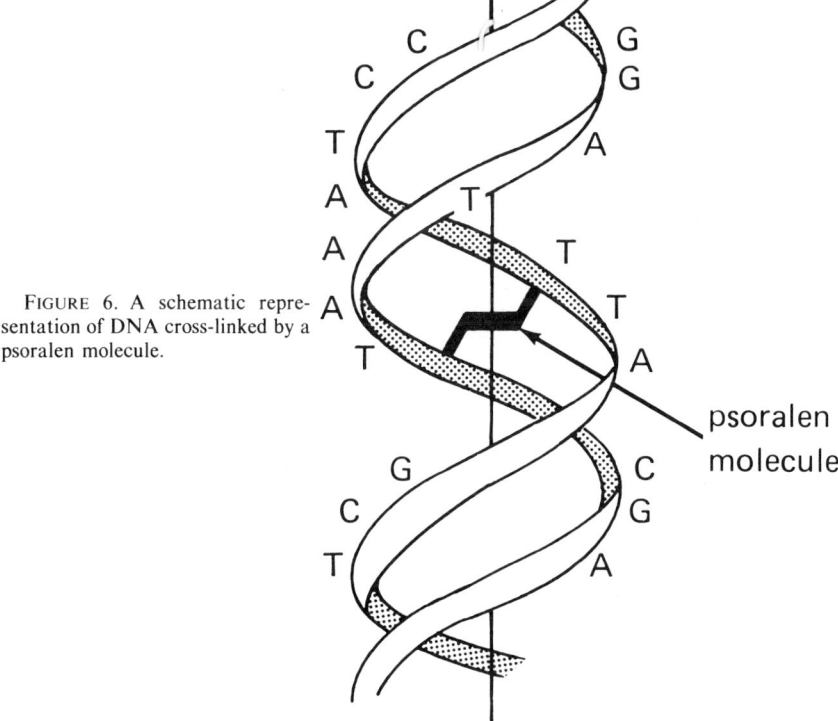

FIGURE 6. A schematic representation of DNA cross-linked by a psoralen molecule.

psoralen molecule

study. Psoralen and 8-MOP appear to be detoxified and excreted as glucuronides and hydroxylated products.[24] Trimethylpsoralen (TMP, FIGURE 4c) gives 5'-carboxy-4,8-dimethylpsoralen (CDP) as a principal metabolite.[31] This metabolite is inactive as a skin photosensitizer; the difference between the cutaneous reactivity of TMP upon topical versus systemic administration is attributed to the metabolic transformation. The reaction TMP→CDP takes place with liver homogenates, but not with skin homogenates (M. A. Pathak, personal communication). Furthermore, 8-MOP induced mixed-function oxidases in mouse liver after administration of a single dose of the drug,[32] but psoralen and TMP failed to induce those enzymes. These findings may also have relevance to our understanding of the differences in clinical effectiveness of these related compounds.

Many models have been used to study 8-MOP phototoxicity. For examining clinical situations, animal experiments are more suitable than *in vitro* models. The guinea pig has been widely used for this purpose; however, either the topical or the intraperitoneal method of administration has generally been used and no significant data on the oral method have been published.

To investigate the different clinical effects occurring after various modes of drug administration, we tested epilated guinea pigs by both the oral and topical methods. 8-MOP (15 $\mu g/cm^2$, in ethanol) was applied topically and the site was then irradiated with 1–5 J/cm^2 of uv-A. This treatment resulted in erythema and necrosis of the skin after 2–4 days, an effect comparable to that obtained in humans. Eight epilated guinea pigs were also tested with oral doses of 2–15 mg/kg and 5 J/cm^2 of uv-A; the minimal phototoxic dose (MPD) is 6.0 mg/kg. The 8-MOP blood concentrations after oral administration were determined by high pressure liquid chromatography (HPLC; μBondapak C_{18} column and methanol/water: 70/30 elution). Concentrations reached a peak between 1 and 4 h and equaled only 40–200 ng/ml (human serum concentrations were of the same magnitude at 0.1 of our dose range), indicating that, in the guinea pig, 8-MOP has a very high detoxification rate, a strong protein binding capacity, or both.

Binding of 8-MOP to human serum albumin has only recently attracted wide attention.[33] It has been suggested that the photoconjugation of 8-MOP is specific to certain proteins.[34] Steiner *et al.*[35] recently reported that serum concentrations of 8-MOP 2 h after oral administration varied considerably in a population of 37 patients, and that no definite correlation between the 8-MOP serum level and the MPD was apparent. Interest in 8-MOP stimulated the development of sensitive quantitative methods for analysis of nanogram quantities of this drug in biological samples. A new bioassay, which uses a culture of *Staphylococcus aureus,* has been developed for the determination of nanogram quantities of 8-MOP in blood, aqueous humor, and the lens (W. Glew, personal communication).

The photosensitizing potency of psoralens strongly depends on their structural characteristics. To date, the ability to sensitize cutaneous tissue to light appears to be a unique characteristic of only the psoralen system. Coumarin and many of those of its substituted derivatives that have been tested were inactive as photosensitizers. Recently, however, Kaidbey and Kligman reported that 6-methylcoumarin (FIGURE 4e) induced photoallergic reactions in humans.[36] In addition, benzodipyrones, which possess two reactive C=C pyrone bonds, have been proposed as potential DNA cross-linking agents and were shown to photoinduce mutation in *Bacillus subtilis.*[37] In subsequent studies, the same investigators reported that 5,7-dimethoxycoumarin

(DMC) (FIGURE 4d) covalently binds to DNA and is lethal to this same bacterial strain.[38,39] This is the only known coumarin derivative with these photobiological properties.

We decided, therefore, to test DMC topically in our guinea pig system; it had no phototoxicity at doses up to 80 times the MPD of 8-MOP. Kinetic studies showed that, although 8-MOP binds to DNA in the ratio of one molecule to 23 nucleotides, the corresponding binding of DMC is only one to 500 nucleotides (P. S. Song, personal communication).† This fact, as well as the inability of DMC to cross-link DNA, might explain the difference in cutaneous behavior of these two related compounds. However, the observation that 7-methoxycoumarin is phototoxic in humans (K. H. Kaidbey, personal communication) makes us aware that much more has to be learned about chemical structure–phototoxicity relationships before definite conclusions can be drawn.

The covalent addition of furocoumarins to DNA is believed to be responsible for the inhibition of DNA synthesis in the proliferating epidermal cells. The mechanism of the therapeutic efficacy of psoralens in photochemotherapy is most probably due to these events. Still, nothing is known about the mechanism of the psoralen-induced melanogenesis, or about many of the other events on the molecular level that are induced by PUVA. Scott et al.[24] proposed that psoralens and uv light act on the level of gene regulation. In addition, DNA synthesis and melanogenesis are reciprocal in a retinal pigment cell culture system.[40] It is possible that uv-induced melanogenesis is a specific instance of differentiation due to suppression of DNA synthesis.

Prostaglandin Involvement in Phototoxicity

Prostaglandins (PGs) have been implicated in many physiological processes. The almost ubiquitous occurrence of the prostaglandin synthetase enzyme system and the presence of its substrate fatty acids in membrane phospholipids of mammalian cells suggest that PGs can be formed within most cell types, where they can act as intracellular messengers.[41]

The role of PGs in cutaneous pathology and inflammation is well established.[42] PGs were found in whole rat skin homogenates; when the epidermis was separated from the dermis, the major portion of the PG activity was located in the epidermis. The realization that PGs are important in cellular control mechanisms has instigated a great amount of research into their possible role in the etiology of cancer.[43]

A tentative pathway of PG formation and its interrelation with the adenylate cyclase system in cutaneous tissue after uv irradiation is shown in FIGURE 7.

Prostaglandins E_2 (PGE$_2$) and F_2 (PGF$_2$) are produced in skin irradiated with uv-B radiation.[42] PGE$_2$ is believed to play a part in the pathogenesis of uv-B–induced tissue injury.[42] This postulated role is supported by several reports documenting that inhibitors of PG synthetase such as indomethacin and aspirin can suppress uv-B–induced erythema.[43] On the other hand, erythema due to psoralen phototoxicity (PUVA) cannot be suppressed with indomethacin[44] and no increase in PG activity is

†During preparation of this manuscript, it was discovered that DMC had been previously tested in six human subjects and was found to be not phototoxic (Marzulli, F. N. & H. I. Maibach. 1970. Perfume phototoxicity. J. Soc. Cosmet. Chem. **21**: 695–715). Ou et al.[38] also stated that the skin sensitizing potency of DMC was yet to be tested.

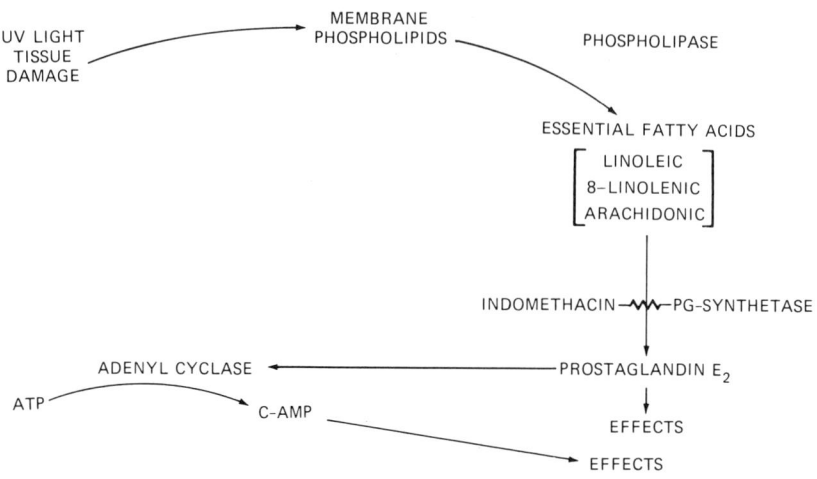

FIGURE 7. A tentative pathway of prostaglandin formation and its interrelation with the adenylate cyclase system in cutaneous tissue following uv irradiation.

demonstrable in exudate from PUVA-inflamed skin.[45] For these reasons, mediators other than PG are likely to be involved in the pathogenesis of PUVA-induced inflammation.

The PGs are rapidly metabolized near the site of their synthesis,[42] increasing the practical difficulties of any study of their role in inflammation. A metabolite of PGE_2, 13,14-dehydro-15-keto-PGE_2 (PGE_2-M), is much more stable and accumulates in plasma, where it can be measured with increased accuracy.[46] The introduction of this specific assay for the measurement of PGE_2-M provided an opportunity to examine, in a relatively noninvasive manner, the systemic levels of PGE_2 after a single acute uv injury. Eight healthy, fair-skinned Caucasians were selected for a study performed at Massachusetts General Hospital, Boston.[47] Before the experiment, individual exposure doses were estimated according to the subject's complexion and results of skin phototesting. Four subjects were exposed to whole-body uv-B irradiation and four to whole-body PUVA irradiation. The PUVA subjects had ingested 8-MOP 2 h before uv-A treatment at a dose of 0.6 mg/kg. The aim was to produce the equivalent of a moderately severe sunburn over most of the body surface. For the PUVA subjects, a less aggressive approach was adopted; it was necessary that the radiant exposure be monitored more carefully, since the dose-response curve for PUVA is steep and phototoxic burns are more painful and persistent than sunburns.

Over a two week period, 18 blood samples were taken from each subject and drawn into heparinized syringes. Plasma PGE_2-M concentrations, including a preirradiation baseline for each subject, were determined by the radioimmunoassay method.[46,48]

Preliminary results showed that plasma concentrations of PGE_2-M were increased significantly in all four subjects treated with uv-B and that, in contrast, PGE_2-M was not significantly increased in any of the PUVA-treated subjects. This finding is consistent with the published data obtained by observing the effects of indomethacin on PUVA-induced erythema.[44] Subsequent animal studies using an increased dose of uv-A could confirm these findings and give valuable information about the proposed different mechanisms of action of uv-B and PUVA phototoxicity.

EPILOGUE

Our knowledge of the photobiology and phototoxicity of the skin is still in its infancy, although substantial progress has been achieved in this field, particularly in the past decade. Strong epidemiological evidence has established that solar radiation is the major factor in the pathogenesis of basal and squamous cell carcinomas (the most common cutaneous neoplasms in man).[49,50]

Our understanding of cellular photobiological events on the molecular level has, also, gone far beyond the pioneering observations of DNA damage and thymine dimer formation. At this date, it is well established that even a single dose of uv radiation can induce changes in proteins, membranes, and lipids and can lead to the formation of a number of heteroadducts within the cell. Furthermore, genetic regulation, genetic differentiation, and the production of a number of regulatory molecules (messengers, hormones, and immunomolecules) can be affected by light.

One of the main objectives of photobiology in the near future will be to shed more light upon the relationship between phototoxicity and photocarcinogenesis, which has been poorly established so far. TABLE 2 shows the major groups of agents that are phototoxic in humans. Of this group of compounds, only the mechanism of action of psoralens is partially understood; the mechanisms of action on the molecular level of the other groups is either only poorly elucidated or not understood at all. It is still generally believed that chronic phototoxicity can lead to carcinogenesis. However, chronic anthracene phototoxicity did not lead to carcinogenesis in hairless mice irradiated with a solar simulator.[51] As a positive control in this experiment, a group of hairless mice treated with 8-MOP under similar conditions developed skin tumors. The investigators suggested that 8-MOP, and, most probably, other furocoumarins, augment photocarcinogenesis through their known covalent addition to DNA upon absorption of appropriate wavelengths of light. Anthracene and some other phototoxic agents may lack this effect; their primary targets in the cell are molecules not directly involved in the transmission of genetic information.

As our knowledge of molecular photobiology increases, we will be able to live in increased harmony with our sun's rays. This knowledge may provide us with a model to help us unveil further two of the basic mysteries of our lives: aging and cancer.

TABLE 2

MAJOR GROUPS OF PHOTOTOXIC AGENTS IN MAN

Psoralens
Sulfonamides
Sulfonylureas
Phenothiazines
Tetracyclines
Coal tar
Anthracene
Pyridine
Acridine
Phenanthrene

ACKNOWLEDGMENTS

I am indebted to Dr. Paul Tobin (Clement Associates, Inc., Washington, DC) for conducting the phototoxicity studies of psoralens and for his participation in preparing this manuscript, to Mr. Albert Giles, Jr. for carrying out all the animal experiments, to Dr. Robert J. Scheuplein for reading and offering useful comments on this manuscript, and to Mrs. Alberta Blair for editorial assistance.

REFERENCES

1. FITZPATRICK, T. B., M. A. PATHAK, L. C. HARBER, M. SEIJI & A. KUKITA. 1974. An introduction to the problem of normal and abnormal responses of man's skin to solar radiation. *In* Sunlight and Man. T. B. Fitzpatrick, Ed.: 3–14. University of Tokyo Press. Tokyo.
2. URBACH, F., J. H. EPSTEIN & P. D. FORBES. 1974. Ultraviolet carcinogenesis: Experimental, global and genetic aspects. *In* Sunlight and Man. T. B. Fitzpatrick, Ed.: 259–83. University of Tokyo Press. Tokyo.
3. BEUKERS, R. & W. BERENDS. 1960. Isolation and identification of the irradiation product of thymine. Biochim. Biophys. Acta **41:** 550 51.
4. WACKER, A., H. DELLWEG & D. WEINBLUM. 1960. Strahlenchemische Veränderung der bakterien-Dexoyribonucleinsäure *in vivo*. Naturwissenschaften **47:** 477.
5. PATHAK, M. A., D. M. KRAMER & U. GUNGERICH. 1972. Formation of thymine dimers in mammalian skin by ultraviolet radiation *in vivo*. Photochem. Photobiol. **15:** 177–85.
6. CLEAVER, J. E. & J. E. TROSKO. 1970. Absence of excision of ultraviolet-induced cyclobutane dimers in xeroderma pigmentosum. Photochem. Photobiol. **11:** 547–50.
7. HART, R. W., R. B. SETLOW & A. D. WOODHEAD. 1977. Evidence that pyrimidine dimers in DNA can give rise to tumors. Proc. Nat. Acad. Sci. USA **74:** 5574–78.
8. LAMOLA, A. A. 1968. Excited state precursors of thymine photodimers. Photochem. Photobiol. **7:** 619–32.
9. KORNHAUSER, A., J. N. HERAK & N. TRINAJSTIĆ. 1968. Mechanism of photosensitized dimerization of pyrimidines. Chem. Commun. **1968:** 1180.
10. KORNHAUSER, A. & M. A. PATHAK. 1972. Studies on the mechanism of the photosensitized dimerization of pyrimidines. Z. Naturforsch. Teil B **27:** 550–53.
11. KORNHAUSER, A., J. B. BURNETT & G. SZABO. 1974. Isotope effects in the photosensitized dimerization of pyrimidines. Croat. Chem. Acta **46**(3): 193–97.
12. HAMMOND, G. S., N. J. TURRO & P. A. LEERMAKERS. 1962. The mechanisms of photoreactions in solution. IX. Energy transfer from the triplet states of aldehydes and ketones to unsaturated compounds. J. Phys. Chem. **66:** 1144–47.
13. SCHENCK, G. O. 1960. Selektivitat und typsiche Reaktions-mechanismen in der Strahlenchemie. Z. Electrochem. **64:** 997–1011.
14. KORNHAUSER, A. & J. B. BURNETT. 1974. Photosensitization of cyclodimerization of pyrimidines. *In* Progress in Photobiology: Proceedings of the Sixth International Congress on Photobiology. G. O. Schenck, Ed.: Paper 013. Deutsche Gesellschaft fur Lichtforschung. Frankfurt am Main, Germany.
15. BADEN, H. P. & M. A. PATHAK. 1967. The metabolism and function of urocanic acid in skin. J. Invest. Dermatol. **48:** 11–17.
16. SMITH, K. C. 1962. Dose-dependent decrease in extractability of DNA from bacteria following irradiation with ultraviolet light or with visible light plus dye. Biochem. Biophys. Res. Commun. **8:** 157–63.
17. TODD, P. & A. HAN. 1976. Uv-induced DNA to protein cross-linking in mammalian cells. *In* Aging, Carcinogenesis, and Radiation Biology. K. C. Smith, Ed.: 83–104. Plenum Press. New York and London.
18. SMITH, K. C. 1974. Molecular changes in the nucleic acids produced by ultraviolet and visible radiation. *In* Sunlight and Man. T. B. Fitzpatrick, Ed.: 57–66. University of Tokyo Press. Tokyo.
19. KORNHAUSER, A., M. A. PATHAK, E. ZIMMERMANN & G. SZABO. 1976. The *in vivo* effect

of ultraviolet irradiation (290–350 nm) on epidermal chromatin. Croat. Chem. Acta **48**(3): 385–90.

20. KORNHAUSER, A. 1976. Uv-induced DNA-protein cross-links *in vivo* and *in vitro*. Photochem. Photobiol. **23**: 457–60.

21. ZIERENBERG, B. E., D. M. KRAMER, M. G. GEISERT & R. G. KIRSTE. 1971. Effects of sensitized and unsensitized longwave uv-irradiation on the solution properties of DNA. Photochem. Photobiol. **14**: 515–20.

22. PATHAK, M. A., D. M. KRAMER & T. B. FITZPATRICK. 1974. Photobiology and photochemistry of furocoumarins (psoralens). *In* Sunlight and Man. T. B. Fitzpatrick, Ed.: 335–68. University of Tokyo Press. Tokyo.

23. MUSAJO, L., G. RODIGHIERO, G. CAPORALE, F. DALL'ACQUA, S. MARCIANI, F. BORDIN, F. BACCICHETTI & R. BEVILACQUA. 1974. *In* Sunlight and Man. T. B. Fitzpatrick, Ed.: 369–87. University of Tokyo Press. Tokyo.

24. SCOTT, B. R., M. A. PATHAK & G. R. MOHN. 1976. Molecular and genetic basis of furocoumarin reaction. Mutat. Res. **39**: 29–74.

25. CHANDRA, P., G. RODIGHIERO, S. BALIKCIOGLU & R. K. BISWAS. 1976. Nucleic acid modification by furocoumarins and light: Some biomedical implications. *In* Photochemotherapy: Basis, Technique and Side Effects. E. G. Jung, Ed.: 25–32. F. K. Schattauer Verlag. Stuttgart, New York.

26. DALL'ACQUA, F. 1977. New chemical aspects of the photoreaction between psoralen and DNA. *In* Research in Photobiology. A. Castellani, Ed.: 245–55. Plenum Press. New York and London.

27. PARRISH, J., T. FITZPATRICK, L. TANNENBAUM & M. PATHAK. 1974. Photochemotherapy of psoriasis with oral methoxsalen and long-wave ultraviolet light. N. Engl. J. Med. **291**(23): 1207–22.

28. WOLFF, K., T. B. FITZPATRICK, J. A. PARRISH, F. GSCHNAIT, B. GILCHREST, H. HÖNIGSMANN, M. A. PATHAK & L. TANNENBAUM. 1976. Photochemotherapy for psoriasis with orally administered methoxsalen. Arch. Dermatol. **112**: 943–50.

29. GILCHREST, B., J. PARRISH, L. TANNENBAUM, H. HAYNES & T. FITZPATRICK. 1976. Oral methoxsalen photochemotherapy of mycosis fungoides. Cancer (Philadelphia) **38**(2): 683–89.

30. STERN, R., L. THIBODEAU, R. KLEINERMAN, J. PARRISH, T. FITZPATRICK & 22 Participating Investigators. 1979. Risk of cutaneous carcinoma in patients treated with oral methoxsalen photochemotherapy for psoriasis. N. Engl. J. Med. **300**(15): 809–13.

31. MANDULA, B. B., M. A. PATHAK & G. DUDEK. 1976. Photochemotherapy: Identification of a metabolite of 4′,5′,8′-trimethylpsoralen. Science **193**: 1131–34.

32. MANDULA, B. B., M. A. PATHAK, Y. NAKAYAMA & S. J. DAVIDSON. 1978. Induction of mixed-function oxidases in mouse liver by psoralens. Br. J. Dermatol. **99**: 687–92.

33. VERONESE, F. M., R. BEVILACQUA, O. SCHIAVON & G. RODIGHIERO. 1978. The binding of 8-methoxypsoralen by human serum albumin. Farmaco Ed. Sci. **33**: 667–75.

34. YOSHIKAWA, K., N. MORI, S. SAKAKIBARA, P. S. SONG & M. NOBUYUKI. 1979. Photoconjugation of 8-methoxypsoralen with proteins. Photochem. Photobiol. **29**: 1127–33.

35. STEINER, I., T. PREY, F. GSCHNAIT, J. WASHUTTL & F. GREITER. 1978. Serum levels of 8-methoxypsoralen 2 hours after oral administration. Acta Derm. Venereol. **58**: 185–88.

36. KAIDBEY, K. H. & A. M. KLIGMAN. 1978. Photocontact allergy to 6-methylcoumarin. Contact Dermatitis **4**: 277–82.

37. HARTER, M. L., I. C. FELKNER, W. W. MANTULIN, D. L. MCINTURFF, J. N. MARX & P. S. SONG. 1974. Excited states and photobiological properties of potential DNA cross-linking agents, the benzodipyrones. Photochem. Photobiol. **20**: 407–13.

38. OU, C. N., P. S. SONG, M. L. HARTER & I. C. FELKNER. 1976. Spectroscopic properties and interactions of dimethoxycoumarin with DNA. Photochem. Photobiol. **24**: 487–90.

39. HARTER, M. L., I. C. FELKNER & P. S. SONG. 1976. Near-uv effects of 5,7-dimethoxycoumarin in *Bacillus subtilis*. Photochem. Photobiol. **24**: 491–93.

40. GARCIA, R. I., M. A. FUENTES, A. KORNHAUSER & G. SZABO. 1975. Comparison of the effect of cyclic AMP and embryo extract on DNA and melanin synthesis in chick embryo retinal pigment cells *in vitro*. The American Society for Cell Biology. Abstract P: 129a.

41. SILVER, M. J. & J. B. SMITH. 1975. Prostaglandins as intracellular messengers. Life Sci. **16:** 1635–48.
42. GOLDYNE, M. E. 1975. Prostaglandins and cutaneous inflammation. J. Invest. Dermatol. **64:** 377–85.
43. SNYDER, D. S. & W. H. EAGLSTEIN. 1974. Intradermal antiprostaglandin agents and sunburn. J. Invest. Dermatol. **62:** 47–50.
44. MORISON, W. L., B. S. PAUL & J. A. PARRISH. 1977. The effects of indomethacin on long-wave ultraviolet-induced delayed erythema. J. Invest. Dermatol. **68:** 120–33.
45. GREAVES, M. W. 1978. Does ultraviolet-evoked prostaglandin formation protect skin from actinic cancer? Lancet **1:** 189.
46. TASHJIAN, A. H., JR., E. F. VOELKEL & L. LEVINE. 1977. Plasma concentrations of 13,14-dihydro-15-keto-prostaglandin E_2 in rabbits bearing the VX_2 carcinoma: Effects of hydrocortisone and indomethacin. Prostaglandins **14:** 309–17.
47. WHITE, H. A. D., L. LEVINE, A. KORNHAUSER & J. A. PARRISH. 1980. Plasma 13,14-dihydro-15-keto-prostoglandin E_{12} levels in humans after ultraviolet irradiation. To be published.
48. LEVINE, L. 1977. Levels of 13,14-dehydro-15-keto-PGE_2 in some biological fluids as measured by radioimmunoassay. Prostaglandins **14:** 1125–39.
49. SCOTT, J., A. W. KOPF & F. URBACH. 1974. Non-melanoma skin cancer among Caucasians in four areas of the U.S. Cancer (Philadelphia) **34:** 1333–38.
50. FEARS, T. R., J. SCOTTO & M. A. SCHNEIDERMAN. 1977. Mathematical models of age and uv effects on the incidence of skin cancer among whites in the U.S. Am. J. Epidemiol. **105:** 420–27.
51. FORBES, P. D., R. E. DAVIES & F. URBACH. 1976. Phototoxicity and photocarcinogenesis: Comparative effects of anthracene and 8-methoxypsoralen in the skin of mice. Food Cosmet. Toxicol. **14:** 303–6.

DISCUSSION

DR. B. S. COOPERMAN: I'd like to ask you a question about tetracycline. Lots of people are taking tetracycline; lots of people are in the sun. Is this an unusual case?

DR. A. KORNHAUSER: That is a very interesting point. There is still little information in the medical literature on the general incidence of drug phototoxicity, as cases are usually sporadic rather than epidemic. Also, the number of cases reported is only a small fraction of those that really occur. In all instances, however, the phototoxic syndrome is strongly dose dependent. Orally administered phototoxic drugs will not produce symptoms until an effective concentration is present in the skin. Tetracycline derivatives vary significantly in their phototoxic potency. Democlocycline is the most potent phototoxic derivative; a daily dose of 600 mg elicits phototoxic responses in most individuals who are exposed to the sun, but smaller doses may also be effective. Tetracycline, on the other hand, rarely evokes phototoxic responses. Furthermore, as in all phototoxic phenomena, the skin type of the individual plays an important role in tetracycline phototoxicity. Fair skin subjects are much more susceptible than pigmented ones. All these factors have to be taken into consideration when one is predicting and clinically evaluating phototoxic phenomena.

Concluding, I must also point out the fact that, in most cases, except for the well known phototoxic agents like psoralens and some photodynamic agents (methylene blue, etc.), the underlying mechanisms, particularly on the molecular level, still remain largely unknown.

STUDY OF THE PHOTOATTACHMENT
OF ESTROGEN RECEPTOR
TO THE NUCLEAR ACCEPTOR SITES
IN HUMAN BREAST CANCER CELLS*

John Kallos and Vincent P. Hollander

Research Institute
Joint Diseases—North General Hospital
Mount Sinai School of Medicine
New York, New York 10035

P. P. Baskevitch and H. Rochefort

Unite d'Endocrinologie Cellulaire et Moleculaire,
U 148 de l' INSERM
34100 Montpellier, France

A model for estrogen hormone action has been in vogue for over a decade.[1,2] For example, the steroid binds to a specific cytoplasmic receptor and the hormone receptor-complex then migrates to the nucleus, where it presumably binds to chromatin to trigger off a specific alteration in gene expression.[3-5] Precisely what happens in the nucleus is still unknown. Although the nature of specific interactions between estrogen receptors and the genetic material has been extensively studied,[3,6] there is, as yet, no evidence for direct contact between the receptor and the DNA in the target cell nucleus.

If there is an intimate contact between the receptor protein and DNA, and if we introduce a short cross-link between the protein and DNA, then the position of this cross-link will identify the point of contact. Our approach to this problem was to study the photochemical attachment of estrogen-receptor complex to bromouracil-substituted DNA (photochemically reactive DNA) in the intact nucleus of human breast cancer cells, MCF-7. We selected MCF-7 cells because they are estrogen responsive and contain estrogen receptor, which can translocate from the cytosol to the nucleus.[7]

Our experiment was designed to follow the effect of irradiation on the extractability of the nuclear receptor as follows:

1. Cells were grown in the presence of bromouracil, so that the bromouracil was incorporated into the nuclear DNA

2. The bromouracil-substituted cells were labeled with ^{3}H-estradiol, so that the cytoplasmic receptor complex translocated to the nucleus

3. The cells were irradiated with near-uv light (~312 nm) to form a covalent cross-link between the receptor and the DNA

*This research was supported by the United States Public Health Service, grant no. P30; the National Cancer Institute, grant no. CA14194; the National Institutes of Health; and by the United States–France (NCI-INSERM) Program on Hormonal Regulation and Cancer.

0077–8923/80/0346–0415 $1.75/1 © 1980, NYAS

4. The cells were homogenized and the KCl extractability of the nuclear receptor was determined.

First, it was necessary to determine whether or not bromouracil, in the absence of irradiation, prevents the *in vivo* nuclear binding of estrogen receptor. Since we have recently demonstrated that estrogen receptor has an enhanced affinity for bromouracil-substituted DNA *in vitro*,[6] we were particularly interested in examining whether or not a similar phenomenon might also operate in the intact cells. MCF-7 cells were grown for five or six days in the presence of bromouracil (5 μg/ml), resulting in a roughly 60% replacement of thymine residues in DNA, without any noticeable effect on cell growth. When the bromouracil-treated cells were homogenized and the nuclear receptor was extracted by KCl, the receptor became more resistant to salt extraction than was that of unsubstituted cells (FIGURE 1). This line of evidence suggests that the receptor binding to bromouracil-substituted nuclei is tighter than the unsubstituted binding—this corresponds well to our *in vitro* binding studies. The *in vitro* DNA binding closely mimics our *in vivo* observations, suggesting that DNA may play an important role in the nuclear binding.

To explore this problem further, the photochemical attachment of estrogen receptor to the bromouracil-substituted nuclei in the MCF-7 cells was examined by following the effect of irradiation on the KCl extractability of the nuclear receptor. When the bromouracil-substituted and ^{3}H-estradiol–labeled MCF-7 cells were incubated in the dark and then subjected to KCl extraction, there was no change in the amount of radioactive receptor recovered as a function of time of incubation (FIGURE 2). However, when the same cells were irradiated with uv light ($\sim$312 nm), there was a time-dependent decrease in the recovery of the receptor complex. About 15% of the radioactive complex could no longer be extracted with KCl (as compared with that

FIGURE 1. The effect of bromouracil on the salt-extractability of the nuclear estrogen receptor in MCF-7 cells. MCF-7 cells were grown for five or six days in the presence of 5 μg/ml bromouracil (control cells were untreated) in NEM medium containing 10% stripped calf serum and insulin. Cells were labeled with 2×10^{-8} M ^{3}H-estradiol (for 45 min at 37° C) and homogenized; then, the specific nuclear receptor was measured by salt extraction (concentration shown on the abscissa) followed by a hydroxyapetite assay. Values have been corrected for nonspecific binding.

Cells with bromouracil: O——O; cells without bromouracil: △——△.

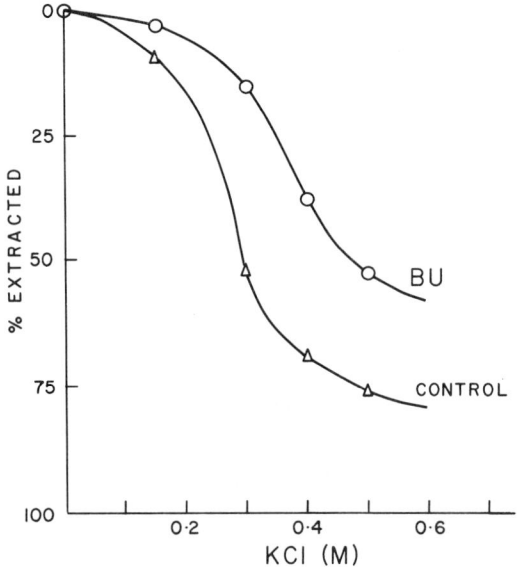

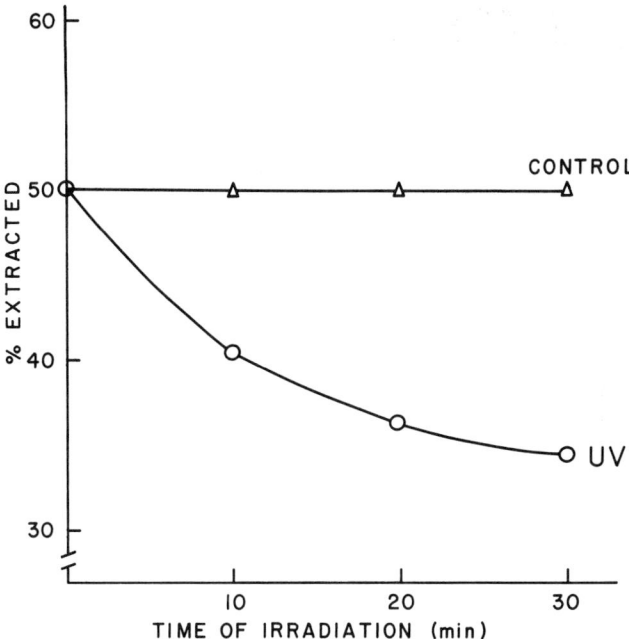

FIGURE 2. The time-dependence of the irradiation on the salt-extractability of estrogen receptor from bromouracil-substituted MCF-7 nuclei.

The bromouracil-substituted and ^{3}H-estradiol-labeled cells were irradiated with uv light (40 W Westinghouse Sun Lamp, approximately 312 nm) for the time indicated and the control cells were kept in the dark. The nuclear receptors were measured by KCl extraction, followed by hydroxyapetite assay.

extracted from the nonirradiated control); this is consistent with the view that portions of the receptor complex become covalently attached to the nucleus after 20 min irradiation. The chemical nature of the nuclear photoproduct, however, remains to be established.

The particular value of photo-cross-linking is to provide a chemical tool for structural study of the locus of that genome which interacts with the steroid receptor. The present data can only be considered preliminary until the photoproducts are identified.

REFERENCES

1. JENSEN, E. V., T. SUZUKI, T. KAWASHIMA, W. E. STUMPF, P. V. JUNGBLUT & E. R. DE SOMBRE. 1968. Proc. Nat. Acad. Sci. USA 59: 632–38.
2. GORSKI, J., D. TOFT, G. SHYMALA, D. SMITH & A. NOTIDES. 1968. Recent Prog. Horm. Res. 24: 45–80.
3. YAMAMOTO, K. R. & B. M. ALBERTS. 1976. Annu. Rev. Biochem. 45: 721–46.
4. GORSKI, J. & F. A. GANNON. 1976. Annu. Rev. Physiol. 38: 425–50.

5. ROCHEFORT, H., J. ANDER, P. P. BASKEVITCH, J. KALLOS, F. VIGNON & B. WESTLEY. 1980. J. Steroid Biochem. **12:** 135–42.
6. KALLOS, J., T. M. FASY, V. P. HOLLANDER & M. D. BICK. 1978. Proc. Nat. Acad. Sci. **75:** 4896–900.
7. HORWITZ, K. B. & W. L. McGUIRE. 1978. J. Biol. Chem. **253:** 8185–91.

EFFECTS OF PHOTOSENSITIVE CHEMICALS ON MALARIA PARASITE CELLS*

Andrew M. Tometsko, J. Donald Hare, Carol R. Tometsko
Patrick Y. Lam, and Debra Lipman

Litron Laboratories, Ltd.
and
University of Rochester Medical Center
Rochester, New York 14620

INTRODUCTION

In recent years, a variety of light-sensitive chemicals have been employed to probe, label, and inactivate biological targets.[1-3] Our own previous work has involved the use of aryl azides and aryl diazonium compounds to study the structural and functional relationships of proteolytic enzymes,[4-7] mitochondrial ATPase,[8] and cellular amino acid transport systems.[9] These experiments indicated that photoprobes will seek out complementary binding sites in biological systems. If the probe is activated while present in the binding site, covalent attachment can occur, resulting in an irreversible loss of biological activity. As a result of these studies, we hypothesized that, under some conditions, it might be possible to employ photosensitive chemicals to inhibit sites in cell systems essential for survival. Essential or vital sites can be defined as those sites that, if inhibited, will cause a loss of crucial biological functions, which will lead to cell death.

In order to test the feasibility of using photoprobes to seek out and destroy vital targets in cell systems, we chose the rodent malaria parasites, *P. berghei* and *P. vinckei,* as model cell systems. The malaria parasite is an exquisitely sensitive pathogen, since mice have no natural defense against it. A few parasites will eventually kill the mouse. The parasites infect the red blood cells and are morphologically distinct following staining. The appearance of drug-resistant strains of the malaria parasite[10] has caused renewed emphasis to be placed on the search for new antimalarial compounds. Generally, drugs are directed against unique targets within the parasite that are essential for metabolic activity. Thus, drug development can be divided into two phases, namely, identification of the targets in the parasite that are essential for survival of the organism and characterization of the binding requirements of a new target site. With proper procedures, photochemical methods could be employed to both identify and characterize vital sites. The general photochemical approach can be adapted for *in vivo* or *in vitro* assay procedures.

In this paper, we present a sensitive, rapid, and economical *in vitro* assay procedure, which is based on the incorporation of radioactively labeled adenosine into a macromolecular fraction of infected red blood cells, a procedure similar to that described previously.[11-17] The *in vitro* assay is then coupled with photoinactivation by 4-fluoro-3-nitrophenyl azide (FNPA) and NAP-nornicotine (SCHEMA 1) to provide

*This research was supported, in part, by the Council for Tobacco Research.

0077–8923/0346–0419 $1.75/1 © 1980, NYAS

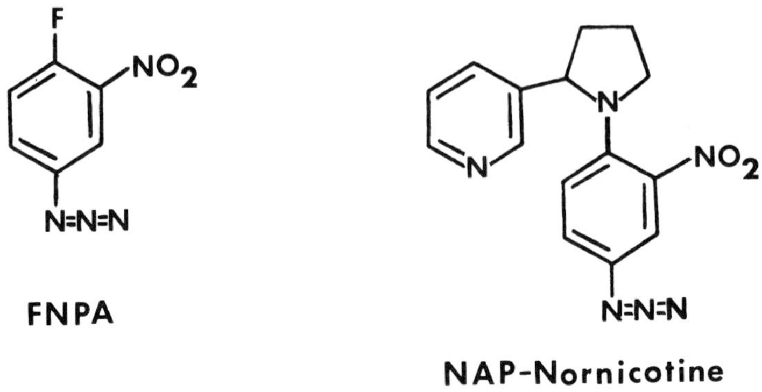

FNPA

NAP-Nornicotine

SCHEMA 1.

evidence for a direct correlation between a light-induced loss of infectivity *in vivo* and a decrease in the incorporation of labeled adenosine *in vitro*.

Experimental results are presented that indicate that these two probes can inhibit sites that are essential to the survival of the rodent malaria parasites. Inhibition of vital sites is shown by (1) the *in vivo* survival patterns following infection with photolyzed blood and (2) the *in vitro* rate of incorporation of radioactive nucleosides into the DNA and RNA of the parasite. The development of new high affinity drugs is discussed.

Finally, we demonstrate the feasibility of using structurally related conventional drugs to protect the vital site against photoinactivation by FNPA. These results suggest that the interaction of photosensitive and conventional compounds with essential target sites in a parasite provides a means of determining the affinity of new derivatives of the photoprobe for those sites, thereby suggesting the structure of potentially useful chemotherapeutic agents.

MATERIALS AND METHODS

Preparation of L-N-4-Azido-2-Nitrophenyl Nornicotine

Nornicotine was obtained from ICN–K&K and purified by eluting 1.0 g samples through 60 g 40–140 mesh silica gel (Baker) with methanol to give 0.79 g pure compound [R_f (methanol) 0.5; PMR (CDCl$_3$) 8.64 (S, ^{1}H), 8.49 (d, J = 6 Hz, ^{1}H), 7.72 (d, J = 8 Hz, ^{1}H), 7.22 (d of d, J = 8, 6 Hz, ^{1}H), 4.11 (t, J = 7 Hz, ^{1}H), 3.06 (q, J = 6 Hz, ^{2}H), 2.38–1.44 (m, ^{4}H, ppm)]. Due to the photosensitivity of the product, the reaction was carried out under subdued light with amber glassware. A solution of FNPA (177 mg; 0.973 mmol) in 2 ml ethanol was added to a mixture of L-nornicotine (120 mg; 0.973 mmol), sodium carbonate (106 mg; 1.70 mmol), and 1 ml water in 2 ml 95% ethanol. A rubber septum was placed on the flask. The reaction mixture was stirred at 50 °C for 10 h. TLC showed that about 10% of L-nornicotine was unreacted. The reaction was worked up by dissolving the mixture in 20 ml water and extracting it with ether (4×). The ether phase was washed with saturated sodium chloride solution and dried with anhydrous sodium sulfate. Ether was evaporated with a water aspirator. The product was purified with preparative TLC (Analab, Silicagel), using a solvent system consisting of petroleum ether/acetone (2:1; R_f = 0.6), and gave an orange oil [R_f 10.6; uv max (0.9% NaCl in H_2O) 265 (7120), 430 (527) nm; ir (neat) 2950 (m), 2850 (m), 2100 (S), 1510 (S), 1330 (S), 1280 (S), 915 (m), 810 (s), 715 (s) cm^{-1}; PMR (CDCl$_3$) 8.72 (S, ^{1}H), 8.62 (d, J = 5 Hz, ^{1}H), 7.73 (d, J = 8 Hz, ^{1}H), 7.50 (d, J = 4 Hz, ^{1}H), 7.35–6.77 (m, ^{4}H), 4.95 (t, J = 7 Hz, ^{1}H), 3.88 (d of d, J = 13, 10 Hz, ^{1}H), 3.08–1.83 (m, ^{5}H); MSR (75 eV) m/e 310 (0.1, M$^+$), 282 (0.5, M − 28), 247 (2.0), 227 (4.0), 135 (9.4, M − 28−247), 88 (8.9), 86 (63.4), 84 (100.0), 51 (3.0), 49 (18.3), 47 (25.4)].

Kinetics of Photolytic Decomposition of NAP-nornicotine

The NAP-nornicotine was dissolved in aqueous 0.9% NaCl solution to make 1.81×10^{-4} *M*. This solution (3 ml) was photolyzed in a Pyrex tube with a Xenon flash lamp (14 pulses per second). The decomposition rate at 265 cm was recorded with a uv spectrophotometer for 30 min. Two maxima, at 260 and 305 nm, started to appear toward the second half of the photolysis. The first order decomposition rate constant for the first part of the photolysis was calculated to be 0.0133 s^{-1} and the half-life, 52 s.

Experimental procedure: P. berghei

Plasmodium berghei was obtained from Dr. A. L. Ritterson (University of Rochester Medical Center). The parasites were maintained by transferring infected blood to fresh mice. Infected blood was obtained by cardiac puncture and was immediately diluted 1:10 with physiological saline solution. A solution of FNPA (2 m*M*) was prepared in physiological saline, and a sample (2 ml) was mixed with an equal volume of infected blood to yield a final concentration of 1 m*M* FNPA. Control blood samples (2 ml) were also diluted with an equal volume of physiological saline. In both cases, dark and light samples were prepared. The dark samples were incubated in subdued light for 10 min; the light samples were photolyzed with a Xenon flash lamp (5000 V: 14 pulses per second) for 10 min.

The resulting four solutions—the controls [infected blood (dark) and infected blood (light)] and the test samples [infected blood + 1 m*M* FNPA (dark) and infected blood + 1 m*M* FNPA (light)]—were then injected i.p. (0.3 ml) into sets of test mice (four in each group). The mice were then tested for parasites in blood smears on consecutive days. Parasites were morphologically distinct within the infected red blood cells, which appeared to be bluer than normal red blood cells. Parasites were observed in mice that received infected blood that had been incubated either in the dark or under photolysis conditions. Parasites were also present in mice that received infected blood that had been incubated with FNPA in the dark. Since no parasites could be detected in mice that received infected blood that had been photolyzed with FNPA, we completed the experiment by determining the survival pattern of this set of mice. Results of the experiment are shown in TABLE 1.

Experimental procedure: P. vinckei

Plasmodium vinckei was received from Dr. David Walliker (Protozoal Genetics Unit, Institute of Animal Genetics, Edinburgh, Scotland) and maintained in the CD-1 mouse strain from Charles River. Infected blood was obtained by cardiac puncture, heparinized, diluted 1:50 to 1:100 in RPMI 1640 buffered with 20 mM Hepes (Grand Island), as suggested by Trager and Jensen,[18] and supplemented with 10% bovine fetal serum (Grand Island). Blood was harvested from infected animals when the proportion of infected red cells reached 60–90%. The parasite was transferred to uninfected mice by intraperitoneal inoculation of 0.1–0.5 ml diluted blood.

Photolysis Conditions.

Diluted red blood cell suspensions were placed in 60 mm plastic petri dishes, the chemicals to be tested were added directly to the cell suspension, and the covered dish was placed under the Xenon flash lamp for 2–10 min. Photolysis was carried out at 14 pulses per second with a 6000 V drop across the lamp. The photolysis unit has been described in Reference 5. Controls were kept in subdued light. Following treatment either in the dark or with photolysis, the viability of the parasite population was

TABLE 1

PHOTOLYTIC INACTIVATION OF *P. berghei* WITH 1.0 MM 4-FLUORO-3-NITROPHENYLAZIDE

Sample	Conditions	Number of Animals	Survivors	Parasitemia
1. Infected RBC	Dark	4	0*	+
2. Infected RBC	Photolysis	4	0*	+
3. Infected RBC + 1 mM FNPA	Dark	4	0*	+
4. Infected RBC	Photolysis	4	4†	−

*Survivors after 1 month.
†Survivors after 6 months.

determined either by i.p. inoculation of mice with 0.4 ml of the various samples or by the uptake of ^{3}H-adenosine into an acid-insoluble fraction of infected red cells.

^{3}H-Adenosine Uptake Assay.

The incorporation of ^{3}H-adenosine (or its metabolic products) into acid-insoluble macromolecules was measured in one of two ways. Triplicate 1 ml samples of the treated red cell suspension were distributed into 35 mm plastic petri dishes and exposed to 3–5 μCi/ml (final concentration) ^{3}H-adenosine directly. In this experiment, the test chemicals were present in the culture medium during labeling. Alternatively, in order to remove the free drug, the treated red cell suspension was sedimented at 800 × g for 5 min, the cell pellet was resuspended in fresh RPMI medium, and triplicate 1 ml samples were exposed to 3–5 μCi/ml (final concentration) ^{3}H-adenosine. The labeled samples were maintained, with occasional agitation, at 37 °C in a CO_2 incubator for varying periods of time. The uptake reaction was terminated by the addition of 0.1 ml formalin, followed by the addition of 0.1 ml hydrogen peroxide (30%) to bleach the hemoglobin, after which the fixed cells were filtered onto GF/A glass fiber filters. The filters were washed with 5 ml water, 5 ml

1% TCA, 5 ml water, and dried with two extractions with methanol (1 ml). The radioactivity on the dried filters was measured in a liquid scintillation spectrometer in an ACS cocktail (Amersham-Searle).

Ribonuclease Digestion.

In order to degrade RNA specifically, labeled, infected red cells were treated with ribonuclease, as previously suggested by Gutteridge and Trigg.[15] A suspension of infected red blood cells was labeled 5 h with ^{3}H-adenosine (4 μCi/ml) and fixed in 10% formalin for 5–10 min. The fixed red blood cells were washed by centrifugation in water, in 1% TCA, in water, and resuspended in 0.1 M acetate buffer (pH 5.1). Duplicate samples were incubated overnight at 37 °C with both RNase A-40 μg/ml (Worthington) and RNase T1-40 units/ml (Miles). Controls were left untreated. Following enzymatic hydrolysis, the pellets were washed with water and 1% TCA, solubilized in 0.5 N KOH, bleached with H_2O_2, and counted in an ACS scintillation cocktail.

RESULTS

Our initial experiments in the study of vital sites in the malaria parasite used *P. berghei*. As mentioned above, mice do not have a natural defense against this parasite. Consequently, severe parasitemia develops; this is shown by morphologically distinct parasitized red blood cells and enlargement of the liver and the spleen of the infected animal. Toward the end of the infection, nearly all the red blood cells exhibited infection: a blood smear stained with Wright's stain had a definite blue cast. Following infection with *P. berghei*, parasites become evident in the blood smears within one week, and the mice die by the third week. This host-parasite system seemed appropriate for probing vital sites, since the number of parasitized red blood cells could be determined by cell counts, providing a quantitative evaluation of the rate of parasitemia. In addition, if vital sites in the parasite were inhibited, we would expect to observe a substantial increase in the survival time of a mouse infected with photochemically treated parasites.

Since previous studies indicated that 4-fluoro-3-nitrophenyl azide is able to inhibit a variety of biological targets,[4-8] we chose this probe to examine the presence of complementary vital sites in the malaria parasite. Experiments were conducted to evaluate the effect of FNPA on the infectivity of the rodent malaria parasite *P. berghei*. Infected mouse blood was incubated either in the dark or under photolysis conditions, both with and without 1 mM FNPA. Photolysis was carried out for 10 min at 14 pps; this has, subsequently, been reduced to less than 2 min. The samples were then injected into sets of normal mice, and the level of parasitemia was followed. As indicated in TABLE 1, parasitemia developed in the mice injected with infected blood that had been incubated with FNPA in the dark or that had been photolyzed in the absence of FNPA. All were dead by the third week. In contrast, those mice that received blood that had been photolyzed with FNPA exhibited no parasitemia—they survived for the entire six month run of the experiment. These results suggest that FNPA is able to seek out and inhibit one or more vital targets in *P. berghei*.

In order to further evaluate the photolytic inhibition of *P. berghei* by FNPA, we carried out a second set of experiments to define the dose response. We employed microscopic inspection of blood smears and measurement of survival times to evaluate the infectivity of the parasites at different FNPA concentrations. The results of these experiments are shown in TABLE 2. Infected blood cells that were photolyzed in the presence of 1 mM FNPA were completely neutralized, and the mice, again, survived for months. Similarly, 0.1 mM FNPA effectively photoinactivated the parasite. The lower limit of effective concentration appears to be about 0.01 mM, since one of four mice survived. As expected, all the mice that received parasites photolyzed in the absence of probe died.

These experiments strongly suggest that photoprobes can be employed to inhibit vital targets in pathogenic organisms. It should be noted further that experiments evaluating the effectiveness of a photosensitive drug could be completely carried out with the blood obtained from a single mouse. This contrasts with experiments in which animals are infected and subsequently treated with massive doses of a drug to maintain a therapeutically effective drug level. Photochemical therapy provides an efficient, effective, low cost means of sensing the importance of cellular targets that complement a specific photosensitive drug.

In order to develop a screening procedure that was more efficient in terms of time and use of animals, we have explored methods to measure the metabolic activity of the parasite in an *in vitro* system. We chose, initially, the uptake of ^{3}H-adenosine (or its metabolic products, such as ^{3}H-inosine or ^{3}H-hypoxanthine) as a measure of the synthesis of RNA and DNA as well as the pathway leading to the synthesis of the purine ribonucleoside and deoxyribonucleoside triphosphates. FIGURE 1 shows a time course of incorporation of ^{3}H-products into acid-insoluble components in uninfected mouse red cells and in red cells infected with *P. vinckei* (maintained in RPMI medium buffered with Hepes and supplemented with 10% bovine fetal serum). Uninfected cells at a dilution comparable to that of the infected cells incorporate low levels of radioactivity. Infected cells show a progressive incorporation of radioactive compounds for several hours. The capacity to incorporate ^{3}H-adenosine does not diminish significantly when the infected blood is incubated 9.5 h at 37 °C prior to the beginning of the labeling period. When incorporation was allowed to continue overnight, a significant additional increment of uptake, which is depicted by the dotted portion of the curve, was noted. However, the same preparation of cultured infected cells, incubated overnight and then labeled for 2 h, displayed a minimal

TABLE 2

PHOTOLYTIC* INHIBITION OF *P. berghei* AT DIFFERENT FNPA CONCENTRATIONS

Test Sample	FNPA Concentration† mM	Parasitemia‡	Survivors
Infected Blood + FNPA	1.0	−	4/4
Infected Blood + FNPA	0.1	−	4/4
Infected Blood + FNPA	0.01	−	1/4
Infected Blood	0.0	+	0/4

*Photolysis was carried out for 10 minutes at 14 pulses per second.
†The FNPA concentration was obtained by mixing infected blood samples with a FNPA solution prepared in sterile saline.
‡Parasitemia was determined by inspection of blood smears that were stained with Wright's stain.

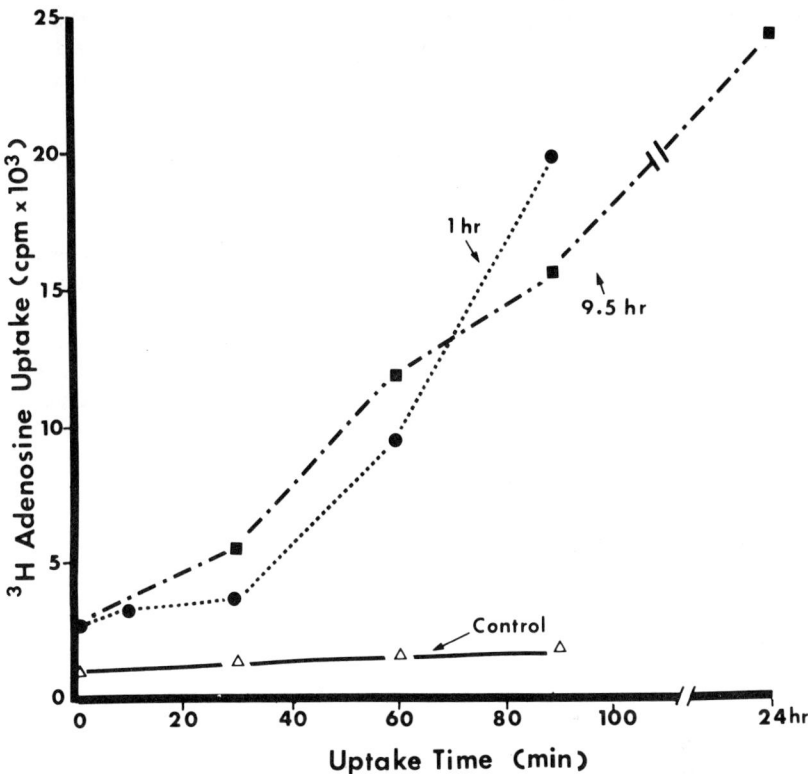

FIGURE 1. The incorporation of ³H-adenosine into nucleic acids of parasitized red blood cells is plotted as a function of uptake time. Cells were incubated 1 or 9.5 h prior to uptake. Control data were obtained with normal red blood cells.

capacity to incorporate radioactive compounds (data not shown). This indicates that the parasites had either failed to survive or continued to differentiate to the schizont stage and released metabolically inactive merozoites. Giemsa-stained preparations revealed few residual infected red cells, but significant numbers of intact normal red cells and structures consistent with free merozoites, suggesting that the parasite had continued to grow *in vitro* with release of merozoites, but that reinfection of normal red cells by merozoites had not taken place.

Incorporation into RNA and DNA

The relative proportion of the radioactive precursors incorporated into RNA and DNA was determined with a culture of infected red cells labeled for 5 h with ³H-adenosine (4 μCi/ml final concentration) and fixed with formalin. Two different methods were used. In one method, the fixed, labeled cells were washed and treated for 18 h with RNase A (40 μg/ml) + RNase T1 (40 units/ml). A control sample was processed in an identical way, but without adding enzymes. Using this procedure, 64% of the radioactivity was hydrolyzed and 36% was RNase resistant, indicating that the proportion of labeled DNA to RNA was 1:2, a figure similar to that found in parasites labeled *in vitro*.[16]

When the second method was used, the relative amount of DNA and RNA was determined by alkaline or acid hydrolysis of the labeled, infected cells. Samples were heated at 90 °C for 20 min in 1% TCA to hydrolyze DNA or at 80 °C for 20 min in 0.2 N NaOH to hydrolyze RNA, neutralized, and precipitated with 10% TCA for counting. If we consider only the radioactivity recovered in the hydrolyzed samples, then the fraction resistant to acid hydrolysis is 21,000 counts/sample (64%; RNA) and that resistant to alkaline hydrolysis is 12,000 counts/sample (36%; DNA), giving a ratio similar to that found with RNase digestion.

The data indicate that the labeled purine base derived from ^{3}H-adenosine is incorporated into both RNA and DNA under these experimental conditions and that,

TABLE 3

AVERAGE DAY OF DEATH OF MICE INOCULATED WITH
P. vinckei–INFECTED RED CELLS TREATED WITH PHOTOACTIVATED FNPA

FNPA Conc. mM	Average Day of Death	Range
0	5	5–6
0.01	5	5–6
0.05	5½	5–6
0.1	7	5–9
0.2	7	6–8
0.5	7	7–8
1.0	11	11–12

NOTE: In each experiment, two CD-1 female mice were inoculated with 0.4 ml cultured red cells from a mouse infected with *P. vinckei* that had been photolyzed 2 min in the presence of the specified concentration of FNPA.

based on the distribution of radioactivity, the relative abundance of the RNA is approximately twice that of the DNA. Furthermore, it was found that the metabolism of the organism could be maintained for at least 10 h in this culture medium, as measured by the rate of incorporation of ^{3}H-adenosine.

Photoinactivation of ^{3}H-Adenosine Uptake and Infectivity by FNPA

Experiments were then performed to determine the effect of photoactivated FNPA on the incorporation of ^{3}H-adenosine into infected red cells and on the infectivity of the treated blood. Samples of the infected red cells from this experiment were inoculated i.p. into two mice and their days of death were recorded. These data are shown in TABLE 3. It is clear that the higher concentrations of FNPA prolong the survival of the inoculated animals. At 1 mM, the survival time was essentially doubled, suggesting that the animals were successfully infected with only a few viable organisms.

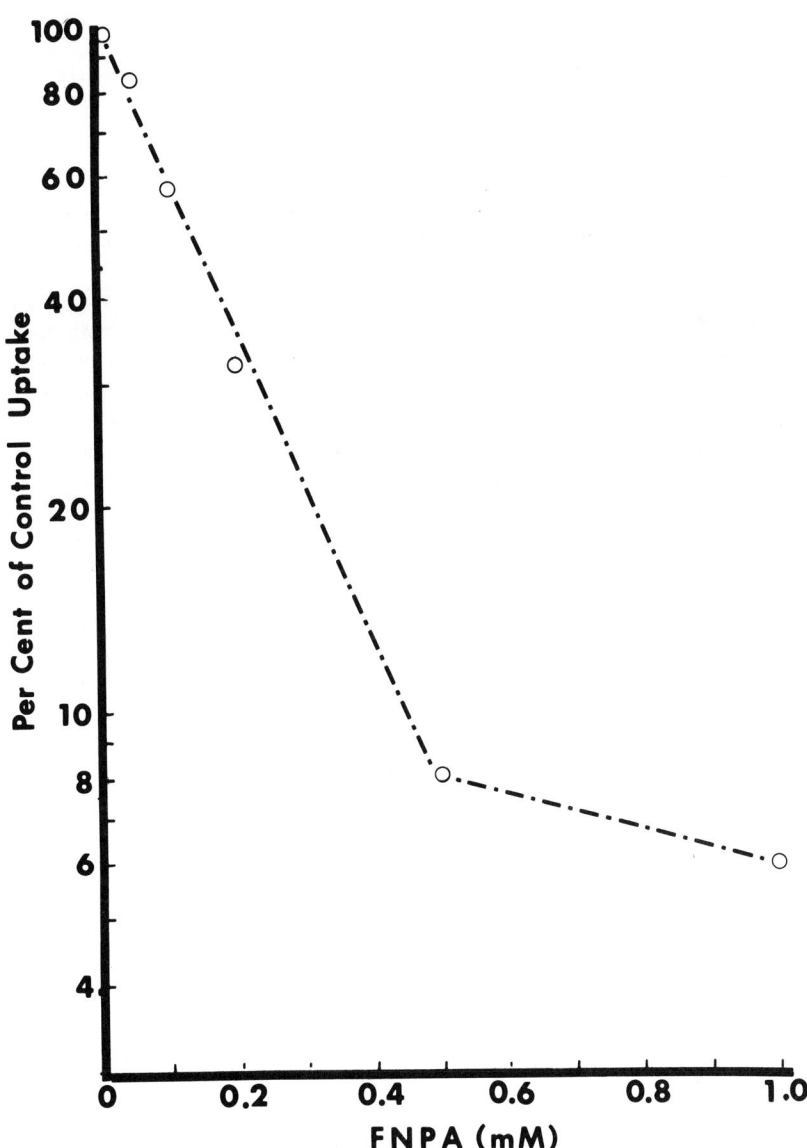

FIGURE 2. The uptake of ^{3}H-adenosine into nucleic acids of parasitized red blood cells is plotted as a function of FNPA concentration. Samples were photolyzed 2 min at 14 pulses per second.

The *in vitro* assay provides a more sensitive indication of photolytic inhibition. FIGURE 2 illustrates the 2 h incorporation of ^{3}H-adenosine into acid-insoluble components following photolysis in the presence of different concentrations of FNPA. This is a concentration-dependent inactivation of the incorporation of ^{3}H-adenosine, with a concentration producing 50% inhibition, which corresponds to 0.14 mM FNPA.

Reversal of FNPA Photoinactivation by DNP

Experiments were then carried out to determine whether the nonphotosensitive chemical, 2,4-dinitrophenol (DNP), would react with the same binding site(s) as FNPA and, thereby, interfere with the FNPA photoinactivation of ^{3}H-adenosine incorporation. In initial experiments (TABLE 4), the two reagents were not removed from the infected red cell suspension but were present during the labeling period. Under these conditions, DNP inhibited the incorporation of ^{3}H-adenosine, thereby masking any protective effect of DNP on photoinactivation by FNPA. Experiments in which the drugs were first removed by sedimenting infected cells and resuspending them in fresh RPMI 1640 medium for an assay of ^{3}H-adenosine incorporation (shown in TABLE 3) were then carried out. Parasitized cells treated with 0.2 mM DNP displayed a capacity to incorporate ^{3}H-adenosine comparable to untreated control cells both dark and photolyzed. This suggests that the effect of DNP on the metabolism of the parasite is fully reversible. The photoinactivation of ^{3}H-adenosine incorporation by 0.1 mM FNPA in this experiment is quite marked (94%) when compared to the effect of the FNPA in the dark (6%). It should be noted that the inactivation of ^{3}H-adenosine incorporation by FNPA is reduced from 94% to 71% in the presence of a one molar excess of DNP. Greater levels of protection against FNPA photoinactivation by DNP could be expected if the ratio of DNP to FNPA were increased.

TABLE 4

PHOTOINACTIVATION OF ^{3}H-ADENOSINE UPTAKE IN *P. vinckei* BY FNPA AND
PROTECTION AGAINST PHOTOINACTIVATION BY DNP

Treatment	Dark Control		Photolysis–2 min	
A. Drugs Not Removed	Uptake	% of Control	Uptake	% of Control
Control	167,230 ± 25,900	100	160,150 ± 11,500	100
DNP–0.2 mM	79,730 ± 23,900	48	74,720 ± 16,200	47
FNPA–0.1 mM	168,510 ± 11,600	101	62,570 ± 1,500	39
DNP + FNPA	68,920 ± 1,100	41	47,450 ± 1,600	30
B. Drugs Removed	Uptake	% of Control	Uptake	% of Control
Control	232,230 ± 14,900	100	223,700 ± 5,500	100
DNP–0.2 mM	265,940 ± 7,100	114	223,780 ± 5,900	96
FNPA–0.1 mM	218,510 ± 2,600	94	13,040 ± 1,200	6
DNP + FNPA	186,020 ± 1,300	80	68,470 ± 5,400	29

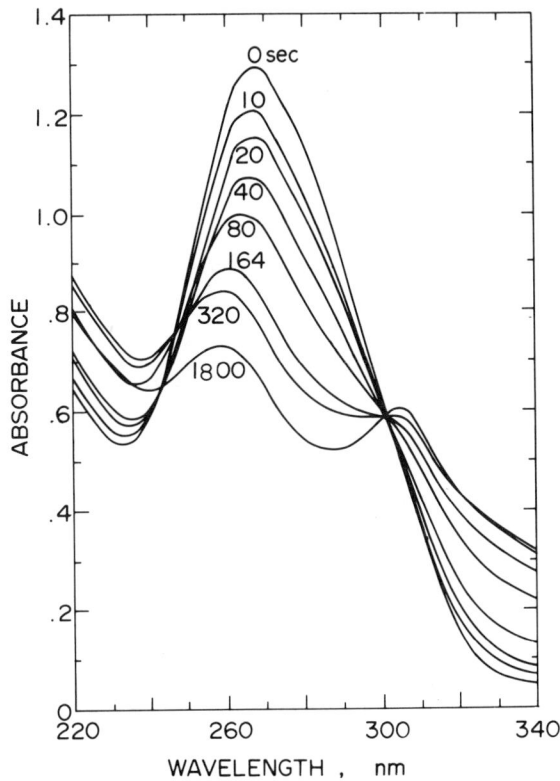

FIGURE 3. The absorbance of NAP-nornicotine is plotted as a function of wavelength for different photolysis times (seconds). The photolysis rate was 14 pulses per second with a Xenon flash lamp.

We next investigated the effect of a new photoprobe, NAP-nornicotine, on *P. vinckei*. This photoprobe provides a cationic probe that was expected to seek out anionic sites in the parasite cells. NAP-nornicotine exhibits substantial photosensitivity, as is shown by the change in absorption at 260 nm (FIGURE 3). The effect of this probe on adenosine uptake is investigated both in the dark and under photolysis conditions (14 pps; 1.5 min). As shown in FIGURE 4, an 80% decrease in adenosine incorporation was observed with NAP-nornicotine at 1.5 m*M*, where the dark effect is negligible. A dark effect was observed at higher concentrations.

DISCUSSION

The results of these preliminary experiments demonstrate that the infectivity of *P. berghei* is completely neutralized by photolysis with FNPA. Thus, vital sites that complement the FNPA structure must be present in the rodent malaria parasite. In experiments with *P. vinckei*, it was demonstrated that the effect on infectivity is directly correlated with a dose-dependent inhibition of the incorporation of ^{3}H-adenosine (or its metabolic products) into the nucleic acids of infected red cells.

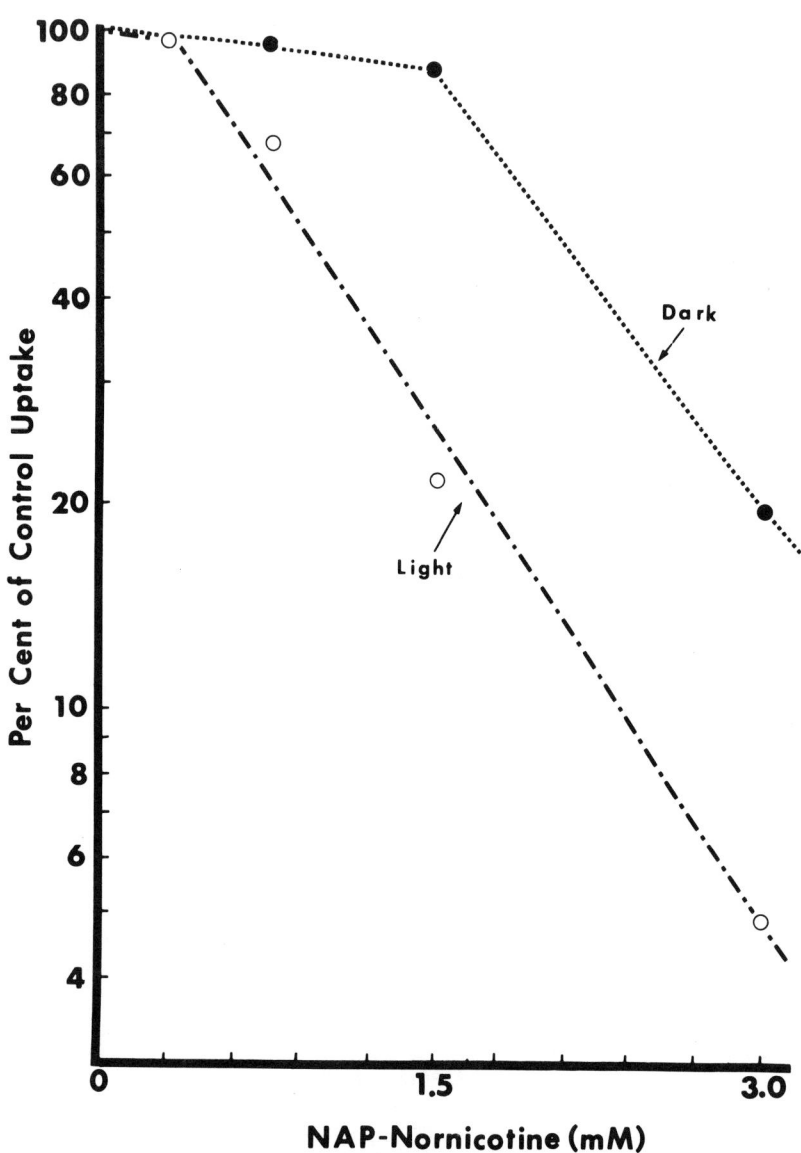

FIGURE 4. The uptake of ^{3}H-adenosine into the malaria parasite, *P. vinckei,* is plotted as a function of NAP-nornicotine concentration (photolysis time: 2 min at 14 pps).

Although our experiments with FNPA strongly suggest that photochemical methods can be employed to identify new vital sites, the application of this methodology to drug design requires some adjustments in the experimental procedure, since it would be impractical to photolyze blood systems to rid them of parasites. We reasoned that, if the photoprobe could be employed initially to identify a vital target, the same reaction could be employed subsequently to develop conventional (nonphotosensitive) drugs, which would inhibit the vital targets with a high affinity. The new procedure would involve screening chemical agents and analogs of the effective photoprobe for those that compete effectively with the probe for the target site. If a chemical is an effective competitive inhibitor, it should protect the parasite from photoinactivation by the photoprobe. The protection would be manifested, *in vivo,* by a decrease in the survival time of the mouse to the control values and, *in vitro,* by an increase in the incorporation of radioactive adenosine into nucleic acids, since a greater number of functional parasites would be present.

To test this hypothesis, we investigated the ability of dinitrophenol to compete with FNPA for binding sites. Through the use of the incorporation of ^{3}H-adenosine as an *in vitro* assay of the effect of FNPA on the metabolism of the parasite, it has been possible to demonstrate that 2,4-dinitrophenol (DNP) partially protects FNPA-sensitive functions of the infected cells against photoinactivation by FNPA (TABLE 4). Additional research is needed to characterize the vital site(s) in the parasite. Although FNPA is a relatively simple molecule, it is able to find complementary sites in a number of different biological targets.

The protective effect of DNP observed in the present case is similar to that found in two other systems that we have studied, in which DNP has been shown to compete with FNPA for target sites. In the first system, described by Senior and Tometsko,[8] both FNPA and DNP increase the activity of mitochondrial ATPase in the dark and photoactivated FNPA strongly inhibits the activity of the enzyme. Significantly, DNP protects the ATPase against photoinactivation by FNPA. These and other data have been interpreted as evidence that FNPA and DNP compete for an allosteric site on the ATPase molecule and that irreversible binding of photoactivated FNPA to this site leads to inactivation of the enzyme.

A second system in which DNP has been found to compete with FNPA for sites related to a specific functional activity is in the transport of nucleosides in resealed human red cell ghosts (Hare, unpublished data). In this isolated membrane system, 0.2 mM FNPA photoinactivates nucleoside transport and 1 mM DNP completely reverses the effect. Since the malaria parasite has the salvage pathways to utilize exogenous purines but not pyrimidines,[13] it is possible that FNPA effects the transport of ^{3}H-adenosine, either in the red cell membrane or in the membrane of the parasite. This would lead to an inhibition of the incorporation of radioactive precursors into nucleic acids by blocking preliminary transport steps.

On the other hand, the drug could also effect more crucial metabolic processes, such as mitochondrial function or nucleic acid synthesis. The fact that higher concentrations of DNP (0.2–1.0 mM), a reversible uncoupler of mitochondrial oxidative phosphorylation,[19] reversibly inhibit ^{3}H-adenosine incorporation (the inhibition is seen only if the drug is left in the medium during the assay period) suggests that the overall process of incorporation into nucleic acids is quite dependent on a normally functioning mitochondrial system. Thus, these data suggest that one mechanism of action of photoactivated FNPA is the irreversible inactivation of mitochondrial function, resulting in the loss of viability and the inhibition of ^{3}H-adenosine incorporation.

A third possible site of action of FNPA could involve binding to DNA. Recent studies have indicated that FNPA exhibits considerable mutagenic activity[20] and it is relatively unique, since it exhibits mutagenic activity against all five test strains of *S. typhimirium* that are routinely used in the Ames test.

The close correlation between concentrations of FNPA that inhibit ^{3}H-adenosine incorporation or destroy infectivity (0.1–1.0 mM) suggests that inactivation of the same target site(s) results in the loss of both functions. Furthermore, the kinetics of the inactivation of incorporation of ^{3}H-adenosine by FNPA (FIGURE 2) suggest a simple one-hit phenomenon, which further supports the importance of the FNPA target site.

The incorporation of ^{3}H-adenosine and its labeled products into both RNA and DNA is similar to that demonstrated previously under a variety of other labeling conditions.[10–17] The extent of this incorporation was as great after 10 h in culture as it was after only 1 h; this suggests that the culture conditions must be capable of supporting continued growth and development of the parasite. Previous work suggested that RNA synthesis in this parasite deteriorated during cultivation *in vitro*.[16] It is not clear what aspects of the experimental conditions of these earlier studies were responsible for the failure of the organism to thrive, as measured by RNA synthesis. The culture conditions chosen for the current studies were suggested by the work of Trager and Jensen[18] and provide an opportunity to study the differential effects of various treatment regimens on the synthesis of DNA and RNA as well as on specific proteins.

These preliminary studies suggest an approach different from that discussed by Lantz and Van Dyke[14] to the development of antimalarial drugs. The first step of this new approach is to identify target sites crucial to the parasite through the use of photosensitive chemical analogs of known antimalarial drugs or nutritional substrates. Secondly, once vital target sites have been identified by their sensitivity to photo-probes, nonphotosensitive analogs of the photoprobe can be constructed; thirdly, their capacity to protect against photoinactivation can be used as a measure of their ability to seek out and interact with the index target site with reasonable affinity.

This approach to the identification of potential targets for chemotherapeutic attack through the use of photosensitive probes in *in vivo* and *in vitro* assay systems provides opportunities to probe vital metabolic processes. It is feasible to measure the differential incorporation either of radioactive purines into DNA and RNA or of radioactive amino acids into specific proteins by using two two-dimensional gel techniques. Studies such as these are currently being developed in our laboratories.

Our experiments verify our initial premise that photoprobes can be employed to identify vital targets in pathogenic organisms. Further developments of this technique could result in a reduction in the cost of developing new drugs and could prove widely applicable.

ACKNOWLEDGMENTS

The authors would like to thank Dr. V. Lisanti for his helpful suggestions and Dr. A. L. Ritterson for his advice in handling the malaria parasites.

REFERENCES

1. KNOWLES, J. E. 1972. Acc. Chem. Res. **5:** 155–60.
2. KATZENELLENBOGEN, J. A. 1977. *In* Biochemical Actions of Hormones, Vol. 4. G. Litwack, Ed.: 1–93. Academic Press. New York.
3. DARFLER, F. & A. M. TOMETSKO. 1978. *In* Chemistry and Biochemistry of Amino Acids, Peptides and Proteins, Vol. 5. B. Weinstein, Ed. Marcel Dekker. New York.
4. TOMETSKO, A. M. & J. TURULA. 1976. Int. J. Pept. Protein Res. **8:** 331–36.
5. TOMETSKO, A. M. & J. TURULA. 1976. Photochem. Photobiol. **23:** 579–85.
6. TOMETSKO, A. M., J. TURULA & J. COMSTOCK. 1978. Int. J. Pept. Protein Res. **12:** 143–54.
7. DeTRAGLIA, M. C., J. S. BRAND & A. M. TOMETSKO. 1978. J. Biol. Chem. **253:** 1846–52.
8. SENIOR, A. E. & A. M. TOMETSKO. 1976. Symposium on Electron Transfer Chains and Oxidative Phosphorylation. E. Quagliarello, *et al.,* Eds.: 155–60. Elsevier. New York.
9. HARE, J. D., G. V. MARINETTI, A. I. MEISLER & A. M. TOMETSKO. 1976. Biochim. Biophys. Acta **443:** 485–93.
10. World Health Organization. 1973. Chemotherapy of Malaria and Resistance to Anti-Malarials. WHO Tech. Rep. Ser. **529:** 30–54.
11. WALSH, C. J. & I. W. SHERMAN. 1968. J. Protozool. **15:** 763–70.
12. VanDYKE, K., C. SZUSTKIEWICZ, C. H. LANTZ & L. H. SAXE. 1969. Biochem. Pharmacol. **18:** 1417–25.
13. VanDYKE K., G. C. TREMBLAY, C. H. LANTZ & C. SZUSTKIEWICZ. 1970. Am. J. Trop. Med. Hyg. **19:** 202–8.
14. LANTZ, C. H. & K. VanDYKE. 1971. Biochem. Pharmacol. **20:** 1157–66.
15. GUTTERIDGE, W. E. & P. I. TRIGG. 1970. J. Protozool. **17:** 89–96.
16. TRIGG, P. I. & W. E. GUTTERIDGE. 1972. Parasitology. **65:** 265–71.
17. COOMBS, G. H. & W. E. GUTTERIDGE. 1975. J. Protozool. **22:** 555–60.
18. TRAGER, W. & J. B. JENSEN. 1976. Science **193:** 673–75.
19. LOOMIS, W. F. & F. LIPMANN. 1948. J. Biol. Chem. **173:** 807–8.
20. McKEE R. M., J. G. TOMETSKO & A. M. TOMETSKO. 1979. Mutation Res. **67:** 183–87.

DISCOVERY AND PHOTOAFFINITY
LABELING OF THE
MITOCHONDRIAL UNCOUPLER-BINDING SITE*

Youssef Hatefi

Department of Biochemistry
Scripps Clinic and Research Foundation
La Jolla, California 92037

INTRODUCTION

A large variety of compounds with unrelated chemical structures, such as substituted phenols, carbonylcyanide phenylhydrazones, salicylanilides, benzimidazoles, fatty acids, as well as dicoumarol, *bis*(hexafluoroacetonyl)acetone, tetraphenylboron, and even azide, share the common property of uncoupling oxidative phosphorylation and all the other energy-linked functions of mitochondria. The unrelated chemical structure of these uncouplers has complicated the study of the mechanism of uncoupling and contributed to the formulation of various theories of uncoupling, including the concept that holds that uncouplers do not have a specific site of action, but simply dissolve in membrane lipids, facilitate proton translocation from one side of the membrane to the other, and thereby collapse the transmembrane electrochemical potential of protons.[1-12] However, the results that other researchers have reported with potent uncouplers[13-16] led us to suspect that uncouplers might have a specific site of action in mitochondria. This possibility was strengthened by the fact that, despite their different chemical structures, all uncouplers bind tightly to bovine serum albumin.

To explore the possible existence of an uncoupler binding site in mitochondria, my colleague, Dr. W. G. Hanstein, designed and synthesized, in radioactive form, a photoaffinity labeling analog of the classical uncoupler, 2,4-dinitrophenol (DNP). The analog, 2-azido-4-nitrophenol (NPA), proved to be a more potent uncoupler than dinitrophenol and sufficiently stable in the absence of intense illumination to allow us to conduct equilibrium binding studies under nonphotolyzing conditions, also.[17] The equilibrium binding studies with radioactive NPA were particularly important in this case, since it was necessary to ascertain whether or not mitochondria contained a specific uncoupler binding site before attempting the less discriminating and more complicated photolabeling experiments.

EQUILIBRIUM BINDING OF TRITIATED 2-AZIDO-4-NITROPHENOL TO MITOCHONDRIA

FIGURE 1 is a plot of [³H]NPA uptake by mitochondria isolated from beef heart (on the ordinate) against the concentration of free NPA (on the abscissa). The open circles show two phases of NPA uptake by mitochondria: an initial high-affinity phase at low levels of added NPA followed by a low-affinity phase at higher levels of added

*This research was supported by grants from the United States Public Health Service, no. AM 08126, and from the National Institute of Science, no. PCM 76-01378.

434

NPA. The latter is due to partitioning of NPA between the mitochondrial and the aqueous domains, and its subtraction from the overall binding curve, A, yielded curve B, which is due to specific NPA binding to a saturable site. The concentration of this site appeared to be comparable to the concentration of mitochondrial ATPase and the more abundant respiratory enzymes, and a Hill plot of the specific binding data (slope = 1.03) indicated uniform NPA binding without appreciable cooperativity, at least up to 90% saturation of the site (FIGURE 2). In addition, it was shown that membranes

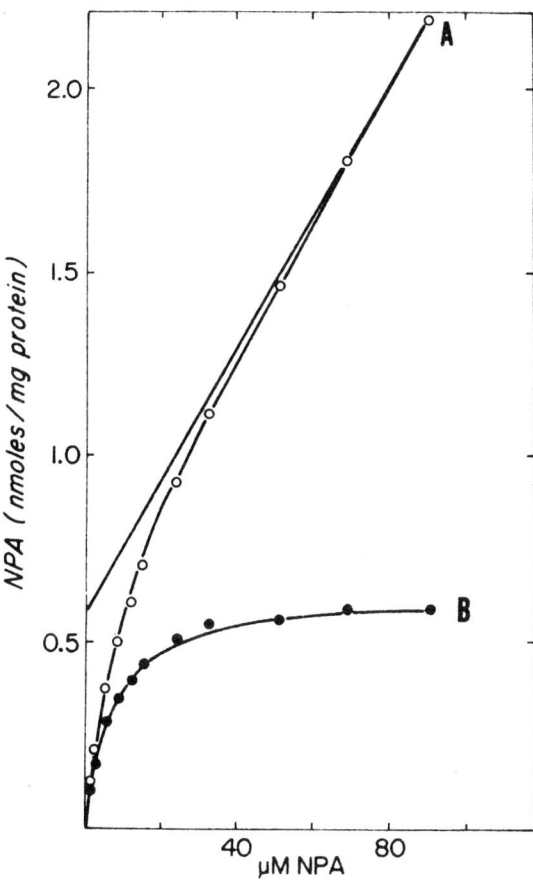

FIGURE 1. Binding of NPA by mitochondria as a function of added NPA concentration. A: total NPA incorporation; B: specific NPA binding. From reference 19.

lacking oxidative phosphorylation enzymes, such as red cell ghosts, did not possess a specific NPA binding site, and exhibited only nonspecific NPA uptake (FIGURE 3), similar to the low-affinity NPA binding by mitochondria shown in FIGURE 1.[18] The specific NPA binding site of mitochondria was characterized further by binding studies in the presence of other uncouplers and various modifiers of membrane function. It was found that all the uncouplers tested (DNP, 2,4,6-trinitrophenol (TNP), pentachlorophenol (PCP), carbonylcyanide m-chlorophenyl hydrazone

(CCCP), 5-chloro-3-*t*-butyl-2'-chloro-4'-nitrosalicylanilide (S-13), tetraphenylboron, dicoumarol, azide) competitively inhibited the specific binding of NPA to mitochondria and submitochondrial particles, while respiratory inhibitors (rotenone, antimycin A, cyanide), phosphorylation inhibitors (rutamycin, dicyclohexylcarbodiimide (DCCD), triethyltin), and specific ionophores (valinomycin + K[+], gramicidin D + K[+]) had no effect.[19,20] These results suggested that the inner mitochondrial membrane contains a specific site for the binding of various uncouplers and provided a basis for photolabeling studies.

RELATIONSHIP BETWEEN UNCOUPLER BINDING AND UNCOUPLING

Before the results of the photolabeling experiments could be meaningfully interpreted, however, it was necessary to find out whether or not uncoupler binding had anything to do with the act of uncoupling and whether or not photolabeling

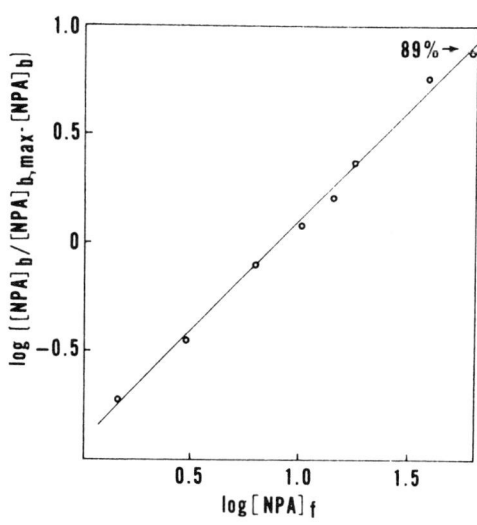

FIGURE 2. A Hill plot of the specific binding of NPA by mitochondria. $[NPA]_{b, max}$: number of binding sites for NPA (nmol/mg protein); $[NPA]_f$: free NPA (μM); $[NPA]_b$: bound NPA (nmol/mg protein). From Reference 19.

occurred at the site identified as the specific uncoupler binding site under equilibrium binding conditions. To answer the first question, a comparison of the potency of various uncouplers (e.g., uncoupler concentrations required for 50% uncoupling, I_{50}) and the dissociation constants (K_D) of these compounds (TABLE 1) suggested a definite relationship between uncoupler binding and uncoupling (see also Reference 21). Furthermore, since the K_D values in TABLE 1 were determined from the competitive inhibition results involving each uncoupler and low concentrations of NPA (i.e., under conditions of predominantly specific NPA binding), it could be concluded that the relationship between uncoupling and uncoupler binding was referable mainly to the specific uncoupler binding site characterized above.

Corroborating evidence was obtained with the use of trinitrophenol[20–22] and, subsequently, tetraphenylborate.[23] These compounds are membrane-impermeable

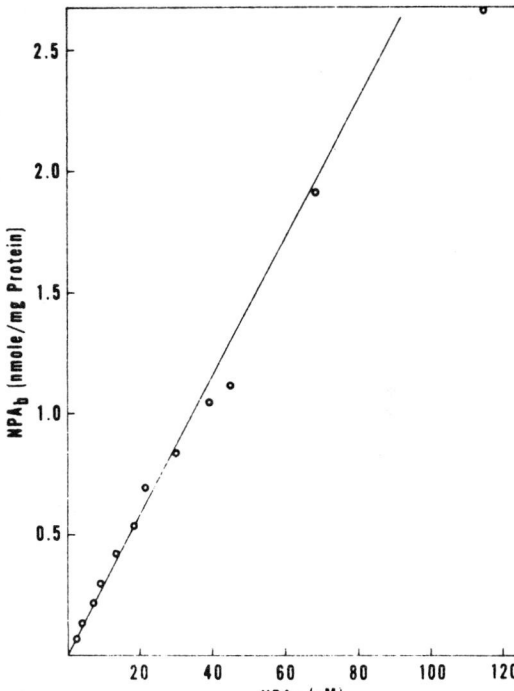

FIGURE 3. NPA uptake by erythrocyte ghosts as a functon of added NPA concentration. NPA_f and NPA_b are free and bound NPA, respectively. From Reference 18.

uncouplers. When presented to mitochondria, they do not penetrate the inner membrane rapidly, do not interact with the specific uncoupler binding site, and do not uncouple. By contrast, when presented to submitochondrial particles, which have an inside-out orientation of the inner membrane, trinitrophenol and tetraphenylborate bind to the uncoupler binding site (which, in the inverted membrane, would be accessible to membrane-impermeable reagents in the medium), and uncouple oxidative phosphorylation and other energy-linked functions (e.g., reverse electron transfer, transhydrogenation from NADH to NADP, and ATP$-^{33}$Pi exchange). The I_{50} of trinitrophenol in the above tests ranged from 40 to 60 μM, while, for tetraphenylborate, the values reported by Phelps and Hanstein were in the range from 4 to 8 μM.[23] We fully appreciate that these results do not unequivocally establish that uncoupler

TABLE 1

COMPARISON OF BINDING AFFINITIES AND UNCOUPLER POTENCIES

Uncoupler	$K_D(\mu M)$	$I_{50}(\mu M)$	K_D/I_{50}
NPA	15–29	5–10	3
DNP	48–73	15–25	3
TNP	121	40–60	2–3
PCP	22–44	4–8	5
Azide	11–15×10^3	3–4×10^3	3.7

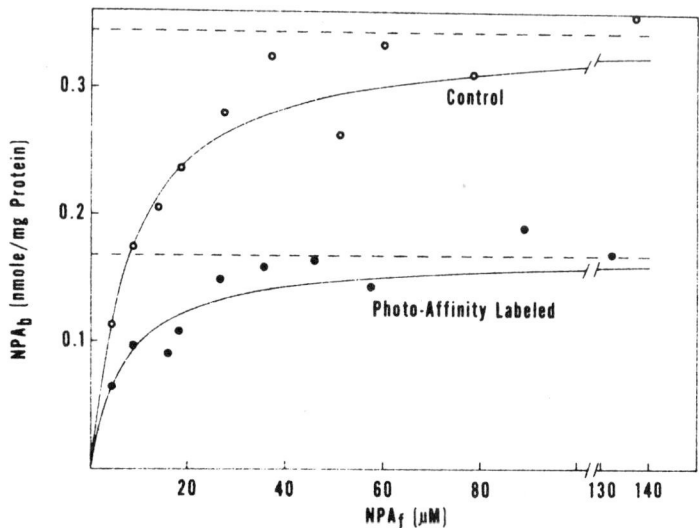

FIGURE 4. Equilibrium binding of NPA by mitochondria and mitochondria photolabeled with NPA. Photolabeling was performed by a 4 min irradiation of the particles in the presence of 20 μM NPA at 4 °C. From Reference 18.

binding is a sine qua non for uncoupling, but it is clear, in the cases of trinitrophenol and tetraphenylboron at least, that, in the absence of binding to the specific binding site of mitochondria, there is no uncoupling.† Further elaboration of this issue is beyond the scope of the present article, but the reader may consult References 20–22.

As regards the relationship between the specific uncoupler binding site identified by equilibrium binding studies and the site(s) occupied by NPA as a consequence of photolabeling, the following results may be cited. Mitochondria were treated with NPA under conditions that resulted in partial photolabeling. They were washed from free and photolyzed products of NPA, then subjected to equilibrium binding studies.[18] Particles treated similarly in the absence of NPA were used as controls. The results, shown in FIGURE 4, indicated that NPA binding to the specific uncoupler binding site was decreased in the particles partially prelabeled with NPA. In other studies, competitive inhibition of NPA binding by increasing concentrations of dinitrophenol was studied both in the dark and under photolyzing conditions. The results showed that dinitrophenol inhibited NPA binding under both conditions. However, it was 50 to 60% less effective in inhibiting NPA binding under photolabeling conditions than in the dark (i.e., under purely equilibrium binding conditions). These results also

---

†Two additional comments are important with regard to trinitrophenol: (1) Although, when added to mitochondria, trinitrophenol does not compete with NPA for binding to the specific uncoupler binding site, it effectively competes with NPA for the low-affinity binding sites of mitochondria (Figure 5 in Reference 22). (2) Trinitrophenyl acetate uncouples mitochondria.[24] This is, presumably, because the uncharged ester can penetrate the inner mitochondrial membrane, become hydrolyzed in the matrix, and the resultant picrate in the matrix can uncouple mitochondria just as it uncouples inside-out particles when added to the medium.

suggested that, under both photolabeling and nonphotolabeling conditions, NPA binds to the same site as DNP, but that, when NPA was allowed to bind covalently, dinitrophenol competition was decreased because it could compete only at the sites that did not contain covalently attached NPA.[18,19]

PHOTOLABELING OF MITOCHONDRIA WITH NPA
AND LOCATION OF THE UNCOUPLER BINDING SITE

FIGURE 5 shows the distribution of radioactivity among the mitochondrial components when whole mitochondria photolabeled with [³H]NPA were subjected to

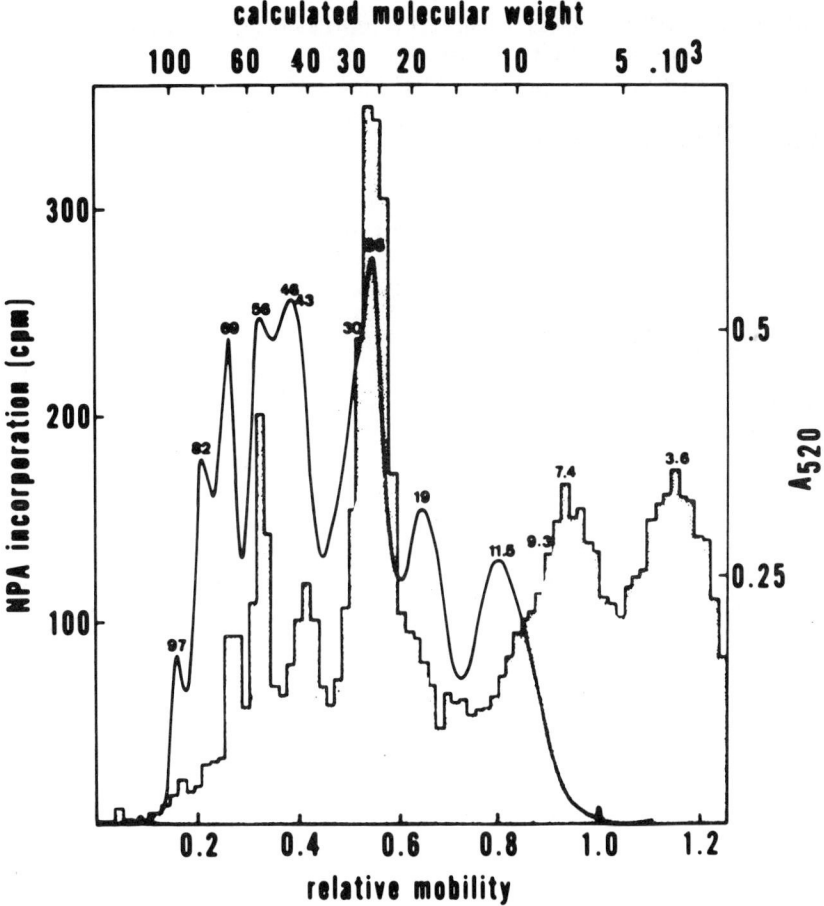

FIGURE 5. The distribution of protein (curved line) and radioactivity (stepped line) after SDS-polyacrylamide gel electrophoresis of mitochondria photolabeled with [³H]NPA. For conditions, see Reference 19.

TABLE 2

SPECIFIC UNCOUPLER BINDING CAPACITY
OF COMPLEXES I, III, IV, AND V

Preparation	Capacity* (nmol/mg protein)
Mitochondria	0.35
Complex I	≤0.05
Complex III	<0.01
Complex IV	<0.01
Complex V	0.81

*The equilibrium binding experiments with tritiated 2-azido-4-nitrophenol were carried out at pH 8.0 and 4 °C.

dodecylsulfate (SDS)–polyacrylamide gel electrophoresis. The curved line shows the protein distribution as shown by Coomassie Blue staining (the peaks are marked by numbers designating the apparent molecular weight, M_r, in kilodaltons) and the stepped line indicates the radioactivity distribution due to [³H]NPA binding. The regions of high specific radioactivity correspond to protein peaks in the approximate M_r regions of 55,000 and 26–30,000. There are also two peaks where little or no protein is present. These results and our data regarding the existence in mitochondria of a specific uncoupler binding site have been confirmed by Cyboron and Dryer, who used NPA with mitochondria from rat and hamster liver and hamster brown adipose tissue;[25] by Kurup and Sanadi, who used NPA with beef heart mitochondria;[26] and by Katre and Wilson, who used the uncoupler 2-nitro-4-azidocarbonylcyanide phenylhydrazone with beef heart mitochondria.[27,28]

To better locate the uncoupler binding site, we examined the equilibrium binding of NPA to the five protein-lipid complexes that comprise the enzymic machinery of the mitochondrial oxidative phosphorylation system. These enzyme complexes are located in the mitochondrial inner membrane and have been described in detail in recent reviews.[29–31] Complexes I (NADH: ubiquinone oxidoreductase), II (succinate: ubiquinone oxidoreductase), III (reduced ubiquinone: ferricytochrome c oxidoreductase), and IV (ferrocytochrome c: oxygen oxidoreductase), plus cytochrome c, make up the respiratory chain. Complex V is concerned with ATP synthesis and hydrolysis. At the level of the respiratory chain, the energy coupling sites are located in Complexes I, III and IV, and, in the isolated state, these three complexes and Complex V (and similar preparations from other sources) have been shown to be capable of energy transduction.[32–37] In addition, Complex V is capable of energy conservation because, in the isolated state, it catalyzes ATP-³³Pi exchange.[38] As with the phosphorylation of submitochondrial preparations (inner membrane vesicles), the ATP-³³Pi exchange activity of Complex V is sensitive to uncouplers, oligomycin, venturicidin, dicyclohexylcarbodiimide, trialkyltins, and valinomycin plus nigericin.

When the uncoupler binding capacities of the above energy-transducing enzyme complexes were examined with [³H]NPA under equilibrium binding conditions, it was found that the uncoupler binding site of mitochondria was absent from the respiratory chain Complexes I, III, and IV, but was present in Complex V at 2–3 times the concentration of this site in mitochondria or submitochondrial particles (TABLE 2).[38] Photoaffinity labeling of Complex V with [³H]NPA showed the occurrence of label in only three regions of the SDS-polyacrylamide gels (FIGURE 6): a small degree of labeling associated with the α and β subunits of F_1-ATPase, extensive labeling associated with a membrane sector polypeptide of M_r about 30,000, and a smaller amount of label near the dye front.[39] Labeling of the $\alpha\beta$ subunits of F_1-ATPase was expected, since phenolate ions are known to bind to the isolated, membrane-bound F_1-ATPase.[40] However, this binding is considerably weaker than the binding of substituted phenols to the mitochondrial uncoupler binding site (TABLE 1). Furthermore, mitochondria can catalyze uncoupler-sensitive energy-linked reactions, such as transhydrogenation and reverse electron transfer, even when the participation of F_1-ATPase is blocked by specific inhibitors. Therefore, we feel that NPA binding to F_1-ATPase may not be concerned with the act of uncoupling.

The occurrence of label near the dye front in FIGURE 6 has not been thoroughly investigated (see also Reference 28). This region of the gels also contains phospholipids that we know, from our studies on mitochondria, are labeled with NPA.[18] Therefore, at this stage of our work, we cannot confidently designate any of the labeled components shown in FIGURE 6 as the mitochondrial uncoupler binding site concerned with the act of uncoupling, although the 30,000 M_r polypeptide might be a

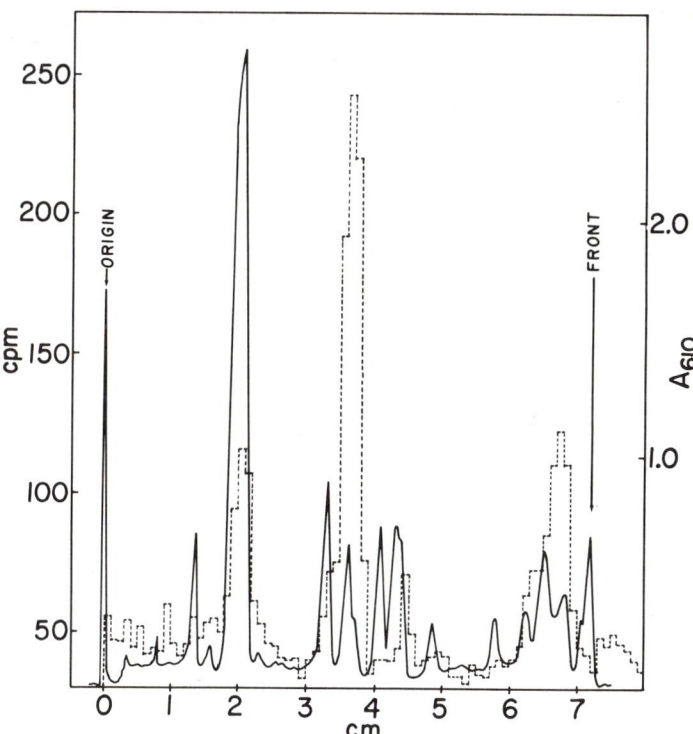

FIGURE 6. The distribution of protein (curved line) and radioactivity (dashed line) after SDS-polyacrylamide gel electrophoresis of Complex V photolabeled with [^{3}H]NPA. For conditions, see Reference 39.

likely candidate. In other studies, we have shown that the ATPase and the ATP-Pi exchange activities of Complex V are inhibited by arginine modifying reagents, such as butanedione and phenylglyoxal. The results have shown the presence of one arginyl residue, located in F_1-ATPase, which is essential for ATP hydrolysis, and another, more reactive, residue, which is essential for ATP-Pi exchange.[41,42] It was also shown that the equilibrium binding of NPA to the specific uncoupler binding site of Complex V is strongly inhibited by butanedione, which suggests that the specific uncoupler binding site of mitochondria might contain an arginyl residue. We plan to perform competitive labeling experiments using [³H]NPA to photolabel phenylglyoxal-treated Complex V and [¹⁴C]phenylglyoxal to label Complex V pretreated with nonradioactive NPA under photolyzing conditions. Suppression of radioactivity bound to any polypeptide, as compared to appropriate controls, should help us identify the Complex V component that bears the mitochondrial uncoupler binding site.

In his keynote address, Dr. Westheimer pointed out that a certain measure of luck is necessary if photoaffinity labeling experiments in biological systems are to yield relatively clear and interpretable results. Considering the enormous complexity of mitochondria, I think we have had an inordinate amount of luck in being able to define the mitochondrial uncoupler binding site to the extent described above. However, I am especially indebted to the organizers of this conference for inviting me here and giving me the opportunity to learn so much from the papers presented at these meetings, because I think it is in what I have learned here that I should seek Dr. Westheimer's important ingredient for the success of our future applications of photoaffinity labeling.

REFERENCES

1. SLATER, E. C. 1966. In Comprehensive Biochemistry, Vol. 14. M. Florkin and E. H. Stotz, Eds.: 327–96. Elsevier Publishing Co. Amsterdam.
2. WEINBACH, E. C. & J. GARBUS. 1969. Nature 221: 1016–18.
3. VAN DAM, D. & E. C. SLATER. 1967. Proc. Nat. Acad. Sci. USA 58: 2015–19.
4. WILSON, D. F., H. P. TING & M. S. KOPPELMAN. 1971. Biochemistry 10: 2897–902.
5. MITCHELL, P. 1966. Biol. Rev. Cambridge Philos. Soc. 41: 445–502.
6. HEMKER, H. C. 1964. Biochim. Biophys. Acta 81: 9–20.
7. MARGOLIS, S. A., G. LENAZ & H. BAUM 1967. Arch Biochem. Biophys. 118: 224–30.
8. TOLLENAERE, J. P. 1973. J. Med. Chem. 16: 791–96.
9. MONTAL, M., B. CHANCE & C. P. LEE 1969. Biochem. Biophys. Res. Commun. 36: 428–34.
10. MCLAUGHLIN, S. 1972. J. Membr. Biol. 9: 361–72.
11. SKULACHEV, V. P., A. A. JASAITIS, V. V. NAVICKAITE, L. S. YAGUZHINSKY, E. A. LIBERMAN, V. P. TOPALI & L. M. ZOFINA. 1969. FEBS (Symposium) 17: 275–84.
12. SKULACHEV, V. P. 1971. In Current Topics in Bioenergetics, Vol. 4. D. R. Sanadi, Ed.: 127–90. Academic Press. New York.
13. HEYTLER, P. G. 1963. Biochemistry 2: 357–61.
14. KAHAK, H. R., J. P. REEVES, S. A. SHORT & F. J. LOMBARDI. 1974. Arch. Biochem. Biophys. 160: 215–22.
15. WEINBACH, E. C. & J. GARBUS. 1965. J. Biol. Chem. 240: 1811–19.
16. WILSON, D. F. 1969. Biochemistry 8: 2475–81.
17. HANSTEIN, W. G., Y. HATEFI & H. KIEFER. 1979. Biochemistry 18: 1019–25.
18. HATEFI, Y., & W. G. HANSTEIN. 1974. In Membrane Proteins in Transport and Phosphorylation. G. F. Azzone, M. E. Klingenberg, E. Quagliariello, and N. Siliprandi, Eds.: 187–200. North-Holland. Amsterdam.

19. HANSTEIN, W. G. & Y. HATEFI. 1974 J. Biol. Chem. **249:** 1356–62.
20. HATEFI, Y. 1975. J. Supramol. Struct. **3:** 201–13.
21. HANSTEIN, W. G. 1976. Biochim. Biophys. Acta **456:** 129–48.
22. HANSTEIN, W. G. & Y. HATEFI 1974. Proc. Nat. Acad. Sci. USA **71:** 288–92.
23. PHELPS, D. C. & W. G. HANSTEIN. 1977. Biochem. Biophys. Res. Commun. **79:** 1245–54.
24. LEADER, J. E. & M. W. WHITEHOUSE. 1966. Biochem. Pharmacol. **15:** 1379–87.
25. CYBORON, G. W. & R. L. DRYER. 1977. Arch. Biochem. Biophys. **179:** 141–46.
26. KURUP, C. K. R. & D. R. SANADI. 1977. J. Bioenerg. Biomembr. **9:** 1–15.
27. KATRE, N. V. & D. F. WILSON. 1977. Arch. Biochem. Biophys. **184:** 578–85.
28. KATRE, N. V. & D. F. WILSON. 1978. Arch. Biochem. Biophys. **191:** 647–56.
29. HATEFI, Y. 1976. *In* The Enzymes of Biological Membranes, Vol. 4. A. Martonosi, Ed.: 3–41. Plenum Press. New York.
30. HATEFI, Y., W. G. HANSTEIN, Y. GALANTE & D. L. STIGGALL. 1975. Fed. Proc. Fed. Am. Soc. Exp. Biol. (Symposium) **34:** 1699–706.
31. HATEFI, Y. & D. L. STIGGALL. 1976. *In* The Enzymes, Vol. 13. P. D. Boyer Ed.: 175–297. Academic Press. New York.
32. RAGAN, C. I. & P. C. HINKLE. 1975. J. Biol. Chem. **250:** 8472–76.
33. LEUNG, K. H. & P. C. HINKLE. 1975. J. Biol. Chem. **250:** 8467–71.
34. WIKSTRÖM, M. K. F. 1977. Nature **266:** 271–73.
35. SERRANO, R., B. I. KANNER & E. RACKER. 1976. J. Biol. Chem. **251:** 2453–61.
36. RYRIE, I. J. 1977. Arch. Biochem. Biophys. **184:** 464–75.
37. KAGAWA, Y., N. SONE, M. YOSHIDA, H. HIRATA & H. OKAMOTO 1976. J. Biochem. (Tokyo) **80:** 141–51.
38. STIGGALL, D. L., Y. M. GALANTE & Y. HATEFI. 1978. J. Biol. Chem. **253:** 956–64.
39. GALANTE, Y. M., S.-Y. WONG & Y. HATEFI. 1979. J. Biol. Chem. **254:** 12372–78.
40. CANTLEY, L. C. & G. G. HAMMES. 1973. Biochemistry **12:** 4900–4.
41. FRIGERI, L., Y. M. GALANTE, W. G. HANSTEIN & Y. HATEFI. 1977. J. Biol. Chem. **252:** 3147–52.
42. FRIGERI, L., Y. M. GALANTE & Y. HATEFI. 1978. J. Biol. Chem. **253:** 8935–40.

THE USE OF PHOTOAFFINITY LABELS IN THE STUDY OF MITOCHONDRIAL FUNCTION*

Maria Erecińska

Departments of Pharmacology and Biochemistry and Biophysics
University of Pennsylvania Medical School
Philadelphia, Pennsylvania 19104

INTRODUCTION

The mitochondrial respiratory chain can be considered as a large multienzyme complex that transfers reducing equivalents from substrates to molecular oxygen with the formation of water and concomitant synthesis of ATP. Most of the building blocks of the respiratory chain, such as flavoproteins, iron-sulfur proteins, and hemeproteins, are tightly bound to, and constitute an integral part of, the inner mitochondrial membrane.[1] A unique position in the respiratory chain is occupied by cytochrome c, a small hemeprotein loosely bound to the outer surface of the inner mitochondrial membrane, which shuttles electrons between cytochrome c reductase and cytochrome c oxidase.[2] In addition to providing an electron transfer pathway between these two large complexes, cytochrome c links one respiratory chain to another in what has been termed an "interchain electron transfer."[3] Molecular mechanisms of cytochrome c–mediated electron transfer reactions have been investigated with a number of different techniques.[2] Recently, a new tool, photoaffinity labeling, has become available for exploring molecular interactions in biological systems. This paper describes the application of this technique to the study of mitochondrial electron transfer and, specifically, to one region of the respiratory chain, that at the level of cytochrome c.

Two important questions were considered:

1. Are association and dissociation of cytochrome c essential to its function?
2. What is the nature of the site to which cytochrome c binds in the inner mitochondrial membrane?

THE EXPERIMENTAL APPROACH

The most useful virtue of cytochrome c lies in the fact that this hemeprotein can easily be extracted from the mitochondria and, subsequently, reincorporated with full restoration of enzymatic activity. This has two important implications. First, cytochrome c can be modified and the electron transfer properties of the modified derivatives can be explored after their reincorporation into cytochrome c–depleted mitochondria. Second, the cytochrome c–depleted membranes contain the "natural," unmodified binding site for cytochrome c. Therefore, one may expect that, if the

*This research was supported by a grant from the United States Public Health Service, no. GM12202.
The author is an established Investigator of the American Heart Association.

0077–8923/80/0346–0444 $1.75/1 © 1980, NYAS

modified derivative binds and is active, it would occupy the same "site" in the respiratory chain as does native cytochrome c in intact mitochondria. Consequently, we have always used cytochrome c–depleted mitochondria as the starting material. Initially, we tested the electron transfer activity and binding parameters of the various photoaffinity labeled derivatives of cytochrome c in the dark. In the next step, we added the labeled derivatives to the cytochrome c–depleted mitochondria, irradiated the samples, and investigated their electron transfer properties. In the final step, we fractionated the irradiated membranes into the various mitochondrial complexes with detergents and salts and explored the location of cytochrome c on the mitochondrial membrane and its relation to the other members of the respiratory chain.

The results of these efforts are summarized below. We have limited the initial presentation to results obtained with three photoaffinity labeled derivatives that we explored. Then, in the final section, we shall include a discussion of the data obtained by other authors.

RESULTS

Characteristics of the Photoaffinity Labels

The photoaffinity labels used to study cytochrome c–mediated electron transfer are shown in FIGURE 1. All the labels react somewhat randomly with the free amino groups of lysine residues located on the surface of the cytochrome c molecule. (For the details of the preparation of the various derivatives, the reader is referred to the original references.[4-8]) However, only the first two, 2,4-dinitro-5-fluorophenylazide (DNAP), which we used,[4,5] and 4-fluoro-3-nitrophenylazide (FNPA), which was introduced by Bisson et al.,[7,8] modify the net charge on cytochrome c. The other two, p-azidophenacylbromide (p-APB),[9] which is linked through 4-mercaptobutyrimidate (4-MBI), and methyl-4-azidobenzoimidate (M-ABI),[10] contain imino groups and maintain the same overall positive charge on cytochrome c. This is shown in TABLE 1, where the relative K_D values are presented, along with the capabilities of the various photoaffinity labeled derivatives to restore the succinate oxidase activity in cytochrome c–depleted mitochondria. It can be seen that all the derivatives are capable of restoring the oxygen uptake. However, the restoration of full activity requires higher concentrations of 2,4-DNAP–cytochrome c and FNPA–cytochrome c, which follows from their increased K_D values. p-APB ($+$MBI)–cytochrome c restores the succinate oxidase activity to about 75%, whereas the behavior of methyl-4-azidobenzoimidate–cytochrome c is almost indistinguishable from that of the native cytochrome c.

Activity of the Covalently Linked Cytochrome C

The next step in our investigation was to establish whether or not cytochrome c that is linked covalently to a site on the mitochondrial membrane is active in electron transport. To test this possibility, cytochrome c–depleted mitochondria isolated from either rat liver or pigeon breast were irradiated in the presence of a slight excess of cytochrome c over cytochrome c oxidase (this depended on the type of the label used: those with unmodified K_D values were used at a ratio of 1–3 cytochromes c per cytochrome a; those with modified K_D values were used at a ratio of 5–8 cytochromes c

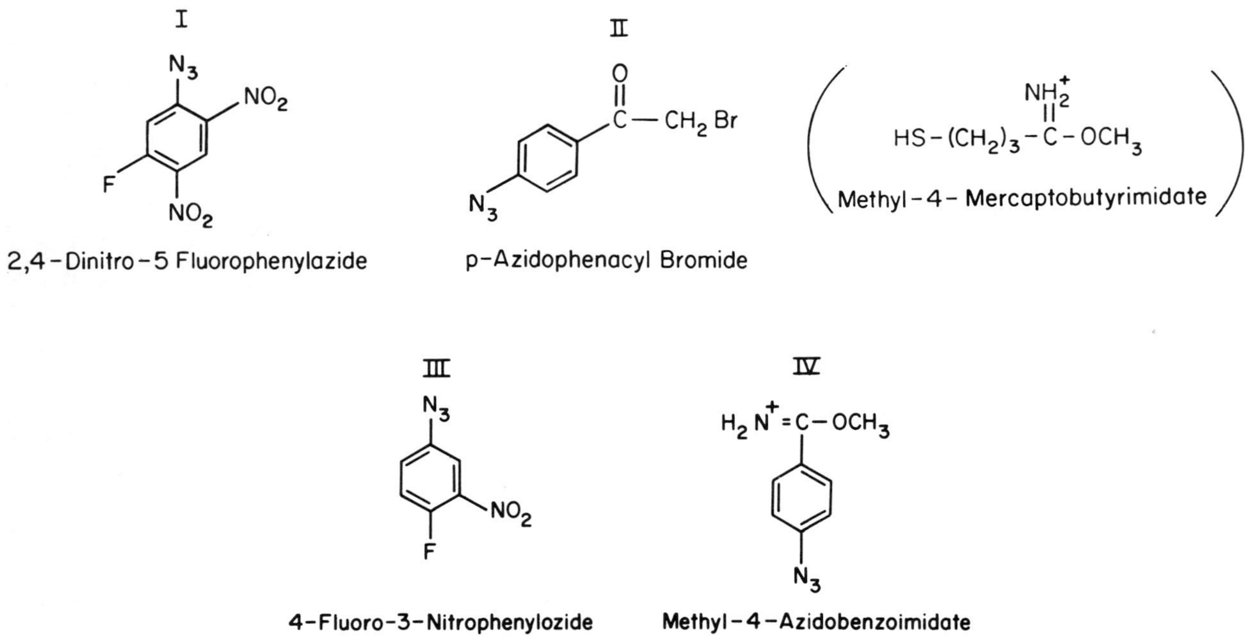

FIGURE 1. Photaffinity labels used to synthesize photoactive derivatives of cytochrome *c*.

per cytochrome a) at a protein concentration that gave the best incorporation of the label in the least time. The irradiated membrane fractions were washed with high concentrations of salts and tested for electron transfer activity.

The different derivatives of cytochrome c covalently linked to the mitochondrial membrane exhibited varying electron transfer activities: 2,4-DNAP had about 15–20% of the succinate oxidase activity and about 40% of the cytochrome oxidase activity measured with ascorbate + TPMD as the substrate, p-APB (+ MBI) had little activity with succinate but about 30–40% of the cytochrome oxidase activity (ascorbate + TPMP was the substrate), and methyl-4-azidobenzoimidate was capable of restoring as much as 50–60% of the succinate oxidase activity. In each case, the addition of native cytochrome c further stimulated the rate of oxygen uptake and was used to establish the maximal rates of respiration. In addition, two types of experiments were carried out in order to establish proper control values. In the first group, the depleted mitochondria were irradiated in the presence of native cytochrome

TABLE 1

K_D VALUES AND ACTIVITIES OF PHOTOAFFINITY LABELED
DERIVATIVES OF CYTOCHROME C

Derivative	K_D Value (Arbitrary Units)	Ability to Restore Respiration (%)	No. of Residues Modified
Native	1	100	0
2,4-Dinitro-5 fluoro phenylazide-cyt c	5–6	100	1–2
4-Fluoro-3-nitro-phenylazide-cyt c	3–4	100	1
(Methyl-4 mercaptobuty-rimidate)-p-azido-phenacylbromide-cyt c	1–2	75	2–3
Methyl-4 azido-benzoimidate-cyt c	1–2	100	3–4

c and then treated as were those irradiated with the photoactive derivatives. In the second, the mitochondria were incubated with the labeled cytochrome c in the dark, washed with salts, and tested for the presence of cytochrome c and electron transfer activity.

In order to confirm these steady-state measurements, we used, in collaboration with Dr. Alan Waring, a low temperature kinetic technique in which oxidation of the various respiratory chain carriers by oxygen was initiated by photolysis of the carbon monoxide–cytochrome oxidase complex.[11] The rates of electron transfer were substantially slowed down at subzero temperatures and could be followed conveniently. FIGURE 2 shows the spectra of control rat liver mitochondria (i.e., intact with native cytochrome c), of mitochondria with covalently linked p-APB (+ MBI)–cytochrome c, and of mitochondria with covalently linked ABI–cytochrome c obtained at -39 °C at various times after the light flash. The baseline in these experiments was the fully reduced spectrum in the presence of carbon monoxide. It can be seen that the

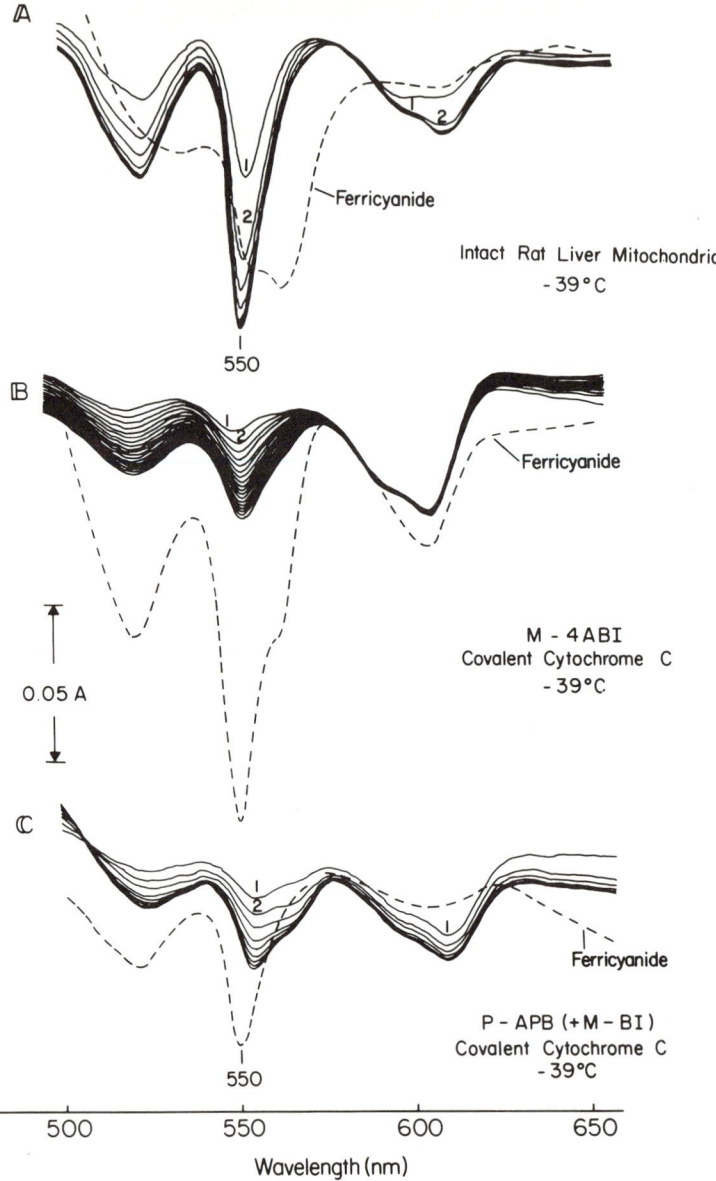

A

Ferricyanide

Intact Rat Liver Mitochondria
- 39 °C

550

B

Ferricyanide

M - 4ABI
Covalent Cytochrome C
- 39 °C

0.05 A

C

Ferricyanide

P - APB (+ M - BI)
Covalent Cytochrome C
- 39 °C

550

500   550   600   650

Wavelength (nm)

FIGURE 2. Absorption spectra of intact rat liver mitochondria and mitochondria with covalently-linked derivatives of cytochrome *c*, which were obtained in a dual wavelength scanning spectrophotometer at −39 °C. The samples were prepared by diluting the mitochondria to a final concentration of 25–30 mg of protein/ml in a medium containing 20% ethylene glycol by volume, the remainder being 0.25 *M* sucrose–0.01 *M* morpholinopropane sulfonate buffer, pH 7.4 at 23 °C. The mitochondria were supplemented with 10 m*M* succinate, allowed to become anaerobic, and saturated with carbon monoxide. The suspension was transferred to a 3.5 mm diameter quartz tube, chilled to −20 °C, and stirred vigorously for a few seconds. At the end of the oxygenation period, the sample was rapidly chilled to about −80 °C. The frozen sample was transferred to the Dewar flask of the spectrophotometer, through which thermoregulated nitrogen was flowing. The reference spectrum is that of the reduced sample with carbon monoxide. The oxidation of the respiratory chain is initiated by the flash-photolysis of CO. (In collaboration with Alan Waring.)

covalently linked derivatives of cytochrome c can be oxidized even at these low temperatures. The main difference between the behaviors of an intact system and of mitochondria with the two photoaffinity labeled derivatives is the extent of oxidation of cytochromes b. Whereas oxidation of cytochrome c precedes that of cytochromes b in intact mitochondria, oxidation of cytochrome b appears to parallel that of cytochrome c in mitochondria with covalently linked derivatives. A detailed kinetic analysis of these experiments is beyond the scope of this article and will be presented in detail elsewhere (Waring and Erecińska, in preparation).

Location of Cytochrome C in Mitochondria

After irradiation, the photoaffinity labeled cytochrome c should remain bound to the neighboring molecules even after the mitochondria are separated into various fractions by treatment with detergents and salts. Therefore, identification of the neighboring components in the cytochrome c binding site can be approached by analyzing the products of the fractionation procedures. Two techniques were used in our studies. The first employed Triton X-100 and KCl[12] and provided a clear separation of cytochrome oxidase ("membranous" pellet) from the cytochrome bc_1 complex (soluble fraction). This procedure is more convenient for the analysis of the oxidase fraction. The second used Triton X-100 plus deoxycholate and ammonium sulfate[13] and yields a cytochrome bc_1 fraction that is free of cytochrome oxidase but contains some succinate dehydrogenase. This procedure is more convenient for the analysis of the cytochrome bc_1 complex.

The results of the fractionation of cytochrome c–depleted pigeon breast mitochondria irradiated in the presence of DNAP–cytochrome c, taken from our earlier works, are presented in FIGURES 3 and 4. The traces in FIGURE 3 show:

A. The very first precipitated mitochondrial pellet after the initial detergent wash. It contains the entire mitochondrial respiratory chain with covalently linked cytochrome c.

B. The "wash" fraction. It contains cytochrome c that was solubilized either with lipids or with proteins containing no heme b or a.

C. The soluble fraction after the first treatment with Triton X-100. It contains mainly cytochrome bc_1 complex and cytochrome c.

D. The fraction solubilized from the cytochrome oxidase pellet by treatment with a higher concentration of Triton X-100. It contains cytochrome c oxidase and cytochrome c.

Since fractions C and D both contained cytochrome c, they were then applied onto an agarose Bio-Gel A-5m column and eluted with a medium containing high concentrations of salts and detergents. It can be seen (FIGURE 4) that, when the fraction containing the cytochrome bc_1 complex (and cytochrome c) was applied to the column, the bc_1 complex was eluted first, followed by cytochrome c. In contrast, cytochrome c oxidase was eluted as the oxidase–cytochrome c complex in which the ratio of the oxidase to cytochrome c was, within experimental error, unity. The overall yield of the cytochrome oxidase–cytochrome c complex was only a few percent.

Mitochondria irradiated with p-APB ($+$ MBI) gave essentially the same labeling

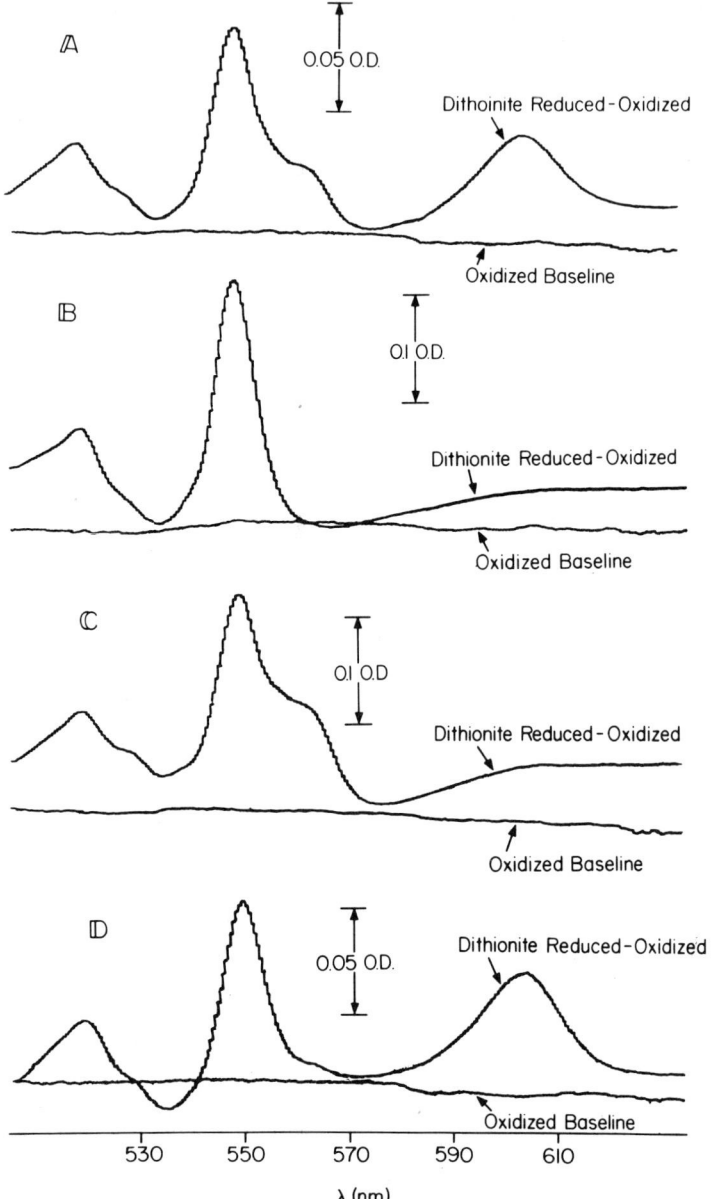

FIGURE 3. Absorption spectra of various mitochondrial fractions obtained by detergent fractionation of pigeon breast mitochondria irradiated in the presence of DNAP-cytochrome *c*. The individual fractions (see the text) were diluted to appropriate concentrations in 0.1 *M* phosphate buffer, pH 7.3, containing 1% Triton X-100. (From Erecińska *et al.*[5] by permission of Academic Press.)

pattern,[6] except that the yield of the complex was higher—as much as 50–60% of cytochrome *c* was found to be incorporated into the complex with cytochrome *c* oxidase. Upon resolution of this cytochrome *c*–containing fraction by chromatography on Bio-Gel A-5m, two complexes were obtained, one of which contained two moles of cytochrome *c* per mole of cytochrome *a* and the second of which contained one mole of cytochrome *c* per mole of cytochrome *a*.

The cytochrome *c*–cytochrome oxidase complex was further analyzed on poly-acrylamide gel electrophoresis in the presence of sodium dodecylsulfate (SDS). Our preliminary results showed that cytochrome *c* binds to one of the smaller subunits of

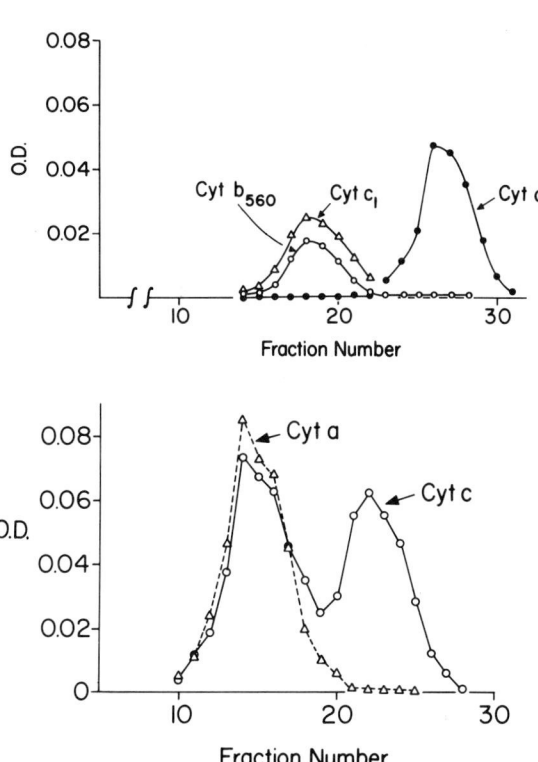

FIGURE 4. Elution patterns of cytochrome bc_1–cytochrome *c* (upper panel) and cytochrome *c* oxidase–cytochrome *c* (lower panel) fractions from the agarose column. An agarose Bio-Gel A-5m column (40 × 2.5 cm) was pre-equilibrated with 0.2 *M* sucrose, 0.1 *M* KCl, and 0.02 *M* phosphate buffer (pH 7.4) containing 1% Triton X-100. The elution was carried out with the same buffer. Two-milliliter fractions were collected and the absorption spectra were recorded using a dual wavelength spectrophotometer. (From Erecińska *et al.*[5] by permission of Academic Press.)

cytochrome *c* oxidase.[6] Recently, we have synthesized a radioactive *p*-APB (+ MBI)–cytochrome *c*, incorporated it into the mitochondria, irradiated it, and fractionated the irradiated membranes with Triton X-100 and KCl. The cytochrome *c* oxidase–cytochrome *c* complex was then subjected to an analysis on a polyacrylamide gel column in the presence of SDS. The same gels were first scanned and then sliced and analyzed for their content of radioactive cytochrome *c*. The preliminary results of these experiments are summarized in FIGURE 5. The upper panel shows the densitometer tracing of the gel containing cytochrome oxidase (control). The lower panel shows the tracing of the cytochrome oxidase–cytochrome *c* complex isolated

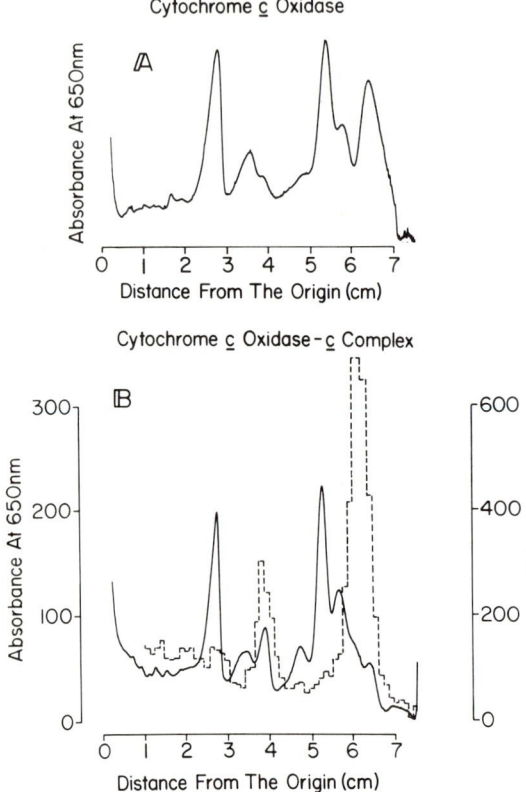

FIGURE 5. Electrophoretic analyses on polyacrylamide SDS-gels of cytochrome oxidase (upper panel) and cytochrome oxidase–cytochrome c complex (lower panel). The cytochrome c–cytrochrome oxidase complex was purified by the Triton X-100 and KCl procedure[12] from pigeon breast mitochondria irradiated with radioactive p-APB (+MBI)–cytochrome c. The same method[12] was used to isolate cytochrome oxidase. The samples were digested with 4% SDS in the presence of mercaptoethanol and loaded on 9% acrylamide gels with an acrylamide:bisacrylamide ratio of 30:1.62. The procedure for the gel electrophoresis was that described by Weber and Osborn.[42] The gels were stained with Coomassie Blue G and scanned at 650 nm (solid lines). The same gels were then sliced in 1 mm slices and the radioactivity in each slice was measured (dotted line).

from irradiated membranes with the radioactivity pattern superimposed on it. It can be seen that a band with a molecular weight of 14,000–15,000, which is clearly visible in cytochrome oxidase, almost disappears in the densitometer trace of the cytochrome oxidase–cytochrome c complex. A new radioactive band appears with a mw of about 28,000, which corresponds to a complex between cytochrome c and one of the smaller subunits of cytochrome oxidase. (A peak of radioactivity corresponding to a band with a mw of about 14,000 is that of cytochrome c that is covalently linked to the lipids of the oxidase.) We have, therefore, concluded, on the basis of these results, that one of the binding sites for cytochrome c on the mitochondrial membrane is cytochrome oxidase itself.

The most puzzling feature of the aforementioned experiments was that, when using either DNAP–cytochrome c or p-ABI (+MBI)–cytochrome c, there was no covalent incorporation of the labeled derivative into the cytochrome bc_1 complex. Very recently, we have synthesized a new photoaffinity labeled derivative of cytochrome c, methyl-4-azido-benzoimidate–cytochrome c, which, after irradiation with the mitochondrial membranes, was capable of high succinate oxidase activity. The irradiated mitochondria were fractionated with salts and detergents; the relevant fractions are shown in FIGURE 6. Spectrum A is that of the oxidase pellet obtained after fractionation with Triton X-100 and KCl. A comparison of this spectrum with spectrum D of FIGURE 3 shows that there is very little cytochrome c in the cytochrome oxidase fraction when methyl-4-azidobenzoimidate is used as the label. (In some experiments, there was even less cytochrome c found in the covalent complex with the oxidase than is shown in spectrum A.) Spectrum B is that of the cytochrome bc_1 complex, a fraction precipitated between 33%–45% saturation with ammonium sulfate in the presence of Triton X-100 and deoxycholate. The spectrum is characteristic of a cytochrome bc_1–cytochrome c complex with an absorption maximum at 550 nm (cytochrome c) and a shoulder at 562 nm (cytochromes b). Cytochrome c remained attached to the cytochrome bc_1 complex during repeated fractionations in the presence of salts and detergents and during chromatography on the agarose Bio-Gel A-5m column. The presence of a small amount of cytochrome c oxidase (absorbance around 605 nm), seen in some spectra of the cytochrome bc_1–cytochrome c complex even after chromatography on the agarose column, may indicate that a bridged complex containing the two large mitochondrial fragments and cytochrome c is formed, albeit in a very low yield.

The most interesting feature of this covalent cytochrome bc_1–cytochrome c complex is its electron transfer activity. Upon the addition of succinate to a suspension of this cytochrome bc_1–cytochrome c complex in the presence of KCN (to inhibit any oxidation of cytochrome c via the minute amount of cytochrome c oxidase present), a prominent absorption peak characteristic of the reduced cytochrome c appeared in the spectrum immediately after mixing. Since cytochrome bc_1 complex prepared by the Triton-deoxycholate procedure contains some succinic dehydrogenase, this immediate reduction of cytochrome c indicates that electrons were able to reach the covalently linked cytochrome c rapidly through the "natural" pathway.

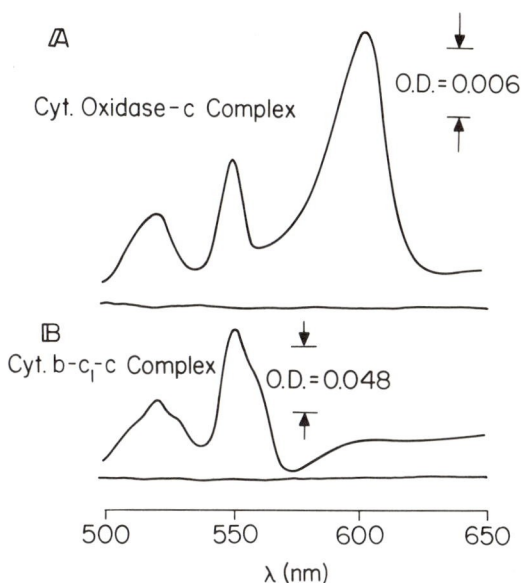

FIGURE 6. Absorption spectra (reduced-oxidized) of the oxidase (A) and cytochrome bc_1 (B) fractions obtained after fractionation of pigeon breast mitochondria irradiated with ABI-cytochrome c.

Spectrum A is that of the oxidase pellet obtained after fractionation with Triton X-100 and KCl. Spectrum B is that of the cytochrome bc_1 fraction precipitated with ammonium sulfate in the presence of Triton X-100 and deoxycholate. The samples were suspended in 0.1 M phosphate buffer (pH 7.3) containing 1% Triton X-100 and oxidized-oxidized difference spectra (flat lines) were recorded in each case. The samples were reduced by the addition of dithionite and reduced-oxidized difference spectra were obtained in a dual wavelength scanning spectrophotometer.

DISCUSSION

Cytochrome c occupies a unique position in the respiratory chain because it links phosphorylation sites 2 and 3 and provides a means for interchain communication between different respiratory chain assemblies.[2,3,14] The immediate donor of electrons to cytochrome c is, most likely, cytochrome c_1,[15] although direct electron transfer from the Rieske iron-sulfur protein cannot be excluded on either kinetic or thermodynamic grounds. The electron acceptor for cytochrome c has been commonly considered to be cytochrome a, based on the kinetic measurements,[16-18] although direct interaction with the visible copper is also possible. In respiring mitochondria,[19] and in mitochondria *in situ,*[20] the oxidation-reduction potentials (E_h) for cytochromes c_1, c, and a; Rieske's iron-sulfur protein; and the visible copper are so close to one another that these electron carriers form an isopotential group. The rates of electron transfer are very fast and give apparent first order rate constants of up to 1000 sec^{-1}.[21] This poses the question of how the respiratory chain is organized on the membrane in order to attain such high electron transfer velocities. Any speculation on this point must involve both the distance and the orientation between the partners that participate in the redox reactions.

Studies on oriented multilayers of cytochrome c oxidase, cytochrome bc_1 complex, and mitochondrial membrane during the past two years showed that the planes of the hemes of cytochrome c oxidase and of the cytochrome bc_1 complex were oriented with their normals approximately perpendicular to the normal of the membrane.[22-25] In contrast, the plane of the cytochrome c heme was found to be oriented at a different angle.[23,24] Measurements of the distances between the fluorescent derivatives of cytochrome c and the hemes of cytochrome c oxidase using a Förster-type energy transfer technique gave rather large values (20 Å or more) for the relevant distances.[26,27] No comparable information is yet available on the distance between cytochrome c and the hemes of the cytochrome bc_1 complex.

It has long been known that most mitochondria contain two cytochrome c molecules per cytochrome a (i.e., per cytochrome oxidase), which are bound to high affinity binding sites.[28-30] However, full restoration of succinate oxidase activity requires only one cytochrome c molecule per cytochrome oxidase.[3,28] The second molecule of cytochrome c may be involved in some way in the interchain electron transfer.[3,14] In order to gain more insight into cytochrome c–catalyzed electron transfer reactions, careful studies have recently been undertaken in a number of laboratories to characterize the binding domains for the cytochrome c oxidase and reductase on the surface of the cytochrome c molecule. Margoliash and coworkers prepared a number of derivatives of cytochrome c in which single lysine residues located in different places on the surface of cytochrome c have been modified chemically.[31-36] The electron transfer activities of these derivatives in their reactions with cytochrome c oxidase and cytochrome c reductase were then analyzed. A modification of this approach entails methylation of a preformed cytochrome c–cytochrome oxidase (or cytochrome reductase) complex and analysis of the methylated lysine residues of cytochrome c.[37,38] The rationale behind the latter approach is that those lysines on the surface of cytochrome c which are in contact with cytochrome oxidase should be protected somewhat against methylation. Both studies have yielded consistent results in that they indicate that the binding site for cytochrome bc_1 complex on the surface of cytochrome c overlaps considerably with that for cytochrome oxidase. These results were interpreted to mean that cytochrome c is quite mobile in the inner mitochondrial membrane and that it transfers electrons from cytochrome c_1 to cytochrome oxidase either by rational or by translational diffusion.

In contrast, our own results with the photoaffinity labeled derivatives of cytochrome c demonstrate that that cytochrome c whose mobility has been restricted by a covalent linkage to its binding site retains the capability to transfer electrons between cytochrome c reductase and cytochrome oxidase. This is consistent with the report of Utsumi and Packer that electron transfer is still active in rat liver mitochondria that have been fixed with glutaraldehyde[39] and with the recent studies of Rosen et al. on cytochrome c cross-linked to reactions center-isolated from Rhodopseudomonas sphaeroides R-26.[40] The latter authors observed fast oxidation of the cross-linked cytochrome c even for the conditions (e.g., high ionic strength) under which the un-cross-linked species showed slow kinetics. Similar high rates of cytochrome c oxidation, independent of the ionic strength, were seen in the detergent-solubilized, ammonium sulfate–precipitated fraction of the membrane fragments from a bacterium, Paracoccus denitrificans, in which cytochrome c seems to be tightly bound.[41] Moreover, studies with the photoaffinity labeled cytochromes c discussed here show that the individual derivatives do not bind randomly to either the oxidase or the reductase, but that some bind only to cytochrome c oxidase and some only to cytochrome c reductase. This is difficult to reconcile with the notions that cytochrome c has the same binding site for both its oxidase and its reductase and that it undergoes major translational motion between the two complexes during electron transfer.

The second important objection to a large, or nonrestricted, mobility of cytochrome c is that the rate of overall electron transfer in mitochondria (and in reaction centers and bacteria) is much higher than the rate of complete dissociation of cytochrome c from its oxidase. How can these apparently conflicting results be reconciled? At least two suggestions can be put forward to explain the discrepancies. The first is that the results obtained from isolated enzyme complexes cannot be extrapolated directly to the situations that exist in intact mitochondria. This seems, however, unlikely, since there is no reason to suspect that electron transfer in the two systems occurs by different mechanisms. The second possibility is that cytochrome c, in intact mitochondria, undergoes only a limited rotational motion between its electron donor and acceptor and is not completely dissociated from its binding site. This would require that cytochrome c reductase and cytochrome c oxidase form a single, continuous binding site for cytochrome c in the mitochondrial membrane. Perhaps the bridged cytochrome bc_1–cytochrome c–cytochrome oxidase complex reflects the existence of such a site.

In addition to its usefulness in evaluating the mobility of cytochrome c in the mitochondrial membrane, photoaffinity labeling has provided us with a unique approach to the analysis of the cytochrome c binding site(s) on the mitochondrial membrane. Thus far, the experiments have yielded the following results: one of the cytochrome c binding sites is on cytochrome c oxidase; the second one appears to be on the cytochrome bc_1 complex. With respect to the first, our studies[4-6] and those of Bisson et al.[7,8] are in agreement, in that they show the formation of a covalent cytochrome c–cytochrome oxidase complex. Our disagreements concern the polypeptide of the oxidase to which the cytochrome c binds. Whereas our own studies indicate that cytochrome c forms a covalent complex with one of the smaller subunits of the oxidase, the results of Bisson *et al.* show that subunit II (mw 22,000) is the site of interaction.[38] It should be pointed out that the complex isolated by Bisson *et al.*, which is formed by irradiation of a detergent-solubilized preparation of cytochrome oxidase with FNAP–cytochrome c, is unable to catalyze electron transfer from ascorbate to molecular oxygen.[7,8] This contrasts with the active complexes we have investigated and described in some detail in this and previous publications.[5,6] This discrepancy may reflect a difference in the topology of cytochrome oxidase between that present in intact mitochondria and that in a solubilized preparation—the formation of the inactive complex might occur at a site that was generated during isolation; the complex would not have to be the same as the "native" (active) site onto which cytochrome c binds in the cytochrome c–depleted mitochondria.

Our recent results on the formation of an active complex between cytochrome c reductase and cytochrome c, only briefly discussed here, open yet another avenue of investigation of interactions of cytochrome c with its neighbors. Future studies should enable us to show how and where cytochrome c binds in such a complex and what its kinetic properties are. But, even at the present stage of our investigations, we can conclude without hesitation that photoaffinity labeling has proven very successful in investigating mitochondrial electron transfer.

ACKNOWLEDGMENTS

I would like to express my sincere thanks to Dr. David F. Wilson, who greatly contributed to the development of ideas discussed here. My thanks are also due Mrs. Jacqueline S. Davis for her expert technical assistance.

REFERENCES

1. WAINIO, W. E. 1970. The Mammalian Mitochondrial Respiratory Chain. Academic Press. New York.
2. FERGUSON-MILLER, S., D. L. BRAUTIGAN & E. MARGOLIASH. 1979. The Electron Transfer Function of Cytochrome C. *In* The Porphyrins, Vol. 7, Part B. D. Dolphins, Ed.: 149–240. Academic Press. New York.
3. WOHLRAB, H. 1970. Biochemistry **9:** 474–79.
4. WILSON, D. F., Y. MIYATA, M. ERECIŃSKA & J. M. VANDERKOOI. 1975. Arch. Biochem. Biophys. **171:** 104–7.
5. ERECIŃSKA, M., J. M. VANDERKOOI & D. F. WILSON. 1975. Arch. Biochem. Biophys. **171:** 108–116.
6. ERECIŃSKA, M. 1977. Biochem. Biophys. Res. Commun. **76:** 495–501.
7. BISSON, R., H. GUTWENIGER, C. MONTECUCCO, R. COLONNA, A. ZANOTTI & A. AZZI. 1977. FEBS Lett. **81:** 147–50.
8. BISSON, R., A. AZZI, H. GUTWENIGER, R. COLONNA, C. MONTECUCCO & A. ZANOTTI. 1978. J. Biol. Chem. **253:** 1874–80.
9. HIXSON, S. H. & S. S. HIXSON. 1975. Biochemistry **14:** 4251–54.
10. JI, T. H. 1977. J. Biol. Chem. **252:** 1566–70.
11. CHANCE, B., N. GRAHAM & V. LEGALLAIS. 1975. Anal. Biochem. **67:** 572–79.
12. SUN, F. F., K. S. PREZBINDOWSKI, F. L. CRANE & E. E. JACOBS. 1968. Biochim. Biophys. Acta **153:** 804–18.

13. ERECIŃSKA, M., R. OSHINO, N. OSHINO & B. CHANCE. 1973. Arch. Biochem. Biophys. **157:** 431–45.
14. CHANCE, B. 1974. Ann. N.Y. Acad. Sci. **227:** 613–26.
15. YU, C. A., L. YU & T. E. KING. 1973. J. Biol. Chem. **248:** 528–33.
16. GIBSON, Q. H., G. PALMER & D. C. WHARTON. 1965. J. Biol. Chem. **240:** 915–20.
17. WILSON, M. T., C. GREENWOOD, M. BRUNORI & E. ANTONINI. 1975. Biochem. J. **147:** 145–153.
18. ANDREASSON, L. E. 1975. Eur. J. Biochem. **53:** 591–97.
19. ERECIŃSKA, M., R. L. VEECH & D. F. WILSON. 1974. Arch. Biochem. Biophys. **160:** 412–21.
20. WILSON, D. F., M. STUBBS, R. L. VEECH, M. ERECIŃSKA & H. A. KREBS. 1974. Biochem. J. **140:** 57–64.
21. NICHOLLS, P. 1976. Biochim. Biophys. Acta **430:** 30–45.
22. ERECIŃSKA, M., D. F. WILSON & J. K. BLASIE. 1978. Biochim. Biophys. Acta **501:** 53–62.
23. ERECIŃSKA, M., D. F. WILSON & J. K. BLASIE. 1978. Biochim. Biophys. Acta **501:** 63–72.
24. ERECIŃSKA, M., J. K. BLASIE & D. F. WILSON. 1977. FEBS Lett. **76:** 235–39.
25. ERECIŃSKA, M. & D. F. WILSON 1979. Arch. Biochem. Biophys. **192:** 80–85.
26. VANDERKOOI, J. M., R. LANDESBERG, W. HAYDEN & C. S. OWEN. 1977. Eur. J. Biochem. **81:** 339–47.
27. DOCKTER, M. E., A. STEINEMANN & G. SCHATZ. 1978. J. Biol. Chem. **253:** 311–17.
28. JACOBS, E. E. & D. R. SANADI. 1960. J. Biol. Chem. **235:** 531–34.
29. ERECIŃSKA, M. 1975. Arch. Biochem. Biophys. **169:** 199–208.
30. FERGUSON-MILLER, S., D. F. BRAUTIGAN & E. MARGOLIASH. 1976. J. Biol. Chem. **251:** 1104–15.
31. FERGUSON-MILLER, S., D. F. BRAUTIGAN & E. MARGOLIASH. 1978. J. Biol. Chem. **253:** 149–59.
32. SPECK, S. H., S. FERGUSON-MILLER, N. OSHEROFF & E. MARGOLIASH. 1979. Proc. Nat. Acad. Sci. USA **76:** 155–59.
33. STAUDENMAYER, N., M. B. SMITH, H. T. SMITH, F. K. SPIES, JR. & F. S. MILLET. 1976. Biochemistry **18:** 3198–05.
34. STAUDENMAYER, N., S. NG., M. B. SMITH & F. S. MILLETT. 1977. Biochemistry **16:** 600–4.
35. SMITH, H. T., N. STAUDENMAYER & F. S. MILLETT. 1977. Biochemistry **16:** 4971–74.
36. AHMED, A. J., H. T. SMITH, M. B. SMITH & F. S. MILLETT. 1978. Biochemistry **17:** 2479–83.
37. PETTIGREW, G. 1978. FEBS Lett. **86:** 14–16.
38. RIEDER, R. & H. R. BOSSHARD. 1978. FEBS Lett. **92:** 223–26.
39. UTSUMI, K. & L. PACKER. 1967. Arch. Biochem. Biophys. **121:** 633–40.
40. ROSEN, D., M. Y. OKAMURA & G. FEHER. 1979. Biophys. J. **25:** 204a.
41. ERECIŃSKA, M., J. S. DAVIS & D. F. WILSON. 1979. Arch. Biochem. Biophys. **197:** 463–69.
42. WEBER, K. & M. OSBORN. 1969. J. Biol. Chem. **244:** 4406–12.

THE USE OF PHOTOCHEMICAL PROBES FOR STUDIES OF STRUCTURE AND FUNCTION OF PURIFIED ACETYLCHOLINE RECEPTOR PREPARATIONS*

Michael A. Raftery, Veit Witzemann, and Steven G. Blanchard

Church Laboratory of Chemical Biology
Division of Chemistry and Chemical Engineering
California Institute of Technology
Pasadena, California 91125

INTRODUCTION

In the studies reported here, we have made use of a variety of photosensitive derivatives for studies of the subunit structure of *Torpedo californica* in its native membrane environment, the detection of cholinergic agonist-induced subunit interactions, the location of the binding site(s) for a cholinergic antagonist, and the identification of a polypeptide that can be labeled with a local anesthetic analog.

AcChR Purified in Membrane Bound Form

Torpedo acetylcholine receptor (AcChR) was first separated into receptor-enriched membrane fractions by sucrose density gradient centrifugation.[1,2] The polypeptide composition of such enriched fractions was initially reported to involve a peptide of M_r 40,000 as well as additional species of M_r 50,000, 60,000, 65,000, and 105,000 (FIGURES 1A and 1B).[2,3] More recently, a further simple purification step has been added to the membrane purification procedure—namely, extraction of nonreceptor polypeptide components by treatment with aqueous base under conditions of low ionic strength,[4,5] as was originally used for selective extraction of red cell membranes.[6] The polypeptide composition of AcChR-enriched membranes following such base extraction is shown in FIGURE 1C. The major species present have M_r of 40, 50, 60, and 65×10^3. Other polypeptide species present in less pure membranes, such as components having M_r of 43 and 90×10^3 daltons, appear to have been either completely or largely eliminated.

PURIFIED SOLUBILIZED AcChR

The polypeptide pattern on sodium dodecylsulfate (SDS) polyacrylamide gel electrophoresis shown in FIGURE 1 is entirely consistent with patterns obtained for

*This research was supported by a grant from the United States Public Health Service, no. NS-10294; by a grant from the Muscular Dystrophy Association of America; and by a grant from the American Heart Association. V. W. received a Fellowship from the Deutscheforschungsgemeinshaft and S. G. B. was the recipient of a National Institutes of Health Predoctoral Fellowship.

0077–8923/0346–0458 $1.75/1 © 1980, NYAS

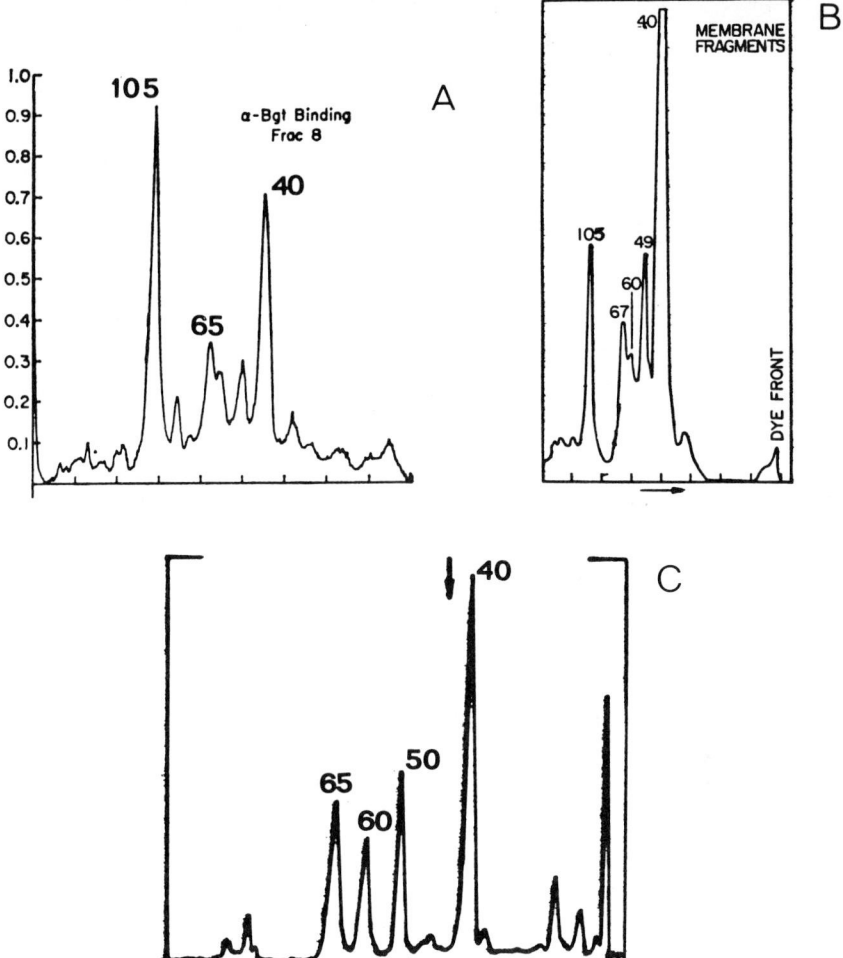

FIGURE 1. Sodium dodecylsulfate polyacrylamide gel electrophoresis of AcChR-enriched membrane fragments. (A) from Duguid and Raftery[2]; (B) from Raftery *et al.*[3]; and (C) from Heubig *et al.*[4] and Elliot *et al.*[5]

Triton X-100 solubilized AcChR purified by affinity chromatographic procedures.[7] Initial analyses reported for *Torpedo* AcChR polypeptides (FIGURE 1A) indicated that species of M_r 42, 35, and 26×10^3 daltons were present.[8] This pattern was shown to result from partial proteolytic degradation during isolation due to Ca^{++}-activated proteases. The first report of the complete polypeptide composition of *Torpedo* AcChR resulted from affinity chromatographic purification of extracts from already highly purified membrane fractions (FIGURE 1B).[3] Several other purification studies have since shown this complex subunit pattern for AcChR preparations from a variety of sources.[9–17]

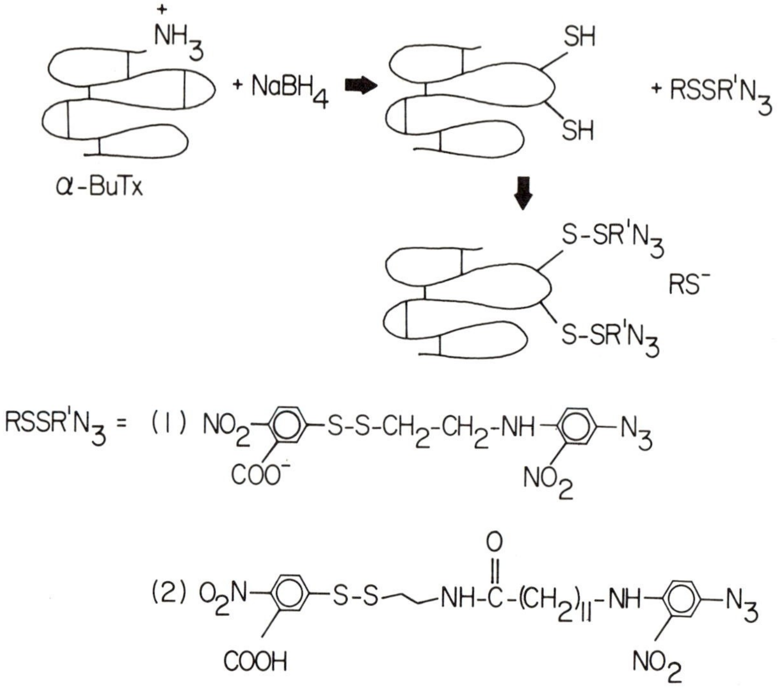

FIGURE 2. A scheme for the selective reduction and formation of photolabile derivatives of $[^{125}I]$ α-bungarotoxin.

SUBUNIT CONTACT

Despite the identical subunit composition of detergent-extracted *Torpedo californica* receptor purified by affinity chromatographic procedures and of the membrane preparations, the questions still remain as to whether or not these polypeptides are in actual physical contact and, naturally, as to whether or not more than one of these is involved in synaptic transmission at the molecular level. We have adopted two main approaches in an attempt to answer these questions.

The first of these is based on the known specificity of α-toxins for the cholinergic receptor and, specifically, for the 40,000 dalton polypeptide.[18–20] We have made use of the selective reduction of one of the five disulfide bonds in α-bungarotoxin (α-BuTx)[21] to introduce covalently, via mixed disulfide bond formation, side chains of varying lengths containing photolabile groups that have the potential of cross-linking the modified α-toxin to neighboring polypeptides upon photoactivation. These reagents were prepared as shown in FIGURE 2, using $[^{125}I]$ α-BuTx. Since one thionitrobenzoate ion is released upon modification of one SH residue, the number of cross-linking reagents covalently attached to the reduced $[^{125}I]$ α-BuTx disulfide bonds could be directly obtained. On the average, about 2 to 3 potential cross-linking groups were covalently introduced into the toxin and, therefore, slightly more than one disulfide bridge per toxin molecule was reduced. The binding properties of the modified toxins were only minimally affected by virtue of the modification and it seemed most likely that the major effect was a decreased lifetime of the receptor-modified toxin complexes.

These derivatives were used to label both 9S and 13S forms[22] of *Torpedo californica* AcChR. The 13S form is the predominant one in the membrane; it is linked by a disulfide bond(s) between two 65,000 dalton polypeptides.[23-26]

Use of Short Cross-Linker

Using AcChR Dimer Preparations

As shown in FIGURE 3B, no significant amounts of radioactivity were associated with any of those components with a defined molecular weight in SDS gel

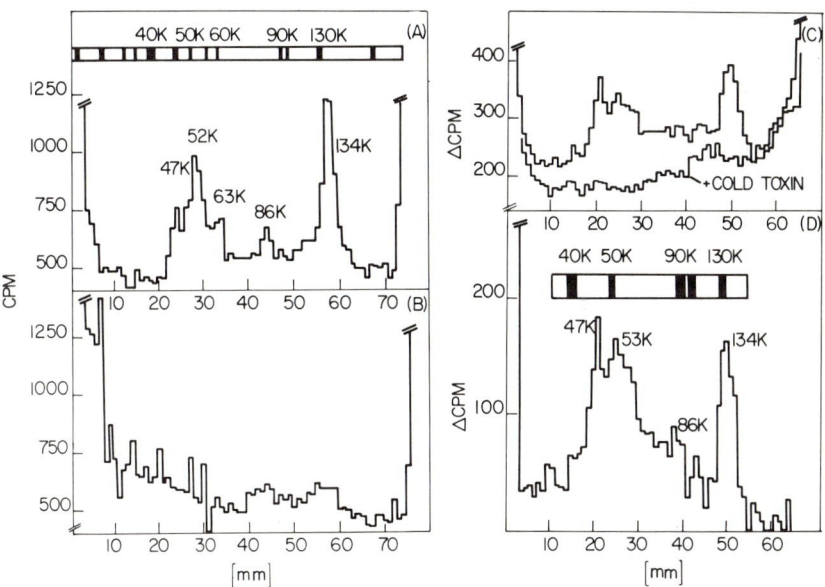

FIGURE 3. (A) SDS gel electrophoresis of AcChR-enriched membrane fragments following cross-linking with [125I] α-BuTx-S-S-R'-N₃. The insert is a schematic of the polypeptide pattern following Coomassie Blue staining. The diagram shows the distribution of [125I] following cross-linking and SDS gel electrophoresis. The apparent molecular weights of cross-linked polypeptides are indicated.
(B) SDS gel electrophoresis of AcChR-enriched membrane fragments that were treated with [125I] α-BuTx-S-S-R'-N₃ but not irradiated prior to electrophoresis.
(C) These membrane fragments were treated with [125I] α-BuTx-S-S-R'-N₃, as in (A), and the distribution of radioactivity upon SDS gel polyacrylamide electrophoresis is shown in the upper graph. The control (lower curve) shows the distribution of radioactivity following gel electrophoresis of membranes that were subjected to the identical cross-linking procedure but that had previously been treated with unlabeled α-BuTx.
(D) This profile shows the difference in radioactivity bound to membrane fragments after cross-linking in the presence and the absence of unlabeled α-BuTx, as analyzed in (C). The insert is a schematic of the polypeptide pattern, indicating the apparent molecular weights following Coomassie Blue staining.

electrophoresis of mixtures of $[^{125}I]$ α-BuTx-S-S-R'-N$_3$ (the short cross-linker) and AcChR in the absence of photolysis. However, when the complex of receptor and modified toxin was irradiated and then subjected to SDS gel electrophoresis, several distinct components were labeled (FIGURES 3A and 3D). These had apparent molecular weights of 47, 52, 63, 86, and 134 × 10^3 daltons. Generation of these labeled components was prevented by pretreatment of the AcChR-enriched membranes with unlabeled α-BuTx before the addition of $[^{125}I]$ α-BuTx-S-S-R'-N$_3$ (FIGURE 3C). It is most likely that the cross-linked component of 47,000 daltons resulted from cross-linking of the modified α-BuTx to the receptor subunit of 40,000 daltons to which it is known to bind.[18-20] Due to the fact that between two and three azido-containing groups were covalently bound to the $[^{125}I]$ α-toxin, several other reaction products could have arisen as a result of (1) two toxin molecules reacting with the same 40,000 dalton polypeptide to yield the component of mw 52,000 daltons; (2) one toxin molecule cross-linking to two 40,000 dalton subunits to yield an ~86,000 dalton component; (3) toxin molecules cross-linking polypeptides other than the 40,000 dalton subunit, such as that of mw 43,000; or (4) cross-linking of polypeptides of differing molecular weight, such as 40,000 and 43,000 dalton components.

In all cases in which labeling was conducted, a major peak of radioactivity was associated with a component of apparent mw 134,000 daltons, indicating that the toxin was probably cross-linked to polypeptides other than the 40,000 dalton component and especially to the dimeric form of the 65,000 dalton polypeptide shown.[23-26]

Using AcChR Monomer Preparations

After conversion of AcChR dimers in the membrane-bound environment to the monomeric form by disulfide bond reduction, followed by alkylation with iodoacetamide (IAcNH$_2$), the labeling experiments using $[^{125}I]$ α-BuTx-S-S-R'-N$_3$ were repeated and analyzed by SDS gel electrophoresis in the absence of reducing agents to prevent cleavage of cross-linked products. The pattern of radioactivity observed in this case is shown in FIGURE 4. The major labeled components of apparent mw 47 and 53 × 10^3 daltons were again observed, with the 47,000 dalton component most likely representing the toxin cross-linked to the 40,000 dalton subunit of the AcChR and the 53,000 dalton subunit perhaps representing two toxin molecules associated with a single 40,000 dalton polypeptide or even labeling of the 50,000 dalton component by a single toxin molecule. The major new features, however, were the almost total lack of a labeled component at 134,000 daltons and the generation of a new cross-linked species of apparent mw 73,000 daltons. Thus, we consider it most likely that this new species represents the 65,000 dalton polypeptide cross-linked to the modified α-BuTx, since the only difference between these experiments and those shown in FIGURE 3 was the conversion of the AcChR to the monomeric form by generation of the 65,000 dalton polypeptide from its dimeric form of 130,000 daltons. The data can, therefore, most readily be interpreted to indicate that the toxin bound to the 40,000 dalton component of the receptor can become cross-linked upon photolysis to the membrane polypeptide of mw 65,000 daltons.

Similar cross-linking experiments were conducted using the modified $[^{125}I]$ α-BuTx derivative, $[^{125}I]$ α-BuTx-S-S-R''-N$_3$, which contains the longer spacers.

Use of Long Cross-Linker

Using AcChR Monomer Preparations

Following the photolysis of those membrane preparations in which the AcChR had been converted to the monomeric 9S form by reduction with dithiothereitol (DTT) and alkylation with IAcNH$_2$, SDS gel electrophoresis profiles demonstrated the unique labeling of a component of apparent mw slightly greater than 65,000 daltons (FIGURE 5A). In this case, only minimal labeling of components with molecular weights smaller than this was observed. Control experiments in which the membrane fragments were first treated with unlabeled α-BuTx prior to addition of [^{125}I] α-BuTx-S-S-R″-N$_3$, followed by photolysis and SDS gel electrophoresis, showed that no cross-linked products were formed. It appeared, therefore, that the longer cross-linking reagent attached to [^{125}I] α-BuTx, that the polypeptide to which the toxin is known to bind, i.e., the 40,000 dalton species, was no longer labeled, and that only a polypeptide that must be within ~33 Å of the 40,000 dalton polypeptide was

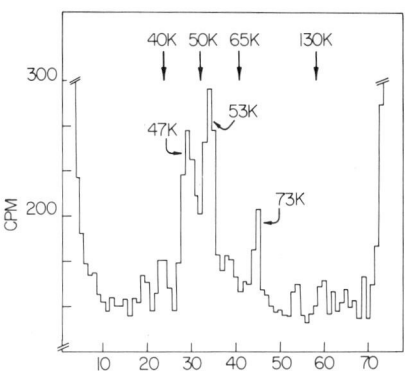

FIGURE 4. SDS polyacrylamide gel electrophoresis without reducing agent of membrane-bound AcChR. Membrane-bound AcChR was treated with DTT and IAcNH$_2$ prior to gel electrophoresis to convert all AcChR to its 9S form. The diagram shows the distribution of cross-linked [^{125}I] α-BuTx-S-S-R′-N$_3$ after SDS gel electrophoresis. The arrows at top indicate the positions of unmodified AcChR polypeptides as shown by Coomassie Blue staining; the lower arrows indicate the apparent molecular weights of radiolabeled products.

uniquely labeled. That this appears to be the AcChR subunit of mw 65,000 dalton is confirmed by the experiments described below.

Using AcChR Dimer Preparations

Highly purified membrane fragments containing AcChR dimers, stabilized by treatment of the membranes with IAcNH$_2$ during homogenization and isolation, were treated with the long cross-linking reagent, [^{125}I] α-BuTx-S-S-R″-N$_3$. Following SDS gel electrophoresis in the absence of a reducing agent, a unique radioactive product of apparent mw 130 × 10^3 daltons was obtained (FIGURE 5C), with little indication of cross-linking of the labeled toxin to any other membrane component. It was especially striking that the component with a molecular weight greater than 65,000 daltons observed with AcChR monomer preparations was essentially absent. This distribution of radioactivity, yielding radiolabeled components of apparent mw 71,000 daltons for AcChR monomer preparations and 130,000 daltons for AcChR dimer preparations,

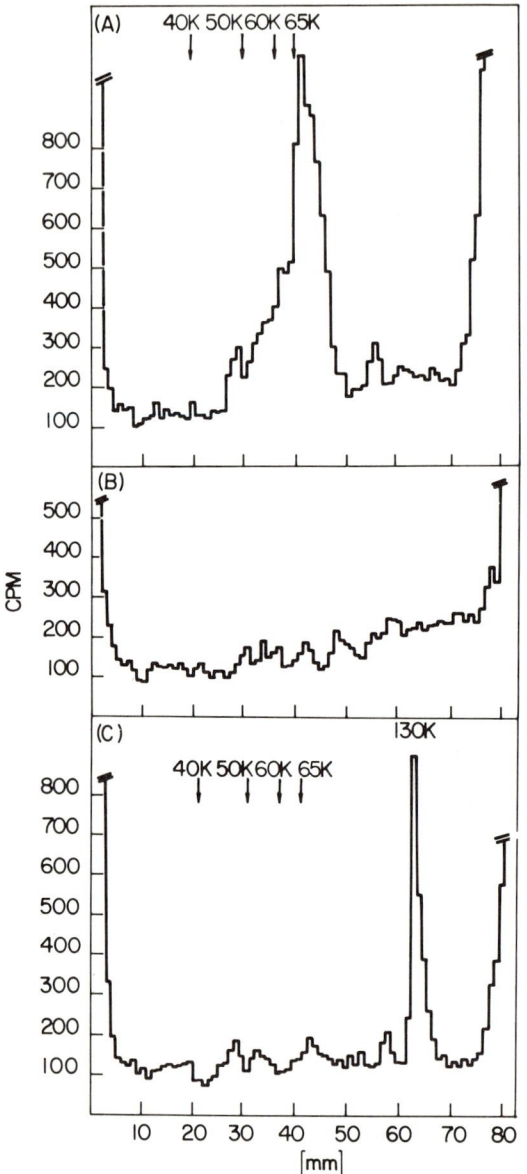

FIGURE 5. SDS gel electrophoresis of products formed upon irradiation of long cross-linker [^{125}I] α-BuTx-S-S-R″-N$_3$ complexes in the presence of AcChR.

(A) The distribution of radioactivity following SDS gel electrophoresis of membrane fragments that were reduced with DTT and alkylated with IAcNH$_2$ during their preparation in order to convert the AcChR to its 9S form, followed by binding of [^{125}I] α-BuTx-S-S-R″-N$_3$ and photolysis prior to electrophoresis.

(B) Same as (A), except that membrane fragments were protected with unmodified α-BuTx prior to the addition of the cross-linking agent and photolysis.

(C) SDS gel electrophoresis of membrane fragments prepared in the presence of IAcNH$_2$ to ensure the stability of the AcChR dimers. The pattern shows the distribution of radioactivity following photolysis in the presence of [^{125}I] α-BuTx-S-S-R″-N$_3$. The arrows in each panel indicate the positions of the AcChR constituent polypeptides corresponding to mw 40, 50, 60, and 65 × 10^3 daltons, respectively.

can best be interpreted as an indication that the toxin derivative was uniquely cross-linked to the AcChR subunit of 65,000 daltons.

In summary, these cross-linking experiments confirm earlier results that showed that the α-toxin binds to the 40,000 dalton polypeptide component of *Torpedo* AcChR.[18–20]

The second interesting result was that the bound α-toxin derivative, [^{125}I] α-BuTx-S-S-R'-N$_3$, was cross-linked to a polypeptide of apparent mw 65,000 daltons when the receptor was in the monomeric 9S form[22] and to a polypeptide of apparent mw 130,000 daltons (FIGURE 3) in the 13.2 S AcChR form.[22] This dimeric form of the receptor appears to be the major naturally occurring form in the membrane-bound environment. The occurrence of a specific disulfide bridge between two 65,000 dalton polypeptides in the dimeric form has been demonstrated in several laboratories.[23-26] The labeling of this polypeptide using [^{125}I] α-BuTx-S-S-R'-N$_3$ was clearly demonstrated (see Figures 3A and 3D). The more dramatic result, however, was obtained with the longer spacer arm attached to [^{125}I] α-BuTx-S-S-R''-N$_3$. In this case, the toxin was no longer cross-linked to the 40,000 dalton polypeptide; the 65,000 dalton polypeptide in the monomeric form of AcChR and its dimer of 130,000 daltons in the dimeric form of AcChR were cross-linked upon photolysis of the bound toxin. Presumably, the longer spacer arm used extended beyond the domain occupied by the 40,000 dalton polypeptide and the photogenerated nitrene reacted in a highly specific manner with the 65,000 dalton polypeptide. Thus, these results, which are based upon a structural approach, strongly imply that a polypeptide of 65,000 daltons is a constituent part of the AcChR in its membrane-bound environment.

SUBUNIT INTERACTIONS

Recently, we have made extensive use of ethidium bromide (ETBr) as a fluorescent probe to monitor cholinergic analogs and other ligands binding specifically to membrane bound AcChR,[27] with emphasis on rapid kinetic events.[28-30] Receptor-bound ethidium undergoes either enhancement or quenching of fluorescence upon ternary complex formation, depending on the nature of the other ligand. In the interest of locating the ethidium binding site, we used [^{3}H] bis-azidoethidium chloride as a photolabile ligand.[20] Using AcChR-enriched membranes, [^{3}H] bis-azidoethidium bromide (ETA) mainly labels the 40,000 dalton polypeptide (FIGURE 6). Upon preincubation of the membranes with carbamylcholine (Carb) to convert the AcChR to a state(s) of high affinity for agonist,[31-33] followed by a similar photolysis, a different pattern was obtained. A striking difference is observed between the two samples when the amounts of radioactivity bound to the individual receptor subunits are compared—an increased incorporation of [^{3}H] ETA of 1.4-, 2.4-, and 5-fold was recorded for the 40,000-, 50,000-, and 65,000-dalton subunits, respectively (FIGURE 6). Qualitatively similar effects on the labeling pattern were observed with another agonist, nicotine, and even antagonists such as d-tubocurarine or bis-(3-aminopyridinium) 1,10-decanediiodide (DAP) (not shown), when the membrane fragments were incubated in the presence of these ligands prior to photolabeling.

H$_{12}$-HTX, a neurotoxin supposedly specific for blocking the cholinergic ionophore, which binds ($K_d = 0.4 \ \mu M$) to AcChR-rich membrane fragments,[34-36] was tested for its ability to interfere with [^{3}H] ETA labeling, since it has been shown to affect AcChR-bound ETBr fluorescence.[37] Solutions of membrane fragments in the low ligand affinity form ($\sim 0.6 \ \mu M$ in toxin binding sites) containing 2 μM [^{3}H] ETA showed no difference between the amount and distribution of [^{3}H] ETA incorporated upon irradiation in the presence and that in the absence of 1 μM H$_{12}$-HTX (FIGURE 7). However, if 1 μM H$_{12}$-HTX was present in addition to 5 μM Carb, the labeling pattern

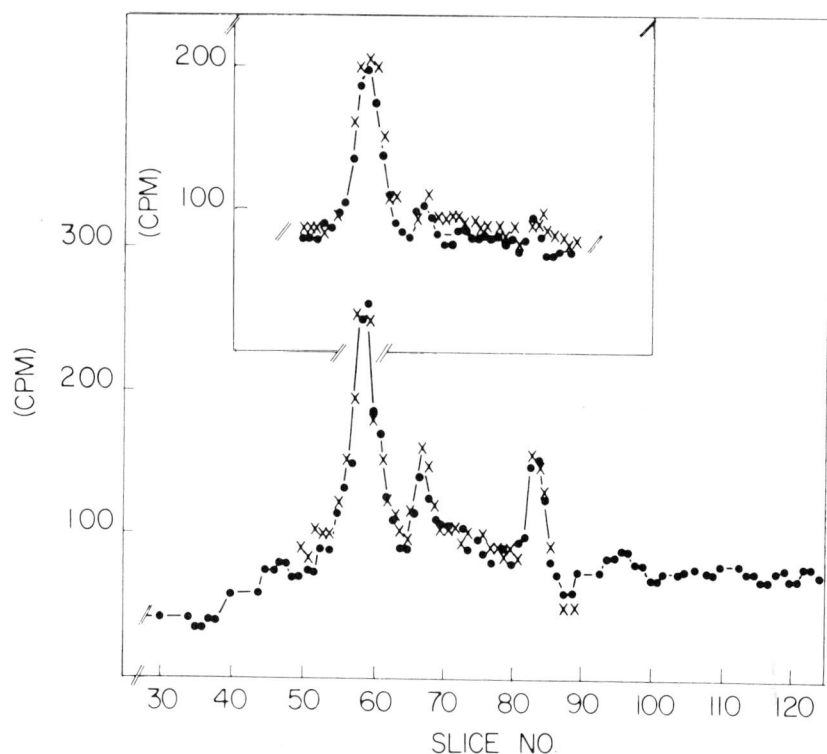

FIGURE 6. The distribution of radioactivity after SDS -polyacrylamide gel electrophoresis of [³H] ETA–labeled membrane-bound AcChR. Upper curve: membrane-bound AcChR (5×10^{-7} M in α-BuTx binding sites) was photolabeled in the presence of [³H] ETA (92×10^{-6} M). Lower curve: membrane-bound AcChR was incubated with 5×10^{-6} M Carb for 10 min to convert the AcChR to the high ligand affinity form prior to irradiation. (Note the increased labeling on the 40,000, 50,000, and 65,000 dalton polypeptides.)

was changed significantly. Radioactivity bound to the 40,000 dalton subunit was decreased to about 30–40% and almost no labeling occurred on the 65,000 dalton subunit, whereas only minor changes were found on the 50,000 dalton subunit.

This result is interpreted as representative of cholinergic ligand-induced conformational changes in the 40,000 molecular weight subunit to which the ligand binds and, in addition, as a demonstration of intersubunit conformational effects involved in structural changes generated at the 40,000 molecular weight subunit and communicated to the subunits of molecular weights 50,000 and 65,000.

Photoaffinity Labeling with a Cholinergic Analog

We have previously shown that the fluorescent cholinergic antagonist, bis-(3-aminopyridinium) 1, 10-decane diiodide, interacts specifically either with purified

AcChR[38] or with AcChR-enriched membranes.[39] It was also determined that this antagonist could form ternary complexes with AcChR-acetylcholine complexes;[39] therefore, it was of interest to locate the binding site for this ligand. A photolabile derivative was prepared—the bis azido derivative, DAPA—and its photodecomposition was studied (FIGURE 8).

Purified AcChR was irradiated in the presence of [³H] bis-(3-azidopyridinium) 1, 10-decane diiodide (DAPA); these photolyzed samples were analyzed by polyacrylamide gel electrophoresis in sodium dodecylsulfate. A polypeptide composition of four major species was observed, as previously found for unmodified receptor, with molecular weights of 40,000, 50,000, 60,000, and 65,000 (FIGURE 9). Only two of these polypeptides, the 40,000 and 60,000 dalton species, were labeled in any great degree (FIGURE 9). The specificity of this labeling was determined by irradiating the receptor and [³H] DAPA in the presence of either α-BuTx or DAP. In both cases, incorporation of radioactivity was dramatically decreased in the 40,000 and 60,000 dalton bands, while the minor labeling of the 50,000 and 65,000 dalton bands was only slightly decreased (FIGURE 9). Carb also afforded some protection at high concentrations (10^{-3} M, ~20-fold in excess of its K_d), but it was not as effective as other ligands. This is, presumably, a reflection of ternary complex formation.

In addition, AcChR-enriched membrane fragments were irradiated in the presence of [³H] DAPA; polyacrylamide gel electrophoresis of these samples was performed in sodium dodecylsulfate (FIGURE 10)—the AcChR subunits were identified by using the polypeptide pattern of an identically treated sample of solubilized purified AcChR as a marker. In analyzing the distribution of the bound radioactivity, it was found that the 40,000 dalton subunit was labeled and, in addition, that about the same amount of radioactivity was associated with the 50,000 dalton subunit, whereas the 60,000 and 65,000 dalton polypeptides showed only minor labeling, barely significant above the background (FIGURE 10). This result contrasts with the findings with purified solubilized AcChR, in which the 60,000 dalton polypeptide was labeled to an extent comparable to that of the 40,000 dalton species. To test the specificity of this photolabeling process, membrane fragments were incubated with α-BuTx to block

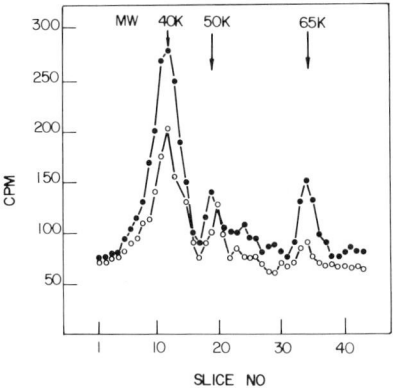

FIGURE 7. Effect of H_{12}-HTX on photolabeling of membrane-bound AcChR. ●: no HTX present; ○: photolabeling in the presence of HTX.

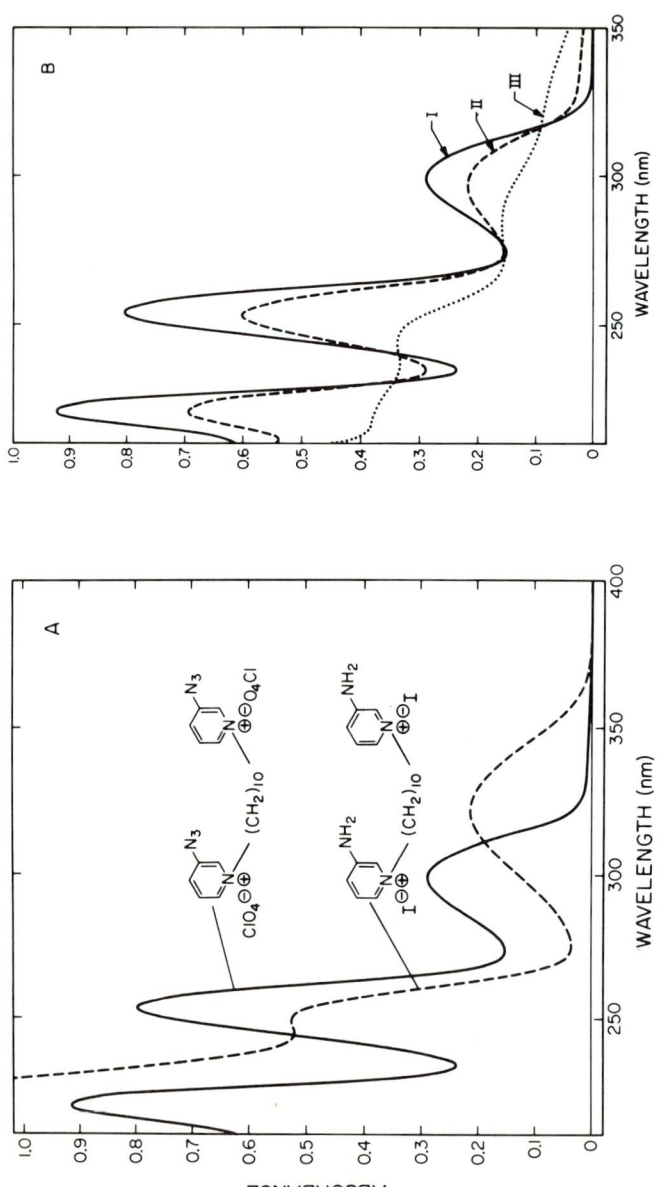

FIGURE 8. (A) Absorption spectra of DAPA and DAP: DAPA (3.2×10^{-5} M) and DAP (3.2×10^{-5} M) in 10^{-3} M sodium phosphate buffer (pH 7.5) at room temperature.

(B) The change of absorption spectrum of DAPA after irradiation. DAPA (3.2×10^{-5} M) in 10^{-3} M sodium phosphate buffer (pH 7.5) was irradiated at room temperature with short-wavelength light. I: no irradiation; II: after 30 s irradiation; III: after 5 min irradiation.

access to all DAP (or DAPA) binding sites. By irradiating [³H] DAPA in the presence of such protected membrane fragments, labeling was almost completely prevented (FIGURE 10). This was true for the 40,000 as well as for the 50,000 dalton subunit. Apparently, no cross-linking had occurred in either experiment, since no radioactivity was bound to higher molecular weight components.

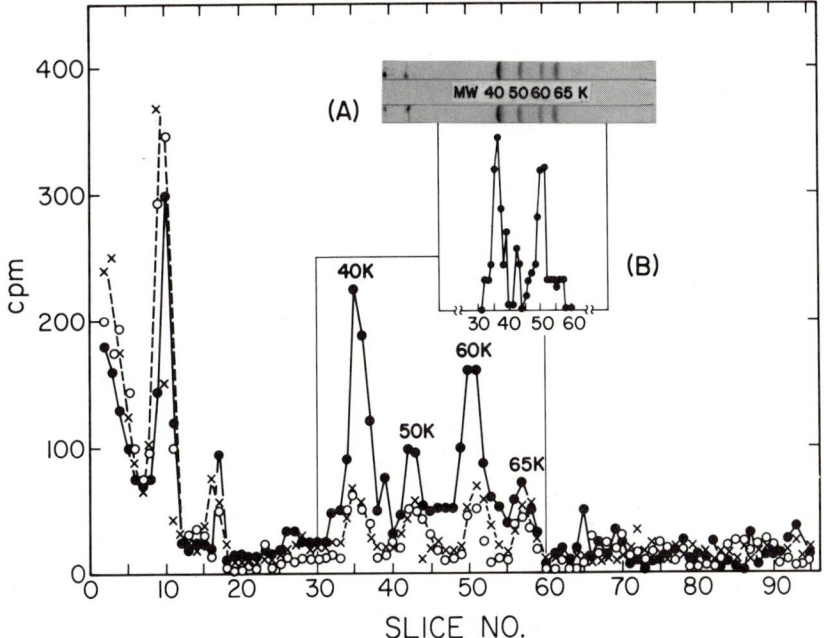

FIGURE 9. The distribution of radioactivity after separation of purified AcChR subunits covalently labeled with [³H] DAPA. Gels were cut into 1 mm slices beginning at the dye front, and radioactivity was measured. The radioactivity next to the dye front (fractions 9–11) was probably due to labeled phospholipids and free azide decomposition products. AcChR (1.2 μM) was photolabeled in the presence of 11 μM DAPA in the absence of other ligands, in the presence of 60 μM DAP ($\times$), or in the presence of 7.5 μM α-BuTx (O).

(Insert A) Top: purified AcChR; bottom: purified AcChR reacted with DAPA.

(Insert B) Shows the radioactivity incorporated into AcChR subunits after the subtraction of nonspecific labeling, which was determined from experiments in which specific labeling was eliminated due to the presence of α-BuTx. The protein bands shown (using Coomassie Blue staining) correspond well with the distribution of radioactivity. Comparing the areas of the radioactivity profile for each subunit and normalizing for the molecular weights showed that the mw 40,000 subunit contained 48% of total AcChR-bound radioactivity, the mw 50,000 subunit, 5%; the mw 60,000 subunit, 43%; and the mw 65,000 subunit, 4%.

The results obtained with [³H] DAPA–labeled membrane fragments strongly support the assumptions that the 40,000 dalton subunit actually carries the specific binding region for DAPA and, therefore, for DAP and that they also reflect structural features of membrane-bound AcChR. Again, a second polypeptide, this time of mw 50,000, was labeled to about the same extent as the 40,000 dalton subunit.

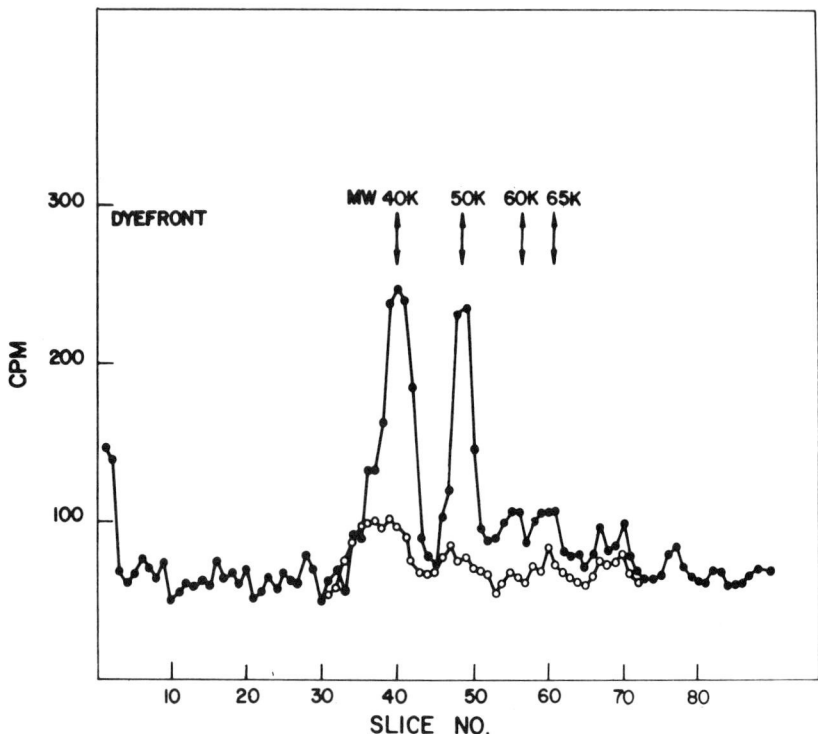

FIGURE 10. Sodium dodecylsulfate gel electrophoresis of photolabeled AcChR-rich membrane fragments. Membrane fragments (5×10^{-6} M in α-BuTx binding sites) in Ringer's solution (pH 7.5) were either irradiated in the presence of DAPA (3×10^{-5} M) (●) or incubated with α-BuTx (3.2×10^{-5} M) for 20 min at room temperature prior to irradiation in the presence of DAPA (○). Photolysis was carried out at room temperature for 2 min using the short-wavelength lamp. The polypeptide pattern of AcChR-rich membrane fragments after SDS gel elecrophoresis is shown; the arrows indicate the corresponding molecular weights and incorporated radioactivity.

Incorporation of radioactivity into both polypeptides could be prevented almost completely if access to the DAPA binding site was blocked by α-BuTx. Since α-BuTx binds, as noted above, to the 40,000 dalton subunit, the specific binding site of DAPA should be located on the same subunit; its reaction with the 50,000 dalton subunit could reflect the structural proximity of this polypeptide to the specific DAPA binding area in the membrane-bound AcChR for the same reasons that apply in the case of solubilized receptor, in which the 60,000 dalton subunit seemed to be closely associated with the 40,000 dalton subunit. The fact that labeling occurred on two different polypeptides, depending on the conformational state of the AcChR, in addition to the common incorporation of [³H] DAPA into the 40,000 dalton subunit, suggests that the specific binding site of this ligand is actually only on the 40,000 dalton subunit. This interpretation suggests that labeling of the 50,000 or 60,000 dalton polypeptides occurred for structural reasons and not because of specific binding sites on both polypeptides. These results imply that the structural arrangement of the AcChR subunits of membrane-bound receptor differs from the purified, solubilized form.

LABELING OF PEPTIDES IN ELECTROPLAX MEMBRANES WITH A LOCAL ANESTHETIC ANALOG

The interactions of various local anesthetics with receptor-rich membrane fragments have been studied by means of inhibition of α-toxin binding[40,41] and by means of extrinsic fluorescent probes.[27,42,43] In the studies reported here, we prepared an azido analog of the local anesthetic procaine amide (I)—namely, procaine amide azide (PAA) (II). This compound was chosen over the procaine derivative because the amide bond is less susceptible to hydrolysis than is procaine's ester linkage. We have previously shown that the membranes contain polypeptides of M_r 40,000, 50,000, 60,000, and 65,000,[2,3] in addition to other major species of M_r ~43,000 and 90,000. Photolysis of [^{3}H] II in the presence of AcChR-rich membrane fragments was coupled with sodium dodecylsulfate gel electrophoresis to demonstrate which polypeptides of the membrane fragment preparation were involved in local anesthetic binding.

$$R-\underset{}{\bigcirc}-\underset{\underset{\underset{H}{|}}{\underset{N}{|}}}{\overset{\overset{O}{\|}}{C}}-CH_2CH_2-\underset{\underset{H}{|}}{N}(CH_2CH_3)_2 \; Cl^-$$

(I): R = NH$_2$ (II): R = N$_3$

When membranes were run on SDS gels 20 cm long, separation between the 40,000 and 43,000 M_r bands was increased. As FIGURE 11 shows, both bands were labeled, with the majority of the radioactivity in the higher M_r band. Photolysis of membrane fragment solutions containing both [^{3}H] PAA and 2–5 μM Carb resulted in decreased incorporation of radioactivity into the 40,000 M_r label (not shown). The M_r 40,000 subunit of *Torpedo californica* contains sites for binding of α-toxins and cholinergic ligands, such as the antagonists, 4-(N-maleimido)-benzyltrimethylammonium iodide and bis-3-aminopyridinium-1-azide, and the agonist, bromoacetylcholine.

Since incorporation of [^{3}H] PAA into the protein of M_r 40,000 was prevented by the presence of Carb, the labeling seen on this polypeptide could be interpreted as being due to PAA bound at cholinergic ligand-binding sites. The identity of the labeled band of M_r 43,000 was less clear. Sobel *et al.* have recently reported the isolation of a particulate protein fraction of this molecular weight from *Torpedo marmorata* membrane fragments.[44] These authors observed that the fluorescence of quinacrine associated with this 43,000 M_r protein decreased upon the addition of HTX in a manner similar to the effects of HTX on quinacrine fluorescence in preparations of intact membrane fragments. It was not possible, however, to equate the protein of

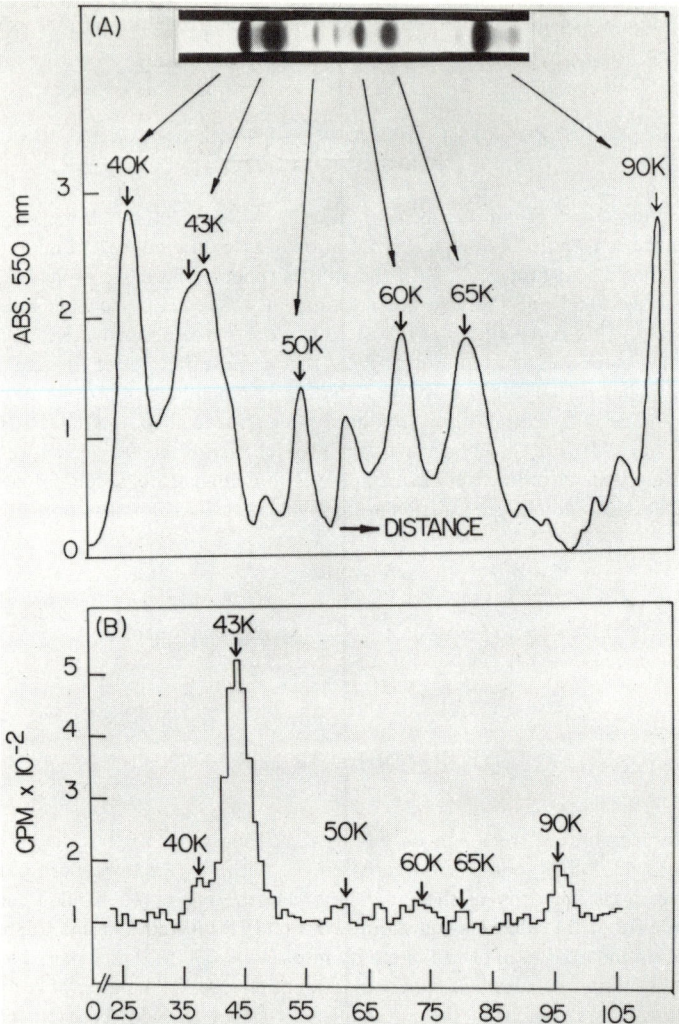

FIGURE 11. Improved separation of membrane components on 1 × 20 cm SDS-polyacrylamide gels.

(A) A scan of Coomassie Brilliant Blue staining intensity. The central portion of a 1 × 20 cm gel was scanned with a Gilford Linear transport accessory with a specially made cuvette and holder. Note that the region around M_r 43,000 contains several staining bands that were not well resolved. The relative amounts of each polypeptide present could not be quantitated, due to the very high absorbance and the fact that the stain did not always penetrate to the center of the gels because of their large diameter.

(B) Radioactivity profile. A total of 2 nmol of [^{125}I] α-labeled α-BuTx sites were placed on the gel. The major amount of radioactivity was incorporated at a position corresponding to a M_r of 43,000, with minor incorporation at M_r 40,000 and 90,000. Each gel slice was 1.1 mm long—there were 152 slices from the dye front to the top of the gel.

Sobel *et al.* with the band of M_r 43,000 labeled by [^{3}H] PAA because the Coomassie Blue staining intensity of high resolution (20 cm) gels of *Torpedo californica* membrane fragments indicated the presence of more than one protein with approximately this molecular weight (FIGURE 11). Because of limitations in the resolution of these gels, we could not unambiguously determine which partially resolved component was labeled by [^{3}H] PAA. In addition, preliminary results showed that the presence of micromolar concentrations of HTX did not decrease the amount of radioactivity incorporated in the 43,000 M_r band when *Torpedo californica* membranes were photolyzed in the presence of [^{3}H] PAA. Conversely, unlabeled PAA displaced membrane-bound [^{3}H]-labeled H_{12}-HTX with an apparent K_i of 500 μM (unpublished data), a concentration two orders of magnitude higher then that necessary to label membrane fragments with [^{3}H] PAA and well above those concentrations that enhance the fluorescence of membrane-bound ethidium bromide. Thus, although HTX and local anesthetics show similar actions both *in vivo* and *in vitro,* they may bind to separate sites on either the same or on different polypeptide chains.

In agreement with these observations, we have recently shown that specific binding of [^{3}H] H_{12}-HTX is associated with AcChR peptides;[37] this has been further confirmed by using membranes depleted of all polypeptides[4,5] except those known to be associated with the receptor.[3]

REFERENCES

1. COHEN, J., M. WEBER, M. HUCHET & J.-P. CHANGEUX. 1972. FEBS Lett. **26:** 43–47.
2. DUGUID, J. & M. A. RAFTERY. 1973. Biochemistry **12:** 3593–97.
3. RAFTERY, M. A., R. VANDLEN, D. MICHAELSON, J. BODE, T. MOODY, Y. CHAO, K. REED, J. DEUTSCH & J. DUGUID. 1974. J. Supramol. Struct. **2:** 585–92.
4. NEUBIG, R., E. K. KRODEL, N. D. BOYD & J. B. COHEN. 1979. Proc. Nat. Acad. Sci. USA **76:** 690–94.
5. ELLIOTT, J., S. M. J. DUNN, S. BLANCHARD & M. A. RAFTERY. 1979 Proc. Nat. Acad. Sci. USA **76:** 2576–79.
6. STECK, T. & J. YU. 1973. J. Supramol. Struct. **1:** 220–31.
7. SCHMIDT, J. & M. A. RAFTERY. 1972. Biochem. Biophys. Res. Commun. **49:** 572–78.
8. SCHMIDT, J. & M. A. RAFTERY. 1973. Biochemistry **12:** 852–56.
9. WEILL, C. L., M. G. MCNAMEE & A. KARLIN. 1974. Biochem. Biophys. Res. Commun. **61:** 997–1003.
10. LINDSTROM, J. & J. PATRICK. 1974. *In* Synaptic Transmission and Neuronal Interaction. M. V. L. BENNETT, Ed.: 191–216. Raven Press. New York.
11. KARLIN, A., C. L. WEILL, M. G. MCNAMEE & R. VALDERRAMA. 1975. Cold Spring Harbor Symp. Quant. Biol. **40:** 203–10.
12. CHANG, R. S. L., L. T. POTTER & D. S. SMITH. 1977. Tissue & Cell **9:** 623.
13. HUCHO, F., G. BANDINI & B. A. SUAREZ-ISLA. 1978. Eur. J. Biochem. **83:** 335–40.
14. RAFTERY, M. A., R. L. VANDLEN, K. L. REED & T. LEE. 1976. Cold Spring Harbor Symp. Quant. Biol. **40:** 193–202.
15. VANDLEN, R. L., J. SCHMIDT & M. A. RAFTERY. 1976. J. Macromol. Sci. Chem. **A10**(1 & 2): 73–109.
16. VANDLEN, R. L., W. C.-S. WU, J. EISENACH & M. A. RAFTERY. 1979. Biochemistry. **18:** 1845–54.
17. DEUTSCH, J. & M. A. RAFTERY. 1979. Arch. Biochem. Biophys. **88:** 735–43.
18. HUCHO, F., P. LAYER, H. R. KIEFER & G. BANDINI. 1976. Proc. Nat. Acad. Sci. USA **73:** 2624–28.
19. WITZEMANN, V. & M. A. RAFTERY. 1977. Biochemistry **16:** 5862–68.

20. WITZEMANN, V. & M. A. RAFTERY. 1978. Biochemistry **17:** 3598–604.
21. CHICHEPORTICHE, R., J.-P. VINCENT, C. KOPEYAN, H. SCHWEITZ & M. LAZDUNSKI. 1975. Biochemistry **14:** 2081.
22. RAFTERY, M. A., J. SCHMIDT & D. G. CLARK. 1972. Arch. Biochem. Biophys. **152:** 882.
23. SUAREZ-ISLA, B. A. & F. HUCHO. 1977. FEBS Lett. **75:** 65.
24. CHANG, H. W. & E. BOCK. 1979. Biochemistry **18**(1): 172.
25. HAMILTON, S., M. MCLAUGHLIN & A. KARLIN. 1979. Biochemistry **18**(1): 155.
26. WITZEMANN, V. & M. A. RAFTERY. 1978. Biochem. Biophys. Res. Commun. **81:** 1025.
27. SCHIMERLIK, M. & M. A. RAFTERY. 1976. Biochem. Biophys. Res. Commun. **73:** 607–13.
28. SCHIMERLIK, M., U. QUAST & M. A. RAFTERY. 1979. Biochemistry. **18:** 1884–90.
29. QUAST, U., M. SCHIMERLIK & M. A. RAFTERY. 1979. Biochemistry. **18:** 1891–901.
30. SCHIMERLIK, M., U. QUAST & M. A. RAFTERY. 1979. Biochemistry. **18:** 1901–6.
31. WEBER, M., T. DAVID-PFEUTY & J.-P. CHANGEUX. 1975. Proc. Nat. Acad. Sci USA **72:** 3443–47.
32. WEILAND, G., B. GEORGIA, V. T. WEE, C. F. CHIGNELL & P. TAYLOR. 1976. Mol. Pharmacol. **12:** 1091–105.
33. LEE, T., V. WITZEMANN, M. SCHIMERLIK & M. A. RAFTERY. 1977. Arch. Biochem. Biophys. **183:** 57–63.
34. ALBUQUERQUE, E. X., E. A. BARNARD, T. H. CHIU, A. J. LAPA, J. O. DOLLY, S.-E. JANSON, J. DALY & B. WITKOP. 1973. Proc. Nat. Acad. Sci. USA **70:** 949–53.
35. ELDEFRAWI, A. T., M. E. ELDEFRAWI, E. X. ALBUQUERQUE, A. C. OLIVERIA, N. MANSOUR, M. ADLER, J. DALY, G. BROWN, W. BURGERMEISTER & B. WITKOP. 1977. Proc. Nat. Acad. Sci. USA **74:** 2172–76.
36. ELLIOTT, J. & M. A. RAFTERY. 1977. Biochem. Biophys. Res. Commun. **77:** 1347–53.
37. ELLIOTT, J. & M. A. RAFTERY. 1979. Biochemistry. **18:** 1868–74.
38. MARTINEZ-CARRION, M. & M. A. RAFTERY. 1973. Biochem. Biophys. Res. Commun. **55:** 1156–64.
39. BODE, J., T. MOODY, M. SCHIMERLIK & M. A. RAFTERY. 1979. Biochemistry. **18:** 1855–61.
40. WEBER, M. & J.-P. CHANGEUX. 1974. Mol. Pharmacol. **10:** 35–40.
41. WEILAND, G., B. GEORGIA, S. LAPPI, C. CHIGNELL & P. TAYLOR. 1977. J. Biol. Chem. **252:** 7648–56.
42. COHEN, J., M. WEBER & J.-P. CHANGEUX. 1974. Mol. Pharmacol. **10:** 904–32.
43. GRUNHAGEN, H. & J.-P. CHANGEUX. 1976. J. Mol. Biol. **106:** 497–516.
44. SOBEL, A., T. HEIDMANN, J. HOFLER & J.-P. CHANGEUX. 1978. Proc. Nat. Acad. Sci. USA **75:** 510–14.

ELECTROPHYSIOLOGICAL EXPERIMENTS WITH PHOTOISOMERIZABLE CHOLINERGIC COMPOUNDS: REVIEW AND PROGRESS REPORT*

Henry A. Lester, Menasche M. Nass, Mauri E. Krouse,
and Jeanne M. Nerbonne

*Division of Biology
California Institute of Technology
Pasadena, California 91125*

Norbert H. Wassermann and Bernard F. Erlanger

*Department of Microbiology
Columbia University Cancer Center/Institute of Cancer Research
New York, New York 10032*

INTRODUCTION

Many small molecules, both natural and synthetic, act on biological membranes by controlling ionic channels in the membrane. Our particular interest is the channel associated with the acetylcholine receptor in the postsynaptic membrane of the nicotinic synapse, where impulses are transferred from a nerve to a muscle fiber or (in some fishes) to an electroplaque. This synapse is a highly efficient electrochemical machine, specialized to function on a millisecond time scale.[1,2] The immediate challenge is to understand the electrical and chemical regulation of receptor channels on this same time scale.

In our experiments, we monitor the number of open channels in the membrane on a millisecond time scale while manipulating the concentration of drugs near receptors, the structure of the drug-receptor complex, or the electric field across the membrane. We employ three classes of drugs known to have distinct effects on acetylcholine receptor channels:

1. Agonists, such as acetylcholine (ACh) itself, which opens channels

2. Antagonists, which prevent channels from opening (for example, curare competes with acetylcholine for a binding site on the receptor and the elapid α-toxins, e.g., α-bungarotoxin, irreversibly block this site)

3. "Open-channel blockers" (local anesthetics are good examples), which block current flow in open channels much as a plug blocks water flow in a drain.

RATIONALE OF THE EXPERIMENTS

Our experiments depend on electrophysiological and photochemical techniques for probing channel activation (FIGURE 1).[3]

*This research was supported by the Muscular Dystrophy Association (fellowship to M.M.N. and grant-in-aid), by the National Institutes of Health (fellowship to J.M.N., RCDA NS-272 to H.A.L., and grant no. NS-11756), and by the National Science Foundation (grant no. PCM-74-02140).

475

Photochemistry

The photochemical techniques derive from the design and synthesis of a class of photochromic (i.e., photoisomerizable) compounds that are active as inhibitors of chymotrypsin[4] and acetylcholinesterase[5,6] and as inhibitors[7] or activators[8] of *Electrophorus electricus* electroplaques. These drugs are azobenzene derivatives capable of assuming either a *cis* or *trans* configuration, the relative concentrations of which can be altered by light of suitable wavelengths. The crucial property of these compounds is the difference between the pharmacology of the two isomers.[9]

These compounds have physical properties well suited for use in our experiments. They absorb light of wavelengths between 300 and 500 nm (FIGURE 2); such light has virtually no effect by itself on electroplaques and can easily be generated by flash lamps and pulsed lasers. This photon absorption leads, with a high quantum yield and within a microsecond, to *cis* → *trans* and *trans* → *cis* isomerizations.[10] There are no long-lived excited states, reactive intermediates, or competing reactions. The photoisomerization properties are not expected to be sensitive to any solvent or binding conditions likely to occur in or near biological membranes.[11–13] The *cis* and *trans* isomers are thermally stable for at least several seconds and, with most of the drugs, for several days. These properties allow us to alter instantaneously (on the time scale of our experiments, 10 μs–10 s) the concentrations of the *cis* and *trans* isomers of various drugs and also to calibrate precisely the magnitudes of these "concentration-jumps."

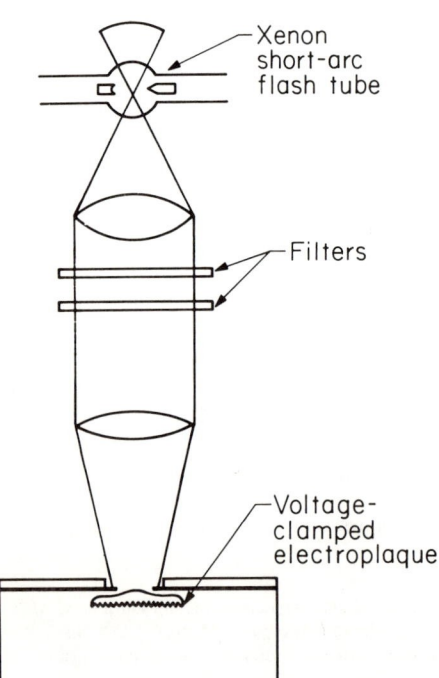

FIGURE 1. A schematic view of our apparatus for measuring the effects of photoisomerizable drugs on membranes. Single electroplaques from the giant Amazonian electric eel, *Electrophorus electricus,* are mounted in the experimental chamber with the innervated face exposed to the small (0.6 ml) upper pool (Pool A). Drugs are added to this pool. (From Nass *et al.*[3])

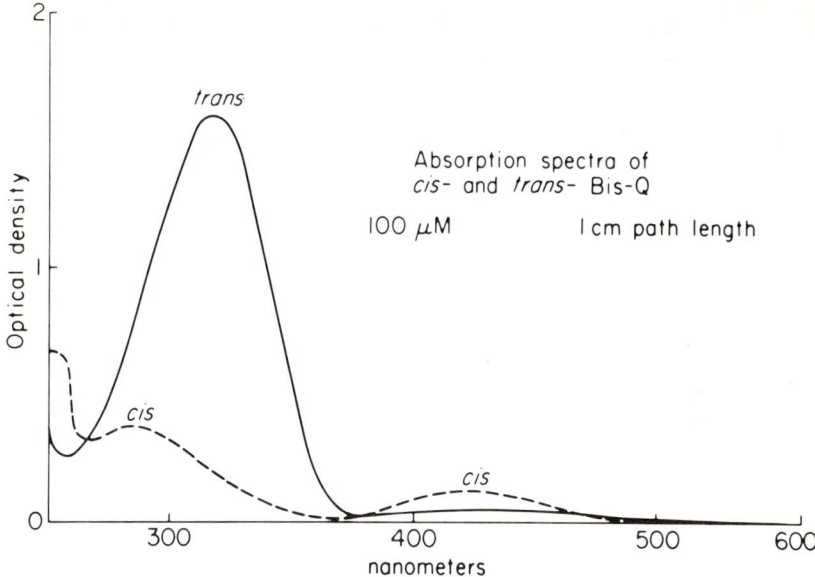

FIGURE 2. Optical absorption spectra for the pure *cis* and *trans* isomers of Bis-Q.

Electrophysiology

To monitor the number of open channels, we employ the voltage clamp. This apparatus fixes, or clamps, the membrane potential to a level set by the experimenter. Electronic circuits generate and measure the amount of current necessary to clamp the voltage. Each open receptor channel contributes an equal increment of current (too small to measure in our studies). The circuit can follow changes in the channel population within 100 μs or so. For experiments on receptor channels in electroplaques, various blocking drugs and subtraction techniques are exploited in order to eliminate the ion currents through other types of channels, such as the electrically excitable Na^+ channels that generate the propagating impulse.[14,15]

AGONISTS

FIGURE 3 presents the structures of two photoisomerizable agonists, Bis-Q and QBr, along with a highly schematic drawing that illustrates how we think they work. The two drugs resemble each other structurally; however, Bis-Q binds reversibly to the receptor[8] while QBr binds covalently to the reduced receptor.[16] The *trans* configuration of each drug is a potent agonist, but the *cis* isomer has little or no activity.[8]

With Bis-Q, we use light flashes to "jump" the agonist concentration.[17] The experiment of FIGURE 3B begins in a solution containing predominantly *cis*-Bis-Q. Because there is only a small concentration of *trans*-Bis-Q, few receptors have agonist molecules bound and therefore few channels are open. A light flash of the appropriate wavelength (peak at 420 nm) converts some of the *cis*-Bis-Q molecules to their *trans*

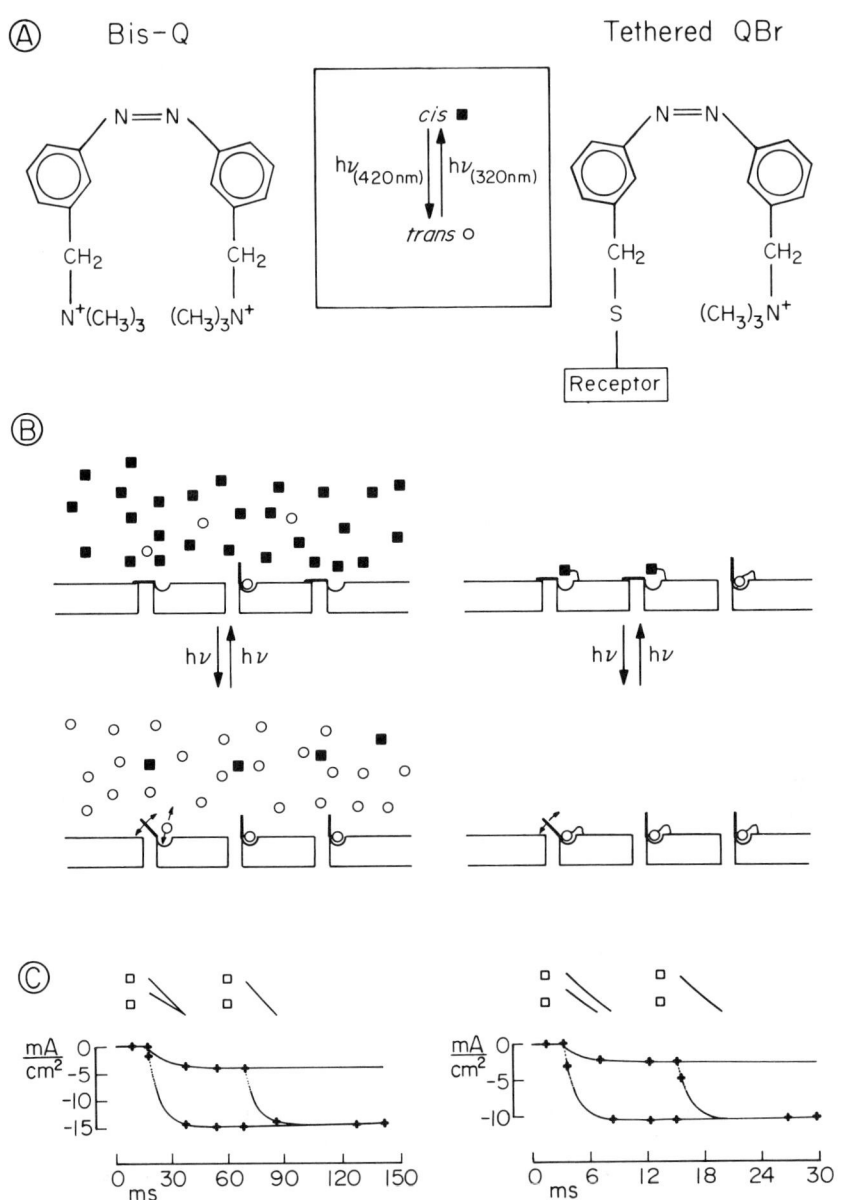

FIGURE 3. The photoisomerizable agonists, Bis-Q (left) and tethered QBr (right).

A: Structures and photoisomerization properties.

B: Bis-Q binds reversibly to receptors; QBr can be linked covalently after reduction of a disulfide bond. The drawing is oversimplified in several respects. For instance, *two* Bis-Q molecules, not just one, are probably required to open a channel; drug molecules may also bind nonspecifically at other sites on the membrane (see text).

C: Voltage-jump and light-flash relaxations. Left panel: Bis-Q (400 n*M*); right panel:

configuration, increasing the [trans-Bis-Q] in solution. After the light flash, each individual receptor is bombarded more frequently by *trans*-Bis-Q molecules. Hence, there is an increased probability that a receptor will have an agonist molecule bound and therefore that channels will be in the open state.[15,18] This increased rate constant for channel opening following an "agonist concentration jump" accounts for the increased relaxation rate constant after the light flash in FIGURE 3C (see legend).

For experiments with QBr, the electroplaque is first exposed to dithiothreitol, which cleaves disulfide bonds.[16,19,20] One of the sulfhydryl groups thus formed is alkylated by QBr. The unreacted QBr is washed away, leaving only QBr molecules tethered to receptors.[8,21] These tethered QBr molecules can be photoisomerized from *cis* to *trans* and vice versa. For instance, in FIGURE 3, the experiment starts with most of the tethered QBr in the *cis*-photostationary mixture; therefore, most channels are closed. A flash photoisomerizes some of the tethered QBr molecules to the *trans* configuration. Channels with tethered *trans*-QBr are more likely to be in the open state than are channels with tethered *cis*-QBr (with any agonist, channels undergo transitions between the open and closed states; the transition rates for reversible and tethered agonists depend on the membrane voltage).[21] Since there is no free agonist, the light flash does not produce a "concentration jump"; instead, the flash produces what we term a "molecular rearrangement."

In FIGURE 3C, the relaxations are faster for QBr than for Bis-Q. Although faster kinetics might be expected because the tethered QBr has eliminated at least one step (see next paragraph) from the activation process, it should be noted that kinetics almost this fast are seen with some reversible agonists, such as carbachol. There is, however, a major qualitative difference between the experiments with Bis-Q and with QBr: the QBr relaxations have the same rate constant before and after the flash. The molecular rearrangement has caused relaxations to scale up in amplitude, but there is no change in the kinetics. There are now more receptors with *trans*-QBr, but each individual receptor is subject to the same opening and closing transitions as the few

---

tethered QBr. Each trial contains three voltage-clamp episodes, taken at intervals of 0.5 s; a light flash occurs about halfway through the second episode of each trial. Traces show agonist-induced currents; leakage and capacitive currents have been subtracted. In the left-hand panel, at the start of the trial, the solution is in the *cis*-photostationary mixture, which contains 60 n*M* *trans*-Bis-Q; the remaining Bis-Q is in the inactive *cis* form. Fifteen ms after the start of each episode, the voltage is jumped from $+51$ to -150 mV. The agonist-induced current increases along an exponential time course (note the semilogarithmic plots that form straight lines; squares define a ten-fold range). For the first two episodes, these voltage-jump relaxations superimpose; the reciprocal time constant is 0.10 ms^{-1}. About halfway through the second episode, the light flash increases the *trans*-Bis-Q concentration to about 243 n*M* (this concentration produces roughly half-maximal activation of the agonist-induced conductance). Following this jump of *trans*-Bis-Q concentration, the conductance increases exponentially to a much larger value with a rate constant of 0.17 ms^{-1}. The third episode occurs in the higher Bis-Q concentration; the voltage-jump rate constant and final conductance equal those for the light-flash relaxation. The temperature is 8 °C. Before the experiment in the right-hand panel, receptors were reduced with dithiothreitol and alkylated by QBr; unreacted QBr was then washed away. The preparation was then exposed to uv light to convert the tethered QBr molecules to the *cis*-photostationary mixture. Thus, as in the left-hand panel, the trial starts with only 15% of the drug in the *trans* form. The voltage-jump and light-flash relaxations all follow an exponential time course, and the rate constant is the same (0.6 ms^{-1}) in all cases. The temperature is 9 °C. (From Lester *et al.*[21])

trans-QBr receptors before the flash. Thus, with reversible agonists, channel activation is governed by a bimolecular agonist-receptor interaction that obeys pseudo-first-order kinetics. With tethered agonists, channel activation is a unimolecular process.

We have found many similarities between the activation of ACh receptors by tethered QBr molecules and by reversible agonists.[21] These similarities include the voltage and temperature dependencies of the equilibria and kinetics. We conclude that the rate-limiting molecular step in channel activation remains the same for reversible agonists and for tethered QBr. Therefore, this step is not the initial, diffusion-limited encounter between agonist and receptor molecules. The rate-limiting step must consist of a subsequent molecular rearrangement. This point is discussed more fully in Reference 21.

Stoichiometry of Receptor Activation with Light-Activated Agonists

Using pure *cis*-Bis-Q, we have explored several other aspects of receptor activation. The experiment of FIGURE 4, for example, was designed to study the dose-response relation at low levels of receptor activation. Each successive flash (2 s apart) incremented the *trans/cis* ratio about 2% towards its value in the *trans*-photostationary mixture (approximately 65% *trans* and 35% *cis*). Thus, each flash produced a roughly equal increment of [*trans*-Bis-Q]. The dose-response relation has a nonlinear start, with a Hill coefficient greater than unity. These results are also obtained with bath application of reversible agonists, and are interpreted as evidence

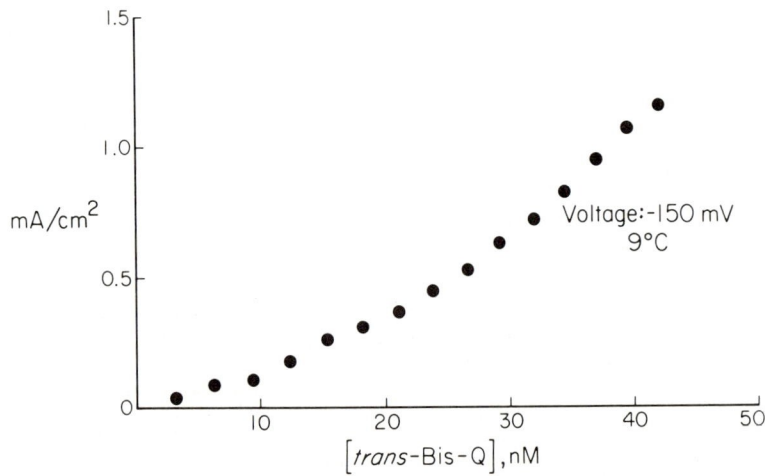

FIGURE 4. A dose-response study with small concentrations of *trans*-Bis-Q. At the start of the experiment, the Ringer solution in Pool A contains 200 nM Bis-Q, more than 99% of which is in the *cis* configuration. Agonist-induced currents are measured in 15 consecutive voltage-clamp episodes at 2 s intervals. During each episode, a flash brings the *trans*-Bis-Q concentration 2.3% closer to its value in the *trans*-photostationary state, which is 65% *trans*.

TABLE 1

STOICHIOMETRY OF THE FUNCTIONAL QBR-RECEPTOR COMPLEX

	Scheme A	Scheme B	Scheme C
Possible combinations of tethered QBr molecules	$trans_a$ cis	$(trans, trans)_a$ $(cis, trans)_a$ $(trans, cis)_a$ (cis, cis)	$(trans, trans)_a$ $(cis, trans)$ $(trans, cis)$ (cis, cis)
Normalized fraction of active receptors, g	t	$2t - t^2$	t^2

t			g_{after}/g_{before}		
				Predicted	
Before Flash	After Flash	Observed	Scheme A	Scheme B	Scheme C
1.0	0.88*	0.87 ± 0.01 (3 cells)	0.88	0.99	0.78
	0.72†	0.70 ± 0.03 (4 cells)	0.72	0.92	0.53
0.15	0.31*	2.0, 2.2	2.10	1.91	4.4
	0.55†	4.0 ± 0.6 (6 cells)	3.66	2.87	13.4

NOTE: Comparison of theory and experiment for three receptor activation schemes. In scheme A, only one tethered QBr molecule is associated with each channel; in schemes B and C, two tethered QBr molecules are associated with each channel. A subscript a denotes the active state of the receptor. The parameter t is the fraction of tethered QBr molecules in the *trans* configuration. Values for t are obtained from actionometric calibrations[3] and from the assumption that the photoisomerization properties of tethered QBr and of free QBr in solution are the same. The measurements employed unfiltered flashes at two different intensities; flashes designated † are fourfold brighter than flashes designated *. The measured value g_{after}/g_{before} is the ratio of agonist-induced current just before the flash to the value after the light-flash relaxation. Mean values are given, ± SEM. Voltage: -150 mV; temperature: 7–11 °C. (From Lester *et al.*[21])

that the open state of the receptor channel is more likely to be associated with the binding of two agonist molecules than with the binding of just one.[1,22]

With tethered QBr, however, a much simpler result is obtained.[21] Although we cannot vary the "concentration" of a covalently bound agonist, we can vary the *cis/trans* ratio of the tethered QBr molecules using light flashes. We have compared the results of such manipulations with the predictions of schemes for receptor activation. Two important assumptions are necessary.

1. QBr molecules tethered to receptors have the same photochemistry as do QBr molecules in solution. That is, they have the same absorption spectrum and quantum yield for photoisomerization.

2. Tethered *cis*-QBr molecules are completely ineffective in opening receptor channels.

TABLE 1 summarizes the data and shows that they fit the scheme in which each receptor channel is regulated by the configuration of a single tethered QBr molecule.

Probing the Nature of Synaptic Delay

Another experiment with pure *cis*-Bis-Q was partly motivated by curiosity about the process of synaptic transmission. The postsynaptic potential begins roughly one millisecond after the impulse has occurred in a presynaptic cell. Although most of this "synaptic delay" is due to events leading to the release of transmitter by the presynaptic cell,[23–25] we wondered whether any part of it derived from agonist-receptor interaction. In terms of our experiments, we wondered how soon we could see channels open after agonist molecules appeared near receptors.[26] The best previous lower limit for this time was 100–150 μs.[23] For this experiment,[27] we employed a pulsed dye laser at 440 nm. A single flash converted more than 50% of the *cis*-Bis-Q molecules to the *trans* configuration within 1 μs. At 23 °C, the first detectable depolarization occurred within 10 μs after the flash (FIGURE 5). These data are limited by several technical factors; the actual delay could well be less than 1 μs. Our "agonist concentration jumps" are still a good deal less impressive than those produced by the nerve itself during synaptic transmission. We can jump the *trans*-Bis-Q concentration from nearly zero to a value roughly three times greater than the apparent dissociation constant for the Bis-Q–receptor interaction. Just after a quantum of acetylcholine appears in the synaptic cleft, however, the local transmitter concentration is at least 100 times greater than the apparent dissociation constant for the acetylcholine-receptor interaction.[1,2] Our results show, nonetheless, that if there is an absolute delay between the appearance of agonist near receptors and the opening of the first channel, this delay is less than 10 μs at 23 °C.

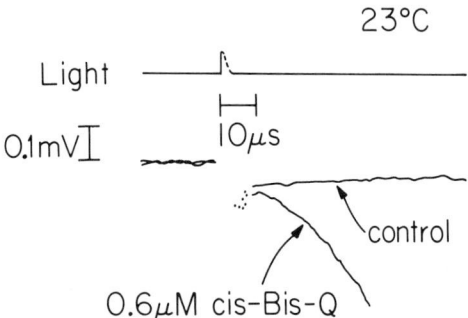

FIGURE 5. Traces from an experiment designed to measure how soon receptor channels begin to open after agonist appears near receptors. Upper trace: output of a photomultiplier tube monitoring the light from a flashlamp-pumped dye laser. The light signal is distorted by the recording system; the flash actually lasts less than 1 μs. Lower traces: voltage across the electroplaque. This is not a voltage-clamp experiment (electrodes are simply placed in the upper and lower pools of FIGURE 1). Therefore, signals are distorted by membrane time constants and do not accurately represent the time course of agonist-induced conductances. The control trace is taken in the absence of Bis-Q. Both the control and Bis-Q traces are obscured by electrical artifacts for several μs; they begin to diverge within 10 μs after the flash. At this point, less than 1% of the receptor channels have been activated. The complete response required several ms and amounted to a depolarization of 20 mV. (From Krouse *et al.*[27])

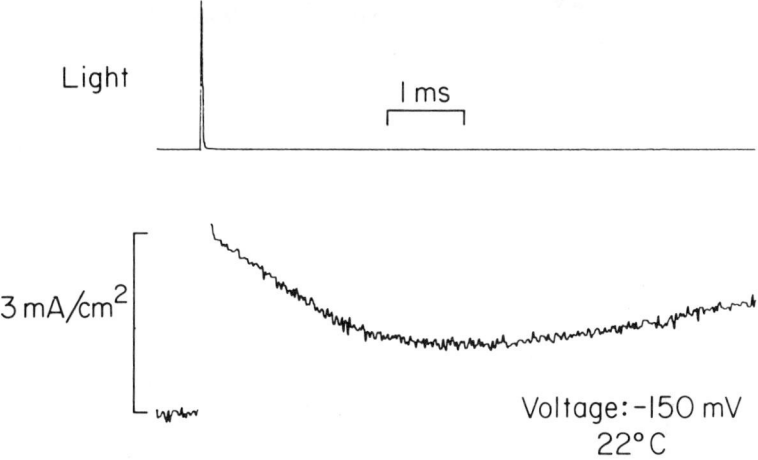

Light

1 ms

3 mA/cm²

Voltage: -150 mV
22°C

FIGURE 6. The response at short times after photoisomerizations of *trans*-Bis-Q molecules bound to receptors. Traces are the average of 16 episodes. In preparation for the experiment, the Bis-Q solution (200 n*M*) is converted to the *trans*-photostationary state by exposing it to many unfiltered flashes. A flash of the same spectral composition (monitored in the upper trace; the flash duration is about 40 μs) also occurs during each episode of the voltage-clamp trial. Thus, though the flashes isomerize individual Bis-Q molecules, they do not alter the concentrations of *cis*- and *trans*-Bis-Q. Nonetheless, the agonist-induced conductance undergoes a sequence of transient changes, eventually returning to the level observed just before the flash. The transients are termed Phases 1–4; the bottom trace, which shows voltage-clamp currents, contains Phases 1 and 2 and the beginning of Phase 3. Phase 1 is a rapid decrease of conductance, revealed as the upward jump. The trace is blanked out for 120 μs during and following the flash because the voltage-clamp circuit is too slow to respond accurately to signals on this time scale. Phase 1 is complete by this time;[3] it is too rapid to be resolved by the clamping circuit. The slower downward deflection is Phase 2, a conductance increase. During the last third of the trace, a slow upward deflection occurs. This is the beginning of Phase 3, another conductance decrease. Phase 3 has a time constant of about 4 ms at 22 °C and is followed by another conductance increase (Phase 4) with a half-time of several seconds.

Phase 1

We have used our techniques to explore the coupling between the agonist binding site and the channel in greater detail. We have been able to address such questions as, "How quickly do events at the binding site affect the channel?" and, "Does the agonist molecule remain bound to the receptor the entire time the channel is open?"

In the experiment of FIGURE 6, bound *trans*-Bis-Q molecules are photoisomerized to the inactive *cis* configuration. As a result, channels close quite rapidly. This relaxation is the fastest we have ever seen with photoisomerizable drugs; we call it Phase 1. Our analysis of this phenomenon is based on the following assumptions.[3]

1. More than one *trans*-Bis-Q molecule may need to bind to the receptor for channel opening. However, if one such bound molecule is isomerized to the *cis* configuration, the channel closes.

2. *Cis*-Bis-Q molecules induce a channel closing rate so great that Phase 1 reaches

completion on the time scale of the flash (50–500 μs). Our clamping circuit had a settling time of 100 μs; therefore, this picture is accurate if *cis*-Bis-Q is such a poor agonist that *cis*-Bis-Q channels have a lifetime of less than 100 μs and very little probability of reopening.

3. As with the experiments on tethered QBr, we assumed that bound *trans*-Bis-Q molecules have the same absorption cross section and the same quantum yield for photoisomerization as do *trans*-Bis-Q molecules in solution.

This theory accounts well for the amplitude and duration of Phase 1. At 10 °C, *trans*-Bis-Q activated channels stay open for about 10 ms.[3,17] But channels close within 100 μs after the *trans* → *cis* photoisomerization. Because this photoisomerization of bound *trans*-Bis-Q molecules closes channels at any time while they are open, we conclude that the agonist molecule remains bound the entire time the channel is open. And, because channels close so soon after the *trans* → *cis* photoisomerization, events at the channel must be coupled very rapidly to those at the binding site.

Since our initial studies on Phase 1, we have found quantitatively similar signals with two other reversible photoisomerizable agonists, the 4-hydroxy and 4-dimethyl-carbamoxy derivatives of Bis-Q. We have also made improvements in the speed of our voltage-clamp, the spectral purity and duration of our flashes, and our knowledge of Bis-Q photochemistry. It would, therefore, be of interest to reinvestigate Phase 1. In particular, we would like to re-examine whether the "cross section" for Phase 1 is one or two Bis-Q molecules per receptor and whether Phase 1 still follows the duration of the flash for very brief flashes.

Open Channel Blockers

Many drugs block membrane excitability by prematurely terminating the open channel. According to present theories,[28–32; but see 35,36] these molecules block transmembrane currents as they bind to sites within open channels. They act like a plug in a drain but with the important difference that the blockade occurs on a millisecond time scale. Open channel blockade seems to underly the action of many local anesthetics and other drugs bearing charged ammonium groups. In our experiments[33,34] with light-activated local anesthetics, we have demonstrated that receptor channels can be blocked by molecules that do not exist until after the channel opens.

The blocking drug we use is *cis*-N-*p*-phenylazophenylcarbamylcholine iodide (EW-1, FIGURE 7).[6] This drug is produced from the relatively inactive *trans* isomer by a light flash. Its action is most simply demonstrated by the effect of the *cis* isomer on the neurally evoked postsynaptic current (PSC). During the growth phase of the PSC, channels open nearly synchronously; acetylcholine then vanishes from the synaptic cleft because of diffusion and hydrolysis. During the decay phase, very few channels open and the time constant for this phase nearly equals the average channel lifetime.[2,37–39] Therefore, if the decay phase is accelerated, this cannot be due to a decreased channel opening rate; it must arise from premature termination of channels.

In the experiment of FIGURE 7, an electroplaque was equilibrated in a solution of *trans*-EW-1. Postsynaptic currents were evoked by stimulating the presynaptic nerves and a flash was delivered during the decay phase of one such response. The decay

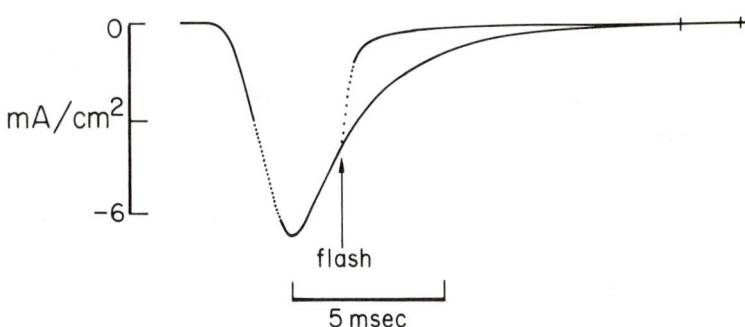

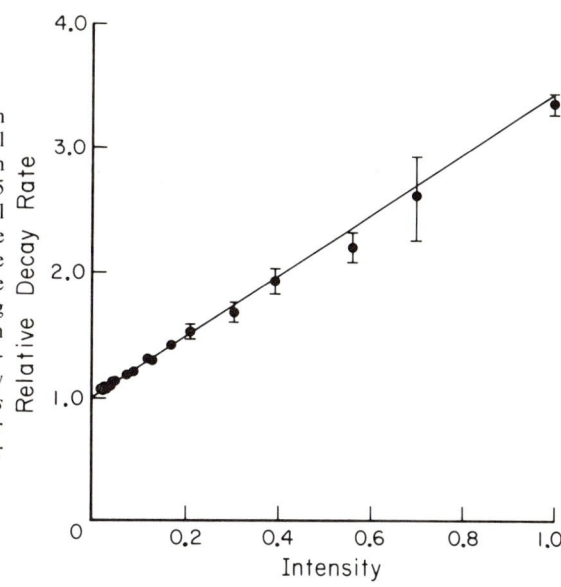

FIGURE 7. A photoisomerizable "open channel blocker," N-*p*-phenylazophenylcarbamylcholine (EW-1). Traces from a light-flash experiment with PSCs in 10 μM *trans*-EW-1. Voltage-clamp currents from two successive episodes, at an interval of 0.3 s. A flash (duration 0.5 ms) occurs during the second episode, isomerizing at least 80% of the *trans*-EW-1 molecules to the *cis* isomer. As a result, the decay phase of the PSC is accelerated. Voltage: -150 mV; temperature: 16 °C. (From Lester *et al.*[33])

FIGURE 8. The effect of flash intensity on "open channel blockade" by EW-1. Data from trials like that of FIGURE 7, in 5 μM EW-1 at 10 °C. The vertical axis is the rate constant of the fast PSC component after the flash, normalized to the value for the immediately preceding episode without a flash. Flash intensity was varied with neutral-density filters; an intensity of 1.0 corresponds to 40% *trans* $\rightarrow$ *cis* photoisomerization. Error bars show $\pm$ 1 s.d. (From Lester *et al.*[33])

phase is accelerated as a result of the flash, thus confirming the hypothesis of open channel blockade.

By varying the flash intensity, we measure a "dose-response" curve for channel blockade by our light flash (FIGURE 8). The relation between the flash intensity and the rate of channel blockade is linear, at least for flash intensities too low to saturate the photochemistry. This suggests that each channel can be blocked by the binding of just one *cis*-EW-1 molecule.

ANTAGONISTS

Membrane excitability is also blocked by drugs that compete with the agonist for the binding site on the receptor, yet do not open channels.[15,40–42] At sufficiently low concentrations, these drugs do not plug open channels.[43] Curare is the quintessential antagonist; its action has been extensively studied at the neuromuscular junction.[44,45] The equilibrium dissociation constant for curare (approximately 0.2 μM) is well known, but its molecular binding rates at the nicotinic receptor have, so far, not been accurately measured.[15,46–48] These rates could be measured from the changes in the kinetics and equilibria of agonist-induced currents following a concentration-jump of antagonist.

Ideally, we would like to have two photoisomerizable drugs. The first would have no activity in the *cis* isomer but would be an antagonist in the *trans* isomer; we could then produce rapid (<1 ms) increases in antagonist concentration. The second drug would have precisely the opposite properties: it would be inactive in the *trans* isomer but an antagonist in the *cis* isomer; with this drug we could produce decreases in antagonist concentration. (Our optical system has only a small output in the 320 nm range, in which the *trans* → *cis* isomerization has a high quantum yield; otherwise, the first drug alone would satisfy our requirements.) The rates of antagonist binding and unbinding would then be obtained directly from the relaxation of the agonist-induced current following these antagonist concentration jumps.

We do not yet possess these two "ideal" drugs. However, we have been working with 2,2'-bis[α-(trimethyl)ammonium)methyl] azobenzene, or 2BQ (2BQ is the 2,2' positional isomer of Bis-Q; see FIGURE 9).[49] Both the *cis* and *trans* isomers of 2BQ are antagonists, though they differ by roughly a factor of three in potency. Their photochemistry is nearly identical to that of Bis-Q. Light in the 420 nm range mainly affects the *cis* → *trans* photoisomerization, while light in the 320 nm range favors the *trans* → *cis* photoisomerization.

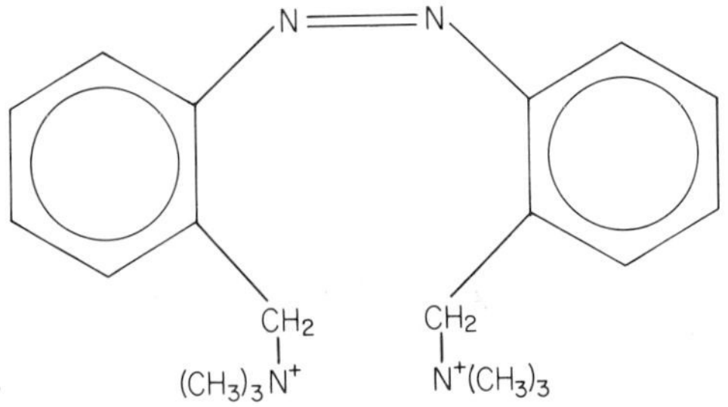

FIGURE 9. A light-activated competitive antagonist, 2BQ (see text).

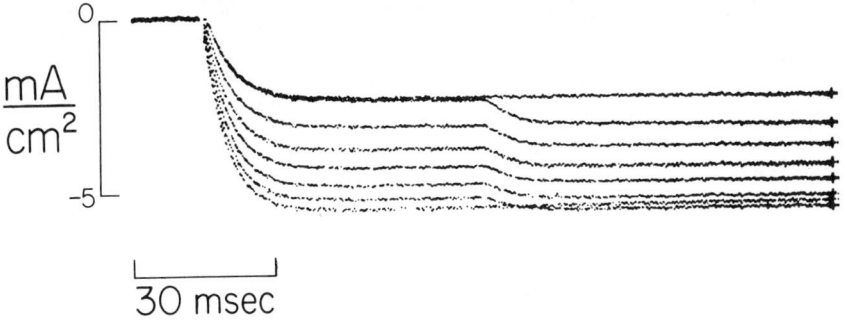

FIGURE 10. Antagonist concentration jump. Voltage-jump and light-flash relaxations in 100 μM carbachol plus 0.5 μM 2BQ. The trial contains eight voltage-clamp episodes. The first and last episodes contain only a voltage-jump from $+51$ to -150 mV; episodes 2 through 7 also contain a light-flash about halfway through the episode. As in FIGURE 3C, traces show agonist-induced currents. The trial begins with the 2BQ in the *cis* photostationary state, which is 85% *cis*-2BQ. Each light flash isomerizes the 2BQ solution about 30% of the way to the *trans*-photostationary state, which is 65% *trans*-2BQ. (By the eighth episode, the 2BQ solution contains 0.3 μM *trans*-2BQ and 0.2 μM *cis*-2BQ.) Both *cis*- and *trans*-2BQ are antagonists; 0.15 μM of the *cis*-photostationary state or 0.4 μM of the *trans*-photostationary state doubles the equilibrium dissociation constant for carbachol. Thus, each light-flash jumps the effective K_I of the 2BQ solution 30% of the way from 0.15 μM to 0.4 μM. After the last flash, the K_I is approximately 0.36 μM. Following each voltage-jump, or K_I-jump, the agonist-induced current increases along an exponential time course. As in FIGURE 3C, the voltage-jump relaxations for the first two episodes superimpose; the reciprocal time constant is 0.16 ms^{-1}. The first light-flash (in the second episode) steps the effective K_I to 0.23 μM (from 0.15 μM). As a result, the agonist-induced current increases along an exponential time course with a reciprocal time constant of 0.21 ms^{-1}. The reciprocal time constants for each light flash relaxation and the next voltage jump relaxation differ by less than 20%. The temperature is 12 °C (see text).

Equilibria

Both *cis* and *trans* 2BQ shift the dose response relation for carbachol to higher concentrations without substantially reducing the maximum agonist-induced current.[50] This shift does not depend on voltage or the number of open channels, suggesting that both *cis* and *trans* 2BQ are competitive antagonists. From the "dose-ratio" method,[47] we obtain an apparent dissociation constant, or K_I, of 0.15 μM for the *cis* isomer and 0.4 μM for the *trans* isomer of 2BQ.

Kinetics

Voltage jump relaxations in the presence of antagonists depend upon the agonist as well as the antagonist.[15] For carbachol in the presence of curare, the relaxations still follow a single exponential time course, but the relaxations are slower than in curare's absence.[15] As the agonist concentration is increased, the voltage jump relaxations become faster, presumably because the agonist competes more successfully for the binding site. We have confirmed these observations for carbachol and 2BQ. In FIGURE 10, the effective inhibition due to antagonist is reduced with each light flash, since *trans* 2BQ is less potent than *cis* 2BQ (the flashes increase the solution's K_I from 0.15

μM in the initial bathing solution to 0.36 μM after the last flash). The reciprocal time constant for the voltage jump relaxation increases from 0.16 ms^{-1} in the first and second episodes to 0.21 ms^{-1} in the last. At 12 °C, the voltage jump and light flash relaxations in 100 μM carbachol and 2BQ follow a simple exponential time course; we conclude that the antagonist equilibrates with receptors much faster than the relaxations shown.[15]

Our data on the kinetics of antagonist binding and dissociation are incomplete. We are limited by the small (factor of 3) difference in potencies between *cis* and *trans* 2BQ and by our optical system's low output in the ultraviolet range. We plan experiments with a nitrogen laser, which will allow us to produce larger "down jumps" in antagonist K_I. A complete description of antagonist interaction with receptors will require a kinetic analysis of relaxations following "up" and "down" jumps in K_I.

CONCLUSIONS

The interpretations presented here are relatively straightforward because the drugs studied have well-defined, immediate, and readily measurable effects upon cellular physiology; they open, prevent from opening, and close ionic channels in the membrane. The experiments underscore the rapid, tight coupling between the binding of a drug to its receptor, or its dissociation from the receptor, and the resultant opening and closing of the channel.

It would be quite interesting to have access to other probes of drug-receptor interaction. With suitable physical methods, it may be possible to detect conformational transitions of receptor proteins or alterations in the membrane environment.

REFERENCES

1. STEINBACH, J. H. & C. F. STEVENS. 1976. Neuromuscular transmission. *In* Frog Neurobiology. R. Llinas & W. Precht, Eds. Springer-Verlag. Berlin.
2. WATHEY, J. C., M. M. NASS & H. A. LESTER. 1979. A numerical reconstruction of the quantal event at nicotinic synapses. Biophys. J. **27**: 145–64.
3. NASS, M. M., H. A. LESTER & M. E. KROUSE. 1978. Response of acetylcholine receptors to photoisomerizations of bound agonist molecules. Biophys. J. **24**: 135–60.
4. KAUFMAN, H., S. M. VRATSANOS & B. F. ERLANGER. 1968. Photoregulation of an enzymic process by means of a light sensitive ligand. Science **162**: 1487–89.
5. BIETH, J., S. M. VRATSANOS, N. H. WASSERMANN & B. F. ERLANGER. 1969. Photoregulation of biological activity by photochromic reagents. II. Inhibitors of acetylcholinesterase. Proc. Nat. Acad. Sci. USA **64**: 1103–6.
6. BIETH, J., N. WASSERMANN, S. M. VRATSANOS & B. F. ERLANGER. 1970. Photoregulation of biological activity by photochromic agents. IV. A model for diurnal variation of enzymic activity. Proc. Nat. Acad. Sci. USA **66**: 850–54.
7. DEAL, W. J., B. F. ERLANGER & D. NACHMANSOHN. 1969. Photoregulation of biological activity by photochromic reagents. III. Photoregulation of bioelectricity by acetylcholine receptor inhibitors. Proc. Nat. Acad. Sci. USA **64**: 1230–34.
8. BARTELS, E., N. H. WASSERMANN & B. F. ERLANGER. 1971. Photochromic activators of the acetylcholine receptor. Proc. Nat. Acad. Sci. USA **68**: 1820–23.
9. ERLANGER, B. F. 1976. Photoregulation of biologically active macromolecules. Annu. Rev. Biochem. **45**: 267–83.
10. ROSS, R. L. & J. BLANC. 1971. Photochromism by *cis* → *trans* isomerization. *In* Techniques of Chemistry. VIII. Photochromism. G. H. Brown, Ed.: 471–556. Wiley-Interscience. New York.

11. BIRNBAUM, P. R. & D. W. G. STYLE. 1954. The photoisomerization of some azobenzene derivatives. Trans. Faraday Soc. **50:** 1192.

12. ZIMMERMAN, G., L. Y. CHOU & U. J. PAIK. 1958. The photochemical isomerization of azobenzene. J. Am. Chem. Soc. **80:** 3528–31.

13. CHEN, D. T.-L. & H. MORAWETZ. 1965. Photoisomerization and fluorescence of chromophores built into the backones of flexible polymer chains. Macromolecules **9:** 463–68.

14. NAKAMURA, Y., S. NAKAJIMA & H. GRUNDFEST. 1965. Analysis of spike electrogenesis and depolarizing K inactivation in electroplaques of *Electrophorus electricus*. J. Gen. Physiol. **49:** 321–49.

15. SHERIDAN, R. E. & H. A. LESTER. 1977. Rates and equilibria at the acetylcholine receptor of *Electrophorus* electroplaques: A study of neurally evoked postsynaptic currents and of voltage-jump relaxations. J. Gen. Physiol. **70:** 187–219.

16. KARLIN, A. & E. BARTELS. 1966. Effects of blocking sulfhydryl groups and of reducing disulfide bonds on the acetylcholine-activated permeability system of the electroplax. Biochim. Biophys. Acta **126:** 525–35.

17. LESTER, H. A. & H. W. CHANG. 1977. Response of acetylcholine receptors to rapid, photochemically produced increases in agonist concentration. Nature **266:** 373–74.

18. SHERIDAN, R. E. & H. A. LESTER. 1975. Relaxation measurements on the acetylcholine receptor. Proc. Nat. Acad. Sci. USA **72:** 3496–500.

19. CLELAND, W. W. 1965. Dithiothreitol, a new protective reagent for SH groups. Biochemistry **3:** 480–82.

20. KARLIN, A. & D. COWBURN. 1973. The affinity-labeling of partially purified acetylcholine receptor from electric tissue of *Electrophorus*. Proc. Nat. Acad. Sci. USA **70:** 3636–40.

21. LESTER, H. A., M. E. KROUSE, M. M. NASS, N. H. WASSERMANN & B. F. ERLANGER. 1980. A covalently bound photoisomerizable agonist. Comparison with reversibly bound agonists at *Electrophorus* electroplaques. J. Gen. Physiol. **75:** 207–32.

22. LESTER, H. A., D. D. KOBLIN & R. E. SHERIDAN. 1978. Role of voltage-sensitive receptors in nicotinic transmission. Biophys. J. **21:** 181–94.

23. KATZ, B. & R. MILEDI. 1965. The measurement of synaptic delay and the time course of acetylcholine release at the neuromuscular junction. Proc. Roy. Soc. Lond. Ser. B **161:** 483–96.

24. KATZ, B. & R. MILEDI. 1965. The effect of temperature on the synaptic delay at the neuromuscular junction. J. Physiol. (London) **181:** 656–70.

25. LLINAS, R., I. Z. STEINBERG & K. WALTON. 1976. Presynaptic calcium currents and their relation to synaptic transmission: Voltage clamp study in squid giant synapse and theoretical model for the calcium gate. Proc. Nat. Acad. Sci. USA **73:** 2918–22.

26. LESTER, H. A., M. M. NASS, M. E. KROUSE, N. H. WASSERMANN & B. F. ERLANGER. 1978. ACh receptor-channels begin to open within 30 μsec after agonist is applied. Soc. Neurosci. Abstr. **4:** 370.

27. KROUSE, M. E., H. A. LESTER, M. M. NASS, J. M. NERBONNE, N. H. WASSERMANN & B. F. ERLANGER. 1979. ACh receptor channels begin to open within 10 μsec after agonist is applied. Soc. Neurosci. Abstr. **5:** 483.

28. ARMSTRONG, C. M. 1966. Time course of TEA^+-induced anomalous rectification in squid giant axons. J. Gen. Physiol. **50:** 491–503.

29. STEINBACH, A. B. 1968. Alteration by Xylocaine (Lidocaine) and its derivatives on the time course of the end plate potential. J. Gen. Physiol. **52:** 144–61.

30. STEINBACH, A. B. 1968. A kinetic model for the action of Xylocaine on receptors for acetylcholine. J. Gen. Physiol. **52:** 162–80.

31. STRICHARTZ, G. R. 1973. The inhibition of sodium currents in myelinated nerve of quaternary ammonium derivatives of Lidocaine. J. Gen. Physiol. **62:** 37–57.

32. ADAMS, P. R. 1975. A model for the procaine end-plate current. J. Physiol. (London) **246:** 61–63P.

33. LESTER, H. A., M. E. KROUSE, M. M. NASS, B. F. ERLANGER & N. H. WASSERMANN. 1978. Light-activated blocker of acetylcholine receptor channels. Abst. Sixth Int. Biophys. Mtg., Kyoto: 294.

34. LESTER, H. A., M. E. KROUSE, M. M. NASS, N. H. WASSERMANN & B. F. ERLANGER.

1979. Light-activated drug confirms a mechanism of ion channel blockade. Nature. **280:** 509–10.

35. BEAM, K. G. 1976. A voltage clamp study of the effect of two lidocaine derivatives on the time course of end-plate currents. J. Physiol. (London) **258:** 279–300.

36. BEAM, K. G. 1976. A quantitative description of end-plate currents in the presence of two lidocaine derivatives. J. Physiol. (London) **258:** 301–22.

37. MAGLEBY, K. L. & C. F. STEVENS. 1972. The effect of voltage on the time course of end-plate currents. J. Physiol. (London) **223:** 151–71.

38. MAGLEBY, K. L. & C. F. STEVENS. 1972. A quantitative description of end-plate current. J. Physiol. (London) **223:** 173–97.

39. ANDERSON, C. R. & C. F. STEVENS. 1973. Voltage clamp analysis of acetylcholine induced end-plate current fluctuations at frog neuromuscular junction. J. Physiol. (London) **235:** 655–91.

40. BROCKES, J. P. & Z. W. HALL. 1975. Acetylcholine receptors in normal and denervated rat diaphragm muscle. II. Comparison of junctional and extrajunctional receptors. Biochemistry **14:** 2100–6.

41. COLQUHOUN, D. & H. P. RANG. 1976. Effects of inhibitors on the binding of iodinated α-bungarotoxin to acetylcholine receptors in rat muscle. Mol. Pharmacol. **8:** 285–92.

42. COLQUHOUN, D., F. DREYER & R. E. SHERIDAN. 1979. The actions of tubocurarine at the frog neuromuscular junction. J. Physiol. **293:** 247–84.

43. KATZ, B. & R. MILEDI. 1972. The statistical nature of the acetylcholine potential and its molecular components. J. Physiol. (London) **224:** 665–98.

44. LANGLEY, J. N. 1905. On the reaction of cells and of nerve endings to certain poisons, chiefly as regards the reaction of striated muscle to nicotine and to curare. J. Physiol. (London) **33:** 374–413.

45. ECCLES, J. C., B. KATZ & S. W. KUFFLER. 1941. Nature of the endplate potential in curarized muscle. J. Neurophysiol. **4:** 362–87.

46. ARMSTRONG, D. L. & H. A. LESTER. 1979. The kinetics of tubocurarine action and restricted diffusion within the synaptic cleft. J. Physiol. **294:** 365–86.

47. JENKINSON, D. H. 1960. The antagonism between d-tubocurarine and substances which depolarize end-plate. J. Physiol. (London) **152:** 309–24.

48. ADAMS, P. R. 1975. Drug interactions at the motor endplate. Pfluegers Arch. **360:** 155–64.

49. WASSERMANN, N. H., E. BARTELS & B. F. ERLANGER. 1979. Conformational properties of the acetylcholine receptor as revealed by studies with constrained depolarizing ligands. Proc. Nat. Acad. Sci. USA **76:** 256–59.

50. GADDUM, J. H. 1937. The quantitative effects of antagonist drug. J. Physiol. (London) **89:** 7–9P.

NITRENES IN PHOTOAFFINITY LABELING: SPECULATIONS OF AN ORGANIC CHEMIST

Walter Lwowski

Department of Chemistry
New Mexico State University
Las Cruces, New Mexico 88003

INTRODUCTION

Recent experience shows that nitrenes[1] are powerful tools for photoaffinity labeling.[2] No single nitrene seems to be best for all the different situations encountered, however. Of the nitrenes known to date, arylnitrenes (including the heteroarylnitrenes) have been used almost exclusively.[2] Their precursors have always been the corresponding azides, which indeed have many advantages. Aryl azides are readily available and methods by which to attach the aryl azide groups to structures with the required biochemical affinities are known. The photochemical behavior of properly substituted aryl azides is quite favorable: They absorb light of wavelengths well above 300 or even 400 nm, with extinction coefficients high enough to capture most of the incident light. This results in short irradiation times as well as in protection of the biomolecules from unrelated photochemical damage—the high absorption by the azide shields the biomolecules, at least for the earlier span of the irradiation time. Nitro-substituted aryl and heteroaryl azides are particularly good in this respect.

The reactivities of arylnitrenes are relatively low, but they can be enhanced by electron-withdrawing substituents on the aryl ring, especially F— and O_2N—. However, arylnitrenes are not altogether ideal: their lifetimes are short and intersystem crossing to the more stable triplet states is usually rapid. (See the article by N. Turro in this volume.) Furthermore, singlet nitrenes undergo rapid intramolecular bond reorganizations,[3-5] all of which might lead both to the formation of several different kinds of covalent bonds and to the depletion of the reactive species by several reaction paths. Depending on their goals, investigators might wish for other nitrenes, combining the virtues of arylnitrenes with those of higher reactivity and longer singlet lifetimes, or lower reactivity and greater selectivity. In cases in which escape of the nitrene from the site of its formation seems unlikely, a selective nitrene of long lifetime might be attractive. In such a situation, a selective nitrene might form just one type of covalent bond, i.e., one product, whose identification in just one fraction of a degradation or sequencing scheme would be relatively easy. A very unselective nitrene might form covalent bonds to many or all of the residues it can reach in the original biomolecule adduct, thus spreading the label over several fractions after degradation. In cases in which escape of the nitrene might occur, or in which the nearby residues are of low reactivity towards electrophiles, reactivities higher than those that can be achieved with arylnitrenes might be needed.

One might hope that cooperation between biochemists and organic chemists eventually will make it possible both to select a nitrene for a given task and to be able to predict in advance what residues in the biomolecule might be attacked and how the

491

0077–8923/0346–0491 $1.75/1 © 1980, NYAS

products of such an attack should be detected in degradation and structure elucidation schemes.

This article will discuss some nitrenes of potential interest in photoaffinity labeling and speculate on future developments of useful nitrenes and useful methods. Many known nitrenes have some properties that might be advantageous, but they or their precursors also have properties that make their application to photoaffinity labeling impossible or restrict the scope of such applications to special cases. The limitations often rest with the precursors, commonly the corresponding azides. It does, however, seem possible to develop alternative precursors with better properties for several nitrenes.

N. Turro, in his article in this volume, has discussed the photochemical principles that operate and the "electronic isomerism" of singlet and triplet states of electron-deficient intermediates. It thus suffices to state here that the nitrenes of interest here are usually generated by direct irradiation in their singlet states. Photosensitization techniques using aromatic ketones allow the generation of triplet nitrenes directly, without the singlet nitrene being formed first. Once formed, the singlet nitrenes usually undergo intersystem crossing to the corresponding triplets at rates that depend on the nature of the nitrene. For covalent bond formation, singlet nitrenes are usually much superior—they acquire an electron pair from their substrate in a single reaction step (often followed by some small change, such as proton transfer). The single step reaction avoids the formation of a paired intermediate, and thus the danger of dissociation of such an intermediate. The electronic nature of triplet nitrenes, however,

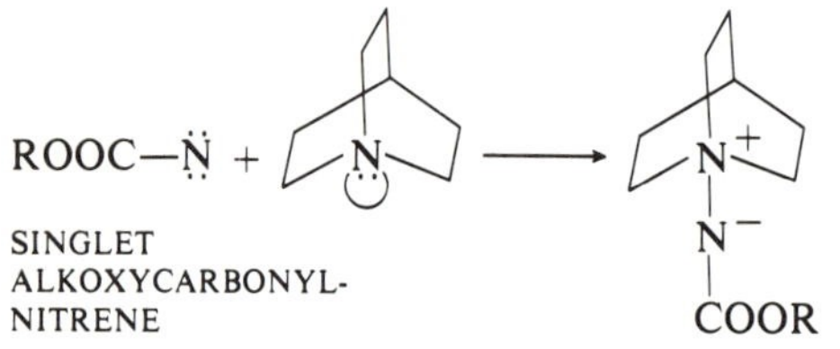

$$ROOC-\ddot{N} + \quad \longrightarrow \quad \hspace{3cm} (1)^6$$

SINGLET
ALKOXYCARBONYL-
NITRENE

1

STABLE YLIDE

2

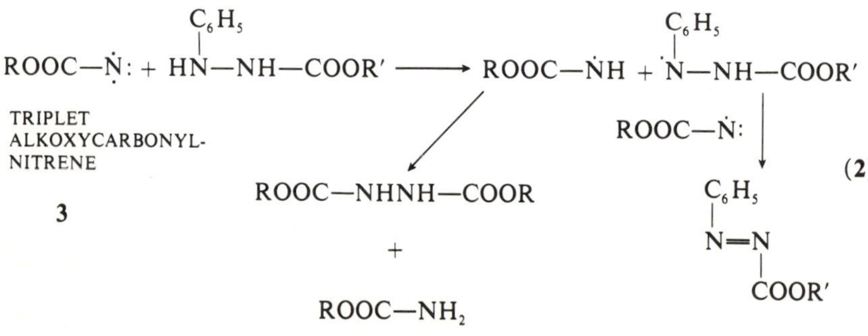

$$ROOC-\dot{N}: + HN-NH-COOR' \longrightarrow ROOC-\dot{N}H + \dot{N}-NH-COOR' \hspace{2cm} (2)^7$$

TRIPLET
ALKOXYCARBONYL-
NITRENE

3

ROOC—NHNH—COOR

+

ROOC—NH₂

4

forces them to undergo two-step reactions in which a covalent bond between the nitrene and its substrate is often made only in the second step. Dissociation of the two moieties then reduces the yield. In useful oversimplification, one can say that singlet nitrenes prefer to undergo concerted electrophilic reactions (such as in Equation 1), while triplet nitrenes tend to undergo two successive radical reactions, in two distinct steps (such as in Equation 2).

Singlet alkoxycarbonylnitrene inserts intermolecularly into C—H bonds with retention of configuration;[8] the corresponding triplet ROCO—N does not react at all with unactivated C—H bonds, but either undergoes radical reactions or dissociates.

Several conditions should be met by a nitrene and its precursor before their use in photoaffinity labeling:

1. The nitrene precursor should have a substituent R of the particular biochemical affinity desired so that the precursor will bind to the receptor site.

2. The nitrene should be generated efficiently and without damage to the target system. The quantum yields of nitrene formation should be high, as should be the extinction coefficient of the precursor. The wavelength of the required light should not damage the system; in most cases it should be long.

3. The precursor should be stable chemically, not react with the system, and not decompose at the temperatures used. Hydrolytic stability is very important.

To meet conditions 1 and 2, it is advantageous if the nitrene precursor has more than just one site to which groups can be attached. That is, a particular type of nitrene (with the desired reactivity and lifetime) should have "handles" to which one may attach a group with the required binding properties and, at a different handle, a group adjusting the photochemical properties in the desired manner. In the arylnitrene series, the aromatic ring positions of the aryl azide provide such handles. As the reactivity of arylnitrenes is strongly influenced by ring substituents, activating substituents can, and usually must, also be attached to the ring. Heteroatoms (S, N, O) on the ring provide universal handles to which a variety of groups can be attached.

Formulas 5 and 6 show the general case and a familiar example. Bayley and Knowles have given a comprehensive list of nitrenes used in photoaffinity labeling.[2] Their successful nitrene precursors conform to 5, with the nitrene center always being aryl or hetaryl. The nitrene center determines the reactivity and other properties of the nitrene (its "type"), which can be modified by substituents within limits depending on the nature of the nitrene center. For example, both the reactivity of arylnitrenes and the photochemical properties of their precursors can be modified greatly. Alkylni-

TABLE 1
VARIOUS TYPES OF NITRENES

Reactivity in Intermolecular Reactions	Properties of the Photo-Precursors (the Azides)		
	Photochemical Properties	Stability of the Precursor	Opportunities for Attaching Handles
AKLYLNITRENES			
Poor. Rearrangement to azomethines predominates.	Poor. λ_{max} at about 287 nm, ϵ about 500. Insensitive to substituents.	Good.	Groups to be attached on the alkyl chain (or ring).
FLUROALKYLNITRENES			
Better. Intermolecular C—H insertion known.[9]	Poor.	Good.	As above.
ARYLNITRENES			
Singlet reactivity medium. Singlet lifetime short. Triplet reacts with C=C and phenyl, but mostly abstracts H·.	Absorption maxima and extinction coefficients very dependent on substituents.[10]	Good.	Attachment of various groups to the aryl ring is generally easy.
FLUOROARYLNITRENES NITRO SUBSTITUTED ARYL-NITRENES			
Electron-withdrawing groups (—NO_2, —F) increase reactivity. More highly fluorinated aryls might prove advantageous in the future.	Nitro-aryl azides absorb strongly between 400 and 500 nm, e.g., $\lambda = 458$ nm with $\epsilon = 4640$.[2]	Good. Variable, but good enough.	Attachment to the ring, often through sulfur or nitrogen.
ALKANOYLNITRENES* R—CO—N			
Very reactive, good singlet lifetimes. Insert into C—H bonds of many types. Cross to the triplet state, which dissociates or abstracts H·. The nitrenes do not rearrange to isocyanates (but their precursors do).[11]	Poor. λ_{max} ~270 nm, ϵ ~30. Substituent effects of absorption are small.	Alkyl—CO—N_3 decomposes at room temperature to give isocyanates only (no nitrenes). Aryl—CO—N_3 decomposes above room temperature. Both aryl and alkanoyl azides are easily hydrolyzed.	On the alkyl chain (or aryl ring).
ALKOXYCARBONYNI- TRENES† RO—CO—N			
Highly reactive, insert into most C—H bonds. React with benzene rings, nitriles, acetylenes, C=C, amines, hydroxy compounds, sulfides, and sulfoxides.	Photochemistry of azide is unfavorable: absorption at 250 nm only 88; at 300 nm, $\epsilon = 2.5$.	Thermally moderately stable, decomposes above 50 or 60 °C. Hydrolytic stability moderate.	Attached to the group R only. Replacing the oxygen in RO by other heteroatoms changes the properties drastically. Substituents on R do not have much influence on photochemistry.

TABLE 1 (*Continued*)
VARIOUS TYPES OF NITRENES

Reactivity in Intermolecular Reactions	Properties of the Photo-Precursors (the Azides)		
	Photochemical Properties	Stability of the Precursor	Opportunities for Attaching Handles
SULFONYLNITRENES‡ R—SO$_2$—N			
Reactivity is high. Insert into C—H bonds, attack aromatic rings.	Light absorption is poor. Wavelengths below 300 nm generally required. Photosensitization gives the undesirable triplet. Arylsulfonyl azides give messy photoreactions; alkylsulfonyl azides are better.	Thermal and hydrolytic stabilities are very good.	Attached at the alkyl group (or the aryl if a suitable photoprecursor for Ar—SO$_2$—N is found).
PHOSPHORYLNITRENES (RO)$_2$P(O)—N			
Reactivities are highest of the known nitrenes. Data limited, only one publication.[12] Will insert into C—H bonds even in the presence of hydroxyl groups.	Generated by short wavelength light; no detailed data.	Very good thermal stability. (RO)$_2$P(O)—N$_3$ is a *very* powerful cholinesterase inhibitor and should be handled with the greatest care.[12]	Presumably through the R groups.
ALKOXY-(N-ALKANESULFONYL)-CARBIMIDOYLNITRENES[14]§ RO—C(=NSO$_2$R')—N			
Reactivities are less than those of carbonylnitrenes. Will not insert into C—H bonds nor attack benzene. Give very good yields in clean reactions with C=C and alcohols.	Give singlet nitrene upon photolysis at 300 nm. No rearrangement. λ_{max} = 231 nm, with ϵ = 9500. At 300 nm, ϵ = 11.	Medium hydrolytic stability. Decomposes at 70 °C.	Handle for affinity through group R; for improved photochemistry probably best through R'.

*Precursors other than azides seem promising. Photolysis of certain heterocycles does produce these nitrenes. These reactions might be adapted to the photochemical requirements for affinity labeling.

†The utility for photoaffinity labeling is limited until other photoprecursors have been developed, but attractive potential precursors exist.

‡Due to the poor photochemical properties of the sulfonyl azides, their use in photoaffinity labeling is quite limited. However, other photoprecursors, similar to those envisioned for carbonylnitrenes, may well be found.

§This type of nitrene seems promising, and better photoprecursors ought to be prepared.

trenes can be made considerably more reactive by fluorination of their alkyl group,[9] but the photochemical properties of alkyl azides are little changed by substitutions in the alkyl group.

The groups responsible for biochemical affinity, for proper photochemical behavior, and for reactivity need not, of course, be separate. It is, however, convenient when they are, so that the biochemical affinity can be changed while the rest of the nitrene precursor is left the same and unchanged in its photochemical properties.

TABLE 1 lists nitrenes one might consider for photoaffinity labeling use if suitable precursors were available. Only the arylnitrenes have been tried extensively. The other entries are speculative with respect to their labeling application. Nitrenes that are known,[1] but seem to hold little promise for photoaffinity labeling use (due to their properties and/or those of their precursors) are omitted.

FUTURE NITRENE LABELS

Of the nitrenes in TABLE 1, only selected arylnitrenes have the hydrolytic stability and the photochemical properties required in most photoaffinity labeling experiments. The span of available reactivities is narrow and the intersystem crossing rate is higher than desired for many potential applications.

The high reactivity of carbonylnitrenes makes them attractive, but the first subgroup, $>$C—CO—N, the alkanoyl- and aroylnitrenes, is saddled with very inconvenient precursors. The alkanoyl azides decompose at room temperature, the aroyl azides at somewhat higher temperatures, and both azides will give only about 50% yields upon photolysis—the rest is transformed into isocyanates. The isocyanate formation is almost completely suppressed in the second group of carbonylnitrene precursors, the alkoxycarbonyl azides. They, too, give highly reactive nitrenes, but the photochemical properties of the azides (and of those carbonyl azides mentioned above) are poor. Thus, one should develop alternative precursors, especially for alkoxycarbonylnitrenes. This task has been given little attention: The organic chemist has the azides, and, for RO—CO—N, a practical and easy α-elimination route (from the base-induced decomposition of RO—CO—NH—OSO$_2$Ar[14]). However, several promising starting points for the development of photoprecursors for photoaffinity labeling exist. Sauer has photolyzed the heterocyclus 7 and obtained aroylnitrenes and aryl isocyanate.[15] If the methods were extended to alkoxycarbonylnitrene, one would presumably get little or no isocyanate. However, the photochemical properties of such a heterocycle, deprived of the aryl group, might be unsatisfactory. Perhaps the substitution of sulfur or imidoyl for one of the ring oxygens would help. A more intriguing class of precursors are aminimides derived from nitrogen heterocycles. Becker has reported the photolysis of 8, giving 41% acetylnitrene, together with methyl isocyanate.[16] Again, one might expect that the corresponding alkoxycarbonyl compound 9 would not give isocyanates, but alkoxycarbonylnitrene, RO—CO—N.

The aminimide route, if it can be developed for photoaffinity labeling use, offers intriguing possibilities. Attaching a group of suitable affinity to the heterocyclus should be possible and the chances for obtaining suitable photochemical properties seem reasonable. In use, the precursor would be bound to some biochemical site and, upon photolysis, the carbonylnitrene would be liberated. Due to its high reactivity, it could then form a covalent bond in the very near vicinity, attaching the group ROCO—N. The heterocyclus and the affinity handle both are part of the leaving group in the nitrene formation, and they would not be covalently bound and, indeed,

$$Ar-\underset{7}{\overset{N-O}{\underset{O}{\bigsqcup}}}\overset{O}{\underset{O}{}} \longrightarrow CO_2 + Ar-CO-N + Ar-NCO \qquad (3)$$

$$\underset{8}{\text{8}} \longrightarrow + H_3C-CO-N \quad (4)$$

$$+$$

$$H_3C-NCO$$

$$\underset{9}{\text{9}} \longrightarrow \qquad (5)$$

$$+$$

$$N-CO-OR$$

might protect the reactive site. One might hope for the binding site to retain its function, so that the nitrene carrier, separated from the nitrene moiety after irradiation, could be exchanged for other substrates, such as natural ones. What would happen to the activity of the biochemical molecule (e.g., an enzyme) would depend on the particular case and the interaction of the newly covalently bound ROOC—N group with the reaction mechanism of the enzyme (or whatever it might be). Degradation would, one hopes, allow one to pinpoint the site of the new covalent bond to N—COOR. If this is bound to one specific building block or fragment, one must conclude that this fragment is close to the binding site. There seems to be no reason why the heterocyclic leaving group of the aminimide nitrene precursor could not itself be the group that provides biochemical affinity. If a biochemically active nitrogen heterocyclus can be converted into an aminimide of the same type as 9, it should be able to carry the alkoxycarbonylnitrene moiety to the binding site, there to release the nitrene upon photolysis. Thus, one has a chance to make a series of photoaffinity labels from the natural substrates of, e.g., enzymes, by attaching to them an aminimide function capable of releasing a nitrene upon photolysis. In some cases, the enzyme so modified might retain some activity, perhaps with changes of its biochemical properties. Formulas 10–13 are speculative examples of alkoxycarbonylnitrenes of this type.

The aminimide approach might well work for nitrenes other than carbonyl- and alkoxycarbonylnitrenes. Sulfonylnitrenes might be suitable.

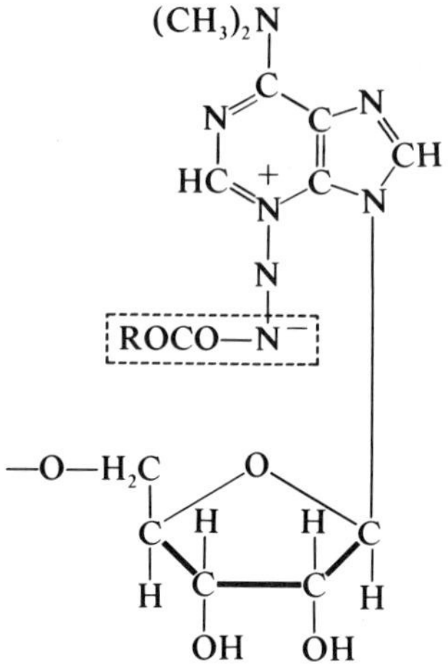

10

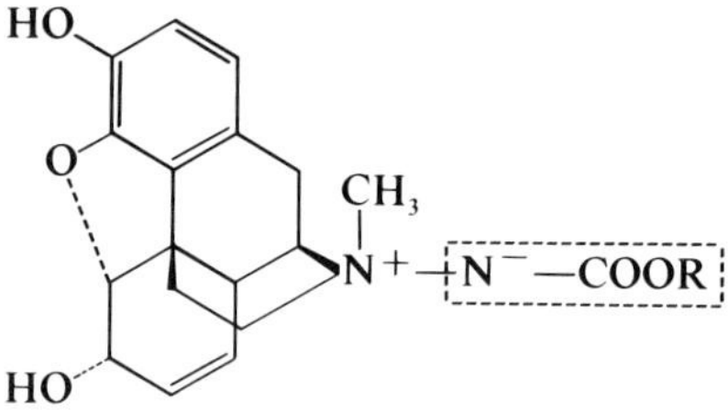

11

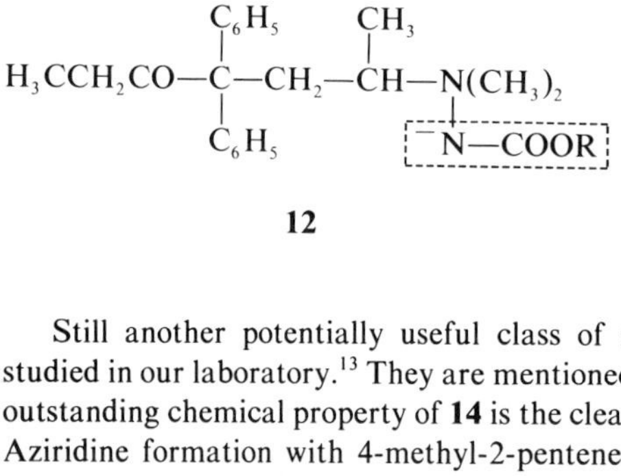

12

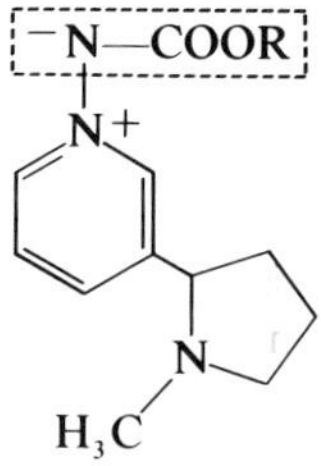

13

Still another potentially useful class of nitrenes are imidoylnitrenes currently studied in our laboratory.[13] They are mentioned above as the last entry in TABLE 1. An outstanding chemical property of **14** is the cleanness of the reactions, e.g., with olefins. Aziridine formation with 4-methyl-2-pentene is stereospecific and proceeds in 85% isolated yield when the olefin concentration is 60 mol%; the reaction still gives a 72% yield when there is only 0.5 mole% olefin in solution. This indicates that the singlet state of **14** is long-lived. The nitrene is also selective and does not attack C—H bonds or benzene rings. Compound 14 reacts cleanly with hydroxyl groups (Equation 6).

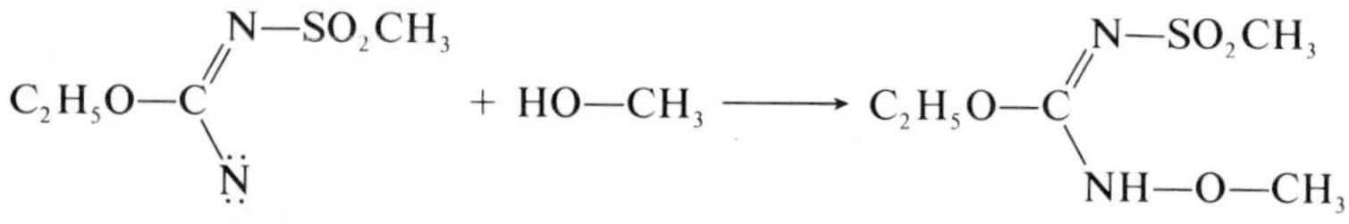

$$C_2H_5O-C\underset{\ddot{N}}{\overset{N-SO_2CH_3}{\big\|}} + HO-CH_3 \longrightarrow C_2H_5O-C\underset{NH-O-CH_3}{\overset{N-SO_2CH_3}{\big\|}} \quad (6)$$

14   **15**

(Isolated in 74% yield)

It might be possible to use analogs of **14** (with the groups of O and S modified to fit the affinity and photochemical requirements) for photoaffinity labeling when good selectivity of the nitrene is desired. The preparation of precursors other than the azide is still being pursued in our laboratory.

PRODUCT DETERMINATION

The location of covalent bonds formed in photoaffinity labeling may be determined at widely varying levels of definition or resolution. The label may be recognized as being bound to fragments ranging from hundreds of thousands of daltons down to a few hundred or to the level of, e.g., a single amino acid or heterocyclic base. Persons far more knowledgeable than this author know of no instance in nitrene photoaffinity labeling in which the new covalent bond has been completely characterized as to its exact nature and location (such as, for instance, "the 6-position of the indole in tryptophane"). The small quantities of the materials dealt with, and the complexity of the systems, make it generally impractical to do such ultimate structural determinations.

In certain cases, investigators might wish for the ultimate resolution in photoaffinity labeling, where the location and new terminus of the new covalent bond is defined to a particular position in the moiety attacked by the nitrene. Planning such experiments would be greatly aided by having a spectrum of nitrenes of graded reactivities and selectivities and by the availability of model studies on the reactions of these nitrenes with various common building blocks encountered in biochemistry (the components of nucleic acids, including the sugars, the amino acids, and so on). The speculations above discuss various old and new types of nitrenes. Studies of nitrene reactions with low molecular weight "bio building blocks" are practically nonexistent. The organic chemists have not even finished with the reactions of rather simple functional groups and bonds, as far as intermolecular nitrene reactions are concerned. However, studying reactions with various heterocycles and other biochemically interesting systems would be quite interesting from the point of view of many organic chemists, and no particular technical obstacles seem to exist, although solubility problems in some (but not in most) might tax the skills of the organic chemist.

After such groundwork has been done, a future biochemist might decide, for example, that, in his system, a nitrene photoaffinity label should or might be located close to a given residue, e.g., tryptophane. Suppose model studies (still to be made) show that there is a nitrene of moderate reactivity that attacks indoles. Suppose the attack occurs at the 6–7 double bond of the indole, giving an azepinopyrrole and from it a mixture of 6- and 7-substituted indoles, bearing the nitrene residue at these two positions. Such a mixture would be hard to separate, the isomers being very similar to each other. It would, however, be easy to separate the mixture of 6- and 7-substituted indoles from other substances. In practice, the nitrene would be generated from a precursor bound to, e.g., an enzyme. Due to its moderate reactivity, the nitrene would not insert into C—H bonds and, if it can't find a reaction partner suitable for singlet reaction, intersystem crossing to the triplet (and finally dissociation) would occur. These would lead only to hydrogen abstraction reactions, not to covalent bond formation. If, however, a moiety of the reactivity of an indole presents itself (such as a tryptophane) and is in reach of the nitrene, the latter could form a covalent bond. If so, the label would "stick" and could be followed down the degradation path to some small fragment, perhaps even the nitrene-substituted tryptophane (whose properties would be known from the model experiments). One might thus enhance the resolution of the method by concentrating the label at one single site and by making the degradative analysis simpler.

In summary, it would be worthwhile for organic chemists to study new nitrenes, new methods to generate nitrenes, and the reactions of nitrenes with the more prominent or interesting building blocks found in biochemistry (and in medicinal chemistry). Such studies of nitrene reactions should be carried out not only under "optimal" conditions, but also in the presence of so very bioinorganic a compound as water.

REFERENCES

1. LWOWSKI, W., Ed. 1970. Nitrenes. Wiley-Interscience. New York; LWOWSKI, W. 1978. Nitrenes. *In* Reactive Intermediates, Vol. 1. M. Jones, Jr. and R. A. Moss, Eds. Wiley-Interscience. New York.
2. BAYLEY, H. & J. R. KNOWLES. 1977. *In* Methods of Enzymology, Vol. 46. W. B. Jacoby and M. Wilchek, Eds. Academic Press. New York.
3. LEHMAN, P. A. & R. S. BERRY. 1973. J. Am. Chem. Soc. **95**: 8614; SUNDBERG, R. J., D. W. GILLESPIE & B. A. DEGRAFF. 1975. J. Am. Chem. Soc. **97**: 6193.
4. SUNDBERG, R. J. & R. W. HEINTZELMAN. 1974. J. Org. Chem. **39**: 2547.
5. DEGRAFF, B. A., D. W. GILLESPIE & R. J. SUNDBERG. 1974. J. Am. Chem. Soc. **96**: 7491.
6. LWOWSKI, W. & R. PALANIAPPAN. Unpublished.
7. LWOWSKI, W. & R. J. MOORE. Unpublished.
8. SIMSON, J. M. & W. LWOWSKI. 1969. J. Am. Chem. Soc. **91**: 5107.
9. BANKS, R. E., D. BERRY, M. J. McGLINCHEY & G. J. MOORE. 1970. J. Chem. Soc. C: 1017.
10. REISER, A. & H. M. WAGNER. 1971. *In* The Chemistry of the Azido Group. S. Patai, Ed.: 446. Wiley-Interscience. London.
11. LINKE, S., G. T. TISUE & W. LWOWSKI. 1967. J. Am. Chem. Soc. **89**: 6308; EIBLER, E. & J. SAUER. 1974. Tetrahedron Lett.: 2569.
12. BRESLOW, R., A. FEIRING & F. HERMAN. 1974. J. Am. Chem. Soc. **96**: 5937.
13. LWOWSKI, W. & O. SUBBA RAO. 1980. Tetrahedron Lett.: 727.
14. LWOWSKI, W. & T. J. MARICICH. 1965. J. Am. Chem. Soc. **87**: 3630.
15. EIBLER E. & J. SAUER. 1974. Tetrahedron Lett.: 2565.
16. BECKER, H. G. O., D. BEYER & H.-J. TIMPE. 1970. Z. Chem. **10**: 264.

Index of Contributors

(Italic page numbers refer to comments made in discussion. The author's affiliation is given at the first appearance of his name.)

502

ANNALS OF THE NEW YORK ACADEMY OF SCIENCES

Volume 347

FORENSIC PSYCHOLOGY AND PSYCHIATRY

Edited by Fred Wright, Charles Bahn, and Robert W. Rieber

The New York Academy of Sciences
New York, New York
1980

Library of Congress Cataloging in Publication Data

Main entry under title:

Forensic psychology and psychiatry.

(Annals of the New York Academy of Sciences; v. 347)
Papers from a symposium held on September 26–28, 1979 by the New York Academy of Sciences and cosponsored by the United States Dept. of Justice, National Institute of Law Enforcement and Criminal Justice.
1. Psychology, Forensic—Congresses. 2. Forensic psychiatry—Congresses. I. Wright, Fred. II. Bahn, Charles. III. Rieber, Robert W. IV. New York Academy of Sciences. V. National Institute of Law Enforcement and Criminal Justice. VI. Series: New York Academy of Sciences. Annals; v. 347. [DNLM: 1. Forensic psychiatry—Congresses. W1 An626YL v. 347 / W740]
Q11.N5 vol. 347 [RA1148] 500s [614′.1]   80–17982

CCP
Printed in the United States of America
ISBN 0-89766-084-6 (Cloth)
ISBN 0-89766-085-4 (Paper)
ISSN 0077-8923

ANNALS OF THE NEW YORK ACADEMY OF SCIENCES

VOLUME 347

June 20, 1980

FORENSIC PSYCHOLOGY AND PSYCHIATRY*

Editors and Conference Organizers
FRED WRIGHT, *Chair*, CHARLES BAHN, and ROBERT W. RIEBER

◆

CONTENTS

* This volume is the result of a symposium entitled Forensic Psychology and Psychiatry, held on September 26–28, 1979 by The New York Academy of Sciences and cosponsored by the United States Department of Justice—National Institute of Law Enforcement and Criminal Justice.

Part IV. The Patient as Offender: Special Problems
Donal E. J. Mac Namara, *Chair*

Part V. "Scared Straight": Panel Discussion
Robert W. Rieber, *Moderator*

Part VI. Violence and the Family
Herman Badillo, *Chair*

Part VII. The Media and Crime
Flora Rheta Schreiber, *Chair*

Part VIII. Human Nature, Crime, and Society
Robert W. Rieber, *Chair*

This project was partially supported by Order Number 9-0695-J-LEAA awarded to the
New York Academy of Sciences by the National Institute of Law Enforcement and
Criminal Justice, U.S. Department of Justice, under the Omnibus Crime Control and
Safe Streets Act of 1968, as amended. Points of view or opinions stated in this docu-
ment are those of the authors and do not necessarily represent the official position or
policies of the U.S. Department of Justice.

PREFACE

Fred Wright, Charles Bahn, and Robert W. Rieber

Department of Psychology
John Jay College of Criminal Justice
New York, New York 10019

Recently, in an effort to further understanding and control of crime and the criminal justice process, behavioral scientists have become active on a practical as well as a theoretical level in addressing a number of the problems involved. Substantial contributions have been made in the following areas: competency to stand trial, issues of psychological evidence, crisis intervention and hostage negotiation, violence and the family, treating the offender, and crime and the media.

This symposium has been designed to provide the people working in these areas with an opportunity to present their techniques, research findings, and theoretical advances to the scientific community as well as to the general public. Investigators include those who work in corrections, probation, parole, police departments, and other criminal justice settings as well as those who work in university, hospital, and other non–criminal justice institutions. It is rarely possible for these practitioners and researchers to talk to each other about their respective contributions and thereby influence and enlarge each other's perspective. It is hoped that this symposium will provide this opportunity as well as provide an opportunity for the synthesis and assimilation of this material within a coherent framework. The symposium will also help to establish the field of forensic psychology as one of the areas in which major and important work on the problem of crime is being undertaken.

We, the organizers, would like to take this opportunity to thank the people and institutions that helped make the symposium possible. We would first like to thank our colleagues at the John Jay College of Criminal Justice for working and struggling to keep that institution alive and healthy, thereby helping to keep alive the notion of dealing with crime and justice in an enlightened fashion. This kind of dedication to the task is illustrated by the presence here today of the president of the college, Dr. Gerald Lynch, who has taken the time to chair the symposium's first session. Other colleagues at the college have also shown similar support and dedication to this symposium, and it is most appreciated.

We would also like to thank the New York Academy of Sciences for sponsoring and helping to fund this event. The staff at the Academy functioned in a highly competent and patient fashion, and that too is appreciated. Dr. William Cain, a member of the Academy, was particularly helpful to us as we developed and organized the program.

Further, we would like to thank the National Institute of Law Enforcement and Criminal Justice of the United States Department of Justice for helping to fund this symposium, and to thank Mr. Henry Dogin, director of the Law Enforcement Assistance Administration, for taking the time and effort to be our keynote speaker at the symposium's subscription dinner. Finally, we are indebted to the symposium participants for the time and effort they have given and are continuing to give in preparing themselves and their material for presentation at this event.

COMPETENCY TO STAND TRIAL: OPENING REMARKS

Gerald W. Lynch

John Jay College of Criminal Justice
New York, New York 10019

I would like to congratulate the organizers of this symposium, for bringing together individuals who are concerned with these very pressing questions in forensic psychology. I really can think of no more pressing issues in psychology than those in forensic psychology because of what is at stake. It is not only the liberty, but sometimes the life, of the individual that we are assessing, diagnosing, or evaluating.

I believe that the area of forensic psychology is one in which there will be breakthroughs in the near future. I think they will make a difference to the fields of criminal justice and psychology.

Probably the reason I'm so hopeful is that I think that the present state of our knowledge is so lacking. We have great difficulty agreeing on the diagnosis in any one case. We fall even farther apart in attempting to explain the reason for the diagnosis, and of course we are at our most vulnerable in trying to predict future behavior. And all these three functions—diagnosis, explanation, and prediction—are what the public and the criminal justice system and the legal system expect of us, and we really haven't been able to provide the answers that we wish we could. I think many who are now in the field are saying that we don't know as much as we perhaps thought we did. But now we are working on it, and systematically we are trying to find the answers, and we are making progress. It is for that reason that we at John Jay College of Criminal Justice established a couple of years ago a Master's Degree in Forensic Psychology and just last year an undergraduate major in forensic psychology.

I see this symposium as a further step in making progress in this crucial field. So I am very pleased to join with you in this symposium.

THE INTERFACE OF THE MENTAL HEALTH AND CRIMINAL JUSTICE SYSTEMS: HANDLING THE VIOLENT RELEASED MENTAL PATIENT

Charles Bahn*

Temple University
Philadelphia, Pennsylvania 19122

Both the mental health and the criminal justice systems have developed around a common problem: how to understand and cope with bizarre, harmful, and socially unacceptable behavior. Both systems have had to define exactly what kinds of behavior fall within their respective purviews, and these definitions show considerable overlap.

An obvious case in point is the definition of insanity.

The mental health system needs a clear definition of insanity for many reasons, the principal one being to determine who should be involuntarily detained and treated in mental hospitals. In recent years, this definition has been subject to very close scrutiny and modification since Szasz (1961, 1963, 1965),[40-42] Scheff (1966),[37] and Goffman (1961, 1963)[16,17] have persuasively argued that those classified as insane are subject to legal disabilities that allow for the possibility of considerable misuse by individuals or by the government. Groeth (1977)[21] reported that eight states have recently enacted mental health statutes that, in effect, limit involuntary commitment to persons who are dangerous to themselves or to others. One such state, the State of California, changed its statutory definitions through the Lauterman-Petris-Short Act to limit involuntary detention and treatment to those who are dangerous to self or others in an active sense or, in a passive sense, to those who are gravely disabled. Gravely disabled was defined as being "unable to provide for one's basic needs for food, clothing or shelter." In the earlier law, the definition of mental illness justifying involuntary detention and treatment was that the individual be "so mentally ill as . . . to require immediate care, treatment or restraint," a tautology that left the specific judgment strictly to the professionals to make, without limitation.

The new criteria allow for 72 hours of involuntary detention and, if needed, an additional 14 days of involuntary treatment. For those who have attempted suicide, yet another 14-day extension is provided for. After this —although there is a possible judicial commitment for another 90 days in those cases where evidence of dangerousness has been presented—if the patients are not gravely disabled, they must be released on demand.

In these states and in several others, statutory limitations on involun-

* Present affiliation: Department of Psychology, John Jay College of Criminal Justice, New York, N.Y. 10019.

3

tary commitment have been a key factor in the trend to deinstitutionalize mental patients.

Another powerful impetus has come from the decision of the United States Supreme Court in *O'Connor* v. *Donaldson*, which Curran (1975)[10] describes as holding that when a patient is not dangerous to himself or others, is mentally ill, and is not currently receiving any treatment, he must be released from custody at his own request. The court refused to deal with the full scope of the question that it could have examined: If a patient is mentally ill and is dangerous, can he be held involuntarily in a mental facility, or indeed a prison, without treatment? Further questions that emerge involve the definition of treatment: Do given procedures and methods require specified outcomes in order to be acknowledged as treatment (Miller, 1977)?[26]

All of these issues, decisions, and questions have contributed to the growing deinstitutionalization of mental patients.

The criminal justice system has its own distinctive needs for definitions of insanity, as Goldstein (1967) explained so clearly in *The Insanity Defense*.[18] If, for example, an individual commits a crime as a result of unconscious and irrational forces over which he has no control, do we wish to hold him responsible?

In 1843, Lord Chief Justice Tindal of the British court declared "not guilty, on the grounds of insanity," one M'Naghten who had shot and killed the personal secretary to Sir Robert Peel.

The acquittal stirred such controversy, whipped up by the newspapers and supported by the queen, that the House of Lords convened a commission of 15 distinguished judges to elucidate the law regarding insanity in a criminal proceeding. The rule that was drawn up stated that:

> to establish a defense on the grounds of insanity, it must be clearly proved that, at the time of committing the act, the party accused was laboring under such a defect of reason, from disease of mind, as not to know the nature and quality of the act he was doing. Or, if he did know it, that he did not know he was doing what was wrong.

Eule (1978) analyzed this position as "the presumption of sanity."[13] Goldstein (1968) pointed out that this derived from a time when mental disease was "not yet an extensive concept, when it was widely assumed that only the exceptional offender was sufficiently mentally disordered to warrant dealing differently with him, and when criminal law was not regarded as a treatment device at all."[19]

Smith and Berlin (1974)[39] have concluded that the M'Naghten rule was difficult, and in some cases impossible, to apply in a courtroom situation. Lawyers, judges, and psychiatrists found the terms of the rule both difficult to bring into testimony and not adequate to cover an expanding concept of mental illness. During the past decades, the concept of "irresistible impulse" has been adopted by some states, and others have been tending toward the provisions of the Model Penal Code of the American Law Institute that provides:

> 1. A person is not responsible for criminal conduct if at the time of such conduct as a result of mental disease or defect he lacked substantial capacity to appreciate the

criminality (wrongfulness) of his conduct or to conform to the requirements of the law.

2. As used in this article, the terms mental disease or defect do not include an abnormality manifested only by repeated criminal or otherwise antisocial conduct.

The expanded definitions, while satisfying our current understanding of mental illness, pose serious questions about the place of legal responsibility in a free society. Goldstein (1967)[18] commented that even while we can recognize the forces that contributed to an individual's behavior, the concept of "blame" may be still necessary.

The concept of "blame" and insanity which is its other side, is one of the ways in which culture marks out the extreme beyond which non-conformity may not go.[18]

The point is the most significant one underlying the discussion of the insanity defense. We are back once again to the attempt of society to define insanity so as to delimit the scope of the criminal justice system.

In actual fact, the insanity defense is pleaded in scarcely 2% of all of the criminal cases that are tried annually in the United States (Eule, 1978).[13] Much more significant, in a practical sense, is the definition of insanity as it relates to the determination of competency to stand trial, or even to participate in plea bargaining. This determination—whether the individual is competent to stand trial, to participate in his defense—is not only a very common issue in criminal proceedings, but some states have enacted legislation that a determination of competency be made in all felony cases.

It is an established principle of the American justice system that the defendant have the capacity to participate rationally and effectively in the legal process, but the proportion of cases in which competency determinations are made varies enormously, as do the criteria for establishing competency and those appointed to make this determination. Roesch and Golding[35] reported that in North Carolina, more than half (56%) of judges surveyed reported that they grant a motion for a competency evaluation immediately, without requesting additional facts not included in the motion. In the same study, it was pointed out that competency evaluations were requested on the bases of advice from arresting officers, requests from the defendant's family, prior history of psychiatric treatment, current alcohol/drug abuse, seriousness of charges, suicide threats or attempts, aggressive behavior in jail, and client distress or depression. The fact that prior history of psychiatric treatment is included in the list signifies the likelihood that former patients of mental institutions are likely to be evaluated for competency. The fact is that less than 10% of all referrals in North Carolina are found incompetent (Roesch and Golding, 1977),[34] although here again, the rate varies considerably in other states.

Egon Bittner (1968)[5] has elaborated on the many ways in which the issue of mental abnormality affects the administration of justice outside the courtroom. The most significant area of impact is in the exercise of police discretion. Banton (1964),[2] Bittner (1967),[4] Goldstein (1960),[20] and La Fave (1965)[24] have all demonstrated that the exercise of discretion is especially prominent in the enforcement of the law with regard to common offenses. Bleicher (1967)[6] pointed out that in many jurisdictions, statutory authorization for police intervention in cases of mental illness pertains, and this is defined as being of a civil rather than criminal nature.

The result is that there are significant issues of police discretion in handling cases that could be regarded as either criminal offenses or as mentally unbalanced behavior.

During the past few years, the continuing deinstitutionalization of the mentally ill has spawned extensive research to determine whether released mental patients have arrest rates that exceed those of the general population. Cocozza, Melick, and Steadman (1978) have concluded that

> the public has little to fear from the mentally ill. Few people released from state mental hospitals are involved in violent crime, and very little of the violent crime that occurs results from such persons.[8]

They have explained away repeated studies showing higher arrest rates for released mental patients than for the general population by arguing that among the patient population, there is a subgroup of those with previous criminal histories and that these individuals are indeed more apt to be arrested after release for violent crimes. Their overall conclusion was that "mental illness and violent crime are most often independent and not interactive."[8]

The conclusion seems premature, at very least, because their study and similar research [Abramson (1972);[1] Brill and Maltzburg (1954);[7] Cohen and Freeman (1945);[9] Durbin, Pasewark, and Albers (1977);[12] Giovannoni and Gurer (1967);[15] Guze, Goodwin, and Crane (1969);[22] Paull and Malek (1974);[30] Rappeport and Lassen (1966);[33] Quinsey (1975);[32] Zitrin, Hardesty, Burdock, and Drosaman (1976)[44]] have used arrest rates and sometimes readmission rates as criteria to determine the dangerousness of the released mental patients. One recent comprehensive study of this genre by Fleming was titled "Interface of the Mental Health and Criminal Justice Systems—An Examination of Pennsylvania's Mental Health Procedures Act of 1976."[14] It explored the possibility that a 1976 statute restricting grounds for initiating and continuing involuntary commitment by requiring proof of dangerousness would result in diversion of "less dangerous" mentally ill persons into the criminal justice system. Arrest and commitment trends before and after the enactment of the 1976 law were examined for Philadelphia County, Pennsylvania, and arrest rates from a small sample of persons for whom unsuccessful commitment attempts had resulted from application of the new law's criteria were analyzed. The expected decrease in the number of involuntary commitments did not take place, but the length of time spent in the hospitals by involuntarily committed persons was reduced considerably. Analysis of county-wide arrest rates provided only "tentative support" for the diversion hypothesis: out of 16 public order offenses, only 2 exhibited the hypothesized increase. There was an increase in the frequency of arrests for violent offenses among the mental health system "reject" sample, but the significance of the increase could not be tested. This study, like most preceding studies, found some increase in arrests, but not in every crime category or in large measure.

Arrest rates, even in combination with readmission rates, may well be an inadequate criterion in determining the potential for violent behavior among released mental patients. A sample of 35 New York City police officers attending John Jay College of Criminal Justice responded to a questionnaire that presented four hypothetical situations in which an individual was described as engaged in assaultive behavior (which, though a simple assault, was a felony by definition) while also engaging in bizarre behavior (such as screaming meaningless phrases) that was indicative of mental abnormality. The respondents were asked how they, as police officers, would actually handle and dispose of these incidents. In two of the cases, the assailant was described as a released mental patient; in the other two cases, this specific identification was not made. More than half of the sample (51.4%) indicated that they would bring all four cases to the emergency room of a local hospital with a psychiatric unit. A third of the respondents indicated that they would attempt to calm the individual and then release him. Only three officers identified arrest as the appropriate method of disposition in any of the four cases, and only one officer would have made an arrest in all four cases. Several respondents commented on the questionnaire form that bringing "mentals" to the emergency room was standard procedure, even for the hypothetical case in which the individual attempted to assault the police officers and had to be physically subdued by them. There were no significant differences between the officers' responses to those cases specifically identified as released mental patients and to those not so identified.

If these results are representative (and obviously the small and localized nature of the sample is a limitation of this survey), we may be better able to understand the relatively small differences between the arrest rates of the general population and those of released mental patients. Part of the explanation may lie in the sizeable proportion of elderly people among released mental hospital patients, a group less likely to be engaged in public disorder or violence. The heuristic value of the survey lies in the implication that arrest rates for released mental patients are low because policemen are reluctant to initiate arrests where the possibilities of trial and conviction are minimal. If so, research on comparative arrest rates is of limited relevance, and the appropriate criterion (although more difficult to accumulate and measure) would be total recorded police contacts with released mental patients, particularly including those that result in transient referral to hospital emergency rooms or to psychiatric facilities although not in commitments.

Bauer (1970) has called mental illness and criminality "two sides of the same coin."[3] Their commonality is in the suspicion or judgment of dangerousness in antisocial or eccentric behavior. A strongly held and persistent notion of the American public is that the mentally ill are dangerous (Nunally, 1961;[29] Steadman and Coceozza, 1978[43]).

The prevention of violence—to self and to others—is a common responsibility of the two systems, a responsibility that has been difficult to fulfill (Koerin, 1978).[25] The problem lies in the prediction of violent behavior. While psychiatric and psychological diagnosis can predict violence at a better than chance ratio, overprediction is still highly prevalent. This means that for every accurate prediction of violence, there will be many inaccurate predictions of violence, or false positives. Ironically, social pressure tends toward even less accurate prediction, because society is much more concerned about the prediction that a given individual will *not* behave in violent fashion when, in fact, he will (false negatives). Thus, a single instance of a discharged or released patient committing a violent crime invariably raises a hue and cry that release procedures be tightened, that screening be stricter, that any remote clue suggesting the possibility of future violence become presumptive evidence that the individual continue to be detained or, if that is illegal, at least that he be observed and monitored (Monahan, 1975).[28]

Peszke (1975)[31] contended that the prediction of dangerousness is not, and should not be, within the competence of medicine, although psychiatrists are competent to judge whether or not the severity of mental illness impairs a patient's competence to make an informed decision. While agreeing to make some of the required judgments, Peszke is unwilling to make the judgments that society most desperately requires, arguing that we simply do not have the knowledge at this time. In a recent article by Saleem Shah (1978) on dangerousness, this point is conceded, in effect, by the conclusion that

> there is abundant evidence to indicate that recidivist offenders account for a disproportionate amount of all crimes leading to arrest . . . if a defendant had five or more arrests prior to the current arrest, the probability of subsequent arrests began to approach certainty . . . defendants that previously committed violent crimes show the highest proportion of rearrests for violent crime.[38]

Dix (1976)[11] reported similar findings for sexual offenders.

It may well be that the most valid and fair prediction of violence or dangerousness at this time is simply an empirical prediction based on past patterns of behavior. Here too, however, all the evidence suggests that we still will be predicting violence for many individuals who will, in fact, not be violent.

Abramson (1972)[1] wrote an article on the criminalization of mentally disordered behavior in which he predicted that the deinstitutionalization of mental patients would lead to placing the care of the mentally ill ultimately in the hands of the police. Monahan (1973)[27] responded with an article entitled "The Psychiatrization of Criminal Behavior" in which he identified the problem as centering on the mentally abnormal offender, who by definition qualifies for entrance into both systems, which leads to each system asserting priority for controlling and correcting him.

Since these predictions were made, it appears that something else has taken place. Rather than a struggle for priority in meeting the needs of society in dealing with mentally abnormal offenders, even those who are potentially dangerous, the struggle has been to refer or divert these individuals elsewhere. The mental health system has engaged in a massive deinstitutionalization of hospital populations without building up adequate community care programs and facilities. The criminal justice system, during the same period, has concentrated on diversion and "community correctional" programs as its court and correctional facilities have become swamped with record numbers of offenders.

This has resulted in informal dispositions made mostly by the police and, sometimes, by prosecutors—referrals that result neither in arrests nor in readmissions. Referrals consist of emergency programs of medication that enable the individual, through sedation, to exert temporary control over his behavior. The contact is a transient one, designed to alleviate the problem briefly; it is a "band-aid" approach. This major interface of the criminal justice and mental health systems is, in fact, one of the sore points of our society. Thus, the estimated 5 to 10% of those apprehended and accused of index crimes (homicide, aggravated assault, rape, and robbery) who are given mental health examinations in order to advise the court about their potential for dangerous behavior really may be only a small proportion of those who actually demonstrate both violent behavior and mental instability (Rubin, 1972).[36]

Obviously, there are other, more positive, interfaces of these two comprehensive service and care systems. The police provide some needed direct mental health services to citizens in their street contacts with them. In many police departments, mental health professionals provide counseling and other mental health services to police officers themselves. Within the juvenile justice system, the treatment model is so prevalent that the principal objective of juvenile courts has been identified as amelioration, if not therapy. Mental health services in corrections, probation, and parole facilities are an intrinsic part of these agencies of criminal justice. Even the most backward states have correctional institutions for the criminally insane—usually those who have committed heinous crimes and show unmistakable evidence of a potential for violence.

A pragmatic overview of the two systems suggests that as the mental health system has been contracting (despite its objective of expanded community care), the criminal justice system has been expanding; this is best demonstrated in growing prison populations. Both systems have been forced by legal challenge to evaluate and monitor the specific formal services rendered to their clientele, particularly when that service is identified as treatment. When these evaluations focus on outcomes in the treatment of mentally abnormal offenders, the conclusion must be that neither system is currently effective in preventing the recurrence of the behavior that brought the individual into the system. We are as far short of "cures" as we are of rehabilitation. Even our definitions and delineations are still inadequate, for in the area of antisocial behavior, we hold widely varying views about what is criminal and what is mental disability. We may agree that some criminals are not insane and that some of the insane are not criminal; but for the great mass of those whose behavior defies simple classification, we have no established way of coping with them or helping them, and are instead shunting them between systems.

REFERENCES

1. ABRAMSON, M. 1972. The criminalization of mentally disordered behavior: possible side effect of a new mental health law. Hosp. Community Psychiatry 23(April): 101–105.
2. BANTON, M. 1964. The Policeman in the Community. Basic Books. New York, N.Y.
3. BAUER, W. 1970. The other side of the coin. Ill. Med. J. 137(February): 158–161.
4. BITTNER, E. 1967. Police discretion of emergency apprehension of mentally ill persons. Social Problems 14: 278–292.
5. BITTNER, E. 1968. The concept of mental abnormality in the administration of justice outside the courtroom. In The Mentally Abnormal Offender. A. de Reuck & R. Porter, Eds.: 201–219. J & A Churchill. London, England.
6. BLEICHER, B. K. 1967. Cleveland-Marshall Law Rev. 16: 93–115.
7. BRILL, H. & B. MALZBERG. 1954. Statistical Report on the Arrest Record of Male ExPatients, Age 16 or Over, Released from New York State Mental Hospitals during the Period 1946–48. American Psychiatric Association–Mental Hospital Service Supplementary Mailing 153, August 1962. New York State Department of Mental Hygiene. Albany, N.Y.
8. COCOZZA, J., M. MELICK & H. J. STEADMAN. 1978. Trends in violent crime among exmental patients. Criminology 16(3): 317–335.
9. COHEN, L. H. & H. FREEMAN. 1945. How dangerous to the community are state hospital patients? Conn. State Med. J. 9(September): 697–700.
10. CURRAN, W. J. 1975. The right to psychiatric treatment: a simple decision in the Supreme Court. N. Eng. J. Med. 293/10: 487–488.
11. DIX, G. E. 1976. Differential processing of abnormal sex offenders: utilization of California's mentally disordered sex offender program. J. Crim. Law Criminol. 67(2): 233–243.
12. DURBIN, J. R., R. A. PASEWARK & D. ALBERS. 1977. Criminality and mental illness: a study of arrest rates in a rural state. Am. J. Psychiatry 134(January): 80–83.
13. EULE, J. M. 1978. The presumption of sanity: bursting the bubble. UCLA Law Rev. 25(4): 637–699.
14. FLEMING, S. 1978. Interface of the Mental Health and Criminal Justice Systems—An Examination of Pennsylvania's Mental Health Procedures Act of 1976. Document No. 78-NI-AX-002. U.S. Department of Justice, LEAA. Washington, D.C.
15. GIOVANNONI, J. M. & L. GURER. 1967. Socially disruptive behavior of ex-mental patients. Arch. Gen. Psychiatry 20(May): 583–591.
16. GOFFMAN, E. 1961. Asylums. Doubleday & Co., Inc. New York, N.Y.
17. GOFFMAN, E. 1963. Stigma. Prentice-Hall, Inc. Englewood Cliffs, N.J.
18. GOLDSTEIN, A. S. 1967. The Insanity Defense. Yale University Press. New York and London.
19. GOLDSTEIN, A. S. 1968. The mentally disordered offender and the criminal law. In The Mentally Abnormal Offender. A. de Reuck & R. Porter, Eds.: 188–201. J & A Churchill. London, England.
20. GOLDSTEIN, J. 1960. Yale Law J. 69: 543–594.
21. GROETH, R. 1977. Overt dangerous behavior as a constitutional requirement for involuntary civil commitment of the mentally ill. Univ. Chicago Law Rev. 44(3): 562–593.
22. GUZE, S. B., D. W. GOODWIN & J. B. CRANE. 1969. Criminal recidivism and psychiatric illness. Arch. Gen. Psychiatry 20(May): 583–591.
23. HALLECK, S. L. 1967. Psychiatry and the Dilemmas of Crime. Harper & Row, Publishers. New York, N.Y.
24. LaFAVE, W. R. 1965. Arrest: The Decision to Take a Suspect into Custody. Little, Brown and Co. Boston, Mass.
25. KOERIN, B. 1978. Violent crime, prevention and control. Crime and Delinquency 24(1): 49–58.
26. MILLER, H. L. 1977. The right to treatment: Can the courts rehabilitate and cure? The Public Interest 46(winter): 96–118.
27. MONAHAN, J. 1973. The psychiatrization of criminal behavior. Hosp. Community Psychiatry 24(February): 105–107.

28. MONAHAN, J. 1975. The prediction of violence. *In* Violence and Criminal Justice. D. Chappel & J. Monahan, Eds. D.C. Heath and Co. Lexington, Mass.
29. NUNALLY, J. D., JR. 1961. Popular Conceptions of Mental Health. Holt, Rinehart & Winston, Inc. New York, N.Y.
30. PAULL, D. & A. A. MALEK. 1974. Psychiatric disorders and criminality. J. Am. Med. Assoc. **228**(June 10): 1369.
31. PESZKE, M. A. 1975. Is dangerousness an issue for physicians in emergency commitment? Am. J. Psychiatry **132/8:** 825–828.
32. QUINSEY, V. C. 1975. Released Oak Ridge patients: a follow-up study of review board discharges. Br. J. Criminol. **45**(3): 264–270.
33. RAPPEPORT, J. R. & G. LASSEN. 1966. The dangerousness of female patients: a comparison of the arrest rate of discharged psychiatric patients and the general population. Am. J. Psychiatry **123**(October): 413–419.
34. ROESCH, R. & S. L. GOLDING. 1977. A Systems Analysis of Competency to Stand Trial Procedures. Department of Psychology. University of Illinois. Urbana, Ill.
35. ROESCH, R. & S. L. GOLDING. 1978. Legal and judicial interpretation of competency to stand trial statutes and procedures. Criminology **16**(3): 420–429.
36. RUBIN, B. 1972. The prediction of dangerousness in mentally ill criminals. Arch. Gen. Psychiatry **77**(September): 397–407.
37. SCHEFF, T. J. 1966. Being Mentally Ill: A Sociological Theory. Aldine. Chicago, Ill.
38. SHAH, S. A. 1978. Dangerousness: a paradigm for exploring some issues in law and psychology. Am. Psychol. **33**(3): 224–239.
39. SMITH, A. B. & L. BERLIN. 1974. Treating the Criminal Offender. Oceana Publications. Dobbs Ferry, N.Y.
40. SZASZ, T. 1961. The Myth of Mental Illness. Harper and Row, Publishers. New York, N.Y.
41. SZASZ, T. 1963. Law, Liberty and Psychiatry. Macmillan Co. New York, N.Y.
42. SZASZ, T. 1965. Psychiatric Justice. Macmillan Co. New York, N.Y.
43. STEADMAN, N. J. & J. J. COCEOZZA. 1978. Selective reporting and the public's misconceptions of the criminally insane. Public Opinion Q. **41**(winter): 523–531.
44. ZITRIN, A., A. S. HARDESTY, E. I. BURDOCK & A. K. DROSAMAN. 1976. Crime and Violence among mental patients. Am. J. Psychiatry **133**(February): 142–149.

PSYCHIATRY ON TRIAL: CLINICAL AND ETHICAL PROBLEMS IN THE PSYCHIATRIC ASSESSMENT OF COMPETENCY TO STAND TRIAL

Henry C. Weinstein

New York University Schools of Medicine and Law
New York, New York 10016

My comments this morning are from a clinical perspective. After a decade of clinical experience, during which I have evaluated thousands of patients as to their competency to stand trial, I find the practice of forensic psychiatry to be a minefield of clinical and ethical problems and conflicts. In my opinion, these clinical and ethical problems and conflicts are so glaring and unacceptable that they cry out for immediate attention and correction. If not, I am afraid that psychiatry will be most harshly judged. This is what I mean by "psychiatry on trial."

The clinical problems are of two sorts. There are the clinical problems that are of general concern in psychiatry—diagnostic reliability and validity, for example. Then there are clinical problems that are specific to the forensic psychiatrist, resulting from the need to apply the findings of the clinical examination to the relevant legal criteria. There are, in addition, special ethical problems, which are ofttimes related to questions of divided professional loyalty or responsibility.

I shall start by making some preliminary remarks about the competency to stand trial process. While competency to stand trial is only one of numerous situations (28 by one count)[1] where a psychiatrist is called to testify in a judicial proceeding in regard to an individual's competency, it is, in my opinion, the most critical interface of psychiatry and the law. This, because it involves the criminal law with its potentially harsh penalties, including the deprivation of liberty, and because it is carried out many times more frequently than the other major criminal law evaluation—that of the insanity defense. As a corollary, many more defendants are involuntarily confined to psychiatric facilities on the basis of questions of incompetency to stand trial than on the basis of having been found not guilty by reason of insanity.

The importance of this issue is highlighted by a consideration of its fundamental rationale. As Stone notes:

> Historically, the legal notion of competency has been thought to serve both ritual and justice. The requirement that the criminal defendant be able to understand the proceedings and aid in his defense flowed from the view that the entering of a plea at trial invoked the judgment of God, sustained the adversarial nature of the court, and aided the discovery of truth.[2]

More specifically, Stone notes that the determination of competency to stand trial serves the following needs of the legal system:

> Guaranteeing the accuracy of the criminal proceedings, especially where competent

12

accused might provide his counsel with crucial facts known only to the accused . . . .

Guaranteeing the fairness of the trial. There is an ineffable sense in which it has long been felt that an accused has not been fairly convicted, no matter what the extrinsic evidence, unless he is able to understand the nature of the proceedings and the basic defense options and consequences . . . .

Maximizing the efficacy of punishment, both in terms of individual deterrence and attributive catharsis of the rest of society.[2]

Before I turn to specific clinical and ethical problems, I'd like to briefly examine the role of the forensic psychiatrist in the competency to stand trial procedure. In our fellowship training program (in psychiatry and the law) at New York University, we use what we call "the fourfold analysis" of forensic psychiatric questions. This analysis can be utilized to clarify the role of the forensic expert witness in any such situation.

The first part of the analysis is the determination of what is the particular legal issue. The legal issue is a yes-or-no question that is required by the legal situation—a legal question. We are dealing here with the legal issue of competency to stand trial. Is the defendant competent to stand trial or not? The ultimate decision, of course, is made by a judge or jury.

The second step of the forensic psychiatric analysis is the determination of the specific legal criteria that are required to resolve the legal issue. The particular legal criteria are set out in statutes, regulations, or case law. It is important to note that the criteria are *legal* criteria—which in turn are used to resolve the legal issue.

The third aspect of this analysis is the clinical examination of the defendant. This is best done by an expert who is familiar with the legal criteria, because the fourth and final part of the analysis is the application of the findings of the clinical examination to the legal criteria. To put it another way, this fourth step involves a determination of whether the specific legal criteria are or are not met by the clinical findings, i.e., whether there is a *causal relationship* between the findings of the clinical examination and the legal criteria. Obviously, the role of the forensic expert is most importantly related to this last aspect of the evaluation, for it is the forensic expert who—cognizant of the legal issue and the legal criteria—applies the specific clinical findings to those legal criteria.

Turning now to some general problems in the psychiatric assessment of competency to stand trial, let us start with this last-mentioned task of applying the clinical findings to the legal criteria. As is always the case, the criteria are stated in legal terms, not medical, psychiatric, or psychological terms. The legal criteria where competency to stand trial is at issue are generally stated as whether the defendant understands the charges against him and whether he can assist in the defense. This brief statement of the criteria was elaborated somewhat by the U.S. Supreme Court in the *Dusky* case, where the criteria are stated as "whether he [the defendant] has sufficient present ability to consult with his lawyer with a reasonable degree of rational understanding, and whether he has a rational as well as factual understanding of the proceedings against him."[3] However, even this somewhat expanded set of criteria does not significantly assist the forensic expert in the complex task of applying the clinical findings to these criteria. How does one move from a specific set of clinical findings to such concepts as "reasonable degree" of "rational understanding," or "a rational as well as factual understanding of the proceedings"?

As an example, let us start with disorders of mood. At what point does a depression or a mania become so severe that a patient is no longer competent to stand trial? At the forensic psychiatric services of the Bellevue Psychiatric Hospital, many patients are referred following a suicide attempt. That a patient might be depressed in the circumstances during which he is assessed for competency would not be surprising. On the other hand, most would agree that an acutely and severely depressed defendant (so depressed that he is suicidal) would hardly be able to adequately participate in his trial and assist in his defense. But, must the patient be actively and unquestionably suicidal to be incompetent to stand trial? At what point on the depression continuum is this particular line to be drawn? To come to an opinion and present this opinion clearly and understandably to the court is the responsibility of the forensic expert.

Similarly, when a defendant is manic, when is he so manic that he is incompetent to stand trial?[4] As with the depressed patient, it is not the adequacy of the defendant's cognitive functions that is at issue, but the effect of his affective disorganization. These issues of clinical judgment are made even more difficult and complicated by the fact that, in reality (as will be elaborated below), the expert's opinion on competency to stand trial is a prediction of how the defendant will be at a trial.

What of disorders of *thinking*? For example, what of a patient who is delusional? It is difficult enough to determine when a particular belief is a "delusion," but to attempt to decide whether the particular delusion itself (not the mere presence of the delusion) affects the patient's understanding of the charges and his ability to assist in his defense is an almost metaphysical question.

I should note that it was not too long ago that it was generally held that any patient who was actively delusional was, ipso facto, incompetent to stand trial. This was based on the rationale that anyone whose mental functioning was so disordered as to be delusional could not function adequately in the legal process. I believe that forensic experts have become more precise since that time.

I turn now from such general problems of applying clinical data to imprecise and broad legal criteria, to some of the special problems presented to psychiatrists in the competency to stand trial evaluation.

Psychiatrists are often in the position to make "dispositional diagnoses,"[2] i.e., the examiner reaches a particular conclusion and presents to the court a particular opinion in order to achieve a particular result. Most frequently, I have found, this is justified on the basis that it will place the patient into a treatment setting. While some will see this as a subtle misuse of the competency process by psychiatrists, it seems rather to highlight the varied interests served by the psychiatrist in the competency to stand trial procedure.[5] Also note here the interfacing of the criminal justice system with the civil psychiatric hospital system—with the psychiatrist in the role of gatekeeper.

Another special problem presented by the evaluation is the fact that although the competency to stand trial criteria presented (for example by the Supreme Court in the *Dusky* case) are generally related to the defendant's "present ability," it is obvious that—since the clinical examination of the patient usually takes place at a time considerably before the start of the trial—the conclusion arrived at is in reality a prediction of how the defendant will be able to function later—either at his trial or at some other time when he is consulting with his attorney. I need not emphasize to this audience the problems in regard to this type of prediction.

Similarly, the landmark case of *Jackson* v. *Indiana* presents this problem very starkly.[6] This case stands for the proposition that if a defendant cannot, within a reasonable period of time, become competent to stand trial, he must be discharged from the criminal justice system. Thus a prediction must be made.

Still another general clinical problem is that of "fragility." There are defendants who, at the time of the examination, are competent to participate in the judicial process but who cannot, in the opinion of the forensic expert, tolerate the stress and tension of a trial. I would find such a patient not competent to stand trial. Professor Brooks of Rutgers Law School seems to disagree. He states that

> some psychiatrists are prepared to characterize as "incompetent to stand trial" a defendant who is so emotionally disturbed that, in the view of the psychiatrist, if he stands trial, might "decompensate," i.e., become psychotic, or otherwise "breakdown" and become more seriously mentally ill. Is this an accepted grounds for determining the fitness of a defendant to stand trial? If not, should a psychiatrist be permitted to testify to this effect? Many do.[7]

It is somewhat hard for me to understand this position. Surely it is not in the interests of either the defendant or the criminal justice system in general to prematurely return a patient to trial if it means that this will only lead to further delay of his trial. Furthermore, although this is a prediction, psychiatrists are uniquely equipped to evaluate this aspect of competency.

The issue of fragility is closely related to the issue of the foreseeability of improvement in therapy, which is part of the overall issue of the changing clinical picture that a defendant may present. In the first place, the defendant may be undergoing treatment during evaluation, i.e., evaluation in a treatment setting, and may be improving. This in itself is the subject (or at least was until recently) of a serious debate, that is, whether someone could be competent to stand trial at the same time that they were receiving psychotropic medication. A number of years ago, one judge went so far as to label this situation "artificial sanity."

On the other hand, it has been pointed out that many participants in the judicial process use drugs. Hollister, in an article titled "Psychotropic Drugs in Court Competency," noting that "ideally, all parties in criminal litigation should be free of drugs," adds tongue in cheek that

> the world not being ideal, such is seldom the case. The prosecuting attorney may take nicotine during recess by smoking, the defense attorney may take caffeine in a cup. And both of these worthies, as well as the judge, may have been recently exposed to beverages containing ethyl alcohol. A woman juror may have taken a proprietary

medication for relief of her headache that probably contains at least three different painkilling or mood altering drugs. A male juror may have taken a sleeping pill the night before and still have the drug in his circulatory system. If the defendant has been incarcerated prior to his trial, he may be more free of drugs than any of the other participants, or at least the drug history may be better documented.[8]

Nonetheless, there are serious concerns in regard to drug therapy where the defendant is awaiting trial. At one point, even here in New York City, it was felt to be improper to return a patient to trial who required tranquilizing medication. This is no longer the case, and a majority of jurisdictions (if not all) accept the principle that a patient on medication may be held competent to stand trial. What of the use of ECT—shock treatment—to make a patient competent or to hasten the process? What of the informed consent necessary for such treatment?

As if this were not complex enough, I will interject at this point Dr. Stone's comment that

> any defense attorney will recognize that one of the best pieces of evidence for convincing a jury that a person was not responsible for his crime is a defendant who is obviously crazy at the trial. That dramatic impression is blunted by the drugs. The effect of such drugs, when unknown to the jury in its appraisal of the defendant's demeanor, has led to a reversal of a conviction.[2]

I will add an even more serious concern of psychiatrists and lawyers. This is the right of the patient to refuse treatment. I shall not review this complex subject but shall merely ask whether, in light of Stone's comment above, the defendant can refuse treatment—any treatment—or whether, if the patient is not competent to make that decision (notice the accumulating complications), his attorney can act on his behalf and insist on this exercise of this "right." Of course, where it is the patient himself who insists on refusing treatment to protect his "crazy" demeanor before a jury, the question of whether or not he is malingering would be properly raised.

Malingering is another very complicated matter and is a special problem on my unit, where an unusually large proportion of the patients are malingering. The clinical assessment of a patient who is believed to be malingering is itself a highly specialized technique, as is the testimony required to support such an opinion. Malingering often takes the form of a feigned amnesia; a patient says, "I don't remember." It is now established, however, that amnesia in and of itself does not render a patient incompetent to stand trial.[9] It is at this point that some would call for the use of special techniques, such as sodium amytal or hypnosis. Thus, many special ethical problems may be raised for the clinician. For example, how does one satisfy the need for "informed consent" from a patient who is suspected of malingering?

I shall now turn to a series of problems that I have broadly labeled "legal problems." There are those who argue that there is no need for professional assessment of the issue of competency to stand trial, that this can be settled on a common sense basis by the judge or the jury. Others say that the best individual to assess competency to stand trial is the defendant's lawyer.[1] One of the many problems with the latter suggestion is that the lawyer, himself an officer of the court, may have tactical interests in regard to the issue of competency to stand trial. Not only the defendant's lawyer, but the prosecuting attorney and occasionally the judge also may use the competency to stand trial issue for tactical purposes, or for purposes of disposition, plea bargaining, etc., rather than to settle the issue of competency itself.

I also list under "legal problems" the misuse of the psychiatric report. We find ourselves unable to protect the confidentiality of the report, and find the information in our reports on competency being used for various purposes at the trial itself. Our New York State statute specifically prohibits this, but research has shown how these reports are misused in this manner.[10]

A well-known problem is the "battle of the experts," where each side "shops around" for a "well-qualified" professional's opinion that will support its particular perception of the facts. Not only do lawyers shop around, but many judges do also—having formed their own opinion as to competency (but for some reason being unwilling to assert it), they send the patient to various court clinics and inpatient facilities until they receive an opinion consistent with their own.

Another troublesome legal problem is the use of the competency to stand trial question for reasons of preventive detention, where under the guise of an unsettled legal issue (the competency question), a patient is kept in detention because he is felt to be too "dangerous" to be at large in the community.

What of the situation where the findings by "impartial" experts are unsatisfactory to the defendant, and he cannot afford to hire an independent expert? The Legal Aid Society, which represents many of our indigent patients at Bellevue, has very limited funds for these purposes. Corrective legislation is being proposed in many jurisdictions.

I can only briefly mention some of the sociological issues related to the assessment of competency to stand trial, such as the effects of class, racial, or cultural differences between the evaluating doctor and the patient, or for that matter between the judge and the patient, or the lawyer and the patient. Some defendants are very sensitive to the matter of labeling and stigma; some would rather be convicted of a crime than categorized as mentally ill. Indeed, some of these patients attempt to "malinger" mental health: "There's nothing wrong with me. I don't belong here."

What of the misuse of psychiatric evaluation by a government? We castigate the Soviet Union in this regard, since it appears that the misuse of psychiatry in the Soviet Union is quite flagrant. There, dissidents are detained and, for all intents and purposes, silenced by means of various psychiatric procedures and incarcerations. Are there misuses of psychiatry for political purposes in the United States? If so, they rarely involve the competency to stand trial issue. One notorious case was that of Ezra Pound, who, following World War II, was incarcerated in St. Elizabeth's Hospital for many years on the grounds that he was incompetent to stand trial for treason. Thomas Szasz argues very powerfully that this was a "political" misuse of psychiatry.[11]

I will list under political problems the need for self-regulation by the profession to insure adequate training and qualification of experts. For example, I regret to say that I am familiar with a number of "experts" whose work belies their narcissism, egocentricity, grandiosity, and lack of self-control, rather than their clinical skills. As a "political" matter, I wonder how long society will permit the profession to tolerate or ignore such matters.

In the brief time remaining, I shall turn to some ethical issues that concern me in regard to the competency to stand trial procedure. One is the "double agent" conflict,[5] which refers to the fact that in certain situations or settings, there may arise conflict between the psychiatrist's role as an evaluator for the government and his role as a physician for the defendant-patient. This is most serious where the competency to stand trial assessment is made in a "treatment setting."

Similar issues arise in regard to confidentiality. The forensic psychiatrist must take precautions to ensure that the defendant is aware of his, the psychiatrist's, role and responsibilities, i.e., that there is no physician-patient privilege and that the psychiatrist will prepare a report for the court. On the other hand, I believe it is incumbent on the psychiatrist to take every precaution to ensure that the report does not include any material that is not strictly necessary for the purposes of the report and that might be adverse to the interests of the defendant.

Karl Menninger has argued that legal issues such as competency to stand trial involve *moral* questions and judgments in which psychiatrists have no particular expertise and, therefore, that psychiatrists should remove themselves entirely from any participation in the legal process.[12] Still others have suggested that the competency to stand trial procedure is so inherently unfair and unjust that it should be abolished entirely.[7] I cannot agree, for I believe that the law seeks the counsel of the behavioral scientist for good reason in these matters. I believe that with proper precautions, reforms, and changes, many of the clinical and ethical problems that I have cited may be obviated.

There are specific legal reforms that are being attempted. The case of *Jackson* v. *Indiana* and recent legislation in some jurisdictions seek to prevent long criminal incarcerations where a patient is not competent to stand trial. Procedural reforms are being instituted to allow a patient to plead the insanity defense even if he is *not* competent to stand trial.[13]

I believe there are a number of ways in which we psychiatrists who participate in this process can contribute to the resolution of some of these problems. First, as for the clinical problems, the clinician must not only be careful and precise in his application of his clinical data to the legal criteria, but most important of all, must present his reasoning to the court—in his report and his testimony—in a clear and coherent fashion.

Second, we must insure that those who participate in the process of assessment of competency to stand trial are made aware of the clinical, legal, social, ethical, and philosophical issues by means of continuing medical education and in-service education. We have done this on my unit by instituting a weekly seminar for our staff titled "Philosophical and Ethical Issues in the Practice of Forensic Psychiatry." This is led jointly by myself and a Ph.D philosopher. This program recently gained support from the Counsel on the Humanities for a "philosopher in residence" to participate in and to run programs not only for the psychiatric staff, but for the Department of Correction, nursing, and other staffs as well.

Third, it may be necessary to separate the evaluation and the treatment functions of the psychiatrist. I believe this is possible even under the most difficult of circumstances.

Fourth, I think that the judicious use of various instruments that have been developed can be helpful.[13] These instruments cannot replace a good clinical judgment or the skill of the forensic expert, but they certainly can help to organize the clinical evaluation as well as the presentation of the material to the court.

Fifth, we must increase research in these areas. We need larger data bases in regard to these patients. We need further tests of the validity and reliability of our clinical evaluations. We need feedback in regard to the results of our evaluations.

Sixth, we need increased training for experts (both psychiatric and psychological) as to their special roles and responsibilities in the legal process. In this regard, I am glad to see the establishment of boards of certification—both psychiatric and psychological—in regard to forensic matters.

Finally, we need more communication between all of those who participate in this process—communication, for example, between psychiatrists and psychologists. This conference goes a long way in regard to providing such increased communication.

REFERENCES

1. SLOVENKO, R. 1973. Psychiatry and Law: 107, 94. Little Brown & Co. Boston, Mass.
2. STONE, A. A. 1975. Mental Health and Law: A System in Transition: 203–213. National Institute of Mental Health. Bethesda, Md.
3. Dusky v. United States, 362 U.S. 402 (1960).
4. Cf., Faber v. Sweet Style Manufacturing Corp., 40 Misc. 2d 212, 242 N.Y.S. 2d 763 (1963).
5. Hastings Center. 1978. In the Service of the State: The Psychiatrist as Double Agent. Hastings Center Report, Special Supplement. New York, N.Y.
6. Jackson v. Indiana, 406 U.S. 736 (1972).
7. BROOKS, A. 1974. Psychiatry and the Mental Health System: 363, 383. Little, Brown & Co. Boston, Mass.
8. HOLLISTER, L. E. 1972. Psychotropic drugs and court competence. In Law, Psychiatry and the Mentally Disordered Offender. L. M. Irvine & T. B. Brelje, Eds.: 14. Charles C. Thomas. Springfield, Ill.
9. KOSON, D. & A. ROBEY. 1973. Amnesia and competency to stand trial. Am. J. Psychiatry 130: 558.
10. Note: 1976. Protecting the confidentiality of pretrial psychiatric disclosures: a survey of standards. N.Y.U. Law Rev. 51: 409.
11. SZASZ, T. S. 1963. Law, Liberty and Psychiatry. Macmillan Co. New York, N.Y.
12. MENNINGER, K. 1966. The Crime of Punishment: 139. Viking Press, Inc. New York, N.Y.
13. Laboratory of Community Psychiatry, Harvard Medical School. 1973. Competency to Stand Trial and Mental Illness. U.S. Government Printing Office. Washington, D. C.

DIAGNOSIS VERSUS DESCRIPTION IN COMPETENCY ISSUES

John E. Exner, Jr.

Department of Psychology
Long Island University
Brooklyn, New York 11201

Most psychologists and psychiatrists would probably agree that the intent of laws pertaining to the issue of competency seems "clear enough." On the surface, the criteria for competency appear to broach the basic question of cognitive functioning or, more precisely, the extent to which cognitive functioning is "minimally adequate" in the areas of word knowledge, recent and remote memory, perceptual accuracy or reality testing, abstraction, and judgment as it is applied to both the personal and social spheres. These laws, derived from English common law, seem to be designed to insure that a defendant has the capacity to defend himself or herself in the court of law. They hold, in effect, that the subject must possess the ability to cooperate in the formulation of his or her defense, that he or she has an awareness and understanding of the nature and objectives of the legal proceedings, and that the subject has an understanding of the potential consequences of the proceedings.

Translated into the context of psychological functioning, these criteria imply some specific minimal level of intellectual functioning, which becomes the basis from which the contents of a stimulus field are received and processed fairly accurately; and that processing is, in turn, translated in such a way as to make decision actions commensurate with the purpose and nature of the legal procedure. It seems logical, then, to assume that this issue of competency would be most relevant in cases where questions of intellectual disability, or "retardation," occur. Surprisingly, however, the bulk of statutes regarding the issue of competency and a clear majority of cases in which the question has been raised focus on the relevant, but often misleading, issue of "mental illness" as the base from which decisions of competency or incompetency will be derived. The mental illness question typically becomes misleading in that courts, counsels, and expert witnesses are often prone to confuse the issue of competency with the very separate and quite different criteria for criminal responsibility.

Competency involves awareness, participation, and understanding, all of which require some intellectual/cognitive operations. This is not, however, to suggest that evaluations of competency should be reduced to some simplistic measure of intelligence, even if there were such a measure available that was uniformly agreed to by the psychological community and found to be acceptable and legitimate by the legal profession. In other words, the issue of competency cannot be settled by an IQ, yet it would be foolhardy to discard standard intelligence tests from among the various techniques employed in the quest for competency answers. Similarly, it would be foolhardy to discard or disavow the issue of mental illness or psychological disability as relevant to this question. But just as the IQ does not contribute significantly to the solution, neither does the assignment of some psychiatric or psychological label. Such an error is most common among the psychiatric, psychological, and legal communities when the term "schizophrenia" is bandied about. Unfortunately, many people, both lay and professional, tend to equate the diagnosis of schizophrenia with some perpetual state of psychosis that reduces a person's level of functioning to that of legal incompetence. Such a conclusion is, at best, an incompetent fantasy or, worse, a severe distortion of reality. It is quite true that during most "psychotic episodes," the subject of that episode is legally incompetent, just as is the epileptic during or immediately after a seizure, or the alcoholic in a drunken stupor. However, not unlike the epileptic seizure or the alcoholic stupor, the disability created by the psychotic state is usually transient, rarely lasting longer than a few hours or a few days except in those instances of the protracted case that involves organic origins or features. Unfortunately, the professional and lay communities typically devote their attention to the schizophrenic who is psychotic, who requires hospitalization, and who is truly disabled. Little attention has been given to the great majority of schizophrenics who are not psychotic, who are not disabled, and who do not require hospitalization. The fact of the matter is that significant numbers of schizophrenics carry on very productive lives—functioning in most every conceivable occupation, including medicine, psychology, and the law—in spite of the limitations that their condition or "illness" imposes upon them. This is not to suggest that all schizophrenics are legally competent. Some schizophrenics are aware, can participate, and do understand. Others cannot and/or do not.

In the same vein, some subjects with a derived IQ of 65 can and do function quite effectively within specific parameters. It is impossible to work with an intellectually "limited" population without encountering the person who adapts to a regular occupational role, saves money, buys clothes, wends his or her way effectively through the chaos of the mass transit system, recites batting line-ups and home-run records, differentiates "rock" from "disco," a "hook" from a "dunk," and a "safety squeeze" from a "sacrifice." This is not to suggest that all intellectually handicapped people are legally competent; but some are very aware, can participate, and do understand. Others cannot and/or do not.

Obviously, any legitimate evaluation for competency will go well beyond the derivation of some number on an ordinal scale that purports to measure intelligence, or some diagnostic category, often agreed to by consensus, that implies a "simple" yes-or-no answer regarding competency. But the obvious is not always achieved with ease. There are several problems involved in bringing a competency issue to closure. Not the least of these is the vagueness and ambiguity of the law itself. Although it is formulated with the best intent, the term used—competency—is much more legal than psychological. Thus, while seemingly designed to focus on intellectual issues, the actual criteria contained in most statutes clearly open the door to the mental illness issue and, more important, permit dialogue pertaining to "degrees" of competence. The latter are often raised when the magnitude of the purported offense is greater. And this issue cannot be brushed aside by using the parallel of "being a little bit pregnant," for there are indeed degrees of competency, which do vary with circumstances. Consequently, any evaluation for competency must include sufficient data from which questions of psychological disability and degrees of competency may be addressed.

Fortunately, there exists a wide array of assessment techniques that can be drawn upon for the task; and the task remains one of assessing cognitive operations. Under optimal circumstances, the assessment approach will include techniques that will insure that the yield of information is valid. To accomplish this goal, it may well be necessary to generate data from multiple sources that are relevant to the same cognitive issue. For instance, if a subject seems unable to recall a brief sequence of digits (as required in most standardized intelligence tests that are administered individually), it would be vitally important to glean more data from other sources from which the functioning of immediate memory could be viewed more thoroughly. Similarly, where subjects manifest evidence of weak or inadequate judgment in response to standardized test items, such as those contained in the comprehension subtest of the various Wechsler scales, other approaches to the study of the logic of the decision process must be included in the assessment routine. This "call" for cross-validation of data may be overly conservative and more time consuming than is preferred, but it is very important to retain an awareness that *if* a subject is determined to be incompetent, he or she is in jeopardy of being denied due process as guaranteed by the Sixth and Fourteenth Amendments. It may be even more important to recognize that the subject who is found to be incompetent may be placed in a facility that is alien and discomforting for an indeterminate period, after which the subject runs the risk of facing the very legal procedure for which he or she deemed to be incompetent to participate in originally. Thus, it behooves us to proceed carefully toward the goal of providing a thorough and valid description of cognitive functioning in all respects.

The major issues to be addressed in a competency evaluation may overlap with, but are not necessarily identical to, those elements addressed in more routine kinds of psychological assessment oriented toward clinical issues. Again, the focus is on cognitive functioning, and the more important aspects of that functioning will concern higher center operations, such as concept formation, decision processes, abstract and social judgment, reality testing or perceptual accuracy, and the extent to which any or all of these are inhibited or altered by emotional input. Thus, while matters of attention and concentration, immediate and remote memory, and the perception of details may be relevant to any final determination of competency, they are far less important to the three criteria specified in the statutes than are the higher center operations.

The description of the cognitive operations should build from the data much like a "logic tree," that is, proceeding from induction to deduction at each point. Thus, if A is true proceed to B, but if A is not true or, more commonly, if A is questionable, then proceed to descriptive subsections concerning A. Probably the best overall starting point will concern perceptual accuracy, or reality testing. This is relatively easy to assess in that it involves accurate, or reasonably accurate, contour identification. Marked distortions in reality testing typically occur only in instances of severe intellectual limitation, of organic deterioration, or of active psychotic states that may be functional or organic in nature. But even the person who is quite deficient intellectually, or the schizophrenic who is not psychotic, can and does function in reasonably adaptive ways in this area.

Possibly the second most important area in creating the descriptive "logic tree" concerns the clarity of thinking. Unlike the issue of reality testing, this is a much more difficult function to assess, as it is multifaceted. For instance, it is not at all uncommon for the subject of a competency evaluation to claim some form of amnesia for the events in question. Unfortunately, amnesia, or the report of amnesia, can arise from any of a variety of cognitive circumstances. It can occur as a result of severe intellectual deficiency; or it can occur as a result of severe distortions in thinking. Either of those could be produced by organic factors, such as cerebral trauma, senile dementia, acute or chronic toxicity, a Korsakoff syndrome, etc. However, it is also clear that when amnesia is provoked by most organic conditions, some process of confabulation, or memory substitution, occurs. Thus, the ruling out or "ruling in" of the organic possibility becomes an important step in the assessment process as it focuses on the issue of the reported amnesia. Similarly, it is not uncommon for a subject about to be evaluated for competence to present an initial picture of perplexed bewilderment, an impoverishment of ideas, a seeming disturbance of associational processes, and a disorientation for time and place. As with amnesia, such a picture can be produced by toxicity, cerebral trauma, infection, organic decay, or by any of the functional psychoses, or in a situation of very severe intellectual deficiency. It would seem simple to suggest that where such an initial picture is present, the "call" of incompetence is warranted. However, many psychological states can be disruptive to the point of creating this form of detachment and disorientation. Severe anxiety states and marked depressions are especially noted for provoking such behavioral pictures for brief periods. Obviously then, it becomes important to track down the origins of the disorientation and also obtain information concerning the permanence or probable duration of the state. Decisions about competency will probably be quite different if a state of behavioral confusion is provoked by intense anxiety, rather than being an integral part of a chronic illness that produces a major deterioration effect to some of the more important cognitive functions. It is important to note here that, as the clarity or coherence of thinking is evaluated, it is critical to avoid overgeneralizations based on unusual thinking patterns. For example, a subject may produce considerable evidence for a valid conclusion that a well-systematized delusional framework is present. But this does not automatically equate with a decision of incompetence. Some delusional operations do interfere with decision processes to the extent that understanding of charges, cooperation with counsel, and/or understanding of the consequences of proceedings is impossible, while other delusional operations may only interfere with areas of functioning that are not relevant to any of the three criteria of the statutes. It is both impractical and unrealistic to describe inappropriate ideational impulse controls without also specifying those areas of ideation that are particularly vulnerable to the control failure.

This same proposition is applicable to descriptive statements concerning the control and display of emotion. Emotion can and does affect memory, attention, stimulus processing, and decision making. It can have a substantial impact on judgment formulations; but this does not necessarily mean that when the control of emotional impulses is inadequate, the product would be so all pervasive as to routinely affect the areas relevant to the statute criteria. Conversely, poor impulse control could precipitate forms of psychological turmoil that might render the subject unable to be aware, participate, and/or understand.

The last major segment of the description of cognitive functioning should focus on the higher center operations of abstraction, or concept formation. These are important processes in the context of all three criteria of the statutes, as they contribute significantly to the capacity to synthesize information into meaningful patterns from which decision operations can proceed. Unlike the issues of thinking and emotion, these operations are more easily assessed. They are functions less prone to interference by the various functional disorders and consequently can often be used as a kind of baseline from which to study the decay or interference that has occurred to other cognitive activities.

Once the cognitive description is "in place," it can be addressed with the objective of evaluating the various operations as they relate directly to specific features of the legal process. For instance, Lipsett, Lelos, and McGarry[1] have provided a checklist of elements that are critical in the legal procedures and for which various degrees of competency in the subject should be present. This list includes such items as an awareness of available legal defenses, the ability to relate to an attorney, the appraisal of the various roles of judge, jury, and witnesses, appreciation of the charges, the capacity to disclose pertinent facts to one's own attorney, the capacity to testify relevantly, etc. Checklists such as these provide the questions about competency, while the description of cognitive functioning provides the data pool from which answers to most or all of those questions may be derived.

This procedure of extensive assessment from which a valid description of cognitive functioning is derived is cumbersome and not perfect. But it does afford the greatest form of protection to the subject, compared to more simplistic and less time-consuming approaches. This is not to suggest that efforts to establish screening approaches for competency should be avoided or abandoned, because several—such as that developed by the Harvard group under McGarry[2]—hold out considerable potential. But screening for, and final decisions about, are two different matters. Thus, if routine screening suggests incompetency, then a more comprehensive cognitive evaluation is essential. Even if routine screening does not yield suggestions of incompetency, those suggestions may be forthcoming from other data sources, such as a history, prison behavior, etc. In those instances, the comprehensive evaluation continues to be warranted.

Unfortunately, the statutes regarding competency are no more precise or any less ambiguous than statutes pertaining to issues of sanity, irresistible impulse, or diminished capacity. Until the statutes are revised to a more precise definition of competent, professionals responsible for these sorts of evaluations must take into account the full measure of cognitive operations as they are applicable to the legal procedure. An ever increasing tendency of lawyers to call upon the issue of competency as a strategy viable to their respective cases increases the likelihood of a greater number of false positives and false negatives in those instances where the more simplistic procedures of intellectual and/or diagnostic categorization are permitted.

A review of 112 cases from the data pool of Rorschach Workshops in which the issue of competency was broached by the legal community indicates that in only 4 instances were the subjects declared incompetent. A review of assessment data in those 4 cases—some of which were collected prior to, and some after, the competency hearing—shows that two subjects were severely retarded and obviously the decision in those cases was well founded. In the remaining 2 cases, the decision of incompetency was based mainly on the diagnosis of schizophrenia. However, in the context of the total data bank available concerning those subjects, probably neither was legally incompetent—both could well understand the nature of the charges, both could interact reasonably well with an attorney in the preparation and conduct of their own defense, and both were clearly alert to the outcome.

As an esoteric exercise, we randomly selected 25 cases from the remaining 108 subjects who had been legally deemed competent to stand trial. We employed three clinical psychologists, all diplomates of the American Board of Examiners in Professional Psychology and all with an expertise in assessment procedures. We provided them, independently, with the raw assessment data on each of the 25 subjects, asking them to create a clear professional description of the cognitive functioning for each of the 25 cases and then, using the checklist of Lipsett, Lelos, and McGarry, to identify those areas pertaining to the legal process for which the subject might be deemed incompetent. Our three experts unanimously checked enough of the items positively in 4 cases that there seems to be no question that they were incompetent by legal standards. In 3 other cases, the number of items checked positive was sufficiently large to raise questions about competency at the time of trial. In the remaining 18 cases, there were uniformed negative checks, indicating that the decision of "competent" was appropriate. But the questionable cases comprise more than 20% of a randomly selected sample. The number is frightening! To be sure, the study itself is not a good one because of the lack of controls and in light of the fact that some of the assessment data in each case were collected after the fact, that is, after the hearing had been concluded. But nonetheless, the data are frightening! It is sad to believe that 4, and possibly 7, people were subjected to legal proceedings that they may not have comprehended. It is equally sad to suspect that others may have been denied the right of those proceedings, when they might well have comprehended easily the nature and consequences of those proceedings.

We are often quite critical of our legal colleagues for their adversary approach and, more particularly, for their seemingly distant attitude toward such issues as competency as they may or may not apply to a client. While some of those criticisms are valid, there is no need to reinforce ignorance with our own brand of incompetence. Let us search for the truth and display it in its full splendor. At least if we err, we do so knowing that we offered our best.

REFERENCES

1. LIPSETT, P. D., D. LELOS & A. L. McGARRY. 1971. Competency for trial: a screening instrument. Am. J. Psychiatry **128:** 105–109.
2. McGARRY, A. L., W. J. CURRAN, P. D. LIPSETT *et al.* 1973. Competency to Stand Trial and Mental Illness. DHEW Publication Number 74–103. National Institute of Mental Health. Bethesda, Md.

PSYCHOLOGICAL ASPECTS OF
COURTROOM TESTIMONY*

Elizabeth F. Loftus

Department of Psychology
University of Washington
Seattle, Washington 98195

In December 1978, the case of *U.S.* v. *Marshall* was tried in Seoul, Korea. The case before the court was rape. The elements in the case were the testimony of the victim and a couple of other witnesses, the testimony of the accused, and the testimony of an expert witness on the reliability of eyewitness accounts. The victim, a young black female soldier, claimed that she had been asleep in the barracks when someone entered her room in the middle of the night, physically assaulted her by striking her in the face with his fists and by choking her, and then raped her. She described her assailant as a black male, but, in part due to heavy drinking, she could not identify the defendant as the person who had raped her.

The defendant, on the other hand, gave a completely different version. He admitted that he had had sex with the victim, but claimed he had been invited. Much to his surprise, the victim then demanded $40. He told her he didn't have the money and would pay her some other time. A witness for the prosecution, a young white woman also living in the barracks, claimed that sometime early that morning she woke up and saw a man standing near her bed. She said, "What are you doing in my room?" to which the man replied something like, "Be cool," and then left. About one month later she identified the defendant as the person who had been in her room, and her version of the events supported the prosecution's contention that the defendant was wandering through the barracks looking for someone to rape, rather than the defendant's version that he had been specifically invited by the victim.

The expert testimony in the case concerned the reliability of eyewitness accounts in general and the specific accounts given in this case. It covered such factors as cross-racial identification and the ability to make an accurate identification after a 32- to 33-day interval of time.

After listening to all the evidence and to instructions from the judge, the jurors retired to deliberate. Shortly thereafter, they acquitted Private Marshall.

As the jurors in a trial (or the judge, if the jury has been waived) listen to testimony, they do more than simply take in the questions and answers. While listening, they construct in their minds an "image" of an incident

* Supported by the National Science Foundation, and by the Andrew Mellon Foundation through its support of the Center for Advanced Study in the Behavioral Sciences where the author held a fellowship during 1978 and 1979.

27

that was, of course, never witnessed by any one of them. If the incident is a crime, their image includes something about the sequence of events, who was involved, and how fleeting or frightening was the crime. If the incident is an accident, their image includes something about what happened, how severe was the accident, and who was at fault. Based on these constructed images, the jurors must then reach a verdict. It is important, then, to understand the factors that influence the construction of an incident in the minds of jurors, as a way of understanding their verdicts.

In every trial, there is a cast of characters, each one of which will impact upon the jury's decision. For each character, it is important to consider both the type of testimony that is presented and the way it is presented.

LANGUAGE AND IMAGE CONSTRUCTION

When a crime or accident occurs, a witness to the event may be asked to recall what happened in as precise detail as possible. Recent research indicates that the language used by the interviewer in questioning a witness can strikingly affect the witness' impression of his or her experience. In one experiment, subject witnesses who had seen a film of an automobile accident were asked about the speed of the vehicles, using one of several question formats. "About how fast were the cars going when they smashed into each other?" led to higher estimates of speed than the same question asked with the verb "hit."[1] Furthermore, witnesses who were queried with the verb "smashed" were later more likely to report that they had seen broken glass, an item that had not existed. The particular words in the question had apparently led the witness to develop a "memory" for the accident that was more severe than the accident actually had been.

Whenever a person experiences an event, some memorial representation is constructed. Postevent information, whether embedded in questions or presented in some other way, can become incorporated into the memory, causing an alteration or distortion in that memory.

If postevent information can so easily alter a person's memory for something that was actually witnessed, it is reasonable to expect that one could alter the construction of an event in the mind of a person who never witnessed that event. Jurors, for example, must construct in their minds a crime or accident that was never witnessed, and must then reach a verdict based upon memorial constructions that are formulated from evidence presented to them. Lawyers have known for some time that the language used in the courtroom can create an impression on the jury. In a 1974 grand jury hearing in which Dr. Kenneth Edelin of Boston, Massachusetts, was charged with manslaughter of a 5- to 7-month-old fetus, the prosecuting attorney used emotionally charged words (e.g., How old was the baby at the time of the abortion? Was the child alive at the time of the abortion?). The defense tended to use less emotional language (e.g., How old was the fetus? Was the fetus viable?). Undoubtedly these versions had very different effects on the construction of the incident in the minds of the jurors.

To study the impact of language in the courtroom, we asked 75 students at the University of Washington to act as jurors, to read some information about a case, and to reach a verdict based on the evidence presented.[2] The incident consisted of a meeting of two men at night at a marina. One man was paying blackmail money to the other. An argument ensued, and the blackmailer ended up in the water and drowned, whereupon the other man was arrested. A witness reported having seen most of the incident. The description of the incident was purposely ambiguous as to whether the blackmailer fell or was pushed in the course of a struggle.

The subject-jurors received one of two versions of the case. One version contained questions with words associated with violence, words intending to evoke emotion, or words that indirectly suggested the blackmailer may have been pushed during a struggle, while the other version contained more neutral language. An example is "How much of the fight did you see?" versus "How much of the incident did you see?"

Jurors who read the emotional version of the case were more likely to return a guilty verdict than those who read the neutral version (41% guilty votes versus 22% guilty votes, respectively). In a follow-up to this study, in which jurors were interviewed individually after returning their verdicts, it was found that those who received the emotional version had a different image of the incident. They tended to think of it as a relatively violent struggle in which the victim pushed the blackmailer over the edge of the pier, resulting in a drowning.

There are many aspects of courtroom language that are worthy of study. For example, the lexical items used by a lawyer can influence the jurors' reactions to evidence. Compare 1 and 2:

1. You testified that the light was red when the car came to the intersection.
2. It was your claim that the light was red when the car came to the intersection.

The language in the first example gives objectivity to the statement that the light was red, whereas the language in the second example gives the impression that the light may or may not have been red. (The statement beginning "It was your contention that . . ." has the same effect.) In a pilot experiment with subjects who played the role of jurors, we found that this simple lexical change influenced how much the jurors believed that the statement was true. Further, in the former case, they were more likely to include a red light in their construction of the accident and to be confident of its existence.

Jurors infer a great deal about lawyers and witnesses from the language they use. For example, during cross-examination, it is common for lawyers to use tag questions of the form: You did X, did you not?, while during direct examination, a more polite form is common: Could you please tell the court what happened on the morning of June 23, 1978? In the courtroom, the tag question is generally very aggressive and leaves the witness little room for formulating an answer. This is often what is desired in cross-examination. Tag questions are not necessarily aggressive and impolite, as when a stranger asks, It's a nice day, isn't it? Juror reactions to aggressive questioning seem to be mixed. Some jurors are impressed by the "strength" exuded by forceful questioning; others are intimidated by the badgering quality of these questions, particularly if the intonation is badgering.

Sociologist Brenda Danet[3] examined the questioning styles of various senators in the Watergate hearings and found that the stance of any particular senator towards the hearing was often given away by the preferred question form. Thus, Senator Sam Ervin relentlessly used tag questions of the form: You did X, didn't you?, while Senator Gurney, the pro-Nixon member of the Watergate committee, frequently used a form like: I am curious to know about X or Could you please tell us about X?, making the hearings sound like a casual conversation between equals, in which one person was inviting the other to fill him in on some details of mere passing interest.

Danet further observed the different tendencies of witnesses to "distance" themselves from some aspect of the situation by using abstract versus concrete terms of reference. Thus, in John Erlichman's testimony before the Ervin committee in the Ellsberg break-in, he referred to the break-in explicitly six different times in a six-minute segment of testimony. But the terms he chose, in sequence, became more and more abstract: (1) "this break-in"; (2) "an activity of this kind"; (3) "an event of this kind"; (4) "this event"; (5) "the thing." Each term is at an increasingly higher level of abstraction, incorporating all previous ones.

There seems to be no doubt that the lexical and syntactic choices that a speaker makes will influence the hearer's ideas, images, and beliefs. John Kennedy recognized this back in 1960 when he was trying to decide whether to run for president. He enlisted the help of Lou Harris and his polls to find out how people felt about politics and religion in general and whether he should openly confront the religious issue in particular. Harris designed some questions specifically to test the depth of religious tension. Example: "Is there a tunnel being dug from Rome so that the Pope can have a secret entrance to the White House if Kennedy wins?" Kennedy was appalled by this question.

"Lou," he asked, "how many people did you poll with this one?"

"About seven or eight hundred people."

"You don't think that's a little dangerous, that you might be planting the idea with some of these people?"

"Well, that's the risk."[4]

In sum, the language that is used in the courtroom and outside of it can reveal a great deal about the speaker. Equally important, it can affect a listener's construction of reality, and thereby influence behavior.

EYEWITNESS TESTIMONY

In a discussion in the House of Lords on March 17, 1973, Lord Gardiner said:

> The danger of identification is that anyone in this country may be wrongly convicted on the evidence of a witness who is perfectly sincere, perfectly convinced that the accused

in the many they saw, and whose sincerity communicates itself to the members of the jury who therefore accept the evidence.[5]

With these words, Lord Gardiner expressed his recognition of the fact that jurors can be influenced by the testimony communicated by a sincere eyewitness. In fact, many lines of evidence converge to demonstrate the soundness of Lord Gardiner's intuitions.

Because of its enormous impact, eyewitness testimony has been successful in causing juries to convict truly guilty people, but its danger lies in the fact that it occasionally leads to the conviction of the innocent. Honest, but mistaken, identification by prosecution witnesses was the prime cause of two recent miscarriages of justice in England. In view of the serious questions raised by those two cases, a committee was appointed to look into the law and procedures relating to identification. The committee, chaired by Lord Devlin, met for two years—between 1974 and 1976—and during this time, the committee examined all lineups that were held in England and Wales during the year 1973. Their analysis produced the following interesting results: there were 2,116 lineups in all, and the suspect was picked out in 45% of these. After being identified in a lineup, 850 people were prosecuted; but in 347 of these cases, the only evidence against the defendant was the identification by one (169 cases) or more (178 cases) eyewitnesses. Of those 347 prosecutions, 74% resulted in a conviction. This figure of 74% indicates that even when no other evidence is available, the testimony of one or more eyewitnesses can be overwhelmingly influential.

Another way to determine the impact of eyewitness testimony is through a simulated trial experiment in which subjects are asked to play the role of jurors, listen to testimony, and reach a verdict. In one study, subject-jurors were given a description of a grocery store robbery in which the owner and his granddaughter were killed. The subjects also received a summary of the evidence and arguments presented at the defendant's trial, after which each juror arrived at a verdict of guilty or not guilty.

Some of the jurors were told that there had been no eyewitnesses to the crime. Others were told that a store clerk testified that he saw the defendant shoot the two victims, although the defense attorney claimed he was mistaken. Finally, a third group of jurors heard that the store clerk had testified to seeing the shootings, but the defense attorney had discredited him by showing that he had not been wearing his glasses on the day of the robbery and that his vision was too poor to allow him to see the face of the robber from where he stood.

With no eyewitnesses, 18% of the subject-jurors felt the defendant was guilty; this rose to 72% when a single eyewitness account was added to the evidence. Interestingly, of the jurors who heard about the discredited witness, 68% still voted for conviction. The study suggests that jurors give eyewitness testimony a great deal of weight, even when that testimony is suspect.[6]

Finally, in an elaborate two-part study, jurors were asked to indicate their impressions of an eyewitness who testified during a mock trial. The study was conducted in two phases, the crime phase and the trial phase.

During the crime phase, subjects (three in each session) sat for a few minutes, whereupon a "thief" entered, posing as a coparticipant. She soon "discovered" a calculator that had apparently been left by a previous subject. She picked it up and put it in her purse, mumbling something about wanting it, and then she left the experimental room. The entire incident lasted just a few minutes. About a half minute after the "thief" left, the experimenter came into the room, gave each witness a questionnaire requesting a description of the thief, and then asked the witnesses to try to identify the thief from a set of six photographs.

In phase two, the trial phase, a new group of subjects—the jurors—were told about the staged theft and the witnesses' identifications. Then the jurors were asked to watch a cross-examination of one of the witnesses who had made an identification and to decide whether the particular witness was or was not mistaken. Some of the jurors watched the testimony of a correct eyewitness, while others watched the testing of an incorrect eyewitness. Finally, the jurors were asked for their reactions to the eyewitness. The results indicated that jurors tended to believe the eyewitness testimony about 80% of the time. What is striking, however, is that these jurors were just as likely to believe a witness who had made an incorrect identification as one who had made a correct identification.

The confidence of the eyewitness was a crucial determinant of believability. Jurors tended to believe witnesses who were highly confident more than they believed those who were not. As a whole, the data from the experiment lead to the conclusion that eyewitness testimony is likely to be believed by jurors, especially when it is offered with a high level of confidence, even though the accuracy of an eyewitness and the confidence of that witness may not be related to one another at all.[7]

In a follow-up to this work, thefts were staged under conditions designed to yield low, moderate, or high proportions of correct identifications of the thief. Again, jurors listened to the testimony of an accurate or inaccurate eyewitness and indicated how much they believed the eyewitness. Jurors changed their rate of belief of witnesses as a function of the theft conditions, but this change was minimal. Instead they responded largely to the confidence that the eyewitness placed in his or her identification. Overall, jurors were overbelieving of eyewitnesses.[8]

The impact of eyewitness testimony was recently compared experimentally to other types of evidence.[9] Subject jurors were presented with testimony in a hypothetical "bad check" case. The defendant was charged with writing a check for the purchase of a television set, a check that had insufficient funds to cover it. The jurors learned numerous details about the case, including one of four critical details. One quarter of the jurors learned that an eyewitness—a clerk who sold the set—had positively identified the defendant as the person who had passed the check. Another quarter of the jurors learned that a polygraph expert had tested the defendant and found that the defendant was lying when he said he had not written that check. One quarter of the jurors learned that a fingerprint expert had examined a print left on the counter by the person who had passed the check; it matched the prints of the defendant. Finally, one quarter learned of a handwriting expert who claimed that the handwriting on the check matched that of the defendant.

After all the testimony was in, the subject-jurors individually arrived at a verdict. Convictions were highest in the case of the eyewitness (78%) and lowest in the case of the handwriting expert (34%). The testimony of the fingerprint and polygraph experts led to an intermediate number of guilty verdicts (70% and 53%, respectively).

Why does eyewitness testimony carry so much weight? In part, this is due to the fact that people in general, and jurors in particular, lack a full understanding of the workings of memory. Some legal writers have tried to argue that

> jurors daily experience the fragility of their own memories. They know recollection fades with time and is affected by the relative significance of the incident. Probably most have experienced on several occasions their own or another's misidentification in social or business relationships.[10]

I disagree. In most of our life experience, truly precise memory is not demanded of us. Errors in recollection often go undetected because they are not particularly important; thus, people do not "daily experience the fragility of their own memories." Furthermore, a recent survey indicates that jurors are not knowledgeable about the operation of a number of important factors that affect their memories.[11] Because they tend to trust their own memories, they also tend to trust the memories of others. Information provided by an eyewitness, particularly a confident witness, is then accepted by the juror and integrated into the mental construction of the incident about which the witness is testifying. Compared to say a handwriting expert, an eyewitness generally gives a fuller account of the events that had transpired. The account typically consists of a rich description of the events and details of these events, thus providing much material for the mental construction in the minds of the jurors. Other experts provide a mere piece of evidence. Perhaps it is easier for jurors to work with a smooth account, modifying it here and there depending upon subsequent evidence, than to take small fragments and weave them together into a coherent image.

Expert Testimony

Rule 702 of the 1975 Federal Rules of Evidence discusses the testimony of experts:

> If scientific, technical, or other specialized knowledge will assist the trier of fact to understand the evidence or to determine a fact in issue, a witness qualified as an expert by knowledge, skill, experience, training, or education, may testify thereto in the form of an opinion or otherwise.[12]

The rule is phrased broadly so that many fields of knowledge may be included. The expert is not viewed in a narrow sense, but as a person qualified in any of a number of ways—by knowledge, skill, and so on. This means that expert testimony is not limited to those with scientific or technical knowledge, such as physicians, psychologists, and economists, but includes those who are occasionally called "skilled" witnesses, such as bankers, or landowners testifying to land values.

The purpose of any evidence, including expert testimony, is to facilitate the acquisition of knowledge by the jury, or trier of fact, thus enabling the jurors to reach a final determination. Because the new federal rules are increasingly liberal in terms of their allowance of expert testimony, it is important to understand what the impact of such testimony is likely to be on the outcome of a trial. A recent study looked at the impact of one type of expert testimony—the testimony of a psychologist about the factors that affect the reliability of eyewitness accounts.[13] Such expert testimony, although relatively new, has already been allowed in numerous states around the country.[14] In this study, experimental jurors were presented with a case modeled after an actual military court-martial that took place during 1977. After reading a summary of the trial, they rendered a verdict. Some of the jurors heard expert psychological testimony, while others did not. The expert testimony described studies that have been conducted, along with experimental results, on people's ability to perceive and recall complex events. Factors that may have influenced the accuracy of the particular identification in the case at bar were related. Individual verdicts were reached. The results indicated that there were fewer convictions when expert testimony was permitted.

In a follow-up experiment, jurors received evidence in a hypothetical crime and then deliberated in "juries" of six to reach a verdict for or against the defendant. Juries who had read about the expert testimony spent much more time discussing the eyewitness account than did juries who had not been presented with expert testimony. Taken together, these studies indicate that one consequence of presenting psychological expert testimony is that it increases the amount of attention that jurors give to eyewitness accounts, perhaps enhancing their scrutinization of those accounts.

It is natural to speculate that other types of experts will similarly affect the amount of attention that jurors give to particular kinds of evidence. Economists undoubtedly increase the attention paid to financial considerations, while physicians enhance the concern for medical injuries. As jurors are constructing mental images of an incident that they hear about, expert testimony can affect the size and shape of the portion that is devoted to a particular aspect of the incident.

Natural shifts in a juror's mental construction will occur throughout the course of a trial as a response to incoming inputs. One particularly powerful phenomenon has been dubbed the "knew-it-all-along" effect.[15] As people come to learn new information, they tend to think that they knew it all along. When a witness is told, either directly or in a more subtle way, that a particular culprit had a mustache or that a given car ran through a red light, it can lead to the belief that this fact was known all along.

Jurors, too, learn information throughout a trial and can come to think that they knew these things all along. This can be worrisome in some trials where it may be necessary to try to restore the jurors to some earlier state of mind. Consider this example. On July 31, 1976, a young man named William Brooks was attending a dental school fraternity picnic at a home on Lake Tapps in the state of Washington. Throughout the day, various students and their companions used different sailboats to sail in the lake. Brooks arrived late at the party, and he and three others took a catamaran sailboat out around 4:00 in the afternoon. While sailing toward the main channel of the lake, the mast of the sailboat came in contact with power lines. The lines carried a current of 12,500 volts, which was transmitted down the mast and through the frame of the boat directly to Brooks. He was electrocuted. A lawsuit was filed by his estate to recover damages for his alleged wrongful death.[16]

The defendants took the position that everyone knows that power lines are dangerous and that death could result if a sailboat makes contact, that Brooks should have known this and should have avoided the power lines, and that the accident was thus his own fault. A critical question then became, Does everyone know that power lines are dangerous . . . ? The jurors who heard this case could not freshly evaluate this question. They were not the same "naive" persons that they had been before the trial began. Rather, they had knowledge that they had not had before; they knew, for example, about this tragic accident. The tendency for people to think that they "knew it all along" undoubtedly caused the jurors to feel that they had known all along a great deal more about sailboats and power lines than they in fact had known. They consequently might have felt that Brooks should have known too.

Can the shifting mental construction be restored to an earlier form? Expert testimony was offered by the plaintiff to try to accomplish this. The testimony took the form of a description and discussion of the "knew-it-all-along" effect. The goal of the testimony was to show how information can change one's state of knowledge, in hopes that the jurors would be less likely to judge the knowledge possessed by William Brooks in terms of the altered knowledge they now possessed.

IMAGE CONSTRUCTION TO VERDICT

In criminal cases in American courts, the burden of proof for determining guilt is the presentation of evidence leading to a belief that is "beyond a reasonable doubt." For civil cases, the standard is a "preponderance of the evidence." These concepts are pivotal. Yet confusion and misunderstanding about the meaning of these terms are widespread. While the courts are haggling the proper meaning of these terms, social scientists are attempting to discover something about the probability judgments that people use in reaching verdicts under these two standards of proof. One study claims that people translate reasonable doubt to mean a probability of guilt higher than 85%;[17] while another claims that under certain conditions, the probability of guilt required by potential jurors is quite low—in some instances as low as 55%—no different from the figure one might expect to find if the jurors were operating under the civil case standard.[18]

The bottom line is, of course, the verdict. Yet to understand how jurors reach verdicts, one must take into account their mental construction of the incidents that they are evaluating. An understanding of these mental constructions will aid in the determination of how much doubt constitutes a "reasonable doubt," or how certain a juror needs to feel that a majority of the evidence favors one party in a lawsuit. The relationship between these images and the final verdicts should become the subject of future research.

SUMMARY

As jurors in a criminal or civil trial listen to testimony, they construct in their minds an "image" of an incident that was never witnessed by them. Many psychological factors influence this mental construction and, consequently, the verdict. Research with experimental jurors has revealed:

1. The images that jurors construct are influenced by the particular words and phrases that are used in the testimony they hear.

2. Jurors tend to be overbelieving of certain types of evidence, such as eyewitness testimony. Jurors are particularly responsive to the confidence with which eyewitnesses relate their testimony, rather than to the likelihood that the testimony is accurate.

3. Expert testimony, particularly on the subject of the reliability of eyewitness accounts, can cause jurors to better scrutinize the evidence they hear.

REFERENCES

1. LOFTUS, E. F. & J. C. PALMER. 1974. Reconstruction of automobile destruction: an example of the interaction between language and memory. J. Verbal Learn. Verbal Behav. **13**: 585–589.
2. KASPRZYK, D., D. E. MONTANO & E. F. LOFTUS. 1975. Effect of leading questions on jurors' verdicts. Jurimetrics J. **16**: 48–51.
3. DANET, B. 1978. Personal communication.
4. HALBERSTAM, D. 1979. The Powers That Be. Alfred A. Knopf, Inc. New York, N.Y.
5. DEVLIN, HONORABLE LORD PATRICK (chair). 1976. Report to the Secretary of State for the Home Department of the Departmental Committee on Evidence of Identification in Criminal Cases. Her Majesty's Stationery Office. London, England.
6. LOFTUS, E. F. 1974. Reconstructing memory: the incredible eyewitness. Psychology Today **8**: 116–119.
7. WELLS, G. L., R. C. L. LINDSAY & T. J. FERGUSON. 1979. Accuracy, confidence, and juror perceptions in eyewitness identification. J. Appl. Psychol. **64**: 440–448.
8. LINDSAY, R. C. L., G. L. WELLS & C. M. RUMPEL. 1979. Juror's Detection of Eyewitness-Identification Accuracy within and across Situations. University of Alberta. Edmonton, Alberta, Canada. (Unpublished manuscript.)
9. LOFTUS, E. F. 1979. Unpublished study. University of Washington. Seattle, Wash.
10. State of Iowa v. James Thomas Galloway, 275 N. W. Rptr. (2nd edit.) 736 (Iowa Supreme Ct. 1975).
11. LOFTUS, E. F. 1979. Eyewitness Testimony. Harvard University Press. Cambridge, Mass.

12. 1975. Federal Rules of Evidence for United States Courts and Magistrates. West Publishing Co. St. Paul, Minn.

13. LOFTUS, E. F. 1980. Impact of expert psychological testimony on the unreliability of eyewitness identification. J. Appl. Psychol. **65**: 9–15.

14. FISHMAN, D. B. & E. F. LOFTUS. 1978. Expert testimony on eyewitness identification. Law Psychol. Rev. **4**: 87–103.

15. FISCHHOFF, B. 1977. Perceived informativeness of facts. J. Exp. Psychol. **3**: 349–358.

16. Brooks v. Puget Sound Power and Light, No. 253270 (Pierce County, Wash., Super. Ct. 1979).

17. SIMON, R. J. & R. J. MAHAN. 1971. Quantifying burdens of proof. Law and Society Rev. **5**: 319–330.

18. NAGEL, S., D. LAMM & M. NEEF. 1978. Decision theory and juror decision-making. Paper presented at the International Society for Political Psychology, New York, N.Y.

COMPETENCY TO STAND TRIAL: DISCUSSION

Discussant: Thomas R. Litwack

Department of Psychology
John Jay College of Criminal Justice
New York, New York 10019

Dr. Bahn's finding that policemen regularly bring assaultive individuals whom they consider to be "mental cases" to hospitals rather than to jails was interesting but not altogether reassuring. Presumably, many such individuals are soon released from the hospitals only to engage again in assaultive behavior. As a citizen, I am not sure that I would not prefer that such individuals be arrested and processed through the criminal justice system, at least initially, even if they were detained—prior to trial, to release on bail, or to some other agreed upon disposition—in a department of corrections hospital rather than jail. At least, then, they would not be released simply to reduce the population of a hospital ward or because they were difficult to manage—as might well be the case now.

However, if such individuals are being brought to hospitals, it should not be surprising to discover—as certain studies referred to by Dr. Bahn suggest—that the patient populations of the psychiatric wards of certain municipal hospitals have higher arrest rates, upon release, than that of the general population. Nevertheless, we have to be careful about how we interpret and present such results. For example, one of the studies cited by Dr. Bahn that found such higher arrest rates for released psychiatric patients was titled "Crime and Violence among Mental Patients."[1] But the patient pool involved was entirely that of Bellevue Hospital patients—hardly a representative sample of "mental patients" generally. Undoubtedly, the title "Crime and Violence among Mental Patients" is likely to stir more interest than the more accurate title: Crime and Violence among Psychiatric Patients Released from Bellevue Hospital. The use of the former title, however, does a great and inexcusable disservice to "mental patients" as a group.

As for the papers of Drs. Exner and Weinstein, I of course agree with Dr. Exner's observation that a particular IQ or psychiatric diagnosis does not render a defendant competent or incompetent—especially since a defendant's competency may depend upon the particular circumstances of the case as well as on his or her state of mind.

In one case that I know of, for example, a defendant charged with murder was found competent to stand trial—and properly so—even though he harbored the delusion that his victims had only *feigned* dying. Since the defendant was willing to allow his attorney to enter a plea of not guilty by reason of insanity, and since the attorney had access to the hospital records necessary to establish that defense, the fact that the defendant was delusional about the events in the indictment would not, and did not, prevent him from receiving a fair trial upon the issue of his insanity.[2] Indeed, his continuing delusions *strengthened* his defense. However, had this same defendant insisted upon going to trial on the sole defense that his alleged victims had not, in fact, died, then he would have been incompetent to stand trial—for then his delusions would have prevented him from rationally and adequately defending himself. (It is also worth noting that, in this case, the defendant's attorney testified on his client's behalf that he, the attorney, needed no further assistance from his client than was forthcoming to adequately defend him on the grounds of insanity. That testimony was crucial—and properly so, I believe—to the ultimate finding of competency. As the court observed, the attorney's testimony regarding the competency of his client was "the most competent source of information on the subject, with the possible exception of the defendant himself.")[2]

Similarly, courts have recognized that a defendant's claimed amnesia for the time period surrounding the crimes with which he or she is charged may or may not render the defendant incompetent to stand trial, depending upon the circumstances. For example, there were reports to the effect that Dan White, who shot and killed the mayor of San Francisco, was claiming amnesia for those events. However, as in that case, when there is no doubt that the defendant had committed the act charged—in other words, when it is clear that no alibi might emerge if the defendant's amnesia should lift (though the defendant's state of mind at the time of the crimes charged might remain in dispute)—then the defendant's amnesia would not interfere with his or her ability to maintain a reasonable defense. Indeed, if such a defendant is claiming some sort of "mental state" defense—either the insanity defense or a defense of diminished responsibility—then his present amnesia is likely to strengthen his claim that, at the time of his criminal acts, he was not "all there."

However, I wish to disagree with Dr. Exner's suggestion that the legal test for competency to stand trial is vague and ambiguous and with Dr. Weinstein's suggestion that the determination of competency or incompetency is often quite difficult. In fact (unlike the various tests for the insanity defense), the criteria for competency (or incompetency) to stand trial are quite clear and precise, and virtually identical from jurisdiction to jurisdiction. Indeed, the criteria for competency are mandated by the Constitution of the United States, since it would be unconstitutional to try a defendant who did not meet certain minimal standards of competency.

In essence, a defendant is competent to stand trial if he is capable of (1) understanding the nature of the charges and the proceedings against him; (2) rationally considering and evaluating the options available to him; (3) cooperating with his attorney in his own defense; and (4) maintaining these functions—and self-control—during a trial. That is *all* that is required for competency, and it is not much. Unless the defendant's mental state would prevent him from receiving a fair trial, the defendant is competent to stand trial—whatever his diagnosis, symptoms, or character defects.

Of course, defendants are often declared incompetent to stand trial when they are in fact competent. But that is because testifying psychiatrists and judges are often ignorant of the criteria for competency; or because—though they know that the defendants at issue are technically competent—mental health professionals and/or judges have decided that certain defendants, for their own good or for the good of society, should be in a hospital rather than in a pretrial detention center or free on bail. In neither case, however, is an erroneous finding of competency made because accurate determinations are difficult to make. In fact, when psychologists are well schooled in the legal criteria for competency, the reliability of their judgments on the subject—even when they are evaluating defendants whose competency is in question—is remarkably high, well over 90%.[3]

Indeed—leaving aside those instances in which defendants may be malingering, i.e., feigning incompetency—it seems to me that the data upon which a defendant's current level of understanding, rationality, and ability to assist his attorney must be judged can always be quickly and simply ascertained. This can be done through questions put to the defendant that directly inquire into the defendant's understanding of his situation,[4] and by questioning the defendant's lawyer as to whether or not the defendant had been able to adequately assist the attorney with the preparation of the defense.

Now this does *not* mean that it will always be easy to ultimately *conclude* whether disturbed defendants are sufficiently informed, rational, and cooperative to be fairly tried. For example, many mentally retarded defendants will have an ability to understand their situation, and to assist their attorney, that is truly on the border line between competency and incompetency. And the determination of whether a defendant has a rational, as well as a factual, understanding of his or her situation may require an equally fine judgment. For example, it may often be difficult to decide whether a defendant who refuses to raise an available defense is acting so irrationally as to be incompetent. But the *data* upon which such difficult judgments must be made will usually be readily obtainable and/or apparent from the facts of the case—the evidence against the defendant and, therefore, the relative likelihood of success of the defenses he is and is not willing to assert—and from the reasons the defendant offers for making his choices.

And whether or not a defendant is sufficiently rational to be tried is *not* an issue for psychiatrists and psychologists to make. Their job is to obtain and describe the data from which the *judge* must determine whether or not the defendant meets the legal criteria for competency. But, of course, mental health professionals can be maximally useful to the court if they present the court with data that are directly relevant to the determination of competency—and *only* with such data.

In fact, it seems to me, traditional psychological tests have no role to play in the determination of competency to stand trial except, perhaps, to aid in the determination of malingering. At least insofar as we are evaluating a defendant's cognitive capacity to stand trial, it would seem that the use of structured interviews that directly assess the defendant's understanding of the legal process and his legal situation would be adequate (assuming, again, that malingering is not in issue). What more information is needed? A broader understanding of the defendant's cognitive capacities—beyond the question of whether or not he understands his legal situation sufficiently well to fairly defend himself—is simply irrelevant.

Thus, I must disagree strongly with the implications of Dr. Exner's finding that, of a sample of cases deemed competent to stand trial, 20% were thought to be incompetent or possibly incompetent by expert clinicians who evaluated the "raw" assessment data—presumably, the results of traditional psychological tests—for each of the 25 cases. Dr. Exner takes those results to mean that numerous defendants who are in fact incompetent to stand trial are, erroneously and unfairly, being declared competent. I take those data only to mean—indeed, to prove—that even expert clinicians cannot validly assess competency to stand trial from "raw" evaluation data—that such data are irrelevant, at best, to competency determinations.

The really difficult problems for mental health professionals (as opposed to judges) in making competency evaluations are (1) determining which defendants are feigning incompetency; and (2) determining which defendants, though presently technically competent, will be unable to proceed to and/or through a trial without suffering an incapacitating breakdown, or worse. More specifically (addressing the second problem first), the fact that a defendant is severely depressed by his predicament does not render him incompetent to stand trial unless he is genuinely too depressed to rationally consider his options or to cooperate with his attorney. But if a depressed patient would be made suicidal by proceeding to trial, then surely he is incompetent to proceed.

Do we have any tools for accurately predicting which disturbed defendants who are presently competent will yet not be able to *remain* competent if forced to undergo the stress of proceeding to trial? I doubt it. So perhaps the only fair way to proceed when a defendant's future competency is in doubt is to give the defendant the benefit of the doubt. That would mean finding defendants incompetent to stand trial when doing otherwise would very possibly cause them grave injury and when they wish such a finding. But it would also mean finding defendants *competent* to stand trial when they are presently competent and wish to proceed, and when the fear that they will not be able to withstand the rigors of a trial is based on less than "clear and convincing evidence."[5] After all, it is usually legally disadvantageous to a defendant who is not incompetent to be found incompetent. Just as no mentally disturbed person's freedom should depend solely upon the demonstrably fallible predictions of psychiatrists,[6] so too a defendant's right to bail, to plea bargain, or to go to trial (perhaps to be found innocent) should not be denied upon mere predictions of incompetence. If it turns out that a defendant cannot, in fact, withstand the pressures of proceeding to or through trial, then of course the judgment of competency can always be reversed.

Moreover, unless a defendant would in fact stand trial—rather than plea bargain—if he or she is found to be competent to proceed, the issue of whether or not the defendant can withstand the stress of a criminal trial, per se, is logically irrelevant to the determination of competency. That is, unless there is good reason to believe that a disturbed defendant's case, if allowed to proceed, will culminate in a trial rather than a negotiated plea, the only legally relevant question becomes whether or not the defendant can rationally understand and participate in the plea-bargaining process.* (Of course, if proceeding to judgment in any manner would engender psychotic or suicidal behavior, then the defendant would be unfit to proceed, regardless of whether a trial or a negotiated plea would otherwise be in the offing.)

As for the issue of malingering, there will no doubt be times when defendants will seek to feign incompetence simply to get transferred from a jail to a hospital; to postpone their trial (when the odds are heavily against them) as long as possible in the hope that witnesses' memories will fade, or the like; or to set the stage for an insanity defense. But at the same time, it should be recognized that the malingering of incompetency will be relatively rare because (with the exceptions just noted) it is rarely in the defendant's interest to successfully feign incompetence. After all, upon a finding of incompetency, the defendant is no longer eligible for bail—since he supposedly needs to be treated in a hospital to be restored to competence—and the prosecutors will lose their incentive to plea bargain. Moreover, unlike the defendant who successfully feigns insanity, the defendant who successfully feigns incompetence is not relieved forever of criminal responsibility for his or her alleged crimes. Once apparent competence returns, the defendant can then be tried. And given how *very disturbed* (or retarded) a defendant must be not to meet the minimal standards required for competency, it is difficult to imagine a defendant feigning for long the overwhelming degree of disturbance that can alone render a person incompetent to stand trial. (The one exception to this would be a feigned claim of amnesia. But, as noted earlier, even true amnesia would not necessarily render a defendant legally incompetent. And the validity of a claim of amnesia can often be determined from a knowledge of the facts surrounding the supposed development of the amnesia and an understanding of the defendant's character structure.) In any case, when the validity of a defendant's apparent incompetency is in doubt, it does little harm to judge the defendant incompetent and to wait and see what develops. The defendant will be hospitalized, and if she or he is malingering, in all likelihood that will soon become apparent.

Finally, I would just like to make one brief comment about Dr. Loftus' paper. If it is true that a witness' recollection of an event is significantly influenced by how she or he is questioned about the event, then the eventual outcome of many trials may well hinge upon who gets to the witness(es) *first,* since people tend to stick to their first account of events. Thus, whether a witness to an automobile accident is first asked (by the plaintiff's attorney) How fast was the other car going when it *smashed* into my client's car? or (by the defendant's insurance company's investigator) How fast was my client's car going when the two cars collided? may well determine how the witness will respond to *either* question in the future.

---

* See Reference 7. Similarly, defendants found incompetent to proceed should not be confined, on the grounds of incompetency per se, for a longer period of time than they would have spent in confinement had they been competent and able to plea bargain.

REFERENCES

1. ZITRIN, A., A. S. HARDESTY, E. I. BURDOCK & A. K. DROSAMAN. 1976. Crime and violence among mental patients. Am. J. Psychiatry **133:** 142–149.
2. People v. Benito Rivera Maldonado, N.Y. St. Supreme Ct. (Preminger, J.)
3. STOCK, H. V. & N. G. Polythress. 1979. Psychologists opinions on competency and insanity: How reliable? Paper presented at the 87th Annual Convention of the American Psychological Association, September 1, 1979.
4. See, e.g., MCGARRY, A. L., W. J. CURRAN, P. D. LIPSETT *et al.* 1973. Competency to Stand Trial and Mental Illness. DHEW Publication No. (HSM) 73–9105. National Institute of Mental Health. Bethesda, Md.
5. Cf., Addington v. Texas, 60 L. Ed. 2d 323 (1979).
6. ENNIS, B. & T. R. LITWACK. 1974. Psychiatry and the presumption of expertise: flipping coins in the courtroom. Calif. Law Rev. **62:** 693–752.
7. STEADMAN, H. 1979. Beating a Rap? Defendants Found Incompetent to Stand Trial: 112–114. University of Chicago Press. Chicago, Ill.

COMPETENCY TO STAND TRIAL:
GENERAL DISCUSSION

Moderator: Gerald W. Lynch

John Jay College of Criminal Justice
New York, New York 10019

H. C. WEINSTEIN (*New York University Schools of Medicine and Law, New York, N.Y. 10016*): We should not fail to note that the vast majority of competency-to-stand-trial questions are determined by the lawyer, using common sense. The lawyer discusses the case with his client and decides—usually, no doubt, without thinking much about the matter—that his client is competent to stand trial. If nothing else comes to the attention of the lawyer or the court, the issue is settled. Thus, relatively few cases come to be evaluated by a psychiatrist.

I would like to add my reaction to a number of points made by my colleagues here this morning. Dr. Loftus' discussion of the eyewitness and the jury reminded me of a point relating to the right to refuse treatment as it relates to the competency-to-stand-trial question. In his textbook, Alan Stone points out that "any defense attorney will recognize that one of the best pieces of evidence for convincing a jury that a person was not responsible for his crime is a defendant who is obviously crazy at the trial. That dramatic impression is blunted by the drugs. The effect of such drugs, when unknown to the jury in its appraisal of a defendant's demeanor, has in fact led to the reversal of a conviction."*†

In other words, there is an argument for not treating a patient while he is awaiting trial. The problem here, of course, is that such a patient would be held incompetent to stand trial under ordinary circumstances. On the other hand, however, there is an argument that the best interests of the patient would be served by proceeding with the trial.

Again, I make the same comment about some of Dr. Exner's data; namely, that the judge may have decided (and we sometimes forget it's the judge who decides this, not the psychologist or psychiatrist) that a particular patient is competent, or rather that he should be tried because of certain realities of the matter. For example, the judge may feel that it would be more advantageous to a particular defendant to be tried and get time served and be freed.

So the findings of the psychologists or the psychiatrists, while relevant, may not be the determining factor in a decision by a judge, and yet the data may have shown that the patient was incompetent. These are called dispositional decisions—where the judge, lawyers, and doctors get together and

---

* STONE, A. A. 1975. Mental Health and Law: A System in Transition. National Institute of Mental Health. Bethesda, Md.
† State v. Murphy, 56 Wash. 2d 761, 768, 355 P 2d 323, 327 (1960).

say, in a low-visibility way, This is what we think is best; and Let's call it this way rather than some other way.

Finally, on the issue of malingering, and particularly the case that was cited of a patient who wanted to go to trial—we call that malingering mental health. The patient who is really quite ill and yet says: I want to go to trial. I don't care what you say about me; I want to go to trial. Well, we have to assess that too. Suppose his reason is really a wish to hurt himself, then how do we find that patient? We remember that the classic case in the literature, Hadfield's case in 1800, was of a man who shot at King George III in a theater in the hope that he would be tried and executed; he acted on the basis of a delusion that if he were tried and executed, the world would be saved. Was he competent to stand trial?

VOCAL INDICATORS OF PSYCHOLOGICAL STRESS

Harry Hollien

*Institute for Advanced Study
of the Communication Processes
University of Florida
Gainesville, Florida 32611*

People have been attempting to assess the presence, absence, and/or magnitude of psychological stress from the speech and voice production of other individuals since primitive man added a cognitive overlay to his repertoire of oral signals. Indeed, it is quite probable that crude assessments of this type were attempted even before organized communicative sounds existed among our species. Quite obviously, these analyses were (and are) attempted for a rather substantial number of reasons, some of which are within the scope of forensic psychology. They include assessment of the presence and magnitude of such emotional states as hostility, aggressive intent, fear, and anxiety; behaviors such as deception or divisiveness; even psychopathological states can be included under this rubric.

There is little question but that emotional and/or behavioral conditions of this type exist and their detection is of consequence. For example, it can be important for monitor personnel to be able to determine the levels and types of stress present in individuals who are physically separated from them—i.e., pilots, astronauts, aquanauts, etc.—irrespective of the message content of the spoken interchange. It is desirable also for a worker at a crisis control center to be able to tell if the caller actually is going to commit suicide from the manner in which he or she communicates. Knowledge of the acoustic/temporal speech clues that correlate with psychosis can be important to clinical personnel. In short, many instances can be cited where information about the behavioral intent or emotional states of an individual could be useful.

Law enforcement personnel, also, would find systems or procedures that could reliably identify the emotions felt by the talker, the presence of lying, or the presence/absence of psychosis helpful in their work. Moreover, if such procedures could be carried out rapidly, on-scene decisions sometimes could be made that currently are not possible. In any case, it would appear that the activities of law enforcement, intelligence, and security agencies all would benefit if the various stress states cited above could be instrumentally identified.

Before any attempt is made to discuss the possible vocal correlates of psychological stress, it will be necessary to clarify a number of terms. The concept of stress is, in and of itself, quite difficult to define. For example, sometimes this term is used to refer to the emphasis patterns an individual uses when uttering a spoken message, and, of course, the ways by which such linguistic emphasis is produced have been studied.[11,30,32,33,49,59] However, these speaking characteristics are only of minor importance to the

47

issues considered in this paper. Admittedly, *some* information about an individual possibly could be deduced by careful analysis of the elements that are stressed within the message. Nevertheless, to date, no very good techniques have been developed for this purpose; i.e., we are not able to predict reliably an individual's emotional state by the way he or she emphasizes specific words within an utterance.

Stress, as it is used in this paper, refers to psychological states, and rather specific ones. Moreover, no matter how psychological stress becomes operative, its presence in a person is the result of some sort of threat;[4] or as Lazarus points out,[48] to be stressed, an individual must anticipate confrontation with a harmful condition of some type. He further points out that the strength of the stress response pretty much results from the magnitude of the threat. Unfortunately, however, a particular stressor, or stressful situation, may result in different responses from different individuals. Nevertheless, a threat ordinarily will create some degree of anxiety, fear, or anger in a given individual. These psychological states are often referred to as emotions, but as Arnold points out,[5] it must be remembered that there are many other emotions (for example, love, joy, happiness) that have little or nothing do to with stress. Hence, the Hicks definition of stress will be adopted for this paper: "stress . . . is a psychological state that is a response to a perceived threat and it will be accompanied by specific emotions."[40] The emotions in this case are, of course, anxiety, fear, and anger; they are consistent with the forensic model.

In the forensic milieu, three types of stress-related situations are of interest. First, it may be useful to obtain insight about the stress-related emotions an individual is experiencing at a given moment. As will be seen below, a few studies have been carried out in this area, and some tentative relationships can be established relative to the particular acoustic and temporal voice/speech features that appear to correlate with some of the emotional behaviors investigated. It would be expected that knowledge of those cues that could be used to predict specific emotional states would be of substantial value to law enforcement and related personnel. Unfortunately, however, clear-cut relationships have not yet been found—and for a number of reasons. For example, in some cases the research is carried out in the laboratory, and the "stress" applied is defined only in terms of the stressor; hence, the results of this type of research often are of only minimal use to individuals working in the forensic area. Other research approaches exhibit weaknesses also. To illustrate, when emotions are studied, actors ordinarily are used to portray them, as it is not often possible to study individuals who have talked first while experiencing powerful emotions and then later when the stress-inducing conditions are absent. Indeed, it is rarely possible to carry out controlled research on individuals who are experiencing actual stress, even though a few studies of this type have been reported. In any event, an attempt will be made to synthesize research results of the types cited above and to suggest at least a few voice and speech characteristics that can be thought to accompany stress.

Second, it should be of use to law enforcement (and related) agencies to be able to determine from the vocal signal alone whether a speaker is suffering from some psychosis—particularly a specific (clinical) disorder, such as schizophrenia. Substantial research has been carried out on the speech/voice correlates of such disorders. However, practically all of this research (except some of the earlier subjective work) has used medicated patients as subjects. Nevertheless, some insight can be gained from reviewing this area, and while the vocal correlates of psychosis are not as central to this paper as are the other two issues, relevant research will be summarized briefly. Nor should it be forgotten that information about clinical conditions sometimes can lead to a better understanding of the behavior of individuals not exhibiting pathology.

Finally, it is obvious that law enforcement, security, and intelligence agencies would benefit substantially from having available reliable systems that could detect lying or other forms of spoken deception. Currently, there are electronic systems in existence that are purported to do just that. They are said to be based on the notion that when a person lies, he or she experiences stress (presumably fear or anxiety) and, in doing so, exhibits certain vocal characteristics that can be measured. However, it remains to be seen whether lying and stress correlate to a high degree and whether there are any simple features that will permit the easy and reliable identification of these states. Nevertheless, lie detection by voice analysis appears to be a stress-related issue, and a very important one. Hence, a review of this area constitutes the third topic addressed by this paper.

VOCAL INDICATORS OF STRESS

There are many commonly held notions about the way speech *should* sound when a person is experiencing stress. Some individuals would argue that anger "should" result in loud, harsh speech; fear in a high-pitched, staccato output. Almost any person will venture at least a tentative identification of the voice and speech characteristics they feel accompany some of the more common emotions. But what information about these issues can be found in the relevant research literature? Do the commonly held stereotypes withstand scrutiny when scientific procedures are applied?

Not nearly enough research has been carried out on the voice/speech correlates of emotion and stress. With respect to emotions, a number of authors have indicated that it is possible to perceptually identify some of them (see, among others, Bonner;[12] Costanzo et al.;[18] Davitz and Davitz;[21] Simonov et al.;[78] and Starkweather[81,82]). For example, Fairbanks and Pronovost[28] report correct identification of simulated emotions of up to 88%, and other authors concur; the Lieberman and Michaels[51] listeners correctly identified emotional content 85% of the time. Of course, it should be stressed that much of the research in question has been carried out on emotions simulated by actors. It is possible that actors caricature emotions, or in some manner accentuate a feature (or features) that is easily identifiable; it may not be as easy to identify the emotions of a person who is actually experiencing them. However, there is some suggestion that identifications of this type can be made also.[84] Thus, if it is possible to perceptually recognize emotions from the paralinguistic elements in voice and speech,[77] it likewise should be possible to identify the relevant acoustic and/or temporal features that lead to these identifications.

Frequency

Speaking fundamental frequency (SFF) and patterns of f_0 usage would appear to be one such feature. In 1939, Fairbanks and Pronovost[28] reported SFF data on six actors simulating anger, fear, grief, contempt, and indifference (the message content was held constant). They reported that the highest mean SFF was observed for anger—with fear a close second—and that contempt and especially indifference showed lower mean frequency levels. These authors further indicated that wide frequency ranges were observed for anger and fear (fear exhibited the widest) and narrow ranges for grief and indifference. Finally, they suggested that changes in SFF are rapid for anger and slow for contempt. Thus, it can be seen that some patterns appear to emerge from data even as limited as these. Later, Williams and Stevens[85] carried out a similar study on simulated anger, fear, sorrow (grief?), and a neutral speaking condition. Their results were reasonably similar to those of Fairbanks and Pronovost, except that they found f_0 to be relatively high for anger and only slightly elevated for fear. It should be noted, also, that in an earlier study, Williams and Stevens[84] found that pilots and control tower operators showed an increase in SFF as a function of increased levels of stress—a finding essentially confirmed by Kuroda *et al.*[47] Since stress probably relates to fear in this case, these results are quite consistent with those cited earlier.

Hicks also has studied SFF as it relates to stress.[40] He defined stress in terms of fear and anxiety, specifically studying the speech of subjects who had stress induced by electric shock and where stress occurred as a result of the subject's making a public speech. He found SFF to be increased somewhat for both stress conditions (especially for the second) but not always significantly so. On the other hand, Markel *et al.* report that they did not observe any increase in perceived pitch to accompany word-induced hostility or anger but, in some cases, they found lowered pitch to relate to depression.[55] Nor did Almeida *et al.* find a consistent trend relating f_0 measures to stress (some subjects raised f_0, others lowered it).[1] In a sense, the data reported by Hecker *et al.*[38] agree with the findings of these authors. Specifically, they required 10 subjects to perform a meter-reading/mathematical task while stress levels were manipulated. These authors report somewhat inconsistent SFF behaviors for their subjects, with some raising f_0 and others lowering it. Finally, the announcer who described the Hindenburg disaster is known to have increased his SFF as a function of emotions he felt during the crash.[84]

In summary, it would appear that—while no definite statements can be made and there is substantial individual variation among subjects—some

TABLE 1

VOICE PARAMETERS THAT APPEAR TO CORRELATE WITH EMOTIONS,
AS CONTRASTED TO NONEMOTIONAL UTTERANCES

Emotion	Feature*		
	Mean SFF Level	Vocal Intensity	Temporal
Anger	+ +	+ +	+
Fear	+	+	+
Grief†	−	−	−
Contempt	−	+	−
Indifference	−	0	+

* + greater than normal; − reduced from normal; 0 not significantly different from normal.
† Sorrow and depression appear to show similar patterns. .

patterns emerge relating SFF to stress and/or to certain emotions;* they may be seen in TABLE 1. Specifically, it would appear that anger and fear probably are accompanied by raised f_o, and grief, contempt, and indifference by lowered SFF. That is, the presence of either of the two emotions closely related to stress in the forensic sense (fear/anger) ordinarily can be expected to result in the individual's raising his or her speaking fundamental frequency. Of course, it should be remembered that this parameter shifts with respect to normal usage patterns. Hence, to be helpful to law enforcement agencies, data based on this metric must be compared with baseline curves for that same individual, obtained from speech produced in a neutral speaking environment. Currently, comparisons of this type are not easily made.

Frequency Variability

The data on frequency variability are not very orderly; hence, very little space will be devoted to this issue. There appears to be some increase in SFF variability for anger but less of an increase, if any at all, for fear.[28,85] Moreover, if the variability findings are summarized under the general rubric of stress, the available data permit almost any position at all to be argued, i.e., SFF variability related to stress (1) may increase;[28] (2) may decrease;[84,85] (3) may not change at all;[40] or (4) may vary from speaker to speaker.[38] Thus, a metric of this type probably would not be of particular use to law enforcement groups, even if it were easily available. A related factor that could prove helpful, however, is the regularity of speaking fundamental frequency (or lack of it). The authors of the above studies (and others) have noted that when talking, stressed individuals exhibit behaviors such as voicing

* The emotions of grief/sorrow, contempt, and indifference are included to permit better understanding of the two emotions of primary interest.

irregularities, discontinuities in f_0 contours, irregular vocal fold vibration, and even vocal tremor.

Intensity

Vocal intensity as related to stress has been investigated by Hicks.[40] Some of his measurements suggest that intensity is raised as a function of stress; the obtained values increased slightly for his group where fear/anxiety was induced by shock and increased significantly for his "public speakers." Since Hicks was able to measure absolute intensity, it is possible that his data are more powerful than most of the other findings in this area. It must be noted, however, that Markel *et al.* reported that they did not find significant increases in perceived loudness for anger but that there was a slight trend for loudness reduction associated with depression.[55] On the other hand, in a previous article,[18] Costanzo *et al.* reported data (a high correlation between perceived loudness and anger) that agree with Hicks—as do Williams and Stevens, who also found some increases in vocal intensity to be associated with anger.[85]

Several other investigators have provided information about vocal intensity–stress relationships. For example, Friedhoff *et al.* reported that intensity tended to increase when their subjects lied and presumably were experiencing stress.[31] On the other hand, Hecker *et al.* did not observe consistent intensity differences between their nonstressed and stressed speaking conditions.[38] Of their 10 subjects, 6 showed small and/or inconsistent differences, 1 exhibited increased intensity as a function of stress, and 3 exhibited decreased intensity. Finally, Huttar used semantic differential scales to study emotions and relate them to acoustic measurements.[43] In most cases, his data are consistent with the generalizable findings relating types/levels of stress to vocal intensity. Probably the best evidence, based on a compilation of all the studies reviewed, is that vocal intensity is increased especially for anger, somewhat for fear and perhaps contempt, but is reduced for grief (see again, TABLE 1). However, as with speaking frequency, these data show inconsistencies, and even where the shifts appear stable, it is necessary to compare the obtained values with those related to subjects' control (unstressed) samples.

Time

The temporal analysis of speech and voice—as it relates to stress and emotions—has led to relatively few generalizations. Not many studies have used the same research protocols or, with the exception of rate, similar metrics. However, based on Fairbanks and Hoaglin,[29] Williams and Stevens,[85] Hicks,[40] Bachrach,[6] Ross *et al.*,[72] and Scherer,[74] at least some relationships can be suggested. It should be noted also that the temporal features column found in TABLE 1 summarizes these findings irrespective of the specific measure. That is, since tendencies only are considered, just the *direction* of the shift—not the type or amount—is indicated. Nevertheless, it can be argued that some intriguing relationships can be found among the time-stress contrasts.

Anger appears to be accompanied by rapid speaking rate and short durations of phonations and pauses;[29] Markel *et al.*[55] agree—at least with respect to rate—as do Williams and Stevens[85] with respect to patterning. According to Fairbanks and Hoaglin,[29] fear is similarly typified, and Bachrach[6] agrees, but Williams and Stevens apparently did not observe parallel relationships (at least they were not systematic). Hicks, also, failed to find that increases in rate correlate with stress (fear/anxiety?). Using another temporal measurement technique, Hicks reported that the number of speech bursts and pauses was significantly reduced as a function of increased stress—a finding consistent with those reported by Fairbanks and Hoaglin, Williams and Stevens, and Hecker *et al.* Specifically, when Hicks carried out a complex analysis of the temporal properties of his subjects' speech (based on the multiple analyses of overall speech patterning), he found significant shifts in his experimental vector accompanying induced stress. Specifically, Hicks' data suggest that when a person is speaking under stress, he or she will exhibit a strong tendency to produce rather long speech bursts—longer, that is, than those to be found in their usual speech rhythms. This particular relationship is one that could be useful to law enforcement personnel in assessing the stress level of a subject. Finally, it is to be noted that nonfluencies may be associated with the speech of individuals who are talking under conditions of stress. For example, Hicks found this to be the case especially for his group where electric shock was the stressor. On the other hand, Silverman and Silverman report that when they threatened to administer electric shock to normal speakers whenever they were nonfluent, their subjects became more fluent.[76] However, these data actually are not in variance with those reported by Hicks as, in this case, the subjects merely demonstrated that they could speak without nonfluencies if they were challenged to do so.

But what of the other emotions? From a synthesis of the findings relative to indifference, it appears that speech rate is somewhat elevated for this emotion. It also appears likely that speech rate and related temporal measures are reduced for contempt and especially for grief (sorrow, depression). In the case of grief, it appears that the reduction in speech rate is due primarily to the prolongation of pauses, particularly between phrases. As stated above, however, these emotions are not as important to law enforcement personnel as are those more closely related to the forensic model. They do provide useful contrasting data, however.

To summarize the acoustic/temporal correlates of stress, the question can be asked, Do the data to be found in TABLE 1 accurately portray the patterns that can be expected in voices reflecting the listed emotions? Unfortunately, only a qualified response can be given to this question. Nevertheless, it is possible to suggest the speech/voice changes that probably would occur when an individual speaks under stressed conditions. Basically, one could expect speaking fundamental frequency to be raised somewhat, vocal intensity to be increased, and, perhaps, the speech rate to be increased slightly. Moreover, there is a very good chance that the stressed individual would exhibit increased nonfluencies and would use relatively long utterances. However, it must be remembered that this description is based on the concept that these features are shifted, or changed, from those exhibited by the same individual in normal or neutral speaking situations. To be of value to more than a very limited forensic model, it will be necessary to specify those acoustic/temporal features that relate directly to stress, since in most instances, a reference profile of a given person's speech probably will not be available. Finally, while some understanding of the speech and voice features that functionally correlate with specific stress and/or emotional conditions is desirable, apparently the parameters identified are not robust enough to be used for the identification of stress and emotions in the field. Indeed, the development of such indicators appears to belong substantially in the future.

Vocal Indicators of Psychosis

There is no question that psychotics experience some form of psychological stress, and there is very good reason to believe that such conditions manifest themselves in the speaking behaviors of these individuals.[15,54] Obviously, then, it is important to identify the vocal correlates of these disorders both for the expected medical reasons and for a reason that is not so clearly recognized, i.e., that information about the relationships of interest possibly can provide useful data concerning the speech characteristics of individuals experiencing short-term stress of a nonclinical type. A secondary purpose for studying the speech of these individuals is one that relates to the forensic milieu: Can a psychotic be recognized as a person who is ill simply by analysis of his or her speech? A brief review of relevant research in this area would appear warranted.†

In order to provide a reasonable structure for this discussion, a system of classifying psychotics has been chosen. It is recognized that there are a number of available and/or acceptable approaches that could be used for this purpose. However, one classification system that would appear defensible divides psychotic states into the following: (1) schizophrenia, with three subcategories according to age: (a) adult, (b) adolescent, and (c) childhood; and (2) affective disorders including: (a) depression (general), (b) involutional depression, and (c) manic-depressive disorders. The present review will use this classification system, in modified form, primarily because most of the reported research uses similar classification categories. The modification will be to reduce these several categories to their two major components: (1) schizophrenia (adult/adolescent) and (2) affective disorders (depression/involutional depression). It is unlikely that organiza-

---

† For a more thorough review of this area, see Darby and Sherk.[20]

tion of the available data into these two relatively gross categories will do violence to the discussed relationships, since very few of the relevant investigators used subject classifications more rigorous than these.

It must be stressed once again that most of the research to be reported was carried out on patients who had been sedated or who were on a course of psychotropic drugs. For this reason, the observed relationships/data may not reflect the true vocal correlates of any particular psychological disorder. Nevertheless, some insight into the area can be gained from a judicious analysis of the available material. Anyway, if a particular psychotic were found in an unmedicated, acute, and (perhaps) violent state, there probably would be little need to carry out any form of speech analysis in order to discover if that person needed help.

Schizophrenia

One of the earliest of the modern investigators was Moses,[60] who attempted to describe the voice of schizophrenics. He reported that his patients' voices were similar to those of children, that they used very high pitches (in male patients, the phonation apparently was typical of that used by females), and that they exhibited "inappropriate" accents and emphasis as well as "rhythmic repetition of vocal patterns." Moskowitz[61] also was interested in this type of patient. He studied the speech of 40 schizophrenics—roughly matched to 40 controls by means of a rating scale—and observed that his patients exhibited "monotonous and weak speech with a flat colorless tone quality." As may be seen, these comments are somewhat anecdotal in nature; nevertheless, they provide some insight into the speech of schizophrenics and form a base for the more precise research that was carried out subsequently.

Ostwald,[65-67] also a pioneer in this area, was particularly interested in adolescents. For example, in 1964, he reported that he had assessed the speech of an adolescent schizophrenic male; this patient showed patterns of rapid frequency shifts and intermittent sound production.[67] In 1966, he and Skolnikoff published their observations of another male adolescent schizophrenic.[68] They reported his speech to be abnormal primarily as follows: (1) voice quality was nasal; (2) articulation was impaired; and (3) breath control was poor. Moreover, this patient's vocal tract was studied by means of a radiographic technique, and the authors report that sometimes the velum did not seal off the nasopharynx, a condition that presumably resulted in the perceived nasality. Time-frequency-amplitude spectrograms were made of the patient's speech signal, and from them, the authors suggest that (1) certain frictional noises of his consonants were missing; (2) shifts occurred in his vowel formants; (3) articulation of the stop consonant was poor; (4) his intonation patterns were inappropriate; and (5) SFF was abnormally high. These observations appear to be in agreement with those of Moses and Moskowitz, especially with respect to the difficulties in articulation, high SFF, muted voice quality, excessive variability in speech rate/rhythm, and, of course, the apparent lack in this type of patient of a finely tuned, integrated control of the vocal apparatus.

Ostwald[65,66] also is responsible for one of those relatively rare instances where a schizophrenic patient was investigated both before and after treatment. In this regard, he has reported observations of a 16-year-old girl who entered the hospital in an acute state of schizophrenia, characterized by withdrawal and apathy. At that time, he noted that she exhibited "monotonous" voice quality and, hence, carried out an acoustic analysis of her voice. Following five weeks of hospitalization, psychotropic medication, and therapy, Ostwald again evaluated this patient and suggested that several speech changes had taken place: (1) her spectral power curve showed a rise in intensity; (2) her vowel formants showed "appreciable change"; (3) her voice showed less "compactness"; and (4) her oral reading had speeded up by an average of 0.06 seconds per syllable. Stated differently, Ostwald interpreted his observations to mean that his patient's speech improved as a function of therapy and showed improvement in speaking intensity level, SFF and intensity variability, and precision of articulatory gestures.

Spoerri reports that he studied a very large population of schizophrenics ($N = 350$).[80] His listing of the voice/speech correlates of schizophrenia is reminiscent of earlier investigators. He typifies the speech of his patient/subjects as exhibiting (1) strain; (2) harshness; (3) register changes (to falsetto); (4) dysarticulation; (5) volume changes (to loud); (6) speed changes with inappropriate alternations; (7) "gloomy, dull timbre"; and (8) monotonous melody. Moreover, Spoerri related voicing irregularities to schizophrenia, and it will be remembered that this characteristic also was found in the speech of individuals experiencing high levels of stress. Later Chevrie-Muller et al. studied 53 hospitalized adolescent schizophrenics (ages 12–23 years) and an age-matched control group.[17] Their only significant finding was that female schizophrenics tended to show a reduction in frequency variability re normal females; the trend for males was similar but not of statistical significance. They also noted that reading time was longer for the schizophrenics, but not significantly so. Since the Chevrie-Muller et al. findings are somewhat in variance with those of most other investigators, they have attempted to explain their data. Basically, they contend that the (phenothiazine) medications administered to their patients possibly biased their results. Finally, Bannister compared 8 adolescent schizophrenics to 17 hospitalized nonpsychotic patients and to a second control population.[7] In this case, the schizophrenic subjects exhibited significantly reduced f_0 variability when compared to the control groups—these results tend to agree with most other published data.

A classic study was carried out in 1968 by Saxman and Burk.[73] They investigated 37 hospitalized schizophrenic females in relation to speaking fundamental frequency level (SFF), fundamental frequency deviation (FFD), and both mean (overall) and sentence reading rates. They contrasted these data to similar observations of a group of 22 female controls. Perhaps most important, they carried out their research 48 hours after psychotropic medication had been discontinued; hence, they are among the very few investigators to study psychotics who were not medicated. Saxman and Burk report that their schizophrenic population exhibited a higher mean SFF than the controls but that this finding was not of statistical significance. The schizophrenic group, however, did show significant differences (from the normal) relative to oral reading rates (slower) and frequency variability (larger FFD). It should be noted that the Saxman and Burk findings of increased FFD are in contrast to most other studies of schizophrenia. However, since they tested their patients after the discontinuation of medication, it is possible that they were recording an acute schizophrenia process obscured in other studies by the medication effect. Perhaps the single variable of medication is controlling in studies of this type. In any case, this particular investigation suggests that a great deal more research is needed before stable relationships will be found with respect to the vocal correlates of schizophrenia.

Several recent investigations provide additional insights of the speech-schizophrenia interface. Denber investigated the voices of 20 male schizophrenics, 31 controls, and 61 depressed patients.[22] He found that speech power, vocal jitter, and SFF differentiated his schizophrenics from the controls but did not find significant differences between his two psychotic groups. Some of Denber's observations are confirmed by Hollien and Darby,[41] who studied 23 schizophrenics, 15 involutional depressives, and 20 controls. These investigators used perceptual identifications, SFF, FFD, reading time, phonation time, and phonation time ratio (P/T) in an attempt to differentiate among their three populations. They found that their controls were (perceptually) identified as nonpsychotic 88% of the time but that their auditors could not systematically separate the schizophrenics from the depressives. Their findings for SFF were nonsignificant, but the noted trend (lowered SFF for the schizophrenics) was somewhat in variance with the findings of most other investigators—except perhaps Scherer,[74] who observed that for his patients, SFF increased as a function of treatment. It should be noted also that the P/T ratios separated Hollien and Darby's two psychotic populations from the controls; however, the meaning of this relationship is not clear.

Unfortunately, robust voice/speech predictors of schizophrenia do not appear to be available. This lack of strong relationships may be due to a number of factors, such as too general a classification system, the effects of medication, and so on. Of course, it could be due to the fact that there simply are no speech/voice features that systematically correlate with schizophrenia; however, the evidence suggests that there probably are such correlates and that ultimately they will be identified. In the interim, it is possible that the noted tendencies can be used to relate speech parameters to schizophrenia in the following manner: (a) fundamental frequency level (SFF) appears to be somewhat higher for schizophrenics than for normals; (b) fundamental frequency deviation (FFD) tends to be reduced for schizophrenics where patients are medicated but increased where they are not; (c) rate and rhythm phenomena may be important—it appears that the prolongation of pause time, elongation of certain words or phonemes, and increased reading times typify schizophrenics (at least if they are medicated); and (d) it is possible that formant features may be abnormal in schizophrenia and may change with treatment; high-low frequency spectra contrasts may be important also.[74]

Affective Disorders: The Depressed

It should be remembered that there are several classes of depressed patients. The most common (other than mixed or general) are the involutional depressives and the manic-depressives. However, this review will collect all types of affective disorders into a single category—that of depression—primarily because, so far, no voice or speech analyses have been able to differentiate among these groups. Indeed, it has not been conclusively demonstrated that depressives speak differently than do normals. It also should be remembered that, as with schizophrenics, virtually all the research carried out on the communicative attributes of these patients has involved speech samples obtained when the subject/patients have been medicated and the acute effects of the disease may have been obscured by the drugs administered. However, a brief review of the relevant research may provide some information about people who are depressed and how it may be possible (eventually) to identify these conditions from speech and voice analyses.

In 1938, Newman and Mather studied the speech of 40 depressed patients whom they classified into several subgroups.[63] Basically, however, they found that the "classical" depressive patients exhibited voice qualities that were "dead or listless"; had narrow pitch ranges; and exhibited slow speech tempo (with frequent pauses and hesitations) and a lack of emphatic accents. Speaking resonance was described as "pharyngeal" and "nasal," and these patients appeared to have limited syntax and a short length of response. Moses characterized the "depressed" voice as one that exhibits uniformity with a regular repetition of the "same gliding down interval."[60] He indicated that when "tone" was lowered, intensity decreased proportionately and that it is this relationship that is responsible for the monotonous voice quality attributed to depressed states. Eldred and Price appear to agree.[26] They report their impressions of the speech and voice patterns of a single patient whom they studied extensively during a 13-month period of psychoanalysis. They suggest that depressed states are accompanied by decreases in pitch, rate, and/or volume and by narrow pitch ranges. However, it is possible that, since their subject was relatively old, some of the voice/speech characteristics they observed could be due to the physiological changes that accompany aging.

Later, Hargreaves *et al.* published a study of 32 psychiatrically hospitalized patients classified as depressed.[36] For this research, they correlated mood ratings and power spectra before, during, and after treatment. Predictions of mood ratings from voice spectra correlated significantly for 25 of the 32 patients, and these correlations were largest for those patients who showed the greatest changes in mood; Helfrich and Scherer[39] also discuss a relationship of this type. Subsequently, the 10 patients who showed the greatest change were tested to discover if there was a uniform voice quality for states of depression. Of the 10, 5 were found to exhibit a "depressed" voice, i.e., reduction in loudness and a corollary reduction "in the higher overtones." The authors suggest that this combination resulted in a "dull, lifeless" voice quality, with diminished inflection (see also Rice et al.[71]). Of the remaining 5 patients, 3 exhibited voices that were actually louder and sometimes higher in pitch during depression than otherwise. The authors suggest that depressive symptoms may result in several different clusters of patterns and that each cluster could be associated with some subclass of the disorder.

After a period during which relatively little speech/voice research on depressed patients was carried out, Darby and Hollien report data on six patients before and after electroconvulsive treatment.[19] Prior to treatment, the voices of these patients were perceptually characterized by a speech pathologist as "dull" and lacking in vitality. Following treatment and with moderate clinical improvement, the voices were judged by the same speech pathologist to have regained some of their normal vitality. Further perceptual analysis resulted in the observation that improvement occurred in articulation and pitch inflection (five patients) and in linguistic stress (four patients). Instrumental analysis also was carried out, but significant trends were not detected in speech power spectra, SFF, FFD, or speaking rate. The lack of significant instrumental findings in this study is of interest. Further, the results would appear to be at variance with those from several other investigations (for example, see Helfrich and Scherer[39]) and especially with Ostwald's[66] findings of increased intensity centered around 500 Hz following electroconvulsant therapy. Possible explanations of these differences could relate to the different methods of analyzing the data. First, Darby and Hollien's subjects were not studied individually but rather as a group, since it is safe to generalize only those relationships that are universal (or pretty much so). Thus, in this instance, the pretreatment spectral curves were averaged and then compared to the mean posttreatment curves. Since no statistically significant differences appeared, the frequency bands centering around 500 Hz were not individually compared, nor were other frequency regions within the overall spectra. Another investigator, Denber,[22] who studied 61 male depressives, 31 controls, and 20 schizophrenics, appears to have found some evidence that a related measure—power—is increased as a function of depression. However, he did not section his spectrograms into high and/or low frequency bands either; and, as a matter of fact, his finding that speech power is increased for depressives tends to run counter to the findings of most other investigators. It also is interesting to note that of Denber's 20 other measures, only the 2 parameters of SFF and jitter differentiated the psychotics from the normals, and jitter alone appeared to separate the groups on a three-way basis.

Finally, two studies have been reported recently. As stated, Hollien and Darby used perceptual ratings, SFF, FFD, reading time, phonation time, and P/T ratios in an attempt to differentiate among their three groups of subjects (15 involutional depressives, 23 schizophrenics, and 20 controls).[41]

It will be remembered that they found the controls could be identified as normal 88% of the time, that the psychotics usually were identified as clinical cases, but that the judges could not differentiate systematically between the two clinical groups. These authors do note, however, that the depressive patients exhibited slightly lower SFF than did the controls (nonsignificant), as well as a slower reading time; the P/T ratios also proved useful in identifying the depressives. Scherer used somewhat smaller groups (9 depressives contrasted to 11 schizophrenics) in order to study the vocal correlates of psychosis.[74] He also carried out speech/voice analyses before and after his subjects received treatment. Of his several measures, only frequency differentiated Scherer's groups; he reports a mean decrease of 9.5 Hz in SFF *following* treatment, and these data are in variance with most other authors. On the other hand, Scherer's reported findings on spectral bands appear to agree with Ostwald and others. In this case, he found an increase in low frequency energy (260–440 Hz) following therapy. Finally, Scherer concludes that treatment causes patients' voices to become more resonant and flexible—a change that, he suggests, is the result of increases in muscle tone.

To summarize, a review of the vocal correlates of affective disorders suggests that such patients probably use different speaking patterns than do normals. While there may be no classical pattern of the speech/voice characteristics of depression, an approximation might be as follows: these patients probably exhibit (1) reduced speaking intensity; (2) reduced FFD, or pitch range; (3) slower speech; (4) reduced intonation; and (5) a lack of linguistic stress. It should be noted also that, with the exception of SFF and its perceptual correlate pitch, this description essentially parallels those for the emotions grief and sorrow. Thus, just as (with certain exceptions) anger/fear appear to correlate with schizophrenia, the vocal correlates of depression suggest related emotional states also. While it probably is somewhat dangerous to push these analogies too far, the suggestion remains that such relationships may have merit, and they may be useful as guides to further research. It must be stressed, however, that all of the relationships suggested in TABLE 2 are tenuous; indeed, conflicting data exist in several instances. Hence, it is necessary to be a little cautious when attempting to generalize the speech/voice characteristics of psychotics for any purpose whatsoever.

LIE (STRESS) DETECTION

As has been pointed out in the preceding two sections, there may be voice and speech attributes that correlate with the emotional or psychological conditions experienced by an individual. Admittedly, the current state-of-the-science makes it difficult to predict precisely which of these factors relate to specific psychological states, and even whether those relationships that apparently have been established can be assumed for all individuals. Nevertheless, the commonly held opinion that high levels of stress produce gross changes in speech rate, vocal intensity, voice frequen-

TABLE 2

PRESUMED SPEECH/VOICE DEVIATIONS (FROM THE NORMAL) OF
TWO BROAD CLASSIFICATIONS OF PSYCHOSIS*

Parameter	Schizophrenia[†]	Depression[†]
Speaking Fundamental Frequency	+	0
Fundamental Frequency Deviation	?	−
Speaking Rate	0	−
Speaking Tempo	+	0
Vocal Intensity	0	−

* Only acoustical and perceptual parameters are included.

† + greater than normal; 0 not significantly different from normal; − reduced from normal; ? conflicting data.

cy, and possibly vocal quality probably is a defensible one. However, for the present, it may be unrealistic for a phonetician or psychologist to claim that he or she can identify behavioral states—such as types of emotion, level of stress, lying, and/or psychosis—solely from an analysis of an individual's speech and voice characteristics. That is, it appears obvious that the speech features correlating with the specific psychological conditions are not robust enough to permit these states to be accurately identified in the field. As stated, development of such indicators appears to be the responsibility of future investigators.

Nevertheless, a number of commercial firms are now marketing equipment that they claim can be used to detect stress, and ultimately lying, from live or recorded samples of a person's speech.[62,79] Chief among them are the Psychological Stress Evaluator (PSE), manufactured by Dektor Counterintelligence and Security, Inc., the Mark II Voice Analyzer, produced by Law Enforcement Associates, Inc., and the Voice Stress Analyzer (VSA), a product of Decision Control, Inc. Several additional devices include the Psychological Stress Analyzer, or PSA (Burns International Security Services), the Hagoth (see Bennett[9]), the Voice Stress Monitor, or ESM-4000 (Security Specialists Marketing Group), and others. Of course, if devices such as these actually were able to detect when an individual was practicing deception, they would be of substantial worth to law enforcement agencies. Even if they were only able to provide some estimation of the level of stress being experienced by a suspect, they would have considerable value. In any case, a number of these devices are being manufactured and marketed. Questions can be raised relative to the principles upon which they are based and as to their accuracy and effectiveness.

Before considering these questions, however, it should be noted that there has been some notoriety associated with voice analyzers, particularly the PSE. For example, analysis of the speech samples associated with the assassinations of both John and Robert Kennedy has led to much sensationalism (see, for example, *Newsweek,*[2] Dick,[24] and O'Toole[64])—as has the processing of speech related to the Patty Hearst kidnapping[25] and the so-called Washington scandals (see, for example, Dick[23] and Haines[35]). Moreover, the fact that the manufacturers claim that their devices can be used to analyze speech transmitted over the telephone, or be used in other covert ways, has resulted in the possibility that their use could lead to abuse of civil rights. Accordingly, in 1976, a congressional committee placed a ban on their use by federal agencies.[3] The proponents of these devices apparently are not deterred by such rulings, and a substantial number of them are in use today throughout the United States. Thus, there is a need to understand the basic premises upon which psychological stress evaluators are predicated and the validity of their output.

It is almost impossible to identify the bases upon which the Voice Stress Analyzer and most of the other systems operate. The manufacturer of the Mark II claims that its characteristics are "different" from those of the PSE, but this unit probably operates in a fashion similar to the PSE. On the other hand, the PSE manufacturers have gone to considerable effort to describe how their unit works. Moreover, their device is somewhat more complex than many of the others—it has several modes of operation, and the operator has to carry out a fairly complex analysis of a graphic trace, whereas many of the other devices use colored lights for readout (green for "the truth" and red for "a lie," of course). As would be expected, no details are given about the actual PSE circuitry. However, analysis of the device (including those elements embedded in molded plastic) reveals that its operational modes probably parallel those of a low-pass filter. Hence, it is necessary to look elsewhere for the theoretical constructs or empirical evidence upon which the operation of this device is based. In this regard, the PSE manufacturers claim that they detect and measure the very slight tremblings (often called microtremors) that occur in the muscles of the human body, in order to accomplish their intended task. That is, they contend that they can evaluate stress, and presumably lying, by demodulating the "subsonic frequencies" that are caused by minute oscillations in the muscles of the vocal mechanism. They argue that these microtremors are normal to *any* voluntary muscle activity but that in the stress situation, they are suppressed. The PSE, then, presumably measures the frequency modulation (FM) of the (vocal) utterance, which is present for normal speech but is reduced (or disappears) for stress (see, among others, Kupec[46]).

There is no question that such microtremors do exist—at least in the long muscles—and at rates varying from 8–14 Hz.[16,52] As noted above, the PSE proponents claim that this tremor exists in the *voice* also, presumably created by some interaction between the laryngeal muscles and the airstream. But do these microtremors exist in the small muscles of the larynx as well as in the large muscles of the extremities? Indeed, it is difficult to understand how an action that is so miniscule as to require sophisticated electromyography (EMG) to be recorded can affect the acoustic speech signal to such a degree that it can be detected in the manner described. In any event, a substantial number of questions such as these can be asked, but, at present, there are very few scientific reports on the subject, and the data reported often appear contradictory.

Perhaps it would be useful to examine first the possibility that microtremors may be present in the muscles associated with the vocal tract.

Four studies appear relevant in this regard. First, Shipp and McGlone, who are highly experienced electromyographists, used hook-wire electrodes embedded in both lip and laryngeal muscles to study this issue.[75] They report that these muscles did not show tremor patterns similar to those of the long muscles and thereby were forced to conclude that if voice analyzers work, their operation has to be based on some other set of principles. In discussing these conclusions, plus additional data that demonstrate this same lack of a relationship, McGlone argues that microtremors of the type in question are most readily found in the large muscles, especially those of the extremities.[57] He further indicates that such tremors are usually associated with isometric contractions, which seldom occur in the small, fast-acting muscles of the vocal tract. On the other hand, Inbar et al. claim that they were able to observe a laryngeal tremor of the type specified.[44] However, they used surface electrodes coupled to a low-pass filtering system in their research. As is well known, surface electrodes will pick up activity created by any muscles in their vicinity, and there is no way of knowing whether the muscle action potentials analyzed are from a single muscle set, from groups of muscles, or simply, perhaps, from some sort of interaction among the muscles. Indeed, when surface electrodes are placed over a structure as complex as the larynx, it even is possible to speculate that the EMG system is triggered by structural movement rather than by action potentials. An EMG study by Faaborg-Anderson appears to bear on this issue.[27] He studied the discharge frequency of the vocalis muscle single motor units for three subjects and found that these rates rose from 10 to 40 per second at the onset of phonation, maintained a 25–39 firing rate during phonation, and fell off to about 15 firings per second after the cessation of sound. While it must be conceded that Faaborg-Anderson did not measure microtremors directly, it also can be argued that microtremors result from neural control of this type. Hence, it is of interest that the firing rate varied as a function of voicing and did not remain at the specified level of 8–14 Hz during phonation. Finally, a comment by Almeida et al. appears germane to this discussion.[1] They indicated that the PSE literature does not restrict microtremor origin to the glottal region. However, they suggest that if such undulations were to originate in the supraglottal tract, "one would have to presuppose a fine synchronization of the discharge frequencies in the different articulator muscles. But since the innervation of different muscles displays continuous phase difference, an acoustic neutralization of [such] possible effects . . . must be expected." Obviously, this relationship also would appear consistent with laryngeal operation and, if true, would negate any potential for a microtremor to occur in the voice. In short, it would appear that the neurological evidence supporting the claims of the PSE proponents is sketchy and contradictory at best; the case they present can hardly be considered as well established.

Studies that have attempted to locate evidence of the microtremor within the acoustic signal itself also have been carried out. McGlone and Hollien[58] report that Dabbs performed fast Fourier transforms on the speech of speakers in stressed and unstressed situations. For the unstressed condition, he found a peak of energy between 10 and 15 Hz, and this peak disappeared in high stress situations; however, peaks also occurred between 0 and 5 Hz in the unstressed speaking condition, and these peaks did not disappear as a function of stress. In an attempt to provide additional data and perhaps clarify these relationships, McGlone and Hollien spectrographically studied the 5–100 Hz frequency band for 30 male subjects producing unstressed speech and compared the obtained results to those from the speech of 10 males stressed by electric shock.[58] They report that there appeared to be no systematic evidence of energy at frequencies below the subjects' speaking fundamental frequency levels for either of their two groups. Almeida et al. report that they investigated this issue also but by means of a somewhat different technique.[1] They analyzed the acoustic output of 14 subjects who were placed in a situation where a lie was required. Examination of time-expanded oscillograms showed that most of their subjects had a tendency to maintain constant f_o throughout all tests and retests. These measurements were subjected to statistical analysis, and the hypothesis that deception causes a modification in the average period duration of an answer was rejected. Further inspection of their measurements demonstrated that subjects react variably to induced stress, that is, with regard to their response patterns. For example, measurement of the average fluctuation values (an FM phenomenon) did not show any significant rise or fall among the answers. This issue is further confused by Inbar et al., who claim to have found evidence of a "tremor" occurring in the third formant of vowels.[44] As can be seen, this statement does little to clarify the controversy. Moreover, it contradicts accepted acoustic theory relative to the operation of the vocal tract, i.e., a very low frequency existing within the signal would modulate the entire signal, not just one resonance region within it. Finally, based on studies in this area, Bachrach concludes that "there appears to be no conclusive evidence that . . . a microtremor exists in the vocal apparatus and the transfer from normal physiological tremor to vocal cords appears unwarranted."[6]

To summarize, currently there appears to be a serious question as to whether the tremor that the PSE and other like units are purported to measure actually is present in the voice and speech of talkers and, indeed, whether the voice analyzers really are not measuring some other feature or event. The very fact that the manufacturers of these units indicate that they can be used over the telephone argues against detection of very low frequencies. That is, if the effects of the microtremor are in the frequency region of 8–14 Hz—and the low-pass cutoff of the telephone is 250 Hz at best—the frequency of interest could not be detected; hence, it must be some other feature that is being measured. In any case, it appears from the above review that all of the propositions suggested by Papcun[69] have been violated, viz., (1) that oscillation occurs in the vocal muscles during speech; (2) that this oscillation is manifest in the acoustic speech signal; and (3) that the oscillation is reduced or modified by psychological stress.

Conceivably, it could be immaterial how a system operates if it does indeed perform the tasks required of it. Unfortunately, the available research does not provide a clear-cut answer about the effectiveness of voice analysis in this regard either. There are some indications that the devices in question can be used to detect stress if the level is high enough[58] but that they are ineffective if the stress level is relatively low.[8,56,57] The above studies would appear to provide useful information, because if it holds that high stress can be detected by voice analyzers and high stress is present during lying, then these devices should be able to detect lying also. However, are these relationships/contentions supported by relevant investigations?

Brenner reports that when he required 24 students to recite a poem before 0–22 spectators, his PSE analyses showed stress to increase as a function of audience size.[13] In this case, it would appear that there were identifiable differences in the PSE patterns and that these patterns correlated with levels of stress. The findings of Leith et al. are not so clear-cut.[50] By PSE analysis, he did find an apparent lowering of stress as his subjects serially made telephone calls, i.e., the adaptation effect was identified. However, the PSE did not discriminate between his two groups: the first were stutterers, who were clearly experiencing severe distress at having to make the telephone calls; and his controls were nonstutterers, who apparently experienced no fear or anxiety as a result of this task. The Vander-Car et al. results are mixed also.[83] In their first study, these investigators correlated PSE analyses with stress measures of heart rate and scores on a test of anxiety. Their subjects were stressed by fear of electric shock and by requiring that they "speak taboo words." In the first study, all three measures were found to reflect the expected levels of stress and to correlate significantly with each other. However, when the study was replicated under only slightly different conditions, the PSE analyses did not correlate with the level of stress or with the other two measures. Thus, VanderCar et al. were forced to conclude that they could not systematically demonstrate the validity of the PSE.

Other conflicting data are available. For example, Brockway et al. report that their obstetrical patients showed similar levels of stress both on the PSE and on a standardized test of stress (anxiety).[14] On the other hand, the data reported by Hollien et al.[42] do not support the Brockway et al. position. This second set of investigators[42] lists data from several studies, one of which involved stress. In that study, a group of young adults produced speech under a high stress condition (as evidenced by experimenter observation, self reports, and high scores on the anxiety scale of the Multiple Affect Adjective Check List) and then under a speaking condition involving little or no stress; a second group of subjects was recorded while speaking under a very low stress condition. PSE traces were made, and three groups of examiners evaluated them. The first group were young adults who received a short training period specifically based on the instructions found in the PSE manual; the second group received substantially more extensive training. The third group was trained in the same manner as was the first but consisted of five scientists who were experienced in analyzing analog traces. The results of this research may be found in TABLE 3. As can be seen from the table, most scores are roughly at chance level; with only the scores of examiner groups A and C for the second unstressed group of talkers above chance.

In short, it does appear the PSE analysis sometimes can provide an in-

TABLE 3

EVALUATION OF PSE TRACES OF STRESSED AND UNSTRESSED SPEECH BY
THREE GROUPS OF AUDITORS*

| | Speech Sample[†] | | | |
Group	Stress	U/S-1	U/S-2	Mean Response
Group A (N = 19)				
Stressed	44			51
Unstressed		45	64	
Group B (N = 10)				
Stressed	35			40
Unstressed		45	39	
Group C (N = 5)				
Stressed	45			53
Unstressed		51	63	

* All values are in percent.
† U/S = unstressed condition.

dication of the presence of stress in speech, that is, if the stress level is *very* high. However, it does not appear to work very well when lower levels of stress are investigated. When these data are considered, perhaps the most important observation that can be made is that PSE analysis apparently does not lead to the correct identification of speech and voice where stress is *not* present or where the stress level is very low. The reason this relationship is so important is that, if nonstress speech is often identified as reflecting stress, a danger exists that unfortunate interpretations of the talker's intent will be made.

Research on stress in voice, perhaps, is somewhat off the point, as the psychological stress evaluator's objective is to detect instances of deception in the utterances of individuals being examined. Since such identification also is the goal of the members of the American Polygraph Association (APA), it is surprising that they have not adopted or endorsed the use of psychological stress evaluators. Quite to the contrary, in 1973, the APA Board of Directors disapproved the use of these devices (specifically the PSE-1) because, in their opinion, (1) they can be used covertly and violate an individual's constitutional rights; (2) their reliability and validity have not been demonstrated; and (3) the training programs and standards for examiners are totally inadequate.[10] The APA further indicated that it would reevaluate its position any time the three cited problems were resolved. It should be noted, however, that the fact that the APA does not support the use of the PSE or similar systems alone does not justify the rejection of these devices. Nevertheless, this group's arguments do lead to the postulation of two very important questions: (1) Does stress accompany lying?; and if so, (2) Will the stress levels associated with deception be high enough to be detected by the voice analyzers? Currently, there appears to be no research that bears directly on the first question; hence, it is impossible to experimentally defend either a positive or negative position in this regard.‡ On the other hand, a stress/lying relationship would be of little importance if the psychological stress evaluators actually measured some voice/speech feature that correlates with lying. Anyway, some research is available on the ability of the voice analyzers to detect lying.

Most of the studies to be reviewed are based on PSE analysis. The performance of this particular device has been the one most often studied, primarily because it is the most visible of the units, its use is most widespread, and its manufacturers are slightly more cooperative than are the individuals who make other devices of this type. As with the experiments on stress, the results of PSE evaluations of individuals who engage in deception or lying are conflicting. For example, Heisse reports having tested the PSE by requiring a group of 12 "trained" evaluators to process 258 "evaluation replies."[37] He claims that his examiners were correct 96.12% of the time. On the other hand, both Barland[8] and Kubis,[45] in independent, scientific studies, have challenged the ability of the PSE to detect lying. In his research, Kubis used 174 subjects in a simulated crime involving a thief, a lookout, and an innocent suspect.[45] In order to determine which of his subjects were lying and which were telling the truth, he utilized the polygraph and two "voice-analyzers" (i.e., the PSE and the VSA), as well as reevaluations of the polygraph records by independent examiners and subjective assessment of the recordings by tape monitoring personnel who were present during the interrogations. The primary accuracy level for the polygraph was found to be 76%; the independent polygraph raters scored 50–60%, and the subjective scores of the monitors were equally as high. On the other hand, the results obtained from the psychological stress evaluation systems (PSE, VSA) were roughly chance, even when the voice-analysis operators were provided with partial information about the subject. In any case, the voice analysis scores were well below those of the polygraph. Kubis argues further that, because his monitors were able to perceptually discriminate among his subjects to a significant degree, it is demonstrated that the task resulted in sufficient emotionality to be valid for its stated purpose. Barland's research was somewhat different than that carried out by Kubis; he studied both low risk and high risk deception.[8] He reports that the PSE analysis was not sufficiently sensitive to detect lies if little jeopardy was involved. In the high risk experiment, the voice analysis technique was compared to the polygraph for a number of criminals who were presumed to be lying (deception was later confirmed in a number of instances). In this case, all 14 polygraph evaluations indicated that the subject was lying; 8 of the 14 PSE evaluations agreed with the polygraph results, and the other 6 were inconclusive. Taken in total, Barland's results were not definitive; however, they do little to support the claims of the psychological stress evaluation proponents.

‡ Many would argue, however, that stress does not uniformly accompany lying—in the case of a sociopath (say), the individual probably would exhibit no stress at all when telling a lie.

We are sensitive to the argument that voice analyzers cannot be adequately tested in the laboratory because only low risk lies can be induced in this milieu and only high risk lies can be detected. However, it is our opinion that this argument is not a valid one. Indeed, we are carrying out a series of studies investigating this issue; one of which recently has been reported by Geison.[34] In this case, 12 individuals (plus 7 controls) with very strong feelings about a controversial social issue were induced to read two statements; one endorsing their position, the other endorsing an opinion completely opposed to theirs. Further, until the experiment was over (and they were informed of its true nature), subjects were led to believe that they would be publicly associated with the lie. Their (high) stress level, associated with the lie, was confirmed by a test of anxiety as well as by direct observation by the experimenter. The obtained tape recordings were processed through the PSE, and three groups of judges evaluated the traces: (1) ten individuals without prior knowledge of the technique, (2) five phoneticians experienced in signal analysis, and (3) three experienced PSE operators; the first two groups received training based on the PSE manual. The correct identifications of the stressed and unstressed samples were found to be roughly at the chance level for all three groups of judges. The PSE operators did score 58.3% correct for the unstressed samples, and the phoneticians 61.7% correct for the stressed; but *overall,* the scores were not significantly different from chance. Thus, it was concluded that "the PSE is not a very good tool for . . . the detection of lies."[34]

To summarize, it would appear that voice analyzers are not very effective in detecting low risk lies;[8,56] for high risk lies, the correct identifications appear to range from chance or a little above[34,42] to very high scores.[37] Kubis,[45] Barland,[8] and Puckett[70] have indicated that these devices constitute not nearly as powerful a tool as does the polygraph—and the limitations of the polygraph are well known. Moreover, no one as yet has tested any of the voice analyzers with speech samples that have been transmitted over a telephone, and research of this type is very much needed.

While it is possible to argue that voice analyzers are both valid and effective as lie detectors, it appears that the much stronger case is to the contrary. Moreover, the negative arguments become more compelling when it is remembered that when claims are made about *any* device, it is incumbent upon the proponents of the system to unequivocally demonstrate the validity of their contentions. Perhaps even more serious are the well-documented fears that these devices will be abused, that civil liberties will be violated by their use (especially over the telephone), and that the right to privacy will be invaded. Finally, even though scientists working in this area are keenly aware of the critical need of law enforcement agencies for a valid tool of this type, the inescapable conclusion is that such an aid does not presently exist.

REFERENCES

1. ALMEIDA, A., G. FLEISCHMANN, G. HEIKE & E. THORMANN. 1975. Short time statistics of the fundamental tone in verbal utterances under psychic stress. Paper read at the Eighth International Congress of Phonetic Sciences, Leeds, England, August 17–23.

2. Anonymous. 1975. Dallas: new questions and answers. Newsweek (April 28): 36–38.
3. Anonymous. 1976. Washington report: house committee calls for ban on government use of polygraph. APA Monitor **1:** 10.
4. APPLEY, M. H. & R. TRUMBULL. 1967. On the concept of psychological stress. *In* Psychological Stress: Issues in Research. M. H. Appley & R. Trumbull, Eds. Meredith Publishing Co. New York, N.Y.
5. ARNOLD, M. B. 1967. Stress and emotion. *In* Psychological Stress: Issues in Research. M. H. Appley & R. Trumbull, Eds. Meredith Publishing Co. New York, N.Y.
6. BACHRACH, A. J. 1979. Speech and its potential for stress monitoring. *In* Proceedings, Workshop on Monitoring Vital Signs in the Diver. C. E. G. Lundgren, Ed.: 78–93. Undersea Medical Society and Office of Naval Research. Bethesda, Md.
7. BANNISTER, M. L. 1972. An instrumental and judgmental analysis of voice samples from psychiatrically hospitalized and non-hospitalized adolescents. Ph.D. Dissertation. University of Kansas. Lawrence, Kans.
8. BARLAND, G. 1973. Use of voice changes in detection of deception. (abst.). J. Acoust. Soc. Am. **54:** 63.
9. BENNETT, R. H., JR. 1977. Hagoth: Fundamentals of Voice Stress Analysis. Hagoth Corp. Issaquah, Wash.
10. Board of Directors. 1973. Resolution Concerning the Dektor Psychological Stress Evaluator (PSE-1). American Polygraph Association. Miami, Fla.
11. BOLLINGER, D. L. 1958. A theory of pitch accent in English. Word **14:** 109–149.
12. BONNER, R. 1943. Changes in the speech pattern under emotional tension. Am. J. Psychol. **56:** 262–273.
13. BRENNER, M. 1974. Stagefright and Stevens' Law. Paper presented at the Eastern Psychological Association Convention, New York, N.Y., April.
14. BROCKWAY, B. F., O. B. PLUMMER & B. M. LOWE. 1976. The effects of two types of nursing reassurance upon patient vocal stress levels as measured by a new tool, the PSE. Nurs. Res. **25:** 440–446.
15. BROWN, B. L., W. J. STRONG & A. C. RENCHER. 1973. Perceptions of personality from speech: effects of manipulations of acoustic parameters. J. Acoust. Soc. Am. **54:** 29–35.
16. BRUMLIK, J. & C. YAP. 1970. Normal Tremor: A Comparative Study. C. C. Thomas. Springfield, Ill.
17. CHEVRIE-MULLER, C., F. DODART, N. SEQUIER-DERMER & D. SALMON 1971. Étude des parametres acoustiques de la parole au cours de la schizophrenia de l'adolescent. Folia Phoniat. **23:** 401–428.
18. COSTANZO, F. S., N. N. MARKEL & P. R. COSTANZO. 1969. Voice quality profile and perceived emotion. J. Counsel. Psychol. **16:** 267–270.
19. DARBY, J. K. & H. HOLLIEN. 1977. Vocal and speech patterns of depressive patients. Folia Phoniat. **29:** 279–291.
20. DARBY, J. K. & A. SHERK. 1979. Speech studies in psychiatric populations. *In* Current Issues in the Phonetic Sciences. H. & P. Hollien, Eds.: 599–608. J. Benjamin, B.V. Amsterdam, The Netherlands.
21. DAVITZ, J. R. & L. J. DAVITZ. 1959. The communication of feelings through content-free speech. J. Commun. **9:** 6–13.
22. DENBER, M. A. 1978. Sound spectrum analysis of the mentally ill. Master's Thesis. University of Rochester. Rochester, N.Y.
23. DICK, W. 1975. Scientific evidence proves Ted told the truth about Chappaquidick. National Enquirer **49** (July 1).
24. DICK, W. 1975. Sirhan was hypnotized to kill Bobby Kennedy. National Enquirer **50** (October 27).
25. DWORKEN, A. 1975. Patty Hearst not guilty. Voice test proves she was forced to lie. National Enquirer **50** (September 23).
26. ELDRED, S. H. & D. B. PRICE. 1958. A linguistic evaluation of feeling states in psychotherapy. Psychiatry **21:** 115–121.
27. FAABORG-ANDERSON, K. 1957. Electromyographic investigation of intrinsic laryngeal muscles in humans. Acta Physiol. Scand. **41**(Supplement): 140.
28. FAIRBANKS, G. & W. PRONOVOST. 1939. An experimental study of the pitch characteristics of the voice during the expression of emotion. Speech Monogr. **6:** 87–104.

29. FAIRBANKS, G. & L. W. HOAGLIN. 1941. An experimental study of the durational characteristics of the voice during the expression of emotion. Speech Monogr. **8**: 85-90.
30. FONAGY, I. 1966. Electrophysiological and acoustic correlates of stress and stress perception. J. Speech Hear. Res. **9**: 231-244.
31. FRIEDHOFF, A. J., M. ALPERT & R. L. KURTZBERG. 1964. An electro-acoustical analysis of the effects of stress on voice. J. Neuropsychiatry **5**: 265-272.
32. FRY, D. B. 1955. Duration and intensity as physical correlates of linguistic stress. J. Accoust. Soc. Am. **27**: 765-768.
33. FRY, D. B. 1958. Experiments in the perception of stress. Lang. Speech **1**: 126-152.
34. GEISON, L. L. 1979. Evaluation of high stress lying by voice analysis. M.A. Thesis. University of Florida. Gainesville, Fla.
35. HAINES, R. 1976. Elizabeth Ray told the truth about the Washington sex scandal: Congressman Hayes did not. National Enquirer **51** (September).
36. HARGREAVES, W. A., J. A. STARKWEATHER & K. H. BLACKER. 1965. Voice quality in depression. J. Abnorm. Psychol. **70**: 218-220.
37. HEISSE, J. W. 1976. Audio stress analysis—A validation and reliability study of the Psychological Stress Evaluator (PSE). *In* Proceedings, 1976 Carnahan Conference on Crime Countermeasures, University of Kentucky, Ky.: 5-18.
38. HECKER, M. H. L., K. N. STEVENS, G. von BISMARCK & C. E. WILLIAMS. 1968. Manifestations of task-induced stress in the acoustic speech signal. J. Acoust. Soc. Am. **44**: 993-1001.
39. HELFRICH, H. & K. R. SCHERER. 1977. Experimental assessment of antidepressant drug effects using spectral analysis of voice. Paper presented at the fall meetings of the Acoustical Society of America, Miami Beach, Fla., December 13-16.
40. HICKS, J. W., JR. 1979. An acoustical/temporal analysis of emotional stress in speech. Ph.D. Dissertation. University of Florida. Gainesville, Fla.
41. HOLLIEN, H. & J. K. DARBY. 1979. Acoustic comparisons of psychotic and non-psychotic voices. *In* Current Issues in the Phonetic Sciences. H. & P. Hollien, Eds.: 609-614. J. Benjamin, B. V. Amsterdam, The Netherlands.
42. HOLLIEN, H., L. L. GEISON & J. W. HICKS, JR. 1980. Stress/lie studies utilizing the PSE. Paper read at the annual meeting of the American Academy of Forensic Sciences, New Orleans, La., February 20-23.
43. HUTTAR, G. L. 1968. Relations between prosodic variables and emotions in normal American English utterances. J. Speech Hear. Res. **11**: 481-487.
44. INBAR, G. F., G. EDEN & M. A. KAPLAN. 1977. Frequency modulation in the human voice and the source of its mediation. *In* Proceedings, 1977 Carnahan Conference on Crime Countermeasures, University of Kentucky, Lexington, Ky.: 213-319.
45. KUBIS, J. 1973. Comparison of Voice Analysis and Polygraph as Lie Detection Procedures. U.S. Army Land Warfare Laboratory. Aberdeen Proving Ground, Md.
46. KUPEC, E. W. 1977. Truth or the consequences. Law Enforce. Commun. **4**: 12-18/42-45.
47. KURODA, I., O. FUJUVARA, N. OHAMURA & N. UTSUKI. 1976. Method for determining pilot stress through analysis of voice communication. Aviat. Space Environ. Med. **47**: 528-533.
48. LAZARUS, R. S. 1966. Psychological Stress and the Coping Process. McGraw-Hill Book Co., Inc. New York, N.Y.
49. LEHISTE, I. & G. E. PETERSON. 1959. Vowel amplitude and phonetic stress in American speech. J. Acoust. Soc. Am. **31**: 428-435.
50. LEITH, W. R., J. L. TIMMONS & M. D. SUGARMAN. 1977. The use of the Psychological Stress Evaluator with stutterers. Paper read to the Convention of the American Speech and Hearing Association, Chicago, Ill., November 2-5.
51. LIEBERMAN, P. & S. B. MICHAELS. 1962. Some aspects of fundamental frequency and envelope amplitude as related to emotional content of speech. J. Acoust. Soc. Am. **34**: 922-927.
52. LIPPOLD, O. 1971. Physiological tremor. Sci. Am. **224**: 65-73.
53. LYKKEN, D. 1974. Psychology and the lie detector industry. Am. Psychol.: 725-739.
54. MARKEL, N. N. 1969. Relationship between voice-quality profiles and MMPI profiles in psychiatic patients. J. Abnorm. Psychol. **74**: 61-66.

55. MARKEL, N. N., M. F. BEIN & J. A. PHILLIS. 1973. The relationship between words and tone of voice. Lang. Speech **16:** 15-21.

56. McGLONE, R. E., C. PETRIE & J. FRYE. 1974. Acoustic analyses of low-risk lies. (abst.) J. Acoust. Soc. Am. **55:** S20.

57. McGLONE, R. E. 1975. Tests of the Psychological Stress Evaluator (PSE) as a lie and stress detector. *In* Proceedings, 1975 Carnahan Conference on Crime Countermeasures, University of Kentucky, Lexington, Ky.: 83-86.

58. McGLONE, R. E. & H. HOLLIEN. 1976. Partial analysis of the acoustic signal of stressed and unstressed speech. *In* Proceedings, 1976 Carnahan Conference on Crime Countermeasures, University of Kentucky, Lexington, Ky.: 19-21.

59. MOL, H. & E. M. UHLENBECK. 1956. The linguistic relevance of intensity in stress. Lingua. **5:** 205-213.

60. MOSES, P. J. 1954. The Voice of Neurosis. Grune and Stratton. New York, N.Y.

61. MOSKOWITZ, E. 1951. Voice quality in the schizophrenic reaction type. Ph.D. Dissertation. New York University. New York, N.Y.

62. NERI, P. A. The Dektor-Psychological Stress Evaluator: an interim report. (Unpublished manuscript.)

63. NEWMAN, S. S. & V. G. MATHER. 1938. Analysis of spoken language of patients with affective disorders. Am. J. Psychiatry **91:** 912-942.

64. O'TOOLE, G. 1975. Lee Harvey Oswald was innocent. Penthouse **6**(8): 45-46 & 124-132.

65. OSTWALD, P. F. 1961. The sounds of emotional disturbance. Arch. Gen. Psychiatry **5:** 587-592.

66. OSTWALD, P. F. 1963. Soundmaking: The Acoustic Communication of Emotion. Charles C. Thomas. Springfield, Ill.

67. OSTWALD, P. F. 1964. Acoustic manifestations of emotional disturbance. *In* Disorders of Communication. D. Rioch & E. Weinstein, Eds.: 450-465. Williams & Wilkins Co. Baltimore, Md.

68. OSTWALD, P. F. & A. SKOLNIKOFF. 1966. Speech disturbances in a schizophrenic adolescent. Postgraduate Med. **12:** 40-49.

69. PAPCUN, G. 1973. The effects of psychological stress on speech. Paper delivered to the fall meeting of the Acoustical Society of America, Los Angeles, Calif., October 30-November 2.

70. PUCKETT, T. 1980. Voice stress analysis procedures vis-a-vis polygraph procedure in real life testing situations. (Unpublished manuscript.)

71. RICE, D. G., G. M. ABRAMS & J. H. SAXMAN. 1969. Speech and physiological correlates of "flat" affect. Arch. Gen. Psychiatry **20:** 566-572.

72. ROSS, M., R. J. DUFFY, H. S. COOKER & R. L. SERGEANT. 1973. Contribution of the lower audible frequencies to the recognition of emotions. A.A.D.: 37-42.

73. SAXMAN, J. M. & K. W. BURK. 1968. Speaking fundamental frequency and rate characteristics of adult female schizophrenics. J. Speech Hear. Res. **11:** 194-302.

74. SCHERER, K. L. Non-linguistic vocal indicators of emotion and psychopathology. *In* Emotions and Psychopathology. C. E. Izard, Ed. Plenum Press, New York, N.Y. (In press.)

75. SHIPP, T. & R. E. McGLONE. 1973. Physiologic correlates of acoustic correlates of psychological stress. (abst.). J. Acoust. Soc. Am. **53:** S63.

76. SILVERMAN, F. H. & E. M. SILVERMAN. 1975. Effects of threat of shock for being disfluent on fluency of normal speakers. Percep. Motor Skills **41:** 353-354.

77. SIMONOV, P. V. & M. V. FROLOV. 1973. Utilization of human voice for estimation of man's emotional stress and state of attention. Aeronaut. Med. **44:** 256-258.

78. SIMONOV, P. V., M. V. FROLOV & V. L. TABGKIN. 1975. Use of the invariant method of speech analysis to discern the emotional state of announcers. Aviat. Space Environ. Med. **46:** 1014-1016.

79. SMITH, G. A. 1974. The measurement of anxiety: a new method by voice analysis. IRCS (Res. Biomed., Technol., Psychiat. Clin. Psychol.) **2:** 1707.

80. SPOERRI, T. H. 1966. Speaking voice of the schizophrenic patient. Arch. Gen. Psychiatry **14:** 581-585.

81. STARKWEATHER, J. A. 1961. Vocal communication of personality and human feelings. J. Commun. **11:** 63-72.

82. STARKWEATHER, J. A. 1956. Content-free speech as a source of information about the speaker. J. Abnorm. Soc. Psychol. **52:** 394–402.
83. VanderCar, D. H., J. GREANER, N. HIBLER, C. D. SPEELBERGER & S. BLOCH. 1980. A description and analysis of the operation and validity of the Psychological Stress Evaluator. J. Forensic Sci. **25:** 174–188.
84. WILLIAMS, C. E. & K. N. STEVENS. 1969. On determining the emotional state of pilots during flight: an exploratory study. Aeronaut. Med. **40:** 1369–1372.
85. WILLIAMS, C. E. & K. N. STEVENS. 1972. Emotions and speech: some acoustical correlates. J. Acoust. Soc. Am. **52:** 1238–1250.

HYPNOSIS AND EVIDENCE: HELP OR HINDRANCE?

Herbert Spiegel*
Department of Psychiatry
College of Physicians and Surgeons
Columbia University
New York, New York 10032

INTRODUCTION

During the past 50 years, there has been a gradual, but definite, emergence of the use of hypnosis in the field of medicine. With this there has been much controversy and, at the same time, an appreciable increase in our knowledge about the phenomenon.[1] More recently, there has been an interest in the uses of hypnosis in the field of forensic medicine. Here the controversies are even more heated, complicated by the intrusion of this controversial subject into legal procedures. Much of the controversy is aggravated and compounded by serious misconceptions about hypnosis itself. In order to minimize the areas of unnecessary friction, it would be well to begin by dealing with the most common misconceptions and clarifying them.

MISCONCEPTIONS

The most common misconception is that hypnosis is sleep. Hypnosis is not only *not* sleep, but is the very opposite of sleep. It is a state of alert, attentive, receptive, integrated concentration characterized by a parallel awareness. That is, the subject in trance can, on the one hand, be aware of a relationship to another person and, at the same time, be intensely involved in another facet of his own life experience. This sensitive capacity to maintain a ribbon of parallel concentration is an indication of extreme alertness, the opposite of sleep. Since the word hypnosis derives from a Greek root meaning sleep, it is an unfortunate term to apply to this phenomenon, but we are historically and traditionally bound to this label.

Another serious misconception is that the hypnotist projects the hypnotic spell onto the subject. This is utter nonsense. The hypnotist projects nothing at all. Instead, he simply taps the natural trance capacity that is inherent in the subject. Trance capacity is a talent that is either genetically determined or learned in an imprint-like manner during early developmental years, or both. The degree of intensity of trance capacity can be measured clinically within 5 to 10 minutes on a 0–5 scale. This measured capability remains stable during adult years except when impaired by some forms of mental illness or by drugs that impair ability to concentrate. A

* Address correspondence to Dr. Spiegel at 19 East 88th Street, New York, N.Y. 10028.

slight reduction of previous capacity can occur with aging, especially by the seventh decade. In everyday life, when a person is highly motivated or highly charged for a specific goal, he is prone to spontaneously shift into his own trance level to facilitate the achievement of a task. What the hypnotist does in formal hypnosis is to simply tap this capacity with the subject's cooperation and compliance.

A third misconception is that only mentally weak or sick people are hypnotizable. This is precisely wrong. It is the mentally healthy population that is usually hypnotizable. For example, psychopaths, persons with character disorders, schizophrenics, the mentally retarded, depressed persons, and persons with neurological deficits that interfere with concentration all have great difficulty concentrating enough in this disciplined way to allow the trance to occur.

Another misunderstanding is that hypnosis occurs only when a hypnotist hypnotizes a subject. We know, of course, that it can occur if the subject cooperates when the hypnotist gives him the signal to go into trance. But more often, hypnosis occurs spontaneously in the person's life, especially under duress or under highly motivating, challenging situations. This fact is especially germane to our topic, which we shall return to later.

A fifth misconception is that hypnosis is dangerous. We now know that hypnosis itself is not dangerous but that the trance state can be used mischievously. One of the features of the trance is that the person goes into such a state of intense concentration that peripheral awareness decreases, customary guardedness decreases, and an assumption of trust—even naive trust—occurs, which makes the subject more vulnerable to deception, exploitation, coercion, or trickery. Such violation of trust by the hypnotist can indeed be dangerous and harmful, but it is not the hypnosis itself that is harmful.

Another misunderstanding about hypnosis is that the hypnotist himself must be some kind of a charismatic, unusual, or weird person in order to evoke a trance state. This is not true. Of course, if the subject perceives the hypnotist as charismatic, that indeed adds to the impact of the interaction; but by and large, any person relating to another person can, if the atmosphere is appropriate, signal a subject to shift into a trance state. Trance induction is simple. It is teachable and learnable; and in a very short time, a novice can be as effective in inducing trance as an experienced hypnotist.

Still another misconception is that women are more hypnotizable than men. Repeatedly, scientific studies have shown that when tested appropriately, there is no difference in distribution of hypnotizability between the adult male and female populations. About 70% of the population is capable of some degree of hypnosis. Roughly, about 15% go into a light trance, which is the peak capacity for that group. Another 15% are capable of very intense trance states, and the remaining are somewhere in the midrange. It is generally observed that whatever capacity a person has can be slightly enhanced by stress or high motivation. With this consideration, it is not an exaggeration to say that well over half of the population is capable of some degree of appreciable trance experience, especially under stress conditions.

ENHANCED MEMORY RECALL WITH HYPNOSIS

The least controversial use of hypnosis is to enhance memory enough to recall simple, circumscribed data that are subject to further corroboration. For example, a witness sees a car or a truck long enough to scan the license number but, on first effort, is unable to remember the numbers. With the enhanced concentration that occurs in the trance state, it is possible to retrieve the memory of the license plate which at first recall was blurred. In a way, this is simply an extension of an everyday experience where on first effort, thinking about some event in the past is somewhat hazy, but with more effort and determination and collateral associations with the event, a clarifying memory emerges. This often occurs spontaneously, but it can also occur in a more structured way with formal hypnotic trance.

A more dramatic use of hypnosis is the uncovering of amnesic periods. For example, often after a head injury, there is an amnesic phase for the victim. Of course if the trauma leads to unconsciousness, the events that occur during the unconscious phase are called "amnesia"; but in fact, because of the unconsciousness, the events never were perceived by the victim in the first place. After consciousness returns, there is first a patch, then continuous recall of life experience. With head trauma, another kind of amnesia often occurs, that is, a "retrograde" amnesia. This means that even though the patient was conscious up to the point of the impact that led to the unconsciousness, when he recovers his consciousness, he is amnesic for a time frame of seconds to minutes prior to the point of impact. This retrograde amnesia is usually of a psychological nature and is very often recoverable. Here is an example of how hypnosis can facilitate this recovery. A 16-year-old young man was in an automobile accident with his father. The father was driving and was killed by the impact of a truck hitting the car from their right. The young man was also struck with a head injury and became unconscious. He recovered consciousness about an hour later in the hospital. Technically, since the boy's father was dead and the boy himself was amnesic to the entire episode, there was no witness to this accident except the driver of the truck. The driver's account went unchallenged. Some time later, it was discovered that the young man was capable of hypnosis; on a 0–5 scale, he scored a 4. Thus, when instructed to go into trance and regress, he was able to recall certain details of how he and his father had dropped off his aunt and had traveled along a certain road up to a certain point. He could then recall the truck coming down from the right and his father saying he was sure the truck would stop because there was a stop sign at the intersection. It was at this point that everything went blank. He came out of the trance with a sense of disappointment, thinking that he had failed. Actually, what he had done was to uncover the retrograde part of the amnesia. These facts were later confirmed by other testimony, and it now meant that there were technically two witnesses to the accident instead of one. With this new situation, the insurance company agreed to settle the issues rather than go to court.

In another case, a woman in her thirties, divorced, and living with her children in a ground-floor apartment was attacked one night by an intruder who entered her bedroom through the window. He ravaged her with a knife in an apparent attempt to kill her. She was wounded, rushed to the hospital, and almost miraculously recovered. For months she had no memory of what she had seen prior to the knife's coming at her. Police investigations focused upon two suspects but with not enough hard information. To enhance her memory, she asked for help with hypnosis; and it was discovered that she was capable of a midrange trance. While in a trance state and with a great deal of emotion, tears, shouting, and reexperiencing of the event in the present tense, she gave enough descriptive information about the features of the intruder to identify her ex-husband as the person. Although in the trance state she gave specific details that identified him, it was only with great reluctance that she acknowledged that it was, in fact, her ex-husband. When she was brought out of the trance state and asked to review what she had recalled, she expressed dismay at the information and hinted that somehow she had known this but had not wanted to admit it to herself. Perhaps, with time and the practical need to pursue the investigation, she allowed this to surface. But it is also possible that this was a self-serving fantasy. Whether or not the assailant actually was her husband must be verified by other data.

In the *Leyra* case,[2] hypnosis was used along with deception and coercion to elicit a confession. Leyra was apprehended and accused of killing his father and mother. After hours of interrogation at the police station, a doctor was sent to treat Leyra in his cell because he had complained of a headache. Along with other treatment, the doctor hypnotized Leyra and told him that he might as well admit to the murders and that he, the doctor, would see to it that the police would "go easy" with him. Leyra then confessed to the doctor. After this, he was taken to the front of the police station, and in the presence of his business partner, Leyra repeated the confession that he had given to the doctor. He was found guilty and sentenced to the electric chair. The appellate court ordered a new trial on learning that the confession had been coerced. On the basis of that confession alone, they could not sentence Leyra to death. At the second trial, he was again found guilty. This time the prosecution used the second confession, which he had made to his partner shortly after the first one. For the second confession, he had not been in a formal trance state. This case went all the way up to the United States Supreme Court; and on a split decision, a new trial was ordered. The majority opinion, written by Justice Black, held that the confession that was repeated a second time outside of the cell had to be regarded as part of a continuum and, therefore, had the same coerced quality of the first confession. At the third trial, the case against Leyra was built largely around fragmented circumstantial evidence, including some bloody clothes and the testimony of a girlfriend. He again was found guilty. On appeal, the court ruled that the evidence was too circumstantial and fragmented for the court to take Leyra's life, and they reversed the decision. Leyra was subsequently freed of all charges. In this instance, the deception used by the doctor to elicit the confession was perpetrated more easily because the victim was in a trance state, with a reduced level of critical judgment. The state of trust enabled the prisoner to feel freer to expose his inner thoughts and memories. It was this feature of coercion and deception that the court seized upon in reversing the lower court. Further, the Supreme Court recognized that the posthypnotic confession exhibited the same feature of coercion as did the original confession.

In the *Miller* case in Connecticut,[3] the issue of hypnosis became critical because its use was not even mentioned during the first trial. Miller was found guilty of transferring a large amount of heroin from one car to another. He was sentenced to 12 years. The prosecution arguments and the jury decision of guilt were based almost entirely upon the testimony of a French-Canadian named Caron, who at first was vague, then somewhat certain, about identifying Miller. But after he returned from an interrogation in Texas dealing with another aspect of the same case, Caron was positive that Miller was the man he had seen and so testified. After Miller was sentenced, the defense—with the prosecutor's agreement—examined the witness Caron. Caron also agreed to be examined with hypnosis. When he appeared for the examination, Caron revealed that he had already been hypnotized before in Texas by a psychologist working with the prosecuting attorney. It was understood that Caron's own pending sentence as an illegal alien would be influenced by the extent of his cooperation with this prosecutor. It turned out that this prosecutor was innocently exploring some other aspects of the case and wanted to find out if Caron could remember a certain license number. While under hypnosis, the prosecution attorneys kept referring to Miller as the guilty man. Miller was a hairdresser, and they would shift from referring to "the hairdresser" and to Miller—and all during the interrogation, there were repeated inferences that Miller was assumed to be guilty. When Caron returned to Connecticut to participate in the trial there, he suddenly became aware that Miller was the man he had seen and so testified. On testing, it turned out that Caron was capable of a moderate capacity for hypnosis; when the case reached the appellate court, Judge Friendly put his finger on this single issue. He asked the Connecticut prosecutor why he had not mentioned that Caron had been hypnotized in Texas regarding this same case. The prosecuting attorney stated that he had not thought it would be important. Judge Friendly asked the prosecutor if he did not think that the defense could have made quite an issue of this with the jury. The prosecutor allowed that this was a possibility. Largely around that point, the appellate court reversed the decision and ordered a new trial. In the second trial, the issue of possible contamination and fixation of memory with hypnosis was introduced. Miller was acquitted.

What is intriguing is that the district attorney in Texas and the psychologist in Texas were in no way attempting to influence Caron. They only coincidentally referred to Miller as the guilty one; but by so doing, they in effect "brainwashed" an intimidated witness to clear his thinking and to posthypnotically assert in court that he was sure that Miller was the man he had seen, even though at no time prior to the Texas experience had he been so clear and positive about Miller.

THE HONEST LIAR SYNDROME

In 1968, in order to explore further this issue of the reliability of information given under hypnosis and its extension after hypnosis, the following experiment took place: A man in his forties—a successful businessman, not a psychiatric patient—volunteered to be the subject. On a 0–5 scale he scored 5, putting him in the top 15% of the highly hypnotizable population. He agreed to appear at the NBC television studios with Frank McGee and myself. The entire experiment was recorded with a movie camera. While he was in a Grade 5 trance, he was told that the communists were taking over the control of the television networks; that this was the real truth; and that no matter who tried to dissuade him of this belief, he would stick to it. In fact, he would even intensify his conviction if he were to be challenged. He was brought out of the formal trance state locked into this premise, i.e., that the communists were taking over the networks. For quite a period of time, Frank McGee challenged him about this. The more McGee pressed him, the firmer he held to the premise. In fact he went so far as to name names, spelling out details of a meeting that had taken place in a loft above a movie house off Sheridan Square where six people had gathered and talked about this plot. He even gave a specific name and described the physical features of the man who was the leader. After he was given the cutoff signal to come out of this trance bind, he had total amnesia for anything that took place. Five months later, he was shown the movie of this event. He was shocked and astounded at what he had said. He had no knowledge of any such person as he had described and had no memory of any meeting having taken place. He experienced the whole sequence as a blackout. He could not deny that he had said these things, because he saw himself doing so in a sound movie. He was baffled and could not understand where all this information was coming from, because he simply had no knowledge of any such event. What is frightening about this experience is that he was a .man whose political orientation is somewhat left of center yet he was talking to Frank McGee as if he, the subject, were an ultraconservative. That is, his allegations and conduct were entirely foreign to his everyday political beliefs. This paradox is critically important to the theme of this paper. During the experiment, in response to the hypnotic signal, the subject created a totally false story to rationalize his compliance. He sincerely believed it to be true. Since he was locked into the hypnotic bind, he suspended his own critical judgment. He lied but did not actually know he was lying. At the time, he was in effect an honest liar.

the charges and sign the confession. He accepted the absence of any firsthand knowledge of the murder as due to "amnesia."

The new information about Peter's personality style and immaturity indicated that his having no memory for the event was not due to amnesia but rather was due to the fact that he had not actually been present and had not, in fact, committed the murder. However, he was unable to withstand the accusatory pressure of the police. This along with other points led to a court decision by the same judge who had presided over the original trial that an injustice had been done, and therefore, a new trial was ordered.

Following that decision, it was learned that exculpatory evidence, placing Peter Reilly five miles from the scene at the time the murder was committed, had been withheld by the prosecution during the first trial. Along with other issues, this led to still another court decision by another judge which dropped all charges against Peter; and he was freed.

Because the HIP indicated that Peter was not hypnotizable and not prone to amnesia, and because it further indicated that his confession was due to his immature and uncertain sense of self, the defense had a potent wedge to align with other issues, which led to vindication.

United States v. Thornton

Thornton was a military policeman charged with the kidnapping, rape, and murder of three teenagers as well as the wounding of another.[7] His defense was not guilty by virtue of insanity. This was in essence documented by a videotaped interview, which allegedly demonstrated that under hypnosis, Thornton revealed a dual personality. The "bad" personality committed acts that the "good" personality was not responsible for.

The HIP revealed a pattern of a person barely able to sustain a trance state. It is well established clinically that multiple personalities all have very high capacities for sustained trance experience.

The HIP was also consistent with the category of a sociopathic personality, capable of destructive acting-out, with guile and deceptive ploys to defend itself. Further, a sociopath usually does not qualify as "lacking substantial capacity" under the American Law Institute guidelines. The jury found Thornton guilty as charged. The defense's psychiatrists did not, at any time, assess Thornton's hypnotic capacity and were thus vulnerable to the charge that the accused had simulated a dual personality to deceive his doctors and the jury in his own desperate defense.

The HIP score was thus able to neutralize the drama of the videotaped dual personality thesis and identified Thornton as an ordinary psychopathic personality, responsible for his own acts.

United States v. Leonora Perez and Filipina Narciso

During the summer of 1975, an unusual number of postoperative patients in the Veteran's Administration Hospital in Ann Arbor, Michigan, suffered respiratory arrests.[8] Some died. Those who survived had patchy or hazy memory or no memory at all of what had occurred. Several of the patients had had memory or psychiatric deficits before their surgery. When respiratory arrest with cerebral anoxia episodes were imposed upon this, it was not surprising that accurate and reliable witnesses were difficult to find. It was suspected that a curare-like substance (Pavulon) had been injected into the intravenous tubings to bring about the respiratory arrests. The FBI was authorized to explore for leads with hypnosis. By agreement and design, all testimony of witnesses was put on record and identified as data prior to the hypnotic interviews. It was clearly understood that data obtained with hypnosis were, at best, possible leads for further evidence but were certainly not to be used alone as direct testimony at trial. If they were to be used, they would certainly be vulnerable to charges of contamination. All interviews with hypnosis were recorded on videotape with time and date recorded simultaneously.

The HIP was administered, and several witnesses were eliminated because the test revealed that they were not hypnotizable. About 12 scored well enough to be interrogated further with hypnosis. New information in fact did emerge, which led to indictments of two nurses (Perez and Narciso). At the pretrial hearing, some of the videotaped material was shown. Arguments ensued. The judge ruled that, in principle, information obtained through the use of hypnosis could be presented to the jury. The government case was entirely circumstantial. The data from hypnosis interviews served only to aid the more customary evidence and testimony. The jury voted both nurses guilty.

Later, the judge denied a motion for judgments of acquittal but did grant the defendants' motion for a new trial. The judge concluded that the misconduct of the government did reasonably affect the jury. However, the term "misconduct" did not refer to the manner in which the hypnosis had been used to elicit information. It dealt with other technical issues of conduct unrelated to the hypnosis. Later, with a new district attorney in office, the government decided to drop the case.

In this case, the HIP was used to scan and identify potential witnesses, who were then interviewed with hypnosis with the expectation that the information elicited would aid in discovering other evidence with which to build the case for presentation.

The Torsney Case

Torsney was a white New York City policeman charged with shooting and killing a young black boy. The police had answered an emergency call in a black neighborhood in Brooklyn where an altercation was allegedly occurring. After investigation, as the police had left the apartment, someone had warned them to "be careful since there was a man out there with a gun." As the officers had walked toward their cars, a young boy had moved forward and asked Torsney a question. Torsney had thought he saw a shining object on the boy, so the officer had quickly drawn his unlocked pistol and shot the young boy.[9,10]

Torsney's defense was not guilty by reason of psychosis due to epilepsy. He was tried in a Brooklyn courtroom with an all-white jury. The HIP indicated that he was quite hypnotizable, not psychotic, and prone to respond to stress with hysterical dissociation. In fact, when tested for his hypnotizability in the presence of the defense counsel and the district attorney, Torsney's trance response was so persistent and intense that extra cutoff signals were necessary to get him out of the dissociated trance state. He was obviously not the controlled, vigilant, secure combat officer that one would expect to see at such an assignment. Torsney conveyed a sense of a sad, not too competent man in the wrong job. His general demeanor usually elicited sympathy. During the trial, he sat staring at the table most of the time. Although his defense was largely based on the diagnosis of epilepsy and resulting psychosis, none of the many tests and examinations done by either side revealed any evidence of his ever having had epilepsy. Nor was evidence of psychosis ever elicited in the psychological tests performed by the psychologists for either side. The prosecution's position was that Torsney was simply a frightened, not very competent police officer, who, under stress, had panicked and shown poor judgment by using his gun in a clumsy effort to protect himself against an imagined threat. This is an act that might even be regarded as within normal range in the average person but is certainly not the response of a trained police officer, who has every reason to expect these emergencies in the course of his everyday work. The jury voted to acquit Torsney by reason of insanity.

Torsney was then committed to a state psychiatric facility for treatment and care. Over a year later, the hospital reported that they had at no time found evidence of epilepsy or psychosis and wanted to discharge him. At first, the trial court agreed. Then the appellate court refused, claiming that the hospital had not treated Torsney for the disabilities decided upon by the jury. By a 4–3 decision, the court of appeals reversed the appellate decision and released Torsney. This highlighted the absurdity of making clinical diagnosis for treatment by means of legal tactics in front of a jury. Further, with the jury decision, Torsney now made claim for medical disability from the Police Department.

However, the Police Department was not legally bound to automatically accept the diagnosis without making its own judicial investigation. Accordingly, another hearing was held, and essentially the same arguments were presented by both sides. The presiding officer was obliged to report a summary of the hearings with a recommendation to the police commissioner. Ultimately, the police commissioner ruled that Torsney was not psychotic and not epileptic; because his actions indicated ineptness, Torsney was discharged from the police force without any medical disability.

In many ways, the Torsney case exemplifies the recurrent weaknesses of our adjudicatory process in determining responsibility for an act. The compassionate concept of not punishing authentically mentally ill persons for actions beyond their control was stretched so far in this case that in a perverted way, the state was using a hospital to "punish" a man for committing a crime. Then the state berated the doctors for not playing the punishment game to comply with the jury decision. The doctors balked by discovering, on their own, that Torsney was not psychotic, not epileptic, and did not belong in a hospital. Clever courtroom tactics had convinced the jury, but the state hospital and eventually the Police Department itself viewed the evidence otherwise. The HIP, a 10-minute clinical test, identified the theme of an inept police officer who panicked under stress. This was ultimately concurred with by the hospital and Police Department.

CONCLUSION

Back to the question posed by this paper, Is hypnosis a help or hindrance in coping with the complex issues of evidence? Clearly, the answer is:

1. Used knowledgeably with appreciation of their limits, hypnosis techniques can be helpful.

2. Knowledge about hypnosis enables us to identify its misuse and abuse.

3. Since hypnosis occurs spontaneously with so many people daily, ignorance about the phenomenon obfuscates the judicious discovery and use of evidence. Therefore, I disagree with my medical, psychiatric, and psychology colleagues who would like to preempt this field and deny its use to other professions. Everyday phenomena like spontaneous hypnosis occur regardless of the territorial claims of various guilds or power groups. I strongly advocate that all professionals dealing with interrogation—this includes qualified police officers, prosecuting and defense attorneys—alert themselves, inform themselves, and become even more knowledgeable about this intriguing phenomenon in order to cope with it more expertly.

SUMMARY

Clarifying misconceptions about hypnosis can reduce confusion about the place of hypnosis in forensic medicine. Hypnosis identifies a person's capacity for attentive, receptive concentration with parallel awareness. While in trance concentration, memory recall under interrogation should not only be subject to all the usual investigative safeguards with checks and balances, but even more so because the leverage effect of hypnotically enhanced memory is achieved at the risk of contamination by external and/or internal cues. This Janus-like feature enables incredibly accurate revivification and recall of perceived events but can also evoke false memories, false confessions, and the "honest liar syndrome." The internal and external factors that account for these contradictory possibilities—and the appropriate safeguards—are considered with case illustrations.

In addition, a new use of trance capacity assessment contributes to clarifying diagnosis and the mental defect/disease issue.

Knowledge of the uses and limits of hypnosis by the interrogating professionals enhances the judicious process of eliciting information and evidence.

REFERENCES

1. SPIEGEL, H. & D. SPIEGEL. 1978. Trance and Treatment: Clinical Uses of Hypnosis. Basic Books. New York, N.Y.
2. Leyra v. Denno, 347 U.S. 556 (1954).
3. U.S. v. Miller, 411 F.2d 825 (2d Cir. 1969).
4. Conn. v. Reilly, 5285 (1973).
5. Reilly v. Conn., 0–24981-5 (1976–6).
6. CONNERY, D. S. 1977. Guilty Until Proven Innocent. G.P. Putnam's Sons. New York, N.Y.
7. U.S. v. Thornton (U.S. Dist. Court W.D. Mo. 1977).
8. U.S. v. Narciso and Perez, Crim. No. 7–80149 E.D. Mich., S.D. (1977).
9. N.Y.C. v. Torsney, 3923 (1976).
10. Dept. Hearing, N.Y.C.P.D. Torsney Case, Hon. Nicholas Figueroa (1979).

THE DETERMINATION OF MALINGERING

Israella Y. Bash*

Psychiatric Associates
Science Park Medical Center
College Park, Maryland 20740

Murray Alpert†

Department of Psychology
New York University Medical Center
New York, New York 10016

INTRODUCTION

The problem of malingering presents a frequent and a difficult challenge in clinical psychology, forensic psychiatry, and many other related areas. Scores of studies have investigated the general problem, but the need for a clearer understanding of what we mean by "malingering" and how to detect it is obvious to anyone who has been confronted with the need to evaluate particular cases. Aside from the general considerations of a philosophical, nosological, or clinical nature, the pragmatic difficulties and consequences relating to the patient's disposition within the criminal justice system make the recognition and accurate detection of malingering an issue of some importance. In the forensic setting (the prison ward), we frequently see patients who present a clinical picture that gives rise to the strong suspicion that they are feigning or exaggerating the symptoms of mental illness in order to escape the probable and undesirable consequences of their criminal behavior, i.e., that they are malingering.

At present, the "state of the art" is such that these suspected malingerers are commonly detected by rather vague clinical intuitions, more or less influenced by observations and interpretations of patient behavior as (perhaps selectively) observed by nursing personnel and by certain exaggerated or incongruous aspects of patient behavior. The present study was designed to test promising objective and reliable techniques to evaluate and diagnose malingering in forensic and/or hospital settings.

There are many who regard malingering as evidence of a mental disease in its own right. Therefore, it becomes significant to ask whether malingerers are distinguishable from nonmalingerers in ways that go beyond the specification in the basic definition—for example, with respect to aspects of their personal, social, and psychological histories, or with respect to other psychological characteristics, and so on. The present study has bearing on these questions insofar as they involve a comparison of

* Present affiliation: Godding Division, St. Elizabeth Hospital, Washington, D.C. 20020.
† Please address reprint requests to Dr. Alpert.

psychiatrically diagnosed malingerers (individuals feigning psychoses and claiming auditory hallucinations) and nonmalingering, nonpsychotic individuals, both groups being drawn from a population about which there is generally little question that they have recently committed some serious violation of law. In a similar fashion, one can develop the question of whether malingerers can be distinguished from psychotics, i.e., Is the person who feigns schizophrenia the same kind of a person as the one who is actually schizophrenic? Again, the present study has bearing on this question.

Several limitations have been accepted for the present study: (1) we have accepted the psychiatric diagnosis as a criterion of malingering; (2) the subjects (S) are all temporary residents of a prison ward of Bellevue Hospital in New York City, sent there by the courts after being indicted for a crime; (3) the diagnosed malingerers do not cover the gamut of the forms of malingering (i.e., all feign schizophrenia with auditory hallucinations), and thus the outcome of this study could not support the hypothesis that malingerers in general constitute a distinctive group of persons; and (4) the present study is constricted with respect to the range of variables included—it concentrates on the malingering act as such. Our question is whether the malingerer is acting out lines and gestures that are laid out for him or whether he is basically acting out a character. It is harder to *live* or *become* the enacted character; it imposes a greater demand on the person's personality than does carrying out a routine. Following this line of thought leads to a major premise on which this study, in its theoretical aspect, is based. The more narrowly constructed the malingering act is, the less is the likelihood that the actor's own personality is involved. The more differentiatedly adaptive the malingering is to a variety of situations, the greater is the likelihood that the malingerer's own personality is involved. It so happens that the variables we have selected as most promising with respect to the primary concerns of the present study are derived from instruments that are widely used for the investigation of personality, i.e., the Rorschach, Bender-Gestalt, Structured Clinical Interview (SCI), and Wechsler Adult Intelligence Scale (WAIS). With the use of these instruments, differences, if any, between malingerers and the comparison groups will be explored.

The idea of expecting differentiating responses from suspected malingerers stems from the notion that a malingerer does not know how a psychotic patient (schizophrenic) will behave in certain situations and, consequently, will respond in a different way than a real psychotic patient. To evaluate this notion, several tests—each of which has been reported in the literature to have relevant features—were employed: WAIS, Rorschach, Bender-Gestalt, SCI, and the Betts test.

In addition, since the most common complaint of the suspected malingerer in forensic settings is auditory hallucinations, the present study investigated this phenomenon. For that purpose, the Perceptual Characteristic Questionnaire (PCQ) and the Listening Task (both developed by M. Alpert, 1970, 1972) were used. The PCQ is a structured questionnaire intended to give a detailed history and clarification of the patient's hallucinations. The

Listening Task represents an attempt to develop an objective and quantitative method for determining when someone is hallucinating. By controlling the input and requiring the patient to report what he hears, one is able to determine the mismatch between input and report.

The present study was designed to explore and investigate the interrelations among various measures (including psychiatric diagnosis) that have been mentioned in the literature for the detection and diagnosis of malingerers.

REVIEW OF THE LITERATURE

Only a small portion of the immense literature on the topic of malingering will be reviewed here. For a detailed review of the literature on this topic, see Bash.[1]

The concept of malingering has been known throughout history. The Bible and the histories of Greece, Rome, and the Middle Ages[2] cite many instances in which the simulation of insanity was used to avoid execution.

Up to this day, there has been no final agreement among the various authorities as to whether or not malingering should be considered a form of mental disease. Support can be found for either of these viewpoints. Furthermore, a review of the literature on the subject of malingering shows a number of difficulties involved in its diagnosis, detection, and classification.

Perhaps the most difficult problem in the study of malingering is one of classification. Are malingerers a special kind of people? If so, should they be classified as schizophrenics? Psychopathic? Mentally defective? Or, in more general terms, mentally sick? These are only some of the questions treated in the literature with respect to the nosology of malingering.

According to Garner, malingering is used in order to avoid pain or frustration.[3] He assumed that malingering to avoid military service, to gain a dependent position, or to avoid some unpleasantness would indicate an inadequate, asocial, or immature personality. Szasz's views are that malingering is not a diagnosis and therefore should be eliminated from the psychiatric and medical fields, especially as a diagnosis of a disease, and that there is no rational explanation for malingering as a psychopathological syndrome.[4]

The view that malingering is a form of mental illness came to the fore particularly during the Second World War. It was believed that only a "crazy" or "sick" person would malinger. This view was especially supported by Eissler,[5] O'Neil,[6] Moersch,[7] and Hunt,[8] who emphasized that malingering is always a disease, sometimes more severe than a mere neurotic disorder because it involves an arrest of the patient's development at an early age. Wertham's views[9] contrast with those of Eissler; Wertham does not view malingering as a mental disease.

Bleuler seems to have been the first to suggest that the simulation of insanity, irrespective of how conscious or unconscious the patient's motives, should be regarded as a manifestation of a mental illness.[10]

A different view was expressed by Davidson, who stated that malingering by itself does not prove a mental disorder.[11] A person faced with a serious charge would be very sane in trying to escape punishment by being committed to a hospital instead. Jones and Llewellyn pointed to the tendency of the malingerers to exaggerate the behavior.[2] Ossipov described the extremes that the malingerer may exhibit.[12] Macdonald pointed out that the suspect who feigns insanity may be insane but motivated to feign insanity because of his lack of insight into his true condition.[13]

In other studies of the simulation of mental illness, projective tests were found to be of value in differential diagnosis. Rosenberg and Feldberg,[14] Benton,[15] Hunt,[8] and Feldman and Graley[16] tried to detect simulation, using the Rorschach test. Their findings showed that the simulators had few responses, rejected numerous cards, had a large number of popular responses, and perseveration and repetition of previous responses were many. Bizarre responses were seldom seen.

A most difficult aspect in the study of malingering is its diagnosis and detection. As early as 1917, Sir John Collie believed it impossible to find symptoms or to lay down rules for the diagnosis and detection of a malingerer.[17] Eissler[5] and Henderson and Gillespie[18] stressed the importance of having the patient's complete case history, to look for contradictions in the patient's story, for discrepancies, and at his general behavior. For the controversial issues of the Ganser syndrome and hysteria, see Bash.[1]

METHOD

Subjects

Four groups of 30 S each were employed. All S were male patients, age range from 19–50, from the prison ward of Bellevue Hospital. Each S was diagnosed as nonpsychotic or as a genuine or feigned schizophrenic with or without concomitant auditory hallucinations, by two psychiatrists. S represent consecutive admissions who met the requirements of the design. The groups were quite well matched with respect to the distributions of age, race, economic status, and education. Group I consisted of 30 S considered to be malingerers ("diagnosed malingerers") who reported auditory hallucinations. Group II consisted of 30 S diagnosed as schizophrenic who reported auditory hallucinations. Group III consisted of 30 S diagnosed as schizophrenic nonhallucinatory. Group IV consisted of 30 S who were referred to the ward for observations, but who were diagnosed as nonpsychotic, and who were not known to have ever been patients in a psychiatric hospital or to have ever experienced auditory hallucinations.

Materials

The following tests were used: the WAIS, the Rorschach, the Bender-Gestalt, the Listening Task, the SCI, the Betts test, and the PCQ. All of the scoring was done blindly by a rater who did not know the group designation of the S. For each test, a special malingering score was devised.

The WAIS

A malingering score was computed based on approximate answers. For **Arithmetic**, the answer given is one above or one below the correct answer (e.g., 4 + 3 = 8 or 6) and was scored + 1 for each instance; for **Block Design**, the answer is correct, except for the placement of one block and this block is 90° or less off and is scored + 1 for each instance; for **Digit Span**, digits are reported one digit above or below the correct number and the answer is scored + 1; for **Picture Arrangement**, all pictures are correct except for one, and this one is placed as the first one or the last one, or S does not change the position of the pictures at all, i.e., he leaves the pictures in the same order as experimenter (E) puts them, and is scored + 1 for each instance; total score is number of picture arrangements scored + 1; for **Information**, "I don't know" (DK) answers to easy items, total score number of DK answers to items 1, 2, 3, 4, 5, 6, 8, 11; for **Picture Completion**, "nothing is missing" answers to more than three consecutive items, total score is number of items so answered.

The total approximate answers score for each subtest was translated into a standard score based on the distribution of all S. The final approximate answers score for each individual was the sum of the subtest standard scores.

The Rorschach‡

The following items were scored: (1) number of responses; (2) number of cards rejected; (3) mean reaction time (for all cards); (4) number of popular responses; (5) perseveration; (6) number of aggressive and anger responses; (7) number of animal and inanimate movement responses; (8) number of bizarre responses (F −); (9) W:M (usually in the form of W > 2 M); (10) M:C (usually the C outweighs M by 2:1); (11) W% (high W%); (12) failure to interpret popular easy plates; (13) number of color responses = C%. The scoring followed the Klopfer system[19] and was developed as follows: **For item 1,** a distribution of all 120 S was computed. S got a + 1 if his score was below the 25th percentile of the combined distribution. **For item 2,** a distribution of all 120 S was computed. S got a + 1 if his score was above the 75th percentile of the distribution. **For item 3,** a distribution of all 120 S was computed. S got a + 1 if his reaction time was in the top 25th

‡ Following are the definitions of the abbreviations used in this paragraph: W = whole or nearly whole blot is used (whole responses); M = human movement responses; C = color responses; F = form level; FM = animal movement responses; m = inanimate responses; and P = popular responses.

percentile of the distribution. **For item 4,** P% was calculated and the distribution for the 120 S was determined; the S then was scored + 1 if his P% was above the 75th percentile of the distribution. **For item 5,** S was scored + 1 if he gave the same response to three or more consecutive cards. A distribution was then done. S got a + 1 if his score was below the 25th percentile of the distribution. **For item 6,** S was scored + 1 for each response that involved killing, attacking, arguing, a rocket going off, or an explosion. Then a distribution of all the 120 S was done. S got a + 1 if his score was above the 75th percentile. **For item 7,** the total number of FM and m responses and the (FM + m)% were determined. Here again, a distribution of all 120 S was computed for (FM + m)%. S got a score of + 1 if his (FM + m)% fell above the 75th percentile of the distribution. **For item 8,** F – % was computed, and S was given a + 1 if his score was below the 25th percentile of the combined distribution of all 120 S. **For item 9,** the W:M ratio was calculated for each subject, and S was given a + 1 if his ratio exceeded the 75th percentile of the combined distribution. **For item 10,** S was given a + 1 if his ratio was above the 75th percentile of the combined distribution of these ratios. **For item 11,** S was scored + 1 if his W% fell above the 75th percentile of the combined W% distribution. **For item 12,** the reference here is to the rejection of popular responses when asked if he can see them in the course of the testing of the limits. The S was given a + 1 for each such popular response that he rejected in the testing of the limits. Then a distribution of all 120 S was done. If S's score was above the 75th percentile, he got a + 1. **For item 13,** it has been reported that malingerers give many color responses as an expression of their emotional state. For each subject $(FC + C + C_n + F/C)$% was computed (C_n refers to a color naming response, and F/C to the arbitrary use of color, e.g., a "pink dog"). Again, S was given a + 1 if the ratio was above the 75th percentile of the combined distribution.

A Rorschach "malingering" score was computed as the sum of the point scores on the preceding 13 items. It was expected that the malingerers would score higher than any of the other groups.

The Bender-Gestalt

The Bender's[20] criteria for malingering were used. They are: (1) the drawings are small and inhibited, since the malingerer—attempting to inhibit his intelligence—succeeds only in inhibiting his impulses; (2) uneven performance—some gestalt functions on high level, others on regressed level; (3) actual pattern properties are exactly indicated, e.g., squares do not become loops, etc., order is maintained although the figures' positions are changed; (4) relationship or direction of parts or details may be altered to the point of apparent disorientation, but actual gestalt function will remain on a high level, e.g., the difficult diamond shape will be reproduced accurately; (5) tendency to simplify symbols, e.g., using a continuous line for a series of dots, but retaining the basic shape of the figure; and (6) more complex drawing elements added. This test had been scored on the above six items plus a seventh item—number of items recalled. This additional item, recall, which was employed here, was not mentioned in the literature but was significant to the present study because of the assumption that the malingerers will say that they can't recall or will recall very few items, since this is the way they perceive that a mentally sick person will respond.

The Listening Task

S's task was to report what he heard and to indicate his confidence. Individual product-moment correlations were calculated between the accuracy and the confidence of the response for each *S*. For a more detailed description of the test, see Bash.[1]

The Structured Clinical Interview (SCI)[21]

All 10 categories were used (e.g., anger-hostility, fear-worry, etc.). Scoring was done as follows: On each category for each item that he answered "yes," *S* got a score of +1. A "no" answer got a zero. The total score for each category was summed separately. Then these raw scores were transformed into standard scores, which are provided in a table, according to age.[21]

The Betts Test

The Sheehan 1967 form was used. All seven modalities were employed. For each modality, *S* was given five items to imagine. *S* was asked to rate the vividness of each image using the following rating scale: 1 = perfectly clear, 2 = very clear, 3 = moderately clear, 4 = not clear but recognizable, 5 = vague and dim, 6 = very vague and dim, 7 = no image present. Some examples of these items are: For the **visual modality**, *S* was asked to imagine some relative or friend and then to rate the vividness of the following: the person's body image, way of walking, different colors of a familiar costume, etc. For the **auditory modality**, *S* was asked to imagine the sound of a whistle of a locomotive, etc. For the **tactual modality**, *S* was asked to imagine the feel of sand, of linen, of fur, etc. For the **kinesthetic modality**, *S* was asked to imagine running upstairs, etc. For the **gustatory modality**, *S* was asked to imagine the taste of salt, etc. For the **olfactory modality**, *S* was asked to imagine the smell of fresh paint, of cooking cabbage, of new leather, etc. For the **somesthetic-organic modality**, *S* was asked to imagine the sensations of fatigue, of hunger, of a sore throat, etc.

The rationale of what we took to be a malingering score was that it was expected that malingerers would attempt to exaggerate the intensity of their imagery, but would have no special reason for doing so more in the context of one of the imagery modalities than in the context of another. Since Sheehan[22] had reported the modality scores separately for a large number of normal S, the presumption was that the malingerers particularly would try to make themselves as different as possible from normals by exaggerating the intensity of their imagery. For this reason, we used the Sheehan findings to generate for each modality a transformation into standard scores with a mean of 50 and a standard deviation of 10 in the corresponding Sheehan distribution. These standard scores were then summed, and the total was taken as a malingering score. The higher the score, the greater was the presumption of malingering. As it turned out, the individual modality means standard scores and the total scores were all very much higher than those obtained in the Sheehan distributions. This difference may be worth pursuing in follow-up studies, but there did not seem to be any reason for not using these scores in the comparisons between the groups of the present investigation.

The Perceptual Characteristic Questionnaire (PCQ)

Scoring was done as follows: (1) duration of hallucination—three years or more; (2) aggressive and hostile messages; (3) visual hallucinations; (4) hallucinations occur many times each day (four or more); (5) nonvocal sounds in addition to voices; (6) source localized outside of patient; (7) more frequent with social isolation; (8) more frequent with emotional arousal (e.g., angry, sad, anxious); (9) more frequent with decreased light; (10) medication did not help in reducing frequency.

Each item was scored *one* if present or *zero* if absent. The total score was the sum of the item scores for the subject. For a more detailed description of this test, see Bash.[1]

PROCEDURE

All S were tested individually in two sessions with each of the tests. In session I, the SCI, Betts, Listening Task, and Rorschach were employed respectively. In session II, the WAIS, PCQ, and Bender were used respectively.

The testing took place in a separate room at the Bellevue Hospital prison ward. Specific instructions for each test were given by E. After reading the instructions for each test, E asked S if there were any questions, making sure that S understood the instructions clearly.

The total time required for each session was approximately 90 minutes.

The same procedure was used with all four groups.

RESULTS

To test the ability of the tests to discriminate between malingerers and the other groups, a one-way analysis of variance (ANOVA), Planned Comparison t-test, and the Student-Newman-Keuls procedure were used for

TABLE 1

MEAN* "MALINGERING" SCORES OF THE FOUR GROUPS

Test	Group I Malingerers	Group II Schizophrenic Hallucinators	Group III Schizophrenic Nonhallu- cinators	Group IV Nonpsychotic	Groups II–IV Combined Mean
WAIS	357.486	280.192	278.876	283.418	280.829
Rorschach	5.367	2.133	2.567	3.066	2.589
Bender	39.367	11.667	12.667	12.000	12.111
Listening	1.354	0.634	0.545	1.060	0.746
SCI	923.967	1042.533	891.433	722.200	885.389
Betts (Total)	1888.072	1437.635	1387.793	1583.044	1469.480

* The means reported above for the WAIS and the Betts are sums of several standardized scores, each with a mean of 50 and a sigma of 10. See description of these scores in the METHODS section.

each test separately. Results are presented in TABLES 1 and 2. As can be seen, our hypothesis was supported for each of the tests except the SCI, and Group I is significantly discriminated from the other three groups on all of the tests except the SCI ($P = 0.001$).

The hypothesis that the PCQ will discriminate between schizophrenic hallucinators and the suspected malingerers was supported. The PCQ was administered only to the malingerers and the schizophrenic hallucinators. As can be seen from TABLE 3, the two groups are effectively discriminated from one another, and, as anticipated, the malingerers scored lower than the schizophrenic hallucinators group.

A separate analysis was done to determine how well the Listening Task and the PCQ can discriminate between malingerers and others. As can be seen from TABLE 4, the Listening Task had only misdiagnosed 4 S (i.e., false

TABLE 2

SUMMARY OF ANOVA FOR FOUR-GROUP COMPARISON ON THE BETTS TEST

Modality	General Between-Groups Comparisons (df = 3/116) F	P	Student-Newman-Keuls Procedure Homogeneous Subsets and Groups*
Visual	16.294	< 0.001	III, II/II, IV/I
Auditory	15.921	< 0.001	III, II/II, IV/I
Tactual	20.675	< 0.001	III, II/IV/I
Kinesthetic	21.197	< 0.001	III, II/IV/I
Gustatory	16.477	< 0.001	III, II/II, IV/I
Olfactory	19.540	< 0.001	III, II, IV/I
Somesthetic-Organic	10.422	< 0.001	III, II, IV/I
All Modalities Combined	26.418	< 0.001	III, II/IV/I

* Members of homogeneous subsets separated by commas; discriminated subsets (at 0.05 significance level) separated by slashes; order of discriminated subsets is from low to high means.

TABLE 3

RESULTS FOR PERCEPTUAL CHARACTERISTICS QUESTIONNAIRE (PCQ)

Group	Means	df	F	P
I. Malingerers	900.633	1/58	9.394	< 0.003
II. Schizophrenic Hallucinators	1161.100			

positive). The PCQ did not do as well. However, when *both* tests were used, the results were fantastic—no misdiagnoses at all (or false positives).

Inspecting TABLE 5, we see that when the battery of tests was used (except the SCI and PCQ), a substantial phi coefficient was obtained (0.8872). There was only one misdiagnosed S. This phi obtained with the composite score is substantially higher than the highest phi obtained for any of the tests individually.

The one-way ANOVA was used to test the overall differences between the four groups on each modality and the overall modalities of the Betts test. As can be seen from TABLE 6, all modalities are effective in discriminating the malingerers from the other three groups. Furthermore, the tactual, kinesthetic, and the overall modalities are even better discriminators, since Group I is significantly different from Group IV and significantly different from Groups II and III.

To test for statistically significant differences between the four groups on all tests that refer to personal characteristics, a one-way ANOVA was used for the WAIS and the Bender. (For results of the other tests, Rorschach and SCI, see Bash.)[1] The results of the subscores of the WAIS—this time using the conventional scores and the conventional way of scoring—are presented in TABLE 7. As can be seen, the malingerers constituted the lowest scoring group on every WAIS score. However, they were significantly lower by both the Planned Comparison test and the Student-Newman-Keuls procedure only on the Information, Comprehension, Arithmetic, Picture Completion, Verbal, and Full Scale scores. They are not discriminated by the Student-Newman-Keuls procedure on Digit Span, Vo-

TABLE 4

CROSS TABULATION OF PCQ AND LISTENING TASK TEST DIAGNOSIS VS. PSYCHIATRIC DIAGNOSIS*

Test	Test Diagnosis	Psychiatric Diagnosis		
		Nonma-lingerers	Ma-lingerers	
Listening Task	Malingerers	4	26	$\phi = 0.7333$
	Nonmalingerers	26	4	sign. at 0.0001
PCQ	Malingerers	9	22	$\phi = 0.4336$
	Nonmalingerers	21	8	sign. at 0.002
Listening Task and PCQ	Malingerers	0	20	$\phi = 0.7071$
	Nonmalingerers	30	10	sign. at 0.0001

* Malingerers vs. schizophrenic hallucinators.

TABLE 5

CROSS TABULATION OF TEST DIAGNOSIS*

	Psychiatric Diagnosis		
Test Diagnosis	Nonmalingerers	Malingerers	
Malingerers	1	26	$\phi = 0.8872$
Nonmalingerers	89	4	sign. at 0.0001

* Based on tests, exclusive of SCI and PCQ vs. psychiatric diagnosis.

cabulary, Digit-Symbol, and Performance scores. They are not significantly different on Similarities, Block Design, Picture Arrangement, and Object Assembly. An explanation for this phenomenon may be that Group I deliberately gave wrong answers in order to appear stupid on the assumption that stupidity characterized schizophrenia. Also, because of their extensive use of approximate answers, Group I's scores are lower.

The Bender test results are also given in TABLE 7, this time using Bender's criteria[20] for diagnosing schizophrenia. As can be seen, the Bender successfully discriminated between the nonschizophrenic groups (I and IV) and the schizophrenic groups (II and III). The Student-Newman-Keuls gave the following divisions: Groups I and IV in one subset and Groups II and III in another. The Bender test is a good discriminator.

DISCUSSION

The basic hypothesis bearing on the ability of the seven tests to detect and, thus, to diagnose malingerers was supported by the findings of the present study. Six of the seven tests successfully discriminated the malingerers

TABLE 6

SUMMARY OF ANOVA FOR FOUR-GROUP COMPARISON OF "MALINGERING" SCORES

	General Between-Groups Comparisons (df 3/116)		Planned Comparison Group I vs. Other Three (df 116)		Student-Newman-Keuls Procedure
Test	F	P	t	P	Homogeneous Subsets & Groups*
WAIS	36.075	< 0.001	10.390	< 0.001	II, III, IV/I
Rorschach	26.770	< 0.001	8.642	< 0.001	II, III, IV/I
Bender	25.061	< 0.001	8.667	< 0.001	II, III, IV/I
Listening	33.604	< 0.001	8.067	< 0.001	II, III/IV/I
SCI	8.815	< 0.001	0.750	N.S.	IV, III/I, II
Betts (Total)	26.812	< 0.001	7.985	< 0.001	II, III/IV/I

* Members of homogeneous subsets separated by commas; discriminated subsets (at 0.05 significance level) separated by slashes; order of discriminated subsets is from low to high means.

TABLE 7

SUMMARY OF ANOVA FOR FOUR-GROUP COMPARISON ON
THE WAIS SUBTESTS AND BENDER-GESTALT

Test	General Between-Groups Comparison (df 3/116)		Planned Comparison Group I vs. Other Three (df 116)		Student-Newman-Keuls Procedure
	F	P	t	P	Homogeneous Subsets and Groups*
WAIS					
Information	5.854	0.001	3.968	0.001	I/II, IV, III
Comprehension	6.932	0.001	3.971	0.001	I/II, III, IV
Arithmetic	3.567	0.016	3.050	0.001	I/II, III, IV
Similarities	.868	0.460 (N.S.)	1.568	0.120 (N.S.)	I, II, III, IV
Digit Span	2.122	0.101 (N.S.)	2.362	0.020	I, II, III, IV
Vocabulary	3.544	0.017	3.091	0.001	I, II, III/II, III, IV
Digit Symbol	2.023	0.115 (N.S.)	2.166	0.032	I, II, III, IV
Picture Completion	4.514	0.005	3.129	0.002	I/III, II, IV
Block Design	1.586	0.197 (N.S.)	1.947	0.054 (N.S.)	I, III, IV, II
Picture Arrangement	1.717	0.167 (N.S.)	1.324	0.180 (N.S.)	I, III, II, IV
Object Assembly	1.537	0.209 (N.S.)	1.331	0.180 (N.S.)	I, III, IV, II
Verbal Score	5.113	0.001	3.699	0.001	I/II, III, IV
Performance Score	2.481	0.064 (N.S.)	2.369	0.013	I, III, II, IV
Full Scale	4.284	0.007	3.441	0.001	I/III, II, IV
BENDER-GESTALT	7.350	0.001	2.593	0.001	IV, I/II, III

* Members of homogeneous subsets separated by commas; discriminated subsets (at 0.05 significance level) separated by slashes; order of discriminated subsets is from low to high means.

from the other three groups. Four of the seven tests, taken together, yielded a multiple correlation of 0.839 with the psychiatric diagnosis. Both the Listening Task and the PCQ significantly discriminated Group I from Group II.

An additional question of interest to the present study was tested: If the S are classified as malingerers or nonmalingerers separately on the basis of each of the five successful tests (exclusive of the PCQ and SCI), on how many of these tests must the S be so classified in order to be safely characterized as a malingerer? Results showed that when our S were characterized as malingerers on the basis of their scores on at least three of the tests and as nonmalingerers if they were so classified on less than three tests, the phi correlation with the psychiatric classification was 0.8872. However, we would hesitate to generalize from this finding without additional supporting evidence.

In general, the overall performance of the malingerers was significantly more exaggerated and significantly different from that of the schizophrenic or the nonpsychotic S. Thus, it may be said that the malingerers are special kinds of people and may be put in a separate classification. There are common patterns in their malingering, which are manifested in areas of behavior that range far beyond the simulation of a mental disease. In a sense, given an incentive to malinger, what unifies the reported findings is a kind of inner logic of such simulation. Malingerers are recognizable by their conformity to the requirements of this inner logic.

Even so, establishing that there is such a common denominator among malingerers that makes them discriminable from others is a far cry from establishing that there is a core of common traits that disposes certain individuals to malinger and that is lacking in others who do not attempt to do so. As indicated, the failure to establish the kind of unity we have found would throw into doubt the distinctiveness of malingerers in the broader sense. Our success, however, does not establish that malingerers do constitute a distinctive group in the broader sense, that is, as a psychologically and psychiatrically meaningful diagnostic category. This issue is dealt with in Bash.[1]

CONCLUSIONS

In reviewing the foregoing, it appears that there is no reason to affirm that malingerers constitute a special class of people, even though we may conclude that they are discriminable from other groups of people. Their difference apparently inheres in what they are doing rather than in what they are. No differences were found between the malingerers and the other subjects that could not be attributed to the act of malingering per se. The nonpsychotic subjects had the same incentive to malinger as did the malingerers, but it is suggested that the simplest explanation of why some individuals malinger and some do not is that the latter are deterred by anxiety about possible consequences of being caught in the deception and by a lack of confidence in their ability to carry it out.

The tests do provide an objective way of detecting malingering, at least in the setting of the prison ward. Apart from their objectivity, the tests may offer the only tenable means of validly diagnosing malingering. Therefore, it is suggested that they should be used whenever possible, especially in a less developed setup.

Finally, it should be noted that the failure to establish distinctive personal characteristics among malingerers in the extreme case of the simulation of psychosis throws some doubt on the likelihood of finding distinctive personal characteristics in other forms of malingering.

REFERENCES

1. BASH, I. Y. 1978. Malingering: a study designed to differentiate between schizophrenic offenders and malingerers. Ph.D. Dissertation. Department of Psychology. New York University. New York, N.Y.
2. JONES, A. B. & J. LLEWELLYN. 1917. Malingering. Heinemann. London, England.
3. GARNER, H. H. 1965. Malingering. Ill. Med. J. 128: 318-319.
4. SZASZ, T. S. 1961. The Myth of Mental Illness. Harper & Row, Publishers. New York, N.Y.

5. EISSLER, K. R. 1951. Malingering. *In* Psychoanalysis and Culture. G. B. Wilbur & W. Muensterbegger, Eds.: 218–253. International Universities Press, Inc. New York, N.Y.
6. O'NEIL, W. 1943. Goldbricks. Hygeia **21**: 426–427. (Quoted in Reference 5.)
7. MOERSCH, F. P. 1944. Malingering: with reference to its neuropsychiatric aspects in civil and in military practice. *In* The Medical Clinics of North America, The Mayo Clinic Number: 928–944. W.B. Saunders. Philadelphia, Penn.
8. HUNT, A. 1946. The detection of malingering. U.S. Nav. Med. Bull. **46**: 249–254.
9. WERTHAM, F. 1949. The Show of Violence. Doubleday & Company, Inc. New York, N.Y.
10. BLEULER, E. 1944. A Textbook of Psychiatry. (Translated by A. A. Brill, 1924.) Macmillan & Company, Ltd. New York, N.Y.
11. DAVIDSON, H. A. 1965. Forensic Psychiatry. Ronald Press Company. New York, N.Y.
12. OSSIPOV, V. P. 1944. Malingering: the simulation of psychosis. Bull. Menninger Clin. **8(2)**: 39–42.
13. MACDONALD, J. M. 1969. Psychiatry and the Criminal. Charles C. Thomas. Springfield, Ill.
14. ROSENBERG, S. J. & T. M. FELDBERG. 1944. Rorschach characteristics of a group of malingers. Rorschach Research Exchange **8**: 141–158.
15. BENTON, A. L. 1945. Rorschach performance of suspected malingerers. J. Abnorm. Soc. Psychol. **40**: 94–96.
16. FELDMAN, M. J. & J. GRALEY. 1954. The effects of an experimental set to simulate abnormality on group Rorschach performance. J. Projective Techniques **18**: 326–334.
17. COLLIE, J. 1917. Malingering and Feigned Sickness. Edward Arnold. London, England. (Quoted in Reference 5.)
18. HENDERSON, D. & R. D. GILLESPIE. 1950. A Textbook of Psychiatry. Oxford University Press. New York, N.Y.
19. KLOPFER, B., M. D. AINSWORTH, W. G. KLOPFER & R. R. HOLT. 1954. Developments in Rorschach Technique. 1. Technique and Theory. World Book Company. Yonkers-on-Hudson, N.Y.
20. BENDER, L. 1938. A Visual Motor Gestalt Test and Its Clinical Use. Research Monograph No. 3. The American Orthopsychiatric Association. New York, N.Y.
21. BURDOCK, E. I. & A. S. HARDESTY. 1968. Structured Clinical Interview (SCI). Springer Publishing Company, Inc. New York, N.Y.
22. SHEEHAN, P. W. 1967. A shortened form of Betts' questionnaire upon mental imagery (QMI). J. Clin. Psychol. **23**: 386–389.

ISSUES OF PSYCHOLOGICAL EVIDENCE: DISCUSSION

Discussant: Murray S. Miron

Department of Psychology
Syracuse University
Syracuse, New York 13210

The papers of this session all represent issues of singular importance to the problems of criminal justice. Lie or stress detection, voice printing, and hypnosis have been eagerly adopted by law enforcement agencies as means for the detection and identification of the criminal. From the caution and circumspection of the laboratory, these techniques have been rushed into the service of the practitioner whose needs and enthusiasm may make him less wary than is justified by the research on these techniques. There can be no doubt that if we are to deal with the permutated increases in crime, we shall have to bring as much of the power of the scientist's laboratory to bear as we can. But it seems to me that at the same time, we must counsel the caution and skepticism that is the hallmark of the scientist to those who would use the fruits of his researches. There is a disturbing tendency to wishfully imagine that there is a "golden key" solution to our problems of rising and increasingly sophisticated crime. When coupled with the glamour of new and "scientific" discoveries, wish and reality may become hopelessly confused.

Unfortunately, even the scientist is not immune to the temptations of such wishfulness. The respect afforded the scientist—in large measure because of his objectivity—may act to make him less circumspect when called upon to offer his expert assistance, precisely because those who seek his advice often have unrealistic expectations. The world of the courtroom, for example, is dramatically and very often disconcertingly different from the world of the laboratory. More than one expert witness has been trapped into an advocative certainty unwarranted by the probabilistic nature of his own research findings. The courtroom atmosphere appears to encourage such advocacy on the part of the expert, in conformity to the legal style of such proceedings. But when the expert becomes an advocate, I think it fair to say that he loses the essential quality that makes him valuable to such court procedures. It is the scientist's uncertainty—his questions more than his answers—that warrants our respect.

The papers of this session all demonstrated the constraint and caution that mark the best of our scientists. Dr. Hollien points to the paucity of data that would support a conclusion of identifying voice correlates of stress, much less the use of a microtremor indicator of lying. Dr. Spiegel, despite the more optimistic tone of his paper, properly warns against some of the more obvious dangers of the use of hypnosis in evidence gathering and self-

100

induced trance states. The paper by Drs. Bash and Alpert on the detection of malingering in criminal patients can be interpreted as an attempt to make such determination more objective than the ex cathedra pronouncements sometimes offered by the forensic psychiatrist.

Taken as a whole, the papers of this session did not offer much encouragement to those who may have sought their own "golden keys." Nor, I suspect, were they found to be particularly newsworthy to the members of the press who were sent to report on the conference. There was much more drama in the newest "discovery" of the Rahway lifers' solution to juvenile delinquency. The session on issues in evidence appeared to have the character of quibbling over old news—the sort of curmudgeonly crankiness the public often associates with the academic. But what was said and what was implied were neither cranky nor unnewsworthy. The message rang loud and clear to anyone who would have cared to listen. There is no glamorous, easy solution to our problems of crime. Beneath the ballyhoo of the technology that has been applied in the service of our forensic needs there lies a soft substrate of too few data too soon extended. That is not to say that the laboratory and its expert custodians have no place in evidentiary proceedings. But it *is* to say that we must continue to counsel caution whenever we export our products into the exotic countries of their much needed application.

As a member of the psychological community who also has become a part of the growth industry spawned by crime and terrorism, I have come to learn firsthand of the dangers of which I speak. Periodically, I like to remind myself of the comment made by that most outspoken iconoclast, Thomas Szasz. In a letter to the editor of the New York Times, in comment on the use of mental health professionals as negotiators and experts on terrorist problems, Szasz asked the rhetorical question: "What do psychiatrists know about terrorism?" His proffered answer was that either this was merely the natural outgrowth of the increasing "psychiatrizing" of human affairs, or psychiatrists were themselves terrorists and hence well qualified as experts in such matters. Despite the obvious polemics of such hyperbole, it is difficult to deny the evidence of the misuses of psychiatric diagnosis that have been reported by those who have escaped the asylums of Russia. Is there not the seed of such abuse in the claims of sure identification of lying, speaker identity, hypnotic memory reconstruction, and malingering? Perhaps exaggerated in this way, the scientist's crankiness becomes a duty rather than an affectation.

With this rather long-winded (and even perhaps cranky) preamble in mind, I should like to turn to an examination of some of the specifics of the papers presented at this session. The authors have spoken eloquently for themselves, and there is little point in repeating what they have said far better than I as discussant could offer. Instead, I shall use my role as discussant to make some personal observations on the issues of each of the papers. So as not to abuse that role, my remarks should not be interpreted as either endorsed by, or even consonant with the views of, the speakers.

Stress, Lying, and Psychological Stress Evaluation

Among the new technologies, none has received more attention than the psychological stress evaluator (PSE). The storm of controversy and advocacy that has swirled around this technique still rages. It seems to me that the issues involved in the theory and uses of the PSE* are generalizably instructive and hence warrant close examination. There is a veritable army of trained and untrained practitioners of the "science" of lie detection daily practicing their trade in the service of criminal investigation, preemployment screening, and even mischief-making—as, it seems to me, are such things as the assertion that Lee Harvey Oswald was not lying when he said, "I didn't kill nobody, no sir." From a $5000 device only marketed with an instruction course in its use, the offsprings of the PSE have devolved to gadgets of less than $250, offered to anyone and for anything. In a recent visit to one of this nation's most prestigious physics laboratories, my rather mundane talk was monitored by one of these hand-held devices, unashamedly thrust under my nose. In New York State, an amendment to the Labor and Industrial Relations Act makes it a misdemeanor to employ PSE devices for the purposes of preemployment screening, and yet to my certain knowledge they are being so used daily.

If one reviews the data on PSE, a curious dichotomy emerges. On the one hand, laboratory studies of the technique find chance or little better accuracy of deception identification. On the other hand, field studies of its application in actual criminal investigations find perfect or near perfect identification. Such discrepancy has prompted more than one advocate of the device to argue that laboratory studies are both artificial and useless as tests of the efficacy of what was meant to be a tool in criminal investigations. Thus, the laboratory researcher is dismissed from the arena of this controversy, and his findings declared irrelevant to the "real world." Such preemptive dismissal is not new. It has plagued every scientist. In defense, some have left the laboratory to join the ranks of their real-worlder critics, others have defensively declared themselves aloof from the mundane, and still others have tried to tailor their research designs to better reflect reality. The criticism may have validity, but I fear that what I detect is the very old infrasonic note of the antiscience antiintellectualism that would make magic and fraud respectable. Fraud and belief in magic are so far removed from the concern of the scientist that he often is sadly naive to their widespread acceptance. There is nothing more pathetic than the hoodwinked scientist, victim of the charlatan.

Routinely, as a part of my university lectures on the statistics of probability and chance, I demonstrate a series of mental effects that I have either purchased from practicing mentalists or have developed on my own. I can, without failure, appear to read any mind in the classroom, make a perfect run through an ESP deck, and relate facts and circumstances of the

---

* It is merely curious rather than significant that PSE is a palindromic permutation of ESP. My use of the acronym PSE is generic rather than specific to any proprietary device.

students' lives. Before and after each demonstration, I carefully point out that the things I am doing are all tricks that my audience can also purchase from such places as Tannens in New York City. I announce that I am a fraud and that I can no more read minds than the least adept among them. What is startling is that these nascent scientists, these members of the future intelligentsia, invariably ask me if I was born with my talent. Despite my protestations, they respond with awe and even fear of what they presume to be my ability to plumb their minds. That is scary. The unquestioned acceptance of PSE is similarly scary.

Out of an admitted bias, born of my psycholinguistics training, I have always considered truth and deception to be linguistic questions. Only propositions have truth value. The merely physical cannot be true or false. Viewed from this lofty linguistic perspective, the notion that there is a physical basis for deception is just plain silly. Consider the following utterances:

1. This administration has been falsely accused of an attempt to cover up certain facts.
2. No aspirin is more effective than Bayer® Aspirin.
3. No heat costs less than oil heat.

All three statements are tautologically true under translation. In the first, the optional deletion of agent specification permitted by the passive voice serves to conceal the source of the assertion. The existence of any false accuser makes the statement true. In the second, the statement merely proclaims that Bayer Aspirin is aspirin. In fact, the commercial goes on to establish that the Bayer product is nothing but aspirin and hence could not hope to be better or worse than any aspirin. In the third, it is clear that no heat costs nothing and that any other heat or anything else for that matter necessarily costs more. As might be expected, such trickery is not either abnormal or unusual in language. It is, in part, the reason that the subject of the polygraph examination is instructed to restrict his answers to yes-or-no, preprepared questions.

As Professor Hollien's paper observes, there are physical voice correlates of stress, even if fewer than we might hope. It is, however, the inductive leap that would functionally relate stress and deception that transcends these physical correlates. Worse, even the logic of this inductive presumption bears scrutiny. Stated baldly, If deception is presumed to cause stress, why is it not equally plausible to assert that stress causes deception? The circumstances of a lie detection test make such speculation not without merit.

By contrast to the carefully evolved procedures of the polygraph examination, the PSE lends itself to significant carelessness. Where the polygraphist uses both control and irrelevant questions in order to establish experimental-like control conditions, the PSE's attraction is that it can be employed clandestinely and hence potentially without proper controls in both senses of that word.

But such argument presumes what is not entirely certain, namely, that there exists anything at all to measure or even abuse. In a publication of my own, which Professor Hollien had not seen, I tentatively concluded that there was some evidence for a microtremor component in the vocal fold tone of speech. That conclusion was based upon two forms of evidence. First, there are a number of studies of sufficient procedural care that indicate that something claimed to represent the 8–12 Hz microtremor component can reliably be identified. Second, the generally accepted account of the demonstrated microtremor in peripheral musculature as having reflex level origins suggests that the condition should be found in at least all larger, striate musculature. Professor Hollien correctly observes in his paper that the very small, fast-acting musculature controlling the action of the vocal folds is sufficiently different in character from the muscles in which the tremor has been found to warrant suspicion as to generalization. I do not disagree; but at the same time, it should be noted that the entire laryngeal mechanism is supported by a network of large and slow-acting muscles, which could—if subject to such microtremor—superimpose their effect upon the vocal fold tone. Thus, those studies of which I am aware that attempt and fail to record the microtremor from electrodes planted in the smaller musculature need not rule out its presence in other muscles associated with the laryngeal mechanism. Until better evidence is available, prudence dictates that any conclusion regarding the PSE and its use in lie detection should be guarded.

Hypnosis and Memory Enhancement

Professor Spiegel's paper reports a number of cases in which he or others have successfully used hypnosis for the purpose of reconstructing past events significant for criminal investigation. It is of interest that Professor Loftus, in a paper delivered just prior to this session, reported on some aspects of witness testimony that are clearly important to the use of hypnotically induced recall. Professor Loftus found that the content of the questions used to elicit recall of an eyewitness significantly influenced the character of the memory. If one asks a witness whether he saw broken glass at the scene of an accident in which the vehicle had "smashed" into another vehicle, the report is more often positive than if the vehicles had only "collided." Such findings well fit the generalized model of conceptual, rather than sensory, memory storage. It is a model in which the human is viewed as an active processor of stimuli rather than as a passive filterer. Such active processing is a sort of analysis by synthesis. That is to say, the processor actively models—hypothesizes—his inputs in a conceptual framework that predicts and extends the incomplete and unorganized inputs given to his senses. The character of the model used for this sensory organization is dependent upon both the past and future experiences of the organism. Previously formed hypotheses about inputs dictate the meaning of present inputs, and later inputs change and modify the stored models to form new hypotheses for current processing. Such a conception readily accounts for the frequent errors in perception and indeed makes such errors normal, rather than abnormal, aspects of both memory and perception. Memory recall in such a model presupposes that the recaller *reconstructs* the sensory events as deductions from the *hypotheses* that were employed in their perception. Such a view significantly differs from one in which sensory inputs are written on a sort of tabula rasa.

It seems to me that hypnotically induced recall assumes something more like the tabula rasa view of memory. It is significant that the probes for such recall under hypnosis often take the form of suggesting that the subject view the past scene like a movie film that may be slowed and even stopped on particular frames. The clear implication is that memory is a sort of blank film, storing latent images that are merely awaiting development. Such a view is not consonant with the well-documented distortions that characterize memory. The practitioner of hypnosis has typically countered such objection with the assertion that the trance state taps processes that are different from those characterizing the normal waking state—processes that are somehow more elemental and basic than those subject to the effects of preconception, bias, and modeling. This is a strong assertion. In my opinion, it fails to be credible from what we know about the hypnotic state. Hypnotic trance has been described as a heightened state of suggestibility. Professor Spiegel, himself, describes it as a heightened state of awareness and concentrated attention normal to the organism—so ordinary, in fact, that Dr. Spiegel warns that self-induced hypnosis may influence any suspect interview. If the state is so pervasive, then one should expect that its processes should be operative in normal memory research, which favors the analysis by synthesis model. Further, if the hypnotic trance heightens suggestibility, is it not the case that one should expect more, rather than less, susceptibility to the effects of bias in memory? Such questions, at the least, suggest that we should view hypnotically elicited memory with some caution.

Professor Spiegel chose to warn us of another danger. He suggests that the results of a suspect interview may be the contaminated fruit of inadvertent or auto-trance induction. Such warning, in my opinion, goes far too far. If one suspects that one can fall into and out of the trance state without will and with the frequency suggested by Professor Spiegel, then we must be talking about a different process than the one that I would reserve for the term hypnotic trance. I am not suggesting that hypnotic trance is necessarily a qualitatively different state from that which characterizes the normal state; but instead, that the term should be reserved for those quantitative enhancements of concentration and suggestibility that differ from those of nontrance states. Rapport, trust, and openness to cooperation cannot, in my view, be used to define the trance state. Although such effects are observed in trance, they are not definitionally discriminating. If they are erected as the criteria of trance, the term becomes empty of meaning.

Insanity, Irresponsibility, and Malingering

The defense of incompetence by reason of insanity is enjoying one of those fashionable cycles in human affairs reminiscent of the hula hoop craze. The disorder of multiple personality has been used far more often as an account of ordinary criminality than its tenuous psychiatric status would predict to be real. The knowledgeable malingerer, however, knows that schizophrenia is far more frequently the diagnosis of choice when the symptomology is vague and variable. That the unknowledgeable confuse multiple personality with schizophrenia is testimony to the pernicious influence of the mass media on our understanding of mental disorders. Nor would I exclude the self-conscious attempts at manipulating public opinion on the part of the mental health professionals. With the certain knowledge that what I am about to say will raise a hue and cry, I am nonetheless moved to observe that the current public emphasis on mental disorder as disease has done as much harm as good in the shaping of public attitudes. My correspondence files literally bulge with letters from critics who protest that they are proud to be self-confessed psychotics. They claim that, like the cancer victim, they *are* victims who must patiently await their cure and, while suffering, require that we absolve them of any and all responsibility for their state or their recovery. Under such conditions, it is not surprising that psychosis should be feigned as defense against criminal responsibility. In all regards, such malingering in the current climate is adaptive and, under such interpretation, the antithesis of insanity.

Thus, the work of Drs. Bash and Alpert in attempting to detect malingering takes on enormous social significance. Their empirical approach to the problem is refreshing, particularly when it is contrasted with the veritable circus of the expert judgments that has recently characterized some of the more notorious criminal prosecutions. The problem of distinguishing malingering from "true" psychosis, however, is not simple. The problem lies in the slipperiness of either label. Bash and Alpert defined the terms by operational invocation of the judgments made by psychiatric professionals. But such definition assumes both that those judgments are independent of the tests employed by the authors and that they are at least reliable, if not valid. With respect to the first point, Drs. Bash and Alpert observe that the psychiatric judgments were not based upon the explicit use of the tests they themselves subsequently employed. Still, one wonders whether the psychiatric judgments could possibly have been entirely free of the content of these tests, which—if they have any validity at all—must capture diagnostic criteria defining the disorders being diagnosed. Thus, there may remain the question of definitional circularity.

With respect to the assumed reliability and validity of such diagnostic judgments, it is difficult not to resurrect the embarrassment of the Rosenhan study.[1] The central finding of the study of the "sane in insane places" is easily dismissed. One surely would hope that any advanced civilization would admit those who sought mental care to the institutions designed for such care. It is the incidental findings of that study that are disconcerting.

The first is that the bona fide residents of these institutions readily detected the pseudopatients, and the second is what transpired after the study was completed. Challenged by his critics, who argued that such failure to detect malingering could not occur in their hospital, Rosenhan suggested that they endeavor to detect the pseudopatients he might send their way. During the following three-month period, of 193 admissions, 41 patients were judged with high confidence to be pseudopatients by at least one member of the staff. Rosenhan reports that in actuality he sent no one.

Malingerers like Garrett Brock Trapnell, with whom I have had some personal dealings, boastfully attest to the ease with which they are able to deceive those who are vested with the responsibility of detecting their subterfuges. In the ghosted book *The Fox Is Crazy Too*, Trapnell records a lifetime of escape from prosecution by claiming insanity.[2]

None of this is meant to imply pessimism or criticism of the speakers of this session. On the contrary, it is precisely the cautions voiced by each of the speakers that are the firm basis for optimism that we can provide contributions to the issues of psychological evidence.

REFERENCES

1. ROSENHAN, D. L. 1973. On being sane in insane places. Science **179:** 250–258.
2. ASINOF, E. 1976. The Fox Is Crazy Too. William Morrow and Co., Inc. New York, N.Y.

FORENSIC PSYCHOLOGY AND HOSTAGE NEGOTIATION: INTRODUCTORY REMARKS

Dorothy Heid Bracey

Criminal Justice Center
John Jay College of Criminal Justice
New York, New York 10019

Hostage taking is an ancient device for strengthening a bargaining position. Military antagonists as well as criminals and political opponents have often used the means of threatening the life and safety of a third party as a way of increasing their leverage in negotiation. The success of the technique has traditionally depended upon the value placed upon the well-being of the hostage or upon the ability to free the hostage by force. Thus, the outcome of a hostage-taking situation depended on a balance of moral, military, or political power.

That analysis of hostage taking changed irrevocably in 1972. Although the growth of international terrorism had made many individuals in government and law enforcement more conscious of the possibility of hostage situations and the need to deal with them, 1972—the year of the attack upon Lod airport and the massacre at the Munich Olympics—marks the period when hostage negotiation came to be deliberately and systematically developed as a technique for countering hostage takers. Since that time, an ever-increasing amount of data has been gathered and exchanged—not only among agencies, but also among nations—and negotiating practices have been rehearsed and refined on a regular basis. It is common to find hostage negotiation units in medium-to-large-size police departments, while even small forces commonly make use of training in negotiation skills. And if terrorist kidnappings have inspired a new approach to hostage negotiation, those dealing with the phenomenon have found the resulting techniques to be applicable also to hostage situations caused by criminals, spontaneous rioters, and the mentally disturbed.[1]

A successful negotiation is one in which the hostage is released, the hostage taker captured, and no deaths occur among hostages, hostage takers, negotiaters, or bystanders. In order to bring about this situation, a large number of factors must be considered and controlled. Among the things to be faced by any agency faced with a hostage situation are (1) agency policy and priorities concerning negotiable items and the well-being of participants; (2) the existence and extent of interagency cooperation and the joint understanding of jurisdictional boundaries; (3) an agreed-upon chain of command; (4) a mutually supportive relationship with the news media, based upon trust and a common concern for the protection of human life; (5) knowledge of and ability to use whatever support services are available—included here are assault teams and precision firearms capability; (6) familiarity with available equipment, such as ambulances, tear gas, and communications devices; and (7) an intelligence-gathering capability that collects accurate and usable information. Deficiencies in any of these areas can defeat a negotiation attempt before it begins or can cause it to break down anywhere in its duration.

Although the absence of any of these factors can destroy a negotiation, their presence does not ensure its success. Success, it has come to be recognized, depends on the ability to understand and respond to the intra- and interpersonal dynamics taking place during the situation.

It was recognized early in the creation of negotiation techniques that the emotional state of the hostage taker was one of the most crucial variables in deciding the outcome of the situation. Included here is the motivation—the criminal who wishes only to escape must be dealt with differently from the ideological terrorist who is willing to die for a cause. The prison inmates with a concise and well-articulated set of demands call for a style of negotiation different from that to be used with an emotionally disturbed individual who calls for a diffuse and unelaborated "justice." The now-common use of psychologists and psychiatrists in the training of negotiators, and their use as consultants in negotiation situations, testifies to the importance attributed to the understanding of the mind of the hostage taker.

The papers presented here, however, are evidence of a much more sophisticated understanding of the role of the mental health sciences in hostage negotiation. One aspect of this is the realization that the emotional situation is a dynamic one and that the negotiation process itself is a factor in changing it. The technique of negotiation as it exists today is not merely bargaining; instead, it is an attempt to change the emotional relationship between the hostage taker and his surroundings so that he becomes willing to release the hostage unharmed. Bargaining—giving the hostage taker something he wants in return for something he will give up—may be part of this process, but it is not the entirety.

Recognition of negotiation as a technique for changing emotional states and relationships gave rise to the realization that the mental and emotional condition of the hostage taker is not the only factor of concern to forensic psychologists and psychiatrists. The corresponding conditions of the negotiators, other law enforcement agents, and hostages themselves must also be understood if the negotiation is to lead to a successful outcome. At some levels, this statement is self-evident; days of work by a patient, trained negotiator can be quickly undone by an aggressive, undisciplined sharpshooter. Other implications were not immediately obvious but have become accepted as the result of study and experience. For example, close relatives of a hostage taker were often brought to the scene to plead and reason; it is now perceived that the emotional relationship between the hostage taker and members of his family may have been among the factors precipitating or underlying the incident. In such cases, the presence of these individuals may exacerbate the situation rather than improve it. And it is only gradually that we are beginning to get some insights into the dynamics of the relationship between the hostage taker and the victim and that we are able to consider the implications of these dynamics for the negotiating process. This is important because changes in one set of psychological relationships may affect the emotional content of other sets. For instance, the negotiator who is ignorant of the "Stockholm syndrome" may be confused, disturbed, and finally angered by evidence of the victim's affection and concern for the hostage taker. Such a negotiator may come to doubt the legitimacy of an effort to save a victim who is perceived as acting less like a victim than like an accomplice and thereby may seriously undermine the success of the negotiating procedure. The ability to understand and predict such reactions on the part of the victims will enable the negotiator to treat them dispassionately and even to make positive use of them.

Unfortunately, it is the very success of psychological and psychiatric research in dealing with hostage takers that forces upon both researchers and practitioners considerations of confidentiality. It is a familiar paradox that the very dissemination of information that enables researchers and practitioners to benefit from each other's findings and experiences also makes that information available to potential hostage takers. In this area, terrorists pose a greater threat than do criminals or the emotionally disturbed. The high levels of intelligence, education, and discipline frequently found in terrorist groups indicate that terrorists are aware of and capable of utilizing the information to be found in scholarly and professional publications and capable of deducing therefrom the strategies and techniques that will be used by law enforcement. At least since the founding of the *Bulletin of the Atomic Scientists,* researchers have been troubled by the use that may be made of their work. The fact that these questions are not new does not make them any the less perplexing. The free circulation of information is not only one of the ethical underpinnings of science, it is also a practical necessity, for only by such circulation are progress and application possible. To confine psychological research concerning hostage negotiation to scientists and laboratories with high security ratings is unthinkable. At the same time, researchers and practitioners in this area must acknowledge their responsibility. There are no easy answers, although writers and speakers might bear the problem in mind as they consider such things as level of specificity and detail, especially in reporting application and policy. Researchers, such as those represented here, face the difficult task of balancing freedom and safety. May their work continue to be used in the interests of understanding and compassion rather than exploitation and abuse.

REFERENCES

1. MAHER, G. F. 1977. Hostage: A Police Approach to a Contemporary Crisis. Charles C. Thomas, Publishers. Springfield, Ill.

VALUES AND ORGANIZATION IN HOSTAGE AND CRISIS NEGOTIATION TEAMS

Harvey Schlossberg

Department of Psychology
John Jay College of Criminal Justice
New York, New York 10019

The use of police officers to defuse crisis situations originated in the late fifties with the introduction of family crisis teams. These were regular patrol officers who were selected for special training in the use of some simple psychological tactics for dealing with people in crisis. Sometimes officers were selected because they had attended college and received at least some introductory psychology. It soon became apparent that much of what is considered routine police work really falls into what could be described as crisis situations. One need only consider almost any contact with the public to see that police are called upon when situations get out of hand. Whether it's a simple fender-bender accident, a broken water main, or a person who has become the victim of a crime, the police are called upon to bring order out of overwhelming chaos. Therefore, the intervention tactics should be simple and general enough to apply to a wide range of situations and to be useful to almost every policeman.

Shortly after the 1972 Olympics massacre in Munich, the nations of the world were confronted with the realization that the terrorism that began in the Middle East shortly after the 1967 Arab-Israeli War no longer had geographical limits. In New York City, the author helped develop a program that ultimately was to serve as a model for much of the world. The Hostage Recovery Program was developed to meet the demands that could be put upon the police as the result of an incident of the proportions of the Munich massacre. It soon proved useful to apply the same principles to domestic situations. The success rate and the resulting positive public reaction, coupled with the simplicity of the tactics, spurred many police departments to reach out for and invest in training in crisis tactics.

Domestic and international hostage taking are very similar and lend themselves to the use of the same tactics. There are two basic premises that underlie the Hostage Recovery Program. First is that the hostage, in and of himself, has no value to the holder. This means that the person who takes the hostage is simply using the hostage as a tool or a device to attract an audience and gain attention. Using a hostage, one can go from total obscurity to international fame in a matter of minutes. For this reason, hostage taking must involve some form of announcement so that an audience will respond. Without an audience, the hostage taking is meaningless. The site selected by the criminal is very carefully chosen for its audience potential. For this reason, any event that will draw press coverage or crowds tends to be a fertile ground for the hostage taker. In many ways, the concept "theater of terror" is quite accurate: that is, the criminal is the star, the hostage is the supporting cast, and the police and public are the audience.

113

An important step is for the police to realize that the hostage taker is using the hostage only in order to attract an audience. The importance of this realization for the police is that they can recognize that any threat or actual physical violence inflicted upon the victim is not done to gain victim compliance, since the victim is usually already fully compliant. Just looking at a hostage situation, we can readily see that the hostage is totally and completely under the criminal's control. Being held hostage is about as close as one can come to being an infant, completely and totally dependent on another. In fact, the relationship between the victim and the criminal sometimes can be described as a parent-child relationship, with the hostage taker becoming the surrogate parent. This phenomenon has been described under a variety of headings, such as "Stockholm syndrome," identification with the aggressor, survival identification syndrome, and transference. These concepts have been devised to explain the strong dependence and cooperation that hostages have demonstrated in almost every situation that has occurred. The reaction extends many months and sometimes years after the hostage situation itself has been resolved. Police must recognize, then, that what is done to the hostage is done in order to gain *police compliance*.

The second basic premise underlying the Hostage Recovery Program is that it is just as much in the criminal's interest as it is in the police' interest not to let a situation become violent. The reason for this is based on simple logic—in any situation that becomes violent, the established authorities must be the victor. Outside of an all-out war, the establishment has the manpower and equipment to effect a victory. The simple truth of hostage taking is that for the criminal, a violent interaction can only result in loss; if he is to profit and enjoy the fruits of his labor, then a negotiated solution is the only alternative. The killing of innocent people cannot go unanswered. In fact, a working hypothesis for the police is that most hostage situations are carefully designed by the criminals in such a way as to avoid the taking of life; if in fact the design were to take life, then probably very little could be done to prevent this from occurring. On the other hand, the police themselves can only be governed by one guideline, that is, that human life is the only important consideration. Unless the protection of life is recognized as a fixed and irreversible boundary, the police tactic would consist of escalating force, which could only result in total disaster.

Bearing in mind the two basic principles already stated, hostage taking can be viewed in an entirely different light. The hostage taker is seen as somebody who has reached a point in life where he is totally frustrated and unable to obtain what he desires; the taking of hostages becomes nothing more than his attempt at problem solving.

In training police how to handle hostage situations, the greatest emphasis is placed on recognizing the problem solving without making judgmental values about the goals that the hostage taker is trying to reach. Rather, hostage taking should be recognized as creative, desperate, and intelligent problem solving. When the police arrive at the scene—and the criminal is ranting and raving, threatening violence, or giving deadlines—it is important that the police remember that they are walking in on this individual's problem solving. With this concept as a frame of reference, hostage taking becomes similar to the problem solving one sees people engaged in during a family dispute. In other words, the same dynamics are at work in a family dispute, a threatened suicide, or hostage taking. Once this assumption is made, crisis intervention techniques become appropriate.

The negotiator is the term generally used in law enforcement for the person who will be intervening in the crisis. We would be just as accurate to call him the therapist, since it is the same role. The goal of the negotiator is to establish himself as a significant "other." He will set an atmosphere similar to what one might find at a therapy session. The therapist will not offer any solutions or advice, but rather will set an atmosphere that is conducive to the patient's working through his own solutions. The same holds true for the negotiator: he will not advise the criminal to surrender nor will he offer possible solutions, since they might trigger a negative outcome or establish a direction that the criminal never thought of. In essence, this is clearly a passive therapy, designed to permit the criminal an opportunity to ventilate and explore various alternatives without the fear of total annihilation. Obviously, the negotiator—like the therapist—will be experiencing stress feelings similar to those that the criminal experiences. In essence, as in therapy, there is a mirror relationship between the feelings experienced by the criminal and by the negotiator. As a result, the negotiator is under great stress—not only because of the mirror effect, but also because he has much at stake in terms of outcome. He has a personal investment in terms of his success as a negotiator, and also in terms of his conscience should anyone be killed while he is negotiating. The criminal in many ways has it easier, since he has the negotiator to help him handle the crisis. Recognizing this, we have introduced a concept of negotiating teams.

While the number of members on a team cannot be clearly delineated—and several combinations are possible, as we will explore shortly—the basic number on a team, regardless of departmental size, should be no less than two individuals. The first man, or primary negotiator, deals as a therapist directly with the criminal. The second negotiator is sometimes called the coach, backup, or secondary negotiator. His role varies depending on how many men are on the team. If he is the only other member, he will help gather and screen intelligence information and select those aspects that may be important to the primary negotiator. He will run interference with supervisors by explaining what is happening so that the primary negotiator need not be disturbed or interfered with. In the event the primary negotiator must leave, the backup will replace him, but only after proper introduction to the criminal by the primary. The real significance of the secondary role is to act as negotiator to the negotiator. In effect, the backup permits the negotiator to ventilate and share some of the stress. It should be pointed out that at no time do the two negotiators deal together with the criminal. If in fact they did, competition would be created and the outcome would be influenced negatively. Since no two hostage incidents are exactly alike, there is no standardized approach, but rather a general, passive stance designed to ease anxieties and tensions not only by what is said, but also through the use of time.

The selection of negotiators is one of the major considerations in forming hostage negotiating teams. The original selection procedures instituted by the New York City Police Department involved volunteers who expressed a belief in nonviolent methods and who were willing to undergo extensive training, which involved personal therapy and dealing with personal feelings. In addition to an intensive medical examination, there were psychiatric interviews and in-depth psychological testing. The tests used were group and individual, i.e., Minnesota multiphasic personality inventory (MMPI), thematic apperception test (TAT), Draw a Person (DAP), and Rorschach. In spite of all the testing and screening, we could not come up with a profile of the ideal negotiator. Experience has dictated that a variety of personalities do equally well. We also attempted to match the negotiator ethnically and by race to the criminal. In reality, this did not work out; no matter what combination was used, we were wrong and the criminal wanted somebody else. Current procedure provides that the first trained negotiator to arrive at the scene will be responsible for negotiating. The negotiators keep in mind the two basic objectives: (1) bargaining with the criminal in order to secure the release of hostages while not doing anything to make the situation worse than it is already; and (2) the ultimate surrender of the criminal. Other personnel at the scene are responsible for the general goals of law enforcement, namely, the maintenance of social order within constitutional limits, protection of life and property, and the enforcing of law. The members of the negotiating team generally have five activities that they must perform. The greater the number of members a team has available, the easier will be the stress upon each individual. The first activity consists of gathering basic information, such as the number of individuals involved, threats, types of weapons, etc. This is done on an ongoing basis; and a log is frequently kept by this negotiator. Depending upon the length of time the operation runs, the depth of information gathering will vary. The second activity involves a negotiator who will act as overall organizer, assigning work to individuals, and who generally is a supervisor in terms of organizational rank. In addition, the supervisor will perform the third, fourth, and fifth activities. These activities include coordination of hostage team with containment team, and maintaining an ongoing analysis of the information that he receives, which will lead to the fifth activity—planning strategy based on that analysis and on a continual assessment of the situation.

In summary, while we cannot specify a particular number of individuals needed to make up an ideal negotiating team, the concept that negotiations should utilize a team approach remains valid. By use of this approach, negotiating functions and tasks can be delegated for greater efficiency. Justification for expending manpower and funds to establish and train these teams is clearly found across the country in the daily news headlines. The incidents may not be of the dramatic international type, but every bank robbery, every family dispute, contains the elements of a nightmare that could sweep innocent people into the center. The problem for the authorities then becomes one of resolving the conflict without the loss of life.

THE DYNAMICS OF THE HOSTAGE TAKER: SOME MAJOR VARIANTS*

Jeanne N. Knutson

The Wright Institute
Berkeley, California 94704

As the phenomenon of terrorism has grown to be a continuing element in modern political behavior, the concurrent phenomenon of politically motivated hostage taking has increasingly impinged on the consciousness and even on the lives of many citizens. Certain categories of citizens are at special risk: government employees—especially those serving outside their country; top officials of transnational companies; individuals (like Patty Hearst) who may be abducted as symbols of political demands and politically motivated rage. Indeed, hostage taking in these high-risk categories has become a big business—not only for the terrorists, who have reaped considerable gains, but also for new transnational corporations selling insurance and security.

Yet, one need not be a member of this high-risk group to be imperiled by the hostage taker, for it is also possible to become an *inadvertent* hostage, someone whose hostage role is determined merely by the chance circumstance of being physically located where the action is. Citizens in this more general category become hostages because they are passengers on a hijacked airplane, because they are present in a government building during a terrorist incident (such as that led by the Hanaafi Muslims in Washington, D.C.), or simply because they are a secretary or a repairman auxiliary to a principal hostage (as in the OPEC raid in Vienna).

As the phenomenon of hostage taking is both discriminating and random, it is of more than academic interest to examine the psychodynamics of the terrorists behind the guns. Various books and papers have been written about negotiating with the hostage taker.[1-4] Other works have focused on the phenomenological experience of the captive.[5-8] However, an exhaustive literature review disclosed no papers that have examined the psychology of the hostage taker and *his* phenomenological view of his captives. Thus, the present paper stands alone and necessarily includes a degree of speculation unconfirmed by other sources. It will attempt to delineate two major types of politically motivated hostage takers and then will provide data to explicate their dynamics.

The data are derived from a long-range research project on terrorists (see Reference 9 for a detailed discussion), in which an attempt is being made to complete in-depth evaluations of all prisoners in U.S. federal

* This project has been supported in part by Dr. David Hubbard of the Aberrant Behavior Center (Dallas, Texas) and in part, through the efforts of Dr. Louis J. West, by USPHS Biomedical Research Support Grant RR05756 awarded to the Neuropsychiatric Institute, University of California, Los Angeles.

prisons who have been convicted of crimes that were politically motivated, and to gather a control sample from prisoners in several other countries. The taped interviews are being conducted in a standardized manner and include administration of both a Rorschach test and the Political Thematic Apperception Measure.[10] As the Symbionese Liberation Army (SLA) has conducted one of the few politically motivated kidnappings thus far in the United States of a specifically targeted, high-risk person, data from this research project have been supplemented by interviews with non–politically motivated prisoners who have taken specifically targeted individuals to achieve a particular goal.

Variants of Hostage Takers

It appears that only a small minority of politically motivated hostage takers are driven by pressing personal needs joined to inadequate psychological resources that cause them to lose an adequate hold on the reality of their personal problems as distinct from the problems of the political system.[11] This small group may seek forced emigration on a hijacked airplane or may make violent threats against the father-president as the solution to their own inner turmoil, or may deliberately abduct another who symbolizes their primitive rage. Because of their numerical insignificance, this paper will not deal with grossly psychologically impaired captors. Instead, it will seek to explicate the dynamics of captors whose actions are mediated by ego functions and directed toward the service of external goals.

Just as hostages can be placed in their captive role on either a deliberate or an inadvertent basis, so the politically motivated hostage taker dons his role of captor in either a deliberate manner (i.e., desiring a particular gain in exchange for his hostage) or casually, through a plan in which hostage taking is an inadvertent or minimal part of the overall scheme. It is the thesis of this paper that this difference in planning and anticipating the responsibility of having hostages reflects a psychological dissimilarity between the two types of captors.

The Reluctant Captor

In the United States, by far the predominant type of politically motivated hostage taking has been of the second, casual type. For example, terrorists have taken airplanes and, in so doing, have also taken hostages. When interviewed, these captors usually are quite aware that they were unwilling and, for most, unable to kill another human being. For them, it was important to take elaborate safeguards for the safety of their hostages and, additionally, to make efforts either to neutralize or, if possible, to convert their hostages to become supporters of their ideological view (and, hence, accomplices and no longer hostages).

These unwilling captors *never employ psychological processes to*

dehumanize their hostages. Before, during, and after the event, they experience their hostages as people—with minds to win over; with emotions
that may be assaulted by the terror of the event and may even go out of control, causing a dreaded act of violence to occur; with bodies that might fail
and, in that way, burden the conscience of the hostage taker. These subjects
experience their captor role as a psychologically stressful burden—a role
that they undertook at great psychic jeopardy. They are not capable of
seriously using another person's life as a poker chip in the pursuit of specific
gains, nor are they capable of comfortably accepting responsibility for
violence toward others or for the death of another human being.

These reluctant captors are motivated by the desire to publicize a cause,
to underline a political demand, to dramatize a political injustice. Often in
opposition to their personal psychology and personal beliefs, they act
violently: they commandeer an airplane at gunpoint; they "expropriate"
money from a bank for their revolutionary cause; they take over a public
building. These subjects are principled individuals whose violence is really
bravado—a facade of strength pressed into the service of what is deemed a
critical political cause. Far from being characteristic of a "criminal personality," reluctant hostage takers usually have neither a criminal record
nor a history of violence. This is not to say that such individuals do not at
times inadvertently cause the death of other people,[9] but rather that they are
not violence prone by nature or characterized by strong or uncontrolled aggressive impulses.†

In their role of hostage taker, these subjects handle the situation in
ways that appear "stupid" or "dumb" to the deliberate hostage taker. If a
passenger desires urgently to leave a hijacked airplane, the person is almost
always allowed to deplane (so that, in an important sense, those remaining
hostages could be described as volunteers). The reluctant hostage taker does
not usually even have a weapon (although one is almost always feigned),
trusting rather to his frequently charismatic personality and his powerful
political vision to provide adequate hostage control, if control becomes a
real issue.

While the reluctant hostage taker is not grossly impaired psychologically, several factors appear to operate frequently to facilitate his becoming a
hostage taker. First, while he possesses considerable ideational resources,
these resources are limited both by poor reality testing as well as by impaired ability to cognitively integrate, analyze, and make sense out of his
ideational world. Thus, these reluctant hostage takers are frequently
typified by lack of logical, systematically goal-directed thinking. Their interview material illustrates this illogical thinking and a lack of adequate
consideration of possible alternatives. These subjects are dreamers—philosophers and ideologues—lacking adequate concreteness and present
orientation in their thinking.

In addition, there is an overreliance on the power of their own will and

---

† For example, their Rorschach protocols do not include aggressive symbols and employ
minimal, if any, color. The color that is employed is adequately form dominated.

that of their cause, which can shade over into a pathological degree of grandiosity. Frequently, these subjects are aware that at the time of their terroristic act, they felt themselves to be invincible and omnipotent. Thus, they felt that no hostage was going to grab for the gun or attempt to take control; and their thinking does not progress to a further consideration that asks, But what if? In the interview, these reluctant hostage takers are frequently asked by what psychological means they were able to avoid the anxiety that a hostage *might* attempt to subdue them or *might* die from a heart attack, or that the bomb *might* go off when someone was around to be harmed. With a measure of surprise, these subjects state that such alternatives had never seriously been considered, since they just *knew* that they could bring the situation to the desired conclusion by the sheer force of their will—a degree of faith unwarranted by the outcome of their actions in numerous cases.

Finally, while hostage takers as a whole are highly likely to have experienced a very close brush with death as a child—perhaps even having been declared dead or dying—this experience is dynamically important in a particular way to the reluctant hostage takers. For this group, a serious illness, the ingestion of rat poison, or long-term immobilization through an accident leads to a reaction formation[12] against feelings of weakness, fragility, or helplessness, which underlies both the bravado of their terroristic act and the lack of adequate plans for self-protection. Their stance involves both a desire to *look* tough and a protection against having to *be* tough (i.e., and thus to be found wanting).

The Deliberate Hostage Taker

Standing in stark contrast to the reluctant hostage taker is the person who purposefully sets out to control the life chances of another human being in order to achieve a desired goal. This person is perfectly willing to execute his hostage, with little or no psychic pain, should the hostage be unwilling or unable to serve as a totally controllable *implement*, an auxiliary facilitative of the hostage taker's threat. For the deliberate hostage taker, the essence of his act is the psychological dehumanization of his hostage, the stripping away of the hostage's human characteristics.

This psychological dehumanization does not imply a lack of awareness of the hostage's feelings and needs. To the contrary, the deliberate hostage taker is often a master of psychological insight, intuitively aware of those factors in his hostage that can be made to work for him, to ensure his control. What the psychological dehumanization does imply rather is a total orientation toward his goal, a total willingness to use psychological insight for purposes of manipulation and control, and a total inability for affective bonding. When push comes to shove, the heretofore friendly and nurturing deliberate hostage taker is quite able to callously sacrifice his victim's life. It is contended here that the well-known Palestinian terrorists, particularly the famed "Carlos,"[13] are the political prototypes of this deliberate hostage taker.

Such psychodynamics obviously contain a large element of psychopathology, particularly a lack of affect and conscience in dealing with others. Few of the deliberate hostage takers who have been interviewed, however, are true psychopaths. Most retain—though deeply buried—a measure of affect and of conscience. However, these characteristics are seen by these hostage takers as hindrances to their work. Therefore, to attempt to arouse their consciences and their caring feelings not only can be counterproductive, it also can be extremely dangerous. The deliberate hostage taker stresses emotional control: he wants his hostages to be in emotional control of themselves at all times, and he demands this of himself as well.

In practical terms, the deliberate hostage taker uses violence as a tool toward his ends. He may capture, execute, and maim—but in a controlled manner, to serve his purposes. As a rule, he is not typified by uncontrolled, violent impulses. He is the epitome of goal orientation. Opposed to the reluctant hostage taker, these subjects are pragmatists whose thinking lacks adequate ability to abstract and to orient to either past or future.

Compared to the complex personalities of the reluctant hostage takers, the deliberate captors' psychodynamics stand forth with simplicity. Lacking the historical experience and the present ability to trust another, to safely care for another, to depend upon another, the deliberate captor trusts only himself and his weapon. He may employ psychological controls ("I don't want to hurt you."; "Sure, you can fix some coffee, honey,"; "Why don't you just lie down now and get a little rest."), but he is constantly aware that it is force that is the key to his scenario. His hostages simply do not exist for him as people; their opinions of him, their children, their lives—all are subsumed under the attainment of his goal.

LET THE CAPTORS SPEAK

In this necessarily brief paper, only limited statements by captors can be given. However, in these brief words, the psychological differences between the majority group in each type is clear. Let us begin with the concerns of the reluctant hostage takers.‡

[S] Well, to tell you the truth, I—I was . . . concerned uh that people—that these particular uh *time* in their life would not uh *damage* them or would not scare them that much that—so that's why I—I went quite a few times from the cockpit to the plane *and* uh *talked* to them and they were drinking. I ordered the stewardess not to give any drinks to—to my—to these friends of mine who were with me nor to any passenger who would uh get himself drunk probably, because we might get into trouble. Other than that, I told these friends of mine, talk to them and uh try to get the situation as relaxed as possible and uh, believe me, that's what it uh—what—what the situation was.

[K] So it sounds like what you were feeling was worried—that every—

[S] Oh, definitely. I was concerned about their uh—their feelings and their being scared. I didn't want them to be scared.

‡ [S] is the subject; [K] is the author.

This subject was concerned about the emotional state of the passengers. He was also concerned about their minds. Literature for his cause was distributed, and various speeches were given. Further, he was concerned about their opinion of him as a person.

[S] I thought uh if everything went smoothly uh we would return from uh from Croatia and land up again somewhere in Europe and—on the way, right there and then I would give up uh and tell the passengers and Captain and everybody else that these things are not real and they—and I would *stand then* on the way ba—that's what I uh had in mind. I would be then at *their* mercy and uh I would try uh to give my message across to them, *now*, without their fearing me, and uh—to tell you the truth, I uh—I *pictured* that return to the United States as somehow uh—uh—happy ending of that dramatic situation, because they wouldn't be a-scared any—anymore. Now they would discover that I wasn't real uh—uh—such animal or uh willing or uh—or being capable to harm them or kill them uh because I couldn't possibly do anything with those things I had on the plane. It's just uh—it's just uh—just uh—just uh—not explosive but kit—plat—kit—kits you play on uh—making all different kinds of . . .

Such a concern was general on the plane. One of this same band of captors subsequently wrote to each passenger from prison, saying in part:

Although I know this letter may not compensate for the feelings of fear and apprehension you suffered during the hijacking I am compelled to at least attempt to explain my seemingly brutal behavior during the hours spent in Paris . . .

And, at the end:

I pray that you can forgive me one day, if you haven't yet, and comprehend my state of mind at the time. As you may know, I will be paying dearly for my actions. During the long years that I will be spending in prison, it would be a great comfort to me to know that you understand that I meant no harm to anyone and am not a brute.

Let us consider the concerns of but one additional reluctant hostage taker:

[S] . . . first of all, let me say when I hijacked the plane to Vietnam, it wasn't a case—any kin—case where I was, you know, ransoming the passengers or attempting to hold hostage or anything like that.

What my intention was, was to take 'em to Vietnam, where they could have seen for themselves what was happening to that country and I figured that the Vietnamese would have showed them around, you know, different hospitals and places bombed and stuff like that and so it would have made not only the initial publicity of the hijacking but then I figured well, later the passengers will return to the United States and they will tell what they've seen, so I—I thought that was the best way—the most—the way that most publicity could be made against the war.

[K] So uh you intended to have your hostages really work with you?

[S] They did. They—well, they weren't hostages. I didn't consider 'em hostages. . . .

[K] Can you tell me a little bit more about what you mean when you say you didn't consider them as hostages?

[S] Well, I mean in the sense that I wasn't holding them for any kind of ransom or any kind of demands, anything like that. I was never—there was never a question of threatening their—their—their lives for any type of demands whatsoever.

[K] A hostage is usually considered somebody who's not free to leave.

[S] Yeah, well, in that sense, they were hostages, but—

[K] Although they seemed to be free to leave. According to what I read, when they asked to go in Los Angeles and in Dallas, you let them go.

[S] Yes, ev—every, single person who asked to leave the plane I allowed them to leave the plane, *including* the crew.

The theme that unites all of the above quotations is clear: hostages are human beings whose lives, feelings, and opinions are of value. Never is violence seriously threatened or feigned threats of violence excused. Never is the responsibility for a successful outcome (idiosyncratically defined as an outcome in which all participants are alive, and experiencing mutual regard, and the political goal is accomplished) shifted from the captor.

The psychodynamics of the reluctant hostage taker are thrown into bold relief when we turn to the views of a deliberate hostage taker. The deliberate hostage taker, by definition, abducts a particular person (or persons) to employ his hostage's life and well-being as a bargaining tool. At the outset, the hostage taker clearly defines the options as "my goal or his life" and thus accepts responsibility, on some level, for the death of another. In the United States, the SLA's abduction of Patty Hearst stands out as an incident of politically motivated, deliberate hostage taking. Elsewhere, the deliberate hostage taker is *the* political prototype. As no politically motivated deliberate hostage taker has been interviewed to date, several interviews were arranged with subjects who had purposefully taken hostages in order to advance a particular goal (escape, ransom, etc.).

The subject whose views are quoted below is a very useful resource—intelligent, creative, and possessing considerable psychological insight into the dynamics of his hostages. His views of his hostages and his personal dynamics are strikingly similar to those of other deliberate hostage takers who have been interviewed. Over a period of time, he has taken a number of people hostage to achieve particular goals. At times, he has dealt considerable bodily harm to noncooperative hostages. It was clinically apparent that it has been favorable circumstances alone that have prevented this subject from killing a hostage.

To begin with, he *planned* to take hostages and to *use* them to advance his goals.

> [S] I know we all went over the plan differently. The way I went over it in my mind was that we would take this guy to a point and uh I never really anticipated a problem from him. Uh—
> [K] Tell me about that. Why didn't you anticipate a problem?
> [S] It's just not—it's just not the nature of, at least American people, to buck—when they've got a loaded gun pointed at 'em. And I figured if he was armed, we would have to get the drop first, so to speak. And uh—but we had continuously planned a backup man with a rifle, when we approached this guy, so we were perfectly safe there. We thought we were . . .
> [K] I'm interested in your saying American people anyway uh are very—if I remember the word you used—passive, submissive, when there's a gun, so you assumed that there was no trouble. It was almost like taking a suitcase.
> [S] Correct.

The view of *others as objects* pervades this subject's material. The dimensions of *projected responsibility* and *control maintenance* are also crucial to understanding his dynamics. He goes on to explain his modus operandi:

> . . . if I like now was to pull a weapon and tell you "don't make no noise; don't do nothin," you know. If somebody comes in this office and I'm u—unable to take them also, I'm gonna kill you, because it's gonna be your fault and—and I would just—

The subject was interrupted and questioned several times as to why if attention were called to him and his hostage by any means whatsoever, the captive would die. Why wouldn't his first impulse be self-protection—a look around to see what danger had been aroused? With growing frustration, he noted that he had a "contract" with his hostages on "a personal basis." In the hypothetical plan we discussed:

> [S] You're thinkin' about two things. You're thinkin' about gettin' out that back gate with your hostage, and you're thinkin' about gettin'—gettin'—n—away—or you're thinkin' about killin' him.
> [K] Well, what you're saying is, you're thinking about revenge. And I don't understand—
> [S] Oh, no; it's not revenge. That's a part of the plan. If I don't make it, I'm gonna kill him. If I don't make it, I *will* kill him. . . . I still have to go back to the thing that I have a plan; right? And a—a part of my plan is killin' him if it messes up.

After several other examples, the issue was joined:

> [K] But what you're saying, it seems to me, is the same thing, that what's *important* is that people obey you.
> [S] Absolutely. You—you have to have control. If I've got—if I've got six hostages and uh—and uh—and one of 'em is causin' dissension in the group, to sacrifice that one will draw the others into line.

The interviewer then noted that a number of terrorists, reluctantly finding themselves in possession of hostages, allowed the frightened or unwilling to leave. This subject commented:

> [S] Now, what I wouldn't do is—like you were talkin' about the terrorist—I wouldn't let *nobody* go . . . No, nobody. Anybody that went would go with a bullet.
> [K] Why?
> [S] Take this with you.
> [K] Why?
> [S] Because I'm not takin' hostages to let 'em go . . . I would let 'em go if my demands were met.
> [K] People I've talked to have let hostages go because they wanted, like you, to keep control of the situation. Like there was an hysterical woman or—
> [S] She's expendable; then she—she goes and takes a bullet with her. That's to enforce my demands.

Just as one would get rid of a malfunctioning appliance, an inedible piece of food, or an unmanageable pet, so the deliberate hostage taker grants his hostages conditional life: minimally, as long as they do not obstruct his plan or, optimally, as they are able to further it.

Like other deliberate hostage takers who have been interviewed, this subject is sensitive to those issues that motivate his captives to be "good" hostages, i.e., perfectly controllable and in control of themselves. One example will have to suffice. It relates to the abduction of a young couple:

> See, once you have a man and wife—'specially if they're young—you can control either one through the other . . . Whatever I want you to do, I can threaten your husband and you'll do it. Whatever I want him to do, I can threaten you, whatever—vice versa. And that was the situation there.

This deliberate hostage taker went on to offer an amazing insight—the obverse of the "Stockholm syndrome," the phenomenon in which hostages are found to become deeply emotionally attached to certain captors.[5,8]

[S] Like we had—we played the age-old game just like the police do, like one of us was uh—was the monster of the group, just growlin' and roarin' and cussin' and threatenin', and uh whoever was like guarding the hostages, one would be like the bad guy and the other one would be the soft-spoken good guy. . . .[Like the police do] The same thing with the hostages, like if you got one guy talkin' about "let's kill 'em, man. We can't wait. The police are gonna be here. Let's kill 'em. They're just gonna testify against us." The other guy sayin' "Man, you know, you don't wanna kill these—look at this little ol' gal. You know. Her and her husband ain't given' nobody no problem in the world." . . . "Man, let's *kill* 'em, you know." . . . "Look, just be cool, man; there ain't no need to hurt these people." And uh, you just become one with 'em.

[K] What purpose does it serve?

[S] As long as they think they got a champion, as long as there's any kind of straw held out to 'em that they can grasp, they're gonna grasp it, before they'll buck the gun.

Many government officials, publicly and privately, counsel potential hostages to "go along" with the Stockholm syndrome. Special note should be taken of the views of this expert captor. When asked if there was safety for the young wife who displayed trusting, dependent behavior, he replied:

No, I wouldn't hurt her . . . I mean, I wouldn't a let her run out the door, or I wouldn't a let her get on the phone, or scream out the window.

[K] So you wouldn't hurt her as long as she was a good hostage?

[S] Let's put it this way. I wouldn't a shot her. I would have dragged her down. I would of . . . maybe hit her with a pistol, if it became necessary.

And if a policeman was alerted by the woman?

[S] Then he would probably be killed immediately.

[K] What about her? What about your rule that if someone—

[S] Well, then—then she has put herself on the other side of the fence and uh she's just as much of a pig as he is then.

CRITICAL DISTINCTIONS

For the deliberate hostage taker, his captive exists as an implement to be used or discarded on the basis of the furtherance of his goals. As a tool, the captive is stripped of those human qualities that normally give pause: psychic pain, personal attachments, weak body organs. These qualities exist in the awareness of the hostage taker, but they are divorced from any *affective* connection to remain only in the rational calculus of his overall plan. After the incident is concluded, the hostage ceases to exist in the memory of his captor as even a two-dimensional person, but only as an attribute of an externally perceived situation. It is thus inconceivable that the deliberate hostage taker would be troubled about the effect of his violence on his hostage, or that he could imaginably write a letter asking for forgiveness!

Further, the deliberate hostage taker is inordinately concerned with the issue of control. He *must* be in command at all times. His words *must* be respected. The urgency of this need for control surpasses the exigencies of the situation to reflect unmet intrapsychic needs of long standing. This is the child who almost died, the child who was never important to anyone, who holds the gun. To him, a "no" echoes with intolerable pain down the corridors of memory as a narcissistic[14,15] injury not to be borne.

The issue of control is not just one of control over the hostage; it is equally the issue of control over self. The deliberate hostage taker quoted above noted how most people instinctively appealed in the name of their children, their spouse, their family. This annoys him—as do tears—because such considerations obstruct the plan in which the hostage is an object. As he remarked, "In case somethin' happens later and I have to shoot this guy, I'd really feel bad, two little kids sittin' there and his wife."

In psychodynamic terms, the deliberate hostage taker is energized by two major forces. First, he is powerfully driven by needs to overcome feelings of weakness and inferiority. He must be tough. He must be consistent. Challenge him, and you will see a violent affirmation of his strength. Always, in his inner awareness, someone is watching whose approval has been painfully withheld because he wasn't tough enough. It is their standards—and not those to which a hostage may appeal—that he emulates in a constant search for affirmation of his worth. Second, he is energized by a need to deny dependency and trust. Here also, offers to act counter to this powerful need—to be soft, tender, trusting—are met with anger. In his psychic economy, the deliberate hostage taker knows—from historical experience and present conviction—that such offers are enveloped with pain and disappointment.

The reluctant hostage taker, on the other hand, is an obviously conflicted person, and the stress of his ever-present conflicts is readily apparent. He needs to be tough ("a freedom fighter"), to be brave ("I never know fear"), to take political actions beyond the approval of most. However, he also needs to be liked, to be accepted, to be seen as nonthreatening. He needs to manipulate and use people for his political goals, but he also needs their approval—their permission, as it were.

Thus, the reluctant hostage taker is burdened by an awesome sense of responsibility to appease both sides of his conflicted self. This need blurs actuality, practical considerations, and logical alternatives. In a pressing inner dialectic, he rapidly cycles from thesis to synthesis and bypasses awareness of the antithetical stance he plays out. His real punishment thus is internal, for whenever he wins (by being tough, by stating his cause dramatically), he necessarily loses (by frightening, hurting, and alienating others).

In the political world today, terrorists encompass both types of hostage takers, with the balance in any one society dependent upon the personal and societal values that they actualize. On the American political scene, idealism and humanitarianism are dominant political forces, and thus, almost all actors play with a very lively concern for acceptance by a liberal, humanitarian public that values the golden rule. Elsewhere (and in certain subsocieties in America), bitterness and intense narcissistic rage are rampant in selected publics and thus provide a tacit—though perhaps unconscious—acceptance of violence and retribution by violent, sociopathic actors. In these societies, the rule of the day is not golden but steel: an eye for an eye, a tooth for a tooth.

All terrorists—whether deliberate or reluctant hostage takers or employing entirely different means toward their political goals—are nurtured by and dependent upon public approval and support. As long as liberalism and humanism typify the American political ideology, the deliberate hostage takers are likely to play only a minor part in the cast of politically motivated captors here.

SUMMARY

This paper represents a unique effort to elucidate the dynamics of two major types of politically motivated hostage takers. The data presented are derived from an ongoing research project that is gathering extensive interview and psychological test materials from prisoners convicted of politically motivated crimes, both within the U.S. and several foreign prison systems.

Data indicate that: (1) *the reluctant hostage taker*, who inadvertently or regretfully possesses hostages, is concerned with the opinions, emotional state, and safety of his captives and is burdened by a sense of responsibility; (2) *the deliberate hostage taker* experiences his hostages as nonhuman objects whose safety and existence are predicated on the furtherance of his goals, is concerned with the issue of control, and projects responsibility for violence onto others. Only a small subset of each type can be considered grossly psychologically impaired and unable to separate intra- and extrapsychic reality. The actions of the majority of each group are mediated generally by ego functions and directed toward the service of external goals.

ACKNOWLEDGMENTS

I wish to express sincere appreciation to Mr. Norman Carlson, Director of the United States Federal Bureau of Prisons, and to his staff throughout this large system who have been uniformly cooperative with my research requirements and supportive of the needs for confidentiality and protection of my subjects' rights of privacy. I would like to especially acknowledge the help at the Atlanta Federal Penitentiary of Mr. Ed Howard and Mr. Ed Watkins in gathering data for the present paper. Finally, I would like to express appreciation to Gail Hellstein and Sally Vamdiver for their patient editing of the research transcripts.

REFERENCES

1. CULLINANE, M. J. 1978. Terrorism—A new era of criminality. Terrorism 1(2): 119–124.
2. KOBETZ, R. W. & H. H. A. COOPER. 1978. Target Terrorism. Bureau of Operations and Research, International Association of Chiefs of Police. Gaithersburg, Md.
3. McKNIGHT, G. 1974. The Terrorist Mind. The Bobbs-Merrill Company. New York, N.Y.
4. MILLER, A. H. 1978. Negotiations for hostages: implications from the police experience. Terrorism 1(2): 125–146.
5. HACKER, F. J. 1976. Crusaders, Criminals, Crazies. Bantam Books. New York, N.Y.

6. JACKSON, G. 1973. Surviving the Long Night. The Vanguard Press, Inc. New York, N.Y.
7. JENKINS, B. 1976. Hostage Survival: Some Preliminary Observations. Report No. P-5637. The Rand Corporation. Santa Monica, Calif.
8. OCHBERG, F. 1977. The victim of terrorism: psychiatric considerations. Terrorism 1(1): 1–22.
9. KNUTSON, J. 1979. Social and psychodynamic pressures toward a negative identity: the case of an American revolutionary-terrorist. Paper presented at the Second Annual Meeting of the International Society of Political Psychology, Washington, D.C., May, 1979.
10. KNUTSON, J. 1973. The new frontier of projective techniques. In The Handbook of Political Psychology. J. Knutson, Ed.: 413–437. Jossey-Bass. San Francisco, Calif.
11. HUBBARD, D. G. 1978. The Skyjacker. Collier Books. New York, N.Y.
12. FREEDMAN, A. M., H. I. KAPLAN & B. J. SADOCK. 1972. Modern Synopsis of Psychiatry. The Williams & Wilkins Co. Baltimore, Md.
13. SMITH, C. 1976. Carlos, Portrait of a Terrorist. Holt, Rinehart and Winston, Inc. New York, N.Y.
14. KOHUT, H. 1971. The Analysis of the Self. International Universities Press. New York, N.Y.
15. KOHUT, H. 1977. The Restoration of the Self. International Universities Press, Inc. New York, N.Y.

VICTIM RESPONSES TO TERROR

Martin Symonds

Psychological Services
Health Services Division
New York City Police Department
New York, New York 10010

In this paper, I plan to share my knowledge and experience of victims' responses to criminally induced terror. Much of my understanding has been derived from my work with sudden, unexpected criminal violence. It is my hope and belief that the insights gained from the unfortunate experiences of these victims can be effectively used in understanding the responses of victims of terrorists.*

In 1971 when I first began my studies of victims of sudden, unexpected, violent crime, I included victims of crimes where there was generally no contact with the criminal, such as the crime of burglary; if violence did occur, it generally was to property and not to person. I also included victims of sudden, unexpected, violent crime where there was minimal contact with the criminal, such as street assault and robbery, popularly known as "mugging," and those victims of sudden, unexpected, violent crime where there was prolonged contact with the criminal—these were crimes of rape, robbery, kidnapping, and hostage taking.

When I reviewed the victims' behavior, I became aware that all victim responses regularly followed certain sequential phases regardless of what type of crime was involved. Only the duration and intensity of each phase was influenced by the nature and quality of contact with the criminal.

Briefly, all victims of sudden, unexpected, violent crime no matter of what kind respond initially with shock and disbelief. This first phase is the phase of denial. This is quickly followed by phase 2, when denial is overwhelmed by reality. These two phases form the acute response to sudden, unexpected violence.

After a varying period of time, the individual enters into phase 3. This is the phase of traumatic depression. It is characterized by circular bouts of apathy, anger, resignation, irritability, constipated rage, insomnia, startle reactions, and replay of the traumatic events through dreams, fantasies, and nightmares. It is also the phase of self-recrimination. Phase 3 can also be called the "I am stupid" phase, since the replay of the traumatic events is evaluated under peacetime conditions after the event is over and the criminal is gone and not under the conditions of criminal-induced terror. (Under the conditions of extensive contact with the criminal, such as prolonged hostage taking, it is highly unlikely that any significant behavior

---

* Much of the material described and quoted in this paper is from unpublished studies by the author.

129

seen in phase 3 would take place. These hostages would, in the active presence of criminal terror, still respond as if they were in phase 2. It is the responses of victims in phase 2 that I will develop in detail later on in this paper.)

It is in phase 3 that prior specific personality patterns and traits exert an influence on the victims' behavior. Those individuals who were excessively love oriented and dependent on others seem to be more prone to develop constricting, depressive behavior. Their fears increase, they develop phobic responses, and they often form hostile, dependent relationships with family and friends. Other individuals—those who were predominantly freedom oriented, detached from others, or power oriented and aggressive—tend to intensify their prior behavior. They may become more removed from people, develop reclusiveness and "short fuse" irritability. In effect they have said, "The world is a jungle and to hell with Mr. Goodguy." Phase 3 is similar to the "survivor syndrome" described by Niederland.[1]

As the individual attempts to integrate and adapt the traumatic experience into future behavior and life-style, he can be said to enter phase 4, which is the phase of resolution and integration. In this phase, the individual develops increased defensive alert patterns to minimize or prevent future victimization. Profound, permanent revision of values and attitudinal changes towards possessions and other people occur in this last phase.

• People whose homes have been burglarized reduce their personal investment and involvement in property, jewelry, watches, TV sets, etc. These items now become objects that can be replaced. No longer does the individual allow himself to be painfully vulnerable to loss by investing a personal sense of self in property.

• A woman ran screaming down the aisle of a plane that was just about to take off. She screamed, "Stop, stop the plane. I left my purse in the airport. Everything is in my purse. My life is in my purse."

These are individuals who are unable or unwilling to accept their victimization and integrate it into their future life-styles. These individuals experience their victimization as a personal affront to their pride compounded by their perceived indifference to their plight. They tenaciously hold on to their feelings of rage and injustice, seeking only reparations and revenge for their victimization, and thus remain psychologically disabled.[2]

In this paper, my focus will be on the acute psychological responses of victims to those crimes where there is prolonged contact with the criminal and thus the acute responses of the victims take place in the criminals' presence. These are the crimes of rape, robbery, and captive and hostage taking. I will particularly focus on the responses of victims to the crimes where the victim is used as instrumental leverage to pressure a third party to satisfy the criminals' demands. These are the crimes of kidnapping and hostage taking.

Criminals use violence or the dramatic threat of violence to induce extreme fright or terror in victims in order to render the victims helpless, powerless, and totally submissive. To fully understand victim responses to criminally induced terror, I found it helpful to explore reactions of people to terror in general. Terror is an affect that the dictionary defines as extreme fright. This past year, I asked a number of people—social acquaintances and colleagues—whether they had ever experienced terror and if so, when and how they had dealt with it. Everyone I asked—they numbered close to 100—said yes. Most recounted episodes related to unpredictable, frightening events and not to people.

- Awakening in a room and finding it filled with smoke.
- Developing a leg cramp while swimming and being unable to get back to shore.
- One person said that while flying to England during World War II, the pilot had announced that the plane was on fire and he didn't think he would be able to land the plane successfully. This man vividly recalled 37 years later that he had just sat still, reviewed his life, and hoped death would be sudden and he wouldn't suffer.

The popular concept that individuals respond to the terror of sudden, overwhelming danger by panicking, screaming, running, or going into a mindless, catatonic state is not supported by actual victim behavior, and not by the literature on catastrophes and disasters—man-made or natural. There are some individuals who exhibit panic terror in response to perceived sudden, overwhelming danger, with mindless running or acts of desperation. This panic-terror behavior generally occurs in situations where physical movement is not completely impeded and there exists the possibility of escape, whether it is realistic or not. Desperate, suicidal acts may occur after prolonged capture when the individual feels hopeless about release.

- Jumping out of a burning building.
- Frenzied behavior of an individual when a bee is in his car.
- Feeling hopeless and running into electrified barbed wire in concentration camps.

In the deliberate act of terror-inducing criminality, the criminal terrorist intends to hold the victim captive and prevent any possibility of his escape. In such situations, where the terrorized victims feel trapped with no exit, they respond to the sudden, overwhelming danger to their lives by a paralysis of affect that I have called "frozen fright."[5]

Years ago I became aware of the phenomenon of frozen fright when I interviewed an 8½-year-old victim of incest. During the interview, she was bright, vivacious, talkative, and very cooperative. At the end of the interview, I said she could go. This youngster took a deep breath, sighed heavily, and said, "I thought I would never get out of here alive." At that time, and even years later with further reflection, I did not see any evidence at all of fright bordering on terror. Since that time almost 20 years ago, after numerous interviews with victims of violent crime, I've been able to identify and confirm the presence of frozen fright behavior in these individuals. It superficially appears to be a cooperative and friendly behavior that confuses even the victim, the criminal, the family and friends of the victim, the police, and society in general. I must emphasize this point. Terrorized, trapped, held-captive individuals, whose only perceived hope of survival depends on the criminal, will exhibit the "cooperative behavior of frozen fright."

This paralysis of affect, with its pseudocalm behavior, is seen in most individuals. Sometimes, youngsters and some immature, dependent, and histrionic individuals will exhibit continual crying, shaking, clinging, and trembling behavior in the presence of the threat of overwhelming danger. Despite the active dramatic behavior, the victim's affect is frozen and unresponsive to any change except the external removal of danger.

- A youngster in a robbery cried, cried, and cried. Despite efforts to shut her up by other fellow victims or by the robbers, she persisted. One robber shot her to death.

- A common experience known to dog owners is their dogs' response to thunder. Many dogs shiver, shake, moan, and cling during a thunderstorm. No amount of assurance allays their response. As soon as the thunder ceases, the dogs stop responding.

Though the affect of the terrorized victims is frozen, the motor and cognitive functions are not. This dissociative phenomenon, which is normally seen in terrorized victims, differs from the splitting of affect from cognitive and motor functions that is seen in people, such as undercover agents, who are involved in dangerous-to-life, high-risk work. In these individuals, who voluntarily accept exceptionally hazardous work, there is a suspension of affect that allows for hyperawareness and hyperalertness. In terrorized individuals, the sudden threat to life causes an acute dissociative response. There is paralysis of affect with narrow constriction of cognitive and motor functions to serve purely one function, namely survival. In their frozen fright, the victims narrowly focus all their energy on survival, exclusively concentrating on the terrorist. This reaction is enhanced by the criminal terrorist's intent to totally dominate the victim. The terrorist creates a hostile environment and thwarts any efforts that would reduce this domination. The victim then feels isolated from others, powerless, and helpless.

The triad of being in a hostile environment, feeling isolated, and feeling helpless produces a profound reaction that Karen Horney has called "basic anxiety."[8] Under conditions of terror, this reaction causes the adult to lose the use of recently learned experience and to respond for survival with the early adaptive behavior of childhood. I have called this response in victims "traumatic psychological infantilism."[9]

This traumatic infantilism compels victims to cling to the very person who is endangering their lives. It accounts for the obedient, placid, compliant, and submissive behavior seen in frozen fright. Even the memory of terror, with the criminal not present, can produce the behavior of traumatic psychological infantilism.

- A supermarket manager was held up by criminals and placed into a meat freezer. He was released four hours later by the police. Six weeks following this incident, he received a phone call at work. He was told,

"Charlie, I am the cat that put you in the freezer. Do you want me to put you in their again?" Charlie said, "No." The criminal said, "O.K. You're a good boy, I want you to take the money from the safe and put it into a brown paper bag. Put it on the take out counter. I'll pick it up. Charlie, remember the freezer." The manager, a battle-honored veteran of World War II, did just that. The detectives couldn't understand how a guy could be robbed by telephone. Charlie, the manager, said, "You don't know what it is to be locked in a freezer and feel you are going to die."

If the atmosphere of terror still persists—and the psychologically traumatized victim perceives that the terrorist, who has the power of life and death over him, is letting him live—profound and persistent attitudinal and behavioral changes occur. He now sees the criminal as the "good guy." This phenomenon is called "pathological transference." I have seen this reaction repeatedly in men, women, and children under the conditions of perceived extreme threat to life.

• A detective undercover agent making a buy of narcotics was held captive for 3½ hours while the criminal gang deliberated whether to "waste him or not." However, the leader of the gang said, "No." Finally the detective's back-up team was able to figure out where he was and rescue him. I interviewed this detective two months later. He kept telling me what a good guy the leader was. For two hours he repeatedly stated, "He could have killed me and didn't." His superiors who were present kept on yelling at him [expletives deleted] what a mean bastard that crook was, but this undercover agent persisted in defending the criminal.

• In another situation, an off-duty detective was held captive when he walked in and interrupted a robbery. When the criminals found out he was a detective, two of the gunmen said, "We'll waste you, you mother fucker." They placed a bag over his head and made him go down on his knees. He later stated, "Silly as it may seem, I was glad it was going to be in the head because I thought it would be quick." He heard the robbers discussing him and then they left. He wasn't shot. Two of the robbers were caught months later. Jerry, the detective, was involved in their capture. The captured robber said to him, "You owe me something. I saved your life." The detective visited the man many times. A close relationship developed, and the detective said to the robber, "If you need me, I'm there for you because you were there for me at that time." When the second robber was caught, the detective related a conversation with his superior, "Chief, this guy has really changed." Jerry went out and bought lunch for him. The third robber is still at large. The detective fantasizes a conversation with him, "Listen Otis what went down, went down; turn yourself in. Believe me I'll work with you. I'm not looking for revenge."

Pathological transference only occurs when someone threatens your life, deliberates, and doesn't kill you. The victim no longer experiences the threat but feels he has been given life by the criminal. Pathological transference doesn't occur—or instantly evaporates—when the person is shot at.

Pathological transference is a consistent finding in individuals held hostage by criminal terrorists. Hostage victims are essentially instrumental victims. They are used and exploited by their captors to exert leverage on a third party, the family, the police, or the government to accede to the captors' demands. The captor expresses the threat of extreme violence to the victim primarily to the third party if the demands are not met. This creates the illusion for the victim that the terrorist captor would not harm him if the third party gave into the captor's demands. This use of the victim as leverage lays the grounds for intense pathological transference. This transference is both accelerated and heightened when the hostage has already been psychologically traumatized by terror. These two components—traumatic psychological infantilism and pathological transference—form the crucial elements in what has been called the Stockholm syndrome.

The Stockholm syndrome has often been viewed as the hostage's identifying with the terrorist. I think that concept doesn't adequately explain hostage behavior. I have found it more useful to view hostage behavior as an attempt to relate to an individual who has first captured the hostage by an act of terror and then used the victim as an instrument to obtain an objective from a third party.

The suffering of the victim is the leverage used for negotiations with a third party. Hostages, in their psychologically traumatized state, never view negotiations for their release as benevolent. The victim would immediately give all for his release, but he interprets and experiences any negotiation as endangering him. He then perceives negotiations, especially if protracted, as indifference, hostility, and rejection—nonloving and life-threatening behavior—by the very people who are negotiating for his release. This reinforces the pathological transference already developed by the prolonged exposure to the terrorist.

Up to now, I have presented the psychodynamics of behavior of victims held captive by criminal terror. An understanding of these dynamics is essential for the effective treatment of hostages from the moment of release. Since 1974, the Karen Horney Victim Treatment Center has utilized the following principles of "psychological first aid for victims of violent crime." They are based on reducing the feelings of isolation, helplessness, and powerlessness that have been induced by criminal terror.

1. Early restoration of power to the victim by asking permission to interview him, e.g., (a) Is this a good time to talk to you?; (b) Do you mind if I ask you some questions?

2. Reduction of isolation by nurturing behavior, thus diminishing the experience of the hostile environment that the victim was subjected to.

3. Diminishing the helpless, hopeless feelings of the victim by having him experience input into determination of his present and future behavior in terms of space and time.

4. To reduce the victim's feelings of having been subjected to the dominant behavior of the terrorist, we encourage the counselor to identify

himself to the victim's satisfaction, to ask for permission even to sit down in the victim's presence, to smoke, etc.

All the foregoing approaches to the victim are based on undoing and reversing the factors that brought about traumatic psychological infantilism.

The rescuers must remember that the sudden release of the victims reproduces an acute phase of crying, clinging, submissive behavior. They still are in the grip of traumatic infantilism. The above methods of nurturing and restoring power are crucial to prevent a second injury, which the rescuers may give the victims. It is important that the victims be allowed to clean up before being restored to familiar surroundings. Debriefing should be delayed. Victims should have privacy without isolation.

Essential both in the treatment of the acute responses after release and, most important, in the treatment of the delayed responses after release is the recognition of the need of the victim to ventilate his feelings of hostility towards the individuals involved in the negotiations for his release, as well as his feelings of the pathological transference towards the terrorist.

During the siege, while the victim is still being held hostage, it is important not to disturb the development of the pathological transference. It must be left alone. Disturbance of the pathological transference while the victim is held hostage would only activate the terror in the victim and may produce hopelessness, which may result in panic-terror behavior in the victim; he may do desperate acts, such as running out even into death. The negotiator must try to reinforce the pseudohelping efforts of the terrorist towards the victim. Rescuers must make no plans to utilize in any way the victim's cooperation in escape plans. Rescuers must remember that to victims of terror, "an open door is not perceived as an open door."

When the victim has been released, pathological transference is still present, and the victim is reluctant to express negative feelings towards his captors and even to participate in their later prosecution. It takes a while for this reaction to subside.

I believe the persistence of the behavior of pathological transference in the victims long after the victims' release is based on a primitive fear that any expression of negative feelings or behavior towards their former captors may result in awesome retaliation. Yet the victims are also aware of the captor's predatory use of their suffering to obtain his demands. This accounts for the persistent, impotent, constipated rage often seen in victims of violent crime. I have used the knowledge acquired from Nazi concentration camp victims who know that they cannot get revenge or even reparations for their suffering from the Nazis. I have encouraged victims to use the concept that "survival, living without fear, is getting even."

Finally, I feel it important to respond to victims of terror by continually reassuring them that their behavior during captivity was fully acceptable; "As long as they are alive, they did the right thing." They did nothing wrong; and it is important to welcome them back as we would a loved one who has recovered from a frightening and painful illness.

REFERENCES

1. NIEDERLAND, W. 1968. Post traumatic symptomatology. *In* Massive Psychic Trauma. H. Krystal, Ed.: 60–70. International Universities Press. New York, N.Y.
2. SYMONDS, M. 1980. Second injury to victims of violent crimes. Evaluation and Change Magazine. (Spring Issue.)
3. OCHBERG, F. 1978. The victim of terrorism. J. Terrorism 1(2): 147–168.
4. STRENTZ, T. 1980. The Stockholm syndrome: law enforcement policy and ego defenses of the hostage. Ann. N.Y. Acad. Sci. (This volume.)
5. SYMONDS, M. 1975. Victims of violence. Am. J. Psychoanal. 35(1): 19–26.
6. LANG, D. 1974. Swedish hostages. New Yorker (November 25): 56–126.
7. BUCKLEY, W. 1974. The kidnapper, the victim and society. Firing Line Program, WKPC-TV, May 15. SECA. Columbia, S.C.
8. HORNEY, K. 1950. Neurosis and Human Growth: 18–19. W. W. Norton and Co., Inc. New York, N.Y.
9. SYMONDS, M. 1976. The rape victim. Psychological patterns of response. Am. J. Psychoanal. 36(3): 27–34.

THE STOCKHOLM SYNDROME:
LAW ENFORCEMENT POLICY AND
EGO DEFENSES OF THE HOSTAGE

Thomas Strentz

FBI Academy
Quantico, Virginia 22135

THE BANK ROBBERY

At 10:15 A.M. on Thursday, August 23, 1973, the quiet early routine of the Sveriges Kreditbank in Stockholm, Sweden, was destroyed by the chatter of a submachine gun. As clouds of plaster and glass settled around the 60 stunned occupants, a heavily armed, lone gunman called out in English, "The party has just begun."[1]

The "party" was to continue for 131 hours, permanently affecting the lives of four young hostages and giving birth to a psychological phenomenon subsequently called the Stockholm syndrome.

During the 131 hours from 10:15 A.M. on August 23 until 9:00 P.M. on August 28, four employees of the Sveriges Kreditbank were held hostage. They were Elisabeth Oldgren, age 21, then an employee of 14 months working as a cashier in foreign exchange, now a nurse; Kristin Ehnmark, age 23, then a bank stenographer in the loan department, today a social worker; Brigitta Lundblad, age 31, an employee of the bank; and Sven Safstrom, age 25, a new employee, today employed by the Swedish government.[2] They were held by a 32-year-old thief, burglar, and prison escapee named Jan-Erik Olsson.[1] Their jail was an 11 x 47 foot, carpeted bank vault, which they came to share with another criminal and former cellmate of Olsson's—Clark Olofsson, age 26. Olofsson joined the group only after Olsson demanded his release from Norrkoping Penitentiary.[2]

This particular hostage situation gained long-lasting notoriety primarily because the electronic media exploited the fears of the victims as well as the sequence of events. Contrary to what had been expected, it was found that the victims feared the *police* more than they feared the robbers. In a telephone call to Prime Minister Olaf Palme, one of the hostages expressed these typical feelings of the group when she said, "The robbers are protecting us from the police." Upon release, other hostages puzzled over their feelings: "Why don't we hate the robbers?"[1]

For weeks after this incident, and while under the care of psychiatrists, some of the hostages experienced the paradox of nightmares over the possible escape of the jailed subjects and yet felt no hatred for these abductors. In fact, they felt the subjects had given them their lives back and were emotionally indebted to them for their generosity.

The Phenomenon

The Stockholm syndrome seems to be an automatic, probably unconscious, emotional response to the trauma of becoming a victim. Though some victims may think it through, this is not a rational choice by a victim who decides consciously that the most advantageous behavior in this predicament is to befriend his captor. This syndrome has been observed around the world and includes a high level of stress as participants are cast together in this life-threatening environment where each must achieve new levels of adaptation or regress to an earlier stage of ego development to stay alive. This phenomenon, this positive bond, affects the hostages and the hostage taker. This positive emotional bond—born in, or perhaps because of, the stress of the siege room—serves to unite its victims against the outsiders. A philosophy of "it's us against them" seems to develop. To date there is no evidence to indicate how long the syndrome lasts. Like the automatic reflex action of the knee, this bond seems to be beyond the control of the victim and the subject.

One definition of the Stockholm syndrome takes into account three phases of the experience and describes it as

the positive feelings of the captives toward their captor(s) that are accompanied by negative feelings toward the police. These feelings are frequently reciprocated by the captor(s). To achieve a successful resolution of a hostage situation, law enforcement must encourage and tolerate the first two phases so as to induce the third and thus preserve the lives of all participants.[3]

Though this relationship is new in the experience of law enforcement officers, the psychological community has long been aware of the use of an emotional bond as a coping mechanism of the ego under stress.

Many years ago, Sigmund Freud forged the theory of personality and conceived three major systems, calling them the id, the ego, and the superego. Their functions are:

The id is man's expression of instinctual drive without regard to reality or morality. It contains the drive for preservation and destruction, as well as the appetite for pleasure.[4]

In the well-adjusted person the ego is the executive of the personality, controlling and governing the id and the superego and maintaining commerce with the external world in the interest of the total personality and its far-flung needs. When the ego is performing its executive functions wisely, harmony and adjustment prevail. Instead of the pleasure principle, the ego is governed by the reality principle.[4]

The superego dictates to the ego how the demands of the id are to be satisfied. It is in effect the conscience and is usually developed by internalization of parental ideals and prohibitions formed during early childhood.[4]

Coping with reality is one function of the ego. The ego in the healthy personality is dynamic and resourceful. One of its functions is the use of defense mechanisms, a concept developed by Sigmund Freud in 1894 when he wrote "The Neuro-Psychoses of Defense." Freud conceived the defense mechanisms as the ego's struggle against painful or unendurable ideas or their effects.[5] The defense mechanisms have been discussed, explained, examined, and defined repeatedly since the last century. They vary in number depending upon the author. However, they all serve the same purpose—to protect the self from hurt and disorganization.[6]

When the self is threatened, the ego must cope under a great deal of stress. The ego enables the personality to continue to function, even during the most painful experiences—such as being taken hostage by an armed, anxious stranger. The hostage wants to survive, and the healthy ego is seeking a means to achieve survival.[7] One avenue open is the use of defense mechanisms. The mechanism used most frequently by hostages interviewed by the author has been regression, which Norman Cameron defines as a return to a less mature, less realistic level of experience and behavior.[8] Several theories have been advanced in an attempt to explain the observable symptoms that law enforcement officials and members of the psychiatric community have come to call the Stockholm syndrome.

In her book *The Ego and Its Mechanisms of Defense,* Anna Freud discusses the phenomenon of identification with the aggressor. This version of identification is called upon by the ego to protect itself against authority figures who have generated anxiety.[5] The purpose of this type of identification is to enable the ego to avoid the wrath—the potential punishment—of the enemy. The hostage identifies out of fear rather than out of love.[4] It would appear that the healthy ego evaluates the situation and selects from its arsenal of defenses that mechanism which served it best in the past when faced with trauma. The normal developing personality makes effective use of the defense mechanism of identification, generally out of love, when modeling itself after a parent.

> Identification often takes place in imitative learning, as when a boy identifies with his father and uses him as a model.[6]

Some authors have called this type of identification "introjection" and use the Nazi concentration camps as an example of people radically altering their norms and values.[9]

According to Coleman:

> Introjection is closely related to identification. As a defense reaction it involves the acceptance of others' *values and norms* as one's own even when they are contrary to one's previous assumptions [italics added].[6]

Coleman goes on to discuss the common occurrence of people adopting the values and beliefs of a new government to avoid social retaliation and punishment. The reaction seems to follow the principle, "If you can't beat 'em join 'em."[6]

Though identification with the aggressor is an attractive explanation for the Stockholm syndrome—and may indeed be a factor in some hostage situations—it is not a total explanation for the phenomenon. This reaction is commonly seen in children at about the age of five as they begin to develop a conscience and have resolved the Oedipus complex. They have given up the dream of being an adult and now begin to work on the reality of growing up. This is usually done by identifying with the parent of the same sex and is generally healthy. However, when this parent is abusive we see the identification serving the dual purpose of protection and of an ego ideal.

The Stockholm syndrome is viewed by this author as regression to a more elementary level of development than is seen in the five-year-old who identifies with a parent. The five-year-old is able to feed himself, speak for himself, and has locomotion. The hostage is more like the infant who must cry for food, cannot speak, and may be bound. Like the infant, the hostage is in a state of extreme dependence and fright. He is terrified of the outside world, like the child who learns to walk and achieves physical separation before he is ready for the emotional separation from the parent.

This infant is blessed with a mother figure who sees to his needs. As these needs are satisfactorily met by the mother figure, the child begins to love this person who is protecting him from the outside world. The adult is capable of caring and leading the infant from dependence and fear. So it is with the hostage—his extreme dependence, his every breath a gift from the subject. He is now as dependent as he was as an infant; the controlling, all-powerful adult is again present; the outside world is threatening once again. The weapons the police have deployed against the subject are also, in the mind of the hostage, deployed against him. Once again he is dependent, perhaps on the brink of death. Once again there is a powerful authority figure who can help. So the behavior that worked for the dependent infant surfaces again as a coping device, a defense mechanism, to lead the way to survival.

DOMESTIC HOSTAGE SITUATIONS

Since 1973, local law enforcement has been faced with many hostage situations. The subject-hostage bond is not always formed, yet case studies show that it is frequently a factor. As such, the Stockholm syndrome should be kept in mind by the police when they face such a situation, plan an attack, debrief former hostages,* and certainly when the subjects are prosecuted.

Hostage situations seem to be on the increase. Today, more than ever, police are responding to armed robberies in progress in a fraction of the time required a few years ago. This increased skill in incident response unfortunately promotes a perpetrator's need to take hostages. In the past, the armed robber was frequently gone before the employees felt safe enough to sound the alarm, but today silent alarms are triggered automatically. Computerized patrol techniques place police units in areas where they are more likely, statistically, to encounter an armed robbery. An analysis of past armed robberies dictates placement of patrol units to counter future at-

---

* In an attempt to gather intelligence about the subject, siege room, status and number of other hostages, etc., the police usually debrief, or carefully interview, victims in hostage situations.

tempts. Progress in one phase of law enforcement has created new demands in another.

The vast majority of hostage incidents are accidental. In cases such as these, it is likely the robber did not plan to take hostages. However, the police arrive sooner than anticipated, and as a new form of flight—a method of escape—the now trapped armed robber takes a hostage in order to bargain his way out.

In his desperation, the armed robber compounds his dilemma by adding kidnaping and assault charges. These considerations are initially minimal to him. His emotions are running high; he wants to buy time, and in this he succeeds. Research has shown that the leader among the abductors has a prior felony arrest.[10] Therefore, though desperate, the hostage taker is not ignorant or inexperienced in the ways of the criminal justice system and realizes the consequences of his new role.

The trapped subject is outgunned and outnumbered, and with each fleeting moment his situation becomes less tenable. Perhaps he takes hostages as a desperate offensive act, one of the few offensive acts available to him in his increasingly defensive position. Whatever his motivation, the subject is now linked with other individuals, usually strangers, who will come to sympathize and in some cases emphathize with him in a manner now recognized and understood.

The stranger—the victim—the law-abiding citizen—is forced into this life and death situation and is unprepared for this turn of events. Suddenly his routine world is turned around. The police, who should help, seem equally helpless. The hostage may feel that the police have let him down by allowing this to happen. It all seems so unreal.

STAGES OF HOSTAGE REACTION

Many hostages seek immediate psychological refuge in denial. According to Anna Freud:

When we find denial, we know that it is a reaction to external danger; when repression takes place, the ego is struggling with instinctual stimuli.[5]

Hostages, in interviews with this author, frequently discuss their use of denial of reality. The findings of denial are not limited.

As I continued to talk to victims of violence, I became aware that the general reactions of these victims were similar to the psychological response of an individual who experiences sudden and unexpected loss. Loss of any kind, particularly if sudden and unexpected, produces a certain sequence of response in all individuals. The first response is shock and denial.[11]

Hostages have also repressed their feelings of fear. Frequently these feelings of fear are transferred from fear of the hostage taker to fear of the police. Research has shown that most hostages die or are injured during the police assault phase.[12] This is not to say that the police kill them.

Denial is a primitive, but effective, psychological defense mechanism.

There are times when the mind is so overloaded with trauma that it cannot handle the situation.[11] To survive, the mind reacts as if the traumatic incident were not happening. The victims respond: "Oh no"; "No, not me"; "This must be a dream"; or "This is not happening."[11] These are all individually effective methods of dealing with excessively stressful situations.

Denial is but one stage of coping with the impossible turn of events. Each victim who copes effectively has a strong will to survive. One may deal with the stress by believing he is dreaming, that he will soon wake up and it will be all over. Some deal with the stress by sleeping; this author has interviewed hostages who have slept for over 48 hours while captive. Some have fainted, though this is rare.

Frequently, hostages gradually accept their situation but find a safety valve in the thought that their fate is not fixed. They view their situation as temporary, sure that the police will come to their rescue. This gradual change from denial to delusions of reprieve reflects a growing acceptance of the facts. Although the victim accepts that he is a hostage, he believes freedom will come soon.[13]

If freedom does not immediately relieve the stress, many hostages begin to engage in busywork, work they feel comfortable doing. Some knit, some methodically count and recount windows or other hostages, and some reflect upon their past life. This author has never interviewed a former hostage who had not taken stock of his life and vowed to change for the better, an attempt to take advantage of a second chance at life. The vast majority of hostages share this sequence of emotional events: denial, delusions of reprieve, busywork, and taking stock. The alliance that takes place between the hostage and the subject comes later.

TIME

Time is a factor in the development of the Stockholm syndrome. Its passage can produce a positive or negative bond, depending on the interaction of the subjects and hostages. If the hostage takers do not abuse their victims, hours spent together will most likely produce "positive" results. Time alone will not do so, but it may be the catalyst in nonabusive situations.

In September 1976, when five Croatian hijackers took a Boeing 727 carrying 95 people on a transatlantic flight from New York to Paris, another incidence of the Stockholm syndrome occurred. Attitudes toward the hijackers and their crime reflected the varying exposures of those involved in the situation.[14] The hostages were released at intervals. The first group was released after a few hours of captivity; the second group was released after a day. The debriefing of the victims in this situation has clearly indicated that the Stockholm syndrome is not a magical phenomenon, but a logical outgrowth of positive human interaction.

TWA flight 355, originally scheduled to fly from New York City to

Tucson, Arizona, via Chicago, on the evening of September 10, 1976, was diverted somewhere over western New York State to Montreal, Canada, where additional fuel was added. The hijackers then traveled to Gander, Newfoundland, where 34 passengers deplaned to lighten the aircraft for its flight to Europe via Keflavik, Iceland, with the remaining 54 passengers and a crew of seven. The subjects, primarily Julianna Eden Busic, selected passengers to deplane. She based her decisions on age and family responsibilities. The remaining passengers, plus the crew of seven, were those who were single, or married with no children, or those who had volunteered to remain on board, such as Bishop O'Rourke. After flying over London, the aircraft landed in Paris where it was surrounded by the police and not allowed to depart. After 13 hours the subjects surrendered to the French police. The episode lasted a total of 25 hours for most of the passengers and about 3 hours for those who deplaned at Gander.[14]

During the months of September and October of 1976, all but two of the hostages and all of the crew were interviewed. The initial hypothesis before the interviews was that those victims released after only a few hours would not express sympathy for the subjects, while those released later would react positively towards the subjects. In other words, time was viewed as the key factor.

The hypothesis was not proven. Instead, it seemed that the victims' attitudes toward the subjects varied from subject to subject and from victim to victim regardless of the amount of time they had spent as captives. Although this seemed illogical, interviews with the victims revealed understandable reasons. It was learned that those victims who had had negative contacts with the subjects did not evidence concern for them, regardless of time of release. Some of these victims had been physically abused by the subjects; they obviously did not like their abusers and advocated the maximum penalty be imposed.

Other victims had slept on and off for two days. This could be a form of defense mechanism of denial, a desperate ego-defensive means of coping with an otherwise intolerable event.[15] These victims had had minimal contact with the subjects and also advocated a maximum penalty. They may not have had distinctly negative contact, but they had experienced no positive association. Their only contact with the subjects had been on three occasions when hostage-taker Mark Vlasic awakened them in Paris as he ordered all of the passengers into the center of the aircraft where he threatened to detonate the explosives unless the French government allowed them to depart.

The other extreme was evidenced by victims, regardless of time of release, who felt great sympathy for their abductors. They had had positive contact with the subjects, which included discussing the hijackers' cause and understanding their motivation and suffering. Some of these victims told the press that they were going to take vacation time to attend the trial. Others began a defense fund for their former captors. Some recommended defense counsel to the subjects, and others refused to be interviewed by the law enforcement officers who had taken the subjects into custody.[14]

Perhaps one of the most self-revealing descriptions of the Stockholm syndrome was offered by one of these hijack victims:

> After it was over and we were safe, I recognized that they [the subjects] had put me through hell and had caused my parents and fiancé a great deal of trauma. Yet, I was alive. I was alive because they had let me live. You know only a few people, if any, who hold your life in their hands and then give it back to you. After it was over, and we were safe and they were in handcuffs, I walked over to them and kissed each one and said, "Thank you for giving me my life back." I know how foolish it sounds, but that is how I felt.[14]

Yet this feeling of affection seems to be a mask for a great inner trauma. Most victims, including those who felt considerable affection for the subjects, reported nightmares. These dreams expressed the fear of the subjects escaping from custody and recapturing them.[14] Dr. Ochberg reports similar findings,[16] as did the psychiatrist in Stockholm in 1973.[2]

Again, the hostages aboard the plane had developed a personal relationship with the criminals. The feelings of one hostage were expressed when she said, "They didn't have anything [the bombs were fakes], but they were really great guys. I really want to go to their trial."[17] This is a very different view from that of New York City Police Commissioner Michael Codd, who said in an interview, "What we have here is the work of madmen—murderers."[18] The interview with the commissioner followed an attempt to defuse a bomb left by the hijackers; the bomb killed one officer and seriously injured three others.[18]

The situation in 1973 in Stockholm was not unique. These same feelings were generated in the Croatian aircraft hijacking and, more recently, in the Japanese Red Army hijacking of JAL flight 472 in September/October 1977,[19] and also in the hostage situation that took place at the German consulate in August of 1978.[20]

ISOLATION

But the Stockholm syndrome relationship does not always develop. Sir Geoffrey Jackson, the British ambassador to Uruguay, was abducted and held by the Tupamaro terrorists for 244 days. He remained in thought and actions the ambassador, the queen's representative, and so impressed his captors with his dignity that they were forced to regularly change his guards and isolate him for fear he might convince them that his cause was just and theirs foolish.[21] Others, such as the American agronomist Dr. Claude Fly, held by the Tupamaros for 208 days in 1970, have also avoided identification with the abductor or his cause.[22] Dr. Fly accomplished this by writing a 600-page autobiography and by developing a 50-page "Christian Checklist," in which he analyzed the New Testament. Like Sir Geoffrey Jackson, Fly was able to create his own world and insulate himself against the hostile pressures around him.[22] According to Brooks McClure:

> In the case of both Dr. Fly and Sir Geoffrey Jackson, and other hostages as well, the terrorist organization found it necessary to remove the guards who were falling under their influence.[13]

In most situations, the Stockholm syndrome is a two-way street.

However, most victims of terrorist or criminal abductors are not individuals of the status of Dr. Fly or Ambassador Jackson, and do not retain an aura of aloofness during their captivity. As yet, there is no identified personality type more inclined to the Stockholm syndrome. The victims do share some common experiences, though.

POSITIVE CONTACT

The primary experience that victims of the syndrome share is positive contact with the subject. The positive contact is generated by *lack* of negative experiences, i.e., beatings, rapes, or physical abuse, rather than by an actual positive act on the part of the abductors. The few injured hostages who have evidenced the syndrome have been able to rationalize their abuse. They have convinced themselves that the abductor's show of force was necessary to take control of the situation, that perhaps their resistance precipitated the abductor's force. Self-blame on the part of the victims is very evident in these situations.

Stockholm syndrome victims share a second common experience; they sense and identify with the human quality of their captor. At times this quality is more imagined than real, as the victims of Fred Carrasco learned in Texas in August of 1974.[23]

On the afternoon of July 24, 1974, at the Texas Penitentiary in Huntsville, Fred Carrasco and two associates took approximately 70 hostages in the prison library. In the course of the 11-day siege, most of the hostages were released. However, the drama was played out on the steps of the library between 9:30 and 10:00 on the night of August 3, 1974. It was during this time that Carrasco executed the remaining hostages.[23] This execution took place in spite of his letters of affection to other hostages who had been released earlier due to medical problems.[24]

Some hostages expressed sympathy for Carrasco.[25] A Texas Ranger—who had been at the scene and had subsequently spoken to victims—stated to the author that there was evidence of the Stockholm syndrome.[26] Though the hostages' emotions did not reflect the depth of those in Sweden a year before, the hostages admitted affectionate feelings toward a person they thought they should hate. They saw their captor as a human being with problems similar to their own. Law enforcement has long recognized that the trapped armed robber believes he is a victim of the police. We now realize that the hostage tends to share his opinion.

When a robber is caught in a bank by quick police response, his dilemma is clear. He wants out with the money and his life. The police are preventing his escape by their presence and are demanding his surrender. The hostage—an innocent customer or employee of the bank—is also inside. His dilemma is similar to that of the robber—he wants to get out and cannot. He has seen the arrogant robber slowly become "a person" with a problem just like his own. The police on the outside correctly perceive the freedom of the hostages as the prerogative of the robber. However, the hostages perceive that the police weapons are pointed at them; the threat of tear gas makes them uncomfortable. The police insistence on the surrender of the subject is also keeping them hostage. Hostages begin to develop the idea that "if the police would go away, I could go home. If they would let him go, I would be free"[20]—and so the bond begins.

HOSTAGE TAKER REACTION

As time passes and positive contact between the hostage and hostage taker begins, the Stockholm syndrome also begins to take its effect upon the subject. This was evident at Entebbe in July of 1976. At least one of the terrorists, one who had engaged in conversations with the hostages from Air France flight 139, elected at the moment of the attack to shoot at the Israeli commandos rather than execute hostages.[27]

A moving account of this relationship is presented by Dr. Frank Ochberg as he recounts the experience of one hostage of the South Moluccans in December of 1975. Mr. Gerard Vaders, a newspaper editor in his 50s, has related his experience to Dr. Ochberg:

> On the second night they tied me again to be a living shield and left me in that position for seven hours. The one who was most psychopathic kept telling me, "your time has come. Say your prayers." They had selected me for the third execution. . . . In the morning when I knew I was going to be executed, I asked to talk to Prins [another hostage] to give him a message to take to my family. I wanted to explain my family situation. My foster child, whose parents had been killed, did not get along too well with my wife, and I had at the time a crisis in my marriage just behind me. . . . There were others things, too. Somewhere I had the feeling that I had failed as a human being. I explained all this and the terrorists insisted on listening.[16]

When Mr. Vaders completed his conversation with Mr. Prins and announced his readiness to die, the South Moluccans said, "No, someone else goes first."[16]

Dr. Ochberg observes that Mr. Vaders was no longer a faceless symbol. He was human. In the presence of his executioners, he made the transition from a symbol to be executed to a human to be spared. Tragically, the Moluccans selected another passenger, Mr. Bierling, led him away, and executed him before they had the opportunity to know him.[16]

Mr. Vaders goes on to explain his intrapsychic experience, his Stockholm syndrome:

> And you had to fight a certain feeling of compassion for the Moluccans. I know this is not natural, but in some way they come over human. They gave us cigarettes. They gave us blankets. But we also realize that they were killers. You try to suppress that in your consciousness. And I knew I was suppressing that. I also knew that they were victims, too. In the long run they would be as much victims as we. Even more. You saw the morale crumbling. You experienced the disintegration of their personalities. The growing of despair. Things dripping through their fingers. You couldn't help but feel a certain pity. For people at the beginning with egos like gods—impregnable, invincible—they end up small, desperate, feeling that all was in vain.[16]

Most people cannot inflict pain on another unless their victim remains dehumanized.[28] When the subject and his hostages are locked together in a vault, a building, a train, or an airplane, a process of humanization apparently does take place. When a person—a hostage—can build empathy while maintaining dignity, he or she can lessen the aggression of a captor.[28] The exception to this is the subject who is antisocial, as Fred Carrasco demonstrated in August of 1974. Fortunately, the Fred Carrascos of the world are in a minority, and in most situations the Stockholm syndrome is a two-way street. With the passage of time and the occurrence of positive experiences, the victims' chances of survival increase. However, isolation of the victims precludes the forming of this positive bond.

In some hostage situations, the victims have been locked in another room, or they have been in the same room but have been hooded or tied, gagged, and forced to face the wall away from the subject.[29] Consciously or unconsciously, the subject has dehumanized his hostage, thereby making it easier to kill him. As long as the hostage is isolated, time is not a factor. The Stockholm syndrome will not be a force that may save the life of the victim.

INDIVIDUALIZED REACTIONS

Additionally, it has been observed that even though some of the hostages responded positively toward their captors, they did not necessarily evidence Stockholm syndrome reactions toward all of the subjects. It was learned, logically, that most of the victims reacted positively toward those subjects who had treated them—in the words of the victims—"fairly." Those hostages who gave glowing accounts of the gentlemanly conduct of some subjects did not generalize to all subjects. They evidenced dislike, even hatred, toward one hostage taker whom they called an animal.

A hypothetical question was posed to determine the depth of victims' feelings toward their captors. Each former hostage was asked what he would do in the following situation: A person immediately recognizable as a law enforcement officer, armed with a shoulder weapon, would order him to lie down. At that same instant, one of his former captors would order him to stand up. When asked what he would do, the victim's response varied according to the identity of the captor giving the "order." If a captor who had treated him fairly hypothetically yelled, "Stand up," he would stand up. Conversely, if he thought it was the command of the subject who had verbally abused him, he would obey the law enforcement officer. This would indicate that the strength of the syndrome is considerable. Even in the face of an armed officer of the law, the victim would offer himself as a human shield for his abductor. As absurd as this may seem, such behavior has been observed by law enforcement officers throughout the world.†

---

† This was observed in the hijacking of a Philippine Airlines flight on September 17, 1978; during a hostage situation in Oceanside, Calif., February 3, 1975; during an aborted bank robbery in Toronto, Canada, in November 1977; and during a hostage situation that grew out of an aborted bank robbery in New York City in August 1976, which was later made into a movie entitled "Dog Day Afternoon."

Whether the incident is a bank robbery in Stockholm, Sweden, a hijacking of an American aircraft over western New York, a kidnaping in South America, or an attempted prison break in Texas, there are behavioral similarities despite geographic and motivational differences. In each situation, a relationship—a healthy relationship (healthy because those involved were alive to talk about it)—seems to develop between people caught in circumstances beyond their control and not of their making, a relationship that reflects the use of ego defense mechanisms by the hostage. This relationship seems to help victims cope with excessive stress and, at the same time, enables them to survive—a little worse for wear, but alive. The Stockholm syndrome is not a magical relationship of a blanket affection for the subject. This bond, though strong, does have its limits. It has logical limits. If a person is nice to another, a positive feeling toward this person develops, even if this person is an armed robber, a hijacker of an aircraft, a kidnaper, or a prisoner attempting to escape.

The victim's need to survive is stronger than his impulse to hate the person who has created his dilemma. It is his ability to survive, to cope, that has enabled man to survive and claw his way to the top of the evolutionary ladder. His ego is functioning and has functioned well, and has performed its primary task of enabling the self to survive. At an unconscious level, the ego has activated the proper defense mechanisms in the correct sequence—denial, regression, identification, or introjection—to achieve survival. The Stockholm syndrome is just another example of the ability of the ego, the healthy ego, to cope and adjust to difficult stress brought about by a traumatic situation.

The application for law enforcement is clear, though it does involve a trade-off. The priority in dealing with hostage situations is the survival of all participants. This means the survival of the hostage, the crowd that has gathered, the police officers, and the subject. To accomplish this end, various police procedures have been instituted. Establishing inner and outer perimeters is a long-standing procedure designed to keep crowds at a safe distance.‡ Police training, discipline, and proper equipment save officers' lives. The development of the Stockholm syndrome may save the life of the hostage as well as the subject. The life of the subject is preserved, as it is highly unlikely that deadly force will be used by the police unless the subject makes a precipitous move. The life of the hostage may also be saved by the Stockholm syndrome, the experience of positive contact, thus setting the stage for regression, identification, and/or introjection. The subject is less likely to injure a hostage he has come to know and, on occasion, to love.[28]

It is suggested that the Stockholm syndrome can be fostered while negotiating with the subject by asking him to allow the hostage to talk on the telephone; by asking him to check on the health of a hostage; or by discussing with him the family responsibilities of the hostages. Any action

---

‡ Perimeters are zones of controlled access. The inner perimeter would be set up to keep out everyone except certain police officials; the outer perimeter would be a zone restricted to police.

the negotiator can take to emphasize the hostage's human qualities to the subject should be considered by the negotiator.

The police negotiator must pay a personal price for this induced relationship. Hostages will curse him, as they did in Stockholm in August of 1973. They will call the police cowards and actively side with the subject in trying to achieve a solution to their plight, a solution not necessarily in their best interest or in the best interest of the community.

Unfortunately, it may not end there. Victims of the Stockholm syndrome may remain hostile toward the police after the siege has ended. The "original" victims in Stockholm still visit their abductors, and one former hostage is engaged to Olofsson.[30] South American victims visit their former captors in jail.§ Others have begun defense funds for them.[14] A hostile hostage is a price that law enforcement must pay for a living hostage. Anti-law enforcement feelings are not new to the police. But this may be the first time it has been suggested that law enforcement seek to encourage hostility, hostility from people whose lives law enforcement has mustered its resources to save. However, a human life is an irreplaceable treasure and worth some hostility. A poor or hostile witness for the prosecution is a small price to pay for this life.

REFERENCES

1. LANG, D. 1974. A reporter at large. New Yorker (November): 56–126.
2. Police Officers. 1978. Interviews with police officers from Stockholm, Sweden, on March 22 and November 8. FBI Academy. Quantico, Va. (Unpublished.)
3. OCHBERG, F. M. 1968. Interview on November 2 with Dr. Ochberg, Acting Director, National Institute of Mental Health, Rockville, Md. (Unpublished.)
4. HALL, C. 1954. A Primer of Freudian Psychology. World Publishing Co. New York, N.Y.
5. FREUD, A. 1966. The Writings of Anna Freud. II. The Ego and the Mechanisms of Defense. revised edit. International Universities Press, Inc. New York, N.Y.
6. COLEMAN, J. C. 1972. Abnormal Psychology and Modern Life. 5th edit. Scott Foresman Co. Glenview, Ill.
7. BELLAK, L., M. HURVICH & H. K. GEDIMAN. 1973. Ego Functions in Schizophrenics, Neurotics and Normals. John Wiley and Sons, Inc. New York, N.Y.
8. CAMERON, N. 1963. Personality Development and Psychopathology: A Dynamic Approach. Houghton Mifflin Co. Boston, Mass.
9. BLUHM, H. O. 1948. How did they survive? Mechanisms of defense in Nazi concentration camps. Am. J. Psychotherapy 2: 3–32.
10. GRAVES, B. & T. STRENTZ. 1977. The Kidnaper: His Crime and His Background. Research Paper. Special Operations and Research Staff. FBI Academy. Quantico, Va.
11. McCLURE, B. 1968. Hostage Survival. U.S. Department of State. Washington, D.C. (Unpublished research material.)
12. JENKINS, B. M., J. JOHNSON & D. RONFELDT. 1977. Numbered Lives: Some Statistical Observations from Seventy-Seven International Hostage Episodes. Report No. P-5905. Rand Corporation. Santa Monica. Calif.
13. Committee on the Judiciary. 1975. Terrorist Activity; Hostage Defense Measures. Hearings before the subcommittee to investigate the administration of the Internal Security Act and other internal security laws of the Committee on the Judiciary. Senate, U. S. Congress. Part 5. 94th Cong., 1st Sess., 1975.

§ This was evident during the hostage situations in Cleveland, Ohio, on October 29, 1975 and in Chicago, Illinois, on August 18, 1978.

14. Victims of Hijacking. 1976. Interviews with victims of hijacking of Trans World Airlines flight 355. New York, Chicago, and Tucson. (Unpublished.)
15. LAUGHLIN, H. P. 1970. The Ego and Its Defenses. Appleton-Century-Crofts, Inc. New York, N.Y.
16. OCHBERG, F. 1978. The victim of terrorism: psychiatric considerations. Terrorism 1(2); 147–168.
17. ALPERN, D. M. 1976. A skyjacking for Croatia. Newsweek (September 20): 25.
18. New York Times. 1976. Skyjackers are charged with murder. September 12: 3.
19. Victims of Hijacking. 1977. Interviews with victims (American citizens) of hijacking of Japanese Airlines flight 472. San Francisco, Los Angeles, and Tokyo. (Unpublished.)
20. Victims of Hostage Situation. 1968. Interviews on August 19 with victims of a hostage situation at the German consulate. Chicago, Ill.
21. JACKSON, SIR GEOFFREY. 1973. Surviving the Long Night. Vanguard Press, Inc. New York, N.Y.
22. FLY, C. L. 1973. No Hope But God. Hawthorn Books, Inc. New York, N.Y.
23. Houston Post. 1974. Murder suicide found in Huntsville case. September 4: 1.
24. HOUSE, A. 1975. The Carrasco Tragedy. Texian Press. Waco, Tex.
25. COOPER, L. 1974. Hostage freed by Carrasco aided prison officials in assault plan. Houston Chronicle (August 5): 4.
26. BURKS, G. W. 1975. Interview in December with Captain Burks of the Texas Rangers. Austin, Tex. (Unpublished.)
27. STEVENSON, W. 1976. Ninety Minutes at Entebbe. Bantam Books. New York, N.Y.
28. ARONSON, E. 1972. Social Animal. W. H. Freeman Co. San Francisco, Calif.
29. Victims of Hostage Situation. 1978. Interviews in March with victims of the Hanafi Muslim siege. Washington, D.C. (Unpublished.)
30. Washington Post. 1976. Swedish Robin Hood. Parade Magazine Supplement, November 14.
31. EITINGER, L. 1964. Concentration Camp Survivors in Norway and Israel. Allen and Unwin. London, England.
32. HACKER, F. J. 1976. Crusaders, Criminals, Crazies. Terror and Terrorism in Our Time. W. W. Norton Co. New York, N.Y.
33. MIRON, M. S. & A. P. GOLDSTEIN. 1978. Hostage. Behaviordelia, Inc. Kalamazoo, Mich.
34. PARRY, A. 1976. Terrorism from Robespierre to Arafat. Vanguard Press, Inc. New York, N.Y.
35. SARGANT, W. W. 1957. Battle for the Mind. Greenwood Press. Westport, Conn.
36. Conference on Terrorism. 1977. Final Report on Dimensions of Victimization in the Context of Terrorist Acts. Proceedings of the Conference, Evian, France, June 3–5.
37. FATTAH, E. Z. Some Reflections of the Victimology of Terrorism. Simon Fraser University. Vancouver, B.C., Canada.
38. HOWELL, A. C. 1975. The hidden crime. Ph.D. Dissertation. Temple University. Philadelphia, Penn.
39. JENKINS, B. M. 1976. Hostage Survival: Some Preliminary Observations. Report No. P-5627. Rand Corporation. Santa Monica, Calif.
40. OCHBERG, F. M. 1978. Terrorism—Is There an Answer? Practical Suggestions to Potential Hostages and to Those Working to Rescue Victims: How to Lead from Strength. Institute of Psychiatry. London, England (Unpublished.)
41. WOLK, R. L. 1977. Psychoanalytical Conceptualization of Hostage Symptoms and Their Treatment. Forensic Services, New York Department of Mental Hygiene. Eastern New York Correctional Facility. Napanoch, N.Y.
42. BROCKMAN, R. 1976. Notes while being hijacked. Atlantic Monthly (December): 68–75.
43. LUNDE, D. T. & T. E. WILSON. 1977. Brainwashing as a defense to criminal liability. Crim. Law Bull. 13(November): 341–382.
44. MILLER, A. H. 1978. Negotiations for hostages: implications from the police experience. Terrorism 1(2): 125–146.
45. SEGAL, J., E. J. HUNTER & Z. SEGAL. 1976. Universal consequences of captivity: stress reactions among divergent populations of prisoners of war and their families Int. Social Sci. J. 28(3): 593–609.
46. SYMONDS, M. 1975. Victims of violence: psychological effects and after effects. Am. J. Phychoanal. 35: 19–26.

HOSTAGE TAKING—THE TAKERS, THE TAKEN, AND THE CONTEXT: DISCUSSION

Discussant: Charles Bahn*

Temple University
Philadelphia, Pennsylvania 19122

Let us begin with the distinction that Dr. Knutson makes between *reluctant* hostage takers and *deliberate* hostage takers. Since we are in the infancy of understanding the phenomenon of hostage taking, the dynamics of the hostage taker, and the dynamics of the hostage, it may very well be helpful to begin with the hypothesis that they are separate phenomena. The circumstances that we're trying to analyze range from a situation in which a crime is in progress, and the perpetrator, the criminal—perhaps even without a weapon and simply by a threat of physical violence—forces a victim to accompany him as part of his escape, to that situation in which a group of people—highly trained, quite deliberate in their actions, assigning roles to each member—set out to and succeed in taking hostages. A significant point that has begun to emerge from the evidence that Agent Strentz presented is that the deliberate hostage taker appears to have a great deal of insight into the dynamics of the situation with regard to the effects of the interaction between hostage taker and victim, whereas the reluctant hostage taker seems to act with a lack of insight into those effects.

Nevertheless, one wonders, for example, where the classical kidnapper would be placed with regard to this distinction. One other point with regard to reluctant hostage takers is that this may be another instance of the factor of contagion in crime. That is, some crimes become fashionable during given periods, perhaps due to the influence of the mass media, perhaps for other reasons as well. Dr. Schlossberg's comments about the craving for attention on the part of the hostage taker—particularly the reluctant hostage taker, who is problem solving and really trying both to solve his problem and gain attention in this way—imply that this really becomes an advantageous tool for such a person, but not a deliberately chosen one. The principal distinction between deliberate and reluctant hostage taking would involve the extent of deliberate and planned depersonalization of the victim from the beginning of the hostage event.

From the victim's perspective, it is not clear that the difference that Dr. Knutson suggested is meaningful. Whether the hostage taker is reluctant or deliberate, I would suggest that from the victim's perspective, the central issue is whether in fact a credible threat to life has been made. More likely, of course, when a deliberate hostage event transpires—particularly a deliberate hostage event with political motivation—we observe that the event generally begins with a kind of initial brutal signature act that makes

* Present affiliation: Department of Psychology, John Jay College of Criminal Justice, New York, N.Y. 10019.

the threat to life fully credible and is undoubtedly intended to bring about the Stockholm syndrome, or victim compliance behavior. This initial terrorization is not unknown in the commission of other violent crimes; studies on the specific interactions between criminals and victims—for example, on what robbers and muggers first say to their victims—show a deliberate terrorization.

Quite often, the first communication is not only depersonalizing, but also a vile insult and an extremely violent threat. For example, "Keep quiet or I'll kill you, mother fucker." Now, in the case of hostage situations, we have something that goes beyond mere terror and is a highly credible threat to life; and once that happens, from the moment that it's not carried out, we have the beginning of the gratitude that builds up on the return of one's life from the individual who made a credible threat and nevertheless is not acting upon it.

So, with some caution, I would identify the possible dichotomy of hostage situations as heuristic, that is, worthy of further analysis and the basis of specific hypotheses to be tested. The general hypothesis is that both the different outcomes in hostage situations and the differing responses by victims, perhaps even the levels of depersonalization, stem from the interaction function of the personalities involved, the specific social interaction that transpires, the extent of conversation or isolation between the hostage taker and the hostage, and perhaps the duration of the incidents.

In other countries, there are studies of the political hostage situations that are retrospective longitudinal studies trying to identify the effects of duration on the dynamics of the hostage situation.

Making the distinction between the reluctant and deliberate hostage taker will help us to respond more clearly as well to those hostage situations that are related to international terrorism. International terrorism usually begins with maximum initial brutality, equalling or surpassing the brutality involved in ordinary crimes.

It is obvious both from a review of the literature and from the papers given by my colleagues that our concentration has been focused primarily on developing an understanding of the psychological state of the hostage taker and secondarily on analyzing the psychological effects of being taken hostage.

We have made studies in both areas, uncovering the need for attention on the part of the hostage taker, the suicidal aspects of his act, and the process of depersonalization of the hostage that enables the hostage taker to exercise control over the hostage and, in some cases, ultimately to kill the hostage.

The more complete description of the Stockholm syndrome that has now begun to emerge points up not only the regressive dependency that dominates the behavior of the hostage, but also the manifold effects on any human being of facing a credible threat of immediate and arbitrary death. Truly, hostages are victims of terror, for a credible death threat is the ultimate terror.

What has been given less attention is the social psychology of hostage taking, and its psychopolitical implications.

To begin with, we must distinguish between those situations in which an individual takes a hostage in the course of committing a crime or during temporary mental derangement and situations in which hostage taking is a tactical component of a terroristic thrust.

In the latter situation, hostage taking is simply one more extreme tactic, often the dominant tactic, used by those who would advance their political cause by means of terror. Other tactics in their array have included bombings, bombings of public places, suicide missions of wholesale killing, and assassinations.

Within this context, hostages taking and the other tactics of terror have in common the fact that they are directed either against innocent people or against those who symbolize the opposing political force. Rather than being directed against the actual foe—against a police force or an army—the terror is directed against a secondary, symbolic target, usually a target that is unprotected and defenseless.

Terror tactics also tend to be carried out with maximum initial brutality, equalling or surpassing the brutality involved in ordinary crimes.

Now, these characteristics of terrorism play a significant role in the way in which terrorism is perceived. Due to its quasi-suicidal nature, political sympathizers view the terrorist as one willing to make even the extreme sacrifice of giving his own life in order to advance the common cause. It thus becomes imperative that sympathizers do not dare to question or criticize the tactics employed because they are, ipso facto, not as committed to the cause as the terrorists, since they have not publicly demonstrated their willingness to lay down their lives for it. They must instead support the activities of the terrorists and provide rationalizations both to themselves and to others that will explain the brutality directed against the innocent.

The general public has a similar imperative problem with terrorism. The tactics of terrorism are so harsh—so much a contradiction to the basic tenets of decency in human relationships, particularly in face-to-face encounters—that the uninvolved observer feels compelled to adduce some extraordinary motivation to explain the act. Thus, because terrorism appears to be spontaneous in nature and to demonstrate an indifference to personal safety, the public is more than willing to believe that the terrorist act is committed by a desperate individual who has no other alternative but death to committing the deed. This quickly becomes elaborated into a belief that the terrorist's desperation undoubtedly derives from grievances that he sees as legitimate, that have been consistently ignored and shunted aside. The terrorist's frustration and desperation have thus driven him to acts beyond the bounds of acceptable social behavior, which will at the very least guarantee the terrorist a hearing, if not actually bring about the amelioration of intolerable conditions.

It is this response by the public, often including members of the government against which the terrorism is directed, that makes terrorism effective. The audience, to make sense of a terroristic act, assumes the terrorist's deep-lying frustration and ultimate desperation.

No doubt, many terrorists are, in fact, people in just such a state. Whether we identify someone as a terrorist or as a freedom fighter is, in some measure, a reflection of our own political position.

However, there are many situations in which other alternatives have not been explored by the terrorists and found useless, and in which the apparent spontaneity of the terroristic acts belies not only an extensive period of planning and training (a preparation not inconsistent with a stance of desperation), but also the involvement of other groups or forces who have no immediate share in the grievance and who are neither desperate nor frustrated but simply malevolent and manipulative.

Surprisingly, even when evidence of funding or training by such Machiavellian outsiders is introduced, the force of the initial explanation of the terrorism as spontaneous outbursts of desperation is so great that the contradictory information becomes difficult to assimilate.

During the past year, we have been confronted with increasingly detailed evidence of linkages between a number of insurgent terrorist movements and the Soviet Union. These linkages go beyond the provision of funding, equipment, and weapons; they are based on common training undertaken on Soviet soil by members of various insurgent groups from different countries, who don't necessarily share a common political ideology or even a common perception of motivating grievances. Two respected former intelligence officials—Dr. Ray Cline, director of the Center for Strategic Studies at Georgetown University, and Robert Moss, editor, The Economist Foreign Report—have testified about Russian training of terrorists, as part of their presentation at the recent Jonathan Institute Conference on International Terrorism (July 1979). They described Russian training camps, one conducted at a base near Moscow, and one at another base in the vicinity of the city of Simperofol in the Black Sea region. These camps were for members of such diverse terrorist groups as the Palestine Liberation Organization, the Popular Front for the Liberation of Palestine, the People's Democratic Front for the Liberation of Palestine, and the Universal Red Army. The course of study included the use of regular and electric detonators, chemical and biological warfare, production of incendiary devices, a study of fuse types, and preparation of antipersonnel minefields.

Nevertheless, in the first issue of the journal *Terrorism* in 1977, when this above-mentioned training was being established, there is an article by (ironically enough) the then "permanent" representative of Iran to the United Nations, in which he approvingly cites a Saudi Arabian statement that contributed to the downfall of a proposed United Nations condemnation of terrorism.

The Saudi amendment suggested that the title of the proposal be amended to include the words,

and study of the underlying causes of those forms of terrorism and acts of violence which lie in misery, frustration, grievance and despair and which cause some people to sacrifice human lives, including their own, in attempts to effect radical change.[1]

This is an almost classical statement of the rationale of terrorism that comes to our minds when we encounter this behavior phenomenon, which seems to violate the most basic tenets of human decency.

Were we able to fully assimilate the meaning of the training programs in which partisans of diverse groups are encouraged to suppress their ideological differences so that they can learn the techniques of hijacking, skyjacking, forays against civilian targets, and bombing of random victims, we should then realize that we have been engaged in what Brian Crozier, director of the London-based Institute for the Study of Conflict, has called "low-intensity" warfare—a secret warfare, sporadic and unpredictable, carried out by zealots who direct their attacks toward random targets, often randomly chosen innocent targets.

In the United Nations debate that led to the downfall of the proposal to condemn terrorism, much was made of the fact that it is difficult to identify the "innocent" in the contemporary political world. Several nations, including Russia, objected to the assumption that some people were innocent and others were not. There are soldiers, they pointed out, without malevolent intentions, while civilians, including women and the aged, may be deeply committed, implacable adversaries of the cause for which terroristic war is being waged.

This semantic debate highlights the difference between spontaneous acts of desperation and covertly developed acts of low-intensity warfare. When a cause eliminates neutrality as a possible stance, it moves beyond just grievance into an area of imposed and rigid ideas of what is right and fair.

The spontaneity of the acts becomes vitiated with the months of intensive training in a foreign country, where only the most rigid fanatic could fail to notice that the host country, in addition to affirming the grievances of the terrorists, is also using their activities to further its own self-interest.

The desperate and almost suicidal quality of the acts, while an implicit aspect of terrorism, fails to explain or illuminate the vast majority of cases. Not only can the terrorist reasonably expect that he will successfully coerce safe pasage away from the scene of his criminal acts to a country where he can find refuge and even acclaim, but he has the added assurance that even if he is caught by one of the western countries—one with a fair judicial and penal system—his compatriots will mount a subsequent terroristic attack whose objective will be to obtain his freedom and safe return.

The existence of countries that provide sanctuary and a hero's welcome to terrorists—and the likelihood that, through a hostage exchange or some other extreme action, an incarcerated convicted terrorist can look forward to release—makes it much easier to contemplate terror without any thought of sacrificing one's life.

It is important for us to understand the individual psychology of the terrorist if we are to deal with it in hostage negotiation. Our comprehension of the plight of the victims of terror, particularly of hostages, can help us both to obtain their freedom and to assuage some of the trauma resulting from their experience.

A deeper understanding of our own need to rationalize terrorism—to understand it and, if possible, to explain it away—can help us to keep both our moral and political balance. If we suspect that our rationalizations are based on inaccurate beliefs, we may be less concerned with vain attempts to redress deeply felt grievances and may admit the possibility that the grievances have been shaped and reinforced by forces whose apparent objectives are the achievement not of justice but of disruption.

REFERENCES

1. 1977. Terrorism **1** (1): 71–85.
2. BURTON, A. 1975. Urban Terrorism. Leo Cooper. London, England.
3. CLUTTERBUCK, R. 1975. Living with Terrorism. Faber and Faber. London, England.
4. ELIOT, J. D. & E. GIBSON, Eds. 1978. Contemporary Terrorism: Selected Readings. International Society of Chiefs of Police. Gaithersburg, Md.
5. LIVINGSTON, M. H., L. B. KRESS & M. G. WANER, Eds. 1978. International Terrorism in the Contemporary World. Greenwood Press. Westport, Conn.
6. SCHREIBER, J. 1978. The Ultimate Weapon, Terrorists and World Order. William Morrow and Co., Inc. New York, N.Y.

THE PLACE OF PSYCHOTHERAPY IN PROBATION AND PAROLE: THE PATIENT AS OFFENDER

Alexander B. Smith and Louis Berlin

Department of Sociology
John Jay College of Criminal Justice
New York, New York 10019

In the past three decades, our evaluation of psychotherapy as a treatment approach in probation and parole has undergone an appreciable change. When the authors began their careers in probation and parole, the prevailing view was that offenders were people suffering from a disturbance in their self-concepts, in their attitudes toward peers and authority, and in their grasp of reality. It followed, therefore, that the basic role of the probation and parole officer was that of corrector of erroneous and unrealistic concepts so that the offender might be put in a position to effect a better adjustment. In this connection, administrators sought out officers who had earned their master's degrees in social work and/or people who had had experience and training in psychotherapy.

A basic assumption of the above orientation was

> the concept that the offense is a symptom; the court must be concerned with treatment of the person. This would involve all that can be learned about his mental and physical condition and the attitudes and external influences which condition his personality and behavior.[1]

After such an in-depth study, the officer classified the offender—who was considered sick—into such categories as neurotic, psychotic, and character disordered. This latter type frustrated the probation and parole officers in their psychotherapeutic endeavors. These offenders were characterized by

> . . . one, an absence of severe neurotic or psychotic symptomotology; two, a lack of development of the superego (the self-control that one expects in an adult is lacking); three, an extremely low frustration tolerance (demands must be met immediately, regardless of future consequences). . . . Unlike the neurotic who may be motivated by his anxiety to seek help, the character disorder tends to "act out" (commits some physical act, usually anti-social), and alleviate his anxiety in this manner.[2]

The faith and confidence in psychotherapy during the decades mentioned were enormous. The one-to-one technique was applied universally and without discrimination. Failures and rejections by the offenders were ascribed to their "resistance" to getting well. When a variation of therapy—such as the Rogerian nondirective approach—was used, the results were frequently disheartening. Particularly was this the case with the so-called character disorders. As a result of the failures expressed in recidivism rates, the reasons were sought not in the nature of the clients, but in the therapists themselves. The literature of the period reflected this self-searching. The one-to-one technique was ineffective because

> the techniques of psychotherapy used today were formulated on a middle-class neurotic

population whose goals, values, and anxieties are entirely different than those of the repetitive offender. . . . The attempt to translate techniques and methods which have been successful on neurotics to the character disorder, including the persistent offender, have been almost a total failure.[2]

Faced with failures of psychoanalytically oriented therapy with its emphasis on the genesis of symptoms, interpretation of dynamics, and imparting of insight, a new orientation towards treatment—disregarding the origin of the condition and concentrating on the way to change behavior—was offered. This psychological modality is behavior modification. Eysenck and Rachman, exponents and practitioners of behavior modification, explain:

Given that a particular behavior pattern, whether neurotic or criminal, has in fact developed, our approach would now be quite ahistorical. We are not particularly concerned, in the majority of cases, with the particular reasons for the emergence of this pattern, but we are virtually concerned with the problem of how this pattern is to be changed. Such change must clearly take the form of deconditioning in the case of dysthymic disorders, and one of reconditioning in the case of the criminal and psychopathic disorders. We do not postulate any underlying complexes or even "neuroses"; in our account, these are unnecessary hypotheses not called for by the facts in question. Thus, our theory and our treatment are purely symptomatic; the symptom in each case is a conditioned, unadapting autonomic or skeletal response, and our task is to abolish this particular, maladaptive pattern of behavior. Once this is accomplished our task is over; there is no anticipation of any recrudescence of the symptom itself, or any emergence of new symptoms, as would be expected if there were any hypothetical complex or underlying cause for the behavior outside the field of conditioning. It is here that the facts must pronounce their judgment as to the adequacy of these two hypotheses.[3]

Introduced into the lexicon of treatment were such terms as behavior modification, operant conditioning, aversive therapy, contractual psychology, and commitment. Probation, parole, and prison workers attempted to utilize this orientation with some successes as well as failures. This orientation was hailed with enthusiasm by probation and parole officers who were not too comfortable or enthusiastic about probing feelings, psychoanalytically or otherwise.

The influx of minorities into probation and parole caseloads—and into the correctional institutions in the 1950s, 1960s, and today—has brought about changes in orientations and techniques in treatment. These offenders were disadvantaged people who needed jobs, housing, health care, and some voice in solving community problems. The primary need of these offenders was for community services. The emphasis in corrections shifted from treating the personality of the offenders to changing the institutions under which they lived.

This new view transforms the way workers assess their clients. The client is now a person whose future depends not only on how well he adjusts and adapts to the environment, but additionally on how well he is linked to social institutions.[4]

Commenting on priorities, the authors of the above take an extreme position regarding concrete services versus counseling: "As members of the helping professions, we have special responsibilities for the delivery of urgently needed services to our clients. Often what they least need is counseling."[4] In addition, these authors express today's view:

Most offenders are not pathologically ill, therefore, the medical (casework) model is inappropriate. . . . Most probation and parole officers are not equipped by education and experience to provide casework counseling even if it is needed.[4]

Though we might accept the assertion that most offenders are not "pathologically ill," counseling is not *thereby* ruled out. One does not have to be "pathologically ill" to need counseling. It is sufficient reason that one has acted out his impulses in an antisocial way, in order for him to be a candidate for counseling aimed at changes in behavior and attitudes. Meeting such needs as jobs, housing, medical treatment, and other concrete needs does not, per se, insure miraculous changes in behavior and attitudes.

Entertaining such views of the nonpathological client and of the psychotherapeutically inept officer, current sociologically oriented correctional theorists assign the officers priority to acting as community resource managers. Some authorities go so far as to encourage officers to become involved in changing institutions:

> The most important activity in which a probation agency can be engaged is, therefore, to provide leadership in the direction of vital social change. Without social change . . . , the most progressive programs will have little effect.[5]

The pendulum has swung to the opposite extreme. The impact of the sociologists, however, has not eliminated the role of counseling but has assigned to it a low priority as compared to the role of resource manager, advocate, and community worker, striving to create new resources and/or helping to coordinate existing resources.

The sociologists, though, have not completely rejected the psychiatric interpretation of crime. However, before presenting their views, it will be helpful to present the classic Freudian view of crime and mental illness. A lucid psychoanalytic presentation of the relationship of mental illness to crime is given by Philip Q. Roche, a Pennsylvania psychiatrist in private practice:

> In meeting stress all of us attempt to maintain a balance and in so doing exhibit what are called symptoms. When such devices are ineffective the balance is shifted and we experience what is called mental illness in some degree. In some persons who have had poor life training, symptoms become fixed in patterns which are called character deformations. We apply various names to them such as "psychopathic personality," "constitutional psychopathic inferior" . . . sociopath. In others we observe symptoms of such intensity and at such variance with common-sense values that we regard and accept the person exhibiting them as psychotically incapacitated. Again, a large number of persons are incapacitated to a degree less than psychotic—we regard them as neurotic. All have in common a tendency to repetitive symbolic destructive behavior directed both outwardly and toward themselves.[6]

Roche notes that the individual who absorbs his antisocial impulses instead of acting them out pays for it in terms of mental illness. "In this light the criminal insures his sanity and maintains an isolation from an awareness of his own 'mental illness.' "[6]

Sociologists generally agree with their colleague Edwin Schur, who holds that deviance does *not* necessarily mean mental illness. He asserts that

> sociologists have often complained that psychiatric interpretations of delinquency and crime have failed to take adequate account of the variation in outlook and behavior patterns that are given social approval in the different socioeconomic strata of our

society. What is considered "normal" in one social class context may be adjudged "pathological" in another. . . . This kind of perspective is increasingly recognized by the more sociologically sophisticated psychiatrists, who nowadays often take into account that the antisocial behavior and outlooks of even a hardened-offender—in terms of the social milieu out of which they developed—are not always evidence of psychic abnormality. Accordingly, new types of psychiatric treatment programs have arisen in which an effort is made to grapple with the group and cultural sources of the antisocial patterns and to create a "therapeutic milieu"—rather than simply attempting to utilize conventional forms of one-to-one psychotherapy.[7]

In this view, sociologists recognize the need to change personal values and attitudes engendered by the group and cultural milieu from which the offender sprang.

In spite of the tide downgrading counseling and other psychotherapeutic approaches, there have been sufficient sober influences to encourage federal funding for community mental health resources. For the officer to engage in therapy while such resources exist is considered a wasteful duplication of services. Probation and parole officers referred their subjects to local city, state, and private psychiatric facilities for evaluation and consultation even at the time when facilities were scarce; but at present, there is greater use of such community mental health facilities. These current practices are helpful to both client and officer. Some corrections agencies boast full-time psychiatrists attached to a court clinic. Others have a "resident psychiatrist" who devotes several days a week to examining and evaluating clients referred to him by the officers. In addition, the psychiatrists meet with probation and parole officers not only for consultation on cases, but to train them "in the techniques of fact gathering, counseling, interpretation and understanding of psychodynamics, as well as providing support for the officers as they developed their own interpretive capabililties."[8] By means of such close cooperation, the clients are serviced and the officers' treatment skills are enhanced. "But by and large, it is the function of the resident psychiatrist to explain to the probation officer what type of mental or emotional disorder the probationer or parolee has, and to offer suggestions as to the best techniques and therapy to be used in effective supervision."[8]

In spite of all the criticisms of the ineffectiveness of psychotherapy in probation and parole, we are of the opinion that psychotherapy and the basic dynamic concepts underlying it can and should be applied in the three basic phases of probation activity—namely, presentence investigation, supervision, and intake—as well as in the precommitment, prerelease, and postcommitment phases of placement on parole. There are various levels of psychotherapy: educating a client about vital facts, such as sex and hygiene information; counseling a client regarding the merits and drawbacks of options in solving problems in family matters and job situations; encouraging a client to ventilate stressful feelings; and lending support to a client in a new and critical situation. These are all forms of psychotherapy in which the probation and parole officer can engage with his clients in a meaningful and helpful way. The officer, during a presentence or preparole interview, is provided with ample opportunity to practice this type of intervention on the various levels mentioned, exclusive of depth analysis. For example, an offender's patent lack of self-confidence may be buttressed by the officer's supportive comments. In addition, an alert, sensitive officer, detecting some confusion in regard to matters of sex and family relationships, may and should utilize the psychotherapeutic technique of clarification and educational exposition. Finally, the offender's conduct and vocational and educational goals can and should be the subject of counseling by the probation and parole officer.

Another way in which psychiatric concepts can and should be applied in this phase of probation activity is the interpretation of the meaning of the offender's act and antisocial behavior. It is not enough for an officer to describe a subject's repeated bickering with his or her employers without the officer's suggesting that such behavior is possibly the acting out of a deep hostility to authority figures. Similarly, misbehavior in school may be attention getting on the part of an offender whose parents were rejecting or neglecting of him or her. If such insights and interpretations were tactfully revealed to the offender, they might contribute to a therapeutic control of his or her future behavior. Most certainly such comments in a presentence report are helpful to the judge in obtaining a deeper understanding of the offender, thus enabling the judge to arrive at a proper sentence.

A sensitive and compassionate description of how trying it is for an offender at his or her referral for a presentence investigation and the role of the officer is contained in this excerpt:

> The appearance before the court, both at the time of referral for presentence investigation, and for sentencing, is a trying and emotional experience for the defendant. It is a time of personal crisis and the role of the probation officer is a significant one. Often he is in court as a reassuring figure and almost always he interviews the defendant immediately after he is placed on probation.[9]

The basic purpose of the precommitment interview is to prepare and lend support to the offender for the new situation with which he or she is confronted. The postcommitment counseling with families most certainly is concerned with counseling on problems rising from incarceration, lending support, and alleviating in a practical manner stresses resulting from the interrupted family relationships. Prerelease counseling is educational in that its purpose is to acquaint the inmate with the conditions of parole supervision, and it is supportive in that the inmate's ventilation of his or her fears and anxieties is encouraged and confronted, and ways of handling these fears are suggested.

Supervision of probationers and parolees provides opportunities for therapy on the levels already mentioned. Differential treatment in terms of counseling to meet differing needs of offenders is desirable.

> A young drug offender, involved in the drug culture as a palliative for family disinterest or rejection, can certainly be assisted by sensitive, supportive counseling by the probation officer. Other offenders, including those with sociopathic tendencies, can and do respond favorably to the more forthright approaches of reality therapy. With additional officers of high capabilities, we have the opportunity to evaluate the effectiveness of different types of counseling with differing offenders.[10]

An interesting question raised by doctrinaire libertarians in regard to probation and parole supervision is, Who has the right to tell anyone what he shall do and how he shall live his life? Such liberals would permit drug addicts and suicidal persons to gratify their needs without coercive restraint by any authority. These same liberals point out that historically, treatment and counseling have been effective only in the absence of authority and coercion.

> The therapist, it was felt, could only operate within a voluntary, permissive framework which included client freedom to accept or reject treatment. Inasmuch as this approach is appropriate to virtually all "helping" situations, treatment in the correctional and juvenile justice field followed suit up until the recent past.[11]

The results were frustrating to the helpers, hence they adopted such techniques as the reality therapy approach of the psychiatrist William Glasser (a technique with which many probation and parole officers are comfortable); the guided group interaction approach devised by the penologist Lloyd McCorkle (a modality adopted by many agencies handling adolescent offenders); and the concepts of positive peer culture; all integrated within an authoritative framework. Another psychiatrist who uses behavioral techniques with sociopaths (antisocial personalities) affirms the authoritative approach, asserting:

> Our Day Treatment Program regularly includes probationers and parolees on an involuntary basis because of our experience that people who break the law usually need to be coerced into treatment initially if meaningful involvement is to be achieved.[12]

Another resolution of the problem of coercion versus self-determination regarding treatment is that of determining whether an offender's crime was related to, let us say, his or her alcoholism and/or mental or emotional problem.[13] If there is this relationship of offense to personal problem, then it would be just and relevant for the court and probation and parole to coerce the offender into treatment. Failure of the offender to heed this condition of probation and parole would then be adequate grounds for citation of a violation.

The officer may use any of several different therapeutic systems on a one-to-one basis. He may practice Rogerian nondirective therapy, Albert Ellis' rational emotive therapy, or Glasser's reality therapy; he may utilize Freudian concepts, such as masculine-feminine conflict, sibling rivalry, identification with parents, severe superego, and others that may be appropriate and understood and accepted by the supervisee. If the officer is trained and skilled, he or she may organize groups and practice the above therapies in a group situation. Further, if the officer is truly creative and experienced, behavior modification principles and operant conditioning may also be used.

Also in supervision, an officer making a referral to another agency (family, job, medical, psychiatric, educational) must utilize therapeutic skills in discussing the offender's need for such community service, and must counsel the offender on what to expect and how to get the most out of the designated program. However, if the supervisee fails to follow through, then the ensuing interviews must and should cover the offender's emotional reaction to the program, some clarification of the realities involved, and some counseling as to alternatives.

In the New York City Family Court, Juvenile Term, there is an intake service where all delinquents are interviewed in an attempt to save them from court action. If either the complainant or the juvenile insists on court action, then the delinquent is moved out of intake. However, if the offender remains in intake, the officer may undertake therapeutic servicing of the youth or make a referral to a community agency. Some considerations entering into such a decision are the case load at the time; the availability of skilled and experienced officers; and the willingness of the delinquent and his or her family to become involved in therapy.

There are probationers and parolees who are so emotionally disturbed as to merit institutionalization or involvement in an intensive therapeutic program with a psychiatrist. Such individuals can be found in any supervision probation and parole case load. These disturbed persons not only require close surveillance, but also some form of therapy, such as supportive counseling. However, should these individuals begin to manifest psychotic symptoms, such as paranoia, hallucinations, or radical mood swings weakening their grasp of reality, the officer must work with members of the family, exercising the therapeutic skills of educating the family members as to the meaning of the erratic behavior, counseling them to the course of action most beneficial to the offender and the family, and, in many cases, working through with them their feelings of guilt, shame, and anger engendered by having a psychotic person in the family. Parolees and probationers who are emotionally disturbed tend to indulge in behavior that violates the conditions of probation or parole. Such behavior may be failure to report, running away from the court's or parole agency's jurisdiction, and acting out of aggressive behavior toward family members or spouses. Though each case is to be treated on an individual basis, the general attitude of the officer is one of interpreting to the court or to the parole agency the deeper, more subtle meaning of the behavior; and where the officer feels the direction of the offender's efforts was generally positive, a recommendation may be made to retain the offender on probation or parole.

An officer who has effected a voluntary or court commitment of a disturbed offender to a mental hospital eagerly awaits the report that will provide him or her with meaningful information on dynamic behavior patterns or significant psychological factors throwing light on the offender's general conduct or criminality. However, in all too many cases, the documents are stereotyped and repeat the information already submitted by the officer in the referral letter. Currently, there are many federally financed community organizations that solicit probationers and parolees who show behavioral and/or emotional problems. Many of these organizations originally focused on drug addicts. With the diminishing number of addicts utilizing their services, these organizations are expanding their target populations, offering in some cases psychiatrists, psychiatric social workers, group therapists, and educational programs to appeal to this emotionally disturbed group. The probation or parole officer, harried by a large case load, may refer his or her charges to these organizations. Some of these therapists send monthly reports and work closely with the officers. Where that is the case, the officer's therapeutic activities are marginal and mainly supportive.

The patient (probationer or parolee) who is undergoing therapy with a private psychiatrist can still become involved, on a lesser level, in a therapeutic relationship with his or her officer. Again, the officer may be supportive and reenforce the insights provided by the psychiatrist. Such intervention depends on the cooperation and sharing of information between the psychiatrist and the officer. Unfortunately, some psychiatrists refuse to work with the officer and accept the offender as a patient on the condition that the psychiatrist will not be "bothered" by the court or parole agency in any way.

The attitude of many psychiatrists treating sex offenders on probation is exemplified by the following:

> Populations convicted of antisocial offenses are generally avoided by most treatment agencies when the persons are paroled from prison into the community or are on probation. Poor motivation for treatment or lack of desire to change generally head the list of reasons why psychotherapy is not offered.[14]

An explanation for this attitude contends that

> most psychiatrists evolve from a culture and training background which emphasizes scholastic achievement as measured by verbal skills. Their dynamic psychotherapy has usually evolved from psychoanalytic concepts developed in a sophisticated verbal culture and attain greatest relevance when the patient and practitioner enjoy a common educational background.[14]

Drawing the obvious conclusions, these psychiatrists organized a group of offender peers from a common background, thus facilitating verbal and nonverbal communication, problem solving, and combating of social isolation more effectively than the one-to-one psychotherapeutic approach.

It is our feeling that a specialized case load in probation and/or parole consisting of between 20 and 30 selected psychiatrically disturbed supervisees would be an effective rehabilitative tool. Such a case load was established in the 1950s in the Kings County Court in Brooklyn, New York. Milton Nechemias, a probation officer, delineated the rationale, problems, and results of intensive casework with the offenders and their families.[15] Establishment of such case loads in probation and parole agencies, especially in urban centers, would drain off these troublesome cases from the run-of-the-mill case loads, enabling the officers to render better services to their regular, nonpsychiatric cases, while the specially trained, skilled officer concentrates on meeting the needs of the disturbed offenders. This arrangement does not rule out referrals to available community resources but will retain the advantage of unfragmented services.

Philadelphia's Adult Probation operates a project known as the Intensive Services Unit. Sex offenders and persons in need of "psychiatric probation" are placed in this unit. Case loads in this project number near 50. An evaluation team from the Georgia Institute of Technology, working with Law Enforcement Assistance Administration funds, noted:

A comparison of rearrest rates between a sample of project clients and a sample of similar clients in caseloads exceeding 100 showed statistically significant lower rates for project clients. However, the project concept calls for a different quality as well as quantity of supervision than that experienced in regular caseloads. In particular, the Intensive Services Unit seeks to take a more psychological psychiatric approach to probation, including a heavy emphasis on assessment.[16]

As indicated above, psychotherapy, though much maligned, is still practiced by correction authorities in probation and parole. Though much faith was invested in the psychological/psychiatric approach for several decades (30s, 40s, and 50s), a disillusioned reaction has set in, severely critical of the medical model and its lack of effectiveness.

Yet, while these assaults on psychotherapy were being mounted, agencies still continued referrals to psychiatrists and encouraged the latter to train probation and parole officers to understand the classical Freudian psychodynamics of behavior and to sharpen their treatment skills. The reason for the persistent life of psychotherapy is that it is useful in corrections. At its best, psychotherapy is effective in changing behavior and attitudes in certain cases; and at its least practical level, it is effective in changing personality. In addition, psychotherapy is humane and helpful in easing stresses and tensions in troubled people who happen to have been placed on probation or parole. Hopefully, in this anxiety-free state of mind, the offenders will refrain from committing other crimes. Probation and parole evolved out of social currents of compassion, and it is only just and right that they utilize techniques of counseling, support, ventilation, and clarification to lighten the burdens of unhappy people caught in the web of the criminal justice system. Psychotherapeutic techniques are not only used in the officer's role of counselor, but can and should be used in his or her roles of community resource manager, advocate, and community worker. It is our feeling that probation and parole agencies should train their officers in the basic tools of psychotherapy so that they will be more competent in using them in all the roles that the officers must fulfill today.

REFERENCES

1. KAWIN, I. 1967. Swing of the pendulum. Federal Probation 31(1): 31.
2. VON WEST, A. 1964. Cultural background and treatment of the persistent offender. Federal Probation 28(2): 17.
3. EYESENCK, H. J. & S. RACHMAN. 1965. The Causes and Cures of Neurosis: 58–59. Robert R. Knapp. San Diego, Calif.
4. DELL'APA, F., W. T. ADAMS, J. D. JORGENSEN & H. R. SIGURDSON. 1976. Advocacy, brokerage, community: the ABC's of probation and parole. Federal Probation 30(4): 41.
5. MACPHERSON, D. P. 1971. Probation and corrections in the seventies. Federal Probation 35(1): 15.
6. ROCHE, P. Q. 1965. Mental health and criminal behavior. Federal Probation 29(3): 15.

7. SCHUR, E. M. 1969. Our Criminal Society: 72. Prentice-Hall, Inc. Englewood Cliffs, N.J.
8. WILKERSON, W. W. 1969. Psychiatric consultation with probationers and parolees. Federal Probation 33(2): 47.
9. GRONEWALD, D. H. 1964. Supervision practices in the federal probation system. Federal Probation 28(3): 20.
10. MCLAUGHLIN, C. 1975. The federal probation system: an inside view. Federal Probation 39(2): 35.
11. STOLLERY, P. L. 1977. Searching for the magic answer to juvenile delinquency. Federal Probation 31(4): 29.
12. PARLOUR, R. R. 1975. Behavioral techniques for sociopathic clients. Federal Probation 39(1): 3.
13. SMITH, A. B. & L. BERLIN. 1979. Introduction to Probation and Parole. 2nd edit.: 163-182. West Publishing. St. Paul, Minn.
14. PETERS, J. J. & R. L. SADOFF. 1971. Psychiatric services for sex offenders on probation. Federal Probation 35(3): 33.
15. NECHEMIAS, M. 1957. Probation supervision of a specialized caseload. Federal Probation 21(2): 23-29.
16. BANKS, J., T. R. SILER & R. L. RADIN. 1977. Past and present findings in intensive adult probation. Federal Probation 41(2): 22.

GROUP TREATMENT OF DELINQUENTS:
A REVIEW OF GUIDED GROUP INTERACTION

Albert Elias

New Jersey Department of Corrections
Trenton, New Jersey 08628

The concept of the primary group, especially the peer group, which plays a significant role in the socialization of children, has been integrated into programs that provide planned, intensive group experiences for juvenile delinquents. In fact, in a relatively brief span of time, this type of experience, in the form of group treatment, has emerged as a major therapeutic tool. It ranks with psychotherapy, behavior modification, and chemotherapy among the major developments in the care of young people with problems.

The peer group, a potentially powerful force in the lives of young people, provides the context for normal growth and development and social and psychological support during a period of rapid physiological and psychological change, role experimentation, and the emergence of a sense of identity. It serves, also, as a testing ground for the adolescent in relation to others, as a source of one's self-image, and as a framework within which to strive for autonomy and independence from parents.[1,2]

Among all of the influences assumed to create delinquency, the peer group has emerged as probably the single most important factor in determining the presence or absence of delinquent behavior.[3] It is not surprising, therefore, that therapists have developed techniques for utilizing the peer group as a corrective experience for many juvenile delinquents.

This article will provide a brief examination of a few of the major approaches to the group treatment of juvenile offenders and a more extensive review of one of these approaches, namely, guided group interaction. Also, this paper will define some of the principal issues that should be addressed by practitioners and others in the field.

Although the concept of treating adolescents in group settings has been in use for many years, it was not until after the Second World War that it gained acceptance on a broad scale in many countries.[4] Currently, group treatment is a principal approach to the problems of a widening range of young people with highly diverse problems. This situation has been accompanied by the development of many different group therapeutic approaches, which vary not only in their underlying philosophies, but also with respect to the planning and conduct of treatment.

Each of the approaches is designed to deal with delinquents who have varying developmental capabilities and problems. Each one in the universe of group treatment methods offers advantages and limitations in working with different groups of juveniles.

One of the most widely used approaches is group counseling. This technique focuses on a particular type of problem—social, educational, vocational, or personal—usually in schools, human service agencies, clinics, and institutional settings. It deals primarily with conscious problems and is oriented toward the resolution of specific, short-term issues.

Group psychotherapy with delinquents, on the other hand, is designed to promote personality and behavior change through interaction in a carefully structured environment that is influenced strongly by the therapist. Delinquent behavior is assumed to arise from serious distortions of family relationships that are treatable on the level of conscious ego functioning. The focus is on the individual intrapsychic conflicts of the juvenile, in a group setting. This approach is heavily dependent on communication and is supplemented with individual sessions. Kaplan and Sadock have labeled it "structured interactional group psychotherapy."[4] There are a number of variations of this approach, depending on the age and the presenting problem of the delinquent, such as activity group therapy, activity interview group therapy, play therapy, and others.[5] Also, the approach presupposes a relatively lengthy period of treatment.

A third major category of group treatment approaches is the behavior therapy model. A basic assumption underlying this model and its variations is that all behavior is learned through reinforcement and that the principles of social learning can be applied to individuals to produce behavioral changes. The focus is on the specific targets for behavioral change that are reflected in the delinquent acts of the juvenile. The treatment method involves defining goals in terms of clearly identifiable, manageable objectives for each group member. Progress is monitored through self-recording and observation of specific behaviors by group members. The group process is used to facilitate change by the establishment of behavioral objectives for the group as a whole, mediation of positive and negative reinforcers by the group, and the modeling function of individual members.[6]

A variant of the behavior therapy model is reality therapy, a system that was developed in a training school for girls.[7] Like other behavioral approaches, it rejects the medical model of mental illness. The core concept of this method is that delinquents are personally responsible for their own behavior and that, by examining it and making value judgments about it, they can achieve a "success identity." The group leader assists by establishing a personal relationship with the group members and by not accepting excuses for irresponsible behavior. The treatment involves the identification of specific behavioral changes that must be made, formulating plans for change, carrying out the change, and evaluating the results.

Guided group interaction, which incorporates some of the elements in the approaches mentioned above, emerged relatively early in the development of group methods. McCorkle, who originated this technique, traces the influence of Wolf, Abrahams, and others on guided group interaction. Like reality therapy, guided group interaction was developed during World War II for use with delinquents in an Army disciplinary center.[8] After the war, McCorkle introduced this approach in the New Jersey correctional system. At that time, it was described by Bixby and McCorkle as follows:

To avoid confusion with the use of group psychotherapy as practiced by psychiatrists, and to avoid any implications that all inmates are mentally abnormal and unbalanced, we decided to call the application of group therapy principles to inmates, Guided Group Interaction.[9]

Pilnick has suggested a more recent definition of this technique as follows:

> Guided Group Interaction is a process of group treatment which directs the dynamics and strengths of the peer group toward constructively altering and developing the behavior of the group members.[10]

Like other approaches to group treatment, variations of the original guided group interaction model have been developed, including positive peer culture and peer group counseling.[11,12] However, since the differences between them are essentially operational and the basic assumptions and core concepts are similar to the original formulation, the discussion that follows will apply to all of them.

Although guided group interaction approaches were developed initially in institutional settings with older male adolescent delinquents, especially at the Highfields Residential Group Center in New Jersey, they have been adopted for use with male and female, early adolescents and young adults as well. Also, the settings have varied from clinics, nonresidential programs, schools, and probation and parole offices to halfway houses, group homes, camps, job corps centers, and others.[13,14] Moreover, the size of the treatment group is fairly constant in each of these settings, in that each group consists, on the average, of 10 members. Larger groups usually develop subgroups, which establish their own goals, norms, and relationships without reference to the objectives of the program.

Another distinguishing feature of this model is the length of participation, which is usually about four to six months. The rationale for selecting this period is based largely on the experience of the practitioners. It appears that prolonged participation in this type of program encourages the development of ritualistic behavior and serves to isolate the group members from stable, routine contacts with the community. Also, release from the program is usually a function of several variables, including (1) an assessment of the member's career in the program by the peer group and the staff; (2) an estimate of the member's ability to function effectively in the community; (3) a review of the member's role in assisting other members with their problems; and (4) a decision by the group and the leader that optimal gains have been achieved at a particular time.[15]

The type of juvenile offender referred to programs employing the group method includes a wide range of offense types. However, the limited available research evidence suggests that the adaptive offender, the individual who gets involved in delinquency in association with others, is best suited to this method. Unsocialized personalities and delinquents who are diagnosed as severe neurotics might not participate profitably in this treatment model.[16,17]

Group structure can facilitate or inhibit group development and the accomplishment of group purposes. Aspects of structure that are important to group treatment approaches, including guided group interaction, are (1) the number of group meetings; (2) how often the group will meet; (3) how long each meeting will last; (4) whether the group will be open-ended or closed;

(5) what degree of control will be retained by the therapist; and (6) the format the meetings will have.[18]

Although it is traditional for other group treatment approaches to meet once a week, in guided group interaction programs, the meetings are held from three to five times each week. However, as in other therapy group situations where the 1- to 1½-hour group meeting has become a standard practice, this method employs the same procedure. Ideally, the duration of group meetings should be related to the problems of the members, the purposes for which the group meets, the format of the meetings, and the capacity of the members to cope with the time span.

The issue of employing an open-ended structure or a closed structure is often related to the interest of the agency that sponsors the group or the therapist. In guided group interaction programs, closed group structure is employed. The basis for assignment is usually determined by the date of admission. It is not necessarily related to any other factors, so that a new member is usually assigned to a group that is in the process of forming. The groups are closed to admissions when there are about 10 members. In this manner, each group develops a history and a culture of its own. Generally, new members are assigned to a group that is beginning to release members. The assignment of new admissions to a functioning group provides them with opportunities to experience the ways in which older members deal with their problems as a group and to learn how to communicate with their peers and the group leader. In many respects, the new admissions learn about the functioning and the format of the group meetings through a process of participant observation. This experience serves also to transmit the culture of the old group, a nondelinquent culture, to the new group.

The issue of control and authority in the group is a crucial one because it determines the climate of the group. Some forms of group treatment require a high degree of control by the therapist, others a low degree, as in client-centered therapy where the leader is viewed as a facilitator and the assumption is made that the group can find its own direction. In guided group interaction settings, as in other settings, an attempt is made to establish sufficient levels of control by the leader to help get the group started and then to transfer power and authority, progressively, as the group is ready to assume it. The role of the leader depends on the nature of the problems confronting the group at a particular time. Generally, however, the leader's role varies from providing support to making interpretations, confronting the group or individual members, and summarizing the interactions.

With reference to the format of the meetings, this is usually related to the intended goals of the group, the problems of the members, the number, frequency, and duration of the meetings, and the degree of capacity of the members for interaction. In some variations of guided group interaction, there is a strict agenda, which includes reporting problems, awarding the meeting to a particular member, attempting to resolve problems, and summarizing the meeting; summaries are made by the group leader, an individual member, or several members. In the original model, however, the agenda varies depending on the stage in the group process at which a group finds itself. The agenda is more flexible and is related to the nature of the problems facing the group or the leader at the time. In either case, the themes that are discussed revolve around "here and now" problems of the members.

Implicit in the structure of this group method are the major assumptions that underlie it. The central assumption is that delinquency is learned behavior that results principally from association with other delinquents in a peer group. Consequently, it follows that the delinquent will change his behavior, in a prosocial direction, only if such conduct is acceptable to the peer group. A second assumption is that change can be achieved effectively if the entire peer group, not just the individual member, is the target of change. In other words, change is most acceptable not only when it receives the confirmation of the peer group, but also when the peer group becomes the major vehicle by which nondelinquent standards are established and problems are solved. A third assumption is that the change will occur through a process of interaction with others who are also changing. If the delinquent can see others changing, then he is more likely to change himself. In a very real sense, a group member changes by helping others to change, not by seeking private solutions to personal and group problems.

A fourth major assumption is that opportunities for reality testing through sharing "here and now" experiences with others provide a means for validating changes that are alleged to have occurred in the group meetings. In total institutions, the social roles played by the inmate represent a serious departure from the roles played before the incarceration. In guided group interaction programs, the opportunity to duplicate delinquent roles learned in the community and to attempt new social roles is crucial for change to occur.[19]

In group treatment approaches, the group process is an important factor in influencing the nature of each member's experience and the role of the leader. It is important, therefore, to have an understanding of this process and its meaning for changing behavior.[20]

The group process can be viewed in terms of a number of dimensions, including the amount and type of participation by the group leader; the themes discussed in the group; the extent to which these themes are introduced by the group leader or emerge from the members; the definition of the group operations in terms of whether the group is individually oriented or group oriented; the degree of analytic orientation that occurs in the group interaction as opposed to concern with current behavior; and the degree to which an accepting climate is generated and maintained or confrontation is emphasized.

The group process that occurs in guided group interaction can be viewed in terms of these dimensions. The developmental process is divided into four phases. Each phase is described in terms of the major problems confronting the group and the characteristic behavior that is found at each phase. In stating that groups have distinct patterns that are observable and predictable, I am making an assumption that is essentially untested—

although it is based to some degree on research evidence and my own and others' participation in and observation of many group meetings.

The first phase can be characterized as a search for structure. Since the members have no common past and no common present relationships outside of the group, there is no identification with each other or with the group leader. The members engage in a considerable amount of random, hostile behavior that involves testing one another and the leader. Each member is involved in a private world in which he is searching for meaning. There is no structure because the members do not know very much about each other, and know even less about the leader. Their problem is to develop a structure, and they do it in a variety of ways. In fact, some groups will attempt to invent a structure by suggesting that a president, vice-president, and secretary be appointed. The themes that emerge are short-lived and almost never discussed in depth. There are long moments of silence and much smoking, whispering, and asking for information from the group leader. Also, there are outbursts of shouting, even laughter, and movements in and out of the meeting.

Later during this phase, the group members communicate by relating stories of how they got into trouble, by describing their escapades, and in other safe, nonthreatening ways. In effect, they are seeking ways to relate to each other. Also, some members take risks and attempt to assume the leadership role.

The objectives of this first stage are to foster and reward interaction, to teach the members that the level of group performance depends heavily on them, to instill confidence in the group, to introduce substantive problems, and to gather information on the members.

The group leader is fairly active in that he poses problems for which solutions must be found and refuses to accept all responsibility for the operation of the meeting. He or she does not provide conclusive answers but encourages discussion of matters of interest to the group.

From the point of view of the individual member, this stage has enabled him or her to introduce to the group substantive problems that exist in the family, the school, and the street; to become aware of differences and problems the members share with each other; to begin to learn to trust the group leader and other group members; and to tell the truth.

The second stage involves principally the formation of subgroupings and friendship pairs. The members of each subgroup sit together, support each other, and attempt to control the discussions of the meetings or perhaps refuse to attend meetings. This is an important experience because it is the point at which the group problems are being identified by the members. Also, they are now in the process of attempting to relate to each other, to take risks, and to begin to trust each other by telling the truth about themselves and their involvement with each other in the daily activities. At the same time, there is a continual struggle among the subgroups for control of the meeting. In effect, there is a public awareness of the existence of each other member since almost everyone belongs to a subgroup that is clearly identified by all.

The group leader, during this stage, is usually stereotyped by the members as all-knowing and omnipotent. The leader attempts to crystallize dilemmas, to encourage the group to explore alternative modes of interaction and behavior, to teach the group to examine problems, and to develop concern for the welfare of the group.

The third stage is concerned with a struggle for survival. This is a crucial period in the careers of the group members because, at this point, they are struggling to survive as a group. They begin to recognize the fact that they are not helping each other by contending for power. Once again, much hostility is expressed. The subgroups begin to fall apart because, in analyzing the bases for their relationships, the members discover that their relationships are not rooted in trust or concern for one another's welfare. In fact, there emerges an awareness of the tenuous character of the clique relationship and that, unless the issue is confronted, the members will not be able to cope with their other problems.

It is interesting to observe the tremendous amount of hostility that is generated between members of subgroups that may have been together for several weeks. Initially, during this third stage, they distrust each other, steal from each other, argue, and even fight on occasion. Unlike the second stage when the discussion is more mechanical and intellectualized, the emotional content in the third stage is very high. It is at this point that a considerable amount of acting out occurs. Hostility is clearly directed toward former friends and the group leader as well. Moreover, group problems are clearly defined at this stage, for there emerges a recognition of the fact that, unless members join together as a total group, they will not be able to address their problems openly, honestly, and directly.

The group leader plays a fairly active role during the third stage, partly because much of the hostility in the group is directed toward him. Also, he plays more of a teaching role at this point. His objectives are principally to help the members understand the group structure and the process, to increase the capacity of the members to see themselves in relation to the group structure, and to help the group become aware of the consequences of factionalism. Also, interestingly enough, at the end of this stage, the power and authority of the leader decreases and begins to be assumed by the group.

The fourth stage is characterized by group solidarity and decision making. During this period, the total group is seen as a special entity, since the subgroups have broken up and the members have reorganized as a cohesive unit. This integration provides the group with the capacity to undertake any of the problems of their members, of the group itself, and of new admissions to the group. The group engages in quiet, deliberate, rational discussions of problems, solutions to problems, and decision making. Also, it is at this point that the group members become the culture bearers for new admissions and share power with the leader in discussions about release from the program and other important issues. Also, the group leader is seen as more of a group member, since others have assumed the leadership role. It is a period of highly cooperative and motivated problem solving. There is greater trust and communication than at earlier stages, and certainly great concern for the group as a whole.

The ultimate test of any group treatment approach is whether changes in attitude and behavior in the group setting will result in long-term, overt behavioral changes in the life-style of the participants. This is a key issue; yet there appears to be relatively little research directed toward it. One of the reasons may be that treatment outcomes cannot be empirically determined by currently available measurement techniques. In the case of guided group interaction, the results of several evaluations generally have neither confirmed nor denied its effectiveness. However, Weeks reported in his study of the Highfields program in New Jersey that recidivism rates for the graduates of this program compare favorably with those for graduates of a state reformatory where guided group interaction was not employed.[16] Furthermore, Stephenson and Scarpetti, in a review of several institutional and community-based programs, found that on the whole, guided group interaction graduates fared better than parolees but not as well as probationers.[21]*

A related issue is the extent to which a group treatment approach lends itself to replication, apart from the therapist who uses it. The systematic character of the method itself to a great extent determines the degree to which the method may be transferred intact under varying conditions. This is an issue that has not been addressed in a systematic way in this field. An attempt was made to replicate guided group interaction programs by providing internships and training experiences for interested persons, many of whom subsequently implemented this approach in other settings. Another technique involved the use of graduates of one program to help establish another one.[23]

A third key issue involves the question of how well group approaches incorporate a thorough understanding of the use of the group process. A major objective of group development is to integrate the dynamics of the individual and the group. In many instances, the potential of the group is either underutilized or neglected.[24] The guided group interaction approach, in contrast to other methods, uses the group as a means for treatment, rather than as the context for treatment, by working on problems through the group process.

Group treatment approaches appear to have great potential for assisting juvenile delinquents with their problems. Each of the several methods that have been developed can contribute to that end. No single approach is the most appropriate therapeutic tool for all types of delinquents. However, when used with awareness of their strengths and limitations, each of the methods presented in this paper has some demonstrated potential for contributing to the resolution of a difficult social problem, namely, the treatment of the juvenile delinquent.

---

*Other evidence indicates that guided group interaction has a positive effect on reducing incidents of school violence and reduces school absenteeism (see References 12 and 22).

REFERENCES

1. JOSSELYN, I. M. 1971. Adolescence. Harper and Row Publishers. New York, N.Y.
2. ERICKSON, E. H. 1968. Identity: Youth and Crisis. W. W. Norton & Co., Inc. New York, N.Y.
3. BERGER, A. 1977. Study of Juvenile Delinquent Behavior. Institute of Juvenile Research. Illinois Department of Mental Health. Chicago, Ill. (Unpublished manuscript.)
4. KAPLAN, H. I. & B. J. SADOCK, Eds. 1972. New Models for Group Therapy. E. P. Dutton and Co., Inc. New York, N.Y.
5. SLAVSON, S. R. & M. SCHIFFER. 1975. Group Psychotherapies for Children. International Universities Press. New York, N.Y.
6. SARRI, R. C. 1964. Behavioral theory and group work. In Individual Change through Small Groups. P. Glasser, R. C. Sarri & R. D. Vinter, Eds.: 50-71. Free Press. New York, N.Y.
7. GLASSER, W. 1965. Reality Therapy. Harper and Row, Publishers. New York, N.Y.
8. ABRAHAMS, J. & L. W. MCCORKLE. 1946. Group psychotherapy of military offenders. Am. J. Sociology 51(5): 455-464.
9. BIXBY, F. L. & L. W. MCCORKLE. 1948. A recorded presentation of a program of Guided Group Interaction in New Jersey correctional institutions. Proceedings of the 78th Annual Congress of Correction. American Correctional Association. College Park, Md.
10. PILNICK, S. 1971. Guided Group Interaction. In Encyclopedia of Social Work. R. Morris, Ed. 1: 181. National Association of Social Workers. New York, N.Y.
11. VORRATH, H. & L. K. BRENDTHRO. 1974. Positive Peer Culture. Aldine Publishing Co. Chicago, Ill.
12. HOWLETT, F. W. & R. G. BOEHM. 1975. School-Based Delinquency Prevention: The Rock Island Experience: 12-14, 40. Justice Systems, Inc. Austin, Tex.
13. MCCORKLE, L. W., A. ELIAS & F. L. BIXBY. 1958. The Highfields Story. Holt, Rhinehart and Winston. New York, N.Y.
14. PILNICK, S. & A. ELIAS. 1966. The Essexfields group rehabilitation project for youthful offenders. In Corrections in the Community 4. California Board of Corrections. Sacramento, Calif.
15. ELIAS, A. 1968. Group treatment programs for juvenile delinquents in New Jersey. Child Welfare 47(S): 286.
16. WEEKS, H. A. 1959. Youthful Offenders at Highfields. University of Michigan Press. Ann Arbor, Mich.
17. WARREN, R. 1965. The Community Treatment Project. Presented at the Annual Conference of the Illinois Academy of Criminology, Chicago, Ill., May 14.
18. LEVINE, B. 1979. Group Psychotherapy. Prentice Hall, Inc. Englewood Cliffs. N.J.
19. RABOW, J. & A. ELIAS. 1969. Organizational boundaries, inmate roles and rehabilitation. J. Res. in Crime and Delinquency (January): 8-16.
20. WHITAKER, D. S. & M. A. LIEBERMAN. 1964. Group Psychotherapy through Group Process: 1. Atherton Press. New York, N.Y.
21. STEPHENSON, R. M. & F. R. SCARPETTI. 1974. Group Interaction as Therapy: 189. Greenwood Press. Westport, Conn.
22. HANNON, J. P. & J. W. WICKS. 1977. Program Evaluation—Peer Culture Development: 5. Report No. 77-114-15. Board of Education. Chicago, Ill.
23. ALLEN, R. F. et al. 1965. Collegefields: 14-15. Special Child Publications, Inc. Seattle, Wash.
24. LEVINSON, H. M. 1973. Use and misuse of groups. Social Work (January): 66-72.

THE VIOLENT PATIENT IN THE COMMUNITY

Maurice R. Green

*Columbia University Physicians
and Surgeons at St. Luke's
New York, New York 10024*

I shall begin with a discussion of violence in America in general, and then proceed to the various categories of patients wherein violent behavior is more frequent and conspicuous; although it must be stressed that most surveys of civil and criminal violence show that less than 20% is associated with a diagnosable mental illness of either a psychotic or neurotic type.[1]

Violence seems to have been increasing steadily over the past several decades, not only in America, but throughout the Western world. The nature of violence, too, seems to have grown more vicious, impersonal, and almost random—such as impulsively pushing someone off a subway platform, or killing someone old and helpless after robbing them. This increased violence has risen in all areas of the country and in all social strata. Certainly it pervades the consciousness of everyone to become a profoundly disturbing social concern. This concern weighs heavily on the raw edge of our consciousness, bidding us to bar our windows, to look warily over our shoulders, and to keep to well-lighted streets when we are out at night.

This ambience of fearful anticipation of violence pervades all our conversation, plans, outings to restaurant and theatre, and even our walking the dog at night. Churches have begun to provide escorts to the elderly for security during their shopping for food and necessities. Violence conditions our lives and social behavior in ways inconceivable to earlier generations. Our drama, popular literature, press, podium, and pulpit and the powerfully persuasive mass media of film, radio, and television all bring the spectre of epidemic irrational violence home to us. Youngsters today apparently take this for granted—not familiar with any other atmosphere. Older folks share nostalgic memories of times, just a few decades past, when no one locked his door in suburbs or rural areas; when no one thought twice about cavorting in Central Park after midnight; when crime and violence seemed far away and sharply limited to the poor, culturally deprived, and politically disinherited population areas of slums and shantytowns. Today violence knows no boundaries; it is in the marketplace, the schools and suburbs, the farms and villages, just around any corner, in our home and community. It is clear now from recent statistical research that the increase is actual and not simply derivative of more thorough record keeping, sampling, and accounting; although for family violence between spouses, parents and children, or siblings, there may be no actual increase, but rather a lessened tolerance for it as reflected in the laws regarding spouse abuse and child abuse.

The complex causes of violence change, to be sure, with the social matrix; with demographic shifts, immigration, urbanization, and the conflicts of subculture; with the alterations in the distribution of wealth and opportunity and the consequent rise of new aspirations and expectations, creating new frustrations and a changed sense of social status and deprivation.[2]

Social attitudes and their subsequent representation in law show a parallel development. New categories of violence, new definitions of crime, come into being with changes in the norms. The legitimate corporal punishment of one era becomes the censurable or punishable abuse of another, properly recorded in the statistics of violence. The kick, cuff, or punch in the nose that was the ordinary accent to an altercation in one era or milieu becomes a reportable assault in another. Only a generation ago, violence between spouses was a popular subject of humor in movies, radio, and the vulgar comic strip. When Jiggs in business suit and spats went drinking with his former working-class cronies, Maggie, the status-hungry, nouveau riche matron, was waiting for him with a "blue collar" rolling pin that said "Pow!" This was considered funny then and not too great an exaggeration of the mores and conflicts of the urban ethnic-immigrant working class. Our sensibilities have changed, the diligent women's movement has flowered, and increasing social and forensic intervention into the affairs of families is providing new insight.

Traditionally, the child-rearing function was the responsibility and near-sacred preserve of the parents: extended family, neighbors, and the church provided supervision and correction, insuring social and moral conformity. Increasingly, with the changes brought about by the human consequences of urban industrial development, the extended family shrank to the nuclear family and, more recently, to the "floating couple" of serial monogamy or the relatively isolated "single parent." Neighborhood and community faded away to a considerable degree in the increasing flux of movement from one place to another, and with the rapid changes in the architecture and character of cities and suburbs. Increasingly, through the 19th century and into the 20th, schools have assumed more and more of the physical, intellectual, and social training of children—and to some extent of parents themselves. And increasingly, throughout the Western world, the authority and influence of the family were weakened as parents became subject to the suasion of educators, social theorists, and the indoctrinating complex of interests and influence that constitute organized public opinion. The Oedipal-incest theories of the Freudians, the writings of the sometimes misguided followers of the great John Dewey, the developmental charts of Dr. Spock, and the stepladder social achievement scale of Eric Erickson have all had their effect—sometimes for the better, often adverse—on the rearing of children and therefore on the integrity of family life. Feminism and the massive entrance of women into the labor force have played their obvious part. So has the army of behavioral scientists marching under the banners of antiauthoritarianism and family democracy.

This egalitarianism, as de Toqueville predicted over a hundred years ago, has become embedded in official and professional rhetoric and has penetrated the family fortress; it feeds the fires of rancorous generational struggles that now reach downward from the college campus to the cradle. Children of all ages today have "rights," asserted by themselves and more convincingly by the attorneys, agencies, and sociopolitical groups that speak for them. Family courts listen, legislation is proposed and adopted, and now the rights of children are respected in due process, however furiously at cross purposes they may be with the wishes, intentions, or requirements of the adults who are called upon to nurture, educate, and somehow govern their children. In the past year I have seen several cases where parents seeking help from the court in coping with a defiant, hostile youngster are met with a counter action by the youngster and the youngster's attorney (paid for by the parents' taxes) of alleged child abuse.

There is little literature on the actual incidence of violence against parents other than the sensational, dramatic accounts of matricide and patricide, which occur relatively rarely. (Although they seemed to be of frequency in the ancient royal families, where these acts were more of a political grab for power than anything else.) An informal survey in the family court in New York City recently showed that about 10% of the family offenses that came to the court were charges against children for assaulting and threatening their parents.

However, most of the participants in these cases of assault never became patients. The population of psychiatric patients as a whole is less violent than the general population. The incidence of violent (or for that matter of *any*) offenses among the discharged-patient population is much less than the incidence among the nonpatient population in the community at large. (A recent survey at Bellevue shows a reversal of this statistic under the so-called revolving door policy of brief hospitalization and early discharge to inadequate or nonexistent community resources.)

During 10 years at Bellevue, Dr. Grace Frank and I studied several children under the age of 11 years who had murdered other children; most of these children showed psychotic signs and symptoms at the time of admission. But children who commit murder do not necessarily show evidence of psychosis or insanity. Many of the children we studied recovered with no further incidence of violent offense or psychosis during a 10-year follow-up. They were treated with medication, individual and family therapy, and supportive guidance in the community and at school.

Of course, since ancient times children under 7 years have been considered incapable of intent, and those between 7 and 12–14 have been held accountable only if proof of intention was very clear and certain. In New York City today, as you all know, the age has been recently lowered to 13 years. Despairing of rehabilitation and treatment, the community is demanding harsher legislation, not only in New York, but throughout the country.

Although most mentally retarded people in the community are not involved with violent or sexually offensive behavior, they are as vulnerable as the rest of the population—a little more so when they are not protected or supported, perhaps. About 30 years ago, I did a random sampling at a center for the retarded and found that out of 100 chosen, the majority of boys were brought to the attention of authorities for help when their aggressive behavior became intolerable to the parents, and the majority of girls were brought for help when their sexual behavior disturbed the family or community. With the increased provision for services obtained by the now-proverbial lobby for the retarded, this situation must be much improved. However, in spite of the improvement, there is still inadequate service for retarded adolescents who, although less than 3% of the general population, make up 10.5% of the delinquent population.

The most commonly diagnosed disorder among violence-prone school children is the attention deficit disorder with hyperactivity. In fact, although learning disorders show no causal link to juvenile delinquency, there is a disquieting statistic that 50% of adjudicated juvenile delinquents manifest a history of learning disability. At any rate, this disorder— previously described under the label of minimal brain dysfunction—responds very well in most instances to medication, psychotherapy, and other treatment when available. A recent study shows that the same group of children not treated with ritalin show the same delay in growth and maturation as evidenced by those receiving it, suggesting a systemic congenital developmental disorder for at least a significant part of this patient population.[3] Special corrective education is required for these children, many of whom show varying signs of mild organic brain impairment. Archie Silver[4] has shown in a seven-year follow-up on children with attention deficit disorders both with and without hyperactivity, and with as well as without any organicity, that corrective educational intervention in the first and second grades was very effective. In fact, in a sizeable sample (150), Silver found a very sharp drop in the incidence of delinquency among the teenage follow-up group.

Another sizeable population of children and youths who become involved in violence in the family and/or the community fall under the rubric of conduct disorders (undersocialized aggressive type and socialized aggressive type), which begin in the primary grades and increase in frequency as these children approach the high school years. This includes the antisocial personality—what sometimes even today is called the psychopath. Walker and McCuble—in Rieber and Vetter's recent book, *The Psychological Foundations of Criminal Justice*—trace the history of the concept back to the 17th century.[5] The concept itself refers to a disorder or group of disorders that does not meet the criteria for more definite forms of mental disorder and is always associated with antisocial conduct. This type of disorder was earlier called moral insanity or moral imbecility. The term psychopathy, which originally meant all mental disorders, came to be used in this restricted way when the German physician Koch used the term "constitutional psychopathic inferiority" because these criminals showed no evidence of insanity in the strict sense. At first, this term included neurasthenia, obsessive-compulsive neurosis, and all sexual deviance.

Sir David Henderson, a Scottish disciple of Adolf Meyer, began the present usage of the term psychopathic disorder—which is more or less synonymous with antisocial personality disorder—which Henderson divided into aggressive and inadequate types.

The other frequent personality disorder of violent aggression, but of a noncriminal type, is the explosive personality disorder in which perfectly law-abiding, conventional, well-mannered people suffer outbursts of exaggerated rage and temper tantrums in response to relatively modest provocation. This diagnostic category has been removed from the category of personality disorders in the third *Diagnostic and Statistical Manual* and placed in the new category of impulse disorders. This category describes individuals who have recurrent and paroxysmal episodes of significant loss of control of aggressive impulses that result in serious assault on another person or destruction of property. There is always genuine regret and self-reproach. Alcohol seems to be a frequent predisposing agent, and there is often a history of hyperactivity in childhood. Using a special activating technique for electroencephalograph (EEG) examination, Russell Monroe found EEG abnormalities among 80% of these episodic impulsive patients.[6] Forty-two of the 70 patients showed aggressive dyscontrol acts towards themselves or others. The epileptoid groups of episodic dyscontrol respond well to a combination of anticonvulsant medication and psychotherapy. The others tend to resent engagement in treatment but need a thorough diagnostic evaluation. Some may do well on lithium; others may do better on benzodiazepines.

Out of 416 patients presenting to a large urban psychiatric emergency service in a two-week period, 62 were classified as violent because of outwardly directed aggressive ideation or behavior, and 63 showed suicidal impulses only.[7] Twenty-five of the 62 were classified as schizophrenic; 18 were classified in a combined category of neuroses, personality and character disorders, and situational disturbances; 7 were alcoholic; 4 were affective disorder with psychosis. Sixty-five percent of the total violent sample showed a major disturbance in perception, cognition, and reality testing that resulted from either psychosis, organicity, or intoxicants.

The criteria for dangerousness—a history of fighting, of the use of weapons, repeated expression of intention to hurt, etc.[8]—were met by most of the violent patients seen. The 65% showing psychosis, organicity, or intoxication could profit from an emergency commitment or voluntary hospitalization. Crisis intervention, short-term hospitalization, environmental manipulation, supportive psychotherapy, and the appropriate medical and psychopharmacological treatments could restore control and help the patient integrate himself safely into the family and community. However, for the group labeled personality and character disorders, or impulse disorders, there may be no treatment or no response or interest in whatever treatment may be available. Such persons may need to be managed within the judicial or penal system. However imperfect these institutions may be, they are more appropriate than psychiatric modes that are inappropriate or ineffective.

Even in institutions, nonpsychotic patients with certain personality and character traits are at a higher risk for assaultive behavior than psychotic patients. The common elements in the violent groups are an intense affect, hostile or depressed; impulsive tendencies with poor capacity for restraint; manipulative behavior with frequent testing of the limits; and regressive childish behavior associated with immaturity, poor judgment, and intolerance of frustration and stress. Transient, very brief psychotic[9] episodes may occur, as well as unpredictable stress-related defensive violence in the form of property destruction and fights with other patients.

A recent study in British Columbia of violent men who raped little girls revealed that very few of these men showed any signs of psychosis, but, like the group above, these men showed neurotic symptoms and personality and character disorders.[10] In general, these violent rapists were characterized by personality traits of hidden inadequacy and impotence, with compensatory violent displays manifested in their cruel sexual assaults on young girls as well as in a fast, reckless, violent life-style associated with excessive drinking, reckless driving of cars and motorcycles, excessive debts, sexual promiscuity, and preoccupation with pornographic materials and fantasy. Incidentally, rapists usually have a history of violent and/or criminal behavior, whereas exhibitionists do not.

In spite of the increase in extrafamilial violence between strangers, by far the greatest amount of violent behavior still occurs between intimates—immediate family, relatives, and neighbors. Although a small percentage, the violent patients who suffer from a manic-depressive illness make up a significant number. It is especially important to recognize this group because treatment is so successful with the use of lithium.

It is useful at this point to have some perspective on the incidence and prevalence of mental disorders among the population of those who commit offenses. Rosner, Wiederlight, Horner-Rosner, and Wieczorek[11] at the New York Criminal and Supreme Courts examined 140 adolescent offenders aged 16-18 and found, as suggested by studies already cited, that by far most (54.9%) were in the category of personality disorders. Eighteen-and-three-tenths percent were found to suffer from schizophrenia, which is about 10 times the incidence and prevalence of this disorder among the same age and socioeconomic group in the general population. However, the Midtown Home Survey[12] reported that about 17.2% of the population in the poverty section were markedly impaired psychiatrically although most had had no contact with a health facility. Nonetheless, 30% of the offenders described by Rosner et al. had had some previous psychiatric hospitalization and/or neurological problems.[11] Robins has shown that 25% of children referred for antisocial behavior were later diagnosed as adult antisocial personalities.[13] Incidentally, a New York State investigative committee showed a high incidence of child abuse in the history of delinquent youths.[14]

Dorothy O. Lewis and her coworkers found that sexual violence among young men is very much a part of a generally violent pattern of behavior:

> sexually assaultive children had been behaving in a variety of violent antisocial ways since early childhood . . . prevalence of psychotic symptoms, major neurological abnormalities, minor neurological impairment and learning disabilities was approximately equal.[15]

Her observations confirm the findings in British Columbia and elsewhere that sexual violence is not a specific entity but simply another manifestation of a generally violent pattern of behavior and life-style.

In contrast to these violent, antisocial adolescents, most violent husbands of battered wives do *not* show antisocial behavior. For most of these men, seen by Janet Geller,[16] there was no evidence of impairment in any area of their lives apart from the marital relationship. All these men were steadily employed, homeowners, good neighbors, and respected, well-liked citizens from a middle-class background. In spite of initial severe resistance, most of them seemed to have profited markedly from a 10-session all-male group experience.

Offer, Marohan, and Ostrov, in Chicago, did a very thorough study of 55 juvenile delinquents referred principally from the juvenile justice system.[17] They screened out all those who exhibited organic brain syndromes, epilepsy, mental retardation, and psychotic or schizophrenic states and selected only chronic offenders who had performed serious offenses, excluding the one-time offender or those who had committed only minor offenses. Hence, the chosen groups were characterized by violent acts against others, associated with attempted murder, armed robbery, burglary, theft, drugs, prostitution, larceny, and property destruction. They found that this group of delinquents would be divided into four subtypes:

1. The impulsive, who is the most violent and antisocial type, has little tolerance for delay and tends to be disliked by teachers and staff.
2. The narcissistic—resistant to any form of psychotherapy—is defensive, denies all problems, and depresses the staff.
3. The empty borderline, always seeking some kind of merger with a parental figure, seems hopelessly passive and incapable of orienting herself to the future.
4. The depressed borderline—trying to evade the painful depressive affect by self-destructive and antisocial behavior—suffers severe superego guilt, has strong internalized values, and was well liked and admired by the staff.

It is clear from the above that any factors that contribute to the following cluster will probably increase the incidence and prevalence of violent behavior in the community: a sense of entrapment; a poor sense of identity, particularly gender identity; sudden loss of status; isolation; and organic impairment of foresight and control due to drugs, infection, heredity, trauma, or alcohol. Therefore, it is practically impossible to predict violent behavior *out of context* for a particular given individual.

Norval Morris has pointed out that the law and psychiatry have failed to come up with actuarial tables—such as the insurance companies have—for categorizing violence.[18] Such an effort would improve the capacity within existing powers better to protect the community from violent recidivists and would lessen the frequency of assimilating all criminals to the prototype of the violent ones.

In actual practice, this assimilation is what is done when we define any particular patient or offender as dangerous. In effect we are saying that this person meets the criteria for membership in the dangerous category. This judgment cannot be made lightly but it must be made—as it is made on inpatient services over and over again when precautions are ordered because a patient is believed to be becoming dangerous to himself or to others. Under the haste to protect innocent patients from undue restriction or detention, the courts were once inclined to insist that an overt violent act or attempted act first must have been made. Evidence beyond a reasonable doubt was insisted upon, as several studies had suggested that 60–70% of those predicted to become violent would not become so. However, clear and convincing evidence is now becoming established as a standard of proof. In *Addington* v. *Texas*,[19] the judge indicated that the protection of the community dictated the sufficiency of clear and convincing evidence, with all regard for due process and judicial review within a reasonable period indicating that there were sufficient safeguards to avoid injustice.

Loren Roth, separating the issue of protecting the community from that of mandating treatment, has proposed a new model commitment law (1979).[20] He urges that brief periods of mental health commitment be permitted on the basis of *parens patria,* the interest of the state in caring for persons unable to care for themselves. However, he insists on the provision that only patients with a specific adjudication of incompetency to consent to or refuse treatment be committed, and for six weeks or less.

This differs from the dangerousness-to-self-or-others type of commitment. When dangerous patients—who are at the same time perfectly competent to consent to or refuse treatment—are forced to have treatment, the physician's identity is degraded and distorted (apart, of course, from emergency situations of imminent danger). Roth insists that dangerousness then must be proved beyond a reasonable doubt, ignoring the *Addington* v. *Texas* ruling; and once proved—and the patient committed as a dangerous, but competent, person—the patient has the right to refuse any or all treatments. Roth envisions the creation of a new type of quasi-penal institution for the long-term detention of dangerous, mentally ill patients who are competent to refuse treatment.

The patient who is dangerous to self falls under both the *parens patria* and the police power of the state, and is not permitted to refuse treatment necessary for his health. Such cases occur in the categories of chronic schizophrenia, alcoholic dementia, and senile dementia with psychosis. The dangerous-to-self approach can also be implemented by effective community care and treatment for the chronically disabled patient.

In conclusion, we see that violence among patients in the community—like violence among the nonpatients of the community—is a community problem, a social problem, as much as it is a psychiatric and legal problem. Patients fall into categories, some of which show a high incidence of violent behavior, as we have reported. Once cooperation is secured, relatively effective modes of treatment are available that are appropriate to the diagnosis of the individual patient—a medically informed, biosocial diagnosis. A large category of character and personality disorders, showing no symptoms or signs of neurosis or psychosis and little, if any, interest in treatment, might respond to innovative approaches or even to some kind of coerced learning experience, as Smith and Berlin indicate.[21] However, there are scant data to warrant much optimism in this area. The majority of violent offenders, like the majority of violent nonoffenders, suffer no diagnosable mental disorder and never become patients. The violence we suffer, fear, and inflict on each other is part of the values, mores, and way of life that most of our population live by.

REFERENCES

1. GUTTMACHER, M. 1960. The Mind of the Murderer. Farrer, Strauss & Cudahy. New York, N.Y.
2. STORR, A. 1968. Human Aggression. Atheneum Publishers. New York, N.Y.
3. OETTINGER, J. R., L. V. MAJOVSKI & W. H. WRIGHT. 1979. Minimal Brain Dysfunction: Effect of Stimulants on Maturation and Growth. Pamphlet No. 175-92174.
4. SILVER, A. A., R. A. HAGEN & R. BEECHER. 1978. Scanning, diagnosis and intervention in the prevention of reading disabilities. J. Learn. Disabil. 2(7): 439–448.
5. WALKER, N. & S. McCUBLE. 1979. In Psychological Foundations of Criminal Justice. R. Rieber & H. Vetter, Eds.1: 144. John Jay Press. New York, N.Y.
6. MONROE, R. 1970. Episodic Behavioral Disorders: 238–246. Harvard University Press. Cambridge, Mass.
7. SKODAL, E. A. & T. B. KARESU. 1978. Emergency psychiatry and the assaultive patient. Am. J. Psychiatry 13(2): 202–205.
8. NANGLE, O. 1976. Dangerousness, reasonable doubt and preconviction psychopath legislation. Southern Ill. Univ. Law J.: 218–236.
9. SOLOFF, P. H. 1979. Physical restraint and the nonpsychotic patient. J. Clin. Psychiatry 40: 302–305.
10. WEST, D. J. 1978. Understanding Sexual Attacks. Heineman. Exeter, N.H.
11. ROSNER, R., M. WIEDERLIGHT, M. B. HORNER-ROSNER & R. R. WIECZOREK. 1976. An analysis of demographic variables in adolescent defendants in a forensic psychiatry clinic. Bull. Am. Acad. Psychiatry Law 4: 251–257.
12. SROLE, L., T. S. LANGNER, S. T. MICHAEL, M. K. OPLER & T. A. C. RENNIE. 1962. Mental Health in the Metropolis 1. McGraw Hill Book Co. New York, N.Y.
13. ROBINS, L. 1966. Deviant Children Grown Up. Williams and Wilkins Co. Baltimore, Md.
14. Pisani Report. 1978. Report on the Relationship between Child Abuse and Neglect and Later Socially Deviant Behavior. Select Committee on Child Abuse. New York State Assembly. Albany, N.Y.
15. LEWIS, O., S. S. SHANOK, J. H. PINCUS & G. H. GLASER. 1979. Violent juvenile delinquents: psychiatric, neurological, psychological and abuse factors. J. Am. Acad. Child Psychiatry 18: 2, 307–319.
16. GELLER, J. 1978. Reaching the battering husband. In Social Work with Groups 1: 1–19.
17. OFFER, D., R. D. MAROHN & E. OSTROV. 1979. The Psychological World of the Juvenile Delinquent: 51–80. Basic Books. New York, N.Y.
18. MORRIS, N. 1969. Should law students encounter the new research techniques. In Law and the Social Order. Ariz. St. Law J.: 55–67.
19. Addington v. Texas, 60 L. Ed. 2d 323 (U. S. Supreme Ct., 1979).
20. ROTH, L. 1979. A commitment law for patients, doctors and lawyers. Am. J. Psychiatry 136: 1121–1127.
21. SMITH, A. & L. BERLIN. 1974. Treating the Criminal Offender. Oceana Publications, Inc. Dobbs Ferry, N.Y.

THE INSANITY DEFENSE, THE MENTALLY DISTURBED OFFENDER, AND SENTENCING DISCRETION

Thomas R. Litwack
Department of Psychology
John Jay College of Criminal Justice
New York, New York 10019

In recent years, proposals for reforming the adjudicatory aspect of our criminal justice system have increasingly stressed two suggestions: (a) that the insanity defense be abolished; and (b) that sentencing discretion on the part of judges be likewise abolished, or at least severely circumscribed.

For example, in New York State, the Department of Mental Hygiene has officially adopted the position that "mental disease or defect" should be abolished as a complete defense to a criminal charge;[1] and a special commission headed by Manhattan District Attorney Robert Morgenthau has advocated significantly curtailing the sentencing discretion now wielded by criminal court judges in New York. Similar proposals have accompanied bills to codify, and amend, the federal criminal code.

Proposals to abolish the insanity defense and sentencing discretion are obviously related in that they both are aimed at reducing the arbitrariness and capacity for error of our criminal justice system and, conversely, at enhancing both the actual fairness and the *perceived* fairness of that system. Indeed, both proposals attack very real and serious problems and, taken individually, have much merit. The points I wish to argue here, however, are (1) that the insanity defense—though it may be very narrowly circumscribed and divorced from the term "insanity"—cannot be completely abolished under the Constitution of the United States; and (2) that in any event, proposals to limit—if not abolish—the insanity defense and proposals to limit sentencing discretion seek to obtain goals that, however laudable, are incompatible with one another. For one of the aims of abolishing the insanity defense is to gain greater flexibility in our capacity to deal with mentally disturbed offenders; but to the extent that limits upon sentencing discretion were rigidly mandated and enforced, much of this sought-after flexibility would be lost.

I shall return to the issue of sentencing discretion and the mentally disturbed offender later in this presentation. For now, however, I would like to amplify upon my first point—that the insanity defense cannot, constitutionally, be totally abolished. This is so, I believe, for a simple reason: the Supreme Court has clearly indicated that it would be unconstitutional to subject to criminal penalties one who has violated the law without *mens rea*, that is, without any awareness of wrongdoing or the ability to control one's wrongdoing.

Consider the example of an individual who genuinely believes that he has heard God speak to him and that God has ordered him to kill another person. Or consider the example of someone who kills another in the delu-

185

sional (and objectively unreasonable) belief that his victim was about to attack him with deadly force. Both these individuals have violated the law, to be sure. They have committed unjustified homicide; but they have done so without any sense or awareness of wrongdoing—without, that is, what the common law referred to as mens rea, or an "evil state of mind."

Under the common law, mens rea was a prerequisite to any conviction for a crime. As one English judge observed during the last century:

> [A] criminal mind, or mens rea, must . . . ultimately be found by the jury in order to justify a conviction, . . . [although] in some cases the proof of the committal of the acts may prima facie, . . . by reason of their own nature, . . . import the proof of mens rea. But even in these cases it is open to the prisoner to rebut the prima facie evidence, so that if, in the end, the jury are satisfied that there was no criminal mind, or mens rea, there cannot be a conviction in England for that which is by the law considered to be a crime.[2]

Or, as one American authority has put it: "An evil deed, without more, does not constitute a crime; a crime is committed only if an evil doer harbored an evil mind."[3]

The Supreme Court of the United States, by its own admission, "has never articulated a general constitutional doctrine of mens rea."[4] I believe, however, that the Court has clearly indicated that mens rea is a constitutionally required element of all offenses defined as criminal and that it would be unconstitutional to punish or label as criminals those offenders who, when they committed their offense(s), wholly lacked mens rea.

For example, in *Powell* v. *Texas,*[4] a case decided in 1968, the Court held that public drunkenness *could,* constitutionally, be subjected to criminal penalties. However, a clear majority of the Court (including three of its present members—Justices Brennan, Stewart, and White) stated that if such behavior were truly uncontrollable, or the result of an "irresistable urge," rather than merely *difficult* to control, then to criminalize such behavior would run afoul of the Constitution's prohibition against cruel and unusual punishment. As the four justices who would have overturned the appellant's conviction explicitly stated in *Powell:* "Criminal penalities may not be inflicted upon a person for being in a condition he is powerless to change."[4] Those justices who affirmed Powell's conviction did so only because they could *not* conclude on the evidence that Powell's compulsions were "completely overpowering." To be sure, a person who commits an act such as murder has done more than just suffer from a condition. But it seems to me that the underlying principle behind the just-quoted statement would apply to our hypothetical cases as well: criminal penalties may not be inflicted upon a person for having acted without having chosen, knowingly, to do evil. After all, the defendant in *Powell* clearly did more than suffer from a condition; he was not only an alcoholic, he appeared while drunk in public places. Yet four judges voted to reverse Powell's conviction, and Justice White—and, apparently, at least two other justices in the majority—refused to do so only because he could not conclude upon the evidence that the defendant "could not prevent himself from appearing in public places," i.e., that his public drunkenness resulted from "completely overpowering urges."

That should hardly be surprising. The notion that individuals should be punished only when they choose to act wrongfully is deeply ingrained in our heritage and traditions. As the Court of Appeals for the District of Columbia stated in the well-known *Brawner* decision (which replaced the Durham rule of insanity in the District of Columbia with the American Law Institute test):

> "free will" is the postulate of responsibility under our jurisprudence. . . . Criminal responsibility is assessed when through "free will" a man elects to do evil.[5]

And since mens rea is an essential element of every crime, defendants are constitutionally entitled to a jury determination of whether or not they acted with mens rea. Thus, proposals that would allow insanity plea defendants a jury trial only on the issue of whether or not they committed the charged act, while leaving it to judges to determine issues regarding the defendant's mental state, likewise run afoul of the Constitution—at least insofar as defendants have a mens rea defense.

The concept of mens rea, it is important to stress, refers to a particular state of mind. It means more than electing to do an act that society views as evil; it means electing to do an act—or, in the case of criminal negligence, not to do an act—with some awareness that society would view that choice as morally wrong. Thus, though a psychopath may commit crimes without any subjective sense of guilt or remorse, he still has acted with mens rea, for he knows fully well that such acts are considered wrong by society. Similarly, if one kills in a premeditative fashion to avenge a previous harm, that murder is committed with mens rea no matter how justified the murderer may feel about having taken the law into his or her own hands. As long as the vengeful perpetrator realizes that society disapproves of such action, mens rea exists. (In such cases, of course, a sympathetic jury might nevertheless find the offender not guilty by reason of insanity.)

But when a crime is committed without such an awareness of wrongdoing, mens rea does not exist. To use our previous examples, if a paranoid individual kills in the delusional belief that he is about to be attacked with deadly force, he has no awareness of wrongdoing. In fact our society would sanction his behavior if his premises were true. Similarly, if one acts illegally in response to the commands of God, one has acted without mens rea, for our society teaches that the word of God is supposed to take precedence over the law of man.

Mens rea must also be distinguished from the words "intentional" and "knowingly" as they are often used in the criminal law. In New York, for example, crimes require conduct to be performed "intentionally," "knowingly," "recklessly," or with "criminal negligence." And, in New York, a person acts *intentionally* with respect to a result or to conduct described by a statute defining an offense "when his conscious objective is to cause such a result or to engage in such conduct";[6] and "*knowingly* . . . when he is aware that his conduct" is violating the law or will cause an illegal result.[7] Thus, a person can "intentionally" commit homicide within the meaning of the New York Penal Law and still lack mens rea, as would be the case with the individual who plans and commits a murder—with intent to kill and with awareness of the consequences of his acts—in accordance with instructions from God.

On the other hand, one can act with less of an evil mind than is conveyed by the words "intentionally" or "knowingly" and still possess mens rea. As Justice Black observed in *Powell* v. *Texas*, states have "wide freedom to determine the extent to which moral culpability should be a prerequisite to conviction of a crime."[4] Indeed, the Supreme Court has upheld convictions that were based upon actions that could only be described as "negligent" or irresponsible.[8] To my knowledge, however, the Supreme Court has never upheld a criminal conviction based upon strict liability, that is, without *any* element of conscious wrongdoing on the part of the offender. Indeed, in *Lambert* v. *California,* the Supreme Court ruled that consistent with due process, an ex-felon could not be convicted for failure to register herself as an ex-felon, under an ordinance requiring her to do so, without proof that she knew of the duty to register or without the probability of such knowledge.[9] Thus, while it is true that "there is no one . . . state of mind which constitutes mens rea,"[10] mens rea requires at least a negligent, that is, an irresponsible, failure to act when one should have acted. To subject an offender who has acted without any mens rea to criminal punishment would appear to violate both the due process clauses and the Eighth Amendment.

Does this mean that some insanity defense is constitutionally required to take into account those offenders who, as a result of a "mental disease or defect," have violated the law without any mens rea? The answer, I believe, is yes. But a very strict insanity test—stricter even than the McNaughton test—would suffice. Specifically, the only insanity test that would seem to be constitutionally required is one that would provide for those defendants who wholly lacked mens rea—those defendants who committed their criminal act without any awareness that what they were doing was wrong and without recklessness or negligence and those defendants who, if they did know what they were doing was wrong, were nevertheless simply unable (and not just "substantially" unable) to conform their conduct to the requirements of the law.

A few things should be noted about this suggestion. To begin with, there is no reason—and no constitutional justification—for limiting this defense to those who have suffered from a diagnosable "mental disease or defect." While that might be one cause of an absence of mens rea, it need not be the only one. I am thinking, for example, of the Torsney case, in which a police officer shot and killed an unarmed youth who, the officer claimed, *appeared* to be drawing a gun.[11] At his trial, Torsney was able to present psychiatric testimony to the effect that he suffered from unusual epileptic attacks and that it was, in part, as a result of one of these episodes that he believed he saw his victim draw a gun. Torsney, of course, was found not guilty by reason of insanity—to the chagrin of many who believed that his claim of insanity was a farce. (And, indeed, during his subsequent commitment for over a year to various civil mental hospitals, no evidence of epilepsy was ever observed or discovered.) But the point is this:

What if, under very trying and frightening circumstances (I believe Torsney was called to the scene of the crime with information that there was an armed and dangerous individual about), Torsney simply panicked? What if he killed his victim because he indeed thought he saw a gun, but his perception was a result of his fright rather than a psychotic "mental disease or defect"? If those were indeed the circumstances, was he any more blameworthy than he would have been if epilepsy, rather than overwhelming fear, caused his misperception? In fact, perhaps so! If Torsney was at all aware of his nervousness or excitability—or of any racial prejudices he was harboring that might have influenced his performance as a policeman— then it may well have been negligent or reckless for him to have continued to work as a policeman and he might well have been legitimately convicted of reckless or negligent homicide.

Thus, while we must have an insanity defense, we need not—and should not—call it the "insanity" defense. Rather we should call this constitutionally required defense the "mens rea defense"—not only because it would be a more accurate description of the defense, but also because it would remove the outdated and confusing term "insanity" from our jurisprudence. Such a step might also forestall the negative misperceptions about the "mentally ill" in general that the public might otherwise derive from reading about cases in which very violent individuals are claiming the "insanity defense." Moreover, I believe it would be wise policy for states to limit their insanity defense to a mens rea defense. For one thing, the more narrow, or strict, the "insanity " defense, the less likely it will be that offenders will be able to successfully feign "insanity." It is one thing to feign having, or having had, a "mental disease or defect," and it is another matter entirely to feign having been completely unable to distinguish between right and wrong or to control one's criminal tendencies.

Similarly, a mens rea defense does not suffer from the vagueness and ambiguity that characterize most other insanity defenses and that make the applicability of such other defenses to particular cases a source of such confusion and disagreement among lay persons and professionals alike. It should be far easier to agree upon the issue of whether a defendant *wholly* lacked mens rea than upon the question of whether he or she "substantially" lacked mens rea—the formulation of the increasingly prevalent American Law Institute test.* I recognize that some sympathetic defendants—for example, wives who have murdered their husbands after having suffered years of physical abuse, and certain police officers—may obtain jury acquittals though they rather clearly did not lack mens rea. However, a basic premise of our society is—and should be—that if one can control one's inclinations toward criminality, then one should exercise such control, however difficult that may be. By adopting a strict mens rea defense in place

---

* Under the American Law Institute test, a "person is not responsible for criminal conduct if at the time of such conduct as a result of a mental disease or defect he lacks substantial capacity either to appreciate the criminality (wrongfulness) of his conduct or to conform his conduct to the requirements of the law."

of the more broadly conceived defenses of "insanity," we may even serve to prevent criminality by reinforcing the notion that the ability to control our criminal tendencies exists and that society expects us to exercise such control, at least whenever possible. (Even if the assumption of the ability for self-control is, in fact, false—even if all our actions are, in fact, determined by forces beyond our control despite our illusion of "free will"—the reinforcement of that illusion via our criminal law may nevertheless be a determinant of behavior, directing behavior towards socially acceptable channels.)

Another major advantage of adopting a mens rea defense in place of the insanity defense is that, by limiting the breadth and ambiguity of the insanity defense, it would more fairly limit the actual and perceived role of psychiatry in the determination of the defendant's guilt.

Actually, the role of psychiatrists in the determination of the claims of insanity has been unfairly criticized. Whatever insanity defense we adopt—and I have argued that we must have at least somewhat of an insanity defense (the mens rea defense)—someone must present to the trier of fact the relevant evidence regarding the mental and emotional state of the accused at the time of her or his crime, i.e., evidence that would allow the trier of fact to determine whether or not a finding of not guilty by reason of insanity would be appropriate. The fact that it is difficult to know how someone thought and felt in the past does not change the fact that we are obligated to do the best we can. Fifth Amendment problems aside (an issue to which I shall return), it would be unfair to require the defendant himself—who may well be barely articulate—to alone present his case to the trier of fact. Therefore, as I said, someone (other than the defendant) must present this information to the jury. While there is no reason in the world why that someone must be a psychiatrist (or even a mental health professional—though the data adduced by a nonprofessional interviewer might well be given less weight than the data adduced by a "professional" interviewer), it is unfair to criticize psychiatrists because they cannot describe more precisely inherently ambiguous psychological processes or because they cannot, in good conscience, make judgments that are beyond their competency. Indeed, it seems to me, psychiatric witnesses get into trouble precisely when they seek to move beyond their range of competency—which is to unveil and describe the relevant mental and emotional state of the interviewee as best they can—and attempt to decide questions that are for the trier of fact to decide. Thus, for example, psychiatrists should *never* be willing to state conclusively whether or not a defendant had or lacked "the capacity to conform his or her conduct to the requirements of the law." Given our present state of knowledge, psychiatrists have no special expertise in making that determination. But, as one court suggested, the psychiatrist should still be free "to describe the defendant's mental condition and symptoms, his pathological beliefs and motivations, if he was thus afflicted, and to explain how these influenced or could have influenced his behavior, particularly his capacity [to] knowingly [commit the crime charged],"[12] while largely leaving it to the trier of fact to determine the ultimate issue of guilt or innocence.

Indeed, even those who would abolish the insanity defense—for example, the authors of the New York State Department of Mental Hygiene Report[1]—often support in its place a rule of "diminished capacity," under which "evidence of abnormal mental condition would be admissible to affect the degree of crime for which the accused could be convicted." Though the authors of that report state that under such a rule, "a psychiatrist would be limited to testimony and documentary evidence of an accused's capacity for culpable conduct,"[1] it seems to me that all the problems with psychiatric testimony that supposedly adhere to the availability and use of the insanity defense would also adhere to the determination of the issue of diminished capacity. The only thing that would be different under the proposed rule is that psychiatric testimony would no longer be able to eventuate in the complete exculpation of defendants.

Perhaps that is what much of the shouting is really about: fear on the part of the public that the existence of the insanity defense allows psychiatrists to convince juries that bad and dangerous people should be treated leniently—too leniently for the public's taste; and fear on the part of the psychiatric profession that that perception will diminish the public's respect for psychiatry and psychiatrists. As I have already suggested, however, that problem largely can be resolved by limiting the insanity defense to a strict mens rea defense. Under such a strict test, the psychiatric witness would not have to engage in determining such ambiguous issues as whether or not a defendant's crime was the "product" of a mental illness (the Durham rule), whether or not the defendant could "appreciate" the wrongfulness of his or her conduct, or whether the defendant was "substantially" unable to conform his or her conduct to the requirements of the law. Under a mens rea test, such vague terms would be abandoned and the only issue regarding the defendant's knowledge would be whether or not the defendant was unaware that he or she was acting in a manner condemned by society. I submit that the answer to that question will almost always be clear from the facts of the case (e.g., whether or not the defendant planned an escape or an alibi) and from the results of the psychiatric interviews. While the question of whether a defendant lacked the capacity to conform his or her conduct to the requirements of the law inherently calls for a more subjective determination, the psychiatric witness always can—and should—make it clear that, while certain apparent facts may have led him or her, for particular reasons, to a particular conclusion on that issue, the issue of when free will is overborne by fear, anger, or desire is essentially a philosophical issue regarding which psychiatrists, as a group, have no special expertise. (That would not prevent the witness—or, during the summation, the sponsoring attorney—from arguing that given the evidence he has adduced regarding the defendant's mental state at the time of the crime, the reasons for crediting that evidence, the other facts of the case, the reasonableness of the witness' basic assumptions about human nature, and the cogency and logic of the witness' integration of all those elements, the witness' conclusion in this particular instance is meritorious and worthy of being adhered to by the trier of fact.)

There is an additional way to ensure that witnesses with professional credentials do not overly sway jurors in cases in which defendants seek to exculpate themselves, in whole or in part, by offering psychiatric testimony regarding their state of mind. Or, looked at from the perspective of the profession, there is another way to get psychiatry off the hook without foreswearing its responsibilities—and its legitimate claims to expertise—altogether. That way is simply for prosecutors to call the defendant himself to the stand for cross-examination when the defendant has offered exculpatory state-of-mind testimony via psychiatrists who have interviewed the defendant subsequent to the alleged crime (unless strategic consideration would make such a move inadvisable). Though at first glance such a policy would appear to violate the defendant's constitutional privilege against self-incrimination, and though I have not had the opportunity to research the issue thoroughly, I wish to argue that such a policy would *not* violate the Fifth Amendment. Consider, first of all, the fact that a criminal defendant waives the privilege when he takes the stand on his own behalf. When a mental health professional testifies, on behalf of a defendant, as to the defendant's state of mind at the time of the crime charged, the mental health professional is often doing little more than repeating to the jury—though perhaps in a more articulate form—the defendant's *own* description of his state of mind. There is nothing wrong with that. However, as the United States Court of Appeals for the Second Circuit has observed, under these circumstances the defendant "is able to get the effective benefit of testifying without doing so by having his experts testify at length as to what he said to them."[13] Thus, why shouldn't the prosecution have the same privilege it would clearly have if the defendant were to testify directly to the court? Indeed, the law is clear in most states that defendants who enter psychiatric testimony on their own behalf *do* waive their Fifth Amendment privilege to the extent that they must then submit to psychiatric examinations by the prosecution's professionals, who are then fully entitled to describe their transactions with the defendant—including the defendant's statements to them—to the trier of fact.[14] Why should that waiver stop at the courtroom door? Looked at from another perspective, What values protected by the Fifth Amendment[15] are served by allowing such defendants *not* to testify? The defendant's right to the privacy of his own thoughts that is protected by the Fifth Amendment is already vitiated by virtue of the fact that prosecution psychiatrists have the right to interview—indeed, interrogate—the defendant and present their findings, including the defendant's verbatim statements, to the trier of fact. Just as the prosecution cannot now use evidence obtained during psychiatric examinations to prove its case that the defendant committed the acts for which he is charged,[16,17] the prosecution would still have to prove its case-in-chief without resort to interrogating the defendant. Thus, the Fifth Amendment's protections against coerced (false) confessions would remain. Moreover, just as the defendant may now present evidence of his insanity and yet refuse to undergo a psychiatric examination, as long as the evidence produced is other than that of a post-offense psychiatric examination,[16] so too defendants should remain able to present nonpsychiatric exculpatory mental-state evidence without having to testify themselves. However, once the defendant does enter into evidence what is essentially his own version of his relevant mental state, he should stand no different from a defendant who directly testifies in his own behalf. To be sure, some truly disturbed defendants will be unable to maintain sufficient composure and coherence under the rigors of cross-examination to be able to adequately defend themselves; some might even suffer breakdowns. Some truly disturbed defendants may be all too willing to admit to powers of reasoning and control that were, in fact, absent at the time of their crimes. But such possibilities go to the issue of the defendant's *competence* to stand trial—as the trial is likely to be conducted. We can all think of defendants who claim a state-of-mind defense—e.g., Dan White, who recently murdered the mayor of San Francisco—who are nevertheless sufficiently capable of undergoing the rigors of cross-examination and sufficiently free of self-punitive motivations to be competent to stand trial even if they would be cross-examined. (If the defendant's competency is in question, the prosecution would have to decide, prior to trial, whether or not to call the defendant to the stand so that the defendant's competence can be determined accordingly. In any event, it would ill behoove the prosecution to call a truly disturbed defendant to the stand; the defendant's behavior on the stand would only argue for the validity of his claim of severe disturbance.)

Finally, a strict insanity test would yield the result that offenders who are seriously disturbed but not wholly lacking in mens rea would not automatically be confined to civil mental hospitals (whether or not that disposition was best for them, for the hospitals, or for the community), as must be the case if such individuals, under a broad or broadly interpreted insanity defense, are found not guilty by reason of insanity. Rather, if such individuals are effectively precluded from entirely exculpating themselves through the defense of insanity, they could be sentenced—if found guilty of some crime—with the flexibility required for reconciling their needs with the legitimate interests of society—to a hospital or community facility, if that is appropriate; to a prison, if the defendant cannot be safely managed elsewhere; and, most important, from one facility to another—within the time limits of the defendant's sentence—as the defendant's behavior and amenability to treatment dictate.

This brings us to the issue of sentencing discretion and the difficulty of reconciling the goals of limiting sentencing discretion with the goal of treating mentally disturbed offenders humanely and therapeutically.

The problem can be simply stated. To the extent that sentencing discretion is abolished, the judiciary will lose the flexibility that is required to deal with mentally disturbed offenders as humanely and intelligently as possible. This problem will be exacerbated if we severely circumscribe the insanity defense (as I have suggested we should), because fewer mentally disturbed defendants than ever will be able to avoid the harshness of criminal sanctions entirely by virtue of a successful plea of not guilty by reason of insanity. Indeed, proposals to abolish the insanity defense are often accompanied by proposals to treat mentally disturbed offenders at the sentencing stage with the flexibility and humanity that their condition deserves and requires.[18] However, to the extent that we allow judges to exercise such discretion in determining an offender's sentence, one of the prime goals of the sentencing reform movement must be sacrificed—the goal of ensuring that an offender's sentence will not be severely affected by the luck (good or ill) of the judicial draw and that similarly situated defendants will not be treated very differently simply because they come before judges of very different temperaments and philosophies. If judges have the flexibility to treat some offenders especially leniently, they also have the discretion to treat offenders unduly harshly; a disturbed offender's fate may then turn more upon the idiosyncracies of the sentencing judge than upon objective, or at least articulated, considerations.

Unfortunately, there is no simple solution to this problem, although it should be noted that even proposals to abolish sentencing discretion would permit judges to sentence offenders to the most appropriate facility available. What would be abolished would be the judge's ability to determine the *length* of the offender's sentence. Still, I think we would all agree that there are offenders who—though not legally insane (or lacking in mens rea)—have committed crimes largely in response to acute emotional stress (rather than out of hardened indifference to the rights of others) and that such offenders should not, and need not, be sentenced to long periods of incarceration, especially when such sentences may have no relation to the likelihood of when such disturbed offenders can be safely returned to the community. Thus, mental health professionals who are concerned with the fair and therapeutic treatment of the mentally disturbed should be wary of proposals to limit sentencing discretion.

Such proposals need not be unduly rigid, however. Indeed, I believe that the Morgenthau commission proposal strikes a proper balance between the goal of limiting sentencing discretion and the goal of allowing judges sufficient flexibility to deal fairly and helpfully with the mentally disturbed offender. Under the commission's proposal, the state legislature would continue to set maximum penalties for each category of crime, but an independent commission would establish guidelines (emphasizing the severity of the offense and the defendant's prior criminal history) that, within a narrow range, would indicate what sentence the judge should hand out in each case. However, and most important, the sentencing judge would be free to depart from the guidelines in unusual circumstances; though when sentencing outside the guideline range, the judge would have to make, on the record, findings of fact justifying his or her deviation from the guidelines, and the sentence would then be subject to appellate review (at the behest of either the defense or the prosecution). Thus, under the Morgenthau commission's proposal, judges would presumably be free to depart from the sentencing guidelines when an offender's criminal behavior was apparently the result of a severe or acute psychological disturbance and when an unusual sentence would best serve to "rehabilitate" the defendant (while still protecting the community).

This leads me to my final topic—the implications of the adoption of such a proposal for the utilization of professional psychological and psychiatric input into the sentencing process.

One thing seems clear to me: the adoption of the Morgenthau commission proposal would increase judicial requests for presentence psychiatric examinations in New York. This is because judges who would be inclined to depart from the sentencing guidelines in the direction of greater leniency, when faced with an apparently disturbed offender, will likely want to obtain professional support for their observations and decision to justify their departure from the sentencing guidelines and to avoid being reversed upon appellate review. (At present, sentencing judges rarely need justify their sentences—however harsh or lenient—to anyone.)

But can mental health professionals genuinely improve the rationality of sentencing decisions? More specifically, Can they determine any better than can judges when confinement is necessary to rehabilitate, or at least deter, particular offenders?; and if so, Can they determine how long such confinement need be? Can they determine—again, any better than judges can without their help—which offenders need to be confined to protect the community and, if so, for how long? These are the hard questions that must be answered before a thoughtful sentence can be imposed. It seems to me that the mental health profession has yet to demonstrate any special competence in answering these questions.

That pessimistic appraisal of the usefulness of presentence psychiatric reports seems, in any event, to be prevalent among judges themselves. Having attempted at least to survey the literature on judicial utilization of presentence psychiatric reports, the findings I have been able to uncover are that while judges frequently request such reports, they are rarely satisfied with the results. Even when judges do find such reports useful, it is usually only because the report has confirmed judicial conclusions about the defendant that were independently indicated by the circumstances of the defendant's crime and by the facts of the defendant's history. As one study concluded:

> It appear[s] that judges hope that psychiatry can tell them which defendants they can safely release to society, which of them will benefit from psychiatric or other rehabilitative treatment, and which are so dangerous that they will need prolonged incarceration. Most judges recognize that they are not given this type of guidance in the psychiatric reports they receive. [Many] judges complained that the reports they receive are too technical, unclear, conclusory, or perfunctory. In fact, there seems to be a widespread feeling that many psychiatric reports merely tell a judge the name of the defendant's mental illness, if any, but do not suggest to him what he should do with the defendant. The dissatisfactions with these evaluations may be due to the unavailability of first rate psychiatric services in some counties. However, it is more likely that the judges' dissatisfaction arises from the fact that the questions they want answered, those concerned with the defendant's dangerousness or potential for rehabilitation, are generally not questions that can be answered by psychiatric evaluation.[19]

It is hardly worth harping on the fact, at this late date, that it is indeed the case that psychiatrists have no special expertise in predicting violence. Indeed, that is now the official position of the American Psychiatric Association. It is not strictly accurate to state, however, that psychiatrists have no ability to predict violent behavior. The studies demonstrating the erroneousness of psychiatric prediction of violence all involved individuals who had not committed violence or threatened violence in the recent past. In such circumstances, presumably, *no one* can accurately predict who will and who will not be violent in the future. In other circumstances, however—for example, when an individual has a recent history of violence, is currently threatening violence, or still harbors delusional beliefs that led to violence in the past—more accurate predictions may be possible. It remains to be demonstrated, however, even in such circumstances, or in any circumstances, that mental health professionals can *better* predict violence or nonviolence than can laymen—including judges.

Probably the most intensive study to date of the use of presentence psychiatric reports is that conducted by Bohmer,[20,21] although her study was limited to the use of such reports in sex offense cases. In any event, she concluded that psychiatric reports had very little effect upon sentencing decisions, though she did find that judges were more appreciative of psychiatric reports that recommended long periods of incarceration than of reports that suggested more risky dispositions. Obviously, such harsher recommendations allowed the judge to impose a long prison sentence with a clear conscience, thus completely taking the judge off the hook. However, it appeared that such sentences were recommended and meted out in cases in which the defendant had a long and/or lurid history of offensive behavior, thus justifying a long period of incarceration (whether in a hospital or a prison) without regard to psychiatric input.

Along the same lines, (former) Judge Marvin Frankel has related the following experience with psychiatric presentence advice:

> An obviously disturbed, inadequate, and troublesome man had called the F.B.I. to tell (accurately) the train he was taking to Washington to assassinate the President. Seemingly "competent" legally despite his imprudence, he pled guilty to a charge carrying a maximum possible prison sentence of up to five years. The report I had requested confirmed that he was disturbed and troublesome, told other things I already knew, and concluded that, "giving serious weight to the nature of the offense and primarily for this reason," the defendant should be given the maximum sentence under the statute. Of course, if there was anything for which the sentencing judge would not be looking to psychologists and other experts outside the law, it was guidance as to "the nature of the offense." Undoubtedly, the vagueness of my inquiry merited no more than this useless response. I have tried since to do better. Sometimes, but rarely, the reports are more helpful.[22]

Judges also request psychiatric reports with some frequency, apparently, when they are confronted with defendants who, though not legally insane, seemingly committed their offense under the pressure of some acute and extreme stress. For example, one prominent judge told me of a case before him in which a man, who had never before had any difficulties with the law, had attempted a robbery—in a manner that suggested he *hoped* to be shot in the attempt—to get some money to pay for his son's upcoming bar mitzvah. A psychiatric presentence report was requested in that case to confirm the judge's suspicion—already formed from the facts presented by the nonpsychiatric probation report—that the defendant was, indeed, not a "bad" man, deeply inclined to crime, but a basically law-abiding citizen who had succumbed to unusual pressures and, given help at least, was unlikely to similarly misbehave again. Following receipt of the report—which, of course, confirmed the judge's perceptions—the judge did mete out an unusually lenient sentence. But again we may ask, Under such circumstances, was such a report really necessary? That is, when a man with a history of well-socialized behavior commits a crime for the first time in his life, and his criminal behavior was apparently triggered by extraordinary pressures, do we really need the opinion of professionals to conclude that such an individual is more amenable to rehabilitative efforts and less dangerous to the community than most offenders who commit superficially similar crimes? Unless such circumstances or similar circumstances exist, is there any basis for assuming that psychiatrists or psychologists can accurately predict which offenders are especially "good risks"?

In sum, let me suggest that there are likely to be few cases in which psychiatric examinations, as such, will produce either data or conclusions that can and will uniquely and validly justify judicial departures from sentencing guidelines. Such departures—whatever their direction—will usually be justified, if at all, by the objective facts of the defendant's crime and history (and by the "common sense" assumptions about human behavior that most judges and mental health professionals share). That does not mean that psychiatric presentence reports are meaningless or valueless. If such reports do no more than ease a judge's mind about acting in other than a rote fashion in certain (unusual) cases, or if they encourage a hesitant judge to take an unorthodox step, that may well justify the expense of such reports. And even if the data and conclusions derived from presentence psychological examinations do no more than confirm a judge's own judgment that unusual or out-of-guideline treatment is called for by the case at hand, such reports will have furthered the goals of sentencing guidelines by helping to ensure that when superficially similar defendants are treated differently from one another, it is not because of the whims of the sentencing judges, but because of the real and meaningful differences among the defendants that lay behind their similarities.

References

1. Department of Mental Hygiene. 1978. The Insanity Defense in New York: A Report to Governor Hugh L. Carey. Albany, N.Y.
2. Regina v. Prince, 2 C.C.R. 154, 163 (Brett, J.; dissenting opinion).
3. 1978. Wharton's Criminal Law. 14th edit. C. E. Torcia, Ed.: 134.
4. Powell v. Texas, 392 U.S. 514, 535 (1968).
5. United States v. Brawner, 471 F. 2d 969, 985 (D.C. Cir. 1972).
6. N.Y. Penal Law, section 15.05–1.
7. N.Y. Penal Law, section 15.02–2.
8. See, e.g., United States v. Park, 421 U.S. 658 (1975).
9. Lambert v. California, 355 U.S. 255 (1957).
10. STEPHEN. 1883. A History of the Criminal Law of England: 95.
11. Matter of Torsney, 420 N.Y.S. 2d 192 (1979).
12. Rhodes v. United States, 282 F. 2d 59, 62 (4th Cir. 1960).
13. United States v. Weiser, 428 F. 2d 932, 936 (2d Cir. 1969).

14. See, e.g., Lee v. County Court of Erie County, 27 N.Y. 2d 432, 318 N.Y.S. 2d 705, 267 N. E. 2d 542, cert. denied, 404 U.S. 823 (1971).
15. See Murphy v. Waterfront Commission of New York, 378 U.S. 52, 55 (1964).
16. See, e.g., Lee v. County Court of Erie County, 318 N.Y.S. 2d 710, 713 (1971).
17. People v. Finn, 406 N.Y.S. 2d 800, 801 (1978).
18. See, e.g., PUGH, D. 1973. The insanity defense in operation. Wash. Univ. Law Quarterly 87.
19. SHAPIRO & CLEMENT. 1975. Presentence information in felony cases in the Massachusetts Supreme Court. Univ. Suffolk Law Rev. 49: 66.
20. BOHMER, C. 1973. Judicial use of psychiatric reports in the sentencing of sex offenders. J. Psychiatry Law 1: 223.
21. BOHMER, C. 1976. Bad or mad: the psychiatrist in the sentencing process. J. Psychiatry Law 4: 23.
22. FRANKEL, M. 1973. Law without Order: 45.

WHEN TREATMENT BECOMES COERCION:
A LEGAL PERSPECTIVE

Alan H. Einhorn

Chayet and Sonnenreich, P.C.
Boston, Massachusetts 02110

INTRODUCTION

The struggle to enforce the rights of the institutionalized mentally ill has focused, in recent years, upon the emergence of the right of the patient to determine whether and when to assent to prescribed medical treatment and particularly upon the patient's "right" to refuse unwanted treatment. Efforts to enforce this "right" to refuse have highlighted the critical need to strike an appropriate balance between the rights and needs of the institutionalized mentally ill and the responsibilities of the state to provide for their care. Available judicial mechanisms have thus far proven incapable of providing that balance. This paper will explore the emerging "right" to refuse treatment in light of judicial efforts to adapt that right to the day-to-day realities of institutional psychiatric care. A mechanism will then be proposed that is designed to balance the rights of the patient and the interests of the state in treatment-refusal situations and to render prompt and responsive treatment decisions when such resolution is necessary.

AN HISTORICAL PERSPECTIVE

The American judiciary has long applied traditional notions of assault and battery to protect the individual against unwanted intrusions upon his physical and emotional integrity. The cloak of security that derives from the common law is extensive. Not only is the intentional touching of another's person without authorization defined as a legal wrong, but the "mere apprehension of a harmful or offensive contact" is also actionable.[1] The protection thus afforded "extends to any part of the body and to anything which is attached to it and practically identified with it."[1]

Applied to the relationship between physician and patient, these same notions of physical and emotional integrity are embodied in the doctrine of "informed consent." According to this doctrine, except in an emergency, a physician must inform his patient of the nature, benefits, and risks of a proposed course of treatment and must obtain the patient's consent to that treatment prior to its administration.[2] The premise of the doctrine is

the concept, fundamental to American jurisprudence, that "every human being of adult years and sound mind, has a right to determine what shall be done to his own body."[3]

While the doctrine of informed consent has been applied with some consistency in cases involving the treatment of physical injury or disability,

199

courts have been considerably more reticent to invoke the doctrine in cases involving the institutionalized mentally ill. This reluctance is the result of several factors, all of which reflect the difficulties inherent in applying rote legal principles to the uncertainties of institutional psychiatric care.

One of these factors is directly related to the competency requirement of the informed consent doctrine. As its foundation, the doctrine of informed consent presupposes that the party consenting to treatment can rationally and meaningfully assess the benefits and risks of a suggested procedure, along with those of alternatives, before choosing to proceed with treatment. Persons suffering from acute mental illness are often incapable of this type of rational assessment, however. According to one commentator:

> . . . in psychiatry the problem [of obtaining informed consent] is not acute, but chronic; not sporadic, but endemic. It is the nature of psychiatry to work with patients who suffer from impaired perceptions of themselves and the world. It is an impairment of the "consenting organ" itself which is being treated.[4]

As a result of this impairment that impedes "informed" consent, a physician responsible for the care of a psychiatric patient is often faced with either foregoing treatment he deems essential to the patient's care; treating the patient without consent; or seeking a declaration of incompetence and appointment of a guardian—a procedure that, as described below, is often unresponsive to the patient's immediate needs. Because strict application of the competency requirement of the doctrine of informed consent would thus create formidable barriers to psychiatric treatment, the courts have generally been unwilling to question the medical judgments of physicians confronted with this dilemma. The usual presumption that an adult is competent until proven otherwise—and that he is therefore entitled, unless adjudicated incompetent, to refuse prescribed treatment—has accordingly often been ignored.[5]

Judicial reticence in applying common-law notions to the institutional setting can also be attributed to the judiciary's reluctance to second-guess medical judgments that a "psychiatric emergency" exists. The concept of psychiatric emergency is critical to the formulation of a right to refuse treatment, because the existence of an emergency relieves the physician of the requirement that he obtain a patient's consent before administering treatment.[2,6] Inasmuch as the patient in effect only retains his "right" to refuse treatment in nonemergent circumstances, the definition of "emergency" establishes the parameters of this right.

Attempts to define "emergency" in the institutional setting have provided little guidance to those seeking to ascertain the parameters of a right to refuse treatment. Part of the problem lies in the nature of the psychiatric emergency itself. Unlike many medical emergencies, a psychiatric emergency often has no clearly identifiable onset or duration.

> In fact it can be said that certain [psychiatric] patients are in a chronic emergency state, either in that violent or dangerous behavior is just barely being kept under control, or that they are so sensitive to stimuli that one must be constantly alert for developing signs of a violent outburst.[7]

Institutionalization only complicates the dilemma. The so-called chronic emergency patient may pose an imminent and continuous threat of serious harm not only to himself, but to those around him by virtue of his confinement with others. Under these conditions, and given the special needs of the seriously mentally ill, the courts have been loathe to restrict the treatment prerogatives of institutional medical personnel.

Still another rationale for the reluctance of the judiciary to enforce the doctrine of informed consent within the institutional setting is the changing character of the inpatient population of state psychiatric facilities. State statutes and court rulings,[8,9] increasingly sensitive to the psychological aspects of criminal behavior, have resulted in hospitalization for many persons who would previously have been incarcerated for antisocial conduct. In addition, virtually every state now requires that a person be considered "dangerous" either to himself or others before he can be committed involuntarily for institutional psychiatric care.* As these developments increased the influx of more seriously ill and dangerous patients into state psychiatric facilities, the introduction and widespread use of psychopharmacological agents, as well as a growing acceptance of the concept of community mental health care, began to reduce the number of treatable and less seriously ill patients in state facilities. The net effect of these changes has been an increasingly volatile and disturbed inpatient population, which has laid added stress on an already overburdened, underfinanced, and understaffed state hospital system. The multiplicity of needs of this patient population, added to the burdens already placed on institutional personnel, have further encouraged judicial restraint vis-à-vis those charged with treatment responsibility.

EMERGENCE OF THE "RIGHT" TO REFUSE

Largely as a result of judicial reluctance to apply common-law principles within the institutional milieu, the scales of justice until recently have tipped decidedly against the interests of the patient. Developments over the last several years, however, have begun to readjust that balance.

The courts have finally begun to reverse the disturbing trend of equating the principles of "commitability" and "incompetency" for purposes of authorizing treatment without consent.† And recent state statutes have specifically distinguished those terms[11] so as to eradicate the presumption that incompetency necessarily flows from commitment.[5]

At the same time, judicial rulings in related areas have evidenced a growing sensitivity to the concepts of human dignity and human choice vis-à-vis the adminstration of unwanted medical treatment.[12,13] Commentators,

---

* In Massachusetts, for example, no person may be committed to a state mental health facility absent a finding that (1) the person is mentally ill, and (2) the discharge of such person from a facility would create a likelihood of serious harm (Mass. G.L.A. c. 123, §8).

† See, e.g., *Winters* v. *Miller.*[10] In that case, the court ruled that a finding of mental illness and commitment to a hospital do not raise even a presumption that the patient is incompetent or unable to manage adequately his own affairs.

including the American Psychiatric Society, have begun to endorse the notion that the involuntary administration of medical treatment is often detrimental to the rehabilitation of the patient and, consequently, to the very purpose of commitment.‡

In conjunction with this increasing sensitivity to the rights and needs of institutionalized psychiatric patients, a growing body of judicial precedent has emerged, reflecting a trend toward the widespread recognition of a "right" to refuse treatment. In *Knecht* v. *Gillman*, for example, the court sustained allegations that the use of an emetic drug on nonconsenting inmates for violations of behavior protocols constituted cruel and unusual punishment.[15] The drug apomorphine had been administered intramuscularly by a nurse as a means to punish undesired behavior. It induced vomiting for periods of 15 minutes to an hour and temporary cardiovascular difficulties. The court enjoined the use of the drug at the facility unless (1) written consent were obtained describing the nature of the treatment proposed, along with its purposes, risks, and effects, and specifically informing the inmate of his right to withdraw his consent at any time; and (2) each treatment administered were authorized by a physician, based upon personal observation, and administered by a physician or nurse.

In *Mackey* v. *Procunier*, the ninth circuit reversed the dismissal of an action brought by an inmate who had been administered succinylcholine as part of a medical experiment.[16] The experiment was designed to ascertain whether behavior could be modified by instilling fear, by inflicting pain, and by psychological suggestion. The court wrote, "Proof of such matters could, in our judgment, raise serious constitutional questions respecting cruel and unusual punishment or impermissible tinkering with the mental processes."[16]

In *Kaimowitz* v. *Michigan Department of Mental Health*, decided the same year as *Mackey*, a Michigan state court enjoined an ongoing experimental psychosurgery program on common-law and constitutional grounds.[17] Although the patient in that instance had actually consented to the surgery, and although the technique had been approved by two hospital committees, the court found that the coercive institutional setting, coupled with the speculative yet irreversible effects of psychosurgery, required the termination of the program. In rendering its decision, the court noted that

psychosurgery is clearly experimental, poses substantial danger to research subjects, and carries substantial unknown risks.[17]

Similar concerns were noted by the court in the landmark case of *Wyatt* v. *Stickney*,[18] in which the Federal District Court for the District of Alabama ruled that institutionalized mental patients have a right to be free

‡ The American Psychiatric Association takes the following position on informed consent: "The American Psychiatric Association is aware of the possibility that the right to adequate care and treatment may be understood and even be used in some cases in a coercive manner. We therefore wish to clearly indicate that our concern is that adequate care and treatment be available. As is the practice generally in medicine, the patient's informed consent for treatment is required except for emergency situations."[14]

from unusual and hazardous treatment procedures, such as lobotomy, electroconvulsive therapy (ECT), and aversive reinforcement conditioning, done without their consent.

While many of the early so-called right-to-refuse cases have recognized such a right only in circumstances involving the use of aversive and intrusive treatment modalities—e.g., psychosurgery, ECT, aversive reinforcement conditioning—or in circumstances where modalities otherwise customarily employed had been used for experimentation or punishment, recent decisions have extended the "right" to refuse to include customary and accepted forms of treatment. Thus, in the case of *In re Boyd*,[19] the lower court dismissed an action brought by an incompetent patient who had refused certain nonessential psychotropic medication on religious grounds. The Court of Appeals for the District of Columbia reversed, indicating that the trial court had failed to give sufficient weight to the patient's religious beliefs. In so ruling, the court acknowledged the principle that medical treatment may not be imposed on a competent person who rejects it, absent a compelling state interest.

Similarly, in *Rennie* v. *Klein*, a federal district court in New Jersey held that involuntary psychiatric patients possess a qualified right to refuse psychotropic medication.[20] And in *Rogers* v. *Okin*, the Federal District Court for the District of Massachusetts ruled that patients confined to psychiatric institutions have the right to be free from forced medication and seclusion in nonemergent circumstances.[21]

The "right" to refuse thus recognized, though perhaps derived from common-law notions of physical and emotional integrity, is based upon a variety of constitutional predicates, including First Amendment freedom of expression, thought,[17] and religion;[6,10,19] the right to privacy under the penumbra of the Bill of Rights;[6,20] the right to be free from cruel and unusual punishment under the Eighth Amendment;[15,16] and the Fifth and Fourteenth Amendment rights to due process protection against invasion of personal liberty.[10]

Enforcing the Newfound Right

Although constitutionally based, the "right" to refuse, like other constitutional rights, is not absolute. If the state can establish compelling reasons for imposing treatment against a person's will, courts will allow treatment to proceed.[5,20] In order to conscientiously enforce the "right" to refuse treatment, therefore, there must exist a mechanism whereby both the rights of the patient and the interests of the state are weighed. Such a mechanism must be capable of promptly and sensitively responding to day-to-day treatment dilemmas, protecting patients' rights, assessing the interests of the state, and authorizing the administration of necessary treatment.

Traditionally, psychiatric treatment decisions were made by the attending physician. In theory, the physician was best suited to advise the patient of treatment choices based upon his firsthand knowledge of the patient's illness, history, and needs and the rapport that he had developed with the patient over time. In addition, the physician had presumably been trained to diagnose the patient's illness, assess the various treatment options available, and choose the most appropriate mode. However, at least with respect to physicians in state psychiatric institutions, irregular staffing patterns and insufficient manpower, along with deteriorating facilities, often preclude any one physician from obtaining firsthand knowledge of a patient's illness or history, or from developing a physician-patient relationship. Indeed, treatment regimens are often administered by inadequately educated or trained nonphysician employees and are used for control rather than treatment. As courts have become increasingly aware of these facts, they have grown reluctant to delegate decision-making authority for a patient's well-being to his treating physician.

Presently available judicial mechanisms for the enforcement of the "right" to refuse treatment have similarly proven to be unworkable. One such mechanism is the statutory guardianship procedure existing under state law. The rationale underlying this procedure is that a patient is competent—and thus has the right to make his own treatment choices—unless he is adjudicated incompetent by a court of law, and a guardian appointed to render decisions for him. The guardianship procedure is an expensive, time-consuming process that is unresponsive to the immediate and changing needs of the institutionalized patient. Moreover, the relief afforded by such a procedure is often unnecessarily broad, given the reasons for its invocation. The procedure provides for a finding of general incompetency and the appointment of a guardian over both the patient's person and estate for an indefinite period of time, when all that may be required is a decision with respect to a particular treatment. In addition, a legal determination of "incompetence" deprives the patient of his basic rights as a citizen, e.g., he may no longer enter into legal relationships. Finally, an adjudication of "incompetence" carries with it a social stigma that may be difficult, if not impossible, to overcome.

The procedure originally employed by the court in *Rennie* v. *Klein* (*Rennie I*)§ to evaluate the plaintiff's refusal to accept psychotropic medication typified the impracticality and inappropriateness of traditional judicial mechanisms for everyday treatment decisions regarding the mentally ill. While the *Rennie* court did not convene a competency/guardianship proceeding, it did provide for a full-scale hearing before a court. In fact, as of November 9, 1978, some 11 months after the case was brought, the *Rennie* court had conducted two full hearings, resulting in two written opinions, regarding treatment decisions involving but one individual and only two specific treatment episodes.

What becomes clear, based on *Rennie I*, is that traditional judicial process—encompassing delays, protracted hearings, expert testimony, and written opinions—does not respond to the need for immediate attention and

---

§ *Rennie I* refers to the proceedings up to and including the decision reported at 462 F. Supp. 1131 (D.N.J. 1979) (Reference 20.)

continuity of care of patients in psychiatric facilities, where tens or even hundreds of refusals of treatment may occur daily. The enormous burden of time, energy, and expense that will befall courts, institutions, and physicians alike if day-to-day treatment decisions are undertaken by the courts, and the potential for harm to patients resulting from unavoidable and interminable delays, hardly justifies the perpetuation of a *Rennie I*-type scenario, as the *Rennie* court later tacitly acknowledged.

An independent, interdisciplinary review board is another mechanism that has been suggested as a means of deciding issues arising from refusals of treatment. Although such mechanisms are presently used in many psychiatric hospitals for review of protocols for experimentation with human subjects, the process has yet to receive judicial sanction for the purpose of monitoring daily treatment decisions. A specific model for such a mechanism was suggested by the Massachusetts Psychiatric Society in its amicus brief filed in the case of *Rogers* v. *Okin*.[7] This model would provide for a three-member review board, independent of the institution, composed of an attorney and two psychiatrists. The attorney, as chairman, would ensure that patients' rights were considered. The psychiatric members of the board would provide the expertise required to evaluate the correctness of the patient's diagnosis, the appropriateness of the suggested treatment, and the availability of less restrictive alternatives to that treatment.

The function of the board would be to review all refusals of treatment that the attending physician deems essential. In the case of such a refusal, the board would hold an informal hearing at which the patient and his attorney could be present. All relevant testimony and evidence would be received. The board would authorize the treatment only if it determined that the patient's refusal resulted from diminished mental capacity attributable to mental illness and that the patient's overall best interests would be served by the treatment, even if it were administered forcibly. Decisions of the review board would be appealable to the courts.

The review board, like its predecessors, has several flaws that render it unfit for its intended purpose. The first is its hearing procedure, which, much like its judicial counterpart, is unsuited to prompt review and immediate decision making. The second is its size; it is unlikely that a board composed of three professionals will be quick enough to respond to the urgency of many refusal situations. In addition, the mere fact that the board would not be located in the facility ensures delay. Finally, there is the inevitable expense attributable to a system that envisions the employment of three professionals, representation by attorneys, preparation of documents, conducting of hearings, etc. Clearly a less cumbersome, more responsive mechanism is necessary.

The most encouraging development vis-à-vis the creation of a mechanism to enforce the "right" to refuse is the recent order of the Federal District Court for the District of New Jersey in the case of *Rennie* v. *Klein* (*Rennie II*).¶

¶ CA No. 77-2624, Sept. 14, 1979 (Reference 20).

Plaintiff-patients in that action petitioned the court for a preliminary injunction to restrain physicians and institutions from administering psychoactive drugs without the patients' freely given consent obtained under procedural safeguards. In rendering its decision, the court reaffirmed its prior finding that the plaintiffs enjoyed a qualified "right" to refuse treatment; ruled that patients are entitled to some due process protection before psychoactive drugs may be administered to them; held that the "right" to refuse can be enforced only if informed consent is obtained prior to treatment; and held that a patient's refusal of treatment can be overriden only if countervailing state interests so required.‖ At the same time, the court issued an order establishing a mechanism for the enforcement of the patient's rights. That order provided for (1) the obtaining of informed consent on written consent forms prior to the administration of medication; (2) a system of patient advocates to analyze instances in which the treating physician certifies that a patient is incapable of providing informed consent (in which case the advocate would be authorized to seek independent review of the physician's treatment decision) and to serve as informal counsel before an informal reviewer; (3) informal review by an independent psychiatrist before an involuntary patient may be forcibly medicated; (4) enforcement of voluntary patients' right to refuse treatment; and (5) forced medication only in emergency circumstances. The court ruled finally that independent lawsuits alleging violations of patients' civil rights would not be barred by its order.

ANOTHER ALTERNATIVE

The *Rennie II* approach is a constructive step in the search for a mechanism that would responsively and responsibly monitor both the rights of the patient and the interests of the state as they relate to treatment decisions in state psychiatric facilities. The *Rennie II* approach does have several shortcomings, however; perhaps the most important is its failure to impose a different standard of review for patients who are deemed by the independent review to be "functionally competent," as opposed to "incompetent," to make treatment decisions. In addition, the court neglected to indicate whether the mechanism would be available in close proximity to the facility on a continuous basis.

In seeking to improve upon the mechanism established by the court in *Rennie II*, any alternative mechanism should satisfy at least the following criteria: (1) it must be capable of providing a prompt resolution of dilemmas regarding consent to treatment; (2) it must be available on a round-the-

---

‖ Factors to be considered when assessing the countervailing state interests involved were stated to be (1) the nature of the physical threat posed by the patient to other patients and staff; (2) the patient's capacity to make a decision relative to his own treatment; (3) the existence of less restrictive treatment alternatives; and (4) the risk of permanent side effects from the proposed treatment.

clock basis; (3) it must be independent of the institution served, the treating physicians, and the patient; (4) its implementers must have appropriate training to assess the patient's condition and the treatment offered; and (5) the resulting decision must have the force of law. Such a mechanism is described below.

The mechanism proposed is similar to that in *Rennie II*. It shall be referred to as the "civil rights officer" (CRO). CROs would be selected from a panel of qualified psychiatrists appointed by the superior court for the jurisdiction in which the facility is located. They would be selected by the superior court judge and assigned to an individual inpatient treatment facility for 8-hour shifts. One CRO would be assigned to each such facility on a 24-hour-a-day, 7-day-a-week basis. The CRO would be a magistrate of the court, employed and salaried by the court, and would have experience and training in the civil rights area.

The sole function of the CRO would be to review and evaluate treatment decisions either when the patient's ability to render such a decision is alleged to be impaired or when the patient has refused treatment that is considered essential to his well-being. Upon being so notified, the CRO would immediately interview the treating physician and the patient refusing treatment. As in *Rennie II*, the patient would be entitled to informal counsel from a patient advocate, also available on a 24-hour-per-day basis and appointed by the state department of mental health. The CRO could seek information from any person who has knowledge pertinent to the patient's case.

Upon completion of this fact-finding function, the CRO would consider the circumstances and the necessity for providing substitute consent and would, to the extent possible, render an immediate decision which would be entered into the patient record. The following factors would be considered by the CRO for purposes of his decision: the apparent capability of the patient to render a reasoned decision regarding treatment; the degree and intrusiveness of the treatment mode suggested; the permanence and severity of the procedure's effects; the existence of less drastic means of accomplishing the same purpose; the reasons for the patient's refusal; the nature of the symptoms for which the treatment is offered; and the effects on the patient and those around him if treatment were not administered. If the CRO determined that the patient did not have the capability to render a rational decision regarding treatment and that his "best interests," on the basis of the factors noted above, would be served by administration of the treatment, such treatment would be administered. If the CRO determined that the patient did have the capability to render a rational decision regarding treatment, the treatment would be withheld unless there were a compelling reason to override the patient's refusal and no acceptable alternative treatment existed. All decisions of the CRO would be subject to appeal to the local court of general jurisdiction. The CRO would be protected from liability for any injury that might result from a good faith decision rendered by him.

CONCLUSION

The recent struggle to enforce the rights of the mentally ill has finally awakened our society and its legal system to the needs of those confined to psychiatric facilities. The response of that system, though cautious at first, has grown increasingly sensitive to patients' rights. The challenge now is to design a process that can balance those rights with the critical need for timely and appropriate treatment in the patients' best interests.

REFERENCES

1. PROSSER, W. 1971. Law of Torts. 4th edit.: 37, 34.
2. Watson v. Clutts, 262 N.C. 153 (1962).
3. Canterbury v. Spence, 464 F. 2d 772, 780 (D.C. Cir., 1972), cert. denied, 409 U.S. 1064 (1974).
4. JONSEN, A. R. & B. EICHELMAN. 1978. Ethical issues in pharmacological treatment. *In* Legal and Ethical Issues in Research and Treatment. D. M. Gallant & R. Force, Eds.: 145. S.P. Medical and Scientific Books. New York, N.Y.
5. PLOTKIN, R. 1977. Limiting the therapeutic orgy; mental patients' right to refuse treatment. N. L. Rev. **72:** 461, 488.
6. Scott v. Plante, 532 F.2d 939 (3d Cir. 1976).
7. Brief of the Massachusetts Psychiatric Society as Amicus Curiae, Rogers v. Okin, CA 75-1610T, U.S. Dist. Ct., Mass., p. 9.
8. Mass. G.L.A. c. 123, § 16.
9. Durham v. United States, 214 F.2d 862 (D.C. Cir. 1954).
10. Winters v. Miller, 446 F.2d 65, 74 (2d Cir.) cert. denied, 404 U.S. 985 (1971).
11. BRAKEL, S. & R. ROCK, Eds. 1971. The Mentally Disabled and the Law. revised edit.: 49-59. American Bar Foundation. Washington, D.C. (From Reference 5.)
12. In re Quinlan, 70 N.J. 10, 355 A.2d 647, cert. denied, 429 U.S. 922 (1976.)
13. Superintendent of Belchertown State School v. Saikewicz, 1977 Mass. Adv. Sh. 2461, 370 N.E. 2d 417 (1977).
14. American Psychiatric Association Task Force on the Right to Treatment. 1977. Am. J. Psychiatry **134:** 3, note 37.
15. Knecht v. Gillman, 488 F. 2d 1136 (8th Cir. 1975).
16. Mackey v. Procunier, 477 F.2d 877 (9th Cir. 1973).
17. Kaimowitz v. Michigan Department of Mental Health, N. 73-19434 AW-(Cir. Ct. Wayne Cty., Mich., July 10, 1973), excerpted in 2 Prison L. Rpts. 433 (1973).
18. Wyatt v. Stickney, 344 F. Supp. 387 (M.D. Ala. 1972), aff'd. sub nom, Wyatt v. Aderholt, 503 F. 2d 1305 (5th Cir. 1974).
19. In re Boyd, 403 A.2d 744 (D.C. App. 1979).
20. Rennie v. Klein, 462 F. Supp. 1131 (D.N.J. 1979) (individual action); Opinion on Plaintiffs' Motion for a Preliminary Injunction (CA No. 77-2624, Sept. 14, 1979) (class action).
21. Rogers v. Okin, D. Mass., CA 75-1610T, Order and Judgment, October 29, 1979.

THE PATIENT AS OFFENDER: PANEL DISCUSSION

Moderator: Donal E. J. Mac Namara
Panel Members: Albert Axelrod, Alan H. Einhorn,
Maurice R. Green, Thomas R. Litwack, and
Alexander B. Smith

D. E. J. MAC NAMARA (*John Jay College of Criminal Justice, New York, N.Y*): I'd like Mr. Einhorn to say a word about society's rights of protection or right to use unattractive alternatives as deterrents against the refusal of treatment.

A. H. EINHORN (*Chayet and Sonnenreich, P.C., Boston, Mass.*): As a practical matter, when you're dealing with issues that involve police power or issues that are controversial in nature, courts will agree that there's a balancing of interests and that society's interest is clearly one that has to be taken into consideration.

In one such case—involving a ward of the state who was absolutely incompetent to understand the fact that he had leukemia and was dying—the question was whether this individual was going to be subjected to chemotherapy, which would have enormous effects on him and which he would not understand. In that case, the court recognized and laid out one mechanism that would weigh and balance the interests of society against the interests of the individual and decided for the individual that treatment could be refused. In the case of venereal disease, tuberculosis, and various other diseases, it's pretty clear by state statute that there is a balancing of interests that would be applied to those circumstances requiring treatment on society's behalf.

UNIDENTIFIED SPEAKER: I would like to ask my question of Dr. Smith, and it's primarily about the role of confidentiality when working along with the criminal justice system as a psychotherapist. It seems to me that when a parole officer acts in the role of therapist, there is an issue of double jeopardy involved.

Usually, a client assumes confidentiality in a therapist, i.e., that the therapist is not going to reveal the things that are discussed in the session. This engenders trust and helps the therapeutic relationship along. I'm not sure that this kind of relationship can be developed with a parole officer.

Also, when a therapist in a mental health center is asked by the court to act as a therapist, the therapist is subject (at least in New Jersey) to be subpoenaed by the court, and the records are also subject to subpoena. That also raises the question of confidentiality in the case—whether or not the client can trust in the therapist when he is acting, at least in part, as an arm of the court.

A. B. SMITH (*John Jay College of Criminal Justice, New York, N.Y.*): That's a good question. Supposing we take the outside agency first. That's easier because the point is that if the outside agency will tell the court in advance that they will not handle the case unless they can maintain confidentiality (as they have this right), then the court may decide whether or not to make the referral. I'm not making this up on the spur of the moment—for a number of years I was attached to the BARO Clinic, which was a psychiatric clinic that was established in Brooklyn in the middle 1950s. The moving force was the then District Attorney Edward Silver, because a clinic of that kind was needed in Brooklyn. There were no agencies that could handle the prepsychotic, the postpsychotic, and the highly disturbed offenders who were placed on probation or parole. These offenders came to the clinic knowing that the ground rules were that confidentiality had to be maintained, that otherwise the clinic wouldn't take the referral.

Now as far as the other situation is concerned, by the very nature of the relationship of a probation officer to the court, or a parole officer to the parole commission, there are certain things that happen between the patient and the officer that must transcend the bounds of confidentiality. Whatever an offender tells a probation officer or a parole officer is not confidential, especially if it has anything to do with the possibility of his committing another crime or the disclosure that he has already committed a crime.

UNIDENTIFIED SPEAKER: I'd like to ask Professor Mac Namara to give us a list of those things that work. Wouldn't it be in the public interest to try to get those things applied?

D. E. J. MAC NAMARA: I would be very hesitant to state dogmatically that any single approach works in a generality of cases. There are some techniques that have been shown in one or more experiments to work with a larger number of offenders than do other techniques that are presently being used, or that have been shown to work better than no technique at all. However, in the opinion of many persons who are concerned with prison reform, inmate's rights, political rights, etc., most of these techniques are considered to be assaultive, aggressive, invasions of privacy, mandatory or coercive treatment when no treatment is wanted, or a hurtful or punitive treatment even though punishment might not be its objective. Those persons have been strong enough in their pressures to disclose these techniques and get further public, shall we say, condemnation of them. They have been strong enough in their pressures to influence a major agency of the United States government to change the entire five-year development plan for a penal institution. They have been strong enough to influence courts to sabotage the Maryland program that was working at least somewhat better than any of the others.

Now my colleague who has just passed away, Robert Martinson—in his book *The Effectiveness of Correctional Treatment,* a very massive study—came pretty much to the conclusion that nothing works very well. But also in the process of doing that study, Martinson made it very clear that nothing much was being attempted and even those things that *were* attempted were done in such a slipshod way, with such poor methodology and such poor controls, that we don't have the documentation that you asked for.

I would like to have an experimental institution in the United States, where we could try out even wild ideas over a period of time until we could discover something that works. Perhaps a United States version of Herstedvester or something of that sort. So, I must admit that I cannot give you a direct answer, but those are some things I'll throw out at you.

UNIDENTIFIED SPEAKER: I'd like to direct my question to Mr. Axelrod. I was wondering whether guided group interaction is given concomitantly with other kinds of treatment.

A. AXELROD* (*Highfields Residential Group Center, Hopewell, N.J.*): To the best of my knowledge, programs utilizing guided group interaction use it solely as a treatment approach. That's generally true in New Jersey and in other programs that I'm aware of.

UNIDENTIFIED SPEAKER: I have a second question for Mr. Axelrod. You state that a basic assumption of the program is that antisocial behavior is learned by association and, conversely, that unlearning of antisocial behavior can be accomplished by association with peers who exhibit social behavior. Now if that were true, then would not the best peer group consist of those adolescents who have persistently exhibited prosocial behavior rather than those who are antisocial?

A. AXELROD: Actually, I think that all juveniles are both social and antisocial, that is, I think that everyone's behavior is prosocial in most aspects. It's only in limited areas that people act antisocially. So if you have a group made up of juvenile delinquents, for the most part they are oriented socially. In terms of making identification with each other, which is an important factor in developing an effective group, I think it's better if the people have something in common, such as identifying themselves as people who have gotten into trouble.

In sum, even though they are delinquent, they have prosocial values and can be effective in helping each other to improve their adjustment to the institutional setting and to the broader society.

D. E. J. MAC NAMARA: I'm going to allot Dr. Litwack 30 seconds to respond to the remark I made about his presentation.

T. R. LITWACK: (*John Jay College of Criminal Justice, New York, N.Y.*): Actually, I'd rather make another comment about something else you said. I'm not so sure that Dr. Mac Namara is correct in saying that the courts, as a result of suits brought by civil liberties lawyers, have significantly constrained the ability of correctional personnel to rehabilitate offenders. For example, Patuxent Institution in Maryland is still functioning—much to the displeasure of civil libertarians—and I'd like Dr. Mac Namara to be more specific about how these suits have forestalled adequate treatment.

As long as I have the microphone, I'd also like to add a few other, very quick points. One is that the Supreme Court ruled just last spring that before individuals can be committed to mental hospitals, there must be clear and convincing evidence that they meet the standards for commitment; so

---

* Mr. Axelrod presented the paper by A. Elias, as the author could not attend the symposium.

presumably it should now be the law that before someone can be forced to undergo treatment, there must be clear and convincing evidence that they need the treatment.

The other point I want to make, in response to Dr. Mac Namara's comments to my paper, was that while it seems to me that we need to reduce sentencing discretion (because some offenders are now incarcerated for too long a period of time and others for too short a period of time), and while the major goal of sentencing should be to protect the community, if you do get rid of sentencing discretion, you will still be left with a problem. Some people—who have really been entirely law abiding all of their lives—will suddenly, as the result of some very acute environmental pressure, go and commit a crime. And if there is no sentencing discretion, those people will be subject to long prison terms despite the fact that (without a finger lifted to rehabilitate them) chances are they would never commit a crime again.

For example, one told to me by a judge, a fellow who had a history of purely prosocial behavior, but who was very strapped for money to pay for his son's bar mitzvah, stuck up a store to get money to pay for the bar mitzvah—and did so under circumstances that suggested that he really hoped he would be killed in the attempt. Do we really want to treat that person like any other offender? And if we have the discretion to treat him otherwise, how do you limit discretion in other cases?

"SCARED STRAIGHT" AND THE PANACEA PHENOMENON: DISCUSSION

Discussant: James O. Finckenauer

School of Criminal Justice
Rutgers University
Newark, New Jersey 07102

Juvenile delinquency is one of the most difficult and intractable social problems facing America today. For example, one of only four priorities for action set by the National Advisory Commission on Criminal Justice Standards and Goals in 1973 was that of preventing juvenile delinquency. "Street crime is a young man's game," the Commission said in support of this priority. Our efforts to prevent and control juvenile delinquency over the past two decades might be described as a search for an elusive panacea. In the words of David Rothenberg of the Fortune Society, "We always seem to seek simple solutions for complex situations." If nothing else, the causes of delinquency are incredibly complex. Delinquency generally results from some combination of the following factors: perceptions of limited opportunities, peer group pressures, normlessness, poor early socialization experiences, social disorganization at home and/or in the community, and negative labeling. Because of the multiple paths to delinquency, it follows that there can be no easy or simple answers. But that doesn't seem to keep us from trying.

Webster defines panacea as a remedy for all diseases; a cure-all. One of the causes *and* effects of our failures and frustrations in dealing with juvenile crime has been a search for a cure-all. This search has been conducted not only by the general public, but by politicians, lawmakers, juvenile-justice officials, and social scientists as well. In this article, I will examine the panacea phenomenon in some detail; look at some of the reasons for our sense of frustration; discuss the "Scared Straight" program as a classic case in point; and suggest some possible implications.

The 1960s and 1970s have been replete with failures in the war on juvenile crime—and these failures were in no small part a result of programs being oversold at the outset. One early example was the massive ($12.5 million) Mobilization for Youth (MFY) project launched on New York's Lower East Side in 1962. This project was designed to combat juvenile delinquency by opening the neighborhood opportunity structure to deviant or potentially deviant youths. It failed largely because it did not account for other causes of delinquency; but responsible persons acted as if it were a surefire answer.

The War on Poverty begun by President Johnson in 1964 was built on the Mobilization for Youth model. Specific aspects such as the Job Corps and Neighborhood Youth Corps were further attempts to combat juvenile delinquency by enhancing legitimate opportunities for youths. These skirmishes against youth crime can be characterized as oversell and underperform. The first is an example of the panacea phenomenon, while the second has certainly contributed to our sense of frustration arising from failure.

The Omnibus Crime Control Act which created the Law Enforcement Assistance Administration (LEAA) in the U.S. Department of Justice has spent millions on crime control and criminal justice since 1968 without reducing juvenile delinquency. The same can be said of the Juvenile Justice and Delinquency Prevention Act of 1974. This is not to say that individual successes have not been achieved through both of these efforts, but rather that the oversell/underperform problem has plagued each of them. In each instance, dramatic breakthroughs were forecast but not realized.

On a more specific level, the diversionary programs and youth service bureaus that were advocated by the National Advisory Commission have, in the words of Bullington and his colleagues, been "widely advertised as a panacea not only for delinquency but also for the inequities and imperfections of the juvenile justice system."[1] Thus, whether it is on the massive scale of MFY, the antipoverty program, or LEAA, or whether it's on the individual program level, the vicious cycle continues. Legislation and programs or projects of various kinds are posed as cure-alls; they fail to live up to expectations which are frequently unrealistic; frustration sets in; and the search for the next panacea begins anew.

Social scientists and researchers also do not seem to be immune to this phenomenon. Here examples can be found when the issue is approached from the opposite direction—namely that of evaluation of treatment efforts. An excellent example is the work of Lipton, Martinson, and Wilks who reviewed 231 treatment studies in corrections—including juvenile corrections—published between 1945 and 1967. This review resulted in Martinson's assessment that "with few and isolated exceptions, the rehabilitative efforts that have been reported so far have had no appreciable effect on recidivism."[2] This became translated into a "nothing works" doctrine with Martinson's statement on a CBS "Sixty Minutes" broadcast that "there is no evidence that correctional rehabilitation reduced recidivism."

Martinson has been criticized for seeking universals in his evaluation, which is another way of saying he was looking for cure-alls. In a recent article, Michael Gottfredson points out that seeking universals is a widely known treatment-destruction technique.[3] He indicates that in seeking universals, an evaluator simply shows that although the treatment method has been found to work with some offenders, it is not effective with others; or that it has not been tried with all offenders. These are simply different versions of the panacea phenomenon.

One of the most recent answers to the juvenile delinquency problem seems to be to scare delinquents or suspected delinquents straight. "Scared Straight" has become the label for the Juvenile Awareness Project at New Jersey's Rahway State Prison. This label derives from the title of an Oscar award-winning film about the project which has been repeatedly aired across the country.

The film was first shown on November 2, 1978 by KTLA, Channel 5 in

Los Angeles. *TV Guide* for that evening carried the following blurb: "SCARED STRAIGHT! Special: Inside a maximum security prison. This hour-long program follows 17 juvenile offenders as they learn, at first hand, about the realities of prison life. Using brutally frank and frequently obscene language, 'Lifers' at Rahway (N.J.) State Prison tell the young people about the ultimate pay-off for their criminality." The film points out that some 8,000 juveniles had visited Rahway and that 80% of them had been "scared straight." Actor Peter Falk narrates the documentary, a factor that seems to enhance the authenticity and drama of the film.

In the time since the first showing of this film, there has been a clamor in some 38 states and foreign countries to create, mandate, and legislate similar programs in everything from local jails to state prisons. This new approach has been touted as the way to stop juvenile delinquency once and for all. Why?

Its appeal seems to stem partly from the fear of crime—juvenile crime—and particularly of the violent young hoodlums who are presumed to stalk the streets. It comes too from a sense of frustration that nothing else works. The ingredients for such a program—convicts, delinquents, and prisons—are readily available everywhere, and it costs little or nothing. Best of all, its success rate is claimed to be close to 90%. It is this unbeatable combination that seems to be responsible for a "Scared Straight" bandwagon, read panacea.

The core of this combination is the success rate. First, what about the 17 youths portrayed in the film? All but one of the 17 are claimed to have been scared straight based on a three-month follow-up. A field survey by the Washington-based National Center on Institutions and Alternatives resulted in a report that for 10 juveniles identified from the film, no involvement in the serious crimes alluded to in the film could be found. Some youngsters reported having committed some minor offenses, but were certainly not hard-core delinquents. Offenses included setting off firecrackers, smoking marijuana, and stealing cookies and candy bars. Some youngsters appearing in the film "Scared Straight" had previously attended the program, contrary to the impression given in the film.

What about the famed overall success rate? Almost from its beginnings, great claims of success for the project have been made by sponsors and supporters and by the lifers themselves. The figures used, however, are so subject to error and inaccuracies as to render them totally invalid. Among the problems with the figures are the following:

a. More than half of the juveniles attending have no record of delinquency. The fact that nondelinquents remain nondelinquent is no great achievement. These are not successes.

b. Some data are collected by means of letters sent to parents/guardians and sponsors within a short time after the juveniles visit the project. These letters ask for information on the subject youngsters' conduct after their visit. This method of collecting data is of the "to your knowledge" variety, and is thus too subjective and haphazard to be valid.

c. Replies to the aforementioned letters are frequently based upon follow-up periods of only days or a few weeks. The most hard-core delinquent may remain crime free over such a short period under any circumstances. Again, these are not successes.

d. Self-selection dictates responses to the letters. Because only some parents and agencies respond, they cannot be considered a representative sample of the whole. It is possible that only some who have good things to say, do so.

e. Recidivism is not defined or uniform for all those reporting. Does it mean rearrest or reconviction? Does it mean further problems in school? Does it mean further incorrigibility? Or, What does it mean? "Recidivism" for a nondelinquent is clearly a misnomer.

Results from a 16-month evaluation of the project, which is the only controlled study to date, show a success rate (no recorded arrests during a six-month follow-up) of 59% for an experimental group of 46 juveniles. A similar group of 35 youngsters who were used for comparison purposes showed a success rate of 89%. This study showed that more of the 46 attenders committed subsequent offenses, and also that they committed more offenses and more serious offenses than did their counterparts in the comparison group. Overall, the project was not successful with any subgroup in the attending sample when outcomes were compared to those of the comparison sample.[4]

Since this study was released in April 1979, an official survey of the records of 67 youths from Mercer County, New Jersey, sent to the project, disclosed that 51 (76%) were subsequently rearrested. Two other surveys reportedly undertaken in New Jersey counties resulted in failure rates of about 40% and 60% respectively.

A recent study by the Michigan Department of Corrections of a project called JOLT (Juvenile Offenders Learn Truth) resulted in its suspension. The project at the State Prison of Southern Michigan was determined to be of "no measurable benefit for those juveniles who toured the prison."[5] It is becoming more and more obvious that it is not possible to simply scare kids straight, at least to those who ever thought that there was a possibility.

The film "Scared Straight" seems to have misled the American public and some officials into thinking this is a miracle cure for juvenile crime. It has misrepresented the lifers' Juvenile Awareness Project by overemphasizing the scare tactics and by giving little or no attention to other aspects of the lifers' approach. It could result in the brutalizing, terrorizing, and traumatizing of youngsters across the country. For example, a report from Pennsylvania about a "scared straight"–type program disclosed that youngsters had been burned and otherwise physically abused by inmates. It may cause the exploitation of inmates and, at the same time, the demise of existing inmate efforts to help youngsters. In the long run, "Scared Straight," the film, could be the worst thing that ever happened to the Juvenile Awareness Project.

Beyond the seemingly inevitable conclusion that it is not possible to simply scare kids straight, we once again face the folly of searching for simplistic solutions—for panaceas. That road seems destined to lead only to further failure and frustration.

REFERENCES

1. BULLINGTON, B., J. SPROWLS, D. KATKIN & M. PHILLIPS. 1978. A critique of diversionary juvenile justice. Crime and Delinquency 24(1): 59–71.
2. MARTINSON, R. 1974. What works?—questions and answers about prison reform. The Public Interest (Spring): 22–54.
3. GOTTFREDSON, M. R. 1979. Treatment destruction techniques. J. Res. Crime Delinquency 16(1): 39–54.
4. FINCKENAUER, J. 1979. Juvenile Awareness Project: Evaluation Report No. 2. New Jersey Department of Corrections. Newark, N.J. (Unpublished.)
5. YARBOROUGH, J. 1979. Evaluation of JOLT as a Deterrence Program. Michigan Department of Corrections. (Unpublished.)

A THEORETICAL PERSPECTIVE ON JUVENILE INTERVENTION PROGRAMS: DISCUSSION

Discussant: Leendert P. Mos

Center for Advanced Study in Theoretical Psychology
The University of Alberta
Edmonton, Alberta, Canada T6G 2E9

It is my intent to sketch a theoretical perspective to evaluate intervention programs aimed at delinquency prevention and/or control, and the results obtained by James Finckenauer and colleagues in their study of Juvenile Awareness Project Help (JAPH).[1,2] Briefly, Finckenauer found that Juvenile Awareness Project Help did not influence juveniles' attitudes towards "justice," "law," "policeman," "prison," "punishment," and "self," or towards "punishment" and "obedience"; however, the project did result in more negative attitudes toward "crime." More importantly, the project did not prevent or control subsequent delinquency. In fact there was some evidence of an increase in delinquency and severity of delinquency following JAPH intervention. While these results may be disturbing to some, they should hardly come as a surprise considering the complexity of human conduct.

Traditionally, human conduct is viewed as normatively regulated. The basic assumption being that in the course of development, individuals internalize norms and values of their culture, community, or primary group and that these come to guide behavior. All education and socialization are based upon this assumption, namely that (prescriptive) beliefs are causally efficacious in conduct. Similarly, from this perspective, deviant behavior is viewed as failure to internalize norms and values or as internalization of deviant norms and values. Several ancillary assumptions are usually invoked to complete this story. The acquisition or internalization of norm and value beliefs and changes in these beliefs frequently require an affective context or relationship; and behavior following from these beliefs must have positive consequences for the individual holding such norm and value beliefs. These qualifications are important because they point out that the internalization of prescriptive beliefs must be supplemented by an account of the acquisition and role of beliefs about the anticipations and behavior of others. Indeed the nature of such beliefs, derived from the perceived anticipations of others, takes on a categorical character for the individual not unlike the prescriptive beliefs internalized during the course of socialization. It is the interactive process concerning prescriptions and anticipations that constitutes the basis for self-definition (self-concept). Presumably, prescriptive beliefs come to influence conduct only after the individual has acquired some beliefs about the anticipations of others, and the latter are probably best understood in terms of felt gratification relative to perceived opportunity. In any case, the claim that human behavior is normatively regulated must be qualified by a recognition that beliefs based on the anticipations and behavior of others might well result in suspension of or change in one's prescriptive beliefs, with a view to rationalizing behavior inconsistent with these beliefs but in some sense appropriate to the perceived anticipations of others.

The conceptual distinction between prescriptive beliefs and beliefs about the anticipations of others—one that is honored in one form or another in psychodynamic, behavioristic, and cognitive theories of personality—is made here for the purpose of evaluating intervention programs only. Thus, programs that are solely designed to change individual or group prescriptive beliefs—attitudes, values, and norms—with the assumption that these changes will result in the modification of behavior consistent with these changed prescriptive beliefs, deal with only one-half of the story. Conforming behavior is not merely a function of acquiring community prescriptions; it is also a function of beliefs acquired about the anticipations of others that may or may not have its basis in, or be consistent with, prescription-guided conduct. In fact, others' anticipations are more likely based on categorical attributions of inadequacy as the result of stereotype, prejudice, or ideology—and always on the basis of felt gratification and perceived opportunity experienced in concrete interpersonal relationships.

The distinction between prescriptive beliefs and beliefs based on others' anticipations can be brought out more forcefully if we consider a two-by-two matrix of beliefs about prescriptions and beliefs about others' anticipations. When prescriptive beliefs and beliefs about others' anticipations coincide, we have a situation where community standards are reflected in the anticipations of significant others and representatives of community institutions. Hence, a situation exists where individuals are "insulated against delinquency." In other words the individual in such a community has maximal opportunity for behaving in a prescribed manner and finds his conformity recognized and gratifying. Instrumental behavior is both appropriate to the anticipations and behavior of others and consistent with internalized norms and values. However, if within a particular community prescriptions are uniform but others' anticipations, for whatever reasons, are quite variable and at variance with prescriptions, we might expect behavior that is deviant from prescribed norms but appropriate to conditions of restricted opportunity and limited gratification. Similarly, if prescriptions are variable for members of the same community but the anticipations of others are uniform (a conflict of prescriptions is characteristic of a pluralistic society), we might expect deviant behavior that is nevertheless appropriate to perceived loss of opportunity and gratification. Finally, when both prescriptions and anticipations are variable, even when these coincide for particular subgroups within a larger socially mobile community, we essentially have a situation where individuals are "sensitized to delinquency."

Of course, an analysis in terms of prescriptions, anticipations, and self-identity is not novel, but the perspective does serve to bring out the complex and interdisciplinary nature of studying human conduct. Thus we might theorize about the psychological mechanisms that mediate prescriptions and anticipations (e.g., dissonance); point to self-identity as the pivotal process (rather than the mere information-processing flow from norms to behavior) for understanding (deviant) conduct; and suggest the relevance of biological considerations in the interaction of cognitive (beliefs) and emotional (gratification) factors in socialization and, hence, the development of self-identity. Furthermore the analysis has the virtue of being primarily social in nature. Self-identity has its roots in the perceived anticipations of others—which in turn are based on the self-identity of significant others and representatives of institutions—and the more formal processes of education, instruction, and nurture of prescriptions. Finally, the relative standing of prescription to anticipation beliefs avoids defining deviant behavior as necessarily against something, and instead views it in terms of self-identity validation. Therefore we might better appreciate the tenacity of the deviant behavior of those juveniles who have little to gain by conformity or much to lose by nonconformity.

Many intervention programs rely on the assumption that deviant behavior is either the result of ineffective internalization of prescriptive norms or effective internalization of deviant norms. Within this context, programs may attempt to change the values and attitudes of individuals or groups through some process of modeling or identification using credible or likable models. Alternatively, individual or group programs may attempt to normalize deviant values and attitudes by demonstrating that behavior following from these restricts individual opportunity and gratification—at least in the long run. It is not my intention to be critical of such programs, only to point out that they fail to recognize the importance of the anticipations (and consequent behavior) of others that constitute the basis of beliefs about opportunity and gratification and, hence, a self-identity that may well be at variance with wider community prescriptions. Conduct that is always selective with regard to self-identity can be most effectively modified by changing conditions of opportunity and gratification, that is, by changing the anticipations of significant others and representatives of community institutions. It is probably not too daring to suggest that programs aimed at delinquency control should probably have as their target representatives of community institutions, while prevention programs are best aimed at those who stand in a primary relationship to juveniles. In terms of the preceding matrix of prescriptions and anticipations, prevention programs are most effective when prescriptions are uniform and anticipations vary and when prescriptions vary and anticipations are uniform, while control programs are best restricted to situations where prescriptions and anticipations are at variance resulting in a sensitization to delinquency.

With respect to the Juvenile Awareness Project Help (JAPH), which is based on the deterrence conception of prevention, my preceding sketch suggests certain criticisms. The intent of the JAPH program is to prevent or control delinquency by impressing upon juveniles certain possible consequences of incarceration—consequences primarily of an aggressive and sexual nature committed by inmates against newly incarcerated juveniles. The impact of the program is presumably heightened by the fact that it was initiated and is conducted by inmates ("lifers") in a prison setting. No attempt will be made here to evaluate the proper application of the conception of deterrence; but it should be noted that the evaluation of potential risk (incarceration and assault) of unintended events (deviant behavior) might affect attitudes towards such events (e.g., Finckenauer did find increased negative attitudes toward "crime"), but they are unlikely to affect behavior that may or may not eventually lead to involvement in crime (*certainty,* not severity of punishment, is the most effective aspect of the deterrence notion). This is not to deny the relevance of the rationality of weighing consequences, but to deny the relevance of these consequences when they are far removed from, or irrelevant to, self-identity-validating (deviant) behavior. Another way of making the same point is to note that beliefs acquired on the basis of the lifers' anticipations are unlikely to affect self-identity because lifers are neither significant others nor representatives of community institutions, and they are themselves unsuccessful in maximizing their opportunities and gratification. It is not surprising then that there were no attitudinal effects relating to "law," "justice," "self," etc., since beliefs about these are acquired either as prescriptions or anticipations. According to the preceding analysis, if the juveniles' attitudes towards the "*self*" had in fact changed, we might then have some basis for expecting attitudes towards "policeman," "prison" and "punishment," etc., to have changed. Also, it is not surprising to find some change in attitudes toward the punishment of criminals if we consider that, despite all the verbal threats expressed by the lifers, they remain what they are, namely, lifers, who are losers and perhaps deserving of some consideration (syntony). In summary, with respect to attitude change as a result of JAPH intervention, we might do better to evaluate attitude changes of the interveners (lifers) than of their juvenile victims.

Without effecting changes in self-identity we would not expect changes in behavior. Nevertheless, exposure to JAPH intervention did appear to increase delinquency ("boomerang effect"). This is a puzzling result that deserves continued investigation. It is perhaps not irrelevant to point out, however, that the *content* of this community-sanctioned program is at variance with community prescriptions! This axiological oddity, which deserves study in its own right, might well serve to reinforce the difficulties juveniles face in attempting to forge culturally normative self-identities on the basis of varying prescriptions and anticipations resulting at best in self-deception and at worst in the deception of others. (The fact that JAPH intervention was more successful with nondelinquents than with delinquents supports this notion insofar as the former might well have better established self-identities and, therefore, are better able to consider distant consequences of their behavior.) Finally, while it is no doubt tempting to expose thousands of juveniles to a project that is economically and politically appealing, the time is past when such intervention programs can be implemented without a firm theoretical basis and a quality evaluation component.

REFERENCES

1. FINCKENAUER, J. O. & J. R. STORTI. 1979. Juvenile Awareness Project Help: Evaluation Report No. 1. Rutgers School of Criminal Justice. Newark, N.J.
2. FINCKENAUER, J. O. 1979. Juvenile Awareness Project Help: Evaluation Report No. 2. Rutgers School of Criminal Justice. Newark, N.J.

A SOCIAL PSYCHOLOGIST VIEWS "SCARED STRAIGHT": DISCUSSION

Discussant: Alfred Cohn

New College
Hofstra University
Hempstead, New York 11550

I have chosen to react to the film and to the lifers' program not in terms of whether the latter "works," a matter which I believe will be amply covered in this discussion, but as an academic social psychologist whose interests include persuasion, propaganda, attitude change, youth and identity, the criminal justice system, and ethics. I wish to raise some general questions from this complex frame of reference.

It is well known that the key to the successful solution of a problem in human behavior is often the definition of the problem. If we define our difficulty in cooperating with a coworker as: "He is an arrogant, self-centered, greedy individual," our action is likely to be very different from what it would be if we defined the problem as: "He is a shy and needful individual." The success of our attempts to alter our relationship hinges on the accuracy of our definition.

The lifers are seeking to deter youngsters from running afoul of the law. Their particular target, at least according to the film, is that group of boys and girls who have been, or appear likely to be, "in trouble." Their method of deterrence includes threats, intimidation, emotional shock, loud and angry bullying, and persuasion. They attempt to persuade their youthful targets, primarily with fear-arousing appeals, to eschew antisocial acts.

Let us speculate for a moment about this. Erik Erikson has suggested that young people are sometimes drawn to delinquency as a means of establishing a sense of self, an identity, albeit a "negative" identity. He writes that a "turn towards a negative identity prevails in the delinquent . . . youth of our larger cities, where conditions of economic, ethnic, and religious marginality provide poor bases for any kind of positive identity. If such 'negative identities' are accepted as a youth's 'natural' and final identity by teachers, judges, and psychiatrists, he not infrequently invests his pride as well as his need for total orientation in becoming exactly what the . . . community expects him to become."[1] A negative identity is described as "an identity perversely based on all those identifications and rules which, at critical stages of development, had been presented . . . as most undesirable or dangerous and yet also as most real."[1]

While the effects of fear-arousing appeals are not fully understood, it does seem that they are more influential if an alternative path is clearly mapped so that the target knows what must be done in order to avoid the dreadful fate depicted for him. It has also been suggested that persons who feel vulnerable to the threat may be so frightened as to feel compelled to deny, derogate, or otherwise reject the persuasive appeal altogether. A person who feels incapable of complying with the fear-arousing persuasion is also likely to reject it. Finally, persons who feel competent will be less influenced by such appeals.[2]

Now to the first point. Those young people who establish the "negative identity" of delinquent (a subgroup of youngsters in trouble) would be placed in a frightening conflict situation to the extent that they find the visit to Rahway pertinent and convincing. The conflict is between maintaining the (negative) identity and facing incarceration, on the one hand, and renouncing the (probably hard-won) identity and minimizing the threat of incarceration, on the other.

It is conceivable that, in response to the threat, one might even seek to strengthen the fragile identity by undertaking more delinquent behavior than one might otherwise have done.

A second point has to do with the desirability of exposing young people to this form of "The Treatment" at all. No psychologist could ethically subject research participants to such an experience. Number Seven of the *Ethical Principles in the Conduct of Research with Human Subjects* states that "the ethical investigator protects participants from physical and mental discomfort, harm and danger. If the risk of such consequences exists, the investigator is required to inform the participant of that fact, secure consent before proceeding, and take all possible measures to minimize distress. . . ."[3]

To be sure, dissuading a young person from criminal activity is a worthy goal. Similarly, involving offenders in humane public service is a worthy goal. However, one cannot but wonder whether these goals justify the procedures used and the stress generated. It is a terrible commentary on our country that we have men and women locked up, often for decades, and subject to the dehumanizing experiences and tensions of prison life. One wishes that our fabled ingenuity had yielded less destructive ways of protecting society and punishing malefactors, and it is gratifying to note recent changes in this direction. To me, it is desirable that the American public be made more aware of the conditions of incarceration so that people can be encouraged to develop viable alternatives. The lifers' program, as depicted in the film, is consistent with the latter goal but seems to encourage the very abuses that prisoners and the public ought to be challenging. The risk, as I see it, of viewers saying, "Look how effective our prison system is," is not to be denied.

To the extent that a macho young man feels humiliated in this frightening situation, and to the extent that his identity is threatened by the humiliation, he may attempt to strengthen his sense of self by reasserting his machismo in some antisocial manner.

To the extent that he feels frightened by the experience and lacks a means of coping with it, he may attempt to discredit what the lifers struggled to impart.

To the extent that he is present involuntarily, he may question the values and ethics of those who subject him to this scary program in order to brutalize him into conformity with society's requirements.

There is no denying that crime among young people is a major problem for all of us. Probably half of the people in this room have been victimized in recent years by offenders of tender years and tough exteriors. But the magnitude of the problem does not justify the reflexlike adoption of such a program as this. The very fact that it is appealing to a public that is fed up with young thugs, the very fact that it provides satisfaction and purpose to persons doomed to spend years in cages, makes it attractive at first glance. It seems useful and, if the film is to be believed, effective. It is inexpensive and, if effective in persuasion, probably cost effective as far as the public is concerned. But it appears to treat heterogeneous young people as being "all alike." It fails to take account of the individual differences among the youths exposed to it. Society seems unwilling to provide sufficient personnel and services to aid young people in trouble. Presentation of the lifers' program as a panacea, as is done in this film, allows us all to breathe a sigh of relief. We can "let the cons do it" and feel virtuous and vindicated.

In other words, we, as a society, are encouraged to "cop out." Perhaps some would-be offenders are deterred by this process of emotional flagellation. But where are the *different* strokes for other folks?

REFERENCES

1. ERIKSON, E. H. 1968. Identity: Youth and Crisis: 88, 174. W. W. Norton & Company. New York, N.Y.
2. MIDDLEBROOK, P. N. 1974. Social Psychology and Modern Life: 168–170. Alfred A. Knopf, Inc. New York, N.Y.
3. American Psychological Association. 1973. Ethical Principles in the Conduct of Research with Human Subjects: 61. American Psychological Association. Washington, D.C.

"SCARED STRAIGHT": DISCUSSION

Discussant: William J. Maguire

Rahway Prison
Rahway, New Jersey 07065

It has been said that the whole concept of the Rahway State Prison lifers' program, their Juvenile Awareness Program, can't possibly work. That it simply isn't possible to scare anybody into or out of anything. It's especially not possible to scare people straight.

It's been said that the hard-core criminals, the real dregs of our society who have been indicted, convicted, and incarcerated for the worst kinds of crimes against our society, are the last people on earth to properly impress any youngster and especially a youngster flirting with a life of crime.

Most pointedly, it has been said that the "Scared Straight" Program is self-defeating, that it possibly could have a romanticizing effect on impressionable young people, and that attempts to scare them straight from a life of crime are doomed to failure. This part of the debate surrounding the lifer's program has had the greatest impact on me. This lofty principle that it simply isn't possible and is indeed dangerous to scare anybody in or out of anything has struck me as the worst sort of argument.

Isn't it true that one of the first object lessons we learn as children is that if you play with fire, you're going to get burned? Isn't it true that we, as adults and parents of impressionable young people, have used the phrase for years? Isn't it true that our alcohol and drug-abuse programs, many funded by agencies of our federal government, at least in part try to scare young people straight by emphasizing the ways alcohol and drugs can adversely affect their lives, much the same as crime can affect their lives?

Isn't it true that our bicycle safety programs try to scare young people into realizing the dangers of two on a bike? Isn't it true that the national defensive-driving program, already attended by fifteen million Americans and compulsory if you have been convicted of moving violations, shows a fatal head-on crash in the first segment of its film? Isn't this an attempt to scare us into driving safely?

In so many ways and in so many areas of our young people's lives, in their impressionable years, we try to scare them straight about drugs, alcohol, bicycles, fire, auto safety, venereal disease, and crime. That's what the lifers' program is about. If we added crime to the above list, which the professionals don't want to do, the lifers' program could be viewed as an adult attempt and an innovation to help and influence young people.

There is nothing so very unique about the program. It's people who are there telling young people they don't want them there. Think about this one too: "Life or breath." How many times a night do you see that on TV? I must assume that most of you work during the day, but you must see it at night. "Life or breath." Scaring us away from smoking. I'm a two-pack-a-day guy, and I'll probably not see 90 years of age.

It's really not the scaring straight, but who is doing the scaring, that boggles the mind of the experts. The experts who have been trying for 200 years and have failed. They cannot accept the fact that the scum of society has come up with a program that works. Fifteen thousand children have gone through the program. Don't tell me it doesn't work. I've talked to too many parents. I've talked to too many children. I've talked to too many other experts. Judge Nicola from Middlesex County, one of the originators of the program, monitored 210 of the kids he sent to Rahway Prison personally, and followed them for one year.

He's an expert. I don't challenge him. I don't challenge Judge Kleiner from Burlington County who has sent approximately 300 children through the program and monitored 100 for a period of six months. He is now working on the second six-month period. I don't challenge his credentials. I don't challenge the credentials of Congressman Ike Williams. After the film was shown, it created such a controversy that people from all over the world were writing to the Rahway State Prison asking penal people, judicial people, and probation people: How do we start it in our own state? How do we start it in our own country?

And lo and behold, 69, 90, 120 days prior to that, the Finckenauer report becomes public. I don't challenge the credentials of Professor Finckenauer. He has the academic credentials to do this kind of work. But I do question both the academic background and the work experience of some of his analysts. That is subject to question. His was the only adverse opinion, from a professional, to come forth. But I have already listed half a dozen others. And I can give you a dozen others if you ask for them, I have their names, whose credentials cannot be criticized. They are professionals.

I'm not a professional. I'm a former mayor, one who had the powers of appointment from my juvenile commission. I'm a former county executive, responsible for the operation of our county jail. I'm now in the New Jersey Assembly on appropriations. So before me every year comes an endless line of money seekers. Every year they are looking for more money, more people, and more space—including my commissioner, William Fowler.

So I have a little bit of experience, but I'm not an expert. I have letters with me from parents, and I have letters with me from children. I tell you the program does work. The bottom line is, Who is doing the scaring? It's our convicted felons. That's why the experts are challenging it. I urge you to support the program. We've had over 15,000 children in this program.

The lifers are booked for the next 90 days, 5 days a week, 9:30 in the morning, and 1:30 in the afternoon. The children keep coming. Penal experts send them, mothers send them, school teachers send them, judges send them, psychiatrists send them, and psychologists send them. Are all of these people wrong? Hell, no! And the nice part about it is that—as a taxpayer you will appreciate this—not one penny of the New Jersey taxpayer's money is used to fund this program. Think of your tax dollars that have been spent on our alcoholic problem and look at the success that even the experts agree is marginal.

Look at the tax dollars that have been spent on the drug-abuse programs. Even the experts admit their success has been marginal. Here we have a program that doesn't cost the taxpayers of the State of New Jersey one lousy copper, and the alleged experts are shooting it down. They'll do it over my dead body.

SOCIAL STRESS AND MARITAL VIOLENCE IN A NATIONAL SAMPLE OF AMERICAN FAMILIES*

Murray A. Straus

Department of Sociology
University of New Hampshire
Durham, New Hampshire 03824

The work of the Family Violence Research Program over the past eight years has accumulated evidence that the family is the most violent institution, group, or setting that a typical citizen is likely to encounter.[27,28,29,33] There are of course exceptions, such as the police or the army in time of war. But the typical citizen has a high probability of being violently assaulted only in his or her own home.

This can be made clear (without, at this point, giving detailed statistics) by pointing out that the Uniform Crime Reports give data on violent crimes in rates per hundred thousand. By contrast, we found it more appropriate to report rates per *hundred,* rather than per hundred thousand or even per thousand.[33]

THE PARADOX OF FAMILY VIOLENCE AND FAMILY STRESS

Family Violence

These data point to the first of many ironies or paradoxes about the family. In this case, the paradox is that the family is also the group to which people look for love, support, and gentleness. The hallmark of family life is *both* love and violence.

Much of the work of the Family Violence Research Program at the University of New Hampshire has been designed to unravel this paradox. We are a long way from a complete explanation. However, some progress has been made. This paper examines one of the several factors that contribute to the explanation: the link between stress and violence.

Stress in Families

Another irony of family life is that, although the family is often seen as a place where one can find respite from the tensions of the world, the family tends to be a group with an inherently high level of conflict and stress.

* This paper is one of a series of publications of the Family Violence Research Program at the University of New Hampshire. The program is supported by the University of New Hampshire and by National Institute of Mental Health Grants MH27557 and T32-MH15161.

229

The theoretical case for this view is presented in detail elsewhere.[6,10] In this paper, there is space to illustrate only two of the stress-producing factors of the family.

First, in addition to the normal differences and conflicts between two or more people, the family has built into its basic structure the "battle of the sexes" and the so-called generation gap.

A second source of stress is inherent in what is expected of families. For example, families are expected to provide adequate food, clothing, and shelter in a society that does not always provide the necessary resources to do this. Another example is the expectation that families bring up healthy, well-adjusted, law-abiding, and intelligent children who can get ahead in the world. The stress occurs because these traits and the opportunity to get ahead are factors beyond the control of any given family to a greater or lesser extent.

The basic argument of the paper is that the second of these stress-producing factors is part of the explanation for the first. Specifically, a major cause of the high rate of violence in families is the high level of stress and conflict characteristic of families. Of course, this is only a plausible argument. Brenner, for example, has shown a clear relationship between stress as indexed by unemployment rate and the rate of assault and homicide in the United States, Canada, and Great Britain.[3] But is it other members of their own families who are assaulted or murdered by the unemployed? This needs to be demonstrated with empirical data. Consequently, a major part of this paper is devoted to such an empirical study.

THE THEORETICAL MODEL

Although the empirical findings will start with the relationship between the levels of stress and violence in families, it is not argued that stress *directly* causes violence. Violence is only one of many possible responses to stress. Among the alternatives are passivity, resignation, or just leaving. University departments, for example, are also stressful environments, but the rate of physical violence within such departments is close to zero.

The absence of a *necessary* link between stress and violence is shown in Brenner's data on the correlates of unemployment.[3] Unemployment is highly correlated with assault and homicide. But it is also correlated with hypertension, deaths from heart attacks, mental hospital admissions, and alcoholism. Similarly, Brown and Harris[4] studied a random sample of women in London, using highly reliable and valid data on life stresses. They demonstrated a clear tendency for these women to respond to stress by *depression* rather than violence.

Mediating Variables

FIGURE 1 suggests that other factors must be present for stress to result in violence. The center box of FIGURE 1 illustrates some of the other variables that must also be present to produce a correlation between stress and violence. For example, people are unlikely to respond to stress by violence unless this is part of the socially scripted method of dealing with stress and frustration—as it is in our society. Therefore, an important part of the model is the existence of norms or images of behavior that depict striking out at others when under stress as part of human nature.

However, these are very general behavioral scripts. They cannot explain *family* violence because they are part of the society's image of basic nature in *all* types of situations. These general scripts may be part of the explanation, but they are not sufficient. To find the additional variables that will lead to a sufficient explanation, one has to look at the nature of the family itself.

Normative Legitimacy of Family Violence

One very simple, but nonetheless important, factor is that the family has different rules about violence than do other groups. In an academic department, an office, or a factory, the basic rule is that no one can hit anyone else, no matter what they do wrong. A person can be a pest, an intolerable bore, negligent, incompetent, selfish, or unwilling to listen to reason. But that still does not give anyone the right to hit such a person. In

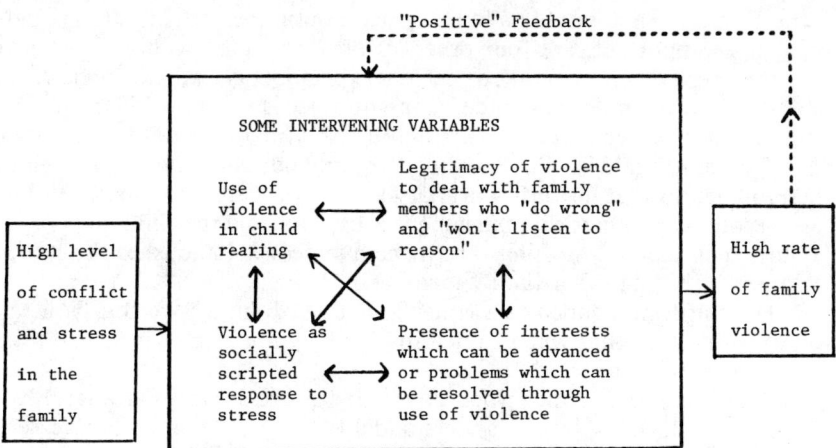

FIGURE 1. Partial model of relationship between stress and family violence. This diagram is labeled as a partial model for two main reasons: The most obvious reason is that it includes only a sampling of the intervening variables that could be included in the center box. Second, the model omits negative feedback loops (i.e., deviation dampening processes) which must be present. Without them the violence would escalate to the point where the system would self-destruct—as it sometimes, but not typically, does. See Reference 27 for a systems model of family violence which includes negative feedback processes and other elements of a cybernetic system.

the family the situation is different. There, the basic rule is that if someone does wrong and won't listen to reason, violence is permissible and sometimes even required.

This is clearly the case in respect to the rights and obligations of parents; but it also applies to spouses. As one husband said about an incident in which his wife threw a coffee pot at him: "I was running around with other women—I deserved it." Statements like that are made by many husbands and wives. In fact, the evidence suggests that a marriage license is also a hitting license.[28,31] Still, that does not explain why or how such a norm arose or why it persists. Here again, there are a number of factors, one of which is the use of violence in child rearing, that is, physical punishment (FIGURE 1).

Family Socialization in Violence

Physical punishment provides the society's basic training in violence but, of course, training that applies most directly to behavior in the family. At least some use of physical punishment is just about universal in American society, typically beginning in infancy.[24] What are the reasons for saying that learning about violence starts with physical punishment?

When physical punishment is used, several things can be expected to occur. Most obviously, the infant or child learns to do or not to do whatever the punishment is intended to teach; for example, to not pick up things from the ground and put them in his or her mouth. Less obvious, but equally or more important, are four other lessons, which are so deeply learned that they become an integral part of one's personality and world view.

The first of these unintended consequences is the association of love with violence. Parents are the first and usually the only ones to hit an infant. For most children this continues throughout childhood.[26] The child therefore learns that his or her primary love objects are also those who hit.

Second, since physical punishment is used to train the child or to teach about which dangerous things are to be avoided, it establishes the moral rightness of hitting other family members.

The third unintended consequence is the "Johnny I've told you ten times" principle—that when something is really important, it justifies the use of physical force.

Fourth is the idea that when one is under stress, tense, or angry, hitting—although wrong—is "understandable," i.e., to a certain extent legitimate.

Involuntary Nature of Family Membership

The last of the mediating variables for which there is space to discuss is the simple fact that the family is only a semivoluntary institution. This is most obvious in the case of children. They cannot leave, nor can parents throw them out, until a legally set age. So leaving—which is probably the most widely used and effective method of avoiding violence—is not available as an alternative in the parent-child aspect of the family.

To a considerable extent the same is true for the marital relationship. Ninety-four percent of the population marries, and anything done by this large percent of the population is not likely to be voluntary. No system of socialization is that effective. In fact, we all know the tremendous informal social pressures that are put on people to get married and stay married. Although divorces are now easier to get, the economic, social, and emotional barriers to breaking up a marital relationship are still extremely strong. Even couples who are living together without a formal marriage find it difficult to end the relationship. In cities like Boston and New York, there is a booming business in marriage counseling for the unmarried.

There are a number of other factors that should be included in FIGURE 1 and in this discussion. Those that have been discussed, however, should be sufficient to illustrate the theory that guided the analysis reported in this paper.†

By way of summary, the theory underlying this paper rejects the idea that people have an innate drive toward aggression, or an innate tendency to respond to stress by aggression. Rather, a link between stress and aggression occurs only if (a) the individual has learned an "aggressive" response to stress; (b) if such a response is a culturally recognized script for behavior under stress; and (c) if the situation seems to be one that will produce rewards for aggression.

SAMPLE

The data used to examine this theory were obtained in January and February of 1976. Interviews were conducted with a national area-probability sample of 2,143 adults. To be eligible for inclusion in the sample, each respondent had to be between 18 and 70 years of age and living with a member of the opposite sex as a couple. However, the couple did not have to be formally married. A random half of the respondents were female and half were male. Interviews lasted approximately one hour and were completely anonymous. Furthermore, interviewers were of the language or racial group that was predominant in the sampling area for which they were responsible. Further details on the sample are given in Straus, Gelles, and Steinmetz.[33]

---

† FIGURE 1 illustrates the general nature of the theory, without listing all of the variables that need to be taken into account. There are two aspects of the model that are included simply to alert readers to their importance, but that are not analyzed. First, this paper will not deal with feedback processes. Second, in the center box the arrows show that each intervening variable is related to the others. They are a mutually supporting system, and interaction effects are no doubt also present. However, in this paper, these and other intervening variables will be dealt with singly.

DEFINITIONS AND MEASURES OF STRESS

There has been a vast debate on the concept of stress.[15,16,18,19,22,23] For example, one issue is whether stress is a property of the situation (such as illness, unemployment, family conflict, getting married, or getting promoted to a new job) or whether it is a subjective experience. For some people a new set of job responsibilities is experienced as stress, whereas for others, *lack* of such new responsibility is a stress.

The definition of stress used here treats stress as a function of the interaction of the subjectively defined demands of a situation and the capabilities of an individual or group to respond to these demands. Stress exists when the subjectively experienced demands are inconsistent with response capabilities. This inconsistency can be demands in excess of capabilities or a low level of demand relative to response capabilities.‡

In fact, there is a gap between the definition of stress given above and data I will actually report. This is because the methodology of this paper *assumes* (a) that some life event, such as moving or the illness of a child, produces a certain but unknown degree of demand on parents; (b) that on the average this is subjectively experienced as a demand; (c) that the capabilities of parents to respond to these demands will not always be sufficient; and (d) that the result is a certain level of stress. On the basis of these assumptions, it is then possible to investigate the relationship between such stressful life events and the level of violence in the family. Obviously, that leaves a large agenda for other investigators to develop a more adequate measure of stress.

As indicated in TABLES 1 and 2, the aspect of stress that is measured in this study is limited to what are called "stressor stimuli." The data were obtained by a modified version of the Holmes and Rahe stressful life events scale.[13] Because of limited interview time, the scale was restricted to the 18 items listed in TABLE 1. (See APPENDIX, Section I.) The scores on this scale ranged from 0 to 18, with a mean of 2.4 and a standard deviation of 2.1. In addition to the overall stress score, we also considered different subgroupings of items. The subscores and their means are given in TABLE 2.

Sex Differences

The first thing to notice in TABLE 1 is that the experiences reported by the men and women respondents are quite similar. The exceptions are events for which men and women have different exposure. Thus, fewer women have paid employment, so it is not surprising that two to three times as many men as women experienced an occupationally related stress, such

---

‡ A more adequate formulation of stress includes a number of other elements. Farrington[6] has identified six components used in research on stress: the stressor stimulus, objective demands, subjective demands, response capabilities, choice of response, and stress level. Important as these six components are, there is no way to investigate them with the data from the sample.

PERCENT EXPERIENCING 18 LIFE STRESSES DURING PREVIOUS YEAR

Life Event	Male (N = 960)	Female (N = 1,183)	Total (N = 2,143)
1. Troubles with the boss	25.8	9.9	17.0
2. Troubles with other people at work	31.4	11.2	20.3
3. Got laid off or fired from work	10.0	5.9	7.7
4. Got arrested or convicted of something serious	1.9	0.9	1.3
5. Death of someone close	41.5	38.8	40.0
6. Foreclosure of a mortgage or loan	1.5	1.6	1.6
7. Being pregnant or having a child born	8.1	15.8	12.4
8. Serious sickness or injury	18.9	16.7	17.6
9. Serious problem with health or behavior of a family member	23.0	29.0	26.3
10. Sexual difficulties	9.0	13.1	11.6
11. In-law troubles	10.9	12.0	11.5
12. A lot worse off financially	15.8	12.1	13.7
13. Separated or divorced	3.6	2.6	3.0
14. Big increase in arguments with spouse/partner	8.1	9.4	8.8
15. Big increase in hours worked or job responsibilities	28.9	16.3	21.9
16. Moved to different neighborhood or town	17.2	16.4	16.8
17. Child kicked out of school or suspended	1.6	1.6	1.6
18. Child got caught doing something illegal	2.7	3.0	2.8

as troubles with a boss or losing a job.§ There are a few other interesting sex differences.

Item 4 shows that twice as many men were arrested or convicted of a serious crime. An interesting sidelight is that to a noncriminologist, an annual arrest or conviction rate of 2 per 100 men seems quite high.

The only other item with a nontrivial difference is item 10, having had some type of sexual problem in the previous year. The rate for women is half again higher than the rate for men (13.1 versus 9.0).

Frequency of Different Stressors

The most frequently occurring stress among the 18 items is the death of someone close to the respondent (item 5). This happened to 40% of our respondents during the year we asked about. The next most frequent stress is closely related—a serious problem with the health or behavior of someone in the family (item 9). This occurred in the lives of about one out of four. For men, however, occupational stresses occurred more frequently. Item 2 shows that about 30% had a difficulty with their boss, and at the positive end about the same percentage had a large increase in their work responsibilities (item 15).

§ The sex difference in item 7 (being pregnant or having a child) is probably due to men misunderstanding the question. It was meant to apply to the men as well as the women in the sample, in the sense of whether the wife was pregnant or had a child in the last year.

TABLE 2

MEAN SCORES ON STRESS INDEXES

Index	Items	Mean Score*		
		Male (N = 960)	Female (N = 1,183)	Total (N = 2,143)
Overall stress index	1 to 18	14.9	12.4	13.5
Occupational stress	1, 2, 15	28.7	12.4	19.7
Economic stress	3, 6, 12	9.0	6.5	7.6
Occupational and economic stress	Occ. + Econ.			27.3
Interpersonal stress	5, 9, 11, 16	23.1	24.1	23.6
Health stress	7, 8	13.3	16.2	14.9
Spousal stress	10, 13, 14	7.1	8.2	7.7
Parental stress	17, 18	2.7	3.1	2.9
Nuclear family stress	Spousal + Parental	14.3	14.2	14.2

* The scores are in percentage form in order to make the scores on each index somewhat comparable. Each is a percentage of the maximum possible raw score. Thus, a mean of 14.9 on the overall stress index means that this group averaged 14.9% of the 18 points that are possible; a mean of 28.7 on the occupational stress index means that this group averaged 28.7% of the three points that are possible on this index. See Reference 35, Chapter 2 for further explanation of percentage standardization.

DEFINITION AND MEASURES OF VIOLENCE

I can deal more adequately—both conceptually and operationally—with violence. This is because violence has been the focus of my research on families for the past seven years, and is the main focus of this study.

The definition of violence that underlies this research treats violence as one type of aggressive act. Therefore, I will first define aggression. *Aggression* is an act carried out with the intention of, or perceived as having the intention of, hurting another person. *Violence* is an act carried out with the intention or perceived intention to cause physical hurt, pain, or injury to another person. Violence, as I am using that term, is therefore synonymous with physical aggression.

Although this is the basic definition of violence used in studies undertaken as part of the Family Violence Research Program at the University of New Hampshire, it is usually necessary to take into account a number of other characteristics of the violent act. These include (a) the severity of the act, ranging from a slap to torture and murder; (b) whether it is instrumental to some other purpose, such as forcing another to do or not to do something, or expressive, i.e., an end in itself; (c) whether it is a culturally permitted or required act, or one that runs counter to cultural norms (legitimate versus illegitimate, or criminal, violence).

To illustrate these three dimensions in relation to violence within the family—a child may be slapped mildly for some misdeed or beaten so severely that medical treatment is necessary; the spanking or beating may be instrumental to teaching the child not to run into a busy street, or it may be done out of exasperation and anger—and the child may be of an age when the legitimacy of parents hitting a child is virtually unquestioned, as compared to the general illegitimacy in our society of hitting an 18-year-old child.

As in the case of the measurement of stress, there is a gap between what this set of definitions demands and what is available for analysis. The technique used is known as the Conflict Tactics Scales.[30] It consists of a check list of acts of physical violence. Respondents were asked about conflicts and difficulties with other family members. They were then asked whether, in the course of such conflicts in the past year, any of the items on the list had occurred. The list starts with nonviolent tactics, such as talking things over, and then proceeds on to verbally aggressive tactics, and finally to physical aggression, that is, violent acts.

The descriptions of violent acts in turn were designed to permit a measure of the severity as well as the frequency of family violence. The list starts out with pushing, slapping, shoving, and throwing things. These are what can be called the "ordinary" or "normal" violence of family life. It then goes on to kicking, biting, punching, hitting with an object, beating up, and using a knife or gun. This latter group of items was used to compute a measure of "severe violence," which is comparable to what social workers call child abuse, feminists would call wife beating, and criminologists would call assaults.

TABLE 3

INCIDENCE RATES FOR SEVERE VIOLENCE INDEX, OVERALL VIOLENCE INDEX, AND ITEMS MAKING UP THESE INDEXES

Conflict Tactics Scale Violence Indexes and Items	Rate Per 100 for Violence By:		Frequency*			
			Mean		Median	
	H	W	H	W	H	W
Wife Beating and Husband Beating (N to R)	3.8	4.6	8.0	8.9	2.4	3.0
Overall Violence Index (K to R)	12.1	11.6	8.8	10.1	2.5	3.0
K. Threw something at spouse	2.8	5.2	5.5	4.5	2.2	2.0
L. Pushed, grabbed, shoved spouse	10.7	8.3	4.2	4.6	2.0	2.1
M. Slapped spouse	5.1	4.6	4.2	3.5	1.6	1.9
N. Kicked, bit, or hit with fist	2.4	3.1	4.8	4.6	1.9	2.3
O. Hit or tried to hit with something	2.2	3.0	4.5	7.4	2.0	3.8
P. Beat up spouse	1.1	0.6	5.5	3.9	1.7	1.4
Q. Threatened with a knife or gun	0.4	0.6	4.6	3.1	1.8	2.0
R. Used a knife or gun	0.3	0.2	5.3	1.8	1.5	1.5

* For those who engaged in each act, i.e., omits those with scores of zero.

It can be seen from this description of the violence indexes of the Conflict Tactics Scales that they take into account the dimensions of intent and severity. However, we do not have data on whether the act was primarily instrumental versus expressive, or on whether the act was one that the members of that family believed to be illegitimate or, in the circumstances, legitimate.

Spouse Violence Rates

The first row of TABLE 3 shows that violence by a husband against his wife that was serious enough to be classified as wife beating occurred as a rate of 3.8 per 100 couples. Violence by a wife serious enough to be classified as husband beating occurred at an even higher rate—4.6 per 100 couples. However, it is important to remember that these data are based on attacks, rather than on injuries produced. If one uses injuries as the criterion, then wife beating would far outdistance husband beating. (See APPENDIX, II.)

What proportion of these attacks were isolated incidents? Our data suggest that this was rarely the case. For those who experienced an assault, the medians in the last column of TABLE 3 show that assaults happened about three times during the year. If the means are used as the measure of the frequency of occurrence, the figure is much higher—about eight or nine times. But this is because of a relatively few couples at the extreme for whom such violence was just about a weekly event.

STRESSFUL LIFE EVENTS AND ASSAULT BETWEEN SPOUSES

For purposes of this analysis, the Stress Index was transferred to Z scores and grouped into categories of half a Z score. Therefore, in FIGURE 2, each horizontal axis category indicates the families who fall within a band that is half a standard deviation wide.

The data plotted in FIGURE 2 clearly show that the higher the stress score, the higher the rate of assault between husband and wife. For the wives, the curve approximately fits a power function. For the husbands the relationship shows a general upward trend, but is irregular.¶

Both the smooth shape of the curve and the fact that the line plotted for the women is above the line for the men at the high stress end of the graph suggest that stress has more effect on violence by wives than on violence by husbands. At the low end of the scale, women in the -1.0 to -1.4 stress group have an assault rate about half that of the men in this group (1.1 per 100 versus 2.2 for the men). But at the high stress end of the

¶ The numbers of husbands and wives, on which each of the rates in FIGURE 2 is based, are: $-1.0 = 361$ and 365; $-0.5 = 459$ and 460; $0.0 = 414$ and 415; $+0.1 = 304$ and 303; $+0.6 = 224$ and 218; $+1.1 = 128$ and 129; $+1.6 = 45$ and 45; $+2.1 = 103$ and 105.

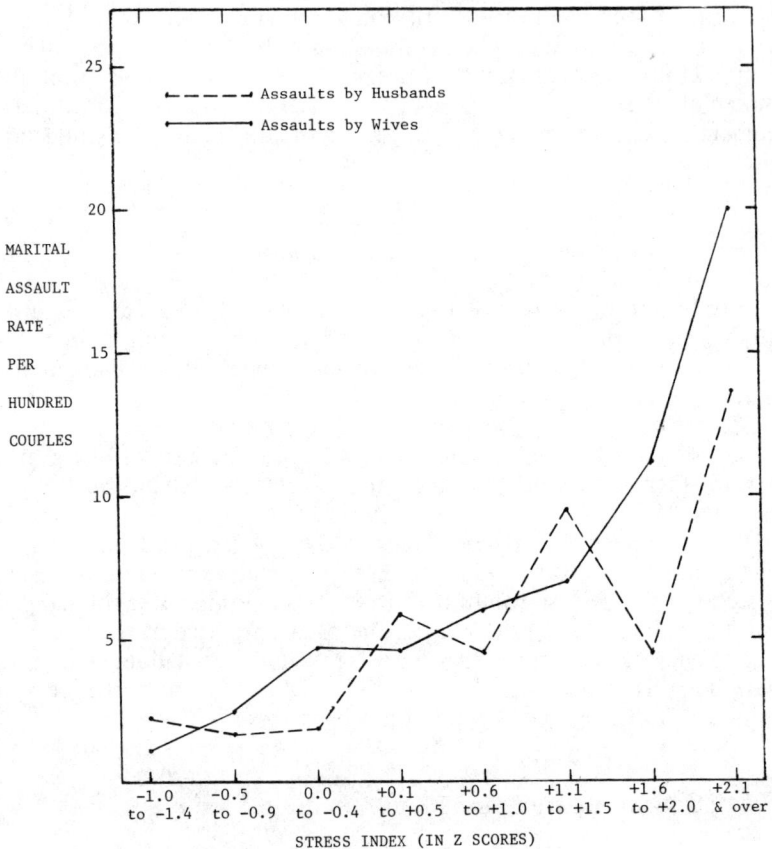

FIGURE 2. Marital assault rate by stress index score.

scale, women in the +1.6 to +2.0 and +2.1 and over categories have assault rates that are, respectively, 150% and 50% greater than the rates for the husbands who experienced this much stress. It seems that in the absence of stress, women are less violent to their spouse than are men, but under stressful conditions women are more violent.

An analysis identical to that in FIGURE 2 was done, except that the dependent variable was not limited to the types of severely violent acts used in FIGURE 2. That is, the measure included pushing, slapping, shoving, and throwing things. Except for the fact that the rates are much higher—they start at 5 per 100 and range up to 48 per 100—the results are very similar.

The importance of this similarity is that it helps establish a connection that is extremely important for understanding serious assaults. Again and again in our research, we find a clear connection between the "ordinary" violence of family life, such as spanking children or pushing or slapping a spouse, and serious violence, such as child abuse and wife beating. Actually, the connection goes further. *Verbal* aggression is also part of this pattern

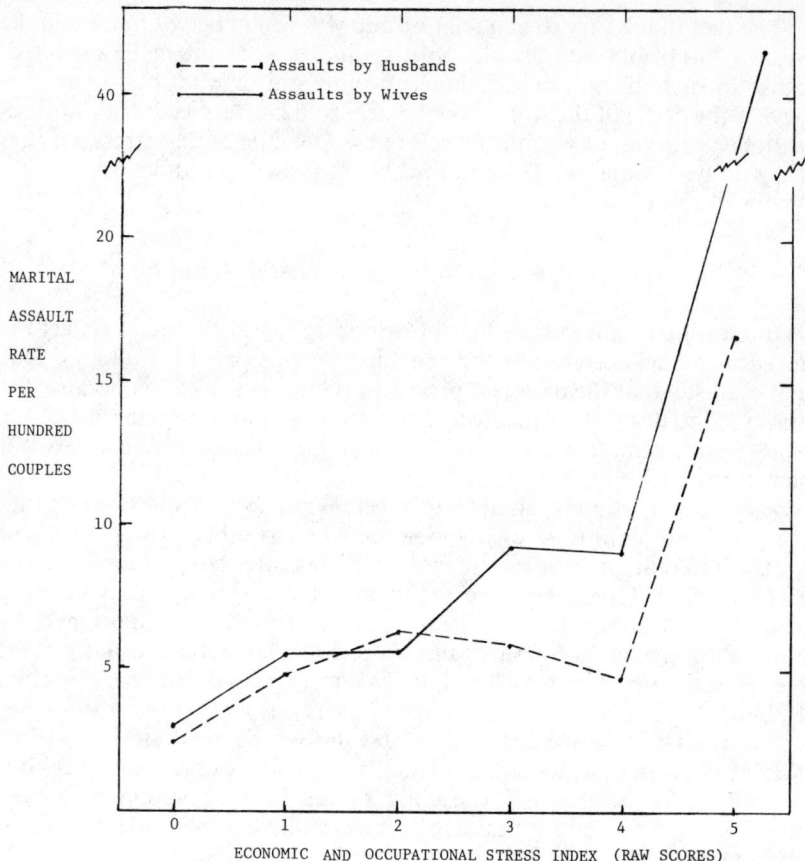

FIGURE 3. Marital assault rate by economic plus occupational stress index.

of relationships. People who hurt another family member verbally are also the ones most likely to hurt them physically.[29] Moreover, the same set of causal factors applies to both the milder forms of violence and acts of violence that are serious enough to be considered child abuse or an assault on a spouse. The similarity of the relationship between stress and the overall violence index and the relationship between stress and serious assaults is but one of many such examples found for this sample.[33]

Types of Stressors and Assaults

The analyses just reported were also carried out using each of the stress subscores listed in Table 2 as the independent variable. In each case, as the amount of stress increased, so did the assault rate. These relationships were strongest for the "spousal stress" and the "economic plus occupational stress" subscores.

The fact that a very strong relationship was found between stress in the spousal relationship and assault on a spouse is what might be expected, because in such cases, the assaulter is lashing out at what he or she may believe is the cause of the stress. The relationship between economic and occupational stress and assault is therefore better evidence that stress per se is associated with violence. This relationship is shown in FIGURE 3.‖

FACTORS LINKING STRESS AND WIFE BEATING

Interesting as are the findings presented so far, they do not reflect the theoretical model sketched at the beginning of this paper (FIGURE 1). One might even say that the data just presented distort the situation because the graphs tend to draw attention away from a very important fact: most of the couples in this sample who were subject to a high degree of stress were not violent.

A critical question is raised by this fact. What accounts for the fact that some people respond to stress by violence whereas others do not? Part of the answer to that question was suggested in the center box of FIGURE 1. The variables included there were selected to illustrate the theory. They were not intended to be a complete list, either of what is theoretically important or of the variables available for this sample. The available data actually cover three of the four variables listed in FIGURE 1 plus a number of other variables.

An analysis was carried out to take into account these intervening variables. This analysis focuses on assaults by husbands on their wives. It is restricted to this aspect of intrafamily assault because, along with child abuse, it is the most serious problem of intrafamily violence, and because of limitations imposed by the length of the paper.

The analysis started by distinguishing husbands in the sample who experienced none of the stressful events in the past year ($N = 139$) from those in the high quartile of the index ($N = 258$). Each of these groups was further divided into those who were in the high quartile of each mediating variable versus those in the low quartile. This enables us to see if the presumed mediating variable was, as specified in the theoretical model, necessary for life stresses to result in violence.

If the theory outlined in FIGURE 1 is correct, the men who had the combination of high stress and the presence of a mediating variable will have a high rate of violence, whereas the men who experienced a similar high amount of stress but without the presence of mediating variable will *not* be more violent than the sample as a whole, despite the fact that they were under as much stress during the year as the others.

‖ The numbers of husbands and wives, on which each of the rates in FIGURE 3 is based, are: 0 = 1,053 and 1,058; 1 = 544 and 548; 2 = 258 and 256; 3 = 135 and 130; 4 = 43 and 44; 5 = 12 and 12.

TABLE 4

EFFECT OF INTERVENING VARIABLES ON THE INCIDENCE OF ASSAULT BY HUSBANDS
EXPERIENCING HIGH STRESS

	Assault Rate per 100 Husbands when Intervening Variable Was:		N*	
Intervening Variable	Low	High	Low	High
A. Childhood Experience With Violence				
Physical punishment after age 12 by mother (0 vs. 4+ per yr)	7.1	6.7	85	89
Physical punishment after age 12 by father (0 vs. 4+ per yr)	7.4	8.4	81	83
Husband's father hit his mother (0 vs. 1+ per yr)	5.4	17.1	167	41
Husband's mother hit his father (0 vs. 1+ per yr)	4.6	23.5	176	34
B. Legitimacy of Family Violence				
Approval of parents slapping a 12-year-old (0 vs. high ¼)	5.9	9.9	34	71
Approval of slapping a spouse (0 vs. any approval)	2.7	15.0	150	100
C. Marital Satisfaction and Importance				
Marital satisfaction index (low vs. high quartile)	12.3	4.9	73	61
Marriage less important to husband than to wife = high	5.9	11.7	17	34
D. Socioeconomic Status				
Education (high vs. low quartile)	6.1	5.4	49	56
Husband a blue collar worker = low	9.2	5.4	284	202*
Income (low ⩽ $9,000, high ⩾ $22,500)	16.4	3.5	122	113*
E. Marital Power				
Power norm index (high = husband should have final say)	4.2	16.3	71	55
Decision power index (high = husband has final say)	5.2	16.1	58	62
F. Social Integration				
Organizational participation index (0 vs. 11+)	10.5	1.7	86	60
Religious service attendance (0–1/yr vs. weekly)	8.9	5.4	79	56
Relatives living near (0–2 vs. 13+)	5.7	11.9	124	118*

* The Ns vary because, even though the intent was for the high and low groups to be the upper and lower quartiles, this was not always possible. In the case of occupational class, for example, the comparison is between a dichotomous nominal variable. In the case of continuous variables, we sometimes wanted to preserve the intrinsic meaning of a score category, such as those with a score of zero, even though this might be more or less than 25% of the sample. Another factor causing the Ns to vary is that the division into quartiles was based on the distribution for the entire sample of 2,143 rather than just the high stress subgroup analyzed in this table. Finally, there are three variables for which the data were obtained from the wife as well as the husband (husband's occupation, family income, and relatives living nearby). The Ns for these variables are roughly double those for the other variables because they are based on the entire sample, rather than only on those families where the husband was the respondent.

Socialization for Violence

The first row of TABLE 4 runs directly contrary to the theory being examined. It shows that the men who were physically punished the most by their mother when they were teenagers were slightly *less* violent under stress than the men who were not or only rarely hit at this age by their mother. On the other hand, having been physically punished on more than just a rare occasion by a *father* does relate to assaulting a wife. Husbands whose father hit them the most have an assault rate against their wives that is slightly higher than do husbands who were under equally high stress that year but who did not experience this much violence directed against them as a teenager. The difference between the effect of having been hit by one's mother versus by one's father suggests that violence by the father against a teenage boy is a more influential role model for violent behavior that the son will later display under stress.

The next two rows of TABLE 4 refer to violence *between the parents* of the husbands in this sample. These two rows show large differences between husbands who are the sons of parents who engaged in physical fights and those who are sons of parents who did not. The assault rate by husbands whose own father had hit their mother was 216% higher than the rate for the men whose father never hit their mother (17.1 per 100 vs. 5.4). Surprisingly, the largest difference of all is in the much greater assault rate by husbands who had grown up in families where their *mother* had hit their father. This contradicts the idea of the same sex parent being a more influential role model. Whatever the intervening process, however, Section A of TABLE 4 shows that the men who assaulted their wives were exposed to more family violence as teenagers than were the men who were not violent despite an equally high level of stress.

Legitimacy of Family Violence

Section B of TABLE 4 reports "semantic differential" scores[20] in response to questions about slapping a child and slapping one's husband or wife. Each score is made up by combining the ratings for how "necessary," "normal," and "good" the respondent rated slapping.

The first row of Section B shows that husbands who approved of slapping a child had a 68% greater rate of assaulting their wives than did the husbands with a score of zero on this index. When it comes to approval of slapping *a spouse,* there is a 456% difference in the predicted direction. These findings are consistent with the theoretical model asserting that the relation between stress and violence is a process that is mediated by social norms, rather than a direct biologically determined relationship. However, since these are cross-sectional data, the findings do not prove the correctness of the model. It is also quite plausible to interpret the greater assault rate by men who approve of violence as an after-the-fact justification. Except for a few variables that clearly occurred at a previous time, such as violence experienced as a child, this caution applies to most of the findings to be reported.

Marital Satisfaction and Importance

The first row of Section C compares men who were low in marital satisfaction with men in the high quartile. The low quartile men had a 151%

higher assault rate. A similar difference is shown by comparing men who rated their marriages as a less important part of their lives than the marriage played in the lives of their wives. Of course, these differences, like a number of others reported in this paper, could reflect the effect of marital violence rather than the cause. Only a longitudinal study can adequately sort out this critical issue. The findings of this study are not inconsistent with the idea that men under stress are more likely to be violent if they do not find the marriage a rewarding and important part of their lives.

Socioeconomic Status

Three aspects of socioeconomic status are examined in Section D of TABLE 4. The first of these, the educational level of the couple, shows findings that many will find surprising. The husbands in the high quartile of education were only slightly less violent than those in the low quartile. This is inconsistent with the widely held view that less educated people are more violent. Actually, a careful review of the available studies fails to support this widespread idea.[31] A number of studies (including an analysis of this sample[7]) suggest there is little or no difference in aggression and violence according to education.

On the other hand, when it comes to indicators of present socioeconomic position, the low groups are, as expected, more violent. The second row of Section D, for example, shows that the assault rate of blue collar husbands is 70% greater than the assault rate of the white collar employed husbands. If the combined income of the couple was $9,000 or less, the rate of assault by husbands on their wives was 368% higher than in families with a more adequate income (16.4 per 100 versus 3.5 per 100).

What could account for the sharply different findings for education as compared to occupation and income? One fairly straightforward possibility is that low income and low status occupations are indirect indicators of even more stress than is measured by the stress index. Low or high education, on the other hand, does not necessarily mean that the couple is currently in an economically bad position, such as is indicated by a total family income of $9,000 and under.

Marital Power

One of the most important factors accounting for the high rate of marital violence is the use of force by men as the "ultimate resource" to back up their position as "head" of the family.[1,12,28,29] Section E provides evidence that this may be part of the explanation for why some men assault their wives when under stress and others do not.

The first row of Section E shows that the assault rate of husbands who feel that husbands *should have* the final say in most family decisions is 288% higher than it is for husbands who are not committed to such male dominance norms. The second row suggests that when this is translated into actual decision power, the differences are almost as great. The husbands who actually did have the final say in most family decisions had an assault rate of 16.1 per 100 as compared 5.2 for the husbands who were also under high stress but shared decisions with their wives.

Social Integration and Isolation

The last set of mediating factors included in this paper explores the theory that violence will be higher in the absence of a network of personal ties. Such ties can provide help in dealing with the stresses of life, and perhaps intervene when disputes within the family become violent.

The first row of Section F shows that men who belonged to no organizations (such as clubs, lodges, business or professional organizations, or unions) had a higher rate of assault than did the men who participated in many such organizations. The same applies to men who attended religious services as compared to men who rarely or never attended services.

The third row of Section F, however, shows opposite results. Couples who had many relatives living within an hour's travel time had a *higher* rate of assault than did couples with few relatives nearby. This finding is not necessarily inconsistent with social network theory. The usual formulation of that theory *assumes* that the network will be prosocial. That is usually a reasonable assumption. However, a social network can also support antisocial behavior. This is the essence of the differential association theory of criminal behavior. A juvenile gang is an example.

In respect to the family, Bott[2] and others have shown that involvement in a closed network helps maintain sexually segregated family roles, whereas couples not tied into such networks tend to have a more equal and shared-task type of family organization and to be less traditional.[25] In the present case, the assumption that the kin network will be opposed to violence is not necessarily correct. For example, a number of women indicated that when they left their husband because of a violent attack, their mothers responded with urgings for the wife to deal with the situation by being a better housekeeper, by being a better sex partner, or by just avoiding him, etc. In some cases, the advice was "you just have to put up with it for the sake of the kids—that's what I did."

SUMMARY AND CONCLUSIONS

This study was designed to determine the extent to which stressful life experiences are associated with assault between husbands and wives, and to explore the reasons for such an associaton. The data used to answer these questions come from a nationally representative sample of 2,143 American couples. Stress was measured by an instrument patterned after the Holmes and Rahe scale. It consisted of a list of 18 stressful events that could have occurred during the year covered by the survey. Assault was measured by the severe violence index of the family Conflict Tactics Scales. This consists of whether any of the following violent acts had occurred in the course of a family dispute during the past year: punching, kicking, biting, hitting with an object, beating up, and using a knife or gun.

The findings show that respondents who experienced none of the 18 stresses in the index had the lowest rate of assault. The assault rate increased as the number of stresses experienced during the year increased. This applies to assaults by wives as well as by husbands but is most clear in the case of the wives. Wives with a stress score of zero had a lower rate of assault as compared to the assaults by husbands with a stress score of zero. But the assault rate of wives climbed steadily with each increment of stress, and gradually became greater than the assault rate of the husbands. Thus, although wives were less assaultive under normal conditions, under stress they were more assaultive than the husbands.

The second part of the analysis was based on the theory that stress by itself does not necessarily lead to violence. Rather, it was assumed that other factors must be present. Several such factors were examined by focusing on men who were in the top quartile in stresses experienced during the year. These men were divided into low and high groups on the basis of variables that might account for the correlation between stress and violence. If the theory is correct, the men who were in the high group of the presumed intervening or mediating variable should have a high assault rate, whereas the men in the low group on these variables should not be more assaultive than the sample as a whole, despite the fact that they were under as much stress during the year as were the other high-stress subgroup of men.

The results were generally consistent with this theory. They suggest the following conclusions:

1. Physical punishment by fathers and parents who hit each other train men to respond to stress by violence.

2. Men who assault their wives believe that physical punishment of children and slapping a spouse are appropriate behavior. Their early experience with violence therefore seems to have carried over into their present normative stance. However, a longitudinal study is needed to establish whether this is actually the causal direction.

3. Men under stress are more likely to assault their wives if the marriage is not an important and rewarding part of their life.

4. Education does not affect the link between stress and violence. However, low income and a low status occupation do, perhaps because these are indicators of additional stresses.

5. Men who believe that husbands should be the dominant person in a marriage, and especially husbands who have actually achieved such a power position, had assault rates from one and a half to three times higher than the men in more equalitarian marriages who were also under stress.

6. Men who were socially isolated (in the sense of not participating in unions, clubs, or other organizations) had higher rates of assault on their wives, whereas men who were involved in supportive networks only rarely assaulted their wives despite being under extremely high stress.

Of course, these conclusions, although consistent with the findings reported in this paper, are not proved by the findings. Many of the findings are open to other equally plausible interpretations, particularly as to causal direction. The question of causal direction can only be adequately dealt with by a longitudinal study. In the absence of such prospective data, the following conclusions must be regarded as only what the study suggests about the etiology of intrafamily violence.

We assume that human beings have an inherent capacity for violence, just as they have an inherent capacity for doing algebra. This capacity is translated into actually solving an equation, or actually assaulting a spouse, *if* one has learned to respond to scientific or technical problems by using mathematics, or if one has learned to respond to stress and family problems by using violence. Even with such training, violence is not an automatic response to stress, nor algebra to a scientific problem. One also has to believe that the problem is amenable to a mathematical solution or to a violent solution. The findings presented in this paper show that violence tends to be high when certain conditions are present; for example, where people are taught the use of violence through childhood experiences and where the need of an individual to dominate a marriage provides a situation that is likely to yield to violence. If conditions such as these are present, stress is related to violence. If these conditions are not present, the relation between stress and violence is absent or minimal.

ACKNOWLEDGMENTS

It is a pleasure to acknowledge the many helpful criticisms and suggestions by the members of the Family Violence Research Program seminar: Joanne Benn, Diane Coleman, Ursula Dibble, David Finkelhor, Jean Giles-Sims, Cathy Greenblatt, Suzanne Smart, and Kersti Yllo; the computer analysis of Shari Hagar; and the typing of this paper by Sieglinde Fizz.

REFERENCES

1. ALLEN, C. & M. A. STRAUS. 1980. Resources, power, and husband-wife violence. *In* The Social Causes of Husband-Wife Violence. M. A. Straus & G. T. Hotaling, Eds.: Chapter 12. University of Minnesota Press.
2. BOTT, E. 1957. Family and Social Network. Tavistock Publications. London, England.
3. BRENNER, M. 1976. Estimating the social costs of national economic policy: implications for mental and physical health, and criminal aggression. Paper presented to the Joint Economic Committee, U.S. Congress, 1976; Revised version to be published as The impact of social and industrial changes on psychopathology, a view of stress from the standpoint of macrosocietal trends. *In* Society, Stress, and Disease. 1979. L. Levi, Ed. Oxford University Press.
4. BROWN, G. W. & T. HARRIS. 1978. Social Origins of Depression: A Study of Psychiatric Disorder in Women. Tavistock Publications. London, England.
5. BULCROFT, R. A. & M. A. STRAUS. 1975. Validity of husband, wife, and child reports of conjugal violence and power. (Mimeographed paper.)
6. FARRINGTON, K. 1980. Stress and family violence. *In* The Social Causes of Husband-Wife Violence. M.A. Straus & G. T. Hotaling, Eds.: Chapter 7. University of Minnesota Press.

7. FINKELHOR, D. 1977. Education and marital violence. (Mimeographed paper.)
8. GELLES, R. J. 1975. Violence and pregnancy: note on the extent of the problem and needed services. Family Coordinator **24**: 81–86.
9. GELLES, R. J. 1976. Abused wives: Why do they stay? Journal of Marriage and the Family **38**: 659–668.
10. GELLES, R. J. & M. A. STRAUS. 1979. Determinants of violence in the family: toward a theoretical integration. *In* Contemporary Theories About the Family. W. R. Burr, R. Hill, I. Nye & I. L. Reiss, Eds. Chapter 21. The Free Press. New York, N.Y.
11. GERSTEN, J. C., T. S. LANGNER, J. G. EISENBERG & L. ORZEK. 1974. Child behavior and life events: undesirable change or change per se. *In* Stressful Life Events: Their Nature and Effects. B. S. Dohrenwend & B. P. Dohrenwend, Eds.: 159–170. John Wiley & Sons, Inc. New York, N.Y.
12. GOODE, W. J. 1971. Force and violence in the family. Journal of Marriage and the Family **33**: 624–636. (Also reprinted in Reference 24.)
13. HOLMES, T. H. & R. H. RAHE. 1967. The social readjustment rating scale. Journal of Psychosomatic Research **11**: 213–218.
14. HOTALING, G. T., S. G. ATWELL & A. S. LINSKY. 1979. Adolescent life changes and illness: a comparison of three models. Journal of Youth and Adolescence **7**(4): 393–403.
15. LAZARUS, R. S. 1966. Psychological Stress and the Coping Process. McGraw-Hill Book Co. New York, N.Y.
16. LEVINE, S. & N. A. SCOTCH. 1967. Toward the development of theoretical models. II. Milbank Memorial Fund Quarterly **45**(2): 163–174.
17. MARTIN, D. 1976. Battered Wives. Glide Publications. San Francisco, Calif.
18. MCGRATH, J. E. 1970. A conceptual formulation for research on stress. *In* Social and Psychological Factors in Stress. J. E. McGrath, Ed.: 10–21. Holt, Rinehart, & Winston, Inc. New York, N.Y.
19. MECHANIC, D. 1962. Students Under Stress: A Study in the Social Psychology of Adaptation. The Free Press. New York, N.Y.
20. OSGOOD, C., G. SUCI & P. TANNENBAUM. 1957. The Measurement of Meaning. University of Illinois Press. Urbana, Ill.
21. PAYKEL, E. S. 1974. Life stress and psychiatric disorder: applications of the clinical approach. *In* Stressful Life Events: Their Nature and Effects. B. S. Dohrenwend & B. P. Dohrenwend, Eds.: 135–149. John Wiley & Sons, Inc. New York, N.Y.
22. SCOTT, R. & A. HOWARD. 1970. Models of Stress. *In* Social Stress. S. Levine & N. A. Scotch, Eds.: 259–278. Aldine Publishing Co. Chicago, Ill.
23. SELYE, H. 1966. The Stress of Life. McGraw-Hill Book Co. New York, N.Y.
24. STEINMETZ, S. K. & M. A. STRAUS, Eds. 1974. Violence in the Family. Harper & Row Publishers. New York, N.Y.
25. STRAUS, M. A. 1969. Social class and farm–city differences in interaction with kin in relation to societal modernization. Rural Sociology **34**: 476–495.
26. STRAUS, M. A. 1971. Some social antecedents of physical punishment: a linkage theory interpretation. Journal of Marriage and the Family **33**: 658–663.
27. STRAUS, M. A. 1973. A general systems theory approach to a theory of violence between family members. Social Science Information **12**: 105–125.
28. STRAUS, M. A. 1976. Sexual inequality, cultural norms, and wife-beating. Victimology **1**: 54–76; reprinted *in* Victims and Society. 1976 E. C. Viano, Ed. Visage Press. Washington, D. C. and *in* Women into Wives: The Legal and Economic Impact on Marriage. J. R. Chapman & M. Gates, Eds. **2**. Sage Publications. Beverly Hills, Calif.
29. STRAUS, M. A. 1977. Wife-beating: How common and why? Victimology **2**: 443–458. Reprinted in Reference 34.
30. STRAUS, M. A. 1979. Measuring intrafamily conflict and violence: the Conflict Tactics (CT) scales. Journal of Marriage and the Family **41**: 75–88.
31. STRAUS, M. A. 1979. Socioeconomic status, aggression, and violence. (Paper in preparation.)
32. STRAUS, M. A. 1980. The marriage license as a hitting license: evidence from popular culture, law, and social science. *In* The Social Causes of Husband-Wife Violence. M.A. Straus & G. T. Hotaling, Eds.: Chapter 3. University of Minnesota Press.
33. STRAUS, M. A., R. J. GELLES & S. K. STEINMETZ. 1980. Behind Closed Doors: Violence in the American Family. Anchor/Doubleday. New York, N.Y.

34. Straus, M. A. & G. T. Hotaling, Eds. 1980. The Social Causes of Husband-Wife Violence. University of Minnesota Press.
35. Straus, M. A. & F. Kumagai. 1979. An empirical comparison of eleven methods of index construction. In Indexing and Scaling for the Social Sciences with SPSS. M. A. Straus, Ed.: Chapter 2. (Book in preparation. A mimeographed copy of this chapter is available upon request).
36. Wolfgang, M. E. 1956. Husband-wife homicides. Corrective Psychiatry and Journal of Social Therapy 2: 263–271. Reprinted In Deviancy and the Family. C.D. Bryand, Ed. F.A. Davis. Philadelphia, Penn.

Appendix

I. Stress Index Modifications

The stress index used in this study departs from the Holmes and Rahe scale in ways other than length. One of the criteria used to select items from the larger original set was the elimination of stresses that have a positive cathexis. Methodological studies show that the negative items account for most of the relationship between scores on the stress index and other variables.[11,21] We modified some items and added some that are not in the Holmes and Rahe scale to secure a set of stressors best suited for this research. The Holmes and Rahe weights were not used in computing the index score for each respondent. This decision was based on research that found the weighting makes little difference in the validity of scales of this type[35] and of the Holmes and Rahe scale specifically.[14]

An important limitation that this stress index shares with the Holmes and Rahe index is that one does not know the time distribution of the stressful events. At one extreme, a person who experienced four of the stressors during the year could have had them spread out over the year, or at the other extreme, all four could have occurred at roughly the same time.

II. Wives as Victims

Although these findings show high rates of violence *by wives*, this should not divert attention from the need to give primary attention to wives *as victims* as the immediate focus of social policy. There are a number of reasons for this:

    a. A validity study carried out in preparation for this research[5] shows that underreporting of violence is greater for violence by husbands than it is for violence by wives. This is probably because an act of violence, so much a part of the male way of life, is typically not the dramatic and often traumatic event that it is for a woman. Physical violence is not unmasculine. But it *is* unfeminine according to contemporary American standards. Consequently, if it was possible to allow for this difference in reporting rates, even in simple numerical terms, wife beating would probably be the more severe problem.

    b. Even if one does not take into account this difference in underreporting, the data in Table 3 show that husbands have higher rates in the most dangerous and injurious forms of violence (beating up and using a knife or gun).

    c. Table 1 also shows that when violent acts are committed by a husband, they are repeated more often than is the case for wives.

    d. These data do not tell us what proportion of the violent acts by wives were in response to blows initiated by husbands. Wolfgang's data on husband-wife homicides[36] suggest that this is an important factor.

    e. The greater physical strength of men makes it more likely that a woman will be seriously injured when beaten up by her husband than the reverse.

    f. A disproportionately large number of attacks by husbands seem to occur when the wife is pregnant,[8] thus posing a danger to the unborn child.

    g. Women are locked into marriage to a much greater extent than are men. Because of a variety of economic and social constraints, they often have no alternative but to endure beatings by their husbands.[9, 17, 28, 29]

VIOLENCE-PRONE FAMILIES

Suzanne K. Steinmetz

Individual and Family Studies
University of Delaware
Newark, Delaware 19711

INTRODUCTION

The intent of this paper is to present an overview of the characteristics of violence-prone families. Given the recent attention paid to family violence, one might believe that this topic has a long, rich research tradition. However, it has only been since the late 1960s that family violence has been identified as a legitimate topic for academic research. Yet, an examination of some of the first written laws suggests that not only did violence between family members exist, but it was an institutionalized, very acceptable way for those in a dominant, superior position to control those in a weaker, subordinate position. Perhaps it is only when that position is questioned, when we become cognizant of the amount and destructiveness of violence within families, that attempts to study the phenomena are undertaken.

The concept of children as property of their parents is illustrated in the Hammurabi Code of 2100 B.C. and the Hebrew Code of 800 B.C., which considered infanticide to be an acceptable practice. The Bible gives us the earliest and best known account of sibling violence, the story of Cain killing his brother Abel.

> and Cain talked with Abel his brother: and it came to pass, when they were in the field, that Cain rose up against Abel, his brother, and slew him (Genesis 4:8)

The Bible also provides us with the dictum "spare the rod and spoil the child," perhaps one of the earliest written accounts of child-rearing philosophy.

A 1646 colonial law attempted to help parents control their rebellious children, noting that unless parents "had been very unchristianly negligent in the education of such children or so provoked them by extreme cruel correction," any child over 16 years of age of sufficient understanding who cursed, smited, and would not obey his natural mother or father "would be put to death."[1]

Colonial custom also demanded that couples cohabit peacefully. However, evidence from court records and diaries suggests that not all spouses were loving. Joan Miller was charged with "beating and reviling her husband and egging her children to healp her, bidding them to knock him in the head and wishing his victuals might choke him."[2] One man in Plymouth Colony was punished for abusing his wife and "kiking her off from a stolle into the fier"; and another man for "drawing his wife in a uncivil manner on the snow."[2]

Concern for protecting children from abuse erupted in 1874 when the story of 9-year-old Mary Ellen who was physically abused by her parents was reported. While protection of animals was available through the Society for the Prevention of Cruelty to Animals (SPCA), there were no laws to protect children. Social workers, by defining Mary Ellen as a member of the animal kingdom, were able to provide help and protection.[2] In 1885, the Pennsylvania legislature considered enacting a bill that would publicly whip wife beaters, as a tax-saving alternative to imprisonment. While the use of violence to control violence is questionable (and not likely to influence the husband to return home as a warm and loving mate), it was an improvement over the 1824 law permitting husbands to chastise their wives with a twig no bigger than their thumb.[2]

The level of violence found within the contemporary family has suggested to some researchers that every role relationship in the American family is characterized by rates of violence that make the problem of violence in the streets pale by comparison.[3] These researchers, summarizing their data from a national sample of 2,143 families, noted that whereas the uniform crime reports for assaults are reported in rates per 100,000, their data were reported in rates per 100. Statistics also indicate that you are at greater risk of injury in your home among family, friends, and neighbors than you are in the crime-ridden streets, and that family members make up the single largest category of homicide victims. Furthermore, domestic disturbance calls are reported to be the most dangerous calls for the police to answer, and more police are injured and killed answering domestic disturbance calls than any other single category of calls.[4]

Frequency of Domestic Violence

One of the more recent studies on child abuse reported 300,000 incidents of abuse; 40,000 cases requiring protective service intervention and 2,000 deaths during 1975.[5] A national sample survey of 2,143 intact families found that 20% hit a child with an object, 4.2% "beat up" a child, 2.8% threatened a child with a knife or gun, and 2.9% used a knife or gun on a child.[6] Furthermore, they predicted that between 1.5 and 2 million children are severely abused each year. These figures are even more disturbing when one realizes that the sample surveyed only intact families (single parents are at higher risk of abuse) and only the parent-child interaction for children age 3-18 (toddlers are at higher risk).

Sibling Violence

Probably the form of family violence considered to be most normal is violence between sibs. One study of college freshmen found that 62% reported that they had used physical violence on a sibling during the last year.[7] Other studies, based on a broad-based nonrandom sample[8] and a random sample,[9] found rates ranging from 63-78%. Straus, Gelles, and

Steinmetz[6] found that during the past year, 75% reported using physical violence and averaged 21 acts per year. Thirty-eight percent of siblings kicked or hit, 14% "beat up," 0.8% threatened to use a gun or knife, and 0.3% used a gun or knife. When we extrapolate these percentages to the 36.3 million children between 3-17 who have siblings, we find that 6.5 million children have been "beaten-up" by a sibling and that nearly 2 million children at sometime during their childhood have faced a gun or knife.

Marital Abuse

The data for marital abuse suggest that violence is unfortunately prevalent in many families. Gelles found that 55% of 80 families experienced marital violence and 21% beat their spouses regularly.[10] Straus reported that 16% of a sample of college freshmen saw their parents engage in marital violence during the past year.[7] Based on a random sample of New Castle County, Delaware, Steinmetz found that 60% of 57 families experienced marital violence.[9] For 10% of the couples, physical violence was a regular occurrence. When these data were combined with police statistics, it was revealed that severe physical abuse was experienced by 7% of wives and 0.6% of husbands.[11] The national survey of family violence[6] reported that during a one-year period, one out of six couples had a violent episode, 5% experienced severe physical abuse, and 4% used a gun or knife.

THE SOCIAL AND PSYCHOLOGICAL CHARACTERISTICS OF VIOLENCE

Psychiatric Conditions

The reporting of statistics on family violence points up the incongruence between the view of the family as the unit that provides love, comfort, protection, and support, and data that indicate the prevalence of violence between family members.

As a result we look for a scapegoat to help us understand the use of extreme violence. It is easy to comprehend why child abusers or wife batterers are labeled as mentally ill—obviously normal people would not behave this way. Likewise, a battered wife is described as having psychiatric defects—Why else would she allow herself to become a victim?

An examination of early studies of child abuse attributed numerous psychiatric defects, such as depression, immaturity, impulsiveness, and dependency, to abusing parents.[12,13,14] Forty-eight percent of the mothers in one British study were described as being neurotic, and a high percentage of fathers in this study were diagnosed as psychopaths.[15] Although the above finding suggests that psychiatric disorders produce child abuse, the evidence to the contrary is overwhelming. Steel and Pollock[14] noted that abusive parents did not exhibit excessive aggressive behavior in other areas of their lives and were not much different from a cross section of the general populations. Kempe and Helfer[15] state that less than 10% of parents who abuse children are seriously mentally ill. Furthermore, electroencephalographic examination of abusive parents found no evidence of a relationship between child abuse and organic dysfunction.[16]

Based on empirical evidence[17] as well as a critical examination of the literature,[18] it appears that, as a group, child abusers are no more or less mentally ill or emotionally disturbed than any randomly selected group of parents. Being identified and labeled as a child abuser appears to be the major distinguishing feature. While there is some evidence of pathology in the profiles of offenders and victims in studies of spouse abuse,[19] the question of cause and effect needs to be raised.

Hilberman and Munson,[20] in their study of 60 battered women, found that almost the entire sample of 60 women had sought medical help for stress-related complaints and many evidenced symptoms commonly associated with the rape-trauma syndrome. Furthermore, more than half had evidence of prior psychological dysfunction, including classic depressive illness, schizophrenia, manic-depression, alcoholism, and severe character disorders. Thirteen of the group had been hospitalized with violent psychotic behavior. There has been an assertion that since certain types of women are more prone to be a victim and since these women often appear to avoid taking steps to resolve their problems, they are at fault for being abused. The assumption is made that all women can control their lives if they choose to. Research describing the personality characteristics of a battered wife often leaves an impression that these victims, by their own weaknesses, had enabled this type of interaction to occur. A woman is likely to become a victim of spouse abuse when she displays the characteristics of a weak, vulnerable woman: she is isolated,[10,20] helpless, and depressed;[25] she has fewer resources;[21-25] she is overcome by anxiety;[21,25,26] and full of guilt and shame.[20,27]

Often it is suggested that by changing the woman's social and economic resources; increasing her education and job skills; teaching her to be less submissive; helping her to have a better self-concept; or teaching her to interpret her husband's moods, the violence can be reduced. While these are valid mechanisms for helping a victim escape from the battering environment, they tend to emphasize the ability of a woman to control her environment, an ability many battered women are lacking. Thus, a profile emerges of a woman who displays a learned helplessness that enables her to be further victimized.[28]

It is suggested that contrary to the notion that these psychiatric conditions cause women to be at risk of being beaten, it is the dynamics of the beating itself that produce these manifestations.[29] This phenomenon is closely related to the processes involved in brainwashing. Isolation from family, friends, and social support systems reinforces the victim's dependency on the abuser for confirmation of her worth. Unfortunately, the confirmation supports the woman's negative self-image, filling her with shame and guilt.

Social Class

While possibly more prevalent among lower classes, family violence is by no means limited to lower-class families. The disproportionate representation of working and lower classes noted by Blumberg,[30] Gil,[17] Holter and Friedman,[13] and Elmer[12] might have resulted from the practice, in earlier research, of utilizing medical facilities to obtain study populations. An underrepresentation of reported violence in middle-class families may be a consequence of the privacy surrounding middle-class acts and the services utilized by middle-class families. Lower-class families usually rely on social control agencies, such as the police, social service or family court workers, and clinics; agencies that keep "public" records. Middle- and upper-class families have access to private social support systems, such as family counselors, private doctors, ministers, and lawyers, that maintain the privacy of the professional relationship.

Blue Collar/White Collar

While the various dimensions of social status show inconsistencies when we use the broad categorization of blue collar/white collar (working class/middle class) classification, the relationship is quite clear. Blue collar status predicts greater levels of family violence for both males and females.[6,9] It may be that the blue collar/white collar category is too broad to clearly discern patterns. However, it may also reflect a broad class-based difference. Middle-class families may have been socialized to sharpen their communication skills because of the desirability of mediation and compromise rather than overt aggression.[31] Since the inability to communicate is highly related to physical violence between spouses,[9,25] this may also contribute to the differences in levels of family violence with respect to social class.

Income

Income is another aspect of social class. Because of the purchasing power associated with it, income provides families with resources useful for mediating many stress-producing and potentially violent situations. Greater financial resources enable parents to procure stress-reducing mechanisms, such as baby sitters, vacations, nursery schools, and camps, which provide them with "time-out" from childrearing/homemaking responsibilities. An examination of the interaction between stress and income and the effect on family violence is provided by the data from the national survey.[6] Increased stress, as rated by 18 items, had no effect on the very poor (family income below $6,000) or on those with family incomes above $20,000 (where income provides a cushion) but did increase the likelihood of child abuse for the middle income group. However, only those families with incomes over $20,000 were immune from the effects of stress-related spousal violence.

When physical or medical problems arise, possessing a higher income enables one to secure medical and psychological help from a private physician. Prescott and Letko[25] found that wives of professional men were four times more likely to have contacted a therapist than wives of men in low-status jobs.

Finally, mothers in higher income families have had greater access to contraception and abortion, thus enabling them to have greater control over family size and spacing, a factor related to family conflict and violence.[31-34] Among Gil's[17] abused families, 40% had 4 or more children, while in Johnson and Morse's[31] sample of 101 abused children, 35% were from families with 4 or more children.

In general there is a consistent decrease in violence as income levels go up. For families with incomes of under $6,000, 53% of families reported abuse between siblings, 22% reported child abuse, and 11% reported for both wife and husband abuse. In contrast, for those families with incomes of $20,000 and over, 41% reported sibling violence, 11% reported child abuse, and 2% each reported husband and wife abuse.

Education

Education is usually considered one of the major components of social class. It defines the range of occupations one is eligible to fulfill and thus is closely linked to income (from the job) and prestige (obtained by working in a given job). Steinmetz[9] found that a husband's education showed a strong negative correlation with spousal violence and father-child violence; a wife's education showed a similar relationship for spousal violence but virtually no relationship (0.04) for the mother-child violence. Gelles'[10] finding of an inverse relationship between husband's educational levels and violence was consistent with that noted by Steinmetz. However, while Gelles noted rather high levels of violence for women college graduates, in the national data there were fewer college graduates who were offenders or victims of spousal violence and college graduates were the least violent parents.

While other studies tended to find a negative relationship between education and violence, the national data[6]—which categorized education into four levels: eighth grade or below; some high school; high school graduate; and college—did not support this finding. For both men and women there was a positive relationship between the first three levels of education and child abuse (11%, 15%, and 18% for men; 12%, 14%, and 17% for women). It was only among those parents who had been exposed to college that a decrease in child-abuse rates occurred (11% for both men and women).

A curvilinear relationship also appeared for spouse abuse, with high school drop-outs having the highest abuse rates (6% each) as well as the highest victimization rates (7% each). The effect of college education on the probability of victimization is noteworthy. While a college education reduces the likelihood of a woman being victimized (2%), it increases the likelihood of victimization for men (5%).

Employment Status

The employment status of the husband/father and satisfaction with occupational/homemaking roles are also predictors of family violence. Unemployment is often perceived by males as incompetency in fulfilling their provider roles. This has been linked to child abuse and wife beating. Gil[17] reported that nearly half (48%) of the fathers in his sample of abusers experienced unemployment during the year preceding the abuse. McKinley[35] found that the lower the job satisfaction, the higher the percentage of fathers who used severe corporal punishment—a relationship that was not affected by social class.

The national survey[6] revealed a consistently lower level of child and spouse abuse among families where the husband was employed full time. Furthermore, part-time employment was more likely to predict family violence than was unemployment. A study of battered women who replied to a request for information in *Ms. Magazine* reported that husbands who were unemployed or employed part-time were extremely violent compared with husbands who were employed full time.[25]

Also related to the use of violence is job satisfaction and perceived inability to fulfill the breadwinner/head-of-household role.[25,36,37] Since middle- and upper-class parents are usually better educated, they are more likely to have fulfilling jobs and have the flexibility to change jobs. They are also likely to reside in larger, more comfortable homes, and have adequate resources for carrying out the homemaker/childbearing role. As a result, parents in the middle and upper classes are less likely to be locked into unfulfilling jobs in the marketplace and in the home.

Occupational Environment

Occupational environment, a concept that focuses on the tasks and ideology inherent in specific occupations, was found to predict, with more accuracy than social class, the parents' use of violence on children.[38,39] This same idea was upheld in studies of the police. These studies found that police showed no evidence of abnormal aggressiveness or rebellious tendencies,[40] sadistic or authoritarian attitudes or behavior,[41] and scored lower on a measure of punitiveness.[42] It appears that it is not the individual who selects law enforcement as a career, but the training and job itself that produce punitive, authoritarian, violent behavior. A recent study found similar results for military personnel in which the ideology and goals of the unit (not just the tasks the individuals actually perform) predicted the levels of violence used.[43]

Isolation

Families who lack close personal friendships and are poorly integrated into the community are likely to experience family violence for several reasons. First, they are lacking the friendship network which could provide support during times of extreme stress, and second, they are not likely to be influenced by the community's expectations of normal social behavior. Merrill[44] reported that 50% of abusive families belonged to no formal group association and 28% had only one such membership. Lenoski[45] found that 89% had unlisted phones. Elmer and Gregg[46] reported that abusive mothers were also found to score higher on an anomie scale.

Gil[17] and Schlosser[47] found that in some instances this isolation results from high mobility, which cuts these families off from kinship and friendship groups. In other instances the isolation results because the abusive families are not fully accepted by their community[44] or are actually rebuffed.[47] There appears to be a certain circularity to this process. The parent who batters the child, or the wife who experiences batterings from her husband, is likely to avoid becoming friendly with neighbors because of embarrassment and fear of discovery. This isolation, however, increases the likelihood of the problems continuing, since the family has no one to discuss problems with or to seek advice and help from. Of course, it is possible that once the aberrant behavior is discovered (most likely when the police are called), the isolation becomes enforced by the community rather than voluntary on the part of the family.

Age and Length of Marriage

O'Brien[37] found that violence was spontaneously mentioned in 64% of longer duration marriages and in 36% of shorter duration marriages. Roy's[24] examination of 150 cases of battered women found that the violence first peaked between 2.5 and 5 years.

In their national study, Straus and his colleagues[6] found that over 80% of those under 30 years of age were more likely to consider the slapping and spanking of 12-year-olds to be necessary, normal, and good. Less than 66% of the group 50 years and older supported this view. Although there is this decrease in the percentage who view the use of physical force on adolescent-aged children as necessary and good, approximately two-thirds of the population over 50 years of age still held a view that is contrary to a large body of research on child rearing, as well as popular advice on child rearing.

This survey reported that the use of violence on children decreased as both the children and parents matured. Eighty-six percent of children 5–9 years old; 54% of children 10–14 years old; and about 33% of children 15–17 years old were hit by their parents during the survey year.

Furthermore, 21% of parents under 30 years of age, 13% of the parents 31–50 years, and 4% of those 51 through 65 used abusive violence on a child. No parent 65 or older used abusive violence on a child, but this may reflect the age of their "child" (a middle-aged adult) rather than a change in child-rearing philosophy. Age appears to be a major influence on spousal violence. While 15% of the couples under 30 years of age used abusive violence on each other, only 4% of those 31 to 50 years and 1% of the group 51 through 65 years of age used abusive violence.

Sex Differences

Lansky, Crandall, Kagan, and Baker,[48] Toby,[49] and Whitehurst[50] found males' behavior to be more violent than females'. This difference has been observed in infants[51] and among Western and non-Western societies.[52] However, when marital and parental roles are examined, the data are not as clear-cut. Women, for example, outnumber men as child abusers.[53] While this is understandable, since women have the major caretaking responsibility, it does suggest that women are not immune from perpetrating violence.

In the national survey[6] men were more likely than women to express the belief that slapping is necessary, normal, and good, but mothers (68%) were more likely to have used violence on the child than were fathers (58%) during the survey year. Furthermore, with the exception of using or threatening to use a gun or knife (admitted only by fathers), mothers used each type of violence more frequently. About 4.4% of mothers kicked, hit, punched, or beat up a child compared with 2.7% of the fathers.

While mothers were more likely to abuse children, it was sons who were at greater risk of abuse: 4.5% for sons versus 2.8% for daughters.

Although media presentations have focused on wife beating as a major problem, husband beating must also be considered. Straus'[7] study of 385 couples showed little difference in the frequency with which husbands and wives committed physically violent acts against each other. Steinmetz,[54] in a comparison of data from five other studies, found that virtually identical percentages of husbands and wives resorted to throwing things, hitting with the hand, and hitting with an object. The only modes that husbands used more frequently than wives were pushing and grabbing—modes requiring superior physical strength—and these differences disappeared in the "high users" group. Furthermore, an examination of husbands and wives who used violence revealed that wives resorted to violence more frequently. Secondary analysis of previously published data revealed that the average violence scores of wives as compared with husbands were all slightly higher in the three studies (4.04 vs. 3.52;[9] 7.82 vs. 6.00;[55] and 7.00 vs. 6.60[8]). The national study[6] found that wives committed an average of 10.1 acts of violence against their husbands during 1975, while husbands averaged only 8.8 acts against their wives. Only Gelles[10] found husbands to exceed their wives in use of physically violent modes. He found that 11% of the husbands and 5% of the wives engaged in marital violence between 2 and 6 times a year, and 14% of the husbands and 6% of the wives used violence between once a month and daily. Wives exceeded husbands in one category, however; 11% of the husbands and 14% of the wives noted that they "seldom" (defined as between two and five times during the marriage) used physical violence against their spouses. Gelles[10] found that husbands exceeded wives in the frequency with which they used violence, but noted that wives tended to slap, throw things, and hit with an object, modes that deemphasize physical strength. The importance of physical strength must not be overlooked; while women and men are nearly equal in their use of violence, women because of smaller size and less strength receive a greater degree of injury. Severe abuse rates, based on a random sample of families and compared to police statistics, suggest that 7% of the women as compared with 0.6% of the men are likely to be severely abused in any given year.[11] Furthermore, battered women, even those with occupational, financial, and family resources, are psychologically trapped—a phenomenon not experienced by men.[29]

Curtis[56] reported that while violence by men against women was responsible for about 27% of the assaults and 17.5% of the homicides, violence by women against men accounted for only 9% of the assaults and 16.4% of homicides. Thus, while women commit only one-third as many assaults against men as men commit against women, the number of cross-sex homicides committed by the two groups is nearly identical. Wilt and Bannon warn that caution should be applied when interpreting the above findings. They note that "non-fatal violence committed by women against men is more likely to be reported to the police than is violence by men against women; thus, women assaulters who come to the attention of the police are likely to be those who have produced a fatal result."[57]

Residence

Like other areas of violence the highest rates of family violence tended to be found in urban (large city) areas. However, data from the national survey[6] did not show a consistent relationship between size of the residential area and family violence. In fact, the family violence rates for wife and child abuse were as high or higher among rural families as among urban families. Furthermore, the rates among rural families for child abuse were higher than rates found in small cities and suburbs. However, urban families and rural families share several things in common: isolation, lower educational levels, and lower incomes all were found to contribute heavily to child abuse and wife beating.

Race

Race was found to predict levels of family violence.[6] While blacks tended to be more violent than whites for child, wife, and husband abuse, they reported lower rates of sibling violence. Those families categorized racially as "other" were consistently highest in all categories except wife abuse (blacks were higher). These groups tend to have more unemployment, lower levels of education and income, larger families producing overcrowding, and to be confined to urban areas that experience higher levels of violent crime.

Pregnancy

Pregnancy is closely related to family violence in several ways. Premarital pregnancy or unplanned pregnancies, which strain limited resources, often result in the child's being resented; this is a precursor to abuse.[13,15,16,58] The financial and emotional stress that accompanies pregnancy has been linked to husbands' frequent and severe physical attacks on their wives.[10,34,27,57] Although many wives reported being the victim of beatings before and after the birth of the child, those that occurred during the pregnancy were described as being considerably more brutal and often included being kicked or punched in the stomach, a phenomenon that Gelles[56] has labeled intrauterine child abuse.

Alcohol

Wertham[59], Gil,[17] and Young[33] found a relationship between the use of alcohol and child abuse. The use of alcohol was also found to be closely linked to wife beating.[10,25,27] MacAndrew and Edgerton[60] suggest that the effects of alcohol on a social behavior are influenced by cultural expectations and socialization. Thus, in some societies the use of alcohol is associated with considerable violence, while in others no relationship exists, or exists only under certain circumstances. Several researchers[2,10,6] have noted that difficulty in ascertaining the actual sequence: Do men drink, lose control, and then beat their wives?; or Do men wish to vent their anger on their wives and drink in order to gain the courage to do so and to provide an excuse for their action?[7] Gelles[10] suggests that the association between alcohol and violence reflects the process of deviance disavowal—men get drunk to give them an excuse for their abusive behavior toward their wives.

Violent Histories

Probably the most important predictor of family violence is a pattern of a history of violence. The axiom, "an abusing parent was often an abused child," has been well documented.[12,14,15,61] Roy[24] found that 81% of husbands who beat their wives were beaten as children or saw their mothers being beaten. However, only 33% of the beaten women reported being beaten or seeing their mother beaten. Being beaten as a child also predicts other types of violence. Owens and Straus,[62] in a secondary analysis of a survey conducted for the Commission on the Causes and Prevention of Violence, found a relationship between experiencing violence as an observer or a victim during childhood and violent behavior as an adult. This finding was supported by Sedgely[63] in a secondary analysis of National Opinion Research Center data. Gayford,[64] in a study of battered wives, discovered that both the batterer and victim had a violent childhood. These patterns were found to continue over several generations in studies of child abuse—a cycle in which the battering parents had experienced abuse from their own parents.[62,65,66,67] Wilt and Bannon[57] note that over one-fourth of the individuals who committed assault or murder reported having had frequent arguments with their parents. Furthermore, their analysis of 90 intra-familial homicides revealed that 62% had been preceded by previous assaults on the same family member. Even in less violent forms, the use of physical force is passed on from generation to generation.[6,8,9] Perhaps one of the more intriguing findings of the national survey[6] is that while the probability of nonviolent parents being violently attacked by their children is about 1 out of 400, the probability of parents who use severe violence on their children being attacked by their children is 200 out of 400.

Based on a study of 34 boys and 39 girls in a family treatment program, Gladston expressed belief that "children who have received significant exposure to violent behavior before the age of two are likely to have identified with this pattern of response in a fashion that proves to be essentially irreversible, although a great deal can be done subsequently to contain it."[68] He notes that intervention before the age of 18 months greatly enhances the possibility of modifying the child's violent behavior.

CONCLUSION

Much of the literature presented has shown the effect of violence in one generation on the behavior of the next generation. However, violence witnessed and experienced by children often is the precursor to violence against society. Experiencing violence during childhood was found to be characteristic in the backgrounds of murderers, assault and batterers, rapists, political assassins, and individuals who commit suicide. Thus none of us are immune from the effects of violence in the family. We experience violence directly within our family or indirectly by having to reside in a violent society caused, in part, by violent socialization practices.

While considerable data have been amassed during the last decade on family violence, we really have only begun to scratch the surface. The evolution of research and theory in this field has produced a questioning of biological-based, instinctual theories or Freudian psychoanalytic theories to explain violence. They have been replaced with theories emphasizing the social/cultural context. The data presented in this article support this theoretical perspective—violence as a learned behavior transmitted from one generation to the next. Obviously this explains only part of the family violence phenomenon.

On the frontier of knowledge, research is focusing on the intricate body processes as a key to violent behavior. Investigation of chromosomal and hormonal influence on violence must not be discounted, especially since trends have appeared across generations.

Research being conducted at the Universities of Maryland and Pennsylvania on organic brain dysfunction is especially exciting. The distinctive brain scan patterns have been found to exist over several generations. This suggests one alternative to social-learning theories as an explanation for family violence existing over several generations.

Personality changes caused by chronic or deteriorating diseases such as diabetes and arteriosclerosis are being examined as a possible link in understanding family violence in certain circumstances.

While social/cultural linkages to family violence will probably predominate at this time, these new areas of exploration will provide additional insights necessary for a more complete understanding of this complex, destructive behavior.

ACKNOWLEDGMENTS

I wish to acknowledge Clella Bay Murray who prepared the references and provided technical editing of this paper. I also want to thank Sarah Roberts Foulke who offered suggestions for improving the manuscript. Finally, I want to express my gratitude to Marge Murvine for her patient typing of numerous drafts (always with my promise that this would be the last).

REFERENCES

1. Brenmer, R. H. 1970. Children and Youth in America: A Documentary History 1: 37. Harvard University Press. Boston, Mass.
2. Steinmetz, S. K. 1978. Violence between family members. Marriage and Family Rev. 1(3): 1-16.
3. Straus, M. A., R. J. Gelles & S. K. Steinmetz. 1978. Physical violence in a nationally representative sample of American families. Presented at the 9th World Congress of Sociology, Uppsala, Sweden, August 14-19.
4. Parnas, R. I. 1967. The police response to domestic disturbances. Wisc. Law Rev. 914: 914-960.
5. Besharov, D. J. 1975. Building a community response to child abuse and maltreatment. Children Today 4(5): 2-4.
6. Straus, M. A., R. J. Gelles & S. K. Steinmetz. 1980. Behind Closed Doors: Violence in the American Family. Doubleday & Co., Inc. New York, N.Y.
7. Straus, M. A. 1974. Leveling civility and violence in the family. J. of Marriage and the Family 36: 13-19.
8. Steinmetz, S. K. 1977. The use of force for resolving family conflict: the training ground for abuse. The Family Coordinator 26: 19-26.
9. Steinmetz, S. K. 1977. The Cycle of Violence: Assertive, Aggressive and Abusive Family Interaction. Praeger Publishers. New York, N.Y.
10. Gelles, R. J. 1974. The Violent Home: A Study of Physical Aggression between Husbands and Wives. Sage Publications. Beverly Hills, Calif.
11. Steinmetz, S. K. 1977. Wifebeating—husband beating—a comparison of the use of physical violence between spouses to resolve marital fights. In Battered Women: A Psychosociological Study of Domestic Violence. M. Roy, Ed.: 63-72. Van Nostrand Reinhold Co. New York, N.Y.

12. ELMER, E. 1971. Studies of child abuse and infant accidents. *In* The Mental Health of the Child. U.S. National Institute of Mental Health. U. S. Government Printing Office. Washington, D.C.
13. HALTER, J. C. & S. B. FRIEDMAN. 1968. Principals of management in child abuse cases. Am. Orthopsychiatry **38**(1): 127–138.
14. STEEL, B. F. & D. A. POLLOCK. 1974. A psychiatric study of parents who abuse infants and small children. *In* The Battered Child. R. E. Helper & C. H. Kempe, Eds.: 89–134. University of Chicago Press. Chicago, Ill.
15. KEMPE, C. H. & R. E. HELPER, Eds. 1972. Helping the Battered Child and His Family. J. P. Lippincott Co. Philadelphia, Penn.
16. SMITH, S. M., L. HONIGSBERGER & C. A. SMITH. 1973. EEG and personality factors in baby beaters. Br. Med. J. **3**: 20–22.
17. GIL, D. G. 1970. Violence Against Children: Physical Child Abuse in the United States. Harvard University Press. Cambridge, Mass.
18. GELLES, R. J. 1973. Child abuse as psychopathology: a sociological critique and reformation. Am. J. Orthopsychiatry **43**: 611–621.
19. SNELL, J., R. ROSENWALD & A. ROBEY. 1964. The wifebeater's wife. A study of family interaction. Arch. Gen. Psychiatry **11**: 107–112.
20. HILBERMAN, E. & I. MUNSON. 1977–78. Sixty battered women. Victimology **2**: 460–470.
21. GELLES, R. J. 1967. Abused wives: Why do they stay? J. Marriage and the Family **38**: 659–668.
22. STRAUS, M. A. 1973. A general systems theory approach to a theory of violence between family members. Social Science Info. **12**: 105–125.
23. STRAUS, M. A. 1977–78. Wifebeating: How common and why? Victimology **2**: 443–457.
24. ROY, M. 1977. Battered Women: A Psychosociological Study of Domestic Violence. Van Nostrand Reinhold Co. New York, N.Y.
25. PRESCOTT, S. & C. LETKO. 1977. Battered: a social psychological perspective. *In* Battered Women: A Psychosociological Study of Domestic Violence. M. Roy, Ed.: 72–96. Van Nostrand Reinhold Co. New York, N.Y.
26. RIDINGTON, J. 1977–78. The transition process: a feminist environment as reconstitutive milieu. Victimology **2**: 563–575.
27. RESNICK, M. 1976. Wife Beating. Counselor Training Manual #1. NOW—Wife Assault Task Force. Ann Arbor, Mich.
28. WALKER, I. E. 1977–78. Battered women and learned helplessness. Victimology **2**: 525–534.
29. STEINMETZ, S. K. 1978. Wife beating: a critique and reformation of existing theory. Bull. Am. Acad. Psychiatry and Law **4**(3): 322–334.
30. BLUMBERG, M. 1964–65. When parents hit out. Twentieth Century **173**: 39–44.
31. JOHNSON, B. & H. A. MORSE. 1968. Injured children and their parents. Children **15**: 147–152.
32. STRAUS, M. A. 1976. Sexual unequality, cultural norms and wifebeating. Victimology **1**: 54–76.
33. YOUNG, L. R. 1964. Wednesday's Children: A Study of Child Neglect and Abuse. McGraw-Hill Book Co. New York, N.Y.
34. FARRINGTON, K. 1977. Family violence and household density; Does the crowded home breed aggression? Paper presented at the Annual Meeting of the Society for the Study of Social Problems, Chicago, Ill., September 5–9.
35. MCKINLEY, D. G. 1964. Social Class and Family Life. The Free Press. New York, N.Y.
36. LEVINGER, G. 1966. Sources of marital dissatisfaction among applicants for divorce. Am. J. Orthopsychiatry **36** (5): 803–807.
37. O'BRIEN, J. E. 1971. Violence in divorce-prone families. J. Marriage and the Family **33**: 692–698.
38. STEINMETZ, S. K. 1971. Occupation and physical punishment: a response to Straus. J. Marriage and the Family **33**: 664–666.
39. STEINMETZ, S. K. 1974. Occupational environment in relation to physical punishment and dogmatism. *In* Violence in the Family. S. K. Steinmetz & M. A. Straus, Eds. Harper and Row, Publishers. New York, N.Y.

40. SKOLNICK, J. H. 1969. Justice Without Trial: Law Enforcement in Democratic Society. John Wiley & Sons, Inc. New York, N.Y.
41. NIEDERHOFFER, A. 1967. Behind the Shield, The Police in Urban Society. Doubleday & Co., Inc. Garden City, N.Y.
42. MACNAMARA, D. E. & E. SAGARIN. 1971. Perspectives on Correction. Thomas Y. Crowell. New York, N.Y.
43. SHWED, J. A. 1979. The military environment and physical child abuse. M. A. Thesis. University of New Hampshire. Durham, N.H.
44. MERRIL, E. J. 1962. Protecting the Battered Child. Children's Division, American Human Association. Denver, Colo.
45. LENOSKI, E. F. 1974. Translating injury data into preventative and health care services— physical child abuse. University of Southern California School of Medicine. Los Angeles, Calif. (Unpublished manuscript.)
46. ELMER, E. & G. S. GREGG. 1967. Developmental characteristics of abused children. Pediatrics 40: 596–602.
47. SCHLOSSER, P. 1964. The abused child. Bull. of the Menninger Clinic 28: 260.
48. LANSKY, L. M., V. S. CRANDALL, J. KAGAN & C. T. BAKER. 1961. Sex differences in aggression and its correlates in middle class adolescents. Child Dev. 32: 45–58.
49. TOBY, J. 1966. Violence and the masculine ideal: some qualitative data. Ann. Am. Acad. Political and Social Sci. 364: 19–27.
50. WHITEHURST, R. N. 1974. Violence in husband-wife interaction. In Violence in the Family. S. K. Steinmetz & M. A. Straus, Eds. Harper and Row, Publishers. New York, N.Y.
51. HOFFMAN, L. W. 1978. Changes in family roles, socialization, and sex differences. In Family Factbook: 59–72. Marquis Academic Media. Chicago, Ill.
52. WHITING, B. 1965. Sex identity conflict and physical violence: a comparative study. Am. Anthropol. 67: 123–140.
53. RADBILL, S. X. 1968. A history of child abuse and infanticide. In The Battered Child. R. E. Helper & C. H. Kempe, Eds. University of Chicago Press. Chicago, Ill.
54. STEINMETZ, S. K. 1977–78. The battered husband syndrome. Victimology 2(3–4): 499–509.
55. STEINMETZ, S. K. 1977. Secondary analysis of data from a United States-Canadian comparison of intra-family conflict. Canadian Conferences on Family Violence, Simon Fraser University, Burnaby, Canada, March 12.
56. CURTIS, L. A. 1974. Criminal Violence: National Patterns and Behavior. Lexington Books. Lexington, Mass.
57. WILT, G. M. & J. D. BANNON. 1976. Violence and the Police: Homicides, Assaults and Disturbances. The Police Foundation. Washington, D.C.
58. GELLES, R. J. 1975. Violence and pregnancy: a note on the extent of the problem and needed services. The Family Coordinator 24(1): 81–86.
59. WERTHAM, F. 1972. Battered children and baffled adults. Bull. N.Y. Acad. Med. 48: 887–898.
60. MACANDREW, C. & R. B. EDGERTON. 1969. Drunken Comportment: A Social Explanation. Aldine Press. Chicago, Ill.
61. WASSERMAN, S. 1967. The abused parent of the abused child. Children 14: 175–179.
62. OWENS, D. J. & M. A. STRAUS. 1975. The social structure of violence in childhood and approval of violence as an adult. Aggressive Behavior 1(2): 193–211.
63. SEDGELY, J. & D. LUND. 1979. Self reported beatings and subsequent tolerance for violence. Public Data Use 7(1): 30–38.
64. GAYFORD, J. J. 1975. Wife-beating: a preliminary survey of 100 cases. Br. Med. J. 1: 194–197.
65. OLIVER, J. E. & A. TAYLOR. 1971. Five generations of ill-treated children in one family pedigree. Br. J. Psychiatry 119: 473–480.
66. SILVER, L. B., C. C. DUBLIN & R. S. LOURIE. 1969. Does violence breed violence? Contribution from a study of the child abuse syndrome. Am. J. Psychiatry 126: 404–407.
67. ZALBA, S. R. 1966. The abused child: a survey of the problem. Social Work 11: 3–16.
68. GLADSTON, R. 1975. Preventing the abuse of little children: the parents' center project for the study and prevention of child abuse. Am. J. Orthopsychiatry 45(3): 372–381.

THE CHARISMATIC LEADER AND THE VIOLENT SURROGATE FAMILY

Fred Wright

Department of Psychology
John Jay College of Criminal Justice
New York, New York 10019

Phyllis Wright

The New York Counseling and Guidance Service
New York, New York 10024

In recent times a new kind of violent behavior has emerged that is both shocking and puzzling. A variety of familylike groups, usually religiously oriented and often headed by highly charismatic leaders, have engaged in unusually bizarre and violent behavior. Generally referred to as cults, they have carried out their activities in a fairly methodical and cohesive fashion. The most dramatic example, of course, is the murder of the United States Congressman Leo J. Ryan and members of his investigating party, as well as the subsequent mass suicide of more than 900 members of the People's Temple, that occurred in Guyana on November 18, 1978. Other examples of violent cults abound. There was the Charles Manson group, which functioned in the early 1970s and which murdered a number of people in California in an unusually grim and sadistic manner. Recently, members of Synanon, a well-known California-based group, originally founded to treat drug addiction and lately reported to be taking on the characteristics of a cult, has been accused of the attempted murder of a prosecutor by putting a rattlesnake in his mailbox. In 1977, a self-styled renegade Mormon prophet named Immanuel David—who, like Jim Jones, had been visited by holocaustic visions—killed himself. The next morning, his wife helped their seven children jump from their eleventh floor hotel room and then followed them. Another renegade Mormon prophet, Ervil Le Baron, who heads a sect called the Church of the Lamb of God, has been convicted of inciting some of his followers to murder his own brother, as well as others, apparently to consolidate his leadership position within his group.

Coercion and violence appear to be a common and an accepted characteristic of many other cults as well. According to reports by the news media,[22] investigating governmental agencies,[28] and ex-members of these organizations,[4] psychological pressure, physical punishment, and/or violent threats are used against those who violate group norms or criticize the cult.

It is the purpose of this paper to develop a clearer understanding of these phenomena by reviewing and discussing the research, theories, and explanations of behavioral scientists that are relevant.

Recently, there has been some empirical research directly related to cult phenomena. Three of the studies reviewed are consistent in their findings regarding the needs of individuals who join cults.[13,24,25] These researchers, working independently of each other, all found that members had experienced significant emotional distress before entering the cult, and that they usually experienced, at least for a time, considerable relief from this distress once involved in the cult. Two of the studies account for this relief by concluding that cult members' hunger for ideology was nourished, for a while at any rate, through membership.[13,25] This has been a frequently given explanation for religious conversion.[5,17] However, the data from the Ullman study[24] of conversion to mainstream religious groups, as well as conversion to the newer sorts of groups under discussion here, don't support this conclusion. Her study was the only one that directly compared converts to regular members on the basis of a search for truth or meaning. She found no difference between the two groups in interest for the search for explanations of topics like the scientific notion of truth or problems of social injustice. She did find that, among the converts, there was a strong need for an accepting authority figure to calm emotional turmoil rooted in childhood. Eighty percent of the experimental subjects, compared to 20% of the controls, had negative feelings about their fathers, or their fathers had been absent while they were growing up. Therefore, Ullman concludes that a high percentage of subjects were looking for father figures and believes that this lends support to Freud's theory that religious conversion, in part, represents a search for a father figure.

In light of Ullman's findings and the fact that psychoanalytically oriented writers have spent a great deal of time and effort exploring the nature of relations between authority figures and subjects via the notion of transference, it would be of value to the purpose of this paper to review that notion as it relates to the topic under discussion. As already noted, Freud accounted for religion-seeking behavior partly as a search for a father figure. He repeats this theme in a number of his books, and also introduces the concept of transference to further explain this kind of behavior.[7-11] According to Freud, people defend themselves against the terrors of life by transferring onto a deity feelings that they had, as children, directed towards their father. In effect, they transfer their dependency needs from their real-world father onto an exalted, heavenly father who will then protect and nourish them if they behave properly, i.e., if they are good children.

Erich Fromm, another leading psychoanalytic writer, developed Freud's views on the transference of authority, particularly in his well-known book *Escape from Freedom.*[12] Here he points out that people have a tendency to give up the independence of their own individual self and to strive to fuse or bind themselves up with somebody or something outside of themselves in order to acquire the strength that they feel they lack.

Fromm focuses particularly on the kind of person he refers to as the authoritarian character. This is the individual who seeks a "magic helper," as Fromm describes it. This helper is a person or personification, such as a principle or God, who will protect, help, and develop the individual; be with him or her always; and never leave the individual alone. When real persons assume this role, according to Fromm, they arc endowed with magic qualities. Those who endow do so out of an inability to stand alone and to fully express their own individual potentialities. They hope to get everything they want from life through the magic helper, instead of through their own actions. This process is illustrated by the Unification Church's practice of having the church leader, Rev. Moon, select marriage partners as well as arrange the weddings for church members.[2]

This kind of dependency can result in an individual's whole life being focused almost entirely on getting the helper to fulfill his or her wishes. People differ in the means they use to achieve this. Some use obedience, some "goodness," while for others suffering is the main means of manipulating the magic helper. This dependency creates a certain amount of security but also results in a feeling of weakness and bondage. In effect, the individual feels enslaved by the helper.

More recently Ernest Becker, in his Pulitzer Prize winning book *The Denial of Death,*[1] has synthesized the notions of a number of psychoanalysts who have discussed transference to authority figures. One aspect of the authority transference, according to him, is in its use as a control device. Through it we are, or believe we are, capable of opposing reality and keeping it ordered or "fixed" so that we can pursue our own expansion and fulfillment. By allying ourselves with another who seems to be made up of all the qualities we feel we are missing, we reduce ambiguity and achieve clarity and boundedness; in short, we believe we have gained control over the world and our fate rather than their controlling us.

Another aspect of the transference to leaders, according to Becker, is that it enables us to overcome our fear of life, of emerging into the world, and of realizing our own individuality, experiencing, and living. By binding ourselves to one person we believe we will tame this terror. For example, by incorporating another's ideology, we hope to free ourselves from the difficult work of having to develop one of our own.

The third use of transference noted by Becker is that through it people believe immortality will be gained. Via transference, the individual fantasizes she or he will overcome even death. That is, in deifying others by placing them on pedestals or by endowing them with extraordinary powers, the believer becomes more powerful. It is as though the more the idealized other possesses, the more the believer possesses and thus feels more secure. This notion helps us to understand the extraordinary mourning and panic that can occur when a leader dies or gets ill. When a leader with whom we have merged our identity and who has become our bulwark against death goes, we too go. We are abruptly faced with mortality at that point, and, most important, our own end comes into sharp focus. The transference object, endowed with supernatural powers, keeps us from perceiving that as long as she or he remains in good health.

Finally, Becker describes an authority transference as an "urge to higher heroism."[1] People need to infuse their life with value so that they can call it good. Transference, thus, is a talent in that it is a form of "creative fetishism," according to Becker. Through it, we take this mystery (our lives and the meaning of our lives) and dispel it by addressing our performance of heroics to another human being who then judges its value. We know if it is bad by the reaction of the idealized other and thus are able to change it. We are now in a position to achieve heroic self-validation, even though it comes through surrender to another's world-view. Thus, the traditional psychoanalytic view of transference as simply unreal projection is rejected. True, it is a distortion of reality but a distortion with two dimensions: distortion due to fears (of loss of control, of life, and of death), but also distortion due to the heroic attempt to assure self-expansion. Thus transference is not necessarily a cowardly maneuver, it can also be seen as a life-enhancing illusion.

Another aspect of transference not discussed by Becker, and yet of relevance to this paper, has to do with the notion of the "transitional object."[26] This is a concept frequently called upon by contemporary psychoanalysts to account for human behavior, and it becomes particularly valuable for this paper in light of the findings[13] of Galanter et al., mentioned earlier. They found that many of their subjects had been in transition at the time of their conversion to the cult. For example, many were ex-college students in the process of moving away from a school setting.

Winnicott was the first to describe transitional objects.[26] He saw them as the "first not-me possession" and referred to such objects as soft dolls, teddy bears, and security blankets. The notion of transitional phenomena grows out of the process of normal infant development. In the beginning , it is thought that children do not distinguish themselves from the mothering one. As development proceeds, however, the mother begins to withdraw her complete support, and the child must adapt to an existence separate from mother. In order to accomplish this separation, a bridge between mother and the outside world must be established. According to Winnicott, a soft object, such as a blanket, becomes the transitional object that enables the growing child to negotiate this separation. This object symbolizes the mother and at the same time is not the mother. It provides an anchor point from which to approach reality and integrate subjective and objective experiences, as well as serving as a defense against anxiety.

Others have indicated that the concept of the transitional object can be broadened to cover a variety of human behaviors other than those of early developmental stages.[16,19,14] For example, Halpern has said "we may define it as applying to any object or habit that a person of any age may use to span the gap between any developmental stage and the one following by carrying the illusion of the previous stage with him until he is ready to stand unaided in the next."[14] These notions enable us then to conceive of the cult leader as a transitional object for certain people who are in a transition. The leader is invested with properties from the member's subjective needs and experiences, as well as retaining part of his or her external identity. The leader-object then enables the person to separate from or leave an earlier developmental stage and move on to something else while at the same time retaining remnants of what was left behind. For example, a young person who joins a cult may separate from the family of origin and simultaneously retain parental and sibling surrogates and, therefore, a family feeling.

Other groups or organizations that may serve the same function are youth gangs, underworld organizations, college fraternities and sororities, encounter groups, psychotherapy groups, or the fan clubs that form around popular entertainers. The gang leader, godfather, housemother, group therapist, or celebrity entertainer serves the same function in fantasy as the cult leader. This may explain, in part, the need of a cult leader like Jim Jones to maintain his heroic, "star" image by, for example, dyeing his hair pitch black and "performing miracles," i.e., faith healing. He could be perceived as doing so, at least in part, in order to retain his position as a glamorous and therefore comforting transitional object for his followers.

Thus far the research reviewed has shown that those who are most susceptible to the appeals of cults are people who are experiencing considerable emotional distress, as well as those who are in a state of transition, or—as Margaret Singer, a psychologist who has also studied modern cults, puts it—who "are between meaningful affiliations."[6]

The Ungerleider et al.[25] study found something else that is of particular relevance to this paper. They assessed hostility and found that those who remained in cults, when compared to those who joined and eventually left, were significantly higher on the variables of "anger at family members" ($P < 0.007$), as measured by the Minnesota multiphasic personality inventory, and "overcontrolled hostility" ($P < 0.05$), as measured on a subscale developed by Megargee.[18] The authors reasoned that the "cults appear to serve as externalized superego substitutes," helping members manage hostile impulses. Thus those who remain in cults appear to be people who are having difficulty managing their aggression. The cult becomes a vehicle through which they can gain control of themselves, and more specifically, it may very well offer them a means to express their anger at family members by rejecting them for another, "better" family and at the same time legitimate their anger. Rev. Moon, for example, describes his church as a "true family" and casts the external world and the family or origin in highly negative terms.[4] These findings suggest that anger at authority figures may be a particular problem for cultists, and yet one that they have not coped with very successfully. Thus another dimension would be added to the cultists' need for the cult leader. That is, the leader helps them in their efforts to govern their own aggression.

It would appear, at least in violent cults, that not only does the leader help members to control their hostility, he also helps members to express it. Wilfred Bion[3] and Fritz Redl[20] have written extensively about this latter phenomenon. As Redl puts it, the leader, or a central person in the group, is unconflicted about matters that the rest of the group members feel inhibited about. Members thus admire this person for being unconflicted about matters they too experience, but feel conflict or shame over. Further, when this unconflicted person initiates an antisocial act, the meaning of that act is changed, freeing others to act because the risk had been taken by the leader. That is, they avoid the guilt or responsibility for acting incurred by the leader and therefore the members can act in a guiltless or nonresponsible fashion. The leader therefore transforms the world for the followers, making it possible for them to do that which they always wanted to do but which was forbidden by internalized norms or repressions, e.g., engage in promiscuous sex or aggression towards others or the self.

Bion extends this notion regarding the "use" people in groups make of leaders.[3] According to him, the leader is as much a creature of the group and its shared emotion, as the group members are his creatures. In fact, he must reflect or mirror their assumptions and feelings in order to qualify for leadership in the first place. Leaders become leaders to particular people because they epitomize or represent in a very concrete way something that is within their followers that the followers are either unable, unwilling, or afraid to acknowledge and express.

The research of Edwin Megargee[18] is also helpful in furthering understanding of this matter. He finds that when comparing offenders who engage in unusually excessive violent behavior (e.g., impulse murderers) to other criminal groups (e.g., moderate aggressors, property offenders, burglars), the violent offenders were assessed as less hostile, less aggressive, and more controlled. In fact, the excessively violent were "overcontrolled." He showed that such people tended to be extremely dependent, submissive, and passive individuals with rigid control over aggressive impulses as long as their dependency was gratified. When the dependency gratification was withdrawn they would become murderously assaultive toward the depriver. The history of these individuals showed that they had had maternal figures who had emphasized conformity to the rules of the social system, and that to gain affection they'd had to deny or repress any hostility. Thus they had never learned how to express hostile feelings. Megargee further hypothesizes that the excessively violent response is not determined by the immediate stimulus but rather that it is a function of the absolute or total amount of instigation to aggression that had been slowly building up over a preceding period of time. This partially accounts for the violent behavior that appears to be all out of proportion to the immediate stimulus (e.g., the response of the People's Temple to Congressman Ryan's investigation).

Megargee suggests as treatment for the overcontrolled a psychotherapy that aims to reduce excessive inhibitions so that the individual can learn to acknowledge and accept his feelings of hostility and learn ways of satisfaction while still not posing too great a threat to society.

Thus far in this paper we have drawn largely on the notions of psychoanalytic thinkers in our efforts to understand abnormal group behavior. However, there are other formulations that can be of use to us as well. For example, susceptibility to suggestion and/or imitation are frequently offered as explanations for hard-to-understand group responses. In fact, those who have analyzed the conversion process in the new religious groups have shown that the recruiters go to great lengths to generate conditions that make it easier for suggestion to take hold. Christopher Edwards, an ex-member of the Unification Church and author of the book on his experiences in this church entitled *Crazy for God*,[4] describes in detail the well-organized technology involved: the chanting, singing, confessions, and group activities that tend to mesmerize and lower the sense of being a separate, independent being; the physical demands and inadequate diet that sap the energy required to thoroughly think issues through; and the constant repetition of the group's ideology coupled with reinforcements contingent upon attitudes and behaviors acceptable to the group.

Stanley Cath, a psychiatrist who had treated ex-cult members, contends, in fact, that there are neurophysiological factors that are being manipulated by technology-wise cult leaders, thereby altering individuals' levels of consciousness and making them far more susceptible to the leader's wishes and influence.[21]

Another explanation for irrational group behavior is presented by Ralph Turner and Lewis Killian in their excellent and comprehensive book *Collective Behavior.*[23] According to them, both psychoanalytic and contagion or suggestion/imitation theories make valuable contributions toward understanding bizarre collective behavior. They qualify their support, however, by indicating that these theories neglect the complexity of people. According to these writers not all members in a group feel and act the same way. They agree with psychoanalytic theory that people have latent or repressed tendencies, but they contend that rather than having only one or a few such tendencies people have several latent tendencies that are relevant to a given situation. If this is the case, then it also becomes important to explain how a group of people with a variety of different urges winds up acting in what, at least to the outside observer, looks like a form of united craziness.

Their explanation lies in what they term "emergent norms."[23] They say that in a particular situation interaction among group members occurs, and that norms then emerge that are specific to the situation. "These 'emergent' norms define those acts that, out of many sorts of behavior that might be possible in the situation, are expected or permitted in this particular crowd. Tendencies to behave in a different fashion are then restrained, and individuals who remain a part of the crowd experience pressure to behave in the manner that has been defined as appropriate."[23] That is, a common or shared understanding as to what sort of behavior is expected in a particular situation develops. This shared understanding encourages behavior consistent with the norm, inhibits behavior contrary to it, and justifies restraining action against individuals who dissent. Since the norm is to some degree specific to the situation, differing in degree or in kind from the norms governing noncrowd situations, it is an "emergent" norm.

They are saying, then, that bizarre group or crowd behavior is similar in many respects to routine crowd or organized behavior. People define their situation, taking into account all the knowledge or information that is available to them at the time, and take on roles or particular functions in their group, for example, becoming leaders and followers. As a result, though the behavior may appear irrational and asocial from outside the crowd, given the fund of information available within the group at that particular time and place and the collective definition of the situation they arrive at as a result of that fund, the behavior members then pursue may seem quite appropriate to them. In effect, an "irrational" group defines the situation differently than the larger group it is part of would define it and, as a result, is governed by norms that are at variance with those of the larger society.

One last point made by Turner and Killian of relevance to this paper has to do with the matter of the significance of anonymity for crowd behavior. They point out that "if crowd behavior is subject to social control under an emergent norm, it is important that the individual in the crowd have an identity so that the control of the crowd can be effective."[23] According to this perspective, the control of the crowd should be greatest among persons who are known to one another rather than among anonymous persons. Therefore, control should be greatest in cults, in comparison to other sorts of crowds or collectives, because people are very well known to each other.

Christopher Edwards confirms this in his account of his life in the Unification Church, where he shows how the proselytizing group went to great lengths to let the initiates know that they were indeed not only well known by the group, but were in fact very highly regarded for their potential to become outstanding supporters of the group's normative system.[4] Where control is great in a group it can be expected that the group as a whole, without dissent or with minimal dissent, will be likely to engage in prescribed behavior regardless of how this behavior appears to people who are not part of that social system.

The last matter to be dealt with in this paper is the cult leaders themselves and their appeal. What information do we have that will enable us to understand these people and the oftentimes enormous influence they have over their followers?

Otto Kernberg,[15] an American psychiatrist and psychoanalyst, describes a personality syndrome that sounds a great deal like that of the various cult leaders who have received public attention in recent times. Specifically, he writes about a subgroup of borderline patients referred to as the narcissistic personality. He describes these patients as presenting excessive self-absorption, usually coinciding with a superficially smooth and effective social adaptation, but with serious distortions in their internal relationships with people. That is, they have serious deficiencies in their capacity to love and to empathize with others. As a consequence, exploitativeness and ruthlessness toward others are also characteristics of these patients.

Further, according to Kernberg, these patients are characterized by various combinations of intense ambitiousness, grandiose fantasies, and overdependence on external admiration and acclaim. They are on a continuous search for gratification of strivings for brilliance, wealth, power, and beauty. Finally, he stresses the presence of chronic, intense envy in these people, and defenses against such envy—particularly devaluation of others, omnipotent control, and narcissistic withdrawal—as major characteristics of their emotional life.

What is the etiology of such a personality type according to Kernberg? First, chronically cold parental figures with covert but intense aggression are a frequent feature in the background of such patients. There is a parental figure, usually the mother or mother surrogate, who functions well on the surface in the home, but with a fair degree of callousness, indifference, and nonverbalized and spiteful aggression. The need for children to defend against the expression of their own envy and hatred in such an environment is obvious, thus leading to the devaluation, control, and withdrawal defenses just mentioned. Another consequence of this childhood environment is the development of a deep conviction of being unworthy, and a view of the world as devoid of nurturance and love.

In addition, the histories of such patients show that they often possessed a quality that could have aroused the envy or admiration of others. For example, unusual physical attractiveness or a special talent became refuge against feelings of being unloved and even hated. Sometimes these patients were used by other family members as a means to garner attention and admiration. Often they were designated the "brilliant" child in the family who was slated to fulfill the family's or a family member's aspiration for greatness. This special position in the family became the source around which the patients' grandiose fantasies became crystallized. Clearly, people with needs and traits like these would be logical candidates for the role of cult leader; such a position or "job" would be highly attractive to them and complement their emotional profile.

Another view of this character type has been explored by Robert Ellwood, a researcher of religious movements. According to him, there are striking parallels between the religious phenomena of primitive shamanism and modern cults. In fact, he says "the cult phenomena could almost be called a modern resurgence of shamanism."[5]

The shaman, in primitive society, provided a variety of valuable services. First, he was usually a person who had gone through a severe emotional disorder of his own, and would probably be defined as mentally ill by ordinary standards. The sickness, however, became the vehicle for explorations of realms beyond the normal perimeters of the human spirit, which put the shaman in a position of healer. That is, through his own personal struggle with, and overcoming of, illness he is in a position to show others the way out of evil or illness. As a result, most shamans are medicine men in their cultures, but not all medicine men are shamans. For shamans usually have special qualities and techniques that enable them to induce mystical, ecstatic experiences. Thus, not only do they heal, they can also provide one with a new spiritual life. Further, Ellwood points out that it is the shaman who, during times of social and spiritual upheaval, breaks free of the traditional bonds and founds new faiths, thereby allowing people to cope with the new experience forced upon them. In summary, the shaman or cult leader's appeal rests in his or her capacity, or apparent capacity, to lead followers out of distress or illness as well as to provide them with a means for survival, even ecstasy, in a difficult and changing world.

Our understanding of the source of the cult leader's power is also furthered by recent research that shows that a person in a position of authority can be highly influential despite consciously striving to be the opposite. Wright, Buirski, and Smith studied graduate-level college students who had formed laboratory groups to study their own group process as well as the nature of group leadership.[27] The authors were surprised to learn the extent to which the group leaders were unknowingly influencing the group members' preferences for, attention to, and attributions about other members. This was measured by responses on a number of research instruments. The leaders themselves strove to conduct themselves in a nondirective and low-disclosing style, and believed they had done so. That is, their conscious intention was to avoid communicating preferences or directing members' attention or attributions. The striking thing about the research is how thoroughly unsuccessful they were in carrying out this intention. Group members sensed the leaders' preferences and interests and followed suit. Apparently, just being assigned the role of leader in a group is enough to profoundly influence the psychological processes of followers.

In sum, a review of the research and literature relevant to cult phenomena was undertaken in this paper in an effort to gain insight into the psychology of cult members, leaders, and the cult itself as an entity. In particular, an attempt was made to understand the sources of the extreme violence engaged in by a number of cults. Results from empirically oriented studies were focused on and related to the theoretical formulations of a number of behavioral scientists for further clarification. Findings indicated that cult members tended to be emotionally distressed people prior to cult membership and that once involved, they obtained considerable relief from this distress at least for a time. Further, research shows that many cult members had been in a state of transition at the time of conversion. People who remain in cults have also been found to be high on the variables of "anger at family members" and "overcontrolled hostility." Cult leaders appear to satisfy a variety of the needs of members as a result of their own personality structure in conjunction with the authority inherent in the role of group leader. Other group-level processes were analyzed in an effort to further account for the phenomena under study.

REFERENCES

1. BECKER, E. 1973. The Denial of Death. The Free Press. New York, N.Y.
2. BERNARD, J. 1979. 700 couples got engaged in the city yesterday . . . and many didn't know each other. New York Post (May 14): 30.
3. BION, W. R. 1959. Experiences in Groups. Basic Books. New York, N.Y.
4. EDWARDS, C. 1979. Crazy for God. Prentice-Hall Inc. Englewood Cliffs, N.J.
5. ELLWOOD, R. S. 1973. Religious and Spiritual Groups in Modern America. Prentice-Hall Inc. Englewood Cliffs, N.J.
6. FREEMAN, M. 1979. Of cults and communication: a conversation with Margaret Singer. A.P.A. Monitor (July/August): 6–7.
7. FREUD, S. 1919. Totem and Taboo. Paul Kegan. London, England.
8. FREUD, S. 1932. Leonardo Da Vinci. Paul Kegan. London, England.
9. FREUD, S. 1934. The Future of an Illusion. Hogarth Press. London, England.
10. FREUD, S. 1934. Civilization and Its Discontents. Hogarth Press. London, England.
11. FREUD, S. 1939. Moses and Monotheism. Hogarth Press. London, England.
12. FROMM, E. 1941. Escape from Freedom. Rhinehart and Winston, Inc. New York, N.Y.
13. GALANTER, M., R. RABKIN, J. RABKIN & A. DEUTSCH. 1979. The "Moonies": a psychological study of conversion and membership in a contemporary religious sect. Am. J. Psychiatry 136: 165–170.

14. HALPERN, H. M. 1968. Transitional phenomena: constructive or pathological. Voices 3: 44.
15. KERNBERG, O. 1975. Borderline Conditions and Pathological Narcissism. Jason Aronson, Inc. New York, N.Y.
16. KOSSEFF, J. W. 1975. The leader using object relations theory. *In* The Leader in the Group. Z. Liff, Ed. Jason Aronson, Inc. New York, N.Y.
17. LIFTON, R. J. 1956. Thought Reform and the Psychology of Totalism. W. W. Norton & Co., Inc. New York, N.Y.
18. MEGARGEE, E. I. 1966. Undercontrolled and overcontrolled personality types in extreme anti-social aggression. Psychological Monographs 80 (611).
19. MURRAY, M. E. 1974. The therapist as a transitional object. Am. J. Psychoanal. 34: 123–127.
20. REDL, F. 1942. Group emotion and leadership. Psychiatry 5: 573–596.
21. SHAPIRO, B., Producer. 1979. Cults: In the Name of God? American Broadcasting Companies, Inc. New York, N.Y. (Television program.)
22. THOMAS, J. & N. SHEPPARD, JR. 1979. Cults in America. New York Times (September 21): 1, 52.
23. TURNER, R. H. & L. M. KILLIAN. 1972. Collective Behavior. Prentice-Hall, Inc. Englewood Cliffs, N.J.
24. ULLMAN, C. 1979. Change of mind or change of heart? Some cognitive and emotional characteristics of religious converts. Ph.D. Thesis. Boston University. Boston, Mass.
25. UNGERLEIDER, T. & D. K. WELLISHCH. 1979. Coercive persuasion (brainwashing), religious cults, and deprogramming. Am. J. Psychiatry 136: 279–282.
26. WINNICOTT, D. W. 1958. Collected Papers: Through Paediatrics to Psycho-analysis. Tavistock Publications. London, England.
27. WRIGHT, F., P. BUIRSKI & N. SMITH. 1978. The implications of leader transparency for the dynamics of short-term process groups. Group 2: 210–219.
28. Attorney General of the State of New York. 1974. Final report on the activities of the Children of God. Charity Frauds Bureau.

PORNOGRAPHY AND VIOLENCE AGAINST WOMEN: EXPERIMENTAL STUDIES*

Edward Donnerstein

Department of Psychology
University of Wisconsin
Madison, Wisconsin 53706

Recently, the National Institute of Mental Health designated that an understanding of the conditions that lead to sexual attacks against women is a major problem area and requires an increased focus. While there are many potential avenues of investigation, one that seems to be of current concern is the role of media effects in the possible elicitation of such aggressive acts, particularly in the area of pornography. Although the 1970 Presidential Commission on Obscenity and Pornography concluded that there was no evidence of a relationship between exposure to erotic forms of presentations and subsequent aggression (particularly sexual crimes), recent criticisms of these findings[1-3] have led a number of investigators to reexamine this issue. Specifically, research by a number of individuals in the social-psychological area has indicated that under appropriate conditions exposure to erotic forms of media presentations can facilitate subsequent aggressive behavior.[4-8] While this research has been directed at the effects of erotic media presentations on behavior, the issue of whether such presentations can in some manner be related to increased aggressive attacks against women has been only recently of concern.[8,9] It is generally believed by a large proportion of the population that many sexual materials can precipitate violent sexual crimes, such as rape.[10] Basic research directed at examining this concern, in regard to erotic forms of media and other presentations that depict women as victims of aggression, is an important goal of social research. The present series of studies was designed to examine this issue.

BRIEF HISTORICAL BACKGROUND

What are the effects of erotic or pornographic materials on antisocial behavior? An examination of recent research and reports in the area would suggest that the effects are, if anything, nonharmful. For example:

It is concluded that pornography is an innocuous stimulus which leads quickly to satiation and that the public concern over it is misplaced.[11]

If a case is to be made against "pornography" in 1970, it will have to made on the grounds other than demonstrated effects of a damaging personal or social nature. Em-

---

* This paper was written while the author was a visiting professor at the University of Wisconsin. Study III and the writing of this paper was supported by a grant from the National Institute of Mental Health, 1 F32 MH 07788-01.

pirical research designed to clarify the question has found no reliable evidence to date that exposure to explicit sexual materials plays a significant role in the causation of delinquent or criminal sexual behavior among youth or adults.[10]

However, recent criticisms of these findings by a number of investigators[2,3] have led to a reexamination of the issue of erotic exposure and subsequent aggressive behavior. While some individuals, like Cline,[2] have argued that there are major methodological and interpretation problems with the pornography commission report, others[12] believe that the observations might be premature. The major reason for this concern comes, in part, from a recent series of experimental studies that suggests that the relationship between exposure to erotic materials and subsequent aggressive behavior is more complex than first believed. The brief review of this research that follows summarizes the current state of this issue.

Aggression-Enhancing Effects of Erotic Exposure

A number of studies in which subjects have been angered, and later exposed to some form of erotic stimulation, have revealed increased aggressive behavior.[4,13] In fact, there is evidence to suggest that the facilitative effects are greater than those attributed to aggressive films.[4,14] Such findings have been interpreted in terms of a general arousal model, stating that under conditions where aggression is a dominant response any source of emotional arousal will tend to increase aggressive behavior.[15] In accordance with this model, aggressive behavior, in subjects who have previously been angered, has been shown to be increased by exposure to arousing sources such as aggressive or erotic films,[4] physical exercise,[16] and noise.[17] It would seem that because of their arousing properties erotic stimuli can have aggression-facilitating effects under certain conditions. Although there has been research indicating that erotic stimuli might increase aggression without prior anger arousal,[18] the majority of evidence to date would suggest that prior anger arousal is an important condition for a facilitative effect of erotic exposure.

Aggression-Inhibiting Effects of Erotic Exposure

A second group of studies[19,20] have shown that exposure to erotic stimuli can actually reduce subsequent aggression. A number of explanations have been suggested for this effect: erotic stimuli are somehow incompatible, in their emotional state, with aggression;[19,21] the level of anger arousal is inappropriate for an aggressive response;[20] or erotic exposure shifts attention away from previous anger arousal.[6] Whatever the explanation, there is sound evidence to suggest that under certain conditions erotic stimuli can reduce subsequent aggressive behavior.

A Reconciliation of the Research

While at first glance such results seem somewhat contradictory, recent studies by Donnerstein *et al.*[6] and Baron and Bell [7] seem to have resolved this controversy. It is now believed that as erotic stimuli become more arousing, they give rise to increases in aggressive behavior. At a low level of arousal, however, such stimuli act to distract a subject's attention away from previous anger[6] or act as an incompatible response with aggression,[7] thus reducing subsequent aggressive behavior. The evidence for this curvilinear relationship between sexual arousal and aggression seems fairly well established. In fact, Baron[22] has shown that this type of relationship also occurs when females are exposed to mild and highly erotic stimuli.

The Issue of Erotic Stimuli and Aggression against Women

While the current theorizing on the relationship of erotic stimuli and aggression seems fairly conclusive, it is interesting to note that all of the aforementioned studies were concerned with same-sex, primarily male-to-male, aggression. Yet, the social implications of this research would be more applicable by an examination of male aggression toward females. For, as noted by the U. S. Commission on Obscenity and Pornography:

> It is often asserted that a distinguishing characteristic of sexually explicit materials is the degrading and demeaning portrayal of the role and the status of the human female. It has been argued that erotic materials describe the female as a mere sexual object to be exploited and manipulated sexually.[10]

In recent years there has been an increasing concern about the relationship of pornography and violence against women. Writers in both the popular media and the scientific community have addressed this issue. Generally, they have taken for granted that pornography and aggression against women are tightly linked:

> We are somewhat educated now as to the effects of rape on women, but we know less about the effects of pornography . . . we can admit that pornography is sexist propaganda, no more and no less. Pornography is the theory, and rape is the practice.[22]

> Pornography is the undiluted essence of anti-female propaganda . . . does one need scientific methodology in order to conclude that the anti-female propaganda that permeates our nation's cultural output promotes a climate in which acts of sexual hostility directed against women are not only tolerated by ideologically encouraged.[23]

> Even when they do not overtly depict scenes of violence and degradation of women at the hands of men, such as rape, beatings, and subordination, the tone is consistently anti-feminist. . . . The intention would seem to be simply to degrade women, and it is noteworthy that in many cases of rape the men involved either act in the same manner . . .[24]

However, what is the evidence regarding the relationship of pornography and aggression against women?

Some studies have attempted to determine whether or not erotica has a differential effect on aggression against men and against women. The general conclusion has been that no differential effects occur. Thus, in one series of studies, Mosher[25,26] found no increase in "sex-calloused" attitudes, aggressive verbal remarks, or exploitive sexual behavior toward females. More recent research by Jaffe *et al.*[5] and Baron and Bell [27] have also indicated that erotic exposure does not differentially affect men's aggression toward males or females.

There are a number of problems with the research that has examined the link between pornography and male aggression toward females. First, there is strong evidence that prior or subsequent anger instigation is critically important in facilitating aggression following erotic exposure. Given the fact that males are usually hesitant about aggressing against females,[28] and that in the above research subjects were not even instigated by their potential victim, it would seem unlikely that a differential facilitation in aggression would occur. In fact, except for the Jaffe *et al.* study,[5] researchers found that exposing nonangered individuals to erotic films tended to *reduce* aggression or maintain it at a level comparable to that of subjects exposed to a neutral film.[19]

Second, previous researchers have found that only under conditions of high sexual arousal does a facilitative effect in aggression occur. Exposure to mild sexually arousing stimuli seems to reduce aggression, even in previously angered individuals.[19,7,6] Again, except for Jaffe *et al.*,[5] the research that has examined the relationship of erotic stimuli and aggression toward females has employed milder forms of sexually arousing stimuli.

It would seem, therefore, that an appropriate test of the effects of erotic stimuli on aggression toward females would need to employ both some form of anger instigation and high levels of sexual arousal. This particular combination of important factors, which seems to account for the facilitative effects of erotic stimuli on aggression, has not, until recently, been investigated in those studies in which females are the victims of aggression from males.

Experiment I

A recent study by Donnerstein and Barrett[8] was designed to examine these issues using the theory and data of past research in the erotic stimuli-aggression area as a framework. Male subjects were exposed to either a neutral or highly arousing erotic film. The type of erotic stimuli employed was similar to those used in previous studies that have indicated facilitative effects for aggression.[4,13] In addition, prior to stimulus exposure subjects were either angered or treated in a neutral manner by a male or female target of aggression. Both aggressive behavior, in the form of electric shock, and physiological reactions of the subject were observed.

Since the procedures in the studies in this series were all similar, a few words regarding the methodology employed are presented. All subjects were male undergraduates who volunteered for the study as part of receiving extra credit in their course work. They believed that they were interacting with another male or female subject in a study on the effects of stress and performance. Our male subjects were first given an opportunity to write an essay with the understanding that the essay would be evaluated by the "other subject" via the delivery of electric shock. If the subject was in a condition where they were to be angered, they received a large number of shocks plus a negative written evaluation of their essay from the other male or female subject. Nonangered subjects received only one shock and a very positive evaluation. This type of procedure is very common in the literature and produces both physiological responses and self-reports that indicate that subjects have, in fact, been angered. Following this procedure, subjects were then given an opportunity to deliver shock to the "subject" who had evaluated their assay. No shock was actually delivered, but subjects assumed that they were in fact administering various levels of shock to this person. At various times in the studies, physiological responses of the subjects in the form of blood pressure, were measured. It should be noted that in addition to various consent forms that were signed by the subject, a complete debriefing as to the nature of the study was given to the subjects at the end of the session.

With this experimental procedure in mind, the first study in this series made a number of predictions based upon previous research in the area: (1) exposure to erotic films should increase aggressive behavior in angered individuals, while (2) no facilitation in aggressive behavior should occur for nonangered subjects. Of more immediate interest, however, were the following questions: (1) Would exposure to erotic stimuli differentially affect aggression toward males and females in subjects who have previously been instigated to aggress? (2) Might there be an increase in aggression toward females even without prior instigation due to implied sexually aggressive cues in the erotic films? and (3) What are the physiological patterns that emerge during film exposure? This third question was of special interest, in that from a theoretical perspective, the interaction of anger arousal and erotic-film-exposure arousal have been employed in an explanatory manner in this area.[4] To date, however, such results were based upon interactions with only male targets of aggression. There is a suggestion from prior research[29] that although males display less aggression toward females following provocation, physiological arousal is maintained at a high level. It seemed important, in terms of past research in this area, to examine further not only the arousal component of anger instigation from males to females, but also its interaction with highly arousing sexual stimuli. Donnerstein and Barrett[8] also examined the effects of anger, erotic stimuli, and sex on a more prosocial or rewarding response. Since it was expected that less social restraints would be present with this reward response than with the shock response toward females, subjects were given an opportunity in this study to administer rewards (money) to their target. The major results for this first study are presented in TABLES 1 and 2. With regard to aggression, as measured by the intensity and durations of shocks administered to the male or female, two interactions were found. The first, anger × sex of

TABLE 1

MEAN INTENSITY* × DURATION AS A FUNCTION OF EXPERIMENTAL CONDITIONS

	Means	
Condition	Anger	No Anger
Anger × Sex of Target		
Male	1.86$_a$	0.95$_c$
Female	1.55$_b$	1.13$_c$
Anger × Films		
Erotic	1.90$_a$	0.93$_c$
Neutral	1.45$_b$	1.15$_c$

* Means with a different subscript differ from each other at the 0.05 level by Duncan's procedure.

target, indicated that angered subjects were more aggressive than nonangered subjects and that subjects angered by a male were more aggressive than those angered by a female. The second, anger × films, indicated that under nonanger conditions there were no effects for the films shown, but, when subjects were angry the erotic film increased aggression. Thus, when subjects were exposed to highly arousing erotic stimuli there was a possibility for aggression to be facilitated. More important to the discussion is the fact that no differential aggression was observed toward females as a function of film exposure. In fact, as has been the case in past studies,[29] less aggression was administered to the female targets. Does this imply, therefore, that erotic films do not influence aggression towards females as suggested by the pornography commission?[10] The physiological data obtained in this study would suggest that perhaps another process was operating with angered subjects. The blood pressure data indicated that higher levels of arousal were obtained with a female rather than a male target after erotic exposure, and that this arousal was still present after aggressing. It might have been expected, therefore, that aggression would have been higher toward females than males. Results, however, tended to indicate just the opposite. Under anger conditions females were aggressed against less than males. It is interesting to note that Taylor and Epstein[29] also found increased physiological arousal in male subjects who were less aggressive toward a female target under attack conditions. One possible explanation for this type of finding, suggested by Dengerink,[28] is that aggression towards females is generally disapproved of, and that this fear of disapproval could act to inhibit aggression. Further evidence that males were inhibited from acting aggressively toward female targets in this study was suggested by the reward data. Under anger conditions a reduction in reward was found for females. It would seem reasonable to suggest that in the context of this study, changes in rewarding behavior would carry less social restraints than delivery of a noxious stimulus toward a female. If these results were a function of inhibitions toward aggressing against females, then conditions allowing

TABLE 2

MEAN CHANGE* IN BLOOD PRESSURE AS A FUNCTION OF
EXPERIMENTAL CONDITIONS AFTER FILM EXPOSURE

	Film	
Condition	Erotic	Neutral
	Mean Blood Pressure	
Anger		
Males	1.8_b	-0.2_b
Females	9.4_a	-3.1_c
No Anger		
Males	8.2_a	-3.9_c
Females	7.2_a	-3.9_c
	Systolic Blood Pressure	
Anger		
Males	2.8_b	-1.4_b
Females	11.3_a	-4.8_c
No Anger		
Males	11.2_a	-5.6_c
Females	8.6_a	-6.2_c

* Means with different subscripts differ from each other at the 0.05 level by Duncan's procedure.

for a reduction in inhibitions might reveal differential aggression toward males and females as a function of erotic exposure.

EXPERIMENT II

The purpose of this experiment was to create a condition in which male subjects would be less inhibited or restrained against aggressing toward a female, in order to examine the effects that erotic exposure would have upon such aggression. While there are many potential strategies to reduce aggressive inhibitions (e.g., aggressive models), the present study adopted a situation similar to that employed by Geen, Stonner, and Shope.[30] These investigators found that when subjects were given two opportunities to aggress against an anger instigator, aggression was higher than in a condition in which subjects were not given this initial aggression opportunity. Furthermore, subjects in the double aggression condition reported less restraints against aggressing than individuals in all other conditions. Additional support for this increase in aggression, following an initial opportunity to aggress, has been provided by a number of investigators (e.g., Reference 31). In the context of the present experiment, it was hypothesized that allowing male subjects an initial opportunity to aggress against a female would act to reduce any aggression inhibitions present. If erotic films are capable of facilitating aggression against females, then the present experiment, by incorporating both anger instigation and highly erotic films in ad-

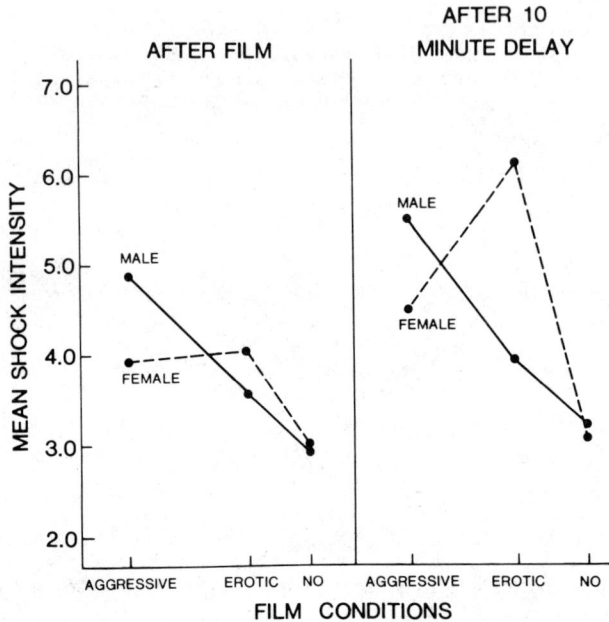

FIGURE 1. Mean shock intensity as a function of film conditions, sex of target, and time of aggression.

dition to a reduction in inhibitions, should allow for a more judicious test of this possibility.

In this study, male subjects were angered by a male or female target prior to being placed into one of three film conditions. Before being given an opportunity to aggress, subjects viewed either a highly erotic film, aggressive film, or no film. After having one opportunity to aggress against the male or female target, subjects waited 10 minutes and were given a second opportunity to aggress.

The results of the present study, as seen in FIGURE 1, would suggest that highly erotic films can act to increase aggressive responses against females under certain conditions. When male subjects were given an opportunity to aggress immediately following film exposure, it was found that highly erotic films did increase aggression beyond that of the no-film controls. This finding corroborates those of other investigators[6, 4] who have found that highly arousing erotica can act as a facilitator of aggression in previously angered individuals. In addition, it was found that during this initial aggression opportunity there was no differential aggression toward males or females. These results are also supportive of previous studies (e.g., References 27, 8, 5) that have indicated no sex-of-target effects following erotic exposure. However, when male subjects were given a second opportunity to aggress against the target, 10 minutes later, aggressive responses were increased against female targets. This finding of an increase in aggression against women in the delayed condition is the first demonstration that this effect can, in fact, occur.

EXPERIMENT III

It has been suggested that a major problem with the conclusion of the pornography commission report[10] was the lack of research on "porno-violence,"or aggressive content in erotic forms of materials.[2] This lack of research was surprising given the results of the National Commission on the Causes and Prevention of Violence,[32] dealing with media aggression and its effect on subsequent aggressive behavior.

Given the nature of most erotic films, in which women are depicted in a submissive, passive role, any subtle aggressive content could act to increase aggression against females because of their association with observed aggression. As noted in the work of Berkowitz,[33] one important determinant of whether an aggressive response is made is the presence of aggressive cues. Not only objects, but individuals can take on aggressive-cue value if they have been associated with observed violence. Thus, in the context of the present research, the viewing of more sexually aggressive films might facilitate aggression towards females because of the aggression-eliciting stimulus properties of the female target from her repeated association with observed violence. This increase in aggression should be especially true for previously angered individuals who are already predisposed to aggress. In the research discussed up to this point the films employed did not contain acts of aggression. If they did, perhaps the results would have differed with respect to female victims.

In order to examine this issue, male subjects in the present study[34] were angered or treated in a neutral manner by a male or female. They were then shown one of three films. Two of the films were highly erotic but differed in aggressive content. While one film was entirely nonaggressive, the other depicted the rape of a women by a man who breaks into her house and forces her at gunpoint into sexual activity. The third film was a neutral (nonerotic and nonaggressive) presentation.

The major results are presented in FIGURE 2. Two interactions occurred which deserve attention. The first, anger × film, indicated that both the erotic and aggressive-erotic film increased aggression, primarily in angered individuals. The largest increase occurred, however, for subjects exposed to the aggressive-erotic film. The second interaction, sex of target × film, indicated that while both types of erotic films increased aggression against a male, only the aggressive-erotic film facilitated aggression against a female, and this level of aggression was higher than that directed against a male. Why would aggression be increased against the female after exposure to the aggressive-erotic film? One potential explanation is that the females' association with the victim in the film made her an aggressive stimulus that could elicit aggressive responses (e.g., Reference 33). The combination of anger and arousal from the film heightened this response and led to the highest

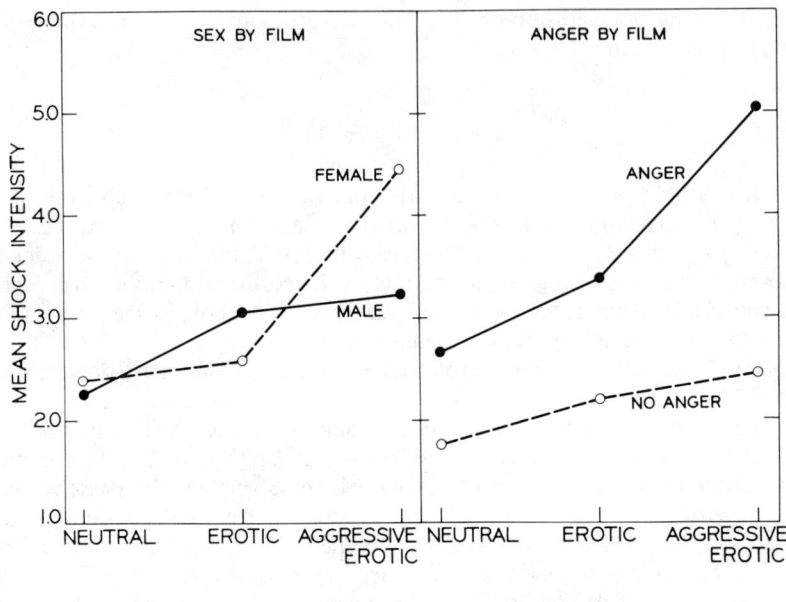

FIGURE 2. Mean shock intensity as a function of sex of target by films, and anger by films.

level of aggression against the female. But, even under nonanger conditions aggression was increased. This was not the case for subjects paired with a male. Under nonanger, the aggressive-erotic film did not influence aggression against the male target. It would seem, then, that the female's association with observed violence was an important contributor to the aggressive responses toward her. If this is the case then it would be expected that films that depict violence against women, even without sexual content, could act as a stimulus for aggressive acts toward women. It seems important, therefore, for future research to begin a systematic investigation into the context of women's association with violence in the media.

CONCLUSION AND IMPLICATIONS

It was the intention of the present research to examine the effects that certain media presentations have on aggression against women. Results from these investigation suggest that films of both an erotic *and* aggressive nature can be a mediator of aggression toward women. In addition to the theoretical implications of these results, there is a more applied question that has been the concern of the present paper. When it is found that (1) 50% of university females report some form of sexual aggression,[35] (2) 39% of the sex offenders questioned indicate that pornography had something to do with the crime they committed,[36] and (3) the incidence of rape and other sexual assaults have increased then the question of what conditions precipitate such actions should be examined. The present research suggests that specific types of media account for part of these actions. Given the increase in sexual and other forms of violence against women depicted in the media, a concern over such presentations seems warranted. There is ample evidence that the observation of violent forms of media can facilitate aggressive response (e.g., Reference 37), yet to assume that the depiction of sexual-aggression could not have a similar effect, particularly against females, would be misleading. Given the findings of the present studies, it seems important for future investigations to begin a systematic examination of the role of the media in aggression against women.

ACKNOWLEDGMENTS

The advice and encouragement of Prof. Len Berkowitz in this research is greatly appreciated.

REFERENCES

1. BERKOWITZ, L. 1971. Sex and violence: we can't have it both ways. Psychology Today.
2. CLINE, V. B. 1974. Another view: pornography effects, the state of the art. *In* Where Do You Draw the Line? V.B. Cline, Ed. Brigham Young University Press. Provo, Utah.
3. DIENSTBIER, R. A. 1977. Sex and violence: Can research have it both ways? Comm. **27**: 176–188.
4. ZILLMANN, D. 1971. Excitation transfer in communication-mediated aggressive behavior. J. Exp. Soc. Psychol. **7**: 419–434.
5. JAFFE, Y., N. MALAMUTH, J. FEINGOLD & S. FESHBACH. 1974. Sexual arousal and behavioral aggression. J. Pers. Soc. Psychol. **30**: 759–764.
6. DONNERSTEIN, E., M. DONNERSTEIN & R. EVANS. 1975. Erotic stimuli and aggression: facilitation or inhibition. J. Pers. Soc. Psychol. **32**: 237–244.
7. BARON, R. A. & P. A. BELL. 1977. Sexual arousal and aggression by males: effects of type of erotic stimuli and prior provocation. J. Pers. Soc. Psychol. **35**: 79–87.
8. DONNERSTEIN, E. & G. BARRETT. 1978. The effects of erotic stimuli on male aggression towards females. J. Pers. Soc. Psychol. **36**: 180–188.
9. DONNERSTEIN, E. & J. HALLAM. 1978. The facilitating effects of erotica on aggression toward females. J. Pers. Soc. Psychol. **36**: 1270–1277.
10. Presidential Commission on Obscenity and Pornography. 1971. U.S. Government Printing Office. Washington, D.C.
11. HOWARD, J. L., M. B. LIPTZIN & C. B. REIFLER. 1973. Is pornography a problem? J. Soc. Issues **29**: 133–145.
12. LIEBERT, R. M. & N. S. SCHWARTZBERG. 1977. Effects of mass media. Annu. Rev. Psychol. **28**: 141–173.
13. MEYER, T. P. 1972. The effects of sexually arousing and violent films on aggressive behavior. J. Sex. Res. **8**: 324–333.
14. ZILLMANN, D., J. L. HOYT & K. D. DAY. 1974. Strength and duration of the effects of aggressive, violent, and erotic communications on subsequent aggressive behavior. Comm. Res. **1**: 286–306.
15. BANDURA, A. 1973. Aggression: A Social Learning Analysis. Prentice-Hall, Inc. Englewood Cliffs, N.J.
16. ZILLMANN, D., A. KATCHER & B. MILAVSKY. 1972. Excitation transfer from physical exercise to subsequent aggressive behavior. J. Exp. Soc. Psychol. **8**: 247–259.

17. DONNERSTEIN, E. & D. W. WILSON. 1976. Effects of noise and perceived control on ongoing and subsequent aggressive behavior. J. Pers. Soc. Psychol. **34**: 774–781.
18. MALAMUTH, N. M., S. FESHBACH & Y. JAFFE. 1977. Sexual arousal and aggression: recent experiments and theoretical issues. J. Soc. Issues **33**: 110–133.
19. BARON, R. A. 1974. The aggression-inhibiting influence of heightened sexual arousal. J. Pers. Soc. Psychol. **30**: 318–322.
20. FRODI, A. 1977. Sexual arousal, situational restrictiveness, and aggressive behavior. J. Res. in Pers. **11**: 48–58.
21. ZILLMANN, D. & B. S. SAPOLSKY. 1977. What mediates the effect of mild erotica on annoyance and hostile behavior in males? J. Pers. Soc. Psychol. **35**: 587–596.
22. MORGAN, R. 1978. Going Too Far. Vintage Press, Inc. New York, N.Y.
23. BROWNMILLER, S. 1975. Against Our Will. Bantam Books, Inc. New York, N.Y.
24. EYSENCK, H. J. & H. NIAS. 1978. Sex, Violence, and the Media. Spector. London, England.
25. MOSHER, D. L. 1971. Pornographic films, male verbal aggression against women, and guilt. In Technical Report of the Commission on Obscenity and Pornography **8**. U.S. Government Printing Office. Washington, D.C.
26. MOSHER, D. L. 1971. Psychological reactions to pornographic films. In Technical Report of the Commission on Obscenity and Pornography **8**. U.S. Government Printing Office. Washington, D.C.
27. BARON, R. A. & P. A. BELL. 1973. Effects of heightened sexual arousal on physical aggression. Proc. 81st Ann. Conv. of the Amer. Psych. Assoc. **8**: 171–172.
28. DENGERINK, H. A. 1976. Personality variables as mediators of attack-instigated aggression. In Perspectives on Aggression. R. Geen & E. O'Neal, Eds. Academic Press Inc. New York, N.Y.
29. TAYLOR, S. P. & S. EPSTEIN. 1967. Aggression as a function of the interaction of the sex of the aggressor and the sex of the victim. Pers. **35**: 474–486.
30. GEEN, R. G., D. STONNER & G. L. SHOPE. 1975. The facilitation of aggression by aggression: a study of response inhibition and disinhibition. J. Pers. Soc. Psychol. **31**: 721–726.
31. GEEN, R. G. & M. B. QUANTY. 1977. The facilitation of aggression by aggression: a study of response inhibition and disinhibition. J. Pers. Soc. Psychol. **31**: 721–726.
32. National Commission on the Causes and Prevention of Violence. 1969. U.S. Government Printing Office. Washington, D.C.
33. BERKOWITZ, L. 1974. Some determinants of impulsive aggression: the role of mediated associations with reinforcements for aggression. Psych. Rev. **81**: 165–176.
34. DONNERSTEIN, E. 1979. Pornography commission revisited: aggressive-erotica and violence against women. (Submitted for publication.)
35. KANIN, E. G. & S. R. PARCELL. 1977. Sexual aggression: a second look at the offended female. Arch. Sex. Behav. **6**: 67–76.
36. WALKER, E. C. 1971. Erotic stimuli and the aggressive sexual offender. Technical Report of Commission on Obscenity and Pornography **8**. U.S. Government Printing Office. Washington, D.C.
37. GEEN, R. G. 1978. Some effects of observing violence upon the behavior of the observer. In Progress in Experimental Personality Research. B. Maher, Ed. **8**. Academic Press, Inc. New York, N.Y.

TELEVISION VIEWING AND AGGRESSIVE BEHAVIOR IN PRESCHOOL CHILDREN: A FIELD STUDY*

Dorothy G. Singer and Jerome L. Singer

Family Television Research and Consultation Center
Yale University
New Haven, Connecticut 06520

Previous Research

For the past two decades, television, "a member of the family,"[1] has been a major influence on the behavior patterns of children. Extensive research by Bandura[2] has indicated very clearly that children imitate observed acts of aggression whether carried out by live adults or filmed models. Television may also reduce some of the sensitivities to pain in others,[3] and provide a basic moral support for violence since in program after program we witness the good guys physically assaulting or shooting the bad guys.[1] Work by Huston-Stein and Wright[4] and Watt and Krull[5] suggests too that the high rate of activity and the arousal value of television may also predispose children to aggressive action. Laboratory studies under controlled conditions (Friedrich and Stein,[6] Noble [7-9]) indicate that children exposed to aggressive films increase their level of aggression.

In a comprehensive report, supported by the Surgeon General's Committee on Television and Social Behavior,[10] accumulated evidence suggests that children predisposed to be aggressive may increase their level of aggression after exposure to violence on television. The data from field studies[11-13] wherein children have been followed up over longer periods of time than in the laboratory studies show a positive correlation on the order of 0.25 between television viewing and incidence of aggressive behavior. While these correlations are modest, they do suggest some evidence that television contributes to some degree to the many possible causes of aggression in children.

An important longitudinal project involved a ten-year follow-up of boys and girls originally studied in the third grade by Lefkowitz et al.[14] Their results indicate that boys who preferred violent television at age nine were the most aggressive both at that time and ten years later. These authors have found that one of the best single predictors at the age of nine of whether a boy will be rated as aggressive by peers or by other criteria ten years later is the amount of *violent* television he watches in childhood. These researchers ruled out possible mediating effects of intelligence, social class, or family background as a means of explaining the correlation for violent television, 0.21 ($P < 0.01$) with concurrent peer-rated aggressiveness

* This study was supported by the Spencer Foundation and by National Science Foundation Grant DAR 6–20772.

and 0.31 ($P < 0.001$) with aggressiveness ten years later. Another study by William Belson[15] in England, following a group of boys between the ages of 12 and 17 over a period of time, indicates that the watching of aggressive material on television, particularly that associated with relatively realistic violent activity such as plays or films in which violence occurs in the context of close personal relations, westerns of a violent kind, programs presenting gratuitous violence, and programs presenting fictional violence of a realistic kind, influences these teenagers to increase their levels of violence. In contrast, he found little or no support for the hypothesis that exposure to sporting programs, science fiction violence, slapstick comedy, or violent cartoons influenced these teenagers to increase their levels of violence.

The Longitudinal Study

One of the objectives of this research was a longitudinal study of the relationship between television viewing within the family setting and possible influences of such viewing on the ongoing patterns of aggression observed during free-play situations in the day-care or preschool setting over a year's time.

Two hundred children from 13 preschool classes in the New Haven, Connecticut area participated in the study. Intelligence, capacity for concept formation, and receptive listening skills were assessed as baseline measures using the Peabody Vocabulary Test, the Do You Know Test (ETS), and Listen to the Story Test (ETS) respectively. In addition, an interview with the child on play activities and television viewing habits was administered.

The children were also observed during their free-play periods for two ten-minute sessions as a baseline for subsequent longitudinal evaluation. Trained observers, working in pairs, simultaneously watched each child and independently recorded all behavior and language. The behavior of the child was then rated independently according to a five-point scale for 20 variables that had been carefully defined in advance. Three such probe periods were conducted during the year's study.

Each family participating in the study kept television log records for a two-week period three times during the year. The log books supplied to the parents consisted of a day-by-day listing of all programs presented by both commercial and educational television stations. Parents were requested to record the degree of intensity and the specific programs watched by the children as well as with whom, if anyone, they viewed each program. Every program recorded in the logbook as having been seen by the child was then coded according to its content.

A detailed informed consent was provided by each family interested in participating in the program. This form follows the guidelines developed by Yale's Faculty of Arts and Sciences Committee. In addition to the consent forms, parents were asked to provide information on the child, some information on family occupational and educational levels (suitable for later use in estimating socioeconomic status), birth order, sex of children, and family size.

Characteristics of the Sample

The eleven participating nursery schools, day care centers, and preschool classes represent institutions that service predominantly lower-middle-class families. Several schools were publicly funded through the state and, in the case of the two public school systems (East Haven and Hamden), through the Federal Title I funds. The structure of each school permitted reasonably unobtrusive observation of the children. The patterns of school activities allowed a sufficient degree of spontaneous free-play behaviors, and the staff were understanding and cooperative.

Pretesting

The following instruments were administered individually to each child involved in the project prior to the observation phase of the first probe: (1) Peabody Picture Vocabulary Test (PPVT) is a nonverbal IQ estimate which requires the child to point to the picture of the item designated by the teacher: e.g., given the word *tackle*, the child points to one of four pictures on the page. (2) Do You Know (Circus, ETS) measures a child's knowledge of facts and concepts necessary for functioning in school and outside. Example: Which of the pictures shows how warm it is outside (thermometer)? (3) Listen to the Story (Circus, ETS) measures the child's ability to listen, understand, and remember information. (4) Interview on imaginative play and television viewing patterns consists of direct questioning of child con-

TABLE 1

SAMPLE CHARACTERISTICS

N = 199	Race: White = 144
Male = 89	Oriental = 2
Female = 110	Hispanic = 6
Age 3 = 50	Black = 47
Age 4 = 149	Primary Language: English = 194
	Non-English = 5

	$\bar{X}$	S.D.
SES Index	3.42	0.94
Peabody PVT (I.Q.)	99.29	19.61
Listen to the Story	13.19	3.51
Do You Know	21.64	4.69
Imaginary Playmate, Part A	6.29	2.40
Stuffed Animals, Part B	8.60	2.91
Total Imaginary Playmate Questionnaire	14.84	4.29

cerning imaginative play tendencies, imaginary companions, favorite television shows, characters on television, as well as patterns of viewing.

TABLE 1 presents the basic data on the sample with respect to the predispositional measures. Overall, the IQ scores, concept level, and listening comprehension were within normal range ($\overline{X}$ = 99.29, S.D. = 19.61).

Observational Variables

In each probe period, children were observed on two separate occasions by two observers who independently recorded everything the child did for a ten-minute period (including verbatim speech). These observers subsequently rated the child independently along a series of 20 variables; Imaginativeness of Play, Positive Affect, Persistence, Evidence of Overt Aggressive Behavior, Motor Activity, Interaction with Peers and Adults, Cooperation with Peers and Adults, Leadership, Fear, Anger, Sadness,

TABLE 2

RELIABILITY OF RATERS ON FIRST AND SECOND OCTOBER OBSERVATIONS 1978

Variable	Observation	Kappa	Variable	Observation	Kappa
Imagination	1	0.72*	Leadership	1	0.64*
	2	0.73*		2	0.64*
Positive Affect	1	0.47*	Fearful	1	0.46*
	2	0.51*		2	0.25†
Persistence	1	0.43*	Angry	1	0.42*
	2	0.59*		2	0.56*
Aggression Towards	1	0.74*	Sad	1	0.42*
	2	0.75*		2	0.54*
			Fatigued	1	0.49*
				2	0.44*
Motor Activity	1	0.58*	Sensory Motor	1	0.46*
	2	0.59*		2	0.60*
Interaction Peers	1	0.56*	Mastery	1	0.58*
	2	0.61*		2	0.65*
Interaction Adults	1	0.54*	Make-believe Play	1	0.64*
	2	0.61*		2	0.78*
Cooperation Peers	1	0.51*	Games With Rules	1	0.49*
	2	0.49*		2	0.66*
Cooperation Adults	1	0.48*			
	2	0.59*			

* $P < 0.00001$.
† $P < 0.00003$.
15 pairs of observers
$N = 198$
Note: Based on D. Cicchetti's interobserver reliability formula

Fatigue, Sensory-Motor Activities, Mastery Play, Make-Believe Play, Games with Rules, Number of Words, and Onomatopoetic Sounds. In effect, these variables represent a priori grouping of behaviors of a general type; e.g., imaginativeness (introduction of make-believe elements into play), positive emotionality (as represented by affects such as interests, curiosity, smiling, laughing, etc.), and persistence at a task for a period of time.

Training of Observers

The observers ($N = 31$), largely Yale undergraduates and graduate students, were selected based on their background in psychology and education.

Observers were provided with 16 typed protocols that were behavioral samples collected in an earlier study and a set of coding instructions. Each variable was discussed in relationship to the instruction booklet. Observers had ample opportunity to discuss reasons for their ratings and a high rate of agreement was attempted on the five-point scale for each variable at each session. During the final sessions, a training tape developed by the Yale Child Study Center was shown that illustrated typical play behaviors in a nursery-school setting. The observers were asked to rate a particular child according to the 20 variables. Observers were given further instructions concerning procedure. Letters of introduction, school etiquette, and actual recording procedures were all discussed in detail.

These sessions were repeated three weeks before the second and third probe for observers who were new to the project. A refresher session was required for those who had participated in previous observations.

Observation Procedures

Observers were told to record in an appropriate place on the record sheet the child's appearance, mannerisms, physical build, time they began and ended each recording, date, sex, and code number of each child. Observations were made only during free-play periods both indoors and out. Observers used a clipboard and stopwatch and tried to be as unobtrusive as possible as they recorded the child's actions and language. Language was recorded verbatim. Observers were instructed not to interrupt behavior, but to accurately record what took place. After the behavior was written down, each observer would then rate the child on the 20 variables, using the five-point scale.

Inter-rater reliability estimates were obtained on the ratings the observers made on the practice protocols and on the actual protocols they collected themselves in the first observational period. Rater reliability was excellent for both training periods, as well as the first probe. Interobserver reliability for all the variables yielded highly significant kappas (TABLE 2).

Development of Logs

The television logs were developed by reviewing the local *TV Guide* and newspaper listing guides for the New Haven area. The daily shows were listed in hour segments of time and recorded on three logging sheets: morning, afternoon, and evening. Space was provided on the sheets for parents to note any programs the child may have watched not listed on the log. A two-week sample of television viewing was obtained for each child; three samples per child throughout the year.

The parents received detailed recording instructions enclosed with the television log packets. They were asked to circle the program watched on the logs. The parents were instructed to note how intensely the child watched a program on a scale of 1 to 5. A rating of "1" meant that the child scarcely watched the program or paid any attention to it, while "5" meant that the child watched with great interest and absorption. In addition, parents were asked to note whether the child watched the program alone, with parents (P), siblings (S), other adults (O), or other children (C) and were instructed to include any combination of people, i.e., other adults and other children.

After each probe period when logs had been returned, the information was transcribed onto a weekly summary sheet. Every show the child watched was noted along with the intensity and with whom it was watched.

Preparation for Statistical Analysis

Time Watched

Each day's viewing was totaled and noted at the bottom of the sheet. A weekly total was achieved by summing all 7 days. The two-week sample was treated as one unit. All statistics are done on a two-week sample. Therefore, when analyzed, if a child watched 5 hours on the first Monday of the logging period and 3 hours on the following Monday, a total of 8 hours was entered for that day. Means and standard deviations were found for the two-week sample, the total sample as well as males and females. Further analysis includes comparisons of a weekday vs. weekend viewing.

Intensity

Finding the mean intensity for each child was based on a half-hour time period. The figure entered would be multiplied by the number of half hours for a show, times the intensity reported on the log. For example, if a child watched an hour and one-half program with an intensity of 4, the intensity would be multiplied by 3. The mean intensity for the sample was achieved by summing all the prorated intensities and dividing by the total number of half hours. As with the viewing time, the mean intensity is based on a two-week period.

Who Watched with Whom

Data on whether the child watched alone or with specific others were based on a half-hour period. Combinations of with whom children watched the shows were entered for analysis. How many hours a child watched television alone, or with parents, and any combination of people were summed for the two-week period and entered for analysis.

Programs Viewed

The programs available for viewing by this group and actually reported on the logs by parents were classified into nine categories and coded:

A. Cartoons, e.g., "Bugs Bunny," "Flintstones."
B. Children's Commercial Shows, e.g., "Captain Kangaroo," "Magic Garden."
C. Educational Shows, e.g., "Sesame Street," "Zoom," "Mr. Rogers."
D. Situation Comedies, e.g., "Happy Days," "I Love Lucy," "Brady Bunch."
E. Game, Variety, Talk, e.g., "Gong Shows," "Mike Douglas," "Jeopardy."
F. Adult Nonviolent, e.g., soap operas, "The Waltons," "Little House On the Prairie."
G. Action-Adventure, e.g., "Wonder Woman," "The Incredible Hulk," "Charlie's Angels."
H. Sports (violent only), e.g., boxing, hockey, auto racing, football.
I. Newscasts and Documentaries.

The categories were divided into the top shows in each category by a quick view of the summary sheets. For example, in Category "A," the shows listed were: "Bugs Bunny," "Scooby-Doo," "Spiderman," etc. If a child watched a show not listed in our program breakdown, it was included under the general category for that type of program, e.g., a special.

The individual programs were combined in categories to determine how many hours children watched a program under the various categories. The programs were also summed individually to determine how many hours a specific show such as "Sesame Street" was watched.

Parametric Characteristics

Our participants' average SES level is in the upper range on the Duncan and Hollingshead-Redlich Scales, clearly a blue-collar to lower-middle socioeconomic status (SES) group. The average Peabody IQ is 99.3; non-whites represent 23–24% of the group; the sample has a somewhat higher number of females than males (110–89), and 4-year-olds predominate over 3-year-olds (149–50).

Predispositional Variables

The children were all administered three types of intelligence tests: the Peabody Picture Vocabulary Test, which yields an IQ based on verbal labeling of pictures; the Listen to the Story and Do You Know scales (newly developed as potentially useful cross-cultural measures of intellectual development by the Educational Testing Service). The scores of our participants on these last two scales were below the currently available normative average although IQs from the PPVT were at the national mean. Subsequent data analyses in this report will be based on the PPVT IQs only, since they have proved to be more reliable with our sample.

In addition to cognitive measures, children were also questioned about imaginary playmates with a scale broken down separately for invisible friends and for stuffed animals.

RESULTS

Patterns of Play and Aggression

As might be expected, certain behavioral variables show significant increases across the probe periods, reflecting particular patterns of growth. Thus, Cooperation and Interaction show steady increases as does Leadership. Aggressive behavior also increased steadily over the year from a mean of 3.01 to a mean of 3.69 [F (2,176), linear trend = 26.6, $P < 0.001$]. This level of aggression is moderately high for such young children.

A factor-analytic examination of the behavioral background and television-viewing variables was carred out. Clearest results emerge from a two-factor principal axis factor analysis with varimax rotation in which the number of hours spent viewing each category of television programming was employed. TABLE 3 presents the results of such a factor analysis across the year with means based on all three probes. The $N = 159$ reflects children from whom full data over the year on all variables were available.

Inspection of TABLE 3 indicates that Factor 1 includes highest loadings for Peer Interaction (0.80), Cooperation with Peers (0.79), Leadership (0.79), Imaginativeness in Play (0.75), and Positive Affect (0.77). This factor corresponds closely with results from our earlier study with middle-class preschoolers[16] and may be labeled *Playfulness*. It essentially indexes a "happy," friendly, and imaginative child. No relationship to television-viewing patterns is in evidence.

The second factor shows its highest loadings for Aggression (0.70) and general Motor Activity (0.68), as well as the affect of Anger (0.52). This factor also reflects sizable loadings for two television variables, the number of hours viewing action-adventure shows (0.44) and game shows (0.36). The

TABLE 3

FACTOR LOADINGS FROM PRINCIPAL AXIS FACTOR ANALYSIS
(VARIMAX ROTATION): TWO FACTOR SOLUTION WITHOUT TOTAL TELEVISION VIEWING

Variable	Factor 1	Factor 2
Sex (1 = M, 2 = F)		− 0.45
IQ	0.32	− 0.37
Age		
SES		
Ethnic Group (1 = white, 2 = nonwhite)		
Total Imaginary Companion Score		
Imaginativeness in Play	0.75	
Positive Affect	0.77	
Persistence during Play	0.50	
Aggression		0.70
Motor Activity		0.68
Peer Interaction	0.80	
Adult Interaction		
Cooperation with Peers	0.79	
Cooperation with Adults		
Leadership	0.79	
Fear	− 0.32	
Angry		0.52
Sad	− 0.38	
Fatigue	− 0.49	
Sensory Motor Play		
Mastery		
Make-Believe Play	0.65	
Games with Rules		
Number of Words	0.74	
Onomatopoetic Sounds	0.31	0.39
Cartoons		
Commercial Children's Shows		
Educational Television		
Situation Comedies		
Variety/Game Shows		0.36
Adult Drama		
Action Shows		0.44
Sports		
News/Documentaries		
Television Viewing Intensity		

Note: N = 159

factor pattern also reflects Sex and IQ loadings (− 0.45 and − 0.37, respectively) suggesting that it is somewhat more characteristic of boys and of children with lower IQs. This factor seems to index the linkage of aggressive and high-arousal programming to overt aggressive or unfocused motor activity as reported in our earlier study with middle-class preschoolers.[17] Examples of action-adventure shows viewed by these children are "Six Million Dollar Man," "Battlestar Galactica," "The Incredible Hulk," and "Wonder Woman." The game shows are characterized by much shouting and hysterical motor activity. This factor can tentatively be labeled *aggression-action television-viewing.*

TABLE 4

CANONICAL CORRELATION ANALYSES OF TELEVISION VIEWING WITH
BEHAVIOR AND PREDISPOSITIONAL VARIABLES*

Variable	Loading of First Canonical Variate	Loading on Second Canonical Variate
Television Variables (Set 1)		
Cartoons	0.32	0.45
Children's Commercial Shows	0.05	0.10
Educational Television Children's Shows	0.51	0.26
Situation Comedies	−0.25	−0.08
Variety-Game Shows	−0.57	0.19
Adult/Family	−0.30	0.26
Action/Detective	−0.50	0.60
News/Documentaries	−0.55	0.51
Behavior and Predispositional (Set 2)		
Imaginative Play	0.02	0.04
Positive Affect	−0.09	0.27
Aggression	−0.08	0.42
Motor Activity	−0.16	0.50
Cooperation Peers	0.17	0.14
Angry	0.14	0.62
Sad	−0.29	−0.09
Fatigue	−0.18	−0.10
Socioeconomic Status	−0.34	−0.03
Ethnicity	−0.82	0.23
IQ	0.49	−0.26
Sex	0.04	−0.61
Age	0.19	−0.07

* Based on an average of three probes. First canonical correlation = 0.65, χ^2 = 199, df = 104, P = 0.00001. Second canonical correlation = 0.50, χ^2 = 114, df = 84, P = 0.02.

Although background variables are not strongly implicated in the principal factor solution, a canonical correlation analysis based on the averages of the three probes over the year does add some new information (TABLE 4). This analysis yields two significant canonical variates when television variables are pitted against behavioral and background variables. The first indicates that nonwhites especially and also lower-SES or lower-IQ children are especially likely to be heavier viewers of action, game, and news shows (or adult-oriented fare, more generally) and less likely to be watchers of educational television [Public Broadcasting Station (PBS) children's shows] or cartoons (canonical correlation = 0.65, χ^2 = 199, df = 104, $P < 0.00001$).

The second canonical variable further confirms the link of action shows to Aggression and high Motor Activity and Anger, indicating also that heavy television viewing of news and cartoons may also relate to action. This relationship again seems especially strong for boys. (Canonical correlation = 0.50, χ^2 = 114, df = 84, $P < 0.02$).

In effect this analysis suggests that while ethnic background and SES or IQ may be strongly associated with viewing preferences for adult (and less

TABLE 5

RESULTS OF MULTIPLE REGRESSION ANALYSES:
STEPWISE PREDICTION OF AGGRESSION VARIABLES AT TIME 2 FROM INDIVIDUAL SHOWS AT
TIME 1 AFTER ENTERING ETHNICITY, IQ, AND SES

Aggression Background Variables	Simple R	F-ratio Unique Contribution	Standardized Beta Weight
Ethnicity	0.06	0.5	0.06
IQ	−0.14	2.95	−0.14
SES	0.19*	3.76	0.14
First Five Television Shows			
"Sesame Street"	0.22†	13.5‡	0.27
"Super Heroes"	0.22†	11.3‡	0.25
"Woody Woodpecker"	0.21†	10.4†	0.24
"I Love Lucy"	−0.14	7.6†	−0.20
"Talk Shows"	0.14	4.3*	0.15
Multiple R	0.51‡		

* $P < 0.05$
† $P < 0.01$
‡ $P < 0.001$

child-oriented) programming, such a relationship does not account for our finding that aggression is tied to viewing of action-oriented television. We cannot explain the fact that more aggressive children are more likely to be watching the more violent programming by asserting that this reflects only a viewing preference of an ethnic or class group whose behavior is already known to show higher levels of motor activity or fighting in preschool periods. If, on the other hand, the type of television viewed is playing some role in stimulating aggression, it is occurring irrespective of the social class or ethnicity of the children.

Another way of looking at this is through partialling out the effect of background factors on the first-order correlation between aggression and action-television viewing. This correlation for the total sample across the three probes is 0.15 ($P < 0.05$). When IQ, SES, sex, and ethnicity are partialled out individually and then in combination, the correlation drops only a total of 0.04 points suggesting that background factors are not in themselves critical determinants of this linkage, and again confirming our earlier work with middle-class children.[16]

While our data cannot be definitive in suggesting a causal link between viewing television and aggression, we can rule out the fact that the linkage is more a reflection of a viewing preference by already aggressive children through examining cross-lagged correlations. We find for example that the correlation between watching action-adventure television shows at Time 1 (October) is correlated + 0.18, $P < 0.05$ with Aggression at Time 3 (April). The correlation of Aggression at Time 1 with action television viewing at Time 3 is only + 0.05. This result again conforms to our earlier findings.[16] The effects of total television viewing we had observed before are not evident here, and our data specifically highlight the action-television and aggression link-up with the indications that possible causality goes from viewing towards behavior rather than the reverse. This is not the case for action television and Motor Activity where the correlations from Time 1–Time 3 are significant but equivalent suggesting no clear possible causal direction.

Specific Programming and Overt Behavior

Our data as presented have focused on general categories of programming because these are more consistent across time and less subject to schedule changes. In this study, however, we also examined the links between specific shows and the behavioral variables. This seems an important step because certain cartoons, for example, may be very full of violence while others are not. Hence any modeling or arousal interpretation of television viewing and behavior may be limited if there are contradictory patterns of content subsumed by combining shows under a general rubric. In the next section we will examine correlations and multiple regression predictions of behavior patterns based on the specific programs our children watched.

Examining which specific shows viewed at Time 1 best predicted aggressive behavior at Time 2 yielded a surprise. It turned out that heavy viewing of "Sesame Street" proved to be especially strongly linked to later aggressive behavior. A multiple-regression analysis of the television shows and background variables predicting later overt aggression (criterion) indicates that heavy watching of "Sesame Street" was the best single predictor of aggression three months later. The correlation of "Sesame Street" with Aggression over the year was 0.22, $P < 0.01$, as a matter of fact.

TABLE 5 makes it clear that specific cartoons that have especially violent content, "Superheroes" and "Woody Woodpecker," are also important predictors of aggression. A situation comedy, "I Love Lucy," proves to be negatively linked to later aggression, a result that may chiefly reflect its attraction for girls who prove less aggressive. This result is contrary to our early findings that this type of programming was tied to overt aggression in girls.

The strong influence of violent cartoons or action shows is also supported when one looks across the year—the best predictors from Time 1 to Time 3 for aggression include viewing of "Scooby-Doo" and the "Six Million Dollar Man." The effect of "Sesame Street" drops off by the third probe apparently because viewing of this show also drops sharply, especially by those children who were more aggressive in the second probe.

If we look at Motor Activity at Time 2 after partialling out the effects of IQ, SES, and ethnicity, the role of very active programming is again clear. "Tom and Jerry" cartoons and "Charlie's Angels" (an action show) both yield significant simple rs (0.21, $P < 0.01$ and 0.28, $P < 0.01$, respectively) and highly significant F-ratios for their unique contributions to the prediction equation. The "Muppets," a much-loved but very active "Sesame Street"-like show, also contributes significantly to the Multiple R while "Laverne and Shirley" and the viewing of "Disney World" are negatively linked to later high levels of Motor Activity. Prediction across the year from Time 1 indicates that early viewing of "Spider Man," another active cartoon, and of game shows are positively linked to later Motor Activity while "Disney World" and "Soap" (a humorous but nonviolent or motor-active comedy series) are negative predictors.

In general, our look at the specific programming tied to later aggression or vigorous activity tends to support a combined modeling-arousal model. "Sesame Street," a program characterized by rapid shifts, arousing and sometimes aggressive content,[18] is linked to aggression along with extremely aggressive cartoons or adventure shows. The shifts in viewing and the schedule changes (or the fact that increased afternoon light for outdoor play cuts out viewing of certain shows) weaken the reliability of the specific programs as measures compared with the categories of programming. Still our findings from the individual shows suggest that those shows especially involving considerable physical motion, rapidity of changes, and violence (as in cartoons, action-adventure, or game shows) are linked to aggression as the more general category of action-adventure.

DISCUSSION

The present study is the first to examine the possible relationships between television viewing and spontaneous behavior in day-care settings for a group of preschool children from lower socioeconomic backgrounds. In general our results support the growing body of findings suggesting that heavier viewing of programs characterized by violent action, considerable rapidity of movement, or related arousing activities may be associated with more aggressive and nonfocused motor activity by preschoolers. Two not necessarily contradictory hypotheses have been advanced in the past for the link between television viewing and aggressive behavior, a generalized arousal effect[5] or the imitation of violent actions.[2] Our findings suggest that the specific category of programming most regularly associated with aggressive activity by these children is *action-adventure*. When we look at *specific* shows we find that aggression is also associated with viewing of particularly aggressive cartoons such as "Superheroes" and "Woody Woodpecker" and also certain game shows known for their hyperactivity, screeching, and a hysterical quality. If there is a causal link between programming and the subsequent behavior of preschoolers, our data suggest that heavy exposure to aggressive and also to rapid-cut content (as in "Sesame Street" or the "Muppets"), or to hysterical behavior by adults (game shows), may work together to produce aggression in children.

Of course our data cannot demonstrate causality definitively. We have attempted to rule out alternative explanations for the association between aggressive behavior and television, however. Partialling out the possible effects of class, IQ, or ethnicity does not affect substantially our correlations. It cannot be argued that children who are aggressive are simply reflecting life-style patterns of a subculture which also watches a good deal of more violent or adult-oriented television. It is the case, as the data from our canonical analysis suggests, that nonwhite and lower SES children do watch more adult-oriented shows and less of the "better quality," PBS, child-oriented shows. But that cannot explain the aggression-action show association which emerges in our second canonical variate.

Our cross-lag analyses also seem to rule out the usual argument that aggressive children simply prefer violent programming. What seems more likely is that there is a subtle interaction effect[16] between viewing, arousal and imitation, and then subsequent preference.

These findings must be viewed in perspective. Our participants were small children who, after all, were not violent. Their aggression consisted of pushing, hitting, knocking over others' blocks, or snatching a toy. It remains to be seen whether such early and consistent aggression is predictive of a later history of antisocial behavior. It is clear that by four years of age children are already confirmed television viewers. The accumulating evidence suggests that those children who are regularly exposed, through parental laxity or ignorance,[16] to violent adult programming or to arousing content are also being put "at risk" for the development of later tendencies to uncooperative, antisocial behavior with peers.

ACKNOWLEDGMENTS

We express our thanks to Paul Christoph for his statistical help and to Richard Gerrig for his editorial assistance.

REFERENCES

1. SINGER, J. L. & D. G. SINGER. 1977. Television: a member of the family. National Elementary School Principal 56(3): 50–53.
2. BANDURA, A. 1973. Aggression: A Social Learning Analysis. Prentice-Hall, Inc. Englewood Cliffs, N.J.
3. CLINE, V. B., R. G. CROFT & S. COURRIER. 1973. Desensitization of children to television violence. J. Pers. Soc. Psych. 27: 360–365.
4. HUSTON-STEIN, A. & J. C. WRIGHT. Children and television: effects of the medium, its content, and its form. J. Res. Dev. Ed. (In press.)
5. WATT, J. H. & R. KRULL. 1977. An examination of three models of television viewing and aggression. Human Comm. Res. 3: 99–112.
6. FRIEDRICH, L. K. & A. H. STEIN. 1975. Prosocial television and young children: the effects of verbal labeling and role playing on learning and behavior. Child Dev. 46: 27–38.
7. NOBLE, G. 1970. Film-mediated creative and aggressive play. Brit. J. Soc. Clin. Psych. 9: 1–7.
8. NOBLE, G. 1973. Effects of different forms of filmed aggression on children's constructive and destructive play. J. Pers. Soc. Psych. 26: 54–59.
9. NOBLE, G. 1975. Children in Front of the Small Screen. Constable. London, England.
10. Surgeon General's Scientific Advisory Committee on Television and Social Behavior. 1972. Television and Growing Up: The Impact of Televised Violence. U.S. Government Printing Office. Washington, D.C.
11. BAILYN, L. 1959. Mass media and children: a study of exposure habits and cognitive effects. Psychological Monographs 73(471).

12. CHAFFEE, S. 1972. Television and adolescent aggressiveness. *In* Television and Social Behavior. J. P. Murray, G. A. Comstock & E. A. Rubinstein, Eds. 3. U.S. Government Printing Office. Washington, D.C.

13. SCHRAMM, W., J. LYLE & E. PARKER. 1961. Television in the Lives of Our Children. Stanford University Press. Stanford, Calif.

14. LEFKOWITZ, M. M., L. D. ERON, L. O. WALDER & L. R. HUESMANN. 1977. Growing Up To Be Violent. Pergamon Press, Inc. New York, N.Y.

15. BELSON, W. A. 1978. Television and the Adolescent Boy. Saxon House. Hampshire, England.

16. SINGER, J. L. & D. G. SINGER. 1980. Television, Imagination and Aggression: A Study of Preschoolers. Erlbaum. Hillsdale, N.J.

17. SINGER, J. L. & D. G. SINGER. 1980. Television viewing, family style and aggressive behavior in preschool children. *In* Violence in the Family: Psychiatric, Sociological and Historical Implications. M. Green, Ed. AAAS Symposium Series. Washington, D.C.

18. SINGER, J. L. & D. G. SINGER. 1979. Come back, Mr. Rogers, come back. Psych. Today. **12**(10): 56–60.

CHILDREN AND AGGRESSION AFTER OBSERVED FILM AGGRESSION WITH SANCTIONING ADULTS

Gilbert J. Eisenberg

Union Free School District 13
Valley Stream, New York 11580

INTRODUCTION

This paper is the result of work done on a dissertation at Fordham University. How and why this study came about are, perhaps, just as important as the results of the study itself.

For decades criticism has been leveled against the social scientist, accusing him of carrying out various scientifically controlled studies, performing black magic under the rubric of statistics, and finally making a statement about this or that variable having a significant effect on another variable—all of which was seen as nonsense by the reader. Such an attitude on the part of the reader often merited consideration, since he dismissed the results of the study because the data were collected from a contrived situation and thus had little or no bearing on the real world. It was the attempt to avoid these pitfalls that led me to the "why" of my study. For looking at the "why" points up the need for continued concern on real-life viewing conditions in the area of media violence and points up the powerful impact that media have on our children.

Hopefully, only a few persons will find fault with the conditions under which the following observations were obtained. The observations were taken within the context of the real world; they are descriptive in nature, which implies some degree of objectivity; and they were the *raison d'être* for the study.

I have been employed as a psychologist in an elementary school in a predominantly white, middle-class, suburban community where material needs are fairly satisfied, where lawns are manicured, homes freshly painted—in essence, a community that personifies the American dream. Children come to school well attired and appear cared for. Parents' concern is evidenced by an active PTA and by the willingness of parents to come to school for the numerous meetings that are requested during the school year.

During my 11 years in the district, it became apparent that television was having an effect on the children. When Evel Knievel was the rage and attempted to achieve his jump from a canyon in the Southwest, I watched daily as many of the boys tried to imitate that jump over makeshift contraptions on dirt paths bordering the expressway and noted the resulting injuries. "Kung Fu" had a similar effect—for months the impact of the program was felt in the school as young children interacted with each other using elaborate kung fu techniques.

Not many months later, a television network aired a two-part program

304

on the Manson murders. After the program was aired, I did an informal survey of the intermediate grades in my building. These children were 9 to 11 years of age. I found that of the children I sampled, over 70% had watched the program and, further, most of them had viewed the program alone or with siblings; few had watched with an adult present. I might add that this program was aired at a time other than the "family hour"—at a time when young audiences supposedly do not view television.

Shortly after this survey, I happened to be walking past a third-grade classroom. The coat rack faced the door, and what I saw absolutely astonished me. On the hooks all along the rack I saw a toy arsenal—toy rifles and pistols staring me in the face as I looked in this classroom—a classroom of children who were eight years of age. I spoke with the teacher later that morning in a sincere attempt to get some sort of explanation; she told me that her children were playing "SWAT." That day on the lunch hour, and on subsequent days, I went out to the playground and watched these little children play. What I saw enacted were hostage situations of the type depicted on the television show "SWAT"; children were shooting and yelling at each other. During the times I observed these children at play, I did not once see any attempt by any of them to resolve the conflict through mediation or even surrender—the resolution was always found in the ultimate "shoot-out," with the children play-acting dead all over the grounds. After some days of watching eight-year-old children imitating the violence and killing they had seen on a television program, my dissertation was born.

Human aggression has been present in every era of recorded history. From early times to the present, the history books provide a steady commentary on man's inhumanity toward man. Many explanations have been proposed in an attempt to understand this phenomenon of aggression, which in some of its manifestations is unique to *Homo sapiens.* Hall finds that destructive fighting is practically unknown among baboons,[1] an animal society that most closely resembles human society.

As in former cultures, the present society must look at the nature of human aggression. It is an issue that takes on increasing importance, partly because of mass media exposure and partly because of the nature of modern technology, which enables man to inflict massive destruction on his fellow man. It is an issue from which one cannot hide. Sagan pointed this out when he said:

> Human aggression, like Dionysus in Euripides' *Bacchae,* will not go away because we deny its existence. Only if we are willing to look at this destructiveness—undisguised—will we succeed in understanding and conquering it.[2]

While there have been several major theoretical bases that have been proposed as explanations for the origins of aggression—i.e., biological and psychoanalytic instinctual theories and the frustration-aggression theory—the author selected Bandura's theory of aggression.

Bandura proposed a social learning theory arguing that the prevailing theories, those concerned primarily with operant or instrumental conditioning, were much too narrow to encompass the scope of human learning.[3] He maintained that many social responses would not be acquired if social training proceeded solely by the method of successive approximation, and he further felt that in terms of human learning, the operant conditioning model was grossly inefficient. Thus, he proposed a social learning theory in which learning was generally labeled "imitation." He defined this as "the tendency for a person to match the behavior or attitude as exhibited by actual or symbolic models."[3]

According to this theory, prior learning is considered a critical factor in determining the amount of violence later displayed. Bandura maintained that aggressive behavior was learned through the same processes by which other forms of behavior are acquired, that is, by observation and direct experience.[4]

In past years there have been numerous investigations in the area of social learning and the modeling of aggressive behavior.[5-8] These studies have typically employed a research paradigm in which one group of children were exposed to adult models who displayed aggressive behavior, while another group of children were exposed to adult models who displayed nonaggressive behavior. The children were then tested for the amount of new learning in a new setting in which the model was not present. Results from these types of studies provided clear evidence that children who were exposed to the aggressive model learned to imitate more verbal and physical aggression than did the children who were exposed to the nonaggressive model.

It has furthermore been demonstrated that children exposed to filmed aggressive models will display subsequent aggressive behavior.[9-14]

In a classic study, Bandura et al. investigated the effects of exposure to filmed aggressive models on children's subsequent aggressive behavior.[9] The results of the study furnished strong evidence that exposure to filmed aggression heightens aggressive behavior in children. Bandura et al. found that the children who were exposed to the aggressive human and cartoon models on film exhibited almost twice as much aggression as did the children in the control group, who were not exposed to aggressive film content.

With the presence of television in almost every home, the role of symbolic models has taken on great importance. In a random sample taken of grades 3–6 in one school in my district, I found that there was not one home without a television. For the third, fourth, and fifth grades, 61% of the sample had three or more television sets in the home. Bandura and Walters maintain that while children in our culture still learn through real-life models, there is an increasing reliance placed on the use of symbolic models, because of the advent of modern technology and the availability of mass media.[15] These symbolic models are provided in films, television, and other audiovisual sources.

In a subsequent publication, Bandura spoke to the power of television.[4] He stated that television provides a rich source of social learning for children; he maintained that through symbolic modeling, audiences of large magnitude can simultaneously be reached and that, as a consequence, the aggression contagion potential of media presentations is greater than that of direct behavioral modeling.

One must ask how important a role television plays in the lives of American children. Nielsen index figures indicate that by the time a child graduates from high school, he has spent more hours observing television than he has spent in the classroom—15,000 hours of viewing as opposed to 11,000 hours of classroom instruction.[16] Waters found that most children under 5 years of age watch 23.5 hours of television a week.[17] It has been reported that by the time the average American child has reached 18 years of age, he will have seen approximately 350,000 commercials and witnessed some 18,000 murders on television. He will have witnessed numerous additional acts of mayhem and "pretend" death. Of these lesser violent acts, he will have seen an average of about one per minute on cartoons, which, for many children under 10 years old, are standard viewing.[18]

On a recent segment of "Bill Moyer's Journal," young children were asked several questions regarding their preference for television as opposed to other things.[19] The first question asked was, "Would you give up your toys for television?"; all of the children said yes. The second question asked was, "Would you give up your friends for television?"; all the children said yes. The third question was, "Would you give up talking with your father for television?"; most children responded yes.

The television industry—under pressure from social scientists, concerned citizens, and the government—devised a concept called "family viewing hour." This would be an evening hour when children along with their parents would watch what the industry considered appropriate family programs. Children, however, were still being exposed to violent television, and, more frequently than not, they watched these programs without the presence of adults.

Waters found the "family hour" to be a complete fiasco. He reported that, by the time the idea had been dropped, Nielsen figures indicated that 10.5 million children under the age of 12 were still watching television after 9 P.M. when the "family hour" ended.[17]

A study carried out by Dillion, shortly after the assassinations of Robert Kennedy and Martin Luther King, disclosed that television networks continued to show violence as entertainment.[20] The study revealed that in a seven-day period, there were 84 killings and 372 acts of violence on television programs. Violent incidents occurred on an average of once every 16.3 minutes during the early evening hours, a time for which network research estimated an audience of 26.7 million children.

How does violent television programming impact on the lives of American children? Numerous studies investigating the effects of television violence on children have found that children who viewed aggressive television programs and filmed violence were more likely to engage in subsequent imitative aggressive behavior than were children who watched nonaggressive programs.[21-26]

Rothenberg reviewed 25 years of research on the effects of violent television on young children.[27] The studies had involved 10,000 children from every possible background. He found that most studies had shown that exposure to media violence produced aggressive behavior in young children.

The evidence, then, clearly suggests that children can and do learn some forms of aggressive behavior through a process of modeling, or imitation. The literature is replete with studies indicating that children will model aggressive behavior not only from live models, but from filmed models, and even from cartoon characters. There is abundant evidence, as well, showing how aggressive television fare to which children are exposed translates into their daily interactions with their peers and society. There have been, however, few systematic investigations that have looked at the possible effects on subsequent behavior of children who have observed film aggression in the presence of sanctioning adults. The distinction between this study and prior studies—and where I hoped to make a contribution—is that this study faces the possibility that violence is not going to disappear from television in the near future and that, therefore, ways must be found to ameliorate the effects of such programs on children. It occurred to me that if children viewed television in the presence of an adult and the adult reacted to the violent content either positively or negatively, this might have an influence on the degree to which the violence affected the children. Consequently, this investigation studied the effects on children's subsequent behavior of adult presence and sanctions during observed film aggression.

In the experiment reported in this paper, children observed a half-hour segment of a current television show on each of two consecutive days. Both shows fell within the top 10% of those shows ranked as most violent by the National Citizen's Committee for Broadcasting.[28] One group of children observed the television program in the presence of an adult who gave positive sanction to the violent aspects of the program; a second group of children watched the television program in the presence of an adult who voiced disapproval at the violent aspects of the program; a third group watched the television program in the presence of an adult who made no comments at all; while a fourth group watched the television program with no adult present—they were, however, observed unnoticed through a window. Immediately following the experimental procedures, the subjects were tested for posttreatment levels of aggression using the Rosenzweig Picture-Frustration (P-F) Study, Children's Form. The P-F Study allows one to classify responses into "direction of aggression," specifically: extrapunitive (E), which is aggression turned outward on the environment; intropunitive (I), which is aggression turned inward on the subject; and impunitive (M), which is aggression turned off in an attempt to evade the situation.

It was predicted that children in the positive-sanction group, where the adult observer sanctioned the televised violence, would score higher levels of outward aggression (E), as measured by the P-F Study, than would children in the other treatment groups. It was also predicted that girls would show levels of outward aggression (E) as high as those of the boys and, further, that the sex of the adult observer would have an effect on children's levels of aggression. Finally, it was predicted that presence or absence of the adult observer would have an effect on subsequent levels of aggression.

As is often the case, the unpredicted findings—the surprises that are part of the exploratory element in every piece of research—match in interest the predicted results; they also provide the grist for generating future studies. In this study, findings relating to the effects on aggression turned inward and aggression evaded fall into such a category.

METHOD

Subjects

The subjects were 80 white males and females, who were seven years of age and from a New York, suburban, public, elementary school. The pupil population of the school was predominantly white. The socioeconomic levels of the subjects included middle to upper-middle class.

Design and Procedure

Preexperimental Assessment of Levels of Aggression

Forty subjects at a time were brought to a room in the school by an experimenter. The subjects were administered the California Test of Personality, primary form, which measures pretest levels of aggression. The children were ranked according to their scores on aggression and were distributed among the cells* so that levels of aggression among cells were similar. The subjects were then randomly assigned to one of four treatment groups. Ten boys and 10 girls were randomly assigned to positive-sanction, negative-sanction, neutral, and control groups. Half of the male subjects in the treatment groups were assigned to a male adult observer, and half of the male subjects were assigned to a female adult observer. Half of the female subjects in the treatment groups were assigned to a male adult observer, and half of the female subjects were assigned to a female adult observer. There were five subjects in each of the smallest cells in the design (TABLE 1). The major analysis was a $4 \times 2 \times 2$ analysis of variance with main effects of treatment, sex of observer, and sex of subject.

Experimental Treatment

One week after the pretreatment, the subjects were taken, according to their assigned groups, to another room where they were exposed to a series

---

* Cell refers to a grouping resulting from a simultaneous classification of subjects according to their sex, their treatment, and sex of their observer.

TABLE 1

SUMMARY OF EXPERIMENTAL DESIGN*

	Male Adult Observer		Female Adult Observer	
	Male Subjects	Female Subjects	Male Subjects	Female Subjects
Positive	5	5	5	5
Negative	5	5	5	5
Neutral	5	5	5	5
Control	5	5	5	5

* $N = 80$.

of filmed segments on a television monitor for a period of one-half hour on two consecutive days. They were instructed to sit in a semicircle around the television monitor where they also had a full view of the adult observer. The subjects were introduced to the adult observer and were told, "Today we are going to watch a television program. When the program is over we will go back to class."

In the positive-sanction treatment groups, each time aggressive behavior was exhibited, either verbally or physically by the characters on the film, the adult observer would indicate approval with such statements as "he deserved that" and "good."

In the negative-sanction groups, each time aggressive behavior was exhibited, either verbally or physically by the characters on the film, the adult observer would indicate disapproval with such statements as "that was terrible" and "he didn't deserve that."

In the neutral-sanction treatment groups, the adult observer said nothing at all.

In the control group, after the subjects were brought to the room and asked to sit around the television monitor, the adult excused herself from the room and the subjects watched the television program without the presence of an adult.

Posttreatment Assessment of Levels of Aggression

On the third day, five subjects at a time were brought to a room in the school where they were given the P-F Study. After the test, the subjects were returned to their classrooms. The experimenters who administered the posttreatment assessment were unknown to the subjects.

RESULTS

Three separate three-way analyses of variance were performed on the data in this investigation. Each analysis was performed to determine the ef-

TABLE 2

ANALYSIS OF VARIANCE OF AGGRESSION SCORES ON THE E FACTOR

Source	df	MS	F
Treatment	3	808.04	4.10*
Sex of Subject	1	84.0	0.42
Sex of Coobserver	1	96.75	0.49
Treatment × Sex of Subject	3	416.29	2.11
Treatment × Sex of Coobserver	3	59.85	0.30
Sex of Subject × Sex of Coobserver	1	1,394.43	7.09*
Treatment × Sex of Subject × Sex of Coobserver	3	290.87	1.47
Within	64	196.63	

* $P < 0.01$.

fects of treatment (positive, negative, neutral, control), sex of subject, sex of observer, and any interaction between sex of subject, sex of observer, and treatment on amount and direction of aggression.

Analysis of variance of the data for the E factor, overt aggression (TABLE 2), reveals a significant difference at the 0.01 level between treatment groups. A Newman-Keuls a posteriori analysis revealed that the subjects in the positive-sanction group scored at a significantly higher level of overt aggression than did subjects in the negative treatment group and that the differences between the mean scores in the negative, neutral, and control groups were not significant.

Further analysis revealed a significant interaction effect between sex of subject and sex of observer (TABLE 3), with male subjects scoring significantly higher levels of overt aggression with the male adult observer than did male subjects with the female adult observer; and with female subjects scoring significantly higher levels of overt aggression with the female adult observer than did female subjects with the male adult observer.

The presence of the adult observer had no effect on the overt aggression scores. The planned comparison yielded a sum of squares of 0.764, which was not significant. The predictions made earlier were verified with respect to outward aggression. At this point, it is of interest to explore some of the unpredicted findings.

Analysis of variance of the data for the I factor, aggression turned inward (TABLE 4), reveals a significant difference at the 0.01 level, between treatment groups, with the subjects in the negative-sanction group scoring significantly higher levels of aggression turned inward than did subjects in the other treatment groups. A Newman-Keuls a posteriori analysis revealed that the differences between scores in the positive, neutral, and control groups were not significant. No interaction effects were obtained (TABLE 5). It appeared as though children were indeed affected by the violent content of the programs, but because of the disapproval of the adult observer, they turned the aggression inward.

The M factor, aggression avoided or evaded, also produced some surprises. The analysis of variance revealed a significant difference at the 0.05 level between treatment groups (TABLE 6). Subjects in the negative, neutral,

TABLE 3

MEANS OF MAIN EFFECTS AND FIRST-ORDER INTERACTIONS FOR E FACTOR SCORES

	Male Observer		Female Observer		Total
Boys	53.80		47.65		50.72
Girls	47.50		58.05		52.77

	Positive	Negative	Neutral	Control	Total
Male Observer	60.30	43.90	49.90	48.50	50.65
Female Observer	59.90	45.70	50.10	55.70	52.85

	Boys	Girls	Total
Positive	61.90	58.30	60.10
Negative	47.10	42.50	44.80
Neutral	49.40	50.60	55.00
Control	44.50	59.70	52.10

and control groups scored at significantly higher levels of aggression avoided or evaded than did subjects in the positive-sanction group. The positive-sanction groups had a significantly lower mean than did the other treatment groups ($P < 0.05$). Upon further examination, it appeared that the statistical significance resulted from the interaction of the female subjects with the sex of the adult, i.e., female subjects scored significantly higher levels of aggression avoided with the male adult observer than did female subjects with the female observer (TABLE 7).

DISCUSSION

The primary purpose of this study was to determine if the modeling of aggression by seven-year-old children, from filmed aggressive models, was influenced by the presence and sex of sanctioning adults.

The findings suggested that while parent presence did not make a significant difference as to the amount of aggression that was modeled, parent sanction did significantly influence how subsequent aggression was expressed. Subjects in the positive-sanction group, where the adult observer

TABLE 4

ANALYSIS OF VARIANCE OF AGGRESSION SCORES ON THE I FACTOR

Source	df	MS	F
Treatment	3	355.24	7.40*
Sex of Subject	1	59.51	1.24
Sex of Coobserver	1	99.01	2.06
Treatment × Sex of Subject	3	124.74	2.59
Treatment × Sex of Coobserver	3	18.37	0.38
Sex of Subject × Sex of Coobserver	1	59.51	1.24
Treatment × Sex of Subject × Sex of Coobserver	3	104.67	2.18
Within	64	47.98	

* $P < 0.01$.

TABLE 5

MEANS OF MAIN EFFECTS AND FIRST-ORDER INTERACTIONS FOR I FACTOR SCORES

	Male Observer		Female Observer		Total
Boys	14.65		18.60		16.62
Girls	18.10		18.60		18.35

	Positive	Negative	Neutral	Control	Total
Male Observer	14.30	21.80	14.50	14.90	16.37
Female Observer	16.70	25.70	17.60	14.40	18.60

	Boys	Girls	Total
Positive	14.50	16.50	15.50
Negative	20.00	27.50	23.75
Neutral	15.00	17.10	16.05
Control	17.00	12.30	14.65

expressed approval of the filmed aggression, showed a significantly higher level of overt aggression than did subjects in the negative-sanction group. In the negative-sanction group, where the adult observer expressed disapproval of the filmed aggression, subjects turned the aggression inward. The subjects in the positive-sanction group scored significantly lower scores of aggression avoided or evaded than did the subjects in the other treatment groups.

That the treatment effect was so strong and pervasive can perhaps be seen in light of the social-power theory of identification.[29] According to this theory, children will tend more to imitate behavior of an adult who controls positive resources than of an adult who is perceived as powerless. The adult observer voicing approval and disapproval of the filmed aggression might well have been perceived by the subjects as an adult having control and power over their future resources. According to the social-power theory, it seems plausible that the subjects in this study identified with the adult observer—whom they perceived as being powerful—and, in so doing, tended to reproduce behavior consistent with the observer's sanctions, thus producing the significant treatment effect.

Much of the recent research in the area of television and modeling be-

TABLE 6

ANALYSIS OF VARIANCE OF AGGRESSION SCORES ON THE M FACTOR

Source	df	MS	F
Treatment	3	405.14	2.99*
Sex of Subject	1	224.43	1.66
Sex of Coobserver	1	296.43	2.19
Treatment × Sex of Subject	3	153.47	1.13
Treatment × Sex of Coobserver	3	25.08	0.18
Sex of Subject × Sex of Coobserver	1	756.50	5.59*
Treatment × Sex of Subject × Sex of Coobserver	3	145.02	1.07
Within	64	135.16	

* $P < 0.05$.

TABLE 7

MEANS OF MAIN EFFECTS AND FIRST-ORDER INTERACTIONS FOR M FACTOR SCORES

	Male Observer		Female Observer		Total
Boys	31.25		33.55		32.40
Girls	34.05		24.05		29.05

	Positive	Negative	Neutral	Control	Total
Male Observer	24.90	33.80	35.50	36.40	32.65
Female Observer	23.20	30.50	32.10	29.40	28.80

	Boys	Girls	Total
Positive	23.10	25.00	24.05
Negative	32.60	31.70	32.15
Neutral	35.50	32.10	33.80
Control	38.40	27.40	32.90

havior has shown that children will model aggressive behavior after exposure to violent television.[22,25,30] While Waters has made suggestions regarding the effect of parent presence on the impact of television on children,[17] the findings of this investigation have shown that parent presence alone has little effect.

In contrast to previous aggression studies where boys were found to be more imitative than girls,[31, 32] the findings of this investigation showed no significant differences between sex of subject in any of the three aspects of aggression examined. This finding might be explained in terms of the type of programs that girls are exposed to today—such as "Wonder Woman," "Police Woman," and "Charlie's Angels"—where the female model is seen in various roles that were, in the past, traditionally male roles. It may also be seen as a reflection of the changing role of women in society. It is felt that this, coupled with the way women are presented in the media today, accounts for the findings in this study, regarding the lack of any significant differences between the sex of the subjects.

Two significant interaction effects were found between sex of subject and sex of observer for the E factor (overt aggression) and the M factor (aggression avoided or evaded). For the E factor, it was found that male subjects who viewed the filmed aggression with a male adult observer showed higher levels of overt aggression than did male subjects who viewed with a female adult observer. Female subjects who viewed the filmed aggression with a female adult observer showed higher levels of overt aggression than did female subjects who viewed with a male adult observer. These findings can be viewed in terms of both dependency and identification behavior. Bandura and Walters suggest that children in the age group used in this study not only seek to identify with the same-sex adult, but also display a great deal of dependency behavior with the same-sex adult.[15] With respect to the concept of identification, Kagan maintains that the child wants to feel and experience that some of the adult characteristics are his; and, thus, the child will try to identify with the adult, if the child is told or made to feel that he and the adult are similar in appearance or temperament.[33]

For the M factor, there was a significant interaction between sex of subject and sex of observer. An examination of the data revealed that the statistical significance resulted from an interaction of the female subjects with the sex of the adult observer. Female subjects who viewed the filmed aggression with the male adult observer showed higher levels of aggression avoided or evaded than did female subjects who viewed with the female observer.

Johnson maintains that once the Oedipal stage has passed, the relationship between a daughter and her father takes on a new dimension.[34] She senses that his love and caring for her depend on her being feminine and attractive. It is suggested that the female subjects might have perceived the male adult observer as the father figure and thus showed high levels of aggression avoided or evaded, feeling that this was expected of them.

CONCLUSIONS

It was concluded that, within the limits of this study, adult presence while children watch filmed aggression on a television monitor has no significant effect on subsequent aggression. The significant differences, however, on the mean scores between treatments clearly suggest that what the adult observer says, in the way of approval or disapproval of the filmed aggression, does have an effect on how the subsequent aggression will be expressed.

Results from previous studies in the area of television and violence have indicated that children learn aggressive behavior from film-mediated aggressive models.[10,22,23,35-38] Based on past research, then, it is fair to assume that some degree of modeling occurred with the subjects in this investigation during their exposure to filmed aggressive models and, further, based on the findings of this investigation, that adult sanction had a significant effect on how subsequent learned aggression was expressed by the subjects.

The adult observers noted an interesting phenomenon that occurred during the experimental trials: more frequently than not, the subjects appeared to be attending only to the more violent aspects of the program being presented on the television monitor. During the program, the subjects talked, laughed, or played with each other. When the background music became intense and loud—usually the cue for a violent sequence—the subjects would stop what they were doing and focus their attention on the television monitor. When the action sequence ended, the subjects tended to return to their talking and playing. This pattern repeated itself the next time the music became intense and loud. It seems, then, that the subjects were selectively tuning out a good deal of the dialogue and were tuning in all the violence. Further research—looking into the possibility that children are selectively attending to the violent aspects of television—should be considered, as this might offer an explanation as to why television violence has such a powerful impact on children.

Unfortunately, few data have been collected on the relationship between children's viewing of aggressive television and parental sanction. Many more data would have to be generated from different age groups, from different socioeconomic levels, and under different conditions before any definitive conclusions could be drawn. The unforeseen findings of this study indicate that there is a possible conflict situation that develops when an adult just says "bad" to the violent content on television. What appears to result is a residue of learned aggression that is either avoided or internalized by the child. Thus, one might conclude that the issue is much more complicated and that brevity on the part of the parent regarding the violence is simply not enough to vitiate the impact of aggressive television fare. While efforts should be made to teach young children to watch television selectively and critically, efforts should also be put forth in the area of parent education. Perhaps as parents are made more aware of the powerful impact of violent television on their children, they can also be educated as to the importance of having lengthy discussions with their children regarding the programs watched on television. Television industry's latest campaign stresses that families watch television together. Together, while important, is simply not enough. What might be critical are family discussions surrounding the substantive issues in the program and how these issues relate to one's life.

ACKNOWLEDGMENTS

With thanks to Dr. Frank Crowley. This paper is based on the author's doctoral dissertation, "Effect on Subsequent Behavior of Seven Year Olds after Observed Film Aggression with Sanctioning Adults," Fordham University, New York, 1978. The author thanks Dr. Belle Wiggens and Carol Eisenberg for their helpful comments; Dr. Thomas Lee, Remo Perini, and the children for making the study possible; and the staff of The Academy their helpful assistance.

REFERENCES

1. HALL, K. R. L. 1964. Aggression in monkey and ape societies. *In* The Natural History of Aggression. J. D. Carthy & F. J. Ebling, Eds.: 17–26. Academic Press. London, England.
2. SAGAN, E. 1974. Cannibalism: Human Aggression and Cultural Form. Harper & Row, Publishers. New York, N.Y.
3. BANDURA, A. 1962. Social learning through imitation. *In* Nebraska Symposium on Motivation: 211–269. University of Nebraska Press. Lincoln, Nebr.
4. BANDURA, A. 1973. Aggression: A Social Learning Analysis. Prentice-Hall, Inc. Englewood Cliffs, N.J.
5. BANDURA, A., D. ROSS & S. A. ROSS. 1961. Transmission of aggression through imitation of aggressive models. J. Abnorm. Soc. Psychol. **63:** 575–582.
6. BANDURA, A. & F. J. McDONALD. 1963. The influence of social reinforcement and the behavior of models in shaping children's moral judgments. J. Abnorm. Soc. Psychol. **67:** 274–281.

7. MAUSNER, B. 1954. The effect of prior reinforcement on the interaction of observer pairs. J. Abnorm. Soc. Psychol. **49:** 65–68.
8. MAUSNER, R. & B. L. BLOCK. 1957. A study of the additivity of variables affecting social interaction. J. Abnorm. Soc. Psychol. **54:** 250–256.
9. BANDURA, A., D. ROSS & S. A. ROSS. 1963. Imitation of film-mediated aggressive models. J. Abnorm. Soc. Psychol. **66:** 3–11.
10. ERON, L. D., M. M. LEFKOWITZ, R. HUESMANN & L. O. WALDER. 1972. Does television violence cause aggression? Am. Psychol. **27:** 253–263.
11. KNIVETON, D. & G. STEPHENSON. 1973. An examination of individual susceptibility to the influence of aggressive film models. Br. J. Psychiatry **122:** 53–56.
12. LIEBERT, R. M. 1972. Television and social learning: some relationships between viewing violence and behaving aggressively (overview). *In* Television and Social Learning. II: 1–42. Surgeon General's Report. Washington, D.C.
13. LIEBERT, R. M. & R. A. BARON. 1972. Short-term effects of televised aggression on children's aggressive behavior. *In* Television and Social Learning. II: 181–201. Surgeon General's Report. Washington, D.C.
14. LOVAAS, O. I. 1961. Effect of exposure to symbolic aggression on aggressive behavior. Child Dev. **32:** 37–44.
15. BANDURA, A. & R. H. WALTERS. 1963. Social Learning and Personality Development. Holt, Rinehart & Winston, Inc. New York, N.Y.
16. KAYE, E. 1974. The Family Guide to Children's Television. Pantheon Books. New York, N.Y.
17. WATERS, H. 1977. What TV does to kids. Newsweek (February 21): 62–70.
18. WILLIAMS, S. & V. CRANE. 1974. Television violence and your child. Paper presented at a lecture series of the College of Marin, California, and the Marin Association for Mental Health.
19. MOYERS, B. 1979. Bill Moyer's Journal. TV program aired July 30. WNET (Public Broadcasting System).
20. DILLION, J. 1968. Violence dominates U.S. summertime TV. Christian Science Monitor (July 25).
21. DOMINICK, J. R. & B. S. GREENBERG. 1972. Attitudes toward violence: the interaction of television exposure, family attitudes, and social class. *In* Television and Adolescent Aggressiveness. III: 314–335. Surgeon General's Report. Washington, D.C.
22. GERBNER, G. 1972. Violence in television drama: trends and symbolic functions. *In* Media Content and Control. I: 28–187. Surgeon General's Report. Washington, D.C.
23. GREENBERG, B. 1974. British children and televised violence. Public Opinion Q. **38:** 531–547.
24. LEFKOWITZ, M. M., L. D. ERON, L. O. WALDER & L. R. HUESMANN. 1972. Television violence and child aggression: a follow-up study. *In* Television and Adolescent Aggressiveness. III: 35–135. Surgeon General's Report. Washington, D.C.
25. LEIFER, A. D. & D. F. ROBERTS. 1972. Children's responses to television violence. *In* Television and Social Learning. II: 43–180. Surgeon General's Report. Washington, D.C.
26. MCINTYRE, J. J. & J. J. TEEVAN. 1972. Television and deviant behavior. *In* Television and Adolescent Aggressiveness. III: 383–435. Surgeon General's Report. Washington, D.C.
27. ROTHENBERG, M. B. 1975. Effect of television violence on children and youth. J. Am. Med. Assoc. **234:** 1043–1046.
28. National Citizen's Committee for Broadcasting. 1977. Newsletter. Washington, D.C.
29. MACCOBY, E. E. 1959. Role-taking in childhood and its consequences for social learning. Child Dev. **30:** 239–252.
30. HANRATTY, M. S., R. M. LIEBERT, L. W. MORRIS & L. E. FERNANDEZ. 1969. Imitation of film-mediated aggression against live and inanimate victims. *In* Proceedings of the 77th Annual Convention of the American Psychological Association: 457–458.
31. BANDURA, A. 1965. Influence of models' reinforcement contingencies on the acquisition of imitative responses. J. Pers. Soc. Psychol. **1:** 589–595.
32. BANDURA, A., D. ROSS & S. A. ROSS. 1963. Vicarious reinforcement and imitative learning. J. Abnorm. Soc. Psychol. **67:** 601–607.

33. KAGAN, J. 1958. The concept of identification. Psychol. Rev. **65:** 296–305.
34. JOHNSON, M. 1963. Sex role learning in the nuclear family. Child Dev. **34:** 319–333.
35. LIEBERT, R. M. 1974. Television and children's aggressive behavior: another look. Am. J. Psychoanal. **34:** 99–107.
36. MURRAY, J. 1973. Television and violence: implications of the Surgeon General's research program. Am. Psychol. **28:** 472–478.
37. MUSSEN, P. & E. RUTHERFORD. 1961. Effects of aggressive cartoons on children's aggressive play. J. Abnorm. Soc. Psychol. **62:** 461–464.
38. SAVITSKY, J. C., R. W. ROGERS, C. E. IZARD & R. M. LIEBERT. 1971. The role of frustration and anger in the imitation of filmed aggression against a human victim. Psychol. Rep. **29:** 807–810.

ADOLESCENT AGGRESSION AND TELEVISION

Leonard D. Eron and L. Rowell Huesmann

Department of Psychology
University of Illinois at Chicago Circle
Chicago, Illinois 60680

Most criminal acts in the United States, at least most violent criminal acts, are committed by young males in late adolescence.[1] There could be many reasons why this is so—biological, psychological, sociological, political, and economic. Empirical studies have uncovered relations between aggression and a number of variables from these classes. Some of these relations are causative, some concomitant or perhaps merely coincidental. One particularly striking finding has been that heightened aggression among adolescents is related to the violence of the television programs they watch.[2] However, the extent and the content of a child's television viewing are inevitably correlated with other potential causes of aggression. For example, most violent crimes are committed in lower-class, ghetto areas by individuals of limited IQ, who have dropped out of school, are unemployed, come from disorganized families, and in general have limited resources for coping with problems.[1] These are also the persons who spend much time watching television and who prefer violent programs.[3,4,5] Thus, on the basis of correlational data alone, it is difficult to attribute cause or effect to either of the variables in question.

Causal relations can be best demonstrated by experimental manipulation or inferred from large-scale observational studies done over time using repeated observations on the same subjects. The studies by Berkowitz and his students with college-age subjects exemplify the former approach, and the studies we have done, following youngsters for periods up to 10 years until late adolescence, illustrate the latter approach. Berkowitz, for example, has demonstrated that exposure of university students to violent films increases the likelihood and magnitude of subsequent aggressive behavior, especially if the viewer is angered or frustrated prior to viewing the film.[6]

In our 10-year longitudinal study, we found that the best single predictor of how aggressive a young man would be at age 19 was the violence of television programs he had watched at age 8.[7] By use of a cross-lagged panel design and partial correlation to control for possible third variables, it was demonstrated that the most plausible hypothesis to explain this relation was that continuous viewing of television violence at the earlier age caused the aggressive behavior that was measured at the later age.

FIGURE 1 describes the cross-lag correlational analyses of our 10-year study. These data have already been published, so we will not dwell on them at any length.[7] You see here the significant difference between the two cross correlations over a 10-year lag. The violence of television programs watched by boys at age 8 is more highly related to their aggression 10 years later than is the aggression of boys at age 8 to the violence of television they watched

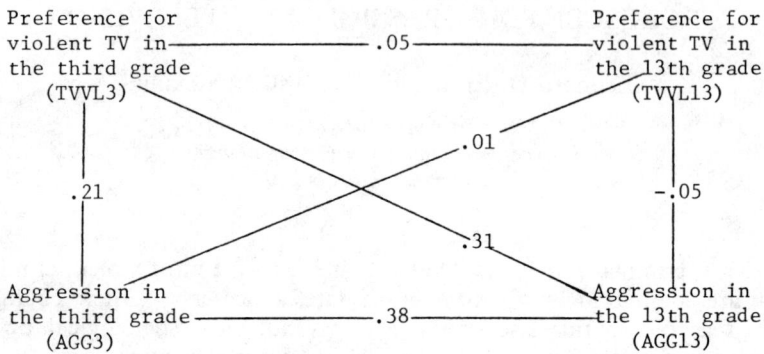

FIGURE 1. Correlations between a preference for violent television and peer-rated aggression for 211 boys over a 10-year lag.

10 years later. This fact, along with other analyses of these data (which are described in Reference 7), reinforces our confidence in the probable causal direction going from violence viewing to aggression. For example, consider those youngsters who at age 8 had been less aggressive but had been watching highly violent television; by the time they were age 19, they were significantly more aggressive than those who initially had been highly aggressive but had been watching less violent programs. This finding contradicts the assertion that it is only highly aggressive individuals or those already predisposed to aggression who are affected by filmed violence.[5]

There can no longer be any doubt that viewing television violence is one important cause of violent behavior among adolescents. The repeated findings of such an effect in rigorously controlled laboratory experiments have been shown to generalize to field investigations in more natural environments.[8] The effect is real. It happens in life, not just in the laboratory. However, not all young people who watch violent television are similarly affected, although a significant number are. The important task for researchers is to isolate and study the relevant mediating variables that determine who the vulnerable ones are, under which conditions, and to devise intervention strategies that will protect those who are susceptible.

One of the mediating variables is gender. Most published studies have shown the television violence effect only for males. For example, in our 10-year study we found there was no relation at all between the violence of programs that girls watched at age 8 and how aggressive they were judged to be by their peers at that age or at age 19.* This obtained difference in results for boys and girls caused us to turn our attention to factors associated with being male or female in our society that might account for the findings. The most obvious factor is the generally higher aggression level in boys. No matter how aggression is measured or what type of aggression is in question,

---

* Actually there was a trend at age 19 for those girls who had been watching violent television to be less aggressive, but this was not statistically significant.

males as a group generally score higher than females as a group. Usually constitutional, hormonal, or other predispositional variables are invoked to explain the differences.[9] However, it cannot be denied that there are some females in our society who are just as aggressive as the most aggressive males and some males who are as nonaggressive as most females. How did these individuals get that way? It is our thesis that they acquired these behaviors, atypical for their gender, at least partially because they were exposed to socialization experiences usually and traditionally reserved for the other sex. In our longitudinal studies of development of aggression in young people, we have continually been confronted by these differences in socialization experiences and by both concomitant and subsequent differences in aggressive behavior.

Another potential mediating variable in the relation between television violence and aggressive behavior might be a child's use of fantasy and the ability to discriminate between fantasy and reality as portrayed on the television screen. Girls may be less affected than boys by television violence because girls may be better able to make this discrimination. In their play and other recreational activities, girls obtain considerable practice in the use of fantasy and have more opportunities to slip back and forth from fantasy to real life than do boys. It is suggested that girls more clearly see television as fantasy and thus are less likely to be influenced by the actions of the characters they observe there.[10] Data we collected in our 10-year study confirm this. In general, girls thought television was significantly less realistic than did boys. Furthermore, the more aggressive a girl was, at both age 8 and age 19, the more realistic she thought television violence was.

Currently we are investigating further these notions about the effect on aggression of differential socialization of boys and girls and how the ability to discriminate between fantasy and reality reduces the effect of television violence on aggressive behavior. We have just completed collection of data in a three-year longitudinal study of approximately 750 children in Oak Park, a suburban Chicago school district, and in two inner-city schools of the Chicago Archdiocese. One-half of these children were in the first grade when we started, and one-half in the third grade. We have not yet completed the three-year longitudinal analyses. However, we do have cross-sectional data obtained from first- and third-grade children in the first wave of the study[11] and some longitudinal analyses from first to second wave. These data are consonant with the interpretation of the previously obtained findings that we have been discussing.

First of all, a positive relation between television violence viewing at home and aggressive behavior was reaffirmed for boys and also emerged clearly for girls. Although the direction of the relation in this study was the same for both sexes, there were interesting differences between the sexes. FIGURE 2 contains cross-lagged correlations obtained across the first year to the second year of our three-year study. The three figures in the top half of FIGURE 2 represent the relation of three measures of television violence to peer-rated aggression in boys over a one-year period, 1977 to 1978. The figure on the left refers to violence of male characters on TV, the middle figure to violence of female characters, and the right-hand figure to sheer frequen-

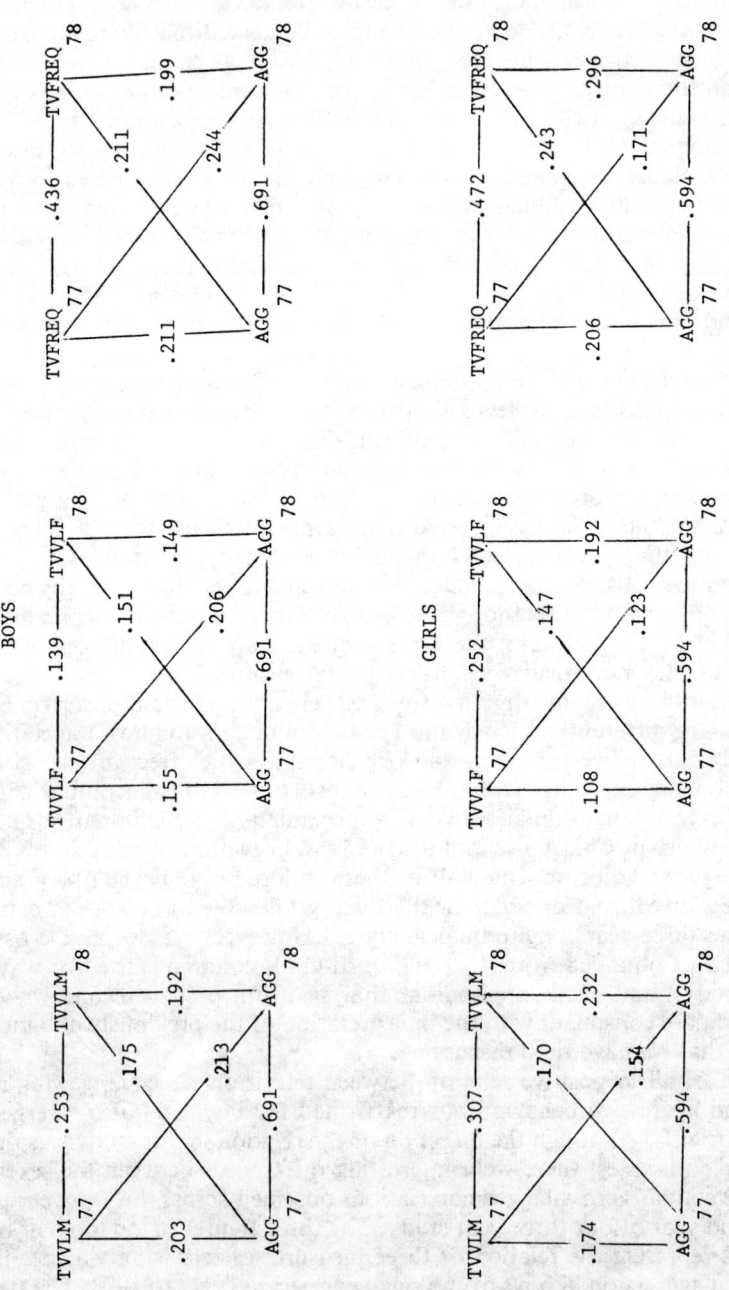

FIGURE 2. Cross-lag correlations. (TVVLM = violence by male characters on TV. TVVLF = violence by female characters on TV. TVFREQ = frequency of TV viewing.)

cy of television viewing. In all cases the correlations are positive, and in all cases the correlation between TV violence in the earlier period and aggression in the later period is greater than the correlation between aggression in the earlier period and TV in the later one. The correlations of course are not great, nor are the differences between the crossed correlations. However, we have always maintained that the effect is cumulative, and it can be predicted that as the years go by, the size of the correlation will increase. Actually, the size of the correlations is of the same order as the contemporaneous correlation in the first wave of our 10-year study.

The cross-lagged correlations for girls are represented in the lower half of FIGURE 2. Here again the correlations are all positive. However, we do not see here the same difference in the cross-lag correlations as is present in the boys' data. Such positive findings for girls were not apparent in our earlier 10-year study and therefore are particularly interesting. Later we will discuss in greater detail the possible reasons for the appearance now of a relation between television violence and aggression for girls when we did not obtain one approximately 20 years ago.

In general, however, this new study of 700 youngsters in a Chicago suburb as well as in the inner city corroborates the findings of our original study done 20 years previously in semirural New York state. We now know that the relation between viewing violence and aggressive behavior has already appeared at age six. Jerome and Dorothy Singer, who observed children's physically aggressive behavior in nursery school over the period of one year, have also recently reported that this behavior was related to the amount of violence that the youngsters, just 3 and 4 years old, viewed on television.[12] By doing a cross-lagged analysis of correlations between aggressive behavior and violence viewing at different times over a year and by partialling out IQ, socioeconomic status, and other background factors—much the same as we did in our 10-year study—the Singers demonstrated that the likely causal direction is from violence viewing to physically aggressive behavior in these three- and four-year-old nursery school children. Their results, based on observed behaviors in nursery school, are even more clear-cut than ours. Interestingly, they also found a positive causal relation for both boys and girls.

TABLE 1 presents the contemporaneous correlations between television violence and aggression in Finland, where our study is being replicated by Kirsti Lagerspetz and where they have now completed the first wave. Our own data are presented again for comparison purposes. Again there are two measures of TV violence and one of frequency of TV viewing. One can see that in both sets of data, the relation of peer-rated aggression to violence by female characters is lower than the relation to male violence. This is true regardless of the subject's sex or age, except for the girls in Finland. The increased effectiveness of the male model is not what we expected. According to modeling theory, female characters should be more salient as models for girls; and it would be predicted that their behaviors would be copied by girls more readily than the behaviors of male characters. In our earlier study conducted 20 years ago, we argued that an important reason for not finding a

TABLE 1

CORRELATION BETWEEN TV VIEWING AND AGGRESSION

	All Subjects	Girls	Boys
Finland 1978			
TVVM*	0.23	0.18	0.14
TVVF†	0.16	0.20	0.07
TVFr‡	0.04	0.09	0.03
USA 1978			
TVVM	0.22	0.23	0.19
TVVF	0.20	0.19	0.15
TVFr	0.22	0.30	0.20
USA 1977			
TVVM	0.22	0.17	0.20
TVVF	0.13	0.11	0.16
TVFr	0.21	0.21	0.21

* TVVM = violence by male characters on TV.
† TVVF = violence by female characters on TV.
‡ TVFr = frequency of television viewing.

TV violence–aggressive behavior relation for girls was that there were far fewer aggressive females on television for a girl to imitate than there were aggressive males for a boy to imitate. This would not seem to be the case, since today we do have aggressive female models on television; and although these models are copied to some extent by girls, the male models seem to be copied more.

It may be that more important than the sex of the model are the behaviors the model is performing and that if masculine activities are intrinsically more appealing to subjects of either sex, then all subjects would be more likely to attend to male characters and imitate their activities. It has been demonstrated that the more powerful the model, the more likely are the model's behaviors to be attended to and copied, regardless of sex.[13] Similarly, it is suggested now that the more appealing are the general activities of the model, the more likely will the observer be to attend to the model and therefore to copy the model's behaviors. Indeed, there is some evidence for this in our data on preference for sex-typed activities among these subjects. Our measure of preference for sex-typed activities comprised a booklet of four pages, each of which contained six pictures of children's activities. Two pictures of each set had been previously rated masculine, two feminine, and two neutral by 67 college students who had designated the activities as popular for boys and girls. The 24 pictures finally used in this procedure were selected with good reliability. The task for the children was to select the two activities they liked best on each page, and the children received a score for the number of masculine, feminine, and neutral pictures they chose. The reason for including a neutral category is that it is much easier for boys to admit to liking neutral activities than to admit to liking feminine ones. Similarly for girls, we anticipated that it would be difficult to admit to liking boys' activities. Here, however, we were surprised. One of our most interesting findings is that *both* boys and girls prefer more traditionally masculine activities as they get older. The mean increase in score is highly significant for both sexes. Therefore, since boys' traditional activities have increasingly more appeal for both boys and girls as they grow older, it is not surprising that male figures stand out as models for both sexes. In Finland, where we have the sole exception to the greater influence of the male model for girls, it is likely that the differentiation between male and female occupational and recreational activities is not as large as it is in this country. Thus for Finnish children, the similarity between model and observer in physical characteristics is more influential in modeling than are the activities in which the male or female model engages.

Furthermore, in this country, the relation between preference for masculine activities and aggression is significant for both boys and girls. Regardless of sex, subjects who score high on preference for masculine activities are likely to be more aggressive. And the relation is stronger from the first to second wave than contemporaneously. The cumulative effect of the socialization experience is obvious. We see the culmination of this socialization experience in FIGURES 3 and 4. These figures describe the results of an experiment by one of our students, Esther Kaplan-Shain,[14] who related scores of men and women college students on scales of masculinity and femininity[15] to performance on an aggression machine. This was an adaption of the Buss-type[16] apparatus, whereby the subject signals a confederate by delivering loud sounds to the confederate's earphones rather than by electric shock—the louder the sound delivered, the more aggressive is the response. Here we see that while masculinity in males has little relation to aggressive responding, femininity in males is significantly negatively related to aggression; similarly, while femininity in females is not predictive of lack of aggression, masculinity in females is positively correlated with the intensity of the aggressive response.[14] Thus it would seem that men—regardless of the masculine attitudes they have—are inhibited from responding aggressively *if* they also have traditionally feminine attitudes and values, while women who subscribe to masculine attitudes and values are facilitated in aggressive

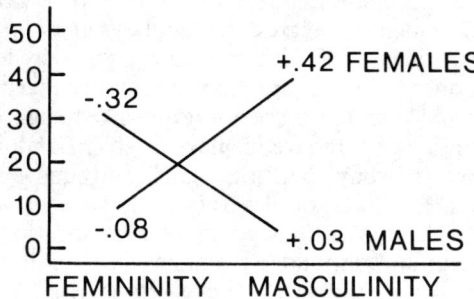

FIGURE 3. Correlations between aggression and masculinity or femininity in male and female college students.

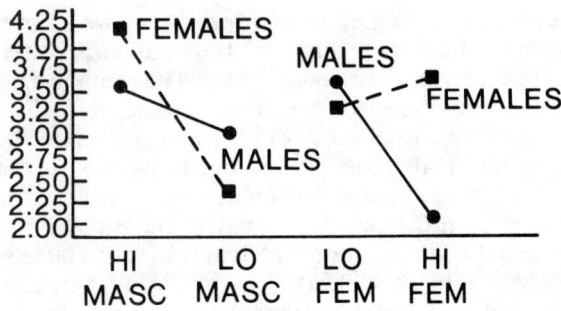

FIGURE 4. Mean aggression scores of high and low masculine and high and low feminine college students (male and female).

responding regardless of their feminine attitudes. FIGURE 4 shows the mean aggression scores according to whether the subjects are high or low masculine or high or low feminine.

There is little difference between aggressive responses of high and low masculine men, but there is a significant difference in the aggressive response of high and low feminine men ($P < 0.02$). Similarly, there is little difference in the responses of high and low feminine women but a large and significant difference between high and low masculine women ($P < 0.01$). The most aggressive responders of all are the high masculine women. Yes, women can learn to be as aggressive as men, despite their low levels of testosterone.

However, within Western societies, women are usually socialized to be nonaggressive, while boys are probably encouraged and reinforced in the direct and overt expression of aggression. Very early in life, girls learn that physical aggression is an undesirable behavior for girls, and so they acquire other behaviors more suitable to expectations for girls. A recent study done with fourth-, sixth-, and eighth-grade youngsters found that while girls endorsed increasingly with age the effectiveness of passive behavior in solving problems, boys increasingly disapproved of such behavior in problem solving.[17] In both of our longitudinal studies and in both the United States and Finland, girls were much less aggressive than boys *at all times*, regardless of how aggression was measured. Since girls do not usually learn physical aggression as a response to instigation, they are rarely either rewarded or punished for such behavior and thus are not responsive to aggressive cues in the environment, including aggressive displays on TV. Bandura's studies have consistently shown that boys perform significantly more imitative aggression than do girls.[18,19] Bandura also found, however, that when girls are positively reinforced for imitating aggressive behavior, they significantly increase such behavior and respond in a manner more similar to boys who are reinforced for the same behavior.[20] The results of Hokanson and Edelman would support this contention that lowered aggression levels in females are a function of lack of reinforcement for aggressive behavior. They found that females did not demonstrate the quickened reduction of physiological arousal after the opportunity to counteraggress against a confederate of the experimenter who had aggressed against them.[21] However, such quickened reduction of heart rate and blood pressure to basal levels was routinely seen in male subjects. Recent studies have shown that the effect of reinforcement on repeated performance of aggressive behavior is relatively independent of the initial modeling of the behavior.[22] What we are suggesting is that different socialization practices have reduced the likelihood that girls will continue to perform aggressive behavior observed on television. In summary, most girls may be trained to be nonaggressive to *such* an extent that aggressive models have little effect on them.

Two related findings are the significant positive relation for girls between aggression and masculine interest patterns as measured by the masculinity-femininity (M-F) scale of the Minnesota multiphasic personality inventory (MMPI) as well as the significant positive relation between aggression scores for girls and the extent to which they watch contact sports on television.[7] Both of these scores related to aggression reflect attitudes and behavior that are normative for boys. For boys, however, there was no relation between viewing contact sports on TV and aggression; nor was there a relation for boys between masculinity on the M-F scale and aggression. It is very probable that the reason for lack of relation with aggression for boys lies in the minimal variability on the other two variables. Most boys, whether low or high aggressive, watch contact sports and also endorse the attitudes and interests comprising the masculinity items on the M-F scale. However, these results indicate that when females are aggressive, some of their interests and activities are deviant from their sex and are similar to the behavior of the male sex group. Parke *et al.* have more recently reported a singular finding in that the level of verbal aggression observed in girls who previously had been exposed to a violent film was higher than that observed in girls who had seen a nonviolent film.[8] However, it should be noted that these girls were incarcerated juvenile delinquents who in the past probably had avoided traditional female values and attitudes and adopted more masculine behaviors.

What about the relation of fantasy behavior to aggression? In our 10-year study, we found that girls who see themselves as masculine at age 19, i.e., those girls who obtain high scores on scale 5 of the MMPI, tend to perceive television as more realistic and also tend to be more aggressive. Thus, the more girls see TV as realistic, the more they are like boys in other respects and the more aggressive they are. We hypothesize that differential ability in using TV as a fantasy experience may account for the difference in the direction of the relation between TV violence and aggression that we found between boys and girls.

In our three-year longitudinal study, we measured each child's fantasy behavior and judgment of TV realism, as well as the variables mentioned previously. The fantasy scales were developed by another of our students, Erica Rosenfeld, from a 45-item questionnaire about daydreams that had been administered to the children.[23] Three major styles of fantasizing were detected in these subjects: "fanciful," in which the youngster daydreams about fairy tales and implausible happenings; "active," in which the youngster daydreams about heroes, achievement, and intellectual pursuits; and "aggressive negative," in which the youngster daydreams about fighting, killing, and being hurt. These styles of fantasy behavior were related to aggression differently for boys and girls.

In the first wave of this three-year study, the major predictors of aggression for boys as indicated by a multiple regression analysis were TV violence viewing, preference for traditional masculine sex-typed activities, and aggressive fantasies. For girls, the best predictors were TV violence viewing, perceptions of TV violence as real, low preference for traditional feminine-type activities, and fantasies about action. In other words, for both sexes TV violence viewing, fantasy behavior, and sex role preference are independently related to aggression, although the nature of the fantasy content that predicts to aggression is different for boys and girls. This is because girls who fantasy about action—heroes and heroines and winning games and achievement—are the most aggressive. For boys, those who fantasy about aggression—beating up other persons—are the ones who are most aggressive. There is no evidence whatsoever in our data that fantasy has a cathartic effect! Especially for boys, those children who *fantasy* about aggressive acts tend to *act* aggressively. Girls, who in general do not score as high as boys on any measure of aggression, also do not daydream much about aggressive themes. However, those girls whose daydreams contain *active* content tend to be aggressive in overt behavior. Active fantasy, it happens, is also generally more characteristic of boys than it is of girls. Thus again we have evidence that girls who are aggressive have interests, values, and attitudes similar to those of boys.

What are the implications of these findings—both from our 10-year longitudinal study and the current studies in Chicago and Finland—for the reduction of aggressive behavior?

Our findings, we believe, point to two areas where efforts can be made that should eventually reduce aggression. The first and most direct is television violence. Significant overall reduction of violence and mayhem on the television screen would, we believe, lower the level of violence in American society. However, we think trying to get any significant change in television programming is like tilting at windmills. Despite the efforts of the American Medical Association, the Parent Teachers Association, and Action for Children's Television, the level of violence on national and local TV has not diminished appreciably. Barring any significant changes in programming, what can be done? For one thing, we can teach parents and children techniques for counteracting the effects of television. Efforts at devising such procedures are going on in at least two places. Dorothy and Jerome Singer of the Yale University Television Research Center are preparing curricula to teach young children and their parents how to be intelligent television consumers; in Chicago we are intervening with groups of children in our longitudinal study to determine the best way to ameliorate the relation between violence viewing and subsequent aggressive behavior in children. It would be nice to report some great breakthrough—the discovery of a vaccine with which we could innoculate children so they would forever be immune to the effects of television violence. However, our first attempts do not appear to have been terribly successful. In the first year of our study, we focused our intervention on teaching children to distinguish between fantasy and reality, e.g., explaining how "Bionic Woman" and "Six Million Dollar Man" simulate the aggressive behaviors and other fantastic actions of these characters and having the children imagine similar feats and how they would simulate them. However, on a criterion test, these children did not distinguish fantasy from reality any better than did a control group of children who had been engaged in different intervening activities. Whether the intervention will have an effect on the relation between violence viewing and subsequent aggressive behavior is still undetermined.

The Singers are having some success in their work with parents—teaching them how to turn off the TV, to monitor the child's watching, to share the viewing experience, to interpret content, to allay fears, and to help the child distinguish real from fantasy figures. Again, the Singers as yet have no data on how these interventions affect the relation between violence viewing and behavior.

However, there is one finding that has obvious implications for the use—or misuse—of fantasy in interventions, and that is the direct positive relation we have found between the extent of aggressive fantasy and the extent of aggressive behavior. It is obviously counterproductive for parents or therapists to encourage their children or clients to engage in fantasy rehearsal of aggressive problem solving in the mistaken assumption that "if you work it out in fantasy, you don't have to work it out in behavior." Such rehearsal often leads to the very acting out one is trying to prevent. We know from simple principles derived from memory studies that the more one rehearses an item, the more apt one is to remember it and therefore to use it in problem solving.

Another finding that suggests a clear direction for intervention is the positive relation between aggression and traditional masculine attitudes and values. The results of our studies to date, as well as those of other researchers, point to differential socialization as crucial in determining the different level of aggression in the two sexes. No matter how aggression is measured or observed, males generally score higher. But not all girls are unaggressive. There are some girls who seem to have been socialized like boys and who are just as aggressive as boys. Thus, although there may be organismically normal conditions, such as sex differences in testosterone level, that are implicated in aggressive behavior, this behavior is not necessarily immutable. Just as some females learn to be aggressive, males could learn *not* to be aggressive. The significant variables are the values and expectations a society holds for the expression of aggressive behavior in one sex rather than another and the rewards it provides or withdraws when that behavior is displayed. We have already discussed the ways in which society discourages aggressive behavior in girls from very early on in their lives and rewards them for engaging in other kinds of activity. We must reexamine what it means to be a man or masculine in our society, since the preponderance of violence in our society is perpetrated by males or by females who are acting like males. It is our contention that if we want to reduce the level of aggression in society, we should also discourage boys from aggression very early on in life and *reward* them for other behaviors. In other words, we should socialize boys more in the manner that we have been socializing girls. Rather than insisting that little girls should be treated like little boys and trained to be aggressive and assertive it should be the other way around. This is where the women's movement has it all wrong. Boys should be socialized the way girls have been traditionally socialized; *boys* should be encouraged to develop socially positive qualities like tenderness, sensitivity to feelings, nurturance, cooperativeness, and aesthetic appreciation. The level of individual aggression in society will be reduced only when male adolescents and young adults, as a result of socialization, subscribe to the same standards of behavior as have been traditionally encouraged for women.

In conclusion, we would like to repeat the old cliché that behavior that is learned can be unlearned; and aggressive behavior is no different—it *can* be unlearned. But how much easier it would be, how much pain and suffering and loss of life and property would be eliminated, if we arranged conditions so that aggression would not be learned in the first place and all youngsters would learn alternative ways of solving problems.

REFERENCES

1. MULVIHILL, D. J. & M. M. TUMIN. 1969. Staff Report to the National Commission on the Causes and Prevention of Violence. **12**. Crimes of Violence. U.S. Government Printing Office. Washington, D.C.
2. CHAFFEE, S. H. 1972. Television and adolescent aggressiveness. *In* Television and Social Behavior. G. A. Comstock & E. A. Rubinstein, Eds.: 31–34. U.S. Government Printing Office. Washington, D.C.
3. COMSTOCK, G., S. CHAFFEE, N. KATZMAN, M. McCOMBS & D. ROBERTS. 1978. Television and Human Behavior. Columbia University Press. New York, N.Y.
4. GREENBERG, B. & J. DOMINICK. 1969. Racial and social class differences in teenagers' use of television. J. Broadcasting **13**: 3331–3334.
5. STEIN, A. H. & L. K. FRIEDRICH. 1975. Impact of television on children and youth. *In* Review of Child Development Research. E. M. Hetherington, Ed. **5**. University of Chicago Press. Chicago, Ill.
6. BERKOWITZ, L. 1973. The control of aggression. *In* Review of Child Development Research. B. Caldwell & H. Ricciuti, Eds. **3**: 95–140. University of Chicago Press. Chicago, Ill.
7. ERON, L. D., L. R. HUESMANN, M. M. LEFKOWITZ & L. O. WALDER. 1972. Does television violence cause aggression? Am. Psychol. **27**: 253–263.
8. PARKE, R. D., L. BERKOWITZ, J. P. LEYENS, S. G. WEST & R. J. SEBASTIAN. 1977. Some effects of violent and non-violent movies on the behavior of juvenile delinquents. Adv. Exp. Soc. Psychol. **5**: 135–172.
9. MACCOBY, E. E. & C. N. JACKLIN. 1974. The Psychology of Sex Differences. Stanford University Press. Stanford, Calif.
10. FESHBACH, S. 1972. Reality and fantasy in filmed violence. *In* Television and Social Behavior. J. P. Murray, E. A. Rubinstein & G. A. Comstock, Eds. **2**: 318–345. U.S. Government Printing Office. Washington, D.C.

11. HUESMANN, L. R., P. FISCHER, L. D. ERON, R. MERMELSTEIN, E. KAPLAN-SHAIN & S. MORIKAWA. 1978. Children's sex-role preference, sex of television model, and imitation of aggressive behaviors. Paper presented at the Third Biennial Meeting of the International Society for Research in Aggression, Washington, D.C., September 22.

12. SINGER, J. L. & D. SINGER. 1978. Television viewing, play and aggression in preschoolers. Paper presented at the Third Biennial Meeting of the International Society for Research in Aggression, Washington, D.C., September 22.

13. BANDURA, A., D. ROSS & S. A. ROSS. 1963. A comparative test of the status envy, social power and secondary reinforcement theories of identification learning. J. Pers. Soc. Psychol. 67: 527–534.

14. KAPLAN-SHAIN, E. 1979. Masculinity, femininity and overt aggression in male and female college students. Department of Psychology. University of Illinois at Chicago Circle. Chicago, Ill. (Unpublished paper.)

15. BEM, S. L. 1974. The measurement of psychological androgyny. J. Consult. Clin. Psychol. 42: 155–162.

16. BUSS, A. H. 1961. The Psychology of Aggression. John Wiley & Sons, Inc. New York, N.Y.

17. CONNOR, J. M., L. A. SERBIN & R. A. ENDER. 1978. Responses of boys and girls to aggressive, assertive and passive behaviors of male and female characters. J. Genet. Psychol. 133: 59–69.

18. BANDURA, A., D. ROSS & S. A. ROSS. 1961. Transmission of aggression through imitation of aggressive models. J. Abnorm. Soc. Psychol. 63: 575–582.

19. BANDURA, A., D. ROSS & S. A. ROSS. 1963. Imitation of film mediated aggressive models. J. Abnorm. Soc. Psychol. 66: 3–11.

20. BANDURA, A., D. ROSS & S. A. ROSS. 1963. Vicarious reinforcement and imitative learning. J. Abnorm. Soc. Psychol. 67: 601–607.

21. HOKANSON, J. E. & R. EDELMAN. 1966. Effect of three social responses on vascular processes. J. Pers. Soc. Psychol. 3: 442–447.

22. HAYES, S. C., A. RINCOVER & D. VOLOSIN. Variables influencing the acquisition and maintenance of aggressive behavior: modeling versus sensory reinforcement. J. Abnorm. Psychol. (In press.)

23. ROSENFELD, E. 1978. The development of an imaginal process inventory for children. Ph.D. Dissertation. Department of Psychology. University of Illinois at Chicago Circle. Chicago, Ill.

THE MEDIA AND CRIME: GENERAL DISCUSSION

Moderator: Flora Rheta Schreiber

Department of Speech and Theater
John Jay College of Criminal Justice
New York, New York 10019

E. DONNERSTEIN (*University of Wisconsin, Madison, Wisc.*): I think we all agreed with each other on the effects of media and violence, that there is an effect on aggressive behavior. I think it's important to note that whether we have correlational, field, or laboratory studies the results are all very similar. I think that's a very important point to make.

L. D. ERON (*University of Illinois, Chicago, Ill.*): Dr. Singer's work is on observations of children in the actual nursery-school situation. Dr. Donnerstein and I have used such things as aggression machines. Dr. Eisenberg used the picture frustration study. Yet they all point to the same kinds of results. I don't think you can quarrel with that anymore.

UNIDENTIFIED SPEAKER: I would like a definition of aggression from Dr. Eron.

L. D. ERON: Aggression has many meanings in society and certainly among lay people, and many of these meanings are positive. For example, for some people aggression connotes achievement, ambition, and pushing ahead, all good middle-class Calvanist ideals.

But this is not the kind of aggression I've been talking about. I define aggressive behavior as behavior that injures another person.

UNIDENTIFIED SPEAKER: How do we teach children the difference?

L. D. ERON: Well, I don't think they have to be inextricably related. There are ways people can get ahead and achieve other than by beating up on other people. Unfortunately, the data that we have show that there's some truth to the lay assumption that these kinds of aggression go together. There's a low-positive correlation between mobility, occupational mobility, aspirations, and physical aggression. But it's certainly not a one-to-one correlation. There is some relationship there. It would seem to me that we ought to be able to devise ways of achieving without beating up on other people.

UNIDENTIFIED SPEAKER: And that should be the job of television, don't you think?

L. D. ERON: I would think so, yes. Television can teach many socially positive, wonderful things, as well as destructive things.

UNIDENTIFIED SPEAKER: If television indeed has such a powerful influence in our society, why don't we have more violence than we do?

L. D. ERON: I have never said that television violence is the only source of aggression in society, and further, there are other factors that tend to ameliorate whatever effect there is. Actually television violence, as far as I can see from the studies I've done, accounts for 10 percent of the variance. Now that's not a great deal, but when you recognize that we have 250 million people and I don't know how many thousands of crimes, 10 percent gets to be big number. Further, not every kid watching television is influenced by it for some of the reasons that Dr. Eisenberg mentioned in his paper. Not everybody that smokes gets lung cancer either, but this doesn't mean that smoking is not a cause of lung cancer. Not all adolescents use drugs, but this doesn't mean we shouldn't be concerned about drug use.

R. W. RIEBER (*John Jay College of Criminal Justice, New York, N.Y.*): I would like to respond to the question that Dr. Morse posed to the panel if that's appropriate for the audience to respond to the audience. I think it might be useful to look at the media and its relationship to aggression in two ways. One way would be to say that it is a reflection of the amount of potential aggression in the society. And as such, has the potential both to precipitate and, perhaps in some instances, actually reduce that potential depending upon the viewers. For example, the question that was raised—Why isn't there more aggression given all of the aggressive television and media?— might be answered by saying, well this is not the cause or even the major precipitating factor. It is simply a reflection of the potential amount of aggression that is available at a given moment if there was an easy release for it. Now, if you approach it in that manner, then you might be able to analyze the kinds of aggressive programs on television or in the media and get some insight into what they mean in terms of perhaps social dreams. I prefer to look at these things as social dreams, a reflection of the unresolved problems society happens to have at any given point in time, just as your personal dreams are a reflection of unresolved problems that you have as an individual. I think if one analyzed the aggressive programs, in fact the programs in general, one can get great insight into the psychosocial distress of which violence is only one aspect in the society at this present time.

Further, Dr. Eron responded to values. This all ties in with values. If we examine the Ten Commandments, referred to in Dr. Mednick's paper, as a guide to values in this society I think we fail on just about every one of them. And a lot of them include potential violence. And this must, in some measure, be a reflection of the value system that we have in a contemporary society. It is important for us to take a look at what kinds of values we give lip service to as opposed to what kinds of values we can actually relate to in terms of our human behavior in everyday life. There's a big discrepancy between the values that we say we believe in and the values in our culture that we actually engage in. And the Ten Commandments are a very good example of that.

So I think there is a tie-in and I think there's a fruitful area for research to investigate the relationship between the two.

F. WRIGHT (*John Jay College of Criminal Justice, New York, N.Y.*): This question is directed to Dr. Eron and his point that it might be better for boys to be like girls. How successful have you been, as a college teacher yourself, in presenting this idea to your students? I'd be interested to hear about your experiences.

L. D. ERON: Well it makes some of my more macho colleagues rather nervous if I talk this way, but actually I have no trouble in presenting these findings and making these recommendations to college students. They all seem to agree with them, at least those college students who are in psychology classes. They think it might not be a bad idea. I do have difficulty though when I talk to PTA groups. Parents say: Well what shall I do when my son comes home? I have to teach him to defend himself. He's got to go out and hit the other guy harder. It's very hard to answer that kind of a question. What has to change is the whole society's values. It has to be done on a societal level. I don't think it can be done on an individual level. For example, notice the terrible overemphasis we have on winning in sports. Take the game of basketball, which is not a violent sport like hockey or football: When a player fouls out, for example, because he's done illegal things such as hurting another player, the sympathy does not go to the player who has had the illegal act committed against him but rather to the guy who fouls out. This is the thing that has to change. Further, we are insisting that girls get the same kind of training. This emphasis on winning is now being extended to 100 percent of the population, whereas before we had it for 50 percent.

UNIDENTIFIED SPEAKER: I want to say that it's not a universal finding that a violent program does increase aggressiveness, at least immediately thereafter. I think it's important to note the effect of the context in which the viewing occurs, as Dr. Eisenberg has pointed out. In short, the context effect may overpower the content effects, and too little study of the former has been done.

The findings I'm familiar with show that there are two kinds of children, very aggressive children (who are also very affectionate) and very withdrawn children. Relating that to adults, it seems that the people who commit the most irrationally violent acts tend to be the most withdrawn. Therefore, if we're concerned about preventing later violence, then maybe we should be concerned with learning how to train withdrawn children to come more in contact with peers, even if it is aggressive contact.

L. D. ERON: Actually, there are studies that have done just what you've said. You're talking about the general activity level of the child. Children who are more active than others will engage in more aggressive acts as well as more acts in general, just because they interact with other kids more. In our studies we controlled for activity level. However, I doubt that the bulk of the criminal acts in this country, or in the world, are committed by these loners who, for example, suddenly up and shoot somebody from the Texas tower. These are really isolated incidents. I don't think they're very prevalent, and that's why they come to our attention. But usually criminal behavior or antisocial aggressive behavior is predictive from early life on, at least according to the studies I'm familiar with.

HUMAN NATURE, CRIME, AND SOCIETY: KEYNOTE ADDRESS*

Sarnoff A. Mednick

*Social Science Research Institute
University of Southern California
Los Angeles, California 90007*

Many months ago, President Carter visited The Bronx in order better to understand the need for urban renewal. His attention was drawn in particular to Charlotte Street, which the *New York Times* had called the worst slum street in New York City. The President duly proclaimed the Charlotte Street Project; it would be a model for national urban renewal programs.

I drove up to The Bronx recently and was rather shocked. The district is almost entirely leveled; buildings that are still half-standing are windowless. The Charlotte Street Project is apparently forgotten.

The experience gave me a sinking, frightened feeling. I spent my childhood and adolescence on Charlotte Street. It was not a rose garden then; but it is still uncomfortable to look for your childhood home and find rubble.

Why did this area disintegrate as so many other areas are disintegrating? Economists and politicians will doubtless propose learned and well-developed reasons. But I can tell you why my family and friends thought they left. A neighborhood boy my age was stabbed to death in front of our apartment house by some cruising youths. Our good friend, the grocer, was held up and shot in the shoulder. Older people hardly dared venture out of their heavily locked doors. It was *danger* that drove them from their homes. And the situation does not seem to be rapidly improving. In 1978, violent crime increased 5%.[15] Most disheartening is the focus of this increase on youngsters; more crimes are now being committed by children under 15 than by adults over 25! In the past 20 years, juvenile crime has increased 1600%.[9] Judging from past experience, these youngsters are not going to be rehabilitated overnight. I don't like to "view with alarm," but many of them are walking time bombs with long criminal careers ahead of them.

I don't know anyone who believes that our methods of dealing with crime have been a blazing success. Perhaps we need to stop and rethink our situation. First, do we want to reduce crime? If so, how? Currently our major efforts to control crime start with individuals *already* delinquent or criminal. We spend fortunes on developing mace, nicer jails, methods of rehabilitation, and faster court systems. Less effort is expended on the primary prevention of crime. I wish to suggest that along with efforts to deal with discovered criminality, we study methods of early intervention to *prevent* the initial onset of criminal behavior.

* The work in genetics is supported by Grant No. MH 31353-02 from the National Institute of Mental Health Center for the Study of Crime and Delinquency.

335

I can imagine three avenues in which primary intervention might be explored:

1. Ecological alterations;
2. Systematic societal change;
3. Individual intervention.

Ecological Alteration

By ecological alteration, I refer to environmental manipulation—such as increasing street lighting, improving supermarket and department store security, and developing defensive architectural design. I will not consider this method further in this paper.

Societal Change

In this century, criminology has been dominated by sociological thinking—and for good reason. It seems quite clear that socioeconomic factors provide the reasons for crime for *most criminals.* Sociological thinking has suggested that the etiology of crime lies exclusively in the structure of society. It is expressly assumed that criminals are normal individuals who have been misshapen by an inappropriately arranged social system. If we improve this system, this should prevent criminality.

A critical assumption of this approach to primary prevention is the essential normality of criminals. To the extent that some criminals have deviant psychological or biological characteristics that help predispose them to antisocial behavior, then societal manipulation *alone* will not be sufficient to prevent crime. (I am, in principle, opposed to arguing for societal adjustment for the betterment of the human condition solely on the promise of reducing crime or mental illness. Human conditions should be improved because we are human. Unrealized promises simply promote reactionary backlash.) Thus, in order to better plan the primary prevention of criminal behavior, we must first consider evidence regarding the possibility that some forms of criminal behavior have individual psychological or biological predispositions.

Individual Intervention

This bioindividual approach to understanding the criminal has been less than popular in the social sciences. Let us take a moment and consider the reasons for this. In the beginning, there was no significant conflict. Auguste Comte in 1855 acknowledged that "the whole social evolution of the race must proceed in entire accordance with biological laws. . . ."[7] Perhaps the problems began 23 years later, when Herbert Spencer applied his phrase "survival of the fittest" to social behavior.[24] His prostitution of the theory of evolution for the preservation of class privilege was an outrage to social reformers. Spencer literally urged the "shouldering aside of the weak by the strong. . . ."[24] Social Darwinism inevitably led to racism. Expedient ethics had their day again in the 1920s in the U.S. in the exploitation of spurious intelligence test results to rationalize discriminatory immigration laws. Nazi ideology did not improve the attractiveness of biosocial interactionism. In the 30s, 40s, and 50s, social science academia simply excluded the consideration of biology from the same context as social factors.

Haller has suggested that part of the reason for this was that many of those who had been pointed to as inferior by our immigration laws had struggled to the top of the social-economic status heap (including the academic heap).[10] Politically and emotionally, these individuals turned away from biology. But perhaps even more telling than these emotional factors was a simple intellectual reason: there was very little compelling, empirical, biological evidence that could help us understand social man or (more specifically) criminality. The evidence for genetic influences on criminality consisted mainly of some relatively inadequate and ignored twin studies (some of which were tainted by having originated in Germany or Japan during the Nazi era). In addition, the literature offered some entertaining, well-written, and inventive analogies to observations of animal behavior. Social scientists found biological factors to be not only affectively repulsive, but coincidentally not intellectually compelling.

Within the last 5 to 10 years, however, there have been research developments that are not totally unworthy of the attention of the criminologist. These research developments may have implications for the planning of primary prevention programs. Consequently I will briefly review evidence relating biological factors to crime. I will first focus on three prospective, longitudinal studies.

THREE PROSPECTIVE STUDIES OF ANTISOCIAL BEHAVIOR

The Wadsworth Study

The first study concerns the delinquents in a "sample of 5362 single-born, legitimate, live births in 1946 occurring between March 3 and 9 in England, Wales and Scotland." Wadsworth described the cumulative, officially recorded delinquency when this birth cohort reached 21 years of age.[26] He then went on to examine the relationship of this delinquency to a childhood measure of autonomic nervous system responses to anticipation of stress. The survey members were subjected to a school medical examination when they were 11 years of age. The period of time during which they waited for this examination was designed to be somewhat stressful. Their pulse rates were measured to assess the effects of this stress anticipation. Those who were eventually registered as delinquents at 21 years of age had had a lower pulse rate increase in anticipation of the stress at age 11. Delinquents in this study were defined as those who "either made a court appearance or were formally cautioned by the police between the ages of 8 and 21 years."[27] The delinquent–not-delinquent differences were substantial for those committing indictable and sexual and violent offenses.

The Wadsworth study also makes an important point relating to the interaction of biological and social factors. Within the group of boys who had experienced broken homes early in life, anticipatory pulse rate did not distinguish the delinquents. Within the boys who did *not* experience broken homes, a small anticipatory pulse rate response did predict well to delinquency. This type of interaction of biological (pulse rate) and social (family disruption) data is predicted by Christiansen[5,6] and Sellin,[23] and has been observed repeatedly in our research in Copenhagen. The biological factors predict best in those areas, situations, or among those groups in which social factors (e.g., stable home, middle-class status) do not "explain" antisocial behavior. In those situations, areas, or groups in which social variables (broken home or lower-class status) do predict to antisocial behavior, the biological variables are less effective in prediction.

The Wadsworth study is important because it is based on a large, national birth cohort. The results must be seen as representative. We should also remember that the data on pulse rate were gathered by hundreds of different physicians in different schools, using rather primitive methods. Not all of these measurements were equally accurately taken. About 10 years intervened between the recording of the pulse rate and the ascertainment of delinquency. Despite these conditions, which in most research do not tend to inflate positive findings, the hypothesized results emerged. Those who did not suffer anticipatory pulse rate increase before the examination were those boys who later were more likely to become seriously delinquent. Perhaps this anticipatory response was also lacking before they committed the act (or acts) that gained them access to the delinquent group.

It may be worth underlining one other feature of the Wadsworth study. The low anticipatory pulse rate was observed 10 years before the delinquency was assessed. It is unlikely that the delinquency experience produced the low pulse rate. The prospective nature of the study establishes low pulse rate in anticipation of a stress as a variable worthy of consideration among the potential etiological factors in delinquency.

How salient a predictive factor is pulse rate? Not very. In the Wadsworth study, it predicts to delinquency about as well as the variable "broken home." It is naive to expect that any variable alone (biological or social) will explain large amounts of delinquency variance. Delinquency is likely to be as complex in its causality as it is in its manifestation. Note, however, that when the *interactive* effect of pulse rate and family factors is assessed, prediction improves considerably.

A Second Prospective Study

Janice Loeb and I have reported on a 10-year follow-up of a group of Danish adolescents.[14] In 1962, we examined their skin conductance (a peripheral autonomic measure); in 1972, we ascertained their registered delinquency from the Danish National Police Register. At 10-year follow-up, 7 boys of the 104 adolescents were noted as having been registered for mildly delinquent acts. The predelinquency 1962 skin conductance level, responsiveness, and recovery of the 7 delinquents was below that of the controls. The mean amplitude of response of the delinquents was one-tenth that of the nondelinquents.

Hare's Study

The third prospective study I will cite was conducted by Hare.[11] In 1964, he examined skin conductance in a group of serious, convicted criminals, all in a maximum security prison. Ten years later, he checked to see how seriously recidivistic the prisoners subsequently became. Skin conductance recovery in 1964 predicted to degree of recidivism 10 years later.

I would make several points relating to these prospective studies.

1. In combination with social and familial factors, such biological characteristics that presage the later development of delinquency might be useful in early detection. The development of such early detection techniques would be an important first step in a program of primary prevention.

2. Studies in Philadelphia by Wolfgang, Figlio, and Sellin,[30] research in Stockholm by Gösta Carlsson,[4] research by West and Farrington[28] in the inner city of London, and our own research on a birth cohort of 32,000 men in Copenhagen have rather reliably indicated that only a very small subgroup of the antisocial individuals is responsible for most of the criminal acts and the more serious criminal acts. The biosocial prediction measures seem to be most appropriate to preidentifying this small group of most serious criminals. A program of intervention focused on such a small number of individuals might prove disproportionately effective in crime reduction.

3. All three of the prospective studies are consistent with a description of the predelinquent and prerecidivistic criminal having somewhat underreactive autonomic nervous systems.

GENETIC AND PSYCHOPHYSIOLOGICAL FACTORS AND ANTISOCIAL BEHAVIOR

I will next discuss evidence that such underreactive autonomic nervous systems are characteristic of criminals. I will also consider the possible origins of this state, including genetic factors. Let us examine the evidence that genetic factors are related to the etiology of antisocial behavior. What is the point of examining the genetics literature? Only one of importance from my point of view. If it can be demonstrated that there is some genetic contribution to some forms of criminality, then consideration of a partial biological predisposition for antisocial behavior would be forced upon us. This would have implications for directions of research. There are three genetic research strategies we will briefly describe—family studies, twin research, and adoption investigations.

Family Studies

It has long been observed that antisocial parents raise an excessive number of children who also become antisocial. In the classic study by Lee Robins, one of the best predictors of antisocial behavior in a child was the father's criminality.[21] In terms of genetics, very little can be concluded from such family data inasmuch as it is difficult to disentangle hereditary and environmental influences.

Twin Studies

Twin studies compare criminal outcomes for identical and fraternal twins. The influence of hereditary factors is assumed to be demonstrated to the extent that the identical twins have more similar outcomes than the fraternal twins. From 1929–1977, I have found 10 twin studies in the literature. The early studies report about 60–70% concordance for crime for identical twins and about 15% concordance for fraternal twins.[5]

The most important study of these 10 was conducted by K. O. Christiansen who investigated the fates of all 7,172 twins born in a well-defined area of Denmark.[6] He used a national, complete criminality register about which Marvin Wolfgang has said: "the reliability and validity of the Danish record keeping system are almost beyond criticism. The criminal registry office in Denmark is probably the most thorough, comprehensive and accurate in the Western world."[29] Christiansen notes that "there are several important characteristics of the Danish law enforcement process that relate to its statutory uniformity regarding treatment of the offender and sentencing by the court. Police officers are legally *required* to report cases if they have a suspect. They are not permitted to make judgements in such matters. . . . The social status of a Danish police officer is comparatively high; they are regarded as being incorruptible."[6]

In this, the largest and best designed of the twin studies of criminality, Christiansen reports 35% concordance for monozygotic (MZ) (male-male) pairs and 13% concordance for the dyzygotic (DZ) (male-male) pairs.[6] (Percents given are pair-wise concordance rates.) In this unselected twin population, the MZ concordance rate is lower than in previous studies. In fact, it is important to note that more cases are discordant than concordant. This suggests that genetic factors control a minor but significant portion of the variance. Nevertheless, the MZ rate is 2.7 times the DZ rate. This result suggests the possibility that there is some genetically controlled, biological characteristic (or set of characteristics) that is identical for the MZ twins and that in some unknown way increases their common risk for being registered for criminal behavior.

The results of the twin studies do not contradict the hypothesis that some genetically transmitted, biological characteristic predisposes to antisocial behavior.

Adoption Studies

The problem with twin studies is that the twins are almost always raised together. There is poor separation of genetic and environmental factors. The adoption design does a better job of this separation. Children adopted at birth share no environment with their biological fathers. If criminality in the biological fathers is related to criminality in their adopted-away children, then this suggests that the criminal biological fathers have genetically transmitted some criminogenic biological characteristic to their children.

Crowe studied a small group of adopted children born to women in prison, as well as control adoptees.[8] The adopted children with *criminal* biological mothers were registered for more crimes than were adopted children with *noncriminal* biological mothers. Cadoret reports that among 246 Iowans adopted at birth, criminality in adoptees and their biological parents was significantly related.[3] (He ascertained criminality by telephone interview of the adoptive parents.)

In Copenhagen, Schulsinger finds excessive amounts of psychopathy among the biological relatives of psychopaths who had been adopted at birth.[22] In this study, Schulsinger identified psychopaths from a population of all the 5,483 Copenhagen County adoptions 1924–1947.

From these same 5,483 adoptions, Hutchings and Mednick ascertained the registered criminality of the male adoptees, their biological fathers, and

TABLE 1

REGISTERED CRIMINALITY IN ADOPTEES AND THEIR FATHERS;
"CROSS-FOSTERING" ANALYSIS*

		If Biological Father Is		
		Not Registered	Minor Crime	Criminal
If Adoptive Father Is	Not Registered	10.5	16.5	22.0
	Minor Crime	13.3	10.0	18.6
	Criminal	11.5	41.1	36.2

* Tabled values are percentage of adoptees criminal.

their adoptive fathers.[12] The results are given in TABLE 1. As can be seen in the table, if neither the biological nor the adoptive father is criminal, 10.5% of their sons are criminal. If the biological father is not criminal but the adoptive father is criminal, this figure rises to only 11.5%. Note that 22% of the sons are criminal if the adoptive father is not criminal and the biological father is criminal. Thus, the comparison (analogous to a cross-fostering comparison) seems to favor a partial genetic-etiology assumption. We must caution, however, that the adoption methodology has a number of drawbacks. These have been discussed by Mednick and Hutchings.[18] In an extension of this study, we have now constructed analogous tables for 7,000 adoptees and 28,000 biological and adoptive relatives; the results replicate. We will soon be reporting results for all 14,435 adoptions in our study. These 14,435 adoptions comprise all the adoptions in the Kingdom of Denmark between 1924 and 1947.

It seems that a partial genetic predisposition for antisocial behavior must be considered a serious possibility. I would again emphasize that the expression of the genetic predisposition depends very heavily on social factors. Thus, in middle and upper classes, the genetic effect is more strongly expressed. In the lower classes, the genetic effect is more weakly expressed. As mentioned above, this is in excellent agreement with Sellin's group resistance theory.[23] In social settings that are highly resistant to crime, individuals who become criminal must have strong individual predispositions. Finally, I would say the obvious—this genetic predisposition must be biological.

The three prospective studies have directed our attention to autonomic nervous system "underreactiveness" as possibly being predispositional to antisocial behavior. Twin studies in our Copenhagen laboratories have suggested that important components of the autonomic response system are heritable.[2]

Autonomic Nervous System of Antisocial Individuals

I will now summarize literature that examines the autonomic responsiveness (specifically the skin conductance response) of antisocial individuals. Much of the research began with consideration of psychopaths. Clinical descriptions of the psychopath include such phrases as: lacks emotion, callous, feels no guilt, no shame, no remorse, incapable of love, fails to learn from punishing experiences, cannot emotionally anticipate consequences. Studies of physiological indicators of emotion have noted that these clinical descriptions fit the objective measurements of the physiology of the psychopath. Interestingly enough, the physiological descriptions also fit criminals, delinquents, and (as we have seen) predelinquents. (See Reference 19 for a review of this work.)

For example, in one type of study, physiological measures of autonomic nervous system functioning are continuously monitored. The subject is told that at the count of 9, he will experience a severe electric shock. The more psychopathic, delinquent, or criminal individual does not evidence anticipatory heart rate, skin conductance, or biochemical indicants of fear. This is true even of psychopathic Swedes studied just before they walked into the courtroom for their criminal trials.[13]

The results in this area of research are remarkably consistent and robust across a variety of experimental procedures, definitions of antisocial behavior, and different national settings. The antisocial groups consistently demonstrate hyporeactive autonomic nervous systems. Recall the three prospective studies that find that these same psychophysiological characteristics predict to antisocial behavior ascertained 10 years later. In view of our twin study results,[2] it is tempting to hypothesize that these physiological characteristics may be a part of the biological predisposition passed on from an antisocial parent. Indeed, in our laboratory in Copenhagen, we have found that a group of children with fathers registered for criminality tends to have the very same physiological signs that have been found to be reliably characteristic of the delinquent, psychopath, and criminal.[16]

Biosocial Interactions in the Learning of Morality

Much of this paper has been devoted to reporting literature that finds some biological factors in criminal behavior. Perhaps it would be useful to close with a specific suggestion as to how such biological characteristics might interact with family and social factors to interfere with the learning of moral behavior. It would do no great harm to begin with a discussion of how we define morality. An early publication may be found in TABLE 2. Note that the major thrust of the message is negative—"thou shalt *not* . . ." While subsequent moral authorities have added *some* positive acts to elaborate the definition of moral behavior (e.g., "love thy neighbor"), they

TABLE 2

THE TEN COMMANDMENTS (EXODUS)*

I am the Lord thy God, thou shalt have no other gods before me.
Thou shalt *not* make a graven image nor bow down or serve them.
Thou shalt *not* take the name of the Lord your God in vain.
Remember the sabbath day and keep it holy.
Honour thy father and thy mother.
Thou shalt *not* kill.
Thou shalt *not* commit adultery.
Thou shalt *not* steal.
Thou shalt *not* bear false witness against your neighbor.
Thou shalt *not* covet thy neighbor's home, wife, maidservant, ox, ass.

* Emphasis added.

have also retained the original, basic, inhibitory definitions of moral acts. There are very few who will denounce you if you do not love your neighbor; but if you seduce his wife, steal from him, and/or kill him, you may be certain that your behavior will be classified as immoral. Thus, putting aside philosophical, poetic, or artistic musing on morality, we might admit to ourselves that the statements of moral behavior that are critical for everyday activities are essentially negative and inhibitory in character. The fact that someone took the trouble to enumerate these strictures—and then carve them onto stone tablets—suggests that at some point, there must have been a strong need for insistence on these inhibitions. People must have evidenced—and perhaps still do evidence—a tendency to exhibit aggressive, adulterous, and avaricious behavior. In self-defense, society has set up moral codes and has struggled to teach its children to *inhibit* impulses leading to transgression of those codes.

How are these inhibitions taught to children? As far as I can see, there are three learning mechanisms that could conceivably help parents teach children civilized behavior: modeling, positive reinforcement, and negative reinforcement. I believe that positive acts—such as loving neighbors, helping old ladies across the street, and cleaning the snow and ice from the front walk—can be learned by modeling; but for the more inhibitory moral commands, modeling does not seem to be a natural method. It is possible to imagine arranging circumstances in some artificial way such that modeling *could* teach children not to be adulterous or aggressive. If our civilization had to depend solely on modeling, however, it is conceivable that things might be even more chaotic than they are today. It is also possible to use positive reinforcement to teach inhibition of forbidden behavior; but again, reinforcing a child 24 hours a day while he is *not* stealing seems a rather inefficient method and not very specific.

Following the excellent exposition of Gordon Trasler,[25] we would suggest that childhood learning of the avoidance of transgression (i.e., the practice of law-abiding behavior) demanded by the moral commandments probably is trained, in the main, via contingent punishment applied by society, family, and peers. The critical inhibitory, morality-training forces in childhood very likely are (1) the punishment of antisocial responses by family, society, and friends; and (2) the child's individual capacity to *learn* to inhibit antisocial responses.

Let us attempt to be specific and to relate how children might learn to inhibit an impulse to steal. Frequently when a child steals from his parents, his peers, his siblings, or a five-and-ten, he is punished. After a sufficient quantity or quality of punishment, just the thought of the act of stealing should be enough to produce a bit of anticipatory fear in the child. If this fear response is large enough, the extended fingers will relax and the stealing impulse will be *successfully inhibited.*

Our story suggests that what happens in this child *after* he has successfully inhibited such an antisocial response is critical for his learning of civilized behavior. Let us consider the situation again in more detail.

1. Child contemplates stealing.
2. Because of previous punishment, he suffers fear.
3. Because of fear, he inhibits the stealing impulse.

What happens to his anticipatory fear?

4. Since he no longer entertains the stealing impulse, the fear will begin to dissipate, to be reduced.

We know that fear reduction is the most powerful, naturally occurring reinforcement that psychologists have discovered. So the reduction of fear (which immediately follows the inhibition of the stealing) can act as a reinforcement for this inhibition, and will result in the learning of the inhibition of stealing. The powerful reinforcement associated with fear reduction increases the probability that the inhibition of the stealing will occur in the future. After many such experiences, the normal child will learn to inhibit stealing impulses. Each time such an impulse arises and is successfully inhibited, the inhibition will be strengthened by reinforcement, since the fear elicited by the impulse will be reduced following successful inhibition.

What does a child need in order to learn effectively to be civilized (in the context of this approach)?

1. A social censuring agent (typically family or peers) *and*
2. An adequate physiological fear response *and*
3. The ability to learn the fear response in anticipation of an antisocial act *and*
4. Fast dissipation of physiological fear to quickly reinforce the inhibitory response.

I have indicated earlier that there is consistent evidence that the antisocial individual does not have an adequate fear response and does not learn adequately to emotionally anticipate negative events. The evidence regarding the final point—rate of dissipation of fear—is unequivocal; the antisocial individual tends to evidence very slow fear dissipation.[19] In terms of this theoretical approach, this suggests that under normal rearing conditions, the antisocial individual is not adequately rewarded for inhibiting antisocial responses.

CONCLUDING REMARKS

In these brief remarks, I have attempted to describe recent evidence that biological factors may play some partial role in the origins of antisocial behavior (or perhaps some forms of antisocial behavior). The biological factors can aid in understanding the conditions leading to antisocial behavior in situations or populations where social-familial factors are less successful at prediction. These include, for example, middle- or upper-class background, recidivistic criminality, female criminality, or crime in rural areas. It is in these situations or individuals that the biological variables show stronger relations with antisocial behavior. In circumstances or individuals where social-familial factors would predict elevated crime (such as lower social class rearing), the biological factors are less effective in prediction.

What the implications of these recent findings may be is far from clear at this point. Certainly no social action would be advised without considerable additional research efforts and replication. Perhaps these findings suggest that we reevaluate our ability to predict early who might later become a serious criminal. The complementarity of the social-familial and biological variables suggests that adding the biological variables to the highly effective social-familial factors[20] in a single predictive study might eventually yield acceptably accurate prediction of serious recidivism.

If excellent prediction were possible, what preventive intervention might shield children or adolescents from a crime career? Perhaps the variables that predict to future serious crime will suggest intervention strategies. Acting on the above-reported reliable findings of low autonomic nervous system arousal in antisocial individuals, Allen *et al.* have begun some pilot research attempting to alter this low arousal state by drug administrations to bring delinquents up to normal arousal states. He reports some success with this method, working with an extremely small group of delinquents.[1] An important problem in such drug intervention is that it may result in long-term, unwanted side effects. It was the danger of such side effects that moved us to reject drug intervention in a primary prevention project in the field of serious mental illness (schizophrenia). We chose the conservative step of an excellent, protective nursery school program.[17]

In this Academy meeting, Professor David Bakan has raised the possibility of using severe punishment (his expression was "to terrorize") on individuals who were identified as possible future criminals. This would certainly seem to be an inappropriate model for intervention. While mild punishment is probably the prevailing method that families, peers, and society use to teach small children to inhibit antisocial conduct, it would not seem a likely or promising technique for pragmatic intervention.

I would record one final thought in this paper. As pointed out above, social scientists have had strong negative emotional reactions to attempts to understand the role that biological factors play in the development of social man. These negative emotional reactions have often been responsive to biological scientists' drawing irresponsible or premature conclusions from fallible correlational research. Such scientific carelessness is especially reprehensible in circumstances where political forces may attempt to use such premature conclusions in justifying repressive social action. Responsible criticism of faulty methods or unfortunate, inadequately grounded conclusions is a necessary and important part of a scientist's work. But I would emphasize the word "responsible." Remember that earlier attempts to silence or retard scientific inquiry by public appeals to emotion or public burning of books have not proven as successful as a single intelligent and penetrating methodological analysis.

REFERENCES

1. ALLEN, H., S. DINITZ, T. FOSTER, H. GOLDMAN & L. LINDNER. 1976. Sociopathy: an experiment in internal environmental control. Am. Behav. Scientist **20:** 215–226.
2. BELL, B., S. A. MEDNICK, I. I. GOTTESMAN & J. SERGEANT. 1977. Electrodermal parameters in young, normal male twins. *In* Biosocial Bases of Criminal Behavior. S. A. Mednick & K. O. Christiansen, Eds. Gardner Press. New York, N.Y.
3. CADORET, R. J. 1978. Psychopathy in adopted-away offspring of biological parents with antisocial behavior. Arch. Gen. Psychiatry **35:** 176–184.
4. CARLSSON, G. 1977. Crime and behavioral epidemiology. Concepts and applications to Swedish data. *In* Biosocial Bases of Criminal Behavior. S. A. Mednick & K. O. Christiansen, Eds. Gardner Press. New York, N.Y.
5. CHRISTIANSEN, K. O. 1977. A review of studies of criminality among twins. *In* Biosocial Bases of Criminal Behavior. S. A. Mednick & K. O. Christiansen, Eds. Gardner Press. New York, N.Y.
6. CHRISTIANSEN, K. O. 1977. A preliminary study of criminality among twins. *In* Biosocial Bases of Criminal Behavior. S. A. Mednick & K. O. Christiansen, Eds. Gardner Press. New York, N.Y.
7. COMTE, A. 1855. The Positive Philosophy of Auguste Comte. (Translated by Harriet Martineau.) Blanchord. New York, N.Y.
8. CROWE, R. 1975. An adoptive study of psychopathy: preliminary results from arrest records and psychiatric hospital records. *In* Genetic Research in Psychiatry. R. Fieve, D. Rosenthal & H. Brill, Eds. Johns Hopkins University Press. Baltimore, Md.
9. GODWIN, J. 1978. Murder USA: The Ways We Kill Each Other. Ballantine Books. New York, N.Y.
10. HALLER, M. H. 1968. Social science and genetics: a historical perspective. *In* Genetics. D. Glass, Ed. The Rockefeller University Press. New York, N.Y.
11. HARE, R. D. 1978. Psychopathy and crime. *In* Colloquium on the Correlates of Crime and the Determinants of Criminal Behavior. L. Otten, Ed. Mitre Corp.
12. HUTCHINGS, B. & S. A. MEDNICK. 1977. Criminality in adoptees and their adoptive and biological parents: a pilot study. *In* Biosocial Bases of Criminal Behavior. S. A. Mednick & K. O. Christiansen, Eds. Gardner Press. New York, N.Y.
13. LIDBERG, L., S. LEVANDER, D. SCHALLING & Y. LIDBERG. 1980. Urinary catecholamines, stress and psychopath—a study of arrested men awaiting trial. Psychosom. Med. (In press.)
14. LOEB, J. & S. A. MEDNICK. 1977. A prospective study of predictors of criminality. 3. Electrodermal response patterns. *In* Biosocial Bases of Criminal Behavior. S. A. Mednick & K. O. Christiansen, Eds. Gardner Press. New York, N.Y.
15. Los Angeles Times. 1979. March 28.
16. MEDNICK, S. A. 1977. A bio-social theory of the learning of law-abiding behavior. *In* Biosocial Bases of Criminal Behavior. S. A. Mednick & K. O. Christiansen, Eds. Gardner Press. New York, N.Y.
17. MEDNICK, S. A. 1979. Risk research and primary prevention of mental illness. Int. J. Mental Health **7:** 150–164.
18. MEDNICK, S. A. & B. HUTCHINGS. 1977. Some considerations in the interpretation of the Danish adoption studies. *In* Biosocial Bases of Criminal Behavior. S. A. Mednick & K. O. Christiansen, Eds. Gardner Press. New York, N.Y.
19. MEDNICK, S. A. & J. VOLVAKA. 1980. Biology and crime. *In* Crime and Justice **2.** N. Morris & M. Tonry, Eds. (In press.)
20. ROBINS, L. H. & K. S. RATCLIFF. 1980. Risk factors in the continuation of childhood antisocial behavior into adulthood. Int. J. Mental Health. (In press.)
21. ROBINS, L. N. 1966. Deviant Children Grown Up. Williams & Wilkins. Baltimore, Md.
22. SCHULSINGER, F. 1977. Psychopath: heredity and environment. *In* Biosocial Bases of Criminal Behavior. S. A. Mednick & K. O. Christiansen, Eds. Gardner Press. New York, N.Y.
23. SELLIN, T. 1938. Culture, Conflict and Crime. Subcommittee on Delinquency. Committee on Personality and Culture. New York, N.Y.
24. SPENCER, H. 1878. Social Statistics. Appleton-Century-Crofts, Inc. New York, N.Y.

25. TRASLER, G. 1972. Criminal behavior. *In* Handbook of Abnormal Psychology. H. H. Eysenck, Ed. G. P. Putnam's Sons. London, England.
26. WADSWORTH, M. E. J. 1975. Delinquency in a national sample of children. Br. J. Criminol. **15:** 167–174.
27. WADSWORTH, M. E. J. 1978. Delinquency, pulse-rates and early emotional deprivation. Br. J. Criminol. **16:** 245–256.
28. WEST, D. J. & D. P. FARRINGTON. 1973. Who Becomes Delinquent? Heinemann. London, England.
29. WOLFGANG, M. E. 1977. Foreword. *In* Biosocial Bases of Criminal Behavior. S. A. Mednick & K. O. Christiansen, Eds. Gardner Press. New York, N.Y.
30. WOLFGANG, M. E., R. M. FIGLIO & T. SELLIN. 1972. Delinquency in a Birth Cohort. University of Chicago Press. Chicago, Ill.

A NEUROPSYCHOSOCIAL PERSPECTIVE OF PERSISTENT JUVENILE DELINQUENCY AND CRIMINAL BEHAVIOR: DISCUSSION

Discussant: Lorne T. Yeudall

Department of Neuropsychology
Alberta Hospital
Edmonton, Alberta,
Canada T5J 2J7

Dr. Mednick[1] has presented strong evidence implicating hereditary influences in the genesis of delinquent and criminal behaviors for some individuals. He and his coworkers have shown that biological differences [quantitative electroencephalograph (EEG) abnormalities, low electrodermal responses (EDRs), and slow electrodermal recovery (EDRec)] that have predictive significance characterize individuals at risk for such antisocial behaviors. At least one of these biological markers (EDRec) has an extremely high heritability index. The theoretical model of antisocial behaviors formulated by Dr. Mednick focuses on the inability to inhibit social responses that are not sanctioned by society and is similar in this respect to a number of hypotheses stressing the role of disinhibition of behaviors. It is also a multivariate model, involving the interaction of the social environment with biological factors (adequate fear response, ability to learn a fear response in anticipation of an asocial act, and fast dissipation of fear and/or quick reinforcement of the inhibitory response). The autonomic abnormalities found in some high risk individuals who commit serious and repetitive antisocial behaviors may be significantly related to brain mechanisms underlying the inhibition of behavior, more specifically, those mechanisms that underlie the fast disruption of the fear and/or quick reinforcement of the inhibitory response. The general focus of his theory is a central theme of many reseachers currently studying persistent criminal and violent behavior, namely, the failure to develop inhibitory controls.

There can be no doubt that learning plays a crucial role in the development of inhibitory controls. The ability to learn, however, hinges on the integrity of the central nervous system. In my opinion, Dr. Mednick's findings are most relevant to this issue: the integrity of the central nervous system. The demonstration of consistent evidence of psychophysiological abnormalities in high risk populations is indicative of dysfunction or impairment of the central nervous system, particularly in those regions of the brain primarily involved in the control and/or regulation of the autonomic nervous system. Disturbed autonomic functioning has been reported on the basis of a variety of complex psychophysiological response measures. However, Dr. Mednick's findings as well as those of other researchers, including my own research group, are not limited to the investigation of autonomic responses but include such assessment techniques as standard

EEG, quantitative EEG, and neuropsychologic. Such multivariate assessment techniques reveal a broader involvement of other regions of the brain. In this context of more generally altered brain function, many other influences in addition to genetic influences on the pre- and postnatal development of the organism may be fruitfully examined.

It appears that there may be an important relationship between the persistent nature of an individual's criminal history and his being identified as a high risk individual. As Dr. Mednick has pointed out from his own observations and from those of Wolfgang, Figlio, and Sellin,[2] a very small percentage (less than 10%) of the criminal offenders are responsible for over 50% of the serious crimes committed in a given catchment area. It is this unique subpopulation that Dr. Mednick feels may have some specific individual characteristics that increase the probability of persistent criminal behavior. If one focuses on the persistent nature of criminal behavior, then there is emerging evidence that altered brain function may be one of these specific individual characteristics.

The association between disturbed brain function or biogenic influences and persistent criminal behavior, particularly in regard to violent-aggressive and psychopathic criminals, has been supported by research involving EEG studies in prison populations.[3-7] There have been similar findings for noncriminal populations in regard to episodic violent behavior and rage syndromes.[8-10] More recently, neuropsychological studies have also found a high incidence of impairments in violent and nonviolent persistent juvenile delinquent populations.[11-16] Over the last seven years, I and several colleagues have focused our research on the so-called persistent offender with an extensive criminal history. Our investigation of persistent (mean convictions, 10.0) male psychopathic criminals convicted of homicide, rape, and physical assault have consistently found a high incidence (76% to 100%) of neuropsychological impairments.[17] Similarly, our studies on persistent adult sex offenders, violent-aggressive criminals, and adolescents with severe conduct disorders have revealed a high incidence of neuropsychological impairments ($\bar{x}$ = 90%).[18,19] The neuropsychological impairments implicated bilateral dysfunction of the frontal and temporal lobes with a dominant hemisphere emphasis in approximately 72% of the cases. In contrast, persistent male criminals with affective disorders, while showing a similar incidence of dysfunction, were found to have a higher incidence of greater nondominant hemisphere dysfunction.[17] A study just recently completed involved neuropsychological and power spectral EEG analyses of 100 consecutive admissions of persistent juvenile offenders without a violent history and 46 age-matched controls.[16] Of the control group, 12% were found to have abnormal neuropsychological profiles in contrast to 86% of the juvenile offenders. In contrast to the previous persistent psychopathic and violent criminals, these juvenile offenders showed a greater involvement of the nondominant hemisphere in 63% of the cases. Spectral analysis of the alpha frequency band of the EEG, which was recorded during the performance of language and visual spatial tasks, revealed that the juveniles had significantly more power in the frontal and temporal lobe regions with a nondominant hemisphere emphasis. Discriminant function analysis of the alpha band for relative power yielded correct classifications of 94.9% and 97.7% for the juvenile offenders and controls, respectively. Thus our results to date have consistently demonstrated a high incidence of neuropsychological and spectral EEG abnormalities that implicate dysfunction of the frontal and temporal regions of the brain.

The brain-behavior relationships of these anterior regions of the brain may be of particular significance to criminal behavior in that they play an important role in the regulation and inhibition of human behavior.[6,10,20-22] For example, Luria points out that the anterior frontal regions of the brain play a decisive role in the formation of plans and intentions, and in the regulation and verification of complex behaviors.[22] These processes are particularly formulated and elaborated via the speech mechanisms of the dominant hemisphere. Nauta similarly views the frontal regions as playing a special role in monitoring and modulating activity in other neocortical and limbic regions of the brain and suggests that "the reciprocal fronto-limbic relationships could be centrally involved in the phenomena of behavioral anticipation."[21] In contrast to the executive and regulatory functions of the frontal lobes, the temporal lobes appear to be more related to subjective consciousness and to play an integrative role in the individual's personal experience as it relates to the awareness of the relationship between information from his external and internal world. As Williams has pointed out, the functions of the temporal lobes "are much more closely identified with the subject himself; they involve his emotional life, his instinctive feelings and activities and his visceral responses to environmental change . . . that is to say, they include his social as well as his physical milieu."[22] Thus the integrity of the cortical and limbic regions of the frontal and temporal lobes would appear to be very important for the acquisition of moral behaviors and the inhibition of transgressions.

The association between persistent criminal behavior and lower socioeconomic status is well known. Ashley Montagu has elucidated the significance of this correlation and has related it to the effects of impoverished environments on the developing brain.[23] He has concluded that lower socioeconomic status associated with deprived environments increases the probability of brain damage at birth and hypothesized that such social environments could result in altered brain functioning, which then renders the individual more vulnerable to the many challenges in his environment. Stott has also emphasized the interactive role of genetic vulnerabilities and adverse environments (of both the child and mother during fetal development).[24] From his studies of maladjustment and delinquency in children, he has concluded that the association between a number of abnormal physical conditions and behavioral disturbance reflected "congenital insult which in some cases was seen both somatically and in impairment of that part of the nervous system controlling behavior."[24] In addition to the suggested effects of the interaction between genetic factors and/or adverse sociological conditions in regard to the developing brain, there remain many other contributing factors (e.g., birth injury, febrile convulsions, head injuries) that result in altered brain function during the early developmental years of the child. For example, Lewis, Shanok, and Balla, in agreement with other studies, found a significant association between perinatal problems and behavioral disorders in seriously delinquent children.[25] In addition, they found that by the age of two years, these children had sustained significantly more and serious head and face traumas.

Male gender is more frequently found to be associated with behavioral disturbances, which in turn are more prevalent in impoverished environments.[24,26-30] It is well known that there is an excess of males relative to females, approximately 5 to 1, in the incidence of behavioral disorders including juvenile delinquency, persistent violent behavior, infantile autism, learning disabilities, developmental dyslexia and dysgraphia, dysphasia, and stuttering. All of these disorders have now been linked to abnormalities of brain function. Thus a plausible assumption is that the male brain may be more susceptible or vulnerable to adverse events occurring during prenatal or postnatal periods of development. Consistent with this hypothesis is a recent comprehensive 30-year study that found an excess of males (3 : 1) with intracranial abscesses.[31] Several authors have suggested that the excess of males in the previously mentioned behavioral disorders is related to gender differences in brain development.[32,33] Genetic neurohumoral mechanisms are considered responsible for hemispheric differences between the two sexes. Flor-Henry has proposed that these hemispheric differences render the sexes differentially vulnerable to disturbances of cerebral development in regard to the dominant and nondominant hemispheres.[34] Males are viewed as having a relatively superior nondominant hemisphere and a more vulnerable dominant hemisphere, whereas females are thought to have a relatively more superior dominant hemisphere and a more vulnerable nondominant hemisphere during the early developmental years. Thus, as I suggested previously, if the male brain in general is more vulnerable than the female brain to adverse developmental events—and in addition, as others have suggested, is more vulnerable to dominant hemisphere injury—then this would be consistent with the well-known excess of males with language-related disorders. The accumulating evidence for the association of dominant hemisphere dysfunction in the previously mentioned male disorders would also account for the clustering of some of these disorders (e.g., juvenile delinquency and learning disabilities). I have suggested elsewhere that the dominant hemisphere dysfunction of the temporal and frontal regions of the brain may play a critical role in the genesis of persistent criminal behavior.[18] More specifically, I have suggested that dominant hemisphere dysfunction disrupts the role of language in the development of foresight or anticipation of the negative consequences of amoral behavior. In contrast to offenders with dominant hemisphere dysfunction, offenders with nondominant hemisphere dysfunction would be susceptible to behavioral disruption as a possible consequence of mood disorders, which have been linked to nondominant hemisphere dysfunction.[35-37]

The findings of several independent studies have demonstrated a high incidence of neuropsychological impairments in persistent juvenile offender populations. These neuropsychological deficits, particularly in the early developmental years of the child and adolescent, could have significant detrimental effects in regard to the functional, emotional, and cognitive adaptive abilities of the individual with such brain dysfunction. Thus high risk individuals who evolve into persistent criminal offenders may be those who have acquired significant neural impairment or brain damage and have the misfortune to be born into an impoverished environment, which typically lacks adequate attention for medical, educational, psychiatric, and legal problems. In contrast, it would be hypothesized that those individuals born into a similar impoverished environment without significant neural impairment would have a dramatically increased probability of coping with their adverse environment, as well as the biological potential to develop normal inhibitory controls.

The importance of primary prevention in regard to the socioeconomic effects on the developing fetus and child has been made clearly before.[23] However, the consequences of sociogenic brain damage and/or dysfunction will most certainly continue to face mankind. The accumulating evidence of a high incidence of brain dysfunction in persistent juvenile and adult criminal populations has implications not only for the possible identification of high risk individuals, but also for alternative approaches to treatment and rehabilitation.[1,6,11,18,38] In conclusion, the emerging relationships between adverse environments, genetic factors, brain damage, altered brain function or dysfunction, male gender, and behavioral disorders in high risk subpopulations strongly suggest that biological factors interacting with the environment play a significant role in the genesis of persistent juvenile delinquency and criminal behavior. As pointed out emphatically by others, these biosocial influences can no longer be ignored, and a multidisciplinary-multimodal approach is needed to effectively deal with the prevention and treatment of high risk offenders.[23,38,39]

REFERENCES

1. MEDNICK, S. A. 1980. Human nature, crime, and society: keynote address. Ann. N.Y. Acad. Sci. (This volume.)
2. WOLFGANG, M. E., R. M. FIGLIO & T. SELLIN. 1972. Delinquency in a Birth Cohort. University of Chicago. Chicago, Ill.
3. HILL, D. 1952. EEG in episodic psychotic and psychopathic behavior: a classification of data. EEG J. 4: 419–442.
4. HILL, D. & D. WATTERSON. 1942. Electroencephalographic studies of psychopathic personalities. J. Neurol. Psychiatry 5: 47–65.
5. MONROE, R. R. 1970. Episodic Behavioral Disorders—A Psychodynamic and Neurophysiologic Analysis. Harvard University Press. Cambridge, Mass.
6. MONROE, R. R. 1978. Brain Dysfunction in Aggressive Criminals. D. C. Heath & Co. Lexington, Mass.
7. WILLIAMS, D. 1975. Studies of persons confined for crimes of violence. In Neural Bases of Violence and Aggression. W. S. Fields & W. H. Sweet, Eds. Warren H. Green. St. Louis, Mo.
8. BACH-Y-RITA, G., J. R. LION, C. E. CLIMENT & F. R. ERVIN. 1971. Episodic dyscontrol: a study of 130 violent patients. Am. J. Psychiatry 127(11): 1473–1478.

9. BLUMER, D. & C. MIGEON. 1975. Hormone and hormonal agents in treatment of aggression. J. Nerv. Ment. Dis. **160**(2): 127-137.

10. ELLIOTT, F. A. 1978. Neurological aspects of antisocial behavior. *In* The Psychopath: A Comprehensive Study of Antisocial Disorders and Behaviors. W. H. Reid, Ed. Brunner/ Mazel. New York, N.Y.

11. BERMAN, A. 1978. Neuropsychological aspects of violent behavior. Presented at the Symposium on Adolescent Murderers at the Annual Convention of the American Psychological Association, Toronto, Ontario, Canada.

12. KRYNICKI, V. E. 1978. Cerebral dysfunction in repetitively assaultive adolescents. J. Nerv. Ment Dis. **166**(1): 59-67.

13. ROBBINS, D., R. PRIES, D. JACOBS, J. BECK & C. SMITH. 1978. A preliminary report on the neuropsychological development of a group of clinic referred juvenile delinquents. Presented at the Symposium on Adolescent Murderers at the Annual Convention of the American Psychological Association, Toronto, Ontario, Canada.

14. SPELLACY, F. 1977. Neuropsychological differences between violent and nonviolent adolescents. J. Clin. Psychol. **33**: 966-969.

15. SPELLACY, F. 1978. Neuropsychological discrimination between violent and nonviolent men. J. Clin. Psychol. **34**(1): 49-52.

16. YEUDALL, L. T., D. FROMM-AUCH & P. DAVIES. 1979. Power spectral EEG and neuropsychological findings in persistent juvenile offenders. (In preparation.)

17. YEUDALL, L. T. 1978. Neuropsychological correlates of criminal psychopathy. I. Differential diagnosis. *In* Human Aggression and Dangerousness. L. Beliveau, G. Canepa & D. Szabo, Eds. Pinel Institute. Montreal, Quebec, Canada.

18. YEUDALL, L. T. 1978. The neuropsychology of aggression. Clarence M. Hincks Memorial Lectures: Psychobiological Approaches to Aggression in Mental illness and Mental Retardation. London, Ontario, Canada.

19. YEUDALL, L. T. & D. FROMM-AUCH. 1979. Neuropsychological impairments in various psychopathological populations. *In* Hemisphere Asymmetrics of Function and Psychopathology. J. Gruzelier & P. Flor-Henry, Eds. (In press.)

20. LURIA, A. R. 1973. The frontal lobes and the regulation of behavior. *In* Psychophysiology of the Frontal Lobes. K. H. Pribra & A. K. Luria, Eds. Academic Press, Inc. New York, N.Y.

21. NAUTA, J. W. H. 1971. The problem of the frontal lobes: a reinterpretation. J. Psychiatr. Res. **8**: 167-187.

22. WILLIAMS, D. 1969. Temporal lobe syndromes. *In* Handbook of Clinical Neurology: Localization in Clinical Neurology. P. J. Vinken & G W. Bruyn, Eds. North Holland. Amsterdam, The Netherlands.

23. MONTAGU, A. 1972. Sociogenic brain damage. Am. Anthropol. **74**(5): 1045-1061.

24. STOTT, D. H. 1962. Evidence for a congenital factor in maladjustment and delinquency. Am. J. Psychiatry **118**(9): 781-794.

25. LEWIS, D. O., S. S. SHANOK & D. A. BALLA. 1979. Perinatal difficulties, head and face trauma, and child abuse in the medical histories of seriously delinquent children. Am. J. Psychiatry **136**(4A): 419-423.

26. FERGUSON, T. 1952. The Young Delinquent in His Social Setting. Oxford University Press. London, England.

27. HUTT, C. 1972. Males and Females. Penguin Books. United Kingdom.

28. LEWIS, D. O. & S. S. SHANOK. 1979. Medical histories of psychiatrically referred delinquent children: an epidemiologic study. Am. J. Psychiatry **136**(2): 231-233.

29. MONTAGU, A. 1971. Touching: The Human Significance of the Skin. Columbia University Press. New York, N.Y.

30. YEUDALL, L. T. 1977. Neuropsychological assessment of forensic disorders. Can. Ment. Health **25**: 7-16.

31. MCCLELLAND, C. J., B. F. CRAIG & H. A. CROCKARD. 1978. Brain abscesses in Northern Ireland: a 30 year community review. J. Neurol. Neurosurg. Psychiatry **41**: 1043-1048.

32. OUNSTED, C. & D. C. TAYLOR, Eds. 1972. Gender Differences: Their Ontogeny and Significance. Churchills. London, England.

33. TAYLOR, D. C. & C. OUNSTED. 1971. Biological mechanisms influencing the outcome of seizures in response to fever. Epilepsia **12**: 33.

34. FLOR-HENRY, P. 1978. Gender, hemispheric specialization and psychopathology. Soc. Sci. Med. **12B**: 155–162.
35. FLOR-HENRY, P. 1979. On certain aspects of the localization of the cerebral systems regulating and determining emotion. Biol. Psychiatry **14**(4): 677–698.
36. GOLDSTEIN, L. 1977. Characteristics of EEG hemispheric asymmetries on psychopathology. *In* Sixth World Congress of Psychiatry. Honolulu, Hawaii.
37. FOLSTEIN, M. F., R. MAIBERGER & P. R. MCHUGH. 1977. Mood disorder as a specific complication of stroke. J. Neurol. Neurosurg. Psychiatry **40**: 1018–1020.
38. JEFFERY, C. R. 1977. Crime Prevention through Environmental Design. Sage Publication, Inc. Beverly Hills, Calif.
39. VAN DEN BERGHE, P. 1974. Bringing beast back in: toward a biosocial theory of aggression. Am. Sociol. Rev.: 77–788.

HUMAN NATURE, CRIME, AND SOCIETY: PANEL DISCUSSION

Moderator: Robert W. Rieber
Panel Members: David Bakan,
Ashley Montagu, and Lorne T. Yeudall

A. Montagu (*Princeton, N.J.*): In the first place, let me say this. When we're dealing with human beings, we're dealing with a very complex series of entities. And to talk about interactionism, namely, the interaction between genes and the environment, has become rather old-hat because by the time we get to the child that is born—whether it is an identical twin, a dizygotic twin, or a singleton—a great many things have happened to the genes, and a great many things have happened to the organism. In the interactionist conception of things, one thinks of the interaction between genes and the environment. This is a rather unsound view to take. What the interaction is, is between the environment and the organism; and the organism is a very different thing from the genotype or the genetic system. An enormous number of things happen. In the first place, in his paper—which I found extremely interesting and well-written and very compellingly so—Dr. Mednick seems to think that monozygotic twins are essentially genetically identical. They are not. No one knows for certain whether they are never so, but the probabilities are very high that they are never genetically identical. They differ in some of their genes at least and sometimes in their chromosomal structure.

Then there are, of course, a vast number of interactions between that growing and developing organism and the environment in the womb. And as you know, in one-egg twins (which should never be called identical twins because they are not identical), often one is larger than the other. When they are born, one may be found to have had its twin's arm around its neck or the amniotic cord twisted around its neck, etc.; the differences between them are very evident.

These differences may be significantly related to the later development of such twins to such an extent that the twins may show considerable differences in their behavior even though they're brought up in the same home. Certainly when they're separated, such twins may show very considerable differences. While we're always citing the remarkable coincidences and concordances in the behavior of twins who have been separated at birth and then subsequently studied, there are differences. Take, for example, Newman and Holzinger's famous case of Phyllis and her sister Gladys, who were separated at birth. One went to college and one did not. As Newman remarked, the benefits that Gladys showed spoke highly in favor of a college education. She showed the advantages of a superior environment. The sister who didn't go to college but was brought up in a lower-class environment showed the lower-class characteristics of such an individual.

356

But what is the point of these remarks to what Dr. Mednick said? Simply this: there is enormous variability in the findings on identical twins and in twin studies. What is often attributed to genes can be very clearly shown to be due in most cases to socioeconomic factors—as for example when Dr. Mednick speaks of low skin conductance level or low pulse level as a good predictor of future delinquency or criminal behavior.

I think it is quite well known that such skin conductance levels and low pulse rates are highly correlated with the emotional condition of the individual at the time of examination. As a child, that individual may have committed no delinquencies whatsoever but still may have been sufficiently emotionally disturbed to show significant changes in his skin conductance and pulse level. Indeed this is what we would expect.

Now to connect this, as Dr. Mednick does, with genetic causes of criminal behavior seems to me an error of scientific methodology. The probabilities indeed are very high that if such children—no matter what their skin conductance levels or pulse rates might be—were removed to an environment that was much more congenial to their healthy development, they would develop as noncriminal, healthy individuals.

This is the long and the short of what I have to say. Let me underscore what I have just said: it is utterly impossible by any method known to me to establish any relationship between genes and criminal behavior.

What we have learned about the interaction of genes in the genetic system is that there is an enormous amount of variability in what happens between genes, that every gene is part of the environment of every other gene, that the interaction between genes and their total environment is very profound indeed, but that no gene ever determines anything. Genes do not make your eyes blue or brown or your skin black or white. What they do is influence the physiological or behavioral expression of a trait. And between the gene and its expression lies a large number of complicating factors.

It is, therefore, my opinion that it is quite impossible with our present knowledge to tease out what part is due to genes and what part is due to environment. It simply can't be done. We just don't have the means of doing this.

So to Dr. Mednick's question as to why it is that people get worried when others begin talking about the genetic determinants of human behavior, the answer is very simple. It is because we have no evidence of any kind that any form of human behavior is genetically determined.

The fact is that everything that human beings come to know and do as human beings they have to learn from other human beings. There isn't a single thing that human beings do—and I don't mean the things they do that they hold in common with other mammals, but the things they do that make them uniquely human—they have to learn from other human beings. And this is not genetically determined. Robert Merton and I wrote a paper about 40 years ago, in the *American Anthropologist,* called "Crime and the Anthropologist" in which we reviewed the first volume of Earnest Hooton's book *The American Criminal,* which was to have appeared in three volumes. As a result of our review, only that one volume was ever published. What Hooton had done was to revive Lombrosianism in a new form. It was not difficult to show how unsound his thesis of inborn criminality was; the crime rates in different societies vary enormously. In New York City last year, there were somewhere in the vicinity of 1800 murders. In England there were somewhere in the vicinity of 300, in Tokyo 50. One can go through a great many examples of such variable statistics. Why the great variation? Is there any genetic difference at work here? The answer surely is that there isn't—that there are socioeconomic, sociocultural factors that are involved here—and that if one really is going to study the origin of criminal behavior, one surely must do this in a wholistic manner.

It is not sufficient to begin with an assumption that genetic determinants are involved in such behavior; I am very well aware that genes are involved in virtually every form of behavior. But the real question we have to ask is: To what extent do genes influence that behavior and especially criminal behavior? I have no doubt that there is some genetic influence responsible in some cases in individuals who have committed criminal behavior. But equally I have no doubt that all of us have genes that under certain conditions would express themselves in the form that Dr. Mednick describes as criminal behavior. We're all capable of criminal behavior. It depends largely on the conditions under which we grow and develop.

D. BAKAN *(York University, Toronto, Ontario, Canada):* May I say something? Dr. Mednick and I have been at it for several times during the day. Perhaps he has changed his position, and that's fine. Maybe for the sake of the *Annals* he's going to rewrite his paper; and maybe for the sake of the *Annals*, when this discussion is published, I'll have rewritten what I have said here. On the other hand, I feel impelled to read at least this, which stimulated part of what I have to say. On page 15 of the manuscript that I received, it goes as follows: "Following the excellent exposition of Gordon Trasler . . . I would suggest that the avoidance of transgression (i.e., lawful behavior) demanded by the moral commandments is probably in the main learned by way of contingent negative reinforcements (punishments) applied by society, family, and peers. I would guess that the critical morality-training forces in childhood are (1) the punishment of antisocial responses by family, society, and friends and (2) the child's individual capacity to learn to inhibit antisocial responses." Okay, so that punishment is certainly the critical factor according to Mednick.

The last thing is in terms of program. Mednick says, I believe, that predelinquents have distinguishing characteristics that could be used to select them for intervention research well before they become serious criminals. Now he says that we're going to intervene, and he says that learning of morality only takes place by punishment. I just put the two things together. If you're going to intervene—and if the critical thing is punishment—it seems to me that there is nothing else that you're going to intervene with except that which you take to be critical. Now I'd like to proceed with my comments.

It is a little-known historical fact that Cleopatra performed some of the earliest experiments on human biological paternity. By controlling the sexual intercourse of women, whom she had imprisoned for the purpose, she was able to explore some of the detailed phenomena of the relationship of sex and childbirth. I mention this because I feel uneasy about the arrogance of the Danish investigators who presume to be knowledgeable about who may be the biological fathers of the children who are put out for adoption. I don't pretend to be an expert on Danish culture or Danish sexual behavior, but I can't believe that the men and women from Denmark are dramatically different from the other Western peoples. Indeed, to this day, we do not have very good data on the gestation period among humans. We have excellent data on thoroughbred dogs, but not on women. So I'm very dubious about the data on the paternity of the children in that study. And I am very concerned that major public policy should be based on such studies.

It is rare for me to find myself in such total and profound disagreement with a paper as I am on this occasion. Indeed, let me say that I even consider the presentation that I have heard to be dangerous.

Let me state what I think are the main points of Mednick's presentation.

The first is that delinquency is to some unspecified extent a function of heredity. The second is that this hereditary defect may be overcome by the use of punishment and the development of anticipatory fear.

Mednick suggests a program of identifying young, predelinquent, hereditarily tainted children and "treating" them. If we take him at his word as to how one learns to be law-abiding, it would seem that the only proper word for his suggested plan is "terrorization."

In response to Mednick, I'd like to make the following three observations.

First, I think that Mednick doesn't understand the proper relationship between statistics, on the one hand, and public policy, on the other.

Second, I think that he is in danger of violating a fundamental principle of legality.

And third, his views are more generally dangerous in connection with public policy.

First, on statistics: Mednick confounds prediction with correlation. They are hardly the same thing. His studies are not predictive. His studies are postdictive, of the past. They describe some presumptive correlations.

Even if it were the case that there were such correlations, there still would be a question as to whether one should use such correlations in connection with public policy in the way that he suggests. The use of presumptive correlation in this way is the essence of unfair discrimination.

Let me give you a very simple example. Suppose we have a test in which more men than women passed. From a statistical point of view, this would constitute a correlation between sex and performance. If one would, on the basis of this correlation, bar women, say, from employment, it would be clearly discriminatory. Similarly, even if most people who display a certain physiological response were later to become criminal, it would be grossly unjust to treat *all* people who display this physiological response as potential criminals.

Consider the basic principle of "innocent until proven guilty." Mednick seems to be recommending a program of large-scale testing to identify potential delinquents, who will then be subjected to some kind of treatment. Mednick would have a needle on an electronic meter not only single people out for suspicion, but subject them to special fear-inducing treatments as well.

I believe that the very notion of such "early detection" of criminality is both heinous—with respect to the individuals that may be so labeled—and mischievous—in connection with public policy. It would be injurious to the individuals, and it would not serve to reduce such delinquency. I would suspect that anyone who might try to implement such a plan would find himself in deep trouble, at least with the parents of children with Mednick's predelinquency signs, those who endowed their children with what Dr. Mednick takes as an unfortunate genetic makeup.

I cannot imagine that the children who are so labeled by Dr. Mednick could develop any respect for the law that might treat them in this manner on the basis of, say, the electrical conductivity of their skins. If such Mednick children were to grow up without any respect for the law, it would be very understandable. The whole thing would constitute an example of the self-fulfilling prophecy.

Let me now speak to the question of the general approach that Mednick seems to be making to public policy. Let me first state what I consider to be a reasonable basic paradigm for apprehending appropriate social behavior. When an individual finds that there's a convergence between the interests of the group of which he is a member and his own interests, then he usually tries to behave well in terms of the norms of that group. On the other hand, when an individual sees his own interests as divergent from those of the group, he may become its enemy. Young people do not become enemies of society of they have hope for a decent life within it. If there is no hope for people, then they can only be controlled by intimidation. However, the limits of the effectiveness of intimidation are set by the limits of the controlling power on the one hand and the amount of courage on the other.

It appears to me that Mednick has not taken either police power or courage into account. Quite the contrary. It appears to me that he has made the assumption that somehow the one that will be carrying out the program he has outlined will have unlimited power and that the target population will be without either power or courage. Mednick has, for example, taken no account of something that is commonplace these days—the power of young people to organize themselves into effective, well-disciplined urban gangs that are capable of returning terror for terror. He has taken no account of justice and fairness as essential ingredients in maintaining the power and credibility of the law-enforcing agencies. I can imagine, for example, the possibility of a pattern of terror loosed on society by some vengeful union of a Mednick-selected group of sluggish-autonomic-nervous-system and low-skin-conductance persons who are outraged against the society that would single them out to be victims of a special fear-inducing program such as Mednick has outlined.

And finally let me mention the following—and this is the deepest paradox associated with the use of punishment at all as a method of social control. Whenever punishment is used as a method of social control, there are always at least two messages involved. The first one is, I am punishing you because you took the cookies out of the cookie jar. That's one thing. But there's always a second lesson. And that second lesson is that it is right and proper to influence another person through the use of force and intimidation; because that is what is modeled when you use punishment. Anytime one uses punishment as a method of control, one is also teaching the person being punished that punishment is a good method of controlling people—at least if one ever gets a chance and if one ever has the power. This means that any kind of use of punishment automatically continues the pattern of terror.

If, then, the Mednick program is ever to be put into effect on the grand scale that he conceives, it would involve the whole society in a massive program of mutual intimidation. There are parts of the world where this has taken place, where everyone is involved in a program of trying to intimidate the others by inducing fear in them.

Indeed, it might well be the tragedy of the world that the program that has been outlined by Dr. Mednick was, in point of fact, put into effect long ago and constitutes the major burden of the modern world. Thank you.

L. T. YEUDALL *(Alberta Hospital, Edmonton, Alberta, Canada):* Thank you. I just have to simmer down a little bit here. It's pretty hard to follow that David; I mean with the adrenalin that is flowing here.

Maybe what I'd like to do is return to a little more sober, scientific attitude. Not that science should be devoid of emotion. But I think one has to pay attention to some of the evidence that's emerging over time.

I find it very interesting that Dr. Montagu is more or less giving the impression that we haven't learned much about genetics and behavior. I don't think that's what he meant really, though possibly he did. But I can't help but think that we've learned something about mental retardation from the genetics of mental retardation. I can't help thinking that we've learned something about the identification of high risk individuals who will become mentally retarded because of genetic structure interacting with developmental fetal environment, which in turn interacts with socioeconomic factors as Dr. Montagu has well pointed out, and as have others before him.

I can't imagine why we have high risk neonatal clinics. Why don't we just scrap them? Because they identify biological markers that will potentially make a life of misery if they're ignored. But now they're not being ignored. Those clinics are increasing the quality of life of individuals both psychologically and physiologically by identifying so-called biological high risk markers.

I find it interesting that when we get into human behavior and start talking about biological markers, everybody gets emotional. But when we talk about physiological factors that don't have psychological behavior associated with them, well that's okay, we can accept that.

I find a similar analogy between neurology and psychiatry. When I'm on a neurosurgery unit or a neurology unit, the doctor goes through the symptoms of temporal lobe lesions and frontal lobe lesions and says, Ah yes, that's an orbital frontal lesion, probably on the left side. If I walk across the hall, I hear the psychiatrist discuss the same symptoms and start talking about dynamics, when the patient is two or three years of age.

Now, there's an interesting parallel here. We have different views of symptoms and behaviors; and what we really have to do, I believe, is examine our own presuppositions, our own belief systems, our own emotional commitments to those belief systems, and then settle down and try to put the picture together in some perspective.

If one looks at human behavior, certainly there are some hints of genetic influences. There are hints of very potent influences during the developmental period, as Dr. Montagu has pointed out in his classic paper entitled "Sociogenic Brain Damage" in the 1972 *American Anthropologist*. There are many factors that interact, not only with the possible genetic structure of the child, as suggested by Stott and others as well as Dr. Montagu, but with the physiological status of the mother and the child, and which covary with a bad environment. We can talk about toxic factors— alcoholism, heavy cigarette smoking, and the list goes on and on—in regard to those things that happen during the prenatal period. Birth injury is another important factor that occurs. The incidence of birth injury, at least in Canada, is phenomenally high. I suspect it's not much lower in the United States. That is, children have their brains injured and become high risk babies for something, whether it's learning disability, juvenile delinquency, stuttering, etc.

The life story doesn't stop. During the child's early development, in those first three years of life, the brain is developing very rapidly. And things happen, such as serious illnesses, convulsions as a consequence of high fevers, battery, and head injuries. As Lewis at Yale has pointed out, the incidence of battering in persistent juvenile delinquents is significantly higher before the age of two, compared to controls.

One other interesting factor is the male gender. The male gender seems to be haunting us in a whole set of disorders. Not only in persistent juvenile delinquency, but in learning disabilities, developmental dyslexia, developmental dysgraphia, developmental dysphasia, stuttering, and hyperactivity, the ratio varies from 5-1 to 10-1, males to females. Ounsted and Taylor at Oxford and Flor-Henry in Edmonton have suggested a male vulnerability hypothesis in regard to dominant brain function. It is a well-known fact that the male is physiologically inferior to the female in a lot of functions and is susceptible to a lot more diseases. I've suggested elsewhere that the male brain in general indeed may be physiologically inferior to the female brain in that it's more vulnerable to adverse developmental effects. Interestingly, a group in Ireland over a 30-year period found that males have brain abscesses at the ratio of 3-1 to females. In addition, there appears to be a greater vulnerability of the left brain—the dominant or language brain—in males that is resulting in disorders pertaining to stuttering, language disorders, learning disabilities, infantile autism (a lack of language), schizophrenia (a thought disorder), juvenile delinquency, and persistent criminality (possibly due to a language disorder, that is, the use of a language to regulate behavior). Thus the evidence indicates that the male-to-female prevalence in pathology involving language disorders is five to one.

There are data to support Dr. Mednick's view about psychophysiological findings of low skin conductance and slow recovery. But there are other data, such as power spectral and quantitative EEG data, from which people are beginning to define characteristics of persistent juvenile offenders and persistent criminal offenders.

There are also neuropsychological data. For example, since around 1972, Dr. Berman from the University of Rhode Island has been consistently demonstrating that persistent offenders have severe neuropsychological impairments—impairments related to cognitive functions involving abstraction and concept formation, as well as anticipation, planning, and organization. Interestingly, all of these functions have been linked to the frontal and temporal lobe system of the brain.

Dr. Pincus and Dr. Lewis at Yale University just recently found that over 94% of violent, persistent juvenile offenders studied had definite neurological disorders. Frank Spellacy in Victoria, Canada, found a similar type of picture with juvenile offenders and violent offenders, that is, a high incidence (over 90%) of neuropsychological impairments. Krynicki and Robbins in the United States have also found similar results. There are lots of data in the literature on persistent chronic offenders, juvenile or adult, that indicate that something is wrong with the offenders' brains.

Now the question is, What percentage of these persistent offenders with brain dysfunction falls into that small group—that 10% that accounts for 60% of the crimes? I don't think we know yet. But my guess is that there may be an interesting relationship between that very small proportion of juveniles who commit a large portion of crimes and brain dysfunction.

Now this links very much to Dr. Montagu's paper, which pointed out that as you go down the socioeconomic ladder, you increase the probability of being born into this world with brain damage, or as I would like to think, altered brain function. It may not be brain damage; it may be altered brain function, which then renders the individual incapable of dealing with the challenges of his environment in the same way as could another child.

Now it's interesting that if you look at the studies of episodic violent people, such as those of Frank Elliott at the Elliott Neurological Institute in Philadelphia, you find that the population of episodic violent adults is very intimately related to damage and dysfunction of the frontal and temporal regions of the brain. And the majority of Elliott's patients came from the middle-class structure—from good homes and good environments. A slight paradox. There is no doubt that the socioeconomic factors are important; however, this could very much depend upon the specific population. For example, it could be that everyone in a given area has primarily a psychosociological reason for their disorder, whereas if you switch to another area, there could be more biological factors operating in regard to the disorder.

Certainly we don't, as you say, know all those influences. But I think we have some parallels in mental retardation where the individual's capacity to learn, to acquire certain things, is diminished. What they can learn, the complexity of what they can learn, and their concept of projecting into the future are impaired. Anybody that's worked with mental retardation knows this. But the retarded are still very amenable to learning and to behavioral techniques. If you focus techniques on what adaptive abilities they have, you can do many, many things indeed. One of the possibilities is that if the persistent offender does have some type of altered brain function, it may indeed be related to the interaction of genetic and developmental influences. But I think it would be unfortunate if we assumed that the persistent offender has the cerebral resources to learn like everybody else. It may not be the case. I don't think we really know yet, but there are some hints that the offenders might be different; and to make that assumption in a sense would be criminal, as it would be to make the assumption that a severely mentally retarded individual could conform in the same way you and I do to the laws of the land or could learn in the same way about the moral laws of the land. I think all we can do is try and find out if indeed that is the case or not. And there are ways of examining those possibilities.

I think the real task is to settle down and try to figure out what are the multivariate possibilities, and then systematically explore those possibilities without getting into the old polemics of the nature versus nurture issue. Let's do the best job we can working together in a multidisciplinary effort, using each other's criticisms and support, and then take the evidence and evaluate it as it comes out. I think those studies have yet to be done; and until we do them, we cannot stand at either end of the polemic pole and say, You're crazy, and I'm right. Thank you.